Adolescence

Ian McMahan

Brooklyn College, CUNY

PEARSON

AB

Boston · New York · San Francisco
Mexico City · Montreal · Toronto · London · Madrid · Munich · Paris
Hong Kong · Singapore · Tokyo · Cape Town · Sydney

Editor-in-Chief: *Susan Hartman*
Senior Acquisitions Editor: *Stephen Frail*
Series Editorial Assistant: *Katharine Motter*
Marketing Manager: *Kate Mitchell*
Production Supervisor: *Elizabeth Gale Napolitano*
Editorial Production Service: *Progressive Publication Alternatives*
Manufacturing Buyer: *JoAnne Sweeney*
Electronic Composition: *Progressive Information Technologies*
Interior Design: *Ellen Pettengell Design*
Photo Researcher: *Rachel Lucas*
Cover Designer: *Joel Gendron*

For related titles and support materials, visit our online catalog at www.pearsonhighered.com.

ISBN-13: 978-0-205-48232-0   ISBN-10: 0-205-48232-5

Library of Congress Cataloging-in-Publication Data

McMahan, Ian.
     Adolescence / Ian McMahan.
            p. cm.
     Includes bibliographical references and index.
     ISBN 978-0-205-48232-0 (alk. paper)
  1. Adolescence.   I.   Title.

  HQ796.M386   2008
  305.235—dc22   2008011600

Printed in the United States of America

10   9   8   7   6   5   4   3   2   1   CIN   12   11   10   09   08

Brief Contents

Contents

Preface

Writing a college textbook that aims to be accurate, comprehensive, up to date, and above all, engaging, is only slightly less challenging than juggling three open soda bottles while perched atop a beach ball. Even so, writing a textbook on adolescence has a major advantage over doing one in, say, geology. Students come to the subject with both a personal interest and a fund of personal experience. All of them have been adolescents themselves, and many are just emerging from adolescence. They want to gain a better understanding of their own development and that of their friends, those they are attracted to, those they find different, strange, even threatening. Most also bring with them a belief that what happens during adolescence is peculiarly important for individuals, their families, and the society in which they live.

I have taken a deep interest in the subject of adolescence throughout my career as both a teacher and researcher. During this same time, I was also actively involved in writing novels and stories *for* adolescents. Looking back, it was inevitable that at some point these two paths would meet and merge, that I would apply my writing skills to the job of presenting the central concepts and findings about adolescence in an attractive and accessible form. The book you are holding is the result of that merger.

KEY THEMES

Two overarching themes are explored throughout this text:

1. Adolescent development involves individual, social, and cultural systems.
2. Positive adolescent development is the norm, though the media and research frequently concentrate on adolescent problems.

Adolescent development does not occur in a vacuum or laboratory, and so this text takes an ecological systems approach to adolescence. For the individual, adolescence brings fundamental changes in biological, cognitive, and self systems, each of which acts upon, and is acted upon, by the others. The individual in turn is situated within embedded social contexts, especially the parents and family, the peer group, the school, the community, and the larger culture. Each of these contexts is potentially affected by the others and by relationships among the others. For example, community beliefs about a particular school can affect a student's self-esteem and cognitive achievement, the peers the student interacts with, and parental commitment to the school and to learning. All of these may in turn tend to confirm or disconfirm the community beliefs.

The adolescent experience today is profoundly affected by cultural diversity and globalization. Some aspects of adolescence are universal or nearly so, but many others are specific to a culture, subculture, or social group. In American society, ethnic diversity has become more a norm than an exception. Adolescents everywhere are affected by the tensions between the specifics of their cultural and historical setting and the influences of globalization. It may seem at first glance that an unbridgable gulf separates a suburban mallrat in middle America, a 12-year-old militia member in Sierra Leone, a street kid in a *favella* of Rio de Janeiro, and a teenage bride in Sri Lanka. All, however, represent important aspects of adolescence at the beginning of the 21st century.

The concept of stage-environment fit is also central to the book's portrayal of adolescence. As adolescents themselves change, so do their relationships with parents, peers, proximate institutions, and the culture. The same parental approach, for example, is likely to meet with very different responses from adolescents of 13, 15, and 17. Often there is a mismatch between adolescent stage and environment. For instance, just as young adolescents begin to strive for greater autonomy and to look for non-parental adult models, they are transferred into schools that typically put greater stress on rules and authority and greater distance between students and teachers.

Much of the research on adolescence, like much of the discussion of adolescence in the media, concentrates on adolescent problems, from drug use, premature sex, and delinquency to eating disorders, depression, and suicide. Certainly it is vital to gain an understanding of these problems and to learn about ways to treat or prevent them. It is at least as crucial, however, to emphasize positive development. How can parents, teachers, and community leaders help adolescents become confident, productive, caring, and involved participants in the life of their family, school, neighborhood, and society? These questions are of critical importance to all of us.

GUIDING PHILOSOPHY

This text implements learning pedagogy that is intended to help students get the most out of their study of adolescent development. My guiding philosophy is that students learn best when they:

1. Practice active learning and deep processing.
2. Focus on the practical applications what they are studying.
3. Think critically and become educated consumers of the research.

Students derive greater educational benefits from active learning and deep processing. When we think about material in more meaningful ways and associate it with information that is already encoded in long-term memory, we remember it better. The more deeply new material (ideas, concepts, facts) is processed, the more likely it is to be recalled later. One of the most effective forms of deep processing is to link new information to oneself. When we engage with new facts and ideas and bring them into relationship with our own personal experience, we give them longer, more complete consideration and organize them more fully. This text makes a strong effort to foster deep processing through illustrative examples that connect to students' life experiences.

An understanding of adolescence has important practical **applications.** Students enroll in adolescence courses for reasons that range from intellectual curiosity and a desire for self-knowledge to a need to satisfy departmental requirements. A great many do so because they aspire to careers working with adolescents, as teachers, counselors, providers of social services, and in other ways. Many also anticipate being parents of adolescents some day and hope that what they learn will help them when the time comes. Throughout the book, the implications that concepts and findings hold for the reader's actual practice are pointed out in the body of the text and explored in greater depth in special boxes.

Students benefit by becoming **educated consumers** of social science. The media continually trumpet astonishing theories, remarkable discoveries, and putative facts about adolescence. How can an ordinary layperson keep a sense of balance under all this buffeting? One important tool is a broad knowledge of the theories and basic findings in the field, which helps the student discern the truly new and significant from the faddish. A second tool, just as important, is an understanding of how research on adolescence really works: What are the strengths and pitfalls of different methods? When is it appropriate to draw personal or policy implications from research results? As students work through these questions, they learn more actively and gain skills they need to understand and evaluate future developments in the field of adolescence.

STRUCTURE OF THE BOOK

The way the book is organized grows directly out of its emphasis on an ecological systems approach.

Part One: Introduction surveys the territory and provides a foundation for the rest of the book. *Chapter 1: Adolescence, Past, Present, and Future,* introduces students to the history of adolescence and describes demographic, economic, and social factors that affect its present and future. *Chapter 2: Adolescence in Theory and Research,* presents the ideas that have most influenced research on adolescence, describes the techniques that are used to gather empirical information about adolescents, and explores ways to understand and critically evaluate research findings.

Part Two: Adolescent Changes presents the biological, physical, and cognitive developments that are common to adolescents in general. *Chapter 3: Puberty and Growth,* describes the hormonal, physical, and sexual changes that help define adolescence and the ways individual adolescents, their parents, and their culture respond to these changes, presents the ways the brain changes during adolescence, and discusses health issues raised by these developments. *Chapter 4: Cognitive Changes* explores approaches to understanding adolescent thinking that include Piaget's cognitive developmental theory and its recent variants, information processing, ideas about intelligence, and metacognition.

Part Three: Adolescent Contexts moves outward from the individual adolescent to the successively embedded contexts in which development takes place. *Chapter 5: Parents and Families* explores the position of adolescents within the family system, the effects of parenting styles, attachment, and conflict, the role of siblings, and family diversity in today's society. *Chapter 6: Peers* examines the growing importance of peers and peer influence during adolescence, explores the nature of social status and popularity, and describes the evolution of social groups such as cliques and crowds. *Chapter 7: School and Work* examines the effects of educational policy, school size and climate, teacher attitudes and expectations, racial segregation, and school choice, describes the role of extracurricular programs and activities, and weighs some plusses and minuses of teen employment. *Chapter 8: Community, Culture, and Media* discusses ways that community values and cultural attitudes affect adolescent development, examines the effects of minority status, social class, and poverty, and describes the rapidly growing impact of media on adolescents.

Part Four: Adolescent Issues takes a detailed look at four social/psychological issues that assume particular importance during adolescence. *Chapter 9: Achievement* explores the ways family, friends, school, culture, ethnic background, and social class affect how adolescents deal with and feel about achievement-related activities. *Chapter 10: Gender* describes current ideas about gender development, examines gender differences in adolescence, and discusses how different social contexts influence gender. *Chapter 11: Identity* discusses the ways adolescence promotes the development of the self concept, self esteem, and a coherent sense of identity, and describes the evolution of moral judgment and a moral identity. *Chapter 12: Intimacy* considers three crucial aspects of personal involvements during adolescence, close friendships, romantic relationships, and sexuality.

Part Five: Adolescent Problems and Prospects presents both difficulties and positive opportunities that are characteristic of adolescence. *Chapter 13: Problems* examines the causes, prevalance, and ways of dealing with externalizing problems, such as delinquency and substance use, and internalizing problems, including eating problems, depression, and suicide. *Chapter 14: Positive Prospects* discusses the importance of coping and resilience, examines the internal and external resources that promote thriving and positive development, and considers the question of how adolescents can become happier.

FEATURES OF THE BOOK

Each chapter includes special features designed to reinforce major themes of the book and make it easier for students to absorb and master the material.

Applications in the Spotlight presents concrete, practical suggestions for putting the ideas and findings of adolescent research to use in the family, the classroom, and the community.

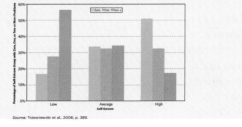

Research in the Spotlight examines in detail a recent study on the chapter topic—the rationale for carrying it out, the methodological concerns, the results, and the implications of those results. This gives students practice in reading and interpreting empirical research while reminding them that our knowledge of adolescence, like adolescence itself, is constantly evolving.

An additional feature, **Writing in the Spotlight,** is incorporated in the book's Study Guide. This is a series of optional assignments that stimulate students to write journals, personal memoirs, poems, stories, interviews, and other narratives keyed to the succession of topics in the course. These can be posted for fellow students to read and discuss and become the basis of class presentations.

Pedagogical features include:

Chapter Outlines and Learning Objectives at the beginning of each chapter, to give students a preview of what they will be reading about and what questions to keep in mind as they read.

Marginal Definitions of key terms, which are also set off in bold type within the text, listed at the end of each chapter, and compiled into a Glossary in the back of the book.

Summing Up, brief descriptions of the content of major sections of chapters, to permit students to review material as they go along.

Connect the Dots, thought-provoking exercises linked to the topics under consideration.

Chapter Summaries at the end of each chapter that are keyed to the Learning Objectives at the beginning of the chapter.

SUPPLEMENTS FOR INSTRUCTORS

The following supplements are available to qualified instructors:

Test Bank

The textbook author, Ian McMahan, wrote the *Test Bank* himself to ensure it reflects the approach and teaching philosophy of the text itself. Multiple-choice and essay questions include both informational and conceptual questions, and are keyed to specific learning objectives and page numbers within each chapter. The *Test Bank* is available in electronic format with an integrated suite of test creation tools for Windows and Macintosh.

Instructor's Manual

Written by Ian McMahan, the *Instructor's Manual* includes detailed outlines, summaries, learning objectives, suggestions for class discussion, and writing topics for each chapter.

PowerPoint Presentations

Written by Ian McMahan, the PowerPoint slides provide a brief lecture outline for each chapter and include the majority of the figures and charts found in the textbook.

SUPPLEMENTS FOR STUDENTS

MyDevelopmentKit (www.mydevelopmentkit.com)

MyDevelopmentKit is an online resource that provides a wealth of study tools for students looking to clarify and deepen their understanding of adolescent development. A range of videos, simulations, and animations expand upon textbook coverage. Self-scoring practice tests and glossary flashcards assist students in their review of textbook concepts. *MyDevelopmentKit* requires an access code; please contact your Pearson representative or visit www.mydevelopmentkit.com for information on how to access this resource.

Study Guide

The *Study Guide* offers students an authoritative summary of the material in the book, together with learning objectives and practice tests.

Acknowledgments

It is a pleasure to thank all those who so ably shepherded this first edition through the publication process, particularly Stephen Frail, Liz Napolitano, Angela Pickard, and Kate Motter at Allyn & Bacon; Marsha Hall at PPA, and photo editor Rachel Lucas. Special thanks go to Edith Beard Brady, who first encouraged me to embark on this long and exciting project. And I would especially like to thank my wife, Jane, and daughter, Selena, for being so consistently and irrationally sure that I could indeed finish writing the book.

I would also like to thank the following reviewers: Carolyn Ashton—California State University, Fullerton; Dave Brueshoff—Concordia University; Richard Cavasina—California University of Pennsylvania; Steve Dennis—Brigham Young University; Jerome Dusek—Syracuse University; Diane Finley—Prince George's Community College; Alice Ganzel—Cornell College; Judith Geary—University of Michigan, Dearborn; Jane Gebelt—Westfield State College; Dawn Gondoli—University of Notre Dame; Stephanie Hewett—The Citadel; Patricia Jarvis—Illinois State University; Erin Kraan—Miami University; Dawn Lewis—Prince George's Community College; Kristin Neff—University of Texas at Austin; Vicki Ritts—St. Louis Community College, Meramec; David Saarnio—Arkansas State University; Debra Sorensen—Utah State University; Nanci Woods—Austin Peay State University.

Finally, a textbook of this sort is in a real sense an ongoing collaboration between the author and those who use it, both faculty and students. I would very much appreciate hearing any comments and suggestions you may have. Please send them to: Adolescence@ianbooks.com.

Part I Introduction

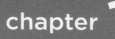
Adolescence: Past, Present, and Future

This first chapter introduces the book, but it is not really necessary to introduce you to adolescence. After all, adolescence is a subject you know a good deal about already. You went through adolescence yourself, whether recently or not so recently. You watched others—friends, siblings, schoolmates, neighbors—go through it. You took in countless articles, stories, movies, and television shows that focused on the trials, pains, perils, and—now and then—the joys of adolescence.

Now you have decided to study adolescence in a more formal and structured way. You want to find out what researchers and scholars know or theorize about the subject. Some of what you are about to learn will fit with and expand on ideas and impressions you already have. Some will surprise you. And some will make you think about what you already know in a different way.

The English word *adolescent* comes from exactly the same Latin root as the word *adult*: *adolescere*, to grow up. However, there is an important grammatical difference between the two terms. *Adult* comes from the verb form that means something that happened in the past and is done with. Adults, in other words, are in the state of having grown up. The verb form of *adolescent*, on the other hand, indicates a process that is actively going on right now, in the present. Adolescents are moving *toward* adulthood. They are growing up. The dynamism that is such a feature of adolescence, the sense of movement and possibilities yet to be achieved, is captured in the word itself.

In the course of this chapter, one question we take up is how to define adolescence. What sorts of characteristics and changes matter? How can we best describe and understand the transitions adolescents go through? How are the successive phases of adolescence different? We next examine the ways adolescents have been thought of and dealt with in various societies across the centuries. Why did some scholars call the 20th century in America the *Age of Adolescence?* What about American teens today? How have they been affected by the changing structure of the family, the growing influence of peers, and conflicting attitudes about sexuality?

Finally, we examine some factors that will have a major impact on adolescents in the coming years, not just in America, but throughout the world. These include population changes, movement from the countryside to the city, migration across national boundaries, and the globalization of industry, entertainment, education, and culture. The increasingly rapid pace of change means that today's preschoolers will reach adolescence in a world that is vastly different from today's world in ways both predictable and unpredictable. What will they need to help them grow up into healthy, constructive adults? And what are the chances that those needs will be met?

First, however, we look at the major themes of this textbook, explain how it is organized, and suggest some ways to use it more effectively.

THEMES AND APPROACHES

▶ **Learning Objective 1.1**
What are the major themes of the book?

As we explore the many aspects of adolescence, you will notice several related themes that help give the material structure and shape.

On the most basic level, we make use of an **ecological systems** approach to adolescence (Bronfenbrenner & Morris, 2006; Lerner, 2006). As adolescents go through fundamental changes in their biological, cognitive, and self-systems, each of these sets of changes acts on, and is acted on, by the others. For example, the physical changes of puberty affect how children think of themselves. These changes in self-image may affect their diet and exercise patterns, which in turn affect their physical development.

Of course, teens are not simply individuals and they do not develop in isolation. They are situated within a series of interlocking *social contexts*. These contexts include their parents and family, peers, school, community, and the larger culture. Each of these contexts may be affected by the others and by the relationships among the others. For example, what if people in a specific geographical area are convinced that certain local schools are superior or inferior? These attitudes are likely to be passed along

Ecological systems The interacting structures both within the adolescent, such as physical, cognitive, and emotional functions, and in the adolescent's surroundings, such as family, peers, school, and the community.

to students in those schools and affect their self-esteem, ambitions, and achievements. Such judgments may also have an impact on the makeup of the student body, the educational expectations of teachers, the level of public funding, and the degree of commitment of parents. In turn, these factors may interact to produce superior results, in the one case, and inferior results in the other, in this way confirming the preconceptions of the community.

The concept of **stage-environment fit** (Eccles, 2004) is also an important tool for understanding adolescence. As adolescents themselves change, so do their relationships with parents, peers, social institutions, and the culture. The same parental approach, for example, is likely to meet with very different responses from adolescents of 13, 15, and 17. Often there is some degree of mismatch between an adolescent's stage and environment. For instance, just as young teens are starting to seek more autonomy and to look for nonparental adult models, they often shift to schools that typically put more stress on rules and authority and greater distance between students and teachers.

The adolescent experience today is profoundly affected by **cultural diversity** and **globalization.** Although some aspects of adolescence are universal, or nearly so, many others vary according to a teen's culture, subculture, or social group. In American society, ethnic diversity has become more a norm than an exception. Adolescents everywhere are affected by the clash between their particular cultural ideas and customs, on the one hand, and those promoted by an increasingly global information and media culture. This book focuses primarily on adolescents in Western cultures, but not at the expense of neglecting those of other backgrounds.

An understanding of adolescence has important practical **applications**. You may be among the many students who take a course in adolescent psychology with the thought of one day working with adolescents as a teacher, counselor, provider of social services, or in other ways. You may also think that one day you may be the parent of an adolescent and hope that what you learn now will help you when that time comes. Throughout this book, the concepts and findings we learn about often have real practical implications for teens and those who deal with teens. These are pointed out in the text and explored in greater depth in special boxes called *Applications in the Spotlight*.

As students, we also benefit by becoming **educated consumers** of social science. The media continually trumpet astonishing theories, remarkable discoveries, and supposed facts about adolescence. How can we keep our sense of balance under all this buffeting? One important tool is gaining a broad understanding of the theories and basic findings in the field. This can help us separate what is really new and significant from what is simply faddish. Just as important, we need to know how research on adolescence really works. What are the strengths and pitfalls of different methods? When are we on safe ground drawing personal or policy implications from research results?

Much of the research on adolescence, like much of the discussion of adolescence in the media, concentrates on adolescent problems, from drug use, premature sex, and delinquency to eating disorders, depression, and suicide. It is certainly important to understand these problems and to discover ways to treat or prevent them. It is at least as crucial, however, to learn more about the potential for **positive development**. How can parents, teachers, and community leaders help adolescents become confident, productive, caring, and engaged participants in the life of their family, school, neighborhood, and society? This book is unusual in its focus on these questions of such critical importance to everyone.

Structure of This Book

The way this book is organized reflects its ecological systems orientation. In Part One, we first take an overview of the history of adolescence and the social factors that affect its present and future. We then examine the principal theories of adolescence and methods for carrying out research. Part Two details developments that adolescents experience in their biological, physical, and cognitive systems.

Stage-environment fit The ways developmental changes in an adolescent interrelate with changes in the adolescent's social environment, such as parental rules and demands.

Cultural diversity The variety of customs, beliefs, expectations, and behaviors that are typical of adolescents from different cultural and ethnic backgrounds.

Globalization The tendency for economic, social, and political events and trends in one part of the world to have an impact on lives in other, distant parts of the world.

Applications Ways of taking knowledge about adolescents that is derived from research and putting it to practical use.

Educated consumers Those whose understanding of the field of adolescence and of the ways knowledge is gathered allows them to judge the strengths and weaknesses of new findings.

Positive development The study of factors that encourage adolescents to develop in a positive direction.

The four chapters of Part Three move outward from individual adolescents to describe their ecological contexts. While parents and family are the most intimate, adolescence sees a rapid growth in the importance of the peer group as well. The lives of most American adolescents are shaped by school, but many also enter the world of work. Beyond these immediate contexts, the community, the culture, and the media all exert a powerful, and often underestimated, influence.

The physical, cognitive, and social transitions of adolescence bring a number of psychosocial issues into high relief. The chapters in Part Four explore some of the most pressing of these. Where do attitudes toward achievement and vocational interests come from? How does gender affect the personality, behavior, hopes, and prospects of adolescents? What goes into developing a sense of personal identity and moral values? How do adolescents deal with concerns about intimacy and sexuality?

Part Five, like Parts One and Two, consists of two chapters. The first examines psychosocial problems in adolescence, which include depression, eating disorders, aggression, delinquency, and drug use. How common are they? What are their sources? How can they be treated or prevented? The final chapter looks at the other face of adolescence. Why are some adolescents able to cope with and overcome difficulties that leave others defenseless? What are the roots of optimism and hope? What resources in the home, the school, and the community can help adolescents find the strength to imagine, and to create, a life worth living?

Learning Strategies

▶ **Learning Objective 1.2**
What strategies will help you gain more from using the book?

Another approach we take in this textbook is to focus on learning strategies. Research has shown that we learn more and retain it better when we engage in **active learning**, or interacting with new information in some way. Reading an interesting or important passage is good; so is underlining or highlighting the key words or phrases. But pausing to think about what a passage said and then trying to put the contents into your own words is better. Better still is making the effort to tell others about it in a way they will understand. Encourage them to ask you questions. You may be red-faced over how much you thought you remembered and didn't, but afterwards the material will be retained much better.

A related strategy for learning is called **deep processing**, or associating new information with material in memory. When we think about material in more meaningful ways and associate it with information that is already stored in our memory, we remember it better. And the more deeply new material is processed, the more likely it is to be recalled later. One of the most effective forms of deep processing is to link new information to ourselves. When we engage with new concepts or facts and bring them into relationship with our own personal experience, we give them longer, more complete consideration and organize them more fully. As they become more relevant to us, they also become easier to retrieve.

Sprinkled throughout this book are suggested exercises entitled *Connect the Dots*. These exercises are designed to encourage active learning and deep processing. When you come to one, stop, consider it, and let your thoughts go in the direction it points. In this way you will think actively and critically about the material. You will begin to draw connections between what you hope to learn and what you already know from your own life experiences.

Active learning Interactions with new information, for example, by rephrasing material or trying to explain it to someone else.

Deep processing The association of new information with material that is already in memory, especially material that has personal relevance.

WHO IS AN ADOLESCENT?

At first, it may seem odd to even ask who is an adolescent. Don't we all know the answer? Yes, of course, but the closer we look at the matter, the more complicated it becomes. Most observers would agree that adolescence is linked to the biological changes of puberty, but what then? Is a 12-year-old girl who has had her first period an adolescent? How about a 9-year-old girl who has entered her growth spurt and

◄ Among preteens, some have already entered adolescence while others are not quite there yet.

started to develop breasts? Or a 14-year-old boy who still has the size, body contours, and smooth cheeks of a prepubescent child?

Suppose, instead, we turn our attention to social and economic factors. If anything, that only adds to the confusion. What do we call a 10-year-old who works full time and contributes to the economic survival of her family? A child? An adult? How about a 17-year-old who is a parent and a wage earner? Is she or he an adult? Then how about a 22-year-old who goes to school full time, lives at home, and is supported entirely by his or her parents?

If we look to the law for an answer to our question, we may end up even more puzzled than before. In most of the United States, young people who want to get a driver's license have to wait until they turn 16. Even then they are not old enough to sign a contract to buy a car or take out insurance. They can get married and vote in elections at 18, but in most states they will not be able to buy beer legally until they turn 21. On the other hand, some who commit crimes are considered mature enough to be tried and punished as adults when they are only 14 or even younger.

Is there a way for us to make some sense of these contradictions? Maybe. A first step would be to keep in mind that adolescence is not something "out there" that we can chase down, capture, dissect, and describe. Instead, it is a name we use to single out a particular segment of the lifespan. It distinguishes this part from those that come before and after. As a concept or category, *adolescence* helps us identify and think about what happens during these years. And like many of the concepts we use every day, it is much more sharply in focus at its center. Toward the edges, it starts to get fuzzy. Unless we agree to make some arbitrary rule about where it begins and ends, we have to put up with the ambiguity that comes from overlapping (and sometimes conflicting) definitions. Some examples of these are given in Table 1.1 on page 8.

Two Sorts of Transitions

Each of the different definitions of adolescence in Table 1.1 represents a particular sort of transition that people go through between late childhood and early adulthood. A *transition* is a period of growth and change that is set off when something disturbs an earlier balance. The "something" may be biological, psychological, cultural, or physical

◄ **Learning Objective 1.3**
How are normative transitions different from idiosyncratic transitions?

Table 1.1   Some Ways of Defining Adolescence
The age boundaries of adolescence are different depending on the area of functioning you look at.

Orientation	From	To
Chronological age	11 or so	20 or so
Physical	Start of growth spurt	Full adult size
Sexual	Appearance of secondary sex characteristics	Ability to reproduce
Familial	Parents grant more freedom	Achievement of independence
Psychosocial	Beginning of quest for identity	Achievement of a sense of identity
Interpersonal	Shift in influence from family to peers	Achievement of intimacy with peers
Educational	Finish elementary school	Finish formal education
Social	Begin to date, enter work world	Leave home, get a job, enter steady relationship

(Riegel, 1976). The transitional phase continues until a new equilibrium is reached. For example, the adolescent growth spurt, which will be discussed in Chapter 3, levels off, or reaches equilibrium, as people reach adult size. They then stay pretty much that size for the rest of their lives. Because even the happiest transitions involve change and instability, they tend to be stressful as well. You may have been terrifically pleased and proud when you graduated from high school. But you may also have had some uncomfortable moments of wondering "What now?" and dreading the possible answers.

Of course, adolescents are not the only ones who have to deal with major transitions; every phase of life has some. The baby goes from total dependency to the relative autonomy of the preschool child. People in early adulthood enter a career, choose a partner, and start a family. Those in middle age adapt to the "empty nest," the physical changes their increasing years bring, and the stresses of retirement. However, the transitions of adolescence are especially varied and far-reaching. They profoundly affect the physical, cognitive, emotional, sexual, and social realms and reach beyond these as well.

Some of these transitions are **normative**, that is, almost everybody in a particular culture can expect to go through them at more or less the same point in their lifespan. Entering puberty, going on a first date, and graduating from high school are examples of normative transitions for American adolescents. Other transitions, while just as important, are more particular to the individual, or **idiosyncratic**. A serious illness, a move to a new town, a parental divorce—these do not happen to most adolescents, and if they do happen, it is at times that no one could have predicted in advance.

We should notice that a particular sort of transition may be normative at one stage of life, but idiosyncratic at others. Having to deal with the decline and death of a parent is a normative transition when it happens during middle age (Havighurst, 1972). Losing a parent while still an adolescent, however, would be an idiosyncratic transition. The impact would probably be greater, and would certainly be quite different, than if the loss had occurred at what is usually thought of as the normal point in the lifespan.

Even when a transition is normative for a particular stage, its timing can affect its impact. For example, in Chapter 3 we look at what happens when children enter puberty earlier or later than their peers. Another area where the timing of normative transitions alters their effects involves the different ways the school years can be structured. What difference does it make whether students leave elementary school after 5th grade for middle school, stay another year before going into junior high, or continue through 8th grade and go directly into high school? As we will see in Chapter 7, the way these transitions are timed has important effects on both self-esteem and academic performance (Eccles & Roeser, 2003; Seidman, Aber, & French, 2003; Simmons & Blyth, 1987).

Normative transitions Changes that most adolescents go through at roughly the same point in their development, such as puberty and entering high school.

Idiosyncratic transitions Changes that take place at unpredictable points during adolescence, such as a parental divorce or a serious illness.

Phases and Tasks

When we consider the question, "Who is an adolescent?" we should also look at the phases and tasks adolescents go through. Most American 7th graders, 10th graders, and college sophomores have a lot in common. They are probably in school, unmarried, and financially dependent on their families. They use language, especially current slang expressions, in similar ways. They are familiar with the same music groups, clothing brands, and snack foods (though their opinions of them may vary). And they are all labeled, and generally treated, as adolescents.

In other ways, of course, they differ widely. This shows up clearly whether we look at physical size, strength, and endurance; at relationships with peers and family members; at personal concerns; or at a long list of other characteristics. Those at the younger end are still close to childhood, while those at the older end are nearly adults.

Because of these differences, those who study adolescence usually see the period as having different phases or stages. **Early adolescence** lasts from around 11 to 14. **Middle adolescence** goes from about 15 to 18. **Late adolescence** extends from around 19 to 22 or later. Some researchers see this last phase as merging into another stage called *youth* (Keniston, 1970) or emerging adulthood (Arnett, 2000). In our society and many other technological societies, these phases fit closely with the division of education into middle or junior high school, high school, and college or university.

According to Robert Havighurst (1972), every period of the life cycle in a given culture brings its own specific **developmental tasks**. These are particular skills, attitudes, and social functions that people are expected to acquire or grow into at that point in their lives. Developmental tasks are set partly by the course of physical and psychological development and partly by society's demands.

During early adolescence, both the body and the mind go through rapid and dramatic changes. The most important developmental tasks involve adapting to these changes and the new social roles they bring, as well as accepting and learning to use one's new physique. In middle adolescence, the focus shifts to achieving psychological independence from parents, developing the ability to have close friendships, and working toward meaningful intimate, possibly sexual, relationships. The developmental tasks of late adolescence include preparing for marriage and family life, considering an economic career, and acquiring a mature set of values. These preparations help the person answer the crucial questions, "Who am I? What will I do with my life?" (Havighurst, 1972).

◄ **Learning Objective 1.4**
What are the three phases of adolescence and how are they linked to different tasks or goals?

Connect the **Dots...**

Make a list of important transitions you remember from your own adolescence. Which ones were normative and which were idiosyncratic? Which of the normative transitions took place at about the same age for you as for your friends and classmates, and which were earlier or later? How do you think the timing affected the way you experienced the transitions?

Early adolescence The period from ages 11 to 14 that roughly coincides with the middle or junior high school years.

Middle adolescence The period from ages 14 to 18 that roughly coincides with the high school years.

Late adolescence The period from ages 18 to 22 that roughly coincides with the college years, often referred to as *emerging adulthood*.

Developmental tasks The skills, attitudes, and social functions that a culture expects members to acquire at a particular point in their lives.

Inventionism The view that the concept of adolescence was promoted in the early 20th century as a way of setting off young people from the adult world.

Summing Up...

The boundaries of adolescence shift, depending on whether we are talking about physical, social, economic, or legal definitions. However we define it, adolescence is marked by major normative and idiosyncratic transitions. The timing of these transitions affects their impact on the individual teen. It is also useful to distinguish among early, middle, and late adolescence. Each is typically linked to particular developmental tasks.

ADOLESCENCE ACROSS HISTORY

Throughout history, people have had many different ways of thinking about and dealing with children and adolescents (Ariès, 1962). Even in the relatively brief history of the United States, approaches to adolescence have gone through major shifts as the society and economy changed (Elder, 1980; Hine, 1999; Kett, 1977).

Some scholars have claimed that the very idea of adolescence emerged as recently as the beginning of the 20th century. This view is known as **inventionism**. It sees laws that banned child labor and established compulsory education as aimed at deliberately setting young people apart from the adult world in a new way. This, it is said, was intended to keep them dependent and prevent them from competing with adults for jobs (Bakan, 1972; Lapsley, Enright, & Serlin, 1985; Musgrove, 1964).

Adolescence today has obviously changed a lot from what it was even 100 or 200 years ago, and it may be that inventionists have a point about the intention of child labor laws in the United States. Still, the historical record shows that earlier societies saw adolescence as a separate stage in development. As far back as our records go, people have treated those between the ages of puberty and full adulthood as a distinct group with its own characteristics and needs (Fox, 1978). The history of adolescence, for all its particularities, reveals some fascinating similarities across cultures and centuries.

Earlier Times

▶ **Learning Objective 1.5**
What are the major similarities and differences between adolescence in earlier times and today?

Some of our earliest information about adolescents comes to us from ancient Athens, in the 4th century BC. There, boys were trained in the three branches of learning—grammar, music, and gymnastics—from the time they reached puberty. When they turned 18, they became *ephebes*, took an oath of allegiance to the city-state, and started military training. After that, they could take part in political deliberations, but they were not considered full citizens until the age of 30 (Golden, 1990). It was also around this age that they usually married. Athenian girls, on the other hand, were educated at home and mostly learned how to manage a household (Katz, 1998). Their childhood ended at 15, when they became marriageable, but legally they remained minors, under the authority of men, their entire lives.

Greek philosophers such as Plato and his one-time pupil, Aristotle, were deeply interested in adolescents. Plato believed that children should study reading and writing from ages 7 to 10, literature from 10 to 13, and music from 13 to 16, because he felt that the abstract nature of music requires more advanced reasoning powers (*Laws* 7.794C–7.810A). As for Aristotle, he suggested dividing formal education into two phases, before and after *hebe*, or puberty, which he set at 14 (*Pol.*, 7.1336b36). He saw adolescence as a period in which the powers of reasoning only gradually become stronger than the passions (*Pol.* 7.1334b25). In his view,

> They [young people] are passionate, irascible, and apt to be carried away by their impulses . . . [T]he young are heated by Nature as drunken men by wine . . . Their lives are lived principally in hope, as hope is of the future and memory of the past; and while the future of youth is long, its past is short (*Rhe.* 12-4.1389a3–1390b12).

Adolescence in the Roman Empire, in the 1st to 3rd centuries AD, was similar in many ways to that in Athens 400 years earlier. Boys of 14 were eligible to marry, but they were not yet considered adults. At 16, they gave up the amulet that marked them as children of citizens and put on the toga worn by men. After a year of military training, they were full citizens (Wiedemann, 1989). Girls were considered marriageable at 12. As in Athens, they never officially became adults, since they stayed under the authority first of their fathers and then of their husbands throughout their lives (Néraudau, 1984).

Preindustrial Europe. Childhood and adolescence in preindustrial Europe are often described in dark terms. French historian Philippe Ariès (1962) asserted that Europeans from AD 1000 to 1700. saw children as tiny adults who deserved no special treatment. Because so many died in infancy and childhood, parents supposedly avoided any emotional involvement, neglecting and even abandoning their offspring (Badinter, 1980; Shorter, 1975). More recent research casts doubt on these claims (Alexandre–Bidon & Lett, 1999; Hanawalt, 1986). Records show that most children in the Middle Ages and Renaissance were just as coddled and cherished as in other eras. If, as happened all too often, they died in childhood, the loss was deeply mourned. In times of famine, parents often left their children at churches and monasteries, but they probably did so not to get rid of them, but to give them a better chance of survival (Boswell, 1988).

Adolescence in preindustrial Europe did have at least one very distinctive feature: **life-cycle service** (Ben–Amos, 1994), or the custom for young people to leave their families at an early age and spend the adolescent years in a different household (Mitterauer, 1992; Modell & Goodman, 1990). For children of peasants, this meant becoming a hired hand or household servant on a larger farm (Kleijwegt, 1991). In towns, boys were apprenticed to tradesmen or craftsmen, while girls became domestic servants or worked at spinning, weaving, and sewing (Alexandre–Bidon & Lett, 1999).

Among the upper classes, too, children were often sent to be raised in other households. This "cross-fostering" helped strengthen personal and political ties among noble families, who were often related by blood or marriage. In troubled times, cross-fostered children also served as hostages to keep unruly rivals in check. You might think twice about besieging your neighbor's castle if you knew your son was inside, at your neighbor's mercy.

Royalty had its own version of this custom. For political and dynastic reasons, princes and princesses were often betrothed or even married while extremely young, sometimes while still babies. The bride-to-be was then sent to her future husband's court to learn the language and customs of her future realm. For example, in 1396, King Richard II of England married Princess Isabella of France. He was 29, and she was 7 (Saul, 1997).

Rousseau and the Enlightenment. The way Western Europeans thought about childhood and adolescence began to change during the 18th century, as part of the intellectual movement called the Enlightenment. A major event in this shift was the publication in 1762 of *Emile* by French philosopher Jean-Jacques Rousseau [1712–1778]. Rousseau put forward the idea that childhood and adolescence are life stages that should be valued for themselves, not simply as waystations in the journey to adulthood. The goal of parents and educators should be to foster children's natural goodness and sensitivity.

Rousseau saw puberty as a particularly difficult time:

> . . . [M]an is not meant to remain a child. He leaves childhood behind him at the time ordained by nature; and this critical moment, short enough in itself, has far-reaching consequences.

> As the roaring of the waves precedes the tempest, so the murmur of rising passions announces this tumultuous change; a suppressed excitement warns us of the approaching danger. A change of temper, frequent outbreaks of anger, a perpetual stirring of the mind, make the child almost ungovernable. He becomes deaf to the voice he used to obey; he is a lion in a fever; he distrusts his keeper and refuses to be controlled
> —ROUSSEAU, 1762/1972, p. 172.

Rousseau's belief that adolescence is an especially tumultuous period was shared by German Romantic poets such as Goethe and Schiller, who spoke of its *Stürm und Drang*, or **storm and stress**. As we shall see, this idea continues to influence many people's thinking to this day.

19th Century America. In the early 1800s, the United States was mostly a nation of farmers. It was also a very young nation. In the census of 1810, fully half of the majority White population was 15 or younger, and more than two-thirds was 25 or younger (Inter-University Consortium, 2001). Most family farms were too small and unproductive to feed extra mouths or to make effective use of their labor. As a result, many children "hired out" when they reached adolescence or even earlier.

For some, this meant working on a larger nearby farm. Others were drawn to the growing factory towns and cities. Beginning in the 1830s, the bustling textile mills of Lowell, Massachusetts, sent recruiters throughout rural New England. They brought back young girls by the wagonload to work the looms.

Life-cycle service The custom in preindustrial Europe that sent young people to live and work away from their families during adolescence.

Storm and stress (in German, "Stürm und Drang") The belief that adolescence is necessarily a very tumultuous period.

▲ Until the reforms of the early 20th century, many American children and adolescents spent their days in bleak factories instead of in school.

▶ **Learning Objective 1.6**
Why was the 20th century called "The Age of Adolescence?"

For many adolescents, hiring out offered a welcome chance to quit their rural isolation and see something of the wider world. At the same time, they were able to make a welcome contribution to their families' economic survival and perhaps save up a little toward their own future. The price, however, was high—long, grueling days in hot, noisy, and terribly dangerous mills and factories.

The growing numbers of adolescents and young adults in towns and cities, beyond the supervision and control of their families, created social problems that included drunkenness and crime. Respectable citizens became alarmed. One wrote, "the class of a large city most dangerous to its property, morals, and its political life are the ignorant, destitute, untrained, and abandoned youth" (Brace, 1872, quoted in Kett, 1977, p. 89). Sunday schools, YMCAs and YWCAs, and moral education courses in public schools were promoted as ways to make up for inadequate parental influence (Kett, 1977).

We should not paint too bleak a picture. Most American teenagers in the 19th century did not spend 14 hours a day working in a dark Satanic mill or join the kids' division of an urban criminal gang like New York's Dead Rabbits. They worked, on the family farm or for local craftsmen and shopkeepers, but they also went to school. A small but growing proportion went on to college. Those still at home formed literary associations, organized dances, and staged performances of popular plays. They went on hay rides and sleigh rides, and got together at church socials, logging bees, quilting bees, and barn raisings (Kett, 1977). And, like teens in other eras, they and their friends certainly had long, earnest talks about what the future might hold for them.

20th Century America

Historians and social scientists have called the 20th century in the United States "The Age of Adolescence" (Kett, 1977; Tyack, 1990). At the beginning of the century, several factors combined to focus attention on those in the teenage years. One was a campaign by reformers to pass laws that restricted child labor and limited the number of hours those in their early teens could work (Kett, 1977). Another was the increasing complexity of modern industry. This called for a more educated workforce. In response, states began to pass laws that made school attendance compulsory. Not just elementary school children, but those of secondary school age as well, *had* to go to school (Tyack, 1990).

Education became known as the best path upward for the children of the working and lower middle classes. Of those 14 to 17, the proportion attending high school climbed dramatically. It grew from about 5% in 1890, to 35% in 1920, to 80% in 1950 (Elder, 1980). The high school years were promoted as a period of essential personal and social growth (Ueda, 1987), what Bruce Springsteen would later call the "glory days."

These developments helped raise **age stratification**, or defining groups on the basis of age, to a new level. Before, adolescents were either the youngest members of the adult workforce or the oldest pupils in schools that mixed children of widely different ages. Now, those between puberty and adulthood were set apart in institutions designed specifically for them (Modell & Goodman, 1990). Because society defined them as a separate group called *adolescents*, they began to see themselves that way. They scoured novels, such as Booth Tarkington's *Seventeen*, published in 1916, and, later, comic strips such as *Archie*, which first appeared in 1941, to learn how teens like themselves were supposed to look, act, talk, and think.

A New Focus on Teens. With the start of the 20th century, adolescence became the object of attention from social scientists [1844–1924]. A two-volume work called *Adolescence*, by psychologist G. Stanley Hall, had a powerful impact on fields as varied as psychology, child study, education, social work, and juvenile justice (Kett, 1977). Journalists and commentators also began paying attention to adolescence. Often, their remarks had the ever-popular theme, "What is wrong with today's kids?"

Age stratification The process of defining groups, such as adolescents, on the basis of their age and treating them differently.

In the 1920s, the "Jazz Age," books, articles, and movies about the excesses of "flaming youth," sprouted faster than speakeasies (Lindsay & Evans, 1925). Cheap cars like the Model T gave young people a new way to evade the watchful eye of grown-ups. Coeducation at high schools and colleges made pairing off easier and more fashionable. Smoking cigarettes and drinking bootleg gin became marks of sophistication. However, the reality was a lot tamer than sensational articles made it sound. When pollsters asked 1920s' adolescents about their views on sex, for example, they were more tolerant of necking and petting than their parents, but otherwise their attitudes were pretty conventional (Lee, 1970).

The "Roaring Twenties" came to a sudden end with an economic collapse that led to the Great Depression of the 1930s. Though the widespread poverty and hardship affected young people as much as anyone, the Depression also had an ironically positive side for some. With no jobs available even for skilled adults, teens were more likely to stay in high school and even to go on to college (Krug, 1971). Many were dismayed by the social problems and inequalities made so obvious by the Depression and became attracted to radical social ideas and political programs. The media, always eager for sensational stories about adolescents, portrayed them as fanatical Communists, called Reds (Buhle, Buhle, & Georgakas, 1998).

Just a few years later, in 1941, the Japanese attack on Pearl Harbor brought the United States into World War II. These same young people enlisted in the armed forces or went to work building ships, tanks, and planes, while their younger sisters and brothers collected newspapers, cans, and scrap metal for the war effort (Brokaw, 1998).

The Baby Boom. The years immediately after World War II saw an extraordinary "baby boom" take place in the United States. Couples who had put off having children because of the insecurities of the Depression and the war now made up for the time they had lost. The children of this boom began entering adolescence in the late 1950s. The effect was startling. During the 1960s the proportion of adolescents in the population increased by as much as 50% (Elder, 1980).

In most ways, this cresting wave of teens was not that different from those of a few years earlier, but that was not the way older Americans saw them. The usual worries about loose sexual morals were topped with concerns about illicit drugs and the pernicious effects of rock and roll. An influential minority of adolescents became active in political protests aimed at ending racial discrimination and opposing the war in Vietnam. This helped set the tone for what came to be called the Woodstock Generation, named for the 1969 rock festival.

In the years that followed, American adolescents seemed to focus less on reforming the world and more on material and career concerns. However, the desire to change things that seemed wrong did not vanish. Teenage girls became active in the women's movement, working to overturn sex discrimination in schools, the workplace, and society as a whole. Gay teens battled to have their right to be different recognized and respected. And adolescents of every variety became more deeply involved in volunteer work and service organizations (Youniss et al., 2002).

American Teens Today

It was the best of times, it was the worst of times, it was the age of wisdom, it was the age of foolishness, it was the epoch of belief, it was the epoch of incredulity, it was the season of Light, it was the season of Darkness, it was the spring of hope, it was the winter of despair . . .

▶ **Learning Objective 1.7**
What major issues do American teens face today?

This famous opening passage from Charles Dickens' *A Tale of Two Cities* was written to describe France just before the French Revolution of 1789. Dickens was making fun of the tendency to see the world around you in the starkest possible terms. This tendency is as alive today as it was in his time, and never is it more alive than when people discuss adolescence.

Here, for example, is a totally unscientific sample of newspaper headlines about adolescents during a single week:

Teens smoking, having sex, but in fewer numbers

Teen Doing Research in Alaska Shares Findings with Others via TV

Man is booked in teen sex case; Suspect met girl on Web

Three teens charged with manslaughter in fatal apartment crash

FIVE TEENS TO BE HONORED AS FUTURE BLACK HISTORY MAKERS

Teen working on mural to be donated to West Island Women's Shelter

ECSTASY USE MOVES FROM RAVE CROWD TO YOUNGER TEENS

Teen Charged With Rape Had Prior Sex Indictment

Teens Display Religious Trend, Report Shows

Teen retreats to boyfriend's house to escape stepfather's abuse

EXPERT DETAILS WARNING SIGNS OF SCHOOL VIOLENCE

Teen steroid abuse prompts new round of TV warnings

LEARNING-DISABLED TEEN HAS PERFECT SCORE ON ENTRANCE EXAM

Deaths of 16-year-old drivers down sharply under new law

VH1 uncovers racist "hatecore" rock

Help for those fighting anorexia

Teen pledges to bridge differences around the world

Teen convicted in fatal beating

Energetic teen group to lobby legislators

17-year-old is being called the next Michael Jordan

Some of the stories apparently hail the strengths of individual adolescents, by highlighting their achievements and involvement in the community. But the overall impression is one of sex, drugs, and violence. Not surprisingly, those same three factors play a major role in the stereotypes many adults have of adolescents (Adelson, 1979; Gilliam & Bales, 2001).

Families in Flux. If adults have trouble keeping up with what is happening with teens, one reason is that the world teens inhabit is changing so rapidly. Fads come and go, hot bands and television shows cool off and disappear, today's slang becomes yesterday's overnight. That sort of change is normal and expected. It was like that when you were 14, and when your parents were 14, and even in your grandparents' day. However, even while fashions fluctuated, the basic institutions stayed much the same from year to year. Today that is much less the case.

For a child, the most basic institution, the one that counts for the most, is the family. During the middle decades of the 20th century, for the White majority, the typical family was seen as a father who brought in the family income, a mother who managed the home, and two or three children. Many of these children lived in the same neighborhood and even the same house throughout childhood. Chances are, some cable channel in your community is still letting viewers enjoy that world by watching reruns (or re-re-reruns) of the hit show from the 1950s, *Leave It to Beaver*. Though a great many families, including many from poor and minority backgrounds, did not fit this description, it became the standard portrait of the American family.

Today, that sort of family is almost as hard to find as a mint 1956 Chevy. Divorce rates rose sharply between 1960 and 1980, as did the number of mothers who work outside the home. The proportion of single-parent families, whether the result of divorce or of childbearing outside of marriage, reached an all-time high (Hernandez,

1997). Nearly half of the parents of today's American teens will experience divorce, and teens will spend several years in a single-parent household (Hetherington, Henderson, & Reiss, 1999). Later, many of these teens will have to make a further adjustment, when they find themselves part of a blended family with a stepparent and stepsiblings. We will look more closely at the changing structure and role of the family in Chapter 5.

The Role of Peers. As family structure has changed, so has the importance of **peers**, or those who are of about the same age or level of development. American teens today spend twice as much time with their friends as with parents or other adults, even when classroom hours aren't counted (Brown, 2004; Larson & Verma, 1999). Teens share their interests with friends and look to them for information, advice, and support. For some, whose parents are absent either emotionally or in reality, peers can even become a sort of surrogate family (Brown & Larson, 2002).

The way teens get along with their peers, whether they are popular, rejected, or ignored, has a long-term impact on their mental health (Rubin, Bukowski, & Parker, 2006). Peers offer companionship and support, but often this comes at a price of conforming to others' attitudes about school, drugs, sex, and antisocial activity (Fergusson, Woodward, & Horwood, 1999).

Another byproduct of peer orientation is **consumerism**: having the "right" athletic shoes, bookbag, MP3 player, or inline skates can become terribly important (Bayot, 2003). One argument that has been made for school uniforms is that they ease the peer pressure students feel to show up at school wearing fashionable clothes they can't afford.

Peers—those people your own age—do not really form a single group during adolescence. Instead, there is an internal structure that changes in important ways across the adolescent years. How do teens find a small group of friends, a *clique*? Why do they become known as part of a larger group, a *crowd*? What effects do these associations have on the way they act and on their sense of who they are? These are some of the questions that are the focus of Chapter 6.

The Issue of Sexuality. American adolescents at the beginning of the 21st century are bombarded with sexual messages. Try to imagine a music video without sexual undertones. How about a movie or television show aimed at teens that has no double meanings, winks, or nudges? And the articles featured in girls' magazines? *He's taken, but he's perfect for me. Are you ready to go all the way? Find out your Sex IQ!*

Obviously, sexual maturation is a basic and universal feature of adolescence. What teens *do* with their maturing bodies, however, is not just a matter of their impulses, emotions, and physical sensations. They are strongly influenced by parents, peers, and the culture as a whole (Brown, Steele, & Walsh-Childers, 2002; Collins, 2005). In today's America, all three of these sources of influence deliver mixed and confusing messages.

Radio talk shows and magazine columnists proclaim that sexual fulfillment is a right and a duty. Meanwhile, sex education classes teach that the only proper way to prevent pregnancy is to abstain from sexual relations. Parents often seem to favor a policy of "Don't ask, don't tell." As for peers, the traditional double standard is still alive and kicking. A girl who is believed to be sexually active may be the target of snide jokes and insults, while a boy who is thought *not* to be sexually active may have his maturity and sexual orientation called into question by other teens.

There have been some positive changes in recent years (Call et al., 2002). The proportion of teens who become sexually active has leveled off, and those who are sexually active are more likely to use contraception (Ozer, Macdonald, & Irwin, 2002). However, American adolescents are still less likely to use contraception than European adolescents (Santelli, Morrow, Anderson, & Lindberg, 2006). Not surprisingly, they also have higher rates of pregnancy and abortion than European teens (Arnett, 2002a).

Peers Those who are of about the same age or level of development.

Consumerism A concern with having or getting the clothes, toys, and other stuff that are currently fashionable.

▲ Sexuality is a major theme in media presentations aimed at teens.

Connect the **Dots...**

Ask friends or relatives of earlier generations about their experiences as adolescents. How did they see their place in society as teens? What problems seemed particularly important? How did they act with parents and peers? How important were the media (music, radio, television) in their lives?

How do today's adolescents deal with the issue of sexuality? Given the risks of pregnancy and dangers of sexually transmitted diseases, why is it so hard to sell teens on the importance of "safe sex"? What role do social institutions, such as schools and government agencies, play in shaping current attitudes and behaviors? We will take a close look at these and many related questions in Chapter 12.

> **Summing Up...**
>
> Societies from ancient times to the present have given adolescents distinct social roles. Social, economic, technological, and population changes have led to dramatic shifts in the lives of adolescents, as well as in the worries adults expressed about adolescents. Issues of particular concern today include changes in family structure, the role of peers, and sexuality.

ADOLESCENTS IN A GLOBAL AGE

Our look at what adolescence has been like in the past can help us understand what it is today. It also gives us clues to what it may be like in years to come. It highlights some of the amazing opportunities and terrible dangers adolescents are likely to encounter in the new century and millennium.

Around the world, the experience of adolescence is changing, just as the world itself is changing (Arnett, 2002b; Larson, 2002). Economic and social factors, environmental problems, population trends, wars, disease—all these have a major impact on adolescents. As traditional ways of life are eroded and washed away by waves of social and economic change, the traditional place of adolescents within those ways of life vanishes as well. They are left adrift, searching for some new landfall that offers them a hope of solid ground.

Even if so many things are in flux, at least one thing is constant in every part of the world: Adolescence is a time of preparation for adulthood. How well are today's children being made ready to be tomorrow's adults? Will they be given the skills, knowledge, and attitudes they need to become good partners, friends, parents, and productive members of their particular society? It is not only their future that is at stake—the future of all of us depends on the answers to these questions. This chapter's "Applications in the Spotlight" looks at how global awareness and understanding can be promoted for adolescents.

Old, Young, and In-Between

▶ **Learning Objective 1.8**
How does the shape of a society's population pyramid affect its adolescents?

In the summer of 2005, the population of the world passed the 6.5 billion mark and is expected to climb to more than 9 billion by 2050 (United Nations, 2004). Of these 6.5 billion, one out of every three is a child or adolescent. But this figure, impressive as it is, tells only a small part of the story. The proportion of young people in the population as a whole varies enormously from one region to another. In the industrialized world, 22% of the population is younger than 18. In Africa and the Middle East, however, the figure is close to or even above one-half (Haub & Rogers, 2002). Table 1.2 makes it clear how much the age makeup varies in different parts of the world.

Many factors are responsible for this wide variation, including public health, nutrition, and medical care. In preindustrial societies, people have lots of babies and die young, resulting in a young population. As conditions improve, people live longer and many more babies survive to adulthood, which temporarily makes the population even younger. However, as parents see that their children are surviving, they stop having extra children as "insurance" and the birth rate falls off. As a result, fewer children are born, more adults survive to old age, and the population as a whole gets older (Fussell & Greene, 2002).

Table 1.2 Proportion of Children and Adolescents, by Region
The proportion of children and adolescents in the population varies widely across different regions in the world.

Region	Younger than 18 (in millions)	% of Total Population
Worldwide	2,147	35
Industrialized nations (North America, Western Europe, Japan)	191	22
Eastern Europe, former Soviet republics	130	27
East Asia (China, Indonesia, Philippines)	604	32
Latin America	195	38
South Asia (India, Pakistan, Bangladesh)	558	41
Middle East & North Africa	153	45
Sub-Saharan Africa	317	51

Source: Haub, C., & Rogers, M. (2002). *Kids Count International Data Sheet.* Washington, DC: Population Reference Bureau.

The Population Pyramid. Take a moment to study Figure 1.1 on page 18, which shows population pyramids for developing and developed countries. A **population pyramid** is a way of graphically illustrating the proportion of people in a society who fall into different age categories. The reason it is so important is that, in the last analysis, the whole of a

Applications in the Spotlight

Promoting Global Awareness and Understanding

Alongside the many similarities that link adolescents from different cultures around the world, an array of differences, some obvious and some quite subtle, distinguish them from one another. How can young people be helped to explore what makes them alike and to appreciate what makes them different? What attitudes, skills, and knowledge will prepare them to function more effectively in an increasingly interdependent world?

Programs to foster global education have a variety of goals, including encouraging students to:

recognize the common features of experiences and perspectives among their peers around the world;

see the diversity of experiences and perspectives among their peers as an opportunity to look at the world in new ways;

understand that multiple versions of ideas, experiences, and perspectives exist and can be mutually accepted and held side by side;

notice that what they have learned about their own community and culture has connections with the issues, realities, and dynamics of nations;

realize that finding out about the world is a generative process in which knowledge is constantly revised in the light of new information and insights (Rennebohm-Franz, 1996).

Achieving these goals means developing a general acquaintance with the major geographical and cultural areas of the world, studying at least one other culture in some depth, and learning how to find and evaluate information about global issues. Learning to recognize cultural stereotypes and biases is critical, as is becoming able to suspend judgment when confronted by information and opinions that are in conflict with one's own understanding and values (Czarra, 2002).

Only a relatively small number of teens can afford to go to another part of the world and live with a family there. However, there are ways to get acquainted with children from other cultures without actually visiting them. Programs that find penpals or "twin" schools in different countries have been around a long time. And, in recent years, the Internet has become an amazing tool for global education. For example, an organization called iEARN (International Education and Resource Network) links more than 15,000 schools in 100 countries via the World Wide Web, at http://www. iearn. org. Through iEARN, as many as *a million students a day* work together online. Their many different collaborative projects range from retelling and studying folktales from many cultures to analyzing the points of view, values, and decisions embodied in media coverage of controversial issues (iEARN, 2003).

Population pyramids A way of showing in graphic form the proportions of people in a society who fall into different age categories.

Figure 1.1 Population Pyramids: Developed and Developing Countries
Typical population pyramids for developed and developing countries.

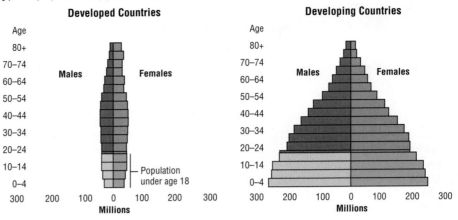

Source: World Population Prospects, 2005.

society depends economically on the group of people who are active and working. Those who work support those who are too old or sick to work, as well as nurture and train those who are still too young to work. In return, they expect that younger groups will take care of them when they retire. This "intergenerational contract" is basic to the way both individual families and society at large function (Fussell, 2002).

When half a country's population is children and teens who have to be fed, housed, clothed, and educated, however, the strain on already scarce resources is overwhelming. Potentially, as these young people reach working age, they will make valuable contributions to their country's economy, but only if they have been given the tools they need and if there is productive work for them to do. Those are both big "ifs." Experts estimate that over the next 50 years, developing countries will have to create almost 2 billion new jobs just to stay at their present levels of employment, which are not very good (Brown, Gardner, & Halweil, 1999).

Adolescents in developed societies that are steadily aging, such as those of Western Europe and North America, face a different set of problems and possibilities (Fussell, 2002). Because there are proportionately fewer, adolescents, they do not have to compete with each other so much for schooling, jobs, and other resources. However, their needs as a group may conflict with the needs of other groups, such as the elderly (Youniss et al., 2002). If elected officials feel they have to choose between supporting education for the young and pensions for the elderly, senior citizens voting in large numbers might well sway the outcome. This is not just a speculative possibility. More than one community has seen construction money for new schools and raises for underpaid teachers voted down by retired people who don't feel they can afford to pay higher taxes.

A Shrinking Globe

▶ **Learning Objective 1.9**
What is meant by *globalization*?

Our world is getting more populous. It is also, in many ways, getting smaller. Information, images, and ideas travel from continent to continent at the speed of light. Products of every sort move by overnight express. People whose parents would have counted a trip to their state capital as the event of the year swap tips on hotels, restaurants, and shops in Rome, Rio, Capetown, and Calcutta. A financial crisis in one region blights the hopes of people half a world away, and disease organisms that until recently were known only in remote, isolated areas strike new victims in every part of the globe.

The Process of Globalization. As we saw earlier in the chapter, this historic trend is known as *globalization* (Arnett, 2002b; Barber, 1995; Schlegel, 2000). Many factors contribute to globalization, including international trade, speedier travel and communications, economic interdependence, and mass migration from one region to another. Of course, all these factors have been around for a very long time. The Romans of 2,000 years ago traded with China, central Asia, and distant parts of Africa. Their empire eventually fell under pressure from waves of new immigrants. One hundred years ago, the telegraph and steamship made relations among widely separated parts of the world both stronger and more immediate. But, like a boulder rolling down a hillside, the process of globalization has continually picked up energy and speed. Today it is a fundamental force that affects the lives of everybody, and especially the lives of adolescents.

Why adolescents in particular? At least two reasons. First, adolescents are still in the process of finding a place for themselves in the world. This may mean they are less locked into traditional ways of doing things and more open to new ideas and possibilities. Second, the flip side of that is the fact that adolescents have not yet settled into an occupation and way of life, which may make them more vulnerable to the impact of social and economic change (Arnett, 2002b).

Branding the World. The most obvious way globalization shows up among teenagers around the world is in the form of consumer goods. Brand names rule, especially American brand names. French teens go after school for *un Macdo et un Coca* (translation: a Big Mac and a Coke). The latest films and music videos are as familiar in Singapore and Buenos Aires as in Toronto or Los Angeles. Children in Indonesia and Tunisia proudly wear Chicago Bulls t-shirts, even if they are not quite sure what game the Bulls play. Nike, Adidas, and other megabrands battle for a place on teenage feet on every continent.

This process is largely driven by commercial interests, of course. Manufacturers and distributors understand that if they can make their product a "must-have" among teens, they will sell a lot of products. Even the most elaborate marketing campaign, however, would flop unless it fit into the needs, desires, and inclinations of its target audience. What are those needs? Why do adolescents around the world so desperately want to wear Levis and Doc Martins, watch Buffy or whoever has replaced her, and listen to this year's hot rock or rap artist?

One of the biggest reasons is the glamorization of the West. The societies of Western Europe and North America, even with all their problems and inequalities, are easily the richest in the history of the world. Their cultural products—television, movies, music, popular magazines, and books—have enormous influence. Those in other parts of the world look at the picture the media presents of the West and see, for better or worse, their own future.

Often enough, the way adolescents in the West are shown in the media is absurdly distorted. American teens do not all have their own rooms with television, computer, and private phone line, a new car, and endless time at the beach. And most adolescents in other parts of the world know or suspect that. Even so, the thought that some *do* have those things, or some of those things, is hugely attractive. If you listen to the same bands or wear the same jeans as those fortunate few, you may get some of their good fortune to rub off on you.

The glamorization of the West is so powerful that clothing manufacturers in East Asia deliberately choose Western-sounding brand names, such as Giordano and Bossini, for their teen-oriented lines. In their advertisements, they show Western models wearing the clothes in Western locales. They even place these advertisements in Western magazines that are imported into Asia, to give Asian teens the (false) impression that the brands are hot in the West (Anonymous, 2001).

Signals to the Crowd

As anthropologist Alice Schlegel (2000) points out, consumer goods are far more than simply things to wear, look at, or listen to. They serve as cultural signals, or badges of membership in the group. How a teen dresses at a party or rock concert links her to others and lets them know she is one of them, even if she doesn't know them. These items give her safe topics to talk about. She has some common ground even with teens she's just met and may not have much else in common with. This is the function of brands of

▶ **Learning Objective 1.10**
Why do teens find it important to be in on current fashions?

Connect the Dots...

Imagine that you are part of a team from another galaxy that is studying the dominant lifeform on the planet Sol-III (otherwise known as Earth). Your assignment is to describe adolescents, using *only* the information you can gather from intercepted television and radio broadcasts. What do these adolescents look like? How do they spend their time? What are their main concerns? What is their place or role in the larger population?

clothing or cosmetics, the latest "cool" technology, movies, television shows, gossip about famous musicians, and the like: to makes it easier to initiate social interactions and keep them going. None of these things matter all that much, but that is exactly the point. People might disagree about important topics, so staying with the trivial is safer.

Trendy consumer goods, whether clothing, music, or video games, also carry implied messages about the way the world works. The continual innovation tells people that whatever is new is automatically better than everything old. If this year's fashionable shoes have rounded toes, that makes shoes with square or pointed toes "so-o-o-o last year!" (And by next year, the rounded toes will probably be branded as square.)

Along with this constant quest for whatever is new and hot goes the concept that people should be free to make their own choices. Why else would so many possibilities be made available to them? Because adolescents in most societies, Western or otherwise, are still largely under their parents' authority, having an area in which they feel free to choose can act as an antidote to their sense of powerlessness. When they make choices that are distinctive, different from what their parents would wear, watch, or listen to, they are announcing to others that they have that freedom to choose (Schlegel, 2000).

> **Summing Up...**
>
> One result of increasingly close ties among different regions of the world is that teens in many countries watch the same television shows, listen to the same music, play with the same electronic gadgets, and wear the same name brand clothes. This serves as a way to show that they know what is new and fashionable and to set themselves apart from those in older generations who don't.

WHERE IS ADOLESCENCE GOING?

▶ **Learning Objective 1.11**
What are the effects on teens of staying in school longer?

As we have already seen, larger social forces helped shape American adolescence during the 20th century and make it into what it is today. In response to changes in the economy, technology, and society as a whole, teens began to stay in school longer. They delayed entering the workplace full time. They put off getting married and having children (Larson, 2002).

One result of this was that teens remained dependent on their parents, economically, socially, and emotionally, longer than in earlier periods. At the same time, because they were grouped with their age-mates in schools and colleges, they began to be seen as separate, apart from grown-up society. This encouraged the growth of a "youth culture," with its own customs, slang, dress, and other characteristics. Similar developments took place in other industrialized societies in Western Europe and East Asia.

Today, similar social forces are at work in every part of the world. To make progress in the global economy, a society has to have an educated population. Its workers have to be at home with the complexities of modern technology. They need to be able to adapt to whatever complexities tomorrow's technology may bring. At the same time, the population explosion in developing countries threatens to overwhelm any economic advances they make (Fussell & Greene, 2002). Any lasting solutions to these problems will depend on the rising generations of adolescents.

Schooling for All?

A trend affecting adolescents worldwide is universal schooling. In the developed countries, practically every child goes through both primary and secondary school. About half then go on to some form of higher education (UNESCO, 2005). The picture is very different in developing countries. Primary education is now essentially universal in Asia and Latin America. In the Arab countries and sub-Saharan Africa, however, only four of five eligible children are in primary school, and among girls the proportion is even lower.

In most developing countries, about half the elementary school students go on to secondary school. This proportion has gone up substantially in recent years (UNESCO, 2005). Those in the other half quit school at 11 or 12. Generally, they cannot afford to go on and their families need the income they could bring in by working. As for college or other higher education, fewer than one in five students in the developing world goes on beyond high school. Even this is a sharp increase over the past (Fussell & Greene, 2002).

Those adolescents who see education as a route to a better life are more likely to stay in school and less likely to get stuck in dead-end jobs. They are also more likely to put off marriage and childbearing. This is especially true for girls. Education opens the way for them to get better paying jobs, and both school and work serve as alternatives to early marriage (Fussell & Greene, 2002). Because women with more education tend to have fewer but healthier children (Jejeebhoy, 1995), making school systems in the developing world more equal for boys and girls would also be a step toward dealing with the population crisis.

Moving to the City

Another social trend that is having a major impact on adolescents throughout the world is **urbanization**, or the trend for young people to move to the cities. In 1999, 47% of the world's people lived in urban areas. The United Nations (UN) projects that by 2030 the proportion of city dwellers will reach 60%, some 5 billion people. Almost all this massive urban growth will take place in the developing countries of Asia, Africa, and Latin America (UNICEF, 2007). Much of it is even more concentrated, in megacities of 10 million or more. Between the years 2000 and 2015, for example, Lagos, Nigeria is expected to grow from 13.4 million to 23.2 million, and Dhaka, Bangladesh, will grow from 12.3 million to 21.1 million (Brokerhoff, 2000). Some of this growth comes from new births, but a major factor is young people who leave the countryside for the city looking for education, work, and a better future (Gibson-Cline, 2000).

Adolescents who move to the city face many new challenges. They leave behind a support system of friends and extended family. Even if they have parents and siblings with them, dealing with a strange setting and culture puts a heavy psychological strain on them (Call et al., 2002). In China, for example, the centrality of family ties has been

▶ **Learning Objective 1.12**
What are the benefits and dangers of urbanization?

Urbanization   The trend for young people, especially those in developing countries, to leave the countryside and move to cities.

◀ Adolescents who grow up in the poorer quarters of cities in the developing world face huge challenges.

a core belief for many centuries. Today, however, urban teens have a weaker sense of family obligation than those still in the countryside (Fuligni & Zhang, 2004).

Urban life also poses serious health risks. The poorer areas of the new megacities usually lack adequate shelter, safe drinking water, and even the most basic sanitation. In the rush to industrialize, pollution controls are brushed aside. As a result, the air in cities of the developing world contains very high levels of dangerous pollutants (World Resources Institute, 2000). In overcrowded shantytowns, epidemics of infectious diseases are a constant danger (Gutiérrez & Kendall, 2000).

The city presents other dangers, too. Poor teens who lack the support of a social network easily fall prey to economic and sexual exploitation (Fussell & Greene, 2002). Worldwide, the number of prostituted children may be as high as 10 million, and it is estimated that a million more children are forced into the sex trade every year (Willis & Levy, 2002). Some are as young as 7 or 8. They are sold by their families, who may believe the promises of traffickers, or lured away, or simply abducted. Often they are smuggled across borders or passed from one criminal band to another. They are kept in line by their illegal status, by their own sense of shame, and by threats of beatings or worse. In many cases they are forced to work for nothing to pay off the "debts" they supposedly owe pimps and traffickers for their food, shelter, and clothing (UNICEF, 2002).

Virtuous and Vicious Cycles

▶ **Learning Objective 1.13 How do virtuous and vicious cycles work?**

Globalization involves much more than movies, music videos, and brand name jeans. As an economic phenomenon, it has altered the lives of billions of people in every corner of the world. More efficient transportation and communication, together with a political climate favorable to international trade, have woven developing countries that Americans used to consider remote into the fabric of the world economy (Weisbrot, Baker, Kraev, & Chen, 2002).

The results are dizzying. The "Japanese" car sold in the United States may have been assembled in Mexico from parts made in the United States, Canada, and elsewhere. The customer service operator you reach when you dial an 800 number may be around the corner from you, or may be in an office building in Ireland or India. The roses sold on the streets of North American cities on Valentine's Day were probably grown in Latin America. And those shirts on sale at your local mall were probably made in Bangladesh, Indonesia, or central Africa.

No one doubts that economic globalization has brought big benefits to some people in developing countries. For those positioned to take advantage of the changes in their local economy, it sets up a *virtuous cycle*. Well-paying jobs open up in technical, communications, management, and service fields. The growing middle class uses some of its increased income to give its children and adolescents better health care, education, and access to technology (Larson, 2002). As the adjoining article indicates, even the very poor often make heavy sacrifices to give their children a better chance in life.

Those teens whose families can afford to keep them in school longer also enter this virtuous cycle. They are more likely to believe they should be free to develop their particular talents and interests, instead of quickly settling into pre-ordained adult roles (Fussell & Greene, 2002). They arrive at adulthood with the intellectual, technical, and economic resources they need to profit from their opportunities. Young women as well as young men enter the working world, and they tend to wait longer before marrying. Once married, they have smaller families, which leaves them well placed to offer even more advantages to their own children.

Many more adolescents, however, fall into a *vicious cycle*. The children of rural or urban poverty, they may never enter school because their parents cannot afford to send them. If they do start school, they leave very early to help support their families (Larson, 2002). Many of them take dangerous or illegal jobs. Girls are even less likely than boys to continue their education (Mensch, Bruce, & Greene, 1998). Instead, girls are sent into domestic service, where they are prey to abuse and exploitation, or they start having babies at an early age (Bellamy, 2002).

India's Poor Bet Precious Sums on Private Schools
by Amy Waldman

MANUA, India — In this democracy of more than one billion people, an educational revolution is under way, its telltale signs the small children everywhere in uniforms and ties. From slums to villages, the march to private education, once reserved for the elite, is on.

On the four-mile stretch of road between this village in Bihar State, in the north, and the district capital, Hajipur, there are 17 private schools (called here "public" schools).

They range from the Moonlight Public School where, for 40 rupees a month, less than a dollar, 200 children learn in one long room that looks like an educational sweatshop, to the DAV School, which sits backed up to a banana grove and charges up to 150 rupees a month, or more than $3. Eleven months after opening, it already has 600 students from 27 villages.

There are at least 100 more private schools in Hajipur, a city of 300,000; hundreds more in Patna, the state capital; and tens of thousands more across India.

The schools, founded by former teachers, landowners, entrepreneurs, and others, and often of uneven quality, have capitalized on parental dismay over the even poorer quality of government schools. Parents say private education, particularly when English is the language of instruction, is their children's only hope for upward mobility.

Such hopes reflect a larger social change in India: a new certainty among many poor parents that if they provide the right education, neither caste nor class will be a barrier to their children's rise.

Even those with little cash to spare seek out these schools. Ram Babu Rai, who farms less than an acre and earns about 1,000 rupees a month ($22), working part time, sends one of his three sons to a private school here. Just sending one boy is a struggle, costing him 2,200 rupees a year ($49), including the 10-year-old's orange and navy blue uniform.

"With my little means, I have to manage my family," Mr. Rai said. "But still, I thought to spare some extra money for the boy, so he will do well in life." A member of the cowherders' caste, Mr. Rai dreams that his son will become a "big officer."

"Since ages, we are doing manual work," said Rehaman Sheik, 35, an illiterate plumber in the Dharavi slum of Bombay. "Why should they?" he said of his sons. "They should have a good profession."

To that end, he spends 400 rupees a month, just under $9, on school tuition and extras like uniforms, out of monthly earnings of 3,000 rupees. He also spends 200 rupees monthly on tutoring, a phenomenon common among parents of government and private school students alike.

SOURCE: "INDIA'S POOR BET PRECIOUS SUMS ON PRIVATE SCHOOLS," BY AMY WALDMAN. *THE NEW YORK TIMES*, NOVEMBER 15, 2003, PP. A1, A5. USED BY PERMISSION.

◀ Indian parents hope that a private school education will give their children upward mobility.

Because they don't have the lengthy and expensive education it takes to get better paying jobs, these adolescents are left behind by their countries' economic progress. Unless conditions change, for example, through programs that make education more accessible to all, their children will likely be left even further behind. This process creates an ever widening and socially dangerous gulf in developing countries between the well off and the poor (Fussell & Greene, 2002). The growing numbers of poor young people, and their growing desperation, pose a threat to the economic development that is the best hope for helping them escape their plight.

The Scourge of HIV/AIDS

▶ **Learning Objective 1.14**
How has the HIV pandemic affected adolescents in different parts of the world?

It is impossible to talk about the future of adolescents around the world without taking a clear-eyed look at the terrible problem of HIV/AIDS. More than 4 million children younger than 15 have died of AIDS since the epidemic began. In 2001 alone, an estimated 580,000 children younger than 15 died of AIDS-related illnesses (UNAIDS, 2001b). As of 2005, more than 2 million children younger than 15 were infected with HIV (UNICEF, 2007), and for those 15 to 24, more than 12 million are living with HIV/AIDS. Another 6,000 are being infected every day (UNAIDS, 2006). This is *half* of all new cases of HIV. The United States has been less affected than many parts of the world, but even so at least 40,000 young people have been infected and more than 10,000 have died of AIDS (NIAID, 2006).

Young people are especially vulnerable because of risky sexual behavior, illicit drug use, and ignorance about prevention. In sub-Saharan Africa, where the epidemic has been most devastating, fewer than three out of ten young people have any detailed knowledge about HIV (UNICEF, 2007). For example, in Mozambique, an island nation off the east coast of Africa, almost two-thirds of boys and three-quarters of girls 15 to 19 are not aware of *any* way to protect themselves (UNAIDS, 2001a).

The AIDS epidemic injures many more than it infects. Around the world, more than 15 million children and young people have lost their parents to AIDS (UNICEF, 2007). In sub-Saharan Africa alone, as many as 12 million children are AIDS orphans (UNAIDS, 2006). Millions more will join them in the next few years. The United Nations forecasts that the number of children orphaned by AIDS will *double* by 2010. In some countries, more than one of every five children will be an AIDS orphan (Wines, 2003). For now, this orphan crisis has had its worst impact in sub-Saharan Africa, but it will soon spread to other regions, such as the Caribbean and South Asia (UNAIDS, 2006).

AIDS also has a catastrophic effect on the economic health and future of affected regions. In Africa, some countries have already been set back in their economic development by as much as 50 years (Call et al., 2002). Some are expected to lose fully half their workforce to AIDS (Stephenson, 2000). These include many of the region's skilled workers, teachers, doctors, and administrators. As a result, even those teens who manage to escape AIDS infection themselves will grow up in countries where even the most basic resources for education, health care, and economic growth are in short supply.

Survival and Growth

▶ **Learning Objective 1.15**
What do adolescents need to survive and flourish?

For societies everywhere, their adolescents are the hope of the future. This is said so often that its meaning starts to wear thin, yet it is literally true. Nations and cultures will survive and grow only if today's and tomorrow's adolescents become active, productive adults. What will that take? What do adolescents need to make a successful passage to adulthood? And what can the larger society do to provide for those needs?

According to the Carnegie Council on Adolescent Development (1995),

> although new social circumstances have vastly altered the landscape for adolescent development, all adolescents continue to have fundamental human requirements that must be met if they are to grow up into healthy, constructive adults. All run the risk of diminished lives if these requirements are not met (p. 49).

These requirements fall into two categories. The first category is "basic survival skills" that all adolescents need, regardless of their life situation. These include:

an ongoing caring relationship with at least one adult;

social support systems (including families, schools, community institutions, health care);

social competence and life skills that allow them to make informed plans and choices about their future;

preparation to become active, contributing members of their communities and nations;

belief in a promising future with real economic and social opportunities to lead a decent life (Takanishi, 2000).

In the second category of requirements are qualities that have become particularly important with the globalization of the economy and the social and political changes that trend has brought. They include:

technical and analytic skills needed to take part in a high-technology, knowledge-rich international economy;

motivation for lifelong learning;

values to live peacefully in a diverse society;

ability to live with uncertainty and change (Takanishi, 2000).

Another way to look at what adolescents need for healthy development is shown in the article below.

As we study adolescents and the institutions that affect their survival and growth, we should keep these lists of requirements in mind. To what extent are social institutions helping adolescents to fulfill them? Do some institutions actually get in the way? What changes might be made—and at what cost—to make society more responsive to the basic needs of its next generation of adults?

Connect the **Dots...**

Consider the list of skills and attitudes today's adolescents need for healthy development. How did you yourself acquire those qualities? What people, settings, and experiences were especially helpful? Were there issues that held you back or got in your way? Can you think of ways to encourage these qualities in adolescents either from less-advantaged segments of our society or in less-developed countries?

What Do Adolescents Need for Healthy Development?

Developmental psychologists Jodie Roth and Jeanne Brooks-Gunn (2000) have devised a clever way to lay out the crucial factors that contribute to healthy adolescent development.

How do the settings in which adolescents live, study, and play enhance (and, in cases, impede) their well-being? The research on the often overlapping worlds of the teenager—the family, peer group, school, work, and neighborhood settings—shows the influence of these different settings.

The important aspects of the family setting are characterized by **TLC:**

TIME,

LIMIT setting, Listening, and Laughter

CONNECTEDNESS/Caring and Communication.

The influence of the peer group lies in **FRIENDs,** offering opportunities for

FRIENDSHIP, risks for not

RESISTING negative influences, chances for developing shared or new

INTERESTS,

EXAMPLES of different attitudes and behaviors (and their consequences), the influential power in

NUMBERS, and the danger of associating with

DEVIANT youth.

The **ABC's** of the school world include the importance of a developmentally

(Continued)

APPROPRIATE school environment for youth, particularly young adolescents, the influence of the

BEHAVIOR of others in the school, and the powerful role of

CONNECTION, to the institution of school as well as to teachers and other students.

The ideal adolescent **WORK**place would offer youth the chance to

WIDEN their horizons, particularly in terms of future careers, develop

ORGANIZATIONAL skills, learn about

RESPONSIBILITY, and gain valuable

KNOWLEDGE.

Source: "What Do Adolescents Need for Healthy Development?" by J. Roth and J. Brooks-Gunn. *Social Policy Report*, XIV (1), 1–11. Used by Permission.

Summing Up...

Economic progress around the world is linked to the spread of education and the migration of young people from the countryside to the city, but not everyone benefits equally. Many teens instead fall victim to economic and sexual exploitation. Another danger is HIV/AIDS, which damages the lives and futures of adolescents both through direct infection and through the loss of parents, family members, teachers, and others in the community.

SUMMARY

Learning Objective 1.1 What are the major themes of the book?

The themes of this textbook include:

An **ecological systems** approach that looks at the ways an adolescent's development affects, and is affected by, changes in the family, the peer group, the school, and broader social and cultural contexts.

The role of **stage-environment fit**, which concerns whether the systems that affect adolescents keep pace with their changing needs and capacities.

The influence of **cultural diversity** and **globalization** on adolescents around the world. Practical **applications** of social science knowledge for teens and those who deal with teens.

The benefits of becoming **educated consumers** of adolescent research by learning about the theories, methods, and basic findings in the field.

The potential for **positive development** among adolescents.

Learning Objective 1.2 What strategies will help you gain more from using the book?

Strategies that can help students learn and retain material more effectively include **active learning** and **deep processing**.

Where we say adolescence begins and ends depends on whether we are considering physical and sexual development, family relationships, educational rules, social customs, or legal codes.

Learning Objective 1.3 How are normative transitions different from idiosyncratic transitions?

Adolescents go through a variety of important transitions. Some transitions, such as puberty or a first date, are **normative**, in that everybody goes through them at roughly the same time. Others, such as moving to a new town or undergoing a parental divorce, are **idiosyncratic**, or particular to that adolescent.

Learning Objective 1.4 What are the three phases of adolescence and how are they linked to different tasks or goals?

Early adolescence lasts from around 11 to 14. **Middle adolescence** goes from about 15 to 18. **Late adolescence** extends from around 19 to 22 and blends into emerging adulthood. Each of these stages is linked to **developmental tasks** that teens are expected to carry through at that point in their lives.

Learning Objective 1.5 What are the major similarities and differences between adolescence in earlier times and today?

In different historical periods, adolescence has had many different as well as similar features. The view that the idea of adolescence emerged as recently as the beginning of the 20th century is known as **inventionism**.

Adolescent boys in ancient Greece and Rome were generally educated to be soldiers and citizens, while girls were trained to be wives and mothers. The Greek philosophers Plato and Aristotle pointed out that adolescents were neither still children nor yet adults and should be treated according to their own particular nature.

In preindustrial Europe, **life-cycle service** meant that many young people left their families to spend adolescence in a different household as apprentices and servants.

The 18th century philosopher Rousseau helped change European attitudes toward children and adolescents by his belief that they should be valued for themselves. He also portrayed adolescence as a time of great **storm and stress**. This idea became widely accepted and is still held by many, although evidence suggests it is a great exaggeration.

As America industrialized, during the 19th century, adolescents made up much of the workforce in the new factories and mills. As teens moved to the cities, where they were less supervised, fears of a "youth problem" led to child labor laws, social welfare organizations directed at young people, and compulsory school attendance.

Learning Objective 1.6 Why was the 20th century called "The Age of Adolescence?"

The 20th century in America has been called the "Age of Adolescence." High school attendance soared, and as teens spent more time with other teens, they began to see themselves as a separate group, with their own pastimes, slang, and ways of dressing. The Baby Boom that followed World War II led to a huge but temporary increase in the proportion of adolescents in the population beginning in the late 1950s. These developments helped raise **age stratification**, or defining groups on the basis of age, to a new level.

Learning Objective 1.7 What major issues do American teens face today?

Today's teens in America confront many social changes and issues. Changes in the ways families are made up, and especially the increase in single-parent families, have an important impact on teens. This is associated with the growing importance of **peers** and the byproduct of consumerism. Of the many troubling issues adolescents must grapple with, few are more urgent than the question of sexuality.

In an increasingly global age, many social and economic factors have a profound influence on how children experience adolescence and how it affects their lives.

Learning Objective 1.8 How does the shape of a society's population pyramid affect its adolescents?

The problems and possibilities that adolescents face are partly shaped by their place in the population. In less-developed economies, children and adolescents typically make up half or more of the population, and their needs place a huge burden on scarce resources. In developed societies, there are proportionally fewer teens, which may mean that their needs compete with those of other age groups and get less attention. A population pyramid graphically illustrates the proportion of people in a society who fall into different age categories.

Learning Objective 1.9 What is meant by globalization?

Learning Objective 1.10 Why do teens find it important to be in on current fashions?

Globalization has meant that ideas, fashions, music and arts, and social changes spread quickly among adolescents in different parts of the world. Wearing, doing, and listening to what is currently hot serve as signals to others that one is part of the group.

Learning Objective 1.11 What are the effects on teens of staying in school longer?

A cycle of social changes that affected American adolescents during the 20th century is having an impact on those in other societies around the world. As teens stay in school longer, they tend to put off marrying until later and have fewer children. Girls with more education enter the workforce in greater numbers and begin to see their social role in more egalitarian ways.

Learning Objective 1.12 What are the benefits and dangers of urbanization?

In less-developed societies, great numbers of adolescents migrate from the countryside to the city or to more developed nations. This urbanization offers many positive possibilities for growth, but also poses serious personal, social, and health risks.

Learning Objective 1.13 How do virtuous and vicious cycles work?

Learning Objective 1.14 How has the HIV pandemic affected adolescents in different parts of the world?

The worldwide epidemic of HIV/AIDS has particularly severe consequences for adolescents, especially in those regions, such as sub-Saharan Africa, that have been hardest hit.

Learning Objective 1.15 What do adolescents need to survive and flourish?

Adolescents are the hope of the future for every society. What they need to flourish is well known, but whether and how well those needs will be met is an unanswered question.

KEY TERMS

Ecological systems (4)	Positive development (5)	Middle adolescence (9)	Age stratification (12)
Stage-environment fit (5)	Active learning (6)	Late adolescence (9)	Peers (15)
Cultural diversity (5)	Deep processing (6)	Developmental tasks (9)	Consumerism (15)
Globalization (5)	Normative transitions (8)	Inventionism (9)	Population pyramid (17)
Applications (5)	Idiosyncratic transitions (8)	Life-cycle service (11)	Urbanization (21)
Educated consumers (5)	Early adolescence (9)	Storm and stress (11)	

Adolescence in Theory and Research

Y ou find yourself stranded in a remote area and you urgently need to build some kind of shelter. As you look around, you realize that almost anything, from mud and clay to palm fronds, tree limbs, and stones, might conceivably be usable. But where to start? To get on with the task, you need some way of deciding which materials are most likely to be useful and how to put them together. You also need to assure yourself that the materials you choose are dependable. If that tree limb you use as a ridgepole turns out to be weak or rotten, you might find the roof collapsing on top of you.

When we set out to construct an understanding of adolescents, the problems we face are similar. In principle, there is no limit to the number and kinds of facts we might gather. Does it matter what a particular teen had for breakfast today? The number and ages of his or her brothers and sisters? The presence of a toxic landfill a quarter mile down the road? The number of students in school classes? The position of the planets at the moment of the adolescent's birth?

To get anywhere in our study of adolescence, we need some way of deciding which facts are most likely to be useful and some guidance on how they fit together. This is a place where theories are helpful. Theories direct our attention to what the theory says is important information. They also alert us to what may be less important or useless. After we decide what information to collect, we need to gather it in ways that make us reasonably confident that it is accurate, objective, and dependable. This is the role of research methodology.

In the pages that follow, we take a familiarization tour of the leading theories about adolescence. We then consider different approaches and strategies social scientists use to find out about adolescence. What issues are raised by the ways research is conducted? And what do students need to know to become educated consumers of research evidence?

THEORIES ABOUT ADOLESCENCE

All of us have picked up a great many facts and observations about adolescence, and all of us have ideas about the subject that help give a structure or shape to what we have learned. Some of these ideas are very general:

- Adolescence happens to living beings, not to rocks or chairs.
- Adolescence comes after childhood and before adulthood.

And some may be fairly specific:

- Adolescents prefer strong sensations, such as loud music, bright colors, and spicy food.
- Adolescents have very unstable emotions, up one minute, down the next.

Ideas or statements of this sort help us connect new information to what we already know. They show us where something fits and alert us if it doesn't seem to fit anywhere. They also allow us to make predictions. Suppose you unintentionally hurt the feelings of a teenage friend. He or she exclaims, "I hate you! I never want to speak to you again!" Based on your understanding of the changeable emotions of adolescents, you may predict that if you apologize and explain, and then give your friend time to cool off, the relationship will soon return to normal.

When we have a number of statements or ideas about a subject that fit together logically, it is called a *theory*. People sometimes react negatively to the word, saying, "I don't need theories, I just want facts." However, we all use theories, and we all need them to make sense of the world. Theories help explain what we already know and help generate predictions about what we do not yet know. Like different filters on a camera lens, they offer ways of looking at the subject that make some features stand out and others fade into the background. They give us a clue to which facts are important and which are not.

Over the last century, some half a dozen formal theories about adolescence have had a major impact on thinking and research in the field. These theories differ in several ways, including:

what aspects of adolescent functioning they set out to explain;

what kinds of explanatory concepts they use;

how much importance they give to different sorts of causes or influences.

The latter is probably the most crucial. You have probably encountered it before, under the heading "nature or nurture" or "genetics or environment." On a closer look, it is a great deal more complicated than that (Larson, 2002; Lerner, 2006).

Consider some of the possible causes a theory of adolescence might appeal to. Adolescents are biological organisms with particular genetic and hormonal makeups. They are the successful product of countless generations of evolutionary history. They are the children of particular parents with their own backgrounds and ideas about child rearing. They live in a particular culture and historical period. They have their own unique sets of experiences and their own ways of understanding and reacting to those experiences. Which of these influences should we pay most attention to? How much weight, if any, should we give to the others? Each theoretical approach has its own variation on an answer to those questions.

In this section you will find an overview of the major theories about adolescence. Most of these approaches are considered in greater detail later on, when we look at the areas of adolescent functioning emphasized by each theory.

Biological and Evolutionary Theories

Adolescence as a scientific field got its start early in the 20th century, with the work of psychologist G. Stanley Hall [1844–1924]. Hall was deeply impressed by Charles Darwin's theory of evolution and by the related ideas of biologist Ernst Haeckel. Haeckel believed that the developing fetus recapitulates, or goes through stages that parallel, the evolutionary history of its species. In his massive two-volume work entitled *Adolescence*, Hall (1904) extended this theory of *recapitulationism* to claim that psychological development, under the control of genetic factors, recapitulates the stages of human history. Babies, in his view, recreate the psychology of the earliest humans, while children are like savages.

◀ **Learning Objective 2.1**
What assumptions do biological and evolutionary theories make about development?

Recapitulationism and Adolescents. Hall saw adolescents as recapitulating the psychology of early civilization. Like the heroes of Homer's epics, they are at the mercy of powerful and quickly changeable passions. They are capable of idealism and pettiness, of friendship and betrayal, of great hopefulness and deep despair. They are also, unlike children, becoming more sensitive to the influences around them. It is therefore urgent for the adult world to make sure they are surrounded only by wholesome influences.

Hall's theory fit well with the thinking of his time. This was the age of empires, when the major European powers (along with the United States) ruled the rest of the world. One defense of this imperialist program was the view that European-American civilization was the highest stage of human cultural evolution. Those who were still at lower stages ("savages") were like children who had to be guided and controlled by parents until they grew up. And if savages are seen as being like children, it is not much of a stretch to see children as being like savages. Hall's theory also influenced those who organized the Boy Scouts in the United States, who saw camping and hiking as a positive way for young adolescent boys to express their "savage" nature (Kett, 1977).

Scientists no longer take Hall's notion of recapitulationism seriously. However, his belief that adolescence is necessarily a turbulent period, filled with *storm and stress*, is still shared by many people, including teachers and parents (Buchanan et al., 1990; Gilliam & Bales, 2001). One current version says that adolescents are at the mercy of

▶ This illustration from *Two Little Savages* by E. T. Seton, a founder of the Boy Scouts, reflects G. Stanley Hall's belief that teens are like "savages."

"Ugh! Heap sassy"

"raging hormones" (Buchanan, Eccles, & Becker, 1992). As we shall see, current research gives little support to this idea.

Evolutionary Psychology. Hall insisted that adolescence had to be understood from the standpoint of evolution. This stance has regained prominence in recent years in the form of **evolutionary psychology** (Buss, 2005a), an approach that tries to understand how current characteristics and behaviors may have been influenced by evolutionary forces. The starting point for this approach is the Darwinian principle of **reproductive fitness**: If some characteristic that is influenced by genes makes it more likely that an individual will pass on his or her genes to offspring who survive, over time the genes for the characteristic will tend to become more widespread in the population. While evolutionary theory has focused mostly on physical characteristics, such as size and coloration, evolutionary psychologists suggest that it can be applied just as easily to psychological traits.

For example, let's suppose that a man who has sex with a lot of women has more children who survive than a man who has sex with only one woman. At the same time, suppose that a woman may improve the chances that *her* children survive if she finds a man who will stay with her and help support the children. Assuming these tendencies are influenced by genetic makeup (a big and controversial assumption), then over a great many generations such a difference would lead to men being more prone to promiscuity and women more inclined to caution and fidelity (Buss, 2005b).

Critics of this approach say that there is no way to show whether an account of this sort is correct (Gould, 2002). Even if all men were promiscuous and all women were monogamous, which is clearly not the case, this could still be, not genetic, but a culturally determined response to the fact that women become pregnant and men don't. And if it is genetic, how do we explain the Na culture of China, in which both men and women are promiscuous and fatherhood is an unknown concept (Hua, 2001)?

Evolutionary explanations have also been criticized for a tendency to drift into **biological determinism**. This is the notion that our genetic makeup dictates what we do. If that were the case, we might still be hunting game on the savannahs of East Africa, where the greatest part of our evolutionary history apparently took place (Stringer & McKie, 1996; Tattersall, 1997). However, as anthropologists have shown, human cultures and institutions vary widely.

Evolutionary psychology An approach that tries to understand how current characteristics and behaviors may have been influenced by evolutionary forces.

Reproductive fitness The Darwinian principle that genetic characteristics that make the survival of one's offspring more likely will gradually become more common in the population.

Biological determinism The idea that what we do is set or determined by our biological or genetic makeup.

Think, for example, of the variation in gender roles around the world and the dramatic ways in which those roles have changed in our own society over the last 100 or even 20 years. The rapid and accelerating pace of social and cultural change, as contrasted to the glacially slow working out of evolutionary processes, suggest that our evolved genetic structure makes possible a huge range of cultural and behavioral possibilities (Bandura, 1998; Gould, 2002). Whether and how those possibilities emerge can be seen as the result of a complex interplay of genetic background and the many levels of experience, both biological and cultural (Lickliter & Honeycutt, 2003).

Psychoanalytic Theories

Unless this is your first psychology course, you have almost certainly spent some time studying the psychoanalytic approach to human development and functioning. This approach had an enormous impact on thinking about psychology throughout the 20th century.

Sigmund Freud. The founder and chief theorist of the psychoanalytic approach was Sigmund Freud [1856–1939]. For Freud, the underlying goal of everything we do is to gratify one of the basic drives we are born with. Of these, the most important is the **libido**, or life-oriented drive, which includes hunger, thirst, and sexual urges (S. Freud, 1938).

In Freud's theory, children go through a regular, biologically based sequence of **psychosexual stages**, or the ways that the sex drive changes its source and target. With each of the first three stages—the *oral, anal,* and *phallic* stages—the source of the drive shifts from one region of the body to another, as does the kind of gratification the child seeks. The conflicts that arise, both within the child and between the child and external reality, also change with each stage.

Of particular importance is a conflict that stems from the phallic stage, the *Oedipus complex*. Named for the central figure of an ancient Greek myth, who unknowingly killed his father and married his mother, the **Oedipus complex** involves the child's passionate desire to have an exclusive sexual relationship with the parent of the opposite sex. This necessarily implies getting rid of the parent of the same sex. The Oedipal fantasy causes the child to fear punishment from the same-sex parent. This in turn leads the child to push these troubling desires out of consciousness and to form a close identification with the same-sex parent. Because Oedipus was a male, this set of events in girls is sometimes called the *Elektra complex*, after the legendary heroine who avenged the murder of her father by killing her guilty mother.

What follows, beginning about age 6, is a *latency* stage in which psychosexual conflicts are mostly kept unconscious. The sex drive is transformed into an urge to acquire physical, mental, and social skills. This delicate balance is upset, however, by the physical and hormonal changes of puberty, which initiate the *genital* stage.

During adolescence, childhood fantasies and conflicts reemerge from the unconscious. These are more urgent and troubling, because sexual maturation gives the adolescent the potential to turn them from fantasies into reality. This leads to a period of inner and outer turmoil that ends only when the adolescent separates emotionally from the parents and focuses his or her desires on a mature relationship with someone outside the family.

Freud never described his ideas about adolescence in detail, however, his theory was further developed by his daughter, Anna Freud [1895–1982], who had a distinguished career of her own, studying and treating children and adolescents. Among her important contributions was a description of how adolescents use certain **defense mechanisms**, or unconscious tools for controlling influences, to keep their burgeoning sexual impulses, and the anxieties they arouse, under control (A. Freud, 1936, 1958). One that is said to be especially common in adolescence is *intellectualization*. This involves taking concrete conflicts and recasting them as abstract issues that obscure the passions fueling them. For example, a teenager who is both drawn to and

◄ **Learning Objective 2.2**
What do psychoanalytic theorists see as the primary tasks of adolescence?

▲ Sigmund Freud, the founder of psychoanalysis, with his daughter Anna, herself a major psychoanalytic theorist.

Libido In Freud's theory, the life force that is responsible for such drives as hunger, thirst, and sex.

Psychosexual stages According to Freud, changes in the source and target of the sex drive during childhood and adolescence that create the oral, anal, phallic, latency, and genital stages.

Oedipus complex The period in which a child develops a desire to gain sexual possession of the opposite-sex parent and to eliminate the rival parent of the same sex; in girls, often referred to as the Elektra complex.

Defense mechanisms According to Anna Freud, unconscious tools for controlling sexual and other dangerous psychological impulses.

Connect the Dots...

What would Freud say is the most important emotional task of adolescence? If an adolescent does not seem to be carrying out that task successfully, what advice do you think a Freudian might give?

anxious about sexual activity might become deeply involved in a moral debate about chastity and free love.

Erik Erikson. Since Freud's day, many psychoanalytic theorists have seen a need to place less stress on the sex drive as such and to pay more attention to the effects of the child's social and cultural experiences (Westen, 2000). The most influential of these, especially in his account of adolescence, was Erik Erikson [1902–1994].

Erikson was born in Germany to a Danish mother. When he was in his mid-20s, he went to Vienna and trained in psychoanalysis with Anna Freud. The rise of Naziism drove him from Europe to the United States, where he spent the rest of his career as a child analyst, professor, and award-winning writer.

One of Erikson's most significant contributions was to point out that Freud's psychosexual stages are accompanied by **psychosocial stages**. At each point in development, new aspects of the person interact with the social environment to create distinctive conflicts or "crises" (Erikson, 1968). For example, the oral stage puts emphasis on taking in nourishment and stimulation from the outside. This dependency raises the issue of whether the infant can trust others to meet its needs. Erikson also widened the focus of the psychoanalytic stage approach. He differentiated Freud's last stage, the genital stage, which begins at puberty, into four successive stages. This yields a total of eight stages across the entire lifespan. These stages and their corresponding issues or crises are shown in Table 2.1.

In his discussions of adolescence, Erikson points out that puberty confronts children with many linked challenges. They must cope with the emergence of new sexual urges and possibilities; come to terms with a rapidly changing body and mind; and deal with the changed way others treat them, no longer as children but not exactly as adults either. All of these raise the crucial questions, "Who am I? What is my place in the world? What do I believe and stand for? Where do I want to go in life?"

Table 2.1   Erikson's Stages of Psychosocial Development
The eight stages of psychosocial development according to Erikson.

Age	Stage/Psychosocial Crisis	Important Events and Influences
0–1	Trust vs. Mistrust	Babies have to trust others to meet their basic needs. If caregivers are unresponsive or inconsistent, the baby may come to mistrust others.
1–2	Autonomy vs. Shame and Doubt	Toddlers learn to take care of themselves, for example, through toilet training. Failure may lead to feelings of shame and incompetence.
3–6	Initiative vs. Guilt	As children take on new activities that may be beyond their capacity, they may come into conflict with parents, leading to feelings of guilt.
6–12	Industry vs. Inferiority	Mastery of academic and social skills leads to self-assurance, but failure creates feelings of inferiority.
12–20	Identity vs. Role Confusion	Adolescents must grapple with and solve issues of personal, social, and occupational identity. Otherwise, they remain confused about their looming adult roles.
20–40	Intimacy vs. Isolation	The priority is forming intimate relationships with friends and partners. Failure leads to a sense of loneliness and isolation.
40–65	Generativity vs. Stagnation	Adults face the task of being productive in their work and supportive to their families. Failure results in a stagnant, self-centered existence.
65–	Ego Integrity vs. Despair	In old age, the person looks back either on a meaningful, productive life or on one of unfulfilled promises and unrealized goals.

Psychosocial stages For Erikson, distinctive ways that developmental changes in the child, adolescent, or adult interact with the social environment to make particular issues more salient.

For Erikson, the most important developmental task of adolescence is to grapple with and ultimately answer these questions. If successful, the adolescent emerges with a firmly grounded sense of identity. The alternative is a sense of confusion about who one is and the part one plays in the scheme of things (Erikson, 1968). We will examine Erikson's theory in greater detail when we take up the issue of identity and the self in Chapter 11.

Cognitive Theories

The physical changes of adolescence are the most easily noticed, followed closely by social and emotional changes. Just as important, but less obvious both to the adolescent and to others, are the ways the adolescent's thinking, or cognition, develops. These changes have been the focus of intensive study by many theorists and researchers.

During the 20th century, the giant in the field of cognitive development was Swiss psychologist Jean Piaget [1896–1980]. Piaget maintained that we do not simply absorb information, instead, we actively work to *construct* an understanding of the world. As we do so, the logical structures that support our thinking change in regular, predictable ways (Piaget & Inhelder, 1969). This progression creates a sequence of four **cognitive stages**. Each of these represents a qualitatively different way of understanding. These stages are outlined in Table 2.2.

The last stage of cognitive development, according to Piaget, is the stage of **formal operations**, which usually begins to appear at around age 12. The advances of this stage give the adolescent new powers to think abstractly, to approach problems more systematically, and to imagine hypothetical possibilities. The implications of these changes for intellectual, social, and moral development are explored in Chapter 4.

Another theorist whose contributions continue to influence thinking about cognitive development is the Russian psychologist Lev Vygotsky [1896–1934]. Vygotsky, who died at the tragically young age of 37, was particularly interested in the way social relationships affect the progress of thinking abilities (Vygotsky, 1962). Formal schooling is important, of course, but so are the practical tasks of everyday life. An adolescent who works to solve a problem cooperatively with peers will probably be intellectually challenged at a level that is difficult but not *too* difficult (Rogoff, 1998).

For Vygotsky, the central feature of cognitive development is acquiring the ability to use the intellectual inventions and tools of one's culture. The chief of these is language, but approaches to logic, math, and memory are important, too (Tappan, 1998). For example, children in our culture often learn math with the help of a digital calculator. In another culture children may be taught by means of an abacus. Their thinking may differ in detail, but in terms of the underlying logic of arithmetic, both groups will be effective in dealing with their particular cultural environment. We will look more closely at Vygotsky's ideas in Chapter 4.

A more recent approach to how we think, **information processing**, is inspired by the analogy of the digital computer (Turing, 1963). In simplest terms, information enters the system through various channels, such as vision, hearing, and touch. It is

▲ Adolescence is a period in which questions of "Who am I?" come to the fore.

◀ **Learning Objective 2.3**
What aspect of adolescent development is the greatest concern of cognitive theories?

Cognitive stages For Piaget, different ways of thinking about and building an understanding of the world.

Formal operations The stage at which adolescents gain new resources for logical and abstract thought.

Information processing The ways information enters the person's cognitive system, gets processed, and is stored for future use.

Table 2.2   Piaget's Stages of Cognitive Development
The four stages of cognitive development according to Piaget.

Stage	Ages	Characteristics
Sensorimotor	0–2	Exploration through direct sensory and motor activities. Development of object permanence.
Preoperational	2–6	Use of symbols, such as words and images. Egocentrism.
Concrete operations	6–12	Logical thought about concrete objects. Development of conservation.
Formal operations	12–	Abstract and hypothetical reasoning.

▶ Vygotsky stressed the way working together with others contributes to intellectual development.

attended to, processed, compared with other information already in the system, and stored. The system may then generate an output (Logan, 2000).

For example, you see and notice something dark and round in your salad. You compare the information about it with what you already know about things that may show up in salads. If it matches the characteristics of an olive, you output the response of eating it. If, on the other hand, it matches the characteristics of a dead bug, you output the verbal response, "Yuck!" If you identify it as an olive and start to eat it, and *then* realize that it matches the characteristics of a dead bug, your output will probably be even more extreme.

The information processing approach began as an attempt to chart the complex elements involved when we think about and know things, recognize, remember, and make decisions. More recently, theorists have also looked at the ways these elements develop. How do they change from childhood, through adolescence, into adulthood? There is a growing body of evidence that the maturation of the brain during adolescence is associated with changes in cognitive ability (Keating, 2004; Spear, 2000). Adolescents also improve markedly in memory, in background knowledge, in the strategies they use to solve problems, and in their awareness of their own thinking processes, or **metacognition** (Keating, 1990, 2004). These changes are examined in more detail in Chapter 3. Developmental theory in the classroom is highlighted in this chapter's Applications in the Spotlight.

Learning and Social Cognitive Theories

▶ **Learning Objective 2.4**
Where do learning and social cognitive theories expect to find the major source of influence on behavior?

The ways we are likely to act in the future are affected by the consequences of our actions. If your friend looks upset after you use a crude expression, you will probably watch your language more carefully next time you are together. The ways we are likely to act in the future are also affected by the consequences we see others receive for their actions. If you overhear a classmate say a cheery "Good morning!" to your usually grumpy professor and see the professor smile in response, you may well start greeting the professor yourself.

The first of these processes, changes in response to the consequences of one's own actions, is the focus of learning or *conditioning* theory. The second, changes as a result of what we observe others do, is a major concern of *social cognitive* theory. These theories are similar in putting great emphasis on the role of rewards and punishments from outside. They are also not concerned with development as such. Instead, the

Metacognition The ability to be aware of one's own thinking processes and to develop more effective ways of using them.

Developmental Theory and Classroom Practice

What is the point of studying all these theories about adolescence? Isn't it practical experience that really matters? Certainly many classroom teachers believe that they have learned more about teaching, learning, and child development from their work than from formal schooling (Richardson, 1996). But what exactly do they think they have learned, how closely do their beliefs agree with research findings, and what are the implications for their students?

These questions were recently discussed in a paper by educational psychologists Denise Daniels and Lee Shumow (2003). They point out that many prospective and practicing teachers in the United States see ability as a major cause of student achievement and believe that a student's ability is a fixed, innate characteristic (Dweck, 1999; Moje & Wade, 1997; Stipek, 2002). In other words, if you do well in school, it is because you were born smart, and if you don't do well, it is because you *weren't* born smart. Many teachers also see the family environment as a major cause of student achievement (National Institute on Student Achievement, Curriculum, and Assessment, 1999). Because neither of these factors can be affected by what the teacher does in

the classroom, those who hold these beliefs, not surprisingly, often feel ineffectual and focus their efforts on classroom control (Midgley, Feldlaufer, & Eccles, 1989).

At the other end of the spectrum, many teachers lean toward a behaviorist perspective. They see their primary role as drilling students in content and basic skills. To accomplish this, they favor extrinsic rewards and penalties as motivational tools (Pajares, 1992; Richardson, 1996). One reason these attitudes are so widespread and persistent is that in a sense, they work. That is, if you define success as getting more of your students to memorize more of the material in the workbook, offering gift certificates at a local fast food outlet as a reward for high scores will probably pay off. On the down side, students in classrooms that operate on this basis often have lower motivation, weaker feelings of competence, and more negative attitudes toward school (Stipek, 2002).

The most important point Daniels and Shumow make is that the way teachers think about their students has a direct effect on how they see their own role, what they do in the classroom, and what they hope to accomplish. As Table 2-A.1 illustrates, the

Table 2-A.1 Views of Child, Teacher Qualities, and Classroom Practices
The qualities that are valued in children and teachers and the way the classroom is run depend largely on the way an educational community thinks about children.

Hypothesized relations between views of child, teacher qualities, and classroom practices			
Views of child	**Valued qualities of teacher (rule)**	**Typical classroom practices**	**Valued qualities of child in school**
Fixed ability	Instructor	Ability groups	Academic achievement
Maturationist	Observer, follower	Prepared classroom, play, exploration	Intuition, self-directed efforts, readiness
Behaviorist	Authority, instructional skills, content knowledge	Didactic instruction, isolated practice, rewards, competition	Knowledge of facts, basic skills, effort
Constructivist (Piaget)	Collaborator, guide, architect, knowledge of cognitive development	Child-choice, guided discovery, cooperative learning	Critical thinking, problem-solving, intrinsic motivation
Social constructivist (Vygotsky)	Consultant, knowledge of cultural and psychological tools and children's domain-specific thinking, intersubjectivity	Community of learners, instructional conversation, authentic tasks	Cultural literacy, collaboration, contribution, metacognition, systematic habits of mind
Personality or stage	Diagnostician, remediator or hands-off	Differential treatment of students	Positive social characteristics
Family influence	Rule model, reporter to parents, knowledge of social learning	Academic emphasis, rewards for good behavior	Achievement, proper social behavior, self-respect
School relations	Nurturer, parent consultant/resource, knowledge of social development	Student-centered, positive classroom climate, social skills curriculum, cooperative learning	Social competence, self-regulation, healthy school adjustment
Cultural influence or ecological	Liaison with parents and community, knowledge of diverse learners, cultural sensitivity, self-aware (biases)	Parent and community involvement, out-of-school activities, cultural instruction	Connectedness, social cognition, cultural awareness, adaptive habits of coping

Views are not distinct, sequential, or exhaustive.

Source: "Child Development and Classroom Teachings," by D. H. Daniels & L. Shumow. *Journal of Adolescent Health, 31,* 122–135. Used by permission.

way that teachers think about their students is directly linked to the theory of child development they find most convincing.

It is understandable that so many prospective teachers adopt either a fixed ability or a behaviorist approach (or occasionally, both at once). These views are part of the commonsense understanding of education in America (Stevenson & Stigler, 1992). That is not to say they are mistaken, but it doesn't mean they are right, either. Those who intend to work with adolescents, in the classroom or in other settings, will have a better chance of being effective and accomplishing their goals if they recognize the implications of what they do. They will understand these implications better if they are familiar with a variety of developmental perspectives and the educational practices that follow from them (Patrick & Pintrich, 2002).

mechanisms that change behavior are seen as basically the same throughout the life-span, from infancy onward.

For much of the 20th century, the most influential approach to basic learning was the **operant conditioning** theory of B. F. Skinner [1904–1990]. In operant conditioning, a behavior that is followed by a *reinforcement*, or, in common-sense terms, a *reward*, becomes more probable. A behavior that is not reinforced gradually becomes less probable, and one that is punished may be suppressed right away (Skinner, 1953). For example, while crossing campus you pass several students whose faces are familiar. You smile at each one. Some smile back, some give no response, and one scowls at you. Next time you are more likely to smile at those who smiled back, or reinforced your smile, than at those who did not reinforce you. As for the one who scowled at you, you certainly won't smile next time and may even look away as you walk past.

Conditioning psychologists suggest that when we try to understand some person's behavior, we should look first at the consequences or reinforcements. Suppose a student is often disruptive in class, in spite of repeated punishments. Is the attention the student receives from classmates serving as a reinforcement? If so, the teacher can try to convince other students to ignore the disruptive behavior, thus removing that source of reinforcement, and at the same time give the problem student other, *nondisruptive* ways to gain attention.

Social cognitive theory (Bandura, 1986, 1997, 2006) focuses on the ways our thoughts and actions are affected by our social environment. We watch what others do, we notice how they react to what we do, and we listen to what they say, about themselves, about us, and about others. Any of this information may change how we think and what we do. A high school freshman in September will probably pay a lot of attention to how juniors and seniors dress, talk, and act. If an influential senior makes a negative comment about teens who wear bright colors, the freshman may well decide to leave that emerald green sweater in the closet until St. Patrick's Day.

Operant conditioning A basic form of learning in which the likelihood of a behavior being repeated is affected by its consequences.

Social cognitive theory An approach that sees observing what others do and what happens to them as important ways of learning.

▶ Social cognitive theory points out ways teens are influenced by the actions and choices of others.

Learning by observation has many practical advantages over direct conditioning. It means we learn from others' mistakes as well as from their fortunate discoveries. Imagine if surgeons had to learn their skills by trial and error! In a sense, all of culture is a matter of observational learning, from Aesop's fables to the descriptions of research results in this book. We learn from what others have done and change our future behavior without having to go through the tedious and possibly dangerous process of learning it directly.

In recent years, social cognitive theory has devoted much attention to the role of internal personal factors that mediate between what the person does and how the environment responds. In particular, self-efficacy, the belief that you have what it takes to master a particular task, makes it more likely that you will try the task and put more effort into succeeding (Bandura, 1997). We will look more closely at the role of self-efficacy in Chapter 9, which deals with issues of achievement.

Social and Anthropological Theories

Adolescents, like everyone else, live embedded in a matrix of social groups. These groups form concentric circles that range in size from the immediate and extended family to neighborhoods, subcultures, cultures, social classes, and societies. Many social scientists have pointed to these social groups as powerful influences in determining how adolescence is experienced and what its later effects are likely to be.

Anthropologists have long studied the question of how adolescence is similar or different from one culture to the next (Schlegel & Barry, 1991). The towering figures in the field were Margaret Mead [1901–1978] and Ruth Benedict [1887–1948]. At the very beginning of her long career, Mead set out to discover if adolescence is necessarily a period of storm and stress, as Hall and many others believed. Her fieldwork in the South Pacific convinced her that Hall was wrong, that it was the attitude and institutions of society that made adolescence either turbulent and stressful or calm and peaceful (Mead, 1928).

In a similar vein, Benedict (1934) drew a distinction between *continuous societies*, in which children gradually and peacefully take on adult roles, and *discontinuous societies*, such as our own, in which there are abrupt and stressful transitions from adolescence to adulthood. The theories and research of Mead, Benedict, and more recent anthropologists are presented in more detail in Chapter 8, when we examine the role of culture in adolescence.

Ecological and Developmental Systems Theories

The effects of the cultural and social environment were also a central concern for Urie Bronfenbrenner [1917–2005]. In his **ecological theory** of development (1979; Bronfenbrenner & Morris, 2006), Bronfenbrenner pointed out that each level of social group in which the developing person functions can be thought of as a system that influences, and is influenced by, systems at other levels. To illustrate this point, an adolescent's family may want him or her to get an excellent education, but what if officials in the town where they live decide to cut taxes rather than pay for superior local schools? If the parents are upset enough by this, they may help organize other parents and influence town officials to change their orientation.

As a rule, the various factors that influence adolescent development are parceled out to specialists in different areas of research. Geneticists study the impact of genes, biologists study physical development, endocrinologists study the effects of hormones, psychologists study mental states and behavior, sociologists study institutions such as families and communities, and so on. How can all these different perspectives be fit together to form a single coherent picture of adolescence?

Developmental systems theory (Lerner, 2002, 2006; Lerner & Castellino, 2002) stresses that development has to be thought of as systematic change in which the adolescent is the center of a network of interacting influences and plays an active role in

Connect the Dots...

Suppose an adolescent is developing problems, such as poor school performance, substance use, or aggressiveness. If you were a social cognitive psychologist, where would you be likely to look first for an explanation of these problems? Why?

◄ **Learning Objective 2.5**
What is the central focus of social and anthropological theories of adolescence?

◄ **Learning Objective 2.6**
How do adolescents interact with the contexts and influences that affect them?

Ecological theory
Bronfenbrenner's view of development, which focuses on the ways an adolescent's social settings interact to influence development.

Developmental systems theory
Lerner's approach, which emphasizes the ways the adolescent plays an active role in dealing with social systems.

Figure 2.1   Lerner's Developmental-Contextual Model of Adolescence
A diagram of Lerner's developmental-contextual model of adolescence.

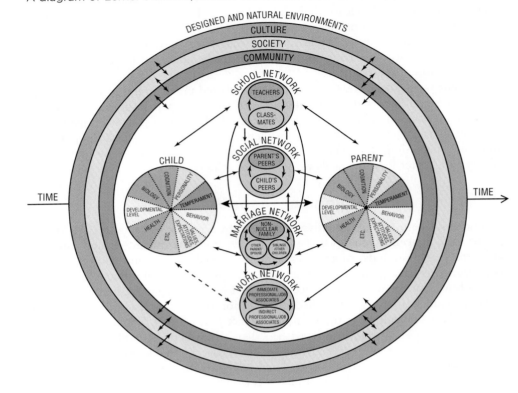

Source: Lerner & Castellino, 2002.

his or her own development. For example, skin color is a genetic characteristic. Discrimination on the basis of skin color is a result of social beliefs and social institutions. The way a particular adolescent reacts to being the target of discrimination will be influenced by the attitudes of parents, peers, teachers, and religious leaders, as well as by individual experiences and broader social forces. Figure 2.1 diagrams how these and other levels of influence affect one another.

Summing Up...

Theories help us make sense of the information we have about a subject and point us toward new information. Some theories about adolescence stress the role of biology and genetics, others focus on emotional development (psychoanalytic theory); the development of thinking (Piaget and Vygotsky); the importance of learning, whether direct or by observation; the role of an adolescent's society and culture; and the ways all these different systems interact on, and are acted on, by the adolescent.

FINDING OUT ABOUT ADOLESCENCE: THE SCIENTIFIC APPROACH

As we saw at the beginning of the chapter, all of us know, or think we know, many things about adolescence, just as we know many things about ourselves and the world in general. But *how* do we know? And if there is something we don't know, how do we find out?

Suppose you meet a 17-year-old who tells you her mother is her best friend. Afterwards, you find yourself wondering about this. Is it a sign of good mental health when a teenager is very close to her mother? Or does it perhaps indicate a problem? How do you decide?

Among other ways of reaching a conclusion, you might:

- go with your "gut feeling" or intuition;
- remember a relevant saying you learned from your parents or others;
- think about people you have known and try to draw some conclusion from what you know about their experiences;
- seek out an authority, such as a philosopher or religious thinker, a poet or novelist, the author of a self-help book, or even someone who gives advice on a television talk show.

All these ways of knowing have a long history and tradition, and all of them can lead us to valuable insights. When you get to know characters in a novel, film, or personal memoir, you may come away convinced that you understand these people, their thoughts and feelings, and what went into making them what they became. You may identify with them and believe that what you learned about them has helped you to understand yourself better, too. Even if you find them very different from you, getting to know them may enlarge your understanding of our common humanity. In a similar way, the wisdom of the past may be a summary of what countless generations of our ancestors learned from their life experiences. Intuition may well tap observations and ways of understanding that complement our rational thoughts (Gladwell, 2005).

However, the emotional power of literary works, the venerability of traditional wisdom, and the directness of intuition all have some important limitations. One of the biggest limitations is that they are subjective—they are a matter of personal feeling and opinion.

In his novel, *Dombey and Son*, Charles Dickens created a memorable and moving portrait of a child rejected by her father. Dickens had experienced painful rejection in his own childhood, and he possessed a fervent and sympathetic imagination. We put down his book (or at least, I did) with the feeling that we have gained a deeper understanding of how a child takes in rejection and what some of its effects are. But how can we be sure? What if the description Dickens gives is wrong or distorted? What if it is accurate only for certain kinds of children and parents, or certain societies and historical periods?

Say we both see the same film. You come away convinced that it is pretentious nonsense. I'm sure it's a masterpiece. Who is right? You? Me? Both of us? Neither? There is no obviously good way to choose. We could look up reviews of the film, but what if the critics disagree? We have the same problem all over again.

This does not mean that the critics, or the authorities, or the old sayings, are wrong, but how do you know whether they are or not? Whichever view I go with, if yours is different, we have no clear way to decide. At best we will probably finish by "agreeing to disagree" and leaving the question unresolved. At worst, those who are willing to be more aggressive may manage to impose their views on the others.

About 400 years ago, a different way of knowing began to gain influence in Western thought. Thinkers such as Copernicus, Bacon, Harvey, and Galileo helped develop and advocate what came to be known as the *scientific approach*. This approach had its earliest successes in the physical realm, in such fields as astronomy, physics, and chemistry. Gradually, investigators began to use it to study people and societies as well. This was the starting point of psychology, sociology, anthropology, and the other disciplines now called the **social sciences**.

"Science" is one of the most potent ideas in the collective thinking of our contemporary civilization. It is also one of the most misunderstood. When the movies or television need to depict a scientist, he (even today, it is still more often than not a "he") is typically shown wearing a white lab coat and fiddling with shiny, sinister apparatus,

Social sciences Fields of investigation and knowledge, such as psychology, sociology, and anthropology, that use the scientific method to study questions about people and their societies.

while rolling his eyes and muttering under his breath. Of course, many scientists do wear white lab coats and use complex equipment. I have even known a few who sometimes roll their eyes and mutter under their breath. Even so, these scenes badly miss the point.

The scientific approach is not about test tubes and microscopes and gigantic particle accelerators; rather, it is about (1) an *attitude* toward knowledge; and (2) a *method* for testing and adding to knowledge. These elements are as useful, even essential, for the study of adolescence as they are in physics or biology.

A Scientific Attitude

▶ **Learning Objective 2.7**
What are the two crucial elements in a scientific attitude?

One of the most basic assumptions of science is that whatever we know about any particular subject, whether it be adolescence or the origins of the solar system, is never final. No matter how strongly we are convinced of something, no matter how obviously true it seems to us, it is always possible that our current understanding is incomplete or even flatly wrong. Because of this, a scientific attitude requires us to examine new ideas, theories, and propositions with an *open mind*.

Keeping an open mind is not always as easy as it might sound. We tend to see the world through lenses that have been colored by such factors as culture, family background, personal experience, race, class, and gender (Stangor & Lange, 1994). The assumptions we make as a result can be so basic to our thinking that we do not even notice them.

Open-mindedness should not be confused with a flabby attitude of, "Yeah, anything's possible." Some propositions are so at odds with solidly based knowledge that we hardly need to take them seriously. Suppose a friend says he's decided that avoiding green vegetables and eating nothing but French fries at every meal builds endurance and prevents acne. You see at once that this goes against everything you've learned about good nutrition. Unless your friend can show you why everything you know is wrong, you have no obligation to give his peculiar notion any further thought.

To be willing to entertain ideas that may differ from our own is the first element in a scientific attitude. The second element, which is just as essential, is to approach these ideas with *skepticism*. Even if a proposition seems to make sense, comes from an acknowledged authority, and is agreed to by hordes of people, we should still ask whether there is evidence to support it. If so, what sort of evidence? Does it consist of empirical facts that can be pointed to, examined, and tested by others? Is it objective, that is, reasonably independent of personal opinions and beliefs (Beutler & Martin, 1999)? How convincing is it?

This dual attitude of openness and skepticism does not apply only to other people's ideas and theories. Like anyone else, scientists generally have some strongly held convictions about the world, and like anyone else, they are often reluctant to alter, much less give up, these convictions. However, when they are operating as scientists, they are expected to stay willing to reexamine their own beliefs and to consider alternatives to them. They are also expected to carry on a continuing search for evidence that confirms, modifies, or disconfirms their own beliefs. While any evidence may be taken into account, the sort that carries the greatest weight in this process is *scientific* evidence.

A Scientific Method

▶ **Learning Objective 2.8**
What are the most important goals of the scientific method?

One of the most important goals of any scientific investigation is to produce clear, accurate, and objective information that bears on the questions that are being asked.

We constantly face questions we'd like answered:

- Will I like this new brand of orange juice?
- Is so–and–so really a friend or just pretending to be?
- Should I plan to go to graduate school, and if so, where?

We gather information we hope will help us answer these questions. We try the juice. We watch how so–and–so acts toward us at a party. We talk to a career counselor and send away for graduate school catalogs. In this sense, we act like scientists every day.

The difference is that over the centuries scientists have developed sets of rules and procedures that are intended to eliminate, or at least lessen, various sources of error. For example, these procedures make it less likely that the information gathered will be affected by subjective factors, such as the investigator's personal beliefs and feelings. If I am carrying out a study, it is likely that I would rather see the results come out a particular way. By using scientific procedures, I deliberately lower the chances that my preference will have a distorting effect on the results.

Scientific investigations are *systematic*. In everyday life, I may decide for or against a new brand of juice after trying one glass. If I wanted to be more scientific, however, I would want to try several glasses, perhaps from different cartons. I might taste it both before and after I brushed my teeth. I would almost certainly want to do a taste comparison against my current brand of juice, without knowing which glass held which juice. At the end of this procedure, however it came out, I would be confident that the results gave me an accurate picture of my reactions to the juice.

When studying a question, investigators often follow a model called **hypothesis** (or prediction) **testing**. Let's say you wonder if a classmate is really your friend. This is the problem to be investigated. Your starting point would be to outline a theory about the problem. As we have seen, a theory is a set of linked statements that helps explain the facts we already know about the topic. A common-sense theory about friendship might include these statements:

- Friends give each other emotional support.
- Friends help each other through difficulties.
- Friends don't betray each other's confidences.

Good theories do more than explain what has already happened, however, they also lead to concrete predictions about what *will* happen in a particular set of circumstances. Such a prediction is called a *hypothesis*. For example, *If Janet is really my friend, and I haven't done my math homework, she'll let me copy hers.*

The next step is to gather information, or *data*, that bears on the hypothesis. You tell Janet you didn't do your math homework and ask to copy hers. You then *analyze* what happens and *draw conclusions*. If Janet says yes, that confirms the hypothesis. You conclude she really is your friend. If she says no, that disconfirms the hypothesis and you conclude she isn't your friend.

But wait. What if she says no, but looks upset and sorry? What if she tells you she doesn't believe in sharing homework, and then offers to do the next assignment with you if you're having trouble? You may begin to think that she *is* your friend after all. But if that's so, your theory of friendship must be incomplete or inaccurate. The information you gathered does not just tell you whether the particular hypothesis is right or wrong, it also gives you leads about *revising your theory* to make it more accurate and powerful.

The process of hypothesis testing, then, involves a sequence of steps:

- Identify the *problem*.
- Outline a relevant *theory*.
- Use the theory to generate a *hypothesis*.
- Gather *data* that bear on the hypothesis.
- *Analyze* the data.
- Draw *conclusions*.
- *Revise* the theory.

Hypothesis testing A model for gaining knowledge that involves using a theory to generate a prediction or hypothesis, and then collecting information that bears on whether the prediction is correct or not.

Research in the Spotlight

Free-Time Activities and Adjustment

The way children spend their time, on work, school, and leisure, varies a lot from one society to another. It also varies a good deal from one social group to another within a particular society. Compared to children in other countries, those in the United States have an unusually large amount of free time (Larson & Verma, 1999). But is this a good thing, a bad thing, or a little of each? Some observers think American children are weighed down by being hustled from one overprogrammed afterschool activity to another (Elkind, 1981). Others suggest that organized activities give children a chance to form social ties and develop new skills (Bronfenbrenner, 1979; Eccles & Barber, 1999).

American children from lower social class backgrounds spend much of their time in unstructured informal activities, such as watching television and playing outdoors. Middle-class children are more likely to play indoor games, read, and take part in organized sports (Posner & Vandell, 1999). Do these differences in how children use their free time have implications for adjustment later on, when they are adolescents? That is the question researchers Susan M. McHale, Ann C. Crouter, and Corinna J. Tucker (2001) decided to try to answer.

Why should organized activities be linked to better adjustment? One theory is that they bring children into contact with people outside the family, both peers and adults, who have similar interests (Kleiber et al., 1986). These relationships in turn encourage feelings of closeness and connectedness that promote self-esteem. In contrast to this scenario, the "child-effects" theory suggests that children themselves select activities that fit their own makeup. In other words, it is not that particular activities lead to better adjustment. Instead, it's that better adjustment inclines a child toward those activities (Marsh, 1992).

The children who took part in the research, 102 girls and 96 boys, were White, first-born, and lived with both parents. They were studied first when they were 10 or 11. Background information, school grades, and measures of conduct problems and depression were collected during a home interview. Then, on seven different evenings over the next 2 to 3 weeks, an interviewer called and asked the children about what they had done that day outside of school. Two years later, the researchers repeated this procedure with the same children, who were now 12 or 13.

As McHale and her colleagues expected, children's activities were linked to their parents' socioeconomic status or SES. Those from lower SES backgrounds spent more time watching television, playing outside, and hanging out, while those from higher SES families spent more time reading and playing organized sports. There were also gender differences. Girls spent more time than boys on hobbies, reading, and outdoor play, while boys spent more time than girls on sports.

Also as expected, the kinds of activities children reported were related to their adjustment. The amount of time spent on hobbies and playing sports was linked to higher grades and lower depression, while time spent playing outdoors or hanging out was related to lower grades and conduct problems. One interesting result: the amount of time a child spent reading was linked to higher grades, but also to more depression.

As McHale and her coworkers point out, because this is a correlational study, it does not let us draw firm conclusions about cause and effect. However, the results do point to a situation in which children's adjustment influences the activities they choose, at the same time that their activities influence their adjustment. As the researchers conclude:

> . . . (T)his pattern of results suggests that the processes linking activities in childhood and adjustment in adolescence are probably reciprocal: bright, energetic, well-behaved children are more inclined to involve themselves in developmentally enhancing activities, and these activities, in turn, promote academic, affective, and behavioral competencies.

Source: McHale, S. M., Crouter, A. C., & Tucker, C. J. (2001). Free-time activities in middle childhood: Links with adjustment in early adolescence. *Child Development, 72,* 1764–1778.

Connect the Dots...

Can you think of a time recently when you used some version of the hypothesis testing approach to try to answer a question? Knowing what you now know about this approach, are there steps you skipped that you should have taken? Does this affect how confident you are about the conclusions you reached?

Hypothesis testing in scientific research involves these same steps. In this chapter's Research in the Spotlight, we see how psychologist Susan McHale and her coworkers follow this process to study the links between children's free-time activities and their emotional adjustment as young adolescents (McHale, Crouter, & Tucker, 2001).

With this example of how researchers carry out an investigation in mind, why not try your hand at developing a research project of your own? The adjoining Applications in the Spotlight explains how.

A Research Project of Your Own

Here are a few typical topics in the field of adolescence:

conflicts between parents and adolescents;

adolescents and risky behavior;

the effects of being a younger sibling;

sources and effects of popularity in high school;

can intelligence be raised?

Choose one that strikes you as especially interesting or important (or another topic that you find even more interesting).

Now imagine that you need to explain what you know about your topic.

Write at least three general statements that would be part of your explanation.

Based on one or more of your statements, develop a hypothesis. In other words, make some sort of concrete prediction about information or relationships that could be observed or measured.

How do you think you might go about testing your hypothesis? What kinds of information would tell you if the hypothesis is correct? What results would *dis*prove your hypothesis? What ways can you think of to gather the information you would need?

Summing Up...

The scientific approach to understanding adolescence starts with an attitude that combines an openness to new ideas with a skepticism that asks what the evidence is for those new ideas or even for old, widely accepted ideas. The scientific method is intended to produce clear, systematic, accurate, and objective information that is not influenced by the personal views of the scientist. One widely used strategy to investigate a problem scientifically is the process of hypothesis testing.

RESEARCH TECHNIQUES

Whatever aspect of adolescence is being studied, whether it is the effects of watching television "reality shows," the reasons some teens become smokers and some don't, or the most effective ways to discourage early pregnancies, when the time comes to collect data, investigators have an assortment of tools or methods they can use. The choice will depend on many factors, ranging from theoretical to practical and ethical.

Types of Research

The major types of research used to gather information about adolescents are historical research, ethnographic studies, observation, case studies, surveys and interviews, correlational studies, and experiments. Before we begin our research we need to consider the following: Who will be studied? About which individuals or groups do the researchers want to be able to make a statement?

◄ **Learning Objective 2.9**
What steps in research make the results more accurate, objective, and dependable?

Populations and Samples. The answer to this question may be very broad, such as "American adolescents" or even "human beings." It may also be very narrow, such as "urban 10th grade girls of Hispanic origin with above average grades in math." Whether broad or narrow, the group that is the focus of the research is known as the **population** of that study.

Researchers hardly ever try to gather information on everyone in a particular population. Instead, they select a **sample**. There are various ways of doing this, but all have the same basic purpose: to make it more likely that the sample is **representative**

Population In a research project, the group that is the focus of the research.

Sample A group, drawn from a population, on which research is conducted.

Representative sample A sample that is basically similar to the intended population.

of the population. If the makeup of the sample accurately reflects the makeup of the population as a whole, then the information gathered about the sample will be **generalizable** to the population.

Suppose a team at a social agency has prepared an educational booklet about sexually transmitted diseases (STDs) to be distributed to high school students. They want to be sure the information is presented clearly and that readers will draw accurate conclusions from it. The population—the group they want to know about—includes every high school student who may read the booklet. However, studying such a large group would take so much time and effort as to be practically impossible. What the team will do instead is give the booklet to a representative sample, one that includes about the same proportions of the various ages, classes, ethnic backgrounds, geographical regions, genders, and so on, as are found among high school students as a whole. If most of those in the sample understand the material, it is reasonable to expect that most of those in the population as a whole will, too.

On the other hand, if a sample is not representative of the population, the information gathered cannot be generalized to the larger group. Say the host of a talk show aimed at adolescents asks listeners to phone in and say how strongly they feel about some controversial topic. Can we expect the outcome to reflect the opinions of adolescents in general? Probably not. First, only a particular subgroup of adolescents may listen to that show. Second, those with strong feelings about the topic may be more likely to call than those who don't much care one way or the other. Because the sample is distorted or *biased*, you cannot assume that the results will hold for the intended population.

Historical Research. How were adolescents of other times similar to those of today? How were they different? What can these similarities and differences tell us about adolescence in general and the effects of historical and cultural factors? Of course, we cannot go back into history and study them directly. However, records of various kinds that have come down to us from the past offer a rich, if often frustrating, source of information.

Joan Jacobs Brumberg (1997) studied the intimate diaries of American girls from the Victorian age down to recent times and found fascinating evidence for a major change in the way girls think about their own bodies. From the written reports of Inquisitors who were searching for heretics in a medieval French village, Emmanuel Le Roy Ladurie (1975) managed to construct a minutely detailed portrait of early 14th century life. Even the headstones in old graveyards can tell us the age at which adolescents in earlier times married, had babies, and died.

Engrossing and valuable as historical research can be, it has an obvious limitation as well. We do not know how far we can generalize from the information we happen to have. Were the girls who kept diaries (and who saved them!) comparable to others of their time who didn't write down their private thoughts or whose diaries didn't survive? As for the village Ladurie studied, we know it was unusual in at least one important way—it drew the concentrated attention of the Inquisition for several years. Even those gravestones may overrepresent the more prosperous families in the community, who could afford markers made of more durable material.

Ethnographic Studies. We have already met anthropologist Margaret Mead. In 1925, barely out of graduate school, she sailed to the island of Samoa, in the South Pacific. During the months that followed, she lived in a small village, taking part in the everyday life of the local people. She filled her notebooks with careful accounts of what she saw and learned. Her description and analysis of the place of adolescents in the traditional culture, *Coming of Age in Samoa* (Mead, 1928), had a powerful impact on Americans' ideas both about adolescence and about the role of culture in general. Even 50 years later, her work continued to attract both harsh critics (Freeman, 1983) and fervent defenders (Holmes, 1987).

Generalizable A description of information gathered from a *representative sample* that can be extended to apply to the population as a whole.

Mead's expedition to Samoa is an example of an **ethnographic study** (Jessor, Colby, & Schweder, 1996). In research of this sort, investigators spend an extended period of time in close contact with the people being studied, often living with them. They observe ceremonies and everyday habits, ask questions, and try to chart the customs, rituals, and shared assumptions that help define a culture or subculture.

Ethnographic studies of adolescence have typically focused on traditional, non-Western cultures, such as the Ijo people of Nigeria (Hollos & Leis, 1989), the Sambia of New Guinea (Herdt, 1999), and the Inuit of Arctic Canada (Condon, 1987). However, the same techniques can be used to gain a deeper understanding of groups closer to home, including ordinary American teens (Phelen, Davidson, & Yu, 1998).

Observation. We all know about observation—you watch what others are doing, maybe without taking part, and try to pick up the information you need about them. Imagine you have been asked to a party by someone you barely know. You find yourself in a room full of strangers. You may very well want to stand on the sidelines a little while to check out the scene.

Scientific observation is basically similar. The biggest difference is that it is carefully structured to yield systematic, objective information that will not be colored by the observer's own emotions, attitudes, and opinions.

Suppose some researchers want to study boy-girl interactions at a 7th-grade party. If they simply go to the party, watch, and take notes, the information they gather will probably consist of impressions that reflect as much about each of them as about the teens at the party. For example, they may, without intending to, spend more time watching certain teens than others, or remember certain kinds of interactions more readily than others.

If the researchers take a more scientific approach, they will probably train themselves ahead of time to recognize and note different kinds of interactions, such as "starts conversation," "rebuffs overture," "teases," "shows off," and so forth. During this training, they will make sure that everyone on the team codes a particular interaction the same way. They may also study photos of the children who will be at the party, so they know them by sight, and work out a detailed schedule to make sure each child is observed the same amount of time. These steps make it more likely that the information they gather will be accurate, objective, and representative of what really went on at the party.

Going to a party is an example of **naturalistic observation**. This takes place in real-life settings—a mall, a playground, a school classroom, a city street, a person's home. This approach has the virtue of giving a picture that is more true to everyday events, but it may also add complications that make the picture harder to understand. If you take a snapshot of a friend, the clutter in the background may draw attention away from your friend's face, even if it gives a faithful impression of your friend's usual surroundings. A skilled portrait photographer would probably place your friend in front of a sheet of seamless paper and adjust the lights to focus all the attention on the face instead. In a similar way, researchers often prefer to bring people into a *laboratory* setting—a fairly neutral, controlled environment that is not expected to affect their behavior—and observe them there.

An interesting twist on observational techniques is the **Experience Sampling Method** (Csikszentmihalyi & Larson, 1984). In effect, this asks the people who are being observed to act as their own observers. The participants are given beepers or cell phones and notebooks. Each time the signal is given, which happens at random intervals during the day, participants jot down where they are, what they are doing, who they are with, and what their mood is. This technique offers an unusual glimpse into the everyday thoughts, feelings, and activities of adolescents. We will look at some of the information that has been gathered using the Experience Sampling Method in later chapters, including Chapters 3 and 6.

Ethnographic study Research in which the investigator spends long periods of time in close contact with the people being studied.

Naturalistic observation Watching and taking notes on people in real-life settings, sometimes without their awareness that they are being watched.

Experience Sampling Method A research approach in which participants record what they are doing, thinking, and feeling whenever they are signaled at random intervals.

Case Studies. A *case study* is an intensive scrutiny of a single individual, often over an extended period of time. Why would a researcher take this approach? The most common reason is that something about the person is unusual or even unique. For example, it occasionally happens that a baby is born with genitals that are not clearly male or female. Before chromosome typing was widely available, a few such babies were wrongly assigned and raised as members of the sex that did not fit their genetic makeup (Money & Ehrhardt, 1972). When these very rare mistakes were discovered, researchers tried to find out as much as possible about the children concerned. Their aim was not only to improve treatment for any similar cases in the future, but also to gain a unique insight into how experience may affect gender roles in the general population.

The case study approach does have at least one big drawback. Because the person being studied *is* unusual, whether in genetic makeup, talents, medical history, family experiences, or some combination of all of these and other factors, we have to be very careful about extending what we learn about that individual to others (Davison, 2000). In other words, it is not clear if the findings can be generalized.

Surveys and Interviews. A professor of mine once gave me a valuable piece of advice: "If there is something you want to find out about teenagers," he said, "go out and ask them. They just might tell you!" This approach is at the heart of two of the most widely used research techniques in the social sciences, the *survey* and the *interview*.

In a survey, participants are asked to respond to a set of questions (a *questionnaire*). They are usually given a preset group of responses to choose from. Say you were taking part in a survey of school athletics. If you were asked, "How frequently do you participate in a team sport?" your choices might be "A. Daily. B. Weekly. C. Once or twice a month. D. Once or twice a year. E. Never." Or the question might be of the sort, "On a scale of 1 (not at all) to 10 (very much), how would you rate your enjoyment of team sports?" This technique lets researchers gather information quickly and easily from a large number of people, whether in person, by telephone, by mail, or over the Internet.

One ambitious example of survey research is the Youth Risk Behavior Surveillance System, or YRBSS, a nationwide assessment of students in grades 9 through 12 (Eaton

► Surveys allow researchers to gather information easily from many teens.

◀ Interview techniques can offer a more detailed look at the experiences and views of adolescents.

et al., 2006). In the 2005 version, 14,000 adolescents in randomly selected classrooms answered questions about smoking, drinking, violence, sexual activity, and other risk-related activities. Among other important findings, the survey revealed that just in the month before responding, 43% had consumed alcohol, 20% had used marijuana, almost 20% had carried a weapon, and 10% had driven after drinking (Eaton et al., 2006).

Interview Techniques. As useful as questionnaire-based surveys are, the fact that the questions and responses are set ahead of time and are the same for everyone can create problems. Important information may be overlooked or left out. Take the question, "What is a friend?" The researchers will certainly have put a lot of thought into choosing the four or five possible responses they offer. Even so, the results are not likely to capture the depth and complexity of an adolescent's thinking about friendship. To do that, a better method would be an open-ended interview.

In an interview, participants respond to questions in their own words and manner and at as much length as they need. The interviewer will have a list of points to cover, but will also be able to pose follow-up questions. Participants may be asked to rephrase statements that are unclear or to say more about some aspect of their response that seems especially significant.

Karin A. Martin (1996) interviewed 55 adolescents, both boys and girls, about their experiences with puberty and sex. Many of the questions, such as, "What difference do you think growing up has made in your life?" were the same for both sexes. Others were specific to girls ("Have you started your period? What happened? How did you feel about it then?") or boys ("How old were you when your voice changed? How did you feel about it?"). Martin recorded the interviews and later studied them to pick out quotations that seemed to capture the important themes on each topic she covered. She also presented tables showing, for example, that girls were less likely than boys to say they were happy with themselves.

Correlational Studies. The purpose of a **correlational study** is to find out how closely two or more factors are related to each other. If the relationship (the "co-relation") is strong, you will be able to use knowledge of one factor to predict the other. Suppose you have noticed that people who wear tie-dyed clothing tend to like classic folk rock. That is, these two factors seem to be correlated. Now you need to buy a gift for some people whose tastes you don't know at all. If you recall seeing them in tie-dyed t-shirts, you might predict that they would more than likely

Correlational study Research in which characteristics of the participants are observed or measured, and then the relationships among these characteristics are examined.

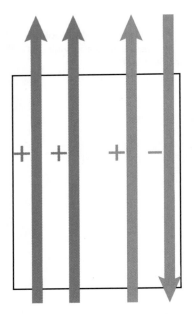

Figure 2.2 Positive and Negative Correlations With *positive* correlations, the variables change in the same direction, while with *negative* correlations, they change in opposite directions.

Connect the Dots...

Have you have come across any examples recently in which a correlation was presented in a way that implied a cause and effect relationship between the correlated factors? Were you misled by it?

Positive correlation A relationship in which the associated factors tend to move in the same direction as one another.

Negative correlation A relationship in which the associated factors tend to move in the opposite direction from one another.

Experiment Research in which some factor is varied and the effect on other factors is observed.

Independent variable In an experiment, the factor that is varied.

Dependent variable In an experiment, the factor that is observed or measured.

appreciate getting a vintage Grateful Dead CD. (Unless they already have it, of course.) You may be wrong, but you will be on much safer ground than if you simply pick a CD at random.

The *strength* of a correlation is what allows your prediction to be more or less firm. The stronger the relationship, the more certain you can be in predicting from one factor to another. The *direction* of the correlation is also of central importance. In a **positive correlation**, the related factors tend to move in the same direction as each other. As one goes up (or down), so does the other. The relationship between the temperature and the amount you perspire is positive: the hotter it is, the more you sweat; the cooler it is, the less you sweat. With a **negative correlation**, the two factors tend to move in opposite directions. As one goes up, the other goes down. The relationship between the temperature and the number of layers of clothing you wear is negative: higher temperatures go with fewer layers, and lower temperatures with more layers. Figure 2.2 is a graphic representation of positive and negative correlations.

One important caution is needed. *Correlation does not imply causation.* If you discover that two factors are correlated, that does *not* tell you that one causes the other. Suppose a researcher finds that aggressive behavior in adolescents is correlated with amount of time spent playing violent video games. If a newspaper then runs a story about the research, the headline might read, "Aggressive Youth Spend More Time on Violent Video Games."

Strictly speaking, such a headline would be fairly accurate. However, a lot of readers will come away thinking that playing violent video games *causes* adolescents to be more aggressive, that is, they will take the correlation as proof of a cause and effect relationship. It may really be the case that playing such games increases aggressiveness, but the correlation does not prove it. There are at least two other possibilities. First, increased aggressiveness may lead the person to like violent video games more. Second, there may be something about the person's personality, background, or setting that causes *both* the aggressiveness and the preference for those games. The correlation tells us that the factors are related in some way, but it does not tell us exactly how. It certainly does not tell us how we might use the relationship to change one or another factor.

Experiments. To pin down cause and effect relationships, we need to adopt a different research approach, the **experiment**. The basic logic of the experiment is straightforward. If you believe that A causes B, you change A, while making sure that no other factors change, and see if B changes. If you think your desk lamp won't go on because the bulb is burnt out, put in a new bulb and see if it lights up. If it does, you were right. If not, there is some other cause for the failure. A, the factor you think is the cause (the bulb), is called the **independent variable**, and B, the factor you think is affected by A (whether the room gets brighter), is called the **dependent variable**.

Suppose you notice that you usually do better on exams if you had a healthy breakfast that morning. To check on this hunch, you do a study. Following an exam, you ask 100 high school students what they had for breakfast that day, then you look at their exam scores. Because you have simply measured what they had for breakfast without doing anything to change it, this would be a *correlational study*.

Let us say you find the scores are positively correlated with the quality of breakfast the student had. Terrific, but remember, correlation does not prove causation. It could be, for example, that students who plan well and study harder are *also* more likely to get up early enough to have time for a good breakfast. In other words, the breakfast itself may not really be what affected their exam scores.

To show a cause and effect relationship, you will need to carry out an experiment. After selecting a group of students, you might give them a test of, say, verbal aptitude, to find out how each one scores before you have done anything to them. Then, on a particular day, you invite them all to show up before school to enjoy a healthy break-

Table 2.3 Carrying Out an Experiment
The most important step in carrying out an experiment is the manipulation of the independent variable.

	Pretest	Experimental Manipulation	Posttest
Experimental Group	Yes	Yes	Yes
Control Group	Yes	No	Yes

fast. Later that day, you give them another test. If their scores go up, you might decide that your hypothesis was correct.

But wait. You changed, or manipulated, the independent variable—what the students had for breakfast—and you measured the dependent variable to see if it changed. But did you also make sure that no other factors changed? Not really. In addition to feeding the students breakfast, you singled them out by giving them two unscheduled tests and an invitation to a special event. It could be that the knowledge of being observed, of being part of a research project, led them to try harder, and do better, on the second test (Guerin, 1986).

Experimental and Control Groups. To control for possibilities of this sort, experimenters use additional groups called, logically enough, *control groups*. The *experimental group* receives the treatment (the breakfast). The control group goes through all the same procedures as the experimental group, *except for* the treatment. In our example, you would give the control group both tests, and in between you would invite them to some event that did not include breakfast. Table 2.3 illustrates the factors involved in carrying out an experiment.

In many ways, the experiment is the most powerful tool in the researcher's toolbox, but like the other tools we have looked at, it has limitations as well. Experimental methods can be used only where the presumed cause, the independent variable, can be manipulated. Often this is impossible, for ethical or practical reasons. For example, you may believe that parental abuse in childhood causes low self-esteem in adolescents. However, even if you had some way to vary the amount of abuse different children suffered, strong moral and ethical considerations would stop you from carrying out such a project.

Strategies for Studying Development

As we have already seen, adolescence can be defined in a variety of ways. However we define it, though, it is a period of immense change. This change is not a repeating cycle, like the seasons of the year, or a set of random fluctuations, like the number of times a day you see a blue car. It is change that moves in a specific direction. We enter adolescence as children and leave it as adults.

Most of the questions we would like to pose about adolescence are not simply what a 12- or 15- or 18-year-old is like, but what happens as the person moves from being 12 to 15 to 18. What characteristics change, and how? Which ones stay the same? How do events at 12, or at an earlier age, affect what happens at 15 or 18 or later still? These are questions about development, or directed change over time. Researchers have developed several strategies for answering these types of questions.

Cross-Sectional Research. The **cross-sectional** approach involves studying different groups of people, each representing a different age, at the same time. Say we are interested in how trust in the political system changes across the early adolescent years. We could give a questionnaire on the topic to a group of 12-year-olds and a group of 15-year-olds, and then compare their responses.

Most studies of changes during adolescence use the cross-sectional approach. One big reason is practical. Once you have taken care of the preliminaries, such as developing

◄ **Learning Objective 2.10**
How do the strategies for studying development differ?

Cross-sectional study Research in which groups representing different ages are studied at the same point in time.

your measures and selecting the people you will study, the actual business of collecting information can be handled very quickly. By choosing appropriate groups, you can gather data on an age spread of 5, 10, or 20 years in a single day. However, this convenience comes at a price.

First, cross-sectional information tells you about age differences, but it does not really tell you about development. You know how those in your groups of 12-year-olds and 15-year-olds responded. What you do not know is how the 12-year-olds may respond once *they* are 15, or how the 15-year-olds would have responded back when they were 12.

Second, your groups don't just differ in age, they also come from different cohorts. **Cohort** is a term used for people born at around the same time, for instance in a particular year. As a rule, members of the same cohort have somewhat similar cultural influences and experiences, which may be different from those of people in other cohorts. For instance, a past political scandal will have had more impact on those who were old enough to follow it at the time than on those who were too young to understand it. If you find a difference in political trust between your 12- and 15-year-olds, you have no way to tell whether it reflects the age difference between them, the difference in experience between their cohorts, or some mixture of both factors.

Longitudinal Research. In a **longitudinal study**, researchers follow the same group of people across the age span of interest. This may be anywhere from a few weeks to an entire lifetime. Suppose you wanted to use a longitudinal strategy to study the development of political trust between ages 12 to 15. You would give your measure of trust to a group of 12-year-olds, and then bring the same individuals back at ages 13, 14, and 15 to be measured again.

The longitudinal approach has some important advantages. Because you are looking at the same people, you can chart the course of development of a factor, not just for the group as a whole, but for each individual separately. This may reveal patterns that are not apparent from cross-sectional research. For example, IQ scores are much the same on average in groups of different ages across the adolescent years. This gives the impression that these scores are stable. Longitudinal studies, however, reveal that during this period some people's scores go up, some go down, some stay steady, and some fluctuate erratically (McCall, Applebaum, & Hogarty, 1973).

Having information from different points in people's lives also makes it possible to see if events and characteristics at an earlier time affect people later on. For example, if you measured impulse control when your group was 10, you can examine whether that predicts various kinds of social behavior at 15 or 18 (Rosnow, 2000).

In spite of its advantages, the longitudinal approach is not that widely used. First, there are practical problems. Longitudinal studies take a long time to complete. If you are studying a 10-year age span, it will take you 10 years to finish. These studies are also expensive to carry out. Someone has to keep track of the people and the information about them over the years. The researchers will also have to cope with problems of *attrition*. With each passing year, more and more of the people in the study will die, move to a distant part of the country, or simply decide not to take part any longer.

There is also a more basic problem with longitudinal research. Differences that are related to age cannot be distinguished from differences that stem from historical events or changes. Suppose you find a steep drop in political trust between ages 13 and 14. This could be related to developmental changes in the way adolescents think about society. It could also be the result of some political crisis that broke out between the times the two measurements were taken. Information from a longitudinal study will not tell you which possibility is correct.

Sequential Research. In recent years, an approach that offers some of the strengths of both cross-sectional and longitudinal research has become more widely used. In a

Cohorts Groups of people who were born at about the same time, such as in a particular calendar year.

Longitudinal study Research in which the same participants are studied at several points over a length of time.

Table 2.4   A Sequential Study
A sequential study combines features of both longitudinal and cross-sectional approaches.

Birth Year (Cohort)	2008	2009	Year Tested (Time of Measurement) 2010
1998	—	—	12 years old
1997	—	12 years old	13 years old
1996	12 years old	13 years old	14 years old
1995	13 years old	14 years old	15 years old
1994	14 years old	15 years old	—
1993	15 years old	—	

sequential study, people from a series of cohorts are observed or measured on several occasions over time (Schaie, 1977). In effect, this means taking the age groups in an initial cross-sectional study and following them longitudinally.

Let us see how this approach could be applied to the example we just looked at, the development of political attitudes between ages 12 to 15. This year, you would give your measure to groups of 12-, 13-, 14-, and 15-year-olds. Next year, you drop the oldest group, who have turned 16, and again test the other three, now 13, 14, and 15. You also add a new group of 12-year-olds. The following (and final) year, you again drop the oldest group, now 16, and retest the other three, now 13, 14, and 15, along with still another new group of 12-year-olds.

If the description in the last paragraph sounds confusing, read it again while looking at Table 2.4. Notice that the vertical columns in the table can be seen as three separate cross-sectional studies, while each horizontal row (except the first and last cohorts, which are tested only once) can be seen as a longitudinal study.

What is the point of all this complication? It allows you to estimate and separate out the impact of both cohort, or year of birth, and time of measurement from changes that are more closely linked to age as such. If the average scores across all ages are different from one year to the next, that suggests that something about the time of measurement—some historical event, for example—is responsible. If people born in different years give different results when tested at the same ages, that suggests some sort of cohort effect. If, however, each yearly wave of testing gives similar cross-sectional results, you can be more confident that you are looking at real age-related changes.

Summing Up...

Research techniques are a set of tools that are meant to make information collected about adolescents more reliable, valid, and objective. Each of these techniques has both advantages and disadvantages, and the information gathered by each technique has both strengths and weaknesses. The choice of a particular approach will be influenced by such factors as the kind of problem being investigated, the kinds of people being looked at, and the resources the investigators have available.

RESEARCH ISSUES AND CONCERNS

Gathering scientific information about adolescents is not simply a matter of choosing a research approach, finding some willing teens, and using the approach on them. Research on human beings raises important, often complex, ethical issues.

Sequential study Research in which participants from different age cohorts are studied at several points over time, in effect combining cross-sectional and longitudinal approaches.

Understanding what the results of that research may mean, and what its limitations are, also poses some difficult questions that are often overlooked.

The Ethics of Research

▶ **Learning Objective 2.11**
What ethical concerns should researchers be sensitive to?

Imagine that you have signed up to take part in a research project. When you arrive, you are told that you will be testing a new computerized measure of emotional intelligence. You are given a series of questions about social situations. After each question, the different choices are ranked from best to worst. Most of the time, your choice turns out to be either "poor" or "very poor."

By the end, you are feeling rather discouraged. You are then asked to complete a questionnaire about your self-image and self-confidence. Afterwards, the researcher tells you that, in fact, the test was preprogrammed to give you a low score, whatever answers you gave. The real goal of the study was not to test a new measure, but to look at the effects of negative feedback on your self-concept.

How would you feel at that point? Amused that you were taken in? Relieved that your performance wasn't really so bad? Irritated or angry that you had been deceived? What if your performance really *was* terrible and the researcher is now trying to make you feel better by telling you it wasn't?

Studies like this, that rely very heavily on deception, used to be common and are still being done (Sieber, Iannuzzo, & Rodriguez, 1995). How did taking part in such a study affect participants? What gave researchers the right to mislead those who took part? Questions of this sort, among researchers, public officials, and others, led to the formulation of codes and standards of ethical research practices (Kimmel, 1996). For psychologists, the basic rules are set forth in the Code of Ethics of the American Psychological Association (1992).

Many researchers in the field of adolescence are based at colleges and universities. In most cases, this means that before they even begin to carry out a study, they must get the approval of an institutional review board. This process gives particular attention to any features of the proposed research that could conceivably cause harm or distress to a participant. It also addresses the question of how the research will benefit participants, either directly or indirectly.

A standard requirement of research on human beings is that they be told what is involved in the experiment, understand the expectations, and freely agree to take part. This is known as giving **informed consent**. In the case of adolescents or children, the informed consent of a parent or legal guardian is generally required as well. Participants are also told that taking part is voluntary. They are free to quit the study at any point and ask that any information they have given up to that point be destroyed.

The use of research techniques to gain new insights about adolescence is important and valuable. Codes of ethics remind us that it is still more important, in fact, essential, always to use these techniques in ways that protect the well-being, dignity, and privacy of the individuals who agree to take part.

Underrepresented Groups

▶ **Learning Objective 2.12**
Why is it important to gather more information about underrepresented groups?

The theorists whose ideas about adolescence were introduced earlier in this chapter disagreed about many points, but most of them had at least three important things in common: they were male, they belonged to the educated middle class, and they were of European origin. Until the latter part of the 20th century, the same could be said about the majority of those who researched, wrote, and taught about adolescence. How this may have influenced our knowledge and ideas is a question with both disturbing and exciting implications.

In principle, science is an enterprise that is unbiased, impartial, and value free. Scientists are supposed to follow wherever the search for truth leads. If a scientific discovery offends someone—even if it offends the scientist who makes it—too bad. Most

Informed consent The ethical requirement that research participants understand what they will be expected to do and freely agree to take part.

scientists accept this principle and try to follow it. However, scientists are also human beings, with characteristics, personal backgrounds, and cultural assumptions that color practically everything they do. It would be astonishing if these factors did not have an impact on their scientific work as well.

Gender, Ethnic, Cultural, and Class Bias. Historically, some major groups of adolescents have been *underrepresented* in both theorizing and research. Among these are females, members of ethnic minorities, and those from lower socioeconomic brackets. In the past, such adolescents were sometimes deliberately left out of samples because researchers saw them as confusing or adding "noise" to the results. When they were included, the ways they were not the same as middle-class white males tended to be interpreted as problems rather than legitimate differences.

The result of this underrepresentation was a sometimes subtle but pervasive bias in the field. By "bias" I do not mean conscious, deliberate prejudice against these groups. Rather, habitual, unexamined ways of thinking and doing research tended to create systematic distortions. As the problem has become more widely recognized, researchers have set out to highlight and correct these distortions (Stangor & Lange, 1994).

Many writers have discussed the effects of **gender bias** on psychological theory and research (Anselmi, 1998; Crawford, 2001). Some of the points that have been made are:

- Males have been thought of as the "standard model" of human being. The ways females may differ have been interpreted as deviations from the standard instead of valid alternatives.

- Areas of psychological functioning that are seen as more feminine, such as empathy and cooperation, have received less attention than those, such as aggression and competition, that are seen as more masculine.

- Gender biases that exist in the larger society influence the direction of research, which in turn may strengthen those biases. For example, it is widely believed that girls are weaker than boys in math. This has led to a hunt for sex differences in mathematical ability that has frequently magnified the significance of any differences found (Galambos, 2004).

These same points can also be applied to **ethnic bias, cultural bias,** and **class bias.** Adolescents from ethnic, cultural, and class minorities have been seen as variations from the "norm" of White middle-class males. Their typical attitudes and behaviors have often been interpreted as problems, rather than respected as legitimate differences. Research efforts have been directed more toward areas of difficulty than their ordinary lives. In extreme cases, the clash of cultural beliefs may lead a child with "deviant" symptoms to be diagnosed and treated as ill (Fadiman, 1997).

Ingroup Bias. A related concern is what social psychologists call **ingroup bias** (Linville & Jones, 1980), or the tendency to see members of our own group more as individuals, while we see those in other groups more in terms of their group membership. For example, Texans may think all New Englanders are basically alike. If you say all Texans are alike, however, they'll start to explain how people from the Piney Woods, the Panhandle, the Gulf Coast, and the Hill Country are very different from one another.

As a result of ingroup bias, those from underrepresented groups tend to be seen as more alike than they really are. Say a research team wants to compare attitudes toward school achievement among Asian American, African American, and White students. They conscientiously recruit equal numbers from each group, give all the students an interview and a questionnaire, and tabulate the differences among the three groups.

Connect the Dots...

Suppose adolescents from various ethnic, cultural, and class backgrounds are different from White middle-class adolescents in some way. Why do you think researchers, policy makers, and others might tend to see those differences as indicating a problem? What impact might that have on programs for adolescents from underrepresented groups?

Gender bias A distortion that results from using habitual assumptions that reflect traditional gender roles. Similar distortions may arise from *ethnic, cultural,* and *class bias.*

Ingroup bias The tendency to see members of one's own group more as individuals and those in other groups more in terms of a social stereotype.

However, the researchers may not pay attention to the fact that their Asian American group includes students of Vietnamese, Taiwanese, Hong Kong Chinese, and Filipino origin, some of whom are foreign born, some first generation, and some from families that have been in the United States for several generations. Similarly, the African American students may be from different parts of the United States or from a variety of other places, such as Haiti, Jamaica, Trinidad, or Guyana, all of which have their own distinct cultures or subcultures. This diversity within the groups, not to mention the differences among individuals within each group, may be ignored or overlooked.

Ingroup bias also leads us to explain the actions of someone from another group as being the result of their group membership. Consider the implications of such sentences as, "Isn't that just like a man!" or "What can you expect from a woman?" The first is obviously spoken by a woman, and the second by a man. In both cases, the speaker is saying that whatever the person did was done more because of gender than because of any individual factors. This is especially likely to happen when the action fits with commonly held stereotypes of the group (Stangor & Lange, 1994).

> ### Summing Up...
>
> Those who carry out research have to be sensitive to the effects what they do may have on the participants. They are also generally required to get the *informed consent* of those who take part. In the past, adolescents who are non-White, non-Western, non-middle-class, and non-male have been underrepresented in research studies, leading to a subtle but pervasive bias. Another source of bias is the tendency to think of members of our own group as individuals, but to see those of other groups in terms of their group membership.

BECOMING AN EDUCATED CONSUMER

It ain't what you don't know that hurts you. It's what you know that ain't so.
—"Mr. Dooley" (Finley Peter Dunne)

The constantly multiplying interconnections in our "wired world" have created an information explosion. New scholarly journals are announced every year. Material that once hid in obscure, dusty archives can now be accessed with a few mouse clicks. Do you want to know what proportion of the population of Cook County (Chicago) is 18 and younger? Two or three clicks at the website of the U.S. Census Bureau at http://www.census.gov/ will tell you. (As of the 2000 census, by the way, the answer is 26.2%.)

At the same time that it has become vastly easier to find a huge array of information about adolescence, it has become much more critical to know how to *evaluate* that information. The mass media—television, newspapers, magazines—are often more interested in striking, dramatic stories than in sound, responsible, but perhaps dull, reporting. The Internet is a source of valuable material of all sorts, but it is also loaded with faulty facts, eccentric ideas, and outright hoaxes.

How do you tell the difference? What questions should you ask that will help you distinguish between information that can be relied on and information that you should be very cautious about taking seriously?

What Is the Source?

One of the skills students learn as they take courses in a field is how to find reliable information about a topic. For example, as part of your course in adolescent psychology, you may be asked to write a research paper on some aspect of the material that particularly interests you. Where do you start?

Connect the Dots...

Have you ever come across some amazing information on the Internet, only to decide later that you simply didn't believe it? What awakened your doubts and what did you do to try to check them out?

▶ **Learning Objective 2.13**
What should students pay attention to when evaluating a source of information?

When a research project generates interesting new information, the investigators make the findings known to others in the field. Initially, this may mean presenting a paper at the annual meeting of an organization, such as the Society for Research on Adolescence (SRA) or the Society for Research in Child Development (SRCD). Next, the researchers will probably write an article explaining what they did, what they found, and what they think the findings mean, and submit it to an academic journal.

Journals are the most important way new research in a field, whether it be genetics, history, or adolescence, becomes known to others. Journals are also an immense, and immensely valuable, storehouse of knowledge about research done in the past. College and university libraries subscribe to journals in a wide range of disciplines and keep archives of journals from the past. In recent years, more and more journals have become available online as well. If you have not yet become familiar with the serials or journals collection of your institution's library, make a point of going over, looking around, and asking questions about what is available and how to access it.

Most academic journal articles are written for readers who already have a background, not just in the field, but in the particular subarea being discussed. They often assume a familiarity with common techniques and use words in a specialized sense that is clear to fellow professionals, but may be confusing to others. As you take more advanced courses in an area, you get a better grasp of the meaning and importance of new discoveries, even when they are expressed in a technical vocabulary.

Once an article is submitted to a journal, it is sent to be reviewed by experts. They look to see if the research was well done and adds something important to knowledge in the field. Often, the reviewers will ask the researchers to revise the report to answer specific questions. This process means that when an article appears in an academic journal, it has already been scrutinized for obvious problems or shortcomings.

Finding Information About Adolescence. Where do you look for research reports about adolescence? First, there are a number of journals that are dedicated specifically to the field, including: *Adolescence, Journal of Adolescent Research, Journal of Early Adolescence, Journal of Research on Adolescence, Journal of Youth and Adolescence,* and *Youth and Society.* Second, there are journals with a broader focus that publish research on adolescents. Among these are *Child Development, Developmental Psychology, Family Relations, Journal of Marriage and the Family,* and *Journal of Personality and Social Psychology.*

Another place to look for reliable information about adolescence is in reference works, such as the *Encyclopedia of Psychology* (Kazden, 2000), the *Handbook of Adolescence* (Adams & Berzonsky, 2002), and the *Handbook of Adolescent Psychology* (Lerner & Steinberg, 2004). Unlike journals, books of this sort do not report on new research; instead, recognized authorities give critical overviews of their particular areas of expertise and summarize the important findings and issues.

Stories about new research on adolescents show up from time to time in newspapers and magazines, and on television and the Internet. Here, the motto to adopt is "buyer beware." The material you find through these channels has not been reviewed for accuracy by experts in the field. It may or may not be trustworthy.

Those who write about adolescence for major newspapers and news magazines, such as the *New York Times,* the *Washington Post, Time,* and *Newsweek,* usually have excellent credentials and backgrounds. Even if they are not professionals, they know enough about the field to evaluate new findings, put them in context, and explain them in a clear and understandable way. This is rarely the case with more sensational publications, however. These publications are much more interested in a shocking headline that grabs potential buyers than in accurate, responsible reporting.

The Internet is an ever-expanding source of information that poses its own peculiar risks to knowledge-seekers. The unmonitored interconnections of the World

Wide Web mean that you can often find fringe views, distortions, and outright false-hoods just a few links away from even the most responsible site. Your best armor against being misled is common sense and an attitude of scientific skepticism. If a statement sounds too weird to be true, there's a strong chance it is.

Is the Finding Reliable?

▶ **Learning Objective 2.14**
What makes a finding reliable?

Woodworkers have a saying, "Measure twice, cut once." They know that sometimes a single measurement will be just inaccurate enough to make the board the wrong length. If you measure twice, it is much more likely that your measurement will be correct, because you will probably catch any error before it is too late.

A similar principle applies to research on adolescence. You can put more confidence in a study if the results are in line with the findings of other studies and build on them. Yes, startling discoveries do come along that turn a field on its head, but not very often. Most of the time, our knowledge grows in fairly small steps. Each set of results adds to and strengthens, or corrects, those that have come before.

For example, it has been widely reported that in early adolescence, girls suffer a drop in self-esteem compared to boys (Rosner & Rierdan, 1994). Suppose that you read a study in which junior high school girls have *higher* self-esteem than boys. As an educated consumer of research information, you will probably wonder why this study is so at odds with many others.

Is there something different about the measure used or the way the researchers defined self-esteem? Is the sample unusual in some way? It could happen purely by chance that the group of girls included some with particularly high self-esteem, or that some of the boys had unusually low self-esteem. This could affect the group averages enough to create the peculiar difference. Until the study has been repli-cated, and its results confirmed, you should probably not put very much confidence in it.

How *Big* Is the Effect?

▶ **Learning Objective 2.15**
How does one judge the practi-cal meaning of an effect?

There is a statistically significant relationship between birth order and IQ test scores (Belmont & Marolla, 1973). On average, first-born children have significantly higher IQs than second-born children, who in turn have significantly higher IQs than their younger siblings. This finding is very reliable. It has been replicated several times (Zajonc & Mullally, 1997). If you do not believe it, you are free to go out and do the research over again. Your results will almost certainly be similar to those of the stud-ies I just cited.

Why do I mention this finding here? Because in presenting it, I used a crucial word in a technical sense that is *not* the same as its ordinary sense. The word is *significant*. In everyday speech, "significant" means more or less the same thing as "important." Not here, however. When social scientists refer to a correlation or difference as sig-nificant, they are using shorthand to indicate that the result has reached **statistical significance**. What that means is that the result is strong enough that it is not likely to be an accident or coincidence.

One way to increase the odds of finding a statistically significant result is to increase the number of people in the study. If the sample is large enough, even very small differences will reach statistical significance. In other words, these differences are almost certainly real. If you do the study again, they will almost certainly show up again. Do they have any *practical* importance? Not necessarily. You have to look beyond statistical significance and judge the size or magnitude of the effect. In the case of IQ and birth order, the difference between first- and second-born children is tiny, much too small to matter in real life. It reached statistical significance, however, because the researchers examined data from almost 400,000 people (Belmont & Marolla, 1973)!

Statistical significance A meas-ure that indicates that a particular result or relationship is strong enough that it is unlikely to be the result of chance or accident.

Can the Results Be Generalized?

As we saw earlier in this chapter, the results of a research project may hold up perfectly well for the adolescents who took part—the sample—but less well for the people we are interested in learning about. In evaluating a study, an important point to consider is how far we can generalize from the people studied to others, and to whom. One rule of thumb is that the more representative the sample is, the more confident we can be about applying the results to the population.

In a large scale survey, such as the Youth Risk Behavior Surveillance System (Kann, 2001), the investigators spend a lot of time, effort, and money to make sure their sample represents American high school students as a whole. But suppose the participants in a study are selected from among the students at a large suburban high school near Dallas. Would the results be similar if the researchers had looked at students in a suburb of Atlanta? What about a suburb of Washington? Cleveland? San Diego? Toronto? Not to mention inner cities, rural areas, and small towns.

Once we become aware of the problem, one thing seems obvious: The more a sample is similar to the group we are interested in, the more likely it is that we can generalize the results. The less similar the tested group and the group of interest are, the more cautious we have to be about generalizing. This *seems* obvious, but it is all too easy to overlook. As we have seen, researchers have too often looked at the attitudes, experiences, problems, and developmental processes of White middle-class American adolescents, and then assumed that what they found applies to all adolescents around the world, regardless of race, class, culture, and ethnic background (Montemayor, 2000).

What About Cause and Effect?

Most of the questions we would like to answer about adolescence are "Why?" questions. As we will see in Chapter 5, teens whose parents go through a divorce tend to have problems such as higher anxiety, school difficulties, and behavioral problems (Hetherington, Bridges, & Insabella, 1998). Once we know that, the obvious next question is, "Why?" What factors *cause* these difficulties? Because we are so eager for an answer, we tend to assume that we already have it. If having divorced parents is related to higher anxiety, it must be the *cause* of the anxiety. After all, it does not seem sensible to think that their child's anxiety causes an adolescent's parents to get a divorce, does it?

As we saw earlier in this chapter, however, finding that two factors are related does not tell us that one causes the other. *Correlation does not imply causality*. Why do social scientists keep repeating that? Because it is so easy to overlook. Imagine a headline, "Memory Problems Linked to Drug Use." Almost all of us will understand that to mean, "Using drugs will cause memory problems." But that is not what the headline says. It says the two things are "linked," that is, correlated. One *may* cause the other, but these results do not tell us that.

To know if a particular set of findings show a cause and effect relationship, the crucial question to ask is this: Did the researchers *change or manipulate* the factor that appears to be the cause, the independent variable? That is, did they conduct an experiment? If so, we can assume that changes in the independent variable caused the changes in the dependent variable. If not, we can't. The results may give us a lead or clue to what causes what, but they are not proof.

◄ **Learning Objective 2.16**
What aspects of a study indicate that the findings can safely be generalized?

◄ **Learning Objective 2.17**
What kinds of research tell us about cause and effect relationships, and what kinds do not?

Summing Up...

In the flood of information available about adolescents today, it is crucial to know how to separate the worthwhile from the worthless. One step is to see if the source is reputable. Another is to ask if a particular finding is in line with other research.

The size of the effect suggests how important a difference or relationship is, and the sorts of participants suggest whether the result can be extended to broader groups. Finally, a correlation does not tell us about cause and effect.

SUMMARY

In our study of adolescence, theories direct our attention to certain facts and tell us how those facts fit together. Research methods help assure us that the facts we gather are accurate, objective, and dependable.

Theories About Adolescence

The theories that have had a major influence during the last century differ in which aspects of adolescent development they set out to explain, what kinds of explanations they offer, and how much importance they give to different sorts of causes or influences.

Learning Objective 2.1   What assumptions do biological and evolutionary theories make about development?

In his biological theory, G. Stanley Hall saw storm and stress as inevitable for adolescents. More current ideas of **evolutionary psychology** try to explain different behaviors in terms of their **reproductive fitness**.

Learning Objective 2.2   What do psychoanalytic theorists see as the primary tasks of adolescence?

Psychoanalytic theories place great importance on the development of the **libido** or sex drive (Sigmund Freud), on the ways the adolescent tries to control this drive through **defense mechanisms** (Anna Freud), and on the **psychosocial stages** that are linked to personal and sexual development (Erikson).

Learning Objective 2.3   What aspect of adolescent development is the greatest concern of cognitive theories?

Cognitive theories emphasize the changes in an adolescent's thinking ability and the implications of those changes. Piaget saw adolescents moving into the stage of **formal operations**, which increases their capacity to think abstractly, systematically, and hypothetically. Vygotsky was more interested in the ways adolescents make greater use of social relationships in their learning. **Information processing** approaches try to chart the steps adolescents take in solving problems and to understand the ways their problem solving becomes more efficient and accurate.

Learning Objective 2.4   Where do learning and social cognitive theories expect to find the major source of influence on behavior?

Learning or conditioning theory focuses on the ways the external consequences of an action change the likelihood that the action will be repeated. **Social cognitive theory**, in contrast, stresses the role of learning by watching what others do and what happens to them.

Learning Objective 2.5   What is the central focus of social and anthropological theories of adolescence?

Social and anthropological approaches concentrate on the ways adolescence is similar and different across widely varying cultures and societies.

Learning Objective 2.6   How do adolescents interact with the contexts and influences that affect them?

Bronfenbrenner's **ecological theory** and Lerner's **developmental systems theory** see the adolescent as developing at the center of a network of interacting influences, being acted on by those influences, but also playing an active role in determining which influences will be most important and what their effect may be.

Finding Out About Adolescence

Among our ways of knowing about the world, the scientific approach has a special place because it is not subjective. This approach combines an attitude and a method.

Learning Objective 2.7   What are the two crucial elements in a scientific attitude?

A scientific attitude assumes that our knowledge of some subject is never final and complete. Accordingly, it requires an open mind to new ideas and propositions. At the same time, both new and old ideas are regarded with a skeptical attitude that asks what evidence there is to support them.

Learning Objective 2.8   What are the most important goals of the scientific method?

A scientific method for gathering information is systematic and objective. One model is **hypothesis testing**, in which a theory is used to generate a prediction, which is then tested against reality.

Research Techniques

Learning Objective 2.9 What steps in research make the results more accurate, objective, and dependable?

Investigators have developed many tools for collecting clear, accurate information about adolescence.

Once the group to be studied, or **population,** has been defined, a **representative sample** is selected. The results from this sample can then be **generalized** to the population.

Historical research uses information from archives and other records.

Ethnographic studies involve spending long periods in close touch with the people being studied.

In an **observational study,** the researcher watches and records what people do, either in a naturalistic setting, such as a playground or classroom, or in a neutral laboratory setting. In the **Experience Sampling Method,** the participants record their own behavior when signaled at random intervals.

A case study is a detailed examination of a particular individual.

In surveys and interviews, the participants respond to questions either by choosing among preset responses or in more free-form fashion.

Correlational studies examine how closely two or more characteristics are related to one another. A **positive correlation** indicates that the two factors tend to move in the same direction, while a **negative correlation** indicates that they tend to move in opposite directions. While a correlational study can document the connection between the factors, it does not prove that a change in one factor causes the other to change.

In an **experiment,** the factor that is thought to be the cause (the **independent variable**) is manipulated or changed, and any corresponding change in the **dependent variable** is observed or measured. If appropriate controls are used, an experiment can show a cause and effect relationship between the variables.

Learning Objective 2.10 How do the strategies for studying development differ?

Several strategies for studying development, or change over time, are used by adolescence researchers.

In **cross-sectional research,** adolescents drawn from different age groups or **cohorts** are studied at the same point in time and compared.

A **longitudinal study** involves looking at the same group of adolescents at several points over time.

Sequential research in effect takes the different age groups in a cross-sectional study and then follows them longitudinally over time.

Research Issues and Concerns

Learning Objective 2.11 What ethical concerns should researchers be sensitive to?

Those who use research techniques to gather information about others need to be alert to the possible effects of the experience on participants and be sure to protect their well-being, dignity, and privacy.

Learning Objective 2.12 Why is it important to gather more information about underrepresented groups?

Until fairly recently, females, members of ethnic minorities, and those from lower socioeconomic groups have been underrepresented in research on adolescence. The result was a subtle but pervasive **gender, ethnic, cultural,** and **class bias** in the ways investigators thought about adolescents and the conclusions they drew.

Ingroup bias is a tendency to think of members of one's own group more as individuals, but to see those of other groups more in terms of their group membership.

Becoming an Educated Consumer

The vast amount of information available in an increasingly wired world makes it essential to learn how to judge the worth, reliability, and importance of reported findings and statements about adolescence.

Learning Objective 2.13 What should students pay attention to when evaluating a source of information?

The most reliable sources are reputable journals and comprehensive handbooks in the field and articles on new developments in major newspapers. The Internet is full of valuable information as well as worthless misinformation.

Learning Objective 2.14 What makes a finding reliable?

Findings that are in line with those of other studies are generally more likely to hold up than those that are new and startling.

Learning Objective 2.15 How does one judge the practical meaning of an effect?

A relationship or difference may be **statistically significant** — that is, likely to be real — and still be so small as to have no practical importance.

Learning Objective 2.16 What aspects of a study indicate that the findings can safely be generalized?

The more the participants in a research project are similar to some other group, the more likely it is that the results can be extended or generalized to the other group.

Learning Objective 2.17. What kinds of research tell us about cause and effect relationships, and what kinds do not?

An educated consumer of research information should know how to recognize a correlational study and keep in mind that the results of such studies do not show cause and effect relationships.

KEY TERMS

Evolutionary psychology (32)	Metacognition (36)	Generalizable (46)	Cross-sectional study (51)
Reproductive fitness (32)	Operant conditioning (38)	Ethnographic study (47)	Cohort (52)
Biological determinism (32)	Social cognitive theory (38)	Naturalistic observation (47)	Longitudinal study (52)
Libido (33)	Ecological theory (39)	Experience Sampling Method (47)	Sequential study (53)
Psychosexual stages (33)	Developmental systems theory (39)	Correlational study (49)	Informed consent (54)
Oedipus complex (33)	Social sciences (41)	Positive correlation (50)	Gender bias (55)
Defense mechanisms (33)	Hypothesis testing (43)	Negative correlation (50)	Ethnic bias (55)
Psychosocial stages (34)	Population (45)	Experiment (50)	Cultural bias (55)
Cognitive stages (35)	Sample (45)	Independent variable (50)	Class bias (55)
Formal operations (35)	Representative sample (45)	Dependent variable (50)	Ingroup bias (55)
Information processing (36)			Statistical significance (58)

Part 2 Adolescent Changes

chapter 3

Puberty and Physical Development

Outline	Learning Objectives
THE BIOLOGY OF PUBERTY	
Hormones in Action	◀ **3.1** How does the endocrine system regulate puberty and growth?
Physical Development	◀ **3.2** What are the physical changes of adolescence for girls and boys?
Sexual Development	◀ **3.3** What are the sexual changes of adolescence for girls and boys?
Menarche and the Secular Trend	◀ **3.4** What is the significance of changes in the age of menarche in recent decades?
RESPONSES TO PUBERTY	
Personal Responses to Puberty	◀ **3.5** Why is puberty a source of pride for some teens and embarrassment for others?
Parental Responses to Puberty	◀ **3.6** Do parents and children become more distant after puberty?
Cultural Responses to Puberty	◀ **3.7** What are puberty rites, and what purposes do they serve?
BRAIN DEVELOPMENT	
The Structure of the Brain	◀ **3.8** What are the principal parts of the brain?
The Developing Brain	◀ **3.9** How do synaptic pruning and myelination help make the brain more efficient?
Behavior and the Brain	◀ **3.10** How is brain development linked to other adolescent changes?
HEALTH ISSUES	
Puberty and Mood	◀ **3.11** Are teens at the mercy of their "raging hormones"?
Body Image	◀ **3.12** What impact do pubertal changes have on body image for girls and boys?
Sleep Needs	◀ **3.13** How much sleep do adolescents need and get?
Nutrition and Exercise	◀ **3.14** Do today's adolescents get proper nutrition and exercise?

"Ready or not, here I come!"

If puberty had a voice, it would probably shout these words. Puberty comes to every child. It comes to those who have been told what to expect and to those whose families and cultures believe in keeping children in the dark. It comes early to some and late to others. It comes to those who are looking forward to it, those who dread it, and those who have never given it a thought. This process, which propels children in the direction of physical and sexual maturity, is a universal feature of our development. "Ready or not…!"

The biological changes of puberty are many, sudden, and far reaching. Sometimes they are a source of joy and excitement. Other times—when you realize you are a head taller or shorter than your best friend, when your back-to-school clothes are too small by Halloween, when the first pimple pops out on your forehead—it is hard to escape the suspicion that you have been taken over by an alien presence.

In this chapter, we look at the major physical changes of adolescence and the effects they have on those who are changing and those around them. The first section focuses on describing the changes themselves, what they are, and how they come about. We get to know the communication and control network called the endocrine system and learn how it sets off and monitors the body's growth. One of the most noticeable aspects of puberty is getting taller, by as much as several inches in a single year, but the growth spurt involves much more than that. Weight, facial and body contours, fat, and muscle change dramatically, too, and they change in different ways for girls and boys. Which brings us to sex.

During puberty, children develop in the direction of becoming sexually mature adults. The organs that are essential to reproduction mature and become functional. At the same time, girls and boys develop a variety of physical characteristics that mark adult females and males. These are the so-called secondary sex characteristics. The sequence of their emergence is pretty much the same from one child to another, but the timing—at what age the process starts and how quickly it goes—varies greatly.

The age at which children enter puberty is influenced by their genetic makeup, but it is also responsive to factors in the child's environment. Diet, health care, physical

▶ Puberty begins the process of physical development from childhood toward adulthood.

labor, even altitude have an impact on when a child enters puberty. As living conditions improve, the average age of puberty goes down. This trend has important implications for children, parents, and social institutions.

Puberty is a major life change, not just physically, but psychologically and socially. In the second section of this chapter, we look at how children respond to the events of puberty. We also examine the personal impact of entering puberty much ahead of or behind friends and peers. As we will see, the effects are quite different depending on whether the child is early or late, a girl or a boy.

When children enter adolescence, it changes their social role in the family and in society as a whole. Both families and the larger culture respond in various ways to the different changes of puberty. These responses may range from looser (or tighter!) household rules, to having to pay adult fares on buses and at the movies, to long, elaborate formal ceremonies that mark the child's transition to adolescence.

The physical and sexual changes may be the most obvious that take place during adolescence, both to adolescents themselves and to those around them, but important changes take place in the brain as well. Recent research has found that these changes affect both the structure of the brain and the ways it functions. These changes, in turn, have been linked to important aspects of behavior, such as judgment, self-control, and risk taking.

The physical changes of adolescence raise some important health issues. Do children become moody and "on a short fuse" after entering puberty? If so, why? Is it a question of "raging hormones," social conflicts, or some combination of these and other factors? As children's bodies change in radical ways, their thoughts and feelings about their bodies change as well, in ways that are sometimes healthy and sometimes definitely *un*healthy. Children's sleep patterns and needs change at puberty, as do their nutritional and exercise needs. We will look at these changes, how they come about, and what their implications are, later in the chapter.

THE BIOLOGY OF PUBERTY

Puberty is, first of all, a biological event. Or rather, it is an entire set of delicately synchronized biological events. The transformation these events bring about is as thorough and as startling as any in the lifespan. On the brink of puberty, a child is just that—a child, with the distinctive size, body shape, skin texture, sweat glands, and undeveloped sexual equipment of a child. A few brisk months later, the same child is closing in fast on the stature, form, and capabilities of an adult. If you have ever been involved in a complicated project, one in which each element had to mesh precisely with many others, you will realize how amazing this process is. The closer you look at the details, the more amazing it becomes. Our discussion of the biology of puberty covers hormones, physical development, sexual development, and the secular trend.

◀ **Learning Objective 3.1**
How does the endocrine system regulate puberty and growth?

Hormones in Action

What sets the changes of puberty in motion and keeps them on track? The most crucial elements are the glands in various parts of the body that make up the **endocrine system**. Endocrine glands work by producing substances called **hormones** and releasing them into the bloodstream. Hormones can be thought of as chemical messengers. When a particular hormone reaches cells that are sensitive to it, those cells respond in a specific way. Figure 3.1 on page 68 shows the most important components of the endocrine system.

The Hypothalamus and Pituitary. The endocrine system is largely controlled by a part of the brain called the **hypothalamus**. Nestled under the cortex, the hypothalamus monitors and directs many bodily functions, including hunger, thirst, and sex (Aron, Findling, & Tyrrell, 2001). It does this by checking and responding to the levels of

Endocrine system A system of glands that produce hormones, as well as parts of the brain and nervous system that regulate hormone production.

Hormones Chemical substances that circulate through the bloodstream and regulate many body functions.

Hypothalamus A part of the brain that monitors and regulates many bodily functions, including hormone production.

Figure 3.1   Components of the Endocrine System
Important parts of the endocrine system include the pituitary and adrenal glands and the gonads (ovaries or testes).

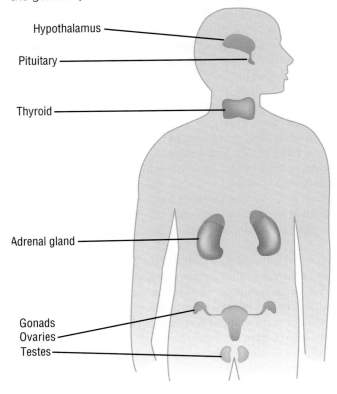

different hormones circulating in the blood. Each hormone has a *set point*, a particular level the system tries to maintain. If the level dips below this, the hypothalamus sends out a signal to produce more of that hormone. If the level rises above the set point, the hypothalamus sends out a different signal to cut down on production.

Just below the hypothalamus, and attached to it by a slender stalk, is a gland called the **pituitary**. Though no bigger than a pea, the pituitary is the master gland of the endocrine system. It controls other endocrine glands by sending out hormones that make them change the way they operate. Among the glands controlled by the pituitary are the **gonads**—the *ovaries* in females and the *testes* in males. The gonads are the major source of sex hormones called **estrogens** and **androgens**. The most important estrogen is *estradiol*, and the most important androgen is *testosterone* (Klein, 1999). We usually think of estrogens as "female" hormones and androgens as "male" hormones, but this is a bit misleading. Both sexes produce both types of hormone. During most of childhood, the levels of estrogens and androgens are very similar in girls and boys (Hopwood et al., 1990).

The HPG Axis.   Together, the hypothalamus, pituitary, and gonads make up the **HPG axis**, named for the initials of the three components. The HPG axis forms what is called a *feedback loop*. We often make use of feedback loops. Suppose you and a friend are cooking dinner together. While you toss the salad, your friend makes stew. You taste it and tell your friend to add more salt. A little later, you taste it again. It still isn't salty enough, so your friend adds a little more salt. The next time you take a taste, it's fine. You say, "Okay, that's it. Enough salt." What your friend does "feeds into" your reaction, and your reaction "feeds back" to control your friend's further actions.

The HPG axis works in a similar way. When the hypothalamus senses that the level of sex hormones in the system is too low, it sends a substance called *gonadotropin-releasing hormone (GnRH)* to the pituitary. In response, the pituitary produces more

Pituitary An endocrine gland that is considered the master gland of the endocrine system.

Gonads The sex glands: the *ovaries* in females and the *testes* in males.

Estrogens Female sex hormones, principally *estradiol*, secreted mainly by the ovaries.

Androgens Male sex hormones, principally *testosterone*, secreted mainly by the testes.

HPG axis A *feedback loop* that regulates the hormones involved in puberty and growth.

luteinizing hormone (LH) and *follicle-stimulating hormone (FSH)*. When LH and FSH reach the gonads, they cause an increased production of sex hormones. LH and FSH also play an important part in reproduction by speeding up development of egg cells in the ovaries and sperm cells in the testes (Brook, 1999; Grumbach & Styne, 2003).

As the gonads produce more sex hormones and release them into the bloodstream, the hypothalamus monitors the rising level. When the level reaches the set point, the hypothalamus lowers production of GnRH, which signals the pituitary to stop producing LH and FSH. This, in turn, causes the gonads to reduce production of sex hormones. The HPG feedback loop is diagrammed in Figure 3.2.

The HPG axis first starts operating well before birth. In males, the production of androgens leads to the development of male sex organs. If androgens are not present, or if their activity is somehow blocked, the sex organs develop in a female direction (Money, 1980). At birth, sex hormones are present at almost adult levels, but they soon decline to very low levels and stay there until the start of puberty (Grumbach & Styne, 2003).

How Puberty Begins.   During childhood, the endocrine system is a little like a dragster at the start line. The engine is all ready to send the car hurtling down the track, but a firm foot on the brakes keeps it from moving. In a similar way, for most of childhood the hypothalamus *suppresses* the production of sex hormones by operating with a very low set point for these hormones (Brooks-Gunn & Reiter, 1990). If it didn't, there is no biological reason toddlers couldn't start puberty. Occasionally, for instance when a tumor damages the hypothalamus, very young children *do* enter puberty (Cacciari et al., 1983).

Normally, the earliest phase of puberty begins long before any outward physical changes. This phase is **adrenarche** *(ad-reen-arky)*, which means the beginning of adrenal involvement. Between the ages of 6 and 9, the *adrenal glands* begin to mature (Susman, Dorn, & Schiefelbein, 2002). Under control of the hypothalamus and pituitary, adrenal glands begin to produce more of an androgen called *DHEA*, or dehydroepiandrosterone (Reiter, 1987). By the age of 10, DHEA levels have reached the low end of the adult range (Hopper & Yen, 1975). This increase in DHEA sets off the first appearance of pubic hair (Hopwood et al., 1990). It has also been linked to changes that take place in the brain during this period (Giedd et al., 1999; Herdt & McClintock, 2000). Lots of children say they had their first feelings of sexual attraction around age 10, before the most obvious changes of puberty, and this too may be an effect of increased levels of DHEA (McClintock & Herdt, 1996).

Along with low levels of sex hormones during childhood, the balance between androgens and estrogens has been about the same in boys and girls (Brooks-Gunn & Reiter, 1990). Now that changes dramatically. The hypothalamus starts to make more GnRH, releasing it in regular pulses. In response, the pituitary makes more LH and FSH. When these hormones reach the gonads, the production of sex hormones ramps up, but unequally in the two sexes. As Figure 3.3 on page 70 shows, in boys testosterone rises to almost 20 times its level before puberty, while in girls it merely doubles. At the same time, estradiol levels double in boys, but increase eight-fold in girls (Nottelmann et al., 1987; Susman, 1997).

The increased levels of sex hormones, together with higher production of growth hormones in the pituitary, the thyroid, and elsewhere, set in motion a whole series of physical changes. The most obvious are the changes in height, weight, body shape, and sexual maturation. We will look more closely at all of these in a moment, but first, what sets the process going? *Why* does the hypothalamus start producing more GnRH? According to one expert, this is "a fundamental problem of developmental neurobiology" (Plant, 1988, p. 1782).

The most immediate cause is that the hypothalamus becomes *less sensitive* to sex hormones. This causes a rise in the set point for these hormones. It is like turning up the dial on a thermostat. Until the temperature in the room reaches the new setting, the furnace keeps running. Or, to use another analogy, the higher the set point, the more estrogens and androgens it takes to make the hypothalamus hit the brakes.

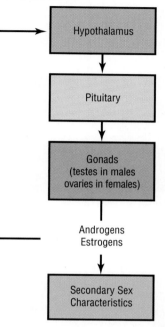

Figure 3.2   HPG Feedback Loop
The HPG (<u>H</u>ypothalamus-<u>P</u>ituitary-<u>G</u>onads) feedback loop controls the production of androgens and estrogens that promote the development of secondary sex characteristics.

Hypothalamus

Pituitary

Gonads
(testes in males
ovaries in females)

Androgens
Estrogens

Secondary Sex
Characteristics

Adrenarche The time very early in puberty when the adrenal glands begin to produce a hormone called *DHEA*.

Figure 3.3   Testosterone and Estradiol Levels During Puberty
During puberty, levels of testosterone and estradiol rise dramatically in both girls and boys.

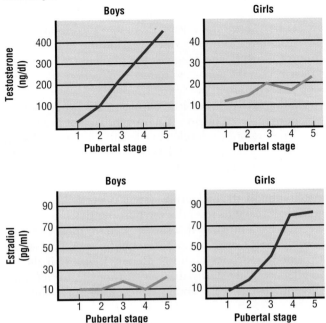

Source: Figure "Testosterone and Estradiol Levels During Puberty," from *Biological Psychological Interactions in Early Adolescence,* by R. M. Lerner and T. T. Foch (Eds.) © 1987. Used by permission.

Connect the Dots...

From an evolutionary standpoint, why might it be an advantage for the first menstrual cycle to be set off by a girl's body weight and proportion of fatty tissue? Would a similar line of reasoning apply to boys as well?

▶ **Learning Objective 3.2**
What are the physical changes of adolescence for girls and boys?

Menarche The time at which a girl has her first menstrual period.

Insulin-like growth factor-I (IGF-I) A substance produced in the liver that may be linked to the onset of puberty.

Leptin A protein secreted by fat cells that may play a role in the timing of menarche.

Adolescent growth spurt A period of rapid physical development that lasts from about 10 to 16 for girls and 12 to 18 for boys.

What changes the set point? One theory is that puberty, in girls at least, is tied to reaching a certain weight and proportion of body fat. Research shows that **menarche** (*men-arky*), or the first menstrual period, usually takes place once a girl reaches a critical body weight of about 47.8 kg (105 lbs.) and about 23% body fat (Frisch, 1984). We know that fatty tissues are able to change androgens, which are produced by the adrenal glands even before puberty, into estrogens (Frisch, 1991). This means that girls with more fatty tissue would potentially have an increased supply of these hormones.

However, menarche comes rather late in puberty, and of course it does not apply to boys. Even if the body weight theory is correct—and there are lots of exceptions (Klein, 1999)—it does not necessarily tell us what sets off puberty. For this, one candidate is a substance produced mostly in the liver, **insulin-like growth factor-I (IGF-I)** (Caufriez, 1997; Dees, Hiney, & Srivastava, 1998; Hiney, Srivastava, Nyberg, Ojeda, & Dees, 1996). Another candidate is **leptin**, a protein secreted by fat cells (Spear, 2000; Styne, 2001). Leptin is known to increase sharply during the weight gains of puberty (Horlick et al., 2000). Still, it is not clear whether this substance helps set off puberty or is itself a side effect of puberty (Archibald, Graber, & Brooks-Gunn, 2002; Susman & Rogol, 2004). Another element that may help explain the start of puberty is the central nervous system, which can directly affect the level of GnRH produced by the hypothalamus (Cameron, 1990; Susman & Rogol, 2004).

Physical Development

One of the dramatic changes that puberty brings is a sudden and rapid increase in size. This is known, logically enough, as the **adolescent growth spurt**. While it lasts, children seem to get bigger by the day. That sweater that fit so well a month ago now has sleeves that don't reach the wrists. The fad for buying jeans so long that they scrape the ground may be a way to avoid showing off your socks. And pity any 12-year-old at a family gathering—some insensitive relative is bound to remark loudly either that they have grown so much or that they *haven't* grown!

Figure 3.4   Change in Height, Age 2-20
The adolescent growth spurt begins about two years earlier for girls than for boys.

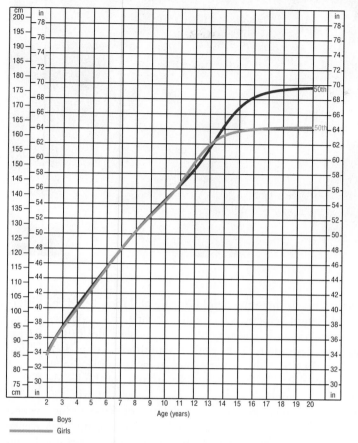

Boys
Girls

Source: National Center for Health Statistics, 2000. Available: http://www.cdc.gov/growthcharts.

The Growth Spurt. For most of childhood, starting at around age 2, children get taller at a fairly slow, steady pace—about 5 cm (2 in.) a year (Klein, 1999). With puberty, however, the rate of change shoots up. Its maximum, or **peak height velocity**, comes about 2 years after the start of the growth spurt. For the few months that this lasts, girls are adding an average of 8 cm (3.25 in.) a year and boys over 9 cm (3.5 in.) a year (Malina, Bouchard, & Beunen, 1988). This is by far the fastest they have been growing since they were toddlers.

Figure 3.4 shows the average changes in height across the childhood and adolescent years. The bump that represents the adolescent growth spurt shows up clearly. What also shows up clearly is that girls start, and finish, the growth spurt about *2 years earlier* than boys (Abbassi, 1998). For girls, the growth spurt starts at about 10, for boys, it's closer to 12. Peak height velocity comes at around 12 for girls and 14 for boys (Malina et al., 1988).

Throughout childhood, boys and girls of the same age have been about the same height (Marshall & Tanner, 1986). Once girls enter the growth spurt, that changes. For a couple of years, between 11 and 13, the average girl is some 4 cm (1.5 in.) taller than the average boy (Ogden et al., 2002). An inch and a half may not sound like much of a difference, but suddenly finding yourself looking over the heads of young people your age or staring at their chins instead of their eyes can leave a lasting impression.

Peak height velocity The fastest change in height, which occurs at around 12 for girls and 14 for boys.

▶ Girls typically start the adolescent growth spurt two years earlier than boys.

Because boys and girls are much the same height during childhood, and the difference in growth rates at peak height velocity is so small—about 1 cm or a quarter of an inch per year—why do males generally end up taller? The answer lies in that 2 year delay. During that time, boys continue to grow at their childhood rate of 5 cm (2 in.) a year. This means that when they start the growth spurt, they are some 4 inches taller than girls were when *they* started it. Those inches make up most of the height difference between adult men and women.

Height is not the only body dimension that changes dramatically—so does weight (Susman et al., 2003). About half of adult body weight is put on during adolescence (Rogol, Clark, & Roemmich, 2002). On average, teens put on weight fastest at about the same age that they get taller fastest, around 12 for girls and 14 for boys (Barnes, 1975; Tanner, 1965).

The adolescent growth spurt ends around age 16 for girls and 18 for boys. By this point, the ends of the long bones in the body finish changing from cartilage to bone, a process called *ossification*. Once this happens, most people do not grow any taller, although their bones do continue to get denser and richer in calcium (Roche, 1986).

"The Awkward Age." The growth spurt in adolescence does not go smoothly and evenly. Different parts of the body change at different times and at different rates. Children who have recently entered their growth spurt sometimes have the feeling their hands and feet aren't where they're supposed to be. The reason is that hands and feet, along with the head, are the first parts of the body to start growing faster at puberty. The arms and legs follow soon after. Growth in the trunk and shoulders comes still later (Tanner, 1972). This **asynchronicity** is responsible for the "gawky," "gangly," or "leggy" look that makes so many early adolescents self-conscious about their appearance.

The hormones that speed up the growth of the body also affect both muscle and fat. Muscle growth follows a course a lot like the ones for height in Figure 3.4. Here, too, boys and girls are very similar until age 11, when girls enter the growth spurt. For the next couple of years, girls have larger muscles than boys of the same age (Tanner, 1972). Then, as boys enter the growth spurt, they quickly overtake the girls. By age 15, boys have about 20% more muscle mass than girls. This is partly because a boy's endocrine system produces more testosterone, which is closely linked to muscle growth (Cheek, 1974). However, boys are also much more likely than girls to exercise regularly during adolescence (Hickman, Roberts, & Gaspar de Matos, 2000). This magnifies their advantage in muscle mass.

Asynchronicity The fact that, during early adolescence, different parts of the body change at different times and different rates.

While boys gain more muscle during early adolescence, girls gain more body fat. Girls add body fat at a fairly slow rate until age 12, when the rise becomes much steeper. Boys actually *lose* some body fat during the time leading up to puberty, then they start putting it on, but at a somewhat slower rate than girls. The result is that by the end of puberty, girls have a ratio of muscle to fat of about 5:4, or barely more muscle than fat. Boys on the other hand, have about *three times* as much muscle as fat (Cheek, 1974; Rogol et al., 2002).

Body proportions change, too. Both boys and girls develop wider hips and shoulders. Typically, boys gain more width in the shoulders than hips, while girls gain more width in the hips than shoulders (Petersen & Taylor, 1980). For many girls in early adolescence, these changes are far from welcome. American society's current ideas about feminine beauty include long legs, slender bodies, and narrow hips. This look is more characteristic of girls just *before* puberty than later on (Faust, 1983). As a result, many adolescent girls are dissatisfied and upset over their changing bodies. Though their growth may be perfectly normal, they become preoccupied with controlling or losing weight (Centers for Disease Control and Prevention, 2006). A small number may go on to develop an eating disorder such as bulimia or anorexia (Hoek, 2006; National Center for Health Statistics, 2005). We will discuss these serious problems later, in Chapter 13.

Other physical differences between boys and girls also emerge during puberty. The size of the heart and lungs increase in both sexes, but the increase is greater in boys (Malina, 1989). The increases in the blood's capacity to carry oxygen and the body's ability to dispose of the byproducts of exercise, such as lactic acid, are also greater in boys (Tanner, 1972). These differences, together with those in size, muscle mass, and body fat, give males an edge in strength and athletic potential that continues throughout the lifespan.

Sexual Development

Just as striking as the physical growth spurt of puberty are the changes that take place in body systems associated with sex and reproduction. In the space of a couple of years, boys and girls go from being children themselves to being physically able to have children of their own. At the same time, their bodily appearance goes through changes that signal to others their new sexual maturity.

◀ **Learning Objective 3.3**
What are the sexual changes of adolescence for girls and boys?

Ovaries and Testes.   At birth, a girl's ovaries already contain up to 472,000 immature eggs or *ova*. (*Ova* is the plural form of the word **ovum**.) Each egg is enclosed in its own separate compartment called a *follicle*. During childhood, the ovaries grow fairly steadily. As we have seen, puberty is set off when the levels of the hormones LH and FSH start to rise. These hormones cause the ovaries to start producing more estrogens and lead the follicles to start developing. (Remember, FSH stands for *follicle-stimulating* hormone.)

The increased estrogens from the ovaries lead the uterus to get longer and change in shape. From its childhood length of 2–3 cm (0.8–1.2 in.), it grows to 5–8 cm (2–3 in.) and becomes rounder (Klein, 1999). The vagina also gets longer, and the external genitals thicken and deepen in color (Crooks & Baur, 2002).

Once regular menstrual cycles begin, a single follicle ripens and bursts each month. This releases the ovum it contains. The ovum moves along the fallopian tube in the direction of the uterus. At the same time, the lining of the uterus swells with blood. If the ovum is fertilized by a sperm, it becomes implanted in the wall of the uterus and starts developing into a fetus. If it is not fertilized, however, both it and the uterine lining are discarded, in the form of menstrual flow.

From menarche, or first menstruation, until menopause, when the process stops, the average woman releases a total of about 400 eggs. This is just a tiny fraction of those she was born with (Macklon & Fauser, 1999).

For many girls, menarche occurs before ova first start to be released. The first few cycles are often irregular and unpredictable. Even when the cycles become more

Ovum The female sex cell, or egg, located in the ovary within a structure called a *follicle*.

regular, a girl may ovulate during some cycles and not during others (Warren, 1983). Because ovulation is unpredictable, so is fertility. This has led to a myth that girls in early adolescence cannot get pregnant. As too many young people have found out the hard way, this is not so. Even a girl who has just reached menarche *may* release an ovum that is potentially fertile. If she is sexually active, pregnancy is a definite possibility. There are even cases of girls who have become pregnant *before* menarche (Jones, 1996)!

A boy's testes grow very little during childhood. Once puberty starts, however, they get bigger very quickly. By the end of adolescence, their volume is as much as six times as great as when puberty began (Klein, 1999). The testes do not contain any **sperm** at birth or during childhood, but once they mature, they produce huge quantities. A single ejaculation, about a teaspoonful of fluid, contains between 200 and 500 million sperm (Crooks & Baur, 2002)!

Interestingly, while girls do not reach menarche until near the end of puberty, boys can start to produce sperm very early in puberty (Klein, 1999). Evolutionary psychologists say this reflects the fact that the biological cost of conceiving a child is quite low for a male, but quite high for a female. Males gain an advantage by starting as early as possible, while for a female it is better to wait until late in the process of maturation, when her body is better prepared for the stress of pregnancy (Geary, 1998).

Stages of Puberty. In both girls and boys, the main sexual developments of puberty follow a fairly regular sequence. Pediatricians and researchers who want to gauge a child's progress through puberty generally use some of the more easily observable secondary sex characteristics as an index. These characteristics are breast development in girls, development of the penis and scrotum in boys, and the spread of pubic hair in both girls and boys. J. M. Tanner, a British expert on puberty and growth, described five successive **Tanner stages** in each of these characteristics (Marshall & Tanner, 1986; Tanner, 1972).

For girls, the first sign of puberty is usually the "breast bud," a slight swelling under the nipple. This may be accompanied by an enlargement of the areola, the flat part of the nipple. In the months that follow, the breasts get larger and take on more adult contours. For a while, the areola and nipple are raised above the curve of the breast. Then, toward the end of puberty, the areola recedes, leaving only the nipple to protrude. Shortly after the breast bud appears, girls start to grow sparse, downy pubic hair. For as many as one-third of girls, this happens *before* the appearance of the breast bud (Biro et al., 2003; Harlan, Harlan, & Grillo, 1980). Like breast development, the growth of pubic hair follows a regular sequence, becoming denser, darker, and curlier as it spreads from the vaginal lips to the pubic area as a whole. These stages are shown in Figure 3.5 on page 75.

With boys, the first sign of puberty is usually the growth of the testes and scrotum. Pubic hair starts to appear soon afterwards, followed by a lengthening and then thickening of the penis. As with girls, boys' pubic hair starts out sparse and downy, and then gets darker, coarser, and curlier as it spreads across the pubic area and onto the inner thighs. These stages are shown in Figure 3.6 on page 75.

About 2 years after boys develop pubic hair, facial hair starts to grow. It appears first at the corners of the upper lip, and then across the whole upper lip. Gradually it spreads to the upper cheeks, the area just below the lower lip, and finally along the jaw and chin (Tanner, 1972). Body hair also appears around this time and continues to spread until well after puberty. How much body hair and where seems to be mostly a matter of heredity (Tanner, 1972). Boys are often upset to notice their nipples and areolas darken in color and get larger. This response to circulating estrogens is a normal part of puberty. About midway through puberty, as many as 70% of boys have some swelling of the breasts. Embarrassing as it may be, this condition, called *gynecomastia*, is almost always temporary (Grumbach & Styne, 1998).

In both girls and boys, armpit hair usually appears near the end of puberty. At about this same time, glands in the skin start producing an oily substance called sebum. This, as practically all teens discover, can lead to blackheads and acne. The sweat glands also

Sperm The male sex cell, produced in huge quantities by the testes beginning at puberty.

Tanner stages A system used to rate the development of secondary sex characteristics during puberty.

Figure 3.5   Tanner Stages, Girls
The Tanner stages in girls range from prepubertal (not shown), in which there is no pigmented pubic hair, to the adult pattern of stage five.

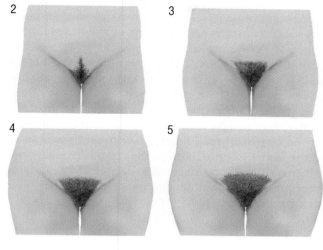

Figure 3.6   Tanner Stages, Boys
The Tanner stages in boys, like those in girls, range from prepubertal (not shown), in which there Is no pigmented pubic hair, to the adult pattern of stage five.

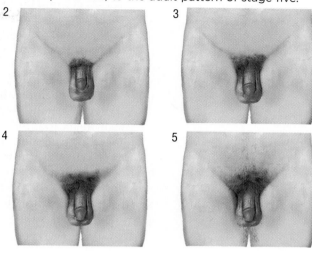

Source: Adapted from J. M. Tanner, *Growth at Adolescence,* 2nd ed. (Oxford: Blackwell Scientific Publications, 1962), as reprinted in H. Katchadourian, *The Biology of Adolescence* (San Francisco: W. H. Freeman, 1977), p. 67.

become more active, especially those in the armpits and pubic area called apocrine sweat glands. These glands produce an oily fluid that is thought to contain **pheromones**, airborne substances that signal emotional states such as fear and sexual arousal. When first secreted, this fluid is odorless, but bacteria on the skin can quickly give it a noticeable smell (Katchadourian, 1977).

Late in puberty, both girls and boys find their voices getting lower in pitch and more resonant. This happens because the vocal cords get longer, the larynx expands, and the resonating spaces in the mouth and nose become bigger (Tanner, 1972). The change in pitch is greater for boys, and so is the potential for embarrassment when the voice "breaks" or shifts uncontrollably between the high and low registers.

Timing of Puberty. As we have just seen, the sequence of events during puberty is fairly regular; not the timing, however. Whether you look at when puberty begins or

Pheromones Airborne chemicals believed to signal emotional states to others.

◀ In boys, facial hair usually appears first on the corners of the upper lip.

how fast it proceeds, you find an enormous range of ages. There are group differences linked to social class, ethnic background, and geographical region, as well as wide individual differences within all of these different groups (Thomas, Renaud, Benefice, de Meeüs, & Guegan, 2001).

On average, girls show the first signs of puberty—either breast budding or pubic hair—at around 10, but this may easily happen as early as 7 or 8 or as late as 13 or 14 (Brown et al., 1998). The length of time between these early developments and menarche, or first menstrual period, is usually about 2 years, but it may be as short as 6 months or as long as 5-1/2 years (Tanner, 1972). This means that some girls will finish puberty before others exactly the same age have even started.

Boys generally go through the stages of puberty a year or two later than girls, but with them, too, there is a lot of variation. The first changes in the testes and the appearance of pubic hair usually occur around age 11, but these changes may start as early as 9 or as late as 14. Once the genitals start to change, they may take as few as 2 or as many as 5 years to reach their mature form (Marshall & Tanner, 1970). As with girls, some boys will already have achieved their adult appearance while others their age are still waiting for the first signs of puberty.

Menarche and the Secular Trend

▶ **Learning Objective 3.4**
What is the significance of changes in the age of menarche in recent decades?

As just mentioned, menarche happens fairly late in puberty, and, of course, it happens only to girls. Even so, it is widely used as a measure of when puberty starts. There is a reason for this. The changes that take place earlier in puberty are mostly gradual. By the time they become apparent, no one may recall exactly when they started. On the other hand, a girl's first menstruation happens at a specific point in time and she can't help but notice it. She may tell others, such as her mother, about it. Later on, she may not be able to say when her breasts began to develop, but even years later she will probably recall how old she was when she got her first period.

Today in the United States, for girls of European or Asian descent the average age of menarche is 12.8 years (Marshall & Tanner, 1986). For African American girls, the average age is somewhat lower, 12.2 years (Herman-Giddens et al., 1997). These figures have stayed about the same for the last 35 years (Lee, Kulin, & Guo, 2001). At the beginning of the 20th century, however, the average age of menarche in the United States was over 14 (Eveleth & Tanner, 1990). Between 1900 and 1960, this average went down steadily by over 2 months every 10 years.

In other countries for which we have historical records, the drop in the age of menarche is even more striking. In Norway in the 1840s, the average girl did not get her first period until she was past 17. Over the next 100 years, the age dropped to slightly over 13 (Eveleth & Tanner, 1990). Other northern European countries showed a similar pattern, as can be seen in Figure 3.7 on page 77. According to the records, the average age of menarche went down by 3 to 4 months every 10 years. This downward shift, known as the **secular trend** (Tanner, 1991), is examined in more detail later in the chapter.

Puberty, Heredity, and Environment. For individuals, the timing of puberty is strongly influenced by heredity (Kaprio et al., 1995; Marshall & Tanner, 1986; Pickles et al., 1998; Rowe, 2000). One of the best predictors of menarche age in girls is the age at which the mother reached menarche (Belsky et al., 2007; Lee et al., 2007). A girl's genetic heritage does not *determine* the timing, however; instead, it establishes a **reaction range** for her, a spread of ages within which puberty is likely to begin. If conditions are favorable, it will come at the early end of the range. If conditions are unfavorable, it will come at the late end.

A number of environmental factors affect the timing of puberty in individuals. The most important factors are nutrition and general health (Garn, 1992). We have already seen that weight and body fat are linked to menarche (Brown et al., 1996; Frisch, 1991). Girls with a greater body mass index at age 3, well before puberty, reach puberty

Secular trend The tendency in recent centuries for puberty to occur at younger ages.

Reaction range A biologically influenced spread in some characteristic, such as height, within which an individual will end up.

Figure 3.7 The Secular Trend in Age of Menarche
The 19th and 20th centuries in Northern Europe and the United States saw a steady decline, or *secular trend*, in the age of menarche.

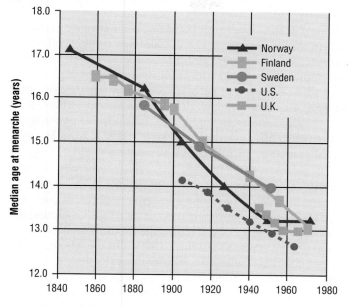

Source: Figure "The Secular Trend in Age of Menarche," from *Worldwide Variation in Human Growth*, by P. B. Eveleth and J. M. Tanner. © 1990 Cambridge University Press. Used by permission.

sooner (Lee et al., 2007). Among girls the same age, those who are taller or heavier tend to reach menarche earlier (St. George, Williams, & Silva, 1994). Malnutrition, on the other hand, delays menarche (Kulin et al., 1982, 1984), as do anorexia nervosa (Irwin, 1981) and food aversions (Smith, 1980). Girls who train intensively, such as ballet dancers and gymnasts, also tend to enter puberty later (Malina, 1985; Pigeon, Oliver, Charlet, & Rochioccioli, 1997; Rogol, Roemmich, & Clark, 2002). It is not clear if this is because of their lower body fat, higher levels of exertion, or both.

Social and psychological factors also influence the timing of puberty. A recent longitudinal study found that adrenarche, the earliest indication of puberty, comes later in girls whose parents are more invested in child-rearing and who have lower levels of marital conflict (Ellis & Essex, 2007). This suggests that girls who feel psychologically safer in their childhood home remain children longer, and that those who feel less safe enter adolescence sooner. Other research supports this suggestion. Girls who experience a lot of family conflict tend to mature earlier (Belsky, 2007; Ellis, 2004; Ellis, McFadyen-Ketchum, Dodge, Pettit, & Bates, 1999; Graber, Brooks-Gunn, & Warren, 1995; Steinberg, 1988). In particular, if the girl's father is not part of the household, she may reach menarche sooner (Bogaert, 2005; Mustanski, Viken, Kaprio, Pulkkinen, & Rose, 2004). The presence of a stepfather may also have an effect on early puberty (Ellis, 2004; Ellis & Garber, 2000; Moffit, Caspi, Belsky, & Silva, 1992; Surbey, 1990).

Why these factors trigger puberty is far from clear. Family conflict certainly creates stress, and that leads to hormonal changes (Susman, 1997, 2004; Susman et al., 2003). However, the specific effect stress hormones have seems to depend on where the person is in adolescence. At early stages, stress tends to delay maturation, but later on it may speed up the process (Kipke, 1999; Susman, 1997).

Another hypothesis is that girls enter puberty sooner if they are often exposed to the pheromones of an unrelated adult male, such as a stepfather (Ellis & Garber, 2000). Pheromones are known to play a role in regulating other reproductive processes (Stern & McClintock, 1998). For example, women who live in close quarters with each other, such as college roommates, tend to have synchronized menstrual cycles

Figure 3.8 Age of Menarche and Social Class
Throughout the world, the age of menarche is linked to social class.

Cuba	urban	12.8
	rural	13.3
Egypt	urban	12.6
	rural	13.9
Hong Kong	better-off	12.4
	worse-off	12.7
India - Punjab	well-off	12.5
	poor	13.7
Mexico	urban	12.6
	rural	14.3
Nigeria	urban	13.8
	rural	14.5
Poland	urban	12.7
	rural	13.4
Romania	urban	13.5
	rural	14.6
Singapore	rich	12.4
	poor	13.0
Sudan	better-off	13.4
	worse-off	14.1
Turkey	well-off	12.4
	poor	13.2
Venezuela	middle-class	12.0
	laborer	12.7
Zaire (Congo)	better-off	13.2
	worse-off	14.7

Source: Eveleth, P. B., & Tanner, J. M. (1990).

(McClintock, 1980). Even close friends who do not live together show this synchrony (Weller, Weller, & Roizman, 1999). Experiments have shown that this is caused by pheromones (Preti, Cutler, Garcia, Huggins, & Lawley, 1986). Pheromones may well help regulate the onset of puberty, too.

Other researchers have looked at the association between father absence and early menarche from a very different angle. Geneticist David Comings and his colleagues (Comings, Muhleman, Johnson, & MacMurray, 2002) have found that a particular gene linked to the X chromosome is associated with impulsivity and multiple sexual partners in males and with father absence and early menarche in females. In other words, men who carry this gene may be more likely to become absent fathers, after having passed the gene on to their daughters, in whom it makes early menarche more likely. If so, the connection between absent fathers and girls' early maturation may have more to do with a shared gene than with stress or pheromones.

Menarche Around the World. Along with individual differences in the timing of puberty, there are big differences between groups of adolescents of different nationalities, ethnic backgrounds, and social classes. In urban areas of developed societies, the average age of menarche may be as low as 12 years, but in the mountains of Nepal or New Guinea it can be as late as 18-1/2 years (Worthman, 1999). On the whole, genetic factors have not been very helpful in explaining these differences (Eveleth & Tanner, 1990). Of much greater importance are environmental factors, such as nutrition, availability of health care, and levels of stress (Morabia & Costanza, 1998).

Differences among ethnic groups often get confused with social class differences. When researchers in Chicago studied menarche in girls from different racial or ethnic backgrounds and different social classes, they found that Latina girls reached menarche earlier than either African American or White girls. When socioeconomic background was taken into account, the Latina girls were still earlier than African American girls. However, controlling for socioeconomic factors wiped out the difference between Latina and White girls (Obeidallah, Brennan, Brooks-Gunn, Kindlon, & Earls, 2000).

Recently, a team of researchers set out to identify the main causes of age variation in menarche in different countries (Thomas et al., 2001). They started by gathering statistics on age at menarche in 67 countries around the globe and found a wide range, from 12-1/2 to 16 years, with a cluster around 13. Next, Thomas and his co-workers looked at how these differences related to geography, living conditions, nutrition, health, and other social and economic factors.

A first finding was that the age at which girls reached menarche is strongly associated with a girl's life expectancy at birth in that society. This suggests that the social conditions that affect longevity also affect the rate of maturation. A closer look revealed two factors that explain variations in age of menarche. One factor is vegetable calorie consumption, which indexes adequate nutrition. The other factor, even stronger, is the rate of illiteracy among adults. This turns out to be closely related to how common child labor is in the society (Parker, 1997; Psacharopoulos, 1997).

In other words, it is not just nutrition that affects menarche, but the balance of energy expended (Thomas et al., 2001). Children who do hard physical labor on a poor diet reach puberty later. This fits well with the finding mentioned earlier that girls who exercise too much in childhood have delayed puberty (Baker, 1985).

Research within countries reveals a similar pattern based on social class and family income. As Figure 3.8 shows, whether we look at the United States, Iraq, South Africa, or elsewhere, girls from poor families tend to reach menarche later than girls from families that are well off (Eveleth & Tanner, 1990). It seems clear that this gap is mostly the result of differences in nutrition and health care. Girls from poor families are also more likely to be set to work at an early age.

Puberty and History. This brings us back to the secular trend. There is good evidence that the age of menarche in Northern Europe dropped from around 17 in the mid-19th century to less than 13 today. But what does this mean? Suppose we tried to project this trend into the past. The figures would have us believe that in 1600, girls did not reach menarche until they were 25 years old. If we project the figures into the future, by the year 2200 menarche would supposedly arrive around a girl's 5th birthday.

We do not need to get too worried about the prospect of pubescent toddlers 200 years from now. In industrialized societies, the secular trend has apparently leveled off (Helm & Grolund, 1998; Lee, Kulin, & Guo, 2001; Nakamura, Shimura, Nonaka, & Miura,1986; Tryggvadottir, Tulinius, & Larusdottir, 1994). As for projections into the past, we can check those against records *from* the past.

As we saw in Chapter 1, in Classical Greece and Rome the usual age of marriage for girls was between 12 and 15. Menarche in those societies typically arrived around 13, in other words about the same age as in Europe and the United States today (Amundsen & Diers, 1969). In Medieval Europe, girls in the aristocracy married *and had children* while they were still in their teens, or even earlier. Mary de Bohun was the wife of Henry of Bolingbroke, who later became England's King Henry IV. Their first child was born when she was 12 and he was 15. This was considered on the young side, but not outrageously so (Bruce, 1986).

The meaning of the secular trend may become clearer when we recall that the 19th century in Europe was a time when vast numbers of people left the countryside for urban slums and when even very young children worked long hours in mines and factories (Colon, 2001; Floud, 1994). The combination of poverty, stress, malnutrition, and grueling work would have pushed the age of puberty to near the upper limit set by our genes. If so, it is no wonder that as living conditions improved over the last century and a half, the age of menarche has declined.

In years to come we can expect to see a similar pattern in developing countries around the world. As the lives of children improve, the age of puberty is likely to drop steadily. It will level off as it nears the bottom of the reaction range set by our common genetic heritage.

Connect the **Dots...**

Economic development is linked to earlier puberty, and, as we saw in Chapter 2, it is also associated with later marriage. What does the conjunction of these two trends suggest about the future of adolescence in developing countries? How do you think more traditional cultures will try to deal with such changes?

Summing Up...

The physical and sexual changes of puberty are set in motion by hormones from the endocrine system. During the adolescent growth spurt, which begins 2 years earlier for girls, children grow taller very rapidly and their bodies change toward adult proportions. At the same time, the reproductive system matures, signaled by changes in the genitals, breast development in girls, and the appearance of body hair. Factors such as nutrition and exercise affect the timing of puberty. The average age of puberty in Western cultures declined over the past two centuries but has now leveled off.

RESPONSES TO PUBERTY

So far, we have been looking at the processes of physical growth and sexual maturation during adolescence. In a literal sense, these make up the definition of puberty and adolescence. In a larger sense, however, they are only part of the story. Think back to your own experience of puberty. What first comes to mind? Some particular physical fact? Probably not. For most people, these take second place to what those facts, or their implications, seemed to *mean*.

The changes that come with puberty do not go unnoticed. These changes call forth a whole series of social and psychological responses. Whether we look at the sudden growth spurt, the new balance of body fat and muscle mass, the changing contours of the body, the development of complexion problems, or any of the other features of puberty, people notice.

Children themselves are aware of the ways they are changing and respond in a personal fashion to them. They also notice and react to the changes in their friends and schoolmates. *Parents* and other adults respond to the different phases of a child's passage through puberty. Different *cultures* have their own ways of marking the milestones of puberty, whether these take the shape of formal rituals or informal traditions.

Personal Responses to Puberty

▶ **Learning Objective 3.5**
Why is puberty a source of pride for some teens and embarrassment for others?

During middle childhood, change seems to come in small, steady amounts. On your birthday, when you stand with your back to the wall to mark how tall you've become, the gain since your last birthday is about the same as the gain the year before. Each year when school starts, you find you can run a little faster, throw a ball a little harder, spell more words, and do more arithmetic problems. You do have a sense of moving forward, but farther along the same road.

Puberty alters that. It is like what physicists call a *phase shift*. When you light a fire under a pot of water, the water gradually gets warmer. The longer you heat it, the warmer it gets. When it reaches 100°C (212°F), however, something new happens. Instead of continuing in the direction it was going, the process itself changes. The water starts to become steam. At some point, there is no more water, only steam.

In a similar way, the start of puberty is also the end of childhood. It means leaving a familiar neighborhood for new, strange, exciting, and possibly dangerous territory. More than that, the process is both inescapable and irreversible. Children turn into adolescents. It happens without regard to whether they look forward to it, hate the idea, or haven't quite figured out how they feel. Once they enter puberty, they cannot turn themselves back into children again. It shouldn't surprise us that such a radical and permanent change often arouses strong responses from those it affects.

Girls and Puberty. Over the last three decades, millions of girls, and quite a few boys, around the age of puberty have devoured Judy Blume's novel, *Are You There God? It's Me, Margaret.* (Blume, 1970). If you were one of them, can you forget 11-year-old Margaret's embarrassing visit to a big department store to buy an unnecessary but socially important "Gro-Bra"? How about the scene in which she and her friends pump their arms back and forth while chanting, "We must—we must—we must increase our bust!"

As we saw earlier in this chapter, breast budding, along with pubic hair, is usually the first sign of sexual development in puberty. Unlike pubic hair, it is also a (semi-) *public* sign (Brooks-Gunn, Newman, Holderness, & Warren, 1994). When a girl starts to develop breasts, others—parents, neighbors, schoolmates—notice. If she doesn't start to develop them at the generally expected time, they notice that. If her breasts seem small or large for her age, they notice *that*, too. And, all too often for the girl's comfort, they comment on what they have noticed (Brooks-Gunn, 1984; Summers-Effler, 2004).

Moving from one phase of life to another is often a source of internal stress, ambivalence, and conflict. The new phase may offer new possibilities, but the old phase had its familiar comforts. No matter how attractive each may be, you cannot have both. This creates an occasion for conflict. Whether you face leaving nursery school for kindergarten, leaving college for the world of work, or leaving the world of work for retirement, you are likely to feel torn. Breast budding is an unmistakable sign of the impending movement from childhood to adolescence. This makes it a potential psychological stressor (Petersen & Taylor, 1980) that may give rise to feelings of loss as well as gain.

The development of breasts represents more than a simple indicator of maturation and change. Breasts are a key sign of female sexuality (Thorne, 1993). For a girl, having breasts announces that she is a sexual creature, while not having them announces the contrary. As the *Song of Solomon* puts it, "We have a little sister, and she has no breasts. What shall we do for our sister, on the day when she is spoken for?" (Cant. 8:8, Revised Standard Version). This means that, along with feelings and attitudes about growth in general, breast budding calls forth feelings and attitudes about sexuality in specific (Rosenbaum, 1979).

Among the few researchers who have studied early adolescent girls' feelings about breast development are Jeanne Brooks-Gunn and her co-workers (Brooks-Gunn et al., 1994). They asked White middle-class girls ages 11 to 14 to remember how they had felt about breast development. The largest group (38%) recalled feeling proud or more mature. Somewhat fewer (31%) said they had felt ashamed, embarrassed, or shocked. A still smaller group (19%) reported mixed or ambivalent feelings. About three-quarters of the girls said they had talked about breast development with their mothers, always at the mother's initiative. Most said these discussions were helpful (Brooks-Gunn et al., 1994).

The biggest source of negative feelings about breast development seems to be the way others react, especially boys. When Karin Martin (1996) interviewed adolescents about their experience of puberty, many of the girls remembered being made to feel embarrassed about their developing breasts.

> *I was really self-conscious 'cause I developed them early, I think it was like fifth grade, and you know guys sometimes would say things.*
>
> — SONDRA

> *I was self-conscious [when I developed breasts]. I still am. I don't know. It's just the boys. Some of them, how they react and stuff, just like if you're bigger you're better and stuff like that, some of the boys, I know some. It's aggravating.*
>
> — WENDY
>
> (MARTIN, 1996, p. 31)

Often this attention from others goes beyond verbal remarks. A common form of teasing in early puberty is snapping the strap of a girl's bra (Thorne, 1993).

Breast development is important, but menarche is generally seen as the decisive turning point in a girl's pubertal development, even though it arrives fairly late in puberty. One reason for this is that it is so definite. Either a girl has had her first period or she hasn't, and either way, she knows. Another reason is the connection to fertility, which, in turn, is an essential component of adulthood. In the closing pages of *Are You There God? It's Me, Margaret*, Margaret, who has kept a box of sanitary napkins hidden in her desk drawer for weeks, discovers blood on her underpants. Her response, after confiding in her mother, is to think, "Now I am growing for sure. Now I am almost a woman!" (Blume, 1970, p. 148).

Research results are in line with Blume's intuitions. In one study, more than 600 girls were asked about their experience of menarche. Nine out of ten said they had immediately told their mothers, and almost three-quarters said the experience made them feel more grown up (Ruble & Brooks-Gunn, 1982). The picture is far from entirely positive, however. Most of the girls admitted to embarrassment, self-consciousness, or physical discomfort, and they also worried about hassles with supplies (Ruble & Brooks-Gunn, 1982).

Most cultures treat menstruation as an extremely sensitive topic (Buckley & Gottlieb, 1988). While those in Western societies do not believe, as the Gisu of Uganda do, that a menstruating woman can cause a potter's wares to crack just by walking past (La Fontaine, 1972), many people still consider menstruation dirty and disgusting (Kowalski & Chapple, 2000; Lee, 1994) or at least deeply embarrassing. This obviously makes it a difficult topic of conversation.

In the not-too-distant past, many parents believed that telling children before puberty about menstruation would damage their innocence. As a result, many girls had no idea what was happening to them when their first period arrived (Greif & Ulman, 1982). A century ago, in 1895, a survey of Boston high school girls showed that 60% of them knew *nothing* about menarche before it happened to them. Understandably, many girls who suddenly discovered they were bleeding were horrified by the thought that they had suffered some kind of internal injury (Brumberg, 1997).

Experiencing terror at menarche is rarer now, but it has not disappeared.

> I can remember [starting my period] distinctly 'cause that was a nightmare for me. My parents had just left to go out to dinner . . . And then I was going to take a bath or a

shower, I can't remember which. I went into the bathroom and I looked down and there was blood and I was just like "What is that?" I thought I was bleeding to death. I was flipping out. I was crying. I had to wait about twenty minutes before I thought they [my parents] would be at the restaurant they were at. I had to call them up. She [my mom] was just like "Don't worry about it. We'll be right home." So she came home. She was like "I guess I should tell you." I was like "Yeah! That would be appropriate right now!"

— (Martin, 1996, p. 22)

What a girl knows or believes about menstruation, what she expects it to be like, helps determine how she experiences menarche (Koff & Rierdan, 1996). If her friends, her mother, or others have led her to think it will be uncomfortable or painful, she will probably find it more unpleasant (Brooks-Gunn & Ruble, 1982). In turn, these perceptions may have a negative effect on how she feels about later menstrual experiences.

Girls who have more preparation for menarche, on the other hand, tend to have more positive attitudes toward menstruation later on (Kieren & Morse, 1992; Rierdan, Koff, & Stubbs, 1989; Scott, Arthur, Panizo, & Owen, 1989). Whether positive or negative, what happens at menarche and shortly afterwards may have a long-lasting impact on feelings about menstruation and sexuality in general (Brooks-Gunn & Reiter, 1990).

Most girls believe they were somewhat or well-prepared for menarche, but about one in ten says she was not prepared (Kieren & Morse, 1992; Koff & Rierdan, 1995). In addition, after menarche many girls say there was quite a discrepancy between what they were told and what they actually experienced (Morse & Doan, 1987).

American girls learn about menstruation from a variety of sources. The most important source is their mothers, but many girls cite girlfriends, sisters, and health providers (nurses and doctors), as well as magazine articles, pamphlets put out by makers of menstrual products, and television (Costos, Ackerman, & Paradis, 2002; Koff & Rierdan, 1995). Not surprisingly, very few girls say they discussed menstruation with males, whether fathers, brothers, or male friends (Koff & Rierdan, 1995).

Another source of information is school. In 1999 about 72% of a representative sample of 5th- and 6th-grade teachers reported that sexuality education is taught in their schools (Landry, Singh, & Darroch, 2000). In line with national guidelines (American School Health Association, 1991), practically all these classes cover puberty. The messages these different sources communicate about menarche may be quite mixed. Girls are usually told it is a natural process that marks their entry into womanhood and that it should be a source of pride. At the same time, they are assured that if they are careful and take the proper precautions, no one will have to know it has happened (Beausang & Razor, 2000; Erchull, Chrisler, Gorman, & Johnston-Robledo, 2002).

Most of the research we have looked at in this section is based primarily on girls who are White and middle class. What about girls from underrepresented groups? Do puberty and menarche have a similar impact on them? Not necessarily. For example, one study found that African American girls are likely to have frank personal talks with their mothers and express positive attitudes about puberty. Mothers of Hispanic girls, however, tend to be more vague, embarrassed, and upset in such discussions, leaving their daughters much less well-informed (O'Sullivan, Meyer-Balberg, & Watkins, 2000). This contrast makes it clear that investigators need to look closely at the ways adolescents from different social and ethnic groups experience similar events in their development.

Boys and Puberty.   You will notice that this section is a lot shorter than the last one. Not that puberty has less impact on boys than on girls, but research on how it affects them psychologically is much harder to find. Here is a striking example: For a boy, the event during puberty that most closely resembles menarche in girls is when he experiences his first ejaculation, but while there are many studies on the effects of menarche, only a handful have looked at boys' first ejaculations.

Researchers do not even agree on the best name for this event. Some prefer "spermarche" (Shipman, 1968), while others argue for "semenarche" (Stein & Reiser, 1994). Whatever it is called—I am going to opt for **spermarche**—there *is* agreement that it usually takes place around age 12-1/2 or 13 (Bell, Weinberg, & Hammersmith, 1981; Downs & Fuller, 1991; Stein & Reiser, 1994). This is very close to the average age of menarche. Given that on average girls enter puberty a couple of years earlier than boys, that may seem odd. Recall, however, that while girls reach menarche fairly *late* in puberty, boys start producing sperm fairly *early*.

One likely reason that spermarche has drawn so little research is that it is a much more private event than menarche. As we have seen, girls usually share the news of menarche with their mothers right away, and later tell their girlfriends. Most boys, however, do not tell anyone, whether parents or friends, about spermarche (Downs & Fuller, 1991; Gaddis & Brooks-Gunn, 1985; Stein & Reiser, 1994). One reason is that boys are generally more reluctant than girls to talk about personal matters, especially those that may reveal a vulnerability (Thorne, 1993).

There is also a more specific reason for this silence. According to one large-scale survey, about one-quarter of boys experience spermarche in the form of a **nocturnal emission** or "wet dream." For more than half, however, it occurs as the result of masturbation (Downs & Fuller, 1991), and the only way most boys (or men, for that matter) will talk about masturbation with their friends is in the form of joking insults that may barely mask anxiety (Lyman, 1987; Martin, 1996).

Earlier research suggested that boys found spermarche a frightening event (Shipman, 1968). More recent studies give a different impression. Boys are usually unprepared and taken by surprise, but unlike girls, they are not embarrassed or fearful. Instead, they report that they felt fairly happy, curious, and more grown up (Downs & Fuller, 1991; Gaddis & Brooks-Gunn, 1985; Stein & Reiser, 1994).

One aspect of puberty in boys that is somewhat public, and that comes before spermarche, is the enlargement of the genitals. For many, this is a source of embarrassment and worry. Most boys are well aware of the emphasis placed on penis size as an indication of sexual adequacy (Crooks & Baur, 2002). For many boys, this leads to "locker room syndrome," a fear that if other boys see them naked, they will make demeaning judgments and hurtful comments. This concern is hardly ever addressed in sexuality education classes at school, nor is it easy to make accurate comparisons. There is a powerful taboo against staring at other guys' bodies—to break it risks even worse consequences. Even if he looks, a boy's own penis almost always looks shorter to him than someone else's, simply because his visual perspective when he looks down at his genitals foreshortens it (Masters, Johnson, & Kolodny, 1988).

Another worry boys have during puberty is being embarrassed by an involuntary erection. Erections are a normal function of the autonomic nervous system in males. They sometimes occur even before birth, and they are fairly common during childhood. Many things can set them off, from fright to a full bladder, from tight clothing to tree climbing. With puberty, however, the higher levels of androgens make them more frequent, while the increased size of the penis makes them more evident. More than one boy has had nightmares about getting an obvious erection when he is called to the front of the classroom or is otherwise the focus of attention. Nor is this simply a bizarre fantasy—now and then, it happens (Sarrel & Sarrel, 1979).

Effects of Pubertal Timing. Puberty comes to every child. When it comes and how long it lasts, however, can vary enormously, as can teens' responses to it. Let's recall some numbers from earlier in this chapter. On average, American girls begin puberty at 10 years, but they may begin as early as 7 or as late as 14. From the beginning to menarche, the process usually takes about 2 years, but it may take as little as 1 or as much as 5 years (Brown et al., 1998).

The range for American boys is just as wide. They usually start puberty at around 11 or 12, but they may start as early as 9 or as late as 14. While the process usually takes about 3 years, it may take as little as 2 or as much as 5 years (Marshall & Tanner, 1970).

Spermarche A boy's first ejaculation of seminal fluid.

Nocturnal emission A spontaneous ejaculation of seminal fluid while asleep; a "wet dream."

To complicate matters further, the age at which girls and boys enter puberty does not seem to predict how long they will take to go through it. An early developer may be average or fast or slow, and so may a late developer. It is entirely possible that a boy or girl who entered puberty early will be overtaken by one who entered late.

As you might expect, the age at which children enter puberty has an important impact on their psychological well-being and social relationships. What is more surprising, perhaps, is how dramatically different this impact is for girls and boys. We turn our attention first to girls.

Girls who mature early tend to suffer for it (Mendle, Turkheimer, & Emery, 2007). They are less popular with their classmates (Aro & Taipale, 1987), have lower self-esteem (Williams & Currie, 2000), and are more anxious and depressed (Ge, Conger, & Elder 1996, 2001; Graber, Lewinsohn, Seeley, & Brooks-Gunn, 1997; Hayward et al., 1997; Stice, Presnell, & Bearman, 2001). Their feelings of depression are stronger when they have higher levels of emotional arousal (Graber, Brooks-Gunn, & Warren, 2006). Early maturers are also more likely to get involved with older boys and to have problems with smoking, drinking, drug use, and sex (Caspi, Lynam, Moffitt, & Silva, 1993; Stattin & Magnusson, 1990; Stice et al., 2001).

One reason for these problems is that early-maturing girls may enter puberty before they have been prepared for it, either by parents or health education classes in school. While practically all adults favor sexuality education in high school or junior high school, less than half think it should be offered in elementary school (Haffner & Wagner, 1999). This has an effect. Even in districts where such classes are given in elementary school, it is almost always in 5th or 6th grade, when students are already 10 or 11 (Landry et al., 2000). This is not likely to be much help to a girl who already entered puberty a year or two earlier.

If early-maturing girls lack support from parents and teachers, they are not likely to find it among their girlfriends, either. The simple fact that they are early means that other girls their age have not yet had to deal with the questions they face and may be unsympathetic or even hostile. In *Are You There God? It's Me, Margaret*, Margaret and her friends relish exchanging nasty rumors about their classmate, Laura Danker, who developed early. Near the end of the story, Laura confronts Margaret.

> "Don't you think I know all about *you* and your friends? Do you think it's any fun to be the biggest kid in the class?"
>
> "I don't know," I said. "I never thought about it."
>
> "Well, try thinking about it. Think about how you'd feel if you had to wear a bra in fourth grade and how everybody laughed and how you always had to cross your arms in front of you. And about how the boys called you dirty names just because of how you looked."
>
> — (BLUME, 1970, p. 117)

Another problem early-maturing girls face is the way they think about their physical appearance. Remember that the onset of puberty is linked to body weight and proportion of body fat, and that one of its effects, especially in girls, is to increase the proportion of body fat (Cheek, 1974). As a result, girls who enter puberty earlier tend to end up somewhat shorter and heavier than those who mature later (Brooks-Gunn, 1991). This is definitely a disadvantage in a culture in which the feminine ideal is to be tall and thin, with a figure like Barbie (Dittmar, Halliwell, & Ive, 2006)!

Not all early-maturing girls face the same degree of cultural and social pressure. Those who attend all-girls' schools, for example, have no more conduct problems than their peers who mature later (Caspi et al., 1993). Apparently, many of the difficulties early maturers have are not the result of early maturation as such; instead, they stem from the way boys, especially older boys, react to their early development. It is worth noting that according to one study, the more friendships with boys an early-maturing girl has, the more likely she is to have emotional problems as well (Ge et al., 1996).

There are also factors that can make the difficulties of early-maturing girls worse. It is easier to handle major life changes when they come one at a time than to be forced to deal with several simultaneously (Coleman, 1974). Puberty is one such change. Another type of change is moving to a new and different sort of school. Elementary school is a more personal, supportive, and nurturing setting than a larger, more impersonal junior high school. Early-maturing girls who make this transition at the 7th-grade level have to cope with two life changes at once—three, if they also start dating at this point. The result is that they have more problems than those who stay in the same school through 8th grade, and then go directly into high school (Simmons & Blyth, 1987).

Researchers have given a lot less attention to late-maturing girls, except to contrast them with those who mature early. Like early maturers, late maturers tend to have more problems with depression than do average maturers (Graber et al., 1997). Before they reach menarche, they worry about being behind the other girls in their development, but by grades 9 and 10, they are more satisfied with their height, weight, and figure than early developers (Simmons & Blyth, 1987). This is not surprising. Because the adolescent growth spurt adds on to whatever childhood growth has already taken place, late developers are likely to end up taller and slimmer than their earlier developing age mates. And, as we have already discussed, in our culture taller and slimmer generally equals more attractive.

Most of the research on effects of the timing of puberty on girls has looked at White middle-class girls. Do the same patterns hold for those from other groups? Maybe not. In one study, early maturers who were White showed more signs of depression than other White girls, but no such differences were found among African American or Hispanic girls (Hayward, Gotlib, Schraedley, & Litt, 1999). Another group of researchers found that self-esteem declined across adolescence among White girls, but not among African American girls (Brown et al., 1998). One reason for this may be that African Americans do not place as high a premium on slimness as other ethnic groups (Flynn & Fitzgibbon, 1996).

For boys, the effects of reaching puberty early or late are quite different than for girls. It has been widely reported that boys who enter puberty earlier have more positive self-images, are more popular with their peers, show more leadership and maturity, and have fewer problems with parents (Jones, 1965; Jones & Bailey, 1950; Mussen & Jones, 1958). This is an impressive list of advantages. You should note, however, that the source of these statements is a longitudinal study of a small group of children that was carried out in California several decades ago, in the first part of the 20th century.

The world has changed since then, but if you are a boy there are still advantages to maturing early (Duncan, Ritter, Dornbusch, Gross, & Carlsmith,1985; Graber et al., 1997; Petersen, 1985). Why should this be? One likely reason is that boys who enter the adolescent growth spurt early become tall and muscular sooner than their age mates. Because they look more mature, they are seen and treated as more mature. They also have an advantage on the athletic field, which matters a lot in early and middle adolescence.

Early-maturing boys do have problems, however (Alsaker, 1995). In particular, boys who enter puberty early experience more hostile feelings and more symptoms of internalized distress (Ge et al., 2001b). They are more likely to develop depressive symptoms (Graber et al., 1997), difficulties at school (Duncan et al., 1985), delinquency (Williams & Dunlop, 1999), and earlier involvement with sex, drugs, and alcohol use (Andersson & Magnusson, 1990; Silbereisen, Petersen, Albrecht, & Kracke, 1989; Wichstrom, 2001). Like their advantages, these disadvantages may be connected to their more mature appearance. Looking older makes it more likely they will hang out with older boys and get involved in their activities (Ge et al., 2002). The finding that early maturation is negative for boys, as it is for girls, shows up in studies of African Americans as well (Ge, Brody, Conger, & Simons, 2006).

Not very much research has focused on late-maturing boys. Compared to those who are on-time, they show more depression and internalizing symptoms such as anxiety, worry, and sleep problems (Graber et al., 1997; Siegel et al., 1999). Their self-image also suffers (Dorn, Susman, & Ponirakis, 2003). On the other hand, late-maturing boys show more social initiative and intellectual curiosity, and as adults they are more creative and insightful (Livson & Peskin, 1980). This may be because their late development forces them to the sidelines of the adolescent social group, which allows them a certain freedom to explore their impulses, ideas, and emotions (Peskin, 1967).

It should be clear by now that entering puberty early or late has a major impact on adolescents, but how can we explain these effects? What causes them? According to the **deviance hypothesis** (Petersen & Taylor, 1980), the fact that you are noticeably different from the others in your peer group is automatically stressful. It is better, more comfortable, to be "on-time" than to be "off-time." According to this explanation, those who enter puberty early *or* late will be affected negatively, but the worst hit will be those who deviate the most from the norm. Because girls generally reach puberty well ahead of boys, early-maturing girls are out of step with other girls *and* with all the boys. In the same way, late-maturing boys are out of step both with other boys and with all the girls.

Another factor to consider is that early puberty may bring childhood to an end before the girl has had time to deal with the normal psychological tasks of childhood. According to this **stage termination hypothesis** (Peskin & Livson, 1972), middle childhood is a time for firming up the authority of the ego and gaining a strong sense of reality. Girls who are plunged into puberty without having finished the process will have a harder time dealing with the changes of adolescence. As for late-developing boys, they may find their adolescence too short to accomplish the developmental tasks that belong to this stage, or they may prolong their adolescence into the young adult years (Erikson, 1968).

Finally, the **adult resemblance hypothesis** (Block, 1984; Faust, 1960) says that those who seem more like adults will benefit more from the status of adults. At first glance this seems to mean that all early maturers will be better off because they are moving toward adult status sooner. As we know, for early-maturing boys this is pretty much true. Then why not for girls? One answer may be the different cultural attitudes about males and females. What is most valued in males is power, independence, and effectiveness—all adult characteristics. In females, however, youth and beauty are much more highly valued. For boys, moving toward adult status is clearly positive. For girls, being seen as adults is more mixed, with negatives that may well outweigh the positives.

Puberty, whether early or late, brings a fundamental change in how individuals are seen and treated. However, while the way others see them matters, how adolescents see themselves also has a profound impact. Whether adolescents *think* they are early or late maturers has more impact on their behavior than whether they really are early or late in their development (Dubas, Graber, & Petersen, 1991). The saying, "You're only as old as you feel," does not apply only to senior citizens. Adolescents, too, tend to act according to how old they feel. In fact, this inner perception often carries more weight than their actual level of maturity (Galambos, Kolaric, Sears, & Maggs, 1999).

We should also remind ourselves that all these findings about the effects of early and late development are based on group averages. There is also a lot of variability within these groups. Adolescents are not simply examples of a particular category, like early or late developers. They are also individuals with their own unique makeups and personal histories. Generalizations based on group membership are no more than a starting point in the process of understanding them. It is at least as important to study how and why they are *different* from others in the same group.

Connect the Dots...

Think about the positive and negative aspects of entering adolescence earlier or later than other young people. How are they different for girls and boys, and why? What aspects of an adolescent's family life or surroundings might turn an advantage into a disadvantage, or vice versa?

Deviance hypothesis The idea that those who enter puberty at a time noticeably different from their peers will be negatively affected.

Stage termination hypothesis The idea that girls who enter puberty early suffer because they did not have time to accomplish the normal tasks of childhood.

Adult resemblance hypothesis The idea that young adolescents who seem more adult-like will be treated more as adults, for better or worse.

Parental Responses to Puberty

Puberty is a major turning point, biologically, personally, and socially (Graber & Brooks-Gunn, 1996). The way children get through the stresses of this crucial transition can affect them for years afterwards. It helps a lot if they see their parents as warm and loving and feel they can count on their support (Wagner, Cohen, & Brooks, 1996). Unfortunately, this is not always the case. For many, puberty is a time when their relationship with their parents becomes less close and more filled with conflict (Laursen, Coy, & Collins, 1998; Montemayor, 1983).

Some of the reasons for this conflict are obvious. With puberty, children are moving into a new stage that makes the usual ways their parents deal with them outmoded. The children probably realize this before the parents. They start to demand more input in family decisions and looser restrictions on their activities, and they are upset when their demands are not instantly met. The bitterest accusation an early adolescent can hurl at a parent is, "You always treat me like a baby!"

Of course, parents recognize that their child is growing up. If nothing else, the physical and sexual changes of puberty make it obvious. Knowing that, however, does not tell them the best way to react to it. The rules and practices they have relied on for years may no longer be appropriate, but developing new ones takes time and effort. In the meantime, the easiest course is to go on using the old ones. This is practically guaranteed to upset the child and arouse conflict. The level of conflict is higher for those who entered puberty early (Laursen & Collins, 1994; Sagestrano, McCormick, & Paikoff, 1999). This suggests that it is the child's maturation, more than age, that is responsible.

Across the adolescent years, conflicts with parents tend to level off or decrease (Laursen et al., 1998). One reason this happens is that most parents give children more autonomy as they get older (Eccles et al., 1991; Paikoff & Brooks-Gunn, 1991). This cuts down on a major source of conflict. However, it does not work quite the same way for boys and girls.

Early adolescents come under increasing pressure from parents and others to act according to traditional male or female roles (Crouter, Manke, & McHale, 1995). This process of **gender intensification** (Hill & Lynch, 1983) pushes boys to be more independent and assertive, and grants them greater autonomy. Girls, on the other hand, are encouraged to be more expressive and compliant (Galambos, 2004). Compared to boys, they have more restrictions put on them, especially in families where the mother has more traditional attitudes about gender roles (Bumpus, Crouter, & McHale, 2001).

Another reason conflicts level off or decrease later in adolescence is that parents and teens spend less and less time together (Laursen & Williams, 1997). This may seem so normal and obvious that it is hardly worth mentioning, but it has inspired an ingenious explanation for the tensions that develop between parents and children at puberty.

The **distancing hypothesis** (Steinberg, 1989) proposes that children who have less contact with their parents as they become sexually mature are less likely to commit incest, with its risks of genetic damage to their offspring. Over many generations, those who had inherited this distancing tendency would produce more and healthier descendents, and the genetic basis for the tendency would become more widespread.

One source of support for this idea is that something similar happens among most species of monkeys and apes. At puberty, young males begin to spend less time with parents and more with age mates (Schlegel, 1995; Steinberg, 1987). However, adolescent females tend to stay close to their mothers and other adult females (Mitchell, 1981). The same is true in most traditional human cultures (Schlegel & Barry, 1991).

If the adaptive basis of distancing is to reduce the risk of incest, it would not much matter if girls stay close to their mothers or boys to their fathers. What would matter is separation from the opposite-sex parent. However, when it comes to avoiding incest, close proximity during early childhood seems to be more important than

◀ **Learning Objective 3.6**
Do parents and children become more distant after puberty?

Gender intensification The process in which young adolescents come under greater pressure to conform to traditional gender roles.

Distancing hypothesis The idea that as children become more sexually mature, they have less contact with parents.

distance during adolescence (Shepher, 1983). The greatest risk of incest is between stepfathers and stepdaughters and between brothers and sisters who did not grow up together (Brown, 1991).

There is other evidence that does not fit well with the distancing hypothesis. For instance, conflict between adolescents and parents does not necessarily lessen their closeness. One study found that while both boys and girls become more distant from their fathers at puberty, they have both more closeness *and* more conflict with their mothers (Claes, 1998). According to another study, while White boys have more conflict and less closeness with parents at puberty, as the distancing hypothesis predicts, Hispanic boys actually grow *closer* to their parents at puberty (Molina & Chassin, 1996). We will look at these issues in greater depth later, in Chapter 5.

Cultural Responses to Puberty

▶ **Learning Objective 3.7**
What are puberty rites, and what purposes do they serve?

Imagine you are walking down the street and you glance in the window of a house. You see balloons, children gathered around a table, a stack of wrapped presents, and a cake with lit candles in it. One child is wearing a shiny pointed hat. Do you have to hear the guests singing "Happy Birthday" to know what is being celebrated? Of course not. The customs that surround a birthday in our culture are familiar to everybody.

It matters when people move from one social role or status to another. It matters to them, it matters to those close to them—parents, relatives, friends—and it matters to the larger social group. To mark these transitions, cultures use various *rituals*. These are events that are deliberately set off from everyday life. These rituals often involve special locations, foods, clothing, music, language, and ways of acting (Turner, 1969). A birthday party is a familiar example, as is a college commencement, a presidential inauguration, or a retirement party.

The most elaborate rituals tend to be connected with the most significant life changes, such as birth, puberty, marriage, parenthood, and death. Like the others on this list, puberty is widely marked by special rites. Anthropologists Alice Schlegel and Herbert Barry, III, surveyed field studies of almost 200 traditional cultures throughout the world. Of those for which information was available, roughly four out of five (79%) held **puberty rites** for girls and two out of three (68%) held them for boys (Schlegel & Barry, 1991).

The What and Why of Puberty Rites. Depending on the culture we look at, puberty rites can last anywhere from a few hours to several months. What the child is expected to do ranges from memorizing a few traditional songs to undergoing repeated and traumatic mutilations (Poole, 1982). Even groups that live in the same region and come into frequent contact with each other may have strikingly different rituals (Herdt, 1982).

Can we make any useful generalizations about something so varied? Fortunately, yes. Puberty rites from all over the world share a similar underlying purpose—they *shape* the process of leaving childhood and achieving adulthood. These rites stamp the imprint of the particular culture on the individual and instill a sense of loyalty to the group (Weisfeld, 1997). The contrast between nature and culture has been called one of the basic ways we understand the world (Lévi-Strauss, 1963). Puberty is a biological fact of nature; marking it with rites transforms it into a cultural fact.

Puberty rites tend to have certain features in common: *separation*, *transition*, and *incorporation* (Gennep, 1909/1960). During the first step, the child is separated from home, parents, and the opposite sex. The next step involves intensive instruction about the beliefs, values, and ceremonial practices of the culture. Rules about personal conduct, especially those that concern sexuality and reproduction, are often stressed. There may be physical or mental ordeals to pass through as well. Finally, the successful boy or girl is welcomed into adult society, usually with feasting and dancing (Ottenberg, 1994).

Puberty rites Cultural rituals such as the Jewish *Bar* and *Bas Mitzvah* or the Hispanic *quinceañero* that mark a child's passage to adolescence.

Puberty Rites for Girls. In most traditional cultures, the customary time to hold puberty rites for a girl is at menarche (Schlegel & Barry, 1991). Because girls reach menarche at different ages, the rites are usually held on an individual basis (Young, 1965). Also, because menarche comes toward the end of puberty, the ceremony generally marks the *end* of the girl's transition from childhood to adulthood.

Among the Navajo people of the American Southwest, a girl's first period is celebrated with a ceremony called *Kinaaldá* (Frisbie, 1967; Lincoln, 1981; Markstrom & Iborra, 2003). A girl's physical maturation lays the groundwork for adulthood, but Navajos believe it is this ritual, rich in symbolism, that gives her the actual power to have children.

For 5 days and 4 nights, the girl's family hogan becomes the First Hogan, from the time when the human race first emerged onto the Earth. At the beginning, the girl is dressed in the ceremonial costume and jewelry of the goddess Changing Woman and massaged by older women of the tribe to mold her into an adult. In the days that follow, she stays inside to greet visitors and grind corn for a huge celebratory cake. She comes out of the hogan only to run a series of ritual footraces with other youngsters.

On the last evening of the Kinaaldá, everyone assembles in the hogan for an entire night of singing and listening to sacred songs and chants. The girl sits on the western side of the circle, facing an open doorway through which the first rays of dawn will strike her. When morning comes, she runs a final footrace. Then she cuts the ceremonial cake, which has been baking all night, and gives a piece to each of the participants. Now she is considered able to marry and bear children. More than that, by re-creating the goddess Changing Woman, she has helped to ensure the fertility of the people as a whole and of the earth that supports them (Lincoln, 1981).

The Kinaaldá ritual is unusual in at least one way, because it *celebrates* the girl's menarche. In a great many traditional cultures, in every part of the world, menstrual blood is considered dangerously powerful (Delaney, Lupton, & Toth, 1976). A woman who is menstruating may have to follow strict rules and restrictions to avoid ruining the crops, sickening the livestock, frightening off game animals, and polluting the starter dough for bread. She may also have to isolate herself in a special menstrual hut throughout her period (Stephens, 1967).

In cultures with such beliefs, one focus of puberty rites tends to be on making sure the girl knows all the taboos she must obey and on controlling her new, and potentially dangerous, sexual potential (Delaney, 1988). The rites are also a way to alert others to the fact that the girl now possesses this power.

▲ As part of the Navajo puberty rite called Kinaaldá, the young adolescent girl runs a series of ceremonial footraces.

Puberty Rites for Boys. As we have seen, there is no specific event comparable to menarche that signals puberty in boys. Maybe as a result of this, boys tend to be initiated in groups rather than one by one (Schlegel & Barry, 1980). Even before puberty, boys tend to spend more time with other boys than girls do with other girls (Mitchell, 1981; Schlegel, 1995). Going through a difficult and painful rite together may strengthen this loyalty to the male peer group. And as a rule, the rites for boys *are* difficult and painful (Schlegel & Barry, 1980; Young, 1965).

Among the Ndumba, in the Eastern Highlands of Papua New Guinea, uninitiated boys of 10 to 12 go through a ceremony to make them into'*ummanra*, or adolescents (Hays & Hays, 1982). The men of the village grab them, carry them off into the woods, and strip them naked. The boys are forced to suffer nosebleeds and are rubbed all over with stinging nettles, then bathed, dressed in new clothes, and led back into the village. After a period of isolation in the men's house, they are decked in ceremonial clothes and led out to a feast at which the men and women of the village dance around them singing songs of celebration. They wear their ceremonial garb for another month, and then change into ordinary clothes. After that, they are treated as adolescents, not children.

Why are puberty rites for boys generally so much harsher and painful than those for girls? One explanation is that boys are being prepared for a physically difficult

▲ Among the Maori of New Zealand, adolescents traditionally tattooed their faces, a custom that is being revived.

adult life of warfare and hunting, while girls are being prepared to be wives and mothers (Buss, 1994; La Fontaine, 1985). Another possibility is that these rites are a tool of social control. Across cultures, adolescent boys are much more likely to act antisocially than adolescent girls (Schlegel & Barry, 1991). Harsh ordeals may help govern their behavior by scaring them into obeying adult authority (Spindler, 1970).

Decline of Puberty Rites. In recent decades, traditional cultures throughout the world have come under heavy pressure from trends toward urbanization, industrialization, and globalization. One result is that even in remote areas, traditional ceremonies marking puberty are rapidly dying out (Richards, 1982). In some parts of the world, however, rituals that were once abandoned are going through a modest revival. For example, among the Maori people of New Zealand, adolescents used to tattoo their faces in elaborate traditional patterns called *moko*. This custom disappeared toward the end of the 19th century, but it has come back in recent years as a way for young Maoris to show their identification with their native culture (Neleman, 1999).

Puberty rites are not common in Western Europe, the United States, or Canada. One reason is that these societies incorporate traditions from so many varied cultures that no single set of customs commands wide loyalty. Another is that adolescents in modern technological societies go through a very long period of education and training. Puberty is still an important turning point, socially as well as biologically, but it has come to signify starting more than finishing.

Some ceremonies marking puberty do survive among particular ethnic and religious groups. In the Jewish tradition, boys at puberty affirm their religious affiliation at a *Bar Mitzvah*, and in recent decades a parallel ceremony for girls, the *Bas Mitzvah*, has become widespread. Many Christian denominations expect young adolescents to study their religion and then announce their formal membership at *confirmation*.

There are also secular events that are roughly comparable to traditional puberty rites, such as the *quinceañero*, a celebration held for young Hispanic girls in the American Southwest, or the similar "Sweet Sixteen" parties. All these events are mainly symbolic, however. Most Hispanic parents do not really expect their daughters to get married right after their quinceañero. When the bar mitzvah boy ritually announces, "Today I am a man," the guests react with affectionate smiles instead of nods of agreement.

> **Summing Up...**
>
> The ways children react to the changes of puberty are influenced by many factors, including their sex, the preparation they have been given, and the degree to which they enter puberty earlier or later than their age mates. Puberty also affects relationships with parents, who may place new stress on traditional gender roles and put more emotional distance between themselves and their adolescent children. More traditional cultures often recognize and confirm the child's new status by some form of puberty rite.

BRAIN DEVELOPMENT

How does the brain change during adolescence, and what significance do these changes have? At one time, the best available way to seek answers to such questions was to wait until someone was dead, and then open his or her skull and take a look. Now, however, evolving techniques of neuroimaging, including *positron emission tomography (PET)* and *functional magnetic resonance imaging (fMRI)*, have led to a rapid growth in our knowledge about how the normal brain develops and what happens when it is in action (Thatcher, Lyon, Rumsey, & Krasnegor, 1996).

The Structure of the Brain

To understand the implications of the changes that take place in the brain at adolescence, we first need to look at how it is put together. The most basic unit of the brain is the nerve cell or *neuron*. A human brain contains as many as 100 billion to 200 billion neurons. Each neuron may be directly linked to hundreds or even thousands of others. This means that the number of interconnections mounts well up into the trillions. At the level of the individual neuron, incoming signals arrive through the many-branched *dendrites*, and outgoing signals are sent through a long fiber called the *axon*. A fatty insulating material called *myelin* wraps the axon and helps make transmission of electrical signals more efficient.

The bud at the end of an axon does not actually touch the dendrite of the next neuron. Instead, there is a tiny gap known as a *synapse*. When an electrical signal flows out along the axon and reaches the end, it causes a chemical called a *neurotransmitter* to be released into the gap. This is picked up by specialized receptors on the dendrite of the next cell, which transform the signal back into an electrical impulse. Among the many neurotransmitters that have been identified so far are *acetylcholine*, *dopamine*, and *serotonin*.

The part of the brain people are most familiar with is the **cerebral cortex** or *neocortex*, the deeply wrinkled layer that covers the rest of the brain. The cortex is responsible for most of the processes we call thinking. It is divided into left and right hemispheres, each of which has several distinct regions called *lobes*. Different functions are carried out in specialized areas. Some areas handle receiving information from the various senses or sending action signals to the muscles. Others, the *association areas*, deal with more complex processes, such as memory, judgment, and planning.

The Developing Brain

When we are born, our brains are already about a quarter of the size they will be in adulthood. By age 10 they have reached 95% of their adult size (Tanner, 1978). During infancy, new synapses form at a furious rate. By age 2, there are a great many more than are needed. A process of **synaptic pruning**, or the elimination of less-used brain circuits, starts up (Huttenlocher, 1999). According to some estimates, neurons lose as many as half their synapses during puberty and adolescence (Spear, 2000). As a result, while the total volume of "gray matter" (neurons and the cells that support them) increases during childhood, it decreases during adolescence (Durston et al., 2001).

Apparently the principle at work here is "use it or lose it." Sensory and motor experiences stimulate and strengthen groups of synapses. Those that do not get enough stimulation are less likely to survive (Greenough & Black, 1999). At the same time, however, ongoing experience makes dendrites continue to branch out and form new synapses (Quartz & Sejnowski, 1997). These changes in the neural network, in turn, make new sorts of experiences possible.

There are other important developments in the brain during adolescence as well. The areas of the cortex that get activated when making a decision are more sharply focused in adolescents than in children (Casey et al., 1997; Galvin et al., 2006; Hooper, Luciana, Conklin, & Yarger, 2004). The right and left hemispheres of adolescents become more able to process information independently (Anokhin, Lutzenberger, Nikolaev, & Birbaumer, 2000). Along with a decrease in the volume of the cortex (Giedd et al., 1999; Shaw et al., 2006) goes an increase in efficiency, as marked by lower energy consumption (Chugani, Phelps, & Mazziotta, 1987). This efficiency may be associated with increased *executive control* (Kuhn, 2006; Rothbart & Posner, 2005), an important aspect of thinking that we look at in more detail in the next chapter.

Another factor that leads to greater efficiency in the adolescent brain is **myelination**, the spread of insulating myelin. Nerve cells that have a myelin sheath on

◄ **Learning Objective 3.8**
What are the principal parts of the brain?

◄ **Learning Objective 3.9**
How do synaptic pruning and myelination help make the brain more efficient?

Cerebral cortex The outermost layer of the brain that is the site of most higher-order brain functions.

Synaptic pruning A process in which brain circuits that are less used are eliminated, leading to a faster, more efficient cognitive system.

Myelination The development of sheaths of myelin insulation along the axons of brain cells, making their operation more sensitive and precise.

their axons are more sensitive and fire faster. They are also more precise in the way they act because the myelin prevents the electrical impulse from leaking to neurons other than those targeted (Bjorklund, 2000). In many parts of the cortex, myelination is complete by early childhood, but in the association areas of the prefrontal cortex, so important to complex cognition, it continues through the adolescent years (Korner, 1991).

A smaller cortex, many fewer synapses, and less energy use: at first, these developments during puberty and adolescence may not sound much like progress. Isn't bigger better?

Not necessarily. An analogy may help explain why. Say you just installed one of those multi-purpose software suites on your computer that does practically everything but brew your coffee. At first, the screen is overloaded with menus and buttons and toolbars, but as you get used to the program, you start pruning. The functions you use a lot, you keep handy. The ones you use occasionally, you hide. Those you never use, you trash. The result is that the program gradually gets smaller, but faster and more adapted to the way *you* work. In a similar way, the increase in cognitive capacity and processing speed during childhood and adolescence may be linked to the gradual loss of synapses, along with the strengthening of those that remain (Casey, Giedd, & Thomas, 2000).

It is important to note that different parts of the adolescent brain change at different rates. In recent years, neuroscientists have found evidence that the "pleasure center" in the limbic system develops more quickly during adolescence than the impulse control systems in the prefrontal cortex (Casey, Getz, & Galvan, 2008). This discrepancy may help explain the fact that teens who should—and generally *do*—know better take risks that endanger their health, their happiness, and even their lives (Steinberg, 2008).

Behavior and the Brain

> **Connect the Dots...**
>
> Research indicates that the prefrontal cortex, a part of the brain deeply involved in assessing risks and making complex judgments, is still developing during the adolescent years. Given that, should adolescents have the same rights and be held to the same standards of responsibility as adults? For example, should they be able to consent to sexual activity or join the armed forces? If they commit an offense, should they be tried as adults?

▶ **Learning Objective 3.10**
How is brain development linked to other adolescent changes?

As we have just seen, along with other physical, cognitive, and emotional changes of adolescence, major developments take place in the structure and functioning of the brain. Because these changes happen during the same period, some people argue that the changes in the brain must *produce* the other changes. If that's so, then the way to understand psychological changes would be to concentrate on what is happening to the brain. This argument is known as **reductionism**.

According to reductionists, if we want to be truly scientific, we should always aim to break down complex events to their more elementary components. For example, learning psychologists have sometimes claimed that the most complicated acts are nothing more than an assembly of simple stimulus-response links (Skinner, 1953).

Psychologists and philosophers have debated this issue for a century or more, and we are not likely to resolve it now. From a practical point of view, I think the question is different. Can we gain a better understanding of some aspect of adolescence by looking at the neurology or biochemistry or brain structure involved? If so, it would be foolish not to do so. On the other hand, we should be careful not to lose important insights by focusing too much on certain details just because they are supposedly more "basic."

An analogy may make this point clearer. Take the experience of color. This involves, among other things, the electron shells of atoms, the biochemistry of cone cells in the eye, and specialized neural assemblies in the thalamus and visual cortex of the brain. But let's imagine we understand all these processes. We know exactly how each is involved in creating the sensation of blue and the sensation of red. Would that allow us to understand the psychological impact of a deep, rich purple? On one level, purple is simply a specified blend of red and blue. On the level that interests us, however, it has a character of its own that we could not predict if we know only about the elements that go into making it up.

Reductionism An approach to scientific explanation that reduces complex processes to more elementary components.

There is another point we should keep in mind. Even if some particular aspect of adolescent psychology can be traced to changes in the brain, that does not mean that it is *determined* by those changes. A person's experiences, behavior, and environment can lead to physical changes in the structure of the brain. These, in turn, can lead to changes in the person's behavior and environment. If we try to single out one element in this dynamic system and say, "This one is the cause, so we should concentrate on it," we are not increasing our understanding, we are hampering it.

Summing Up...

The more advanced parts of the brain continue to develop across adolescence. The process of synaptic pruning cuts down on neuronal connections that are little used, while the process of myelination makes the transmission of nerve impulses faster and more precise. These changes improve complex processes such as judgment and executive control.

HEALTH ISSUES

The physical, psychological, and social changes that take place during adolescence are dramatic, rapid, and far-reaching. It's no wonder these changes raise important health issues for young adolescents. Among the most noticeable issues are problems with mood and body image. This is also a time when young people form health habits that will affect their well-being for years to come. These habits include getting enough sleep; eating a balanced, nutritious diet; and exercising regularly (American Medical Association, 2003). These health-enhancing behaviors do not come about automatically, they are strengthened when adolescents understand their effects, both immediately and in the long run, and when their parents and friends model healthy behavior (Jessor, Turbin, & Costa, 1998).

Puberty and Mood

One of the most common stereotypes of adolescents is that they are subject to wild emotional swings, going from exhilaration to deep despair and back again at the least excuse. Long before G. Stanley Hall (1904) popularized the idea of adolescence as a period of "storm and stress," Shakespeare was depicting such moody, unpredictable teenagers as Romeo, Juliet, and Prince Hal. In recent years, a scientific-sounding explanation has become attached to this stereotype. The mood swings and emotional storms that teens supposedly experience are now said to be the result of **"raging hormones"** (Buchanan, Eccles, & Becker, 1992; Petersen, 1985).

Mood Swings in Adolescents. Are adolescents moodier than children or adults? And if they are, why? Is it in fact linked to shifting hormone levels? Is it, as some have said, the result of a "pileup" of stressful life changes (Simmons & Blyth, 1987)? Or some combination of these factors?

There is evidence that early adolescents are more emotional than those younger or older than them (Buchanan et al., 1992; Dahl, 2004; Hunt, 1999). Moods change faster around puberty than later in adolescence (Bence, 1990). Reed Larson and Maryse Richards (1994) used the Experience Sampling Method, described earlier in Chapter 2, to look at the everyday lives of teens. The participants wore beepers that went off at random times during the day and evening. Each time this happened, they noted who they were with, what they were doing, and how they felt. Adolescents reported extreme states of emotion—positive *and* negative—more often than their parents. A related study that followed a group of teens across 4 years found that the range of emotional ups and downs gradually narrows from early to late adolescence (Larson, Moneta, Richards, & Wilson, 2002).

◄ **Learning Objective 3.11**
Are teens at the mercy of their "raging hormones"?

"Raging hormones" The belief that many of the problems of adolescents can be traced to their changing hormone levels.

So far, the popular stereotype seems fairly accurate. When we try to tie this emotionality directly to hormones, however, the picture gets a good deal murkier. Both estrogen and testosterone have been linked to greater excitability and more rapid response to stimulation (Buchanan et al., 1992). The rise in level of these hormones early in puberty might then make children likely to react more quickly and more extremely to situations, whether positive or negative. We should also remember that during puberty, hormone levels not only increase quickly, they fluctuate erratically. It takes the body time to get used to these changes and for the changes themselves to become more stable. The greater emotionality in early adolescence may stem from these rapid and unpredictable changes in hormone levels, rather than from the particular level reached (Buchanan et al., 1992).

Hormones and Life Events. Hormones can directly affect emotions, that is clear, but hormones and emotions may be related in other ways as well. First, an emotional state can bring about a change in hormone levels. For example, psychological stress leads to increased production of the hormone *cortisol*. Hormones and emotions can also affect each other, in a sort of feedback loop. Hormones can also affect other factors, such as excitability or physical appearance, that in turn affect emotions (Susman et al., 2003).

Hormones also interact with life events to have an impact on emotions. In other words, a particular life event may have a greater or lesser effect, depending on hormonal levels at the time it takes place. In one study that directly measured hormone levels in young girls, higher levels were associated with greater negative feelings, but the link was not very strong (Brooks-Gunn & Warren, 1989). Social factors carried greater weight, and so did the relationship of negative life events and hormone levels (Brooks-Gunn & Warren, 1989). This complex interaction of biological, environmental, and social influences is discussed in this chapter's Research in the Spotlight.

Early adolescence is a time of many stressful but expected transitions—going through puberty, changing schools, gaining greater independence. It also brings an increase in unpredictable events. These may include changed relationships with peers, romantic involvements, school difficulties, new tensions with parents and siblings, and issues related to sex and drugs (Larson & Ham, 1993). Not only do young adolescents have more negative life events to cope with, they also seem to be more vulnerable to them (Brooks-Gunn & Warren, 1989; Compas & Phares, 1991; Larson & Ham, 1993). That is, each of the larger *number* of events they experience has a greater *impact* as well. This double whammy makes it easy to see why their emotions might swing wildly.

One reason for this increased vulnerability may be simple lack of experience. Puberty propels children into new, unexplored territory. When something happens to them, they don't have a built up stock of information to use for comparison and evaluation. The first time a friend passes along something you said in confidence, your sense of being betrayed may be much greater because you don't yet have similar experiences to measure it against. The sentiment, "I never felt this way before," can easily slide over into, "No one ever felt this way before!" If a parent or older sibling tells you to take it easy, you'll get over it, a likely response is to wail, "You don't understand!" and rush sobbing from the room. At that point, somebody will probably murmur, "What can you expect? Must be raging hormones."

Connect the Dots...

Can you recall an occasion during early adolescence when you found yourself wildly elated or deeply upset, only to have others, such as parents, minimize or dismiss your feelings? Looking back, to what extent do you think your mood swing was a response to particular life events or to the newness of those events? What about the idea that your emotional state was set off or magnified by factors, such as "raging hormones," that you were not aware of?

▶ **Learning Objective 3.12**
What impact do pubertal changes have on body image for girls and boys?

Body image The ways people perceive, think of, and feel about their bodies.

Body Image

The physical changes that take place during puberty find a reflection in **body image**, the way adolescents perceive, think of, and feel about their bodies. Like a funhouse mirror, however, this reflection is often distorted. Girls are especially prone to criticize their own appearance. They see themselves as overweight, even when they are not (Benedikt, Wertheim, & Love, 1998), and are particularly dissatisfied with their hips, thighs, and waists (Attie, Brooks-Gunn, & Petersen, 1990; Rosenblum & Lewis, 1999). These areas of the body, of course, are particularly affected by puberty.

How Does Puberty Affect Adjustment in Girls?

As we have seen, puberty is an event (or a set of events) that is both biological and social. How an adolescent adjusts to puberty depends partly on the timing and rate of physical and hormonal changes. However, adjustment is also affected by the ways parents, friends, and society at large interpret and respond to those changes (Brooks-Gunn, Graber, & Paikoff, 1994; Susman, 2004). Lots of research has documented these associations between puberty and various measures of adjustment, but much less is known about the nature of the connections. What are the specific pathways that link physical and hormonal events with psychological states?

Pinning down the ways the timing of puberty and the hormonal changes are associated with psychological adjustment is not easy. For one thing, researchers have generally relied on self-reports to measure timing. Girls are asked to recall how old they were when they started developing, or when they had their first period, or whether they were ahead, behind, or even with other girls their age. This can be valuable information about a girl's *perception* of puberty, but it is hard to tell how accurate it is. As for hormonal changes, if people are aware of them at all, it is only because they may notice some of their psychological effects, such as moodiness. But that link, between hormonal changes and psychological effects, is just what investigators want to find out about. Any information already based on it is not likely to be helpful.

One way around these difficulties is to measure physical development and hormone levels directly, as children are going through puberty. This is the approach taken by Julia Graber, Jeanne Brooks-Gunn, and Michelle Warren (2006), in a study

entitled "Pubertal effects on adjustment in girls: Moving from demonstrating effects to identifying pathways." The participants were 100 White middle-class girls aged 10 to 14. Each was examined by a doctor or nurse who used the Tanner scales (Marshall & Tanner, 1969) to rate the girl's stage of breast and pubic hair development. A blood test revealed levels of two important hormones, estradiol (an estrogen produced by the gonads) and DHEAS (an androgen produced by the adrenal gland). A self-report scale was used to measure the psychological variables of emotional arousal, attention difficulties, negative life events, depressive feelings, and aggression.

As the researchers expected, each of the three predictors—pubertal timing, estradiol level, and DHEAS level—had connections to depression, aggression, or both. However, the precise nature of the connections was different in each case. As Figure R3.1 shows, depressive feelings were linked directly to estradiol levels; indirectly, by way of emotional arousal, to early puberty; and not at all to DHEAS levels. In contrast, aggression was linked indirectly to both estradiol and DHEAS, by way of stressful life events, but was not significantly linked either directly or indirectly with pubertal timing (see Figure R3.2).

Beyond the specific findings made by Graber and her colleagues, their study highlights the way biological and hormonal changes during puberty are interwoven with social and psychological factors in a dense fabric of causes and effects. As we learn more about the process, we may also find ways to make it less stressful and more productive for those who are about to go through it.

Figure R3.1   Connections with Depressive Effect
Depressive feelings were linked both to estradiol levels and to emotional arousal connnected with the timing of puberty, but not to DHEAS.

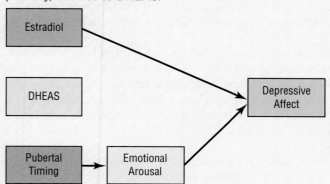

Source: "Pubertal Effects on Adjustment in Girls," by J. A. Graber et al. *Journal of Youth and Adolescence, 35*, 391–401, Figure 1. Used by permission.

Figure R3.2   Pubertal Variables and Aggression
Aggression was linked to estradiol and, by way of stress, to DHEAS, but not to pubertal timing.

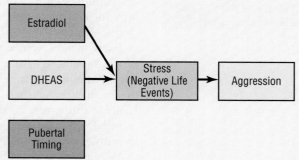

Source: "Pubertal Effects on Adjustment in Girls," by J. A. Graber et al. *Journal of Youth and Adolescence, 35*, 391–401, Figure 1. Used by permission.

Interestingly, how dissatisfied girls are with their bodies has little to do with how attractive others—adults and other teens—find them (Rosenblum & Lewis, 1999). When girls describe an ideal girl's body, they make it much thinner than boys do when *they* describe an ideal girl's body (Thompson, Corwin, & Sargent, 1997). Adolescent girls aren't alone in this. Adult women also overestimate how much thinness is valued by others (Cash & Henry, 1995; Wiseman, Gray, Mosimann, & Ahrens, 1992).

Body dissatisfaction does not have that much to do with actual weight, either. According to recent surveys, some 16% of adolescent girls in the United States are overweight (Ogden, Carroll, Curtin, McDowell, Tabak, & Flegal, 2006). But almost 40% of adolescent girls, two and a half times as many, *think* they are overweight, and 60%, a clear majority, are actively trying to *lose* weight (Centers for Disease Control and Prevention, 2006).

Along with dissatisfaction goes *objectification*. Instead of being "okay inside their skins," many girls come to think of their body as something divorced from the self, an alien contraption that has to be worked on, punished, or conquered (Martin, 1996). As one girl put it:

> I'm tired of it [my body] being this big. I want to get it in shape. I'm gonna have to start taking it to the gym.
>
> — DANIELLE
> (MARTIN, 1996, p. 41)

Most adolescents, girls and boys, think they can control their weight and body shape, if only they exert enough willpower (Ferron, 1997). These expectations are unrealistic, however. Both weight and body type are influenced by genetic as well as environmental factors (Grilo & Pogue-Geile, 1991). When their efforts do not succeed, the result is feelings of inadequacy and lack of self-control (O'Dea & Abraham, 1999).

A major source of dissatisfaction for many girls is the images conveyed by the media (Polce-Lynch, 2001). The teenage girls who are featured in magazines and on television tend to be unusually tall and thin. Not only that, they have been getting *thinner* in recent years (Guillen & Barr, 1994; O'Dea, 1995). Not surprisingly, teens who watch more television and read more teen-oriented magazines are more dissatisfied with their own bodies (Hofschire & Greenberg, 2002). One study found that among girls 15 to 18 who used diet pills or laxatives for weight control, most also read health and fitness magazines (Thomsen, Weber, & Brown, 2001). Among younger girls, 9 to 14, those who want to look like media stars are more likely to be concerned about their own weight (Field et al., 2001).

It is not just girls who are affected by media images. The males who are featured in magazines and television shows for teens are uniformly broad shouldered and hipless, with bulging pecs and washboard abs. The male action figures marketed to younger boys are even more extreme, with bigger muscles than even champion bodybuilders (Pope, Olivardia, Gruber, & Borowiecki, 1999). The more boys buy into ideals of muscularity, the more dissatisfied they are with their own bodies (Jones, 2004).

Early in adolescence there is not that much difference in level of body dissatisfaction between boys and girls (Rosenblum & Lewis, 1999). For both boys and girls, the best predictor of change efforts is their sense of being pressured by parents, peers, and the media, rather than their personal feelings (Jones, 2004; Ricciardelli, McCabe, Holt, & Finemore, 2003). Across the adolescent years, however, boys become more satisfied, while girls become more *dis*satisfied (Gardner, Friedman, & Jackson, 1999; Rosenblum & Lewis, 1999).

We can understand this better when we consider what happens to boys and girls during puberty. Boys tend to get taller and more muscular, bringing them closer to the cultural ideal. Girls, however, tend to put on weight, especially in the hips and thighs. In other words, they are moving farther away from cultural ideals of beauty. In addition, girls come under pressure from parents, peers, and the media to lose

Connect the Dots...

Recently the fashion industry in several European countries has talked of not using as models young women who are so thin that they appear to suffer from an eating disorder. Do you think measures of that sort will have an impact on the body image problems of adolescents? What other steps might be helpful?

weight, even when their actual weight is normal (Benedikt et al., 1998; Byely, Archibald, Graber, & Brooks-Gunn, 2000; Cauffman & Steinberg, 1996; Ricciardelli & McCabe, 2001).

An interesting exception: in one study, girls who were rated as more attractive at age 13 were more satisfied with their bodies at age 18, even if their attractiveness ratings went *down* between the two ages (Rosenblum & Lewis, 1999). It seems that if enough people think you are attractive early in adolescence, you develop defenses that help you resist the effects of social pressure and a negative body image later on.

We should also note that most of the teens who took part in the studies cited here were Whites of European descent. Studies of African American adolescents yield a different picture. Most African American girls—some 70%—say they are satisfied with their bodies, and nearly as many think it is better to be a little overweight than a little underweight (Parker et al., 1995). In this, they agree with African American boys, men, and adult women, who tend to find larger female bodies attractive (Thompson, Sargent, & Kemper, 1996).

This chapter's Applications in the Spotlight on page 98 discusses some approaches to helping young adolescents maintain a more positive body image.

Negative body images lead to widespread unhappiness among teens. For some, the consequences are even more drastic and can include crash and fad diets, use of untested and risky "nutritional supplements," steroid abuse, and eating disorders, as well as depression and other psychological disorders. We will look more closely at these later, in Chapter 13.

Sleep Needs

> Early to bed and early to rise
>
> Makes a man healthy, wealthy, and wise.

Benjamin Franklin's famous maxim may or may not be true of adults, but certainly doesn't apply to adolescents. It would be much more accurate to say,

> Early to rise and early to bed
>
> Makes a teen grumpy and slow in the head!

Most American adolescents do not get nearly enough sleep. Experts say they need 9 or more hours a night, but only a small minority get that much. Almost half get 7 hours or less, and the figure goes down steadily across the teen years (Carskadon, 2002; Wolfson & Carskadon, 1998). One reason for this decline—no surprise here—is that teens stay up later than preteens, and older teens stay up later than younger teens (Carskadon, Harvey, & Duke, 1980; Snell, Adam, & Duncan, 2007). Teens also socialize later in the evening (Allen, 1992), and their parents are less likely to set and enforce early bedtimes (Mercer, Merritt, & Cowell, 1998).

It is not just the amount of sleep that matters, its timing is also crucial. Puberty brings about a change in daily body rhythm. When adolescents have a chance to set their own sleep schedules, such as on weekends and during vacations, they stay up later at night and get up later in the morning (Carskadon, Vieria, & Acebo, 1993; Laberge, 2001). If free to choose, most would go to sleep around 1:00 A.M. and wake up around 10:00 A.M. (Carskadon, Acebo, Richardson, Tate, & Seifer 1997). This pattern, called a *delayed phase preference*, is probably related to a shift, with puberty, in concentrations of the sleep-related hormone *melatonin* during the nighttime hours (Salti et al., 2000).

The irony, of course, is that the school day typically starts *earlier* for middle schoolers, who are going through puberty, than for younger children. High school usually starts earlier still, often before 8:00 A.M. (Wahlstrom, 1999, 2002). The predictable result is that many middle school and high school students are sleepy during their first few classes (Carskadon, Wolfson, Acebo, Tzischinsky, & Seifer, 1998). True, they do

▲ Since her first appearance in 1959, Barbie has helped give young girls an unrealistic view of what adult bodies should look like.

◀ **Learning Objective 3.13**
How much sleep do adolescents need and get?

Helping Middle Schoolers Develop a Healthy Body Image

At age 10, it seemed I woke up to a body that filled the room. Men were staring at me, and the sixth-grade boys snapped the one bra in the class. Home after school, I'd watch TV and pace. Munching chips. Talking to the dog. Staring out the window. Eating macaroni. Eating soup. Eating...

— **MARYA** (McKnight Foundation, 1994, p. 9)

Among the important personal and social processes during the middle-school years, the development of body image has a special place. The physical changes of puberty, the increasing importance of acceptance by peers, early steps toward establishing a sense of personal identity—all these help shape the way preteens think and feel about their bodies. A positive body image can help promote self-confidence, self-esteem, good peer relationships, and good health habits (Levine & Smolak, 2001; Mussell, Binford, & Fulkerson, 2000). On the other hand, dissatisfaction with one's body is the strongest single predictor of eating disorders (Archibald, Graber, & Brooks-Gunn, 2002).

What can teachers, school counselors, parents, and others who are in contact with middle-school children do to help them develop positive body images? According to Patrick Akos and Dana H. Levitt (2002), quite a lot. Effective interventions can be carried out on a number of levels, from the individual child and the peer group to the school and the community. With a proactive wellness orientation, the primary goal becomes forestalling body dissatisfaction and preventing disordered eating patterns, rather than waiting to treat them once they develop.

One element in reducing body image distortions is making students more aware of physiological factors such as:

the range of normal body types and the influence of both genetic background and environmental factors;

the normal physical and psychological changes of puberty and how they affect body size and configuration; and

the role of proper nutrition, moderate exercise, and adequate sleep in maintaining good health.

On a more social and psychological plane, students can be encouraged to explore influences on their body image, from assumptions about the attitudes of peers to cultural and media messages about the overriding importance of appearance. While peers are often a large part of the problem, they can also be enlisted as part of a positive response. An ongoing group of students committed to improving their body image can offer mutual support that helps members resist external peer pressures and norms (O'Dea & Abraham, 2000). Through games, discussions, and role playing, they can learn to feel better about themselves while helping the others in the group to feel better about themselves.

No matter how devoted adults may be to helping students develop more positive body images and acknowledge diversity, their efforts take place in a cultural environment that teaches a very different lesson, that there is a single ideal based on, "You can never be too thin." Parents, teachers, or school counselors cannot hope to change popular culture single-handed, but that does not mean they are helpless. For example, they can push to

have the school cafeteria offer healthy alternatives to fattening meals and snacks;

make staff members more aware of the importance of body image;

see that the school library contains magazines, booklets, and other materials that promote healthy nutrition and exercise;

take concrete steps to discourage and censure verbal harassment based on physical appearance; and

circulate information about puberty, body image, and a healthful lifestyle to parents through PTA meetings or orientation materials given to parents of incoming middle-school students.

Steps of this sort can have an impact on the culture of a school and the community it serves.

become more awake as the day wears on. By 3:00 P.M., most of them are fully alert, but by then, school is over!

Stress, whether related to family, friends, school, or other issues, has an impact on sleep patterns. In turn, problems with sleeping are themselves a source of additional stress. One interesting idea is that the sleep-wake system has two very different ways of responding to stress. Under acute stress, the "turn-on" mode leads to trouble getting to sleep and staying asleep. If stress is continuous and unavoidable, however, the system may shift over to a "shut-off" mode, in which sleep is longer and deeper (Sadeh & Gruber, 2002). If you have a tough exam coming up the next morning, your worrying may make it hard to get to sleep, but if you've been stressed for weeks about those papers you have to write, the urge to take a nap may be overwhelming!

Adolescents who don't get enough sleep are more likely to have other problems as well, including being overweight, depression, low self-esteem, anxiety, irritability, fearfulness, and emotional instability (Fredriksen, Rhodes, Reddy, & Way, 2004; Morrison, McGee, & Stanton, 1992; Sadeh & Gruber, 2002; Snell et al., 2007). Their academic performance suffers, too. When researchers compared students who were doing poorly in high school with those who were doing well, they found that students with C and D averages got almost half an hour less sleep per night than students earning A's and B's. They were also more tired and depressed during the day (Wolfson & Carskadon, 1998). Contrary to what most teens believe, sleeping late on weekends does *not* make up for sleep lost during the week. If anything, having a very different sleep schedule on weekdays and weekends makes it harder to fall asleep during the week and leads to even more problems (Laberge, 2001).

Nutrition and Exercise

Good nutrition and regular physical exercise are terrifically important not only for adolescents, but for the adults they will become. Poor diet and physical inactivity account for at least 300,000 deaths per year in the United States, more than any other preventable cause except smoking (McGinnis & Foege, 1993). The health habits formed in childhood and adolescence have a lasting impact (Jessor et al., 1998). Those who are overweight as adolescents, for example, are more likely to be overweight as adults (Guo, Roche, Chumlea, Gardner, & Siervogel, 1994) and to be at greater risk for heart disease, stroke, diabetes, and other serious conditions (Public Health Service, 1988).

◄ Learning Objective 3.14
Do today's adolescents get proper nutrition and exercise?

Nutrition. The importance of a well-balanced diet and regular exercise is something "everybody knows." Parents, teachers, and government agencies at every level try to encourage children to pay attention and develop healthy habits. With puberty, however, other forces weigh in. First, the dramatic physical changes of the adolescent growth spurt create new and intense energy needs. In a fairly short period of time, body mass almost doubles. At the same time, as we have seen earlier in this chapter, the ratio of muscle and fat to total mass also changes, as does the **metabolism**, the rate at which the body uses energy.

The result of this astonishing growth is that teenaged boys and girls need more calories and nutrients than they will at any other stage of life. There are also growing differences in energy needs and expenditures between boys and girls (Bitar, Fellmann, Vernet, Coudert, & Vermorel, 1999). At age 10, the average boy consumes about 200 calories more per day than the average girl. By the time they are 18, the boy will need to take in 600-800 more calories every day than the girl (Department of Health, 1991).

The federal government's *Dietary Guidelines for Americans* urge everyone to eat a variety of foods, eat plenty of fruits, vegetables, and grain products, and follow a diet low in fat and moderate in sugar and salt (U.S. Department of Health and Human Services, 2005). If teens followed this advice, even while upping their calorie intake by as much as 50%, there would be no problem. Most of them, however, don't. More than 84% eat too much total fat, and more than 91% eat too much saturated fat, the worst kind from a health standpoint (Lewis, Crane, & Hubbard, 1994). Over half of teens eat less than one serving of fruit a day, and 29% eat less than one serving of vegetables a day—unless we decide to count French fries as a vegetable (Krebs-Smith et al., 1996)!

Part of the problem is that, while young adolescents are going through their growth spurt and experiencing a rapid increase in appetite, they are also starting to eat away from home more often and on more irregular schedules (Troiano & Flegal,

Metabolism The rate at which the body uses energy.

▶ Fast food is an everyday fact of life for American teens.

1998). A lot of the time, that means skipping meals and loading up on snacks and fast foods, which tend to be high in fats, sugar, and salt, and low in important nutrients (Dwyer et al., 2001; Jahns, Siega-Riz, & Popkin, 2001; Siega-Riz, Cavadini, & Popkin, 2000). On any given day, nearly one-third of U.S. youngsters eat fast food (Bowman, Gortmaker, Ebbeling, Pereira, & Ludwig, 2004). Grabbing something quick that will fill the yawning hole in your middle takes priority over sound nutrition. And if all your friends are having pizza or burgers after school, are you going to hold out for a green salad with sprouts?

In recent years, the proportion of American adolescents who are obese has more than *doubled.* By the mid-1990s, it stood at over 11% across race and sex, and at over 16%—one in six—for African American girls (U.S. Department of Health and Human Services, 2001). More recently, a study of almost 30,000 adolescents in industrialized countries found that about 15% of American 15-year-olds were obese, and another 30% were overweight (Lissau et al., 2004). These were the highest percentages of any country studied. Also, a recent study found that girls who are overweight during childhood are many times more likely to be obese as young adults and to develop higher cardiovascular risks (Thompson et al., 2007).

While the teen penchant for fast food surely contributes to this problem, it is not the whole story. In recent years, the total calorie intake for teens changed very little, and the amount from fat actually dropped a little, though it is still much too high (Troiano, Briefel, Carroll, & Bialostosky, 2000). What this suggests is that the problem is not just what or how much adolescents eat, although there is plenty of room for improvement there. The real problem is what they are doing when they are not eating—which is, as we discuss in the next section, not much of anything (Krishnamoorthy, Hart, & Jelalian, 2006).

Exercise. To be blunt, more and more teens are turning into couch potatoes. Adolescents may talk about working out, buffing up, and pumping iron, but for most of them, it is simply talk. One large-scale study found that fewer than half of male adolescents, and fewer than one-quarter of female adolescents, met minimum standards of physical activity (Gordon-Larsen, Nelson, & Popkin, 2004). Even this understates the problem, because across the teen years the proportion who remain active, as well as the amount of activity they engage in, drops steadily (Nelson, Gordon-Larsen, Adair, & Popkin, 2005).

One reason for this drop is that organized physical activity in school is becoming less common. In 1991, 42% of students had a daily physical education class, but by 1999 this figure had dropped to 29% (Kann et al., 2000). Among those who did have physical education classes in 1999, almost one-quarter said they got less than 20 minutes of exercise in class anyway (Kann et al., 2000).

Both sex and ethnic background are linked to activity level. Boys are consistently more active than girls, though both become more sedentary as they get older (Bradley, McMurray, Harrell, & Deng, 2000). African American girls are particularly inactive. When surveyed, about 20% report that they have not taken part in *any* vigorous or moderate activity during any of the 7 days before the survey, compared to half that proportion—10%—of Caucasian girls (U.S. Department of Health and Human Services, 2000).

It would be hard to overstate how much regular exercise contributes to good health. Exercise increases the body's metabolic rate, helping it burn off extra calories more quickly, and in moderate amounts, it lowers appetite as well. In other words, it is an effective tool to control weight (Mensohik, Ahmed, Alexander, & Blum, 2008). Exercise promotes cardiovascular fitness, builds muscle strength, and reduces sports-related injuries (Sothern, Loftin, Suskind, Udall, & Blecker, 1999). It may also strengthen the immune system (Nieman & Pedersen, 1999) and increase levels of serotonin, which has an antidepressant effect (Nash, 1996). Research shows that even as little as 10 minutes of jumping exercises three times a week in early adolescence significantly increases bone mass and strength and may help prevent brittle bones later in life (MacKelvie, Khan, Petit, Janssen, & McKay, 2003).

Exercise has also been linked to better relationships with parents, better academic performance, and lower drug use (Field, Diego, & Sanders, 2001). This does not necessarily mean that a teen can raise his or her grades and reduce family conflicts by starting to work out. Cause and effect may also run in the other direction. One important factor in helping teens to stay with an exercise program is a feeling of support from parents and friends (Sallis, Prochaska, Taylor, Hill, & Geraci, 1999; Smith 1999). Those who are doing well in school and staying off drugs may have the sort of positive self-image that makes them *want* to keep fit through exercise.

Summing Up...

The physical, psychological, and social changes of adolescence raise important health issues. New issues and experiences, along with hormonal shifts, can create mood swings and heightened emotionality. Unhappiness with one's changing body is common, especially among girls who read teen-oriented magazines, and can lead to serious eating problems. Many adolescents are chronically sleep-deprived. Too many skip meals and rely on high-fat fast food, resulting in an epidemic of teen obesity, and too few get even a minimum of physical exercise.

SUMMARY

Puberty is the beginning of a process of physical and sexual development that has far-reaching psychological and social effects as well. The biological changes of adolescence also raise important health issues.

Puberty is a set of interconnected biological events that affect practically every aspect of the individual, from height to lung capacity to facial and body hair.

Learning Objective 3.1. How does the endocrine system regulate puberty and growth?

The changes of puberty are set in motion and controlled by the system of **endocrine** glands that produce **hormones**. Particularly important are the **hypothalamus**, the **pituitary**, and the **gonads**—testes in males and ovaries in females. These make up the **HPG axis**.

Puberty begins when, signaled by the hypothalamus, the pituitary sends a message to the gonads to produce more sex hormones—**estrogens** and **androgens**. These, in turn, set off processes of physical and sexual development.

Learning Objective 3.2. What are the physical changes of adolescence for girls and boys?

One dramatic aspect of puberty is the adolescent **growth spurt**, which begins about 2 years earlier for girls than for boys. This period of very rapid growth affects not only height and body proportions, but the balance of muscle and fat and other biological systems.

Learning Objective 3.3. What are the sexual changes of adolescence for girls and boys?

Sexual development during adolescence generally follows a regular sequence, described by the **Tanner stages**. For girls, the earliest stage is usually breast development, followed by the growth of pubic hair and changes in the genitals. For boys, changes in the genitals are followed by the appearance of pubic hair.

The timing of puberty is affected by many factors, from social class and geographic region to nutrition and exercise. In Western societies, girls usually show the first signs of puberty around age 10, but some begin as early as 7 or 8 or as late as 13 or 14. For boys, the earliest signs generally appear around age 11, but may come as early as 9 or as late as 14 or 15.

Learning Objective 3.4. What is the significance of changes in the age of menarche in recent decades?

During the 19th and 20th centuries, the average age of **menarche**, a girl's first menstrual period, dropped steadily in Northern Europe and America, in what is called the **secular trend**. This is most likely the result of improved nutrition and living conditions.

When a child enters puberty, people notice and react. Children have personal responses to their own development and that of friends and peers. Parents respond to the changes they see in their children. In many cultures, the larger society also marks the transition, with formal or informal rituals.

Learning Objective 3.5. Why is puberty a source of pride for some teens and embarrassment for others?

For girls, breast development is usually the first sign of puberty and sets off complex feelings about movement to a new stage of life and about sexuality. The reactions of peers, especially boys, often lead to embarrassment and self-consciousness. Menstruation is also often a source of mixed feelings, depending in part on how prepared the girl is.

For boys, their first ejaculation is typically the result of a **nocturnal emission** or masturbation and is generally experienced positively. The enlargement of the genitals, however, often leads to self-consciousness and a fear of social comparison.

When an individual child enters puberty has an impact on their well-being and social relationships.

For girls, maturing early is linked to a number of negative effects, including low self-esteem, depression, and problem behaviors. Late-maturing girls have fewer negative effects and are generally more satisfied with their bodies.

Early-maturing boys are more popular with peers and have fewer problems with parents, but are more likely to get involved with sex, drugs, and alcohol. Boys who mature late suffer from anxiety and poor self-image, but tend to be more intellectually curious and creative.

Timing effects may result from being noticeably different from one's peers (the **deviance hypothesis**), from having to enter a new stage before completing the tasks of the earlier stage (the **stage termination hypothesis**), from being treated differently by others because of looking more mature (the **adult resemblance hypothesis**), or from some combination of these factors.

Learning Objective 3.6. Do parents and children become more distant after puberty?

Parents often react to a child entering puberty by giving the child more autonomy, which cuts down on family conflict, and by putting greater stress on acting according to traditional gender roles. They also tend to spend less time with their children.

Learning Objective 3.7. What are puberty rites, and what purposes do they serve?

Especially in traditional cultures, a child's entry into puberty is generally marked by special events called **puberty rites**. For girls, these generally include instruction on adult roles and rules, taboos, and sexual matters. Boys are often subjected to difficult and painful ordeals.

Learning Objective 3.8. What are the principal parts of the brain?

At puberty, the brain contains many billions of neurons, each linked through synapses to hundreds or thousands of others. The **cerebral cortex** is particularly important.

Learning Objective 3.9. How do synaptic pruning and myelination help make the brain more efficient?

During adolescence, as many as half of the synapses are lost to **synaptic pruning**, making the cortex, which is deeply involved in judgment, executive control, and other complex functions, faster and more efficient. **Myelination**, which insulates nerve cells and makes them faster and more sensitive, spreads to the advanced areas of the prefrontal cortex.

Learning Objective 3.10. How is brain development linked to other adolescent changes?

Scholars disagree about the degree to which changes in behavior during adolescence should be seen as the effect of changes in the brain.

The dramatic and far-reaching changes of adolescence raise important health issues for young people.

Learning Objective 3.11. Are teens at the mercy of their "raging hormones"?

Young adolescents tend to be more emotional and to undergo more rapid mood shifts than either children or older adolescents.

This is often attributed to **"raging hormones,"** but may also reflect the stresses posed by big transitions and other life events.

Learning Objective 3.12. What impact do pubertal changes have on body image for girls and boys?

Physical and sexual development during puberty may lead to a distorted or negative **body image**, especially in girls, who tend to see themselves as overweight even when they are not.

Learning Objective 3.13. How much sleep do adolescents need and get?

Most adolescents get far too little sleep, and the sleep they do get often comes during the wrong part of their daily biological rhythm. One result is that many teens are sleepy through most of their hours in school.

Learning Objective 3.14. Do today's adolescents get proper nutrition and exercise?

During the adolescent growth spurt, teens need more calories and nutrients than at any other stage of life. Most, however, take in too much fat and sugar and far too little healthy fruits and vegetables, leading to an epidemic of adolescent overweight and obesity. The problems created by the typical adolescent diet are compounded by a sharp decline in healthful physical exercise, due in part to less organized physical activity in school.

KEY TERMS

Endocrine system (67)
Hormones (67)
Hypothalamus (67)
Pituitary (68)
Gonads (68)
Estrogens (68)
Androgens (68)
HPG axis (68)
Adrenarche (69)
Menarche (70)

Insulin-like growth factor-I (IGF-I) (70)
Leptin (70)
Adolescent growth spurt (70)
Peak height velocity (71)
Asynchronicity (72)
Ovum (73)
Sperm (74)
Tanner stages (74)
Pheromones (75)

Secular trend (76)
Reaction range (76)
Spermarche (83)
Nocturnal emission (83)
Deviance hypothesis (86)
Stage termination hypothesis (86)
Adult resemblance hypothesis (86)
Gender intensification (87)

Distancing hypothesis (87)
Puberty rites (88)
Cerebral cortex (91)
Synaptic pruning (91)
Myelination (91)
Reductionism (92)
"Raging hormones" (93)
Body image (94)
Metabolism (99)

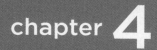
Cognitive Changes

Whe have just looked at the far-reaching physical changes adolescents go through. Across these same years, radical changes also take place in how adolescents think. This process is known as **cognitive development** and it affects not just school work, but every aspect of life, from personal relationships to beliefs about the universe.

Teens pick up a lot of new information during adolescence, whether in school, with friends, or simply by going through daily life. But learning more information is the least of it. Adolescents approach intellectual tasks with a better grasp of logic than children. They deal with *what if?* questions in ways that would have eluded them just a couple of years earlier. They become able to pay attention to more aspects of a situation, or to more than one situation, at the same time. Perhaps most important, they gain a better understanding and control of their own mental processes.

We begin this chapter with a close look at the ideas and research of a giant in the field of cognitive development, Jean Piaget. Piaget's theory of cognitive stages and his description of adolescent thinking have been around for half a century and more, but they continue to shape both research and its application to such areas as education. Others, inspired by his approach, have explored ideas about why adolescents can be so acutely self-conscious and at the same time so seemingly blind to risks.

A more recent approach to cognitive development is inspired not by Piaget, but by the computer. Can we understand adolescents better if we imagine their minds as devices that process information? What strengths do these devices have? What limitations? How do they get "upgraded" across the adolescent years? Do our findings point to ways we can help teens use their "wetware" more effectively?

For the last 100 years, researchers have explored ways to measure the abilities of children and adolescents and to compare them to one another. The best-known product of this effort is the IQ test. What do these tests actually measure? Is intelligence something fixed about a person or can it change? Where do ethnic and class differences in IQ scores come from? We will also look at some alternative ways of thinking about intelligence.

Researchers aren't the only ones who think about thinking. Adolescents do, too. Their ideas about the nature of thought and knowledge change, as does their ability to monitor and guide their own thinking processes. These developments, in turn, give adolescents the potential to think critically and scientifically.

PIAGET'S APPROACH

Beyond any doubt, the most important psychologist in the last 100 years to examine how children think and how their thinking changes as they get older was *Jean Piaget* (pronounced *Pee-ah-ZHAY*) [1896–1980]. Piaget's observations and ideas shaped the study of cognitive development for most of the 20th century. His ideas continue to have a profound influence on theorists and researchers throughout the world.

Piaget took an early interest in the world of nature and published his first scientific paper, about sighting a rare albino sparrow, when he was only 10. By the time he was in his teens, his articles on shellfish were appearing regularly in scientific journals. He continued to study biology in college and graduate school, and earned his Ph.D. when he was 21. By then, he had developed a strong interest in philosophy and psychology as well. He went off to Paris, enrolled in psychology courses at the Sorbonne, and took a job at the laboratories founded by Alfred Binet, who had developed the first modern intelligence test.

Piaget's assignment was to standardize a new test of logical reasoning. This meant giving the test to elementary school students and charting how many items those of different ages got right. Soon, however, Piaget was paying more attention to the items children got *wrong*. He asked probing questions, trying to understand what led them astray. Gradually, he became convinced that the younger children gave different

Cognitive development The ways the thinking process changes with age and experience.

answers not because they reasoned *poorly*, but because they reasoned *differently*. For them, thinking as they did, the "wrong" answers were actually reasonable.

This implied that what changes in children's thinking is not just how much they know, but how they think about what they know. This concept became the core of Piaget's theory. He concluded that the way children think shifts in a regular pattern from one system of logic to another. Each of these logical systems gives rise to a different **cognitive stage** (Piaget & Inhelder, 1969).

Piaget saw these cognitive stages as *universal* and *invariant*. Every child goes through the same set of stages, in the same order. Why should this be so? A result of maturation? Not for Piaget. Instead, he saw cognitive development as the product of an active *interaction* between the child's cognitive level and the environment. The child continually tries to *construct* a better, more adaptive understanding of the world. Because all children live in the same world and approach this task with the same basic mental tools, it is not surprising that they follow similar paths of development. Maturation is important, but what it does is "open up new possibilities . . . which still have to be actualized by collaboration with the environment" (Piaget, 1971, p. 21). The potentialities that a child possesses become realized only as the child acts on, and is acted on, by the physical and social world.

Piaget described two linked processes as central to the way a child (or an adolescent or adult) adapts to new problems and experiences. **Assimilation** involves trying to understand the new information in terms of one's existing knowledge. For example, when snowboarding first became popular, most people probably thought, "Oh, that's just like skiing." That is, they tried to *assimilate* the new activity to an existing concept. **Accommodation**, in turn, is a matter of changing one's existing concepts in response to those parts of the new experience that can't be easily assimilated. One sight of an expert snowboarder's aerial stunts is enough to broaden anybody's concept of what can be done while sliding down a snowy slope.

Stages of Cognitive Development

We already had a quick look at Piaget's description of the cognitive stages in Chapter 2. To review, babies spend the first 2 years of life in the **sensorimotor stage**, or experiencing the world mostly as a matter of sense impressions and motor actions. Gradually, they realize that objects in their environment exist separately from them. This helps them to acquire the beginnings of a capacity for internal thought.

During the **preoperational stage**, from about ages 2 to 7, children develop the ability to make something, such as a word, a mental symbol, or an object, stand for something else. The word "horse" can represent a large animal, but so can a broomstick. This *symbolic function* makes it possible to deal mentally with things that are not physically present, but preoperational children tend to confuse the way things look with their underlying qualities. For example, if you show them two rows of six pennies that are lined up evenly, they will say each row contains the same number of pennies. If you then stretch out one of the rows, they will tell you the longer row now contains more pennies (Piaget, 1952).

The next stage, **concrete operations**, lasts from about ages 7 to 11. Children become able to think about more than one dimension of a problem or situation at the same time. They also realize that just because something looks different, it may not have changed. This understanding is known as *conservation*. For example, if you flatten a ball of clay into a pancake without adding or taking away any clay, a child who has achieved concrete operations will realize that it still contains the same amount of clay. Concrete operational children are also able to step back from their own view of a situation and imagine how it looks from another person's point of view. This *perspective-taking* ability has important implications for their social relationships and moral thinking.

With concrete operations, children become better able to think logically (Flavell, Miller, & Miller, 2002). If you give them the problem, "All elephants are gray. Jumbo

◀ **Learning Objective 4.1**
How do earlier cognitive stages lead up to the stage typical of adolescence?

Cognitive stage In Piaget's view, a distinctive way of thinking, typical of a particular age and based on a particular system of logic.

Assimilation Piaget's term for the process by which one tries to understand a new experience by making it fit with existing knowledge or understandings.

Accommodation For Piaget, the process of changing one's cognitive structures in response to new information or experiences.

Sensorimotor stage The stage Piaget says is characteristic of infancy, in which experience of the world is based on perceptions and motor activity.

Preoperational stage The second of Piaget's stages of cognitive development, marked by the emergence of an ability to represent objects and events symbolically.

Concrete operations Piaget's third stage, in which those in middle childhood become able to think about more than one aspect of a problem at a time and to solve it through mental operations.

is an elephant. What color is Jumbo?" they can easily conclude that Jumbo is gray. However, when they try to extend their reasoning from the real and concrete to the possible, they run into problems (Markovits et al., 1996). If you say, "All elephants are pink with polka dots. Jumbo is an elephant. What color is Jumbo?" they may protest that that's impossible. Elephants are *not* pink!

The Logic of Formal Operations

▶ **Learning Objective 4.2**
Why is hypothetical thinking important during adolescence?

The fourth and last of Piaget's stages is **formal operations**, which children enter during early adolescence, around ages 11 or 12. This is the stage that most concerns us. The central change that takes place in moving from concrete to formal operations is that thinking comes to be based on an abstract system of formal logic. Adolescents can now perform mental operations on ideas and propositions, and not just on tangible objects, as at the earlier concrete operational stage. This means they can think just as easily about what *might be* as about what *is*.

As an example, take what is called a *transitivity problem*. Elementary school students often wrestle with such questions as, "If Tim is taller than Mary, and Mary is taller than Bob, who is taller, Tim or Bob?" As long as the elements in the problem—Tim, Mary, and Bob—are real objects that might be present, concrete operational children can usually reach the correct answer. They do so by mentally comparing Tim and Mary, then Mary and Bob, and putting them in order of height.

Once children reach formal operations, however, Piaget says their approach changes. They act as if they solve the problem on the level of abstract *propositional logic*. That is,

If A is greater than B, and B is greater than C, A is greater than C.

Notice that this statement is *necessarily* true. It doesn't matter what A, B, and C stand for. The letters can be Tim, Mary, and Bob, but they could just as easily represent classic rock groups, or the yuckiness of different main dishes in the school cafeteria, or the rights to life, liberty, and the pursuit of happiness. They can be concrete or abstract, real or unreal. Adolescents will still be able to reach the logically correct conclusion (Miller, Custer, & Nassau, 2000).

Hypothetico-Deductive Reasoning. The ability to work with abstractions is one of the central elements in formal operations. Another is an approach that Piaget (1972) called **hypothetico-deductive reasoning**. In its simplest form, this involves reasoning that moves from a *hypothesis* or premise to a *deduction* or conclusion. One place this reasoning flourishes is in detective stories: "Either Lisabetta or Lazlo committed the crime. If Lazlo is guilty, he must not have an alibi for the crucial 5 minutes. If he does have an alibi, either it is false and he may be guilty, or he is innocent and Lisabetta is the culprit." The detective then sets out to learn if the suspect has an alibi and if the alibi stands up to inspection.

Formal operations The fourth stage according to Piaget, which enables adolescents and adults to use an abstract system of logic to understand the world.

Hypothetico-deductive reasoning A way of reasoning in which a person makes a logical prediction based on some supposition, and then checks the prediction against reality.

Competence-performance gap The fact that people do not consistently do as well at some tasks as they are capable of doing.

Hypothetico-deductive reasoning is closely related to the approach used by scientists that we looked at in Chapter 2. Faced with the task of explaining some event or set of events, the scientist (like the adolescent) imagines the various possible explanations, deduces what outcome each explanation would lead to, and looks for empirical information that will confirm or disconfirm each hypothesis.

Even when adolescents show that they are able to use formal operations, whether they do so successfully in a particular instance is influenced by factors such as the content of the problem (Janveau-Brennan & Markovits, 1999). This means we have to keep in mind the difference between their *competence*, what they can do, and their *performance*, how well they do in a specific situation (Overton, 1990), which is known as the **competence-performance gap**.

Many different factors may contribute to this competence-performance gap. The person may have a limited amount of attention to devote to the problem (Cowan, 2001), the material in the problem may be unfamiliar or complex, or may be hard to retrieve from memory (Markovits & Barrouillet, 2002). Adolescents (and adults, too) are generally more successful in reasoning about matters that are familiar and personally relevant (Ward & Overton, 1990).

Personal beliefs about the world also have an impact on how effectively people reason. When adolescents are given evidence that fits with their own views, they are less likely to notice its logical flaws than if it conflicts with their beliefs (Klaczynski & Narasimham, 1998; Kuhn, Garcia–Mila, Zohar, & Anderson, 1995). This may be because they have more trouble processing information that does not fit with their own thinking. They may also be trying to protect their personal views from being disproved. In this chapter's Research in the Spotlight on page 110, we take a closer look at a study (Klaczynski, 2000) that addresses this particular issue.

From Particular to General. Being able to use formal operations helps adolescents become better at what logicians call **inductive reasoning**, or the process of going from a collection of particular facts to a general conclusion. On the other hand, hypothetico-deductive reasoning involves going from a general hypothesis to a particular conclusion, as we have just seen.

To make the contrast clearer, here are examples of each type of reasoning. Hypothetico-deductive:

A. If all dogs are four-legged furry animals;

B. And Rex is a dog;

C. Rex is a four-legged furry animal.

Inductive:

A. If Barkley, Fido, and Spot are similar-looking four-legged furry animals;

B. And Barkley, Fido, and Spot are dogs;

C. And Rex is a four-legged furry animal that looks similar to Barkley, Fido, and Spot;

D. Rex is a dog.

The thing to notice about these examples is they lead to very different levels of confidence. You are much surer about the conclusion in the first one. In fact, if A and B are true, C *has* to be true. You don't need to know anything in particular about Rex, dogs, or animals to reach that conclusion. You don't even need to know what animals are. It is purely a question of logic.

With the inductive example, however, the best you can say is that the conclusion is *likely* to be true, rather than that it has to be. You will have more confidence in your conclusion if it is based on more examples, but you are still dealing with probabilities. Even if you have seen 100 or 1,000 four-legged furry animals, and every single one of them is a dog, you can't be certain that all such animals are dogs. It is always possible that Rex is some other sort of furry four-legged animal, such as a wolf or coyote, that happens to look like a dog.

Children can successfully use inductive reasoning techniques to extend their understanding of the world, but they may place more faith than they should in the conclusions they draw (Pillow, 2002). With adolescence, they come to realize that conclusions drawn from inductive logic, such as extrapolating from a small number of cases to a general principle, are provisional and could well be wrong (Byrnes, 2002). They also become more aware of problems with drawing inferences about characteristics that have low versus high variability (Jacobs & Narloch, 2001).

Suppose you meet two 4th graders from a particular school and learn they are both 10. You might be willing to infer that most 4th graders at the school will be 10. But what if they are both wearing a certain brand of sneaker? Would you infer that most other 4th graders wear that brand? You would probably reason that there is not much variability in age-grade relations. Favorite brand of sneaker, however, seems likely to have higher variability, so inferring from a small sample is riskier. As adolescents

Inductive reasoning The process of drawing a general conclusion from particular facts or instances.

Analytic and Heuristic Reasoning

The ability to think rationally and logically has often been seen as the high point of cognitive development during adolescence. An important part of this is dealing with questions from an unbiased, impartial point of view. People have personal beliefs and experiences, but these should not get in the way when they consider an argument or course of action. They should use the same standards and logic to weigh the evidence, whether it supports or opposes their own position.

Let's say you and I disagree about some proposal—say, offering children a $1 reward for each book they read. You think it's a terrific idea, and I think it's awful. We discuss the question and try to reach a reasonable conclusion. But suppose that when I'm presented with evidence that supports my viewpoint, I accept it without question. If it opposes my viewpoint, I look at it much more critically, trying to find flaws in it. Meanwhile you, from your standpoint, are doing the same thing. What happens? Instead of arriving at a logical solution we can both accept, we find that we're further apart than before. Not only that, we are each more convinced than ever that the evidence is on our side.

To explain events of this sort, cognitive psychologists suggest that we have two different systems for reasoning. One, the system studied by Piaget, is logical, rational, and analytic. The other, called *heuristic reasoning*, is more intuitive. It relies on unquestioned assumptions, stereotypes, and vivid examples. Using the analytic system is a conscious and deliberate decision. The heuristic system, on the other hand, works quickly, effortlessly, and outside of conscious awareness to give judgments that "feel right" (Epstein, 1994; Sloman, 1996; Stanovich, 1999).

Paul Klaczynski (2000) has put forward a model for how adolescents treat new information that bears on their personal beliefs. If the information fits with what they already think, it is routed through the heuristic system and quickly, uncritically accepted. If it does not fit, however, the person looks at the new information closely, trying to find flaws or reasons to discount it. The main purpose is to protect existing theories and beliefs. However, some adolescents may be more interested in acquiring new knowledge than in preserving their theories. These "knowledge-driven" teens would be more open-minded and use analytic processing on new information, whether it agrees or disagrees with their personal theories.

To test this model, Klaczynski studied two groups of early and middle adolescents from middle-class families. For one group, the focus was their beliefs about social class. For the other, it was their beliefs about members of their religion. For example, they were asked whether belonging to their religion makes people good parents. They were asked similar questions about the effects of being in the upper middle class, as opposed to the working class. The questions about religion were assumed to be personally relevant. Those about social class, however, which did not concern the participants' own class, were presumably seen as not personally relevant.

A few days later, the participants were given a series of descriptions of experiments and asked to evaluate them. In the religion group, the results of some of the experiments were favorable to the participants' own religion, while others had results that were unfavorable or neutral. Similarly, in the social class group, some experiments came out favorable to the upper middle class, some were favorable to the working class, and some were neutral.

Each experiment had logical flaws built into it. For instance, a psychologist who is studying social class and stress has working-class students give a speech to their school class. Upper-middle-class students are told to ask a friend to steal something. Measures of stress are higher for the upper-middle-class students. The psychologist concludes that being from the working class makes students better able to handle stress. The flaw is that the two groups were asked to do different things. Any difference between them could have been because of that difference, rather than their different social class backgrounds.

The results showed that the middle adolescents were better scientific reasoners than the early adolescents. However, the effect of bias on their reasoning was just as strong at both ages. In the social class condition, the experiments with results that fit the participant's beliefs were easily accepted, while those that went against the participant's beliefs were carefully scrutinized. This was even more so in the religion condition. Participants were more likely to detect logical flaws in studies that went against their own religious group than in those that favored their religious group.

Participants who were more "knowledge-driven," based on their answers to earlier questionnaires, showed better scientific reasoning and greater balance in using their abilities. This was not because they were more wishy-washy in their beliefs. In fact, their range of beliefs was as great at the outset as it was for those who were more "belief-driven."

This research suggests that biased use of reasoning is not just a question of general intellectual ability or analytic skills. People who use their skills to poke holes in conclusions they disagree with may leave those same skills unused when they agree with the conclusions. The results also raise big questions about the idea that people are irrational because they are doing the best they can with limited resources. The older adolescents in this research had more cognitive resources than the younger ones, but they didn't use them any better.

Finally, what about the teens who saw searching for truth as more important than protecting their personal beliefs? Their reasoning was less biased and more rational. Does this have implications for the educational system and the goals of the society as a whole?

Source: Klaczynski, P. A. (2000).

become more alert to possible problems with inductive reasoning, they begin to put greater confidence in conclusions supported by deductive reasoning than in those that are the result of inductive reasoning (Galotti, Komatsu, & Voelz, 1997).

Logic in Everyday Life

Piaget's theorizing, like his research, focused mainly on how children and adolescents develop and use abstract systems of thought and logic. As a result, the topics he dealt with leaned toward such questions as how children understand space, time, quantity, and the laws of chance. However, the same capabilities that help adolescents cope with a problem in geometry, algebra, or physics also show up in their thinking about personal and social issues.

Hypothetical Alternatives. Imagine someone who is observing the activity in the school cafeteria at lunchtime. "Hmm . . . There's Caitlin. Now if she sits with Louise, she must have apologized to Barbara for what she said yesterday, because Louise and Barbara are pretty tight. But if Caitlin sits with Jessica and her bunch, she must still be mad at Barbara, because Jessica and Barbara can't stand each other." The problem is one of social relations rather than the physical world, but the hypothetico-deductive approach is the same.

Because adolescents become able to take a step back from concrete reality and think about the world in more abstract terms, they are better at thinking about possibilities—or even *im*possibilities. Have you ever wondered what you would be like if you had grown up in a different place, or with different parents, or even at a different point in history? Many adolescents entertain this sort of fantasy. One reason is simply that they can. They begin to look at *what is* as one particular case of *what might be*.

This fascination with hypothetical alternatives to current reality extends far beyond the personal. Children tend to accept things as they are, but adolescents can question the present. They can measure it against abstract concepts such as fairness, justice, and human rights, and see where it falls short. They can imagine ways in which the world could be different and better. When others—parents, adult authorities—seem blind to both the flaws and the possibilities, they may become frustrated and angry. Both the recent actions against violence and economic globalization, as well as the student movement of the 1960s and 1970s reflect this process. For Piaget (1970), youthful idealism is a natural consequence of the new reasoning powers that come with formal operations.

Understanding Multiple Meanings. Suppose you tell a friend that you have a big exam coming up next week, but you don't intend to start studying until the day before. Your friend shakes his head and remarks, "You know what they say. A stitch in time saves nine." What is *that* supposed to mean? Your exam is in English, not in sewing!

Of course, you know perfectly well what your friend meant. But if you ask concrete operational children to explain the proverb, they are likely to say, "Well, if something is starting to rip, like a sweater, and you sew it up right away, the rip won't get bigger." In other words, they stay with the literal, concrete meaning of what was said. Teens, however, understand that alongside the literal meaning is another, figurative meaning. The figurative meaning of the saying is its real point. It isn't about sewing, it's about the wisdom of dealing with any sort of problem early on, before it gets worse.

Because adolescents gain the ability to step back from the obvious features of a statement, object, or situation, they develop a new appreciation of *metaphor*. Metaphors make an unspoken, implicit comparison between the thing that is said and something else that is left unsaid. For example, two sentences ago I said adolescents "step back from" the features of a statement. You had no trouble understanding that this did not literally mean moving away. Instead, the physical action was used to suggest some features of the mental process.

Connect the **Dots...**

Can you think of instances during adolescence when you made inferences based on a few cases and later realized your conclusions were incorrect? How might this sort of inductive reasoning contribute to to the development of stereotypes about social groups of which an adolescent encounters only a few members?

◄ **Learning Objective 4.3**
How do formal operations affect the everyday thinking of teens?

▶ The ability to understand multiple meanings gives teens a new appreciation for irony and satire.

On a basic level, children begin to understand and use figurative expressions very early (Power, Taylor, & Nippold, 2001). A toddler who runs around with a broomstick, pretending it is a horse, is expressing a metaphor. Understanding complex metaphors requires much more, though. The person has to be able to compare the explicit and implicit meanings on a mental level. Adolescents have this ability to a degree that younger children do not (Franquart-Declercq & Gineste, 2001).

The ability to keep more than one meaning in mind shows itself in other ways, too. Suppose that one chilly fall day you decide to wear your new jacket for the first time. It's in a hot new style that hasn't caught on yet at your school, and you wonder if it's a little too radical. As you walk in, an acquaintance eyes you and says, "Nice jacket." How does that make you feel?

You probably object that you cannot answer the question without a lot more information. Is your relationship with the other person generally positive, negative, or neutral? What was his or her tone of voice? How about facial expression? Any rolling of eyes? Were others on hand? If so, did the comment seem to be aimed more to you or to them? How did they respond? With smiles? Laughter?

Why do you need to know all this? Because you recognize that the literal message may mean exactly what it says. On the other hand, it may be meant to communicate a very different message. Said in a deadpan voice and with lifted eyebrows, "Nice jacket" is understood to mean, "You look like a total dork" (Kreuz & Roberts, 1995).

Even 6- to 8-year-olds sense that this sort of *sarcasm* is meant to be "mean" or "funny" (Creusere, 1999; de Groot, Kaplan, Rosenblatt, Dews, & Winner, 1995). By early adolescence they understand the implied meaning and the speaker's intent better (Capelli, Nakagawa, & Madden, 1990). Because they now have a clearer grasp of how sarcasm works, they are also more likely to use it when they are talking to each other (Eder, 1995; Gibbs, 2000).

Adolescent Egocentrism

One of the important concepts in Piaget's description of children's thinking is **egocentrism**. This is the failure to make a distinction between one's own point of view and someone else's (Piaget & Inhelder, 1969). For example, a child who is retelling her day at kindergarten may assume that her parents know all the other children, not just by name but in as much detail as she does.

◀ Learning Objective 4.4
How does adolescent egocentrism show itself in the imaginary audience and the personal fable?

Everybody, young and old, is egocentric from time to time. The reason is simple. We see and experience the world from our own point of view, both literally and figuratively. To see it from another person's point of view involves at least two steps. The first is what Piaget calls *decentration*, that is, mentally putting our own perceptions to one side. Next, we must try to *imagine* how the other sees things.

Young children who are still at the preoperational stage are egocentric partly because they don't quite grasp that other people *have* a different point of view. By the time they reach the stage of concrete operations, they understand that and become better able to put themselves in the other person's shoes. So why would adolescents, who are well past the preoperational stage, have a problem with egocentrism?

According to Piaget (1971), formal operations make it easier for adolescents to think about their own thinking. This *reflective abstraction* gives them the power to consider what they know and to extend it to new problems and situations. However, it may also lead to a mood of self-absorption and self-consciousness. As they ponder the workings of their minds, adolescents may have trouble distinguishing between thoughts about their own thinking and thoughts about the thinking of others. In other words, they develop a form of egocentrism. It is certainly more complex than that found in 6-year-olds, but it is egocentrism just the same.

David Elkind (1967, 1978, 1985) elaborated on Piaget's account of adolescent egocentrism. He described two major ways it might show itself. He called these the *imaginary audience* and the *personal fable*.

The Imaginary Audience. Early adolescence, as we know, is a period of rapid and enormous changes. Those who are going through these changes are acutely, often painfully aware of them. How can they think that others aren't just as attentive? They create an **imaginary audience** that is as involved and concerned with them as they themselves are. This audience watches their every move, cheering when something goes well, but ready to pounce on even the tiniest mistake or fault. Try to convince a 13-year-old that no one will notice the pimple that has just erupted on his or her nose or recall that weird comment in history class.

The concept of the imaginary audience has been used to explain many aspects of early adolescence: acute self-consciousness, of course, but also conformity to fads and fashions, susceptibility to peer pressure, a heightened need for personal privacy, and even noisiness. Elkind writes,

> A good deal of adolescent boorishness, loudness, and faddish dress is probably provoked, partially in any case, by a failure to differentiate between what the young person believes to be attractive and what others admire. It is for this reason that the young person frequently fails to understand why adults disapprove of the way he dresses and behaves.
>
> (ELKIND, 1967, p. 1030)

Elkind (1967) suggests that this egocentric pattern begins to fade by 15 or 16. Adolescents gradually come to know the difference between their own self-conscious awareness of themselves and what they believe others may think. As they learn more about the reactions of their friends, who make up their *real* audience, they are able to pay less attention to the fantasy of the imaginary audience. They begin to realize that, on the whole, most other people are simply not that concerned with them. However, like egocentrism, the imaginary audience may never vanish completely. Even adults are often nervous that everybody they meet must notice the spot on their clothes or their face.

Egocentrism For Piaget, the process of assuming that other people's points of view are the same as one's own.

Imaginary audience For Elkind, an aspect of adolescent egocentrism that involves believing that one is the focus of others' attention and involvement.

The Personal Fable. A second way adolescent egocentrism shows itself, according to Elkind (1967), is in the belief that one's thoughts, feelings, and experiences are unique. He calls this conviction the **personal fable**. Once they reach the stage of formal operations, adolescents develop a new capacity to examine and ponder their own mental processes. This leads them to think of the newness and differentness of what they think and feel as unique to them.

One reason the personal fable comes into being is the fact that adolescents do confront so many feelings, situations, and challenges that are absolutely new to them. The first time you fall in love, the first time a friend drops you, the first time you see your parents as ordinary and fallible, is unique to you. It never happened to you before. It is just a short step from the realization, "*I* never felt like this before," to the conclusion, "*No one* ever felt like this before." If someone then pats your shoulder and says, "I know how you feel," the only possible response is an emphatic, "No, you don't. You *can't!*"

The personal fable is also linked to the imaginary audience. After all, why would everybody be so aware of your every move if you weren't different, unusual, and uniquely important? The failure to distinguish between one's own point of view and the point of view of others, which is the core of egocentrism, leads to a failure to distinguish between those characteristics that are unique and individual and those that are shared by many people or even by everybody.

One possible result of the personal fable is a deep-seated sense of loneliness and isolation. What is the point of trying to share your feelings with others if you know they can't possibly understand them? What comfort can they give you? Another, more sinister, result is the belief that, since you are unique, you are exempt from consequences that others might suffer. The laws of probability do not apply to you. Unprotected sex may lead to pregnancy or STDs for others, but not for you. Lots of people get into terrible accidents when they drive drunk, but that can't possibly happen to you. You are unique and invulnerable—the usual rules do not hold (Alberts, Elkind, & Ginsberg, 2007; Arnett, 1992). On a more positive note, a belief in one's uniqueness may give an adolescent the inner strength to pursue a talent or calling, even if those around are less than supportive.

Other Views on Egocentrism. Ever since Elkind first published his description of adolescent egocentrism, a great many people learned about it and thought, "Aha! So *that's* the explanation!" Once it is pointed out, the idea seems so obviously correct, not to mention enlightening. As we know, however, the test of a psychological theory is not only whether it sounds convincing. What does research show? Are early adolescents especially egocentric? Are they more likely than children or older adolescents to think others are watching and judging them?

Some studies have found the predicted pattern (Alberts et al., 2007; Elkind & Bowen, 1979; Enright, Lapsley, & Shukla, 1979; Enright, Shukla, & Lapsley, 1980), but others have found no age differences (Goossens, Seiffge–Krenke, & Marcoen, 1992; Lapsley, Milsetead, Quintana, Flannery, & Buss, 1986; Vartanian, 2001). Age differences are also hard to find on measures of the personal fable (Lapsley et al., 1986; Quadrel, Fischoff, & Davis, 1993). In fact, it is sometimes adults, not adolescents, who are more likely to believe they are invulnerable (Millstein, 1993)!

Much of this research asks people to imagine themselves in various situations and to say how they would react. Suppose you just got a terrible haircut. Would you go out and not worry about it? Sit where people won't notice you? Stay home altogether? As Vartanian (2000) points out, there is nothing imaginary about the audience in cases like this. What these questions seem to measure is not so much egocentrism—*imagining* that people are watching you—as self-consciousness—being *aware* that people are watching you (Cohn et al., 1988).

After all, the peer group becomes increasingly important—some would say all-important—in early adolescence (Csikszentmihalyi & Larson, 1984; Steinberg & Silverberg, 1986). Young adolescents pay close attention to how their peers look,

Personal fable In Elkind's view, believing that one's experiences are unique and that one is exempt from the usual consequences of one's actions.

dress, and act (Brown, Mounts, Lamborn, & Steinberg, 1993), and they gossip about one another a lot, often in disparaging terms (Parker & Gottman, 1989; Talbot, 2002). If those in their early teens believe their peers are watching and judging them, this may not be a cognitive distortion—they may be absolutely right (Bell & Bromnick, 2000)!

Questions have been raised about the personal fable as well. Teens do tend to believe that bad things are more likely to happen to others than to them (Quadrel, Fischoff, & Davis, 1993). However, other studies show that teens are aware of the dangers attached to risky behaviors such as drug use, unsafe sex, and drunk driving (Beyth-Marom, Austin, Fischoff, Palmgren, & Jacobs–Quadrel, 1993; Halpern-Felsher & Schinnerer, 2002). Even so, teens are more likely to engage in risky behaviors. Why?

One explanation is that they want the excitement of risky behavior more than they fear the possible consequences (Arnett & Balle-Jensen, 1993; Miller & Byrnes, 1997). Another possibility is that they want to avoid the regret they would feel if they were to miss out on something by taking the safer choice (Amsel, Bowden, Cottrell, & Sullivan, 2005). In other words, their risk taking may be more a question of their motivations and emotions than of some problem with their thinking (Reyna & Farley, 2006). There is also increasing evidence that the brain systems involved in controlling risky behavior mature more slowly than those that push toward risky thrills (Steinberg, 2007, 2008).

We should also note some important gender differences in adolescent egocentrism. Girls generally show more of the self-consciousness associated with the imaginary audience (Rankin, Lane, Gibbons, and Gerrard, 2004). At the same time, boys are more likely to believe in their own uniqueness, invulnerability, and omnipotence (Alberts et al., 2007; Goossens, Beyers, Emmen, & van Aken, 2002).

Summing Up...

The work of Piaget has profoundly influenced ideas about cognitive development. Adolescents enter the stage of formal operations, marked by a capacity to think hypothetically and abstractly. Their grasp of multiple meanings gives them a better understanding of metaphor and sarcasm, but their self-reflection may lead to a form of egocentrism that shows itself both in self-consciousness about an imaginary audience and in the misplaced feelings of uniqueness known as a personal fable.

BEYOND PIAGET

For well over half a century, researchers around the world have been testing different aspects of Piaget's theory (Flavell, Miller, & Miller, 2002). Not surprisingly, some parts have not held up as well as others. In his later years, even Piaget himself raised questions about aspects of his earlier thinking (Beilin & Fireman, 2000; Piaget, 1972).

Many of Piaget's basic ideas still shape our understanding of cognitive development. Among these are:

the concept of children and adolescents as active agents in their own development;

the goal of explaining, rather than simply describing, developmental change;

the focus on high-level cognitive performance; and

the search for mental structures that are reflected in many seemingly unrelated areas of functioning (Brainerd, 1996; Flavell, 1996).

On the other hand, Piaget's model of universal cognitive stages has been widely questioned. Instead of four dramatically different ways of thinking, researchers have found gradual age trends that roughly conform to Piaget's descriptions. In particular, young children seem to be more competent than Piaget thought, and older children seem to be *less* competent (Flavell et al., 2002)!

A related problem is especially pertinent to adolescents. Piaget maintained that all adolescents reach the stage of formal operations at about the same age (Inhelder & Piaget, 1958). However, research has uncovered wide individual differences. Depending on the particular test that is used, the domain that is involved, and the person's experiences, as many as 40–60% of late adolescents and adults fail to show formal operational thinking (Keating, 1991).

Even when people have shown that they are *capable* of using formal operational reasoning, they don't necessarily do it (Piaget, 1972). As we saw earlier in this chapter, there is often a gap between their competence (what they *can* do) and their performance (what they actually do in a particular situation). For example, when adults in a supermarket were asked which of two sizes of a product was a better buy, fewer than 30% used the proportional reasoning approach that Piaget would have predicted (Capon & Kuhn, 1979).

One way to explain this is to argue that many situations in everyday life do not really demand a formal-operational approach (Gray, 1990). Suppose I want to watch television. I press the power button on the remote control, but nothing happens. In theory, at that point I should make a mental list of all the factors and combinations of factors that might be responsible for the failure. Having done that, I should proceed to test each one, while holding the others constant, until I establish which factor is at fault.

I *could* do that. I understand how to form such a plan and I have the mental capacity to carry it out. What I probably *will* do is press the power button harder while also jiggling the sliding door to the battery compartment and aiming the infrared bulb more precisely at the television. If that works, I won't know exactly why it worked, but I won't much care; the television went on. If it doesn't work, I'll get up and press the power button on the set itself (and hope that the remote somehow fixes itself). Only if the set still stays dark am I likely to launch a serious, formal-operational campaign to find out why.

New Directions and Theories

In recent years, psychologists working in the tradition of Piaget have extended his approach to take into account new ideas and new research findings about the thinking of children and adolescents. One of these psychologists is Kurt Fischer (1980; Fischer & Bidell, 1998). In Fischer's view, the basic unit of development is what he calls a *dynamic skill*, "a capacity to act in an organized way in a specific context" (Fischer & Bidell, 1998, p. 478).

The skills a child develops, such as the ability to solve a particular kind of problem, are determined both by the child's optimal level of performance at that time and by the support and encouragement the child gets from the environment. If parents, teachers, and others in the child's social environment encourage a range of different skills equally, the child's development will be smooth and even. In most cases, however, some skills get more encouragement than others. As a result, different children will show different patterns of skills. A particular child will have acquired some advanced skills and some that are less advanced. This contrasts sharply with Piaget, who held that a concrete operational child would be concrete operational across the board.

With development, skills get coordinated with other skills to produce new systems of skills. This progress follows an ordered sequence of tiers, much like Piaget's stages, from *sensorimotor* to *representational* to *abstract*. These tiers, however, are not about the person, they are about the skills. Adolescents are prepared, by their optimal level of performance, to acquire abstract skills, but whether they do so, and to what extent, will depend on how much those skills are supported by their social environment.

Society, Culture, and Cognition. Fischer's views have a lot in common with the sociocultural approach of Lev Vygotsky (1978). Vygotsky was a Russian psychologist whose writings date back to the 1920s and 1930s and who died young. In recent

Connect the Dots...

In view of the possibility that performance and competence may not always be the same, does it make sense to judge the competence of adolescents based on their performance? Can you think of approaches that might narrow the gap between competence and performance?

▶ **Learning Objective 4.5**
How do social factors influence cognitive development?

◄ Teens with more skill in an activity use scaffolding to pass along their social knowledge to others.

decades his ideas have gained increasing recognition. Where Piaget focused on the individual child interacting with the surroundings, Vygotsky saw the child's *social* interactions as much more crucial to development. In particular, he distinguished between *everyday concepts*, which children can acquire on their own, and *scientific concepts*, which require help from someone with more expertise. For example, a child who visits the zoo may spontaneously notice the similarity between lions, tigers, and ordinary cats. However, even a very bright child will need instruction to arrive at the concept of the phylogenetic ladder.

When children and teens play or work at something, they usually do it around others, some of whom are more skilled than they. In the process, the social knowledge of the more skilled participants gets passed along. Think about something as commonplace as playing a card game. How did you learn? By studying the subject on your own? Probably not. No, some friend, who may have been a little older than you, said, "Let's play 'Go Fish.'" (Or bridge, or gin rummy, or whatever.) When you said, "I don't know how," your friend said, "It's easy. I'll show you." Pretty soon, you did know. In the process, you acquired more than just the rules of that particular game, you also picked up something about rules in general, and strategies, and the social importance of taking turns, and maybe even some basic notions about probability.

Vygotsky would say that this experience affected you because it took place in your **zone of proximal development**. This is the region that lies between the best you can do on your own and what you could do if guided by a more skilled adult or peer. Consider two children who try to do cartwheels. Neither one succeeds. On the basis of their performance, you would probably say they are at the same level. But when you tell and show them how to do a cartwheel, one "gets it" and the other doesn't. You now realize that they were not at the same level. For one, cartwheels were within the zone of proximal development—the skills he or she was ready to be helped to acquire—but not for the other. As children acquire new skills and understandings, their zone of proximal development moves to a new level, making still further progress possible (Chaiklin, 2003).

One aspect of social interactions that makes learning and growth go more smoothly and efficiently is **scaffolding**. This refers to the way those who are more expert adapt

Zone of proximal development Vygotsky's term for tasks that children cannot yet accomplish on their own but could succeed at with help from someone more skilled.

Scaffolding For Vygotsky, adapting one's guidance and support to the current level of knowledge and understanding of the learner.

their guidance and support to the current level of the learner. For example, a parent who is helping a child learn to ride a bike might start by running alongside, holding the back of the seat, and keeping the child from wobbling too much. As the child begins to achieve a sense of balance, the parent might let go of the seat but continue to stay close enough to help avert a fall. More generally, as a learner gains in skill and understanding, the teacher modifies the scaffolding to keep the learner at a level near the upper end of his or her current capabilities.

A contemporary psychologist who has been deeply influenced by Vygotsky's ideas is Barbara Rogoff (1990, 1998). She points out that when children and teens try to acquire the knowledge, skills, and thinking patterns of their culture, it is very much like visiting a foreign country. If you're smart (or lucky), you will find a guide who is sensitive to what you already know and don't know. You will pay close attention, not just to what your guide points out, but to how your guide hails a cab, chats with a friend, or orders something in a café. For Rogoff, social interactions among children, teens, and adults form an "apprenticeship in thinking." Those who are less experienced improve their understanding through participation with more skilled partners.

The Role of Mental Resources. For Piaget, the basic reason adolescents can solve problems that baffle even very bright children is that the adolescents have constructed a cognitive structure that is more adequate and logical. More recent theorists, influenced by the growing interest in information processing, have reinterpreted this idea to suggest that children's mental resources are more limited than those of adolescents (Demetriou, Christou, Spanoudis, & Platsidou, 2002; Demetriou & Roftoupoulos, 1999; Halford, 1999; Pascual-Leone & Johnson, 1999). Just as the personal computers of 5 years ago have evolved (so to speak) into models that are much faster, more powerful, and more versatile, so the thinking ability of children becomes less limited, more powerful, with maturation and experience.

One of the most influential researchers to merge Piaget's insights with those of information processing approaches was Robbie Case (1992, 1998). In his view, the developmental changes that Piaget charted are the result of changes in processing capacity and processing efficiency. Along with improvements in how many things a child can hold in mind at once, there are changes in the *kinds* of things the child can hold in mind. Adolescents reach what Case calls the *vectorial* or *abstract dimensional* stage. This enables them to handle such tasks as proportional reasoning and verbal analogies.

As children's thinking develops, they become better able to use **executive control structures** to solve problems. These structures include mental representations of the goal or outcome and of different approaches and strategies that might work. Adolescents are better than children at solving problems because they are able to represent the situation more accurately and coordinate a greater number of options. This ability is partly the result of maturation, including the development of the frontal lobes of the brain (Case, 1998; Kuhn, 2006).

Because individual children have to deal with different tasks, some easier, some harder, they may differ in how mature their executive control structures are (Bjorklund, 2000). Another factor in creating individual differences is practice. As you repeat an activity, it becomes more automatic and less effortful. This frees mental capacity for other activities. A child learning to play the piano has to concentrate on hitting the right notes. With practice, playing the notes becomes more automatic. Now the child can focus attention on other aspects of the music, such as phrasing and dynamics. In the same way, a skilled basketball player can concentrate on the strategy of the game without worrying about the mechanics of dribbling.

In its emphasis on stages of problem solving, Case's work was very much in the tradition of Piaget. It was also heavily influenced by approaches that look at adolescent thinking in terms of how information is gathered and processed. We will now take a closer look at those approaches.

Executive control structures
Mental representations of goals, outcomes, and strategies that make it possible to approach problems more effectively.

Figure 4.1 Cognition as Information Processing
One influential model of cognition interprets it as steps in information processing.

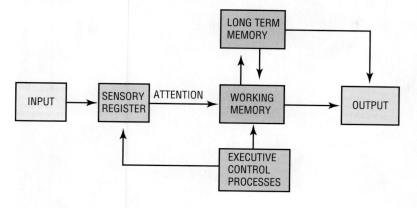

Information Processing

No single information processing theory dominates the field of cognitive development the way Piaget's theory used to (Bjorklund, 2000; Miller, 2001; Siegler, 1998). Instead, researchers share some basic assumptions. First, and most obvious, people process information. The mind can be seen as something like a computer. It does things to information that comes in from outside or that is already stored in the system. The information may be retrieved, stored, coded, decoded, discarded, compared with other information, combined with other information, and so forth. This processing is what we usually refer to as *thinking*.

A second assumption is that the system's capacity is *limited*. We only have room to handle a certain amount of information at a time. Suppose you are taking a brisk walk and singing a favorite song. Suddenly you remember a problem you need to think through. You will almost certainly stop singing while you grapple with the problem. You may even slow down or stop walking. Why? Because the extra burden of thinking about the problem pushed the system beyond its capacity. Like the power grid on a hot summer day, it had to shed some of its load to keep operating.

The information processing system can be thought of as a set of elements or components that work together (Atkinson & Shiffrin, 1968). Researchers generally agree on how to describe the major components (see Figure 4.1). Let's say you are taking a walk and you pass a piece of paper on the ground. This visual information becomes part of your environmental *input* and enters the *sensory register*.

The sensory register can take in a lot of information, but it cannot hold it for more than a tiny fraction of a second. After that, the information is pushed out as more information flows in. But if something about the visual information catches your *attention*, the information is passed along to *working memory*. Working memory does not have room for very much information, but it can retain it for several seconds or even longer while processing it.

Suppose the piece of paper is about the size and color of a $10 bill. That captures your attention all right! An *executive function* now brings information about what money looks like from *long-term memory* into working memory. There, it is compared with the information already there. If there's a match, you will stop and pick up the piece of paper. If not, you'll walk on and probably forget the incident soon afterwards.

Information processing approaches are not specifically about developmental change. The basic system presumably works the same way for everybody. However, nobody doubts that adolescents reason and solve problems better than children (Raven, Court, & Raven, 1982; Wechsler, 1981). The system, then, must be working better—faster, more efficiently, more accurately. How and why? To answer that question, researchers have looked at different components of the system, especially

◀ **Learning Objective 4.6**
How does information processing change with adolescence?

▶ Divided attention, the ability to do more than one thing at once, improves from childhood to adolescence.

attention, speed of processing, and working memory. In what ways do they improve with age?

Attention. "Pay attention!" We've all heard that, more times than we care to remember. The use of the word *pay* is significant. We think of attention as a scarce resource, like money. We have to budget it among different needs. If too much attention goes to one thing, there may not be enough left for others. You listen to a bird singing outside the classroom window while the teacher is explaining the homework for tomorrow. Later, you realize that you have no idea what your assignment is.

Researchers have studied many aspects of children's attention (Bjorklund, 2000). One aspect is how well they can focus on one task or stimulus while excluding others, called **selective attention**. I have always been impressed with people who manage to study or write papers in the cafeteria. Somehow they block out the clatter and, even harder, the chatter, while continuing to pay attention to their task.

In one study of selective attention (Ridderinkhof, van der Molen, & Band, 1997), the participants reacted to a series of colored rectangles that were tilted at different angles. For some, the task was to pay attention to color and ignore angle of tilt. Others had to pay attention to tilt and ignore color. For both groups, the results clearly showed that "as children grow older, they are less susceptible to interference from irrelevant information" (Ridderinkhof et al., 1997, p. 322). In other words, they are better able to block out what doesn't matter and pay more attention to what does.

Adolescents are often proud of their ability to attend to more than one thing at once. This is called **divided attention**, and, like selective attention, it improves from childhood to adolescence (Hamilton, 1983; Schiff & Knopf, 1985). How many of us insisted, at 15, that we studied better with the television or stereo on? The wonder was not whether we studied better, but that we were able to study at all! Recent research suggests that the total amount of available attention does not increase from childhood to early adolescence. What does improve is the ability to control how that attention is allocated (Irwin-Chase & Burns, 2000).

Working Memory. *Working memory* has two related jobs: to keep a limited amount of information actively in awareness, and at the same time process that or other information

---

Connect the Dots...

As an adolescent, did you usually study or read with music playing in the background? How do you think a psychologist with an information processing perspective would evaluate that practice? What points might support it, and what points might argue against it?

Selective attention Concentrating on one task or experience while blocking out awareness of others.

Divided attention Attending to more than one stimulus at the same time.

(Baddeley, 1992; Swanson, 1999). The part that keeps information active is often called *short-term memory* (Engle, Kane, & Tuholski, 1999).

Adolescents do better than children both on the amount of information they can keep active and the speed with which they process it (Gathercole, Pickering, Ambridge, & Wearing, 2004; Kail & Hall, 2001). When kindergarten children listen to a string of numbers or words, and then try to repeat them back, they typically recall only about four items. By the time they reach adolescence, their memory span has practically doubled, to seven or eight items (Ferguson, Bowey, & Tilley, 2002). Adolescents also have much faster *processing speed* than children (Kail & Ferrer, 2007). Whether it is a matter of choosing an object of a particular color or shape, picking out a target letter, doing mental addition, or mentally rotating an object, the amount of time the task takes goes down steeply between middle childhood and early adolescence. Then it starts to level off.

Evidence is piling up that the age-related boost in processing speed is the main reason working memory improves with age. The improvement in working memory, in turn, is closely linked to increases in what is called *fluid intelligence*. This is roughly the same thing as reasoning ability (Fry & Hale, 2000). These three characteristics form a *developmental cascade*. Change, like a river, flows from one level or system to the next, as Figure 4.2 illustrates.

But *why* does processing speed improve so dramatically between middle childhood and adolescence? One likely contributor that we looked at in the last chapter is the physical changes that take place in the brain during this period (Shaw et al., 2006; Spear, 2000). These changes are thought to speed up the transmission of nerve impulses, especially in the associative, or "thinking," area of the cortex.

Adolescents also have advantages over children in the way they use working memory. For example, they are better at *not* remembering information if it is not relevant to what they are doing (Lorsbach & Reimer, 1997). Suppose you read children and adolescents a list of words to learn. Halfway through the list, you tell them to forget the words up until then and learn only the ones that follow (Bjork, 1989). When asked to recall the words, children produce more of the ones they were told to ignore than do adolescents (Wilson & Kipp, 1998). Two factors may contribute to this. One factor is that adolescents are better able to stop rehearsing information once they find out that it will be irrelevant. The other is that when it comes time to recall the information, they are better at keeping themselves from producing the irrelevant parts.

Fuzzy Traces and Rules of Thumb.   In an earlier section of this chapter, we saw that there is often a gap between competence and performance. Teens who are perfectly capable of reasoning about a problem and reaching a logically correct conclusion often don't.

For example, suppose you are touring colleges, looking for one you will want to attend. A survey of students at College A shows that 65% of students rate the instructors as interesting and challenging. That sounds very attractive, but during your visit to College A you attend two classes. You find one of them boring and the other pretty low level. What will your impression be of College A?

Both Piaget's formal operational thinker and a computer-like information processor would probably give College A a high score. After all, the students who are actually enrolled there have been to lots of classes, while you saw only two. That means their experience is much more representative than yours, so logically, you ought to give it greater weight. Chances are, however, that you won't. Instead, you will follow the rule of thumb that says "seeing is believing" and decide against College A.

So why are we not always strictly logical? One explanation is that we prefer to think and solve problems using more intuitive processes, because these are faster, use less mental energy, and often give answers that are just as good as a logical analysis, or even better. According to **fuzzy-trace theory**, the ways we store information in memory can vary all the way from a precisely literal, verbatim representation to an inexact and fuzzy trace (Brainerd & Reyna, 1990, 2001; Reyna & Brainerd, 1995). As an example,

Figure 4.2   Developmental Cascade
Faster processing speed creates a *developmental cascade* that leads to improved fluid intelligence.

Fuzzy-trace theory The theory that we often store information in memory in inexact traces that preserve only the gist of the information.

think of the difference between the transcript of a speech that gives every word and sentence and a reporter's summary that provides the gist of what the speaker said.

One reason we prefer to use fuzzy traces is that they are easier to store, retrieve, and use (Miller & Bjorklund, 1998). Fuzzy traces are also less likely to be forgotten. Let's say you're shopping on the Web for a certain CD. You find three music sites that have it. On one, the price is $18.70. On another, it is $18.75. The third is charging $19.60. A computer would store this information in verbatim form, but you probably won't. Instead, you'll keep a fuzzy trace that tells you the first two sites are in the same ballpark and the third one is overpriced. A week from now, you are not likely to recall the exact price at any of the sites, but you will almost certainly remember which one's prices were out of line.

Young children seem to be more likely to remember information in verbatim form and less able to extract and use the gist of it (Brainerd & Gordon, 1994; Marx & Henderson, 1996). During the elementary school years and early adolescence, however, they switch over to relying more on fuzzy traces (Bjorklund, 2000). Because this leads to faster processing that uses less working memory, it leaves more resources available for other tasks.

The work of Paul Klaczynski (2001, 2005) supports the idea that we often approach problems more intuitively than analytically. As we saw earlier in this chapter, Klaczynski finds that adolescents and adults have two distinct processing systems. One system consciously applies traditional logic to abstract, "decontextualized" representations of the problem. The other uses *heuristics*, or rules of thumb, and operates on the edge of awareness to produce what Klaczynski (2001) calls "cognitively cheap" solutions. This is the source of what we ordinarily call "gut feelings" or intuitions (Gladwell, 2005).

Suppose you are told that Jennifer and Andrea are friends and that Andrea and Joyce are friends. You will probably conclude that Jennifer and Joyce are friends (Markovits & Dumas, 1999). A logician, however, would say that your conclusion does not follow. The friendship relationship is not linear. It does not have the transitive property that, say, "equal to" and "greater than" have. If you were applying your analytic skills to the problem, you would have to say that you can't tell whether Jane and Joyce are friends. Instead, you use a rule of thumb that says, *A friend of a friend is probably a friend* (Heider, 1958).

Klaczynski's approach, along with fuzzy-trace theory, may help explain a puzzling problem. Adolescents who have to make decisions in real-life situations often choose an illogical option, even though they have the capacity to reason logically. This seems strange, but if they have two different cognitive systems for dealing with problems, and only one of them follows traditionally logical rules, it makes more sense. We can better understand their choices by studying the rules of thumb they actually use in making them.

> **Summing Up...**
>
> One alternative to Piaget's approach is Vygotsky's theory, which stresses the role of others, such as older peers and adults, in promoting cognitive development. Another alternative examines how adolescents process information to solve problems and how their ability to deal with information improves during the adolescent years. Important improvements include more efficient control of attention, faster processing, more effective use of memory, and the development of quick, if sometimes inaccurate, heuristics or rules of thumb.

INTELLIGENCE IN ADOLESCENCE

We have just taken a look at ideas about adolescent thinking that range from Piaget's and Vygotsky's theories of cognitive development to information processing approaches. For all of these, the main goal of researchers has been to arrive at general principles about cognition and its development. How do people in general think? How can we describe the typical course of development? One child may progress through Piaget's stages at a different pace than another, and one person may deal with information faster or slower than another, but this is seen as a side issue. The main focus is on understanding the normal process, as it shows itself in people in general.

Figure 4.3 Normal Distribution of IQ Scores
IQ tests are designed to yield scores that form a *normal distribution.*

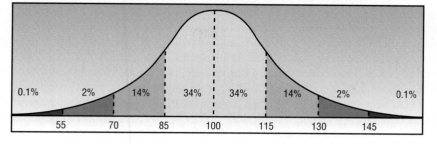

In everyday life, however, we are often more concerned with how one person differs from another. Does Eric take longer than Susan to catch on to a new concept in arithmetic? Compared to her classmates, is Jennifer ahead or behind in reading? Are students in your local school peforming at grade level? Who in your social organization is best at coming up with a plan to deal with some problem? Who is best at getting everybody on board once a plan has been decided on? (Not necessarily the same person.)

Questions of this sort are about *individual differences*—comparing one person with another, or with group averages. Providing answers to them is the goal of the *psychometric* ("measuring the mind") approach to cognition.

Measuring Intelligence

Early in the 20th century, the French government appealed to a leading psychologist, *Alfred Binet* (*bee-NAY*), for help. Could he come up with an objective, scientific way to predict how well or badly children would do in school? In response, Binet and his co-workers developed a set of measures of how children performed in school-related areas such as vocabulary, logical reasoning, and memory. They were able to show that scores on these measures did a good job of predicting success in school.

The way a child did on the Binet test was scored in terms of *mental age.* This was based on the average age of children who performed at the same level as the child being evaluated. Soon, however, researchers started using a scoring system that reflected the *relationship* of a child's mental age to his or her chronological age. This became known as the **intelligence quotient (IQ)**, and the tests that measure it were (and are) called *IQ tests.*

IQ tests are no longer scored in terms of mental and chronological age. Instead, someone's performance is compared with that of others of the same age to calculate what is called a *deviation IQ.* The tests are *standardized* to give an average score of 100. Those who perform worse than the average for their age group get scores below 100, and those who perform better than average get scores higher than 100. Figure 4.3 shows an idealized distribution of scores on such a test. As you see, most people—just over two-thirds—get scores between 85 and 115. The farther above or below 100 a score is, the smaller the number of people who are likely to receive it.

Does Intelligence Change with Age?

Are older adolescents more intelligent than younger adolescents? What we have learned about formal operations and improvements in information processing tells us that the answer has to be "Yes." On the other hand, the average IQ score at age 17 is 100, just as it is at age 12. Not only that, if you know the score a child got at 12, you can do a good job of predicting the score he or she will get at 17 (Sternberg, Grigorenko, & Bundy, 2001). So which is it? Does intelligence change or doesn't it?

Development of Intelligence. As usual, with questions of that sort, the best answer is "Well, yes and no." Figure 4.4 on page 124 charts how mental abilities change from

◄ **Learning Objective 4.7**
What is IQ and how is it measured?

◄ **Learning Objective 4.8**
What are fluid and crystallized intelligence, and how do they change during adolescence?

Intelligence quotient (IQ) A score that represents how a person's performance on measures of school-related skills (or *IQ tests*) compares with the performance of others who are similar in age.

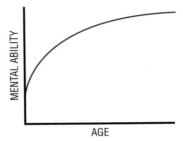

Figure 4.4 Changes in Overall Mental Ability with Age
Overall, mental ability increases across childhood and adolescence, then levels off.

birth to adulthood. The curve goes up sharply and steadily to about age 16, and then starts to level off. That tells us that the absolute level of intelligence increases a good deal during adolescence. However, at each age many children stay in pretty much the same *relative* position within their age group. Because relative position is what IQ scores are based on, someone can gain a lot in knowledge and reasoning ability during adolescence and still end up with the same IQ score.

We should also remember that an IQ score represents a kind of average of someone's performance on a wide variety of tasks. One widely-used test, the Wechsler, is made up of 11 different subtests that range from answering questions about general information to reproducing block designs. Each of these has its own developmental course. In general, verbal abilities seem to increase continuously across late adolescence into adulthood, but scores on the performance scales, which involve speed as well as accuracy, peak in early adulthood (Bayley, 1968).

These growth patterns for different mental abilities may reflect the distinction between fluid intelligence and crystallized intelligence (Cattell, 1998; Horn, 1998). **Fluid intelligence** is roughly equivalent to processing speed or the efficiency of working memory (Swanson, 1999). **Crystallized intelligence**, on the other hand, refers to the knowledge and critical judgment that people accumulate as a result of education and experience (McArdle, Ferrer-Caja, Hamagami, & Woodcock, 2002). As Figure 4.5 illustrates, fluid intelligence peaks during adolescence, while crystallized intelligence continues to increase across the adult years. Because traditional IQ scores reflect both sorts of intelligence, their curve splits the difference and ends up looking level.

You have probably heard comments like, "So-and-so has a really high IQ." It should be clear by now that this statement is based on a misunderstanding. IQ is not something a person *has*, like brown eyes or a nice smile. It is a score on a particular test taken at a particular time, under particular circumstances. While it is true that many people get similar scores over the years, many others show substantial changes, and not always in the same direction.

Look at the five curves in Figure 4.6 on page 125. Each curve represents a group of children who took intelligence tests regularly from ages 2 to 17. As you can see, while some stayed fairly level, others went down and then up, or up and then down, or down and then up and then down again. In this study, the *average* gap between a child's lowest and highest IQ scores was more than 28 points (McCall, Applebaum, & Hogarty, 1973)!

Fluid intelligence The ability to reason quickly and effectively about novel problems.

Crystallized intelligence The ability to draw on accumulated knowledge and judgment.

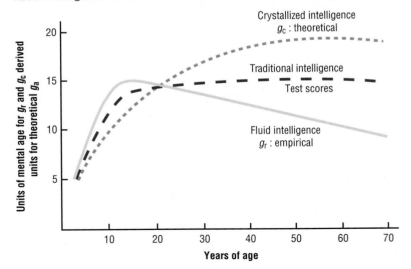

Figure 4.5 Development of Fluid and Crystallized Intelligence
Fluid intelligence is thought to peak during adolescence, then decline, while crystallized intelligence continues to increase across the adult years.

Source: Figure "A Theoretical Description of Life Span Curves of Intellectual Abilities," from *Intelligence: Its Structure, Growth and Action* by R. B. Cattell. © 1987 by Elsevier. Reprinted by permission.

Figure 4.6   Different Trajectories of IQ Scores Over Age
Individual IQ scores follow many different trajectories over age.

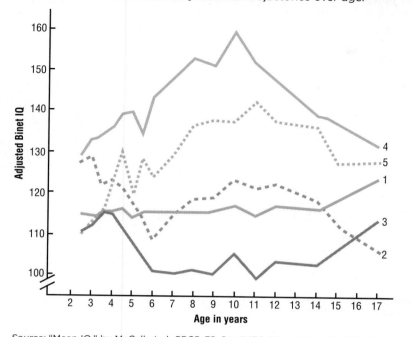

Source: "Mean IQ," by McCall et al. *SRCD 38*, Ser # 150, Figure 5, p. 48, 1973. Used by permission.

Social Class, Ethnicity, and IQ. One of the bitterest and longest-running disputes in social science concerns the origins and significance of class and ethnic differences in IQ scores. As a group, children from working-class families score 10 to 15 points lower on average than their middle-class peers (Helms, 1997). Ethnic differences are also notable. The average IQ scores of Black and Native American children are about 12 to 15 points lower than those of White children. The average scores of Hispanic children fall in between those of Whites and Blacks, while those of Asian American children average about the same as those of Whites, or slightly higher (Neisser et al., 1996). There is evidence that these class and ethnic differences have narrowed in recent years (Williams & Ceci, 1997), but they are still substantial and worrying.

Where do these group differences come from? Three general explanations have been offered:

Cultural bias. The tests may be more oriented toward the knowledge and experiences of White middle-class children and underestimate the abilities of those from poor and minority backgrounds (Helms, 1992).

Genetic background. Group differences in IQ scores may reflect hereditary differences in intellectual potential (Herrnstein & Murray, 1994).

Environmental factors. The lower average scores of children from poor and minority backgrounds may be a result of growing up in family, neighborhood, and school settings that are less favorable to intellectual growth (Duncan & Brooks-Gunn, 2000).

Those who favor the cultural bias explanation point out that middle-class and White children are more likely to have picked up the sorts of skills and information that IQ tests measure. For example, vocabulary and sentence construction scales might put Black and Hispanic children, who have been exposed to different ("nonstandard") varieties of English, at a disadvantage (Helms, 1992). On the other hand, when researchers have used *culture-fair tests* that are equally novel to children from

Figure 4.7 Within-Group and Between-Group Differences
Genetically-linked differences within groups do not necessarily show that between-group differences are genetically linked.

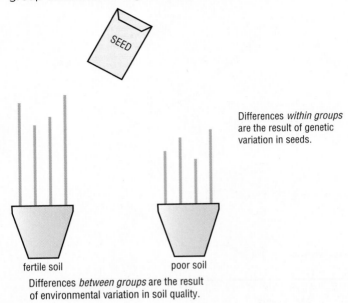

Differences *within groups* are the result of genetic variation in seeds.

fertile soil

poor soil

Differences *between groups* are the result of environmental variation in soil quality.

different groups, middle-class Whites continue to have higher average scores (Jensen, 1980). Even if cultural bias does play a role, then, as it very well may, it does not appear to be the whole story.

As for the genetic hypothesis, there is plenty of evidence from twin studies, adoption studies, and other sources that differences in intellectual performance among children *within* a particular group are influenced by heredity (Rowe, 1999; Scarr & Weinberg, 1983). However, odd as it may seem, this does not help us at all to understand differences *between* groups. To see why this is so, consider the analogy shown in Figure 4.7 (Lewontin, 1976).

Suppose we take flower seeds from a box of mixed seeds and plant them in two pots, one filled with fertile soil and the other with poor soil. Within each pot, some flowers will grow taller than others. Because the environment of the pot is the same for all the seeds in it, these differences must reflect genetic variation or heredity. At the same time, we notice that the flowers in the pot with fertile soil grow taller on average than those in the pot with poor soil. Because the genetic mix is the same in both pots, this average difference must be the result of the difference in environment. This suggests that even when we find consistent group differences in some characteristic, we cannot conclude that they are genetically determined (Neisser et al., 1996; Sternberg, Grigorenko, & Kidd, 2005).

Support for the environmental hypothesis comes from several lines of evidence. Low-income and ethnic minority parents are often poorly educated themselves and may not have the resources to give their children an intellectually stimulating environment (Klebanov, Brooks-Gunn, McCarton, & McCormick, 1998). When parents in these groups *do* encourage learning and provide mastery challenges, their children do much better on IQ tests and in school (Gottfried, Fleming, & Gottfried, 1998; Klebanov et al., 1998). In other studies, Black and mixed-ethnicity children who were adopted into White middle-class families obtained IQ scores above the average for children as a whole and well above the average for comparable children raised in low-income Black communities (Scarr & Weinberg, 1983; Waldman, Weinberg, & Scarr, 1994). It is also worth noting that the IQ test performance of today's ethnic minorities in the United States is similar to that of other ethnic minorities a century ago, before they became assimilated to the majority culture (Sowell, 1978).

More generally, there are many reasons to believe that experiences such as going to school have a direct effect on measured intelligence (Ceci, 2003). Research on Swedish boys who had comparable IQ scores at age 13 showed that dropping out of high school cost almost two IQ points for each missed year of schooling (Härnqvist, 1968). When, during the 1960s, a Virginia county shut its public schools to avoid integrating them, Black children in that county showed a loss of about six IQ points per year of missed school, compared to similar Black children in a neighboring county (Green, Hoffman, Morse, Hayes, & Morgan, 1964). Results of large-scale studies prove what parents and classroom teachers have often suspected: with each summer month away from school, children lose ground from their end-of-year scores on intellectual and academic tests (Hayes & Grether, 1982).

Other Views of Intelligence

IQ tests are based on the idea that intelligence is a matter of knowledge and reasoning ability and that people can be ranked according to how much of these qualities they have. On the other hand, most of us can think of people who are bright in English but hopeless in math, who can reason their way through fiendish puzzles but not notice when a friend is upset, or who have marvelous "street smarts" but barely get by in school. For example, Brazilian street children who failed math in school can be quick and accurate at doing the calculations they need as street peddlers (Carraher, Carraher, & Schliemann, 1985). Is "intelligence" really a single thing, or are we better off seeing it as several or many abilities?

Sternberg's "Triarchic Theory." One attempt to answer the question of intelligence is Robert Sternberg's (1985, 1988) **triarchic theory of intelligence**. Sternberg groups different abilities under three main headings:

Contextual or practical intelligence includes the ability to size up practical situations and respond flexibly to them. Intelligent behavior in one setting may be anything but intelligent in a different setting. If a particular setting is a poor fit, contextual intelligence helps the person adapt, for instance, by reshaping the situation or leaving it for a better one.

Experiential or creative intelligence allows people to solve problems either through well-learned automatic procedures or by combining information to arrive at new and useful insights and approaches. It has a lot in common with what we ordinarily call creativity.

Componential or analytic intelligence is the common core of mental processes that are important in any context. These include defining a problem, retrieving relevant information, and devising a strategy for solving the problem. Componential intelligence is roughly the same as the kind of abilities measured by traditional IQ tests.

Sternberg (1997) has found that because people have different strengths in these three kinds of intelligence, they learn best when there is a good fit between the teaching approach and their own strengths. In one study (Sternberg, Torff, & Grigorenko, 1999), advanced 8th graders were taught introductory psychology. Some were in a traditional course; for others, the course stressed critical thinking. The rest were given a "triarchic" course that included the three elements of practical, creative, and analytical thinking. The triarchic group learned significantly more (and enjoyed the course more) than those in either the traditional or the critical thinking groups. Other studies that applied a triarchic approach to large, diverse groups of students also found this approach more effective than conventional instruction (Grigorenko, Jarvin, & Sternberg, 2002).

In recent years, Sternberg (1997; Sternberg & Williams, 2002) has placed increasing emphasis on what he calls *successful intelligence*, the ability to choose and succeed at personal goals. To be successfully intelligent, a person has to recognize and capitalize on personal strengths, as well as recognize and compensate for weaknesses. This involves finding an individual balance of practical, creative, and analytic abilities. Depending on the circumstances, the person may choose to adapt to an environment,

◄ **Learning Objective 4.9**
How are Sternberg's and Gardner's views of intelligence similar and different?

Triarchic theory of intelligence
Sternberg's notion that practical, creative, and analytic intelligence represent different, independent abilities.

such as a new school; modify the environment to make it a better fit, for example, by choosing different classes; or change environments altogether, such as transferring to a more appropriate school (Sternberg, 2002).

Gardner's "Frames of Mind." For Howard Gardner (1983, 1993, 1999), "intelligence" is not really one thing. Instead, he sees it as being made up of **multiple intelligences.** His original list of these included:

> linguistic intelligence;
>
> logical-mathematical intelligence;
>
> musical intelligence;
>
> spatial intelligence;
>
> bodily-kinesthetic intelligence;
>
> interpersonal intelligence; and
>
> intrapersonal intelligence.

Linguistic and logical-mathematical intelligence are familiar because they are basically the same as what IQ tests measure. Musical intelligence shows itself in the performance and composition of music, and spatial intelligence concerns perceiving spatial relationships and moving effectively through the physical environment. Bodily-kinesthetic intelligence shows itself in effective control of one's physical movements. Interpersonal intelligence concerns awareness and understanding of others, and intrapersonal intelligence involves self-awareness and insight.

More recently, Gardner (1999) has suggested three more candidates for the list. *Naturalist intelligence* involves understanding other living beings and how they are interconnected. *Existential intelligence* shows itself in reflections on the meaning of life and the place of humans in the universe. *Spiritual intelligence* concerns perceptions and intuitions about our relationship to the spiritual realm.

In Gardner's view, these different abilities are not facets of a single intelligence, but separate, independent modules. For example, a gifted athlete or surgeon might be very high in both spatial and bodily-kinesthetic intelligence and still be only average (or even below average) in others. He also believes that all of us have some potential for each variety of intelligence, potential that can be brought out by appropriate education, training, and experience.

▶ Howard Gardner would say that playing football and playing in the band tap different kinds of intelligence.

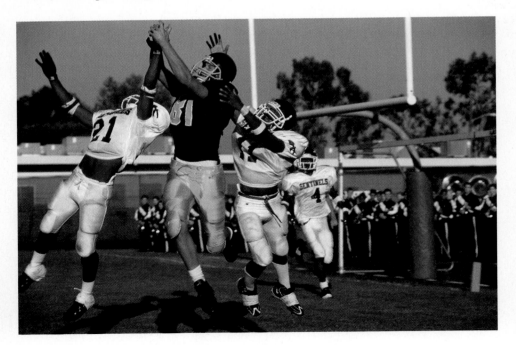

Multiple intelligences In Gardner's view, different abilities that are specific to particular domains and that are not necessarily closely related to one another.

One piece of evidence Gardner cites for his theory is what is called *savant syndrome*. Occasionally, someone who is autistic or developmentally disabled shows an unusual ability in a particular narrow area. One such person, for instance, is not able to handle his daily needs, but he knows more than 7,600 books by heart, as well as every area code, zip code, and numbered highway in the United States (Treffert & Wallace, 2002)!

Gardner's theory of multiple intelligences has attracted a lot of attention over the past 20 years. Many educators see it as a useful corrective to the stress our society places on linguistic and logical-mathematical skills. So far, however, there has not been much direct research evidence to support Gardner's ideas. It is not even clear how to decide whether something is an "intelligence," as opposed to a talent (Bjorklund, 2000). Still, by highlighting the variety of ability areas, Gardner reminds us that people can be gifted in many ways, some of which do not show up on SAT or IQ scores.

Are Teens Getting Smarter? The other day, a colleague of mine complained bitterly that most of his undergraduate students did not know when the American Civil War took place. I was reminded that when I was a college freshman, a professor lamented the fact that so few of his students had had more than two years of Latin in high school. In both cases, the implication was that the younger generation was less smart and less educated than the older generation.

One piece of evidence for this perennial complaint was a gradual decline, over several decades, in average SAT scores (Kaplan & Saccuzzo, 2001). In 1994, the SAT's developers tried to address the problem by changing the norms used for scoring the test. They were widely attacked for "dumbing it down." This complaint overlooked an important fact—the earlier norms were based on a much smaller, more select group of college-bound students than those who take the test today. It is as if you compared the running speed of a 1940 champion high school track team with the running speed of all the teens taking physical education classes in 2000 and announced that the world is getting slower.

If, instead of SAT scores, you look at how average IQ scores have changed over time, you discover a very different picture. On average, these scores have shown a steady *increase* of about three IQ points every 10 years for the last 60 years. This is called the **Flynn effect**, after the researcher who has done the most to investigate it (Flynn, 1987, 1999). The Flynn effect is not just some quirk of IQ tests. A similar increase in performance turned up among French adolescents on measures of Piagetian formal operations (Flieller, 1999).

What can be the reason for such remarkable gains? Several explanations have been put forward. One explanation is that better medical care and nutrition have made today's youth healthier than their parents and grandparents. Another is that more children are staying in school for more years (Neisser, 1998). Even the wider use of interactive video games has been nominated (Greenfield, 1998). More generally, both Piagetian and information processing views would agree that the complexities of life in a modern society push adolescents to develop skills they might not have needed in an earlier time.

Summing Up...

IQ tests are designed to measure individual differences among adolescents in skills and abilities linked to school performance. The average IQ score stays much the same across adolescence, but many teens see their scores rise, drop, or both. Persistent class and ethnic differences in average IQ have been explained in several ways, including test bias, genetic differences, and differences in environment. Recently, theorists such as Sternberg and Gardner have argued that some important aspects of intelligence are not represented on standard IQ tests.

Flynn effect The trend for average scores on standardized intelligence tests to increase steadily over time.

Applications in the Spotlight

Self-Regulated Learning in the Classroom

We often think of learning as a matter of applying the appropriate cognitive resources to a problem. In this view, if we can simply teach students effective cognitive strategies, their learning will improve. What happens all too often, however, is that the student who learns a strategy in one context fails to use it when the context changes. The toolbox may be full, but that is not much help if the lid stays closed.

From the perspective of self-regulated learning, the missing ingredients are motivation and emotion. An effective, self-sustaining learner is one who has fused cognition, motivation, and emotion—*skill*, *will*, and *thrill* (Paris & Paris, 2001). This fusion generates the ability and willingness to exert effort, to persist in the face of difficulty, to aspire to challenging but realistic goals, and to feel pride and a sense of efficacy about one's accomplishments. Creating such a fusion is an enterprise to which teachers, parents, and others who interact with adolescents can contribute greatly.

One important factor is the way tasks are structured. Rote learning and peer competition tend to make students focus on simply getting the task done, often in a superficial manner, but tasks that are varied, challenging, and meaningful promote the use of deeper learning strategies (Blumenfeld, 1992). Students are more likely to get immersed in tasks that connect to their intrinsic interests, allow for collaboration, give them a sense of possessing the product or result, and communicate high expectations (Marks, Doane, & Secada, 1996). Projects that are more open-ended give students a chance to choose and control what they work on, how they work, and what end they work toward (Turner, 1995). In the process, they gain confidence in their ability to generate plans, formulate solutions, and monitor their progress toward their goal.

Educational psychologists Scott Paris and Alison Paris (2001) have described a series of principles teachers can use to design

THINKING ABOUT THINKING

One of the exciting developments that takes place in the thinking of adolescents is that they become increasingly aware of what they know and how they know it. They also come to recognize what they *don't* know and to develop more effective strategies for finding out. This ability to "think about thinking" and "know about knowing" is called **metacognition** (Flavell et al., 2002; Kuhn & Franklin, 2006; Moshman, 2005).

To illustrate metacognition in action, imagine that you are studying for an exam.

As you read the text and look over your notes, you *monitor* your comprehension. Do you understand all the words and concepts? Do you have all the information you need? If not, do you know where to find it?

Next, you decide on an approach or *strategy*. Can you break the material down into more manageable chunks? What procedures do you know that may be useful? Outlining? Highlighting key words? Making flashcards?

Once you have made these decisions, you put them into effect, while keeping an eye on your progress. Are you overlooking any important material? Are your study aids helping? What if you take a practice test to assess your progress, and then use the results to refine your strategy?

In these ways, you are using your *declarative knowledge* (the information you have on hand), your *procedural knowledge* (the things you know how to do), and your *conditional knowledge* (your understanding of when to use a particular skill or approach) (Kuhn, 1999). As a result, your studying is both more thorough and more efficient.

Metacognition The ability to think about one's own thinking and reflect on the mental tools one has available for learning and solving problems.

Self-regulated learning Exercising personal control over the steps that lead to developing skills and improving understanding.

Metacognitive strategies are a core element in **self-regulated learning** (Zimmerman, 2000). As the term implies, this stresses the student's ability to exert autonomous control over activities that move toward personal goals of acquiring information, developing skills, and improving the self (Paris & Paris, 2001). While self-regulation can be seen as a developmental process that emerges from experience, it is also a set of skills that can be explicitly taught to adolescents, helping them become strategic, motivated, and independent learners. This chapter's Applications in the Spotlight discusses some of the ways self-regulated learning can be fostered in the classroom.

activities that promote self-regulated learning in their students. Among them:

Examining personal learning styles and strategies deepens personal awareness of self-regulation.

Evaluating what you know and what you don't know makes effort allocation more efficient.

Regular self-assessment promotes monitoring of progress and feelings of self-efficacy.

Self-management of thinking, effort, and feelings encourages flexible, strategic, and goal-oriented approaches to problems.

Managing time and resources through planning and monitoring is basic to setting priorities, overcoming frustration, and persisting to completion.

There are at least three ways students can develop a better grasp of self-regulated learning (Paris & Paris, 2001). The first is from repeated experiences. As they apply cognitive strategies, monitor the results, and realize that the strategies work, they incorporate them into their self-understanding. The second is through direct instruction, in which the teacher describes and models a strategic approach to a problem. The third is through engagement in tasks that require self-regulation, such as collaborative learning projects.

Paris and Paris (2001) conclude that:

...Direct explanations about cognitive strategies, metacognitive discussions, and peer tutoring can all help increase students' use of effective learning strategies. SRL [self-regulated learning] is also more likely when teachers create classroom environments in which students have opportunities to seek challenges, to reflect on their progress, and to take responsibility and pride in their accomplishments. SRL then is a combination of knowledge about appropriate actions coupled with motivation to pursue goals supported in environments that allow students to be autonomous. (p. 99)

Ideas About Knowledge

Another important development during adolescence has to do with **personal epistemology**, or how people understand what knowledge is (Hofer & Pintrich, 1997, 2002). Researchers have found a regular sequence of stages. Children believe in *objectivism*. The truth is out there. Authorities know it, or if they don't yet know, they can observe and determine it. With early adolescence, a shift takes place to *relativism*. Because different people have different points of view, there may be many versions of truth, and each one is as valid as the next.

In late adolescence and early adulthood, relativism gradually gives way to *rationalism*. From this perspective, while absolute truth may be difficult or impossible to know, there are meaningful ways to evaluate different points of view and choose among them. Not every idea is equally good or correct (King & Kitchener, 2002). Science, which includes the social sciences, takes a rationalist position on knowledge. Scientists do not all hold the same ideas—far from it. They do, however, agree that scientific statements need to be backed by evidence, and they generally agree on what counts as evidence and what doesn't.

Look at the following statements, adapted from David Moshman (2005):

$2 + 2 = 4$

Chocolate ice cream is better than vanilla ice cream.

Einstein's theory is better than Newton's theory.

As objectivists, children see knowledge as being like the first statement. Why does 2 plus 2 equal 4? Because it does, that's all. If you are silly enough to doubt it, you can count on your fingers and see for yourself.

For early adolescents, as relativists, the second statement is more typical of knowledge. You like vanilla better? Okay, then for you it *is* better. Personally, I think chocolate is better. Who is correct? Both of us. It all depends on your point of view.

As rationalists, late adolescents assume that much of our knowledge is *not* simply a matter of taste. There are sound reasons to say that Einstein's theory is preferable to Newton's. And if Newton, whose own approach to knowledge was scientific and rationalist, were still around, he would almost certainly agree.

Thinking Critically

Earlier in this chapter, in presenting Howard Gardner's theory of multiple intelligences, I mentioned a man with savant syndrome who has memorized thousands of books word for word. If we think of knowledge as the accumulation of lots and lots of facts, someone

◀ **Learning Objective 4.10**
How do adolescents understand knowledge differently from children and adults?

Personal epistemology The different ways children, adolescents, and adults think about what knowledge is and what it is based on.

▶ Through critical thinking, teens analyze what they learn and coordinate it with other things they know.

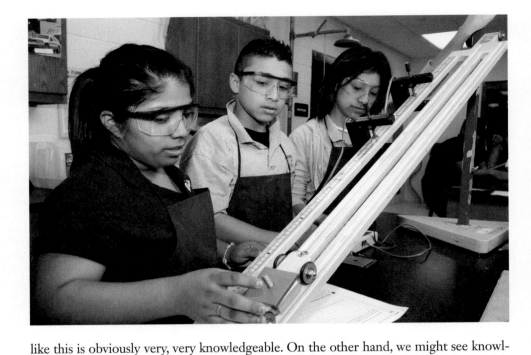

like this is obviously very, very knowledgeable. On the other hand, we might see knowledge as a resource that helps us understand the world and make effective decisions. In that case, knowing a lot of facts is only one of the necessary ingredients. If you want to make pancakes, you have to have flour, but if a bag of flour is *all* you have, you are out of luck.

The rationalist approach to knowledge that emerges during adolescence is an important contributor to the development of **critical thinking** in adolescents. What is critical thinking? One definition would be *purposeful thinking that involves transforming knowledge* (Keating & Sasse, 1996). You do not simply retrieve what you know and apply it. You analyze it, judge whether it is correct and relevant, and coordinate it with other things you know.

Say you are now reviewing this section. Maybe you have an exam coming up, or maybe you want to be sure you understand it before you move on. You could memorize the definition I just gave. You would then know more than you did before, but you would *not* have engaged in critical thinking. Suppose, instead, you mull over what the definition means. Can you think of examples from your own experience? How does the concept fit with other concepts you find valid and useful? Does it apply to the way you approach your classwork? How about other aspects of your life?

Psychologist Daniel Keating (1996, 2004; Keating & Sasse, 1996) sees critical thinking as having three major components. *Conceptual flexibility* involves making connections among different aspects of a concept, coming up with related concepts and ideas, and applying a particular concept in a new way. *Reflective thinking* is a process of systematically evaluating ideas, whether new or old. This may use formal logical reasoning, but it also involves testing theories against practice. *Cognitive self-regulation*, which we touched on earlier, helps mobilize the other two and bring them to bear on a problem (Winne, 2001; Zimmerman, 2002). For example, as you study a new subject, do you keep track of what you understand and what you don't? Do you look for clarification of material that seems vague or unclear? Or do you simply assume that you learned it until that awful moment you try to put it to use and realize that you didn't learn it after all?

Adolescence is a vital period for developing critical thinking. There are several reasons for this (Keating, 1990, 2004; Keating & Sasse, 1996):

By adolescence, many basic cognitive processes have become automatic (Case, 1998). This frees cognitive resources for other uses.

Adolescents know more, about a broader range of subjects. This gives them the knowledge base they need to make comparisons.

Adolescents can think about more than one aspect of what they know at the same time. This makes it more likely that they will arrive at new, creative solutions to problems.

Critical thinking Connecting new information with existing understanding, analyzing points of agreement, and using the result to make effective decisions.

Adolescents are more likely to use their cognitive tools spontaneously. They do not need to be prompted.

Adolescents have a new understanding that knowledge is relative and uncertain. This makes them more likely to ask questions, rather than accept information and ideas on authority.

While adolescents have important resources they will need to become critical thinkers, the process is not automatic. What happens in their lives, in and out of the classroom, will either help or hinder (Byrnes, 2002). Too often, school experiences hinder (Steinberg, 1996). Several factors contribute to this (Keating & Sasse, 1996). One is the idea that if it won't be on the test, it's not important. (And, of course, once you've taken the test, none of it is important!) Another is that to develop critical thinking, you need opportunities to ask questions, discuss, and even argue. Given the demands on teachers and students in most high school classes, this does not happen as often as it should. In addition, the idea that knowledge is tentative runs directly counter to the idea that the teacher is the authority. Too often, this means that adolescents who are trying to become critical thinkers are instead seen as disrespectful and even subversive.

> **Connect the Dots...**
>
> Are there steps that schools could take to encourage metacognition, self-regulated learning, and critical thinking in their adolescent students? What sorts of practices might tend to favor these developments? Can you recall examples of each from your own experience?

> **Summing Up...**
>
> Adolescents become increasingly able to use metacognition and self-regulated learning to plan and monitor their skill development and problem solving. They also develop a more advanced understanding of what knowledge is and how to assess it. This makes it more possible for them to develop critical thinking, in which they make connections among different ideas and areas of knowledge, evaluate what they know, and put these abilities to use in learning and developing creative solutions to problems.

SUMMARY

Adolescence is marked by far-reaching changes in cognition or thinking. While teens learn a great deal about themselves and the world, the ways they are able to take in, analyze, and understand this information change as well.

A major influencer on studies of **cognitive development** during the 20th century was Jean Piaget.

Learning Objective 4.1. How do earlier cognitive stages lead up to the stage typical of adolescence?

According to Piaget's theory, cognition develops across childhood and adolescence by way of universal **cognitive stages**. These stages represent different systems of logic and ways of thinking. Development results from an active interaction between the child's cognitive level and the environment. This adaptation is propelled by the linked processes of **assimilation** and **accommodation**.

Learning Objective 4.2. Why is hypothetical thinking important during adolescence?

After passing through the **sensorimotor** (0–2), **preoperational** (2–7), and **concrete operational** (7–11) stages, young adolescents enter the stage of **formal operations**. As a result, they can perform mental operations on abstract ideas and propositions, and they can engage in hypothetical or "what if" thinking.

Learning Objective 4.3. How do formal operations affect the everyday thinking of teens?

Adolescents can reason both from a general premise to a specific conclusion (deductive) and from a group of specific facts to a general conclusion (inductive). They can also understand multiple meanings, for example, metaphors and sarcasm.

Learning Objective 4.4. How does adolescent egocentrism show itself in the imaginary audience and the personal fable?

As adolescents think more about their own thinking, they may confuse their thinking with that of others. According to Elkind, this can result in adolescent **egocentrism**. Their self-conscious awareness may lead adolescents to think that others, in the form of an **imaginary audience**, are just as aware of and concerned with them. They may also develop a **personal fable**, the belief that their thoughts, feelings, and experiences are unique and that they are exempt from consequences that others might suffer.

Other researchers point out that teens really do watch and notice one another; the audience may not be so imaginary. Also, teens may realize the possible consequences of risky behaviors, but go ahead anyway for fear of missing out on something exciting.

Some of Piaget's basic ideas have held up well, but others have not. One that is widely questioned is that of dramatically different stages. Gradual age trends may describe development better. And even adolescents who are capable of using formal operational logic may not always do so.

Learning Objective 4.5. How do social factors influence cognitive development?

Vygotsky's sociocultural approach places greater stress on the role of others in encouraging development. The **zone of**

proximal development is the region between what you are able to do on your own and what you could do with guidance from a more skilled peer or adult. With **scaffolding**, those with greater skills adapt to the current level of the learner, for example, by simplifying their explanations.

Case and others suggest that adolescents develop more effective ways of representing problems and planning strategies to solve them. With practice, their cognitive controls become more automatic, freeing mental capacity for other activities.

Learning Objective 4.6. How does information processing change with adolescence?

In recent years, the analogy of the computer has inspired an information processing approach to adolescent thinking. Cognition is analyzed as a matter of taking in information, paying attention to it, comparing and combining it with other information, and generating a response to it.

Many of these processes become faster and more efficient during adolescence. Adolescents are better able to direct their attention to relevant information while blocking out what is irrelevant. They can keep more information active and process it faster than children. These improvements are thought to be linked to changes in the cerebral cortex.

Adolescents also become less literal in their thinking, using **fuzzy traces** and heuristics to solve problems. These are faster and use less mental energy than more formal logic and often give results that are just as useful.

Intelligence testing is concerned with measuring an adolescent's abilities and performance and comparing them with those of others.

Learning Objective 4.7. What is IQ and how is it measured?

The most widely used tool for doing this is the IQ test, which is designed to give an average **intelligence quotient (IQ)** of 100. About two-thirds of the population get scores between 85 and 115. Mental abilities climb sharply from birth through middle adolescence, and then level off. At each age, many stay in the same relative position within their age group, but both gains and losses are common.

Learning Objective 4.8. What are fluid and crystallized intelligence, and how do they change during adolescence?

Fluid intelligence, or processing speed, peaks during adolescence, while **crystallized intelligence,** or accumulated knowledge and judgment skills, continues to increase across the adult years.

Substantial and consistent differences in average IQ score have been found among different social classes and ethnic groups. These are often explained as a result of cultural bias, genetic background, or environmental factors.

Learning Objective 4.9. How are Sternberg's and Gardner's views of intelligence similar and different?

While IQ tests focus on verbal and quantitative skills that are important to school performance, other approaches see "intelligence" in terms of a broader range of abilities and skills.

Sternberg's **triarchic theory of intelligence** suggests that abilities should be understood as reflecting individual differences in practical, creative, and analytic intelligence.

For Gardner, there are **multiple intelligences**, ranging from linguistic to intrapersonal. A particular adolescent may be strong in some, weak in others, and average in still others.

Research suggests that in recent decades, adolescents have become increasingly intelligent. This **Flynn effect** may reflect improvements in nutrition, health care, and education.

Adolescents become increasingly able to reflect on their own knowledge and thinking processes, in what is termed **metacognition**.

In **self-regulated learning,** adolescents choose personal goals, develop strategies for moving toward those goals, and monitor their progress.

Learning Objective 4.10. How do adolescents understand knowledge differently from children and adults?

Across adolescence, concepts of knowledge, or **personal epistemology,** change from objectivism (what is, is), through relativism (to each his own), to rationalism (some ideas are better than others).

Learning Objective 4.11. What is critical thinking and why is it important?

The cognitive changes of adolescence contribute to the development of **critical thinking.** This involves connecting different concepts and ideas, evaluating these logically and practically, and bringing them to bear on projects and problems.

KEY TERMS

Cognitive development (106)
Cognitive stage (107)
Assimilation (107)
Accommodation (107)
Sensorimotor stage (107)
Preoperational stage (107)
Concrete operations (107)
Formal operations (108)
Hypothetico-deductive reasoning (108)

Competence-performance gap (108)
Inductive reasoning (109)
Egocentrism (113)
Imaginary audience (113)
Personal fable (114)
Zone of proximal development (117)
Scaffolding (117)

Executive control structures (118)
Selective attention (120)
Divided attention (120)
Fuzzy-trace theory (121)
Intelligence quotient (IQ) (123)
Fluid intelligence (124)
Crystallized intelligence (124)

Triarchic theory of intelligence (127)
Multiple intelligences (128)
Flynn effect (129)
Metacognition (130)
Self-regulated learning (130)
Personal epistemology (131)
Critical thinking (132)

Part 3 Adolescent Contexts

chapter 5

Families

Outline	Learning Objectives

ADOLESCENTS IN THE FAMILY SYSTEM

Families as Dynamic Systems
◄ **5.1** How does adolescence change the family system?

Changing Functions and Expectations
◄ **5.2** What functions does a family serve, and how do these change?

Extended Families
◄ **5.3** What is the impact of an extended family on adolescents?

PARENTS AND PARENTING

Parenting Dimensions and Styles
◄ **5.4** What are the dimensions and styles of child rearing?

Ethnic and Cultural Differences
◄ **5.5** Is there a best way to raise children?

Autonomy and Control
◄ **5.6** Why are issues of autonomy and control important?

Attachment in Adolescents
◄ **5.7** What is attachment and how does it affect relationships?

Parent-Teen Conflict
◄ **5.8** Are parents and teens bound to come into conflict?

Families and Behavioral Genetics
◄ **5.9** How does genetic background interact with the family environment?

SIBLINGS AND ADOLESCENCE

The Sibling Relationship
◄ **5.10** How do sibling relationships affect adolescents?

Only Children
◄ **5.11** Are only children at a disadvantage?

FAMILY DIVERSITY

Divorce and Adolescents
◄ **5.12** How does parental divorce affect adolescents?

Remarriage and Stepfamilies
◄ **5.13** What problems do adolescents in stepfamilies face?

Dual-Earner Families
◄ **5.14** What are the effects of living in a dual-earner family?

Lesbian and Gay Families
◄ **5.15** How does being raised by lesbian or gay parents affect teens?

Movies and novels sometimes portray children who spend their adolescence on a tropical isle, totally cut off from the adult world, but that is not the way it is. Adolescents are deeply embedded in a social context of people and institutions that affect them and are affected by them. The most fundamental of these institutions, the one that has the most direct impact on teens, is the *family*. In this chapter we look at the family across adolescence. What functions does it serve? How does it carry them out? What happens when it doesn't work as well as it might?

We can think of the family as a system and the people in the family as interconnected elements. Any time one of the elements changes in a major way, it sets in motion corresponding changes in the other elements and in the system as a whole. A child's passage through puberty and into adolescence is such a major change. It forces other members of the family to make adjustments in their relationships with the adolescent and with one another.

Across families, parents differ widely in their rules, attitudes, beliefs, and approaches to discipline. Researchers have described these differences as reflecting a small set of parenting styles. What are these parenting styles, and how are they connected to the ways adolescents turn out? Is there a single approach that produces the best results?

How do different cultures and ethnic groups differ in their approaches to child rearing, and what effects do these differences have? Should parents expect to exercise control over their adolescent children, and if so, what kind? Is conflict between parents and teens inevitable? These are among the questions about parent-adolescent relationships that we will examine. We will also look at the role of siblings in a teen's development, as parents aren't the only members of the family who affect adolescents.

In recent decades, American society has changed profoundly, and so has the American family. More parents of teens divorce, some remarry, and some don't. Some parents were never married. In families with two parents, it is more common for both parents to work full time outside the home. Families in which the parents are lesbian or gay have become more visible. In the last section of the chapter, we will see what researchers have learned about the impact of these changes in family structure on adolescents.

▲ Families are a central institution in the lives of adolescents.

ADOLESCENTS IN THE FAMILY SYSTEM

What do families do and what are they for? There are so many ways to answer these questions. As *economic* units, families work together to produce and consume. As *social* units, they promote the survival, comfort, and mutual support of their members. As *generational* units, they provide a way to accumulate the skills and knowledge of older people and ensure that these skills are passed along to those who are younger. As *structural* units, they link people to one another and to the broader community. But the most important role of the family, the one most people would call central, is to bear, care for, raise, and train children.

In any human society, parents and families are chiefly responsible for seeing that their children acquire the essential values, beliefs, and aspirations of the culture. This process is called **socialization** (Maccoby, 2006). Through socialization, children learn to control their impulses, interact with others, and become competent and well-adapted members of their culture. Even if society does not always give families the support they need to accomplish this task, the family generally gets the blame if the child goes astray.

According to Robert LeVine (1974), families in every society have the same three basic goals for their children. The first is to make sure they *survive* to adulthood. The second is to give them the *skills and attitudes* they will need to support themselves economically as adults. The third is to encourage *other social values*, such as achievement, social advancement, creativity, and self-fulfillment.

Socialization The process through which children acquire the attitudes, beliefs, behaviors, and skills that their parents and culture consider appropriate.

LeVine sees these goals as forming a sort of staircase. Economic concerns come to the fore only after it is clear the child will live, and self-expression has a lower priority than being able to make a living. Parents are not necessarily aware of this ranking, which is seldom spelled out. This can lead to misunderstandings and conflicts. Say an adolescent comes home with a new stud in her nose. The parent's first thought may be the risk of infection. Even if that worry is allayed, what if having a pierced nose lowers the chances of success in a career? The teen's view, that her friends think studs are cool and it is, after all, her nose, may carry less weight with the parent than the imagined impact on the child's physical and economic survival.

Families as Dynamic Systems

Parents, and adults in general, often think of child rearing as a one-way process in which the parents mold the child's behavior and attitudes. This view overlooks some important points. First, while parents certainly influence their children, children also influence their parents (Bell, 1979; Cook, 2001). Second, these influences are not simply one-to-one. Instead, families form complex *social systems* of relationships that are constantly responding to changing circumstances (Cox & Paley, 1997; Minuchin, 1988).

To illustrate these points, Figure 5.1 on page 140 diagrams a family of two parents and one adolescent. The red arrows indicate that each of the three family members has a direct influence on each of the others. In addition, each *dyadic relationship* between two of the members has an indirect effect on the third member, indicated by blue arrows. That member, in turn, has an influence on that relationship. Each of these relationships has a reciprocal effect on each of the other relationships, as shown by the green arrows.

If this seems hopelessly complicated, an example may make it clearer. Suppose a father tells his 14-year-old son to clean up his room. When the boy puts off doing it, the father gets irritated and resorts to threats. This makes the boy more defiant, which increases the father's exasperation. So far, only the father-son dyad is active. Each is influencing the other. But now the growing tension in that relationship leads the mother to get involved. When she tries a more conciliatory approach, the father accuses her of spoiling the son. In other words, the relationship between mother and son has a negative impact on the parents' relationship. This, in turn, may affect how each of them relates to the boy and how he relates to them.

◄ **Learning Objective 5.1**
How does adolescence change the family system?

Figure 5.1 Lines of Influence in a Family System
Lines of influence in a family system form a complex web.

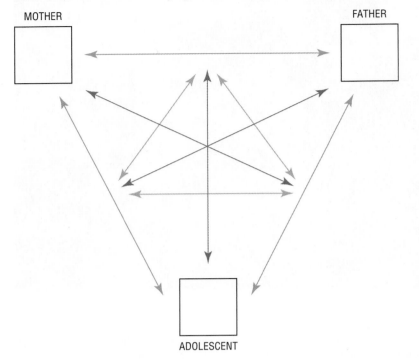

MOTHER

FATHER

ADOLESCENT

Positive and Negative Feedback Loops. The cycle of anger and defiance between father and son that we just looked at is an example of what is called a **positive feedback loop.** The increase in anger leads to an increase in defiance, which leads to an increase in anger, and so on. Each person's response tends to amplify the other's response. This is like what happens when someone holding a live microphone steps in front of the loudspeaker. Because the amplified sound is carried by the microphone back into the amplifier in a continuous loop, it sets off an unearthly screech that has everyone clapping their hands over their ears.

Interactions in a relationship can also become part of a **negative feedback loop.** Suppose the father, seeing the son's reluctance to clean his room at that moment, rephrases his request in a way that lets the son comply without feeling he is giving in. In that case, the increase in negative emotion in the son sets off a response from the father that leads to a *decrease* in defiance (see Figure 5.2 on page 141). Notice that this technical usage of the term "negative feedback" is very different from the everyday sense of "criticism."

In general, negative feedback tends to keep a system stable, while positive feedback tends to change it (Granic, Dishion, & Hollenstein, 2002). The balance and tension between these two processes helps give the system its dynamic character (Granic, 2000). For example, the mother of an early adolescent girl may react to the child's greater involvement with peers by keeping a stricter watch on who her daughter spends time with. This would be a negative feedback loop. The parent's reaction to the child's expanding social horizons tends to contract them. The net effect is to keep things much as they are.

Now, suppose the girl asks to stay significantly later than usual at a party. The mother agrees, but says the girl should call in during the evening and be sure to be home at a certain time. This makes the child feel more mature, responsible, and trusted. As a result, she is careful to follow her parents' conditions exactly. This, in turn, makes the parents feel that she can be trusted with still greater freedom and responsibility. This is an example of a positive feedback loop. If the cycle continues, the effect will be to give the child an ever-increasing degree of autonomy; that is, the ability to act independently and take responsibility for one's actions.

Positive feedback loop A system in which an increase or decrease in one connected factor leads to a change in the same direction in the other connected factor.

Negative feedback loop A system in which a change in one connected factor leads to a change in the opposite direction in the other connected factor.

Figure 5.2   Positive and Negative Feedback Loops
Example of positive and negative feedback loops.

A. Positive Feedback Loop

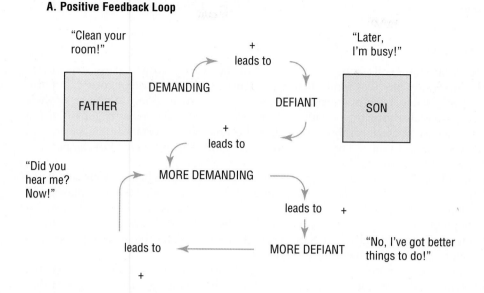

B. Negative Feedback Loop

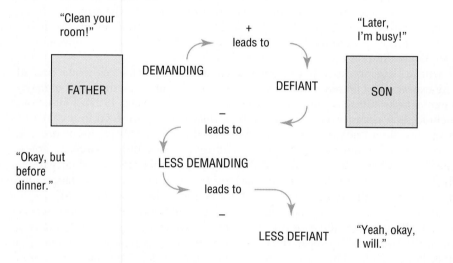

Disequilibrium and Phase Transitions. Any time there is a significant change in a family member or in a dyadic relationship, it creates an imbalance or **disequilibrium** in the family system (Minuchin, 1988). One important example of such a change is puberty. As we saw in Chapter 3, puberty forces both the parents and the child to make major adjustments in their attitudes, behaviors, and ways of relating (Gutman & Eccles, 2007). As the ways of getting along that worked in childhood start to change, interactions between parents and adolescents become more variable and less predictable (Granic, Hollenstein, Dishion, & Patterson, 2003). This can create a sense of insecurity in both the parents and the teen.

Periods like this, when old patterns are breaking down and new patterns are emerging, are called **phase transitions** (Lewis, 2000). During phase transitions, even minor events can have a strong impact on the path development takes (Lewis & Douglas, 1998). Take the girl we talked about in the previous section. What if she comes home from that party half an hour late? Even if she has some sort of excuse, there is a chance her parents will decide they were wrong to trust her. The restrictions they impose as a result may lead the girl to start misleading them about where she goes and what she

Disequilibrium In a family system, a situation in which there is significant change in a family member or in a relationship between family members.

Phase transition A period of change in a family system during which minor events may have far-reaching consequences.

does with whom. If they find this out, their level of trust will sink even lower. The cycle of distrust and deception will intensify. In effect, coming home either on time or half an hour late has led to a major and enduring difference in the entire family system.

Changing Functions and Expectations

▶ **Learning Objective 5.2**
What functions does a family serve, and how do these change?

While children are still young, the functions of the family unit are pretty straightforward. The family provides food, shelter, clothing, and health care, of course, but also warmth and safety, both physical and emotional. Parents not only take care of their children, they also give them skills and knowledge they will need to get by in the world. Once children start school, the school becomes an important influence as well, but they still *live* at home. The family, under the guidance and control of the parents, is the central focus of their lives.

With adolescence, this changes. The child's social interests begin to move outside the family, even to exclude the family. Friends and age mates take on new importance. Those family weekends in the country or days at the beach used to be such a treat, but now they become occasions for tears and protests. Don't the parents understand? If they miss their best friend's party Saturday night they won't be able to show their faces in school for the rest of the year!

Children and parents have a long history of interacting with each other, but the rapid changes of early adolescence bring a lot of their assumptions and expectations about each other into question (Collins, 2001). Each may act in ways that are surprising, even dismaying, to the other. When an expectation about someone turns out to be wrong, it has both cognitive and emotional consequences. On the cognitive level, it means that whatever ideas about the person led to that expectation are at least partly wrong and need to be reexamined. Emotionally, the result may be disappointment, or even anger, depending on the kind of expectation involved.

As we will see later in this chapter, questions of autonomy are a frequent source of conflicting expectations. Parents and adolescents generally agree on the order of major developmental tasks during adolescence (Decovic, Noom, & Meeus, 1997). These tasks might include such changes as going alone to a club, getting involved in a romantic relationship, handling one's own money, seeing the doctor without a parent present, and having personal opinions about political and moral questions. However, adolescents expect to be able to handle issues of this sort at an earlier age than their parents expect they should (Decovic, 2002). These clashing expectations can lead to disappointment and a feeling on the adolescent's part of not being respected and trusted.

Issues of authority and control also become more troublesome in early adolescence (Laursen & Collins, 1994). Teens begin to expect to have more say in family matters, while the parents may still expect their decisions to be accepted without question (Gutman & Eccles, 2007). This collision of expectations can lead to tense and unpleasant conversations. One aspect of this is that when discussing family issues, early adolescents interrupt their parents more often and agree with them less often than children do (Beaumont, Vasconcelos, & Ruggeri, 2001). These discussions are also less likely to lead to a consensus decision (Ullrich & Kreppner, 2002).

Traditionally, parents and the family help prepare adolescents to function as adults. In the past, teens often learned household and occupational skills by working side-by-side with their parents and older siblings. In today's society, however, that function has been taken over more and more by institutions outside the home, such as schools, peers, and the Internet. Parents may not even *have* the particular knowledge their children need. Margaret Mead (1978) pointed out that as the pace of social and technological change increases, the skills, customs, and knowledge of older generations become less and less relevant to the young. This leaves parents wondering whether they have any important role left to play. I can teach my child how to change a typewriter ribbon or adjust the idle speed on a carburetor, but what would be the point? Both typewriters and carburetors are obsolete, and so is my hard-earned knowledge of how to deal with them.

Connect the **Dots...**

At the same time that children enter adolescence, many parents are approaching or entering their "midlife" years. How do you think this might affect family relationships?

◄ In extended families, grandparents offer children an additional source of emotional support.

Extended Families

The most widespread American concept of family, the one we all know from television shows, stories, and novels, is the **nuclear family**. This term refers to a single set of parents and their children, who may have only infrequent contact with other relatives. In other cultures around the world, however, the most common model is the **extended family,** in which parents and their children live with or near grandparents, aunts and uncles, and other kin (Schlegel & Barry, 1991). The extended family is also more common among African Americans, Asian Americans, Mexican Americans, and other ethnic minorities in the United States (Fuligni, Tseng, & Lam, 1999; Suarez-Orozco & Suarez-Orozco, 1996; Taylor, 1997).

Being in close contact with family members beyond the parents offers adolescents an additional source of emotional support. In fact, teens in traditional cultures often say they feel closer to their grandparents than to their parents (Schlegel & Barry, 1991). Grandparents in America sometimes joke that they get all the fun of child rearing without any of the work. This has more than a grain of truth in it. Typically, it is the parents who have to deal with discipline, while the grandparents can concentrate on being warm, nurturant, and supportive.

Members of the extended family can give support to parents, too. This is particularly important for those who are under psychological and economic stress. Single mothers, for example, are more likely to cope well and be more sensitive parents when they can count on psychological support and child care relief from relatives (Coley, 1998; Taylor & Roberts, 1995). This is linked, in turn, to better outcomes for the children and teens, who are better adjusted psychologically, do better in school, and have fewer behavior problems (Salem, Zimmerman, & Notaro, 1998; Taylor, 1996).

One reason adolescents in the American majority culture have less contact with relatives outside the nuclear family is that middle-class White Americans move around a lot. If your parents relocated to St. Louis from Philadelphia, and your grandparents stayed back in Pennsylvania, you are not likely to see very much of them. While even occasional visits may give you a strong emotional tie to them, it is not at all the same as the regular, even daily interactions you might have had if you lived nearby.

Another reason for less contact with relatives is that extended families don't extend as much as they used to. The average number of children in families dropped steadily during the 20th century (Mortimer & Larson, 2002). This decline has

◄ **Learning Objective 5.3**
What is the impact of an extended family on adolescents?

Nuclear family A single set of parents and their children.

Extended family A family that includes grandparents, aunts and uncles, and other kin, as well as parents and children.

dramatically cut back on the number of aunts, uncles, and cousins most American adolescents have.

Compared to Americans, adolescents in Europe have much more extensive contact with their extended families (Alsaker & Flammer, 1999), partly because relatives tend to live closer to each other geographically. It is also a question of tradition. People tend to think of their native region as home, however far away they may move. Children are often sent to stay with the grandparents during school vacations, where they have a chance to bond (or quarrel!) with cousins who may live at the other end of the country.

> **Summing Up...**
>
> Families function to protect children, to give them the skills they need to support themselves as adults, and to pass along the beliefs and values of their culture. The family can be seen as a dynamic system in which each member affects the others and their relationships. With adolescence, divergent expectations about autonomy, authority, and control may lead to family stress. Some adolescents, especially in more traditional settings, find support in their extended families.

PARENTS AND PARENTING

So far we have been looking at processes and issues that concern every family that includes adolescents. All families have to find ways to deal with the changing roles and needs of their members and the changing relationships among them. They all have to address questions raised by these changes. What topics are family matters, and what are personal? How are family decisions made? Who has the last word? How does the system adapt?

Along with these questions about how families in general work, however, we can also ask about the ways parents and families differ. Think about the people you knew during adolescence, your friends and schoolmates, and the ways they talked about their families. Some said their parents were warm and affectionate. Others saw their parents as more cool and distant. Some complained that they hardly ever saw their parents. Others said their parents were constantly in their faces. Some felt free to object when they didn't like some family decision. Others turned pale at the thought of even seeming to disagree with their parents.

Is every family different? Or can we sort families into different categories that help us see how those within each category are similar? What is it the parents in each group do, and how do these typical ways of behaving affect their adolescent children? Can we say there is such a thing as a *best* way to raise teenagers?

Parenting Dimensions and Styles

▶ **Learning Objective 5.4**
What are the dimensions and styles of child rearing?

Over half a century's worth of research on the attitudes and actions of parents has shown that we can capture a lot about what goes on by looking at two aspects or dimensions of the way parents treat their children (Maccoby & Martin, 1983; Steinberg, 2001). This is more than just a handy way to describe parents or assign them to types. Where parents fall on these dimensions has been consistently linked to important psychological characteristics of their children.

Parenting Dimensions. The first of these parenting dimensions is **acceptance/responsiveness.** Praising and encouraging the child is an important part of this quality, as is expressing warmth and affection. This does not mean the parents take an attitude of, "Whatever you do is fine." In fact, they can be quite critical when the child does not live up to their expectations. However, the criticism is always within the context of accepting, valuing, and loving the child.

Responsiveness is just as important. Parents who score high on this dimension pay attention to children and respond to their signals (Kerr, Stattin, Biesecker, &

Acceptance/responsiveness A dimension of child rearing that includes giving praise, warmth, and affection and paying attention to children's wants, needs, and concerns.

◀ Parents who are high in acceptance/responsiveness greet their children's accomplishments with warmth and praise.

Ferrer-Wreder, 2002). In other words, they *listen*. Because children feel able to express their feelings and concerns, they gain a sense of control over what happens (Seligman, 1975). The sense that you can have an impact has positive psychological effects, even when it is not entirely accurate. Take a child who is asked at snacktime to choose between apple juice and orange juice. Factually, the parent is determining what the child will have (no sugary cola drinks allowed!). The child, however, *does* choose, is listened to, and feels at least partly in control.

In contrast, parents who are less accepting and responsive are likely to criticize their children in a belittling, hostile way. They may brush aside a child's attempts to communicate or may not notice them. The message, intended or not, is that the child does not deserve their attention or affection. It is not hard to imagine why such a family atmosphere has been linked to depression, poor relationships with peers, and other psychosocial problems later on (Ge, Best, Conger, & Simons, 1996; MacKinnon-Lewis, Starnes, Volling, & Johnson, 1997).

The other dimension of parenting is **demandingness/control.** This is just what it sounds like. Parents who score high on this dimension set more rules and regulations. They also keep a closer watch to make sure their demands are met. In contrast, those who score low on this dimension impose fewer restrictions on their children and are less likely to set strict goals. Their children are given a lot of room to decide for themselves what they want to do.

Parenting Styles. Researchers have found that the two dimensions we just looked at, acceptance/responsiveness and demandingness/control, are relatively independent of each other (Maccoby & Martin, 1983). Parents who are responsive may be demanding or undemanding. The same is true for parents who are unresponsive. This creates four possible combinations, which are shown in Figure 5.3 on page 146. These combinations make a close fit with the four *parental styles* described by Diana Baumrind (1978, 1991, 2005).

Authoritative parents are both demanding and responsive. They set clear standards and goals for their children that take the child's abilities, needs, and level of development into account. They listen to the child's perspective, but make it clear that ultimately they are in charge. They are also willing to explain the reasons for the rules

Demandingness/control A dimension of child rearing that includes setting rules, stating expectations clearly, and monitoring the child to make sure that rules are followed and expectations are met.

Authoritative parents Those who are both responsive and demanding.

Figure 5.3 Responsiveness, Demandingness, and Parental Style
The dimensions of responsiveness and demandingness interact to form four parental styles.

	DEMANDING	**UNDEMANDING**
RESPONSIVE	Authoritative	Indulgent
UNRESPONSIVE	Authoritarian	Indifferent

they set and to adapt the rules as the child matures. They encourage the child's autonomy within an atmosphere of warmth and acceptance.

Authoritarian parents are also demanding, but the context is "Do as you're told... Because I said so." Authoritarian parents expect prompt, unquestioning obedience; respect; and conformity. Punishment for breaking the rules is strict, harsh, and often physical. They do not show much affection for their children. Some may simply not feel any. Others may worry that letting warm feelings show will undermine their authority.

Indulgent parents are warm and responsive, but they do not place many demands on their children. On the whole, the children are allowed to do as they please. Discipline is rare and inconsistent. When disagreements come up, the children are encouraged to feel like equal partners with an equal voice. Indulgent parents often believe that imposing goals, rules, and restrictions will hamper the development of the child's creativity and self-expression.

Indifferent parents spend hardly any time and energy on their children. In some cases, this results from active rejection. For example, the child may stem from an unwanted pregnancy or be a vivid reminder of a disliked former partner. Others may be so overwhelmed by their own problems that they simply don't have the resources to be involved with their children. Indifferent parents show little interest in what their children do or where they go and do not show much affection or concern for them. The rules and goals they set, if they set any, are primarily meant to keep the children from bothering them.

Adolescent Outcomes. Many researchers have looked at the links between different styles of parenting and the way children and adolescents turn out. For the most part, these studies have led to similar conclusions (Steinberg, 2001).

> Adolescents from *authoritative* families consistently show the most favorable outcomes. They do better in school, they are more independent and self-assured, they are less anxious and depressed, and they are less likely to get involved in delinquency and drug use.

> Adolescents from *authoritarian* families are more dependent and passive. They are less self-assured and have weak self-esteem and communication skills.

> Adolescents from *indulgent* families tend to be more immature and irresponsible. They are also more influenced by their friends and peers.

> Adolescents from *indifferent* families have the hardest time. They show little interest in school or work and are more likely to get involved in delinquency, early sexual activity, and drug use.
>
> –(Fuligni & Eccles, 1993; Kurdek & Fine, 1994; Slicker, 1998; Steinberg, Lamborn, Darling, Mounts, & Dornbusch, 1994)

What is it about authoritative parenting that apparently works so well? The central elements of this approach have been described as acceptance/involvement, supervision/control, and psychological autonomy-granting (Roberts & Steinberg, 1999). Of these, involvement seems linked to the teen's overall sense of well-being. Autonomy-granting is related to the teen's feelings of self-competence and self-esteem, as well as to achievement motives. It also seems to act as a shield against anxiety and depression.

Supervision/control is the trickiest component. Researchers (like parents and adolescents themselves) see an important difference between *behavioral control*,

Authoritarian parents Those who are demanding, but not responsive.

Indulgent parents Those who are responsive, but not demanding.

Indifferent parents Those who are neither responsive nor demanding.

which involves setting standards, providing guidance, and monitoring the child's actions, and *psychological control*, which blocks the development of autonomy and self-regulation (Barber, 1996). As we might expect, these different forms of control are linked to different outcomes (Pettit, Laird, Dodge, Bates, & Criss, 2001). We will look more closely at the complications of parental monitoring and control later in this chapter.

Who Affects Whom? Descriptions of child rearing often use words like *make*, *facilitate*, *enable*, *engage*, *foster*, *enhance*. Whether intentional or not, this way of speaking gives the impression that parents do things and the child is affected. Parenting is the cause, and the way the child turns out is the effect. Of course, what parents do has an effect on their children; however this overlooks an important point. What children do, and what they are like, affects parents as well.

As we saw earlier in this chapter, the family can be thought of as a system with reciprocal effects (Collins, Maccoby, Steinberg, Hetherington, & Bornstein, 2000; Kerr et al., 2002; Kuczynski & Parkin, 2006). What parents do affects the children, and at the same time what children do affects the parents. This creates a loop or circuit of cause and effect that links the parents and children together.

For example, adolescents who are cheerful, easy-going, responsible, and self-assured may draw out qualities of warmth, support, and flexible guidance from their parents. These parental qualities, in turn, would encourage a sense of being trusted and valued in the teens. On the other hand, teens who are hostile and defiant may not respond to attempts to reason with them. This may lead the parents to try harsh discipline and become more authoritarian, or to give up on them and become more indifferent. Either of these responses could lead to an increase in hostility and defiance from the teen (Kim, Conger, Lorenz, & Elder, 2001).

The examples in the last paragraph start with a description of the adolescent. I do not mean this to imply that a child's characteristics somehow come first in the cycle. Those cheerful, self-assured adolescents may be that way partly because of the kind of parenting they received as children. The kind of parenting they received at that stage may have been affected by the way they responded to their parents as toddlers and babies, *and* by the way their parents responded to them.

Parents do not simply react to their children, any more than children are simply clay in the hands of their parents. Even before they become parents, people have ideas about how children should be raised and what they should be like when they grow up (Alwin, 1988). Once they are parents, they try to put these ideas into practice. At that point, however, the child's characteristics start to play a role (Clark, Kochanska, & Ready, 2000; Hastings & Rubin, 1999). For example, parents who are patient but firm have toddlers who become more willing to follow expectations over time. At the same time, however, toddlers who are very stubborn gradually elicit more coercive parenting (Kuczynski & Kochanska, 1995; Ritchie, 1999).

What seems to matter here is the **goodness of fit** between the parents' attitudes and expectations and the child's temperament (Thomas & Chess, 1986). If the fit is not too bad at the beginning, and if the parents are reasonably responsive and adaptable, it starts a cycle in which the child and parents become increasingly attuned to one another's needs, desires, and goals. If the parents are less adaptable, however, and there is a big discrepency between them and the child, a cycle may be set off in which the child's difficult temperament is amplified by the parents' response (Park, Belsky, Putnam, & Crnic, 1997; van den Boom, 1995).

Ethnic and Cultural Differences

Many of the studies that show the advantages of authoritative parenting have involved mostly White middle-class American families. This raises an important question: Do the experiences and assumptions of mainstream America apply to those who are somewhat apart from it?

Connect the **Dots...**

Why do you think adolescents with indulgent parents tend to be more influenced by friends and peers? Can you recall examples from among adolescents you have known?

◀ **Learning Objective 5.5**
Is there a best way to raise children?

Goodness of fit The relationship between the demands and expectations of parents and the temperament of the child.

When researchers look at parents of different ethnic and cultural backgrounds, they find some distinctly different attitudes and beliefs about parents and families (Garcia Coll, Meyer, & Brillon, 1995). Hispanic, Native American, and Asian American parents are all more likely than European Americans to stress the importance of obeying parental authority. Children are expected to show polite, respectful attitudes and behavior toward parents and elders (Fuligni, Yip, & Tseng, 2002; Greenberger & Chen, 1996; Harwood, Schoelmerich, Ventura-Cook, Schulze, & Wilson, 1996; MacPhee, Fritz, & Miller-Heyl, 1996). African American parents also put great stress on parental authority (Smetana, 2000; Smetana & Chuang, 2001). Parents do not feel they need to explain the reasons for their decisions; the fact that they are the child's parents is considered reason enough to be obeyed.

Partly as a result of this cultural difference, fewer parents in ethnic minorities are classified as authoritative, and more are classified as authoritarian (Chao, 1994, 2001). However, the *effects* of authoritarian parenting do not seem to be as negative for minority teens (Lamborn, Dornbusch, & Steinberg, 1996). Unlike European Americans, Asian American youngsters with authoritarian parents tend to do well in school (Fuligni, 1997; Huntsinger, Jose, & Larson, 1998). African American teens whose parents demand strict obedience and use harsh discipline do not develop the sorts of social problems seen in European Americans with this type of parenting (Brody & Flor, 1998; Deater-Deckard & Dodge, 1997).

Why is this? It may be that sometimes, in some circumstances, authoritarian parenting may actually be more adaptive. If you are trying to bring up children in a dangerous neighborhood, you want to make sure they strictly obey the rules you set to keep them safe and away from bad influences. Keeping them safe will probably strike you as more urgent than fostering their sense of independence (Ogbu, 1994). If harsh punishment is the only form of discipline that seems to work, that is what you will use. The children may not resent the restrictions or the punishment as much, because they sense that these are meant to protect them.

▶ Parents in difficult environments may rely on authoritarian measures to keep their children safe.

A Fifth Parenting Style. Some scholars argue that the categories of authoritative and authoritarian do not apply well to people whose cultures or ethnic groups have different ideas about parents, children, and families (Chao, 1994). Parents in traditional cultures do place a heavy emphasis on parental authority, but they often combine this with a lot of parental warmth (Kakar, 1998).

On the one hand, this pattern does not fit the usual picture of authoritative parenting, as the important qualities of responsiveness and autonomy-granting are missing. However, the element of warmth means it does not quite fit the usual description of authoritarian parenting, either. Diana Baumrind (1987), whose research laid the groundwork for the study of parental styles, has suggested that this combination of warmth and a reliance on unquestioned parental authority should be called *traditional parenting*.

When we turn our attention from North America and Europe to other parts of the world, we find that this traditional parenting style is the most common pattern (Schlegel & Barry, 1991; Whiting & Edwards, 1988). This is not surprising when we consider that most of the *societies* in these parts of the world are also more traditional. These societies are likely to stress the role of custom and tradition as guides to behavior and to see a person's obligations to the community as taking priority over individual rights and needs (Triandis, 1995).

In such a traditional society, an adolescent who has received traditional parenting may fit in better than one with authoritative parents. There may be a cost, however. As we saw in Chapter 1, the trend toward globalization is changing the world politically and economically. Those who have been brought up to see conformity to tradition and obedience to authority as central values may have trouble when they need to adapt to new customs and circumstances (Arnett, 1995; Barber, 1995).

Authoritative Parenting for Everyone? At the beginning of this chapter we looked at three basic goals parents have in raising their children. These are, first, to help the child live to adulthood; second, to give the child the attitudes and skills needed for economic survival as an adult; and third, to promote the development of moral, artistic, religious, and personal values. Those who follow traditional parenting styles would probably agree with these goals just as readily as those who use authoritative parenting. Where they differ may be in how they understand the second and third goals and what tools they have to help them achieve them.

If we compare working-class and middle-class American parents, we see that the working-class parents put more stress on obedience and respect for authority, use more authoritarian discipline, and talk to and reason with their children less often (Maccoby, 1980; McLoyd, 1998). Why do working-class parents adopt this traditional, even authoritarian, parenting style? One reason relates to goal two, economic survival. Working-class parents may emphasize obedience and respect for authority because they think these are qualities their children will need to get by in their working lives (Arnett, 1995). In addition, the parents themselves were probably brought up to think of obedience to authority as a moral virtue. Making sure their children acquire it too is also part of goal three.

There is another factor as well, which concerns the resources parents have available. Economic hardship creates psychological stress. The conditions of life of working-class parents may leave them too edgy and drained to be warm, supportive parents (Conger, Ge, Elder, Lorenz, & Simons, 1994). You've just put in a hard day at work, your boss has been on your case, and you're worried about making this month's car payment. It won't be easy to find the emotional energy to explain to your 12-year-old why she can't go to a late movie on Saturday. Instead, you simply lay down the law. And she had better not argue if she knows what's good for her!

It is understandable that some parents rely on more traditional and authoritarian techniques in dealing with their children. However, it is becoming clear that American adolescents whose parents take a more authoritative approach have more positive outcomes, no matter what their racial, ethnic, or class backgrounds (Steinberg, 2001). This is true even among teens who have committed serious juvenile offenses (Steinberg, Blatt-Eisengart,

& Cauffman, 2006). Studies in other Western cultures lead to a similar conclusion (Adalbjarnardottir & Hafsteinsson, 2001; Goosens & Beyers, 2002; Wolfradt, Hempel, & Miles, 2002). Increasingly, research in the non-Western world is also showing the benefits of authoritative parenting (Dmitrieva, Chen, Greenberger, & Gil-Rivas, 2004; Feldman, Rosenthal, Mont-Reynaud, Lao, & Leung, 1991; Khaleque & Rohner, 2002; Shek, 1996; Stewart et al., 2000). In his presidential address to the Society for Research on Adolescence, Laurence Steinberg (2001) summed up the matter this way:

> There is no question that authoritative parenting is associated with certain developmental outcomes, not all of which are adaptive in all contexts. But in present-day, contemporary, industrialized societies, the characteristics fostered by authoritative parenting—self-reliance, achievement motivation, prosocial behavior, self-control, cheerfulness, and social confidence—are highly desired and highly desirable. Unless these characteristics become maladaptive in our society (a highly unlikely possibility) parents who do not raise their children with these goals in mind are placing their children at a disadvantage.
>
> –(STEINBERG, 2001, p. 13)

In this chapter's Applications in the Spotlight, we take a look at a widely used program that helps families with young adolescents develop the skills and practices they need to stay on track.

Applications in the Spotlight

Strengthening Families

The physical, psychological, and social changes of early adolescence often conspire to widen the emotional distance between parents and young teens. At the same time, the examples set by peers take on increasing importance. Even if those examples include problem behaviors such as alcohol, tobacco, and other substance use, antisocial activities, and precocious sex, the impulse to go along can become overwhelming, especially if there is not a strong parental influence to provide a counterweight (Dishion & Owen, 2002).

Most parents would very much like to give their young adolescents the guidance and support they need to avoid substance use and other problem behaviors. Many, however, feel lost and confused over *how* to give it. Others are convinced they do know how, even when the approach they take has just the opposite effect they want. Still others, discouraged by sullen resentment or escalating defiance from their kids, eventually give up and withdraw.

Among the many programs that work with parents and adolescents to reduce problem behaviors (Child Trends, 2004), one that has been shown to be effective is the *Strengthening Families Program* (SFP). This is a brief curriculum for parents and their 10- to 14-year-old children, originally developed by researchers at Iowa State University (Molgaard, Spoth, & Redmond, 2000).

An SFP program meets once a week for 7 weeks and enrolls from 8 to 13 families. At each session, parents and adolescents meet separately for the first hour, then come together for the second hour. Parent and teen segments are designed to have parallel content that is then practiced and reinforced during the family segment.

> . . . For example, while the parents are learning how to use consequences when youth break rules, youth are learning about the importance of following rules. In the family session that follows, youth and parents practice problem solving as a family for situations when rules are broken.
>
> (MOLGAARD et al., 2000, p. 2)

Parent sessions in SFP begin with a videotaped presentation that includes scenes of typical family interactions, both positive and negative. This is followed by group discussion, role playing, and other exercises designed to build parenting skills. Meanwhile, the adolescents are taking part in group discussions, activities, and games intended to encourage social bonding and skill practice.

For parents, the presentations focus on understanding adolescent development, dealing with everyday interactions, setting and maintaining appropriate limits, and communicating beliefs and expectations about alcohol and drug use. To help participating families hold onto what they have learned, booster sessions on handling stress, communicating when you don't agree, and dealing with peer pressures are offered several months after the program finishes.

The *Strengthening Families Program* has a measurable effect on the families that take part. In one study, adolescents who had gone through SFP were followed for the next 4 years. Compared to equivalent groups of teens who had not done SFP, they measured lower on both initiation and current use of alcohol, tobacco, and marijuana (Spoth, Redmond, & Shin, 2001). Other studies showed significantly fewer conduct problems and school-related problem behaviors, less affiliation with deviant peers, and lower levels of hostility in interacting with parents, up to 4 years after participants were in the program (see Figure A5.1) (Molgaard et al., 2000).

According to an old saying, "An ounce of prevention is worth a pound of cure." Based on the reported benefits, the *Strengthening Families Program* and other family-focused intervention programs that target young adolescents offer good proof of the saying's validity. More detailed information can be found on the program's website: www.strengtheningfamiliesprogram.org.

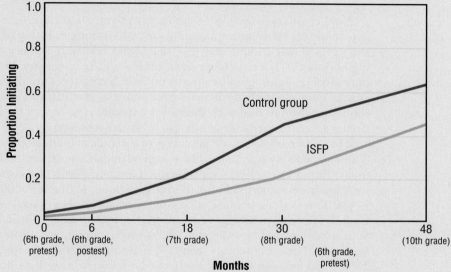

Figure A5.1   Alcohol Use Without Parental Permission
Intervention programs that strengthen families lead to lower levels of alcohol use without parental permission.

*ISFP youth compared with youth who did not attend the program.

Source: Mogaard et al., 2000, p. 9.

Autonomy and Control

"Please, Mother, I'd rather do it myself!"

This tagline from a classic television commercial captures a universal issue families face during adolescence. How can adolescents achieve a healthy, mature sense of **autonomy**? And what *is* healthy and mature, anyway? Does it mean having to cut the emotional ties with the parents? Is family life a prison and adolescence is jailbreak time? Or are there ways teens can balance becoming more their own person and still maintaining a close emotional connection to their parents?

Two Sorts of Autonomy. Parents also face a dilemma. How do they encourage their children's development and still guide them and protect them from danger? It is a little like helping a child learn to ride a bicycle. Stay back too far, and the child may fall over, get hurt, and lose confidence. But hover too close, ready to grab the handlebars at the first sign of trouble, and the child may miss that magical moment when the bike stops wobbling and seems to stay upright all by itself.

As this analogy suggests, children's movement toward greater autonomy starts long before adolescence. A 3-year-old in a store may wander and explore, glancing back at the parent now and then for reassurance. However, the physical, cognitive, and social changes of puberty move the question of autonomy much higher on the family agenda. Adulthood is now more than an eventual possibility, suddenly it seems just around the corner, and it has to be prepared for.

◀ **Learning Objective 5.6**
Why are issues of autonomy and control important?

Autonomy An ability to act independently and a willingness to take responsibility for one's actions.

The concept of autonomy is many-sided, but it is useful to think of it as having two major components: emotional and behavioral (Hill & Holmbeck, 1986; Steinberg, 1990).

Emotional autonomy implies developing sources of emotional strength within oneself. An adolescent who is emotionally autonomous no longer has to depend on parents for comfort, reassurance, and a sense of security, the way a child does. An important step in this direction is to begin to see the parents as people with their own needs, who are as fallible as anyone else.

Behavioral autonomy is the ability to make one's own decisions about important questions. This implies taking responsibility for one's actions and their consequences. Behavioral autonomy also shows itself in such everyday matters as making sure you have a supply of clean socks and setting the alarm before you go to sleep (and getting up on your own when it goes off!).

Neither of these aspects of autonomy comes all at once or easily. Sometimes an apparently trivial dispute will send young adolescents storming off as if it is the end of the world. Their parents may give each other baffled looks or mutter, "Must be raging hormones." There is, however, a psychological explanation. Moving toward autonomy involves fighting on two fronts at once. Young teens are pushing their parents to change long-established roles and procedures to give them more of a say. At the same time, they have to deal with their own temptation to stay in the child role. After all, having someone take care of you can be greatly comforting.

The degree of autonomy parents give their teens is affected by a variety of factors. These include age, of course, but also gender, cultural expectations, and parental attitudes (Eccles et al., 1991; Silverberg & Gondoli, 1996). Girls often have more input into family decisions than boys (Bumpus, Crouter, & McHale, 2001; Fuligni & Eccles, 1993). This may be because adolescent girls are generally seen as more mature than boys the same age (Brooks-Gunn & Reiter, 1990). Teens in Asian or Asian American families do not get, or expect to get, as much autonomy as European Americans the same age (Greenberger & Chen, 1996; Rothbaum, Poll, Azuma, Miyake, & Weisz, 2000). And, not surprisingly, mothers who hold traditional gender role attitudes give their adolescent daughters less autonomy (Bumpus et al., 2001).

Behavioral and Psychological Control. Back in the 1960s, psychologist Earl Schaefer (1965) pointed out that different parents use different forms of control, and that these are linked to different outcomes in their children. It is not solely *how much* control that matters, that plays a role, but the *kind* of control is even more crucial. For a quarter of a century or so, this insight was relatively neglected. The reason may have been that researchers were so busy studying parental styles (Barber & Harmon, 2002). As they began asking *why* different parenting styles have the effects they do, however, the question of control came back onto the agenda (Roberts & Steinberg, 1999; Steinberg, 2005).

We can distinguish between two sorts of control: behavioral and psychological (Barber, 1996, 2002; Steinberg, 1990).

Behavioral control concerns parents setting rules, restrictions, and limits on their child's activities. For example, curfews, chores, and good manners would all fall under this heading. As the name implies, the focus is on guiding and controlling the child's *behavior.* An important facet of behavioral control is *monitoring* (Dishion & McMahon, 1998). This involves both *structuring* the child's daily environments—at home, at school, on evenings and weekends—and *tracking* the child's behavior in those environments (Capaldi, 2003).

Psychological control involves attempts by parents to control their children by manipulating their thoughts, feelings, and attachment to the parents (Barber & Harmon, 2002). This includes inducing guilt feelings in the child ("You don't know how much it wounds me when you disagree with me") and using love withdrawal as a punishment (for example, the "silent treatment"). Psychological control is *intrusive.* By not acknowledging the child as a separate individual, the parent invades the child's psychological world.

Behavioral and psychological control have been found to predict very different outcomes in adolescents. *Low* levels of behavioral control are linked to externalizing problems such as drug use, truancy, and antisocial behavior (Barber & Harmon, 2002;

Emotional autonomy The ability to function without having to rely on others, such as parents, to provide a sense of comfort and security.

Behavioral autonomy The ability to make one's own decisions and take responsibility for them.

Behavioral control The rules and limits parents place on their child's activities.

Psychological control Trying to control children by acting on their thoughts and feelings.

Barber, Stolz, & Olsen, 2005). In contrast, *high* levels of psychological control are linked to internalizing problems, including anxiety, depression, and withdrawn behavior (Barber & Harmon, 2002; Barber et al., 2005; Rogers, Buchanan, & Winchell, 2003; Silk, Morris, Kanaya, & Steinberg, 2003).

The relationship between psychological control and adolescent problem behaviors is not limited to mainstream American families. It also shows up in African Americans and Hispanic Americans (Bean, Bush, McKenry, & Wilson, 2003; Smetana & Daddis, 2002) and in cultures as varied as Australia, India, Israel, Mexico, and Palestine (Barber & Harmon, 2002; Barber et al., 2005).

Why is psychological control consistently linked to such negative effects? The reasons seem clear. If parents do not respect a child's individual thoughts and feelings, they interfere with the development of feelings of competence and autonomy. Where behavioral control is meant to control the child's behavior, psychological control aims to control the child's sense of self (Nucci, Hasebe, & Lins-Dyer, 2005).

With behavioral control, the picture is slightly less clear. Many studies have linked parental monitoring with less delinquency; less drug, alcohol, and tobacco use; and less frequent risky sex (Galambos, Barker, & Almeida, 2003; Kerr et al., 2002). The usual explanation is that parents who keep track of what their children are doing, where, and with whom, are able to step in and take charge if a problem starts to develop. They may also be more interested and involved.

But how do parents *know* about the activities of their children? From private detectives or hidden video cameras? Not as a rule, I hope! No, they know because the children tell them, either spontaneously or when questioned (Crouter, Bumpus, Davis, & McHale, 2005; Kerr & Stattin, 2003). While parents and teens differ about how much teens should disclose to their parents, they do agree that issues involving prudence and safety should be disclosed (Smetana, Metzger, Gettman, & Campione-Barr, 2006). This suggests that monitoring works, at least in part, because there is already an atmosphere of openness, trust, and closeness in the family. That atmosphere itself may be as important to adolescent adjustment as having parents who closely monitor their children (Finkenauer, Engels, & Meeus, 2002; Kerr & Stattin, 2003; Laird, Pettit, Dodge, & Bates, 2003).

Recent research shows that parental responsiveness, high behavioral control, and low psychological control all have links to adolescent self-disclosure (Criss, Pettit, Dodge, Bates, & Williams, 2006; Soenens, Vansteenkiste, Luyckx, & Goossens, 2006). These factors combine to create a family atmosphere of supportiveness, openness, and trust (Henry, Robinson, Neal, & Huey, 2006). Where such an atmosphere does not exist, teens who are engaged in problem behaviors either don't tell their parents or lie about their activities. In turn, their parents' lack of knowledge keeps them from taking steps that might make the situation better (Tilton-Weaver & Marshall, 2003).

Attachment in Adolescents

What holds a family together? According to British psychiatrist John Bowlby (1969; 1988), it is the emotional bond or **attachment** that develops between parents and children. In Bowlby's view, the need to be close to parents, especially in times of distress, is built into our biological nature. The sense of security this gives is rewarding to both parents and children.

Until recently, studies of attachment have concentrated on parents and infants. Based on reactions to strange situations and brief separations from the caregiver, researchers find that most babies have formed a *secure attachment*. They use the parent as a base for exploring and seek contact with the parent when distressed. Some, however, show a form of *insecure attachment*, either *resistant*, *avoidant*, or *disorganized/disoriented* (Ainsworth, Blehar, Waters, & Wall, 1978; Hertsgaard, Gunnar, Erickson, & Nachmias, 1995).

The most important influence on infant attachment is the sensitivity and responsiveness of the parent or caregiver (De Woolf & van IJzendoorn, 1997). Babies whose parents are reasonably sensitive, affectionate, and attentive tend to form secure attachments. Those whose parents are insensitive, inconsistent, impatient, neglecting, or

Connect the Dots...

Think about the four parenting styles described earlier. Which do you think is most likely to be linked to behavioral control? Which to psychological control? Why? Does this shed any light on the ways these parenting styles affect adolescents?

◀ **Learning Objective 5.7**
What is attachment and how does it affect relationships?

Attachment The emotional bond that develops between parents and children; may include *secure, resistant, avoidant,* and *disorganized/disoriented* attachment.

abusive are more likely to end up with an insecure attachment (Carlson, 1998; Isabella, 1993; Isabella & Belsky, 1991).

Attachment Experiences and Working Models. According to attachment theory, experiences in infancy lay the groundwork for a person's **internal working models** (Bowlby, 1988; Bretherton, 1990). These models are basic concepts children form about other people and themselves, which they use to understand what happens in their personal interactions. Our internal working models help us form expectations about what will happen in human relationships.

A securely attached child who receives responsive, affectionate care develops a positive working model of others ("The people who care for me are dependable."). At the same time, the child's ability to attract the caregiver's attention helps generate a positive working model of the self ("I'm important, I matter."). Insensitive or inconsistent care, however, leads to a negative working model of others ("You can't count on them."), while neglect fosters a negative working model of the self ("I'm worthless, I don't matter.").

In Bowlby's view, the working models of the self and others that begin to develop in infancy continue to affect the person's relationships throughout life. The way an adolescent relates to a close friend, a romantic partner, or a teacher (or, of course, a parent) will be affected by the way he or she experienced attachment relationships in infancy and childhood. In turn, important life events, such as the loss of a parent, a parental divorce, or the experience of abuse, can change the person's working models (Waters, Weinfield, & Hamilton, 2000).

One interesting way of working out this idea is shown in Figure 5.4. According to this, it is the *pattern* of working models that generates the different ways teens approach close relationships. Those who have positive working models of both themselves and others will be secure in their relationships. Those who have positive models of the self, but negative models of others, will downplay the importance of emotional ties. Those with a negative model of the self, but a positive model of others, will be preoccupied with establishing relationships, but at the same time pessimistic about the possibility of them working out. Those with negative working models of both the self and others will be fearful of emotional bonds (Bartholomew & Horowitz, 1991).

Continuity of Early Attachment Beliefs. Suppose you know whether someone was securely or insecurely attached as a baby. Will that help you predict their working models of attachment as adolescents? On the whole, yes, it will. That statement is based on several longitudinal studies (Hamilton, 2000; Lewis, Feiring, & Rosenthal, 2000; Waters, Merrick, Treboux, Crowell, & Albersheim, 2000; Weinfield, Sroufe, & Egelund, 2000). These studies looked at how various groups of babies behaved in attachment situations. Then, years later, when the babies had grown up into adolescents and young adults, the researchers studied their attitudes about attachment and relationships.

Generally, there is a link between attachment behavior as a baby and later attitudes about attachment. Those who acted securely attached as babies hold more positive working models later on. Those who were insecure as babies hold more negative working models later on (Hamilton, 2000; Waters et al., 2000a). There were also some people who went from being securely attached as babies to having insecure attitudes as young

Figure 5.4   Working Models and Relationship Styles
Working models of the self and others are linked to different relationship styles.

Working Model of Self	Working Model of Others	
	Positive	Negative
Positive	Secure	Dismissive
Negative	Preoccupied	Fearful

Source: Bartholomew & Horowitz, 1991.

Internal working models The basic positive or negative concepts that children form about other people and about themselves.

adults. These people are more likely to have experienced the divorce of their parents (Lewis et al., 2000), to have been mistreated as children, or to have had mothers who suffered from depression (Weinfield et al., 2000).

Why are a person's working models apparently so stable, even over a span of 15 or 20 years? One reason may be that they help create *self-fulfilling prophecies*. A child who expects others to accept her may act in a way that makes it more likely they will. When they do accept her, it confirms and strengthens her positive working models of herself and others. If some are rejecting—you can't win 'em all—her positive working model helps buffer her from taking the disappointment as a reflection on her personally.

In contrast, a child who expects to be rejected may not approach others at all. If he does make an overture, he may do it in a way that sets the stage for rejection. Even if some others *are* open to friendship with him, his negative working models may keep him from noticing and taking advantage of the opportunity.

This is not just a made-up example. Evidence is mounting that working models are indeed connected to the peer relationships of adolescents. The conclusions teens drew earlier in childhood about themselves and others later predict both their choice of friends and how well they relate to them (Biesecker & Easterbrooks, 2002; Schneider, Atkinson, & Tardif, 2001). This chapter's Research in the Spotlight provides an example.

Research in the Spotlight

Parents, Peers, and Attachment Style

According to attachment theory, the working models of the self and others that develop early in childhood lead to distinctive attachment styles that endure into adolescence and adulthood. Those who are *securely* attached feel worth being cared about and believe those they are attached to are dependable. Those who are *insecure-dismissing* tend to shy away from attachment relationships because they distrust others. Those who are *insecure-preoccupied* long to have such relationships, but do not believe they are really worthy of them.

Research on attachment generally shows that across the adolescent years, peers gradually replace parents as the targets of a child's intimate relationships. On average, older teens are more upset about separations from best friends and boy/girlfriends than from parents. They also confide more in friends and romantic partners than in parents. However, intimacy is not quite the same thing as attachment, which has more to do with feeling able to rely on someone if things go wrong. A lasting and powerful attachment may be taken for granted, or even overlooked, as long as no distressing situation comes along to activate it.

What impact does an adolescent's attachment style have on attachments to parents and peers? This question was explored by psychologists Harry Freeman and B. Bradford Brown (2001). They reasoned that those with secure attachment styles would continue to see parents, especially mothers, as their most important attachment figure. Insecurely attached teens, however, would be more likely to look to peers—friends and romantic partners—for attachment support. This would be particularly so for those with a preoccupied style. Dismissing teens, on the other hand, might avoid attachment to both parents *and* peers and prefer to rely on themselves.

The participants in the study, high school juniors and seniors, were classified as secure, preoccupied, or dismissing, based on a measure of attachment style. About 44% of them were secure, 28% preoccupied, and 26% dismissing. They were asked to name the person in their life they relied on most for emotional support and to rate the amount of attachment support they got from their mothers, fathers, best friends, and boy/girlfriends. The results clearly confirmed the researchers' predictions. In the secure group, 80% named a parent, usually the mother, while in the two insecure groups, over 60% named a peer. Particularly striking, over a quarter of the dismissing group named themselves as the person they relied on most.

In their discussion of the results, Freeman and Brown point out that durability is a vital quality of a supportive attachment. In adolescence, relationships with friends and romantic partners tend to be fairly unstable. Conflict or absence can quickly erode them. Relationships with parents are felt to be more enduring and secure. As one participant put it,

> I can go to [my mom] with my problems, I can rely on her to be there for me, I know that she won't get mad at me for you know, for like a mistake or something like that . . .

(FREEMAN & BROWN, 2001, p. 666)

However, this feeling of security is linked to a secure attachment style. Teens with an insecure attachment style are more likely to look outside the family, to friends and boy/girlfriends, for a sense of support. Even if they think they have found it there, a distressing measure of dependency and unpredictability may come with it.

Attachment to parents is linked to better social skills, competence in friendships, and emotional adjustment (Allen et al., 2002; Engels et al., 2002; Engels, Finkenauer, Meeus, & Dekovic 2001). Attachment to parents is also connected to a lower level of problems, such as depression (Marsh, McFarland, Allen, Boykin McElhaney, & Land, 2003) and substance abuse (Bogenschneider, Wu, Raffaelli, & Tsay, 1998). Working models for relationships with parents and friends are related to working models for relationships with romantic partners as well (Furman, Simon, Shaffer, & Bouchey, 2002; Mayseless & Scharf, 2007). We will look at some implications of these connections later, when we discuss the development of peer relations (Chapter 6) and intimacy (Chapter 12).

Connect the **Dots...**

Can you think of ways that adolescents might be helped to overcome negative working models of the self or of others that may date back to infancy or early childhood?

Parent-Teen Conflict

▶ **Learning Objective 5.8**
Are parents and teens bound to come into conflict?

While working on this chapter, I dropped by a large bookstore and browsed in the Parenting department. The books were arranged by age. On the first shelves, I noticed such titles as, *The Magic Years*, *How to Raise a Happy Baby*, and *Kids Are Worth It*. The covers featured cute, smiling babies and attractive, smiling parents.

Then I moved a few feet to the right, to the Adolescence section. Some of the titles caught my eye:

The Roller Coaster Years
How to Keep Your Teenager Out of Trouble
How to Stop the Battle With Your Teenager
How to Keep Your Teenager From Driving You Crazy
Yes, Your Teen Is Crazy!

Clearly, the idea that adolescence has to be a time of "storm and stress" is alive and well and living at Barnes & Noble!

As we saw in Chapter 2, this conception of tumultuous adolescence has a long and distinguished history, going back to G. Stanley Hall (1904) and even to Aristotle. Psychoanalytic theorists such as Anna Freud (1958) claimed that children are so wrapped up emotionally with their parents that at adolescence the only way they can move forward is to break away. This process of **detachment** is assumed to set off conflict and tension, but Freud saw that as healthy and necessary. In her view, if an adolescent *doesn't* go through a period of storm and stress, it is a bad sign.

But the fact that prestigious people held an idea does not necessarily mean it is correct. How does it stand up to being tested against experience?

Research on Conflict. Since the 1960s, many researchers have taken close looks at the question of whether conflict between parents and adolescents is a defining feature of this stage of life. The results can be summed up in the title of an article that reviewed dozens of these studies: "Parents and adolescents in conflict: All families some of the time and some families most of the time" (Montemayor, 1983).

Parents and teens do squabble and bicker, and they do so more often than they did earlier, when the teens were still children. On average, they come into conflict even more often than married couples who are having problems (Montemayor, 1986)! One reason has to do with changing roles and lines of authority. Adolescents are likely to challenge, or at least question, parental power and to push for a greater say in decision making (Helwig & Kim, 1999). While parents generally agree that their teens should have more of a say, often their attitude comes down to, "Yes, of course, but not just yet."

Adolescents and parents may quarrel; however, they tend to agree on the big issues, including their love and respect for one another (Moore, Guzman, Hair, Lippman, & Garrett, 2004; Steinberg & Silk, 2002). Where they disagree most is over apparently minor issues, such as clothing, curfews, music, neatness, and time management (Collins, 1990; Hill & Holmbeck, 1987; Steinberg, 1990). As we will see a little later,

Detachment The process by which adolescents break away from their parents.

◄ Parent-teen clashes often occur over seemingly minor issues such as clothing choices.

this often happens because parents and teens have clashing ideas about what *is* a minor issue. In addition, young adolescents tend to be better at resolving conflicts with age mates than with parents (Borbely, Graber, Nichols, Brooks-Gunn, & Botvin, 2005).

We should not exaggerate the degree of conflict in the typical family. A large majority of teens think highly of their parents, want to be like them, and enjoy spending time with them (Moore et al., 2004). Similar results have been found for African American, Asian American, Mexican American, and Filipino American teens (Fuligni, 1998; Smetana & Gaines, 1999). While parents tend to *expect* a lot of conflict when their children enter adolescence (Buchanan, 2003), they often report that in fact adolescence has brought them closer to their children (Shearer, Crouter, & McHale, 2005).

Some families do have high levels of parent-teen conflict. However, most of these also have family problems that date back to when the teens were still children (Rutter, Graham, Chadwick, & Yule, 1976). This does not lend much support to the idea that family conflict occurs because the children have entered adolescence (Steinberg, 2001).

Conflict Across the Adolescent Years. The conflicts that do occur between parents and adolescents are most frequent early in adolescence (Gutman & Eccles, 2007; Laursen, Coy, & Collins, 1998). This is when various sources of conflict—physical, cognitive, social—first come into play. Not only is there more conflict, but early teens report being less helpful and feeling less affectionate toward their parents (Eberly & Montemayor, 1999).

Young adolescents disagree more often with their mothers than with their fathers (Laursen, 1995). This probably reflects the fact that they see more of their mothers than their fathers (Larson & Richards, 1994). These conflicts with mothers are more frequent and more intense for daughters than sons (Graber & Brooks-Gunn, 1999), especially if the mothers are restrictive in their parenting and the daughters react strongly to stress (Villanueva-Abraham, 2002).

From early to late adolescence, the number of conflicts between adolescents and parents drops steadily (Laursen et al., 1998). This parallels a drop in the amount of time teens and parents spend together (Larson, Richards, Moneta, Holmbeck, & Duckett, 1996; Laursen & Williams, 1997). It seems likely that the disagreements drop off simply because parents and children are together less (Laursen et al., 1998). The emotional intensity of conflicts, however, goes *up* from early to middle adolescence (Laursen et al., 1998). One reason may be that the issues involved become more serious (Arnett, 1999).

Stereotype and Reality. If, as research results indicate, conflict and turmoil do *not* define most parent-teen relationships, why does the stereotype hang on so doggedly? What makes parents buy all those books about how to cope with their stormy teens?

First, there is a *contrast effect*. Compared to the school-age children they so recently were, young teens *are* stormy. Their moods swing more widely and more often (Larson, Moneta, Richards, & Wilson, 2002; Larson & Richards, 1994). In the emotional life of an ordinary 12-year-old, the highs are really high, the lows are really low, and the alternations from one to another are dizzying. If one of these swings comes after a parent-teen dispute, it is easy for parents to see the conflict as deeper and more significant than it may seem to the teen.

Questions of parental authority and adolescent autonomy also enter the picture. Parents and adolescents generally agree that parents have the right to make rules on *moral*, *conventional*, and *safety* issues. They also agree that *personal* issues are the teen's domain (Smetana & Asquith, 1994).

But what issues belong in which category? Is the way you dress a personal issue? Most adolescents would say yes, and say it loudly, but for parents, looking "decent and respectable" may be a social, a moral, or even a safety issue that clearly falls under their authority. The scene that follows a statement such as, "You are not leaving the house looking like that" is sure to strengthen the parents' belief that adolescence is a time of turmoil.

An adolescent who has just been ordered to change into a less hole-y pair of jeans or a less revealing top may wonder, "What's the big deal anyway?" Parents do not always explain what lies behind their reactions (Arnett, 1999). They themselves may not be fully aware of their reasons. So when they say, "I don't like you hanging around with those kids," they mean, "Those kids look like druggies." "Why don't you invite your new (boy/girl)friend over sometime when we're home," means, "I don't know what might happen if we let you two be alone in the house." Even, "Be home no later than twelve," may contain the unspoken message, "I want you to leave the party before that kid who's driving you home gets tanked up and wraps his car around a tree."

There is still another reason parents may see their relationship with their adolescents as full of conflict. They find it harder to shake off the upsetting effect of an argument (Steinberg, 2001). Long after a teen has forgotten about some heated exchange, the parents may still be brooding about it (Dekovic, 1999). Is their child on a path that leads toward disaster? Will he or she grow up, move away, and never call home? Have they somehow failed as parents?

The next stop is the nearest bookstore.

Families and Behavioral Genetics

▶ **Learning Objective 5.9**
How does genetic background interact with the family environment?

Genotype A person's genetic makeup, as contrasted with *phenotype*, or the way that genetic makeup is expressed in the person.

Behavioral genetics A method for inferring the influence of genes and environment by studying people who are genetically related.

Twin study Research that compares identical and fraternal twins to assess the effects of nature and nurture.

"The fruit never falls far from the tree." This old saying reminds us that parents affect their children in ways beyond styles of parenting, ways of exercising control, and even ties of affection and attachment. Parents are also the source of their children's **genotype**, or genetic makeup. If adolescents resemble their parents in various ways, or if they seem to have been shaped by their parents, it may be a result of what the parents have *done*. It may also be a result of what the parents *are*; that is, of the genes they have passed along to their children.

In recent years, many scholars have set out to understand how development is affected by the combination of genetic heritage and experience. One important approach to this effort is **behavioral genetics**. Behavioral geneticists do not study the actual genes people possess; instead, they look for statistical similarities and differences among people who share different *proportions* of their genes, such as parents and children, twins, siblings, stepsiblings, and so on. From these relationships, they infer the relative influence of genetic background and environment in producing individual differences among people.

Two basic strategies are common in behavioral genetics research. In a **twin study** (for example, Deater-Deckard & O'Connor, 2000), the degree of similarity in pairs of *identical twins*, who have all their genes in common, is compared to the degree of similarity in *fraternal twins*, who share only 50% of their genes. If the identical twins turn out to be more similar, this is interpreted as a result of genetic influence.

An **adoption study** (for example, O'Connor, Plomin, Caspi, & DeFries, 2000) follows a slightly different logic. Adopted children are compared with their *biological* parents, with whom they share 50% of their genes, but none of their environment, and with their *adoptive* parents, with whom they share their environment but none of their genes. To the extent the children are like their biological parents, it must be an effect of genetic factors. To the extent they are like their adoptive parents, it must be an effect of environment or experience.

Shared and Nonshared Environments. Both twin studies and adoption studies give an estimate of how much genetic factors contribute to differences on some characteristic. They also allow researchers to estimate the strength of two sources of environmental influence. *Shared environmental influences* are those aspects of experience that tend to make siblings *similar to* each other. *Nonshared environmental influences* are those that tend to make siblings *different from* each other (Plomin & Daniels, 1987).

An important point to remember about shared and nonshared environmental influences is that they are usually defined by their *effects*. Suppose the parents of two adolescents get a divorce. The divorce is clearly an environmental influence. If both teens respond similarly, for example, by withdrawing socially, that makes it a shared environmental influence. But what if one withdraws and the other becomes more focused on peers? Then the divorce turns out to be a *nonshared* environmental influence, because it is linked to different effects (Turkheimer & Waldron, 2000).

For a while, many researchers thought that shared environmental influences were much less important than nonshared environmental influences (Plomin & Daniels, 1987; Rowe, 1994). This led to claims that what parents do has little effect on the way their adolescents turn out (Harris, 1998). These claims attracted a lot of attention from the media. As more evidence has accumulated, however, it becomes clear that there is more of a balance between shared and nonshared environmental influences (Collins, Maccoby, Steinberg, Hetherington, & Bornstein, 2000; Reiss, Neiderheiser, Hetherington, & Plomin, 2000; Rutter, 2002). What parents do matters, but they do not always do the same things to different children (Conger & Conger, 1994; Feinberg & Hetherington, 2001).

Genotype and Environment. We often think of heredity and environment as factors that work independently of each other. This is misleading in at least two ways. First, our genetic makeup can influence the environments we are exposed to (Scarr, 1993). Second, environmental factors can affect how, or even whether, various genetic tendencies get expressed (Rutter, 2002).

Suppose you know an adolescent who is a hotshot skier. Is that a matter of genetics or environment? The best answer is, "Both." But how? Behavioral geneticist Sandra Scarr (1993) has described three ways a person's genotype and environment may be related.

Passive genotype-environment correlations occur because parents (who, of course, are genetically related to their children) *provide* home environments that are influenced by their *own* genotypes. Parents who are genetically inclined to be athletic pass this inclination on to their children *and* create a home setting that encourages interest in sports.

Evocative genotype-environment correlations occur because a child's genetically influenced characteristics *call forth* particular responses from others. A child who takes to skis like a duck to water will get more encouragement, support, and trips to the slope than one who would rather stay inside the ski lodge and read a mystery.

Active genotype-environment correlations occur when people actively *seek out* environments that fit best with their genetic predispositions. An athletic teen may hang out mostly with others who have the same interests, watch ESPN instead of MTV, and save up for a trip to a famous ski resort instead of buying lots of CDs. This is often called *niche-picking*; that is, the teen hunts for a social/environmental niche that is compatible with his or her genetic tendencies.

Adoption study Research that compares adopted children with their biological and adoptive parents to assess the effects of nature and nurture.

Passive genotype-environment correlation A situation in which parents create environments that are associated with their own genetically influenced traits, which are similar to those of their child.

Evocative genotype-environment correlation A situation in which a child has genetically influenced traits that evoke particular responses from others.

Active genotype-environment correlation A situation in which children seek out settings that are congenial to their genetically influenced traits.

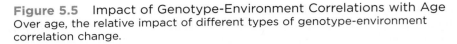

Figure 5.5 Impact of Genotype-Environment Correlations with Age
Over age, the relative impact of different types of genotype-environment correlation change.

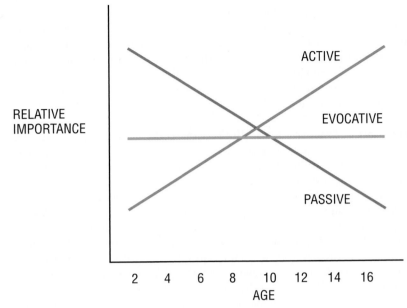

Source: GeneXEnvir correl, after Scarr & McCartney, 1983.

According to Scarr (Scarr & McCartney, 1983), the relative importance of these three processes change during childhood and adolescence (see Figure 5.5). During early childhood, passive genotype-environment correlations count the most. Young children more or less take whatever environment their parents provide. As they get older, and especially as they enter adolescence, they start to choose their own friends and interests. This gives active genotype-environment correlations greater importance. Evocative genotype-environment correlations, the ways being attractive, or athletic, or irritable, affect how others react to the person, stay important right across the lifespan.

Sometimes people with a particular set of genetic tendencies react one way to one environment but a different way to a different environment, and sometimes a particular environment has different effects on those with different genes. These are examples of **gene-environment interaction** (Maccoby, 2000).

In one striking case, a large-scale Finnish study looked at adopted children. Some had birth mothers with schizophrenia, which has a strong genetic component. If these at-risk children grew up in healthy adoptive families, they did not develop psychiatric problems. Children who were adopted into dysfunctional families did develop problems, but only if they carried the genetic risk (Tienari et al., 1994, 2003). This interaction between genetic risk and environmental risk is diagrammed in Figure 5.6.

Gene-environment interaction
A situation in which a particular genetic predisposition is expressed in one environment but not in another, or in which a particular environment has a certain effect on those with one set of genes but not on those with a different set.

Figure 5.6 Incidence of Schizophrenic Symptoms in Adopted Children at Risk
Schizophrenic symptoms in adopted children reflect an interaction of genetic risk and the characteristics of the adoptive family.

Adopted Child's Genetic Risk of Schizophrenia	Characteristics of Adoptive Family	
	Healthy, Supportive	Dysfunctional
High	Low symptoms	High symptoms
Low	Low symptoms	Low symptoms

Source: Tienari et al., 1994, 2003. *American Journal of Psychiatry*, 160, 1587–1594.

There is still a lot to be learned about how gene-environment interactions work (Moffitt & Caspi, 2007). One possibility is that environmental factors change the way genes produce proteins, which, in turn, changes the structure and function of the brain (Reiss & Neiderheiser, 2000). Animal studies have shown that very early stress can permanently alter the activity of genes that control stress-related hormones (Plotsky & Meaney, 1993; Suomi, 2000). In humans, when mothers are trained to respond better to their baby's irritability (a genetically-influenced trait), easily distressed babies develop less avoidant attachment (van den Boom, 1995).

> **Summing Up...**
>
> Parenting can be described in terms of acceptance/responsiveness and demandingness/control. Together, these dimensions generate four parenting styles: authoritative, authoritarian, indulgent, and indifferent. Each parenting style is linked to particular adolescent outcomes, with authoritative parenting leading to the most positive results. The type of control the parent uses and the adolescent's attachment beliefs are also important. So is the way the adolescent's genetic heritage relates to the family environment.

SIBLINGS AND ADOLESCENCE

So far in our discussion of families, we have concentrated on adolescents and their parents. Of course, this is central, but it leaves out another important element of family life: brothers and sisters. Siblings are a fact of life. In recent decades the average size of families has declined in the United States and Canada, as in most other industrialized societies, but the great majority of American children still grow up in households with at least one sibling (U.S. Bureau of the Census, 2006).

The sibling relationship contains a peculiar mix of equality and hierarchy, of closeness and conflict. Grade school children say their siblings matter to them as much as or even more than their close friends. At the same time, they admit they quarrel with them more (Furman & Buhrmester, 1985). One moment siblings are sharing secrets, the next they are bickering over who sits where or who got a bigger piece of pie.

Adolescents often act as caregivers for younger brothers and sisters. In many societies around the world, older siblings are the *main* caregivers (Schlegel & Barry, 1991; Weisner, 1989). Industrialized societies like our own have generally turned this role over to schools and other institutions. Still, bigger children, especially girls, are often expected to take care of the littler ones. This gives them experience at being responsible and in charge (Zukow-Goldring, 2002). It can also be a rare opportunity to exercise power and boss someone around.

Siblings influence one another in many different ways. They are models, teachers, partners, and critics. They are also sources of valuable feedback. Your best friend won't tell you how lame your new haircut looks or what a jerk your new romantic interest really is, but you can usually count on a brother or sister for painfully frank comments. Siblings also influence one another indirectly, by way of the parents. If an older brother or sister gets along well with others and does well in school, the parents are likely to be more confident and relaxed with the younger siblings. If the older child gets in trouble, however, the younger child often feels the effects (Brody, Kim, Murry, & Brown, 2003).

Getting along with a sibling on a daily basis is an important socializing experience (Seginer, 1998; Teti, 2002). It teaches negotiating skills, the art of compromise, and the ability to stand up for oneself without being obnoxious. Good sibling relationships also serve as a "bridge" to making close friends outside the family, because they involve the same social and emotional skills (Bigelow, Tesson, & Lewko, 1999; Dickson, 2002). In particular, sibling relationships provide an ideal context for developing the self-disclosure skills that are so important for adolescent and adult relationships (Howe, Aquan-Assee, Bukowski, Rinaldi, & Lehoux 2000).

▲ Teens often act as caregivers to younger brothers and sisters.

Siblings also promote the development of gender roles (McHale, Crouter, & Whiteman, 2003). Older same-sex siblings serve as both instructors and examples of these roles (McHale, Updegraff, Helms-Erikson, & Crouter, 2001). In mixed-sex pairs, sisters may learn control tactics from their brothers that they can then use in their friendships. Less often, brothers pick up intimacy skills from their sisters (Updegraff, McHale, & Crouter, 2000). In early adolescence, when sex segregation is so pervasive, brothers and sisters offer one another a unique chance to learn and practice relating to the opposite sex (Updegraff et al., 2000).

The Sibling Relationship

▶ **Learning Objective 5.10**
How do sibling relationships affect adolescents?

One unusual feature of the sibling relationship is that it can be both *complementary*, like the parent-child relationship, and *reciprocal*, like the more equal relationship between friends (Dunn, 1993). This duality shows up in the kinds of support siblings give one another. On issues that involve social life, schoolwork, and risky behavior such as sex and drugs, it is the older siblings who are likely to give advice and support. On family issues, however, siblings tend to play equally supportive roles (Tucker, McHale, & Crouter, 2001). This makes good sense. On wider issues, older siblings are probably more experienced, but both siblings have had a lifetime of exposure to their family situation.

Younger siblings often take their older brothers and sisters as models, especially if the two have a warm, close relationship and the older sibling's experience is seen as positive (Whiteman & Buchanan, 2002). This is not universal, however. Sometimes, especially if siblings are close in age, they may deliberately define themselves as *different* from each other (Feinberg & Hetherington, 2000). This process, called **de-identification,** may help cut down on rivalry, envy, and possible resentment (Schacter, 1985; Updegraff et al., 2000).

Sometimes the modeling process between siblings has unfortunate results. Siblings may influence the development of problem behaviors (Conger, Conger, & Scaramella, 1997). For pairs of sisters as well as pairs of brothers, an older sibling's delinquency predicts delinquency in the younger sibling as well (Slomkowski, Rende, Conger, Simons, & Conger, 2001). One explanation for this is **sibling collusion**, in which the siblings form coalitions that promote deviant behavior (Bullock & Dishion, 2002, 2003). As each sibling eggs on the other and provides praise and admiration for deviant acts, it creates a positive feedback loop that can lead to more and more extreme behavior.

Connect the **Dots...**

Some siblings are close in age, but others are separated by several, or even many, years. How do you think these differences might affect their relationship and their effect on one another?

Like conflict between adolescents and their parents, conflict between siblings peaks early in adolescence (Brody, Stoneman, & McCoy, 1994; Buhrmester & Furman, 1990). Along with all the other changes young teens have to deal with, putting up with either an older sibling, who pretends to know it all, or a younger sibling, who seems to be such a baby, can fill the cup to overflowing.

As adolescence goes on, sibling relationships generally become calmer and more equal, but they also become more distant. One longitudinal study found a drop in both negative *and* positive interactions across the teen years (Hetherington et al., 1999). Of course, as we have seen, teens spend less time with their families as they get older (Larson et al., 1996). That includes their brothers and sisters.

▶ **Learning Objective 5.11**
Are only children at a disadvantage?

Even so, siblings who were relatively close as children remain fairly close as adolescents (Dunn, Slomkowski, & Beardsall, 1994). This is particularly so for same-sex siblings (Kim, McHale, Osgood, & Crouter, 2006). They continue to see each other as important and intimate relations and to turn to each other for companionship and support (Furman & Buhrmester, 1992). They also continue to influence each other, in a reciprocal relationship (Cook, 2001). Those who fought a lot as children, however, not only continue to fight, but are at greater risk for anxiety, depression, and delinquent behavior (Stocker, Burwell, & Briggs, 2002).

De-identification A process in which siblings deliberately define themselves as different from one another by taking up different interests, activities, friends, and so on.

Sibling collusion A situation in which siblings form coalitions that encourage deviant or problem behavior.

Only Children

Our discussion of sibling relationships leaves out one fairly sizable group of adolescents. What about those who have no brothers or sisters? Did they miss out on an essential part of their development? Do they turn out to be spoiled, pampered, and selfish, as the stereotype has it?

In a word, no. On the whole, only children are friendly, competent, and well-adjusted (Falbo, 1992). One reason may be that they have not had to share the attention of their parents with other children. Another may be that they have always had to deal with peers as equals instead of lording it over a younger brother or sister or being bossed around by an older sibling.

> ### Summing Up...
>
> Siblings have a significant influence on one another, offering support, advice, and practice in getting along with others. Conflict among siblings peaks in early adolescence, and then declines along with sibling interactions in general. As adolescents, only children do not seem to have any special problems.

FAMILY DIVERSITY

For most Americans in the years that followed the end of World War II in 1945, the word *family* called up the same image: a married couple, generally White and native-born, with two or three children. The husband worked and the wife stayed home to look after the house and the children. On holidays, grandparents (also married) and other relatives might put in an appearance. Divorce and unwed parenthood were spoken of in an undertone, working mothers were criticized or pitied, and even only children felt somewhat odd and left out.

This social norm was reinforced by movies, television shows, and the cover illustrations of widely read magazines. While it was never 100% accurate, even for the White majority, neither was it such a gross distortion. In 1960, 91% of families with children under 18 were headed by married couples (U.S. Bureau of the Census, 2001a). Even as late as 1986, in well over a third of married couples with children under 18, only the husband worked (U.S. Bureau of the Census, 2003).

What is different in the first decade of the 21st century? The list is very long. Most striking is a change in the basic structure of the American family. "Traditional" families, like television's Cleavers and Simpsons, a married couple with children in which only the husband works, now represent only 7% of American households (U.S. Bureau of the Census, 2000). What happened?

During the 1970s and 1980s, the divorce rate soared, as did the number of children born outside of marriage (Hernandez, 1997). These trends combined to make single-parent families much more common. In 1960, 9% of children under 18 were living with one parent. By 2005, the proportion had climbed to 28%, more than one out of four (U.S. Bureau of the Census, 2006). Another 5% of children are living without either parent, with other relatives or with nonrelatives. Both the divorce rate and the proportion of children in single-parent families are now higher in the United States than in any other industrialized country (Hernandez, 1997; Hetherington et al., 1999).

Along with the rising number of divorces came a rising number of remarriages. As a result, more adolescents than ever are living in stepfamilies. These may be simple, as when the child's custodial parent remarries to someone who is childless. They may also be more complex, with various combinations of siblings, stepsiblings, and half-siblings in the same family.

Economic changes have also had an important impact on family diversity. As more married mothers take jobs, dual-earner families have become the norm. For many women, pursuing an occupation is a personal choice that has a positive effect on their self-esteem and life satisfaction (Silverberg & Steinberg, 1990). Others have no choice, especially if they are single mothers or divorced. They need whatever they can earn to keep the family afloat.

An emerging aspect of family diversity concerns the sexual orientation of parents. Recent years have seen a greater openness among lesbian and gay adults. This has led to increased visibility for families in which one or more of a child's parents identify as lesbian or gay (Patterson, 2002). Many such families involve children from a previous marriage. In others, the children were born or adopted after the parents identified as gay or lesbian.

Divorce and Adolescents

▶ **Learning Objective 5.12**
How does parental divorce affect adolescents?

One way to get a clearer picture of how divorce has increased since the 1960s is to look at a few statistics. Today, one out of five first marriages ends in divorce within 5 years. By the time 10 years have passed, the proportion rises to one of three (National Center for Health Statistics, 2002). Every year, new divorces affect another *one million* American children and adolescents (Hetherington et al., 1998). This figure does not include the children of the many couples who separate without divorcing, nor those whose parents never married in the first place. According to one estimate, 60% of all children born in the 1990s will spend at least some of their childhood or adolescent years living in a single-parent household (Bumpass & Raley, 1995).

Effects of Divorce. Clearly, divorce affects the lives of a great many, maybe even the majority of, children and adolescents, but what effects does it have? Is divorce always bad for the children? Are children and adolescents whose parents get a divorce worse off than those whose parents stay together? If so, in what ways? And why?

In recent decades, questions of this sort have inspired scores of research projects. On the whole, the results have been consistent. Compared to those who live with both biological parents, teens whose parents are divorced run a greater risk of developing problems such as drug and alcohol use, depression, anxiety, and earlier sexual activity (Amato & Keith, 1991; Buchanan, 2000; Cherlin, 1999; Hetherington & Stanley-Hagan, 2002). They do worse in school and are less likely to go to college (Astone & McLanahan, 1991, 1995). As adults, they are more likely to have marital problems and get divorced themselves (Hetherington, 1999).

Differences of this sort show up time and again, but we have to be careful how we interpret them. First, on average, the effects are rather small. They may be getting even smaller as divorce becomes more widespread and less of a social stigma for the children (Amato & Keith, 1991). Second, the great majority of teens from divorced families, about 75% to 80%, recover with time and show healthy patterns of adjustment (Chase-Lansdale, Cherlin, & Kiernan, 1995; Hetherington et al., 1998).

By way of comparison, among teens raised in nondivorcing homes, about 90% show no long-term adjustment problems (Hetherington, 1998). This suggests that divorce is responsible for an extra 10% to 15% of adolescents who develop psychological and behavior problems. That is certainly an important increase, but it is still a small fraction of the entire group of teens who have experienced a parental divorce.

Another question is why these problems develop. Do they result from the divorce itself? From the changes that follow divorce? From some of the conditions that *led to* the divorce? Dissolving a marriage is a weighty decision, especially if there are children involved. Whatever pushed the parents to that point may well have had an ongoing effect on the children as well.

Staying Together for the Sake of the Children? Parents who are unhappy in their marriage often wonder if they should tough it out until the children are grown (Hetherington & Kelly, 2002). It is only common sense to believe that divorce presents risks to the children. Wouldn't it be kinder and less selfish to avoid those risks by staying together? This is as personal a decision as anyone can be called on to make, but what researchers have found may offer some guidance.

At least some of the difficulties that teens from divorced families experience start to show up *before* the divorce, even years earlier (Cherlin et al., 1991; Sun, 2001). One longitudinal study (Sun, 2001) looked at over 10,000 high school students in 10th grade and again in 12th grade. Of these, 798 went through a marital disruption in between the two surveys. Their responses from both before and after the disruption could be compared to those of teens with undisrupted families.

◄ Open conflict between parents threatens a child's belief in the security of the family.

The researcher summarized the results this way:

> [A]dolescents from families that subsequently dissolve exhibit more academic, psychological, and behavioral problems than peers whose parents remain married. Families on the verge of breakup are also characterized by less intimate parent-parent and parent-child relationships, less parental commitment to children's education, and fewer economic and human resources.
>
> **(Sun, 2001, p. 697)**

The results also indicated that the later effects of the divorce were almost totally predictable from pre-divorce factors. In itself, the divorce seemed to cause little additional damage to the children (Sun, 2001).

Helpful as these results are, they do not answer the question about staying together, because they concern families that did *not* stay together. There may have been other parents in the study who managed to conceal or put aside their marital problems in order to stay together. Marital conflict that is out in the open is more harmful to teens than when it is covert (Harold & Conger, 1997).

Overt conflict has such negative effects, most importantly because it threatens the child's belief that the family is secure. However, it does more. Adolescents who have witnessed hostility between their parents also seem to interpret *parent-child* conflict as more hostile or threatening (Harold, Fincham, Osborne, & Conger, 1997). This may make them feel less secure in their own relationship with their parents (Cummings & Davies, 1994). They may also blame themselves, with resulting emotional problems (Buehler, Lange, & Franck, 2007).

This suggests that a decisive factor is how openly hostile the parents are while they are together. When there is a high level of ongoing conflict between the parents, teens do better in the long run if their parents separate or divorce (Amato, Loomis, & Booth, 1995; Booth & Amato, 2001; Emery, 1999; Jekielek, 1998).

In some families, on the other hand, there has been little overt conflict before a divorce, even though the parents may not have been close or committed to the marriage. In those cases, the divorce can have much more negative consequences on the children, who see it as unexpected, uncontrollable, and the source of a series of devastating life changes (Booth & Amato, 2001).

Remarriage and Stepfamilies

The great majority of adolescents who go through a parental divorce will also experience living in a stepfamily (White & Gilbreth, 2001). Most divorced custodial parents, as many as three out of four, remarry or cohabit within 3 to 5 years of the divorce (Hetherington, 1998; U.S. Bureau of the Census, 2006).

Connect the **Dots...**

Based on what you have learned about the effects on adolescents of family conflict and divorce, what advice would you give to parents who are considering divorce? What would you tell their adolescent child?

◄ **Learning Objective 5.13**
What problems do adolescents in stepfamilies face?

For many teens, who are already trying to cope with puberty, the transition to secondary school, major changes in peer relationships, and the aftermath of their parents' breakup, adjusting to a new sort-of parental figure and maybe to one or more new sort-of siblings is more than they can handle. Adolescents in single-parent homes have more short-term problems, such as delinquency, depression, and low school achievement, than those in intact families, but those in stepfamilies have more still (Hetherington, 1999; Hetherington & Kelly, 2002).

Adapting to a Stepfamily. Several factors conspire to make it hard to adapt to a stepfamily. One is simply that it represents one more family transition on top of those the child has already confronted (Capaldi & Patterson, 1991). To be in a position to handle a remarriage, a child must have already dealt with the effects of the parents' divorce (Brody & Neubaum, 1996). If you are still off balance from an earlier event, a new stress may easily knock you down.

Another factor is the effect on the amount of parental attention the adolescent receives (Coleman, Ganong, & Fine, 2000). The mother, after all, is busy trying to adjust to her new marriage. At the same time, the divorced father may have less to do with the children once there is a new man in the household (Furstenberg & Harris, 1992; Hetherington et al., 1998). As for the stepfather, he may adopt a more distant, less parental role and leave questions of discipline to the mother (Hetherington & Stanley-Hagen, 2002).

Then there is the potential for *role confusion*. Over time, families develop sets of implicit rules and expectations. A newcomer can't be expected to know these right away, nor is the newcomer's place in the system clear (Buchanan, Maccoby, & Dornbusch, 1996). If a new stepfather suggests that the teen help with some household chore, the reply might be a cold, "You can't tell me what to do. You're not my *real* father!"

Problems and Adjustment. In the short run, a parent's remarriage is harder on early adolescents than on either school-age children or older adolescents (Bray & Kelly, 1998; Hetherington et al., 1999). The accumulation of major transitions makes it harder to deal with still another set of changes. It may also be that younger children have more at stake in making the new family work (Hetherington et al., 1998).

On average, girls have more trouble interacting with stepfathers than do boys (Vuchinich, Hetherington, Vuchinich, & Clingempeel, 1991). Having an unrelated adult male in the home may pose tricky questions about their developing sexuality. They may also have developed a closer relationship with the mother after the divorce (Koerner, Jacobs, & Raymond, 2000) and resent what feels like its loss to an interloper.

Getting used to living in a stepfamily is not easy. Still, one point is worth emphasizing—the great majority of adolescents overcome any initial problems and make a good adjustment (Emery, 1999). A crucial factor is the way the parent and stepparent relate to the child. As we have seen, the authoritative approach is linked to better child outcomes in general. It is even more important with teens who have been through their parents' divorce and remarriage.

Consistent, supportive discipline that is sensitive to the teen's changing level of development makes healthy adjustment more likely (Hetherington et al., 1999; Hetherington & Stanley-Hagan, 2002), as do warm, close relationships with either the stepfather, the biological father, or preferably both (White & Galbreth, 2001).

As for adolescents who find themselves in an uncongenial stepfamily situation, they have an option that isn't open to younger children—they can disengage. Adolescence is a time when activities outside the home and family assume greater importance in any case (Larson & Richards, 1994). If being home means criticism, conflict, and bad feelings, spending as little time there as possible may seem like a better choice.

As many as one-quarter to one-third of adolescents in divorced and remarried families *do* choose to disengage (Hetherington & Jodl, 1994). This often has negative consequences, such as academic problems and antisocial behavior, but it does not have to. If the teen develops a relationship with a caring adult, such as a relative, teacher, coach, or parent of a friend, disengagement may be a reasonable solution to a disrupted family life (Hetherington, 1993).

Figure 5.7 Proportion of Married Couples with Children in Which Both Parents Work
The proportion of married couples with children in which both parents work has increased in recent decades.

	1975	1986	2002
Married couples with children under 18	47%	59%	67%
Married couples with children 6–18	55%	66%	73%

Source: Bureau of the Census, Bureau of Labor Statistics.

Dual-Earner Families

Divorce and remarriage are not the only reasons fewer American adolescents today grow up in a "traditional" family. Families in which the father is the breadwinner and the mother is the homemaker are also getting harder to find. Among married couples with children under 18, 70% of the wives work outside the home, and when we look at couples with school-age children, between 6 and 18, the proportion rises to 76% (U.S. Bureau of the Census, 2003). Figure 5.7 shows how these proportions have increased over recent decades.

◄ **Learning Objective 5.14**
What are the effects of living in a dual-earner family?

Stereotypes of Dual-Earner Families. Any social trend that is at odds with long-accepted views can be expected to set off controversy and debate. Here, for example, is the beginning of a news report.

Study Links Working Mothers to Slower Learning
by Tamar Lewin

Adding fuel to the debate over mothers who work, a new analysis of the largest government child-care study has found that early maternal employment has negative effects on children's intellectual development . . .

(LEWIN, 2002b)

Follow-up articles pointed out that other researchers, looking at the same data, had found *no* difference in cognitive ability between children who spent long hours in child care and those whose mothers cared for them at home (Cheever, 2002; Lewin, 2002a). But did everyone who saw the original headline also read the follow-ups?

There is less controversy about the effects on older children and adolescents of having both parents employed. In general, any negative effects are few and small (Galambos & Ehrenberg, 1997; Harvey, 1999; Lerner & Noh, 2000). A recent meta-analysis looked at 68 studies of the effects of maternal employment on children's achievement (Goldberg, Prause, Lucas-Thomson, & Himsel, 2008). Overall, the children of mothers who worked were not significantly different from those whose mothers were not employed, although those whose mothers worked part time had slightly higher achievement scores than those whose mothers worked full time. For girls, having a mother who works is linked to higher self-esteem, higher career aspirations, and less stereotyped views of male and female roles (Hoffman, 1989; Richards & Duckett, 1994). Presumably, the mother serves them as a model of an active, achieving woman.

For boys, the picture is cloudier. Middle-class boys whose mothers work full time tend to get lower grades and achievement scores than those whose mothers are not employed (Bogenschneider & Steinberg, 1994; Bronfenbrenner, 1986). Teenaged boys with working mothers also get into more arguments with parents and siblings (Montemayor, 1984). One reason for this may be that when both parents work, more household chores fall on the children, and boys accept this with less grace than girls (Gottfried, Gottfried, & Bathurst, 2002).

Latchkey Teens. Adolescent children in dual-earner families are often expected to take care of themselves for long periods outside of school and on vacation days. Unsupervised self-care or **latchkey teens** have a lot of opportunities for getting into trouble. A particularly risky time for deviant activity is in the afternoon between the end of school and the parents' return home from work (Pettit, Bates, Dodge, & Meece, 1999).

Latchkey teens are somewhat more likely to show emotional, academic, and adjustment problems than those who have a parent at home during their free hours (Marshall et al., 1997; Pettit, Bates, & Dodge, 1997). Those who live in poor neighborhoods, where there are more chances to hang out with deviant or delinquent peers, are at even greater risk (Posner & Vandell, 1994).

Not surprisingly, a crucial factor in whether latchkey teens develop problems is the degree of parental monitoring (Jacobson & Crockett, 2000; Pettit et al., 1999). Those who are more closely supervised, for example, by calling a parent when they get home from school, get higher grades, are less depressed, and are less likely to become involved in problem behaviors (Jacobson & Crockett, 2000). Adolescents whose dual-earner parents manage to maintain a warm, responsive relationship with them, in spite of the stresses and pressures of their work lives, usually manage to function well (Crouter, Bumpus, Maguire, & McHale, 1999; Vander Ven, Cullen, Carrozza, & Wright, 2001).

Lesbian and Gay Families

▶ **Learning Objective 5.15**
How does being raised by lesbian or gay parents affect teens?

Another aspect of family diversity in today's America is a growing number and variety of lesbian and gay families. Most of the children in these families were born to mixed-sex couples before one or both partners identified as gay or lesbian. There are also increasing numbers of lesbians and gays who choose to become parents, most often by means of donor insemination or adoption (Patterson, 2002; Patterson & Hastings, 2006). Gay or lesbian parents may be single, or they may have same-sex partners. If there are partners, they may or may not develop stepparenting relationships with the children.

How many American children and adolescents live with parents who are lesbian or gay? Estimates range as high as 1 to 5 million (Patterson, 2002), but no one really knows. Many lesbian and gay adults, especially those who are parents, are careful to hide their sexual orientation because of fear of discrimination.

There is reason for this fear. Until very recently, and still to some extent, being known to be lesbian or gay could have serious negative consequences. Anyone who was openly gay or lesbian was often considered inherently unfit to be a parent (Armesto, 2002; Savin-Williams & Esterberg, 2000). In a divorce, this could mean loss of custody and even of visitation rights. It could also mean being automatically shown the door by adoption agencies. In such a situation, gays and lesbians who wanted to have a family, or to keep the one they had, would have needed to be very brave, or very foolish, to admit their sexual orientation to pollsters, social science researchers, or anyone else.

America's widespread and visceral aversion to tolerating gay and lesbian families was rooted in a tangled knot of worries and speculations. First, that lesbian and gay lifestyles are unhealthy and would create adjustment problems in any children exposed to them. Second, that the children would be rejected by others because of their parents' orientation. And, probably the most potent, that children raised by gay or lesbian parents would grow up to be gay or lesbian themselves (Bailey & Dawood, 1995).

Over the last couple of decades, research evidence has started to accumulate that bears on these concerns (Patterson, 2006; Savin-Williams & Esterberg, 2000). On balance, it gives no support to these concerns. Some points to notice:

Gay and lesbian parents know at least as much about good child-rearing practices as heterosexual parents do, and are just as committed to following them (Flaks, Ficher, Masterpasqua, & Joseph, 1995).

Both partners in lesbian and gay couples are generally attached to the children and share in caregiving (Bigner & Jacobsen, 1989; Patterson, 2002). If anything, parenting responsibilities tend to be more equally shared than in heterosexual couples (Chan, Brooks, Raboy, & Patterson, 1998; Tasker & Golombok, 1998).

Latchkey teens Adolescents who are without adult supervision after school and on vacation days, usually because parents work outside the home.

◄ Marcus McLaurin, 7, was sent home from school as punishment for telling a classmate that he had two mothers.

Children of gay and lesbian parents are just as mature and well-adjusted, on average, as children of heterosexual parents (Golombok et al., 2003; Patterson, 2006).

Comparisons of adolescents living with parent couples who are same-sex and other-sex show similar levels of self-esteem, school achievement, functioning with peers, involvement in romantic relationships, and problem behaviors (Wainwright & Patterson, 2006, 2008; Wainwright, Russell, & Patterson, 2004).

The huge majority of children of gay or lesbian parents, over 90%, develop a heterosexual orientation as adults. This is essentially the same percentage as in children raised by heterosexual parents (Bailey & Dawood, 1998; Golombok & Tasker, 1996; Gottman, 1990; Tasker & Golombok, 1997).

There are a couple of differences worth noting between children being raised in lesbian and gay families and those in heterosexual families. In many places these children still run a risk of being stigmatized because of their parents' orientation and lifestyle (Gartell, Deck, Rodas, Peyser, & Banks, 2005). In 2003, for example, a 7-year-old boy in Louisiana was given detention and sent home from school as punishment for telling a classmate his mother was gay (Moller, 2003). Another difference is that, while children raised in gay and lesbian families are no more likely to develop homosexual preferences as adults, they do find it easier to *imagine* doing so. More of them also say that if their sexual orientation did change, they would be more likely to act on it (Golombok & Tasker, 1996).

As we will see in Chapter 12, the development of sexual preferences is a very complicated matter, with many riddles still to be solved. If it were as simple as children copying their parents, we would have a lot of trouble explaining the fact that most gays and lesbians grew up in families with heterosexual parents! One thing, however, is becoming clear. There is no objective reason to deny someone's right to be a parent because of sexual orientation. As the American Psychological Association has stated, the adjustment and development of children is unrelated to parental sexual orientation. Children of lesbian and gay parents are as likely as those of heterosexual parents to flourish (APA, 2004).

Summing Up...

Family structure in Western cultures is becoming more diverse. Parental divorce and remarriage affect a great many children, as does an increased number of single-parent households. More mothers, whether in a partnered relationship or not, work full time outside the home. Families in which one or more parents identifies as lesbian or gay have become more visible as well.

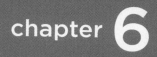

Peers

Outline	Learning Objectives

Just as family relationships change dramatically during adolescence, so do relationships with other adolescents. There is a rough symmetry to these changes. Children generally look to their parents for help with decisions, or comfort when things go wrong, or simply ideas for interesting activities on a rainy afternoon. With adolescence, they are more and more likely to turn to other teens to meet all these needs (Dumont & Provost, 1999). The family doesn't lose its importance, but the peer group, or age mates, gradually becomes an important and independent source of influence (Brown, 2004).

An array of biological, cognitive, and social factors operate in different ways to encourage adolescents to turn from the family to the peer group. Where do adolescents look when they need to decide what to wear, what to read, what musicians to listen to, what movies are hot, or even what to think? Most of the time, they turn to other adolescents. Another way of putting it is that teens use other teens as their *reference group*. Peers serve as a source of information, as a standard of comparison, and as a source of praise and criticism. Sometimes peer influence clashes with the goals and values of a teen's parents. How do adolescents deal with these *cross-pressures*, and how does their approach change with increasing maturity?

As the peer group takes on greater importance, so does the *status* of the individual within the group. Researchers have charted the relationships within adolescent groups and identified different status categories. Why does someone end up in a particular category, and what implications does that have? Why is it useful to separate being *liked* and being *popular*? An ugly fact about adolescent peer groups is that very often some members are victimized by others. What factors are responsible for *bullies* and *victims*, and what can be done to create a social atmosphere that discourages victimization?

Any good-sized body of adolescents, such as a school class, contains a variety of informal social groupings. One sort of group, the *clique*, is a small, intimate group of teens linked by friendship and common activities. Another group, the *crowd*, is based more on reputation and interests. Both serve as ways to understand the social structure and find one's place within it. They can also act to stereotype, stigmatize, and exclude those who do not fit the accepted mold.

THE IMPORTANCE OF PEERS

Who is a **peer**? The term comes to us from an Old French word, "pair," which means *even* or *equal*. In Britain, for example, a peer is someone with a title of nobility, who is considered the social equal of every other titled lord (and, of course, the superior of any mere commoner). Modern social scientists have adopted the term to refer to those who are at roughly the same level in age, social status, or level of functioning.

This is a fairly elastic definition. It expands and contracts as a function of similarities, contrasts, the number and kinds of people around, and the range of differences among them. At a big family gathering, everyone from 2 to 20 may be considered one of "the kids." In a different context, a 13-year-old may spurn an 11-year-old as a baby. At school, a sophomore and a senior will probably not think of each other as peers, but at an away game with a rival school, they may.

The fact that relationships with peers involve equal status gives them a special significance for children and adolescents. Families do not, as a rule, offer children much experience with social equality. Instead, power, knowledge, skills, and privileges tend to be *asymmetrical*, or one-way. Parents perch at the top of the ladder, older siblings are on a higher rung, and younger siblings are lower down. Those above you get to tell you what to do, show you what they consider the right way to do it, and get on your case if you try to do it some other way.

Peers are less bossy and critical. They have to be, otherwise they face the dreaded question, "Just who do you think you are?" Because they are more open, they create a space for exploration and experimentation. New ideas, skills, and roles can be tried out in relative safety. Is there a danger that you'll do something dopey or reveal an area of

Peer Someone who is at roughly the same level in age, social status, or level of functioning with another.

◄ At mixed-age gatherings, all those who are not adults may act like peers to one another.

ignorance? So what? Peers, those of equal status, are less likely to come down too hard on you. They know it is just a question of time before they commit some silly blunder themselves and need *your* tolerance.

Children start interacting with other children when they are still babies, as early as the middle of the first year (Rubin, Bukowski, & Parker, 2006; Vandell & Mueller, 1995). By the time they are toddlers of 2 or 2-1/2, the way they play together shows clear imitation and complementary roles (Eckerman & Didow, 1996). A typical exchange might be, "You run, I catch you." "Okay, now I catch you."

Over the preschool and elementary school years, the social complexity of these interactions with other children increases steadily, as does their importance to the participants. Group activities help children learn about teamwork, cooperation, compromise, taking turns, sharing, and other essential social skills (Hartup, 1983). By the time they arrive at puberty, most of them are already well-prepared to spend more time and invest more emotional energy in interactions with their age mates.

It would be hard to exaggerate the amount of time American adolescents spend with other adolescents. During the school year, most of the weekday is spent in class, in the lunchroom, or in the halls, all settings in which teens far outnumber adults. Afterschool activities, whether formal (sports, clubs, and so on) or informal (hanging out with friends), mostly involve other teens. A good part of the evening may be spent studying at friends' houses, talking to them on the phone, or exchanging instant messages via computer or cell phone.

When vacation comes, the picture stays much the same. Whether you go off to camp or hang on the corner or at the mall, the essential point is that you are with those of your own age. In all, American adolescents spend from *two to four times* as many of their waking hours interacting with peers as with parents, siblings, or anyone else (Brown, 2004; Csikszentmihalyi, Larson, & Prescott, 1977; Larson & Verma, 1999).

The sheer quantity of time spent together is just the beginning of the story. As everyone who remembers adolescence knows, relations with other adolescents are a source of moments of both great joy and deep distress (Larson & Richards, 1994). During adolescence, others the same age develop into a more important source of advice and emotional support than parents (Furman & Buhrmester, 1992; Youniss & Smollar, 1985). Weekends, and the chance to spend even more free time with other teens, become the emotional high point of the week (Larson & Richards, 1998).

Peers Across Cultures

▶ **Learning Objective 6.1**
What factors make peers become more central during adolescence?

The way teens in America and Western Europe become progressively less involved with parents and other adults, and more involved with age mates, is not unique. In some ways, it reflects features common to practically all human societies. In other ways, and just as importantly, it is influenced by specific social and historical trends.

Social scientists Alice Schlegel and Walter Berry III (1991) surveyed information on adolescence in 186 different societies outside the industrial West, representing every major geographical area and cultural type. Here is how they summarized their findings about the way adolescents associate with their peers:

> Such groups take on a special meaning in adolescence, when young people are temporarily released from intense identification with a family. In childhood, people depend for their very life on the natal family; in adulthood, they are responsible for the well-being of spouses and children and for pursuing the interests and position of the marital family. For the brief period of adolescence, they are neither so dependent as they were nor so responsible as they will be. It is then that peer relations can take on an intensity of attachment that they lack at other stages of the life cycle . . .
>
> (SCHLEGEL & BERRY, 1991, p. 68)

In the traditional societies that were the focus of Schlegel and Berry's investigation, there are widespread gender differences in the ways adolescents relate to their age mates. Boys are more oriented toward peers, and away from parents, than girls are. Adolescent boys spend much of their time hanging out with other adolescent boys. Girls, on the other hand, are more likely to be part of groups that include girls and women of various ages. In particular, adolescent girls spend more time with their mothers than boys do with their fathers or mothers. Girls also have a smaller number of same-age, same-sex friends than boys. While groups of boys are more activity-oriented, when girls get together with peers it is mostly to relax (Schlegel & Berry, 1991).

Human beings are not the only species that shows this sort of pattern—it also turns up in research on other primates. In most species of apes and monkeys, young males at puberty start spending less time with parents and more with other juvenile males (Schlegel, 1995; Steinberg, 1987). Females, however, continue to spend much of their time with the mother and other females of different ages (Mitchell, 1981).

As we saw in an earlier chapter, some theorists interpret this development as a biological device that cuts down on the risks of incest and inbreeding (Steinberg, 1989). Other theorists offer a different explanation. Adolescent males are sexually mature enough to be possible rivals to adult males, but they are not yet strong enough to defend themselves against a jealous adult. Given this, it makes good evolutionary sense for them to keep a safe distance from adult society and band together for mutual protection (Spear, 2000).

From Family to Peers. In more traditional societies outside Western Europe and America, teens continue to spend much of their time with parents, other adults, and younger children (Larson, Wilson, Brown, Furstenberg, & Verma, 2002). In India, for example, teens are with other family members for almost half their waking hours (Larson & Verma, 1999). The disappearance of traditional home-based occupations has meant that fewer adolescents work side-by-side with their parents, but at the same time an increased stress on education leads parents to supervise their teenage children more closely (Bianci, 2000; Verma, Sharma, & Larson, 2002). Even so, the trend is for teens around the world to spend more and more of their free time with other teens (Booth, 2002; Santa Maria, 2002).

Contemporary Western societies have seen this trend carried to an extreme. American and European teens spend more time with peers than with family members or other adults (Brown, 2004; Larson & Verma, 1999). Between the ages of 10 and 18, the proportion of waking hours teens spend with other family members drops from 35% to 14% (Larson, Richards, Moneta, Holmbeck, & Duckett, 1996). That means 86% of teens' waking hours are spent *away* from family members. Of course, some of those hours are spent alone, listening to music, surfing the Web, reading, or simply musing about life, but a great many hours are spent with friends outside the home (Rubin et al., 2006).

Many factors have contributed to this shift from family to peers, including:

The trend toward smaller families, which gives children and adolescents fewer siblings to be with.

The trend toward dual-earner families, which means that much of the time parents are not on hand.

Social trends such as urbanization, which create a larger pool of accessible children who are similar in age.

Segregation by Age. Left to themselves, children and adolescents spend as much time with children who are a year or more older or younger than themselves as with those their own age (Ellis, Rogoff, & Cromer, 1981; Gray & Feldman, 1997; Kerr, Stattin, Biesecker, & Ferrer-Wreder, 2002). However, in American society today, children and adolescents spend most of their time with a narrow group made up of those who are almost exactly their own age. One big reason for this is that they are *not* left to themselves. Children's activities are increasingly organized—some would say bureaucratized—by adults. This imposes more and more adult-created constraints on how children and teens use their time and with whom. It is not too strong to call this a system of **age segregation**.

Historically, the institution that most obviously promotes age segregation is the school system. During the late 19th and early 20th centuries, growing numbers of adolescents continued their education into and through high school. This had the effect of deepening the social gap between adolescents and adults and creating a new sense of group identity among adolescents (Angus, 1988).

Across the 20th century, American schools adopted policies of *age grading* and *social promotion*. Under age grading, children started school only if their birthday fell within a particular 12-month span. From that point on, social promotion meant that they were passed along through the system with the same age group they had started with.

These policies fostered a strict social segregation by age *within* the population of children and teens. Suppose you were born in August and your community schools used a September 1 cut-off date. During your whole school career, right through high school and even college, you would always be a grade ahead of the child down the block who was born just a few weeks later than you. Children who live near one another and who are close in age might ordinarily become friends, but the fact that they are separated socially in school makes that much less likely (Allen, 1989).

Out of School. Age segregation carries over into out-of-school activities, too. In informal neighborhood games, such as pickup basketball, sandlot baseball, and four-square (a popular pickup game among girls), anyone who knows the moves is usually accepted, whatever their age. That changes when formal organization moves in. Like the schools, sports leagues for young people rely on age grading with strict cut-offs. In youth soccer, for example, there are different teams and leagues for each 1-year slice. If you were born on July 31, you'd be the youngest on your team. A friend born just 1 day later would have to play in the next younger league. Organizations such as the Boy and Girl Scouts also have rules of this sort.

However convenient these social and organizational regulations may be for adult administrators, they have the effect of creating a rigid separation by age among children and teens. This is so pervasive that we tend to think of it as natural, if we notice it at all. But try this: Make a list of the people who were personally important to you in junior high and high school. Now, focus on those who were also adolescents at the time. Chances are, you will discover that most of them were in your own grade (Blyth, Hill, & Thiel, 1982).

Connect the Dots...

What do you think is the main reason teens spend less time with their families? Would they simply rather be with their peers? Does the pace of modern life make quality family time less available to them? What other factors might play an important role?

Age segregation The social custom of grouping people, such as children and adolescents, on the basis of their chronological age.

Figure 6.1   Adolescents as a Proportion of the U.S. Population
The proportion of adolescents in the U.S. population has varied widely over recent decades.

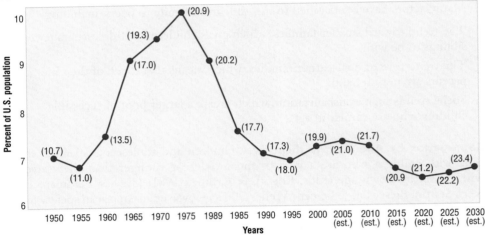

Source: UN Population Bureau, U.S. Bureau of the Census, 2001.

A Generation Gap? Adults have fretted and grumbled about the morals, tastes, and conduct of youngsters at least since the dawn of history and probably before. In ancient Athens, one of the charges made against Socrates was that his ideas encouraged young people to stray from the ways of their elders.

Why should this urge to criticize the younger generation seem so universal? Some reasons are straightforward. As we develop ways of thinking and doing things, they become habitual. We begin to see them as right and natural, rather than one particular option among many. If you grew up eating salad at the beginning of dinner, you may be upset when someone waits to serve it after the main course, European style.

Adolescents, by the simple fact that they are younger, have had less time to form set habits. Their developing cognitive abilities also enter the picture. Because hypothetical thinking comes more easily to them, they can imagine doing things in ways different than they've been taught. At the same time, their new social status—no longer children, if not yet adults—gives them some degree of freedom to act on what they imagine. A desire to construct an identity separate from the one they were assigned as children makes it more alluring to do things in ways that are distinctive.

These elements work together to make adolescents more open to new styles, trends, and ideas, especially if they see other teens adopting them. To the extent these new ways clash with the ways of older generations, members of those older generations are likely to deplore and criticize them. That may even be part of the attraction.

These factors are not limited to any particular society or point in history. However, some developments in American society during the 20th century led to increased worry about a **generation gap**—or a sharp divide between the values of adolescents and adults—and its effects. One such development was the baby boom in the years after World War II. As we saw earlier, the boomer babies started hitting adolescence early in the 1960s. The result, as Figure 6.1 shows, was that the proportion of teens in the population went up sharply. Between 1950 and 1975, the absolute number of teens in the United States practically doubled.

In the 1960s, the visibility of adolescents soared along with their numbers. Major magazines featured photos of "typical" teens on their covers. The Beatles and the Rolling Stones made star appearances on the staid, middle-of-the-road *Ed Sullivan Show*. Commentators agreed that whatever was going on with the young people, it was new and important, and perhaps deeply disturbing. One observer was sociologist James Coleman, whose book, *The Adolescent Society* (1961), described a monolithic world of adolescents that had its own value system directly *against* adult values.

Generation gap The idea that there is a sharp divide between the value systems and goals of adolescents and adults.

Parents saw learning and doing well in school as top priorities for teens. The teens themselves, however, turned up their noses at academic success and especially at *striving* for academic success. Letting others find out you were smart counted as a really dumb move—what mattered was being popular and athletic.

Hardly anyone will deny that parents and their adolescent children often have different, even conflicting, priorities. Just wait until the most popular teen in class throws a big party the weekend before an important exam and listen to the arguments that break out all over the neighborhood! As we saw in the last chapter, however, conflicts between parents and teens most often involve matters of preference and taste—how to dress, how to spend time, who to spend it with. On the big questions, such as personal beliefs, goals, and values, adolescents tend to hold views that are quite similar to those of their parents (Moore et al., 2004).

Culture and the Pace of Change

When we looked at the history of adolescence, in Chapter 1, we saw how social, economic, and political changes in society have an impact on the ways adolescents are regarded and treated. The emergence of a youth culture in today's world reflects both technological changes and the rate at which those changes take place. Because modern society is increasingly complex, young people need a longer period of training to cope with it. Because they are still in school, they are set apart from the working world of adults, and because the things they are taught—the concepts, the techniques, the tools—are themselves changing rapidly, what they learn may be more up-to-date and more relevant than what their elders learned a generation ago.

◄ **Learning Objective 6.2**
How does the pace of social change alter relations between generations?

Generational Relations. Anthropologist Margaret Mead (1978) foresaw this situation. She described the ways that the pace of social and technological change could alter the relations between generations. She also gave names to the different cultural forms that result: postfigurative, cofigurative, and prefigurative.

In societies where change comes slowly, **postfigurative cultures** hold sway. Those who are older know most of what their children will need to know, because they themselves learned it as children. Whether the subject is rites, customs, songs, farming techniques, or how to make shoes, the traditional ways are passed along from generation to generation. This makes respect for elders, who are the repositories of important knowledge, a strong cultural value.

As the pace of change picks up, **cofigurative cultures** emerge. Some of the old ways are still relevant, but many others are not. How do adolescents sort out which is which? One way is by comparing notes with each other. If I tell my daughter she would enjoy music by Debussy or Thelonius Monk, she might or might not give it a try, and she might or might not like it. But if she *wants* a recommendation, she is at least as likely to ask a friend her own age. Chances are, the friend will recommend some musician I have never heard of.

As the pace of social and technical change increases still more, Mead predicted the development of **prefigurative cultures**. These cultures would come about when the *younger* generation possesses the knowledge and skills that the *older* generation needs to acquire. Instead of children learning from their parents, parents would have to learn from their children. This role reversal would also lead to a drastic shift in social power and prestige. Older would no longer mean wiser, but past and out of touch.

A television commercial from a few years ago captures the notion of a prefigurative culture. Half a dozen bankers in their 50s, in formal business garb, are trying to follow the technobabble of a casually dressed 20-something who wants them to fund his dot-com startup. Finally, to his obvious surprise, they say they will give him all the money he needs. They clearly have no idea what he is planning to do, but their incomprehension makes them all the more convinced that it must be new and important.

Over the last century or two, starting roughly with the Industrial Revolution, Western societies have moved from being primarily postfigurative to mostly cofigurative.

Postfigurative culture A culture in which social change is slow and younger generations need to acquire the knowledge and skills of their elders.

Cofigurative culture A culture in which social change is fairly rapid and both older and younger generations come to have knowledge and skills that the other needs to acquire.

Prefigurative culture A culture in which social change is very rapid and older generations need to replace obsolete knowledge and skills with those of the younger generation.

► In a culture with prefigurative aspects, it is often the young who teach their elders how to use new technology.

Connect the **Dots...**

In Mead's terms, how would you describe Western cultures today? How have different factors in society, such as the spread of information technology, affected the relations between adolescents and adults?

Customs, skills, and values are no longer transmitted in only one direction, from older to younger generations. Social influence has become more of a two-way street. In matters of style, as well as cutting-edge technology, youth rules. There may even be emerging elements of prefigurative culture. It is teens, for example, who have pioneered sending each other short text messages via cell phone. Now they are teaching their elders how to do it.

One Youth Culture or Many?   Any general statement that starts off, "Kids these days . . ." is likely to be inaccurate and misleading. Adolescents are simply too various to catch them all in one net. Most of them do have some things in common, of course. The biological, cognitive, and social changes they are going through are similar enough to make the idea of a separate and coherent **youth culture** plausible. To adults who observe the group from the outside, the similarities among its members may be more obvious than the differences. Teens also feel internal and external pressures to dress and act and think the way they believe "people like you" are supposed to.

Some of the external pressures are commercial. Worldwide, adolescents make up a vast market with wads of discretionary cash (Barber, 1995). If a recording, movie, clothing fashion, or electronic gadget can be turned into a "gotta-have-it," the marketers who get there first will make a lot of money very quickly, but they need to be swift on their feet. The teen market is as fickle as it is enthusiastic—what's new and hot today can turn old and cold by tomorrow.

Western styles have an overpowering influence on adolescents in today's "global village" (Schlegel, 2000). The same films, CDs, clothing, cosmetics, and even slang expressions turn up in the high schools of Ankara and Atlanta, Houston and Hong Kong, Peoria, Paris, and Prague. This does not mean, however, that teens worldwide give their allegiance to a single youth culture. The uniform of jeans, t-shirt, and name-brand sneakers may look the same, but goals, values, cultural assumptions, and beliefs about the world vary widely.

Even within American society, the ways adolescents differ from one another are at least as important as the ways they are similar (Stone & Brown, 1998). For example, it is obvious that music is a very big element in youth culture, but what *kind* of music? Hip hop, techno, salsa, 'sixties, trance, heavy metal, country, Christian, disco, folk . . .? Is the music really a force that draws teens together into a common alternative culture? Or something that pushes them apart, into separate, noncommunicating subcultures?

Someone who knew about American adolescents only from the media might think they all spend spring vacation at South Padre Island or Cancun, cavorting on the beach. A bunch of them do, but many others spend the vacation working together to

Youth culture The idea that adolescents as a group have customs, values, and beliefs that separate them from the culture of adults.

build houses for poor people. And what about the ones who are in the library studying for AP exams, out practicing a sport, or at home looking after younger brothers and sisters? Or around the corner, getting high? All of them are "typical," and all of them are influenced in their behavior by peers.

Summing Up...

With adolescence, more time and emotional energy are invested in relationships with age mates. This trend is amplified by age segregation in and out of school. While worries about a serious generation gap appear unfounded, the increasing pace of social and technological change is altering the relations between generations.

PATHS OF PEER INFLUENCE

"You are *not* leaving the house dressed like that!"

"But Mom, this is what all the kids are wearing!"

"And I suppose if all the kids jumped off a bridge, you'd jump too?"

(Pause.) "Well, if everybody else jumped, I'd look like a total wuss if I didn't! You don't want that, do you?"

This dialogue is imaginary. It just *sounds* like some exchanges you took part in when you were an adolescent, or perhaps more recently if you are the parent of an adolescent. One of the things "everybody knows" about teens is that they pay close attention to other teens and are strongly influenced by them.

To what extent is this common idea correct? Why and how do adolescents influence one another? When is that influence a positive or negative force? What about parents? Can they successfully counter the influence of "a bad crowd" on their child? These are some of the questions to be tackled in the next few pages.

Conformity and Social Influence

In a classic study of peer influence by Solomon Asch (1953), a college student found himself in a lab with several other young people. Their task was to judge which of three lines was the same length as a comparison line. The first few rounds were easy. Everybody agreed on the obvious response. Then came a problem to which the answer looked just as obvious. This time, however, the other participants all gave what seemed like the wrong answer. What did the student do?

You may have come across this study before now. If so, you know that it was not really about judging line lengths, it was about conformity. The other "participants" were working for the researcher. On the target problem, they deliberately gave the same wrong answer, to see what the real subject would do. You probably recall that a majority of the subjects answered the way the rest of the group had done, even if they realized the answer was incorrect (Asch, 1953). In other words, they *conformed* to what the others did.

A dictionary might define **conformity** as complying with the actions or attitudes of others. Those who took part in the Asch study certainly did that. Why? Apparently they felt under some pressure not to disagree with the rest of the group. As an old saying announces, "If you want to get along, you've got to go along."

Now suppose you are walking across campus. You notice a handful of students looking up into the branches of a tree. You pause and look also. Is that an act of conformity? It meets the definition. But did you do it out of a feeling of being pressured? Probably not. A more likely reason is that you wanted to find out what they were all staring at.

◄ **Learning Objective 6.3**
Why distinguish between normative and informational social influence?

Conformity Doing as others are doing or as others urge one to do, whether or not it fits with personal inclinations, values, and beliefs.

Both these situations involve being influenced by others, but the underlying reasons are different. What happened in the Asch study is an example of **normative social influence**: you act a certain way because you know a social norm or rule says you are expected to. If you're in a stadium when a wave comes around, you might prefer to stay in your seat, but you will probably stand and raise your arms with all the others because you know that is what you are supposed to do.

On the other hand, suppose several friends tell you a new movie is awesome. If you decide to go see for yourself, they certainly influenced you, but not because of a social norm. Instead, the *information* they gave you affected your behavior. This is known as **informational social influence** (Deutsch & Gerard, 1955). Stopping to see what everyone is staring at in that tree is another example of this. The actions of the other students communicate the information that something interesting is up there.

These two varieties of social influence can occur together and often do. Some New York subway stations are so far underground that they have elevators to carry passengers between the track level and the surface. Some of these elevators have doors at both ends. I've noticed that people who are unfamiliar with the station usually face the door they came in—the "front." Those who *know* which door will open next face that one. By the time the elevator makes its trip up or down, almost everyone is facing the correct door. I see this as partly normative (everyone in an elevator is expected to face the same way) and partly informational (you follow people who seem to know what they are doing).

Or consider the flurry of phone calls before a school dance, as teens compare notes on what they are planning to wear. Finding out that everyone is dressing a certain way is vital information that tells you the general level of dressiness. It is also a source of implicit pressure to meet the expectation that you will dress like the others, whether you really want to or not.

Peers as Reference Groups

▶ **Learning Objective 6.4**
What roles do peers play as a reference group?

At first the concept of peer influence may seem rather vague and even mysterious, pervasive and yet unseen. Even after we accept the idea that peers influence attitudes and behavior, we are still faced with questions about how and why. By detailing the processes involved in peer influence, we can take away some of the mystery and get closer to answering our questions.

A useful way to think about how peer influence works is called **reference group theory** (Singer, 1981). This approach says that in social situations, people look to various groups to gain important information. One sort of information is *normative*. What actions, attitudes, and values are expected and normal? How are you supposed to act? Another sort of information is *comparative*. What is the usual level or standard of performance? How should you evaluate yourself, relative to others? Reference groups also serve as an *audience* that observes, evaluates, and reacts to what the individual does and says. Or, as a former mayor of New York liked to ask passersby, "How'm I doin'?"

In practice, this means that we may have a number of reference groups that serve different functions. A member of the high school tennis team might use top-seeded players and international stars as a normative reference group. If players she admires favor a particular brand of equipment or clothing, this will influence her purchases. If they display notably bad or good manners on the court, that too will influence her.

For a comparative reference group, however, she would be more likely to look to others at her level. The way she feels about her game will probably not depend on whether she is as good as this year's Davis Cup winner. It *will* be affected by how she plays against those in her own league. As for an audience reference group, one that attends her matches, cheers her on, and offers critiques, this would probably include her coach, teammates, friends, and family.

What makes adolescents orient to one or another reference group? One factor is their own social links and affiliations. If they are active in Scouting, other Scouts will

Normative social influence
Acting like others because there is a social norm that prescribes doing as others do.

Informational social influence
Acting like others because of a belief that others have better information about the correct thing to do.

Reference group A set of people that someone looks to for information about what to do and what constitutes doing well, as well as evaluative comments and praise.

be an important reference group. If they live for skateboarding, they will be influenced by other 'boarders. In these examples, the affiliations are self-chosen. Other affiliations are not. For example, being from a particular ethnic or religious or social class background tends to make teens pay more attention to reference groups with similar backgrounds than to those with different backgrounds.

Connect the Dots...

Can you speculate how recent changes in social communication, such as Internet chat rooms, may alter or broaden the selection of reference groups that adolescents have available? What effects do you think that might have on teen attitudes and behaviors?

Models, Wannabes, and Alpha Pups.   Those who make up a person's normative reference group serve as *models* for how to act, what to value, what attitudes to hold, and so on. Observing what they do makes it more likely that the person will imitate their behavior. Social cognitive theory (Bandura, 1989) has generated a long line of research on factors that predict which models are imitated more. High on the list are:

Similarity. We are more likely to observe and imitate those who seem to be like us.

Status. We are more likely to observe and imitate those who are admired or successful.

Social power. We are more likely to observe and imitate those who control resources that are important to us, such as praise and criticism.

These factors sometimes work together and sometimes work in opposition to one another. For example, a 9th grader may see 10th graders as both similar and of high status and therefore regard them as a reference group. On the other hand, that same 9th grader may think of seniors as so dissimilar that they are placed in a different category and have less impact, even though they have more status than 10th graders.

Sometimes the high status of a reference group counts for more than the degree of similarity or dissimilarity. An adolescent who is not particularly popular, for example, may take the most popular teens as a normative reference group. If rock musicians are looked up to in a school, some teens who are not the least bit musical will copy their hairstyle, dress, language, and attitudes. Presumably they hope that some of the rockers' high status will rub off on them. Those who orient toward a high-status reference group in spite of a big similarity gap are often referred to as *wannabes*.

People who want to sell products to adolescents are very aware of the importance of normative reference groups. If they can get those with high status and social power to adopt a new fashion or snack food or rock group, normative social influence and word of mouth will take care of the rest. But how do you find them?

In one technique, market researchers try to identify the young trendsetters they call *alpha pups*, or leaders of the pack (Tierney, 2001). They approach random teens in the target population and ask, "Who is the coolest kid you know?" They then track down those who were named and ask them the same question. This process continues up the ladder of coolness until they finally reach someone who says, "Why.... Me, I guess!" The teens singled out in this way are then given the product, in the hope that they will infect others with the urge to try it. This is known, picturesquely enough, as *viral marketing* (Tierney, 2001).

Social Comparison and Self-Reinforcement.   Do you recall what it was like in school when the teacher handed back a test or report? Kids craned their necks to see the marks on other students' papers, while a murmur of "How'd you do?" ran around the room. The reason that they acted this way is that for most of them, the rest of the class was serving as a comparative reference group. They needed to find out how their own performance compared to those of others, because that told them how to react to their own score.

How should you feel when you see a 79 in red ink at the top of your quiz? Proud? Disappointed? So-so? It depends partly on whether the marks on this quiz were generally high, low, or middling. It also depends on how you see your performance in comparison to that of *your particular reference group*. For some, the reference group will be the class as a whole. Others will look to a subset of students that they take to be similar in ability or attitude to themselves. For still others, the reference group may be a fairly abstract concept, such as top students who earn straight A's. This process is called social comparison (Suls & Wheeler, 2000).

Social comparison is an essential element in the way we evaluate an action or event and figure out how to respond to it emotionally. The process works something like this:

You do something.

You compare your performance to a standard.

If your performance meets or exceeds the standard, you feel pride (reward yourself).

If your performance doesn't come up to the standard, you feel shame (punish yourself).

In this sequence, the source of the standard is the person's own comparative reference group. This means that if two adolescents who perform at exactly the same level have different reference groups, one may come away feeling terrific, while the other feels awful. Because this is a process of providing consequences (emotional rewards and punishments) to oneself, it is often referred to as **self-reinforcement** (Bandura, 1989).

The process of social comparison becomes more differentiated with age, as teens come to make finer distinctions in their selection of reference groups (Pomerantz, Ruble, Frey, & Grenlich, 1995). Social comparison operates in many other areas in addition to school achievement, from body image to sports performance to being invited to the "right" parties. Because it plays an important role in molding adolescents' self-esteem, we will discuss it in greater detail in Chapter 11, when we take up the question of how adolescents arrive at a sense of self.

Boosters and Critics. From our earliest days, we often find ourselves, or *put* ourselves, in front of an audience. Playgrounds echo to the cry of, "Look, Mommy, look, Daddy! Look what I can do!" The cheers and boos we receive from an audience reference group have a double function. They provide evaluative feedback that *guides* us toward more adaptive behavior. They also serve as emotional rewards and punishments that *motivate* more adaptive behavior. As children move into adolescence, parents and other important adults continue to be an audience reference group, but increasingly the reference group that counts most as an audience is other teens.

Sometimes, as we saw in Chapter 4 on cognitive development, this is an *imaginary audience* (Elkind, 1967). All too often, however, the audience is all too real (Vartanian, 2000). Think back to, say, 8th grade. It is the first day of school. You walk into your homeroom for the first time. Most of the other students are still strangers or at most casual acquaintances. You are sure they are scanning you, studying your clothes, your shoes, your hair, your face, your posture, or your style. Even the label on your backpack may get a glance or two. And, of course, you, as a member of *their* audience reference group, are busily scanning them, too.

Social comparison The process of comparing one's status or performance to that of a particular reference group.

Self-reinforcement Rewarding or punishing oneself for what one considers a good or bad outcome of one's actions.

▶ As an audience, peers provide both evaluative feedback and emotional rewards.

Both positive and negative responses serve to teach and enforce the standards of the reference group. Those who threaten the group's cohesion by deviating from those standards are quickly brought into line. The conformity that this fosters makes the group more unified. It may also make the members value it more, because they are paying a higher price to belong (Festinger, 1957). As for outsiders, they may become targets of sarcasm and ridicule, as a way of strengthening the distinction between ingroup and outgroup (Erikson, 1959).

Who Cares What They Say? The preceding sections give us some idea of how peer influence works, but still leaves the question of *why* it works. If your peers could take away your food or whip you through the streets, you would probably pay very close attention to how they expected you to act. Fortunately, peer groups in modern Western societies do not usually have that kind of power over individuals.

What if you show up at school wearing something you really like but your class-mates think is outlandish? What is the worst that can happen? Someone may laugh, point, and make rude remarks. Big deal! So what is it that keeps you from wearing whatever catches your fancy?

One answer is that adolescents, and indeed all of us, have a powerful **need to belong** (Newman & Newman, 2001). According to this view, young adolescents are driven to be part of the group because the alternative is feeling unwelcome, isolated, and lonely. The group also provides a ready-made sense of identity. People express pride in the group they belong to and tend to idealize other members of the group, especially in contrast to those who are not part of the group (Reicher, Levine, & Gordijn, 1998; Tajfel, 1981). One curious illustration of this: When a school's team wins an important game, teens who never even show up to watch a game go around chanting, "We're Number One!"

What is the source of this powerful need to belong? One suggestion is that our sense of self is based, at least in part, on the way our peers see and respond to us (Harter, 1999; Mead, 1934). If they react negatively, it poses a direct threat to our self-esteem. If they exclude us, we feel inadequate, isolated, and ashamed (Lashbrook, 2000). Keeping on the good side of the peer group, then, is a matter of psychological self-protection.

Staying on good terms with the group can sometimes be a question of physical self-protection as well. Evolutionary psychologists point out that in earlier times, those who were part of a group were more likely to avoid predators, resist aggressors, and survive to pass on their characteristics to a new generation (Caporael & Baron, 1997; Smith, Murphy, & Coats, 1999). In many troubled parts of the world, and in gang-ridden neighborhoods in America, this may still be the case.

Peers and Parents

As part of a television campaign against teen smoking, several young adolescents are shown making comically desperate attempts to avoid a parental lecture on the dangers of tobacco. The scene switches to a playground, where a boy's schoolmates offer him a cigarette. "No, thanks," he says. The voiceover spells out the message. Your teens may not seem to hear you, but what you tell them matters in the end.

The script for this little drama conveys some other messages that may not have been intended. It takes for granted that peer influence and parental influence are opposing forces, battling for the allegiance of the adolescent. It also takes for granted that the intended audience, parents and other adults, knows this already and does not need to be persuaded.

Is there a built-in conflict between the norms, goals, values, and approved behaviors of parents and peers? If there is, does one source of influence carry more weight with adolescents? If there *isn't* such a conflict, why are so many people convinced that there is? These are some of the questions we will look at in this section.

◀ **Learning Objective 6.5**
What are cross-pressures, and how much of a problem are they?

Need to belong The drive to be part of the social group and to feel accepted by others.

Figure 6.2   Conformity to Peer Pressure
Conformity to peer pressure peaks in mid-adolescence.

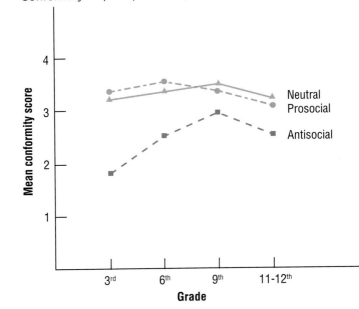

Source: "Conformity to Peer Pressure," by T. J. Berndt. *Developmental Psychology* 15, 608–616. © 1979. Used by permission of the American Psychological Association (APA).

Conformity, Autonomy, and Parents. You are walking home from school with some classmates. As you pass a closed-down factory building, one child picks up a rock and says, "I bet I can hit a window from here." Soon the others are throwing rocks at the building, too. When they notice that you aren't, they call you a wuss and say you probably can't even throw that far. You are not sure if you should do it. What would you *really* do?

In a classic study of conformity, psychologist Thomas Berndt (1979) asked children and adolescents from 3rd grade to 12th grade about situations like this, in which their inclinations or preferences clashed with what their peers urged them to do. Some of the situations involved antisocial acts, such as cheating, stealing, and damaging property. Others were neutral, for example, deciding whether to go bowling, as your friends want, or watch a movie, as you'd prefer. A third category was prosocial activity. For example, your friends say you should help your little brother with homework, but you want to go cheer up a sick friend. In a second part of the study, Berndt also asked children how they would react in neutral and prosocial situations if their *parents* wanted them to do something other than what they themselves wanted.

For all three types of situations, conformity to peers went up between 3rd and 6th grade and down between 9th and 12th grade. As Figure 6.2 shows, this pattern was most striking for antisocial acts. Those in 9th grade (roughly 15-year-olds) said they would give in to peer pressure a good deal more often than either 6th graders or older adolescents.

And parents? Not surprisingly, the degree to which children said they would conform to their parents' wishes went down, slowly but steadily, from 3rd grade to 12th grade (Berndt, 1979). This parallels a drop in the amount of closeness and engagement between parents and children, and a rise in the amount of conflict (Collins, 1990; Laursen, Coy, & Collins, 1998; Paikoff & Brooks-Gunn, 1991).

Why should peer conformity rise in early adolescence, peak in middle adolescence, and decline in late adolescence? One explanation is that this represents the changing balance between two forces, peer pressure and the teen's push toward greater *autonomy*. Peer pressure increases steadily across the early and middle adolescent years (Gavin & Furman, 1989), but so do feelings of self-reliance (Steinberg & Silverberg, 1986).

Following the lead of their peers may help young adolescents find the strength to become less dependent on their parents (Steinberg & Silverberg, 1986). Maybe to a 12- or 13-year-old, "Everybody in my class watches this show" feels like a more convincing argument than, "I like this show and want to watch it." As the old saying tells us, there is safety in numbers. Then, as teens gain confidence in their ability to make their own decisions, they become more able to resist pressures to conform from parents *or* peers.

Parental Style and Peer Orientation. While all adolescents have to deal with pressures to conform to peers and parents, they handle these pressures in different ways. One factor that is linked to the approach they adopt is the kind of parenting they received as children and the kind they continue to receive as they enter adolescence.

From what we learned about parental styles in Chapter 5, it should come as no surprise that teens with warm, accepting, and moderately controlling parents are more competent in dealing with peers and have better peer relationships (Dekovic & Meeus, 1997). In particular, girls who feel more accepted by their fathers have closer peer relationships, as do boys who feel more accepted by their mothers (Updegraff, Booth, & Thayer, 2002).

Some adolescents, on the other hand, have overly strict parents who limit their ability to make their own decisions. Psychologists Andrew Fuligni and Jacqueline Eccles (1993) found that this lack of opportunity to become more independent is linked to a more extreme orientation toward peers. These teens place such importance on their peer relationships that they are willing to take time away from things they ought to do, act dumber than they are, and break parental rules to keep in good with peers. They are also more likely to seek advice from their peers than from their parents (Fuligni & Eccles, 1993).

Overly strict parents are not the only ones whose young adolescents turn away from them. Teens whose parents are overly permissive or neglecting are also more likely to seek advice from peers and to be influenced by them (Bronfenbrenner, 1967; Steinberg, 1987b). In these cases, the adolescent is apparently trying to make up for a lack of parental structure and support, rather than reacting against too much parental structure.

The sort of extreme peer orientation just described—a willingness to spend too much time on peers, to play down one's abilities or talents, and to break parental rules—has consequences. In a later follow-up to the study by Fuligni and Eccles (1993), those who had shown this orientation as young adolescents had more problems with aggression, property damage, and drug and alcohol use later in adolescence (Fuligni, Eccles, Barber, & Clements, 2001). One reason is that the peers they are most likely to turn to tend to engage in deviant and risky behavior themselves (Bogenschneider, Wu, Raffaelli, & Tsay, 1998; Mayeux & Cillessen, 2007).

Interestingly, seeking advice from peers instead of parents in early adolescence did not lead to later adjustment problems (Fuligni et al., 2001). The reason may be that support from an age mate, in the form of friendship and advice, can help make up for a lack of emotional support from parents (Gauze, Bukowski, Aquan-Assee, & Sippol, 1996; Hartup & Stevens, 1997).

These links between the way parents act and the way their children turn out do, however, raise the familiar problem of what leads to what. Is it their parents' authoritarian attitudes that drive children to rebel and turn to peers for support? Or do parents notice that their children are rebelling and hanging out with "undesirable" peers, and crack down in the (probably futile) hope of straightening them out?

Quite possibly, both these processes are at work. As Figure 6.3 shows, problem behavior in the child may lead to more autocratic behavior in the parents, which, in turn, leads to more problem behavior in the child (Vuchinich, Bank, & Patterson, 1992). Unless something interrupts this vicious cycle, the parents may finally give up on the child as a hopeless case (Kerr, Stattin, Biesecker, & Ferrer-Wreder, 2002). If they stop trying to exert control and withdraw their emotional support, where else can the adolescent turn except to peers?

Figure 6.3 Cycle of Problem Behavior and Parental Response

Teen problem behavior and The parental response to it can set in motion a "vicious circle."

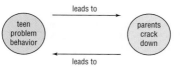

Cross-Pressures. Sooner or later, we all have the experience of being pulled in different directions by important people in our lives. The particular issue may seem fairly trivial, such as *Which set of relatives do we spend Thanksgiving with?* However, because significant relationships are involved, coping with such dilemmas can be very difficult. There is often more at stake than appears on the surface.

One popular idea about adolescence is that it is generally a period of strong **cross-pressures**, or competing social influences from different sources. If the values and goals of the peer group are at odds with those of parents and the world of adults, many of the choices a teen makes will inevitably go against someone important. Some theorists see this opposition as both necessary and helpful. If the child is too intertwined with the parents, breaking loose may *require* an outright rebellion, preferably with a little help from rebellious friends (Freud, 1958; Steinberg & Silverberg, 1986).

For most teens, cross-pressures turn out to be less troublesome than we might expect. One reason is that parents exert a lot of influence, both direct and indirect, over the peers their children are actually exposed to. The most obvious example is parents who decide to live in a particular community or neighborhood and send their child to a particular school because they think the other children there will be a better influence.

A more subtle effect involves parental styles and attitudes. Parents who are warm, engaged with their children, and neither too firm nor too lax have children who are attached to them and who share their central values (Kerr et al., 2002). These children, in turn, are likely to choose friends who have similar values and to shy away from those whose attitudes are too much at odds with those of their family (Bogenschneider et al., 1998; Galambos, Barker, & Almeida, 2003). They are also more likely to pay attention if the parents give them a heads-up about a particular peer. As a result, the influences they are subject to from parents and peers do not usually clash. On many questions, peer influence even tends to *reinforce* parental influence (Brown, 2004).

Some teens do get involved with antisocial peers and engage in behaviors that bring them into serious conflict with parents and other adults (Brendgen, Vitaro, & Bukowski, 2000; Broidy, et al., 2003; Dishion & Owen, 2002; Laird, Jordan, Dodge, Pettit, & Bates, 2001; Mayeux & Cillessen, 2007). However, even this can be thought of as a result of indirect parental influence. If interactions with the parents leave the child with negative feelings, these may generalize to other adult-led, structured settings, such as school. To avoid these feelings, the child may seek out other peers who are fleeing adult influences (Kerr et al., 2002).

Both overly strict parents and those who fail to monitor their children have teens who are especially susceptible to peer influence (Kerr et al., 2002). These teens are also more likely to *select* deviant peers as friends (Bogenschneider et al., 1998; Dishion & Owen, 2002). Once they do so, they and their peers may egg one another on into more and more deviant activities (Dishion, McCord, & Poulin, 1999). Not surprisingly, this combination of selection and influence is linked to doing poorly in school, both socially and academically, and to higher delinquency rates (Kerr & Stattin, 2000).

Parents do, of course, worry about the possible influence of their children's friends. They make efforts to encourage the friendships they see as positive and discourage those they see as negative (Tilton-Weaver & Galambos, 2002, 2003). They also ask more questions about friends. These peer-management techniques have mixed results. Parents who are less disapproving have teens who increasingly choose prosocial friends. Parents have less success influencing negative friendships. If anything, their vocal disapproval leads to more conflict, which, in turn, is linked to increases in negative friendships (Tilton-Weaver & Galambos, 2002).

It is also important to remember that adolescents are not merely passive targets of cross-pressures. To some extent, they can *decide* whether to pay attention to some people and not others. When it comes to seeking advice, for example, they do make distinctions. If the question concerns recreation, styles, relationships, and other

Cross-pressures A situation in which someone is subject to competing social influences from different sources, such as parents and peers.

day-to-day issues, they are likely to turn to their peers. On matters that are more future-oriented, such as scholastic goals and professional ambitions, and on questions of right and wrong, they are more likely to consult parents and other significant adults (Sebald, 1986; Young & Ferguson, 1979).

Unfortunately, as we have seen, it may not always be clear which category a particular issue belongs in. For example, a teen who is urged to try a supposedly harmless drug may see this as a personal matter to be talked over with friends. The teen's parents, on the other hand, may feel strongly that the potential consequences, including any possible risk of long-term or permanent damage, make it a question they should have a say about.

> **Summing Up...**
>
> For teens, peers serve as a crucial reference group. They exert normative and informational social influence as models, as sources of praise and criticism, and as an audience. Conformity to peers peaks in early adolescence, giving way to greater autonomy in late adolescence. While peer influence is often seen as being in conflict with parental influence, this is not necessarily so. Teens, especially those with authoritative parents, often select friends with values that are similar to those of their parents.

STATUS, ACCEPTANCE, AND POPULARITY

The purest treasure mortal times afford
Is spotless reputation.

—SHAKESPEARE, *RICHARD II*, I, 1

According to sociologist Max Weber (1946), a central motive in humans is the desire for social status. Weber defined this as including *honor*, *prestige*, and *power*. There is no period in the lifespan about which this is more accurate than adolescence. Who likes or dislikes whom, who has or hasn't been invited to a particular party, and who gets to sit at which table in the cafeteria are constant topics of earnest conversation. Reputation and popularity rise and fall like shares on the stock market, and, as with any social game, some people are winners and some are losers.

Studying Social Status

How do we find out an adolescent's place in a social group? This is the goal of **sociometric techniques**. These are various ways of asking people in a group how they see or assess other members of the group. The information they provide is then analyzed to determine the status of each member.

Over the years, one of the most widely used sociometric techniques has relied on nominations (Terry & Coie, 1991). Each child in a group, such as a school classroom, may be asked to name three children he or she really likes and three he or she really *doesn't* like. Once the positive and negative votes for each child are tallied, they can be used to calculate two aspects of the child's status.

Social preference is measured by subtracting the number of negative nominations (named as *disliked*) from the number of positive nominations (named as *liked*). Children with high positive scores are liked by a lot of peers and disliked by few. Those with high negative scores are disliked by many and liked by few.

What of those with scores around zero? This could come about in several ways. It may be that no one likes *or* dislikes them, or that a few people like them and a few dislike them, but it could also mean that they received lots of positive *and* negative nominations. To distinguish these very different cases, the positive and negative nominations are added up and used as a measure of **social impact**.

◄ **Learning Objective 6.6**
What are the different categories of social status?

Sociometric techniques Research tools used to study the structure and inner connections of social groups.

Social preference In nomination studies, the degree to which a person is chosen as liked (and not chosen as disliked) by others in the social group.

Social impact The degree to which a person is chosen either as liked *or* disliked.

▲ Rejected-aggressive teens are quick to believe others are hostile and to retaliate.

Popular In nomination studies, a label for those who are high in both social preference and social impact.

Rejected In nomination studies, a label for those who are low in social preference, but high in social impact.

Neglected In nomination studies, a label for those who are very low in social impact and neutral in social preference.

Controversial In nomination studies, a label for those who are very high in social impact, but neutral in social preference.

Average In nomination studies, a label for those who are near the middle on both social preference and social impact.

Hostile attributional bias A tendency to assume that ambiguous actions by others are the result of hostile intent and to respond in a hostile fashion.

Status Categories. The scores on these two dimensions of status, social preference and social impact, allow researchers to place everybody in the group into one of five categories (Coie, Dodge, & Coppotelli, 1982):

Popular or accepted children receive many positive nominations and few negative nominations. As a result, they are high in both social preference and social impact.

Rejected children receive many negative nominations and few positive ones. This makes them high in social impact, but low in social preference.

Neglected children get few mentions as either liked or disliked. This places them very low in social impact, but near the neutral point on social preference.

Controversial children are those who get many nominations both as liked and as disliked. This makes them very high in social impact, but near the middle in social preference.

Average children get some positive and negative nominations, but not a lot of either. As a result, they are near the middle on both social impact and social preference.

While much of the research on sociometric status has focused on elementary school children, these same categories turn up in studies of adolescents (Parkhurst & Hopmeyer, 1998).

When teachers and classmates are asked to describe those who are in the *popular* or accepted category, they use words like calm, friendly, cheerful, outgoing, attractive, warm, funny, and smart (Coie, Dodge, & Kupersmidt, 1990; Kennedy, 1990; Rubin, Bukowski, & Parker, 2006). What's not to like?

Rejected children tend to fall into two subgroups. Those who are *rejected-aggressive* are disruptive, hostile, and antisocial. Those who are *rejected-withdrawn* are socially immature, shy, timid, and lonely (Downey, Lebolt, Rincon, & Freitas, 1998; Gazelle & Ladd, 2003; Zakriski & Coie, 1996).

Children in the *neglected* category also tend to be shy and passive, but while they hold back from trying to connect to peers, they don't seem to be particularly lonely or upset about their social status (Coie et al., 1990; Crick & Ladd, 1993; Rubin et al., 2006).

As for *average* children, they are, well, average.

Status and Stability.   That leaves those who fall into the *controversial* category. Less research has been devoted to them. One reason is that there are not that many of them, maybe 5% of those in a typical classroom. Another reason (which may also explain their scarcity) is that theirs is a rather unstable status. Instead of staying controversial, they tend to move fairly quickly into one of the other categories (Newcomb & Bukowski, 1984).

The other categories are more stable. Popular children usually stay popular, average children usually stay average, and rejected children almost always stay rejected (Rubin et al., 2006). In part, this is because of the way they act. Rejected-aggressive adolescents develop what is called a **hostile attributional bias** (Crick & Dodge, 1994, 1996). That is, they are on the lookout for hostility from others. They are quick to attribute what others do to a hostile intent and they retaliate in a hostile way.

Those in their peer group also develop an attributional bias about these rejected teens that contributes to keeping them rejected. If a rejected-aggressive child does something antisocial, others will tend to attribute it to the rejected child's mean, nasty character. If the same child tries to make a friendly or prosocial gesture, however, others will assume it is manipulative and insincere and disregard it (Hymel, Bowker, & Woody, 1993). Both rejected-aggressive and rejected-withdrawn children and teens are at risk for social and psychological problems (Brendgen, Vitaro, Bukowski, Doyle, & Markiewicz, 2001; Deater-Deckard, 2001).

What factors make it more likely that a child will be in one category or another? Fairly high on the list are physical attractiveness, intelligence, and social skills (Becker & Luthar, 2007; Hartup, 1996). Children and adolescents who are more attractive are liked better, and those who are noticeably unattractive are liked less (Kennedy, 1990).

Intelligence also matters. Children who do well in school and on IQ tests are more likely to be in the popular or average category than in the rejected category (Bukowski, Gauze, Hoza, & Newcomb, 1993). That may seem surprising. The general impression is that nerds and wonks are near the bottom of the social ladder. The problem with nerds and wonks, however, is not that they are smart, but that they are both smart *and* socially clueless (Kinney, 1993). As a rule, those with above average general intelligence have above average social intelligence as well.

Parental styles and attitudes also make an important contribution to children's sociometric status. Parents who are warm, sensitive, and moderately controlling, while encouraging the child's autonomy, have children with strong social skills who are well-liked and accepted (Mize & Pettit, 1997). Adolescents whose parents are highly accepting also have more positive peer experiences (Kan & McHale, 2007).

Being Liked and Being Popular

As we have just seen, the sociometric approach to measuring social status asks how much each child is liked and accepted or disliked and rejected by the others in the group. Because this is what we usually mean by the term *popularity*, calling children who come out with many positive and few negative votes "popular" makes sense. But is that what children and adolescents themselves mean when they say someone is popular?

Another approach would be to find out how children *perceive* the others in the group. As well as asking them to name three children they like best, we could ask them to name the three children they think are the most popular.

This may seem like a very minor change in procedure, but it can lead to strikingly different results. In a study of 7th and 8th graders by Jennifer Parkhurst and Andrea Hopmeyer (1998), most of those who came out high on sociometric popularity were *not* perceived as very popular, although their schoolmates did see them as kind, trustworthy, unaggressive, and not stuck-up. The ones who were seen as popular, on the other hand, were considered dominant, aggressive, stuck-up, and not kind or trustworthy. They were also not well-liked.

A wry definition of a *celebrity* is somebody who is famous for being famous. For young adolescents, it seems that being popular means having everyone think you are popular, even if not many of them actually like you. How could such a paradoxical situation come about?

One illustration comes from two longitudinal studies of girls who were cheerleaders in 7th and 8th grade (Eder, 1985; Eder & Kinney, 1995). At the beginning of 7th grade, when the girls first became cheerleaders, they were generally well-liked. Their new position carried high visibility and prestige, and lots of other girls started trying to make friends with them. In response, the cheerleaders became very picky and stand-offish. They said they didn't even have enough time for the people who were already their friends. They were also concerned that if they associated too much with lower-status girls, it might damage their own prestige.

Soon the cheerleaders were mostly hanging out with one another. More and more they snubbed those who were not part of their little circle. This gave them a growing reputation for being stuck-up. Other teens stopped trying to be friends with them and began to dislike them instead. However, even as the general dislike of the cheerleaders grew, so did their reputation as being "popular."

Model Kids and Tough Kids. The concept of popularity already has this curious sense by late elementary school. Preadolescent boys who are rated as popular fall into two different categories (LaFontana & Cillessen, 2002; Rodkin, Farmer, Pearl, & Van Acker, 2000, 2002). Both types are described as athletic and cool. However, *model boys* are also seen as leaders and as cooperative, studious, and unaggressive. *Tough boys*, while considered just as popular, are seen as disruptive boys who get into trouble and start fights. As for girls, the characteristics that are linked to being considered popular,

Connect the Dots...

Think of people you knew in high school that you would have labeled popular, neglected, rejected-aggressive, and rejected-withdrawn. What in their characteristics, attitudes, and behaviors do you think would help explain their differences in social status?

◀ **Learning Objective 6.7**
What is relational aggression and how does it affect popularity?

but not necessarily well-liked, include physical attractiveness, lots of spending money, and a penchant for bullying and excluding others (Adler & Adler, 1998; Lease, Kennedy, & Axelrod, 2002).

In both sexes, the popular/not well-liked adolescents are considered aggressive bullies who are disengaged from school, while those who are popular *and* well-liked are seen as friendly, helpful, and academically engaged (de Bruyn & Cillessen, 2006). Unsurprisingly, for teens who are not aggressive, popularity is linked to improving academic performance across 9th and 10th grade. Among aggressive teens, just the opposite pattern emerges. The more popular they are, the more their grades decline across the 2 years (Gorman, Schwartz, Nakamoto, Abou-ezzeddine, & Toblin, 2003).

Just as sociometric popularity (being liked) and rejection (being disliked) are quite stable across the early adolescent years, so are being *seen* as popular or unpopular (Mayeuex, Bellmore, & Kaplan, 2002). If you know a child's status in 6th grade, you can be fairly sure of what that status will be in 8th grade.

Our understanding of social status continues to evolve. In this chapter's Research in the Spotlight, we look at a research project that goes beyond the usual questions of sociometric and perceived popularity to ask what children themselves think their popular and unpopular peers are like.

Research in the Spotlight

How Do Teens Themselves See Popular and Unpopular Peers?

The discussion in this section of status and popularity leans heavily on information from two somewhat different, but related research approaches. The *sociometric* approach asks teens to name peers they like or dislike, uses those nominations to put people in various categories, and looks to see how those in one category are different from those in other categories. The *sociological* approach asks teens to name those peers they think are popular, leaving it up to each one to decide what "popular" means, and then looks to see how the more popular teens are different from less popular teens.

Both these approaches focus on those who are placed in a particular category because others in the group point them out as liked or popular. In the language of person perception, they are *targets*. But what a researcher discovers about a target is not necessarily what those in the group—the *perceivers*—think about the target. Suppose a researcher found that teens who are well-liked are more manipulative than average kids. That doesn't mean other teens like them *because* they see them as manipulative. On the contrary, they may like them because they've been manipulated into thinking they are sincerely friendly.

Kathryn LaFontana and Antonius Cillessen (2002) conducted a study of social status that concentrated on the perceivers instead of the targets. Their objective was to learn what characteristics children themselves associate with being popular and unpopular. The participants, 4th to 8th graders in an ethnically mixed school, were asked which children in their grade were popular, which were unpopular, and which they personally liked and disliked. They were also asked which were athletic, smart, prosocial, physically aggressive, relationally aggressive, and withdrawn. The researchers did not stop at counting the "votes" each child received, however, they also analyzed the patterns in the votes each child *cast*.

How did this work? Suppose a child named exactly the same classmates on the "liked" question as on the "smart" question. This would mean that for her, being smart was linked to being liked. If, in response to "who is popular" and "who is prosocial," she named totally *different* classmates, this would indicate that she did not perceive being prosocial as important to being popular.

What did the results show? Athletic ability was more closely linked with being popular, while prosocial behavior was more closely linked with being liked. Academic ability was associated about equally with being popular and being liked. As for physical and relational aggression, both types of aggression were linked with being popular, on the one hand, and being *dis*liked, on the other.

Preadolescents and early adolescents have complex perceptions about popular and unpopular peers. They associate both prosocial and antisocial behaviors with being popular and make a distinction between seeing a peer as popular and liking that person.

Source: LaFontana, K. M., & Cillessen, A. H. N., 2002.

Popularity and Aggression. As more researchers focus attention on perceived popularity, one finding keeps showing up. Teens who are seen as popular are often seen as aggressive, too (Hawley, Little, & Card, 2007; LaFontana & Cillessen, 2002; Mayeux et al., 2002; McDougall, Vaillancourt, & Hymel, 2002). Yet, aggressiveness is usually associated with being *dis*liked (LaFontana & Cillessen, 2002; Newcomb, Bukowski, & Pattee, 1993). Is this another example of the paradox discussed in the last section? In a way, yes, but it also shows why it is useful to distinguish between two sorts of aggression.

Everybody knows about physical aggression. Researchers who want to measure it use items such as "hits, kicks, or punches others" and "starts fights and calls other kids names." But consider such behaviors as "gets even by keeping a person from being in their group of friends," "spreads rumors about people and talks behind their backs," and "ignores people or stops talking to them." Actions like these are meant to harm somebody, so we can certainly call them aggressive, but they are different from a punch in the nose. The aim is to damage the other person's personal and social relations. For that reason, this is known as **relational aggression** (Crick & Grotpeter, 1995).

Researchers who have looked closely at aggressive youth find two distinct groups. One group consists of young people who do not do nice things for others, have poor friendship adjustment, and are high in open, physical aggression. As one might expect, they are disliked and rejected by others. The second group, however, apparently has few adjustment problems. They are seen as being nice to others *at the same time* that they are high in relational aggression. Far from being disliked and rejected by others, they are well liked by many and seen as popular (Cillessen & Rose, 2005; Keisner & Pastore, 2005; Prinstein & Cillessen, 2003).

How to Stay Popular. The picture that emerges is this: Adolescents who are popular, as distinct from well-liked, *use* relational aggression as one way to keep their position at the top of the social heap (Hawley et al., 2007; Merten, 1997). In one study, both popular and well-liked adolescents were viewed as being athletic, smart, cooperative, and outgoing. However, the well-liked adolescents were rated as *low* in both physical and relational aggression, while the popular adolescents were rated as *high* in both (LaFontana & Cillessen, 2002). A longitudinal study found that from ages 10 to 14, relational aggression increasingly predicted *high* social prominence but *low* social preference (Cillessen & Mayeux, 2004).

Here is a glimpse of relational aggression in action. Abby, Brenda, and Gretchen, 7th graders, have a grudge against Sherry. To get at her, they work to turn Sherry's friend, Wellsley, against her. As Wellsley recalls,

> That day, Abby and Brenda got mad at me because I was hanging around Sherry. I go, "Abby, what's wrong, why are you mad?" She goes, "Well you're choosing Sherry over me and Brenda, but that's OK because we don't need you." Gretchen goes, "Why are you hanging around with Sherry so much?" I go, "Because I think that's kind of mean what you guys are doing to her." Gretchen goes, "Well, Wellsley, you know what she used to say about you and your house?" I go, "No, what?" Gretchen goes, "Once she wrote me a note and said that when she was over to your house that your little brothers were all brats." I go, "Right, prove it." The next day she brought a note and it was Sherry's handwriting. She always talks behind my back, so I don't really hate her or anything, but I don't hang around her as much.
>
> —(MERTEN, 1997, p. 183)

One detail about this incident jumped out at me. Did Gretchen just *happen* to save the note Sherry wrote about Wellsley? Or was she busily compiling dossiers on her classmates, in case she needed to use the information against them later?

In recent years, concern about relational aggression among children and adolescents has spread from researchers to teachers, parents, and others. Most of this concern has focused on relational aggression by girls and its effects on other girls (Owens, Shute, & Slee, 2000; Owens, Slee, & Shute, 2000; Simmons, 2002;

▲ Spreading nasty rumors about someone is a common form of relational aggression.

Relational aggression Trying to hurt someone by attacking their personal and social relationships, for example, through ridicule, exclusion, and malicious gossip.

Wiseman, 2002). A widely circulated article was entitled, *Girls Just Want to be Mean* (Talbot, 2002), and a 2004 film, *Mean Girls*, grossed more than $100 million (Berger, 2007).

Why girls and not boys? One reason is that the very idea of aggressive girls strikes many adults as shocking. As long as aggression was defined as physical and overt, adolescent girls looked much less aggressive than boys, but adding relational aggression to the picture changes that dramatically. As one observer noted,

> Unlike boys, who tend to bully acquaintances or strangers, girls frequently attack within tightly knit friendship networks, making aggression harder to identify and intensifying the damage to the victims. Within the hidden culture of aggression, girls fight with body language and relationships instead of fists and knives.
>
> —(Simmons, 2002, p. 78)

There is a good deal of evidence that overt aggression is more common among boys than girls (Coie et al., 1982; Crick & Grotpeter, 1995), while relational aggression is more common among girls than boys (Crick, 1997; Crick & Grotpeter, 1995). However, the *link* between aggression and social status is similar for boys and girls (Cillessen & Rose, 2005). Young people of both genders use rumors, hurtful jokes, insults, and excluding as ways of establishing, showing, and holding onto their own social standing (Pellegrini & Long, 2002; Savin-Williams, 1979). If I put you down, and you let me get away with it, that pushes me up.

Understanding Peers

Social status, popularity, and peer acceptance are daily concerns for most adolescents. After all, they interact with their peers every day and for most of the day (Csikszentmihalyi & Larson, 1984). Understandably, making these interactions work out well is a central task for adolescents (Berndt & Savin-Williams, 1993). In the course of trying to do that, they find themselves facing one sticky question after another: "Why is she acting so mean?" "Does he really want to be friends, or does he just want to copy my homework?" "What will she think when she finds out I was hanging with somebody she doesn't like?" "What can I do to make him like me?" The answers adolescents arrive at in turn have a direct effect on how they feel and what they do.

Dealing with questions of this sort requires **social cognition**, the capacity to reason about people and social relationships. Like cognition generally, social cognition scores some important advances during the adolescent years, including

Adolescents can think about social situations more logically and more abstractly.

They have a more subtle, sophisticated understanding of how people function.

They can look at more than one aspect of a social situation, or at connected aspects of different situations, at the same time.

They can think about possibilities and work out likely paths from where they are to where they want to be.

They become more aware of their own psychological processes and how these affect their relationships with others.

These advances affect many aspects of an adolescent's life, from concepts of the self to relationships with parents to ideas about society. Nowhere is this impact more profound than on the ways a teen interacts with other teens.

We saw in Chapter 4 that two approaches, cognitive developmental theory and information processing, have shaped much of the recent research on adolescent thinking. These same two approaches have strongly influenced work on social cognition. The cognitive developmental approach is the basis of research on *social perspective taking*, the ways people become aware of the viewpoints of others. The information processing perspective is at the core of research on *social problem solving*, the ways adolescents analyze and respond to particular problems that arise in social interactions.

Connect the Dots...

Imagine you are telling a friend about relational aggression, and the friend asks you to give an example. Can you recall an incident from adolescence that would help make the concept clear? If not, can you make one up? What in particular about the incident makes it a case of relational aggression?

▶ **Learning Objective 6.8**
How does the ability to understand others change during adolescence?

Social cognition The ability to reason effectively about people and social relationships.

Social Perspective Taking. An important concept in Piaget's description of children's thinking is *egocentrism*, a failure to distinguish between your own point of view and someone else's (Piaget & Inhelder, 1969). To some extent, we are all subject to this. For example, we may assume that people from a different culture see the world the same way we do. When we find out that they don't, we are astonished.

During childhood and adolescence there are major advances in **social perspective taking**, the ability to move past egocentrism and look at situations from the viewpoint of another person. Psychologist Robert Selman (1980; Yeates & Selman, 1989) has charted these developmental changes by presenting children with interpersonal dilemmas and analyzing their responses. For example, a girl who is really good at climbing trees is asked by a friend to rescue a kitten that is trapped in a tree. The problem is, after she took a tumble earlier, the girl's father made her promise not to climb trees anymore. What should she do?

By looking at how well children understood the viewpoints of the girl, the friend, and the girl's father, Selman was able to describe a series of stages in the development of perspective taking (Selman, 1976). At the earliest stage, preschool and kindergarten children usually assume that the girl will save the kitten because she (like them) likes kittens, and that the father will be glad because *he* likes kittens. In other words, they see everyone's viewpoint as the same as their own.

By the time they reach early adolescence, teens have come to realize that people can have different points of view and that others are also able to understand that. The girl may decide to climb the tree because she thinks her father would understand that she wasn't just disobeying, that she did it because she thinks he would let her if he knew about the kitten. In everyday life, a teen would be able to understand, for instance, how two classmates are at odds because each of them is misinterpreting the viewpoint of the other.

The most complex level of perspective taking is usually reached during middle to late adolescence. Adolescents try to understand the perspectives of others in terms of the social system they operate in. They realize that everyone's perspective taking, including their own, is imperfect, and that it may be distorted by factors they are not even aware of. For instance, these might include stereotypes and unexamined assumptions about race, social class, gender, and power relationships.

The central concerns of Selman's work are the abilities adolescents have to analyze and understand social situations and how those abilities develop. A second approach focuses more on how adolescents *use* their abilities when they face a particular social situation or problem.

Social Problem Solving. Sometimes, interacting with peers is straightforward and rewarding. Often, however, it brings daily hassles (Bowker, Bukowski, Hymel, & Sippola, 2000). For example,

> Two students in class are talking quietly. One glances at you, and then quickly looks away. Are they talking about you? If so, is what they're saying positive or negative? How should you react? Should you react at all, or try to ignore them?

> A schoolmate whom you don't really know, who is kind of a loner, invites you to a party. Do you go? If not, what do you say when you refuse?

> You and a friend get into an argument. The next time you pass each other in the hall, your friend doesn't seem to notice you. What do you do?

> A couple of students walk past you in the cafeteria and one bumps into your tray. They keep on going. Do you call after them? *Go* after them? Shrug it off?

Situations of this sort have several features in common. First, they involve social relationships, or dealings with others. Second, it is not quite clear what's going on. Third, you need to figure out how to feel or what to do. In other words, the interactions present *social problems* that you need to *solve*.

Research on social problem solving or *social information processing* (Crick & Dodge, 1989, 1994) looks at the process of coping with social situations and interactions. What can go wrong and why? What are the consequences to the teen's social relationships

Social perspective taking
The capacity to infer or imagine the thoughts, perceptions, and emotions of other people.

and adjustment? Can adolescents be helped to develop more positive and productive ways of handling their relationships?

Important elements of dealing with a social situation include interpreting social cues, selecting a goal, deciding on a response, and carrying out the response (Crick & Dodge, 1994). Each of these steps can lead to problems. An adolescent who feels unattractive may be more alert for cues that signal rejection than for those that indicate interest. The way an adolescent interprets cues may also cause distortions. An example we have already encountered is *hostile attributional bias* (Crick & Dodge, 1994, 1996), in which rejected-aggressive teens tend to see what others do in a hostile light and retaliate with hostility. Those who lose sight of their goal, or who do not have adequate social responses at their disposal, are also less likely to solve social problems successfully.

The choice of a response is affected by *outcome expectations* and feelings of *self-efficacy* (Bandura, 2006). What is the result of a particular response likely to be? How much confidence does the adolescent have about being able to carry it out? If you are convinced you will meet with rejection, or that you will trip over your words when you try to make friends with someone, it may seem easier not to make the overture at all.

Bullies and Victims

▶ **Learning Objective 6.9**
Who is likely to become a bully or a victim?

For many children and adolescents, their interactions with peers are neither happy nor safe. At least 1 of 10 children is the victim of severe or frequent **bullying**—or deliberate victimization—and many more suffer less intense victimization (Berger, 2007; DeVoe et al., 2003; Hanish & Guerra, 2002; Haynie et al., 2001; Nansel et al., 2001; Rodkin, 2004). The harassment they endure ranges from verbal insults to social exclusion to physical assaults. This is not just a matter of a few unpleasant incidents that can be easily brushed off. The school setting forces victims and bullies into close contact day after day, and longitudinal studies show that the same children tend to be victimized year after year (Paul & Cillessen, 2003). Even witnessing harassment leads to increased anxiety among those who are not themselves victims (Nishina & Juvonen, 2005).

The most obvious targets of bullying are those who are already near the bottom of the social ladder. They tend to be withdrawn, depressed, insecure, fearful, physically weak, and socially immature, with poor social skills (Craig, 1998; Fox & Boulton, 2006; Olweus, 1993; Smith, Shu, & Madsen, 2001). They also have problems managing confrontations (Champion, Vernberg, & Shipman, 2003), and the more they are picked on and rejected, the more lonely and isolated they feel (Graham & Juvonen, 2001; Kochenderfer-Ladd & Wardrop, 2001).

Many who are victimized blame themselves for their plight and try to avoid social encounters. This, in turn, makes them even more likely victims (Hodges & Perry, 1999). Having a best friend can help protect someone from this vicious circle (Fox & Boulton, 2006; Hodges, Boivin, Vitaro, & Bukowski, 1999), but this kind of support is not always available. Others often shy away from victimized peers, out of fear that if they are friends with a victim, they will become targets of bullying, too (Merten, 1996).

Being victimized has been linked to serious and long-lasting problems (Hawker & Boulton, 2000). These problems include depression, anxiety, loneliness, anger, sadness, poorer school performance, and poor self-esteem (Bellmore & Cillessen, 2006; Cillessen & Nukulkij, 2002; Giang, Ghavami, Gonzalez, & Wittig, 2002; Hoglund, 2007; Schwartz, Gorman, Nakamoto, & Toblin, 2005). These problems are even more severe when the general level of aggressiveness in the classroom is higher (Cillessen & Nukulkij, 2002). Some approaches to dealing with the effects of aggression and bullying are discussed in this chapter's Applications in the Spotlight.

And what of the bullies? Not surprisingly, they tend to be aggressive, hostile, and domineering (Craig, 1998; Olweus, 1995). They also tend to think of themselves as attractive and popular (O'Moore & Kirkham, 2001), when, in fact, they tend to be disliked (Veenstra et al., 2005). Some, however, are popular with other bullies (Pellegrini, Bartini, & Brooks, 1999), and others manage to get along well with peers who, though mostly nonaggressive themselves, tacitly support their bullying (Farmer et al., 2002; Garandeau & Cillessen, 2006).

Bullying The deliberate victimization of another person through verbal, social, or physical attacks.

Applications in the Spotlight

What to Do About Bullying

In the fall of 2003, a high school freshman in a small town in Minnesota took a pistol to school and shot two other students. Both died. Afterwards, schoolmates said the boy had been constantly bullied and teased about his acne condition (Robertson & Vaishnav, 2004). This is not an exceptional case. In the aftermath of the Columbine High School shootings, the U.S. Secret Service carried out an exhaustive study of school violence. The investigators found that bullying contributed to almost 3/4 of the school shootings they looked at (Vossekuil, Fein, Reddy, Borum, & Modzeleski, 2002). In fact, bullying was practically the only element that was common to most of the cases.

Bullying affects more than just the victims and their attackers. In schools where it occurs, a psychological climate can develop in which no one feels safe and learning suffers. Other students come to see bullying as normal and acceptable. Some start to take part in it themselves. Others avoid school because they fear becoming victims (Olweus, 1993).

There are practical and effective ways to prevent bullying. A major effort to curb bullying and victimization in schools was carried out in Norway and Sweden in the 1980s (Olweus, 1993, 1995). Within 2 years, bullying had dropped by 50% and continued to drop the longer the program went on. Truancy, vandalism, and theft also declined. This Olweus program, named for its developer, has since been adapted to North American conditions (Olweus, Limber, & Mihalic, 1999).

The core of the Olweus approach to bullying prevention is a set of rules that apply to all students, not just those who are actively involved in bullying:

We do not bully other students.

We try to help students who are bullied.

We make a point of including all students who are easily left out.

When we know someone is being bullied, we tell a teacher, parent, or adult we trust.

Steps to implement the approach on a *schoolwide* level include:

giving out an anonymous questionnaire to determine the nature and extent of the problem;

holding a conference day to acquaint school personnel with the program and involve them actively in putting it into effect;

forming a schoolwide committee to coordinate anti-bullying efforts;

meeting with parents to make them aware of the need for the program and to explain how it will make the school a safer and more positive learning environment.

On a *classroom* level, interventions include:

helping students to develop classroom rules against bullying and to take responsibility for conforming to them;

creating positive consequences for prosocial behavior and sanctions for bullying, malicious teasing, social exclusion, and other forms of harassment;

holding regular class meetings to discuss and evaluate the success of the program.

On an *individual* level, the program targets specific students who are involved in bullying, either as bullies or victims.

Bullies are given a clear, strong message that bullying is unacceptable, that it carries serious consequences, and that their future actions will be closely watched.

Victims are told how the school staff intend to deal with the bully and are urged to report any new bullying episodes immediately (Olweus, Limber, & Mihalic, 1999).

Parents of both bullies and victims are brought into the process and encouraged to support the school's efforts to avert any further episodes of bullying.

No intervention program or campaign by school personnel or other concerned adults is likely to wipe out bullying completely. What such interventions can do, however, is change the psychological climate to make bullies aware of the general disapproval of their schoolmates and give victims a sense of sympathy and support. And that, as evaluation research has shown, is enough to cause a considerable reduction in bullying. More information on this program can be found at www.clemson.edu/olweus/.

Bullies learn that they can get what they want without the usual social skills of negotiation and compromise. In the short run, this may seem like an advantage, but the long-term consequences are quite negative. Bullies run a greater risk of becoming delinquents, criminals, and substance abusers (Baldry & Farrington, 2000; Loeber & Dishion, 1984). One study found that children who had been identified as bullies in childhood were five times more likely to have serious criminal records by the time they reached age 30 (Olweus, 1993). More recently, research on a representative

Figure 6.4   Bullying in School by Grade
Bullying in school, is most frequent in the middle-school grades.

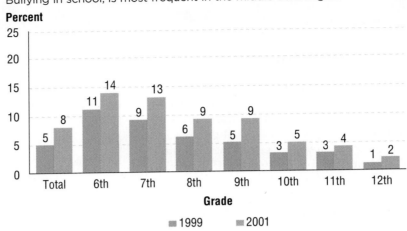

Source: U.S. Department of Justice.

sample of almost 16,000 American adolescents showed a strong link between bullying and violent behaviors (Nansel, Overpeck, Haynie, Ruan, & Scheidt, 2003).

We have been talking about bullies and victims as if they are two distinct groups. However, a good many children who are victimized also victimize others. These *bully/victims* turn out to be particularly at risk. They have higher rates of problem behavior, lower self-control and social competence, and poorer school functioning than either pure bullies or pure victims (Andreou, 2000; Haynie et al., 2001; Olafsen & Viemero, 2000). In the light of such events as the Columbine High School shootings, it is chilling to learn that bully/victims are more likely to carry a weapon to school in the belief that it will give them protection from their enemies (Isaacs, Card, & Hodges, 2000).

Bullying and victimization reach a peak during the early adolescent years, and then decline, as shown in Figure 6.4 (DeVoe et al., 2003; Nansel et al., 2001; Pellegrini & Long, 2002). One reason for this may be the transition from elementary to secondary school, which thrusts young people into new social settings. They have to claim their place in the new group, and one way to do that is through bullying others (Pellegrini & Long, 2002). Once a new dominance hierarchy or "pecking order" has been established, the need to bully becomes less pressing. At the same time, the broader social scene of high school makes it more possible for victimized teens to keep a safer distance from the people who have been victimizing them. Interestingly, students in classrooms and schools that are more ethnically diverse are less likely to feel vulnerable and victimized, because there is more balance of power among different ethnic groups (Graham, 2006).

Encouraging Social Competence

Some children enter adolescence with an impressive set of social skills already in place (Englund, Levy, Hyson, & Sroufe, 2000). Others aren't so fortunate. Whether they are sad and withdrawn, aggressive and hostile, or simply odd and out of step with the rest, they run the risk of being rejected by their peers. Peer rejection, in turn, is a risk factor for a long list of psychological problems and disorders, ranging from delinquency and drug use to anxiety, depression, and fantasies about suicide (Deater-Deckard, 2001; Dodge & Pettit, 2003; Sandstrom, Cillessen, & Eisenhower, 2003).

What can be done to help adolescents who have difficulty relating to their peers? A good place to start is to increase awareness and concern on the part of adults in their lives, especially parents, teachers, and school officials. Too often, problems such as isolation, rejection, bullying, and victimization are minimized or shrugged off as a normal part of growing up (Smith & Brain, 2000).

Beyond that, psychologists and educators have developed a great variety of school-based programs to teach children and adolescents the skills they need to avoid

Connect the Dots...

Suppose you knew an adolescent who was being victimized by a bully. What advice would you offer to improve the situation? Given what you have learned about bullies and victims, explain why you think following your suggestions would help.

▶ **Learning Objective 6.10**
What can be done to help teens get along better with peers?

victimization or stop bullying (CASEL, 2002; Frey et al., 2005; Smith, Pepler, & Rigby, 2004; Taylor, Liang, Tracy, Williams, & Seigle, 2002). While they differ in detail and approach, most of these programs try to teach children self-control, confidence, responsibility, cooperation, problem-solving skills, and conflict avoidance techniques. They also stress the importance of a positive school and classroom climate.

When 6th graders who had been through one such program were asked what they had learned, they said,

> I learned to speak out.
>
> I learned that it is important to share your feelings with others when they are bothering you and you don't like it.
>
> I learned how to cope with annoyance.
>
> Count to 10 to calm down.
>
> If you have a problem, you should sit down and talk about it instead of getting into fist fights. It's a better way to communicate.
>
> —(TAYLOR et al., 2002, pp. 267–268)

By now, there is plenty of research evidence that social skills training programs can help a wide variety of children and adolescents to get along better with peers (Deater-Deckard, 2001). However, the long-term effects of these programs are not yet clear (Hundert et al., 1999). Do teens retain the social skills they have learned? Or do they gradually slip back into their earlier, less effective, ways of relating?

Summing Up...

An adolescent's social status—popular, rejected, neglected, controversial, or average—is based on a combination of social preference and social impact. For most, this status is fairly stable. Some teens are seen as popular, but are not well-liked; they tend to be high in relational aggression. Across adolescence, the ability to understand peers improves as a result of more effective social cognition and social perspective taking. Bullying and victimization, of and by peers, peaks in early adolescence. Many teens are victimized, and those who are both victims and bullies are at particular risk. Intervention programs that encourage social skills can reduce peer rejection and victimization.

SOCIAL GROUPS IN ADOLESCENCE

Tomorrow afternoon, you go past a middle school or high school just as the teens come spilling out the front entrance. Recalling what you've read so far in this chapter, you nod wisely and murmur, "Aha—the peer group." Okay, so some are boys and some are girls, some are tall and some are short, and there's a mixture of different ages, ethnic groups, and styles of dress, but what they have in common—their social status as teenagers—stands out more than their differences.

Now imagine that you look young enough to pass for 15. With the permission of school officials, you register as a transfer student and spend the next couple of months as a high school freshman. You go to classes, join some clubs, and hang out with other students after school. Of course, when no one is looking, you take careful notes. This procedure is called participant observation, and it has a lot in common with the way anthropologists study a different culture. In this case, the "culture" is the other students, the ones who really are adolescents.

You will quickly discover, if you didn't know it already, that what looked from a distance like an undifferentiated mass of teens is actually a fine-grain structure of interlocking social groups. If there were a motto carved over the door, it might read, "A place for everyone and everyone in his or her place," or maybe, "When in Rome, do as the Romans."

Social groups take on a greater importance for adolescents than they have for children or, in most cases, for adults. Several factors converge to make this happen (Brown, 1990, 2004; Brown & Klute, 2002):

Puberty. Physical and sexual maturation is usually accompanied by a heightened and changed interest in others one's own age, as well as by a withdrawal of interest from adults and particularly parents.

The quest for identity. A changing body and changing cognitive abilities raise the question, "Who am I?" One place to look for an answer is in the ways others who are like us see and respond to us (Harter, 1999; Mead, 1934).

Social cognitive development. Adolescents become able to look past surface traits to intentions, norms, beliefs, and personality dispositions. This makes it more likely they will seek out others who fit with their needs and values.

Social structures. The transition from elementary to middle or junior high school usually means going from a self-contained classroom of familiar peers and a familiar teacher to a shifting array of semi-strangers and teachers who may barely know your name. A group of familiar peers is a source of much-needed stability and support.

Compared to the social world of children, adolescent social groups change in important ways (Brown, 1990, 2004).

Adolescents *spend much more time* on interactions with peers. They are together at school, they hang out together after school and on weekends, and when they aren't together they communicate by phone, e-mail, and instant messaging.

These interactions take place *with less adult guidance or control.* A big lure of the mall is that adolescents are on their own. Even when a teen's friends come over, the group usually goes off to the teen's room and shuts the door.

Adolescents start to draw closer to *peers of the opposite sex*. The gender segregation that is such a feature of childhood begins to erode.

Social groups get bigger, expanding from the small neighborhood-based groups of late childhood to larger groups based on norms, personality traits, and behavior patterns.

Social scientists describe two types of social groups that are especially typical of adolescence in America, the *clique* and the *crowd* (Brown, 1990; Brown & Klute, 2002). We will take a look at each in turn.

Adolescent Cliques

▶ Learning Objective 6.11
What are cliques and how do they change across adolescence?

A **clique** is a small, tightly knit group of friends who spend as much time together as they can manage. Cliques start to form in late preadolescence, but they flourish most in the early to middle adolescent years. A clique may have as many as a dozen members or as few as three, but the average is five or six—small enough so that all the members know each other well.

As a rule, those in a clique are the same age and sex, in the same school class, and from similar economic and ethnic backgrounds (Graham & Juvonen, 2002). They may be drawn together by a common interest or simply by interlocking friendships (Brown & Klute, 2002). Best friends are almost always in the same clique (Ennett & Bauman, 1996; Urberg, Degirmencioglu, Tolson, & Halliday-Scher, 1995). If for some reason they aren't, it places quite a strain on their friendship.

Not all adolescents belong to cliques, although to a teen who isn't in one, it may feel that way. In fact, a study of 9th graders found that fewer than half of them— 44%—were members of a clique (Ennett & Bauman, 1996). The rest were divided fairly evenly between two very different categories. *Liaisons* are socially active teens who have friends in two or more cliques, but do not belong to any themselves. They help bridge the gaps between groups that otherwise might not communicate. *Isolates*, in contrast, have few friends either within cliques or outside of them.

Figure 6.5 on page 201 charts the different relationship patterns in a group of teens. An arrow between two people means that one of them named the other as a best friend.

Clique A small, close-knit group of friends, generally of the same age, sex, and social status.

◄ Members of a clique are usually of the same age and sex and share similar ethnic and class backgrounds.

A double-headed arrow indicates that each of the two picked the other. Notice how closely interwoven the members of the cliques are. This web of connections helps make cliques quite stable. Across the school year, one or two new members may join and one or two old members leave, but the structure stays pretty much the same (Degirmencioglu, Urberg, Tolson, & Richard, 1998).

The biggest plus to being part of a clique is the social and emotional support members give each other. Even before you arrive at a party, you know you'll have friends there. Afterwards, they will tell you what you did right and what you did wrong, and expect you to do the same for them. They will be there to applaud your triumphs and console you over disappointments.

One study of young adolescents found that for girls, being a clique member or a liaison was linked to better peer relationships and school adjustment, as well as to

Figure 6.5   Social Network in a Group of Teens
Friendship patterns among teens include cliques, liaisons, and isolates.

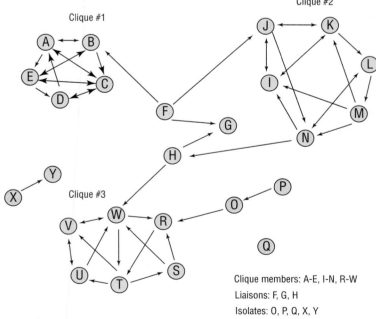

Clique members: A-E, I-N, R-W

Liaisons: F, G, H

Isolates: O, P, Q, X, Y

Source: Ennett, S. T., & Bauman, K. E. (1996). Adolescent social networks: School, demographic, and longitudinal considerations. *Journal of Adolescent Research, 11,* 203. Used by permission.

▶ In early adolescence, cliques of boys and cliques of girls start paying attention to each other.

fewer behavior problems (Henrich, Kuperminc, Sack, Blatt, & Leadbeater, 2000). Interestingly, these effects were not found for boys. This may be because status for boys tends to be based more on personal skills, such as in sports, while for girls popularity and interpersonal relationships are paramount (Eder, 1985).

At the same time that cliques provide important benefits, they also put intense pressure on members to conform to the group's norms. This is especially so of high-status cliques. Befriending someone outside the clique, dating the wrong person, or even wearing the wrong brand of clothing can result in teasing, ridicule, and the threat of expulsion from the clique (Adler & Adler, 1998; Brown & Klute, 2002).

Cliques have a life cycle of their own (Dunphy, 1963). In early adolescence, there are cliques of girls and cliques of boys, and seldom the twain do meet. A year or so later, girls' cliques and boys' cliques of similar status start to hang out, if not together, at least in the same area. Imagine the sidewalk outside a middle school, with separate little clumps of boys and girls pretending not to notice each other but surreptitiously checking to make sure the other group is noticing *them*.

In the third stage, according to Dunphy, this sex segregation starts to break down as the leaders of cliques begin dating. As other clique members follow their lead, mixed-sex groups take over some of the functions of the clique (Cooksey, Mott, & Neubauer, 2002). Toward late adolescence, these groups too become less important, as teens pair off and spend more of their leisure time in couples and sets of couples.

Adolescent Crowds

Connect the Dots...

Were you part of a clique as an adolescent? If so, in what ways were you similar to others in your clique and in what ways different? How did the clique form in the first place, and how did it evolve?

▶ **Learning Objective 6.12**
What are crowds and what are some typical crowds in high school?

The **crowd** is as much an idea as it is a group. While cliques are based on concrete relationships among specific people, a crowd is defined by abstract notions, such as reputation and stereotypes, along with observable characteristics, such as school grades, clothing, interests, and activities (Brown, 1990; Brown & Klute, 2002; Stone & Brown, 1999). If you come to school in spiked hair, combat boots, torn jeans, a studded leather wrist band, and a black Metallica t-shirt, everybody will assume that you belong to a certain crowd. It doesn't matter if you hang out with others in that crowd or not. You may not even know any of them. If you look like a duck, talk like a duck, and dress like a duck, everybody figures you must be a duck. And a lot of the time, *so do you* (Prinstein & La Greca, 2002).

The concept of the crowd offers teens a way to understand the social structure and to place themselves and others within it. It gives them a social identity, however partial, along with a rough and ready way to recognize potential friends and foes (Stone & Brown, 1999; Urberg, Degirmencioglu, Tolson, & Halliday-Scher, 2000). The more they identify with a particular crowd, the more that crowd begins to replace adolescents in general as their primary *reference group*. They evaluate "their" crowd more positively and view other crowds more negatively (Tarrant, 2002). As a result, they start to dress and act like others in the crowd and use the same slang. They develop similar attitudes toward such issues as sexual activity and substance use (Henry, Schoeny, Deptula, &

Crowd A social category for which membership is based largely on observed characteristics, reputation, and stereotypes.

◄ Teens who are not seen as belonging to a particular crowd often feel excluded.

Slavick, 2007; La Greca, Prinstein, & Fetter, 2001). Any new friends they make usually come from within the crowd, too. If they have to choose a fellow student for a school activity, they are likely to choose one from a high-status crowd, especially if they see themselves as belonging to such a crowd (Horn, 2006).

Labels vary from place to place and year to year, but the basic crowd structure of American high schools stays pretty much the same (Brown & Klute, 2002; Urberg et al., 2000). Some typical crowds, along with their supposed identifying marks, are:

Jocks—swagger, play on teams, like to party

Populars (preps, trendies)—fashionable, snobbish, run the school

Brains—use big words, make all A's, study even on weekends

Normals—ordinary teens who don't particularly stand out

Nerds—weird clothes, weird hobbies, socially clueless

Druggies—turned off, tuned out, usually stoned

Headbangers—studs, heavy metal, attitude

Nobodies—withdrawn, confused misfits

These probably sound familiar to you, even if some of the names are not exactly the ones you recall from high school days. It is also not news that crowds vary enormously in social status. Jocks and populars are at the top, and nobodies are at the bottom (Garner, Bootcheck, Lorr, & Rauch, 2006).

The Columbine shootings in 1999 caused many Americans to think about adolescent crowds and the effects they may have. In the newspaper article on page 204, a *New York Times* reporter visited a suburban high school in Arizona and describes the crowd situation she found there.

It is worth pointing out that not too many teens fit perfectly with the image of any single crowd. Many have interests and attitudes that bridge different crowds. A particular teen may be seen as a member of one crowd by some people, as a member of a different crowd by others, and as a member of *both* by still others (Brown, Mory, & Kinney, 1994). I remember my confusion, at age 14, when I discovered that a classmate who had always struck me as a total jock was not only quite bright but also a skilled and sensitive flutist.

The Life Cycle of Crowds. The cognitive changes that take place during adolescence gradually give teens a more differentiated view of the world. What used to look either black or white now reveals a spectrum of grays. As a result, the structure of crowds

Arizona High School Provides Glimpse Inside Cliques' Divisive Webs
by Tamar Lewin

SCOTTSDALE, Ariz., April 30—Look around the sprawling Chaparral High School campus at lunch time, and the social geography of the 1,850 students is clearly mapped out.

The football players and their friends have the center table outdoors, at what everyone calls the ramada. In back of them, the picnic tables are filled with popular students, too: an attractive, preppy array of cheerleaders, lesser jocks, and members of the student government and the All Stars, a service club.

"You wouldn't dare come sit out here if you didn't know the people," said Lauren Barth, a sophomore cheerleader. "But once you're in with the girls, everyone is really friendly to you. When I made cheerleader, it was like I was just set."

Inside, in the cafeteria, there are more braces and glasses and hair that doesn't quite have a shape. These tend to be students with less social status, the skateboarders, the nerds, those who say they are just regular, the freshmen who have not yet found their place in the sun. There are many other lunchtime domains: a bunch of art students eat in the studios, some band members gather by the music building, and dozens of drama students—and others attracted by their nonconformist clothes and easy acceptance—in the theater building. But for all the choices, a few students still have no niche, eating upstairs or alone outside the library, or just wandering, their heads low as they pass clumps of noisy schoolmates.

. . .

[T]he popular students who lunch outside were far more likely than the ones sitting inside to say that they love the school, and feel connected to at least one teacher.

A group of freshmen eating inside nodded vigorous agreement as Catherine Hodge discussed her sense of Chaparral.

"I don't like this school and I don't know anybody who does," she said. "A lot of it is that football is such a big part of school and so many people take the whole popularity thing out of control . . ."

At Chaparral, where violence is almost unheard of, the Colorado shootings came the week after a student assaulted a baseball player with brass knuckles, and some members of the baseball team retaliated by smashing the attacker's car with their bats. The principal . . . says the incident was a fight over a girl, but many students describe it in more tribal terms, as a reflection of long-simmering tensions between athletes and others—the same discomforts surrounding the Colorado shootings.

Chaparral's athletes do not see it that way. "I don't see the team treating people badly, or people resenting us," said Grant Simpson, a sophomore football player. "It's true that if you mess with someone, you're messing with all their friends."

"Brass knuckles isn't supposed to happen here and it did, so you sort of think maybe anything can happen here," said Jillian Sitto, a freshman who loves Chaparral . . . "It scares me to death because people are so cliquey here, and there's so much emphasis on who you're friends with. I looked around and tried to think if I could imagine kids feeling so angry here and I could. There are kids who get picked on a lot. It's usually a whole lot of little comments that add up. I try to be nice to everybody. And after the shootings I tried to be really really nice, because you never know."

SOURCE: LEWIN, T., 1999, MAY 2.

becomes more differentiated as well. In one Midwestern community, the middle school had only two crowds, a small, high-status group of trendies, and everybody else, the dweebs (Kinney, 1993, 1999). With the transition to high school, the dweebs evolved into several different crowds. Some of these had almost as much status as the trendies. By the end of high school, still more differentiation had taken place, and the barriers between some of the groups became easier to cross (Horn, 2003). This process is diagrammed in Figure 6.6 on page 205.

Being seen as part of a particular crowd by others is not always the same as personally identifying with that crowd. Both, however, have a similar and wide-ranging impact on adolescents. Crowd affiliation has been linked to self-esteem, school achievement, psychological adjustment, substance use, delinquency, and a range of

Figure 6.6 Evolution of Crowd Structure Across Adolescence
Across adolescence, crowd structures become more differentiated.

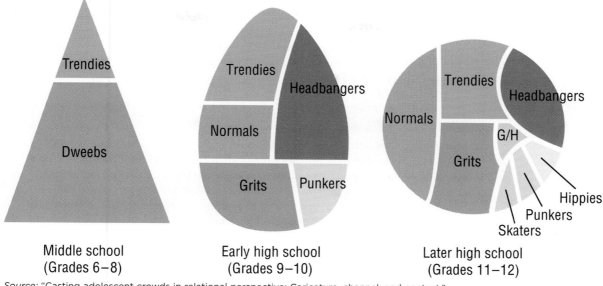

| Middle school | Early high school | Later high school |
| (Grades 6–8) | (Grades 9–10) | (Grades 11–12) |

Source: "Casting adolescent crowds in relational perspective: Caricature, channel, and context."
Advances in adolescent development: Vol. 6. Personal relationships during adolescence, by R. Montemayor,
G. R. Adams, and T. P. Gullotta (Eds). © 1994 by Sage Publications. Used by permission.

health risk behaviors (La Greca et al., 2001; Urberg et al., 2000). What is more, these linkages continue into young adulthood (Barber, Eccles, & Stone, 2001).

To some extent, the links between crowd membership and behavior are the result of a selection process. Obviously, someone who uses drugs is more likely to be classified as a druggie than someone who doesn't, just as someone who gets consistently high grades is more likely to be seen as a brain than someone who just scrapes by academically. However, there is also a process of social influence at work. Belonging to a crowd *channels* the teen toward the activities that are typical of that crowd (Eccles & Barber, 1999; Henry et al., 2007; Iervolino et al., 2002; Stone, Barber, & Eccles, 2002). If the teens you hang with spend every Saturday night getting drunk, your chances of leading a sober lifestyle are fairly slim.

Crowds and Ethnic Minorities. Most of the research we have just been looking at was done in schools where most of the students were White. What about other ethnic groups? The answer depends largely on whether we are looking at ethnic minorities within a mostly White school, or at schools in which most of the students are non-White.

Studies carried out in mostly non-White schools have found crowds of jocks, populars, brains, partiers, druggies, and so on, just as in mostly White schools (Brown & Mounts, 1989; Fordham & Ogbu, 1986). This shouldn't surprise us. The concept of crowds grows out of a need to figure out the social structure and to place oneself and others within it. This need is at least as urgent in an inner-city school with few Whites as in a suburban school with few non-Whites.

A different picture emerges in multi-ethnic schools. There, ethnic identifications tend to come before, or modify, crowd identifications. That is, teens will talk of an African American crowd (the "bros," for example), an Asian crowd, or an Hispanic crowd *alongside* the jocks, populars, and what have you. In one Midwestern school, researchers found both a "Black crowd" of African Americans and a "wannabe Black" crowd, students of varying ethnicity who adopted hip hop styles, slang, and attitudes (Stone & Brown, 1999).

These ethnically defined crowds generally contain more specific subcrowds. In a large multi-ethnic school, you might find Asian populars, Hispanic jocks, African American nerds, and so on. However, those *within* a particular ethnic group are more likely to recognize these distinctions than those outside it (Brown & Mounts, 1989).

This reflects a phenomenon we encountered in an earlier chapter, called *ingroup bias* (Rudman, Feinberg, & Fairchild, 2002). We all tend to notice differences among people in our own group, whatever it may be, But when we look at those in other groups, we see them more in terms of their group membership. A Latino student, for example, may be aware of all sorts of important distinctions among fellow Latinos, but think all White students belong to the "Anglo" crowd. Meanwhile, those White students are very aware of big differences among various White crowds, but tend to see all Hispanics as part of the Hispanic crowd.

Summing Up...

Social groups are particularly important during adolescence. The clique, a small, close-knit group of friends who are usually similar in age, sex, and background, is a source of social and emotional support as well as of pressure to conform to the clique's norms. Crowds, such as jocks, brains, and nerds, are larger groups that are based largely on reputation and shared characteristics. Membership in a crowd is a source of social status as well as social influence.

SUMMARY

Biological, cognitive, and social factors all operate in different ways to encourage adolescents to turn from the family to the peer group.

American teens spend two to four times as much of their waking day with **peers** as with parents or siblings. In other cultures, too, both traditional and Westernized, the peer group takes on special significance during adolescence. Boys spend much of their time during adolescence with groups of other boys. Girls are more likely to divide their time between same-age friends and adult female relatives.

Learning Objective 6.1 What factors make peers become more central during adolescence?

In Western societies, trends toward smaller families, more dual-earner families, and larger pools of accessible peers contribute to the shift from family to peers. Another factor that fosters peer relationships is **age segregation**, both in school and in extracurricular activities such as organized sports. The styles, trends, attitudes, and behaviors that adolescents acquire from their peers make up a **youth culture** that may be at odds with the values of the adult culture. This leads to the perception of a **generation gap**.

Learning Objective 6.2 How does the pace of social change alter relations between generations?

The pace of social, economic, and political changes in society affects the relationships between adolescents and adults. In traditional or **postfigurative cultures,** younger generations learn most of what they need to know from older generations. In **cofigurative cultures,** social change is more rapid and adolescents learn from one another as much as from their elders. In **prefigurative cultures,** very rapid social and technological change means that younger generations have knowledge and skills that their elders need to learn.

Adolescents are strongly influenced in their actions by what their peers do, say, and think.

Learning Objective 6.3 Why distinguish between normative and informational social influence?

In **normative social influence,** teens are affected by others because there is a norm or expectation of doing as others do. In **informational social influence,** they are affected by others because these others seem to have better information about what to do.

Learning Objective 6.4 What roles do peers play as a reference group?

Teens look to their peers, or to a particular subsection of their peers, as a **reference group**. Reference groups provide information about what is normal and expected, offer a baseline for judging one's performance, and serve as a knowledgeable audience. **Social comparison** is the process of using a reference group as a standard to evaluate oneself. **Self-reinforcement** involves feeling good or bad about oneself, depending on how such evaluations come out.

One reason the peer group wields so much social influence during adolescence is the **need to belong**. Teens find a source for a sense of identity in group membership and dread being excluded from the group.

Learning Objective 6.5 What are cross-pressures, and how much of a problem are they?

The influence peers have on adolescents is often seen as clashing with the influence of parents. During early adolescence, conformity to parents' wishes decreases slowly but steadily, while conformity to peers increases and then declines across later adolescence. With the growth of self-confidence and a sense of autonomy, teens become better able to resist pressures to conform both from parents and from peers.

The peer orientation of adolescents is linked to parental style. Teens with warm and accepting parents have better peer relationships. Those whose parents are overly strict often place extreme importance on keeping on good terms with peers. Teens with overly permissive or neglecting parents also tend to look for advice, structure, and support from their peers. **Cross-pressures** arise when the goals and values of parents and peers are at odds. Many teens, however, share their parents' central values and gravitate toward peers with similar orientations.

Social status is measured by looking at how an adolescent is regarded by peers.

Learning Objective 6.6 What are the different categories of social status?

A **social preference** score indicates how often the teen is named as liked, versus how often as disliked. A **social impact** score indicates how often the teen is named as liked *or* disliked. Those who are liked by many and disliked by few are considered **popular** or accepted. Those who are disliked by many and liked by few are considered **rejected**. Those who are neither liked nor disliked are considered **neglected**. Those who are liked by many *and* disliked by many are considered **controversial**. Those who are liked by some and disliked by some are considered **average**. These categories, with the exception of controversial, are fairly stable across adolescence.

Learning Objective 6.7 What is relational aggression and how does it affect popularity?

Some adolescents are considered popular by their peers, without necessarily being well-liked. This has been linked to the use of **relational aggression** as a means to maintain high status.

Learning Objective 6.8 How does the ability to understand others change during adolescence?

Understanding one's peers is a function of **social cognition**, which becomes more mature and effective during adolescence. An important aspect of social cognition is **social perspective taking**, the ability to look at situations from another person's viewpoint. Middle to late adolescents generally reach the most complex level of this ability. *Social information processing*, which involves noticing and interpreting social cues and deciding how to respond to them, becomes more efficient and accurate during adolescence.

Learning Objective 6.9 Who is likely to become a bully or a victim?

Bullying is widespread during childhood and adolescence. It has a negative impact not just on bullies and their victims, but on those who witness harassment as well. Victims of bullying tend to be withdrawn, insecure, and socially isolated, while bullies tend to be aggressive, hostile, domineering, and disliked by peers. Some who are victimized themselves also victimize others. These bully/victims are at particular risk for problem behavior.

Learning Objective 6.10 What can be done to help teens get along better with peers?

Programs that encourage social competence, self-control, conflict avoidance, and other social skills have been found to reduce bullying and help teens get along better with peers.

Social groups take on increased importance during adolescence. Two typical adolescent social groups are the clique and the crowd.

Learning Objective 6.11 What are cliques and how do they change across adolescence?

A **clique** is a small, tightly knit group of friends who are usually similar in age, sex, and social background. Cliques offer adolescents social and emotional support, but also demand conformity to the group's norms.

Learning Objective 6.12 What are crowds and what are some typical crowds in high school?

A **crowd** is a social group that is largely defined by reputation, interests, and activities. Crowds common to most high schools include populars, jocks, brains, druggies, and nerds. Most adolescents identify with their crowd as their primary reference group, evaluate it more positively, and view other crowds more negatively. Schools that are mostly non-White have a similar crowd structure to those that are mostly White. In multi-ethnic schools, there are often crowds that are defined by ethnic background, as well as those defined by reputation and interests.

KEY TERMS

Peer (174)
Age segregation (177)
Generation gap (178)
Postfigurative culture (179)
Cofigurative culture (179)
Prefigurative culture (179)
Youth culture (180)
Conformity (181)

Normative social influence (182)
Informational social influence (182)
Reference group (182)
Social comparison (184)
Self-reinforcement (184)
Need to belong (185)
Cross-pressures (188)

Sociometric techniques (189)
Social preference (189)
Social impact (189)
Popular (190)
Rejected (190)
Neglected (190)
Controversial (190)
Average (190)
Hostile attributional bias (190)

Relational aggression (193)
Social cognition (194)
Social perspective taking (195)
Bullying (196)
Clique (200)
Crowd (202)

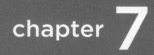

School and Work

Outline	Learning Objectives

The social institution that has the most direct impact on the daily lives of adolescents is school. It is there they spend much of their time, make and meet friends, acquire new skills, and come into contact with the ideas, issues, and concerns of the larger world of adults. For adults, schools are seen as a critical tool for shaping upcoming generations to fit the ideals and changing needs of society. As a result, debates about educational policies—who to teach, what to teach, how to teach—continue today as they have for the last century or more. Should schools be larger, to offer more facilities? Smaller, to offer more intimacy? What about class size? Does it matter enough to devote scarce resources to making classes smaller? And what of the question of middle school versus junior high school? Is there good reason to group the grades one way or another, or is it simply a matter of doing things the way they've always been done?

People often talk about school as if the setting and the experience are similar for all adolescents. Far from it. Schools differ in many significant ways. Some stress how well the best students perform, while others put more emphasis on individual improvement. Some group students by measures of ability, others do not. In some schools, the atmosphere leads students to look forward to Monday mornings, while in others children spend their weekends dreading the week to come. Some schools offer their students a haven from the uncertainties of the outside world, but in others, students are so concerned about getting through the day safely that they have little attention left for anything else.

In this chapter, we look at some of the ways school policy, school transitions, school climate, and school safety affect teens today. We also look at how extracurricular activities and after-school programs help adolescents feel more closely involved in their community of students. More and more adolescents are finishing high school and going on to college. What concerns are raised by this trend? And what of the decreasing, but still important, proportion of adolescents who drop out? What leads them to this course, and what can be done to help them? Finally, whether they are still in school or not, many American teens work. What do we know about the ways employment affects their family, school, and personal life?

ADOLESCENTS AND SCHOOL

American youngsters spend more of their time in school than anywhere else except home. Yet, while the experience is practically universal, the details vary widely. Schools may be big or small, intimate or impersonal, strict or lenient, safe or dangerous. Teachers may be inspiring or boring, brilliant or dull, their students' friends and mentors or their jailers.

The results vary just as widely. Some students catch fire, others have any spark in them extinguished. Some pick up good study habits, others pick up bad drug habits. Some become aware of their own potential, others become convinced that they have none. Some look back on their school years with nostalgic affection, others are amazed that they even made it through. And a substantial number *don't* make it through—alienated, discouraged, or terminally bored, they drop out.

How should we think about all the complicated ways schools affect adolescent development? One useful approach is to see schools as part of an interlocking system with different levels. What happens in an individual classroom matters enormously, as does what happens at the local school board, in the state legislature, in Washington, and even on the world stage. Each of these levels affects students both directly and in combination with other levels (Eccles & Roeser, 2003).

At the most general level, school systems are a vital part of their local communities. These communities, in turn, are embedded in the larger society. Policies, directives, and trends at the state and national level have an impact, direct or indirect, on how the local system is run, as do the attitudes of parents, voters, and local officials. Within school systems, individual schools tend to develop their own character and reputation.

One school may be known for its chorus, another for its test scores in math, and a third for the number and attitude of the hall monitors. The most direct and sustained contact between adolescents and the educational system takes place inside the classroom, with teachers and fellow students. How do teachers see their role? How effective do they feel? What do they expect of their students, academically and socially?

These factors help determine how teens experience and respond to their teachers, their schools, and their education as a whole. In the sections that follow, we will examine these factors more closely.

School Systems and Educational Policy

What should secondary schools teach, and how should they do it? These questions have aroused passionate discussion and disagreement since before the birth of the United States. They are still argued over by educators, social thinkers, political leaders, and ordinary citizens and parents. And of course students and teachers, who are most directly concerned, have their own views about them.

Back in colonial times, Benjamin Franklin criticized the existing Latin grammar schools, which offered a classical education in Greek and Latin to children of the wealthy. In their place, Franklin proposed academies that would teach all worthy students, of any social class, such useful subjects as arithmetic, accounting, navigation, modern languages, and gardening (Krug, 1966). By the time of the Civil War, a century later, over 6,000 academies were in operation, enrolling a quarter of a million boys and girls (Butts, 1978).

Franklin's academies were a pioneering attempt to meet three basic goals of secondary education. Americans expect that high schools will:

prepare graduates to take on their responsibilities as citizens in a free, democratic society;

give all students the skills they need to fill useful roles in the economy and promote the nation's growth; and

provide educational oportunities that will allow individuals to get ahead socially and economically after graduation (Labaree, 1997).

These goals do not always fit together well. If schools focus on individual social mobility, they may create a competitive environment that pushes a few students ahead at the expense of the rest. Responsible citizens need to have a common culture and sense of community, but this may be undermined by the aim to fit students into particular slots in the working world. Should the educational system primarily serve students as individuals or the society as a whole? Who decides what best serves either students or society?

At the beginning of the 20th century, fewer than 5% of adults had a high school degree or the equivalent. By the end of the century, that figure had soared to almost 90% (Snyder & Hoffman, 2002; U.S. Bureau of the Census, 1999). This astonishing shift forced educators and public officials to rethink the mission of high schools time and again.

In the first decades of the 20th century, climbing enrollments and a more diverse student body led educators to embrace the idea of the **comprehensive high school.** Entering high school students were channeled into college prep, vocational, or general education tracks, based on what were assumed to be their future roles in the economy (Preskill, 1989). Critics of this system, such as the philosopher John Dewey, pointed out that too often the real basis of assignment was the wealth and status of a student's parents. Instead, Dewey and his colleagues said that high schools should promote the goal of democratic equality and citizenship by having students of different racial, ethnic, and economic backgrounds study common subjects together, in the same classroom. This approach came to be known as **progressive education** (Krug, 1966).

These contrasting views became the poles in a debate that continued through the rest of the 20th century and is far from over today. Those on one side are alarmed that schools are not giving adolescents what they consider a solid traditional education.

◀ Learning Objective 7.1
How have policy debates shaped secondary education?

Comprehensive high school High schools that try to educate the whole pool of adolescents by placing them in different *tracks* according to their presumed abilities and future economic roles.

Progressive education An approach that saw equality and democratic citizenship as central goals of the educational system.

Those on the other side worry that much of what goes on in school is rote learning that is foreign to the real needs and concerns of adolescents. Over the last 50 years, the seesaw of educational policy has swung now one way, now the other.

In practice, most of the tilt has been toward the traditional side. In the 1950s, the Soviet Union launched the world's first artificial satellite, Sputnik I. Alarmed that their country was falling behind in the "space race," many Americans blamed progressive education and its supposed neglect of science and math. The federal government pushed for a more rigorous science curriculum in high schools. Academically oriented students with an interest in science got a boost from this effort, but many others began to feel overlooked and ignored.

During the 1960s and 1970s, a growing number of adolescents started to call for more relevant education (Church, 1976). Critics urged educators to give students more freedom and respect (Holt, 1964, 1967; Illich, 1971). One author described the typical high school as having "a repressive, almost prison-like atmosphere" (Silberman, 1970, p. 349). Even as some educators tried to come to terms with these criticisms, a report called, *A Nation at Risk* (National Commission on Excellence in Education, 1983) warned of a "rising tide of mediocrity." Scores on the Scholastic Aptitude Test (SAT) were declining steadily. Many high school graduates lacked basic skills. The achievement levels of American students were dismal compared to those of students in other industrialized countries; nor has the situation changed much since the 1980s. Table 7.1 shows some results from more recent international comparisons.

One prescription for these problems that gradually gained powerful support was standards-based education. Instead of focusing on material covered or credits earned, **standards-based education** involves setting statewide or nationwide standards in each basic subject that all students are expected to meet. Regular performance assessments check if the standards are being met, and low-scoring schools and districts are penalized (George & Alexander, 2003). This approach was the inspiration for a far-reaching federal program called *No Child Left Behind* (Bush, 2001).

Critics of the standards-based approach say the combination of high-stakes testing and harsh penalties for failure gives schools a powerful incentive to "teach to the test." Instead of being encouraged to explore a subject, students may be urged to drill and cram the particular information that is likely to be on the test (Diamond, 2007; Kohn,

Standards-based education An approach that sets society-wide educational standards that all schools and students are expected to meet.

Table 7.1 Recent Achievement Scores Around the World
The United States fares poorly in international comparisons of adolescent achievement scores.

Literacy		Advanced Math		Physics	
Finland	546	France	557	Norway	581
Canada	534	Russian Fed.	542	Sweden	573
New Zealand	529	Switzerland	533	Russian Fed.	545
Australia	528	Australia	525	Denmark	534
Ireland	527	Denmark	522	Slovenia	523
United Kingdom	523	Cyprus	518	Germany	522
Sweden	516	Lithuania	516	Australia	518
Austria	507	Greece	513	*Int'l average*	*501*
France	505	Sweden	512	Cyprus	494
Norway	505	Canada	509	Switzerland	488
United States	**504**	*Int'l average*	*501*	Latvia	488
Int'l average	*500*	Slovenia	475	Greece	486
Switzerland	494	Italy	474	Canada	485
Germany	494	Czech Republic	469	France	466
Czech Republic	492	Germany	465	Czech Republic	451
Greece	474	**United States**	**442**	Austria	435
Russian Fed.	462	Austria	436	**United States**	**423**

Source: NCES, 2000, 2002.

2000). Whether standards-based education will bring the benefits its sponsors promise or the problems its critics foresee is still up in the air. What is clear is that this approach currently has widespread support among legislators, parents, and the public.

Supersizing and Downsizing the Schools. In the half century between 1940 and 1990, the population of the United States increased by 70%. During this same period, the number of public schools in the United States *declined* by 69% (Howley, 1994). This dramatic contrast was the result of a steady trend toward consolidating smaller schools and constructing bigger ones, especially at the high school level. Today, high schools with 2,000 to 3,000 students are common. Some of the largest have neared and even passed the 5,000 mark. The same upsizing tendency, on a somewhat smaller scale, is showing up in middle schools as well. Middle schools typically have 900 to 1,400 students, and many have 2,000 or more (George & Alexander, 2003).

The trend toward larger secondary schools got a boost in the 1950s. In an influential book, *The American High School Today* (Conant, 1959), James Bryant Conant, then president of Harvard University, argued that larger high schools with more highly trained teachers would produce more of the scientists the country needed. The case for larger high schools also argues that they use resources better. Every high school needs a cafeteria, library, chemistry lab, gym, and so on. A facility that serves a certain number of students may, for not much more in construction costs, handle two or three times that number.

Larger schools can offer a wider variety of courses, including those on more specialized topics. They also have the resources to offer advanced placement courses that carry college credit. In many areas, the local high school is also a socially important center of the community. Faced with a choice of expanding it or creating a new high school that lacks its history and school spirit, parents and community leaders often opt for supersizing (Gregory, 2000).

Advantages of Smaller Schools. Those who favor smaller schools point out that students in small high schools are more likely to get personalized attention from a teacher or mentor (Elder & Conger, 2000). In smaller schools, somebody knows who the students are. The result is that students feel less alienated (Fine & Somerville, 1998), and this helps them become more attached to the school and to their teachers (Crosnoe, Johnson, & Elder, 2004). Parents are also more enthusiastic about small schools. They say teachers are more likely to help struggling students and that they themselves feel closer to the school community (Public Agenda, 2002).

Smaller schools are safer schools. Students are much less likely to be victims of theft and violence, and their schools are less likely to impose invasive security measures, such as metal detectors and drug sweeps (Kaufmann et al., 2000). Smaller high schools have academic advantages, too. Attendance and passing rates are higher, and dropout rates are lower, than in large high schools (Stiefel, Latarola, Fruchter, & Berne, 1998; Wasley et al., 2000). Students in smaller high schools also have higher grades and achievement test scores, even after individual and family backgrounds are taken into account (Elder & Conger, 2000; La Sage & Ye, 2000). What's more, studies indicate that attending a smaller high school has an especially positive effect on achievement for ethnic minority students and those from low-income families (Cotton, 2001; Howley & Bickel, 2000; Lee & Smith, 1997; Raywid, 1997).

Even some apparent advantages of bigness are not always what they seem. A large high school may have many more clubs, interest groups, sports teams, and student publications; however, students in small high schools are much more likely to *take part* in extracurricular activities (Barker & Gump, 1964; Crosnoe et al., 2004; McNeal, 1999). This is especially true for students who aren't doing that well in school. In big schools, they are more likely to watch from the sidelines, instead of getting involved.

One reason for this is simple probability. Take a senior yearbook. It needs only one editor-in-chief, whether the senior class has 150 students or 1,500. This makes a student's chances of becoming editor-in-chief 10 times greater in the smaller school.

Connect the **Dots...**

Was the high school you attended small, medium, large, or supersize? Make lists of things you liked and disliked about your school experience that had a connection to the size of the school. How did your experiences compare with the factors discussed in this section of the chapter?

And while the yearbook in a big school may have a bigger staff, it is unlikely to have 10 times the number of staffers. The same holds for the soccer team, band, dramatics association, and boosters club. This is important because students who are active in extracurricular activities develop a stronger sense of connection to their school (Elder & Conger, 2000; McNeely, Nonnemaker, & Blum, 2002).

How small is small? Some experts conclude that 400 to 900 students is the best size (Lee & Smith, 1997, 2001; Williams, 1990). They also point out that downsizing in itself is not a recipe for instant success—what matters is the climate that is created. Ideally, students, teachers, and administrators in smaller schools come to know and care about one another more than is possible in large schools. Parents are more likely to know the principal and teachers, to keep track of how their children are doing, and to take part in school activities. The resulting sense of community gives students a feeling of control, influence, and efficacy that leads them to take greater personal responsibility for their learning.

Class Size. Even though researchers have concluded that reducing school size is enormously important, this message has not gotten through to most parents or teachers (Johnson, 2002). Instead, members of the public, like government officials, have focused their attention on reducing *class* size. More than half the states in the United States, along with countless individual school districts, have started programs to reduce class size (Finn, 2002). Calls for smaller classes are heard in other countries as well, including Canada, Australia, and Britain.

One reason this idea has so much appeal is that it is easy to grasp. Teachers, like the rest of us, have only a limited amount of attention and energy. If they divide it fairly, then the smaller the class, the more individual attention each student will receive. Smaller classes are also reputed to have less noise and disruptive behavior, which allows teachers to encourage more discussion and other positive interactions among students (Ehrenberg, Brewer, Gamoran, & Willms, 2001). The conclusion seems obvious: children in smaller classes should do better in school—but do they?

One ambitious attempt to answer this question experimentally was Tennessee's Project STAR (Student-Teacher Achievement Ratio), carried out in the 1980s (Mosteller, Light, & Sachs, 1996). Children entering kindergarten were randomly assigned to a small class of 13 to 17 students, a regular-size class of 22 to 26, or a regular-size class with both a teacher and a teacher's aide. Whichever type class they were assigned to, they stayed in through 3rd grade. Then in 4th grade, all the children went into regular classrooms.

The results were impressive. Children who were assigned to small classes did better every year in every subject. These benefits were particularly strong for minority and inner-city students, which narrowed the usual achievement gap between Whites and minorities. In follow-up studies, the gains continued after the students moved into full-size classes. Even in 8th grade, those who had been in the small classes were as much as half a school year ahead of their schoolmates in both reading and mathematics (Finn, Gerber, Achilles, & Boyd-Zaharias, 2001). So smaller classes do make a difference, at least in the early grades. What about later on?

No one has yet tried the experimental approach of Project STAR with adolescents, but studies have looked at how class size relates to school achievement in the higher grades. In general, the studies find very little difference between high school classes with 25 students and those with up to 35 (Bennett, 1998; Goldstein, Yang, Omar, Turner, & Thompson, 2000; Rutter & Maughan, 2002). The reason seems to be that classes of 25 and 35 are run pretty much alike. The teacher lectures, asks students questions, and gives written work to the whole group. Reducing the class to 23 (or enlarging it to 32) does not do much to alter the classroom dynamic.

This suggests that smaller classes can make a difference, but only if they are small enough to allow a different approach to teaching and learning. Take a senior seminar with eight or ten students. In a way, it shares some important features with kindergarten, where we know class size makes a difference. It is a small group, its functioning depends on the personal relationships among the participants, and the members

◄ Smaller seminar-like classes allow a different approach to teaching and learning.

are engaged in individual hands-on projects (Ehrenberg et al., 2001). Maybe instead of trying to reduce high school classes from, say, 30 to 22, school officials should consider leaving most of the classes at 30 and using the money saved to give every student a chance to take part in a small learning group as well.

Moving from Grade to Grade. How should school systems organize the 12 years of schooling from 1st grade to 12th grade? In particular, what should they do with adolescents? Over the years, several approaches have been tried. The reasons for them range from historical accident to educational theory to administrative convenience. More recently, social scientists have contributed the findings of empirical research to this ongoing discussion.

In 19th and early 20th century America, many students finished their education with the 8th grade, the last of what was called primary school. Some then went on to 4 years of secondary or high school, either to gain a high school diploma and enter the workforce or to prepare for college. This created what is called the 8–4 system: 8 years of primary schooling followed by 4 years of secondary education (Pulliam & Van Patten, 1995).

In the 1920s, educational theorists began pushing for separate schools based on the special needs of young adolescents. They proposed combining grades 7 and 8 from the primary school and grade 9 from the high school to create a **junior high school.** This helped with some practical problems, too. As the population expanded and secondary education became more compulsory, school enrollments soared. Hard-pressed officials realized that expanding the existing 8–4 system would mean building new elementary schools *and* new high schools. By establishing a junior high school, they could make do with only one new institution (George & Alexander, 2003).

By the middle of the 20th century, the great majority of students in the United States were in a 6–3–3 system: 6 years of elementary school, 3 years of junior high, and 3 years of high school, but even as this approach won out, dissatisfaction with it grew. One criticism was that junior high schools were too much like high schools. Teachers who were organized by subjects didn't get to know their students well. The abrupt shift from the self-contained elementary school classroom to ever-changing teachers and groups of classmates set students adrift and led to adjustment problems.

Critics also argued that 7th and 8th graders were physically, socially, and psychologically more like 6th graders than 9th graders. As a solution, they proposed to give 9th grade back to high school and create a **middle school** that included grades 6

Junior high school Typically, a school that includes grades 7, 8, and 9, intended to meet the special needs of young adolescents and be a bridge between elementary and high schools.

Middle school A school that typically includes grades 6, 7, and 8, and that has become more common than junior high school in recent years.

Table 7.2 How Do Middle Schools Stand Apart?
Middle schools differ in many ways from both elementary and high schools.

Aspect	Elementary School	Middle School	High School
Student-teacher relationship	Parental	Advisor	Choice
Teacher organization	Self-contained	Interdisciplinary team	Department
Curricular goals	Skills	Exploratory	Depth
Schedule	Self-contained	Block	Periods
Instruction	Teacher-directed	Diverse	Student-directed
Student grouping	Grade level	Supportive	Subject
Organization	Single classroom	Team or house	Department
Teacher preparation	Child-oriented generalist	Flexible resource	Academic specialist

Source: Table "How Do Middle Schools Stand Apart?" in *The Exemplary Middle School*, 3/e, by P.S. George and W.M. Alexander. © 2003 by Wadsworth. Used by permission.

through 8 (Eichhorn, 1966). Middle schools were intended to be different from either elementary or high school in ways that are described in Table 7.2.

From a handful of schools in the 1960s, middle schools, and the 5-3-4 system they are part of, spread dramatically. By the beginning of the 21st century, they had become the most common form of early secondary education in the United States (George & Alexander, 2003).

Surviving School Transitions. Any sort of transition can pose a risk of uncertainty and stress. Whether you are moving to a new town, going from elementary to middle school, or leaving college for the working world, you are probably wondering exactly what the change will mean. You may find the prospect exciting, but you may also worry that it could turn out badly.

For those who make the transition from elementary to middle or junior high school, there is also the pain of what can be called the "small frog in a large pond syndrome." Back in June, they were at the top of the heap, the biggest, oldest, and most prestigious kids in their school. Now, just 2 months later, they find themselves demoted to lowest of the low, clueless newbies in an expanded world of blooming, buzzing confusion. For many, the stress of this transition is piled on top of the physical, psychological, and social stresses of puberty. In the words of one 6th grader, "Being in middle school is just like a bird being kicked out of its nest by its mother" (Gootman, 2007, p. A1).

▶ Middle school students are at an age when issues of identity and self-concept become more pressing.

The new school environment may also clash with the changing social and cognitive abilities of young adolescents (Eccles & Roeser, 2003). Just when they could use some guidance and support from adults, their teachers see their role more as teaching course content. At a time when students are becoming better able to reason, consider alternatives, and make choices for themselves, their teachers are putting more emphasis on classroom control and discipline (Feldlaufer, Midgley, & Eccles, 1988). At an age when self-concept and questions of identity are coming to the fore, teachers place less focus on mastering tasks and more on competition, relative ability, and social comparison (Midgely, Anderman, & Hicks, 1995).

One result is that school grades and achievement scores go down from the last year of elementary school to the first year of middle or junior high school (Alspaugh, 1998; Seidman, Allen, Aber, Mitchell, & Feinman, 1994; Simmons & Blyth, 1987). Also, interest in school goes down (Eccles et al., 1993) and school-related anxiety goes up (Wigfield & Eccles, 1989).

What about the move into high school? Although not that many studies have focused on this shift, it seems to amplify problems as much as the earlier one (Barber & Olsen, 2004; Benner & Graham, 2007; Lee & Smith, 2001). The average high school is, if anything, more bureaucratic, intimidating, and impersonal than middle school, especially for new students. Students and teachers do not have many chances to get to know each other. As a result, they tend to distrust one another (Eccles & Roeser, 2003). Students evaluate the school environment more negatively and have a weaker sense of belonging (Barber & Olsen, 2004; Benner & Graham, 2007). As they get accustomed to the new setting, many of them recover. For those who were having difficulties before, however, the added stresses may be more than they can handle, and they may drop out (Alspaugh, 2000; Fine, 1991).

One way to reduce the problems brought on by school transitions might be to cut down on the number of transitions students have to make. In other words, to go back to an 8-4 system. Children would stay in elementary school through 8th grade, then go directly into high school. Studies have found that students in such a system have better feelings about themselves and about their connection to school than those who shift first to middle or junior high school, then later to high school (Eccles et al., 1997; Seidman et al., 1994; Simmons & Blyth, 1987). Students in an 8-4 system have fewer changes to adjust to, and when the transition does come, most of them will have already dealt with the stresses of puberty. Ironically, today's research suggests that the educators of 100 years ago may have had the right idea about how to organize schooling for adolescents (Seidman, Aber, & French, 2003).

In School

While policies at the level of the community, the state, and the nation have profound effects on the education of adolescents, so does the way their particular school functions. The actions and attitudes of administrators, teachers, and students help create an atmosphere that encourages or discourages an individual's desire to learn, sense of belonging, and positive development. Among the particular factors that make a difference are the kinds of goals that are stressed, the ways students are channeled into different classes, and the psychological climate of the school. What are the students like? Are they motivated to learn? Do they feel safe at school and on the way to and from school?

Performance and Mastery. A basic goal of schools is to get students to learn—but how? One traditional and widespread approach is to single out those students who perform best for special attention. The hope is that rewarding good students will encourage others to emulate them. Many schools print the names of those who make the honor roll in the school newspaper or stage a special honor assembly at the end of the year. Some schools compile class rankings and cite them on a student's report card,

Connect the Dots...

Short of reorganizing the school system, as the last paragraph suggests, can you think of steps that might be taken to help adolescents cope with the stresses of school transitions? What would it take to implement them?

◄ **Learning Objective 7.2**
What are the effects of school climate and school membership?

and the very top students may be singled out at graduation as the class valedictorian and salutatorian.

According to psychologists who study the impact of different educational practices, this approach creates a school-wide environment that affects what students think about themselves as well as how they act (Eccles, 2004; Maehr & Midgley, 1996; Roeser, Midgley, & Urdan, 1996). The emphasis on who is smarter than whom and who gets higher grades generates an ability-goal or **performance orientation** (Anderman & Anderman, 1999)—that is, students focus on success and interpret their outcomes as reflecting their ability or lack of ability. Because even a teen whose grade point average is a remarkable 3.85 will be overshadowed by one who gets a 3.9 or 4.0, the system creates a tiny handful of winners and a huge majority of losers.

In contrast, schools that reward academic effort and improvement and downplay competition and social comparison encourage a task-goal or **mastery orientation** (Anderman & Anderman, 1999). Practices such as cooperative learning, in which groups of students investigate problems and present their conclusions to the rest of the class, promote a focus on learning and mastering a task, as opposed to simply doing well or getting the right answer (Marzano, Pickering, & Pollock, 2001). As a result, students not only learn more, but come away with a stronger sense of personal efficacy and a deeper interest in the subject matter (Nichols, 1996).

The orientation of the school, toward performance or mastery, makes a difference (Urdan & Schoenfelder, 2006). Students who see their school as performance oriented have lower educational values, achievement, and self-esteem (Meece, Anderman, & Anderman, 2006). They are also more likely to show anger, depression, truancy, and delinquency (Eccles, 2004; Fiqueira-McDonough, 1986; Roeser & Eccles, 1998). If the orientation shifts from mastery to performance across grade levels or school transitions, both motivation and achievement suffer (Urdan & Midgley, 2003). In Chapter 9, we will look more closely at these two orientations and why they have such different effects on adolescents.

On and Off the Track. In most American secondary schools, students are assigned to harder or easier classes and class sequences. These assignments are based on such criteria as previous grades, perceived ability, and teacher recommendations. Some students end up taking mostly honors courses, others non-honors college prep courses, and still others vocational or general courses. Until the late 1960s, this sorting process usually took the form of **tracking**.

Most high schools assigned students to a particular track when they entered and expected them to stay in that track. If you were placed in the vocational track as a freshman, you knew you would be taking vocational courses for the next 4 years. This system was widely criticized as promoting social inequality, in part because it was so rigid. Once students were placed in a lower track, it was rare for them to manage to change to a higher track (Dornbusch, 1994).

In response to this criticism, most high schools have abandoned formal tracks. Instead, individual courses are labeled as honors, basic, remedial, and so on. In principle, a student may take an honors history course, a general English course, and remedial math. A few do. Most, however, end up mostly in courses at a particular level. Formal tracks may have faded, but students and institutions still follow their traces (Lucas, 1999).

The main educational argument for this ability grouping is that students are more motivated to learn when they study material that fits with their level of accomplishment. For students who get placed in gifted or high-ability groups, this may be so (Fuligni, Eccles, & Barber, 1995; Pallas, Entwisle, Alexander, & Stluka, 1994). Those assigned to low-ability and non-college classes, however, have lower school achievement and involvement, even when their initial ability levels are taken into account (Bennett & LeCompte, 1990). These students are also at greater risk for a variety of problems, including school misconduct, substance use, and delinquency (Oakes, Gamaron, & Page, 1992).

Performance orientation A focus on competitive success and a tendency to interpret outcomes as a sign of ability or lack of ability. Also called ability-goal orientation.

Mastery orientation A focus on learning and mastering tasks and on personal improvement. Also called task-goal orientation,

Tracking The practice, now less common, of assigning students to a particular curriculum or set of courses on the basis of their presumed abilities.

Why is ability grouping linked to negative effects for those in the lower ability tracks? One reason is that these students generally do not get as good an educational experience. More experienced teachers prefer to teach more advanced classes, and they teach them with an expectation that their students will do well (Eccles & Roeser, 2003). Teachers whose students have already been labeled as low in ability, however, tend to hold lower expectations and set lower goals. The system also affects the kinds of friends an adolescent makes (Crosnoe, 2002). In effect, it collects students with achievement or adjustment problems in one place, where they are more likely to influence one another in a negative direction (Dishion, McCord, & Poulin, 1999).

A further problem is that minority youth, particularly Hispanic and African American boys, are more likely to be placed in low-ability and non-college-prep courses (Oakes et al., 1992). In many cases, these placements are incorrect, even by the criteria of the system (Dornbusch, 1994). Middle-class parents whose children have been assigned to lower-level classes are likely to realize what a disaster this may turn out to be. They are also more likely to know how to buck the system and get their children reassigned to higher-level courses. Meanwhile, the children of poor and minority parents, who do not know their way around the education bureaucracy, are kept in the less-demanding classes. In this way, the system tends to reinforce existing inequalities.

The Role of School Climate. As we have just seen, the kind of goal orientation a school fosters has an important impact on its students. Whether or not the school makes wide use of ability grouping also matters. On a more general level, both of these contribute to a general atmosphere or **school climate**. What is it like to attend? Do students take their work seriously? Do they expect to be able to learn? Do they find their classes involving? Do they think of their teachers as sources of support? Not surprisingly, the answers to questions of this sort play a big role in determining how strongly students connect to the school and how well they learn (Eccles & Roeser, 2003; Haynes, Emmons, & Ben Avie, 1997; Rutter, 1983). A positive school climate can also help protect vulnerable youngsters from developing psychological problems (Kuperminc, Leadbetter, & Blatta, 2001).

A great many elements help create a positive school climate, including:

strong leadership;

a staff with shared vision and goals;

an attractive and safe working environment;

clear and fair rules about order and discipline;

clear curricular goals;

positive expectations for achievement;

constructive, nurturing feedback;

involvement of students in taking responsibilities;

respectful and democratic student-teacher interactions; and

opportunities for all students to participate in school activities

(ECCLES, 2004; RUTTER & MAUGHAN, 2002; VIENO, PERKINS, SMITH, & SANTINELLO, 2005).

We can sort most of the items on this list into two broader categories: *demandingness* and *responsiveness*. Students in a demanding school understand that they are expected to perform up to their potential and to show self-reliance and self-control. In a responsive school, they believe that the teachers and staff respect their opinions and feelings, take them seriously, and want to involve them in the life of the school (Bateman, 2002).

The dimensions of demandingness and responsiveness ought to sound familiar. We introduced these terms earlier, in Chapter 5, when we looked at ways to describe effective parenting (Baumrind, 1978, 1991). The same pattern that is most effective for parents is most effective for schools, too. Like authoritative parents, a school that is both

School climate The general learning atmosphere in a school, including attitudes of students and staff, order and discipline, and student participation.

demanding and responsive works well. Its students behave better, are more motivated, and achieve more (Wentzel, 2002).

Some schools, however, make discipline the top priority, without giving much consideration to the needs and opinions of students. Because these schools are demanding but not responsive, they are more like authoritarian parents. Still other schools, which lack leadership, clear goals, and organization, resemble indulgent or indifferent parents. Just as these styles of parenting are linked to less favorable outcomes for children, so these types of schools are linked to less favorable outcomes for their students (Wentzel, 2002).

The concept of *stage-environment fit* (Eccles et al., 1993) can help us understand how school climate affects students. How well does the structure of a child's environment match the child's level of development? Does the environment adjust as the child develops? Authoritative parents, as we know, strive to give their children privileges and responsibilities that are appropriate to their stage of development and individual personality. These change, of course, as the child becomes more mature. In a similar way, effective schools adapt their curriculum, teaching style, and modes of control, not just to student needs and areas of competence, but to the ways those needs and competencies change as students get older.

How might this work in practice? In adolescence, students become more able to reason abstractly and think about hypothetical situations. A teaching approach that calls on these developing abilities is more likely to get them involved than one that focuses on storing up information (Anderman, Maehr, & Midgley, 1999). Adolescence is also a time when the ability to weigh various factors and make careful, mature decisions is developing. By giving students more say about what courses they take and how they organize their academic work, the school can acknowledge these developments, as well as respect their growing need for autonomy. When students feel the school promotes their personal autonomy and competence, they become more engaged and they achieve more (Zimmer-Gembeck, Chipuer, Hanisch, Creed, & McGregor, 2006).

Connectedness. Most of the research on effective schools has focused on student achievement—grades, test scores, and the like (Anderman, 2002). This is not surprising. Education is, after all, the primary job of the school system. If schools cannot manage to develop intellectual skills and pass along knowledge, they waste the time of their students and the resources of society. Wisely or not, the usual measures of success are such statistics as graduation rates, test scores, and grade point averages.

In recent years, researchers have started to look at how schools can foster the mental health of students, as well as their academic achievement. This is a worthwhile goal in itself, and it also contributes to student performance (Wenglinsky, 2002). One factor that makes a big difference is how much teens have a sense of **school membership** (Smerdon, 2002). Do they believe the teachers and staff care about them? Do they feel connected to the school? To their fellow students? Are they committed to the school and to their academic work?

Adolescents who can answer these questions with a "Yes" come out ahead on a number of measures of mental health. These students earn higher grades and have a lower risk of developing psychological problems (Anderman & Freeman, 2004; Lohman & Newman, 2002). They are less likely to use substances, engage in violence, or get involved in sexual activity at an early age (Anderman, 2002; McNeely, Nonnemaker, & Blum, 2002). They are less likely to drop out of school (Crosnoe, Erickson, & Dornbusch, 2002). Moreover, the positive effects are found across different ethnic groups (Faircloth & Hamm, 2005; Sirin & Rogers-Sirin, 2005).

Why does membership have such a powerful impact? The need to belong may well be a universal human motivation (Baumeister & Leary, 1995; Deci, Vallerland, Pelletier, & Ryan, 1991; Newman & Newman, 2001). In any social setting, people are driven to establish and maintain positive social relationships with those around them. If they succeed, they feel they belong—they are members in good standing. Because

School membership The sense that students have of being connected and committed to their school and its positive functioning.

they feel they belong, they tend to have positive attitudes about the group, its activities, and those who are part of it (Festinger, 1957). If they fail to achieve positive social relationships, however, the result is alienation from both the setting and the people they associate with it. It is an easy step from, "My teacher doesn't like me" to "I hate school!"

Several attributes of schools have been linked to school membership or connectedness. When teachers are empathic, supportive, and consistent, and when they encourage self-management, the students develop a stronger feeling of being part of the school and learn better (DeGroot, 1997). Disciplinary policies matter, too. The harsher the discipline, the less students feel connected to the school (McNeely et al., 2002). At schools that practice "zero-tolerance," imposing harsh penalties such as expulsion for a first offense, students have an especially low sense of membership.

School size and participation rates in extracurricular activities make a difference. On average, students in smaller schools feel more attached to their schools than those in larger schools (Lee & Smith, 1997; McNeely et al., 2002), as do those who take part in school clubs, teams, and organizations (Elder & Conger, 2000). These two factors are connected, but each makes its own separate contribution. As we saw earlier in this chapter, students in smaller schools are more likely to take part in school activities, and teachers in smaller schools are more likely to develop warm, supportive relationships with their students. This generates the sort of classroom climate that fosters a sense of school membership.

The age and grade level of students also affect their connectedness to school. As students get older and move through the system, they become less and less likely to feel cared for, respected, and valued by their schools (Benson, Scales, Leffert, & Roehlkpartain, 1999; Larson, 2000; Whitlock, 2002). By the time they are seniors, they are often skeptical and even cynical about their relationship to school as an institution (Whitlock, 2002). This "senioritis" often shows up in the form of frustration, power struggles over school rules, and disengagement. As Figure 7.1 illustrates, over the last couple of decades, 12th graders have found school increasingly less interesting, meaningful, and important to their futures (NCES, 2002).

Classmates and Friends. In the last chapter, we looked at some of the many ways adolescents are influenced by their peers and friends. Not surprisingly, their attitudes

Figure 7.1   Twelfth-Graders' Interest in School
Interest in school among 12th-graders has declined steadily in recent decades.

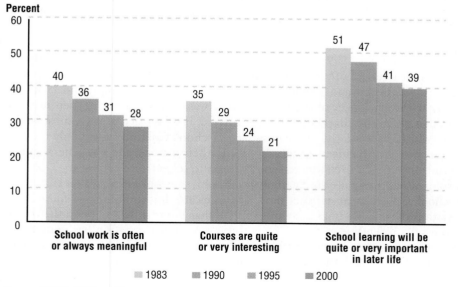

Source: NCES, 2002, p. 72.

toward school and education are strongly affected by their schoolmates. If they attend a school where most teens have high educational aspirations, they are likely to be more engaged in school and to have more positive self-concepts (Murdock, Anderman, & Hodge, 2000). If their friends are motivated to succeed in school, they tend to be motivated, too (Kindermann, McCollam, & Gibson, 1996; Ryan, 2001).

The attitudes of schoolmates can also have a negative influence. In schools where a high proportion of students have low motivation and dislike school, they reinforce these attitudes in the rest of their classmates (Dishion et al., 1999). These students also affect the general climate or culture of the school. When many students misbehave, oppose teacher authority, and hold antisocial attitudes, this creates a social norm. The cool kid is the one who acts up and gets away with it (Rodkin, 2004). In response, teachers and school officials give top priority to discipline and control. This in turn makes students feel more estranged and less like members of a caring community.

When teachers are constantly forced to deal with disruption, they cannot possibly do as good a job of teaching because they are too busy trying to stay in charge. Their students lose out, and so do they. The constant stress leads to rapid burn-out. As a result, experienced teachers tend to transfer out of such high-maintenance schools or avoid them in the first place. This means that students who most need the help and encouragement of a skilled teacher are often taught by new, inexperienced, and sometimes unqualified instructors (Hughes, 2002).

A classic study of an inner-city high school offers a striking description of peer influence (Fordham & Ogbu, 1986). The researchers found that African American males put pressure on one another *not* to succeed in school. The explanation was that they saw formal education as an enterprise imposed on minorities by the dominant White majority. Doing well in school was interpreted as rejecting their ethnic identity by "acting White."

Many educators and social scientists believe that this social pressure not to succeed helps explain the lower school achievement of minority students (Roscigno, 2000). However, this explanation remains controversial. Peers do have an impact on engagement and achievement in school, but so do neighborhoods, families, and the schools themselves (Cook, Herman, Phillips, & Settersten, 2002). Teachers, too, often expect lower achievement and more disruption from minority males (Crozier, 2005; Diamond, Randolph, & Spillane, 2004). As well as harmful, this stereotype may be simply wrong. Some studies find that, far from being less engaged than Whites or Hispanics, African American students are more engaged and report trying harder in school (Ainsworth-Darnell & Downey, 1998; Johnson, Crosnoe, & Elder, 2001).

Safety in School. In 1999, two students at Columbine High School in Littleton, Colorado, murdered 12 other students and a teacher, and then turned their guns on themselves. Americans, and people throughout the world, were deeply shocked. One especially troubling aspect of the terrible event was that it did not happen in some gang-ridden inner-city Blackboard Jungle. Instead, it took place in what most would have described as an orderly, well-run suburban school. Columbine was only the first of a series of violent incidents at schools. Teens, their parents, and the general public began to worry. Was it even safe to send children to school?

In some ways, the answer is clearly that school is safe—or at least, safer than away from school. Government statistics show that teens are almost three times more likely to be victims of violent crimes away from school than either at school or on the way to and from school (DeVoe et al., 2002), and the rate of victimization has gone down sharply in recent years. Between 1992 and 2003, the rate of violent crime at school decreased by 42%, and the crime rate away from school also dropped (NCES, 2006).

Figure 7.2   Percentage of High School Students Carrying Weapons to School
Percentage of students in grades 9–12 who reported recently carrying a weapon to school, by race or ethnicity.

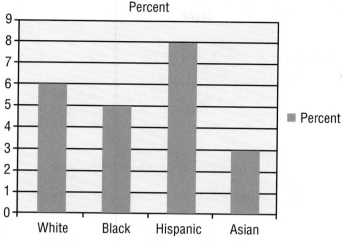

Percent

■ Percent

White   Black   Hispanic   Asian

Source: NCES 2006.

On the other hand, weapons such as guns, knives, and clubs are still all too common in school. In 2005, 6% of high school students admitted bringing a weapon to school at least once in the previous 30 days. This is a sizable drop from the 1993 figure of 12%, but it still represents more than 1 of every 20 students. Males were almost four times as likely to bring a weapon to school as females—in 2005, 10% versus less than 3% (Dinkes, Cataldi, Kena, & Baum, 2006). The proportions for most ethnic groups were basically similar, as Figure 7.2 shows.

Students who carry weapons often say they do so for self-protection (Sheley & Wright, 1998). However, when children are armed, even minor disputes can easily escalate into violence. In 2001, almost 1 in 10 high school students said they had been threatened or injured with a weapon at school (DeVoe et al., 2002). Here, too, there was a big gender difference: 12% of males reported being threatened or injured in the previous year, compared to 7% of females. Some 6% of students say they are afraid of being attacked at school and that they stay away from some school activities as a result (Dinkes et al., 2006).

Students are not the only ones who are victims of violence in school. During the 2003–2004 school year, over 250,000 teachers were threatened with injury by a student, and 130,000 were physically attacked by a student (Dinkes et al., 2006).

Educators, social scientists, and public officials agree that making schools safe for learning is a high-priority task. There is less agreement on how to carry it out. Security measures often include metal detectors, locker checks, security cameras, security guards or police officers, adult supervision in hallways, and badges or picture identification for students (Dinkes et al., 2006). However, research suggests that aggressive use of such measures can alienate students, increase distrust and misbehavior, and disrupt the school environment by interfering with learning (Beger, 2003). Research also indicates that for middle-school students, those in classes and schools that are more ethnically diverse feel safer and less likely to be harassed by peers (Juvonen, Nishina, & Graham, 2006).

One controversial measure, already mentioned, is a policy of "zero tolerance." A student who is found with a weapon at school is automatically suspended or expelled, no matter what the circumstances. One strike and you're out. This approach does relieve school officials of the burden of making judgments that may be second guessed or attacked as discriminatory, but it can also lead to absurd results, such as the incident described in the newspaper article on page 224. As a result, lawmakers in several states have backed away from such inflexible rules.

▲ Many adolescents are haunted by the fear that a violent incident could take place at their own school.

Sharp Calculator Leads To Student's Suspension

Blade Inside Broke Zero-Tolerance Rule

by Joe Humphrey

BRANDON—Angela Saffold's calculator can't help her figure the Hillsborough County school district's zero-tolerance policy on weapons.

It just doesn't add up, she said.

Her 13-year-old son, Burns Middle School sixth-grader Cortez Curtis, is serving a 10-day suspension for taking his mother's calculator to school. Hidden within the James Bond-esque calculator are tools such as a screwdriver, a magnifying glass and—the contraband that led to his suspension and arrest on felony weapons possession—a 2-inch knife blade.

Curtis was not brandishing the weapon or threatening a classmate.

"That would be something totally different," Saffold said, acknowledging those would be legitimate grounds for discipline.

But she said the punishment is too severe for just taking the calculator to school Friday.

"He didn't do anything wrong," Saffold said. "He didn't threaten anybody."

District policy is clear: Weapons are weapons. Whether butter knife or machete, 2 inches or 2 feet, policy dictates an automatic 10-day suspension. Curtis also might be permanently banished from Burns, as the policy also suggests placement in an alternative school or possible expulsion.

"That's what zero-tolerance means," said district spokesman Mark Hart.

Superintendent Earl Lennard would not address any specific situation, but he said state and federal mandates require the district to apply a zero-tolerance approach in dealing with weapons possession. He said the district tries to use "common sense."

Saffold said she bought the calculator at a roadside stand for about $5. Curtis asked to borrow it the night of March 5 to do homework. He took it to school Friday without Saffold's knowledge, she said, and when he dropped the calculator, the knife blade was exposed.

Curtis said he put the knife back inside the calculator, but another student had told the teacher. She asked Curtis for the calculator but could not find the knife until he showed it to her.

She reported him to administrators, triggering the suspension, arrest and a trip to juvenile detention.

"It's a shame, but the way things have been in our society," said sheriff's Deputy Jeff Massaro, the school resource deputy. "The bottom line is he had a weapon."

SOURCE: "SHARP CALCULATOR LEADS TO STUDENTS' SUSPENSION: BLADE INSIDE BROKE ZERO-TOLERANCE RULE," BY JOE HUMPHREY. *THE TAMPA (FL) TRIBUNE*, MARCH 12, 2003. USED BY PERMISSION.

In Class

▶ **Learning Objective 7.3**
How do teacher expectations affect students?

The general climate of a school matters a lot, but in the end the classroom is the place where education really happens or doesn't happen. In class, students become engaged or disengaged in learning. They relate, positively or negatively, to their teacher and classmates. As a result of their classroom experiences, their sense of themselves as competent becomes stronger or weaker.

The experiences, motivations, and aptitudes students bring with them at the start of the school year are of enormous importance. Once in class, however, the teacher's beliefs, attitudes, and practices have as much impact on learning as the students' backgrounds (Wenglinsky, 2002). A good teacher can help students overcome huge difficulties. An ineffective teacher can magically transform eager interest into resentful boredom.

In this section, we look at teachers in the classroom from three angles. What do teachers think about themselves? What do they think about their students? And how do they interact with their students (Eccles, 2004)?

Teachers and Efficacy. Many teachers feel confident that they have the knowledge and skills they need to help their students advance. Many others have doubts about their ability to accomplish their goals in the classroom. These differences in teachers' sense of personal efficacy (Bandura, 2006) have an impact on how their students perform, behave, and feel about themselves, the teacher, and school in general (Lee & Smith, 2001; Roeser, Eccles, & Sameroff, 1998).

Teachers who have a strong sense of efficacy believe they can reach even the most difficult students. They are sure they can make a difference in their students' lives. As a result of these beliefs, they put more effort into their relationships with students and persevere longer when their efforts do not pay off right away. They communicate their high expectations to their students, which builds up their students' confidence that they have what it takes to succeed if they only try hard enough (Eccles, 2004).

On the other hand, teachers who have little confidence in their ability to be effective may communicate low expectations to their students and give up quickly in the face of difficulty. This strengthens student feelings of incompetence and alienation. These feelings, in turn, reinforce the teacher's lack of confidence (Roeser, Eccles, & Freedman-Doan, 1999).

Both the positive and negative effects of teacher efficacy are examples of a self-fulfilling prophecy (Merton, 1948). This occurs when people's expectations (the prophecy part) lead them to act in ways that make what they expect more likely to happen (the self-fulfilling part). Say I have to cross a brook by walking a narrow log. If I'm sure I'll fall, I may become more hesitant in my movements. This in turn may make it more likely that I will fall. What I prophesized has come to pass, not through a miracle, but as a result of my own actions.

How might this process work in the classroom? Suppose a student makes a comment or asks a question that is interesting but a bit off topic. Teachers who are confident about their knowledge and teaching skills will be comfortable following the question where it leads or explaining why they'd rather deal with it later. The result is that the student feels competent and acknowledged. Teachers who lack confidence, however, may be so rattled by a question they feel unable to handle that they squelch it. They may even leave the student with the impression that it was a stupid question. As a result, the student feels angry, disengaged, and helpless (Roeser et al., 1999).

Compared to elementary school teachers, junior high and middle school teachers generally have less confidence in their teaching efficacy (Midgley, Feldlaufer, & Eccles, 1989). One reason for this is that many of them accept the widely held stereotype that young adolescents are less teachable because of their "raging hormones." Instead of meeting difficulties with an increased effort, they may shrug them off as unavoidable. Secondary school teachers also tend to pull back from getting involved with their students' social and emotional problems, just at a time when teens have an increasing need of adult support and guidance (Roeser & Midgley, 1997; Simmons & Blyth, 1987).

Differential Expectations. Teachers with a strong or weak sense of efficacy have an impact on everyone in their classes, because of the expectations they hold about their own effectiveness. Another influential factor is the expectations teachers hold about different students in their classes (Wentzel, 2002). This child is smart, that one is not so smart, this one is a cut-up, that one is a model student, and so on. These expectations may then lead teachers to treat students differently without even realizing they are doing it.

Let's say a teacher is calling on individual students with questions. When a "bright" student fails to give the right answer, the teacher may pause and probe. When a "dull" student doesn't answer, however, the teacher is likely to move on quickly to someone else. The message to the first student is that trying harder will lead to success.

The message to the second student is that there is little hope (Dweck & Elliot, 1983). We should not be surprised if the first student's performance improves and the second student's performance gets worse.

A landmark study by Robert Rosenthal and Lenore Jacobson (1968) brought these teacher expectancy effects to public attention over three decades ago. Since then, many researchers have shown how expectations can lead teachers to treat some students in ways that enhance their achievement, while in effect undermining others (Eccles & Wigfield, 1985; Madon, Jussim, & Eccles, 1997). Even if two students start off with similar ability and motivation, the one whose teacher has low expectations is likely to do worse than the one whose teacher is more positive (Jussim & Eccles, 1992).

A particular concern is that these expectations are often linked to a student's gender, racial/ethnic background, and social class, as well as personal attractiveness (Eccles, 2004; Ritts, Patterson, & Tubbs, 1992). Researchers have found that low teacher expectations have small but definite negative effects on girls' achievement in math and science and on the achievement of minority and poor children in all subject areas (Eccles & Wigfield, 1985; Ferguson, 1998). The impact of teacher expectations is not spread equally among students. Girls, African American teens, students from poorer homes, and low achievers as a group tend to be more sensitive to both the negative effects of low teacher expectancies and the positive effects of high teacher expectancies (Jussim, Eccles, & Madon, 1996; Madon et al., 1997).

Relating to Students. Just as schools develop psychological climates, so do individual classrooms within schools. Even a troubled school may have a class all the students know is terrific, and the most effective school may have a class everyone knows to avoid if possible. The particular mix of students contributes to this climate, and so does the match or mismatch between students and teacher, but the most powerful factor is the way the teacher relates to students.

The climate of a classroom plays a critical role in determining how the motivation, engagement, self-esteem, and academic achievement of students develop (Anderson, Hamilton, & Hattie, 2004; Eccles, 2004; Roeser et al., 1996). In order to learn, and to want to go on learning, students need teachers who give them trust, concern, and respect. Studies show that students who believe their teachers support them and care about them feel better about themselves and their school experience, show more interest in class, and try harder to succeed (Patrick, Ryan, & Kaplan, 2007; Roeser & Eccles, 1998; Roeser et al., 1996; Wentzel, 1998).

There is more to running a class well than providing trust and support, crucial though these are. Effective teachers also manage their classrooms well. They are clear about rules, they keep track of how students are doing and give them regular feedback, and they hold students accountable for keeping up with the work. These measures pay off. When a class functions smoothly, predictably, and efficiently, students learn better and behave better (Eccles, 2004).

As this description makes clear, good teachers are a lot like authoritative parents. They project high expectations for both achievement and discipline and give positive feedback when students meet those expectations. They strike an age-appropriate balance between controlling the class and giving students individual autonomy. They give students a sense of warmth, responsiveness, support, and openness to communication (Haynes, Emmons, & Ben-Avie, 1997; Wentzel, 2002). Not every teacher can be expected to live up to this list of qualities all the time, but the closer they come, the more their classes encourage their students' emotional growth, as well as their academic achievement (Phillips, 1997; Rowan, Chiang, & Miller, 1997).

Connect the **Dots...**

Who was your best teacher in high school? Who was just so-so? Who was the worst? Looking back, how would you say they were different (or similar) in terms of their goal orientation, feelings of self-efficacy, expectations for students, and ability to control the classroom? Do you think the qualities that made your best teacher the best can be taught to aspiring teachers? How?

▶ **Learning Objective 7.4**
What are the issues around school diversity, school choice, exceptional students, and the dropout problem?

Some Current Issues in the Schools

The history of education is filled with controversy, and no wonder: the subject is too important, and too riddled with uncertainties, for everyone to agree. The adolescents of today will be the citizens, producers, and voters of tomorrow, and the education they receive will have a direct impact on the political, social, and economic future of their nation and world.

There are many vital issues that are currently hot topics of discussion. We will concentrate on four of these:

how to promote racial and ethnic integration and diversity;

whether and in what ways parents should be able to choose their children's school;

how the educational system should deal with students whose talents or needs fall outside the usual range; and

how to encourage teens to stay in school.

Racial Segregation. Half a century ago, in the landmark decision *Brown v. Board of Education* (1954), the U.S. Supreme Court ruled that segregated schools are inherently unequal. During the years that followed, communities tried a number of approaches to meet their obligation to desegregate their school systems. Some relied on parent choice, for instance, by creating "magnet schools" intended to attract White students to mostly Black areas. Others used mandatory measures, such as **busing** students of different racial groups from one neighborhood to another to bring about racial balance.

The process was hardly ever without controversy. Desegregation programs often aroused strong opposition, especially from Whites and especially if they required busing. Some writers even argued that mandatory school desegregation *increased* segregation by driving Whites away from urban areas with large Black communities into more segregated suburbs (Rivkin, 1994).

By 1990, movement in the direction of integrated schools had essentially stopped and reversed course. Figure 7.3 shows the percentage of Whites in schools attended by the average Black student. Notice how this rose steadily during the 1970s, and then fell just as steadily during the 1990s.

Data from the 2000–2001 school year show that the average White student attended a school where the great majority of the student body was White, and about 17% of the nation's Black students—25% of Black students in the Northeast and Midwest—attended schools that had *99% or 100%* minority enrollment. These were often schools in areas with enormous poverty, limited resources, and social and health problems

Busing The practice of shifting students of different racial backgrounds from one neighborhood to another in order to increase racial balance in schools.

Figure 7.3   Whites in Black School
The average Black student attends a school that enrolls fewer than one-third White students.

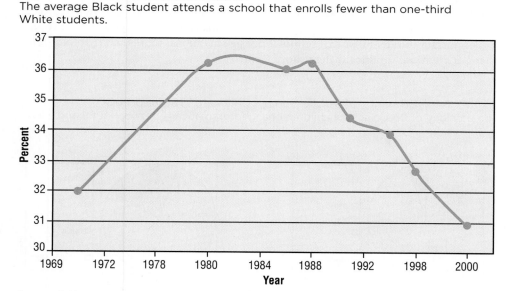

Source: "Whites in Black Schools," by E. Frankenberg, C. Lee, and G. Orfield. The Civil Rights Project, Harvard University. Used by permission.

of many types (Frankenberg, Lee, & Orfield, 2003). In recent years, the suburbs have become more racially and ethnically diverse, but there, too, segregated schools are the rule rather than the exception (Reardon & Yun, 2001).

Most Americans support the principle of racial, ethnic, and cultural diversity in the schools, even if they do not always agree with the measures used to bring it about. A survey taken in 1999 found that 59% of Americans believed that we need to do more to integrate the schools. In the same survey, 68% saw integration as improving education for Blacks, and 50% said that it made education better for Whites (Gallup, 1999). Another survey, a year earlier, found that 60% of Blacks and 34% of Whites said it was "absolutely essential" for schools to "have a diverse student body with kids from different ethnic and racial backgrounds" (Farkas, Johnson, Immerwahr, & McHugh, 1998).

Given this public support for integration, why has segregated schooling become more common rather than less? One reason is that courts have become less willing to force school districts to desegregate (Orfield, 1999). But the most important reason may be demographic changes. Recent decades have seen a major shift in the racial and ethnic makeup of American adolescents. There simply aren't as many White teens in public school as there used to be, and the ones there tend to live in mostly White suburban communities (Iceland, Weinberg, & Steinmetz, 2002). In six states, including the country's two most populous (California and Texas), White students are a *minority* of the enrolled public school population.

In 1968, the great majority—80%—of children in public schools were White, Blacks represented about 15% and Hispanics 5%, with much smaller percentages of Asians and Native Americans. By the year 2000, the number of Blacks enrolled in public school had increased by 29%, while the number of Whites had dropped by 17%. Most striking, the number of Hispanics practically tripled (Frankenberg et al., 2003), bringing the number almost up to that of Blacks. There was also a steep increase in the number of Asian students. These changes are shown in Figure 7.4.

Because of these population shifts, growing numbers of students attend **multiracial schools**, that is, schools in which three or more different racial groups each make up at least 10% of the enrollment. Three out of 10 Black students, 4 out of 10 Hispanic students, and fully three-quarters of Asian students are in multiracial schools. The figure for Whites is much lower, less than 15%, but as Table 7.3 on page 229 shows, that too almost doubled during the 1990s (Frankenberg et al., 2003).

In the early years of the movement toward desegregation, many people hoped that the experience of integrated schools would help erase the gap in school achievement and test scores between Black and White students. On the whole, they were disappointed. The gap did not go away (Entwistle, 1990; Weinberg, 1977). We will look at some of the ways social scientists have explained this result in Chapter 9. Meanwhile, it is important to remember that school is not just about test scores and that long-term changes are more significant than short-term.

Multiracial schools The increasingly common schools in which three or more different racial/ethnic groups each make up at least 10% of the enrollment.

Figure 7.4 Ethnicity of Public School Children, 1968 and 2000
The ethnicity of public school children changed dramatically between 1968 and 2000.

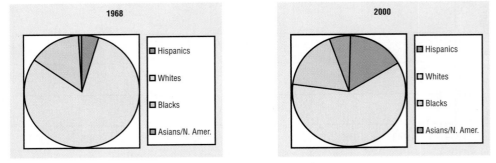

Source: "Ethnicity of Public School Children," by E. Frankenberg, C. Lee, and G. Orfield. The Civil Rights Project, Harvard University. Used by permission.

Table 7.3 Percentage of Students in Multiracial Schools by Race, 1992 and 2000
More and more students in the United States attend multiracial schools.

	White	Black	Hispanic	Asian	Native American
1992–93	7.8	16.3	26.6	41.0	16.2
2000–01	14.3	28.9	38.8	75.0	24.9

Source: 1992-3, 2000-1 NCES Common Core of Data.

For example, one study looked at thousands of poor Chicagoans, almost all minorities, who were moved to mostly White suburbs. After a initial period of adjustment, their children were more likely to take college-track classes, to graduate high school, and to go on to college. They were also more likely to have both Black and White friends (Rosenbaum, 1995). Other studies indicate that Black students who attend racially mixed high schools are better prepared to succeed in college and to take on leadership roles in their careers and communities as adults (Adan & Felner, 1995; Eaton, 2001; Wells & Crain, 1994).

In the coming decades, the United States will continue in the direction of a more multiracial society. At the same time, the worlds of business, education, science, and the arts are predicted to become more global in their reach and focus. Those whose school experience has made them comfortable interacting with people from different cultural and racial backgrounds will have an obvious advantage (Eaton, 2001; Schofield, 2001). Can the American educational system change course and offer that advantage to a larger proportion of its students? That is still an open question.

School Choice. Nine out of 10 American children attend public school. This proportion has stayed much the same for several decades (Alt & Peter, 2002). And parents seem to be reasonably satisfied with the education their children are getting. In one nationwide poll, 71% of public school parents gave their child's school a grade of A or B (Rose & Gallup, 2002). When asked about problems the public schools face, inadequate financial support, cited by 23%, topped the list. Overcrowding and lack of discipline were tied for second place, well behind at 17%.

Many educators and policymakers are not so satisfied. Beginning with the report, *A Nation at Risk* (National Commission on Excellence in Education, 1983), America's public schools have been lambasted for not doing their job. As evidence, critics point to poor student performance on international tests, declining SAT (Scholastic Aptitude Test) scores, increasingly poor science achievement, watered down curricula, and too little time devoted to classroom study and homework.

One widely recommended remedy is increased **school choice**. The idea is that if schools have to compete for students, they will be forced to improve. In a sense, those who can afford to go live somewhere else have always had wide school choice. Homes in communities with highly regarded public schools command a premium price. Most families, however, do not have this option. To give them greater choice, many school systems have made it easier for students to transfer from one public school to another. In 1999, for example, 16% of public school students attended a school the family had chosen, up from 12% in 1993 (Alt & Peter, 2002).

Another strategy to promote choice is the creation of **charter schools**. These are schools that are supported by public funds, but have a degree of independence from local school boards. More than 2,600 charter schools, serving almost 700,000 students, have opened since 1991 (Rimer, 2003). Their freedom from bureaucratic constraints is meant to encourage innovation and greater responsiveness to student needs. So far, however, it is not clear that students benefit more than they would have in traditional public schools (Goldhaber & Eide, 2002).

A more controversial approach to school choice is to offer parents publicly funded **education vouchers** to help pay the cost of private school. Americans are split down the middle about vouchers. In the poll already mentioned, 46% of adults supported an

School choice An approach that makes it easier for parents and students to change from one public school to another.

Charter schools Publicly financed schools that function outside the ordinary public school structure.

Education vouchers An approach that allows parents to use public education funds toward the cost of placing their children in private schools.

education voucher program and 52% opposed it (Rose & Gallup, 2002). So far, only a few places around the country have started offering education on vouchers. One issue is that the great majority of private school students—82% in 2003–2004— attend schools that are affiliated with particular religious denominations (NCES, 2006). The question of using public funds to pay for religious education went all the way to the U.S. Supreme Court, which in June 2002 ruled 5 to 4 that education vouchers are constitutional (*Zelman v. Simmons Harris*).

Some parents answer the question of school choice by deciding not to send their children to school at all. As of 2003, 1.1 million students, about 2.2% of the school-age population, were in **home schooling**, most of them full time (NCES, 2005). Three-quarters of home-schooled students were White, from two-parent families. When parents were asked why they chose home schooling, the most important reasons were concern about safety, drugs, and negative peer pressure in school, a desire to give special religious or moral instruction, and dissatisfaction with the academic instruction in the schools (NCES, 2005).

What about the results of parents taking their children out of the public school system? Do students at private schools get a better education? On the whole, the evidence says yes. Average scores on achievement tests in reading, mathematics, and science are higher for private school students. Private schools also tend to have stiffer requirements for graduation. As a result, their graduates complete more advanced courses in science, mathematics, and foreign language than public school graduates (NCES, 2002). Private school students are also much more likely to go on to finish college than those who attended public school. This holds even for students from poor families. Looking at students in the lowest 25% socioeconomic bracket, 24% of those who attended private school went on to earn a bachelor's degree, but only 7% of those who attended public school did (Alt & Peter, 2002).

A number of reasons have been suggested for this advantage. One is that economic status is a major predictor of academic achievement (Gutman & Eccles, 1999), and on average private school students are better off. Over 40% of public school students are poor enough to be eligible for free or reduced price lunches, as compared to 10% of private school students. One-half of private schools do not have *any* eligible students (Alt & Peter, 2002). Another reason is that private schools demand a greater commitment from both parents and students. Sociologist James Coleman has noted that in Catholic schools, which enroll 46% of all private school students (NCES, 2006), parents, teachers, and students all share similar attitudes and values (Coleman & Hoffer, 1987).

What happens in school matters too, of course. One extensive study of Catholic high schools found that teachers, administrators, and staff were all committed to the

Home schooling A situation in which parents educate their children at home, generally with some oversight from local or state education authorities.

▶ Students at private schools often receive more intensive and personalized instruction.

academic, spiritual, and social development of students. They communicated high expectations, provided extra help when it was needed, and created an atmosphere of mutual respect among everyone in the school (Bryk, Lee, & Holland, 1993). As we saw earlier in this chapter, this is the sort of school climate that encourages student achievement, whether the school is public or private, religious or secular (Benveniste, Carnoy, & Rothstein, 2002; Rutter & Maughan, 2002).

Exceptional Students. So far, we have been looking at school and the school experience in terms of that mythical creature, the average American adolescent. Why mythical? Because teens differ from one another in so many ways, even if they happen to be identical twins. But there are some adolescents whose differences are more striking, in ways that have a particular impact on their education. Some, who have unusually strong talents or abilities, are called **gifted**. Others, who have physical, cognitive, or developmental problems that interfere with their success in school, are called **disabled**. Both groups present challenging issues to schools and educators.

The usual rule that is used to label a student gifted is an IQ test score of 130 or higher. On average, only two or three people out of 100 score this high or higher. Some schools also look at unusual talents, for example in music or art. Once a student is considered gifted or talented, the next question is, "Now what?"

In some school systems, gifted students are channeled into separate, enriched classes. Elsewhere, they are assigned to regular classrooms and perhaps given extra, more challenging assignments. There are even a few highly selective public high schools around the country, like New York's famed Stuyvesant High School and Bronx High School of Science, that admit only gifted students (and only some of them!). In addition, three-quarters of high school students attend schools that offer at least one higher-level Advanced Placement or **AP class**, and 22% attend schools that offer four or more AP courses (NCES, 2005). These courses are generally open to any student who can handle the work, not just to those officially labeled as gifted. Students who do well on the nationwide AP exam in a subject area may be granted an exemption or course credit when they reach college.

Along with those students who have unusual gifts, there are also students with unusual problems and educational needs. Many kinds of problems and special needs can hinder an adolescent from coping successfully with school, including physical dysfunctions, such as visual or hearing impairments; mental retardation; learning disabilities; and other developmental disorders (Hallahan & Kauffman, 1999). An increased awareness among parents and teachers has made learning disabilities, such as dyslexia and attention deficit hyperactivity disorder (ADHD), the fastest-growing category (O'Shea, O'Shea, & Algozzine, 2002).

In the past, children and adolescents with disabilities were often placed in separate schools or classrooms, or put in regular classes but not given the help they needed to adapt successfully. Some were even excluded from school altogether as "ineducable." Then, in 1975, the U.S. Congress passed a law that requires school districts to give children with special needs an education comparable to what other children receive in the "least restrictive environment." Many school districts interpret that phrase to mean integrating those with disabilities into regular classrooms. This practice, known as inclusion, or **mainstreaming**, has grown rapidly. In 1988–1989, only 31% of students with disabilities spent 80% or more of the school day in a regular education classroom. By 2004, practically half—49.9%—did so (NCES, 2005).

How well does mainstreaming work? The most accurate answer seems to be, "So-so." When mainstreamed special-needs students are compared on academic outcomes to those placed in separate special education classes, sometimes they come out ahead and sometimes they do not (Manset & Semmel, 1997). An analysis of studies that looked at the effect on students' self-concept of different kinds of placement—regular class, resource room, self-contained class, and special school—did not find any particular advantage for mainstreaming (Elbaum, 2002).

▲ Programs for gifted students offer chances to go well beyond the usual schoolwork.

Gifted Those students who are considered to have unusually strong talents or abilities that make more challenging educational efforts advisable.

Disabled Those students who have physical, cognitive, or developmental problems that interfere with their progress in school.

AP class An intensive high school class that leads to a nationwide Advanced Placement exam in a subject; students who do well may get course credit in the subject when they reach college.

Mainstreaming The practice of integrating students with disabilities into regular classrooms.

▲ Students with disabilities benefit from being included in classrooms that stress cooperative learning.

Mainstreamed students do benefit, both academically and socially, when they are included in classrooms that stress cooperative learning (Stevens & Slavin, 1995). One recent study looked at students with mild disabilities in a high school history class. Some received teacher-directed guided notes, while others took part in peer tutoring. Those in the peer tutoring group did significantly better on the exam at the end of the quarter, as well as on measures of reading comprehension and learning strategies. They also said that the time they spent tutoring one another made the academic quarter feel like one of their shortest quarters ever (Mastropieri, Scruggs, Spencer, & Fontana, 2003).

The Problem of Dropouts. So far in this chapter, we have been talking as if all adolescents of high school age are in high school. Not quite. Some leave school before they graduate. A few decades ago, **dropouts** who left high school without a diploma could often step into a good-paying full-time job in the mill, or down the mine, or with the local streetcar company. Today, however, those who lack a high school education pay a steep price. A high school diploma is a minumum requirement for most jobs. In 1998, the unemployment rate for dropouts was 75% higher than for high school graduates (NCES, 2000, 2001). The ones who do have a job earn much less than those who graduated high school—27% less for males, and 30% less for females (NCES, 2002).

The proportion of teens who drop out has gone down over the last 30 years, from 15% in 1972 to 10% in 2004. The sharpest decline was among Blacks. As of 2001, their dropout rate was 11%, down from 13% a year earlier and 21% in 1972. The rate for Hispanic students, however, at 27%, was 2-1/2 times that of Blacks (NCES, 2003). Not having English as one's first language is a major predictor for dropping out. In fact, the 2001 dropout rate for Hispanics who were born outside the United States was 43%, almost three times that of Hispanics born in the United States (NCES, 2003).

While the overall dropout rate has declined in recent years, the problem is still especially severe in 200 to 300 schools in the 35 largest cities in the United States. In half of the high schools researchers looked at, 50% or fewer of the students who enrolled in 9th grade graduated. The schools with the lowest graduation rates were those with more than 900 students and in which 90% or more of the students were non-White (Balfanz & Legters, 2001). However, we have to be careful about the conclusions we draw. Students in large, inner-city high schools are not only mostly non-White, they are mostly from families in poverty as well, and under a lot of stress as a result. When the family's socioeconomic status (SES) is taken into account, the dropout rates for different ethnic groups become much the same (Rumberger, 1995).

Socioeconomic status is only one of the factors that predict a teen's risk of dropping out. Girls who get pregnant are at high risk for dropping out, even after controlling for family background (Geronimus & Korenman, 1992). Both academic and social problems also make a big difference (NCES, 2006). In one study, Michael Newcomb, of the University of Southern California, and his co-workers followed over 700 8th graders through high school (Newcomb et al., 2002). The most powerful predictor of dropping out was lack of academic success. Students who had poor grades and test scores in 8th grade were more likely to leave school before graduation. As expected, low family SES predicted dropping out, and so did general deviance. Eighth graders who showed aggressive or defiant attitudes toward teachers, delinquent behavior, and tobacco use by age 14 were less likely to finish high school.

More than half of those who drop out of high school do sooner or later go back and finish or pass an equivalent *General Education Development* (*GED*) test (NCES, 2000). Both government agencies and private organizations have developed programs to increase this number and to encourage teens who are at risk not to drop out in the first place. One problem is that at-risk students generally start having academic difficulties well before they reach high school (Rumberger, 2001). At what point should—or can—an intervention program intervene?

Dropouts Teens who leave high school before graduating and receiving a diploma.

On the middle and high school level, one approach that seems to work is to create smaller, self-contained academies within a school for students who are in danger of dropping out. These create a non-threatening environment for learning that promotes student engagement and a sense of membership. It is also important to combine high standards with ways for students to recover from failure without the risk of being held back (McPartland & Jordan, 2001).

> ### Summing Up...
>
> Schools are expected to educate children as individuals, future citizens, and contributors to the society and economy. How to do this best is an ongoing discussion. An earlier trend toward larger schools is starting to reverse. Many educators and others are concerned about effects of large classes and the number and placement of school transitions. Within the school, goal orientation, school climate, and school safety all contribute to student outcomes. In the classroom, teacher attitudes and expectations are crucial. Other vital issues include promoting racial integration in schools, allowing parents and students greater school choice, giving students with exceptional abilities or needs an appropriate education, and encouraging students to stay in school.

INFORMAL EDUCATION

Education is not something that takes place only in the classroom, during class hours, and following the announced subject being taught. Adolescents learn quite a lot from the other things they do, both during and after school. In this section, we examine the role of extracurricular and after-school activities.

During School

Imagine that somebody asked you to name half a dozen peak moments in your high school career. What would make it to your list? An algebra test? A class discussion of the causes of the Civil War? Just barely possible, if that was the only time in 4 years that you aced a math test, or if you held your own in a hot discussion about the role of slavery in setting off the war. But there are some far more likely candidates for big moments. How about scoring the winning point for your team? Getting a juicy part in the school play? Working right up to the deadline to put the yearbook together? Persuading student council to adopt a controversial resolution?

What all these have in common is that they are **extracurricular activities**. They are school-based and school-sponsored, but they are not part of the formal educational curriculum. Extracurricular activities are such a familiar part of American secondary schools that it comes as a small shock to find out that they are fairly rare in Europe (Hamilton & Hamilton, 2003). In the United States, around two-thirds of high school students take part in at least one school-based club or activity, and more than one-half play a team sport (Eccles & Barber, 1999). Participation does vary a good deal. As we saw earlier in the chapter, smaller schools have a higher percentage of students who take part than larger schools (Crosnoe et al., 2003). Those of lower socioeconomic status and those getting lower grades are less likely to participate, as are Hispanic students (Feldman & Matjasko, 2006). Participation levels tend to decline as teens get older, in part because taking part in activities such as team sports or band calls for specialized skills and prior experience (Pederson, 2005).

Voters and policymakers sometimes see extracurricular activities as pleasant but useless frills, or even think they take time away from "real" schoolwork (for example, Herszenhorn, 2003; Landis, 2002). When money for schools gets tight, art and music programs are often the first hit, and athletic teams (other than glory sports such as football) are not far behind. This is unfortunate. Researchers have linked participation

◀ **Learning Objective 7.5**
What are the benefits of extracurricular activities?

Extracurricular activities School sponsored and supported voluntary activities that are not part of the formal educational curriculum.

in extracurricular activities to a long list of educational, personal, and social benefits (Feldman & Matjasko, 2005).

Compared to those who are less active, adolescents who take part in extracurricular activities:

are more engaged in school, spend more time on homework, and earn better grades;

spend more time talking to teachers outside of class and more time talking over school concerns with their parents;

have higher educational aspirations;

are less likely to drop out of high school and more likely to go on to college;

have higher self-esteem and are less depressed;

have better initiative and social skills; and

show less delinquency, problem behaviors, and substance use.

(BARBER, ECCLES, & STONE, 2001; BARTKO & ECCLES, 2004; BROH, 2002; DARLING, 2005; DWORKIN, LARSON, & HANSEN, 2003; EANES, FLETCHER, & BROWN, 2002; FREDERICKS & ECCLES, 2005; MAHONEY & CAIRNS, 1997; MARSH, 1992; McNEIL, 1995)

Beyond the specific gains adolescents make from extracurricular activities, they generally find them involving, challenging, and interesting. As Figure 7.5 shows, teens are more motivated and involved during extracurricular activities than in class or hanging out with friends (Larson, 2000). And because extracurricular activities are voluntary, if they stop being interesting, you can stop doing them!

One longitudinal study (Mahoney, Cairns, & Farmer, 2003) followed 695 students all the way across the adolescent years, from ages 12 to 20. The results of this project are described in this chapter's Research in the Spotlight on page 235.

Connect the **Dots...**

In your experience as an adolescent, what extracurricular activity had the greatest impact on you, whether positive or negative? What aspects of the activity do you think were most important in creating that impact? If you were asked to design a program of extracurricular activities, what features would you say are essential, and what would you be most concerned to avoid?

Figure 7.5 Interest Levels During School and Extracurricular Activities
Extracurricular activities generate higher levels of intrinsic motivation combined with concentration than either school or being with friends.

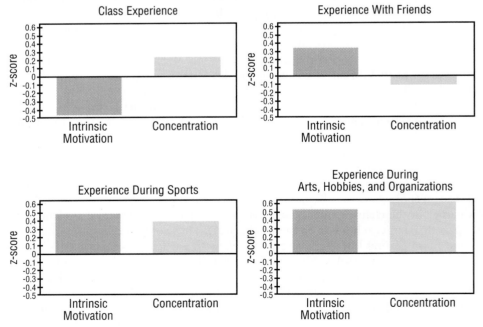

Source: "Toward a Psychology of Positive Youth Development," by R. W. Larson. *American Psychologist 55*, 170–183, Figures 1 and 2. © 2000. Used by permission of the American Psychological Association.

Extracurricular Activities and Academic Success: What's the Connection?

More and more evidence supports a link between taking part in extracurricular activities and doing better in school. Teens who participate in sports, clubs, publications, arts activities, and so on, get higher grades, have higher aspirations, and are more likely to finish high school and go on to college than those who do not participate. This is an impressive list of positive outcomes, but strong as it is, the evidence is *correlational*. It tells us that participation and academic success are connected, but not exactly how.

Some possible explanations include:

- The connection to a team or club may give kids who otherwise might drop out a reason to keep coming to school, pass their courses, and get their diploma.
- School performance may affect a student's decision to get involved in extracurricular activities. For instance, a student gets a good mark in English and is encouraged to try out for the school paper.
- Participation may affect something else that in turn affects school success. For example, an athlete who is having trouble in a subject may get informal tutoring from teammates who have already taken that course.
- The qualities that make success in school more likely—talent, motivation, family background, or whatever—may also make an interest in extracurricular activities more likely.

An added wrinkle: all of these explanations may be partly true. They may hold for some students but not others, or even for the same students at different times in their school career.

How can we choose among all these possibilities? While correlational data do not *prove* cause and effect, if you have information on the same people from different times—*longitudinal* data

—there are ways of deciding whether a particular cause-and-effect sequence makes sense.

Joseph Mahoney, of Yale University, and Beverley Cairns and Tom Farmer, of the University of North Carolina at Chapel Hill, interviewed the same 695 adolescents every year from 7th to 12th grade and again when they were about 20. Each year, the students' teachers rated their social behavior, including aggression and popularity. Information about extracurricular participation was collected from yearbooks.

Mahoney and his co-workers reasoned that because extracurricular activities are usually voluntary, structured, and challenging, they help develop an adolescent's *interpersonal competence*. While taking part, teens have the chance to form positive relationships with schoolmates and adults, such as faculty advisors and coaches, outside the classroom. When you're working side-by-side with people on some project you're all interested in, you get to know them and they get to know you. The more consistently you participate, the greater the effect.

The researchers used a technique called *path analysis* that looks at the relationships among different variables over time. They proposed that extracurricular participation leads to higher educational attainment by affecting both interpersonal competence and educational aspirations. This model is shown in the diagram, which includes the results of the path analysis. The number next to each arrow indicates the relative strength of that connection. As the researchers suggested, extracurricular participation in early and middle adolescence was linked to interpersonal competence in middle adolescence, educational aspirations in late adolescence, and educational status at age 20.

Source: Mahoney, Cairns, & Farmer, 2003.

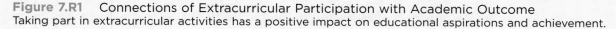

Figure 7.R1 Connections of Extracurricular Participation with Academic Outcome
Taking part in extracurricular activities has a positive impact on educational aspirations and achievement.

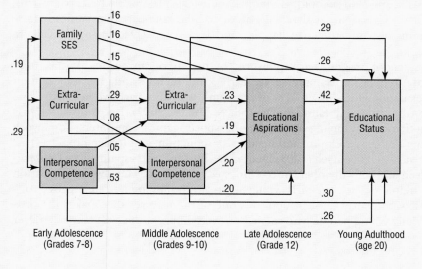

After School

► **Learning Objective 7.6**
How do after-school programs help teens?

As more and more parents work, more and more young adolescents are left on their own during the hours after school lets out. According to the U.S. Census Bureau, almost 5 million 12- to 14-year-olds, 42% of the total, spend an average of 10 hours a week in what is called **self-care** (Smith, 2002). The government does not collect this information about older teens, but we can reasonably assume that even more of those over 14 are unsupervised after school.

Some of these young people go straight home after school to do their homework or look after younger brothers and sisters. For others, this is the time to go over to a friend's house or hang out down on the corner or at the mall (Carnegie Council on Adolescent Development, 1992). The stereotype is that most of these "latchkey kids" are lower-income inner-city minorities. The facts are rather different. In reality, only about 30% of Black and Hispanic youngsters, and of those with family incomes below the poverty level, are in self-care. For Whites, however, and for those with family incomes of more than twice the poverty level, the figure is nearly 50% (Smith, 2002).

Worries about how children spend the after-school hours have been around for over 100 years—in fact, ever since the majority of children in the United States started going to school instead of to work (Halpern, 2002). One recent report announced that the period from 3:00 PM to 6:00 PM on school days is "prime time for juvenile crime." It went on to claim that during these hours, teens are most likely to be in or cause a car crash, be killed by household accidents, get hooked on cigarettes, experiment with other dangerous drugs, engage in sexual intercourse, get pregnant, and become addicted to violent video games (Newman, Fox, Flynn, & Christeson, 2000). Some of these statements were backed up with evidence such as FBI crime reports. Others were based on polls that may not meet usual scientific standards (Ericson, 2001). Whether these concerns are exaggerated or not, they are widespread and deeply felt.

The impact of after-school activities depends very much on what those activities are and where they take place. Even unstructured hangout time is not necessarily a bad thing. One study followed over 400 children across the early adolescent years. The children who were most at risk for problem behaviors were those who lived in less safe neighborhoods, spent more unsupervised time with peers, and had parents who did not pay as much attention to where they were and what they were doing (Pettit, Bates, Dodge, & Meece, 1999). However, as Figure 7.6 on page 237 shows, those in safer neighborhoods were at less risk for problems, even if they did spend more unsupervised time with peers and had parents who did not watch them closely.

After-school activities are not just about avoiding risk. They also have many positive effects (Eccles & Gootman, 2002; Scott-Little, Hamann, & Jurs, 2002). Students who take part in after-school programs say they feel more competent, pay closer attention in class, and skip school less often. They are also less likely to start drinking (Grossman, 2003; Grossman et al., 2002). Students who take part in organized after-school programs also say they are happier and less bored (Dadisman, Vandell, & Pierce, 2002).

Many after-school programs are sponsored by private organizations. The Boys & Girls Clubs of America, for example, serve nearly 3 million boys and girls at more than 2,000 facilities nationwide. About 70% of the youth who take part live in urban areas and 56% are from minority families (Deutsch & Hirsch, 2002). Local Boys & Girls Clubs offer activities that include arts and crafts, sports, games, computers, homework help, and programs on developmental needs, risk reduction, and leadership.

Psychologist Nancy Deutsch (2003; Deutsch & Hirsch, 2002) spent 4 years observing the children and staff members at one Boys & Girls Club. Her own participation ranged from helping coach the girls' volleyball team to judging a "cutest baby" contest. In her view, the fairly loose structure is one of the features that makes the program work. Many young people who spent 3 or more hours at the club every day after

Self-care Adolescents who are left unsupervised during the hours after school lets out.

Figure 7.6   Parental Monitoring, Neighborhood Safety, and Peer Involvement
Parental monitoring, neighborhood safety, and peer involvement interact to affect externalizing problems.

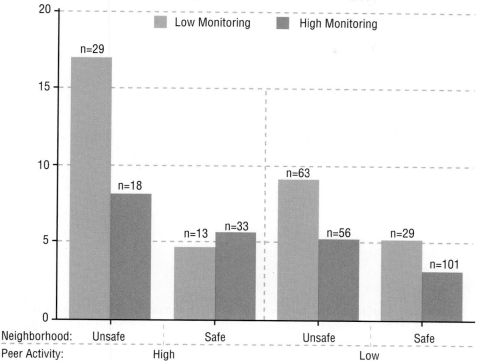

Source: The Impact of After-School Peer Contact on Early Adolescent Externalizing Problems Is Mediated by Parental Monitoring, Perceived Neighborhood Safety, and Prior Adjustment. by G. S. Pettit, J. E. Bates, K. A. Dodge, & D. W. Meece. (1999). *Child Development, 70,* 768—778. Figure 1, p. 775. © 1999. Used by permission.

school told her they would stop coming if it became structured more like school. What attracted them to the club was that they could be themselves. Explaining why the club felt like home to them, one teen said, "When I come here everybody treats me the same as other people." Another added, "People here always listen to you and help you if you have problems" (Deutsch & Hirsch, 2002).

> **Summing Up...**
>
> Adolescents who take part in extracurricular activities feel more connected to school, get better grades, talk more with teachers and parents about their studies, are more likely to finish school and go on to college, have higher self-esteem and better social skills, and show fewer problem behaviors. Organized after-school programs carry many of the same benefits. Together these non-academic activities offer adolescents a way to explore new interests, learn new skills, and develop social competence with other teens in a safe, supportive environment.

IS THERE LIFE AFTER HIGH SCHOOL?

It is a magical moment when a high school senior flips the tassel on that funny square hat from one side to the other. However, extraordinary as it is, it is not the end of adolescence, merely of one very big chunk of it. Contrary to what some pop songs proclaim, the world does go on turning after high school graduation. And most teens take that next step into the unknown, nervous but eager just the same.

Figure 7.7   Median Income by Educational Level
The education level a person reached has a marked effect on median income.

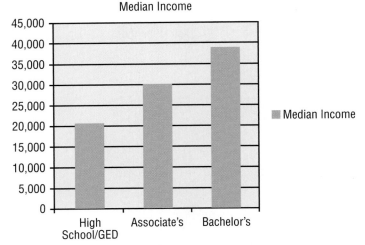

Median Income

Source: U.S. Census Bureau, 2006.

Off to College

► **Learning Objective 7.7**
What proportion of adolescents go to college and how many stay in?

A century ago, a college education was out of reach for practically all American adolescents. Of every 100 young people of college age, only four actually went to college. The rest could only read about college life in popular novels for teens, such as those that followed Dink Stover's exploits at Yale (Johnson, 1912), in much the way a teen today might read a magazine article or watch a television show about sports heroes and media stars. College attendance gradually rose, but even by 1950, only 20% of young people were enrolled in college (Church, 1976).

Today, in contrast, 88% of 8th graders expect to continue their education after high school—and this is not simply wishful thinking. About 63% of students do enroll in college immediately after finishing high school, and within 2 years the proportion has climbed to 70% (Venezia, Kirst, & Antonio, 2003). One reason so many go to college is that both teens and their parents realize that in today's economy, a college education pays off in more than intellectual, social, and personal growth. It also leads to higher income. Take a look at Figure 7.7. In 2004, workers 18 and over with only a high school diploma or GED earned a median income of $20,733. Those with an associate's degree earned $30,026, and those with a bachelor's degree earned $38,880 (U.S. Bureau of the Census, 2006). That amounts to an 88% annual bonus for having put in 4 successful years at college.

Figure 7.8   College Enrollment, by Sex

In recent years, more women than men have enrolled in college.

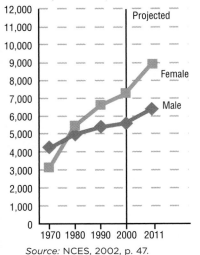

Enrollment (in thousands)

Source: NCES, 2002, p. 47.

Until the 1970s, more males than females went to college. Since then, the number of females has increased much more rapidly than the number of males (see Figure 7.8). Today, about 57% of those who earn bachelor's degrees are women (NCES, 2002). Family income and racial/ethnic background also make a big difference in college attendance. Those from poorer families and those of color are less likely to go to college, as Figure 7.9 on page 239 illustrates (Venezia et al., 2003), and are even less likely to finish college. The proportion of kindergarten children who grow up to earn a bachelor's degree ranges from 49% for Asian Americans and 29% for Whites down to 10% for Latinos (Education Trust, 2001).

One factor that has a strong effect on college attendance by teens from economically disadvantaged families is the attitude of their parents. Parents who are less optimistic about their children's educational chances push their children less, while those who are more optimistic help buffer their children from the effects of their situation (Crosnoe, Mistry, & Elder, 2002).

Getting In. Compared to other industrialized countries, the United States has a much more open system of higher education. There are 2- and 4-year colleges; public

Figure 7.9   Going to College, by Family Income and Race
Low-income students and students of color are less likely to go to college directly after finishing high school.

CHART A

PERCENTAGE OF HIGH SCHOOL COMPLETERS WHO
WERE ENROLLED IN COLLEGE THE OCTOBER AFTER COMPLETING
HIGH SCHOOL, BY FAMILY INCOME* AND RACE/ETHNICITY, 2000

100%						
75%						
50%						
25%						
0%	63	50	59	77	66	55	53

	LOW	MIDDLE	HIGH	WHITE	BLACK	HISPANIC
Total (All Students)	Family Income*			Race/Ethnicity		

Source: NCES, 2003, p. 6.

and private; secular and religious; liberal and technical; small, large, and in between; each with its own characteristics and rules. In some European countries, in contrast, a central authority looks at student goals and qualifications and matches them to a particular institution. In the United States, high school students can apply anywhere they like and go anywhere they are admitted (provided they can afford the tuition or get enough financial aid).

This openness creates wider possibilities for students. At the same time, however, the lack of coordination between high schools and colleges creates problems for them (Karen, 2002). In one recent study, less than 12% of high school students knew what courses they needed to take to be admitted to public colleges in their state. Many believed, wrongly, that simply meeting the requirements for high school graduation would prepare them for college (Venezia et al., 2003). A good counselor could probably steer them toward an appropriate college and guide them through the application

◀ The college tour has become a familiar ritual for many American high school students.

process, but many high school counselors are too overburdened to give students that kind of individual attention.

Staying In. A lot of teens think that getting into college is the hardest part. Not necessarily. About half of all students entering college have to take one or more remedial courses, even if they did well in the subject in high school. This is often a shocking blow to the student's self-confidence at an already vulnerable time, and the effects can be far-reaching. Students who have to take even one remedial course are less likely to finish college (NCES, 2001).

A startling number of students who enter college drop out. Among those who start at a community college, about half do not come back for their second year. As for first-year students at 4-year colleges, about one-quarter do not return for the second year (American Council on Education, 2002). One explanation for this is that many high schools do not really prepare their students for college-level study. In fact, the best predictor of whether a student will stay in and finish college is the quality and intensity of that student's high school education (Adelman, 1999).

We shouldn't be too gloomy here. Yes, for many adolescents, maybe even most, the transition from high school to college has some very scary aspects. It may involve moving away from home for the first time. It will probably mean parting from lifelong friends, at least until winter break, and having to find one's way among a whole new group of people. It may threaten to break up an intense romantic relationship. At the same time, though, it is a big step away from childhood and dependency toward adulthood and independence. For most adolescents, that makes it a thrilling moment.

Off to Work—Or Not

As we saw in the last section, 63% of American adolescents enter college right after they finish high school. Another 7% enroll in college within the next 2 years (NCES, 2002). That leaves about 30%, a little less than one in three, who graduate from high school, but do not go on to college. What happens to them, and what can be done to improve their situation and prospects?

These teens are sometimes referred to as the **forgotten half.** The term comes from the title of an influential report produced by a panel of experts in the late 1980s (William T. Grant Foundation, 1988). The report pointed out that, with the shift in the United States from a manufacturing economy to one oriented more toward information and service industries, many of the well-paying jobs that used to be open to high school graduates, especially males, no longer exist.

This trend has continued and even accelerated in recent years (Halperin, 1998). Between 1980 and 2000, young men with a college degree saw their median income go up 11%. During that same period, the median income of young men with only a high school diploma dropped 18% (NCES, 2002)! And those are the ones who find a job—over 12% do not (U.S. Bureau of the Census, 2001).

One part of the problem is that American society puts so much stress on the importance of a college education. No one questions that college is valuable, but the emphasis it receives has meant that the 30% who finish high school but are not college bound are neglected. The courses they are steered toward are less rigorous and leave them with weaker skills, and high schools typically do little to help prepare them to look for, find, and hold down a worthwhile job.

For example, among the basic skills adolescents need to succeed in today's and tomorrow's economy are the ability to read and do math at least at a 9th-grade level (Murnane & Levy, 1997). However, more than one-third of 12th graders do not have even a basic level of math skills, and 23% do not have basic reading skills (NCES, 2000, 2002). Most of those who do have these skills go on to college instead of directly into the workplace. As a result, potential employers come to think of a high school diploma not as evidence of skills, but as evidence of lack of skills. In turn, as word gets around that a diploma doesn't buy much, students still in high school lose some of their motivation to do well.

Connect the **Dots...**

Imagine that a neighbor or younger sibling who is still in high school asks you for advice about choosing a college, getting in, and staying in. What are the most important points you would want to make? What warnings do you think it would be important to offer?

▶ **Learning Objective 7.8**
What problems face teens who finish high school but do not go on to college?

Forgotten half A term used to describe those adolescents, currently about one-third, who finish high school but do not go on to college.

One way that has been suggested to improve the prospects of high school graduates is to develop closer cooperation between the schools and the working world. College-bound students are given counseling at school (though often not enough of it). Why shouldn't non-college-bound students also get improved counseling, in the form of information and advice about training and career opportunities? As we will see later in this chapter, other industrialized countries have well-established job training programs that begin while students are still in high school (Hamilton & Hurrelman, 1994). By the time the participants graduate from high school, they already have useful skills, experience at a real job, a clearer understanding of how to deal with the working world, and often a job waiting for them.

The Role of Mentors

In Homer's *Odyssey*, when Odysseus has to leave his home and family to join the war against Troy, he asks a trusted friend to watch over the upbringing and education of his young son, Telemachus. The friend, who faithfully carries out this task, is named Mentor. Ever since, the term **mentor** has meant an adult whose connection with a young person includes teaching new skills, actively promoting personal and social competence, and providing guidance and support (Hamilton & Hamilton, 2003). A mentoring relationship is more than just getting together to talk or being shown how to do something. While instruction and challenge are important, encouragement, mutual commitment and respect, and the emotional bond that develops over time are even more important (Beam, Chen, & Greenberger, 2002; Liang, Tracy, Taylor, & Williams, 2002).

◄ **Learning Objective 7.9**
What are mentors and how can they be more effective?

You can probably bring to mind someone who acted (or still acts) as a mentor to you. When college students in one study were asked to name the most important people in their lives before they entered college, 82% included at least one adult outside their family (Hamilton & Darling, 1996). Often, teens find mentors on their own, or they find each other. The mentor they find may be a neighbor or family friend, a coach, a teacher, a co-worker, a member of the clergy, or an older member of a social or faith-based organization. For others, an organization such as Big Brothers/Big Sisters pairs them with someone who, with good training and a certain amount of luck, becomes a mentor to them (Parra, DuBois, Neville, & Pugh-Lilly, 2002; Rhodes, 2002).

Benefits of Mentors. For adolescents, mentors have something in common with both parents and peers. Like peers, they are chosen, not decreed by fate, and like parents, they are sources of information, adult attitudes and skills, and even wisdom. They offer the teen a living model of how adults act and shape the teen's own actions through their praise and criticism (Darling, Hamilton, Toyokawa, & Matsuda, 2002; Zimmerman, Bingenheimer, & Notaro, 2002). Mentors also serve as a source of what is called **social capital** (Coleman, 1990). This is the web of social and professional relationships that make it easier to be productive or accomplish one's goals. For example, a mentor who is not up on a teen's special field of interest may know of someone who is and arrange for the teen to meet that person.

Having a mentor helps teens whose environment puts them at risk to get through their difficulties more safely. One study of 770 adolescents in a large Midwestern city found that those — about half of the group — who had someone they saw as a mentor were less likely to smoke marijuana or get involved in delinquency and had more positive attitudes toward school (Zimmerman et al., 2002). Other studies confirm that teens with mentors are less likely to be involved in misconduct, even if their close friends are (Greenberger, Chen, & Beam, 1998).

Volunteer Mentors. Unfortunately, at-risk adolescents who may need a mentor the most are often the ones who have the most trouble finding one. Changes in American society have cut down on the availability of adults who traditionally served as leaders and role models. This is especially a problem in urban centers (Rhodes, 2002). In response, programs that provide volunteer mentoring have become more widespread. Big Brothers/Big Sisters is probably the best known of these.

Mentor A non-familial adult who provides a young person with guidance and support.

Social capital A network of personal and social relationships that makes it easier to be effective in accomplishing one's goals.

There is plenty of evidence that volunteer mentoring programs help the adolescents who take part. One study used the long waiting lists for Big Brothers/Big Sisters to conduct a true experiment. Teens were chosen randomly to be matched with a mentor or to stay on the waiting list for 18 months. At the end of the 18 months, those who had been assigned a Big Brother or Big Sister were less likely to have started using drugs and alcohol, had better school attendance and grades, and said they were getting along better with peers and family members than those who had been kept on the waiting list (Tierney, Grossman, & Resch, 1995).

Researchers find that the positive impact of mentoring grows as the relationship matures (Parra et al., 2002). The trusting and supportive relationship with a mentor helps the teen achieve more positive, trusting relationships with parents and peers, a greater sense of school competence, and more positive self-worth (Rhodes, 2000; Grossman, Resch, & Zand et al., 2008). However, if the mentoring relationship breaks off after too short a time, far from helping, it may even have a negative effect on the teen (Grossman & Rhodes, 2002; Spencer, 2007).

Are there ways to help someone be a more effective mentor? We take a closer look at this question in the adjoining Applications in the Spotlight.

Applications in the Spotlight

Mentoring Adolescents

Mentoring programs could not operate without the adults who contribute their time, energy, and talents to serve as mentors. Those who volunteer typically come to these programs because they want to help young people overcome disadvantages, and as a rule, they *do* help. Sometimes, however, the match between an adult mentor and a teen simply doesn't work out, a valuable opportunity goes to waste, and both the would-be mentor and the adolescent may leave the experience too discouraged to try again.

Researchers who evaluate mentoring programs have discovered some important differences between adults who are effective mentors and those who are less successful. The most basic of these is the way the adult understands the mentoring role. Mentoring depends on building a relationship of trust between two people who start off as strangers. This is not easy in the best of circumstances. It may be even more difficult for the new mentor. Many of the teens who come to these programs have a history of being let down by others. It is too much to expect them to lower their guard just because some program staff member tells them this new adult is now their mentor.

Mentors who realize the crucial need for mutual trust and are willing to put in the time to develop it are more likely to succeed than those who set out to change the kids they're working with right away. Mentors who push too hard and too soon—for example, trying to talk about the teen's problems before the teen is ready—may awaken passive or active resistance. The likely result is sullen defiance from the teen, frustration for the mentor, and an early end to their association.

Beyond their determination to create a relationship of mutual trust, effective mentors share a number of qualities:

They are committed to being a dependable presence in the teen's life.

They realize that it is basically up to them to keep the relationship going. Teens often test adults to find out if they really will be there when needed. A mentor should be proactive. This means, for example, not waiting for the teen to set up the next meeting.

They show respect for young people's points of view by listening to what they say and paying attention to what they think matters.

They make sure the teen is involved in deciding how to spend their time together. This means learning about the teen's interests and offering choices, rather than planning out everything ahead of time.

They respect the teen's need to have fun. Sharing enjoyable moments is a valuable part of any positive relationship, and a mentor may be able to offer fun experiences the teen's family cannot provide.

They get acquainted with the teen's family and try to enlist their support of the mentoring relationship.

To summarize, adults who become effective mentors tend to see themselves as caring, supportive, and resourceful friends. A major challenge for mentoring programs is to recruit volunteers who either come in with this attitude or are open to developing it.

Source: Sipe, 2003.

Summing Up...

Almost three-quarters of U.S. adolescents enroll in college after finishing high school, but few high school students know as much as they should about what college involves and requires. As a result, many find themselves assigned to remedial courses, and many drop out after their first year. Those who do not go on to college often find that high school has not given them the preparation they need to look for and get a worthwhile job. Teens who are lucky enough to find a mentor, an adult who offers advice, encouragement, and support are more likely to avoid problem behaviors and overcome difficulties.

ADOLESCENTS AND WORK

If you go to your local mall or fast-food restaurant any afternoon during the school year, or at any time of day during the summer, you will almost certainly see teenage students working in the stockroom, behind the counter, at the cash register, and on the floor. Students with part-time jobs are such a common sight in the United States that hardly anyone even notices. In a larger perspective, however, they are remarkable. In most of the world, an adolescent either works or goes to school, but not both at the same time. Until fairly recently, that was the case in America, too. In this section we look at how that changed, in what directions, and what the costs and benefits have been. We also examine some ways society might help prepare young people better for adult careers.

From Work to School and Back to Work

In 1890, only 1 of 20 adolescents of high school age was a full-time student. Most of the rest had left school before they were 15 to become full-time workers (Elder, 1980; Horan & Hargis, 1991). Across the first half of the 20th century, the proportion who went to high school climbed steadily and steeply. It reached 35% in 1920 and 80% in 1950. The proportion who worked dropped just as steeply. By 1940, only 1 out of 20 high school students worked during the school year (U.S. Department of Commerce, 1940). It was the end of the Depression, jobs were scarce, and in any case people assumed that a student's job was to study—that's why they called it schoolwork.

The decades between 1940 and 1980 saw a dramatic shift. As the economy changed from industrial toward postindustrial, more and more jobs could be handled by low-wage part-time employees (Ginzberg, 1977). Teenagers moved in to fill them. By 1980, about two-thirds of high school seniors had worked part time while in school (Lewin-Epstein, 1981). By 1997, almost the same proportion of 14-year-olds reported that they had worked for pay at some point (U.S. Department of Labor, 2000). During any given week of the school year, 9% of 15-year-olds, 26% of 16-year-olds, and 39% of 17-year-olds have a paying job (U.S. Department of Labor, 2000). The percentage for 15-year-olds would probably be higher if it weren't for legal restrictions on the kinds of work those under 16 are allowed to do.

What, Where, How Long? What sorts of jobs do adolescents do? It depends a lot on how old they are. Younger teens are more likely to work on an informal basis, doing occasional babysitting (mostly girls) or yard work (mostly boys). Between ages 14 and 15, teens start to shift from these casual freelance jobs to working on a steady basis for a particular employer. For most, that means working in a restaurant or store. Averaging across boys and girls, about one-quarter work in food preparation and service and another quarter in retail sales. Almost all the rest do other service, sales, and clerical jobs or, in the case of boys, general labor (U.S. Department of Labor, 2000).

◄ **Learning Objective 7.10**
How many teens work, how much of their time, and for how much money?

▶ Most American teens who work have jobs in retail sales and food service.

Government statistics consider any teen who works at least 1 hour a week for pay to be employed. Most work a good deal more than that. During the school year, over half of those with jobs work 15 or more hours a week. Some 10% work 30 hours or more (U.S. Department of Labor, 2000). Considering that school takes up 30 or 35 hours a week, not including homework, this does not leave much time for eating, sleeping, or hanging with friends. As you might expect, during the summer months many more adolescents work full time or close to.

As for pay, most teens who work earn more than the minimum wage, but not by much. In 1998, when the minimum wage was $5.15, the median earnings for 15- to 17-year-olds were $5.57 an hour (U.S. Department of Labor, 2000). A large majority of teens earned between $5 and $6 an hour, or very close to the median.

Teen Employment, Race, and Family Income. Employment among adolescents varies a lot by family income and across racial/ethnic groups. However, the nature of the differences may not be what you would predict. Teens from higher income families are twice as likely to work as those from lower-income families, and White teens are twice as likely to work as Blacks or Hispanics (U.S. Department of Labor, 2000).

Why these dramatic differences? One factor may be accessibility. The sorts of jobs that are open to adolescents tend to be in the suburbs, which are generally more White and prosperous than urban areas. Teens also have to get to and from work. This can be very hard to manage if public transportation is sparse, they can't afford a car, and their parents can't drive them. It is worth noting that, while proportionately fewer poor and minority teens have jobs, those who do have them tend to work longer hours (Brown, 2001; U.S. Department of Labor, 2000).

The unemployment picture mirrors the employment picture. Looking only at those who are considered in the labor force—either working or actively looking for work—roughly 17% of White adolescents are unemployed. For minority youth, unemployment is much higher, 30% for Hispanics and 35% for Blacks. Breaking the figures down by family income gives a similar result. For teens in the labor force whose family incomes are in the top quarter, only 12% are out of a job. Among those with family incomes in the lowest quarter, 31% are unemployed (U.S. Department of Labor, 2000).

▶ **Learning Objective 7.11**
What do teens gain or lose by working while in school?

Plusses and Minuses of Teen Employment

Work ethic The belief that working brings positive personal benefits, such as a strengthened character, in addition to whatever goods the work produces.

The **work ethic**—the belief that work is a positive virtue and that "idle hands are the devil's workshop"—has a very long history in American culture. In 1641, families in the Massachusetts Bay Colony were ordered to make sure their children worked industriously (U.S. Department of Labor, 1968). More recently, various government panels, such as the National Commission on Youth (1980), have announced that part-time work is vitally important in helping adolescents make the transition to adulthood. Work, it is said, encourages independence, develops a greater sense of responsibility and self-respect, and promotes positive attitudes and good work habits.

The results from research give a more mixed account (Larson & Verma, 1999; Vondracek & Porfeli, 2003). Working does not seem to have much impact one way or the other on self-esteem or general mental health (Mihalic & Elliot, 1997; Marsh, 1991; Mortimer, Finch, Ryu, Shanahan, & Call, 1996; Steinberg, Fegley, & Dornbusch, 1993). It is, however, linked to school misconduct, delinquency, and greater use of tobacco, marijuana, and alcohol (Mortimer et al., 1996; Steinberg et al., 1993). A study that looked at over 70,000 teens also found relationships between part-time work and aggression, not getting enough sleep, skipping breakfast, and not getting enough exercise (Bachman & Schulenberg, 1993).

As for school achievement, the number of hours worked is more influential than the simple fact of having a job. Those who spend more than 15 or 20 hours a week at work tend to get lower grades, be less involved in school, and have higher dropout rates (Bachman & Schulenberg, 1993; Steinberg & Cauffman, 1995). They also take fewer challenging math and science courses (Singh & Ozturk, 2000) and score lower on standardized tests (Singh, 1998). However, one study found that teens who work a moderate amount earn better grades than either those working more than 20 hours or those who don't work at all (Mortimer et al., 1996).

Jobs and Family Life. When adolescents begin to work, their place in the family often changes in complex ways. They may begin to form connections to the adult world that are independent of their parents. Some parents appreciate their children's greater independence as a step toward maturity. Others find it a threat to their authority. On the whole, teens who work may have better communication and more emotional closeness with their parents (Shanahan, Mortimer, & Krüger, 2002; Steinberg & Cauffman, 1995). However, here again the amount teens work is an important factor. Teens who work less than 20 hours a week see their parents as more caring and trusting than either those who work more than 20 hours or those who don't work (Pickering & Vazsonyi, 2002). They also rate their communication with their parents as better.

Working also has an impact on family time (Mihalic & Elliott, 1997; Mortimer & Shanahan, 1994). How many parents have suggested some family activity, only to be told, "Sorry, I have to work that weekend." Certainly adolescents who work *believe* their jobs interfere with family life, even when the amount of time they actually spend with their family is about the same as for teens who don't work (Pickering & Vazsonyi, 2002). This is not necessarily a contradiction. The pressure of juggling school, job, homework, and friends may make what contact they do have with their parents feel less like "quality time."

Where Does the Money Go? One of the benefits adolescents are said to gain from working is a better understanding of the value of money. A child's allowance might as well fall from heaven, but a paycheck clearly represents a certain amount of time and energy that could have been used in other, probably more pleasant, ways. That exchange— the employee's work for the employer's money—gives the employee an excellent reason to plan, budget, save, and make prudent decisions about expenses. Or not. For most working teens, not.

Hardly any teens with jobs save much of their earnings to pay for their education or contribute to household expenses. If they save at all, it's for renting a stretch limo on prom night. In fact, having a working teen in the family increases some household expenses, including transportation, meals out, entertainment, and housing (Johnson & Lino, 2000). Not many American parents really expect their teens to help out with the family budget or even to put money aside for college. One researcher found that nearly

Connect the Dots...

As an adolescent, did you work part time while going to school? Imagine you are talking with someone from a country where it is less common for students to work during the school year. How would you describe the experience? What would you say you learned from your work life? Do you expect that what you learned will be of value to you in your intended career as an adult? Why, or why not?

half of those between the ages of 12 and 18 were expected to spend all their earnings any way they liked (Meeks, 1998).

How do teens like to spend their earnings? You can probably write out the list without reading any further. More than half of teen spending is on clothing and entertainment (Klein, 1998). Teens who work spend 36% more on clothing every year than those who don't work (Johnson & Lino, 2000). As for entertainment, that includes movies, CDs, electronic gadgets, pizza with friends, and for many, alcohol and drugs (Greenberger & Steinberg, 1986). Teen spending is described in the following newspaper article excerpt.

What Recession? Teens Still Spending
by Kurt Blumenau

Pat Allen isn't afraid to spend money.

Three or four times a month, the Catasauqua High School senior sees a shirt, a music CD, or something else that catches his fancy. He doesn't hesitate to buy it, using money he earns working 20 hours a week at the Yocco's restaurant on Hamilton Boulevard in Allentown.

"I go ahead and put it on my debit card," Allen said.

SOURCE: *ALLENTOWN (PA) MORNING CALL*, MAY 4, 2003.

One observer argues that American adolescents with jobs are suffering from **premature affluence** (Bachman, 1983). They have a lot of money to spend and few hesitations about spending it, mostly because they know their basic necessities are taken care of. Later, when they are out on their own and paying for a place to live and food to eat, the spending habits they learned as teens may get them into deep financial trouble. Far from teaching them the value of money, adolescent employment teaches them that it's cool and easy to buy stuff. Not that they should be blamed too much for these materialistic attitudes. As we will see in the next chapter, a whole industry of highly skilled, highly paid adult marketers is devoted to helping them learn exactly that lesson.

Bridging the Gap Between School and Work

▶ **Learning Objective 7.12**
How can social programs ease the transition between school and work?

Many American adolescents who are employed develop a cynical attitude toward work (Greenberger & Steinberg, 1986). One big reason is that most see little connection between what they do at work and their personal goals, ambitions, and dreams for the future. A lucky few land a job that fits with or awakens their interest in some field that they want to explore. For the rest, those 15 or 20 hours a week are primarily about chatting with co-workers and getting the money to buy stuff. Nine out of 10 adolescents hope to continue their education after high school (Venenzia, 2003). Not many of them intend to pursue a degree in flipping hamburgers, raking lawns, refolding and shelving sweaters, or ringing up housewares purchases.

From what we have seen of the research, it seems clear that the American custom of encouraging teens to work part time after school does not give them an understanding of and preparation for the world of adult work. Nor does it do much for their skills, self-esteem, or commitment to developing and using their potential in ways that benefit themselves and society. Are there other models that may do the job better?

One approach experts often point to is the **apprenticeship** system in some European countries. From the time they are 14 or 15, young people split their time between school and on-the-job training. When they finish, usually at 19, they take a comprehensive exam. If they pass, they receive a government diploma that leads to a full-time career-oriented job in their field or, for some, further training at a technical college (Haefeli, 2000; Hamilton & Hamilton, 2003; Kerckhoff, 2002). About two-thirds of all youth in Germany and Switzerland complete an apprenticeship in fields that range from banking and insurance to medical technology and hotel management (Haefeli, 2000; Shanahan et al., 2002).

Premature affluence The experience of having disposable income with few responsibilities, which may give adolescents unrealistic attitudes toward money.

Apprenticeship A system in which adolescents divide their time between school and on-the-job training, leading to a certificate or diploma in their chosen career field.

To be successful, apprenticeship programs rely on close cooperation among the business, labor, government, and educational sectors, not to mention adolescents themselves (Hamilton & Hamilton, 2003). These programs also expect teens to be willing to make important career decisions at an early age. Critics question whether these qualifications fit well with American society (Kantor, 1994). Even so, in the 1990s the U.S. government funded a 5-year program called *School-to-Work*. Its purpose was to explore ways to strengthen connections between school and work. One of these was apprenticeships. Others included *cooperative education* and *internships* (Hamilton & Hamilton, 2003).

Cooperative education, which enrolls mostly vocational students, involves a semester or year of classroom learning combined with paid practical training in a workplace. The school plans and supervises a student's program and gives academic credit for work experience. Often the program and placement are customized to the individual student's needs and interests. *Internships* also combine school-based and work-based learning, but they are usually less formal than cooperative education. An intern may or may not be paid, may or may not receive school credit, and may or may not be closely supervised. Both internships and cooperative education are more flexible than apprenticeships, but unlike apprenticeships, they do not lead to a widely recognized certification or credential (Hamilton & Hamilton, 2003).

Those who run school-to-work programs have devoted most of their efforts to the "forgotten half," teens who get out of high school and look for a job instead of going to college to prepare for a career. Certainly, as we saw earlier in the chapter, these teens do not usually get the attention and help they need. However, the challenge of finding a vocation that is personally fulfilling is one that confronts all adolescents, whether they are college-bound or work-bound (Vondracek & Porfeli, 2003). If their job experience while still in high school can be made more meaningful, it may help them to meet that challenge successfully.

Summing Up...

American adolescents generally work part time at some point while in school. Most work in food preparation and service, retail sales, and clerical jobs. Over half of those with jobs put in 15 or more hours a week at barely more than the minimum wage. Teens from higher income and White families find it easier to find jobs. Working during adolescence has some benefits, but drawbacks include poor school performance and more problem behaviors. The money earned goes mostly for clothing and entertainment and may lead to bad spending habits. The jobs American teens hold while in school seldom have much relevance to their adult interests and goals. School-to-work programs, such as apprenticeships and internships, try to connect adolescent employment with the skills needed for adult careers.

SUMMARY

School is the place where adolescents spend much of their time, interact with friends and peers, acquire new skills, and come to grips with the concerns and expectations of adult society.

Learning Objective 7.1 How have policy debates shaped secondary education?

Educational issues often arouse heated controversy. Across the 20th century, high school enrollment soared from a small minority of teens to practically all of them. The **comprehensive high school** offered different tracks that reflected the presumed abilities and future employment of students. In contrast,

progressive education saw the role of high schools as promoting equality by having students of many backgrounds study the same subjects together.

Learning Objective 7.2 What are the effects of school climate and school membership?

Standards-based education involves setting performance goals that all students are expected to meet. Until recently, the trend has been to make secondary schools larger. Those who favor smaller secondary schools argue that students get more personal attention, feel safer, and are less likely to drop out.

For adolescents, smaller classes do not seem to have much effect.

Moving from one school level to another is a source of stress for students. Common models in the United States include 6-3-3: 6 years of elementary school, 3 years of **junior high school**, and 3 years of high school, and 5-3-4: 5 years of elementary school, 3 years of **middle school**, and 4 years of high school. Studies suggest that students may be better off in an 8-4 system, 8 years of primary school and 4 years of high school.

Learning Objective 7.3 **How do teacher expectations affect students?**

The way a school functions affects students' desire to learn, sense of belonging, and positive development. Some schools stress competition and high grades, which encourages a **performance orientation**. Other schools stress personal effort and improvement, which encourages a **mastery orientation**. Many schools assign students to different levels of courses according to their grades and presumed ability. This may take the form of **tracking** or of looser ability grouping. Ability grouping may benefit students who are placed in higher level courses, but has negative effects on those assigned to low-ability and non-college-prep classes. Minority youth and those of lower socioeconomic status are more likely to be assigned to low-ability courses.

School climate is affected by both the demandingness and the responsiveness of the school. In demanding schools, students know they are expected to perform up to their potential and to show reliance and self-control. In responsive schools, students feel that teachers and staff respect their opinions and take them seriously. A good stage-environment fit between a school and its adolescent students promotes personal autonomy and competence. A strong sense of **school membership** contributes to the mental health as well as the academic performance of students. Students in smaller schools, and those who participate more in school clubs, teams, and organizations, feel a greater sense of school membership.

Teachers with a strong sense of personal efficacy put more effort into their relationships with students, communicate high expectations, and persist longer when their initial efforts do not succeed. Middle school and junior high school teachers tend to have less confidence in their teaching efficacy than elementary school teachers. They are also less likely to get involved with their students' social and emotional problems. Teacher expectations for their classes and for individual students can create a self-fulfilling prophecy. Students who are expected not to perform well may be treated in ways that make it more likely they will not perform well. Teachers' expectations are often linked to a student's gender, race, social class, and personal attractiveness.

Good teachers, like authoritative parents, set high expectations, give praise when these expectations are met, strike a balance between autonomy and control, and project a sense of warmth, responsiveness, and support.

Learning Objective 7.4 **What are the issues around school diversity, school choice, exceptional students, and the dropout problem?**

Current issues around education include racial integration and diversity, greater school choice, students with exceptional abilities or educational needs, and encouraging teens to stay in school.

Over the last half century, racial integration in public schools first increased, then decreased. The average White student goes to a school where the great majority of students are White, and many Black students go to schools that are almost entirely Black. There are fewer White students in public school than in years past and more of them live in mostly White suburbs. During the same period, the proportion of Hispanic and Asian students in public schools increased sharply. More and more students attend **multiracial schools** in which three or more racial groups each make up at least 10% of the student body.

School choice makes it easier for students to transfer from one public school to another they think is better. **Charter schools** are publicly funded schools that are exempt from many regulations in the hope of encouraging innovation. **Education vouchers** use public funds to help parents meet the cost of sending their children to private and religious schools. In **home schooling**, parents take on the responsibility of educating their children, usually with some guidance and regulation.

Some students, called **gifted**, have unusually strong talents or abilities. Others, called **disabled**, have problems that interfere with their school success. Gifted students may be channeled into more advanced or enriched classes, such as Advanced Placement or **AP classes**. In many schools, those with disabilities or special needs are placed in regular classrooms, a practice called **mainstreaming**.

About 1 in 10 adolescents leave high school without graduating. These **dropouts** have much higher unemployment than high school graduates and earn much less if they do find a job. Dropout rates have declined in recent years, especially for Blacks, but remain high for Hispanics, particularly for those born outside the United States. Predictors of dropping out include lack of academic success, pregancy, low family socioeconomic status, delinquency, and having a first language other than English. Students at risk of dropping out may be helped by small academies within schools that promote learning and a sense of school membership.

Extracurricular and after-school activities contribute to the educational experience of most American adolescents.

Learning Objective 7.5 **What are the benefits of extracurricular activities?**

Taking part in a school-based club, activity, or team sport is linked to a long list of benefits, including increased motivation and involvement, a stronger sense of school membership, better grades, higher educational aspirations, better self-esteem, and fewer problem behaviors.

Learning Objective 7.6 **How do after-school programs help teens?**

The daytime hours after school are often considered high risk, especially for unsupervised teens in **self-care**. Students are attracted to after-school programs by the chance to be with peers, the opportunities to explore new activities, and an unschool-like setting that allows them to relax and be themselves.

Most American high school students expect to go on to college.

Learning Objective 7.7 What proportion of adolescents go to college and how many stay in?

About two-thirds of high school graduates enter college. Teens from poorer families and those from minority ethnic backgrounds are less likely to enter college and much less likely to finish college. The United States offers an enormous range of choices in higher education, but most high school students suffer from a lack of information and individual counseling. About half of those who enter college have to take remedial courses, and many do not return after their freshman year.

Learning Objective 7.8 What problems face teens who finish high school but do not go on to college?

College education is increasingly a requirement for most well-paying jobs. The one-third of teens who finish high school but do not enter college, the **forgotten half**, typically get little in the way of information, training, and advice about making their way in the working world.

Learning Objective 7.9 What are mentors and how can they be more effective?

Adolescents who have a **mentor** to give them advice, guidance, and support have more positive attitudes toward school and are less likely to get involved in misconduct.

Learning Objective 7.10 How many teens work, how much of their time, and for how much money?

A majority of American adolescents work. Younger teens mostly do occasional babysitting (girls) or yard work (boys). Those 15 and over are likely to work on a steady basis in offices, restaurants, and stores. Over half of those with jobs work 15 or more hours a week during the school year and more during the summer. A large majority are paid at or close to the minimum wage. White teens and those from higher income families are twice as likely to find work as those from minority and lower income backgrounds.

Part-time work while still in school is common among American adolescents.

Learning Objective 7.11 What do teens gain or lose by working while in school?

Adolescents with part-time jobs generally expect to spend their earnings any way they like. More than half of teen spending is for clothing and entertainment. This **premature affluence** may lead to unrealistic and harmful attitudes about money.

Learning Objective 7.12 How can social programs ease the transition between school and work?

Efforts to strengthen the connection between school and work and smooth the transition include **apprenticeships**, cooperative education programs, and internships.

KEY TERMS

Comprehensive high school (211)
Progressive education (211)
Standards-based education (212)
Junior high school (215)
Middle school (215)
Performance orientation (218)

Mastery orientation (218)
Tracking (218)
School climate (219)
School membership (220)
Busing (227)
Multiracial schools (228)
School choice (229)
Charter schools (229)

Education vouchers (229)
Home schooling (230)
Gifted (231)
Disabled (231)
AP class (231)
Mainstreaming (231)
Dropouts (232)
Extracurricular activities (233)

Self-care (236)
Forgotten half (240)
Mentor (241)
Social capital (241)
Work ethic (244)
Premature affluence (246)
Apprenticeship (246)

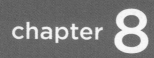

chapter 8

Community, Culture, and the Media

So far we have looked at adolescents in settings that are close at hand—their families, their friends and peers, their schools, and their workplaces. These settings affect the teen directly, and the teen affects them directly as well. In the language of Bronfenbrenner's (1989) ecological systems theory of development, which we encountered in Chapter 2, they all help to make up the adolescent's *microsystem*.

There are other aspects of a teen's world that have just as great an impact, but are more impersonal. The local community where the teen lives is part of what Bronfenbrenner calls the *exosystem*. How does the exosystem affect teens? Here is an example: In one community, adults may think of adolescents as a precious resource to be fostered. In another community, they may see them as a potential threat to be watched and kept down. The contrasting atmospheres and policies these attitudes encourage will affect all the adolescents in each community, whether they did anything to inspire them.

Communities, in turn, are embedded in the *macrosystem*, the broad ideology of the adolescent's culture, subculture, or social class. This is a system of beliefs that sets forth, among other things, how children should be treated, how they should behave, what their proper place is in the social world, and what their goals in life should be. These beliefs are passed along to younger generations both by individuals—parents, teachers, neighbors—and by institutions such as schools, government agencies, and the media.

A great many of the people who study adolescence think of themselves as social scientists. One of the traditional goals of social science has been to develop theories that describe, explain, and predict what human beings *in general* think, feel, and do. Consider how many of the statements, descriptions, and ideas in this book refer to "adolescents." In principle, that means any adolescent, anywhere.

At the same time, we all know that human beings are enormously diverse. Individuals are different from one another, often widely different. So are families, groups of friends, school student bodies, generations, communities, ethnic groups, social classes, linguistic communities, regions, nations, and groups of nations.

Each group, from the most particular to the most inclusive, has its own attitudes, customs, and beliefs. These are rooted in its history, its position within larger groups, its access to education, information, and opportunity, and so on. These attitudes and beliefs are far from fixed. As circumstances change, people and groups change, too—and they don't necessarily all change in the same direction. For example, in response to globalization, some people and groups in more traditional societies become "Westernized." Others cling more tightly to local traditions, even to some that were on the point of disappearing. Still others try to create a blend of local and global ways of living, or to move back and forth between the two.

In this chapter, we take a close look at some of the ways social groups and social forces have an impact on adolescent development. We turn first to communities and the different ways adolescents connect to them. Next, we examine the role of culture and cultural differences in the lives of adolescents. Finally, we assess the influence of what many see as the defining force of our era, information technology and the media.

ADOLESCENTS AND COMMUNITY

What comes to mind when you try to imagine a good way of life? For a great many Americans, this question calls up a nostalgic vision of life in a small town about 75 years ago. Everybody knows everybody else. People say "hi" and pause to chat as they walk to work or to the store. The local cop helps children cross the street and occasionally stops traffic to let a stray dog or a family of ducklings cross safely.

After school and on weekends, teens roller skate, ride their bikes, and get together to play a game or build a tree house in the woods. If a teenager has problems, some kindly teacher or neighbor will notice and help out. There is always something to do—social clubs, fraternal organizations, bowling leagues, churches, and schools sponsor one event after another. If all else fails, you and your friends can decide to put on a play in someone's garage.

◄ The sense of community in small town life has broad nostalgic appeal.

Of course, this is a fantasy. It has been fostered over the years by films, television shows, and "Main Street USA" attractions in theme parks. It isn't hard to find very different descriptions of small-town life, ones that depict a world of racist divisions, petty feuds, nosy neighbors, and stifling pressure to conform. The question, however, is not whether the fantasy is realistic, but what makes it so attractive.

The Need to Belong

In the last chapter we came across the idea that all of us naturally have a *need to belong* (Baumeister & Leary, 1995; Deci, Vallerland, Pelletier, & Ryan, 1991; Newman & Newman, 2001). In any social setting, be it a club, a classroom, a workplace, or even an elevator stuck between floors, people want to feel that they have positive social relationships with those around them. One of the most chilling playground threats is, "I'm not going to talk to you any more!"

A Sense of Community. The strength of the small-town fantasy is that it offers a **sense of community**. In this imagined environment, people feel intimately connected to one another and to the group as a whole. Social divisions—between generations, social classes, genders, ethnic groups—may exist, but they are less important than the sense of common membership and common purpose that unites people. In particular, children and adolescents see themselves as an acknowledged, valued, and protected part of the larger community. In return, they acknowledge, respect, and value the community.

We all know that life is not like that today, if it ever was (Putnam, 2000). More and more Americans live in suburban areas where the closest thing to a Main Street is the local shopping mall. Instead of living down the street or a few blocks away, teachers, doctors, and other significant figures in the community may have to drive half an hour or more just to get home after work. Children grow up with no clear idea of what their parents do during the workday, and parents are just as unclear about what their children do at, and after, school.

◄ **Learning Objective 8.1**
What is a sense of community and why is it important to teens?

Sense of community The feeling of close connection and shared purpose that unites the person with others in the group.

▶ Poor inner-city neighborhoods place multiple stresses on teens and their parents.

Along with lack of knowledge and connection comes lack of confidence. The age segregation described in earlier chapters leaves both teens and adults with inaccurate, unflattering, and often alarming stereotypes of one another. The social bonds that could unite the community are replaced by social distance and distrust. To passing motorists who have watched too much sensational television, those teens hanging out on the corner look like gang members and drug dealers. The result of this distrust is that adolescents become *disaffected*. They stop caring about the welfare of the community, because they do not think the community cares about their welfare.

The Left Out. Achieving a sense of belonging is even more difficult for those growing up in inner-city neighborhoods (Hart & Atkins, 2002). The many stresses, including poverty, unemployment, inadequate housing, and dysfunctional schools, help foster a sense of being disregarded, unimportant, and powerless. This is so for teens *and* for many of the adults they look to for guidance. Inner-city teens are less likely to belong to a team or club, in part because there are proportionately fewer adults in the neighborhood to serve as coaches and advisors (Hart & Atkins, 2002). We should not be surprised to learn that *social trust*—in neighbors, shopkeepers, police officers, and people in general—is lower in racially and socially diverse urban areas than in more homogeneous suburbs (Saguaro Seminar, 2001).

An additional problem is that feelings of powerlessness tend to perpetuate themselves. Suppose the basketball court in a particular neighborhood is in bad shape. In a middle-class neighborhood, the teens who use the court or their parents will probably know how to find out which town official to approach for repairs. They will expect that their request will be listened to, and if it isn't, they will become indignant. They may organize a committee, circulate a petition, get neighbors involved, and generally make life difficult for town officials until the court is resurfaced. In a disadvantaged neighborhood, however, adolescents are less likely to expect help or attention from authorities in the first place. They may not even ask to have the court fixed. If they do and are turned down, instead of pressing the issue, they may see this as confirming and strengthening their sense of themselves as powerless and unimportant.

Community Engagement

What can be done to help adolescents feel more like active members of the community, instead of like outsiders looking in? How can they achieve a better understanding of their rights, responsibilities, and relationships with those around them? According to experts in the field, these crucial developments get a major boost from

Connect the **Dots...**

When you were growing up, were you aware of feeling connected to your community? If so, how did it show itself? What factors helped bring it into being? If not, were you aware at the time of not having such a sense of community? Were there aspects of your life that made you feel separate from the community? Did you believe you were missing something important that your peers had?

▶ **Learning Objective 8.2**
What can be done to build a stronger sense of community?

participation in local community organizations (Flanagan, 2003; Youniss, McLellan, & Yates, 1997). As teens exercise their rights as members and take on responsibilities in the organization's activities, they begin to feel that their contribution is important and their views count. They matter.

Benefits of Community Organizations. Community organizations for adolescents are sometimes seen, by both supporters and opponents, as little more than a way to "keep kids off the street and away from drugs." Research suggests that in fact these groups can have a significant place in an adolescent's development. Specifically, these organizations help teens identify with the common good and become engaged in their community. Psychologist Constance Flanagan (2003) points to several factors that help this come about.

The way teens become accepted and trusted by the group is through working toward common goals and getting past differences that might divide the group. This encourages the development of a collective identity, an "us" orientation instead of a "me" orientation.

In families and schools, power and authority are top-down, but in democratically organized youth groups, everyone has a similar chance to speak up and take a leadership role. This helps build an identification with the group and its goals. As they work with others toward a group goal, adolescents realize that people have different points of view. Getting anywhere, or just keeping the group together, usually requires everyone to be willing to bargain and compromise. Individuals learn to make the organization's well-being a goal alongside their personal goals. At least sometimes, that means putting the organization first. You may really want to speak for the group at a community meeting, but if you know that another member will be more effective, you step aside for the good of the group and its goals.

Taking an active part in a community organization has another benefit as well. It helps adolescents develop positive, ongoing relationships with concerned, caring adults. In America today, the only adults most teens interact with regularly are parents and teachers (Larson & Richards, 1994). Adding a coach or group advisor to that list broadens the adolescent's knowledge of adult society and access to it. And those adults who give their time and energy to work with teens also serve as good models of positive community involvement.

The benefits are not all on one side. The energy and enthusiasm young people bring to community organizations can inspire new efforts and new achievements. By insisting that they have a meaningful voice in the decisions of the organization, they may give new life to the organization's internal life. Because they don't know that some project "can't be done," they may push the boundaries of what the organization is willing to attempt and able to accomplish (Flanagan, 2003).

What Values? In describing how adolescents gain a sense of community from taking part in youth organizations, we have assumed that these groups are run along democratic lines and embrace such values as trust, tolerance, equality, and compassion (Flanagan, 2003). These values are at the heart of American civil society, but they are not peculiar to North America. Adolescents around the world endorse the concepts of free speech and democratic procedures (Helwig, Arnold, Tan, & Boyd, 2003; Torney-Purta, Lehmann, Oswald, & Schulz, 2001), and the United Nations Convention on the Rights of the Child stresses children's right to free expression and self-determination (Limber & Flekkoy, 1995).

Even so, we should recognize that youth organizations, like young people themselves, are strongly affected by the values of the larger community. The most murderous tyrannies in recent history had the enthusiastic support of huge popular youth organizations (Erikson, 1950; Lerner, 1992). The anthem of Mussolini's Fascists, *Giovinezza* ("Youth"), hailed "Youth, youth, Springtime of beauty!" The Hitler Youth of Nazi Germany, like the Red Guards of Maoist China's Cultural Revolution, eagerly persecuted those they had been taught to see as the enemies of the state. The reason was not that they were mean, nasty people (though some undoubtedly were!).

They were told, and they believed, that they were fighting for the social goals of admired adult leaders and the good of the community. They also gained a sense of identification and solidarity with their fellow teen members and with the community as a whole. When they paraded through the streets, adult spectators cheered.

We can draw important lessons from these historical experiences. The same characteristics that make young people such a precious resource for the community—their idealism, their energy, their readiness to throw themselves into a project—can be subverted, turned to antidemocratic ends. It is not enough that a community organization has the support and involvement of adolescents. We also have to look closely at the values the organization fosters in its members, both through what it says and what it does.

"Winning Isn't Everything"

▶ **Learning Objective 8.3**
How do organized teen sports help or hinder the growth of a sense of community?

One of the most popular categories of community activities for young people is athletics. In the United States, tens of millions of young people take part in organized, community-based sports such as Little League baseball, soccer and hockey leagues, swimming, tennis, and basketball (Poinsett, 1996). In fact, the game of basketball got its start at a YMCA in New England as a way for adolescents to stay active in winter, when it was too cold for outdoor sports. Taking part in athletics has a long list of potential benefits for teens, including physical fitness and better coordination, of course, but also increased motivation, self-control, discipline, and self-esteem. Playing an organized sport can give valuable lessons in teamwork, cooperation, and sportsmanship. It is also a way to form closer ties with peers, adults, and the community at large.

Unfortunately, the reality is often different. In today's society, the lure of a trophy or title often counts for much more than the pleasure of playing the game. Too many youth coaches and parents have adopted, and passed along to young athletes, the view expressed by pro football coach Vince Lombardi: "Winning isn't everything, it's the *only* thing!" Generally this hyper-competitive attitude gets public attention only when supporters of children on opposite teams assault one another (for example, "Parents of Hockey Players Accused of Attacking Third Parent" [Associated Press, 2003]). The atmosphere it generates, however, poisons the experience for everyone playing. Youth sports leagues have a shortage of volunteer referees, who get fed up with fans who yell "Kill the ump!" or try to slug them over a controversial decision (Still, 2002). In recent years, doctors have started seeing young adolescents with the sorts of serious knee injuries that are usually associated with professional athletes (Kolata, 2008).

According to psychologist William Damon (1997), this "win at any cost" orientation turns youth participation in sports away from its original goal, which was to help build moral character as well as physical fitness. Hardly any of the teens who take part in organized sports will go on to become professional athletes. Why let an exaggerated stress on winning ruin their enjoyment of the activity? To help make organized sports a more positive experience for adolescents, Damon (1997) urges communities to adopt a "youth charter." This would include a pledge of public support for youth sports, an emphasis on sportsmanlike conduct, and measures to promote broader participation by average players as well as exceptional athletes. Some leagues, for example, have adopted a "no-cut" policy. Everyone who signs up and attends practice regularly gets to play on a team.

Summing Up...

Adolescents need to feel that they are connected to family, friends, and neighbors and that they matter. Recent social changes have made it harder to achieve this sense of community, especially for those growing up in poverty. Participation in community organizations can help by fostering a sense of being accepted and listened to and by offering experience in working with others in a democratic setting. Most community organizations embody positive social values, but some communicate messages, such as winning at any cost, that undermine their effect.

THE ROLE OF CULTURE

Alle Menschen werden Brüder

(*All men will become brothers*)

— SCHILLER, *Ode to Joy*

Oh, East is East, and West is West, and never the twain shall meet.

— KIPLING, *Ballad of East and West*

Try this quiz. For each of the following statements, indicate how much you agree or disagree:

1	2	3	4	5	6	7
Strongly Disagree				Strongly Agree		

1. True happiness comes from making those around you happy.
2. Don't hide your light under a bushel—if you've got it, flaunt it.
3. Respect for authority is what holds a society together.
4. The greatest thrill is being singled out as a winner.
5. Young people should follow their parents' advice about educational and career plans.
6. The key to self-respect is being able to stand on your own.

Now look over your responses. You probably see them as indicating something about your personal view of the world. And, of course, they do. But they also say something about your background. If you grew up in North America or Western Europe, chances are you agreed more with the even-numbered than the odd-numbered items. If you grew up in Korea, Japan, or China, however, just the opposite pattern is likely.

The explanation for this difference is that people in various parts of the world have different ideas about what personal attitudes are most desirable. Adolescents in these different regions, while similar in some ways, vary widely in many of their attitudes, beliefs, and behaviors. If you ask a classmate to go to a movie, and he or she nods in reply, you probably assume that means yes. In most parts of the world, it does, but in Japan, it may mean nothing more than, "I've heard and understood your question." And in some places, such as certain areas of Greece and Turkey, it means "No" (Matsumoto, 2000)!

So which poet is right? Schiller, who foresaw universal brotherhood? Or Kipling, who saw an unbridgeable gap between peoples? In this section, we examine some of the differences and similarities across different societies. How do they come about? What implications do they have for adolescent development? What about groups, such as immigrants, racial/ethnic minorities, and different social classes, that may exist *within* a particular society but have different attitudes and behaviors? How do teens with these backgrounds adapt to the larger society, and how does the society as a whole adapt to them?

What Is Culture?

Scholars have been trying for a century or more to agree on a good definition of *culture*. One said that "culture is to society what memory is to individuals" (Kluckhohn, 1954). Others have described culture as "what has worked in the experience of a society, so that it was worth transmitting to future generations" (Triandis & Suh, 2002), or simply as the shared way of life of a group of people (Berry, Poortinga, Segall, & Dasen, 1992). For our purposes, we can think of **culture** as a relatively stable system of norms, beliefs, values, attitudes, and behaviors that is shared by a group and transmitted across generations.

▶ **Learning Objective 8.4**
How can the study of cultures help us understand adolescence?

Culture A relatively stable system of shared norms, beliefs, values, and behaviors that is passed along across generations.

There are several things to notice about this definition. First, cultures are only *relatively* stable. As a rule, they do not change very quickly or easily, but they do change. For example, 50 years ago, the culture of the American South required Whites and Blacks to use separate eating places, restrooms, and water fountains. Today, most Americans, especially those too young to have grown up in that culture, find this practice, and the racist beliefs that inspired it, bizarre and repugnant.

Second, cultures are not just a grab-bag of random customs, they are *systems*. The values, beliefs, norms, and behaviors of a particular culture interconnect and work together. Take the question of whether teens address adults by their first or last name. This behavior has links to cultural beliefs about hierarchy, equality, and the place of adolescents in society; to norms of deference; to cultural values such as respect and intimacy; and so on.

Third, while the elements of a culture are shared by a group, there are also individual differences. Not everyone in the group adheres equally to all the culture's elements. Many, perhaps most, are mainstream in their core beliefs, values, and behaviors. However, there are also those who differ, some in small ways and some in large. "Loose" cultures tend to be tolerant of these deviations, while "tight" cultures enforce strict conformity to cultural rules (Pelto, 1968).

Why Study Culture?   According to an old saying, fish do not know about water because it is all around them all the time. Something similar can be said about one's own cultural beliefs and practices. They seem so ordinary, so normal, so natural, that they usually go unnoticed. If you happen to come across people who think or behave differently, you may be inclined to see them as *extra*ordinary, *ab*normal, and *un*natural. It will probably not occur to you that they may find you just as peculiar as you find them.

This is an example of **ethnocentrism**, the tendency to interpret the world from the standpoint of one's own cultural values and assumptions (Matsumoto, 2000). All of us have this tendency, just as all of us have a tendency to see things from our own personal standpoint. After all, we live within our own skins and within our own cultures. It takes an act of will and imagination to step outside these ever-present contexts and look from a different vantage point.

This is just as much the case for social scientists as it is for poets, politicians, or plumbers. Even the assumption that social science is an important way to understand people has its roots in Western culture. As a result, the great bulk of social science research, including research on adolescence, has been carried out in America and Western Europe, by American and Western European scholars, who test American and Western European theories, by studying Americans and Western Europeans. The consequence of this semi-monopoly is that the way most Western people behave is often assumed to be the norm for everybody everywhere. If people from another culture act in ways that depart from that norm, they may seem shocking, irrational, or even dangerously immoral.

For example, consider the custom of dating. The majority of Americans take it for granted that at some point in early or middle adolescence (or even *before* adolescence), boys and girls start going to movies, parties, and other social events in heterosexual pairs. It is also assumed, if not stated, that this is a sort of training for emotional and physical intimacy. Dating is not only considered acceptable, it is practically an obligation. If it doesn't happen more or less on schedule, both parents and the teens themselves start to worry.

However, while dating is an ordinary feature of life for American teens today, it would be quite misleading to think of it as a normal part of *adolescence*. In North America, and to a lesser extent in Western Europe, teen dating is considered "normal" (Alsaker & Flammer, 1999). In many parts of the world, however, dating is considered an exotic, faddish import from the West. And in some societies it is condemned as a serious violation of basic cultural and religious values and beliefs.

If everyone is ethnocentric to some extent, does that mean we are doomed to misunderstand people from other cultures and groups? Not necessarily. For a start, we can recognize that we tend to interpret the world from a particular point of view, and that other views are also possible. Second, we can realize that just as we may

Ethnocentrism The tendency to see the world from the standpoint of one's own cultural values and assumptions.

misunderstand people from other cultural backgrounds, they may also be acting on the basis of misunderstanding *us*. Third, we can make an effort to learn about and comprehend the assumptions, beliefs, and values of other cultures. That way, when an issue comes up, we will have the information we need to understand how the situation may look from the other person's standpoint.

Psychology and Culture. Cultural differences in customs and habits can be easy to spot. Some people eat with forks, some with chopsticks, and some with fingers. Some people sleep on beds, some on mats, and some in hammocks. Some people cover practically their whole body, some wear shorts and t-shirts, and some wear nothing at all. *Psychological* differences based on culture are more subtle and more easily missed. Even if someone looks different, dresses different, and acts different, we may still take it for granted that we are all the same under the skin. But that assumption may be wrong.

Here is an example of how psychological processes can be affected by cultural factors (Rubin, 1998). Even as toddlers, some children are more inhibited and socially reticent than others, apparently because of a pattern of biological differences (Fox, Calkins, Schmidt, Rubin, & Coplan, 1996; Kagan, Reznick, & Snidman, 1987). Their shyness with peers often leads to rejection. By early adolescence, they may develop feelings of social ineptness, loneliness, and depression (Boivin, Hymel, & Bukowski, 1995; Rubin, Chen, McDougall, Bowker, & McKinnon, 1995). This is a sad but perfectly logical outcome.

The studies that uncovered this sequence of events, however, looked at children in North America and Western Europe, where assertiveness is expected and valued and the shy child is at a disadvantage. In China, on the other hand, children who are shy, quiet, and reticent are considered particularly well behaved. As adolescents they think well of themselves and their social relationships, and their teachers and peers see them as achievers and leaders (Chen, Rubin, & Li, 1997; Chen, Rubin, Li, & Li, 1999). The biological basis may be the same, but the contrast in cultural values leads to a very different outcome.

Another example comes from a research project that compared how Canadian and Chinese children evaluate telling the truth and lying (Lee, Cameron, Xu, & Board, 1997). The children, who were 7-, 9-, and 11-years-old, heard four brief stories. Two stories were about children who did a good deed, such as secretly giving money so that a classmate could afford to go on a class trip, and then either admitted or denied doing it when asked by the teacher. The other two stories were about children who did something harmful, such as knocking down a classmate, and then either admitted or denied doing it. After hearing each story, the children were asked to evaluate both the action of the child in the story and the child's telling the truth or lying about the action.

◄ Cultural values affect adolescent attitudes in many sometimes surprising ways.

Figure 8.1 Lying About a Good Deed
Cultural values affect whether teens think it is wrong to falsely deny having done a good deed.

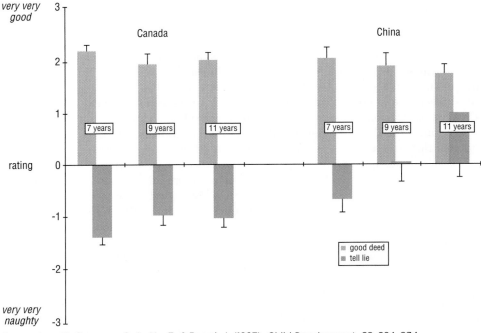

Source: Lee, K., Cameron, C. A., Xu, F., & Board, J. (1997). *Child Development, 68,* 924–934. Used by permission.

On many points, the Canadian and Chinese children agreed. It is good to help a classmate and bad to knock someone down. If you do knock someone down, it is very good to admit what you did and very bad to lie about it. But what about admitting or denying a *good* deed? Figure 8.1 shows an interesting cultural difference. At each age, the Canadian children said that taking credit for a good deed is a good thing and falsely denying you did it is a bad thing. The youngest Chinese children said the same. But the 9-year-olds, while still very positive about taking credit for a good deed, also said denying it was good. The 11-year-olds evaluated *not* taking credit more favorably than taking credit. For these early adolescents, the value their culture places on modesty and self-effacement carried more weight than the prohibition against lying (Lee et al., 1997).

These studies are examples of cross-cultural research. In **cross-cultural research**, participants from different cultures are given the same task or situation or asked the same questions about some aspect of their lives. If the results are similar for the different cultural groups, it suggests that the psychological process being investigated is the same across cultures, or *universal*. If differences are found, it suggests that the process is *culture specific*. Often, as in the study we just looked at by Lee and colleagues (1997), the results reveal both differences and similarities.

We need to use caution when we interpret cross-cultural studies. First, there is the problem that a task or question may not have the same meaning in different cultures (Shweder, 2000). Adolescents in a tribal culture may be baffled by verbal analogy problems, but whiz through complex kinship relationships that would leave American genealogists scratching their heads in puzzlement. Even apparently simple psychological terms may have subtly different connotations in different languages (Triandis & Suh, 2002).

Second, any time we compare two things, we have a tendency to conclude that one is better than the other, instead of simply recognizing that they are different. When it is two cultures that are being compared, and one of them is your own, this is especially tempting. Is it better to take credit for a good deed you've done? The Canadian children said yes, and probably most in the United States would agree. Does that mean the Chinese 11-year-olds were dumb to say you shouldn't take credit? Not at

Cross-cultural research Research that involves comparing how the same process or phenomenon is expressed or experienced by people from different cultural groups.

all. In fact, their responses show a sophisticated understanding of what their culture's value system says one should do when two positive values, truth-telling and modesty, come into conflict.

Individualism and Collectivism

In both the studies we just looked at, Asian children and teens placed a high value on modesty and reticence, while children and teens in North America valued assertiveness more. What does this difference tell us about the cultural systems of the two groups? Many scholars would say that it reflects a more fundamental distinction between cultures that embrace the contrasting worldviews of **individualism** and **collectivism** (Markus & Kitiyama, 1991; Triandis, 1995).

In *individualistic cultures*, people are thought to be unique, separate, and autonomous individuals with their own personal rights, goals, and needs. These may fit with the interests of the group, but if they clash, it is considered normal to put one's personal goals first. The personal characteristics that are highly valued include assertiveness, competitiveness, individual achievement, and self-expression. People think of themselves as *independent*.

In *collectivistic cultures*, people are seen in terms of their relationship to groups such as their family, tribe, religious co-believers, or country. Their activities are guided by the goals, norms, and beliefs of the group. If a conflict comes up between personal and group goals, they are expected to set their personal goals aside and act in the interest of the group. Cooperativeness, modesty, obedience, self-control, and sensitivity to others are highly valued. People see themselves as *interdependent* (Shweder et al., 2006).

A particular culture may contain both individualistic and collectivistic elements. For example, in the United States, a person is under no legal obligation to help someone else. If you see someone collapse in the street and walk on by, you may suffer pangs of conscience later, but you won't get in trouble with the law. In France, however, which would also be considered an individualistic culture, *fraternity* is valued as highly as *liberty* and *equality*. One way this shows itself is that you can be sent to jail for the crime of "failure to render aid to a person in danger."

We should also be aware that many societies in which the majority culture is individualistic have minorities with collectivistic cultures. The North African minority in France, the Turkish minority in Germany, Indian and Pakistani minorities in Britain, and Hispanic and Asian American minorities in the United States are all considered more collectivistic in their cultural orientation than the majorities in these countries. Later in the chapter we discuss adolescents whose family's culture differs from that of the majority culture and look at some of the ways they deal with this situation.

The concepts of individualism and collectivism have been widely used to describe, explain, and comment on the ways values, customs, and psychological processes differ from one society to another (Brewer & Chen, 2007; Triandis & Suh, 2002). The collision between these two worldviews has even been cited as an underlying cause of international tension and conflict (Huntington, 1993). At the same time, critics have said that these concepts are incomplete, inadequate, or misleading (Baumrind, 1998; Briley & Wyer, 2001; Spiro, 1993; Turiel, 2002).

Traditionally, social scientists have seen cultures as unified and harmonious systems whose shared values, beliefs, and practices complement and support one another (Benedict, 1934; Erickson, 2002; Triandis, 1996). What this leaves out, according to critics, is the existence of conflict and opposition in society. What if particular cultural beliefs and practices benefit some segments of society at the expense of others?

One example is the inferior position of girls and women in many traditional societies. The list of cultural practices that they are subjected to around the world includes imposed marriages even as children, genital mutilation, forced seclusion, denial of education and health care, physical and sexual abuse, and "honor killings." A recent film, *Starkiss*, portrays girls in India, some as young as 4, whose debt-ridden families

▶ **Learning Objective 8.5**
How are collectivistic and individualistic cultures different?

Connect the **Dots...**

You are getting ready to leave for a friend's birthday party when your aunt calls you up. She isn't feeling well and asks you to go to the drugstore to pick up some medications. If you agree, you will miss most of your friend's party. What do you do? How is your choice relevant to the distinction between collectivistic and individualistic values?

Individualism A worldview that focuses on the uniqueness and independence of autonomous individuals and stresses the importance of personal rights, goals, and needs.

Collectivism A worldview that focuses on the connectedness of the person to the family or group and stresses the importance of upholding the goals, norms, and beliefs of the group.

have sold them to a traveling circus. Their acrobatic training is grueling and danger-ous, but they are grateful for it, because they know the most likely alternative is being sold into prostitution (Holden, 2003).

Some cultural psychologists maintain that people in collectivistic societies do not share Western standards of individual rights and egalitarian values. They value order and tradition, and they believe in their society's hierarchical structure. If a wife dis-obeys her husband, for instance by going to a movie alone, she will agree that he is morally right to give her a severe beating (Shweder, Mahapatra, & Miller, 1987). Critics respond that too often, cultural psychologists talk to the wrong people, name-ly spokesmen for the particular culture (Wikan, 1991). When those in disadvantaged positions, such as girls and women, are interviewed in situations where they feel free to speak their minds, they often have no difficulty complaining about the injustices they face every day (Turiel, 2002).

For instance, an anthropologist who lived with a Bedouin tribe in rural Egypt found that women and girls certainly noticed and resented their inferior status. One young woman pointed out that the men "make women work hard and don't pay attention to them. Even if the woman is ill, the man won't lift a finger to help, not even to pick up a crying baby" (Abu-Lughod, 1993, p. 239). In a study carried out in southern India, Hindu 10-, 15-, and 20-year-olds were asked about situations in which a husband and wife want to fulfill conflicting personal desires (Neff, 2001). Hindu girls are tradition-ally taught from childhood that a wife's duty is to treat her husband as a lord whose desires are law. Even so, the children and adolescents who took part in the study showed a *mixture* of collectivistic and individualistic ways of reasoning. When the person's desire seemed important, they gave priority to personal autonomy over inter-personal responsibility for husbands *and* wives (Neff, 2001).

Transmitting Culture

► **Learning Objective 8.6**
How do teens acquire the norms and attitudes of their culture?

A few pages ago, in defining culture, we said that it is *transmitted across generations.* That much seems obvious. We are not born knowing the ways of any particular cul-ture. But by the time we reach adulthood we have acquired a whole complex of rules, attitudes, and behavior patterns. The culture a person is raised in even affects brain functioning during simple judgment tasks (Hedden, Ketay, Aron, Markus, & Gabrieli, 2008). What transmission process accounts for this?

In response to this question, cultural anthropologists and psychologists traditionally rely on two closely related concepts: socialization and enculturation. **Socialization** refers to learning the social norms, rules, and behaviors of the *society*. **Enculturation** refers to adopting the underlying psychological aspects of the *culture* (Matsumoto, 2000).

According to this approach, first parents, then siblings, other family members, peers, teachers, religious leaders, and others in the community teach young people the culture's values and customs. They reinforce appropriate behavior, correct mistakes, and serve as models of the accepted way to think, feel, speak, and act. Symbolic mod-els also have a powerful influence. These models include characters in traditional tales, religious sagas, stories, and media presentations. Gradually, over many years and countless interactions, children and adolescents become thoroughly adept in whatever culture they were born into.

The concept of enculturation suggests that a culture is a fixed system "out there," and the child's task is to bring it "in here." An analogy might be learning the alphabet. A child may use blocks, songs, picture books, repetition, Sesame Street skits, or any combination. Whatever the method, the goal is clear: to learn exactly the same ABCs, in exactly the same order, as everyone else in the culture.

If the task of children is simply to fit themselves into a culture, however, how can a culture ever change (Erickson, 2002)? A different approach to cultural transmission is closer to the cognitive theories of Piaget and Vygotsky. In this view, children *construct* an understanding of their culture by testing their ways of thinking and acting against the reactions of others. What they acquire is not a "culture," but an interrelated set of

Socialization The process by which children and adolescents acquire the social norms, rules, and behaviors of their family and society.

Enculturation The process by which children and adolescents acquire the attitudes, beliefs, and psychological aspects of their culture.

practices that allow them to live and function in a particular social community (Brenneis, 2002; Schieffelin, 1990). One implication of this is that people are able to choose from among their repertoire of attitudes and behaviors, instead of blindly following whatever the culture prescribes.

This approach also leaves open the possibility that some understanding children and adolescents construct for themselves clashes with some aspects of their culture. Consider the young Americans who took part in the civil rights movement of the 1960s. The cultural institution they opposed and fought to overcome, racial segregation, had deep roots in American history and everyday life. They opposed it, not because they rejected American culture, but because they were committed to what they saw as basic American values ("We hold these truths to be self-evident, that all men are created equal . . .").

The constructivist view of culture also implies that we go on developing the ability to function in various cultural "communities of practice" all our lives (Bakhtin, 1981; Erickson, 2002; Holland, Lachicotte, Skinner, & Cain, 2001; Rogoff, Turkanis, & Bartlett, 2001; Wenger, 1998). Our families, schools, peers, local communities, and colleagues at work, as well as the media, all give us exposure to different cultures and subcultures. This allows us (or even forces us) to put together varying systems of thinking and acting that work in each community of practice. In this sense, we could say that everybody is multicultural (Glazer, 1997).

Social Diversity

The people of North America have been a diverse lot for centuries. Even in colonial times, many different groups of Native Americans and newcomers from an array of national and religious backgrounds existed alongside one another, not always easily. Today, *ethnic and cultural diversity* among American adolescents is at a record high. The proportion of children in the United States and Canada who belong to ethnic minorities has grown steadily and continues to grow. According to the 2000 U.S. Census, minorities account for 39% of the under-18 population, as compared with 28% of the adult population. Of these, the largest single group of minority children is Hispanic, with 17% of the child population, up from 12% just 10 years earlier (O'Hare, 2001).

◀ **Learning Objective 8.7**
How do teens who belong to an ethnic minority function within a culture?

One reason for this trend is that minority parents tend to have larger families (Ventura, Martin, Curtin, Menacker, & Hamilton, 2000). Another contributing factor is immigration. Immigrants are typically young adults, who are more likely to bring children with them when they immigrate or to have children soon after they arrive (O'Hare, 2001). Of today's American teens, 19%, practically one in five, were born in other countries or are the children of recent immigrants (Forum on Child and Family Statistics, 2002). And unlike the early 20th century, when practically all immigrants were from various regions of Europe, today's new Americans come from every part of the globe. Immigrant children enter U.S. schools speaking over 100 different languages (OBLEMA, 2000).

Many immigrant and ethnic minority adolescents struggle with the additional stresses of family poverty. While minority youth are disproportionately affected by poverty (McLoyd, 1990), almost 1 in 10 White adolescents are poor as well (Forum on Child and Family Statistics, 2002). The United States is often billed as the richest nation in the history of the world. In such a setting, those who have to grow up poor face special obstacles.

Culture and Ethnicity. An **ethnic group** is a group of people who share characteristics such as race, religion, national origin, linguistic background, cultural heritage, and customs. This set of characteristics is known as *ethnicity*. By this definition, all of us belong to at least one ethnic group, and many of us to more than one. The U.S. Census Bureau uses just five ethnic categories: Hispanic, Black (non-Hispanic), White, Native American, and Asian/Pacific Islander. But that is a matter of administrative convenience. Each of these labels covers many groups. The Asian American

Ethnic group A group of people who share characteristics such as race, religion, national origin, linguistic background, cultural heritage, and customs.

category alone can be divided into as many as 29 distinct ethnic groups (Liu, Pope-Davis, Nevitt, & Toporek, 1999).

Many Americans who are part of the White majority have some attachment to their ethnic roots. They may celebrate St. Patrick's Day, eat lutefish, cholent, polenta, or kielbasa, and encourage their children to learn the music, dances, language, and customs of their group of origin. For most of them, however, their ethnic membership is less central than it is for those who belong to ethnic minorities (Waters, 1990). They are not constantly forced to deal with differences between their ethnic group and the majority culture, or even discrimination by the majority culture, because they have been accepted as *part of* the majority. For this reason, most of the research in the United States and Canada on ethnic membership and adolescents has concentrated on people of color: Blacks, Hispanics, Asian Americans, and Native Americans.

It is helpful to separate out three aspects of ethnicity, on the level of the individual, the group, and the society. First, individuals can have a stronger or weaker sense of membership in the group, or *ethnic identity*. Second, each ethnic group has its own *cultural identity*—those attitudes, values, and behaviors that distinguish it from other groups. Third, on the level of society, ethnic minorities are often forced to live with a greater or lesser degree of prejudice, discrimination, and a sense of exclusion from the majority (Phinney, 1996; Williams et al., 2002).

Earlier in the chapter, we saw that children and adolescents take on the psychological aspects of their culture through a process of *enculturation*. Those who have to deal with two or more cultures, such as that of their ethnic group and that of the larger society, face a more complicated task called *acculturation* (Berry, 1995). Do they turn their backs on their ethnic heritage and adopt the majority culture? Do they reject the ways of society and cling to their minority status? Or do they try to hold onto their ethnic background while also taking part in the dominant culture? The way adolescents respond to this problem has important implications for their sense of personal identity, as we will see in Chapter 11.

Majority Relations. Social scientists used to assume that acculturation automatically led to divided loyalties (Stonequist, 1935). Members of ethnic minorities sometimes make the same assumption. This is shown by the contemptuous terms sometimes used for peers they suspect of "acting White." These terms include the Hispanic "coconut" (brown on the outside, white on the inside), the African American "Oreo," the Native American "apple," and the Asian American "banana." The implication is that the only way you can fit into the majority culture is by renouncing your ethnic background.

This is not necessarily so. According to cross-cultural psychologist John Berry (Berry, Kim, Minde, & Mok, 1987), there are four distinct ways immigrants and members of ethnic minorities can relate to the majority culture:

Assimilation—giving up their own culture and identifying with the majority culture;

Marginalization—rejecting both their own culture and the majority culture;

Separation—identifying only with their own group and rejecting the majority culture;

Integration—retaining their identification with their own ethnic group while *also* identifying with the majority culture.

Those people who identify with both their ethnic group and the majority culture are said to become **bicultural**. Research suggests that they have fewer psychological problems than those who assimilate, marginalize, or separate themselves (Berry et al., 1987; Farver, Narang, & Bhadha, 2002; Sam & Berry, 1995).

One way researchers track the process of acculturation is to ask children with immigrant backgrounds what ethnic labels they use for themselves. For example, a study of 7th graders of Mexican descent revealed that among first-generation students, almost two-thirds referred to themselves as Mexican. About one-quarter called

---

Connect the Dots...

How would you describe your own cultural or ethnic background? What experiences helped you to understand and accept your culture? What aspects of your culture's attitudes and values do you identify with most closely? Are there some that you question or reject? If so, at what point did you begin to be aware of that?

Assimilation A process in which members of an ethnic minority renounce their culture of origin and identify with the majority culture.

Marginalization A process in which members of an ethnic minority reject both their culture of origin and the majority culture.

Separation A process in which members of an ethnic minority identify only with their culture of origin and reject the majority culture.

Integration A process in which members of an ethnic minority retain their identification with their culture of origin while *also* identifying with the majority culture.

Bicultural A term for adolescents who have successfully integrated their identifications with both their culture of origin and the majority culture.

◄ Bicultural teens identify with both their own ethnic group and the majority culture.

themselves Mexican American, and the rest used such labels as Hispanic, Chicano, or Latino. By the second generation, however, fewer than one in five used the label Mexican, and the percentage who called themselves Mexican American jumped to 60% (Buriel & Cardoza, 1993).

Minority Parents and Teens. As teens from ethnic minorities deal with the task of acculturation, they also have to deal with the distance between their parents' values and attitudes and those of the majority culture. This is particularly true for children of immigrant families. Children generally acculturate more quickly than their parents (Buki, Ma, Strom, & Strom, 2003; Phinney, Ong, & Madden, 2000; Portes, 1997). Many adult immigrants have had the experience of taking their teenage child along to act as a guide and interpreter with a doctor, a government agency, or the phone company.

As we saw earlier in the chapter, most immigrant groups in the United States, Canada, and Western Europe come from cultures that stress such values as parental authority, conformity, interdependence, and subordinating one's own needs to the needs of the family (Kwak, 2003). These values are also more widespread among African Americans than in the majority White culture (Gaines et al., 1997; Harrison, Wilson, Pine, Chan, & Buriel, 1990). What happens when these parental values and expectations come into contact with the more individualistic outlook adolescents acquire in Western cultures?

One study looked at over 700 families in Southern California (Phinney et al., 2000). The families included Armenian, Mexican, and Vietnamese immigrants, as well as African American and European American non-immigrants. Parents and adolescents alike were asked how much they agreed that children should obey their parents, look after them when they need help, share the work at home without pay, and live at home until they get married. The results are shown in Figure 8.2 on page 266. In every group, the parents believed more strongly in these family obligations than their teenage children did. In the immigrant groups, the longer the families had been in the United States, the *bigger* this gap was between parents and teens. As expected, immigrants endorsed family obligations a good deal more than European Americans, with African Americans in between (Phinney et al., 2000).

The sorts of family obligations that ethnic minority parents rate as particularly important stress the interdependence of family members. At the same time, gaining a sense of personal autonomy is often seen as a central task of adolescence (Kroger,

Figure 8.2 Cultural and Generational Differences in Views of Family Obligations

Parents' and children's views of family obligations differ according to cultural background and amount of time in the United States.

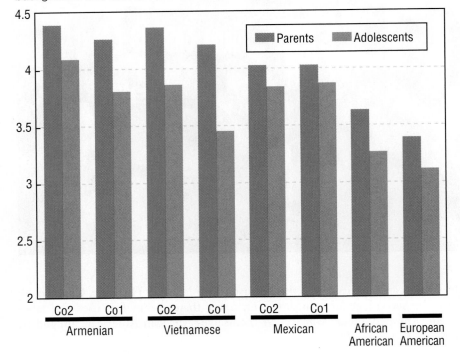

Source: Phinney et al., 2000, p. 535.

1998; Steinberg & Silverberg, 1986). Are ethnic minority teens who set out to achieve this goal bound to clash with the more family-oriented views of their parents? Not necessarily. As Turkish psychologist Cigdem Kagitcibasi (2003) points out, autonomy is not at all the same thing as being separate or distant from others. Adolescents and their parents may disagree over issues of autonomy and still agree on the value of close family ties (Kwak, 2003). This chapter's Research in the Spotlight on page 267 presents a study that explores how a child's sense of obligation toward the family affects school achievement in American teens of European, Asian, and Latin American origin.

In Western societies today, young people often have to make their own decisions about personal, educational, and career choices. At the same time, the social support they receive from their immediate and extended family, and from their ethnic community, can give them a much-needed sense of security (Blair, Legazpi Blair, & Madamba, 1999; Kwak & Berry, 2001). The need for autonomy and the need for family closeness and support may come into conflict, but they do not have to. Parents, too, may see their children's autonomy and relatedness as conflicting goals, but they may also view them as connected and mutually supporting (Tamis-LeMonda et al., 2008). It is possible to integrate these two years in what Kagitcibasi (2003) calls the "autonomous/related self."

In a similar way, the goals and values of an ethnic minority culture may come into conflict with those of the majority culture, but they do not have to. Adolescents may instead manage to integrate the two and become bicultural.

A key element in becoming bicultural is language. A recent study looked at 474 adolescents in the United States from Armenian, Mexican, or Vietnamese backgrounds (Phinney, 2003). Some adolescents were U.S.-born children of immigrants and others were foreign-born who had arrived in the United States before the age of 7. For the foreign-born, whose first language was not English, the better their English, the stronger their *American* identity. For the U.S.-born, on the other hand, the better their command of their parents' language of origin, the stronger their *ethnic* identity.

Culture and Family

Compared to those of European background, Asian and Latin American parents in the United States put a good deal of stress on a child's duties and obligations toward the family. To a great extent, their adolescent children agree with these views (Fuligni, Tseng, & Lam, 1999). Chinese, Filipino, Mexican, and Central and South American teens in the United States believe they should help more around the house, make sacrifices for the family, and respect the wishes and opinions of parents and older family members. And they see these duties to the family not just as a child's duties, but as lifelong obligations.

One important way Asian and Latin American teens think they can help their families is by doing well in school. Often, their parents emigrated to the United States specifically to give their children a better start in life and see education as a key factor in accomplishing this. The children hope success in school will lead to a better career that will put them in a position to support the family in years to come (Zhou & Bankston, 1998). Many teens say that, considering the sacrifices their parents have made, they would feel guilty if they didn't try hard and take advantage of the opportunities they have been given (Suárez-Orozco & Suárez-Orozco, 1995).

How is a sense of family obligation linked to academic motivation? To answer this question, UCLA psychologist Andrew Fuligni and his co-workers carried out a longitudinal study of about 1,000 adolescents from immigrant and native-born families with Asian, Latin American, and European backgrounds (Fuligni, 2001; Fuligni et al., 1999). The research began when the students were in 6th grade and continued through the high

school years. The measures included various aspects of family obligation and academic motivation. The researchers also had access to the school grades of the participants.

One notable finding was that family obligation was strongly linked to the value of success and the usefulness of education in general math and English, but not to *intrinsic* interest in math and English. Those with a stronger sense of duty to their family valued school success more but didn't find their studies any more (or any less) interesting than those with a weaker sense of family obligation.

As Figure R8.1 shows, the transition to high school brought a steep decline in school motivation that continued through 12th grade. However, this drop off was considerably less steep for those with a higher sense of family obligation. While they were affected by the disillusionment with education that is such a feature of high school life, these students still held on to a stronger sense of the importance of doing well.

What this tells us about the motivations and school achievements of students from different ethnic groups is that love of learning for its own sake is no more or less common among Asian or Latin Americans than among those of European background. However, some minority students have an edge because they believe that doing well in school is important to their own and their families' future. This gives them a compelling reason to work hard, study, and persist even in the face of difficulties and failure.

Source: Fuligni, A. J., 2001, pp. 61–75.

Figure R8.1   Changes in Teens' Value of Academic Success According to Level of Family Obligation
Teens who feel a strong sense of family obligation place a higher value on academic success.

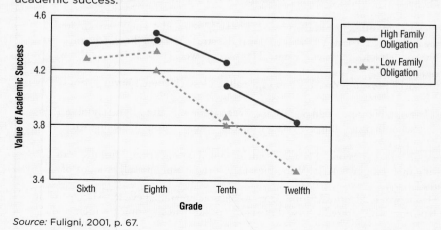

Source: Fuligni, 2001, p. 67.

Bicultural teens often adapt and merge customs from the two cultures. For example, what high school ritual is more typically American than the prom? The following newspaper article describes how teens from one cultural minority both adapted to this custom and changed it to better fit their own customs and values.

▲ A girl planning to attend the all-girls Muslim prom checks out her new gown.

For the Muslim Prom Queen, There Are No Kings Allowed
by Patricia Leigh Brown

FREMONT, Calif., June 7. The trappings of a typical high school prom were all there: the strobe lights, the garlands, the crepe pineapple centerpieces and even a tiara for the queen. In fact, Fatima Haque's prom tonight had practically everything one might expect on one of a teenage girl's most important nights. Except boys.

Ms. Haque and her friends may have helped initiate a new American ritual: the all-girl Muslim prom. It is a spirited response to religious and cultural beliefs that forbid dating, dancing with or touching boys, or appearing without a hijab, the Islamic head scarf. While Ms. Haque and her Muslim friends do most things other teenagers do—shopping for shoes at Macy's, watching *The Matrix Reloaded* at the mall, or ordering Jumbo Jack burgers and curly fries at Jack in the Box—an essential ingredient of the American prom, boys, is off limits. So they decided to do something about it.

"A lot of Muslim girls don't go to prom," said Ms. Haque, 18, who removed her hijab and shawl at the prom to reveal an ethereal silvery gown. "So while the other girls are getting ready for their prom, the Muslim girls are getting ready for our prom, so we won't feel left out."

Non-Muslim students at San Jose High Academy, where Ms. Haque is president of the student body, went to the school's coed prom last month—renting cars or limousines, dining at the Sheraton, going to breakfast at Denny's and, for some, drinking. Ms. Haque, meanwhile, was on her turquoise cellphone with the smiley faces organizing the prom. She posted an announcement on Bay Area Muslim Youth, a Yahoo news group scanned by young people throughout the San Francisco Bay area, home to one of the country's largest and most active Muslim communities.

"We got so close, we wanted to hang," said Fatin Alhadi, 17, a friend, explaining the farewell-to-high-school celebration, which involved cooking, shopping, and decorating the room, rented with a loan from Ms. Haque's parents. "It's an excuse to dress and put makeup on. Everyone has so much fun at the prom."

Ms. Haque and her Muslim girlfriends dwell in a world of exquisite subtlety in which modesty is the underlying principle. Though she wears a hijab, Ms. Alhadi recently dyed her black hair auburn. "Everyone asks me why, because nobody sees it," she said. "But I like to look at myself."

Ms. Haque, who will attend the University of California at Berkeley in the fall, is one of a growing number of young Muslim women who have adopted the covering their mothers rejected. Islamic dress, worn after puberty, often accompanies a commitment not to date or to engage in activities where genders intermingle.

Ms. Haque's decision to cover herself, which she made in her freshman year, was nuanced and thoughtful.

"I noticed a big difference in the way guys talked," she said. "They were afraid. I guess they had more respect. You walked down the street and you didn't feel guys staring at you. You felt a lot more confident." Her parents were surprised but said it was her decision.

But the social pressures on Muslims, especially in less-cloistered settings, can be intense.

"I felt left out, big time," said Saira Lara, 17, a senior at Gunn High School in Palo Alto, of her school's prom. But she gets a vicarious taste of dating by talking with her non-Muslim friends.

"The drama that goes on!" Ms. Lara said, looking dazzling at the Muslim prom in a flowing maroon gown. "The Valentine's Day without a phone call or a box of chocolates!"

Ms. Haque would like the Muslim prom to become an annual event. "My goal is an elegant ballroom with a three-course dinner—no paper plates—women waiters and a hundred girls," she said.

Tonight, the prom room was filled with promise as the young women whirled around the dance floor, strobe lights blinking. "Show off whatever you've got!" Ms. Lara exhorted the throng, sounding like a D.J. "Come on, guys. This is the most magical night of your life!"

Source: *New York Times*, 2003, June 9, pp. A1, A24.

Social Class

When social scientists want to describe someone's place in society, the terms they use are **social class** or *socioeconomic status (SES)*. One clue to social class, the one often used in U.S. government statistics, is family income; but class is about more than money. Among other things, social class involves living conditions, social prestige, access to resources, knowledge about how institutions work, and the ability to affect those institutions.

Think about the terms "blue collar" and "white collar." Miners, factory workers, laborers, and so on, are called blue collar because their work is physical and often dirty, and blue shirts don't show the dirt as much. Someone in a white-collar occupation, such as a salesperson, receptionist, or data processor, may actually earn less than a factory worker, but because their job is less physical and cleaner, it is considered a social step up from a blue collar job.

On the whole, ethnic minorities in the United States have lower SES than the White majority. It is true there are some senators, college presidents, network commentators, and corporate executives whose background is Black, Hispanic, or Asian American, but they are even more an exception in their ethnic groups than their White counterparts are among Whites in general. Most minority families have more limited access to educational and occupational opportunities and community resources than do White families.

The problem is still worse for immigrants, who may have problems coping with the language and customs of their new home. The old-fashioned political machine was one response to this. At election time, you supported the local ward captain. In return, if a problem came up with your landlord, your employer, or some government agency, the ward captain knew who to call and had the clout to get heard. Today, an effective community advocacy group can serve a similar function, but not all communities have them.

For better or worse, all adolescents are affected by their family's income, education, and position in society. However, the impact of socioeconomic status is particularly negative and severe for teens who grow up in poverty (Bornstein & Bradley, 2003).

Growing Up In Poverty. What is it like to grow up poor? Millions of American adolescents know the answer to that question from their own experience. It means:

Having other children make mean comments about your discount-store sneakers and hand-me-down clothes from your cousin.

Living in a cramped apartment with peeling walls, dripping faucets, and a battered old television that never stops flickering.

Making lame excuses when your friends decide to stop for a snack or go to a movie you can't afford.

Putting up with a sore tooth because there's no money for a dentist visit.

Blowing a test because the street noise kept you from studying, and then having the teacher be kind about it, as if he never expected you to pass.

Having to tiptoe around at bill time because your parents are on such a short fuse.

Above all, it means looking at the kids on television, in magazines, and in other neighborhoods, and knowing you cannot have the designer clothes, electronic gadgets, private rooms, cars, and expensive vacations that they seem to take for granted. And

◄ **Learning Objective 8.8**
How does growing up in poverty affect adolescents?

Social class A person's place or status in society, as indicated by wealth, income, education, living conditions, prestige, and influence.

Figure 8.3 Children Living in Relative Poverty

The percentage of children living below the poverty line is sharply higher in the United States than in most other developed countries.

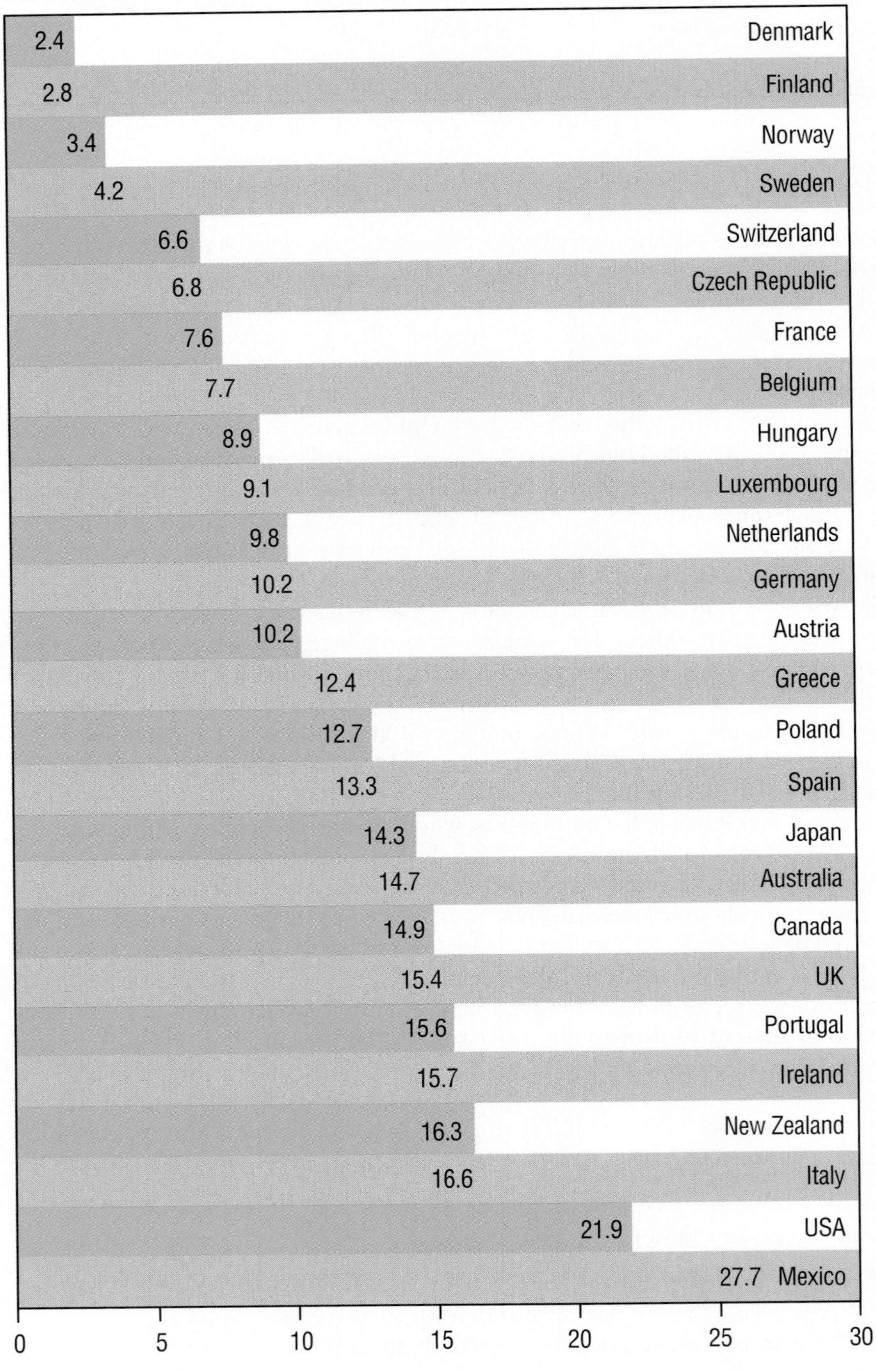

Denmark	2.4
Finland	2.8
Norway	3.4
Sweden	4.2
Switzerland	6.6
Czech Republic	6.8
France	7.6
Belgium	7.7
Hungary	8.9
Luxembourg	9.1
Netherlands	9.8
Germany	10.2
Austria	10.2
Greece	12.4
Poland	12.7
Spain	13.3
Japan	14.3
Australia	14.7
Canada	14.9
UK	15.4
Portugal	15.6
Ireland	15.7
New Zealand	16.3
Italy	16.6
USA	21.9
Mexico	27.7

Source: UNICEF, 2005, p. 4.

perhaps feeling ashamed that, for some reason you cannot figure out, you don't *deserve* to have what they have.

How Widespread Is Poverty? Over 13 million American children under 18 live in poverty. That totals more than 18%, or nearly one in every five children. For minority children, the percentages are much higher: 29% for Blacks and 24% for Hispanics

(U.S. Bureau of the Census, 2006). Of these, a great many—6% overall, 14% of Blacks, and 9% of Hispanics—live in *extreme* poverty, with family incomes less than half the official poverty level. These figures have improved a bit over the last couple of decades, but they still place the United States behind almost every other developed nation in the world (see Figure 8.3 on page 270).

Why do so many young people in the United States grow up poor? One reason is that the economy changed during the last part of the 20th century. Well-paid blue-collar jobs became scarcer. The new jobs that were created tended to be in far-off suburbs and required clerical skills that poor parents didn't have. At the same time, a shift in political attitudes led to a sharp reduction in government programs to assist the poor (Huston, McLoyd, & Coll, 1994).

Another reason family poverty is so widespread is wage inequality. Compared to those in most other developed countries, many workers in the United States earn a good deal less than the median wage, even though they work full time. As Figure 8.4 shows, the percentage of those in these poorly paid jobs is closely linked to the percentage of children in poverty (UNICEF, 2000).

Effects of Poverty. Growing up poor has been linked to a long list of negative consequences (Brooks-Gunn, Duncan, & Maritato, 1997; Conger, Rueter, & Conger, 2000; McLoyd, 1998). Among these consequences are low academic achievement, juvenile delinquency, teenage pregnancy, anxiety, and depression. Drawing on an ecological systems approach to development, we can see these problems as the result of interacting factors on several levels (Leventhal & Brooks-Gunn, 2003; Sampson, 2002). These factors include:

The community. Impoverished neighborhoods typically have fewer positive resources, such as libraries, parks, and community centers, and weaker social controls. As a result, poor adolescents are more exposed to such risks as delinquency, violence, early sexual activity, and illegal or harmful substances. They are also *less* exposed to successful adult models who might inspire them to stay in school and avoid these risks (Leventhal & Brooks-Gunn, 2000).

Figure 8.4   Wages and Child Poverty
Child poverty is closely linked to the percentage of low-wage workers in a country.

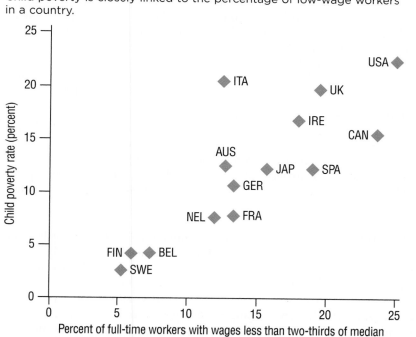

Source: UNICEF, 2000, p. 14.

▶ Community resources are scarcer and less well maintained in poorer neighborhoods.

School. As we saw in Chapter 7, schools with a high concentration of impoverished students face a very difficult task. Just maintaining order takes much of the staff's energy. The facilities that schools in wealthier communities take for granted, such as libraries, labs, and computers, may be obsolete or totally lacking. The message this transmits to poor teens is that they and their education are simply not that important to the larger society.

Peers. In disadvantaged neighborhoods, the lack of organized activities and weaker social controls gives adolescents more unstructured, unsupervised time to spend with peers who may be deviant or antisocial (Leventhal & Brooks-Gunn, 2000). Unsupervised hang-out time with friends has been linked to risk behaviors such as drug and alcohol use and delinquency (McHale, Crouter, & Tucker, 2001; Osgood, Wilson, O'Malley, Bachman, & Johnston, 1996). And not all peers are friendly. Teenage gangs are an unavoidable fact in impoverished areas.

Parents. Low-wage jobs, the threat of unemployment, and the constant struggle to make ends meet take a serious toll on the mental health of low-income parents and make it harder for them to be sensitive and supportive to their children (Ceballo & McLoyd, 2002; Conger et al., 2002; Mistry, Vandewater, Huston, & McLoyd, 2002). They may resort to harsh and inconsistent discipline, made even harsher because they know the dangers their children face and are frustrated that they can't protect them better (Simons, Johnson, Beaman, Conger, & Whitbeck, 1996).

The individual adolescent. Growing up poor has a direct negative impact on an adolescent's physical, cognitive, emotional, and behavioral development (McLoyd, 1998). Poor nutrition, inadequate health care, exposure to environmental toxins such as lead, and chronic stress take a toll. So does the sense of being powerless and having no way out. The anxiety and depression these conditions encourage make it harder for the teen to cope with everyday difficulties, much less imagine and work toward a better future.

Overcoming Poverty. Every poor adolescent faces some or all of these hazards. Even so, some manage to overcome them. They do well in school, avoid drugs, delinquency, and early pregnancy, and go on to create a life for themselves that is productive and fulfilling. A crucial factor in their success is the social support they get from parents, extended family members, teachers, mentors, and friends (Ceballo & McLoyd, 2002). Parents and other adults strengthen a feeling of competence and a willingness to aim high by their praise and respect for the teen's accomplishments. Ambitious and supportive peers are both models to emulate and sources of advice and encouragement.

Some adolescents growing up in poverty are fortunate enough to have these resources available and to profit from them. Most, however, do not (Hart & Atkins, 2002). For them, organizations such as Big Brothers/Big Sisters, Boys & Girls Clubs, 4-H Clubs, and community-based mentoring programs can be a lifeline. Later, in Chapter 14, we take up the critical question of how we as a community, a nation, and a species can further the positive development of the adolescents who represent our future.

Connect the **Dots...**

One frequent assumption in individualistic cultures is that people are responsible for what happens to them. How do you think that idea would affect adolescents growing up in poverty? How might it affect the beliefs and attitudes of other, more economically secure, adolescents toward their poorer classmates?

Summing Up...

A culture is a system of beliefs, attitudes, values, and behaviors that are shared by a particular group. People often look at the world through the lens of their own culture's values, but cross-cultural research helps point out both differences and similarities across cultures. An important difference in orientation is between individualism, typical of Western cultures, and collectivism, found in East Asia and many other parts of the world. Children and adolescents acquire the rules and values of their culture, but also construct understandings of the various subcultures they are exposed to. This is especially so for immigrants and members of ethnic minorities, who must find ways to relate to both their culture of origin and the majority culture. Social class also has a major impact on adolescents, particularly on those who grow up in poverty.

LEISURE AND THE MEDIA

A striking fact about adolescents in developed societies is how much leisure they have. According to one estimate, during the school year American teens enjoy an average of 6-1/2 to 8 hours of free time a day, and European teens slightly less (Larson & Seepersad, 2003). For both groups, their hours of free time add up to more than the total amount they spend on schoolwork, at paid jobs, and helping around the house. In effect, half of their waking hours are their own to do with as they please.

What they do with this time varies somewhat from one country to another. Adolescents in Germany, Norway, and Switzerland spend twice as much time playing musical instruments as those in the United States or other European countries (Flammer & Schaffner, 2003). American teens spend more time than others partying, dating, and hanging out with friends (Larson & Seepersad, 2003). Teens in Korea and Japan don't have as much choice as the others. Most of them spend several hours after school at "cram schools" that prepare them for the fiendishly difficult university entrance exams (Lee, 2003; Nishino & Larson, 2003).

In spite of these and other differences, one generalization holds equally well across North America, Europe, and East Asia. However much leisure time adolescents have, they spend the larger part of it, 6 or more hours a day, engaged with some form of mass **media**, such as television, radio, CDs, the Internet, or video games (Roberts & Foehr, 2004), and often with more than one at the same time. Teens routinely multitask—they surf the Internet, listen to a CD or streaming audio, check their e-mail, exchange instant messages with friends, and give an occasional glance to the television across the room, all at the same time (Foehr, 2006; Lenhart, Madden, & Hitlin, 2005).

The Impact of Media

Parents and community leaders throughout history have worried about the impact of new communication technologies on young people (Comstock & Scharrer, 2006). Fifty years ago, the concern was comic books; a century ago it was "penny dreadful" novels for teens; and if we go back to ancient Greece, Plato thought storytellers should be banned as subversive. More recently, pop and rap lyrics, movies, television shows, video games, and even Harry Potter books have been denounced and threatened with various kinds of government regulation. In 2003, for example, the U.S.

◀ **Learning Objective 8.9**
How much time do teens spend on media?

Media The various means, such as books, magazines, radio, television, films, and the Internet, by which information, experiences, and entertainment are communicated to the public.

▶ Teens across the developed world routinely multitask.

Supreme Court ruled (*U.S. v. American Library Association*) that a law forcing public libraries to block access for minors to sex-related websites did not infringe on the right of free speech.

In recent years, many serious questions have been raised about the impact the media may have on adolescents, including:

How much of their time do teens spend on media involvement? Does that keep them from other activities that might be more beneficial?

Is the view of the world adolescents get from the media harmfully distorted?

What effect does exposure to the media have on teens' attitudes and behavior in such sensitive areas as aggression, sexuality, substance use, and body image?

How does the primary goal of commercial media, which is to sell stuff to young people, affect the information and values that are presented?

And, not to be overlooked, what are the positive effects of adolescent involvement with media?

In the pages that follow, we will try to get provisional answers to some of these questions.

How Much Time Do Teens Spend on Media? One of the current stereotypes of adolescents is that they all have calluses on their ears from the headphones of their iPod, and that doing homework means lying on the floor in front of the television with a book somewhere nearby. Scientific surveys show that this stereotype is pretty accurate. Figure 8.5 on page 275 charts the *average* daily use of various media by those in early, middle, and late adolescence. The total, not shown on the chart, is already above 7 hours for 8- to 10-year-olds, climbs to almost 8 hours at 12 or 13, then drifts down to just over 7 hours for the 15- to 18-year-olds (Roberts, Henriksen, & Foehr, 2004). Put another way, the amount of time teens spend on media is not much less than what adults consider a standard workday of 8 hours.

Until age 13 or 14, television dominates children's media exposure. One reason is that more than two-thirds of U.S. adolescents have a television in their bedroom, and more often than not, that is where they go to watch (Foehr, 2006). Another reason is that having a television on is not necessarily the same as watching it attentively. Many teens keep track of what's going on on the screen, maybe with the volume down, but only stop to watch when something grabs their attention (Comstock & Scharrer, 2006).

Figure 8.5   Average Daily Media Use by Age
Total media use is about the same across adolescence, but the balance among different media changes with age.

	Age group		
	8–10 years	**11–14 years**	**15–18 years**
Television	3:19	3:30	2:23
Videos	:46	:43	:37
Movies in theaters	:26	:19	:09
Radio, CDs, tapes	:55	1:43	2:38
Books, magazines, newspapers	:54	:42	:37
Video games	:31	:26	:21
Computer	:23	:31	:26
Total leisure media	7:13	7:55	7:11

Source: Roberts et al., 2004.

Music, Books, and Computers. Across adolescence, music steadily gains in importance. Plenty of teens wake up to a favorite rock station, carry around an iPod with hundreds or even thousands of songs downloaded to it, and get together with friends after school to listen to a hot new CD or watch music videos. Everyone who was ever an adolescent knows that you can't retreat to your room to brood about something without putting on some music to help you brood. By late adolescence, music has overtaken television as the biggest use of time.

About four out of five adolescents report that they read something for pleasure at least 5 minutes a day. *What* they read changes with age. Younger teens are more likely to read books and older teens are more likely to read newspapers and magazines. As a result, leisure reading as a whole declines, from about an hour a day for 8- to 10-year-olds to half an hour for 15- to 18-year-olds (Roberts & Foehr, 2003).

The numbers shown in Figure 8.5 for computer use, roughly half an hour a day for each of the age groups, may be misleadingly low. Practically all U.S. teenagers have used a computer at least occasionally, three-quarters go online fairly often, and over one-half use a computer on a daily basis (Kaiser Family Foundation, 2001; Lenhart, Madden, & Hitlin, 2005). Those who do use a computer daily generally have access to a computer at home and spend as much as an hour a day on it (Roberts & Foehr, 2003).

We should keep in mind that a relatively recent technology like the personal computer is a moving target. Each year more adolescents gain easy access to computers and the Internet. Almost every week some new use becomes available, be it streaming audio and video, music downloads, instant messaging, or whatever the next big thing turns out to be. One recent survey found that over half of teens who are online have contributed content, such as a webpage or blog (Lenhart & Madden, 2005). As computers become more available and take over many of the functions of other media, we can expect that adolescents will spend even more time and do more things on them (Roberts & Foehr, 2003).

Differences in Media Use. The averages shown in Figure 8.5 tell us a lot about media use, but they hide some important distinctions. A few examples:

Boys watch more television than girls, and girls listen to music a lot more than boys.

Boys play video and computer games more than girls, but otherwise both sexes use computers about equally.

Socioeconomic status is linked to media exposure, at least for younger adolescents. Compared to those from higher income and more educated families, teens with lower income backgrounds spend more time on television, video games, and music, but not on computer use.

Ethnic background also predicts media use. African American adolescents are exposed to about 9 hours of media daily, as compared to 8 hours for Hispanic teens and 7 hours for White teens (Roberts & Foehr, 2003).

Not surprisingly, young people from families in which the television is on most of the day, including during meals, and in which there are few if any rules about viewing, tend to be particularly heavy television viewers (Comstock & Scharrer, 1999).

On the topic of heavy television viewers, more than 20% of U.S. adolescents say they watch more than 5 hours a day. About one of three, however, watches only 1 hour or less, and 20% report no exposure to television at all (Roberts & Foehr, 2003). In general, those who use one medium a lot tend to use others more than the average as well. For example, teens who do not use computers on a daily basis are exposed to about 6 hours of other media, but those who use computers more than an hour a day say they also use other media *9 hours* a day (Roberts & Foehr, 2003).

The Internet. By the time children are 10, they are already more likely to use the Internet than adults at any age over 25. As Figure 8.6 shows, just between 1998 and 2001 Internet use increased dramatically among children, adolescents, and young adults (U.S. Department of Commerce, 2002). Another survey found that between 1999 and 2004, the proportion of time devoted to computer use almost doubled (Roberts, Foehr, & Rideout, 2005). Those in the 10- to 13-year-old group most often use the Internet for schoolwork (77%), sending and receiving e-mail (64%), and playing games (65%). Among 14- to 17-year-olds, games drop off slightly to 61%, while schoolwork (86%) and e-mail (82%) continue to climb (U.S. Department of Commerce, 2002). The older adolescents are also about twice as likely as the younger group to use Internet chatrooms.

Internet use among teens is strongly linked to family income and ethnic background. Only about one-half of adolescents in the two lowest categories of family income use the Internet, while in the highest category, only 12% *don't* go online (see Figure 8.7 on page 277). Not surprisingly, higher SES teens are likely to use the Internet both at home and at school. Many poorer teens can only go online at school (or perhaps at the public library), because they don't have a computer at home.

Figure 8.6 Internet Use by Age
Internet use increases steadily across the adolescent years.

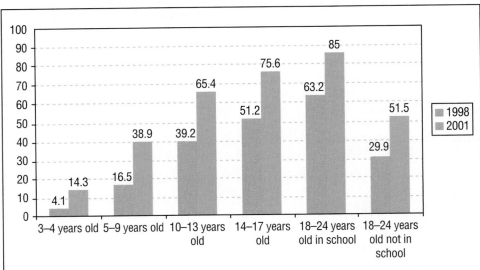

Source: U.S. Department of Commerce, 2002, p. 43.

Leisure and the Media **277**

Figure 8.7 Internet Use, by Family Income
Family income is strongly linked to Internet use among teens.

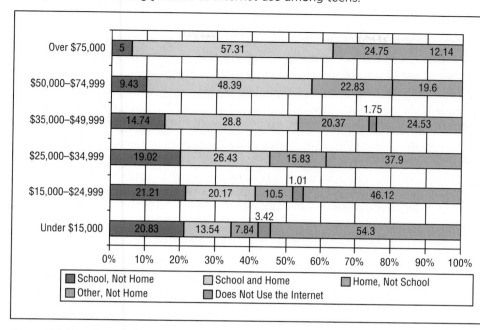

Source: U.S. Department of Commerce, 2002, p. 50.

A similar pattern shows up for different ethnic groups. Among Hispanics and Blacks, about half do not use the Internet at all. Those who do are more likely to log on at school than at home. Among Whites and Asian Americans, in contrast, some 80% use the Internet, and very few—1 in 10—do so only at school (U.S. Department of Commerce, 2002). Again, this most likely reflects a lower proportion of Black and Hispanic homes with computers.

What's the Attraction?

It should be clear by now that adolescents are very heavy media users. But why? What do they get out of it? Asked directly, a typical teen may say, "It's fun," or "I like it," or even "It gets me through the day." That's a start, but it does not tell us why adolescents make the particular media choices they make. Both the promoters of commercial media and their critics sometimes assume that teens are a passively receptive audience that will eat any garbage shoveled in their direction. This is partly true. Most of the time, adolescents first decide to "watch television," and *then* look to see if there is anything interesting on (Comstock & Scharrer, 2006). Even so, adolescents are capable of actively *deciding* what to do with their media time. With the spread of CDs, DVDs, cable television, and online music and video, the range of choices available to them is limited only by their awareness of what's out there.

Uses and Gratifications. A helpful approach to understanding how adolescents make their media choices and how those choices affect them is known as **uses and gratifications** (Rubin, 2002). What *uses* do teens expect a particular movie or television show or CD to serve? What *gratifications* do they get from the experience? There are obviously many possibilities. Among them might be having a good laugh or a good cry, keeping up with what the other kids are talking about, taking your mind off your problems, becoming suave and sophisticated, learning the basic moves of being an alligator wrestler, and many others.

Connect the **Dots...**

At what age did you and your friends start using computers and the Internet? What did you use them for? Where — at school, at home, at the library?

◄ **Learning Objective 8.10**
What do teens expect to get from media?

Uses and gratifications An approach to understanding how adolescents choose which media to attend to and what they get from their choices.

▲ Adolescents are drawn to media experiences that offer high sensation.

The long list of possible uses and gratifications can be condensed into a few broader categories (Dominick, 2001):

Diversion. Teens use media to relax, have fun, relieve boredom, entertain themselves, and manage their moods.

Cognition. The media communicate information on everything from what letter comes where in the alphabet to the social habits of wombats.

Social utility. Going to a movie, watching a video, or listening to music with friends is the norm for adolescents (Roberts et al., 2004). Even those who watch or listen alone can chat about the experience with friends the next day.

Withdrawal. Put on your earphones, press "Play," and you shut out the rest of the world.

Personal identity. Adolescence is a time to grapple with issues of personal values, attitudes, goals, and ambitions. Real people known through the media and admired fictional characters offer possible answers to such questions as, "What kind of person do I want to be?"

A sixth category that is especially relevant to adolescents is *high sensation* (Arnett, 1995). Teens, more than adults, seek out experiences that provide what movie ads call "heart-pounding excitement." Car chases, sudden explosions, graphic fight scenes, and grisly killers who jump out of closets sell tickets, particularly to adolescent boys. And everybody knows when your favorite song comes on, you crank up the volume to 11!

What Uses? Which Gratifications? The media choices adolescents make often serve more than one use and offer more than one gratification. A movie may present an interesting story, a favorite actor, a chance to hang with friends, and an excuse to get out of the house, all at once. We should also notice that teens who make the same media choice may do so with different uses in mind. Some people watch MTV for the music, some for the dancing, some for the costumes, and some simply to go along with their friends who want to watch. And sometimes a media choice leads to unexpected gratifications. A show that was tuned in just to kill time may turn out to be deeply moving or to speak directly to a teen's personal concerns (Roberts et al., 2004).

Even if a particular movie, song, or television show appeals to many adolescents, it does not say the same things to them all. When teens are intensely focused on some particular issue, such as sexuality, peer popularity, or relationships with parents, that can shape how they interpret the meaning of a media experience (Brown, 2002). In a sense, each spectator sees a different performance because of what he or she brings to it.

One study looked at the reactions of young adolescent girls to sexual material in the media, such as nudity in ads. Those who had not yet reached menarche tended to find the depictions "gross." Those who had reached menarche, but were not yet sexually active, were often fascinated, even clipping photos of models for their bedroom walls. And those who were already involved in sexual relationships found the mainstream depictions less interesting than more "oppositional" material (Brown, White, & Nikopoulou, 1993).

Effects of Media Exposure

▶ **Learning Objective 8.11**
How does exposure to violent media affect teen aggression?

Involvement with the media influences adolescents, that much is clear. Whenever a pop star sets off a new craze in clothing, jewelry, gestures, or catch phrases, the evidence is there for everyone to see. But *how* does this influence work psychologically? Do the media pose a threat to the physical and mental health of adolescents, especially in the areas of aggression and sexuality?

Public discussions of media effects often assume that adolescents follow the saying, *Monkey see, monkey do.* If they are allowed to watch a sexually suggestive scene, or see a photo of someone using drugs, or hear lyrics about assaulting police officers, next thing you know they'll all be doing it. Occasionally evidence turns up to support this idea. After a movie showed a character lying down in the middle of a busy road on a dare, a teenage boy was killed copying him. Both television "reality shows" and car commercials that feature dangerous stunts routinely warn viewers not to "try this at home," as if, without the warning, some would. Accounts of the 1999 school shootings at Columbine High School in Colorado often highlight the parallels between the actions of the two teenage killers and their favorite video game, "Doom."

Fortunately, adolescents do not blindly imitate what they see in the media. If they did, imagine what would happen when *Silence of the Lambs* played on cable television or millions of spectators came out of the latest *Terminator* movie! What adolescents choose to watch, how they interpret what they see, and what (if anything) they incorporate into their own attitudes and behavior are all affected by their individual histories, psychological makeups, and life situations. A focus on direct imitation may even lead us to downplay or overlook very real, if more subtle, effects of the media on adolescents.

Theories of Media Effects. How, then, does contact with the media affect adolescents? Media researchers most often rely on three approaches to understanding the process (Roberts et al., 2004):

Cultivation theory (Gerbner, Gross, Morgan, Signorielli, & Shanahan, 2002). The media constantly retell a selective and biased set of myths and ideologies that help define social thinking in a particular society. The more people watch, the more the experience "cultivates" a shared set of ideas about the world. For example, teens who watch a lot of soap operas are more likely to believe that single mothers have an easy time of it (Larson, 1996).

Social cognitive theory (Bandura, 2002). People learn from what they see others do. What they learn and perform depends on many factors, such as whether the model is rewarded or punished, how attractive and similar the model appears to be, and whether the situation seems relevant to the watcher's own needs. For example, teens cite the media as an important source of information about sex (Sutton, Brown, Wilson, & Klein, 2002). Sex on television is generally presented as glamorous, unplanned, unmarried, unprotected, and without negative consequences (Ward, 2003). As a result, adolescents store this version of reality and rely on it later (Brown & Steele, 1995).

Schematic information processing theory (Berkowitz, 1990; Shrum, 2002; Zillman, 2002). People form mental representations, such as schemas or scripts, and use them to interpret situations. This affects social judgments and behavior. The media are a powerful source of new schemas and a means of activating and modifying those schemas a person already has. For example, a crude joke about a character's weight will evoke different schemas in viewers if the context is a sitcom, with loud laugh track, or a sensitive drama about eating disorders. If these viewers then encounter someone with a weight problem, they will tend to interpret the person's situation according to whichever schema is uppermost in their minds.

Media Violence and Aggression. Adolescents can and do have access to what some in Hollywood refer to as "torture porn." According to an authoritative report by the U.S. Federal Trade Commission, films with a level of violence that earns an R rating are routinely advertised on websites with lots of teen users, and unrated violent material is often a touted feature on "special version" DVDs. In tests, almost half of teens were able to buy tickets to R-rated films and almost three-quarters managed to buy unrated or R-rated DVDs (Federal Trade Commission, 2007).

What effects do all this exposure to media violence have? Over the years, researchers have carried out well over a thousand studies on this question. The results lead to several conclusions (Comstock & Scharrer, 2006):

Watching violence in the media helps generate cognitive schemas that may serve as guides to action in later situations. If the hero reacts to verbal rudeness by knocking the offender to the ground, the viewers acquire the schema that rude people deserve to be taught a severe (physical) lesson.

The way adolescents react to viewing a particular violent incident in the media varies a lot depending on their own experiences, interests, needs, and situations.

The way an incident is interpreted depends on such factors as whether it is shown as effective, successful, and justified. When the heroic government agent pushes the villainous terrorist off a rooftop, thus saving the city from destruction, those in the audience cheer. Nobody thinks about how horrible it must be to fall 50 stories to your death.

Several consequences follow from exposure to media violence. The most obvious is that some children—though not all—become more aggressive. For example, a large-scale longitudinal study showed that for children who were more involved with television as preschoolers, watching violent shows predicted their aggressiveness as teens (Anderson, Huston, Schmitt, Linebarger, & Wright, 2001). Another longitudinal study showed a link between time watching television as teens to later aggressive behavior. This link held up even after such factors as earlier aggressiveness, childhood neglect, and neighborhood violence were taken into account (Johnson, Cohen, Smailes, Kasen, & Brook, 2002).

Other effects, though less noticeable, are also important. Watching violence leads to an increased acceptance of aggression and a decreased sensitivity to the suffering of others. The first time people, especially children, see a violent scene in the media, they are scared and anxious (Cantor, 2000). But repeated exposure desensitizes them and leaves them with a desire for stronger ("more exciting") doses. Once you've seen a car crash into a lamppost a few times, you're bored unless it rolls over, bursts into flames, and goes through the front window of a Starbucks.

What this implies is that while only some children may *act* more aggressively as a result of exposure to media violence, the effects on others create a psychological climate in which aggression is seen as normal and unremarkable. This cuts down on the peer disapproval that is one of the major brakes on antisocial behavior.

We should also notice that the *amount* of violence children and adolescents see in the media is totally out of line with reality and gives them a very distorted view of the world (Gerbner et al., 2002). By the time children finish elementary school, they will have seen some 8,000 murders and more than 100,000 other acts of violence, just on network television (Huston et al., 1992). When you throw in cable, movies, videotapes, and computer games as well, the numbers are staggering—and terribly deceptive. For example, FBI records show that murders make up two of every 1,000 reported crimes. On crime dramas such as "FBI," however, fully *half* of the crimes shown are murder (Oliver, 1994). As film critic Michael Medved points out,

About 350 characters appear each night on prime-time TV, but studies show an average of seven of these people are murdered every night. If this rate applied in reality, then in just 50 days everyone in the United States would be killed and the last left could turn off the TV.

—(quoted in Bushman & Anderson, 2001)

Is the Case Proven? Not everyone agrees that media violence is a serious problem. Critics point out that while there are hundreds of studies linking media violence and increased aggressiveness, most of them are correlational (Freedman, 1984). As we all know, correlations can suggest cause and effect, but they do not prove it. Media representatives sometimes deny that watching media violence affects viewers at all (for example, Moore, 1993). This seems odd, considering that they turn around and charge advertisers tens of thousands of dollars a minute based on the supposed impact of their commercials on those who watch.

Researchers Brad Bushman and Craig Anderson (2001) point out that the strength of the statistical link between media violence and aggression is very nearly as strong as that between smoking and lung cancer. It is actually *stronger* than the link between condom use and reduced HIV infection. However, like the effects of smoking or not using a condom, the effects of media violence are not the same for everyone and may not always be obvious, especially in the short run.

One cigarette won't kill you. One episode of unprotected sex may not give you AIDS. Watching one violent television show may increase your aggressive thoughts, feelings, and behaviors, but the effects usually wear off in an hour or so (Bushman & Huesmann, 2001). In all these cases, it is the cumulative effects that can be so severe. Someone who smokes a pack of cigarettes a day for 10 or 15 years runs a seriously higher risk of lung cancer and heart disease. Someone who repeatedly has unprotected sex with multiple partners runs a seriously higher risk of contracting (and transmitting) HIV. And someone who watches violent media a couple of hours a day over a 15-year period runs a seriously higher risk of becoming habitually aggressive or even a violent offender (Huesmann, Moise-Titus, Podolski, & Eron, 2003).

Video Games. Those who worry about the effects of television violence on adolescents worry even more about the effects of violence in video and computer games (Anderson & Bushman, 2001; Roberts et al., 2004). The reasons for their concern include:

Prevalence of violence. An analysis in 2001 of the 70 top-selling video and computer games found that 89% of them contained violence, 41% required violence to do well, and 17% made violence the primary focus of the game (Children Now, 2001).

Explicitness. The violence in video games is often more graphic and extreme than anything on television. Poking out an opponent's eye, cutting off his head, or tearing the heart out of his chest, all with appropriate screams and spurts of blood, are ordinary. Even sports games tend to involve more violent action than actual sports (Hafner, 2003).

Involvement. Unlike television, in which the watcher has to identify with a character in the show, with video games the player *is* the character who commits the violent acts and is then directly rewarded by winning points (Roberts et al., 2004).

Popularity. More than two-thirds of children ages 2–18 live in a home with a video game system, and one-third of them have video game systems in their bedrooms. On any given day, 44% of boys and 17% of girls report playing computer or video games (Kaiser Family Foundation, 1999).

Lack of diversity. An analysis of top-selling video games revealed that two-thirds of the characters were male. The others were either nonhuman (19%) or female (17%). Almost 9 of 10 heroes were White, and in seven top-selling games for children, *all* the human characters were White (Children Now, 2001).

In spite of these concerns, the impact of computer and video games is still a topic of debate. Some argue that for most young people, playing violent video games allows them to explore their feelings, master their rage, and empower themselves against life's challenges (Jansz, 2005). However, experiments show that rewarding violent actions in video games increases hostile emotion, aggressive thinking, and aggressive behavior (Carnagey & Anderson, 2005). Brain imaging studies have shown that playing violent video games causes changes in brain activity that are linked to aggression (Weber, Ritterfeld, & Mathiak, 2006). In one recent study, college students played violent or nonviolent video games for 20 minutes, and then saw a video that showed real-life violence. Those who had been playing a violent game had lower physiological reactions to watching the real violence (Carnagey, Anderson, & Bushman, 2007). In other words, the video game had *desensitized* them to violence.

A meta-analysis that compiled the results of some three dozen research studies of violent video games reached this conclusion:

> Exposure [to violent video and computer games] is positively associated with heightened levels of aggression in young adults and children, in experimental and nonexperimental designs, and in males and females.
>
> —(ANDERSON & BUSHMAN, 2001, p. 358)

This chapter's Applications in the Spotlight discusses attempts to come up with effective, informative ratings for television shows, music, video games, and other media.

Applications in the Spotlight

Rating the Media

The findings we have reviewed in this section make the case that exposure to violence in the media promotes aggressive attitudes and behaviors and that exposure to the sort of sexual content found in most media promotes unhealthy attitudes toward sexuality, love, and marriage. What can, or should, be done to give adolescents some degree of protection from these hazards?

In the United States, the usual pattern since the late 1960s has been that a public clamor develops over the level of sex and violence in media such as films, television shows, and video games. This is followed by talk of some kind of government regulation. The media industry in question then offers to set up a rating system to help parents decide which programs, movies, or games they want their children exposed to (Federal Trade Commission, 2007).

One result of this approach is shown in Table A8.1. Currently there are at least seven commonly used rating systems, covering movies, broadcast television, premium cable television, recordings, home and arcade video games, and Internet sites (Bushman & Cantor, 2003). *Descriptive* ratings (for instance, V for violence or AL for adult language) give some information about the content of a program. *Evaluative* ratings (such as PG-13 or TV-14) recommend which age groups should or should not watch. Two of the systems, for television shows and video games, combine both sorts of ratings. The rest give only one or the other. In most cases, ratings are assigned by the producer or distributor of the show or game.

Parents pay attention to ratings, but many do not understand the meaning of the various symbols in the different systems. While adolescents and adults generally know what movie ratings such as PG and R mean, only about half of parents know what TV-MA means, and only 5% realize that D stands for sexual dialogue (Kaiser Family Foundation, 2001).

How much difference do ratings make? As adolescents get older, they increasingly watch films and television and play electronic games either alone or with friends and not with parents (Roberts et al., 2003). When friends come over to watch a video, more often than not it is R-rated. In fact, teenage boys find movies and shows with restricted ratings more attractive, the so-called "forbidden fruit" effect (Bushman & Cantor, 2003).

Critics of the current media ratings situation (to call it a system would be too much of a stretch) point out that if parental guidance is the best alternative to some form of censorship, parents need valid, reliable, and easily understandable information about what is in the media their children may be exposed to (Bushman & Cantor, 2003; Walsh & Gentile, 2001). A unified system would be a major step forward, especially if it used explicit criteria, gave descriptive information about content, and relied on raters who didn't have a financial interest in the product they were rating. Realistically, however, this is not likely to happen any time soon. Meanwhile, parents, and the public generally, can try to master the alphabet soup shown in Table A8.1.

Table A8.1   Guide to Most Common U.S. Rating Systems
The most commonly used media rating systems in the United States.

Evaluative ratings	Content indicators	Assignment
Motion Picture Association of America ratings		
G: general audiences PG: parental guidance suggested PG-13: parents strongly cautioned R: restricted—under 17 requires accompanying parent or adult guardian NC-17: no one 17 and under admitted	None: reasons for ratings of recent films available at www.mpaa.org and on some movie posters and advertisements	Assigned by a paid panel of parents, a movie's producer may appeal the panel's decision to an industry appeals board
TV Parental Guidelines (V-chip ratings)		
TV-Y: all children[a] TV-Y7: directed to older children[a] TV-G: general audience[a] TV-PG: parental guidance suggested[a] TV-14: parents strongly cautioned[a] TV-MA: mature audiences only[a]	FV: fantasy violence[a] V: violence[a] S: sex[a] I: coarse language[a] D: sexual dialogue or innuendo[a]	Self-assigned by the producer or distributor; designed to be applied to all programming except news and sports
TV: Premium channel content codes		
None	MV: mild violence V: violence GV: graphic violence AL: adult language GL: graphic language BN: brief nudity N: nudity AC: adult content SC: strong sexual content RP: rape	Assigned by the channel showing the movie
Music advisories		
Parental advisory: explicit content	None	Self-assigned by the producer or distributor
Video games: Electronic Software Ratings Board ratings		
eC: early childhood, ages 3+ E: everyone, ages 6+ T: teen, ages 13+ M: mature, ages 17+ Ao: adults only	Variety of phrases [e.g., animated violence, comic mischief, strong language, mature sexual themes]	Assigned by a rating board on the basis of a submitted tape and questionnaire
Arcade games: Parental Advisory System		
None	Animated violence, lifelines violence, sexual content, language (three levels of each: green, suitable for everyone; yellow, mild; red, strong)	Self-assigned by the producer or distributor
Internet Content Rating Association		
None	Violence, nudity, sex, offensive language, intolerance, alcohol, tobacco, drug use, and so forth	Computer-generated rating based on a questionnaire filled out by the producer

Source: Adopted from www.jconnscontor.com.

[a]Definitions are usually not given with the abbreviated ratings.

The Media and Sexuality

▶ **Learning Objective 8.12**
What roles do media play in sexual socialization?

A couple of generations ago, adolescents who wanted to find out about sex had only a couple of choices. They could try looking up sexually related words in the dictionary [*Sex: anything connected with reproduction. Reproduction: the process by which animals and plants produce new individuals.*]. Or they could try to understand the often wildly inaccurate accounts of their friends.

Today, their task is a lot simpler—all they need to do is turn on the television, read a teen magazine, or surf the Web (Sutton, Brown, Wilson, & Klein, 2002). In one poll, 29% of U.S. teens named television as their principal source of information about sex, as compared to 7% who cited parents, and 3% who mentioned sex education courses (Stodghill, 1998). And no wonder. One analysis found sexual content in more than two-thirds of all television shows, with suggestive or explicit intercourse in 1 of every 10 programs (Kunkel, Cope, Farrar, Biely, Farinola, & Dornerstein, 2001). Magazines aimed at adolescents now devote dramatically more space to sexual topics (Walsh-Childers, Gotthoffer, & Lepre, 2002). And almost three out of four teenage computer users have come across pornography online, if only by accident (Kaiser Family Foundation, 2001).

Public concerns about the media and adolescent sexuality are as widespread and deep as concerns about media violence. Less is known on the topic, however, because many fewer studies have been done (Ward, 2003). Even so, the picture that emerges is consistent with what we know about media effects on aggression.

Sexually charged media experiences have a measurable impact on how teens think and feel about sex and, to a lesser extent, on what they do (Ward, 2003; Zillman, 2000). In one experiment, young men and women saw television episodes in which the men were sex-driven, the women were sex objects, and dating was a competitive game. Later, the women, but not the men, endorsed these stereotypes more than those in control groups (Ward, 2002).

Connect the **Dots...**

In 2007, a U.S. federal court struck down a law that made it a crime for websites to allow children to gain access to "harmful" material, chiefly pornography. The ruling said the law was too broad, ineffective, and at odds with free speech rights. Given what you have learned about the effects of media exposure on adolescents, what do you think about this law, similar efforts to limit sexually explicit material, and the court's ruling?

Critics worry about the way sexuality is portrayed in the media (Malamuth & Impett, 2001). Sexual relationships are generally between unmarried people, who may have met only recently, who do not maintain a relationship afterwards, and who do not use contraception or protect against sexually transmitted diseases (Brown, 2002). The idea that sex can be an important part of an ongoing, committed, and responsible relationship is rarely presented (Ward, 2003). As a result, teens tend to develop cynical attitudes about love and marriage and come to believe that promiscuity is the norm (Zillman, 2000). The more teens watch popular prime time shows, the more they endorse sexual stereotypes and the more likely they are to be sexually experienced (Ward & Friedman, 2006). An analysis of programs that are specifically teen-oriented also found evidence for a double standard, in which girls were punished more often than boys for sexual behavior, especially if they made the first move (Aubrey, 2002).

The sexual socialization of adolescents involves much more than their encounters with sexuality in the media, of course. As we will see in Chapter 12, it is affected by countless messages, direct and indirect, verbal and nonverbal, that go all the way back to the earliest days of life (Ward, 2003). However, the media have a special role to play. One of the major developmental tasks of adolescence is adjusting to sexual maturation and to the emotional and social changes that accompany it. However, our society treats these topics as particularly sensitive. Just when teens need to discuss, explore, and ask questions, parents and other adults in their lives tend to shy away.

To some extent, the media can make up for that lack (Chapin, 2000). In other parts of the world, the media have played an effective part in encouraging sexual responsibility (Keller & Brown, 2002). For example, three of four European adults say they have learned about sexually transmitted diseases from the media. In the United States, however, the proportion is only one in four (American Social Health Association, 1996; Brown, Steele, & Walsh-Childers, 2001).

Here is how experts sum up the situation:

One of the paradoxes of U.S. culture is that sexual desire is used to sell everything from motorcycles to ice cream while the sexuality of youth is denied. As the federal government increases funding for abstinence-only-until-marriage sex education in the public schools, sexually transmitted disease rates among young people soar. The media could be an important source of information and models of healthy sexuality for young people. Unfortunately, a number of barriers exist primarily because the media are first and foremost profit-making entities that are reluctant to take on controversial issues that may alienate viewers and advertisers.

(KELLER & BROWN, 2002, p. 71)

▲ Media concepts of attractiveness are linked to body dissatisfaction in teens.

Body Image and the Media

◀ **Learning Objective 8.13**
How is body satisfaction in adolescents influenced by media images?

Closely connected to the topic of sexuality in the media is the question of how media concepts of physical attractiveness affect adolescents. As was mentioned in Chapter 3, for many teens the physical changes of adolescence are accompanied by a disturbance in *body image* (Cash & Pruzinsky, 2002). In simple terms, girls decide they're too pudgy and boys decide they're too scrawny (Clay, Vignoles, & Dittmar, 2005; Smolak & Stein, 2006). One obvious source of their dissatisfaction is the images they find in the media. The women held up as ideals in fashion magazines and on television are taller and thinner than a healthy average woman (Fouts & Burggraff, 2000; Thompson & Smolak, 2001), and the men are taller and more muscular (Labre, 2002).

After our discussion of media effects on aggression and sexuality, it should not come as a surprise to learn that girls who read fashion magazines that feature thin models and watch television shows with thin female stars are more dissatisfied with their own bodies (Harrison, 2001; Harrison & Cantor, 1997). Even brief exposures can have an impact. In one experiment, female undergraduates waited in a room supplied with either fashion or news magazines. They then filled out a questionnaire about dieting (Turner, Hamilton, Jacobs, Angood, & Dwyer, 1997). Those who had been browsing through fashion magazines jammed with photos of thin models expressed more dissatisfaction with their weight than those who had looked at news magazines.

Television watching has an impact on girls' body satisfaction as early as age 5 (Dohnt & Tiggemann, 2006). Prolonged exposure increases the effects. Three years after television was introduced to the island of Fiji, in the South Pacific, the percentage of teenage girls with symptoms of eating disorders more than doubled (Becker, Burwell, Herzog, Hamburg, & Gilman, 2002). Before the arrival of television, the cultural ideal was a robust body and a healthy appetite. After 3 years of exposure to television, 74% of girls said they felt too fat and 69% admitted they had dieted to lose weight.

In Chapter 13 we will look in more detail at body image disturbances and eating disorders. We will also ask why some teens seem able to shrug off the influence of media stereotypes of attractiveness.

Now For Some Good News...

◀ **Learning Objective 8.14**
What are some positive effects of teen media involvement?

It is perfectly normal and even admirable for adults to be concerned for those who are young and vulnerable. It makes sense to worry over whether new features of our world may damage them. As we have just seen, there are plenty of good reasons to worry about the impact of today's ever-present media on adolescents. However, if we focus only on the problems the media raise, real and serious as they are, we miss a very large and very important part of the picture.

Today's adolescents have wider and easier access to the riches of human culture than anyone could have imagined even 50 years ago. The collections of the world's great libraries and museums are only a mouse click away. Any music that has been recorded and any film that has been preserved are probably available on CD, DVD, or videotape, and if not, an Internet newsgroup may help you find a collector who has a copy. Passionate about needlework, reptiles, Moroccan cooking, or dirtbike racing? There are magazines, websites, and cable channels eager to help you deepen your knowledge and keep up-to-date.

On a more personal level, chatrooms, instant messaging, and sites such as Facebook and MySpace make it possible to stay in touch with your best friend, that neat kid you met at camp last summer, and someone you haven't even met face-to-face, all at the same time (Valkenburg & Peter, 2007). Adolescents whose background, interests, attitudes, or sexual orientation leave them feeling isolated and desperately lonely can discover others in the same situation and develop an online relationship of mutual support, although of course they should be cautious in dealing with people they do not know (McMillan & Morrison, 2006; Wolak, Mitchell, & Finkelhor, 2003).

As they say on late-night infomercials, "Wait, there's more!" Today's teens are not limited to being passive, or even active, consumers of media. Advances in digital technology make it possible for them to become producers of media as well (Lenhart & Madden, 2005). Around the world, adolescents are recording CDs, putting together videos, compiling blogs, editing zines, building websites, and swapping their creations with like-minded young people who may live half a dozen time zones away. In the process, they are reaching across cultures to lay the foundations of a global community rich with possibilities for the future.

Summing Up...

Adolescents in the modern world spend huge amounts of their free time involved with media. Across adolescence, television watching declines and music listening increases. New uses of computers and the Internet, such as blogs and social websites, draw in more and more teens. The media offer teens diversion, information about the world, and social experiences. Negative effects of media exposure on adolescents can include increased aggression, cynical or unrealistic attitudes about sexual activity, and distorted body image.

SUMMARY

Adolescents are powerfully affected by the communities in which they live, by the culture in which their community is embedded, and by the media to which they are so constantly exposed.

Learning Objective 8.1 What is a sense of community and why is it important to teens?

A community is much more than a set of buildings in a particular location. It is adults and children who are joined by their common setting, activities, goals, attitudes, and values. Growing physical and social distance between adults and adolescents, encouraged by suburbanization and age segregation, makes achieving a **sense of community** more difficult. Inner-city teens are particularly likely to feel left out, unimportant, and powerless.

Learning Objective 8.2 What can be done to build a stronger sense of community?

Community organizations for adolescents can play a critical role in fostering a sense of engagement and identification with the common good and the development of positive social values.

Learning Objective 8.3 How do organized teen sports help or hinder the growth of a sense of community?

Organized sports offer many benefits to teens, but an overemphasis on winning can undermine these and diminish their enjoyment of the activity.

Cultures are systems of norms, beliefs, values, and behaviors that are shared by a group and passed along to new generations.

Learning Objective 8.4 How can the study of cultures help us understand adolescence?

We often interpret the world from the standpoint of our own cultural assumptions and think of others' cultural practices as peculiar. This tendency is called **ethnocentrism**. A knowledge of different cultures, gained through **cross-cultural research**, can help create a more sympathetic understanding of those from other backgrounds.

Learning Objective 8.5 **How are collectivistic and individualistic cultures different?**

One widely used approach to understanding cultural differences relies on concepts of **individualism** and **collectivism**. Individualistic cultures, such as those of the United States, Canada, and Western Europe, focus more on the rights, goals, and needs of independent individuals. Collectivistic cultures, such as those of China and India, focus more on the norms, beliefs, and goals of the group and the duty of interdependent individuals to act in the interest of the group. Critics of these concepts cite findings that adolescents across cultures develop similar concepts of universal human rights.

Learning Objective 8.6 **How do teens acquire the norms and attitudes of their culture?**

Children and adolescents may acquire the rules and traditions of their culture through **socialization**, or instruction from parents, peers, teachers, and community leaders, and through **enculturation**, in which the psychological aspects of the culture are passed along through traditional stories, sagas, and media presentations. They may also construct an understanding of the social practices that allow them to get along in their community.

Learning Objective 8.7 **How do teens who belong to an ethnic minority function within a culture?**

The United States, Canada, and Western Europe have become much more culturally diverse in recent decades, largely because of immigration from other parts of the world. Teens who are members of minority cultural or **ethnic groups** develop various relationships to the majority culture. Those who **assimilate** give up their own culture to identify with the majority culture. Those who **marginalize** themselves reject both their own culture and the majority culture. Those who **separate** identify only with their own culture and reject the majority culture. Those who **integrate** retain their identification with their own culture while also identifying with the majority culture. These teens are called **bicultural**. Bicultural teens have fewer psychological difficulties than those in the other groups.

Adolescents from ethnic minorities may develop goals and values that are different from those of their parents. In general, immigrant parents believe more strongly in family obligations than their adolescent children do.

Learning Objective 8.8 **How does growing up in poverty affect adolescents?**

Adolescents are deeply affected by their family's **social class** or SES, which involves wealth, income, education, and place in society. Almost one in five American children under 18 live in *poverty*. The percentages are especially high for minority children, many of whom live in extreme poverty. Growing up poor affects adolescents at every level of their experience, from stressed-out parents to deviant peers, inadequate school facilities, and deprived, often dangerous, neighborhoods.

Adolescents in developed societies have a great deal of free time, much of which they spend engaged with some form of the **media**.

Learning Objective 8.9 **How much time do teens spend on media?**

In early adolescence, television takes up the most time. Across adolescence, music steadily gains importance, as does use of a computer, especially time online. Internet use among teens is strongly linked to family income and ethnic background. Higher SES and White adolescents use the Internet much more, both at school and at home.

Learning Objective 8.10 **What do teens expect to get from media?**

Among the reasons adolescents use media so much are diversion, excitement, gathering information, and keeping up with the interests of friends and peers.

Learning Objective 8.11 **How does exposure to violent media affect teen aggression?**

The effects of media exposure can be understood in terms of the *understanding* of the world communicated by the media, the *models* for behaviors and attitudes that are presented, and the *scripts* or social judgments that are provided or encouraged. A major concern is how exposure to *violence* in the media affects children and adolescents. Research indicates that watching media violence causes some children to become more aggressive and leads many others to be more accepting of aggressiveness. Violent video games arouse special concern because the violence is so pervasive and explicit and because players are involved in first-person violent activities.

Learning Objective 8.12 **What roles do media play in sexual socialization?**

Another concern is the effects on adolescents of exposure to sexuality in the media. Almost one in three U.S. teens name television as their main source of information about sex, and almost three of four have come across pornography online. The media generally presents a recreational view of sexual relations that leads to cynical attitudes among teens.

Learning Objective 8.13 **How is body satisfaction in adolescents influenced by media images?**

The images of physical attractiveness presented in the media have been linked to body dissatisfaction, disturbed body image, and eating disorders among adolescents.

Learning Objective 8.14 **What are some positive effects of teen media involvement?**

Along with attention to the negative effects of media exposure on teens, it should be noted that through the media those growing up today have wider and easier access to the riches of human culture than any previous generation.

KEY TERMS

Sense of community (253)
Culture (257)
Ethnocentrism (258)
Cross-cultural research (260)
Individualism (261)

Collectivism (261)
Socialization (262)
Enculturation (262)
Ethnic group (263)
Assimilation (264)

Marginalization (264)
Separation (264)
Integration (264)
Bicultural (264)
Social class (269)

Media (273)
Uses and gratifications
  (277)

Part 4 Adolescent Issues

Achievement

Not enjoyment, and not sorrow,

Is our destined end or way;

But to act, that each to-morrow

Find us farther than to-day...

Let us, then, be up and doing,

With a heart for any fate;

Still achieving, still pursuing,

Learn to labor and to wait.

—LONGFELLOW, *"A Psalm of Life"*

The issue of **achievement**—what we do and how well we do it—is one that makes an early appearance and never really goes away. Parents brag (or worry) about their children's first steps and first words. Report cards start almost as soon as school itself. Even young children compare their skills and abilities with one another. At the other end of the lifespan, some people stay active in their professions into their 80s and 90s. And a bridge or checkers tournament in a retirement community can generate strong involvement and fierce competition. In between, activities and evaluations are an inescapable part of life. From transcripts and resumes to sports trophies and scrapbooks, the records of our achievements are an important part of what we point to when someone asks who we are.

During adolescence, the question of achievement is particularly high on the agenda. There are several reasons for this. In today's technological societies, people need advanced knowledge and skills. These go well beyond what children can be expected to learn. It is during adolescence that young people start to acquire this knowledge and these skills, or fail to acquire them.

Compared to children, adolescents are expected to make many more choices, both in and out of school. Do they elect to take vocational, college-track, or AP courses? How do they balance schoolwork, sports practice, part-time work, and hang-out time with friends? Do they aim for college or decide to look for a job after high school?

Along with the greater range of choices adolescents face, the choices they do make have more far-reaching implications. A teen who decides not to take science courses in high school because they are said to be dry and tough has probably closed off a whole range of college majors and future careers. If you make a wrong turn, the longer you keep driving, the harder it is to get back on the right road.

The more advanced cognitive abilities adolescents develop allow them to imagine hypothetical futures based on their abilities, interests, and limitations ("Since I like to draw, maybe I should be an artist or designer."). They can also reason through the logical and practical steps that link today's choices to long-range goals ("If I want to become an architect, I'll need to take lots of math courses.").

In this chapter, we look first at how an adolescent's family, friends, school, ethnic background, and culture affect achievement orientation. We then examine some of the ways individual adolescents deal with achievement. Finally, we discuss the process of occupational and career development during adolescence.

INFLUENCES ON ACHIEVEMENT

My friend's son, Matteo, discovered light switches even before he could walk. Whenever his parents brought him into a room, he scanned the walls and reached for any switch he saw. He would then gleefully turn the lights on and off until someone called a halt to the game. If put down, he would crawl to the nearest lamp or appliance and hunt for a way to turn it on.

This enjoyment in controlling events and having a visible impact on the world around is called **competence motivation,** and it starts to show itself in earliest

Achievement The accomplishment of a goal, generally by using personal skills and resources to overcome difficulties.

Competence motivation The desire to control events and have an impact on the world that begins to show itself in early childhood.

childhood (Elliot & Dweck, 2005; White, 1959). Parents, teachers, and other adults often worry about how to get young people involved in achievement, but they may be on the wrong track. The question they might ponder instead is how to make sure young people don't *lose* the involvement they started out with.

By the time children reach adolescence, they have already had a long history of confronting achievement issues and a long list of influences on the ways they deal with them. Not surprisingly, the family, peers, school, and the broader culture all play important roles. In the pages that follow, we will see what research can tell us about these influences.

Home and Family

Suppose you decide to try some new activity. How likely is it that you will do it really well the first time? Not very. To explore and learn new skills, children need to feel comfortable about accepting challenges, taking risks, and occasionally falling on their faces. Several elements in the parent-child relationship can help build this feeling of confidence.

Parents and Self-Assurance. We saw in Chapter 5 that an essential element in creating this sense of safety is the child's *attachment* relationship with the parents (Bowlby, 1969, 1988). Children who were securely attached as babies start school with greater curiosity, self-assurance, and problem-solving skills (Waters, Wippman, & Sroufe, 1979). And those who enter school with secure attachments tend to perform better and remain more self-assured all the way into adolescence (Jacobsen & Hofmann, 1997).

Along with attachment, key elements are **independence training** and **achievement training,** encouraging children to do things on their own and do them well. In one classic study (Rosen & D'Andrade, 1959), preadolescent boys who measured either high or low in achievement motivation worked at difficult tasks while their parents watched and offered any suggestions they liked. The parents of the high-motivation boys set high standards, offered helpful hints, and praised good performance. Parents of the low-motivation boys, however, tended to jump in and tell their sons what to do and got irritated at the slightest setback.

Another factor that matters a great deal is how parents praise or criticize their children's achievements. Parents who praise successes and are not too upset by an occasional failure have children who welcome challenges and enjoy trying to do things well. In contrast, parents who do not react positively to their child's successes and who come down hard on failures have children who become anxious and helpless when faced with achievement tasks (Burhans & Dweck, 1995).

◄ **Learning Objective 9.1**
How do parents help children become motivated achievers?

Independence training
Encouraging children to do things on their own.

Achievement training
Encouraging children to strive to do things well.

◄ Parents of highly motivated children are both warm and encouraging.

To sum up, the parents of highly motivated and successful children and adolescents are *warm, encouraging, firm, fair,* and *involved* (Gonzalez, Doan Holbein, & Quilter, 2002; Juang & Silbereisen, 2002; Wentzel, 1998). If this set of characteristics sounds very familiar, it should. We heard about it earlier, in Chapter 5, as a description of the *authoritative* parenting style (Baumrind, 1991). Achievement, then, is still another area of functioning in which teens with authoritative parents have an advantage.

One study of high school students related parenting styles, as perceived by the students, to the students' goal orientations (Gonzalez et al., 2002). Those teens who saw their parents as authoritative were more interested in learning new skills and enhancing their understanding. Those with authoritarian or permissive parents, however, were more concerned about proving their ability by outdoing others and avoiding failures that would bring negative judgments of their competence.

Parent Involvement. To say, as we did in the last section, that parents of motivated adolescents stress independence and achievement does not mean they simply shove their children out into the world with a hearty, "Go in and win!" Their encouragement and support are generally more helpful and tangible than that. For example, they try to arrange life at home to provide a suitable place and adequate time for schoolwork, even at a cost to their own convenience. Aside from its practical value, this demonstrates the high priority they place on achievement and encourages the child to do the same (Grolnick & Slowiaczek, 1994).

Effective parents offer more than encouragement and support. They also communicate a sense that learning is important and a belief that the teen has what it takes to learn well. For example, several studies have found that adolescents whose parents see math and science as important *and* believe their children can do well in these areas show more interest and perform better in math and science courses (Bhanot & Jovanovic, 2005; Bouchey & Harter, 2005; Tenenbaum & Leaper, 2003).

Parents of motivated adolescents are also likely to be involved more directly in their child's education, especially during early adolescence (Gregory & Weinstein, 2004; Kohl, Lengua, McMahon, & Conduct Problems Prevention Research Group, 2000; Muller, 1998; Spera, 2006). Their involvement can show itself in a number of ways, such as:

- monitoring their child's progress in school;
- communicating with teachers;
- helping with schoolwork;
- giving advice about course choices;
- attending school functions; and
- taking part in parent-teacher organizations.

This factor of parental involvement gives one more advantage to teens from White middle-class families. Their parents are likely to understand the school system better, feel more confident about intervening in case of a problem, and have more time to take an active role (Crosnoe, 2001; Csikszentmihalyi & Schneider, 2000; McGrath, Swisher, Elder, & Conger, 2001).

An interesting point is that across adolescence, measures of parental involvement tend to go down (Stevenson & Baker, 1987). One likely reason is that older teens generally want, and usually get, a greater degree of autonomy. Another is that parents may feel less capable of giving help. Most adults are reasonably comfortable with middle-school arithmetic, for example, but even those with college degrees may find today's version of 10th-grade math daunting (Muller, 1998; Steinberg, Brown, & Dornbusch, 1996).

Parents also adjust their level of involvement to their children's needs and progress (Muller, 1998). Those whose teens are doing well in school will not feel the same need to monitor their progress, communicate with teachers, help with schoolwork, or attend school functions. It is when students start having problems that their parents are more likely to get involved (McNeal, 1999; Sanders, 1998).

Parents are not the only family members who matter. One recent study looked at conversations between adolescent siblings. The most frequent topics were extracurricular activities, media, and academics. Siblings talk with each other a lot about academics, and the more they do so, the more they are also likely to say they feel competent academically (Tucker & Winzeler, 2007).

Peers

Early adolescence is marked by a drop in school grades, achievement scores, and interest in school, along with a rise in school-related anxiety (Alspaugh, 1998; Eccles et al., 1993; Lee & Smith, 2001; Wigfield & Eccles, 1989; Wigfield & Wagner, 2005). At the same time, early adolescence is marked by a rise in the amount of time spent with, and the importance given to, friends and age mates (Brown, 1990; Larson & Verma, 1999). For many parents, as well as teachers, policymakers, and other adults, the inference seems obvious. The reason their teens aren't doing as well as they did when they were younger must be the negative influence of those other teens they are hanging around. (And, of course, the parents of those "other" teens are probably thinking the same thing!)

To some extent, those who draw this connection have a point. Peers do have an important impact on the school-related attitudes, motivation, and achievement of adolescents (Barber, Eccles, & Stone, 2001; La Greca, Prinstein, & Fetter, 2001; Ryan, 2001; Urberg, Degirmencioglu, Tolson, & Halliday-Scher, 2000). However, this impact is by no means all negative. Those teens with less-motivated and lower-achieving friends do tend to do worse themselves, but those whose friends value education and do well in school tend to be more engaged with school and to do better (Crosnoe, Riegle-Crumb, Field, Frank, & Muller, 2008; Steinberg, Brown, & Dornbusch, 1996; Zimmer-Gembeck, Chipuer, Hanisch, Creed, & McGregor, 2006).

Two processes that help account for the impact of peers on achievement are **selection** and **socialization.** Adolescents tend to *select*, or choose, friends who are similar to them. At the same time, friends tend to *socialize*, or influence, one another to become more similar, through reinforcement, modeling, and shared norms (Ryan, 2001). If the other teens in your clique think that studying hard and doing well make you a teacher's pet, your study time is likely to drop off, along with your grades. But if they enjoy learning and think education is important, your achievement is likely to improve.

In school, adolescents typically operate with more than one sort of goal (Wentzel, 2000). Of course, intellectual achievement may be one of the goals, but obeying the rules, gaining the approval of the teacher, living up to a reputation (whether positive or negative), and conforming to the norms of one's classmates and friends may be just as important or more important. If a student's goals fit with the motivational environment

◄ **Learning Objective 9.2**
What impact do peers have on school-related attitudes?

Selection A process by which adolescents tend to choose to associate with friends who are similar to them.

Socialization A process by which friends tend to influence one another to become more similar.

◄ Teens whose friends enjoy learning and think education is important have higher achievement themselves.

of the classroom, that will encourage achievement. But if there is a clash between the student's goals and the school's, achievement is likely to suffer (Eccles et al., 1993).

One study (Ryan, 2001) identified the members of different friendship groups in the fall of 7th grade and followed them across the school year. Because of selection, members of each particular group tended to have similar levels of motivation and achievement at the beginning. Even so, group attitudes in the fall predicted changes in both intrinsic motivation and school grades for its members. On average, *everyone's* grades and motivation went down during 7th grade, but those whose friendship group consisted of high achievers showed less of a decline than those whose friends were low achievers (Ryan, 2001). We take a more detailed look at this interesting study in this chapter's Research in the Spotlight.

Research in the Spotlight

Friends and Achievement

Birds of a feather flock together.

There is plenty of research to bear out what old sayings and common sense lead us to suppose. By and large, adolescents tend to associate with others who have similar backgrounds, interests, values, and attitudes. At the same time, however, they are influenced by the attitudes, values, interests, and activities of the people they associate with. The saying might be more accurate if we were to add: And birds who flock together become more of a feather.

Because selection—joining a group of people who are like you—and socialization—becoming more like the people whose group you join—operate together, they are hard to disentangle. When we recall that those in a group are both sources of influence and targets of influence, figuring out what leads to what may start to seem like an impossible task.

This is the task that Allison Ryan (2001) took on in her study, "The peer group as a context for the development of young adolescent motivation and achievement." Her starting point was to map the social networks in the 7th grade of an urban middle school with an economically and ethnically diverse student body. Early in the school year, more than 300 students were asked to list the teens they "hang around with and talk to the most." A sophisticated computer program charted these friendship patterns and identified 52 separate groups of students who interacted more with one another than with those in other groups. The groups ranged in size from 2 to 11 members, with an average of around 5. Practically all were single-sex, and the majority drew members from only one ethnic background.

Ryan focused on three aspects of motivation. Students were asked to rate their expectancy of success ("How well do you expect to do in school this year?"), their intrinsic interest ("How much do you like doing schoolwork?"), and the utility value of schoolwork ("In general, how useful is what you learn in school?"). To measure achievement, Ryan gathered students' grades in academic core subjects for the last quarter of 6th grade and the first and last quarters of 7th grade. Each of the peer groups was then given a score for the three motivation measures and for achievement, based on the average of the members' scores in the fall quarter.

Not surprisingly, the data indicated that adolescents tend to hang out with others who have similar levels of motivation and achievement. This represents the selection part of the process. Probably as a result of this selection, groups that were high on one aspect of motivation were high on the others, and on achievement as well. The central question, however, was whether students are also socialized by the group they belong to. To answer this, Ryan made use of a complex statistical technique called hierarchical linear modeling. In effect, this asks whether the characteristics of the group contribute to changes in those who belong to the group, even after taking into account the initial level of the individual members.

The results of the study showed that participants were affected by the kind of friendship group they belonged to, but not across the board. As is typical of early adolescence, the average levels of intrinsic interest in school and grades went down. However, those who belonged to groups of teens who liked school and got good grades showed less of a drop, and those whose friends disliked school and got lower grades showed a greater drop. This documents the effect of socialization and shows that "peer groups have the potential to bring about both positive and negative changes" (Ryan, 2001, p. 1146).

On the other hand, even though being in a particular group affected actual achievement, it had only a minor impact on students' expectancies of success. As for the usefulness or importance of schoolwork, peer group membership did not seem to influence students' opinions at all. This reminds us that even when motivational characteristics are closely related, they may still be influenced by different factors. An adolescent's specific peer group is important, but so are parents, teachers, school climate, cultural atmosphere, and, of course, the adolescent's personal experiences and ways of understanding those experiences.

Source: Ryan, A. M., 2001, pp. 1135–1150.

While many parents may believe they need to counteract the influence of their child's friends and peers, in many ways parents and peers work together (Brown, Mounts, Lamborn, & Steinberg, 1993; Cook, Herman, Phillips, & Settersten, 2002; Gonzalez, Cauce, Friedman, & Mason, 1996). First, parents play a role in their child's selection of friends, by encouraging friendships they see as positive and discouraging those they see as negative (Tilton-Weaver & Galambos, 2002). Second, parents who are warm, engaged with their children, and neither too firm nor too lax, have children who are attached to them and who share their central values (Kerr, Stattin, Biesecker, & Ferrer-Wreder, 2002). These children, in turn, are likely to choose friends who have similar values (Bogenschneider, Wu, Raffaelli, & Tsay, 1998). If those values include a positive attitude toward school and achievement, that fact will be reflected in the way the group of friends behaves.

School Climate

Just as the attitudes of parents and friends help shape an adolescent's motivation for achievement, so does the psychological climate of the school and classroom. Which students are most valued, praised, and rewarded? In what ways? And for what kind of achievement? As we saw in Chapter 7, schools that stress ability, grades, and competition encourage *performance goals* (Eccles, 2003). What comes to matter to students is winning, or at least not losing in a way that seems like evidence for low ability. The question on everyone's mind is, "Will this be on the test?" If the answer is no, the idea or information is tossed away as useless.

In contrast, schools that reward effort and individual improvement and play down competition for grades encourage *mastery goals* (Anderman & Anderman, 1999). The same distinction extends to classrooms and individual teachers. Those who emphasize performance goals over mastery goals produce students who are more likely to handicap themselves and less likely to ask for needed help (Turner et al., 2002). As young adolescents quickly discover, middle schools are more likely than elementary schools to stress performance goals (Kumar, 2006).

There is another significant difference between settings that favor performance goals and those that favor mastery goals. In performance-oriented schools, the problem is not simply that students are graded on their work. In the right context, grades can provide valuable feedback as well as welcome encouragement. The competitive approach, however, means that good grades are made into a *scarce* commodity (Covington, 1992, 2002). Praise and rewards are given on a comparative rather than absolute basis. You may have mastered the material that is being studied and improved your understanding, but you get that A only if you perform *better* than your classmates. This generates a pervasive feeling of lack of control that works against putting in the necessary effort to learn. We take a more detailed look at differences in goal orientation among adolescents later in this chapter.

Even something as seemingly slight as the kinds of questions a teacher puts to a class can affect student attitudes toward achievement (Kaplan & Maehr, 2002). Consider a teacher who asks, "Who commanded the Union troops at Gettysburg?" What messages does this question convey?

There is a particular *right* answer;

Any other answer is *wrong*;

The teacher *knows* what the right answer is;

The student's job is to *learn* it by heart and *produce* it on demand.

What if, instead, the teacher asked, "Why was Lee willing to risk so much by invading the North?" This question suggests that the teacher and students are involved together in a process of *creating* knowledge, rather than merely memorizing knowledge that someone else created.

Mutual involvement among teachers and students contributes to achievement in other ways as well. When students feel supported in their efforts by teachers and fellow

Connect the **Dots...**

When you think back to high school, did you and your circle of friends have similar attitudes about school, studies, going to college, and other achievement-related topics? Did they receive grades similar to your? Would you say that you chose one another in part because you seemed similar? Do you think you influenced one another in your attitudes toward achievement?

◄ **Learning Objective 9.3**
How are students affected by a competitive school atmosphere?

students, they become more engaged with the class, more oriented toward mastery goals, and more convinced that they have what it takes to succeed both academically and socially (Patrick, Ryan, & Kaplan, 2007; Wentzel, Monzo, Williams, & Tomback, 2007).

Culture

▶ **Learning Objective 9.4**
In what ways do cultural beliefs influence individual achievement?

How is adolescent achievement affected by cultural attitudes and practices? For American researchers and educators, this question has taken on some urgency in recent years, as one international comparison after another put the United States well behind other industrialized countries (Stevenson & Stigler, 1992; TIMSS, 1997). This trend has continued. A report by the U.S. Department of Education shows that 8th graders in the United States score lower in math, science, and reading than those in other major nations such as Canada, Japan, Russia, and England (Sherman, Honegger, & McGivern, 2003).

Declining Scores: Why? This mediocre showing does not seem to be the result of penny-pinching. In absolute terms, the United States spends more on secondary education—over $6,000 per student in 1998—than other industrialized countries. Even as a proportion of gross domestic product (a measure of the size of the economy), U.S. spending on secondary education ranks around the middle, lower than France and Canada, but higher than Germany and Japan (Sherman et al., 2003).

Harold Stevenson, a leading investigator of school achievement across cultures, suggested that one reason American students do poorly is that that American schools spend less time on basics than schools in other countries (Fuligni & Stevenson, 1995). At least as important, American parents, teachers, and students are more likely to see achievement, high or low, as indicating native ability, while those in East Asia are more likely to stress the importance of effort and persistence (Chen & Stevenson, 1995; Stevenson & Lee, 1990). As we will see later in this chapter, this pattern has a profound effect on achievement attitudes. Students who see their own low ability as the cause of their failures are likely to become discouraged and quit. Those who see their failure more as the result of inadequate effort are encouraged to persist and try harder.

Not everyone agrees with Stevenson's analysis of the problem. Critics argue that adolescents in different cultures understand concepts such as ability and effort in different ways (Elliott & Bempechat, 2002). They also differ in the value they see in high achievement. You may believe that working hard is the key to doing well, but if you do not see doing well as very important, your achievement level will stay low. Students in the United States may even believe they *are* working hard, based on those they see around them, though comparisons with those in other countries show they are not (Elliott, Hufton, Illushin, & Willis, 2003)!

The Culture of Achievement. Are there particular features of different cultures that encourage or discourage achievement in young people? David McClelland, one of the founders of achievement motivation theory, certainly thought so. In his book, *The Achieving Society* (1961), he put forward the idea that if cultures stress self-reliance and encourage children to seek out challenges and do things well, younger generations will develop higher levels of achievement motivation. That encouragement will, in turn, favor more achievement and economic progress.

McClelland came up with an ingenious way to test this idea. He looked at children's books from 23 countries around the world and measured the amount of achievement imagery they contained. He then showed that by charting how frequent these achievement themes were in each country during the 1920s, he could predict the country's economic growth from 1929 to 1950 (McClelland, 1961). This was not simply an odd coincidence. In a second study that looked at 39 countries, McClelland showed that the level of achievement imagery in children's readers in 1950 predicted their country's economic growth between 1952 and 1958 (McClelland, 1961).

Figure 9.1   Self- and Other-Referenced Motives Vary Across Countries
Both self-referenced and other-referenced motives vary across countries.

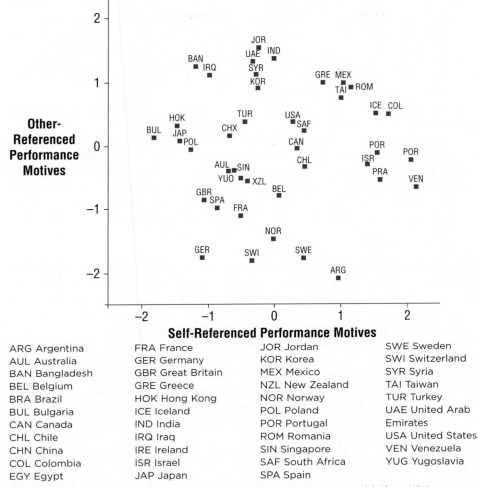

Source: Figure 1, "Position of 42 Countries on the Independent Dimensions of Self- and Other-Referenced Performance Motives," by E. Van de Vliert and O. Janssen. *Journal of Cross-Cultural Psychology 33,* 380–397. © 2002. Used by permission.

While cultures differ in the stress they put on achievement, there is reason to think that some of the same psychological processes support achievement across cultures. Recently, investigators studied performance goals and satisfaction among students in 42 countries (van de Vliert & Janssen, 2002). To what extent do young people measure their success against their own past performance or against the performance of others? This contrast is roughly the same as the distinction we drew earlier between mastery and performance goals.

As Figure 9.1 shows, both self-referenced and other-referenced motives vary widely from one country to another. South American countries are relatively stronger in self-referenced motives, Arab countries have relatively high other-referenced motives, and Western European countries have relatively weak other-referenced motives. The United States and Canada are near the middle on both dimensions. However, in spite of these important differences, the *relationships* between motives and satisfaction turn out to be similar across cultures. Self-referenced performance motives are linked to greater satisfaction, and other-referenced performance motives are linked to less satisfaction (van de Vliert & Janssen, 2002). From Singapore to Switzerland and Bulgaria to Bangladesh, if you judge your successes by your own past performance, you gain more satisfaction from achievement than if you rate yourself according to the performance of competitors.

Ethnicity and Class

▶ **Learning Objective 9.5**
Why is there an achievement gap between different social classes and ethnic groups?

One of the most consistent findings about adolescent achievement in the United States is that, on average, White and Asian American students get markedly higher grades and higher scores on standardized tests than Black and Hispanic students. National assessments have documented this gap at both the 8th- and 12th-grade level and in a variety of school subjects, including math, reading, geography, and history (National Center for Education Statistics [NCES], 2000, 2003). A similar gap shows up between teens from middle-class and working-class backgrounds (Felner et al., 1995). Low-income and minority youth are at the greatest risk for school failure, with boys at even greater risk than girls (Gutman, Sameroff, & Eccles, 2002; Leventhal & Brooks-Gunn, 2004; Orfield, Losen, Wald, & Swanson, 2004).

These achievement gaps have sparked a heated and ongoing controversy. Everyone admits they exist, but there is disagreement about *why* they exist. Is there something about White middle-class teens that helps them to perform better? Is there something about poor and minority teens that causes them to perform worse? Or are both of these at work? How do high-achieving Asian American adolescents, many of them from poor and immigrant families, fit into the picture? We will take up these points one by one.

White and Middle-Class Advantages. Some of the more obvious advantages White middle-class children enjoy begin even before they enter elementary school. On the whole, they are better fed, better housed, and get better medical care. Their parents are more likely to encourage educational toys, games, and television. Once the children enter school, their parents are better positioned to learn about educational opportunities, be able to cope with the school bureaucracy, and have the time, confidence, and inclination to take part in school affairs (Crosnoe, 2001; Csikszentmihalyi & Schneider, 2000; McGrath, Swisher, Elder, & Conger, 2001). In addition, White middle-class parents are more likely to adopt an authoritative approach to parenting and provide the sort of independence training that encourages the development of high achievement motivation. The benefits of these practices continue through childhood and into adolescence.

Young people from White middle-class backgrounds also have an advantage because they typically reach adolescence with more cultural capital than those from poor and minority backgrounds (Bourdieu, 1997; Dumais, 2002). **Cultural capital** refers to the advantages young people gain from being introduced to art, music, libraries, museums, and other cultural resources. Middle-class parents are likely to see music lessons, art classes, visits to museums and libraries, summer camp, travel, and such as normal and valuable features of childhood, and to find the resources to provide them even if it is a strain. The culture, in turn, expects that children will acquire the knowledge and skills that experiences of this sort help develop.

Having more cultural capital has been linked to higher achievement among adolescents, not just in the United States, but in industrialized countries in general (UNESCO, 2003). Unfortunately, American public schools, under pressure from tightened budgets and the need to prep students for high-stakes tests, are less and less likely to offer the classes in art and music that could extend these benefits to non-middle-class and minority children (Herszenhorn, 2003). Increasingly, if the children don't get it at home, they don't get it.

Poor and Minority Disadvantages. One important roadblock to achievement for adolescents from poor and minority backgrounds is that the schools they attend are simply not as effective. In schools with higher percentages of students who are eligible for free or subsidized lunches (a common measure of poverty):

> teachers have less experience;
>
> fewer teachers are certified in their subjects;
>
> the schools are larger;

Cultural capital The advantages young people gain from being introduced to art, music, libraries, museums, and other cultural resources.

Figure 9.2   Poverty, School Characteristics, and Student Math Achievement
Student poverty is connected with math achievement and school characteristics.

	% students in school eligible for free or reduced price lunch				
	10% or less	11–25%	26–50%	51–75%	75%+
1. Math Achievement Scores	243	234	228	218	207
eligible for subs. lunch:					
Yes	#	218	219	209	201
No	244	238	233	228	212
2. School characteristics					
% students w/ very positive attitude toward achievement	80%	46%	34%	28%	29%
% teachers certified in math	27	40	38	31	22
% teachers w/ 2 yrs or less exper.	13	12	13	14	16
% schools w/ serious/moderate physical conflicts among students	2	10	11	22	22
% schools w/ enrollment of more than 1000 students	1	5	2	4	9
% teachers who leave before end of school year	6	10	30	29	35
% of schools in which more than half of parents participate in parent-teacher organizations	60	38	20	11	5

too few cases to tabulate.

Source: NCES, 2003, Tables 12-1 & 12-2.

students are absent more frequently;

classes are disrupted more often; and

teachers are more likely to quit.

—**(NCES, 2003)**

Given all these problems, it is no surprise that as the proportion of low-income students in a school goes up, achievement scores go down. And this is not only a matter of students from poverty backgrounds doing badly. As Figure 9.2 illustrates, the scores of students who are *not* eligible for subsidized lunches also go down as the proportion of low-income students in their school goes up (NCES, 2003).

Going to an inferior school is not the only risk factor that particularly affects minority teens. Other factors include growing up in a single-parent household; the education level, employment, and mental health of parents; being the victim of violent crime; family economic stresses, such as having a parent laid off or unemployed; and living in a low-income, high crime area. The more of these risk factors adolescents have to deal with, the lower their academic achievement (Gutman, Sameroff, & Eccles, 2002). However, other factors, such as consistent parental discipline, can help protect teens from these effects (see Figure 9.3 on page 302).

Minority children also face the hazards of outright discrimination on the part of teachers and peers. A recent study followed over 600 African American teens from the beginning of 7th grade to the end of 8th grade. The more day-to-day discrimination they reported, such as not being picked for activities by peers or being graded more harshly by teachers because of their race, the more their grades, sense of academic ability, and valuing of school declined (Eccles, Wong, & Peck, 2006).

Stereotype Threat. Minority and non-middle-class adolescents may also be held back by the low expectations the larger society holds for them. In general, those who are members of groups such as Blacks, Hispanics, women, or children of manual

Connect the **Dots...**

Can you recall any clear instances of racial or ethnic discrimination in the classroom? How do you think these instances affected the target of discrimination (or you, if you were the target)? What about others in the class? How did they respond, either at the time or later on?

Figure 9.3   Risk Factors, Parent Discipline, and School Grades
Students whose parents are consistent in their discipline are better able to deal with multiple risk factors.

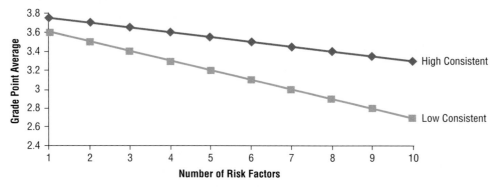

Source: "Risk Factors, Parent Discipline, and School Grades," by L. M. Gutman, A. J. Sameroff, and J. S. Eccles. *American Journal of Community Psychology 30*, 367–399. © 2002. Used by permission.

workers are very much aware of the negative stereotypes the majority culture holds about their group. As a result, evaluative situations, such as tests, create a **stereotype threat** (Aronson & Good, 2002; Croizet & Claire, 1998; Steele, 1997; Steele & Aronson, 1995; Steele, Spencer, & Aronson, 2002). Those affected by stereotype threat worry that if they fail, they will simply be confirming the majority's negative opinions about their group. This fear leads to performance anxiety that interferes with success. This anxiety may even temporarily lower the student's cognitive capacity (Schmader & Johns, 2003). Brooding about the likelihood and implications of failure uses up attention and memory resources that could better be applied to the task.

More and more evidence confirms the role of stereotype threat. In one study, for example, Black and Hispanic preadolescents who were aware of negative stereotypes about their ethnic groups were given an achievement task under one of two conditions. Those who were told the task measured general ability did worse on the task than White students. Those who were told it was a game, however, did *better* than White students on the same task (McKown & Weinstein, 2003).

There may be effective ways to help minority adolescents resist the effects of stereotype threat. In a recent experiment, African American college students were encouraged to see intelligence as malleable rather than fixed. Follow-ups showed that they became more engaged in their studies, enjoyed them more, and earned higher grades than students in comparison groups (Aronson, Fried, & Good, 2002).

The Burden of "Acting White." While the expectations others hold about poor and minority adolescents may generate stereotype threat, the expectations adolescents themselves hold also matter. Anthropologist John Ogbu (2002; Fordham & Ogbu, 1986) studied minority students in both inner-city and affluent suburban settings. In his view, the awareness of discrimination leads minority teens to think that school success is pointless. They may even see it as a form of giving in to the majority culture. This negative expectation leads to the emergence of an **oppositional peer culture** that rejects the goals and values of the school and the majority culture. Instead of doctors and judges, minority teens may choose hustlers and gangsta rappers as role models. Those adolescents who do accept the school values and try to achieve, for example, by using standard English and participating in class, may find themselves resented and rejected for "acting White."

Ogbu's explanation has aroused controversy for a decade and more (Lee, 2002). Some critics feel it verges on "blaming the victim" for the problem. They point to surveys that find Black students have *more* favorable attitudes toward education, hard work, and effort than Whites (Ainsworth-Darnell & Downey, 1998; Downey & Ainsworth-Darnell, 2002). In response, supporters of Ogbu's position point out that low-income and ethnic minority students typically give overly optimistic responses to surveys about school and achievement (Farkas, Lleras, & Maczuga, et al., 2002). They

Stereotype threat A factor that may interfere with the performance of those who belong to groups that are the target of negative stereotypes by arousing anxiety that they will fail and in this way confirm the stereotype.

Oppositional peer culture The rejection of values and goals of the majority culture based on a belief that discrimination makes it pointless to try to conform to the majority.

may favor hard work more than their White classmates, but it turns out they actually spend *less* time on homework (Mickelson, 1990).

Another element of Ogbu's hypothesis is less controversial. Even in 1st grade, African American children show that they know about racial factors in the workplace and consider stereotypically "Black" jobs less desirable and of lower status (Bigler, Averhart, & Liben, 2003). This tendency is more general than simply knowing about social relationships as they are now. In a recent study, children and young adolescents were told about a number of occupations they had never heard of before, some real and some invented. They were then shown pictures of people performing those occupations. If those pictured were African American, the participants rated the occupation as having lower status than if those in the picture were White (Bigler, Averhart, & Liben, 2003).

Ethnic Identity and Achievement. Being aware that one's racial or ethnic group is the target of negative stereotypes and discrimination does not always affect adolescents unfavorably. Psychologist Daphna Oyserman and her co-workers (Oyserman, Brickman, & Rhodes, 2007; Oyserman, Gant, & Ager, 1995) have outlined ways in which ethnic identity can *promote* academic achievement. Three aspects of ethnic identity are especially important: feeling connected to one's racial-ethnic group, knowing that others may not value one's group, and believing that doing well in school is part of being a good group member.

One recent study (Altschul, Oyserman, & Bybee, 2006) looked at a randomly selected group of African American and Latino adolescents in low-income urban schools. The teens answered questions about their racial-ethnic identity at four times between the fall of 8th grade and the spring of 9th grade, and their scores were analyzed in relation to their grade point averages. The results indicated that those whose racial-ethnic identities were stronger earned higher grades at each point in time. This relationship held for both Blacks and Latinos and for both boys and girls.

Another recent study, of almost 600 9th graders from Mexican, Chinese, and European backgrounds (Fuligni, Witkow, & Garcia, 2005), led to similar conclusions. The more strongly the participants identified with their ethnic background, and the more positive they felt about their ethnic group, the more they valued school success, saw it as important to their future, and believed they had the personal resources they needed to succeed. Doing well in school calls for more determination and effort for those from immigrant and ethnic minority backgrounds (Fuligni, 2001). One source for this extra push may be a sense of loyalty to one's group and a desire to prove that negative stereotypes are wrong. Being aware that one may face future discrimination can also lead to stronger determination and greater effort in school (Eccles et al., 2006).

The Asian Exception. On average, Asian American students do better in school than students from other minority groups (NCES, 2003). Why is this? Several factors have been cited as responsible. One is their belief that doing well in school and continuing their education is the best way—maybe the *only* way—for them to succeed in American society (Kao & Tienda, 1995; Sue & Okazaki, 1990). Success, in turn, is seen as an obligation to their parents and families (Fuligni, 2001). These linked beliefs give them very good reasons to work hard, study, and persist even in the face of difficulties and failure.

Another factor is that Asian cultures tend to regard ability or intelligence as something that can be molded by experience and effort (Stevenson & Stigler, 1992). Hard work, more than native (that is, fixed) ability, is seen as the key to achievement. The right way to respond to setbacks is not to give up, but to try harder. Given these cultural attitudes, it is not surprising that Asian American students spend more time studying and less time in leisure activities than their classmates from other ethnic groups (NCES, 2001; Steinberg et al., 1996). These extra efforts pay off in higher grades.

In short, Asian American teens expect to be able to do well because they believe the key to success is trying harder. They put a high value on achievement because they believe it will help them reach important goals and live up to their family obligations. As we will see in the next section, these beliefs combine to give them higher personal motivation to achieve, even if they have no more *intrinsic* interest in their schoolwork than teens from other ethnic backgrounds. Moreover, motivation and success can set in motion a "virtuous circle," in which motivation increases success and success increases motivation (Fuligni, 2001). As a result, the successes that follow their higher efforts make further successes more likely.

Summing Up...

Adolescents whose parents are warm, encouraging, and involved approach achievement with more confidence and enthusiasm. Having friends who value accomplishment is another source of encouragement, as is going to a school that stresses mastery goals. Cultural beliefs and values also have an impact on both performance and satisfaction. In the United States, factors that lead to lower achievement scores of low-income and minority youth include family and neighborhood stresses, inferior and troubled schools, stereotype threat, and an oppositional peer culture, as well as the effect of middle-class advantages.

UNDERSTANDING ACHIEVEMENT

However much we learn about the social factors that influence adolescent achievement, we have to recognize that in the end, it is the individual teen who does or does not deal with achievement situations effectively. Some overcome difficult home, peer, and school backgrounds to do well and enjoy doing it. Others who would seem to have everything going for them agonize over every quiz, handicap themselves, or withdraw altogether. And some who seem to meet all the usual standards of success take no personal pride in their achievements and even say they dread the moment when the world finds out how hollow their accomplishments are.

In this section, we look at some of the ways individual adolescents differ in their approach to achievement. Among the questions we explore are:

What to do? Why do teens *prefer* tasks that are easy, difficult, or in between?

Why do it? What are the different incentives that lead teens to *undertake* achievement-related tasks?

What does it mean? How do teens *understand* and *evaluate* the results of their efforts?

What is it like? How do teens *experience* their engagement with an achievement task?

We then attempt to bring these different facets together into an integrated description. How can adolescents best approach learning, achievement, and the exploration and development of their potentials? And how can others, such as parents, teachers, and counselors, encourage such development?

Motives, Expectancies, and Values

▶ **Learning Objective 9.6**
What personal and external factors help predict achievement behavior?

The common-sense view of achievement places *motivation* central to the understanding of achievement. Why does a teen do well at something? He or she is really motivated! Why do some do badly? They must lack motivation! Simple as it is, this view has been the starting point for more complex explorations of the process of achievement. According to one classic view, the essential elements of motivation are a person's *motives*, *expectancies*, and *values* (Atkinson, 1964).

Motives. We can think of a **motive** as a fairly stable, long-term psychological need for a particular kind of emotional consequence. For instance, someone with a strong *affiliation motive* will look for chances to make positive, warm, and fuzzy connections to others. Someone with a strong *power motive*, on the other hand, will seek out opportunities to exert control over others. Achievement situations call forth at least *two*

Motive A stable, ongoing personal sensitivity to a particular sort of emotional consequence.

◀ Students who are high in motive to succeed seek out courses that are neither too easy nor too hard for them.

motives. One, the **motive to succeed (M_s)** involves wanting to *get* the positive feelings that follow a success. The other, the **motive to avoid failure (M_af)** involves wanting to *avoid* the negative feelings that follow a failure.

We all have both these motives; what matters is their relative strength. For example, those whose motive to succeed is stronger ($M_s > M_{af}$) will tend to prefer tasks of *intermediate difficulty* and stay away from those that are either very easy or very hard (Atkinson & Feather, 1966). Easy tasks practically guarantee success, but because they are easy, you don't get much pride from succeeding at them. If you succeed at a very hard task, you can feel a lot of pride, but because it is so hard, you probably *won't* succeed. Tasks in the middle, however, offer you both a good chance of succeeding *and* a good deal of pride when you do succeed.

How about those whose motive to avoid failure is stronger ($M_{af} > M_s$)? They could choose easy tasks because that reduces their chances of failing—and so they do. They may even try to avoid achievement situations altogether because any task, no matter how easy, poses some risk of failing. However, paradoxically, they may instead select the *hardest* tasks (Atkinson & Feather, 1966). At first glance, this seems very odd. After all, it does practically guarantee failure. However—and this is the crucial point—it also practically eliminates the negative feelings that usually *come with* failure. If you try to do something that's really, really hard, and you don't succeed, how bad do you have to feel?

Expectancies. An **expectancy** is a person's subjective belief that taking some action will lead to a certain consequence. Thinking that some task is going to be easy, hard, or in between is an example of an expectancy. For instance:

If I study hard, I have a good chance of acing the final.

If I play tennis with that guy, he'll probably beat me.

If I take on this project, it's a toss-up whether I can do a decent job.

These examples concern some form of success or failure. However, teens also hold expectancies about other types of actions and consequences, such as:

If I eat this piece of cake, my face is sure to break out.

If I hang out with that new kid, we'll probably have fun.

If I tell people at school I believe in UFOs, most of them will think I'm really weird.

Expectancies help guide adolescents toward areas where they think they can succeed and also help energize their behavior. Generally, when people think they can

Connect the Dots...

Based on what you have learned so far in this chapter, what sorts of experiences as a child or in the classroom do you think would be likely to give someone a high motive to succeed? How about a strong motive to avoid failure?

Motive to succeed (M_s) A need or sensitivity to the positive feelings that arise from succeeding at a task.

Motive to avoid failure (M_af) A sensitivity to the negative feelings that arise from failing at a task and a need to avoid those feelings.

Expectancy A subjective estimate of the likelihood that a particular action will lead to a particular result.

succeed at something, they put in more effort and perform better. However, crucial as expectancies are, there is another vital piece to the puzzle. Consider these statements:

■ If I took a course and did the work, I could learn to read and write Ancient Egyptian.

■ I have the time, energy, and tuition money to take a course in Ancient Egyptian.

But what if I don't particularly *want* or *need* to learn the language of the Pharaohs? Yes, I could take a course, and if my expectancy is accurate, I would succeed. But why do it? In another lifetime maybe I would enjoy being an Egyptologist. For now, though, I can't see that learning hieroglyphics would be of much interest or use to me. What we have left out, then, is the incentive or personal *value* of an outcome.

Values. Sometimes the only consequences of succeeding or failing at something are whatever feelings we get from the success or failure. Mostly, however, the tasks we choose and the way we perform them have other consequences as well. A kindergartner who makes an intricate collage or block construction will probably feel pride in success, but the praise from parents and teacher and the admiration of friends also count for a lot. If you take a difficult class in an unfamiliar field, you may be pleased that you even understood enough of the material to pass the final, but no matter how hard you worked for that C–, it will not do much for your GPA. Whether you find your job easy, difficult, or somewhere in the middle, regular paychecks are part of what keeps you showing up.

Achievement motivation researchers Jacquelynne Eccles and Allan Wigfield (Wigfield & Eccles, 2000; Wigfield, Eccles, Schiefele, Roeser, & Davis-Kean, 2006) describe four kinds of incentives or values that are commonly found in achievement situations:

Attainment value. How important do you feel it is to do well on the task?

Intrinsic value. How much enjoyment do you get from doing the task?

Utility value. How useful to you are the consequences of doing the task?

Cost. What other activities do you have to give up to do the task? How much energy do you have to put into it? What are the emotional costs?

The balance among these values will be different from one situation to another. If you're in the dentist's waiting room, doing a crossword puzzle may have some intrinsic value (you enjoy doing it) and some utility value (it helps pass the time and distracts you from worrying about that cavity). But if you do the same crossword puzzle when you know you should be reading the assignment for a class tomorrow morning, the cost factor may outweigh the positive consequences.

Intrinsic and Extrinsic Motivation

▶ **Learning Objective 9.7**
How are intrinsic and extrinsic motivation related?

So far we have been looking at motivation and achievement in terms of results. Does an adolescent expect to succeed or fail at a task? What is the outcome? What values or incentives are linked to the outcome? Sometimes, however, the activity itself is engaging, interesting, or fun, regardless of the outcome. Books about the American Civil War are consistent best sellers, even though few readers expect to take an exam on the material. Playing a round of golf or a game of chess can be a pleasurable experience whether you win or lose. And how many people watch television quiz shows partly because it's such fun to try to guess the answers before the contestant?

Psychologists Edward Deci and Richard Ryan, of the University of Rochester, have spent over three decades studying the different reasons or goals that give rise to an action (Deci, 1975; Deci & Ryan, 1985, 2002; Ryan & Deci, 2000). They draw a basic distinction between **intrinsic motivation,** doing something because it is inherently interesting or enjoyable, and **extrinsic motivation,** doing something because it leads to an outcome that is not built into the activity. In their view, one of the biggest

Intrinsic motivation Undertaking an activity for the sake of the interest or enjoyment that the activity brings.

Extrinsic motivation Undertaking an activity for the sake of the expected outcome or consequence.

drawbacks to extrinsic motivation—the carrot and the stick—is that it can make the person feel forced to do the activity. This, in turn, can lead to lack of interest, resentment, and resistance.

In a classic British movie, *The Loneliness of the Long-Distance Runner* (1962), a teenage boy steals a car and is sent to reform school. There, his one source of pleasure is cross-country running, which he is allowed to practice because the warden hopes to take the trophy at a big meet. On the eve of the meet, the boy is told he had better win, or else. During the race, he easily leads the other runners until he is almost at the finish line. Then he stops and lets the others pass him, ignoring the urgent and furious shouts from the warden. Faced with heavy extrinsic pressure to succeed, he reasserts his personal autonomy by deliberately refusing to win at something he ordinarily enjoys.

Some Curious Effects of Rewards. Not many adolescents go to such extremes. However, offering a tangible extrinsic reward for succeeding at an activity, or threatening punishment for failure, can *undermine* intrinsic motivation for the activity (Deci, Koestner, & Ryan, 2001). In one pioneering study (Deci, 1971), participants were asked to solve an interesting puzzle. Half were told in advance that they would be paid for their efforts, and the other half were not. When the participants later had access to the puzzle during free time, those who were expecting to be paid spent less time trying to solve it.

Why should being paid to do something make it seem less intrinsically interesting? Apparently, we come to interpret the extrinsic reward as the main reason for our actions (Deci & Ryan, 1985; Lepper, Greene, & Nisbett, 1973). We stop noticing whatever pleasure we get from the activity and come to believe we are doing it for the money. So why do it during free time, when no extrinsic reward is available?

This explanation has some rather disturbing implications about the way education is usually structured for adolescents. Starting in middle school and continuing through high school and into college, there is an increasing focus on grades, class rankings, prizes, and other extrinsic consequences. Across these same years, the level of student interest in coursework drops steadily (Gottfried, Fleming, & Gottfried, 2001; Lepper, Corpus, & Iyengar, 2005). It is hard to escape the thought that the stress the system places on competition and grades is undermining whatever intrinsic motivation students feel toward their studies.

Even verbal praise sometimes undermines intrinsic motivation, especially if it focuses on ability rather than effort (Henderlong & Lepper, 2002; Mueller & Dweck, 1998). Telling students how smart they are when they perform well may make them feel they have to go on proving their intelligence by receiving high scores. The result may be that they stay with what they know is safe and avoid learning opportunities that pose the risk of making mistakes (Elliot & Dweck, 2005).

Work or Play? Intrinsic and extrinsic motivation reach well beyond the classroom. Teens who are avid painters, rock climbers, bridge players, or musicians, often invest as much time, energy, and resources, or more, in their interests as in their schoolwork. The same adolescent who spends hours happily doing crossword puzzles or playing Scrabble with friends may complain about half an hour of vocabulary homework for English class. The reason seems to be that the degree of choice or constraint makes one activity feel more like *play* and the other more like *work*, even when the two activities have a lot in common (Lepper & Greene, 1975).

In Mark Twain's classic novel, *Tom Sawyer*, Tom is about to enjoy a carefree Saturday morning when his Aunt Polly tells him he has to whitewash the fence. He is sure his day is ruined—then he has an inspiration. When his friends come by, he pretends to be having a great time. His friends beg him to let them join in, even offering bribes for a turn with the whitewash brush.

Most readers probably see this episode as evidence that Tom was shrewd and his friends were gullible, but the concept of intrinsic motivation puts it in a very different

▲ Intrinsic motivation involves doing activities that are inherently interesting or enjoyable.

' AIN'T THAT WORK?

▲ Tom Sawyer thought he tricked his friends into doing his work, but for them it was fun.

light. In reality, Tom didn't take advantage of his friends. They really did have fun painting the fence because what was a *chore* to Tom was a *game* to them. Because he had to do it, he overlooked or devalued the enjoyable aspects of the activity.

This leads to a startling conclusion:

The more we see ourselves doing something for *extrinsic* reasons, the more we think of the activity as *work*.

The more we see ourselves doing something for *intrinsic* reasons ("for its own sake"), the less we think of the activity as work and the more we think of it as *play*. (McMahan, 1996, p. 168)

Still more startling is the implication that adolescents (and adults!) may be able to learn *not* to overlook their intrinsic reasons for doing something, even when there are also extrinsic rewards or penalties.

When Can Extrinsic Motivation Be Helpful? We have just seen how extrinsic rewards can undermine people's intrinsic interest in an activity. But what if their interest was low to start with? For many students, much of what they study in school is not a subject of deep intrinsic interest—it is simply a hurdle they've been told they have to get over. In that case, extrinsic rewards may keep them doing the work until they either reach their external goal or discover some intrinsic interest they did not feel at first (Pintrich, 2000). For example, when children first start lessons on a musical instrument, many of them have to be coaxed or bribed to practice, but some eventually reach the point where they *enjoy* playing and begin to do it for its own sake.

According to Deci and Ryan (1985; Ryan & Deci, 2000), extrinsic motivation comes in different varieties with different results. Take two students in a high school class that both find intrinsically dull and boring. One, however, sees the class as a necessary step toward some personal goal, such as having a choice of colleges. The other is simply concerned to avoid criticism and penalties from parents. Both are extrinsically motivated, but the first student has accepted the activity as personally relevant and sees doing it well as a personal choice. For the other, the extrinsic reasons are the whole story. If those reasons vanished, so would the student's inclination to continue the activity.

Causes of Success and Failure

▶ **Learning Objective 9.8**
How do adolescents explain their successes and failures?

Motives, expectancies, values, and intrinsic motivation are psychological processes that lead up to an activity or that operate during the activity. However, one influential approach to achievement focuses on what happens *after* the activity. According to Bernard Weiner's (1985, 1992) **attribution theory,** once people have done something (such as take a test) and evaluated their outcome, they try to understand *why* that outcome happened. That is, they *attribute* their success or failure to one or more causes. The explanations they arrive at, in turn, affect their feelings about the outcome, their willingness to do the activity again, and their expectancies for future attempts.

Four causal factors are particularly central to achievement attributions: *ability, effort, task ease* or *difficulty,* and *luck* (Weiner, 1992). For example, an adolescent who has just received a high grade in history might explain this outcome in various ways:

"I have a talent for the subject." [Ability]

"I worked hard in the course." [Effort]

"This teacher is an easy grader." [Task]

"Most of my guesses on the final were right." [Luck]

Attribution theory An approach to achievement that focuses on the causes people see as responsible for their successes and failures.

Locus of causality A belief that the cause of an outcome is something about the person (internal) or about the situation (external).

Similarly, a teen's explanations for a failure might include low ability, not trying hard enough, a really tough course, and guessing wrong.

These four factors can be arranged according to two causal dimensions (see Figure 9.4 on page 309). **Locus of causality** concerns whether the cause is seen as internal or external. **Causal stability** refers to whether the cause is thought to be open to

Figure 9.4 Causal Attributions for an Achievement Outcome
Causal attributions for an achievement outcome (and how you might explain doing well on a quiz).

Locus of Causality

Stability	Internal Cause	External Cause
Stable Cause	*Ability* "I'm pretty smart in English"	*Task difficulty* "All the quizzes in this course are pretty simple."
Unstable Cause	*Effort* "I studied hard for the quiz."	*Luck* "Most of my guesses turned out to be right."

change or stay basically the same over time. So ability, for instance, is *internal*, because it is something about the person, and *stable*, because we tend to think that ability doesn't change, at least in the short run. A third dimension, *controllability*, is not shown in Figure 9.4, but as we shall see, it too plays an important role (Weiner, 1994).

How do people decide what caused a success or failure? To some extent, everyone uses similar common-sense rules. For example:

If I usually succeed, and I succeeded this time, the likely cause is internal (i.e., ability and/or effort).

If I usually succeed, and I failed this time, I probably didn't try hard enough, or I may have had bad luck.

If I succeed, and so does everybody else, the reason is that the task was easy.

If I sometimes succeed and sometimes fail, and I try just as hard each time, my outcomes are mostly a question of luck.

However, people do not always explain their outcomes the same way, even in what appear to be similar situations. Take two adolescents who both do badly on the first quiz in a course. One attributes the failure to insufficient effort, signs up for tutoring, and cuts down on television to put in more study time. The other attributes the failure to lack of ability for the subject and decides to drop the course. They earned the same low score on the quiz, but their different attributions lead to very different results (Graham & Weiner, 1996).

Some Effects of Attributions. As we saw in the last illustration, the explanations an adolescent gives for successes and failures can powerfully affect self-esteem, emotional state, and future outcomes. For example, a recent study of almost 10,000 high school seniors found that one of the best predictors of earnings in young adulthood was whether the teen believed luck or effort determines success in life (Deke & Haimson, 2006). Weiner traces the specific effects of particular attributions to the different causal dimensions.

The *stability dimension* has its greatest impact on *expectancies*. If you think an outcome was the result of stable causes, you will expect a similar outcome next time. For example, if you attribute a success to high ability, you can reasonably expect to succeed again. But if you decide an outcome was the result of unstable causes, such as effort or luck, you have less to go on in forming an expectancy for the future, because an unstable cause might change next time.

Causal stability A belief that the cause of an outcome is relatively stable or variable.

Figure 9.5   Weiner's Attribution Theory of Achievement
In Weiner's view, both the locus and the stability of causal attributions have impact on later achievement behavior.

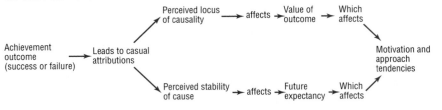

Connect the **Dots...**

One common piece of advice is, "If at first you don't succeed, try, try again." Another is, "Don't beat your head against a wall." What are the implications of these two sayings in terms of attributions and expectancies? Could you put them together to come up with sound advice about how to choose tasks and when to persist at them?

In contrast, the *locus of causality dimension* has an impact on the *emotional value* of the outcome and on *self-esteem* (Alderman, 2003). If you think a success is the result of internal causes, such as high ability or effort, you feel prouder of it than if you think it was produced by external causes. If you think you failed because of low ability or lack of effort, you feel worse than if you think it was because of a hard task or bad luck. Figure 9.5 summarizes the ways stability and locus of causality affect motivation.

Responsibility for Achievements. **Controllability,** the third dimension in Weiner's account, is the belief that the cause of an outcome is something that the person can deliberately affect. This is not shown in Figure 9.5. Consider the difference between ability and effort. Both are internal, and ability is stable while effort is unstable. In addition, we think of effort as something we can control and see ability as outside our control (Weiner, 1994). This distinction leads to the proposition that *controllability* has impact both on the *emotional value* of the outcome *and* on *expectancies.*

Take two teens who do equally well at some activity. The one who interprets the success as the result of hard work is likely to feel more pride than a classmate who has some talent but didn't put in much effort. The first teen *owns* the success and feels *responsible* for it in a way that the second can't.

As for a failure, if it is seen as the result of uncontrollable factors (such as a handicap or a lack of talent), the person will feel less responsible for it. No failure feels good, but one that you couldn't help is felt as less shameful. If the cause was controllable, however, such as deciding to goof off the night before a big exam, the responsibility, or blame, for the failure falls squarely on the person.

This implies that if you fail at something and see the cause as lack of effort, a controllable internal factor, you will feel particularly bad. Someone once said that the saddest sentence in the English language is, "It might have been." A close runner-up has to be, "I could have succeeded, if only I had tried a little harder." However, the picture is not entirely bleak. Because effort is seen as controllable, attributing a failure to lack of effort, no matter how bad it feels, may also raise both expectancies ("*If* I try harder, I *can* succeed.") and motivation ("I *intend* to try harder.").

Goal Orientations

▶ **Learning Objective 9.9**
How do mastery and performance goal orientations differ?

In Chapter 7, and earlier in this chapter as well, we looked at the different goal structures adolescents find in their families, classrooms, schools, communities, and cultures (Urdan & Schoenfelder, 2006). What gets more emphasis by parents, teachers, and other adults? Exceptional performance or individual improvement? Children and adolescents respond to these features of their social environment by developing their own personal goal orientations. These orientations profoundly affect the way children and adolescents approach achievement (Anderman, Austin, & Johnson, 2002; Dweck, 1999).

Researchers have described two contrasting goal orientations:

Mastery orientation. Achievement situations are treated as opportunities to increase competence, acquire new skills, and extend mastery. Those with a mastery orientation believe that abilities can be improved (the *incremental* theory) and tend to attribute their successes to both ability and effort and their failures to insufficient effort.

Controllability A belief that the cause of an outcome is something the person can deliberately affect.

Mastery orientation A tendency to see achievement situations as opportunities to become more competent and acquire new skills.

Performance orientation. Achievement situations are viewed as opportunities to show how smart you are and to outperform others. Ability is seen as a fixed trait (the *entity* theory) that is reflected in both success and failure. This makes it especially important to avoid failure because failing would imply a low ability that could not be changed by practice or greater effort. If failure does occur, it may lead to **learned helplessness,** a tendency to give up because of a belief that further efforts will not lead to success.

We can also make a distinction between *performance-approach* and *performance-avoid* orientations (Elliot & Church, 1997; Harackiewicz, Pintrich, Barron, Elliot, & Thrash, 2002; Midgley et al., 1998; Pintrich, 2000). Those with performance-approach goals engage in achievement tasks because they want to build up their self-esteem by outdoing others. An example would be the teen who refuses to share notes from the day you were out because you might then get a higher score on the next test (Midgley, Middleton, Gheen, & Kumar, 2002). For those with performance-avoid goals, on the other hand, the most important thing is not to fail because failing would make the person feel and look stupid.

Effects of Goal Orientation. How does having these different orientations affect adolescents? A *mastery* goal orientation has been linked to an array of positive outcomes, including higher levels of interest, more long-term learning, and the use of deep cognitive strategies (Anderman, Austin, & Johnson, 2003; Harackiewicz, Pintrich, Barron, Elliot, & Thrash, 2002; Pintrich, 2000). A *performance-approach* goal orientation, on the other hand, has been shown repeatedly to predict higher grades (Harackiewicz et al., 2002).

This contrast is illustrated by a study of college students in introductory psychology classes. Those who held *mastery* goals at the start of the semester had higher levels of *interest* in the material at the end of the semester, while those who held *performance* goals at the start of the semester earned higher *grades* for the term. Mastery goals did not predict grades, and performance goals did not predict interest. This pattern continued. In later semesters, the students with mastery goals took more psychology courses, but those with performance goals earned higher grades (Harackiewicz, Barron, Tauer, Carter, & Elliot, 2000).

What about teens with a *performance-avoid* goal orientation? As we said earlier, their overriding need is to keep from looking and feeling dumb. This can lead to an assortment of defensive, and generally harmful, strategies. Adolescents with this orientation are less likely to ask for help when they need it because asking for help strikes them as an admission of inferiority (Ryan, Pintrich, & Midgley, 2001). They are also more likely to engage in **self-handicapping.** This involves putting obstacles in the way of successful performance so that the cause of failure is deflected away from their ability (Martin, Marsh, & Debus, 2001; Middleton & Midgley, 1997). For example, an adolescent who goes out partying the night before a big exam has a good excuse for blowing the exam. This helps keep an ego-wounding attribution to low ability at bay.

Goals, Grades, and Intrinsic Motivation. Recently, a hot debate has broken out over the relationship of goal orientation to intrinsic motivation. We saw earlier that extrinsic rewards tend to undermine intrinsic motivation, at least under some conditions. What about grades and high-stakes tests? If someone who starts out with an intrinsic interest in a subject adopts a performance-approach goal—that is, works mainly for a high grade or test score—what does that do to intrinsic interest? Those on one side of the debate (for example, Midgley et al., 2002) say that students who focus on grades will be distracted from the inherent value of the activity. Those who disagree (for example, Harackiewicz et al., 2002) argue that mastery and performance goals add up. Having both, they say, benefits the person more than having either alone.

This is not a question of dry, abstract theory. The system of grading schoolwork, usually on a competitive basis, is practically universal in the Western and

Performance orientation A tendency to see achievement situations as opportunities to show superiority by outperforming others.

Learned helplessness A condition that may follow failure if the person comes to believe that the outcome is uncontrollable and that further efforts are pointless.

Self-handicapping Placing obstacles in the way of one's performance in order to avoid having to attribute a possible failure to low ability.

Westernized world, and high-stakes testing is becoming more and more common. If this approach undermines student interest and encourages superficial learning, cheating, reluctance to cooperate with schoolmates, and general grade-grubbing (Midgley et al., 2002), it is certainly worth spreading the word widely and working to change the system. If, on the other hand, feeling a desire and pressure to excel leads to superior performance, and grades are a major way students assess their progress (Covington & Müeller, 2001), then efforts to reform the grading system are misguided.

The ongoing debate over the effects of performance and mastery goals also reflects a division between researchers whose main interest is describing what *is*—whether trying to outdo others leads to higher grades—and those who are more concerned with what *ought* to be—whether educators should be trying to encourage more mastery-oriented values (Roeser, 2004). It may be, then, that both sides are correct in their own way. There is solid evidence linking performance-approach goals with higher grades *and* solid evidence linking mastery goals to greater interest and deeper learning (Anderman et al., 2003; Harackiewicz et al., 2002). If the objective is higher grades and test scores, encouraging performance-approach goals may be the way to go. If the purpose is to foster student interest, a more mastery-oriented structure may be indicated.

Some aspects of a mastery orientation may improve grades as well as interest. A recent study of 7th graders found that those who believed intelligence is malleable (an element in mastery orientation) improved over the junior high years, while those who believed intelligence is fixed did not (Blackwell, Trzesniewski, & Dweck, 2007). When another group of 7th graders was taught that intelligence is malleable, their motivation and grades went up, while those of a control group went down.

One question that has been somewhat overlooked in this discussion is what happens when those with performance-approach orientations *don't* outperform others. What if they fail? Because they tend to believe that intelligence or ability is a fixed trait (Dweck, 1999), and that trying harder signifies a lack of ability, they may well switch to performance-avoid goals or give up after even a relatively minor failure (Molden & Dweck, 2000). Consider the plight of adolescents who make grades their most important priority in high school, and then go off to a selective college. After the first few weeks, they realize that they are now competing for grades against an entire freshman class whose high school records are just as impressive as their own. A sudden passion for computer games or late-night movies might give them an excellent excuse to fall back on if they tumble from the top of the heap.

Flow

▶ **Learning Objective 9.10**
What is flow and when is it likely to occur?

So far in this section we have concentrated on how teens cope with such practical questions as success, failure, and the consequences of such outcomes, but achievement is much more than a result. Achievement is an active *process* that sometimes—not always—leads to a state of deep involvement and enjoyment. Athletes talk of getting "in the zone" where the game seems to play itself. Writers describe becoming so immersed in a story that the characters take over. Psychologist Mihaly Csikszentmihalyi (1990; Nakamura & Csikszentmihalyi, 2002) has spent many years studying this state, which he calls "flow."

What is **flow** like? It includes:

A feeling of being *carried along* by the activity.

A merging of *action* and *awareness*.

A reduced sense of *self-consciousness*.

A *narrowing of attention* to the activity itself.

A sense of *being in control* of one's actions and setting.

A feeling of profound *pleasure* and *fulfillment*.

—(CSIKSZENTMIHALYI, 1990)

Flow A state of deep involvement and enjoyment that may occur when a task calls for solid skills and presents high but realistic challenges.

Figure 9.6 Skill, Challenge, and Flow
Flow is most likely to occur when someone with developed skills takes on a reasonably challenging task.

Perceived Skills	Perceived Challenge	
	HIGH	LOW
HIGH	FLOW	BOREDOM
LOW	ANXIETY	APATHY

Source: Brophy, 1998.

▲ The state of flow provides the thrilling experience of being carried along by an activity.

One element of flow is solid *skill*. To feel in control and at the same time let yourself be carried along, you need to have the basics of the activity down cold. How can you achieve flow in a basketball game if you constantly need to think about how to dribble and pass? Imagine trying to write a creative story in a new language, if both your grammar and vocabulary are shaky! Another element is *challenge*. Flow becomes more likely when an activity seems challenging, but success seems possible.

Skill and challenge interact to generate different emotional states (Brophy, 1998). As Figure 9.6 illustrates, when both skill and challenge are high, a likely result is the experience of flow. A teen who is skilled but takes on an unchallenging task is more likely to be bored. As for those who think their skill level is low, they will probably experience either anxiety or apathy, depending on whether they see the task as challenging or unchallenging.

There is a subtle but important distinction between flow and the concept of intrinsic motivation we discussed earlier. Intrinsic motivation involves doing something because it is pleasurable, exciting, or enjoyable. Flow, on the other hand, refers not to the reason for doing it, but to the experience *while* doing it. Unless an activity is intrinsically interesting, it is unlikely to lead to flow. However, intrinsic motivation does not have to be the only, or even the most important, reason for the activity. Skilled professionals, from artists and athletes to surgeons and chefs, can experience flow, even when they have plenty of extrinsic reasons for doing what they do.

Connect the Dots...

Have you ever experienced a state of flow? If so, did it fit with Csikszentmihalyi's description? Why do you think it happened at that particular time, in that situation? What might you do to encourage it to happen again? And if you haven't yet experienced flow, in what area of your life do you think it is most likely to happen? Why?

The Capable Self

A former U.S. Secretary of Education once commented that there are three things to remember about education: motivation, motivation, and motivation (Maehr & Meyer, 1997, p. 372). Because motivation is so central, the ideas and research we have been examining are much more than interesting intellectual exercises. They have vitally important implications for the ways adolescents can best approach and cope with learning, achievement, and the development of their abilities, skills, and knowledge.

What if an adolescent combined the positive attitudes, habits, and personal characteristics achievement researchers have uncovered? What would that be like? One description has been called the **capable self** (McMahan, 1996). Its core is a generalized sense of *self-efficacy*, the belief that one has the abilities, skills, energy, and resources needed to have an impact on events of personal importance (Bandura, 1997).

Starting from this core belief in self-efficacy, the capable teen:

Approaches achievement tasks expecting to be able to affect the outcome.

Chooses reasonably challenging tasks that make effective use of effort and abilities, develop skills, and hold the possibility of achieving flow.

◄ **Learning Objective 9.11**
What are the psychological attitudes that make up the capable self?

Capable self An integrated description of the attitudes, habits, and characteristics that have been shown to positively affect achievement.

Tries to avoid wasting time on tasks that are either much too easy or much too difficult.

Thinks of tasks in terms of their intrinsic interest and rewards and their relevance to long-range goals.

Judges success and failure in terms of personal progress and mastery rather than external competition.

Sees successes as the result of both lasting and temporary internal factors (ability and effort) and failures as primarily due to insufficient effort, temporary external factors, or the choice of an inappropriately difficult task.

Enjoys the positive feelings that come with success and thinks of failure as a source of information and motivation for future successes.

Some would object that the world doesn't work that way (Urdan, 2004). From high-stakes testing to college admissions, the contexts of adolescent achievement seem structured to encourage competitive performance goals and threaten dire consequences for failure. The race is to the swift, and the devil take the hindmost.

As the accompanying Applications in the Spotlight on page 315 details, however, it is possible to restructure classrooms and schools to stress mastery goals. Capable teens will seek out settings that favor their approach to achievement. Even if they are temporarily stuck in an unfavorable situation, their positive attitudes will help them make the best of it until they are able to move on.

Summing Up...

Achievement actions, such as choosing an easy or difficult task, vary partly because adolescents differ in sensitivity to success and failure, expectancies of success, and the way they value outcomes. Extrinsic consequences of an activity, such as rewards, often undermine intrinsic interest. The ways teens explain or attribute their successes and failures affect feelings about these outcomes as well as future expectancies. Personal goal orientations toward performance or mastery also have an impact on levels of interest and accomplishment. When teens undertake challenging tasks for which they have practiced skills, they may experience flow, a state of deep interest and involvement. A particularly capable teen could combine positive elements from each of these approaches to achievement.

CAREER DEVELOPMENT

The changes of adolescence help push the question of, "What will I do for a living?" to a higher spot on the agenda. For those who drop out of high school or who move directly from high school into the working world, the question is immediate, and, as we saw in Chapter 7, the choices available to them are often limited. In 21st century America, however, dropouts are a minority. Most teens expect to go to college or pursue other advanced training after high school, and many will not start full-time employment until they are well into their 20s (Kerckhoff, 2002). For them, the question is more, "What do I *want* to do for a living?" and it may seem much less important than, "How do I get into the college of my choice?"

Even so, the choices teens make about school and work have a lasting impact on their achievements, satisfactions, and life courses. In this section, we first examine how adolescents make occupational decisions. We then look at helping adolescents orient toward careers that fit their interests, values, and talents. We see the importance of beliefs teens hold about themselves, their abilities, and their potentials. Finally, we look at the role parents and schools can play in helping teens develop a thoughtful approach to occupations and careers.

Encouraging Mastery Goals in the Classroom

Students who believe that mastery goals are stressed in their classroom adopt mastery goals themselves, have stronger self-efficacy beliefs, use more effective learning strategies, cope better with failure, and feel more positive about school (Kaplan & Maehr, 2002). To foster these advantages, researchers urge educators to move toward *mastery goal structures* in the classroom (Ames, 1992; Kaplan & Maehr, 2002; Patrick, 2004). That is, what takes place in the classroom should be deliberately structured in ways that encourage students to adopt mastery goal orientations. How can this be done?

According to the late Carol Midgley and her team of researchers at the University of Michigan (Midgley et al., 2002), some of the elements that contribute to building a more mastery-focused classroom are:

- cooperative learning;
- grouping students by topic and interest;
- grading students on progress and improvement;
- an emphasis on learning for its own sake;
- self-scheduling and self-regulation;
- viewing mistakes as a part of learning;
- allowing students to redo work;
- providing challenging classwork and homework; and
- peer and cross-age tutoring.

Another way to describe classroom practices that encourage a mastery goal orientation is the **TARGET** framework (Ames, 1992). This acronym stands for **T**asks, **A**uthority, **R**ecognition, **G**rouping, **E**valuation, and **T**ime.

- *Tasks* are meaningful, challenging, and varied enough to accommodate a range of skill levels.
- *Authority* and responsibility for rules and decisions are shared with students.
- *Recognition* is based on effort and improvement and is available to all students, not just top performers.
- *Grouping* is flexible and based on interest rather than ability.

- *Evaluation* is noncompetitive, criterion-based, and private rather than public.
- *Time* is used flexibly so that students can pace themselves.

These recommendations place most of the responsibility for classroom goal structures on the teacher's educational strategy, and certainly the attitudes and orientations of teachers have a powerful impact, even in the first weeks of class (Patrick, Anderman, Ryan, Edelin, & Midgley, 2001; Patrick, Turner, Meyer, & Midgley, 2003). However, for students, and particularly for adolescents, the classroom is at least as much a *social* setting as an achievement setting. Their social experiences in class directly affect their motivation and involvement in schoolwork (Patrick, 2004). Do they feel supported by teachers and classmates? Is there an atmosphere of mutual respect? Do they see the teachers as fair? Are they encouraged to interact and cooperate with one another? All these factors are linked to their interest in and liking for school. Along with the TARGET practices, teachers who intend to create a mastery-oriented classroom will want to encourage a positive social environment.

Are reforms of this sort possible? If so, would they accomplish the intended aims? Tim Urdan (2004) points out that while mastery goals have been linked to a long list of intellectual benefits, they do not necessarily produce better grades (Harackiewicz et al., 2000). At a time when politicians and school administrators place ever greater stress on raising test scores and holding schools and teachers "accountable" for results, should teachers risk an approach that may produce better learning but lower scores? And when the culture stresses competition and rewards performance, is it even fair to students to encourage them to adopt mastery goals? What if the result is that their more performance-goal-oriented schoolmates get higher grades, are admitted to more prestigious colleges, and are propelled into more successful careers? These are issues that affect, not just educators and researchers, but everyone who is concerned about the place and future of learning in our society.

Career Stages

For much of the 20th century, a towering figure in the field of career development was Donald Super. Super (1957, 1990) went well beyond asking how people choose their work to describe a cycle of life stages, charted in Figure 9.7 on page 316. Within this cycle, careers emerge from the ongoing interaction between a person's developing skills, interests, personal values, and sense of identity, on one hand, and the shifting requirements of the workplace, the economy, and the society on the other hand.

During the **growth stage** of childhood and early adolescence, the self-concept becomes increasingly complex and accurate at the same time as the child develops

◄ **Learning Objective 9.12**
What are the stages of career development during adolescence?

Figure 9.7   Life Stages and Career Development
Super sees the adolescent years as a time for growth and exploration of career interests.

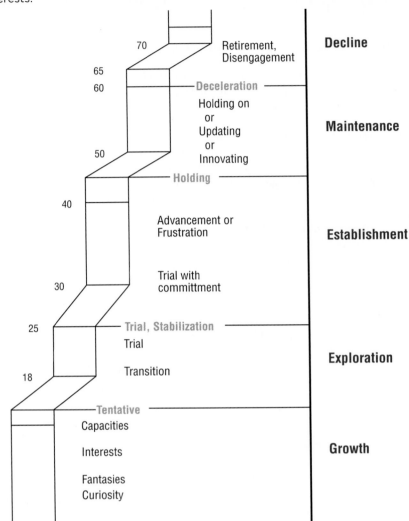

Source: Adapted from Super, 1990.

knowledge of and attitudes toward work in general and particular occupations. During the elementary years, the driving force is fantasy role-playing (cowboys, firefighters, ballerinas). As adolescence approaches, the focus shifts to occupations that relate to personal interests, likes, and dislikes. In the later years of this stage, around 13 or 14, young people begin to consider their own talents and abilities and relate these to the requirements of different jobs.

The **exploration stage** lasts from mid-adolescence to the mid-20s. It begins with a phase of *crystallization*. Teens begin to translate their knowledge and ideas about themselves into general occupational leanings. A girl who realizes that she really enjoys finding things out may begin to think about a career as a scientist (or as a detective!). The boy everybody asks for help when a computer acts up may wonder about a career in information sciences. The adolescent whom classmates turn to for advice and emotional support may consider going into a "people profession" such as counseling or psychology.

The next phase of the exploration stage, from about 18 to 21, involves *specification*. At this point, young people begin to move from general inclinations to more specific occupational aims. Declaring a college major, for instance, is a question of gathering

Growth stage For Super, the period during childhood and early adolescence that involves acquiring knowledge of work in general and particular occupations.

Exploration stage For Super, the period from mid-adolescence to young adulthood that involves translating knowledge and ideas about oneself into career leanings and occupational aims.

information, consulting preferences, balancing alternatives, and making a decision that may have a lasting impact.

Finally, in early adulthood comes an initial try at *implementation*. Having chosen what seems to be an appropriate occupation, the person tries out a job in that area. However, the sense of commitment to the occupation is still tentative. Positive experiences on the job will strengthen and confirm the person's commitment. If the work does not meet expectations, however, the person may change goals and repeat the cycle of crystallization, specification, and implementation with a new occupation.

As Figure 9.7 on page 316 indicates, Super's theory describes stages that continue past adolescence and young adulthood to cover the whole lifespan. Briefly, the years from 25 to 45 make up the *establishment stage*, the years in which the person settles in a chosen occupation. The years from 45 to 60 make up the *maintenance stage*, in which the person holds onto the chosen position and tries to stay up with new developments. The last of Super's five stages is the *decline stage*, which involves a disengagement from one's occupation, leading to retirement.

An important aspect of Super's approach is the concept of **career maturity.** This refers to a person's readiness to make informed, age-appropriate career decisions (Patton & Lokan, 2001). How career maturity expresses itself depends on the person's age, career development stage, and situation. For an early adolescent, talking to adults about what they do and perhaps visiting them at work would show a high degree of career maturity. A high school student with high career maturity might choose electives that relate to a field of interest and try to find part-time work or an internship that offers a chance for hands-on experience. Career maturity has been linked to academic motivation, feelings of self-efficacy, work commitment, career decidedness, and having a career role model (Creed & Patton, 2003; Flouri & Buchanan, 2002).

Super's approach continues to influence both researchers and career counselors (Patton & Lokan, 2001). It has also been the subject of criticism (Vondracek & Porfeli, 2002). Like Erikson's (1968) approach to identity development and Piaget's (1970) approach to cognitive development, Super describes a series of stages that everyone supposedly goes through at pretty much the same age. However, it becomes more and more clear that many people do not fit so neatly into this scheme.

Today, many adolescents in Western and Westernized societies extend their education into their mid-20s and put off making firm decisions about either an occupation or marriage until well past the age that Super would expect (Arnett, 2004; Mortimer, Zimmer-Gembeck, Holmes, & Shanahan, 2002). Structural changes in the American and world economy and the rapid pace of technological change have also had a major impact on career development. In the typical career Super describes, a young adult chooses an occupation, goes to work for a company or organization, and gradually moves through the ranks until retirement. That sort of career has become more and more the exception. Many of today's adolescents can expect to change, not just their employers, but their entire career orientation at least once and maybe more than once during their working lives (Murnane & Levy, 1997).

Vocational Inclinations

Super's theory of career development tries to describe the process by which an adolescent or young adult chooses one occupation or another. But *why* does someone (or why *should* someone) lean toward one occupation rather than another? This question is addressed by another classic approach to career development, the **vocational type theory** of John Holland (1973; 1987; 1996).

Holland's Vocational Types. In Holland's view, people enjoy work more and are more successful at it when they choose an occupation that is a good match for their personality. The first step in doing this is to find out an individual's personality type. For Holland, the six basic personality types can be represented by the points on a

◄ **Learning Objective 9.13**
How can teens find out what vocations they lean toward?

Career maturity A person's readiness to make informed, age-appropriate career decisions and depends on age, stage of career development, and situation.

Vocational type theory The idea that people enjoy a career more and are more successful in it if their occupation is a good match with their personality and interests.

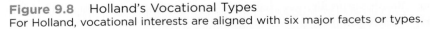

Figure 9.8 Holland's Vocational Types

For Holland, vocational interests are aligned with six major facets or types.

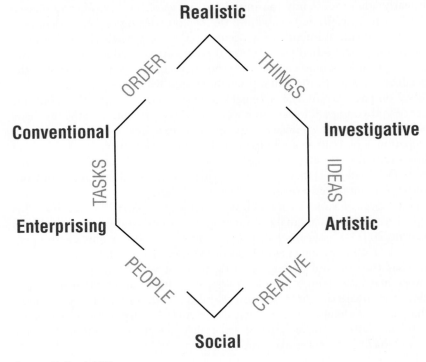

Source: Holland, 1973.

hexagon (see Figure 9.8). Those types that are closer to one another on the hexagon are more similar, and those that are farther away are less similar.

Holland's six vocational types are:

Realistic. These people like working with real things more than with ideas or people. They are good with their hands, but may have trouble expressing themselves in words or dealing with others. They like to see practical results from their work.

Investigative. These people enjoy solving abstract problems but are not particularly interested in working with others. They prefer ambiguous challenges to very structured work.

Artistic. These people look for opportunities for self-expression. They tend to be original, independent, and unconventional, and prefer to avoid highly structured or routine problems.

Social. These people get along well with others and are concerned about their welfare. They express themselves well, like attention, and prefer to solve problems through discussion and compromise.

Enterprising. These people are good with words and enjoy selling, convincing, and leading others. They have energy, self-confidence, and an attraction to power, status, and social control.

Conventional. These people prefer very ordered activities in which they know exactly what is expected of them. They fit well in clearly structured organizations, but do not try to take leadership roles.

Self-Directed Search. A measure of vocational type that yields a "Holland Code" representing the person's three most important types.

Assessing Vocational Types. To find out someone's type, vocational counselors in schools and colleges often use a measure called the **Self-Directed Search** (Holland, 1997). This measure presents a long series of questions about how people see themselves, what they like to do, what occupations they feel positively about, and what skills they have. It is even possible to take it online and receive a lengthy analysis of the

Table 9.1   Items Similar to Those in Holland's *Self-Directed Search* Questionnaire
These items are similar to those in Holland's *self-directed search* questionnaire.

Are You:	Can You:	Do You Like to:
____Practical	____Read a blueprint	____Work outdoors
____Straightforward	____Pitch a tent	____Use your hands
	R	
____Athletic	____Fix electrical things	____Build things
____Inquisitive	____Solve math problems	____Explore ideas
____Observant	____Think abstractly	____Work independently
	I	
____Precise	____Understand physics	____Read scientific articles
____Creative	____Sketch, draw, paint	____Go to concerts and plays
____Intuitive	____Play a musical instrument	____Take photographs
	A	
____An individualist	____Design posters, leaflets	____Work on crafts
____Helpful	____Teach or train others	____Take part in meetings
____Outgoing	____Mediate disputes	____Help people with problems
	S	
____Insightful	____Lead a group discussion	____Do volunteer work
____Self-confident	____Initiate projects	____Meet important people
____Assertive	____Give talks or speeches	____Win a leadership award
	E	
____Persuasive	____Sell things or promote ideas	____Be elected to office
____Accurate	____Do a lot of paperwork quickly	____Follow clear procedures
____Methodical	____Work well within a system	____Work with numbers
	C	
____Well groomed	____Keep accurate records	____Be responsible for details

SCORING: Count the number of items checked in each of the six categories. Your Holland Code consists of the letters for the top-scoring category, followed by the next-highest and third-highest.

Source: Based on Holland, 1973. The full *Self-Directed Search* may be taken online, for a fee, at www.self-directed-search.com/aboutsds.html.

results practically at once. Some items similar to those on the Self-Directed Search are shown in Table 9.1.

After the measure is scored for each of the six types, the top three categories or themes are identified. Hardly anyone is a pure type. Instead, while one category may stand out, others will also be fairly strong. The three highest scores are used to generate a "Holland Code." For example, a student whose highest score is in the Enterprising category, followed by Social, and then Conventional, would be assigned a Holland Code of ESC.

Recently, investigators looked at the interest scores of over 6,600 adolescents representing each of the major U.S. ethnic groups. The pattern of interests was stable from 8th grade to 12th grade, but there were ethnic group differences in the level of interests. Minority teens showed greater interest in Social, Enterprising, and Conventional activities, all of which are more oriented to people than to things (Tracey & Robbins, 2005).

Over the years, Holland and his co-workers have compiled 3-letter codes for thousands of different occupations. The most recent listing is over 750 pages long (Gottfredson & Holland, 1996). These codes are based on the way those who hold a particular job respond to the Holland questionnaire. If firefighters, for instance, tended to get high scores on the Realistic, Social, and Conventional scales, that occupation would be included (along with many others) in the RSC listing.

▲ As adolescents explore their interests and talents, it helps to connect with adults who have similar interests and talents.

Once a person has taken the Self-Directed Search and been given a Holland Code, the next step is to consult the list of occupations that have that specific code. We just mentioned a student with a Holland Code of ESC. Dozens of job titles are said to fit this code, including director of student affairs, college registrar, sightseeing guide, and school-crossing guard. Holland does *not* say that the student would necessarily be successful in these occupations. The Self-Directed Search is not an aptitude test. However, because the student's interests are similar to the interests of those who already hold such jobs, he or she could be expected to find the work environment interesting and satisfying.

It makes good sense to say, as Holland does, that people should think hard about their talents and interests when they choose an occupation. Someone who enjoys being outside working with machinery and animals is not likely to be very happy or successful as office manager for a big law firm. However, practically any occupation is likely to attract, for different reasons, people with a range of characters and interests. Some physicians are passionate about medical research, some are deeply involved in their patients, some are wrapped up in their own highly developed skills, and some went into medicine mainly to please their parents. Each, in his or her own way, may have a successful and socially useful career.

We should also recognize that what draws a person to an occupation is not necessarily what they find once they are in it. What people do in their job changes them, just as they may change the way the job is done. Some grow into a profession that they were not well-suited to at first. Others eventually find that what once attracted them to a job no longer satisfies them. Paying attention to one's interests, strengths, weaknesses, and personal likes and dislikes at a particular moment in life can certainly help in choosing a career. However, the hunt for a perfect match between personality type and occupation leaves out the possibility that both the person and the job will change.

Self-Efficacy and Vocations

▶ **Learning Objective 9.14**
Why are career-related self-efficacy beliefs important?

One criticism that has been made of Holland's approach to career choice is that it stresses the role of people's interests, but does not take into account their expectations and beliefs about themselves. For example, a vocational test may tell me that my interests are very much like those of judges, or professional athletes, or best-selling novelists. I may very well be attracted to one or more of those occupations, but if I don't believe I have what it takes to *become* a judge, or a pro athlete, or a famous novelist, I am not likely to strive for it. And if I don't strive for it, it is a sure thing that I won't achieve it!

This line of argument has led a growing number of researchers to look at vocational choice from the viewpoint of social cognitive theory (Bandura, Barbarabelli, Caprara, & Pastorelli, 2001; Lent & Brown, 2002; Pinquart, Juang, & Silbereisen, 2003; Turner & Lapan, 2002). As we saw earlier, an important element in this theory is the concept of *self-efficacy*. To what extent do people believe they have the abilities they need to initiate, organize, and successfully carry out whatever has to be done to achieve a particular goal (Bandura, 1997)? How do an adolescent's self-efficacy beliefs shape vocational aspirations and achievements? Where do those beliefs come from?

There are several ways self-efficacy beliefs have an impact on occupational development:

> The higher people's perceived efficacy to fulfill educational requirements and occupational roles, the wider the career options they seriously consider pursuing, the greater the interest they have in them, the better they prepare themselves educationally for different occupational careers, and the greater their staying power in challenging career pursuits. People simply eliminate from consideration occupations they believe to be beyond their capabilities, however attractive the occupations may be
>
> Bandura et al., 2001, p. 188.

Research confirms that those who believe more strongly in their own efficacy have higher aspirations, choose more challenging careers, and are more successful in meeting the educational requirements of their chosen field (O'Brien, Friedman, Tipton, &

Linn, 2000). This holds even when differences in ability and earlier academic achievement are taken into account (Lent et al., 2001).

Career-related self-efficacy beliefs are important even in early adolescence, when students are just beginning to think seriously about possible occupations. Those who are more confident that they can search out information about careers and plan their own educational and vocational futures will consider a wider range of occupations, as will those who are more confident that they have the qualities they need to succeed in various occupations (Lapan, Kardash, & Turner, 2002). This may encourage them to aim for careers that otherwise might have seemed out of reach (Turner & Lapan, 2002).

In a study carried out in Germany, adolescents between ages 12 and 15 were asked about their self-efficacy beliefs (Pinquart, Juang, & Silbereisen, 2003). They were later contacted at 18, the age at which most German youth apply for career apprenticeships, and again at 21. Those with high self-efficacy beliefs as young adolescents were less likely to become unemployed and more likely to be satisfied with their jobs as young adults. One reason high self-efficacy helped was that it reduced the level of stress during the process of applying for apprenticeships. Another was that those with high self-efficacy were more likely to seek out jobs that were a good fit with their interests and aptitudes. Those with low self-efficacy beliefs, in contrast, approached the application process with dread and tended to settle for whatever work they could get.

A positive career orientation has broader benefits as well. A recent longitudinal study of 7th- to 12th-grade students in the Northeastern United States found that those who valued work as a means of self-actualization and saw school as a way to prepare for a satisfying future career had fewer problem behaviors a year later (Skorikov & Vondracek, 2007).

Parents and Career Choice

Self-efficacy beliefs, personal interests, and career maturity are all clearly important, but we still face questions about *why* adolescents orient toward one occupation over another. You may be sure you have what it takes to do well in some occupation. You may have reason to think it is an occupation that attracts people who have similar interests to yours. Even so, you may end up pursuing something quite different. How does that happen? What factors encourage adolescents to move toward a particular vocation instead of another?

Both theory and research, as well as common sense, point to parents as a major influence on occupational choice (Bryant, Zvonkovic, & Reynolds, 2006; Eccles, Barber, & Jozefowicz, 1998; Jodl, Michael, Malanchuk, Eccles, & Sameroff, 2001). There are a number of interconnected reasons why this should be so. First, parents are a child's earliest and closest models of people who go out into the working world. The kind of work they do, their involvement or lack of involvement in it, the way they talk about their work experiences when they are home, all these help shape the child's view of and orientation toward work. Even the way other children react to the statement, "My mom or dad is a _____," may have a lasting effect.

When parents and teens have a warm, close relationship and the parents make their work sound interesting and involving, adolescents tend to be attracted to similar fields. This can be seen as a facet of the adolescent's identification with the parent, or more simply as a case of reasoning, "If my parent likes this work, and I'm similar to my parent, I'll probably like it too." If the parent seems to *dislike* his or her job, however, or find it unrewarding, a parallel line of reasoning can lead even an adolescent who feels close to the parent to choose a widely different vocation.

Second, parents influence the occupational goals of their child by the ways they interpret, explain, and respond to the child's abilities, inclinations, and experiences (Eccles, 1993). Statements such as, "I can see you really like [drawing, soccer, math, etc.]" place a particular event in a more general framework. Over time, this helps mold the child's self-concept and feelings of efficacy, which, in turn, affect occupational aspirations (Jodl et al., 2001). For example, if a teenage girl's parents respond more positively to a good grade in English or history than to one in algebra, they communicate the message that non-technical pursuits are more appropriate for her (Barber & Eccles,

Connect the Dots...

What do you think should be the most important considerations in choosing a career direction? Interests? Talents and skills? Job opportunities and future prospects? Financial possibilities? Family wishes and traditions? What advice about career choice would you give to a younger brother, sister, or friend? Is there any advice you wish someone had given you during your teen years?

◄ **Learning Objective 9.15**
In what ways do parents help shape teens' career choices?

▲ Parents help children explore possible vocational paths by providing experiences and resources that are linked to their interests.

1992). One recent study found that parents believed that science is less interesting and more difficult for girls than for boys, and that these beliefs predicted their children's interest and self-efficacy beliefs in science (Tenenbaum & Leaper, 2003).

Third, parents help shape their child's vocational interests by actively offering career-related experiences and resources (Young, 1994). This might involve visits to the office or workplace and leisure time activities as well. If a teen expresses curiosity about marine biology, the parents might make time for a weekend visit to the aquarium or pass up a favorite television show to watch a *Nature* special on dolphins together. Parents who regularly read to their young children, for example, and make a point of getting them a library card when they are older, encourage an interest and involvement in intellectual pursuits, whereas those who volunteer to coach their child's soccer team encourage more athletic interests (Jodl et al., 2001).

Fourth, parents provide emotional support and encouragement for their adolescent's vocational explorations (Caspi, Wright, Moffitt, & Silva, 1998; Kracke, 2002). Parental support has an impact on several critical aspects of vocational development, including interest level, self-efficacy, career expectancies, and the values attached to different occupations (Ferry, Fouad, & Smith, 2000; Lapan, Hinkelman, Adams, & Turner, 1999; McWhirter, Hackett, & Bandalos, 1998). A study of a multi-ethnic group of middle-school adolescents found that their perceptions of parental support predicted feelings of self-efficacy across all six Holland career categories (Turner & Lapan, 2002).

Fifth, parents can be a valuable source of vocational information and contacts. For example, middle-class parents are likely to have friends and acquaintances who know about educational programs, internships, and other career-related opportunities. A parent in a skilled trade may know ways to get an apprenticeship and earn a union card. Teens with musical or literary ambitions have a much better chance of being "discovered" if their parents know people in the arts and can approach an agent, editor, or producer on their behalf.

Finally, parents affect the vocational interests of their adolescents by the priorities and social values they communicate. How important is it to gain power and status? To contribute to progress? To help others? To make a lot of money? To express yourself creatively? To have job security? To be your own boss? To exercise the full scope of your talents and abilities? To have enough time for yourself and your family? The answers adolescents give to questions of this sort will lead them to put some occupations high on their list and cross others off completely. A teen who sees independence as an important value will not be drawn to a factory job or a place in a corporate hierarchy, while one who values clear instructions and a secure position will not want to go into the arts or start a small business.

School Career Counseling

▶ **Learning Objective 9.16**
What is the role of school counselors?

Ideally, the role of parents and the role of school counselors should go hand in hand in helping young adolescents in their career development (Turner & Lapan, 2002). School guidance programs are intended to help students make informed and mature decisions about their educational and vocational choices by offering information, resources, and materials that the students (or their parents) would have trouble finding on their own. Adolescents who are helped in this way to develop the skills and self-confidence to carry out career-related tasks, such as finding out job requirements and making long-range plans, are likely to widen the range of occupations they think of as possible (Lapan, Kardash, & Turner, 2002).

Unfortunately, this is an ideal that few schools achieve (Mortimer et al., 2002). Most of the time, school guidance counselors are overworked, burdened with non-counseling chores, and taken up with advising students about which high school courses to take and the nuts and bolts of applying to college. If asked, they might find time to administer the Holland Self-Directed Search, score it, and print out a list of job titles that match the student's category. That is certainly something, but it falls far short of meeting the needs of most adolescents, as the comments in this chapter's second Applications in the Spotlight on page 323 indicate.

A **Applications in the Spotlight**

How Students Experience Vocational Counseling

Reports on school counseling often focus on statistics: how many students used the counseling office, how many tests and assessments were administered, what proportion of graduating seniors went on to college, and so on. But what is the counseling process like for students? As part of a longitudinal study that began in 9th grade, sociologist Jeylan T. Mortimer and her colleagues interviewed a group of participants in their mid-20s about how they had made decisions about vocation and work. One of the topics discussed was the influence of high school guidance counseling.

On the whole, the comments were less than enthusiastic:

Case 1173, Female:

I had a guidance counselor in high school, but, yeah, I wouldn't call that a relationship at all. I basically, they would say, you're doing a great job and we're very proud of you and this is, I think, you should go here or, you know, I don't know. I don't remember if they really guided me in any direction . . .

Case 208, Male:

The counseling program wasn't all that great at (my high school) ... Like I think I had three different advisors over four years and they didn't seem in tune other than making sure that my class slate was filled and everything . . .

Case 934, Female:

I graduated with a class of 360 and unless you took yourself to the guidance office they weren't coming to search you out.

Case 1150, Female:

I don't remember being told that [going to a counselor] was an option for me. You know, like, come in speak to a counselor, and I always thought that bad kids needed to talk to counselors, and at home I never had problems, so I never had to go into the office of the principal or talk to a counselor.

Case 834, Female:

I remember taking tests telling me, like the tests to see what you might want to do, but I remember while taking those tests, answering according to not what I really was interested in, but what I think would be cool to be interested in . . . I was kind of manipulating the results in some kind of form because it's like you want it to look good . . .

Source: Mortimer et al., 2002.

Thanks to the Internet, important resources, such as the Occupational Outlook Handbook (Bureau of Labor Statistics, 2006b), are now available to anyone who has Internet access. For teens, the federal government offers a fun and informative website called "What Do You Like?" (Bureau of Labor Statistics, 2006a). For these resources to be helpful, however, a student has to know they are there and how to find them, and those who need them most are probably the least likely to have this information.

It is not that hard to come up with a list of recommendations for programs to offer adolescents more effective vocational counseling. In fact, such lists have existed for years (for example, College Board, 1986; William T. Grant Foundation, 1988), but it is unclear if schools and communities in the United States can find the will and the resources to carry out such programs. At a minimum, those who plan to teach or work with adolescents ought to have a basic knowledge of the processes and procedures of career development and should understand why it is so important to pass that knowledge along to the teens they work with.

Summing Up...

Choosing a future career becomes increasingly important across adolescence. According to Super, adolescents move through the growth and exploration stages of career development and benefit from increased career maturity. In Holland's view, a teen's personality, skills, and interests describe a vocational type that suggests the occupations he or she would find satisfying. Another factor is self-efficacy, the belief that one has the necessary talent, skills, and determination to succeed in a particular career. Both interests and self-efficacy beliefs are affected by the attitudes, actions, and encouragement of parents. School guidance programs could be a valuable resource for teens who are exploring career possibilities, but too often these programs are overburdened and understaffed.

SUMMARY

The issue of **achievement** is high on the agenda during adolescence. Teens are expected to learn advanced skills and to make crucial choices about their educational path. In addition, their more advanced cognitive abilities let them consider possible selves, imagine hypothetical future careers, and plan necessary steps toward long-range career goals.

The ways adolescents approach achievement issues are influenced by parents, peers, teachers and schools, and the broader culture, as well as their personal history and experiences.

Learning Objective 9.1 How do parents help children become motivated achievers?

Through **independence** and **achievement training**, parents encourage children to do things on their own and to want to do them well. Parents of highly motivated adolescents adopt a warm, encouraging, and authoritative style. They are more involved in their teens' education, monitoring their progress and helping with schoolwork.

Learning Objective 9.2 What impact do peers have on school-related attitudes?

Peers influence achievement, for better or worse, both because teens tend to select similar friends and because friends encourage similar attitudes and habits in one another.

Learning Objective 9.3 How are students affected by a competitive school atmosphere?

Schools that stress ability, grades, and competition encourage *performance goals* that are linked to higher grades but lower interest. Schools that reward effort and individual improvement and play down competition for grades encourage *mastery goals* that are linked to greater interest.

Learning Objective 9.4 In what ways do cultural beliefs influence individual achievement?

Different cultures put more or less stress on achievement and interpret the causes of success and failure differently, leading to different attitudes and behaviors among adolescents. However, the links between motives and satisfaction are similar across cultures.

Learning Objective 9.5 Why is there an achievement gap between different social classes and ethnic groups?

Within the United States, White and Asian American students get higher grades than Black and Hispanic students, and middle-class students get higher grades than low-income students. These gaps are explained in various ways.

White middle-class children enjoy many advantages, including more **cultural capital** gained from art and music lessons, library and museum visits, and opportunities to travel. Poor and minority children suffer from many disadvantages, including poorer nutrition and health care, family economic stresses, rundown neighborhoods, inadequate schools, and discrimination.

Teens who know that their economic or ethnic group is held in low regard may suffer from **stereotype threat**, in which their anxiety about failing interferes with performance. Expectations that prejudice will block success may create an **oppositional peer culture** that rejects the goals of the majority culture and sees trying to succeed as "giving in" and "acting White."

Minority teens who identify strongly with their ethnic group and who feel that doing well is part of being a good group member have improved achievement. Asian American students tend to do better than those from other ethnic minorities. This has been explained as a result of cultural beliefs favoring high effort, a high value placed on achievement, and a need to do well as a duty to one's family.

Individual adolescents differ in their feelings, attitudes, and beliefs about success and failure and in the ways they experience situations that involve achievement.

Learning Objective 9.6 What personal and external factors help predict achievement behavior?

Teens with a high **motive to succeed (M_s)** want to get the positive feelings that come with success, while those with a high **motive to avoid failure (M_{af})** are concerned with avoiding the negative feelings that come with failure. Those whose motive to succeed is stronger ($M_s > M_{af}$) tend to choose tasks they find fairly challenging, while those whose motive to avoid failure is stronger ($M_{af} > M_s$) tend to prefer either very easy or very hard tasks. Deciding on what task to try is also affected by the person's **expectancy** of success and the subjective *value* of the outcome.

Learning Objective 9.7 How are intrinsic and extrinsic motivation related?

An activity may involve **intrinsic motivation** (the interest or pleasure of the activity itself), **extrinsic motivation** (some outcome or incentive that is not built into the activity), or both. In many situations, extrinsic rewards tend to lead teens to devalue their intrinsic motivation for the activity.

Learning Objective 9.8 How do adolescents explain their successes and failures?

After doing something, adolescents **attribute** their success or failure to causes such as ability, effort, the difficulty of the task, and luck. The particular causes a teen sees as responsible for an outcome have impact both on expectancies for future efforts and on the emotional value of the outcome.

Learning Objective 9.9 How do mastery and performance goal orientations differ?

Adolescents differ in their personal goal orientation. Those with a **mastery orientation** treat achievement situations as chances to improve their skills and acquire new ones. Those with a **performance orientation** see achievement situations as chances to prove their ability by outperforming others. Teens with a mastery orientation tend to develop greater interest in their subject and more long-term learning. Those with a performance orientation tend to earn higher grades. Some teens with a performance-avoid orientation are concerned mostly with avoiding looking stupid and may engage in **self-handicapping** that deflects the cause of failure away from their ability.

Learning Objective 9.10   What is flow and when is it likely to occur?

When teens are doing an activity for which they have solid skills and which is moderately challenging, they may experience **flow,** a state of deep involvement and enjoyment.

Learning Objective 9.11   What are the psychological attitudes that make up the capable self?

Adolescents who have developed the set of characteristics called the **capable self** believe they have the abilities and resources to accomplish something, choose reasonably challenging tasks, see success or failure in terms of personal mastery, and relish the positive feelings that come with success, while looking on failure as a learning experience.

With adolescence, the question of career intentions and aspirations takes on growing importance.

Learning Objective 9.12   What are the stages of career development during adolescence?

According to Super, adolescents move from the **growth stage** of career development, in which they explore personal interests and talents, to the **exploration stage,** in which they translate their self-knowledge into general occupational leanings.

Teens with a higher level of **career maturity** are more likely to make informed, age-appropriate career decisions.

Learning Objective 9.13   How can teens find out what vocations they lean toward?

The **vocational type** approach of John Holland focuses on how an individual's interests and skills fit with the personalities of those in different vocations.

Learning Objective 9.14   Why are career-related self-efficacy beliefs important?

Self-efficacy, the belief that one has the qualities needed to succeed in a career, is linked to consideration of a wider range of occupations and higher aspirations.

Learning Objective 9.15   In what ways do parents help shape teens' career choices?

Parents are a major influence on occupational choice. They offer examples of ways to approach a career, opportunities to explore different activities, emotional support and encouragement, valuable information and contacts, and a sense of social values and priorities.

Learning Objective 9.16   What is the role of school counselors?

School guidance programs are potentially a valuable source of career counseling, but often are overburdened and ineffective.

KEY TERMS

Achievement (292)	Oppositional peer culture (302)	Extrinsic motivation (306)	Self-handicapping (311)
Competence motivation (292)		Attribution theory (308)	Flow (312)
Independence training (293)	Motive (304)	Locus of causality (308)	Capable Self (313)
Achievement training (293)	Motive to succeed (M_s) (305)	Causal stability (309)	Growth stage (316)
Selection (295)	Motive to avoid failure (M_{af}) (305)	Controllability (310)	Exploration stage (316)
Socialization (295)		Mastery orientation (310)	Career maturity (317)
Cultural capital (300)	Expectancy (305)	Performance orientation (311)	Vocational type theory (317)
Stereotype threat (302)	Intrinsic motivation (306)	Learned helplessness (311)	Self-Directed Search (318)

Gender

Outline	Learning Objectives

The animals went in two by two
The elephant and the kangaroo
And they all went into the ark
For to get out of the rain

—**American Nursery Rhyme**

No one hearing the biblical account of the Flood, or the nursery rhyme based on it, has to be told why Noah's ark carried two of each species, and not one, or three, or seventeen. We all immediately understand that one of the two was male and the other was female. These categories are so basic to our thinking about the world that in cartoons even fish, machines, pieces of furniture, and kitchen equipment are given gender-typed characteristics. A talking saucepan with a moustache is a man, but if it has long eyelashes, it's a woman!

Unlike saucepans, humans are *born* female or male. But how is this biological fact linked with the broad range of similarities and differences we see between girls and boys or women and men? Social scientists have put forward a variety of explanations. They point to factors that include our evolutionary history; the examples offered by other people; the social rewards and punishments for fitting or not fitting into expected roles; cultural messages transmitted by parents, peers, and the media; and the changing ways children and adolescents think about and understand sex and gender. In the first section of this chapter, we examine some influential sets of ideas about gender and see where they agree, where they differ, and where they overlap.

Next, we look at some of the major gender similarities and differences among adolescents. Why do so many teenage girls come to dislike and fear math? Why do self-concept and self-esteem become bigger problems in adolescence and how does this contribute to gender differences in emotion and mood? How do adolescent males and females differ in the ways they interact with friends and peers? What impact do cultural and ethnic factors have on gender roles?

Finally, we examine the social contexts in which gender-related ideas, attitudes, and behaviors develop. What are the relative influences of parents, siblings, and peers? How do the media affect teens' concepts and expectations about gender? Where are gender roles going? Have adolescents in Western societies started to move beyond traditional ideas of what is masculine or feminine? If so, what implications do these changes have for them now and in the future?

UNDERSTANDING GENDER DEVELOPMENT

Social scientists today tend to use the word *sex* to indicate the fact of being biologically male or female and the word *gender* to refer to characteristics that may be the result of developmental and social experience (Galambos, 2004; Lippa, 2002). In line with this, calling something a **sex difference** usually implies that it is rooted in biology, while calling it a **gender difference** suggests that cultural and social factors are involved. For instance, the fact that more men than women are bald is a *sex difference*, the result of the action of a sex-linked recessive gene. The fact that in our society (like many others) girls and women generally wear their hair longer than boys and men is a *gender difference*, based on cultural expectations and ideas about what is proper and attractive in men and women. Men could let their hair grow down to their waists, and women could adopt crewcuts, but by and large they don't, for social and cultural reasons.

Every culture has a great many ideas about how males or females are supposed to look, act, think, and feel. The whole set of these shared cultural expectations about gender is called a **gender role.** Gender roles differ, sometimes very greatly, from one society to another. Consider, for example, that in some cultures women routinely work as long-distance truck drivers, while in other cultures they are forbidden to drive at

Sex difference A difference between males and females that is thought to be based mainly on biological factors.

Gender difference A difference between males and females that is thought to be based mainly on cultural and social factors.

Gender role A set of shared cultural expectations that outlines the attitudes and behaviors a typical male or female should display.

◀ Gender roles change as societies change.

all. Gender roles also change from one era to another. The American mainstream culture, for instance, has gradually become more accepting of a woman who goes to West Point and becomes a career army officer or a man who leaves a high-pressure job to stay home and look after his young children.

How does someone come to have the characteristics of his or her gender role? This process is called **gender typing,** and it has been the subject of much discussion among scholars who give different accounts of how it works. Some believe that *biology* plays the biggest role. Others maintain that *socialization*, the sum of the experiences children and adolescents have, is most important. Still others hold that *cognition* is a central factor in gender typing. We will now look at these contrasting approaches and some of the research results that underlie them.

Biological Approaches

From the moment of conception, males and females are genetically different. These genetic differences, in turn, affect the production of hormones such as *testosterone* that play a role in organizing the structure and functioning of the body, the nervous system, and the brain (Susman, 2004). One of the most obvious ways this shows itself is in what a baby's external genitals look like at birth. High levels of prenatal testosterone during the early weeks of gestation lead to male-seeming genitals and low levels lead to female-seeming genitals. Because the link between genes and genitals is by way of prenatal testosterone, it can happen, though very rarely, that the genitals do not match the baby's genetic makeup (Herdt, 1990).

Genes and hormones affect gender-linked characteristics in less obvious ways as well. Researchers are just beginning to understand ways in which prenatal hormone levels may affect the development of brain structures such as the amygdala, which plays a major role in an individual's reactions to threats, and the prefrontal cortex, which is linked to planning, judgment, and self-control (Hines, 2002, 2004). Brain-imaging studies show differences in these structures between males and females (Breedlove, 1994), but it is unclear to what extent these are the result of prenatal hormones, experiences in infancy and childhood, or some combination of these and other factors.

Sex Hormones. As one would expect, on average, prenatal testosterone levels are much higher for male than for female fetuses. However, *within* each sex the levels can vary a good deal from one fetus to another. These levels can be measured during

◀ **Learning Objective 10.1**
How do genes and hormones affect gender development?

Gender typing The process by which children come to take on the gender roles expected in their society.

pregnancy, both in the mother's blood and in the amniotic fluid, as part of regular pre-natal medical care. In one recent study, girls who were exposed to higher levels of prenatal testosterone showed greater involvement at age 3-1/2 with masculine toys, games, and activities—those that are more typical of boys (Hines, Golombok, Rust, Johnston, & Golding, 2002). Other studies have also linked prenatal exposure to testosterone to more masculine activities and interests in girls (Berenbaum, 1999, 2002; Cohen-Bendahan, Buitelaarc, van Goozend, Orlebekee, & Cohen-Kettenis; 2005), as well as to poorer social relationships in both girls and boys (Knickmeyer, Baron-Cohen, Raggatt, & Taylor, 2005).

One source of evidence about the effects of prenatal hormones is studies of children with *congenital adrenal hyperplasia* (CAH). This is a genetic disorder that causes the adrenal gland to overproduce androgens, or male sex hormones, beginning well before birth. Boys with CAH seem relatively unaffected, probably because their testes produce less androgen as compensation for the overproduction from the adrenal gland (Wudy, Dorr, Solleder, Djalali, & Homoki, 1999). In girls, however, CAH caus-es the genitals to develop in a masculine direction. Most often, both the appearance of the genitals and the hormone imbalance itself are corrected soon after birth, but other effects apparently remain.

Research shows that, compared to other girls, those with CAH tend to like boys' toys more and girls' toys less, to show a greater preference for boys' activities, and to play more with boys (Hines, 2002, 2004). They also perform better than other girls on some spatial tasks that usually favor boys, such as throwing a ball or dart at a target, though not on others, such as mental rotations (Hines et al., 2003). As adults, these girls report more dissatisfaction with being women and less sexual interest in men than do those not affected by CAH (Hines, Brook, & Conway, 2004). Could it be that parents and other family members had some lingering reaction to knowing about these girls' condition and somehow pushed them toward more masculine activities? It is certainly possible, but parents of girls with CAH seem quite positive that they did no such thing (Ehrhardt & Baker, 1977). It is at least as plausible to suggest that the pre-natal exposure to high levels of androgen "masculinized" influential parts of the brain (Hines, 2004).

Genetic Factors. Another approach to understanding the biological aspects of gender involves estimating the relative influence of genetics and environment on different traits and behaviors. As we saw earlier, in Chapter 4, one way to do this is by comparing identical and fraternal twins. This technique has been used to look at young children whose gender behavior is *atypical*; that is, boys who are regarded as very feminine and girls who are regarded as very masculine. One such study found that genetic factors accounted for a large part of the variability in the children's gender behavior (Coolidge, Thede, & Young, 2002). However, other studies that looked at atypical gender behavior in twins found that both genetic and environmental factors made significant contributions and that environmental factors were more important than genetic background (Iervolino, Hines, Golombok, Rust, & Plomin, 2005; Knafo, Iervolino, & Plomin, 2005).

Biological influences on gender do not mysteriously stop working at the moment of birth, of course. The hormonal changes of puberty, and the many physical and psy-chological changes that follow, have an enormous impact on gender roles and gender differences. These changes have already been described in some detail in Chapter 3, so one example may be enough to make the point. The release of adrenocortical hor-mones early in adolescence has been linked to the emergence of a child's first roman-tic interest in another person (McClintock & Herdt, 1996). Because gender-typical characteristics are considered particularly attractive—in fact, they are practically a working definition of what's considered attractive—the result of this new interest is often an intensification of gender-typed behavior (Hill & Lynch, 1983). Girls start to worry about their looks and figures, and boys begin studying their biceps and search-ing for traces of fuzz on their upper lips.

Socialization Approaches

Socialization refers to all the various ways other people and society as a whole have an impact on development. Those who consider socialization the crucial factor in gender development point out that children and adolescents, from their very earliest days, are affected by a broad network of gendered social influences (Bandura & Bussey, 2004; Bussey & Bandura, 1999). Some gender differences are rooted in biology, of course, but most of the attitudes, roles, and constraints that define gender are passed along by social institutions and practices.

Agents of Socialization. Parents, teachers, siblings, and peers serve as models of gender-linked attitudes and behaviors (Fagot, Rodgers, & Leinbach, 2000). They also provide both direct and indirect praise and criticism for behavior that is considered gender-appropriate or gender-inappropriate (Leve & Fagot, 1997; Martin & Fabes, 2001). Sources of social information, such as books, television shows, music videos, and other media, are saturated with vivid examples of gender standards and values (Aubrey, 2004; Clark, Almeida, Gurka, & Middleton, 2003; Signorielli & Kahlenberg, 2001).

The socialization of gender roles begins even before birth, when expectant parents decorate the baby's room. As a visit to a baby store shows, everything from crib sheets to diapers comes coded by gender. Flowers, kittens, and anything pink is for girls, while boys get toy trains in blue. The ways parents handle babies, the amount of time they spend talking to them, the activities they encourage, all are affected by whether the baby is a girl or a boy (Lippa, 2002; McHale, Crouter, & Whiteman, 2003). When talking to their children, parents tend to make more supportive comments to daughters than to sons and issue fewer orders to sons than to daughters, encouraging closeness in girls but independence in boys (Leaper, Anderson, & Sanders, 1998). Even picture books offer implicit lessons in gender roles, depicting males as more active, mothers as nurturing, and fathers as largely invisible (Anderson & Hamilton, 2005; Hamilton, Anderson, Broaddus, & Young, 2006).

By the time they are 3, children spend more time playing with others of the same sex and favor gender-typed toys, games, and activities. This provides still more opportunities to learn and practice the skills and attitudes that society considers appropriate to their gender (Leaper & Friedman, 2006).

Bandura's Social Cognitive Theory. How does gender socialization work? What factors help or hinder the transmission of gender standards to the developing child? One influential account is the *social cognitive theory* of Albert Bandura (1986; Bussey & Bandura, 1999). In this model, personal factors, such as thoughts, desires, and feelings, interact with learned behavior patterns and social influences to produce tendencies to act in particular ways. Adolescents, like children or adults, observe what others do in a situation and what the consequences are, and then use this information to help them decide on ways of acting that seem likely to bring them closer to their goals. For instance, during the first days of starting at a new school, a teen will probably pay close attention to how others of his or her gender dress, talk, and act, and then try to model those behaviors as a step toward fitting in.

We do not simply copy what we see others doing, however. As a result of their own experiences, individuals develop a personal set of gender-role standards that sometimes override the influence of the immediate situation. Imagine a girl who has been brought up to believe that getting your clothes dirty is unladylike. What does she do when the children she's playing with decide to roll down a grassy or dusty slope? She may refuse to join them. She may even feel proud that she has behaved properly by keeping her clothes clean, though she may also wish she could be part of the fun.

Another important element in the social cognitive account of gender is *self-efficacy*, the belief that one has the resources to carry out some behavior or achieve some goal (Bandura, 1997, 2001). For example, a teenage boy may believe that playing football is a sign of masculinity, but whether he tries out for the team, or even joins a game of

◀ **Learning Objective 10.2**
How do others model and shape gender-related attitudes and behaviors?

Connect the **Dots...**

A common-sense view of gender differences is that they are built in. As the saying goes, "Boys will be boys." If parents and other adults really believe that, why do they go to such lengths to gender type children from birth, for example, by putting hair ribbons on a baby girl's bald head? What of children and teens who are seen as gender atypical? They generally come under a lot of pressure to conform to traditional roles. What does that suggest?

Socialization The processes through which children acquire the attitudes, beliefs, behaviors, and skills that their parents, peers, and culture consider appropriate.

touch with guys in the neighborhood, will depend largely on whether he thinks he can do so successfully. In this way, self-efficacy beliefs shape people's development by channeling the sorts of activities and social environments they choose. These, in turn, affect the models and reward structures they are exposed to and pay attention to (Bandura & Bussey, 2004).

Cognitive Approaches

▶ **Learning Objective 10.3**
Why are gender identity and gender schemas important?

The ways children and adolescents think about the world and try to understand it change dramatically over the years. Part of what they are trying to understand is themselves and their place in the world, including the significance of their sex and gender. Those who advance a cognitive explanation of gender typing see this process of thinking and understanding as critical to the development of gender roles.

Kohlberg and Gender Identity. One theorist who did a great deal to highlight the place of cognition in gender typing was Lawrence Kohlberg. As part of his effort to bring the insights of Piaget's work to bear on social and personality development, Kohlberg (1966) proposed a *cognitive developmental theory* of gender. His starting point was the apparently simple question: How do children at different stages of development *think about* gender? The answer turns out to be rather complex. While even 3-year-olds can correctly label themselves as boys or girls, only later do they understand that gender is stable over time—that boys grow up to be men and girls to be women. **Gender consistency,** the realization that gender is consistent or invariant—that a boy who dresses like a girl and plays girls' games is still a boy—comes later still. These understandings, not surprisingly, are linked to other aspects of cognitive development, such as the achievement of conservation (Martin, Ruble, & Szkrybalo, 2002).

In Kohlberg's view, these elements—self-labeling, gender stability, and gender consistency—are the essential elements for constructing a coherent **gender identity.** Once a girl realizes that she will still be a girl even if she cuts her hair and plays with guns and trucks, and that when she grows up, she will be a woman, she *identifies* with the social role that goes with that identity. This causes the underlying motivation for gender-typed behavior to shift from outside to inside. Before developing a stable gender identity, she might have reasoned, "I do girl things because people like it when I do and don't like it when I don't, and I want people to like what I do." Once a stable gender identity is in place, however, she thinks, "Since I'm a girl, I *want* to do girl things and I want to find out how to do them better, because when I do I feel more like myself."

Gender Schema Theory. The process of developing a sense of gender identity also plays a central role in another cognitive approach to gender, **gender schema theory** (Bem, 1981; Martin & Halverson, 1981, 1987). This approach puts particular stress on the ways children, adolescents, and adults gather and process information about gender. In effect, it views the individual as a detective who is actively trying to solve the puzzles presented by the social world and his or her place in that world.

A first step in understanding the world is to construct categories or *schemas*. These are mental structures that allow the child to group objects in the world as being similar to one another and different from other objects. It turns out that one of the earliest and most basic distinctions children make is between male and female. Just as adults, on hearing that someone has had a baby, usually ask "Boy or girl?", children who are shown a new toy want to know if it is a girl toy or a boy toy. Almost anything can be the object of this gendering process. Pink is for girls, blue is for boys; baseball is for boys, softball is for girls; dogs are for boys, cats are for girls; the sun is male, the moon is female; and by now everybody knows about Venus and Mars!

Children start noticing and attending to gender cues at an amazingly early age (Martin & Ruble, 2004). By their first birthday, babies are able not only to distinguish between male and female faces, but also to link each type of face with a corresponding

Gender consistency A person's awareness that gender is a permanent or invariant characteristic of an individual.

Gender identity Those aspects of a person's sense of self that relate to masculinity or femininity.

Gender schema theory A set of ideas that concerns the ways children, adolescents, and adults gather and organize information about gender, and then use this information to guide their attitudes and actions.

voice (Poulin-Dubois, Serbin, & Derbyshire, 1998). Not long afterwards, they show the beginnings of knowledge about the kinds of household activities typical of men and women (Poulin-Dubois, Serbin, Eichstedt, Sen, & Beissel, 2002). Children's gender knowledge is not purely literal, it is metaphorical as well. Toddlers of 18 months already associate males with bears, fir trees, and the color blue (Eichstedt, Serbin, Poulin-Dubois, & Sen, 2002)!

Gender schemas involve more than understanding and forming expectations about others—they also have personal implications. Along with the recognition that there are two mutually exclusive gender groups, even young children are aware that they belong to one and not the other (Kane, 2006; Ruble, Martin, & Bernebaum, 2006). This has immediate and long-lasting consequences. Children begin to prefer their own group to the other and to think of it as better (Powlishta, 2004; Ruble et al., 2006). By age 3, they tend to play mostly with others of their own sex (Martin & Fabes, 2001). They also start to see both their own group and the other group in stereotypical terms. For example, children who find out that one boy prefers a particular toy think that other boys will also prefer that toy and that girls won't like it as much (Martin, Eisenbud, & Rose, 1995).

Once a sense of gender identity emerges, children start to process gender-related information differently. They pay more attention to information about their own gender and remember it better. In one study, boys and girls were shown several unfamiliar gadgets, such as a pizza cutter, and told that some were boy things and some were girl things. The boys spent more time playing with what they thought were boy things and remembered them better a few days later, while the girls spent more time with the girl things and remembered *them* better (Bradbard, Martin, Endsley, & Halverson, 1986). Children (and adults) may also distort information so that it fits their gender schemas better. For example, children who hear a story about a boy cooking or sewing may later recall it as being about a *girl* performing these gender-typed activities (Martin & Halverson, 1983).

Similarities and Differences. Both Kohlberg's cognitive developmental theory and gender schema theory propose that children who have achieved a stable gender identity are intrinsically motivated to learn and practice the skills, activities, and attitudes that "go with" their gender (Martin & Ruble, 2004). There are, however, some important differences between the two approaches. For Kohlberg, identification with one's gender role and the intrinsic motivation to conform to it develop once the child achieves a full understanding of gender constancy, at around age 6 or 7. In contrast, gender schema theorists see this process as beginning with the earliest emergence of gender identity, during the preschool years or even toddlerhood. By age 5 or 6, rigid either/or stereotyping reaches a peak, followed by a phase of more flexible ideas about gender (Trautner et al., 2005).

Both of these approaches see the child's acquisition of a sense of gender identity as the central event in the development of gender typing. Recently, however, researchers have suggested that gender identity may consist of several different components (Egan & Perry, 2001; Yunger, Carver, & Perry, 2004). These include:

knowing that one belongs to a particular gender;

feeling like or unlike others of one's gender;

being content or satisfied with one's gender;

feeling under pressure from others to conform to the stereotype of one's gender; and

believing that one's own sex is better than the other one.

These facets of gender identity may develop at different ages and have different implications. Essentially all children over the age of 2 or 3 know whether they are boys or girls, and most tend to think their own sex is better than the other one. However, a teenage boy who knows perfectly well he is a boy and thinks boys are better than girls may still believe that he is not as good at doing boy things as other boys. Similarly, a teenage girl who knows she is a girl and likes being a girl may feel she is not as good as other girls at doing girl things. Not surprisingly, this view of the self as not measuring up leads to low self-esteem. If an adolescent also feels under strong pressure from others—parents, peers—to conform to the traditional gender stereotype, he or she may become withdrawn and depressed as well (Yunger et al., 2004). Recent research also indicates that the particular attributes that are considered positive for each sex may vary across racial and ethnic groups (Corby, Hodges, & Perry, 2007).

Integrating Varying Approaches

▶ **Learning Objective 10.4**
How can different views be combined to understand gender development?

All of us are at the same time biological, social, and psychological beings. Any attempt to explain gender roles would have to take this obvious fact into account. Over the years, the different approaches we just looked at have evolved in the direction of acknowledging and incorporating insights and research findings from other approaches into their own analyses. The social cognitive approach stresses the importance of models, rewards, and punishments in shaping gendered behaviors, but also gives emphasis to such cognitive factors as expectations, self-regulation, and feelings of self-efficacy (Bandura & Bussey, 2004). Researchers in the cognitive developmental and gender schema traditions point out that the *content* of children's gender roles—the particular attitudes and activities they see as appropriate to those of their sex—is passed along by parents, peers, the media, and other agents of socialization (Martin, Ruble, & Szkrybalo, 2004). While biological theorists agree that genetic heritage, hormones, and other biological factors establish a firm foundation for gender roles, many would add that what is built on that foundation is strongly influenced by both culture and individual psychology (Susman, 2004).

Are these different ways of looking at gender development moving toward a single overarching, integrated conception (Galambos, 2004)? If so, it may well make use of *developmental systems theory* (Lerner, 2002; Lerner & Castellino, 2002). In this view, a person's individual characteristics—physical, intellectual, emotional, and so on—act on *and* are acted on by the contexts in which the person is embedded. These contexts include the family, peer group, community, and broader culture. The person is an active participant in these interactions, bringing his or her own history, gender-linked characteristics, abilities, expectations, and goals to them. To understand developmental trajectories, we need to consider how the interconnected and evolving aspects of the adolescent relate to the various and changing features of the adolescent's environment.

Connect the **Dots...**

To what extent would you say your own attitudes and interests as a young adolescent were typical or atypical of your gender? Can you recall instances in which others—parents, siblings, friends—tried to push you either toward gender typical activities or away from gender atypical activities? If so, how did you respond? How do you think you would respond now?

An example may make it clearer how the developmental systems orientation might account for a particular teen's gender role and attitudes. Imagine a young adolescent boy who is skinny and bright. Both body type and intelligence are affected by biological factors as well as by early experience. The boy will learn that in our culture an important aspect of the traditional masculine gender role is athletic prowess. He will also realize that he is less endowed in that department than most of his male peers. What does he do with this understanding and what impact does it have on his further development?

The answer to these questions will largely depend on his other characteristics, as well as the features of the social environment he finds himself in. He may feel inferior to other guys and become withdrawn and depressed. He may embark on a body-building program and even start abusing steroids in an attempt to compensate for his constitutional makeup. He may develop an interest in a sport for which his slim build is an advantage. He may notice that scientific and technical skills are also part of the traditional masculine gender role, work on developing those skills, and start hanging with a crowd that values academic success and looks down on jocks. If the mismatch between his personality and his school is extreme, and if he feels support from family and friends, he may actively work to transfer to a school that provides a more congenial setting for someone like him.

▲ A teen's body type and other biological characteristics interact with gender roles and the social environment.

Gender Intensification

The theories of gender development we just looked at focus much of their attention on the period from birth (or, for biological approaches, even before birth) through middle childhood. The reason for this is straightforward: By the time children are 7 or 8, they show that they basically understand their culture's gender roles and prefer to conform to them (Martin et al., 2004). Events during adolescence, however, make their own unique contribution to gender development. Just as early adolescence brings far-reaching physical and social changes, it may also increase the external and internal pressures to think, feel, and act in ways that are considered gender-appropriate. This possibility is known as the gender intensification hypothesis (Hill & Lynch, 1983).

The **gender intensification hypothesis** states that the physical changes of puberty alert parents, teachers, peers, and the world at large that a child is beginning the transition to adulthood. This gives new urgency to acting more like an adult, and especially acting like an adult of one's own sex. Parents start to worry when, or if, their child will "grow out of" interests and activities they see as inappropriate (Crouter, Manke, & McHale, 1995). Young adolescents start to see themselves more in gender-typed terms and show less tolerance of cross-gender behaviors (Carr, 2007; McHale et al., 2003). Once teens begin dating, conforming to traditional gender roles becomes even more urgent. Those who are considered most attractive are generally the more "feminine" girls and the more "masculine" boys (Feiring, 1999).

The arguments for gender intensification are persuasive, but finding clear evidence for it has proved more difficult. One study found that differences in gender role attitudes between boys and girls widened from 6th to 8th grade (Galambos, Almeida, & Petersen, 1990). In another study, gender-linked differences in expressive behavior became more pronounced over the adolescent years (Polce-Lynch, Myers, Kliewer, & Kilmartin, 2001). Other research, however, suggests that at least some gender-stereotyped attitudes are already well-established by middle childhood and do *not* get stronger during adolescence (Jacobs, Vernon, & Eccles, 2005). The fairest conclusion may be that different adolescents follow different trajectories (Bartini, 2006). The degree of gender intensification depends on the individual teen, the social context he or she is in, and the particular aspect of gender-related development that is being looked at (Galambos, 2004).

◀ **Learning Objective 10.5**
What is gender intensification?

Summing Up...

Gender roles are cultural standards for how males and females are supposed to look, act, and think. They are transmitted to new generations by way of gender typing. While genes and hormones have an important effect, parents, siblings, peers, and the wider culture offer examples of accepted attitudes and behaviors and positive or negative consequences to those who fit or don't fit the expected model. The child's own realization that gender is a consistent part of personality leads to adopting a gender identity and constructing gender schemas that affect perceptions and preferences. A developmental systems approach integrates these diverse factors to describe how an adolescent's gender characteristics act on and are acted on by personal, social, and cultural contexts.

GENDER DIFFERENCES IN ADOLESCENCE

At the heart of our ideas about gender is the conviction that males and females are different in important ways. If that were not the case, there would be no reason for this chapter. But as with many aspects of the world that we think we know a lot about, some of what we think we know is correct, some is sort of true, and some is flat wrong.

In most respects, males and females are much more alike than they are different (Hyde, 2007). A landmark study that followed a representative sample of healthy U.S.

Gender intensification hypothesis The proposal that, with the approach of adolescence, children come under increased pressure from others to conform more closely to expected gender roles.

children from birth to young adulthood found very few gender differences on cognitive tasks (Waber et al., 2007), but it is more the differences that people tend to notice and consider significant. In this section, we look at some major areas of functioning in which males and females have been *found* to differ or are generally *believed* to differ. Are girls and boys different in their intellectual abilities and achievements, and if so, how, how much, and why? How do differences in self-esteem develop? Are girls more emotional? Are boys more aggressive? What are the implications of the different ways girls and boys interact with their peers and friends?

Achievement

▶ **Learning Objective 10.6**
How does stereotype threat relate to gender differences in achievement?

A memorable feature of my life in 5th grade was the weekly spelling bee. If nothing else, it gave us a welcome chance to stand up and move around, instead of being stuck sitting at our desks. I felt a mixture of excitement and dread as Mrs. Norman worked her way inexorably down the two lines in my direction. Would I get an easy word? An impossible one? If I spelled it wrong, would I at least come close? As I walked back to my seat, would the other children cluck sympathetically or make fun of my cluelessness?

You may have noticed that I referred to two lines of students. This probably calls for an explanation. In those days, it was thought only natural that a spelling bee, or almost any school competition, was structured as "the girls against the boys." Many weeks, once the words got tougher, I found myself the only boy still standing, while across the room four or five girls waited confidently for their turn to spell *rhythm* or *confident*. My feelings about this were very mixed. On the one hand, I was proud to be upholding the honor of my team. On the other, I could not dodge the well-known fact that a real boy *shouldn't* be able to spell as well as the girls.

One of the things "everybody knows" about gender and school achievement is that girls do better in English and boys do better in math. This is considered so normal that it usually doesn't merit comment. Only the exception—the girl who is a math whiz, the boy who can spell and likes to read—seems to need explaining. Children pick up this stereotype early and hang onto it through adolescence and into adulthood (Jacobs et al., 2005; Meece, Glienke, & Burg, 2006). Their belief seems confirmed by even a casual look at the adult world. The more a profession involves mathematical skills, such as science and engineering, the more likely it is to be overwhelmingly male (National Council for Research on Women, 2002). Women, on the other hand, are more likely to be found in teaching, library science, and other occupations that favor verbal skills and that, on the whole, do not pay as well or enjoy as much prestige as more "masculine" careers (Galambos, 2004).

Gender in the Classroom. School, then, is a setting in which one's gender matters. Many scholars have argued that it is also structured and conducted in ways that are unfair to either males or females (Koch, 2003). One widely circulated report accused U.S. schools of short-changing girls, especially as they approach adolescence (American Association of University Women, 1992). For example, teachers interact more with boys and give them more instruction and help, while girls sit quietly and wait their turn (Sadker, Sadker, & Zittleman, 2008). By adolescence, girls show less confidence in their ability to succeed on school tasks than boys, even when their actual performance does not differ (Crandall, 1969; Eccles, Wigfield, & Byrnes, 2004; Klassen, 2002).

Does this mean that boys have it easy, then? Not at all. Think about the behaviors that are valued and taught in elementary school. These behaviors include following rules, raising your hand instead of speaking out, keeping your desk and notebook neat, and working quietly at your seat instead of running around. In terms of traditional gender roles, these are a much better fit for girls than for boys (DeZolt & Hull, 2001; Maccoby, 1998). The fact that most elementary school teachers are women deprives boys of same-sex academic role models and adds to the impression that the classroom is a "feminized" setting. Perhaps as a result, boys are more likely than girls to be put in remedial programs, be the target of disciplinary actions, and end up as underachievers

(Eccles et al., 2004). Not surprisingly, they are also more likely to drop out or be expelled before finishing high school (National Center for Education Statistics, 2003).

Perhaps the fairest conclusion about the relationship of gender to school is that the school experience is tough on everyone, but males and females face different sets of disadvantages (Eccles et al., 2004). These, in turn, produce different patterns of achievement that have further effects, not just during adolescence, but into adulthood. One pattern that has broad implications, and that is found in developed countries throughout the world, is the underrepresentation of females in scientific and technical fields (UNESCO, 2003). In the next section, we look at some of the factors that contribute to this pattern.

Gender, Math, and Science. In 1992, the manufacturers of Barbie dolls introduced a deluxe version called "Teen Talk Barbie" that came with a repertoire of spoken comments. One of Barbie's observations about the world was, "Math class is tough!" (Associated Press, 1992). Howls of protest forced the makers to delete the remark, but they were not really telling children anything they did not already believe. As we have seen, there is a widely held stereotype that boys have higher ability for math than girls (Jacobs et al., 2005; Skaalvik & Skaalvik, 2004; Wilgenbusch & Merrill, 1999). Widely held, yes; but is there any truth to it? Many of the psychological differences that are supposed to exist between males and females have turned out on closer examination to be cultural myths (Maccoby & Jacklin, 1974). For example, girls are not more sociable or suggestible than boys, and boys are not more logical or analytic than girls. But what about math? Is it the case that boys really have higher ability in math than girls? To answer this question, we need to take a step backward and look at another, related, skill area.

The Role of Spatial Abilities. There is at least one cognitive difference between males and females that has been documented over and over. By early adolescence, boys on average perform better than girls on tests of spatial abilities such as *mental rotation* (Linn & Petersen, 1985; Nuttal, Casey, & Pezaris, 2005; Siegel-Hinson & McKeever, 2002). This involves being able to look at an object, such as an assembly of blocks, and to imagine how it would appear in other orientations (see Figure 10.1).

Spatial ability has been linked to levels of testosterone in young adolescents, both boys and girls (Davison & Susman, 2001), so it shouldn't surprise us that the boys' relative advantage emerges around puberty, the same time that their testosterone levels increase more sharply than those of girls (Kerns & Berenbaum, 1991). We should also notice that this difference is not universal. A recent study found that while middle-class boys did better than middle-class girls on a spatial ability task, there were no performance differences between low-income boys and girls (Levine, Vasilyeva, Lourenco, Newcombe, & Huttenlocher, 2005). Another major study found a gender difference on a perceptual analysis task, but not on a perceptual reasoning task (Waber et al., 2007). And in Iceland, high school girls actually do *better* than boys on spatial tasks (Lemke et al., 2004).

Pubertal hormones are far from being the only factor at work. Childhood experiences also have an important role. For example, children who play more with three-dimensional toys, such as Lego blocks, do better on tests of spatial ability, whether

Figure 10.1 Mental Rotation Task
Mental rotation: Which of the objects on the right is identical to the one on the left except for its orientation in space?

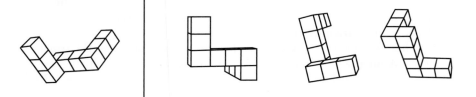

they are boys or girls (Brosnan, 1998; Tracy, 1987). Construction toys of this sort—Legos, Tinkertoys, Erector sets—are generally stereotyped as masculine and shelved on the boys' aisle of the toy store. Because they are seen as boy toys, boys tend to like them and play with them more than girls do. This may help explain why boys eventually show better spatial abilities. It may also be that prenatal testosterone gives boys a stronger predisposition toward activities of this sort (Davison & Susman, 2001).

Remarkably, a recent experiment demonstrated that playing action video games for as little as 10 hours greatly decreased the gender difference in mental rotation scores (Feng, Spence, & Pratt, 2007). Ordinarily, of course, games of this sort appeal much more to boys than girls (Quaiser-Pohl, Geiser, & Lehmann, 2006). However, these results suggest that if action video games were developed that girls, too, enjoyed, the gender difference in spatial relations might wither away.

The gender difference in spatial abilities has implications well beyond seeing how to turn a big, awkwardly-shaped package so it fits into the back seat of a car. During elementary school, girls are just as good as boys at understanding mathematical concepts and are actually better at computational skills (Ruble et al., 2006). As a result, they tend to get higher grades than boys in math (Kenney-Benson, Pomerantz, Ryan, & Patrick, 2006; Kimball, 1989). Children notice this, too. When researchers in a recent study asked 4th and 5th graders about gender differences in school performance, both boys and girls said the two sexes do pretty much the same in math (Heyman & Legare, 2004).

Beginning in early adolescence, however, boys start doing somewhat better than girls on tests of arithmetic reasoning (Halpern, 2000; Hyde, Fennema, & Lamon, 1990). For example, the National Assessment of Educational Progress found *no* gender differences in math among 4th graders. In grades 8 and 12, however, the boys had higher math scores than the girls (National Center for Education Statistics, 2003). Boys also get higher average scores on the quantitative section of the Scholastic Aptitude Test (SAT), taken in late adolescence, than do girls, though not by much (Delisi & McGillicuddy-Delisi, 2002). One of the biggest sources of this growing advantage is the gender difference in spatial abilities (Nuttall et al., 2005). In fact, when differences in spatial ability are taken into account, boys score no better on the SAT than girls do (Casey, 1996).

The Role of Math Stereotypes. Why was no one very surprised (offended, maybe, but not surprised) when Barbie announced that math class is hard? From this brief look at the facts, we can see that on average girls do not do worse in math than boys, except for the small difference in spatial abilities (Eccles et al., 2004). Even that difference may not show up until adolescence. As Figure 10.2 on page 339 illustrates, the size of the difference is trivial. Yet the commonly accepted view is that there is a vast gulf, with girls over there, on the hopeless side, and boys over here, with differential equations dancing in their heads.

Even adolescents whose personal experiences might have led them to know better seem to be affected by this gender stereotype. Girls who have shown high ability and interest in science during high school often shift onto nonscientific paths when they reach college (Adamuti-Trache & Andres, 2002; Jacobs, Davis-Kean, Bleeker, Eccles, & Malanchuk, 2005). In high school, girls make up almost half of those taking physics courses, but at each step farther up the academic ladder the proportion of females among physics students gets smaller (Ivie & Stowe, 2002).

In college, mathematically gifted young women are about half as likely as mathematically gifted young men to get a degree in math (Benbow, Lubinski, Shea, and Eftekhari-Sanjani, 2000). Even when technical and scientific programs are deliberately designed to be woman-friendly, the women gradually lose their confidence and do more poorly, while the men's confidence and performance improves (Hartman & Hartman, 2002). Women who endorse the stereotype do worse in math courses and are less likely to want to seek a math-related career (Kiefer & Sekaquaptewa, 2007; Schmader, Johns, & Barquissau, 2004). Moreover, even many college women who are majoring in math-related fields implicitly associate *math* with *maleness*, and the

Connect the Dots...

Suppose you were asked to design a program to increase interest and achievement in math and science among middle school girls. What approach would you take? What elements would you think it particularly important to include?

Figure 10.2   Male and Female Math Performance
These two distributions differ about as much as the average gender difference in math performance.

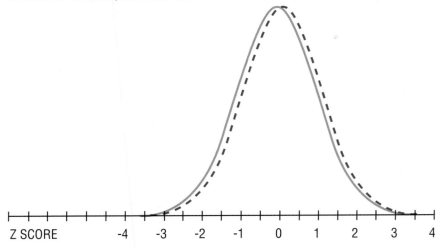

Z SCORE   -4   -3   -2   -1   0   1   2   3   4

Source: Figure 1, "Two Normal Distributions," by J. S. Hyde, E. Fennema, and S. J. Lamon. *Psychological Bulletin 107,* 139–155. © 1990. Used by permission of the American Psychological Association (APA).

stronger the association, the weaker their self-identification with math and the lower their math SAT scores (Nosek, Banaji, & Greenwald, 2002).

Expectancies, Values, and Learned Helplessness. A number of interlocking processes can help explain the gap between what girls may actually be able to accomplish in math and science and how they think of their capabilities (Eccles, 2004; Lips, 2004). Girls tend to have lower expectancies for success in technical fields (Jacobs et al., 2005; Skaalvik & Skaalvik, 2004). These lower expectancies affect both their interest in such fields and their willingness to invest effort in them. And the best predictors of going on in math are interest and feelings of self-efficacy (Stevens, Wang, Olivárez, & Hamman, 2007). If you don't think you can succeed at something, why do it? If you're forced to do it—because of a school requirement, for example—why try hard, given that it's unlikely to help anyway? Of course, putting in less effort is likely to lead to worse performance, which was the expected outcome to begin with.

Girls also tend to see their accomplishments in math and science as having less personal importance or value (Wigfield, Eccles, Schiefele, Roeser, & Davis-Kean, 2006). People often place a lower value on activities in which they feel less competent, as a way

◄ Gender stereotypes make many girls less willing to take courses in the sciences.

of preserving their self-esteem (Major, Spencer, Schmader, Wolfe, & Crocker, 1998). Because girls rate their competence in math lower than do boys (Fredricks & Eccles, 2002; Kurman, 2004), it should not come as a surprise that they tend to devalue the field as well. Their competency beliefs also contribute to a sort of vicious circle, in which successes are explained as the result of temporary factors, such as good luck, while failures are seen as a natural consequence of low ability. As we saw in Chapter 9, this pattern of explanations or attributions results in a feeling of *learned helplessness* (Dweck, 1999).

Competition and Stereotype Threat. Recent research suggests that psychological climate also plays an important role. Specifically, males may be stimulated by a competitive atmosphere, while females react more negatively to it. In one study of students at a very selective engineering school in Israel, the men's performance improved as the level of competition went up, but the women's performance did not (Gneezy, Niederle, & Rustichini, 2003). This effect was even stronger in mixed groups than in all-male or all-female groups. Another recent study, which looked at American college students, found that women shied away from a competitive situation, even when it would have been to their advantage to choose it. Men, in contrast, preferred the competitive situation even when they would have been better off in the noncompetitive situation (Niederle & Vesterlund, 2005).

Still another factor that may help explain the gender gap in scientific and technical fields is *stereotype threat*, which was introduced in Chapter 9. Girls are well aware that as a group they are not expected to be as competent as boys in math. The more they are reminded of this negative stereotype, and of the way it applies to them, the more they develop performance anxiety and think negative thoughts about the task (Cadinu, Maass, Rosabianca, & Kiesner, 2005; Steele & Ambady, 2006). These negative thoughts, in turn, reduce their ability to focus on the task and get in the way of doing well (Davies & Spencer, 2005; Schmader & Johns, 2003). One recent study of young women taking very advanced college courses in mathematics found that even they performed worse under conditions linked to stereotype threat (Good, Aronson, & Harder, 2008).

Even something as simple as being the only female in a group with males can be enough to interfere with solving math problems (Ben-Zeev, Fein, & Inzlicht, 2005). In a recent experiment, male and female science and engineering majors watched a video of a summer conference meeting in their field. For some, the male–female ratio in the video was balanced, and for others, there were noticeably more males than females. This difference had no impact on men, but women who saw the unbalanced video were less interested in taking part in the conference (Murphy, Steele, & Gross, 2007).

This chapter's Applications in the Spotlight on page 341 suggests some ways the classroom experience might be changed to reduce stereotype threat.

Self-Esteem

▶ **Learning Objective 10.7**
What effects does gender have on teen self-esteem?

School achievement is not the only area in which the impact of adolescence is more negative for girls than for boys. A number of studies have shown that girls suffer a decline in self-esteem during the early adolescent years and that this decline is sharpest in those who are farther along in their development (Simmons, Blythe, Van Cleave, & Bush, 1979). As a result, they have lower self-esteem on average than boys the same age (Kling, Hyde, Showers, & Buswell, 1999; Robins & Trzesniewski, 2005).

Puberty and Body Changes. Why does this difference develop? One contributing factor is the impact of puberty on body image, which is one of the strongest predictors of self-esteem for adolescents (DuBois, Tevendale, Burk-Braxton, Swenson, & Hardesty, 2000; Tolman, Impett, Tracy, & Michael, 2006; Williams & Currie, 2000). For boys, entering adolescence means becoming taller and more muscular, in other words, more masculine (Smolak, Murnen, & Thompson, 2005). For girls, however, the weight gain that comes with puberty is more likely to be a source of unhappiness (Galambos, 2004).

Applications in the Spotlight

Countering the Effects of Stereotype Threat

Research over the past few years has made it clear that one of the biggest reasons girls perform below their potential in math-related areas is the effect of *stereotype threat*. When something in a testing situation reminds girls of the negative stereotype that girls aren't good in math, their performance tends to suffer (Ryan & Ryan, 2005; Steele, 1997). This can happen even when they do not believe the stereotype applies to them personally and even if they expect to succeed on the test. But why does it happen?

Investigators have offered several explanations for the effects of stereotype threat. If girls start to worry that by doing badly they will confirm the negative stereotype about their group, this concern may distract them from concentrating on the task (Schmader & Johns, 2003). In addition, the belief that they are in competition with boys and that their performance will be seen as an indication of their native ability creates what is called a *performance-avoid* goal orientation (Pintrich & Schunk, 2002). The girl becomes preoccupied with staving off a negative judgment of her ability. This distraction, as we saw in Chapter 9, has consistently been linked to lower levels of performance (Harackiewicz, Pintrich, Barron, Elliot, & Thrash, 2002).

What can teachers and others who work with young people do to help girls overcome the effects of stereotype threat? It is unrealistic to expect that anyone can reach adolescence in our society without "knowing" that girls are supposed to be weaker in math (even though they get higher grades in the subject!). And, of course, girls and boys know they are girls and boys. However, just as making the category of gender *more* salient increases stereotype threat and leads girls to perform worse than boys (Aronson & Good, 2002), making gender *less* salient may

reduce stereotype threat. For example, girls perform better when tested in an all-girl group than when boys are present (Inzlicht & Ben-Zeev, 2000). Even something as simple as leaving off a question about the person's sex on the test sheet might well help.

On a more proactive level, questions designed to direct attention to individual characteristics instead of group membership have been shown to reduce stereotype threat and increase math performance (Ambady, Paik, Steele, Owen-Smith, & Mitchell, 2004). If girls are led to believe that a task measures personal improvement, rather than a fixed ability, they are more likely to adopt a *mastery* goal orientation and avoid the effects of stereotype threat (Good, Aronson, & Inzlicht, 2003). Research with college students has found that young women who endorse gender stereotypes and traditional roles are more affected by stereotype threat (Schmader, Johns, & Barquissau, 2004). This suggests that learning more about the ways males and females are more alike than different (Hyde, 2005) may serve to reduce stereotype threat.

Even more direct, in one recent study college women were given a brief explanation of stereotype threat and then told, "If you are feeling anxious while taking this test, this anxiety could be the result of these negative stereotypes that are widely known in society and have nothing to do with your actual ability to do well on the test." They did just as well on the test as their male fellow students, while other women who did not receive the explanation performed worse than the men (Johns, Schmader, & Martens, 2005, p. 176). It would seem, then, that this is still another situation in which "knowledge is power."

Compared to boys their age, adolescent girls are dissatisfied with their bodies (Barker & Galambos, 2003; Davison & McCabe, 2006), and those who are more advanced physically are more dissatisfied (Tobin-Richards, Boxer, & Petersen, 1983). It is hard to feel good about yourself if you dislike the way you look, or if you think others dislike it. The greater stress put on being physically attractive as children enter adolescence magnifies this effect (McHale, Corneal, Crouter, & Birch, 2001), as does the increasing focus on what others, especially other adolescents, think about you and the way you look (Frederickson & Roberts, 1997).

We saw in Chapter 6 how one's relationships with peers take on increasing importance during adolescence. This is even more the case with girls than with boys (Brown, 2001; Rose & Rudolph, 2006). In line with traditional gender roles, a major source of a girl's sense of self-esteem is her success in building and maintaining close personal relationships (Cross & Madson, 1997). Often, however, keeping a relationship going seems to require hiding one's own thoughts, needs, and desires and presenting a "false self" (Harter, 2006). Imagine, for instance, a teenage girl who is dating a passionate fan of NASCAR racing or whose best friend adores a particular heavy metal group.

Whatever her real feelings about loud cars and loud music, she may be strongly tempted to pretend to share those interests as a way of holding onto the relationships.

Personal relationships may be crucial to self-esteem, but personal relationships built on silencing or disguising one's self also pose a threat to self-esteem by making it harder to create authentic connection with others. Even if people seem to like you, if you believe the "you" they like isn't the *real* you, their liking will not make you feel more positive about yourself or your relationships. It may even confirm your conviction that no one could possibly like you if they really knew you. Given this, it is no surprise that a sense of inauthenticity has been linked to low self-esteem in adolescent girls (Harter, Marold, Whitesell, & Cobbs, 1996).

Carol Gilligan and "Loss of Voice". One researcher who has devoted a great deal of attention to the ways girls silence their own needs for the sake of preserving relationships is Harvard psychologist Carol Gilligan (1982, 1993; Brown & Gilligan, 1992). Based on intensive interviews with preadolescent and adolescent girls, Gilligan wrote that girls are particularly aware of and interested in human relationships. As they reach adolescence, however, they begin to realize that this sensitivity to others is not very highly valued by society. Instead, the greater rewards go to those—more likely boys— who are practical, solve problems, and get things done.

Once girls recognize this situation, they face some difficult choices. If they repress their interest in intimacy and become more "objective," they may achieve more, but at a cost that includes feeling less authentic and being seen as less feminine. If, instead, they maintain their passionate interest in emotions and relationships, they are seen as caring and selfless, but are passed over in favor of higher-achieving boys. Gilligan says that this dilemma undermines the confidence girls feel in their own insights and makes them begin to doubt themselves. They become more tentative, more likely to defer to the opinions of others, and they silence their distinctive "voice" (Ryan, 2003).

Gilligan's views on the predicament of adolescent girls aroused a lot of interest and helped inspire a widely read book, *Reviving Ophelia* (Pipher, 1994). Her views also became a topic of controversy. Some critics were bothered that Gilligan relied on interpreting what girls said in interviews, without comparable information from adolescent boys. This, they felt, may have led her to see greater gender differences than exist in reality. Others suggested that what Gilligan says about girls in general may really apply only to some girls, and to some boys as well. In one study, there was no overall gender difference in voice, but those girls with a more typical feminine gender orientation did show a loss of voice, as did both girls and boys who did not feel that important others supported their self-expression (Harter, Waters, Whitesell, & Kastelic, 1998).

There is no reason to doubt that puberty and adolescence create problems for the self-esteem of boys as well as girls (Sommers, 2000). Both boys and girls receive the message that they are expected to conform to practically unattainable physical ideals as well as stringent gender-linked psychological ideals (Olivardia, Pope, Borowiecki, & Cohane, 2004; Yunger, Carver, & Perry, 2004). To the extent that they fall short of these goals, or believe they fall short of them, their self-esteem suffers (Chu, Porche, & Tolman, 2005; Frost & McKelvie, 2004). As a result, measured self-esteem drops during adolescence for both boys and girls; however, it drops *more* for girls (Robins & Trzesniewski, 2005). Why?

Gilligan and those who share her perspective point out that the particular goals set by traditional gender roles are obviously different for girls and boys. Physically, girls are supposed to look like Barbie and boys like GI Joe. These contrasting, but equally impossible, ideals push girls in the direction of eating disorders and boys in the direction of steroid abuse. Psychologically, boys are expected to be independent, assertive, and emotionally stoic, while girls are expected to be sensitive, sympathetic, and noncombative (Ruble et al., 2006). In effect, a boy is told to stand up for what he believes, even when he doesn't believe anything in particular, while a girl is told to be soft-spoken and responsive to the needs of others, even when she feels like screaming! To the extent, then, that adolescents accept and try to conform to traditional gender roles, girls will silence their voice, and boys will not (Tolman et al., 2006).

Emotion and Mood

According to the usual gender stereotypes, girls and women are more emotional than boys and men. They supposedly feel and express more distress, sadness, guilt, and fear than males, and more happiness as well (Plant, Hyde, Keltner, & Devine, 2000). Males, on the other hand, are stereotyped as feeling and expressing more anger. For college students and adults, at least, these stereotypes are fairly accurate (Kring, 2000; Kring & Gordon, 1998). Studies of babies and young children, however, find few or no important gender differences in emotions (Else-Quest, Hyde, Goldsmith, & Van Hulle, 2006). These contrasting findings suggest that differences in emotionality emerge during childhood and adolescence as a result of the different experiences girls and boys have with parents and peers (Brody & Hall, 2000; Ruble et al., 2006). Girls not only display their vulnerable emotions more often than boys do, they also expect to get more positive responses from others than boys do (Shipman, Zeman, & Stegall, 2001).

A classic study hints at one way these emotional differences might develop. Adults were shown a film of a baby reacting to a jack-in-the-box. Some of them had been told the baby was a girl, and others that it was a boy. Those who thought they were watching a boy tended to describe the baby's reaction as angry, but those who thought they were watching a girl were more likely to describe the baby's reaction as fearful (Condry & Condry, 1976). Even though boy and girl toddlers can be equally difficult, mothers respond differently to difficult daughters and difficult sons (Maccoby, 1998).

The most frequent emotional problem that adolescents experience is *depression*. This shows itself most obviously in frequent or prolonged bouts of feeling sad, unhappy, or "blue," but it may also lead to apathy, pessimism, and physical symptoms such as sleep problems and loss of appetite (Graber, 2004). It is also where one of the more striking gender-related differences shows up. During childhood, boys are just as likely as girls, or even slightly more likely, to experience depressive symptoms. Starting with puberty, however, about twice as many girls as boys become depressed (Petersen et al., 1993; Twenge & Nolen-Hoeksema, 2002; Wade, Cairney, & Pevalin, 2002). As Figure 10.3 shows, this difference continues into and through adulthood (Lewinsohn, Rohde, Seeley, Kling & Gotlib, 2006).

◄ Learning Objective 10.8
How does gender relate to emotion and mood in adolescence?

Figure 10.3 Gender Differences in Depressed Mood
The difference in depressed mood between girls and boys increases across adolescence.

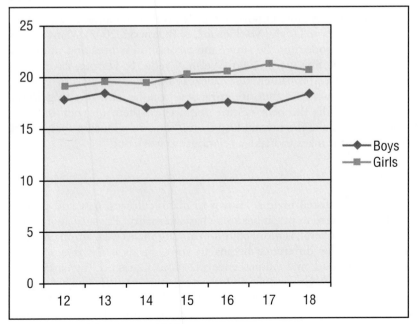

Source: Ge, Natsuak, & Conger, 2006.

► During adolescence, girls are twice as likely as boys to fall victim to depression.

What is responsible for the big rise in depression among girls? Researchers have offered several explanations. One element is low self-esteem, which is both a source and a symptom of depression. Some of the same factors we just looked at that contribute to lower self-esteem in adolescent girls, such as body image problems and a sense of inauthenticity, also help account for depression (Tolman et al., 2006). More generally, the stresses of puberty, concerns about appearance and popularity, and social pressures to fit into appropriate gender roles (Yunger, Carver, & Perry, 2004) are more intense for girls than for boys (Graber, 2004).

Girls also tend to handle emotional stresses in a different way from boys. From early childhood, girls are trained to be more aware of their emotions. Parents talk about emotions more with girls than with boys, and girls are able to display their vulnerable emotions, such as sadness, more easily than boys (Brody & Hall, 2000). One result of this is that under stress, girls are more likely to brood about their problems and turn them inward, in a process called *rumination*. Boys are more likely to try to push away their negative feelings and distract themselves with activities (Seiffge-Krenke & Stemmler, 2002).

Still another factor is the greater importance girls give to romantic relationships and intimacy (Brendgen, Vitaro, Doyle, Markiewicz, & Bukowski, 2002). Many events can trigger a depressive episode, but the single most common is breaking up with a romantic partner (Davila & Steinberg, 2006; Welsh, Grello, & Harper, 2003). The emotional distress of a breakup is bad enough, but it is amplified for girls by the way it can cause them to doubt whether they are attractive, popular, and able to gain the qualities and master the skills the peer culture requires of them (Joyner & Udry, 2000). It is all too easy to make the mental leap from, "This relationship didn't work out" to "I don't have what it takes to make a relationship work out!"

Aggression

► **Learning Objective 10.9**
In what ways are teenage boys more aggressive than girls and in what ways not?

The stereotype of the two-fisted male is known to many cultures, past and present (White, 2001). Like many stereotypes, it has some basis in reality. Physical aggression, like antisocial behavior in general, is more common among males than among females (Hartup, 2005). This gender difference begins to show up as early as age 3 and continues through childhood and adolescence (Dodge, Coies, & Lynam, 2006; Zimmer-Gemback, Geiger, & Crick, 2005). One recent study that looked at longitudinal information on children and teens in the United States, Canada, and New Zealand found that even girls who are chronically aggressive are notably less aggressive than chronically aggressive boys from the same background (Broidy et al., 2003).

This average difference between boys and girls in physical aggressiveness, real as it is, obscures a more complicated situation. Among boys, researchers find a small group that is consistently aggressive starting in childhood and continuing into adolescence, and a much larger group that is consistently *non*aggressive from childhood into adolescence (Broidy et al., 2003; Tremblay & Nagin, 2005). Still other boys are moderately aggressive as children, but become less so as they move into adolescence. Similar groupings show up among girls. There is a small group that is consistently aggressive, a much larger group that is consistently nonaggressive, and a group that becomes less aggressive from childhood to adolescence. There are, however, two important differences: the girls who become less aggressive as teens become *much* less aggressive; and the levels of aggressiveness of the girls are much lower than those of the boys across all the groups (Broidy et al., 2003).

As long as observers kept their attention fixed on physical aggression, it seemed very clear that boys are more aggressive than girls. In recent years, however, more and more studies have focused on indirect or *relational aggression* (Crick & Grotpeter, 1995; Vaillancourt, 2005). This form of aggression, which was described earlier, in Chapter 6, involves harming others by damaging their social relationships. For example, a relationally aggressive teen might spread nasty rumors about a classmate or try to turn the other person's friends against him or her. Because adolescent girls form tighter social groups than boys, and because they are more concerned about preserving intimacy, relational aggression poses a bigger threat to them (Rose & Rudolph, 2006). For example, one recent study found that girls expect the highest level of aggressive responses when something goes wrong in close one-to-one relationships (Benenson, Sinclair, & Dolenszky, 2006).

When relational aggression was discovered by the public, it was often described as something peculiar to girls (Simmons, 2002; Wiseman, 2002). An early chapter in one popular book was entitled, "Why Girls are Prone to RA" (Dellasega & Nixon, 2003), and people flocked to watch the film, *Mean Girls* (2004). Certainly there is a common gender stereotype of girls whispering behind one another's backs while boys slug it out on the playground, but is this really the case? Are girls more relationally aggressive than boys? The evidence is mixed (Underwood, 2003). Some researchers find more relational aggression among girls than among boys (for instance, Salmivalli, Kaukiainen, & Lagerspetz, 2000; Zimmer-Gembeck et al., 2005). Other researchers find no difference (for instance, Pakaslahti & Keltigangas-Jarvinen, 2000). There have even been studies in which the *boys* used more relational aggression (David & Kistner, 2000; Peets & Kikas, 2006). What is clear is that the *proportion* of relational to other forms of aggression is higher for girls. When girls want to do harm to someone, they are much more likely to use indirect means, such as rumors or exclusion, than to throw a punch or insult the other person to his or her face (Crick, Casas, & Nelson, 2002).

Personal Relationships

Imagine that a friend of yours who teaches 8th grade asks you to help out on a class trip. You are in the middle of this chapter on gender, so you seize the opportunity to carry out an observational study. In other words, you watch the teens and take mental notes on the ways boys and girls act similarly or differently. Several things are likely to catch your attention right away. The boys and girls mostly hang out in separate groups, and the groups of boys are generally larger and looser than the groups of girls—half a dozen boys in a group, versus two or three girls. As for the ways they act, there are not many similarities for you to note, and lots of differences. The boys are horsing around, trading jokes, mock insults, and mock punches, while the girls are deep into what look like intense private conversations with one another.

These are gender stereotypes, of course, and of course there are many exceptions. Girls do laugh and kid around, and boys do have serious heart-to-heart talks, but in this case, as in others, the stereotypes turn out to have a solid basis in fact. From childhood, girls care more about personal relationships, and put more energy into them,

◄ **Learning Objective 10.10**
Why are personal relationships closer for girls?

than boys do. The kinds of stresses peer relationships create are different for girls, and so are the emotional benefits girls gain from those relationships (Galambos, 2004; Rose & Rudolph, 2006). Each of these differences deserves a closer look.

By early adolescence, girls are more likely than boys to see the goals of relationships as friendship, support, and mutual involvement (Murphy & Eisenberg, 2002; Rose & Asher, 2004; Strough & Berg, 2000). More than boys, they want to feel close and interdependent with others, to keep their relationships intact, and to resolve problems as they come up (Henrich, Blatt, Kuperminc, Zohar, & Leadbetter, 2001; Rose & Asher, 2004). Because they place such importance on personal relationships, girls are more likely than boys to worry about hurting others, losing friends as a result of getting angry, and being rejected and lonely (Henrich et al., 2001).

The ways girls behave in peer relationships reflect the importance they give them. They spend more time in social conversation, and they disclose more personal information about themselves in these conversations, than boys do (Buhrmester & Furman, 1987; McNelles & Connolly, 1999; Rose, 2002). It is not that much of a caricature to say that girls talk about feelings and friends, and boys talk about cars and sports (Tannen, 1990). Girls are more sensitive to distress in others and show more empathy than boys (Tucker, Updegraff, McHale, & Crouter, 1999), and they are more likely to act in a prosocial way when conflicts arise (Sandstrom & Cillessen, 2003; Storch, Brassard, & Masia-Warner, 2003).

Connect the **Dots...**

On average, girls are more likely than boys to deal with problems in their personal relationships by talking them over with friends. What advantages do you see to this approach, and what disadvantages?

Boys and girls generally experience about the same level of conflict in their friendships, but girls are more likely to experience more of other kinds of friendship stress, such as being dropped or betrayed by a friend (Rose & Asher, 2004; Rudolph, 2002). When something bad does happen in a relationship, girls are more likely than boys to talk about their problems and look for support from other close friends (Bowker, Bukowski, Hymel, & Sippola, 2000; Hunter & Boyle, 2004). This often takes the form of **co-rumination,** in which friends dwell on and hash over their problems and the thoughts and feelings set off by the problems (Connor-Smith, Compas, Wadsworth, Thomsen, & Saltzman, 2000; Rose, 2002; Starr & Davila, 2008). This way of coping with difficulties may be effective, but it is linked to depression, which, as we saw a little earlier, becomes much more common in girls than in boys during adolescence (Stone & Hankin, 2007).

Compared to boys, girls gain a lot from their peer relationships, including more affection, closeness, trust, and acceptance (Rose & Rudolph, 2006). The price for these advantages is a greater risk of developing emotional problems, such as low self-esteem and depression, that are connected to feelings about status, popularity, and acceptance. In addition, the very intensity of their friendships make them more fragile, as is pointed out in this chapter's Research in the Spotlight on page 347. By contrast, the ways boys relate to one another may put them at greater risk for behavioral problems such as aggression, but at the same time give them some defenses against emotional problems (Rose & Rudolph, 2006).

Aside from whatever benefits they may bring, *why* do these gender differences in ways of relating to peers develop? Some differences can be seen even in early childhood, but it is clear that the differences become more pronounced with adolescence (Rose & Rudolph, 2006). We have seen that puberty brings increased social pressure to conform to traditional roles, and that the female role stresses intimacy and emotionality in a way that the male role does not.

Co-rumination A process in which friends talk about their problems and negative feelings at length, sometimes prolonging or amplifying the feelings.

Homophobia A pronounced attitude of fear or distaste for feelings of sexual attraction toward one's own sex or for those who are thought to have such feelings.

There are also strong cultural pressures that actively discourage and even punish close friendships among boys. Widespread **homophobia**—a fear and loathing of feelings of sexual attraction to others of one's own sex—makes any intimacy between boys personally and socially risky. Well before puberty, and before boys have any clear notion of sexuality in general or homosexuality in particular, they know that being called a "faggot" is a terrible insult to be avoided at almost any cost (Pascoe, 2005; Poteat & Espelage, 2007). If the cost includes keeping one's emotional distance from other boys, so be it. As the (very masculine gender-typed) saying has it, "He travels fastest who travels alone."

Gender and the Fragility of Close Friendships

One thing that is clear about same-sex friendships is that adolescent girls have closer relationships with one another than do adolescent boys. As we have seen, girls spend more time talking about personal matters, such as friends, hopes, and feelings, and in the process they share self-related information on a more confidential and intimate level. Does this greater intimacy mean that girls' friendships are stronger and more lasting than those of boys? Apparently not. A recent study by psychologists Joyce Benenson and Athena Christakos shows just the opposite. According to their findings, girls' relationships with their closest friends are actually more *fragile* than boys' closest friendships.

The participants in the study were boys and girls in the 5th, 7th, and 9th grades in a lower-middle-class area of Montréal, Québec. To get more detailed information about the children's closest friendships, the investigators interviewed each child individually. The questions included how often the child interacted with his or her closest friend, how long they had been friends, and how bad the child would feel if the friendship ended. Participants were also asked to tell about earlier close friendships that had ended.

Boys and girls spent about the same amount of time talking or hanging out with their closest friend. However, as Benenson and Christakos had predicted, the girls' closest friendships were a good deal newer—that is, had lasted less time so far—than the boys' closest friendships. When asked how they would feel if the friendship ended, the girls imagined that they would feel much worse than the boys did and said that their lives would be changed more. At the same time, more than twice as many girls as boys confided that their closest friend had *already* done something that threatened or damaged their friendship.

In addition, a good many more girls than boys told the researchers about someone who had once been their closest friend but who was no longer a friend. Boys and girls felt equally bad about having such a close same-sex friendship come to an end, but the girls said their lives were changed more by the breakup than boys did.

Why are close friendships more precarious and more dangerous for girls than for boys? Benenson and Chirstakos offer a couple of possible explanations. One is that the greater intimacy in girls' close friendships creates greater possible risks (Crick & Grotpeter, 1995). If I know your deepest, most personal secrets and we come into a conflict, I just might be tempted to divulge what I know to someone else, as a way of getting back at you. And if I do yield to that temptation, you will probably find the betrayal very, very hard to forgive and forget. Boys, in contrast, are more likely to deal with conflicts with friends by a direct confrontation that may be easier to get over.

Another factor that makes girls' close friendships more vulnerable is also connected to their greater intimacy. Boys' friendships tend to exist in the context of a larger group of buddies, while those of girls are more likely to occur in isolation. When conflicts come up, others in a group can serve as allies, mediators, and even alternative friends. Loyalty to the group also offers a good reason to keep a conflict from going too far. Without these moderating influences, girls may find that misunderstandings and arguments can quickly escalate beyond the point at which the relationship can be saved.

Source: Benenson, J. F., & Christakos, A., 2003, pp. 1123–1129.

Ethnic and Cultural Differences

In 2006, the Dutch government commissioned a film about their culture to be shown to people, mostly from Third World countries, who want to immigrate to the Netherlands. The treatment of gender standards included footage of men and women at a nude beach. This alone would have made the film illegal in some parts of the world, so a second version was also made, leaving out the nude shots. What was the point of the film? According to a spokeswoman for the Ministry of Immigration, "People do need to know what kind of country they are coming to. You have to know a little about the values here, like the fact that men and women have the same rights" (Crouch, 2006, p. A4).

Those who live within a particular culture often take it for granted that their culture's gender roles are "natural" or built in (Liben, 2004). In fact, different cultures vary, sometimes quite widely, in what is accepted or prescribed for males and females. Consider, as the Dutch filmmakers did, the question of proper dress, especially for females. In some countries, a girl or woman who reveals anything more than her face is thought of as indecent. In others, including the United States, the fashion among

◄ **Learning Objective 10.11**
What is the impact of culture and ethnicity on gender roles?

▶ Girls in more traditional societies are often faced with a clash between different cultural values and customs.

teenage girls, and even preteens, is to reveal as much of the body as possible without getting in trouble with parents and school officials (Trebay, 2003).

Social scientists describe the gender beliefs of cultures in broad terms as *traditional* or *modern*. In traditional cultures, men are seen as more important than women, and it is considered appropriate for men to dominate and control women. In modern cultures, women and men are said to be equal in their rights, educational and occupational opportunities, and social position (Best & Thomas, 2004). A major cross-cultural study of university students found that those in European countries such as the Netherlands, England, and Italy scored highest in modern attitudes, while those in African and Asian countries such as Nigeria, Pakistan, and Malaysia scored highest in traditional attitudes. Interestingly, the United States fell squarely in the middle (Williams & Best, 1990).

Ethnic Differences. Why didn't the American students in this study end up more clearly in either the modern or traditional group? One explanation is that *within* American culture, there are substantial and complex differences in gender roles and gender-related attitudes that are linked to people's race, ethnicity, and social class (Kane, 2000). Until recently, research on gender development in American adolescents has focused mainly on those from White middle-class backgrounds, which makes it hard to say very much with certainty about those from underrepresented groups (Galambos, 2004). Even so, we can point to some important ways in which the gender differences we have just examined do not necessarily take the same form among non-White or non-middle-class teens.

As an example, take self-esteem. As we saw in an earlier section of this chapter, girls have lower self-esteem than boys from early adolescence on. A major contributor to this is that girls are more dissatisfied with the way their bodies look, and in particular tend to think that they are overweight (Smolak, 2004). However, although African American girls generally have a heavier build than their European American peers (Dawson, 1988), they are also more satisfied with their bodies and have higher self-esteem (Kelly, Wall, Eisenberg, Story, & Neumark-Sztainer, 2005; Turnage, 2004). This reflects the different standards for female attractiveness in the African American community (Perry, Rosenblatt, & Wang, 2004; Thompson, Sargent, & Kemper, 1996). It is not universally so, however. Those African American girls who identify more closely with the majority culture also show more distorted body images (Abrams & Stormer, 2002).

Hispanic Americans and Gender. The gender role attitudes of Hispanic American adolescents also reveal a tension between the standards of their ethnic background and those of the majority culture. Hispanic Americans are diverse in their origins, from those whose families have been in the United States for generations, to those more recently arrived from a variety of countries in Latin America. However, they share traditions that emphasize family relationships, childbearing, respect for those higher on the social ladder, and strong gender role divisions. Men are supposed to be strong and independent, and women are expected to be chaste and submissive (Mayo & Resnick, 1996). Children—especially daughters—are raised to take in and uphold these values (Raffaelli & Ontai, 2004).

These traditions are still current. Hispanic Americans generally hold more traditional gender-related attitudes than African Americans or European Americans (Kane, 2000). However, the longer their families have been in the United States, the more their attitudes are like those of mainstream Americans. Their generation matters, too. Second-generation Hispanic women are less traditional in their gender attitudes than those of the first generation (Leaper & Valin, 1996; Valentine & Mosley, 2000). More education, better command of English, and having non-Hispanic friends also predict less traditional gender attitudes (Phinney & Flores, 2002). What this suggests is that more exposure to the mainstream culture weakens attachment to traditional gender values, especially for girls and women attracted by the idea of having more personal freedom.

A recent study of Arab American adolescents makes a similar point. Those who try to conform to Arab cultural values find themselves at odds with the dominant cultural norms in the United States, and those who try to fit in with the majority culture are seen as challenging Arab cultural values (Ajrouch, 2004). The conflict is perhaps sharpest for girls, who are even expected not to have any contact with boys outside their family, but it poses problems for boys as well. For example, brothers are expected to protect their sisters and make sure they do not break the gender rules. But what is a boy to do if he notices his sister talking to a male classmate, rebukes her, and is told to go mind his own business? Is what she does his business, or isn't it? The answer depends on which set of cultural standards each of them is appealing to.

Summing Up...

In adolescence boys begin to get higher math grades and test scores than girls. The reasons advanced include hormone effects, parent and teacher expectations, and stereotype threat. Girls' self-esteem declines more than boys' during early adolescence, partly in response to greater body dissatisfaction. Differences in emotionality also emerge during adolescence. Girls suffer more from depression, in part because they invest more in close personal relationships. Gender attitudes are in part a function of culture and ethnic background and range from very traditional, in which males dominate, to more modern, which stress gender equality.

SOCIAL CONTEXTS OF GENDER DEVELOPMENT

As a child, I came to realize that men were expected to take off their hats in the presence of women. That particular gender role standard gradually died out, in part because most American men stopped wearing hats. A culture, or a subgroup within a culture, may have clear ideas about how males and females should be and act, but for those gender role standards to survive, they have to be passed along successfully to the next generation of children and adolescents. How does this happen? Social scientists generally agree that the answer involves an ongoing interaction between the individual child and the social contexts he or she takes part in (Lerner, 2002). Among the most influential of these contexts in affecting gender-related attitudes and behaviors are the *family*, *peers*, and, increasingly, the *mass media*. Let's look at each of these in turn.

Parents and Siblings

► **Learning Objective 10.12**
How is gender typing affected by parents and siblings?

▲ In many American families, gender stereotypes dictate who does which household chores.

If you ask people why boys and girls are different, one answer you will often hear is that their parents treat them differently. This is certainly true in some obvious ways. Pay a quick visit to the children's section of a clothing store and look at the racks of frilly pink garments on one side and sturdy blue duds on the other. Surprisingly, however, when researchers observe parents and children, they find that when it comes to many areas of social behavior, such as cooperation, aggression, and independence, parents mostly treat boys and girls similarly (Lytton & Romney, 1991; McHale, Crouter, & Whiteman, 2003).

One way in which fathers and mothers do treat children differently concerns involvement and communication. In families that include both girls and boys, parents spend more time with the child of their own sex (McHale et al., 2003). Mothers talk to their children more and in more supportive ways, while fathers ask more questions, provide more information, and give more directions (Leaper, Anderson, & Sanders, 1998). Along with the content of these interchanges, parents are also giving children a chance to watch and compare the contrasting ways an adult male and adult female interact with others (Tannen, 1990).

Children notice gender-typed features in the relationship between their parents, too. Who does the dishes? Who makes up the grocery list? Who is the main breadwinner? If both parents work and they come home equally tired, who makes sure that dinner gets on the table? One study of young adolescents found that in families where the parents followed a more traditional division of labor, the girls became increasingly involved in housework, while the boys spent more and more time on male-type chores such as washing the car (Crouter, Manke, & McHale, 1995).

In addition, parents are swayed by gender stereotypes in the activities they encourage their children to take up. A girl is more likely to be offered dance lessons than boxing lessons, and just the opposite for a boy. In one recent study, parents were asked to teach their young adolescent children several science tasks. The boys and girls were similar in their science grades and level of interest, but the parents were likely to think that the girls were both less interested and less able in science (Tenenbaum & Leaper, 2003). Another interesting finding from the study was that fathers used more complicated language and concepts when teaching boys, which suggests that they did not expect a girl to understand the material as easily. A related study looked at low-income mothers who were playing with a set of magnets with their children. The mothers used more science-related talk with sons than with daughters, and the proportion of such talk predicted how well the children understood science texts 2 years later (Tenenbaum, Snow, Roach, & Kurland, 2005).

Brothers and sisters who are close in age are also powerful influences on one another. Outside of school, they are one another's most frequent companion (McHale & Crouter, 1996). While together they serve as models; teachers; sources of praise, criticism, and advice; social partners; and sometimes sparring partners. They also offer each other a chance to watch how their parents treat the other child, and children watch this very carefully indeed. Few things in family life can set off indignation like the impression that a sibling is getting favored treatment, especially if the favoritism seems to be based on gender. One woman I know still bristles when she recalls that in her family, her older brother always got the bigger lamb chop because he was a boy and older.

Siblings have such an impact on one another that they are more consistently similar to each other in their gender-linked attributes than they are to their parents. However, the current of influence runs stronger from the older to the younger child (McHale, Updegraff, Helms-Erikson, & Crouter, 2001). Research on school-age siblings in a free play situation found that the sex of the older sibling largely determined the ways they played. Younger girls and boys with an older brother played more with balls, cars, and toy weapons, while those with an older sister were more likely to get involved in art projects, doll play, or playing house (Stoneman, Brody, & MacKinnon, 1986). This study also showed that both boys and girls who had an older sibling of the other sex held less stereotyped gender role concepts than those with a same-sex older

Connect the **Dots...**

Do you have siblings of the other sex, either older or younger? If so, how do you think that affected your own gender role development and theirs? Can you think of particular occasions that support your conclusions?

sibling. Apparently, it is harder to develop a stereotyped view of either your own or the other sex when you are interacting on a daily basis with a sibling of the other sex.

Peers

We saw earlier in the chapter the many ways in which gender roles affect peer relationships (Rose & Rudolph, 2006). At the same time, peer relationships have an important effect on gender roles (Maccoby, 2002). From around age 3 until early adolescence, children choose to spend most of their free play time exclusively with others of their own sex, and the ways they spend that time are decidedly different. Groups of boys engage more in competitive games, conflicts, dominance efforts, and rough and tumble play, while groups of girls, usually smaller in number, tend to talk and act reciprocally and in group harmony (Maccoby, 1998). In the process, the members of the groups are both modeling and responding to gender-typed behaviors—more competition for the boys, more intimacy for the girls (Rubin, Bukowski, & Parker, 2006).

With adolescence, gender-typed attributes and behaviors take on added importance as ways to impress and attract those of the other sex. As has already been mentioned, young adolescents generally consider more "feminine" girls and more "masculine" boys to be most attractive (Feiring, 1999). It is a cliche that the girl who at 10 was the most daring tree-climber in the neighborhood turns timorous and demure at 13, trading her worn jeans and t-shirt for more feminine garb, but the cliche is based in reality (Carr, 2007). In a similar way, young adolescent boys who start arm-wrestling or trading mock insults check surreptitiously to make sure the girls nearby are noticing. Chances are, the girls *are* noticing, even if they pretend not to.

On the whole, adolescents who feel more gender-typical and more able to succeed at gender-typical activities have higher self-esteem, while those who feel under greater pressure to conform to typical gender roles have bigger adjustment problems (Egan & Perry, 2001; Yunger, Carver, & Perry, 2004). Boys judge gender nonconformity more harshly than do girls, and nonconforming boys are judged much more harshly than nonconforming girls (Bayly, Sippola, & Buchanan, 2006). This does not necessarily mean that teens *must* adopt stereotyped gender identities to be socially accepted and psychologically healthy. Those gender nonconformists who are looked down on and excluded by their peers have a rough time of it, but those who are *not* excluded for their nonconformity do not suffer for it (Smith & Leaper, 2006). Because adolescents have at least some freedom to choose or construct their own reference group of peers, those who do not fit traditional gender stereotypes may eventually succeed in finding other teens who tolerate, accept, or even admire them.

◄ **Learning Objective 10.13**
How do adolescents respond to peers who are more or less gender typical?

The Media

The amount of exposure adolescents have to mass media, and the freedom they have to decide what they expose themselves to, are something quite new in human history (Comstock & Scharrer, 2006). Just 50 years ago, an average American adolescent had access to a radio, probably a television, perhaps a record player, and whatever papers and magazines came into the home. All of these were usually in the living room or family room, where parents could keep tabs on how much and what their children were watching, listening to, and reading. Today, according to surveys, almost two-thirds of teens have a television in their room, 88% have a CD player, 86% a radio, 45% a video game console, 36% a VCR, and 22% a computer (Roberts & Foehr, 2004). These figures do not include DVD players or iPods, which became widespread after the survey was done. Nor does all this equipment sit there gathering dust. Adolescents spend some 2-1/2 hours a day watching television and over 6 hours a day in total media exposure (Comstock & Scharrer, 2006).

◄ **Learning Objective 10.14**
What impact do images of gender roles offered by the media have on teens?

Functions of Media. One of the important functions the media play in teens' lives is to give them information about other people, social relationships, and the world in general. Some of this information is conveyed directly, but much of it is more implicit.

Not surprisingly, given how pervasive gender roles and gender concerns are in modern society, much of this information is about males, females, and the relationships among them. Much of it, whether in dramas, comedies, or commercials, relies heavily on gender stereotypes, rather than accurate reflections of reality. Women are underrepresented, especially in positions of power, leadership, or decision making. They are underrepresented in another sense too, because most of the women who *do* appear are unrealistically young, beautiful, and above all, thin (Galambos, 2004; Ganahl, Prinsen, & Netzley, 2003). When women who are not pencil-thin are depicted, they often get negative comments about their weight from male characters, comments that are reinforced by the show's laugh track (Fouts & Burggraf, 2000).

Media, Gender, and Body Image. How does prolonged exposure to this misinformation about gender affect adolescents? Correlational studies have repeatedly connected the amount of television viewing to more gender-typed views and attitudes (Signorielli, 2001). In particular, more television watching has been linked to poorer body image in adolescent girls and boys (Anderson, Huston, Schmitt, Linebarger, & Wright, 2001; Polce-Lynch, Myers, Kliewer, & Kilmartin, 2001). Nor is television the only source of effects like these. In one clever experiment, female undergraduates sat in a waiting room with either fashion magazines or news magazines, and then completed a questionnaire about dieting. Those who had been exposed to the fashion magazines said they were more unhappy about their weight and more afraid of getting fat than those who had seen the news magazines (Turner, Hamilton, Jacobs, Angood, & Dwyer, 1997).

Music videos are another widely popular source of stereotyped information about gender that is aimed directly at adolescents. In a typical music video, scantily dressed girls shimmy, shake, and do whatever else they can to attract the attention of the cool, powerful male musician, who often seems more interested in his microphone or guitar (Arnett, 2002). In one recent study, African American high school students were asked about their music video viewing habits and their gender role attitudes. Then they were shown either four gender-stereotyped videos or four non-stereotyped videos. As the researchers expected, more frequent music video watching was linked to more traditional gender role standards. In addition, those who saw the stereotyped videos in the lab expressed more traditional views about gender than those who saw the non-stereotyped videos (Ward, Hansbrough, & Walker, 2005). Even watching for a quarter of an hour or so, it seems, can have a measurable impact on teens.

The media have indirect as well as direct effects on the gender attitudes of adolescents. One study measured the magazine preferences and body dissatisfaction of 7th and 10th graders in two successive years. Reading appearance magazines, such as *Seventeen* and *Fitness*, did not directly predict a poor body image. However, boys who

Connect the **Dots...**

During the next few days, have a notepad and pen nearby when you watch television. Keep track of the proportion of lead characters who are male and female. How do they interact? What about them is the audience supposed to admire? Are there characters who are made fun of? If so, on what basis, and does it vary with their gender?

▶ Music videos have a powerful impact on the gender role attitudes of teens.

read such magazines talked more to their friends about muscle-building, and girls who read them talked more to their friends about dieting, and these social behaviors *were* linked to more body dissatisfaction (King & Jones, 2006).

Where Are Gender Roles Going?

During the 1970s, an upsurge of interest in gender roles and the place of women in society led some social scientists to take a closer look at the way gender roles had usually been thought of (Bem, 1977; Spence & Helmreich, 1978). One thing they noticed was that the concepts of masculinity and femininity were generally treated in either/or terms, as opposite ends of a single dimension. In other words, a person who was considered high in feminine traits (nurturing, sensitive, expressive . . .) was automatically expected to be low in masculine traits (assertive, analytical, independent . . .), and vice versa. But was that necessarily so? Or could it be the product of a particular way of *thinking* about gender? What would happen if people's "masculine" and "feminine" characteristics were measured *separately?*

The answer to that question is diagrammed in Figure 10.4. Some people (mostly males) are high in masculine and low in feminine traits, and others (mostly females) are high in feminine and low in masculine traits. Some score low on both sorts of traits. The interesting group, however, is the fourth one. These, males and females, are high in *both* masculine and feminine characteristics and are said to display psychological **androgyny.** In one classic study of college students (Spence & Helmreich, 1978), about two-thirds of the men scored as masculine and two-thirds of the women as feminine. Fewer than 1 in 10 were in the undifferentiated group. The rest, some 30% of the men and women fell in the androgynous category. More recent research on college students found that even higher proportions, 45% of the women and 34% of the men, were classified as androgynous (Morrison & Shaffer, 2003).

Those who developed the concept of psychological androgyny also suggested that androgynous individuals are better off than those stuck in a rigid gender type because they are more flexible in their social responses and more responsive to the demands of a situation (Bem, 1977). They can be independent and assertive when that is called for, and nurturing and sympathetic when that is appropriate (Harter, Waters, Whitesell, & Kastelic, 1998). Androgynous children and adolescents do seem to be better adjusted and have higher self-esteem than those with more traditional gender roles (Allgood-Merton & Stockard, 1991).

At the same time, there are reasons to think that being androgynous may have more favorable results for girls than for boys, at least once they reach adolescence (Galambos, 2004). Girls continue to have a wider range of attitudes and behaviors available to them, while boys continue to come under considerably more social pressure from parents and

◄ **Learning Objective 10.15**
What is psychological androgyny?

Androgyny Having both typically masculine and typically feminine psychological characteristics.

Figure 10.4   Gender Role Orientations
Together, levels of masculinity and femininity generate four gender role orientations.

		Femininity	
		High	Low
Masculinity	High	Androgynous	Masculine sex-typed
	Low	Feminine sex-typed	Undifferentiated

▲ Androgynous girls, who are high in masculine as well as feminine traits, are accepted and admired.

peers to fit into traditional masculine roles (Bayly et al., 2006; Egan & Perry, 2001). In other words, what works socially may not be androgyny so much as masculinity, and it works for girls as well as for boys. Androgynous girls, who are high in masculine as well as feminine traits, are accepted and admired, and boys who are high in masculine *but not* feminine traits are accepted and admired (Massad, 1981). Apparently what has changed in the last half century, then, is not that society has moved beyond traditional gender roles, but that girls and women have received permission to express their more masculine side, as long as they also hold onto their femininity. Adolescent girls can take up rock-climbing and run for class president, but adolescent boys are still expected to hide any feelings of weakness, sadness, fear, or tenderness (Pollack, 1998).

Does this mean that traditional gender roles are a permanent feature of human society, at least for males? Not necessarily. What seems to produce the best adjustment in children is a combination of feeling pretty much like other children of your sex and *not* feeling under strong social pressure to conform to traditional gender roles (Carver, Yunger, & Perry, 2003). This suggests that if the range of observed and accepted attitudes and behaviors becomes wider, more children with more different ways of being will be able to see themselves as gender typical and therefore okay. We know that the content and flexibility of gender roles have been different in different eras and different cultures (for example, Mead, 1935). What we don't know is what future generations of adolescents will consider to be typical and appropriate gender roles, or even if they will consider the question to be very important.

Summing Up...

Parents and siblings are powerful influences on gender roles, both as models and as sources of praise and criticism. Teens, too, model and respond to the gender-typed behaviors of their peers. Those who are more gender typical are generally considered more attractive and have higher self-esteem. The media's message that males are active and aggressive, while females are thin and attractive, fosters gender-typed attitudes and poorer body image in both boys and girls. Psychological androgyny—having both masculine and feminine positive traits—has been linked to better adjustment, but may be more beneficial for girls than for boys.

SUMMARY

Gender is one of the basic categories that adolescents use to understand themselves and others.

Shared cultural expectations about how females and males should look, act, think, and feel—**gender roles**—are passed along to new generations by the process of **gender typing**. Several approaches to understanding gender typing are current.

Learning Objective 10.1 How do genes and hormones affect gender development?

Biological approaches stress the ways genetic and hormonal differences between males and females affect physical and neurological development.

Learning Objective 10.2 How do others model and shape gender-related attitudes and behaviors?

Socialization approaches stress the importance of gendered social influences, including the models of gendered behavior that parents and peers present and the ways other people respond to gender typical and gender atypical attitudes and behaviors.

Learning Objective 10.3 Why are gender identity and gender schemas important?

Cognitive approaches stress the ways a child's understanding of gender leads to the achievement of **gender consistency** and the construction of **gender schemas** and a coherent **gender identity**.

Learning Objective 10.4 How can different views be combined to understand gender development?

An ecological systems approach offers an integrated account of how a person's sex and gender act on and are acted on by the social contexts in which the person is embedded.

Learning Objective 10.5 What is gender intensification?

Although accounts of gender development focus mainly on infancy and childhood, the physical and psychological changes of puberty may lead to **gender intensification,** increased social pressures during early adolescence to conform to traditional gender roles.

Males and females are much more similar than different, but the differences, real or supposed, tend to draw more attention and research.

Learning Objective 10.6 How does stereotype threat relate to gender differences in achievement?

In school, girls are widely believed to do better in verbal areas, whereas boys do better in math. There is a gender difference in math performance, but not until early adolescence. Explanations include testosterone levels, childhood experiences with spatial toys, parent and teacher expectations, and stereotype threat.

Learning Objective 10.7 What effects does gender have on teen self-esteem?

During early adolescence, self-esteem declines more sharply for girls than for boys. One reason is that girls experience greater body dissatisfaction than boys. Girls' self-esteem and confidence may also suffer as they realize that their interest in and sensitivity to human relationships is not as highly valued by society as the practical problem solving more typical of boys. This is said to lead to them silencing their distinctive "voice."

Learning Objective 10.8 How does gender relate to emotion and mood in adolescence?

During adolescence, gender differences in emotionality also emerge. Girls display both happiness and fear more openly, and boys display anger more easily. During childhood, depression is equally frequent among boys and girls, but from puberty and into adulthood, girls are twice as likely to become depressed. One explanation is that girls tend to brood about their problems while boys tend to distract themselves from negative feelings.

Learning Objective 10.9 In what ways are teenage boys more aggressive than girls and in what ways not?

Boys are more physically aggressive than girls throughout childhood and adolescence. Relational aggression is found among boys as well as girls, but makes up a larger proportion of aggressive behavior for girls.

Learning Objective 10.10 Why are personal relationships closer for girls?

Adolescent girls place more importance on close personal relationships than do boys. They spend more time in conversations, disclose more about themselves, and show more empathy to others than do boys.

Learning Objective 10.11 What is the impact of culture and ethnicity on gender roles?

All cultures define gender roles, but the content of these roles varies greatly across cultures and even within cultures. Broadly speaking, more traditional cultures see men as more important than women and more modern cultures adopt a goal of gender equality.

Children and adolescents acquire a knowledge and acceptance of gender roles as they interact with the social contexts in which they find themselves.

Learning Objective 10.12 How is gender typing affected by parents and siblings?

Mothers and fathers tend to talk differently to boys and girls, to divide household duties along gender typical lines, and to encourage gender-typed interests and activities. Those with siblings of the other sex hold less stereotyped gender concepts and interests.

Learning Objective 10.13 How do adolescents respond to peers who are more or less gender typical?

Young adolescents consider more feminine girls and more masculine boys to be most attractive. Gender nonconformity in adolescence is judged harshly, especially by boys.

Learning Objective 10.14 What impact do images of gender roles offered by the media have on teens?

For teens, a major source of information and influence on gender roles is the media. The media portray adults in heavily gender-stereotyped ways. Men are strong, active, and effective, and women are young, beautiful, dependent, and thin. Television watching and reading teen magazines have been linked to gender-stereotyped attitudes and poor body image in adolescent boys and girls.

Learning Objective 10.15 What is psychological androgyny?

Adolescents who have both masculine and feminine typed characteristics are said to exhibit **androgyny**. Androgynous teens often are better adjusted and have higher self-esteem than those with more traditional gender attitudes.

KEY TERMS

Sex difference (328)
Gender difference (328)
Gender role (328)
Gender typing (329)

Socialization (331)
Gender consistency (332)
Gender identity (332)
Gender schema theory (332)

Gender intensification
  hypothesis (335)
Co-rumination (346)
Homophobia (346)

Androgyny (353)

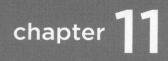
Identity

BIFF. I just can't take hold, Mom. I can't take hold of some kind of a life.
—ARTHUR MILLER, *Death of a Salesman*

This race and this country and this life produced me, he said. I shall express myself as I am.
—JAMES JOYCE, *Portrait of the Artist as a Young Man*

I yam what I yam.
—Popeye

Adolescents ask themselves questions that never occurred to them when they were children. To begin with, the far-reaching biological, social, and psychological changes of adolescence raise new questions: Why is this happening? What does it mean? Where is it leading? Will it ever stop?

At the same time, the cognitive progress adolescents achieve makes it possible for them to pose more complex questions, for example, the sort that start with, "What if . . .?", and to come up with more complex answers. Among these complex questions, none are more typical of adolescence than: What kind of person am I? What are my good and bad qualities? Where do I want my life to go? What do I believe in? What do I think is the right thing to do?

In this chapter we look at how adolescents pose these questions, how they answer them, and what their responses mean for their development.

SELF-CONCEPT AND SELF-ESTEEM

Just consider all the terms in common use that rely on the idea of self. We could start at *A*, with self-awareness, and work our way through the alphabet, by way of self-blame, self-control, self-disclosure, and self-efficacy, to self-verification, self-worth, and self-zeal. Let's not overlook *self-help*, a concept so popular that it has its own category in lists of best-selling books. The difficulty is that the term *self-* has come to be used to mean so many different things that it is often hard to know just what it is supposed to mean in a particular case.

Conceptions of the Self

▶ **Learning Objective 11.1**
How does the self-concept change during adolescence?

Over 100 years ago, William James (1890) pointed out that the self has two contrasting sides to it. There is the psychological process that allows us to think and know about ourselves, which he called the *I*. This is what people experience as the "something" inside their heads that thinks their thoughts, feels their feelings, and is the core of who they really are (Olson, 1999). But, just as important, there is also what James called the *Me*—the sum total of what a person knows or believes about himself or herself. This is the self people think about when they face questions such as, "Who am I?" or "What am I like?"

The two sides of the self that James described, the self as experiencing subject (the I) and the self as beliefs about oneself as object (the Me), continue to be widely studied (Harter, 2006; Leary & Tangney, 2002). Social scientists today also place increasing stress on understanding the self as *executive function*. This is the cognitive process that we met in Chapter 4 and that handles ongoing planning, priority setting, and decision making (Baumeister, 1998). During adolescence, far-reaching changes take place in each of these aspects of the self.

Developing a Sense of Self. Do newborn babies have any inkling that they are separate from the world around them? It is not at all clear that they do (Harter, 2006), but certainly such a sense starts to develop very early. During the first year babies begin to react differently to images of themselves than they do to images of others (Rochat & Striano, 2002). By age 2, they can recognize their own image in a mirror (Lewis & Brooks-Gunn, 1979), even if their culture has not given them any earlier experience with mirrors (Priel & deSchonen, 1986).

If you ask preschoolers, "Who are you?" they have no trouble describing themselves in individual ways. Their answers, however, generally stay with concrete categories such as age, sex, physical characteristics, achievements, and personal likings: "I'm 3-years-old . . . I have blue eyes . . . I know all of my ABCs . . . I like pizza . . ." (Harter, 1999, p. 37). Only toward early adolescence do more psychological terms begin to show up in self-descriptions: "I'm old-fashioned . . . I try to be helpful . . . Mostly I'm good, but I lose my temper . . ." (Montemayor & Eisen, 1977, p. 318).

The Self-Concept in Adolescence. With adolescence, major changes take place in the **self-concept**, or the way teens think about, understand, and describe themselves. Over the course of the teenage years, the self-concept becomes:

more *complex*;

more *differentiated*;

more *abstract*; and

more *integrated*.

The *complexity* of an adolescent's self-concept shows itself in the sheer variety of personal and interpersonal traits that show up in self-descriptions, from friendly and obnoxious to tolerant, popular, rebellious, and responsible. It is important to note that the list often includes both positive and negative traits. This too is a sign of more complex thinking. Teens also go beyond apparent external characteristics ("I'm tall . . . I play soccer . . .") to describe personal beliefs, attitudes, motives, and emotions. This requires them to turn their gaze inward on those aspects of the self that are private and really known only to themselves. They may also have to keep in mind any discrepancies between the ways they feel privately and the ways they present themselves to others.

Adolescents make more, and more subtle, *differentiations* when they describe themselves. They are more sensitive to the ways situations interact with their internal states. Instead of making a global statement like, "I am cheerful," as a 10-year-old might, someone who is 15 would be more likely to say, "I am cheerful *unless* my parents have been getting on my case," or "I am cheerful *except* when I'm stressed by schoolwork, then I turn into a real grump." In other words, they are able to notice more than one aspect of their behavior—their habitual characteristics *and* the circumstances that alter those characteristics—and to think about these different aspects at the same time.

Another way in which the self-concepts of adolescents become more differentiated is that they become more aware of possible contradictions between how they see

Self-concept The organized set of thoughts, ideas, and perceptions that people hold about themselves.

◀ Adolescents spend a lot of time pondering their actions and internal states.

themselves and how they believe others see them (Harter, 1999). A straight-A student might say, "All the kids think I'm so smart that I just breeze through school. And I let them think that, too. I'd probably hate it if anybody knew how much I shake inside every time we have a test!" Teens also become more aware of the ways they may act differently with, and be thought of differently by, people in different sectors of their lives, such as parents, teachers, school friends, camp friends, and so on.

Abstraction and Consistency. When adolescents are asked to describe themselves, rather than respond to the specific items of a questionnaire, they often include not just concrete descriptions of the ways they typically behave, but higher-order, more *abstract* generalizations as well. For example, teens who notice that they are usually friendly, able to get along with different sorts of people, and willing to consider others' points of view may fit these fairly concrete behaviors together by thinking of themselves as *tolerant* (Harter, 1990). Even though this is an abstract generalization, rather than something that can be directly observed, the inclusion of "tolerant" in the self-concept may help influence the way the adolescent responds in future situations.

As teens come to recognize the discrepancies, contradictions, and role differences in their self-concept, they also feel a need to develop an internally consistent, coherent idea of who they are. Otherwise, how can they know, among so many possibilities, which is the "real me" and which is phony? This *integration* process may make use of several strategies. In one, the adolescent resolves the apparent clash between two characteristics by introducing a higher order idea. For example, "How come I can be so happy sometimes and then be so down in the dumps? I must be a very sensitive, emotional person." Another strategy involves taking the position that behaving differently in different roles is not only common but desirable: "It wouldn't be normal to act the same way with everyone; you act one way with your friends and a different way with your parents, that's the way it should be" (Harter, 1988, p. 23).

Dealing with Discrepancies. A study by Susan Harter and Ann Monsour (1992) documents some of the processes we just examined. The participants, who were 7th, 9th, or 11th graders, were asked to describe the way they were with parents, friends, teachers, and romantic partners. They then went through these self-descriptions again, looking for discrepancies and contradictions, and indicated how bothered they were when they found them. The results are shown in Figure 11.1. The 7th graders

Figure 11.1 Perceptions of Opposing Self-Attributes
Ninth-graders are most likely to see themselves as having opposing attributes and to feel confused about this.

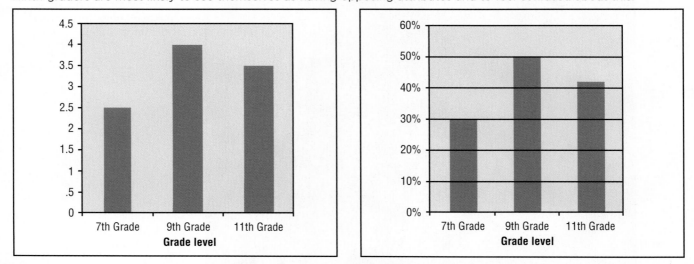

Source: Adapted from S. Harter & A. Mansour, 1992, "Developmental analysis of conflict caused by opposing attributes in the adolescent self portrait," *Developmental Psychology, 28,* p. 225. Used by permission of the American Psychological Association (APA).

did not notice many discrepancies and were not particularly bothered when they did notice them. The 9th graders noticed the largest number of inconsistencies *and* were most disturbed by them. Those in the oldest group also noticed a lot of discrepancies, but were less bothered by them, presumably because they were farther along in developing an integrated view of the self that allowed for or explained discrepancies of this sort.

The Role of Possible Selves. The abstract reasoning powers that come with adolescence make it easier to move beyond "Who am I?" to consider "Who *could* I be?" Alongside a sense of self that is based on present characteristics, teens begin to construct a sense of their **possible selves**, or the various selves they might become (Oyserman & Fryberg, 2001). These possible selves then play a role in planning, setting priorities, and self-regulation. For example, an adolescent who considers becoming a doctor an attractive and possible future self would probably choose to study for a biology exam, while one whose most important self goal is to win a lacrosse scholarship might spend the time practicing instead.

Constructing possible selves is a dynamic process that involves both expanding the range of possibilities, through hypothetical thinking, and narrowing the range, through critical thinking. As William James (1890) pointed out over a century ago, we all have to give up some of our dreams when it becomes clear they cannot be realized. Those who give up their dreams too soon, however, or who never entertain them in the first place, may be placing unnecessary boundaries on their future. These are particular risks for low-income, rural, and ethnic minority teens, who may be unaware of positive possibilities or may see poverty and discrimination as placing impassible roadblocks to achieving those possibilities (Oyserman & Fryberg, 2006).

Cognitive and Social Factors. So far we have looked at *how* self-concept develops across childhood and adolescence. But *why* does it develop that way, and in particular, why does adolescence bring such far-reaching changes? In response to these questions, social scientists point to events in both cognitive and social development. Some of the expressions in the previous sections should have sounded familiar, such as, "able to notice more than one aspect, and to think about these different aspects at the same time," "higher order abstraction," or "hypothetical thinking." We saw earlier, in Chapter 4, that with adolescence comes an increased capacity to think logically and abstractly, to understand the points of views of multiple parties in a situation, and to keep different aspects of a situation in mind simultaneously. These abilities are preconditions for the development of a more differentiated and integrated self-concept. They also make that development more likely. A teen who *can* notice personal inconsistencies eventually *will* notice them, and will be motivated, and able, to do something about them.

The word "self" has a solitary sound to it, but the way the self-concept develops is anything but solitary. From the *working models* that infants form to the complex integrated self-concept of late adolescence and adulthood, our knowledge of the self is powerfully influenced by our social relationships. This realization has a long history in social science. Over a century ago, sociologist Charles Horton Cooley (1902) introduced the term **looking-glass self** as a way of indicating that we learn to know ourselves by interacting with others and observing how they respond to us. Another pioneering sociologist, George Herbert Mead (1934), elaborated on Cooley's approach by suggesting that we pool the responses and opinions we've observed into what he called the **generalized other** and then, in effect, carry it around with us. As we saw in Chapter 6, during late childhood and early adolescence, the peer group gains more and more social importance as a source of attitudes, behaviors, and values. Cooley and Mead would add that peers, by the way they respond to an adolescent, also have a crucial influence over that adolescent's evolving self-concept.

Connect the **Dots...**

What were the most important possible selves you entertained as an adolescent? Were there some that you gave up because they seemed impractical or impossible? Were there any that you now think you may have given up too easily? To what extent was your present life course predicted or shaped by earlier possible selves?

Possible selves People's sense of the different selves they might become under various circumstances and with various courses of action.

Looking-glass self Cooley's term to indicate that we find out about ourselves by observing the way others respond to us in our interactions.

Generalized other For G. H. Mead, someone's internalized summary of the ways others have responded to that person in social interactions.

▶ Much of what teens know about themselves is learned from their interactions with others.

Self-Esteem

Suppose you asked a 15-year-old what leads her to like or dislike herself as a person. A typical response might sound something like this:

> Well, I like some things about me, but I don't like others. I'm glad that I'm popular since it's really important to me to have friends. But in school I don't do as well as the really smart kids. That's OK, because if you're too smart you'll lose your friends. So being smart is just not that important. Except to my parents. I feel like I'm letting them down when I don't do as well as they want. But what's really important to me is how I look. If I like the way I look, then I really like the kind of person I am . . . There's another thing about how much I like the kind of person I am. It matters what other people think, especially the other kids at school. It matters whether they like you. I care about what my parents think about me too. I've also changed. It started when I went to junior high school. I got really depressed. I thought it was going to be so great, like I'd feel so grown-up, and then I saw all of these new, older kids who really had it together and I didn't. So I felt terrible. There was this one day when I hated the way I looked, and I didn't get invited to this really important party, and then I got an awful report card, so for a couple of days I thought it would be best to just end it all. I mean, why bother getting up the next morning? What's the point? I was letting my parents down, I wasn't good-looking any more, and I wasn't that popular after all, and things were never going to get better. . . .
>
> —(HARTER, 1990, pp. 364–365)

One point to notice about this narrative is that while many of the statements are about how the adolescent sees herself, or her *self-concept* ("I'm popular . . . "), the focus is on how she *feels* about the way she sees herself, or her **self-esteem** ("I'm *glad* I'm popular . . .") (King, 1997). This distinction between self-concept and self-esteem may seem like a fine point, and researchers do not always follow it strictly, but it has some important implications, as we'll see.

Baseline and Barometric Self-Esteem. Notice that the most general statements in the passage just quoted are in the present tense ("I'm glad . . ." "I really like . . ." "I care . . ."). Some, however, such as "I felt terrible," get more specific and switch to the past tense. This grammatical twist reflects a crucial distinction between two aspects of self-esteem (Rosenberg, 1986). One, known as **baseline self-esteem**, is the level of positive or negative feelings about the self that is fairly stable over time (Trzesniewski, Donnellan, & Robins, 2003). Those who have high self-esteem at one point, relative

Self-esteem The set of positive or negative evaluations and feelings that people hold about themselves.

Baseline self-esteem A level of positive or negative feelings about the self that is fairly stable over time.

Figure 11.2   Baseline Self-Esteem Across the Lifespan
At puberty, self-esteem drops much more for girls than for boys.

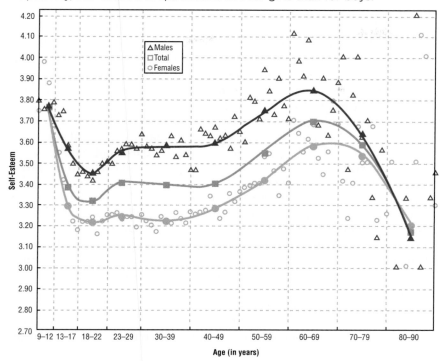

Source: R. W. Robins, K. H. Trzesniewski, J. Tracy, S. D. Gosling, & J. Potter, 2002, "Global self-esteem across the lifespan," *Psychology and Aging, 17*, p. 428. Used by permission of the American Psychological Association (APA).

to others their age, tend to have high self-esteem even years later as well, and similarly for those whose self-esteem is low for their age group.

At the same time, however, particular incidents—an unexpected compliment from a friend, an unusually low or high score on a quiz, stumbling over a word while giving an oral report in front of classmates—can temporarily make what's called **barometric self-esteem** move above or below the baseline. These swings in barometric self-esteem are wider and more frequent in early adolescence than in either childhood or later adolescence (Rosenberg, 1986), as a result of all the personal and social changes that take place during this period.

Early adolescence also marks a major change in the average level of *baseline* self-esteem. Take a look at Figure 11.2, which is based on information collected over the Internet from more than 300,000 people of all ages (Robins, Trzesniewski, Tracy, Gosling, & Potter, 2002). During late childhood, self-esteem is relatively high, but it drops sharply during early and middle adolescence. It then levels off during late adolescence and rises a little in early adulthood.

Researchers offer several explanations for this dramatic decline going into early adolescence. One explanation is that before adolescence, children have unrealistically positive views of themselves that bump up against hard facts as they move through the grade school years. Puberty, as we have seen, brings its own problems, and the ability to think more abstractly about the self may make missed opportunities and failed expectations loom larger. In addition, as we saw in Chapter 7, the transition from grade school to the more remote, challenging, and socially tricky setting of junior high school has a powerful effect on self-concept and self-esteem (Eccles, 2004; Robins & Trzesniewski, 2005).

Figure 11.2 also offers a graphic illustration of a point that was discussed earlier, in Chapter 10. The drop in self-esteem that takes place in early adolescence is markedly more severe for girls than for boys. In fact, the gender gap that opens up around the age of puberty continues on through the adult years (Kling, Hyde, Showers, & Buswell, 1999). The factors responsible for this, as we have already seen, include

Barometric self-esteem
Temporary changes in positive or negative feelings about the self that occur in response to particular incidents.

academic and social stresses, as well as gender differences in body image ideals and probably some other factors that we are still unaware of.

Contributors to Self-Esteem. The evaluations adolescents give themselves in different domains, such as school performance, athletic skill, physical appearance, and social acceptance, all contribute to their global sense of self-esteem, but they do not contribute equally. Overall, the single most influential factor is physical appearance (Harter, 2006). Teens who think they are attractive have higher self-esteem, and those who think they are unattractive have lower self-esteem.

Feeling socially accepted by peers is the second most significant factor. Especially in early adolescence, social support from peers promotes a positive sense of self-worth that, in turn, is linked to more effective coping and better adjustment (DuBois et al., 2002). Scholastic and athletic abilities have less impact, as do good behavior and staying out of trouble. One odd note is that acceptance by classmates has even more influence over self-esteem than the personal regard of close friends (Harter, 1999). Apparently close friends are *supposed* to be supportive, so their evaluations are not given as much weight as reactions from those who aren't particular friends.

Keep in mind that the findings we just looked at are about the average adolescent. There is plenty of room for individual variations in the way self-esteem is constructed. As William James (1890) pointed out, the way you evaluate yourself in a particular area will not have much impact on your self-esteem unless success in that area is important to you. For instance, I know very well that my gymnastic ability is very weak (well, to be honest, nonexistent). But since I never claimed to be a gymnast or set out to be one, admitting that shortcoming does not really make much difference in the way I feel about myself.

For some teens, how they rate their intellectual ability or their ability to make and keep close friends has more impact on their self-esteem than winning a beauty contest or a school election. For others, being chosen for the team and playing well are the only things that really make them feel worthwhile. Still others stake much of their feeling of self-worth on their romantic appeal. If that doesn't seem to be working the way it should, they are not consoled by having good friends, a seat on student council, a blemish-free complexion, or a high GPA.

Ethnic Background and Self-Esteem. The question of how an adolescent's ethnicity relates to self-esteem has drawn increasing attention from researchers in recent years. As was discussed in Chapter 1, the teen population in North America and Western Europe is becoming more diverse in ethnic and cultural background as a result of demographic changes and flows of migration. Along with the awareness of being part of a minority, those from ethnic minority backgrounds often have to cope with economic disadvantages, prejudice, and discrimination. What effects do these pressures have on adolescents and their sense of self-worth?

One view is that the dominant group in a culture defines what is considered valuable and generally favors its own characteristics, which leads to a devaluation of minority groups (Jones, 1999). If so, African Americans, with a long history of being targets of racism and discrimination, should suffer from particularly low self-esteem (Scott, 1997). However, this is not the case. Among adolescents, Blacks in fact have *higher* self-esteem than Whites, who in turn score higher than Hispanics, Asians, and American Indians (Greene & Way, 2005; Twenge & Crocker, 2002). Why should this be? One factor is the strong support Black teens receive from parents and other adults in the Black community, in part because of their shared experience of racism (Gray-Little & Hafdahl, 2000; Greene & Way, 2005).

Self-esteem is also closely linked to the person's sense of ethnic identity. This connection has been documented in many different ethnic groups (Bracey, Bámaca, & Umaña-Taylor, 2004). Those minority teens who are more closely identified with their ethnic group generally feel more positive about themselves (Oyserman, Brickman, & Rhodes, 2007; Umaña-Taylor & Fine, 2004). Because Black adolescents

Connect the **Dots...**

Can you recall people you knew during adolescence who seemed to have everything going for them but had low self-esteem? What factors do you think may have been responsible for that discrepancy?

◄ Teens who identify with their ethnic background feel more positive about themselves.

tend to have a particularly strong sense of ethnic identity (DuBois, Burk-Braxton, Swenson, Tevendale, & Hardesty, 2002), this may help explain their higher self-esteem as a group. We will take a more detailed look at the topic of ethnic identity later in this chapter.

Consequences of Low Self-Esteem. In the 1980s, the state of California funded a task force with the goal of raising the self-esteem of Californians. This effort, it was claimed, would more than pay for itself by reducing such supposed consequences of low self-esteem as crime, delinquency, underachievement, drug abuse, and teen pregnancy (Mecca, Smelser, & Vasconcellos, 1989). Unfortunately for this plan, it turned out to be very hard to show that raising self-esteem would have any impact on the social problems low self-esteem was said to cause (Baumeister, Campbell, Krueger, & Vohs, 2003).

There is definitely a link between self-esteem and school achievement, for example (DuBois & Tevendale, 1999), but which way does it run? Does feeling better about yourself lead you to do better in school, or does your success in school make you feel better about yourself? Both may be correct, of course. The two processes may even amplify each other. But if your goal is to improve your academic performance, would it make more sense to sign up for a class in self-esteem or in, say, study skills?

The issue of whether self-esteem has life consequences, and if so, what they are, is hotly debated by social scientists. One very comprehensive review of the research evidence concluded that raising self-esteem does *not* lead to good school performance, better personal relationships, less aggression, or fewer problem behaviors such as substance abuse (Baumeister et al., 2003). In fact, the only important benefit the authors cited was that higher self-esteem leads to greater happiness (not that that should be sneered at). On the other side of the debate, recent reports find strong connections between *low* self-esteem and problems such as aggression and antisocial behavior (Donnellan, Trzesniewski, Robins, Moffitt, & Caspi, 2005; Trzesniewski et al., 2006; Ybrandt, 2008). One report, which uses longitudinal information to examine links between self-esteem in early adolescence and a variety of problems in adulthood, is the subject of this chapter's Research in the Spotlight on page 366.

This debate will no doubt continue, and lead to more and better research along the way, but we should note the possibility that both sides could be correct. Low self-esteem in early adolescence does indeed seem to be a serious risk factor for later problems. So far, however, the evidence does not give much hope that programs aimed specifically at raising self-esteem help to avert those later problems. One answer to this dilemma may be to develop interventions that focus more on the *sources* of low self-esteem than on feelings of self-worth as such. For example, we know that poor social relationships lead

Long-Term Consequences of Low Self-Esteem

Scholars disagree about whether self-esteem is useful for predicting future adjustment. Many suggest that high self-esteem promotes goals, coping mechanisms, and behaviors that make success in work and personal life more likely, while cutting down on the likelihood of mental and physical problems, substance abuse, and antisocial behavior. Others argue that high self-esteem is more a consequence of positive behaviors than a cause. If things are going well, self-esteem is high, and if they aren't, it is low.

One way to get closer to settling this disagreement would be to follow a representative group from childhood, across adolescence, and into adulthood. One recent study did just that. The participants included practically everyone born in the town of Dunedin, New Zealand, between April 1972 and March 1973. They have been assessed at regular intervals from birth through to adulthood. Vast amounts of information were collected, including measures of self-esteem, psychological problems, fitness, IQ, and educational and occupational outcomes.

The researchers created an adolescent self-esteem score from measures given at ages 11, 13, and 15, and then used that to predict a variety of outcomes in adulthood. These included aspects of mental health, physical health, economic prospects, and criminal convictions. Each of these analyses took into account the possible effects of adolescent depression, IQ, social class, gender, and childhood body mass index, which is linked to later health outcomes.

As adults, compared to those with high self-esteem as adolescents, those with low self-esteem were:

more likely to develop major depression disorder;

more likely to develop anxiety disorder;

more likely to be dependent on tobacco;

more likely to have poor cardiorespiratory health;

more likely to rate their health as poor;

more likely to be convicted of a violent crime;

more likely to be convicted of *any* crime;

more likely to drop out of high school;

more likely to have financial problems; and

less likely to go to university.

All of these relationships held up after gender, IQ, social class, and so on were taken into account.

Another way to look at these results is to count the number of problems each participant developed as an adult and chart them in terms of their earlier self-esteem. Figure R11.1 shows the result. Those with low self-esteem in early adolescence were likely to have multiple adjustment problems as young adults, those with high self-esteem in early adolescence were likely to have no adjustment problems in early adulthood, and those in the middle were in the middle.

While it is important, as always, to keep in mind that finding a relationship between two factors does not prove that one *causes* the other, these results do make it clear that a young adolescent with low self-esteem is at a higher risk for serious problems later on.

Source: Trzesniewski et al., 2006.

Figure R11.1 Problems of Low Self-Esteem
Lower self-esteem is associated with a greater number of problems.

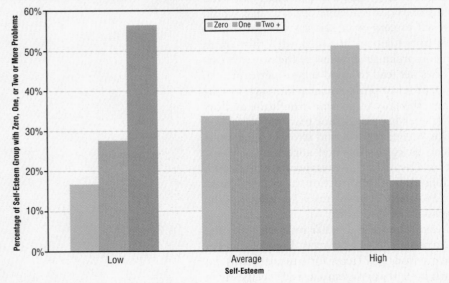

Source: M. B. Donnellan, K. H. Trzesniewski, R. W. Robins, T. E. Moffitt, & A. Caspi, 2006, "Low self-esteem is related to aggression, antisocial behavior, and delinquency," *Psychological Science, 16,* 328–335. Used by permission of the American Psychological Association (APA).

to low self-esteem. Given that, providing young adolescents with social experiences that help build their interpersonal skills as well as their confidence may lead to more positive results than simply trying to boost their confidence (DuBois, Lockerd, Reach, & Parra, 2003). Some current efforts along these lines will be examined in Chapter 14.

Summing Up...

With adolescence, the self-concept—an awareness of being separate and different from others—becomes more complex and includes psychological as well as physical characteristics. Teens notice interactions of their internal states with situations and discrepancies between the way they believe they really are and the way they present themselves. Self-esteem, the way people feel about themselves, declines during early adolescence, especially for girls. The most important contributors to self-esteem during adolescence are appearance and social acceptance. Athletic and scholastic abilities have less impact. Low self-esteem may lead to problem behaviors, but it also seems likely that problem behaviors lead to poorer feelings of self-worth.

FORGING AN IDENTITY

If we had to choose a single word to describe the experience of adolescence, one of the top candidates would have to be *change*. Change, rapid change, occurs in each of the areas we have looked at so far: physical, neurological, and sexual developments following puberty; cognitive capacities; relationships with parents, siblings, and peers; and social status in school, the workplace, and the community. Childhood, however treasured it may have been, recedes into the past, and up ahead, approaching with mind-numbing speed, looms adulthood, with its dimly sensed promises, challenges, and demands.

These changes come accompanied by newly urgent questions: What kind of person am I? What do I believe in? What do I want to do with my life? What is my place in the world? These are questions about **identity**, the psychological structure that allows us to keep a sense of personal continuity from the past, through the present, to the possible future, and that gives a sense of meaning, purpose, and direction to life (Chandler, Lalonde, Sokol, & Hallett, 2003). According to Erik Erikson (1968), asking oneself such questions and arriving at satisfactory answers to them are the most important developmental tasks adolescents face.

We looked briefly at Erikson's theory in Chapter 2. Based on his observations as a child psychoanalyst, he proposed that everyone goes through a series of eight life stages (Erikson, 1963). Each of these stages brings a particular psychosocial issue or "crisis" to the fore. For example, the total dependence that babies have on their caretakers sharply poses the question of whether other people can be trusted. The answer a baby's experiences lead to will have a long-lasting effect on feelings about the self, interactions with others, and the outcomes of later stages.

◄ **Learning Objective 11.3**
Why is adolescence considered the period of the identity crisis?

Identity The psychological structure that gives people a sense of personal continuity across situations and across their individual history.

Identity crisis For Erikson, an adolescent's response to the tension between the need to explore what is unique about oneself and the wish to become someone who will get respect and validation from family, friends, and community.

The Identity Crisis

During the adolescent years, the psychosocial issue that becomes most pressing is that of *identity versus identity diffusion*. This sets off what Erikson called the **identity crisis**. In today's world, the number of directions a teen *might* go in is practically endless, whether we are talking about occupations, interests, friendships, political views, social allegiances, religious beliefs, or sexual orientations. Among all these dizzying possibilities, the adolescent must not only choose some, but at the same time reject others. And these choices are not purely personal. They take place in the context of the adolescent's society and partly in response to society. There is a constant tension between the need to explore what is unique and different about oneself and the need to develop an identity that will be respected and validated by one's friends, family, and community.

▲ A psychosocial moratorium offers teens the freedom to explore different aspects of identity.

As a follower of Freud, Erikson (1963) held that children unconsciously *identify* with their parents' personalities, beliefs, and values, as well as the ways their parents view them. These identifications may or may not be a good fit with the character, interests, talents, and desires of the child. When young adolescents start questioning what they have always taken for granted about themselves and their place in the family and the world, it puts a strain on them as well as on those around them. After all, the assumptions they are wondering about are their parents' assumptions, too, and few people enjoy having their basic views put in question, whether by their children or by themselves.

For many teens, this questioning process is made less of a strain because they benefit from what Erikson refers to as a **psychosocial moratorium**. This is an unspoken pact that frees teens from heavy responsibilities that might frustrate their ability to develop their talents and interests. At the same time it protects them from harsh penalties for unconventional attitudes and behaviors. An adolescent can show up for dinner in a ripped t-shirt, proclaim the virtues of a vegan diet (or of eating meat, if the parents happen to be vegan), and make a snide remark about the parents' favorite politician, without having to fear being sent to bed hungry. The psychosocial moratorium encourages active exploration of identities by making the process, if not totally risk-free, at least much less risky. It is a little like being able to take an important segment of life on a pass–fail basis.

Who Benefits from Moratorium? Erikson firmly believed that all adolescents *should* have the freedom to experiment and explore different roles that a moratorium makes possible. Without it, there is less chance they will discover their real interests, examine their most important beliefs, and find a career that allows them to use their talents and develop their potentials. Erikson also realized that for vast numbers of adolescents, such a moratorium is an unaffordable luxury. Those growing up in more traditional cultures often find that their occupations, social roles, attitudes, and religious beliefs have been prescribed for them from before they were born. If these are not a good fit, breaking out of them may require a desperate struggle. As for teens in Westernized societies, they are frequently urged to stay in school through and past their adolescent years, which offers a sort of moratorium at least on the level of choosing a major and a vocation. This is not much use, however, to those who have to drop out and take whatever job they can find to help support their family, nor to those whose parents relentlessly push them toward a particular role or career without regard for their inclinations.

Successfully resolving the identity crisis is not something that happens all at once. Each of the important domains, such as choosing and preparing for a career; reevaluating one's moral, political, and religious beliefs; and adopting social, interpersonal, and sexual roles, can have its own timetable for *experimentation* during a moratorium period, followed by *choice*, *commitment*, and *consolidation*. Even when an adolescent achieves a clear sense of identity in one or all of these domains, it does not represent the final word on the subject. The world changes, often at a dizzying pace, and careers, relationships, and social roles change with it. The healthy adult is able to be flexible and open to these changes while staying faithful to his or her core identity.

Foreclosure, Diffusion, and Negative Identity. For Erikson, adolescents who have passed through the identity crisis and achieved a coherent sense of identity gain a general sense of well-being. They feel comfortable with themselves, their past histories, the futures they project, the people who matter to them, and the world at large. But this is not everyone's experience. There are several ways the process of identity development can take a wrong turn.

If a teen is not given the freedom to experiment and explore, or if the thought of questioning the certainties of childhood identifications is too threatening, the result may be a premature and unconsidered shutting off of possibilities called **identity foreclosure**. Here are two examples of identity foreclosure: Just a couple of generations ago in America, many girls were brought up to believe that their destiny in life was to get married, have children, and keep house for their families, just as their mothers had done. Many of them accepted that identity, not because they had explored other paths

Psychosocial moratorium A period in which adolescents are given a degree of freedom to explore their impulses, talents, interests, social roles, and beliefs without fear that minor offenses against convention will bring drastic consequences.

Identity foreclosure A process in which adolescents commit themselves to the identities assigned to them by their parents and community, while shutting off other possible paths of development.

and decided that it was the one that best suited them, but simply because they knew it was what everyone expected of them and they didn't see any other choice. In today's America, many middle-class teens have no quiet time to think about who they are and what they want from life. They are kept too busy taking AP classes, going to SAT prep sessions, playing sports, taking music lessons, and doing "volunteer" work, all to better their chances of making the cut at the selective college of their parents' dreams.

Identity foreclosure involves accepting a rigid definition of the self that is taken in from outside. In contrast, **identity diffusion**, which Erikson (1968) also called *identity confusion*, reflects a failure to construct any coherent sense of self. Adolescents can be psychologically paralyzed by the many options today's society offers and baffled by the task of fitting all their varied and clashing thoughts and feelings, all their past and present moments, into the frame of a single continuous person. Cut off from a future that belongs to some self they don't even recognize, they may sink into a state of apathy and depression or waste their time in meaningless and possibly dangerous activities. Some may even find it hard to think of a convincing reason to go on living (Chandler et al., 2003).

One way out of identity diffusion is to adopt what Erikson called a **negative identity**. As the old saying has it, "I'd as well be hanged for a sheep as a lamb." In other words, if you feel the world doesn't acknowledge your existence, instead of meekly accepting invisibility, give the world a poke in the eye with a sharp stick. The preacher's son, unable to be righteous enough to live up to his family's standards, pierces his eyebrow, wears only black and chains, and mutters about alliances with dark powers. The daughter of work-obsessed conventional parents starts skipping school to hang out with members of a biker gang. If you can *force* people to look at you, even if they wear expressions of disgust, the fact that they are looking helps prove that you really do exist. For these adolescents, that is precisely the point that seems to be in doubt.

Research on Erikson's Theory

Erikson's books and essays about the identity crisis introduced the term and concept to world culture and had a profound influence on the way people think about adolescence. In recent decades there has been an explosion of studies on identity (Bauman, 2001; Côté, 2006b). A great deal of this research has made use of an approach based on Erikson's ideas and developed by James Marcia (1966, 1980).

Marcia classifies an individual's identity development by examining two processes, exploration (or *crisis*) and commitment, in three areas of activity, *occupation, beliefs and values*, and *interpersonal relations*. **Identity exploration** involves searching out and examining alternatives in a particular area. **Identity commitment** is a matter of choosing a belief or course of action and making a personal investment in it. Researchers use information from interviews and questionnaires to assess the degree to which someone has engaged in exploration and made a commitment. This allows them to place the person in one of four categories of **identity status** (see Figure 11.3).

After our discussion of Erikson's ideas about identity, the categories of identity status will be familiar. They are:

Identity diffusion. The status of someone who has not devoted energy to exploration and has not made a commitment. "How do I want to make a living? Who knows? I'll think about that when I have to."

Figure 11.3   Categories of Identity Status
The processes of exploration and commitment generate four categories of identity status.

		Exploration	
		No	Yes
Commitment	No	Identity Diffusion	Moratorium
	Yes	Identity Foreclosure	Identity Achievement

◀ **Learning Objective 11.4**
How are identity exploration and identity commitment linked to identity status?

Connect the Dots...

Among people you have known, can you think of any who seem to be examples of identity foreclosure? How about identity diffusion? Negative identity? What about each of them leads you to classify them that way?

Identity diffusion A reluctance or refusal to consider identity issues; also called *identity confusion*.

Negative identity Acting in ways that are guaranteed to arouse disapproval, but that also guarantee attention and concern.

Identity exploration For Marcia, examining alternatives in a particular area of activity, such as occupation or beliefs and values.

Identity commitment Choosing a belief or course of action and making a personal investment in it.

Identity status For Marcia, the presence or absence, in different areas of activity, of *exploration* efforts and *commitment*.

Identity foreclosure. The status of someone who has made a commitment in some area, but without going through a process of exploration. "I've always known I'd go into my mom's business when I grow up, so that's what I'll do."

Moratorium. The status of someone who is in the process of exploring options in some area, but who has not yet made a commitment. "I've thought about being a doctor, but I wonder if it's what I really want. I'm planning to volunteer in a clinic this summer and see how I like it. I hope that will help me decide."

Identity achievement. The status of someone who, after going through a period of exploration and examination, has made a personal commitment to particular goals or beliefs. "I was doing pre-law, but I've always loved the horn. I've been taking lessons and playing in the school orchestra right along. After some long talks with my teachers, I decided to try to make a career in music. I don't know what my parents will say, but I do know this is what's right for me."

On the whole, the results from research that uses Marcia's approach fit well with Erikson's theory. The personality characteristics that are associated with each status are in line with Erikson's descriptions (Meeus, Iedema, Helsen, & Vollebergh, 1999; Schwartz, 2001). Those in the *diffusion* category are generally apathetic and uninterested, are not close to peers, and may be at risk for school failure, depression, and substance abuse (Marcia, 1980, 1993; Meeus & Dekovic, 1995). Those in the *foreclosure* status tend to be closed-minded, rigid, and somewhat authoritarian, with a tendency to resist change (Marcia, 1980). Those in *moratorium*, on the other hand, are more open-minded and thoughtful, but also more anxious (Berman, Schwartz, Kurtines, & Berman, 2001). Finally, those in the *achieved* status have more balanced thinking, more effective decision-making skills, and deeper relationships with others (Boyes & Chandler, 1992; Marcia, 1993; Waterman, 1999, 2007).

The Role of Identity Styles. Another approach to identity status is to examine the different ways individuals deal with information about identity-related questions. Michael Berzonsky (2003a, 2004a) has described three of these **identity styles** and linked them to different identity statuses. Those with a *diffuse-avoidant* processing style, who are typically in the diffusion status, try to avoid dealing with personal problems, conflicts, and decisions by putting them off and letting situational demands dictate what they do. Those who are foreclosed use a *normative* processing style. They are conscientious and agreeable, but have a low tolerance for ambiguity and a high need for structure. They are very closed off to information that may put their personal belief systems in question. In sharp contrast, those in moratorium, as well as those in the identity achieved category, display an *informational* processing style. They deliberately seek out self-relevant information. They are ready to look skeptically at their own views, suspend judgment, and reevaluate their conclusions about themselves when confronted with discrepancies.

One source of these different identity styles is the type of parenting the adolescent received (Berzonsky, 2004b). If we think back to Baumrind's descriptions of parenting approaches, in Chapter 5, the correspondences that have been found make perfect sense. Adolescents with permissive parents tend to have a diffuse-avoidant identity style and diffusion status. Those with more authoritarian parents are more likely to have a normative style and a foreclosed status. Those whose parents took a more authoritative approach have an informational style and an achieved identity status.

These different informational styles have consequences, too. A recent study of college freshmen found that students with an informational style had a clear sense of purpose, a high level of academic autonomy, good social skills, and good grades. Students with a normative style also had a clear sense of purpose, but were less tolerant and less autonomous. Those with a diffuse-avoidant style were at a disadvantage on a number of counts, including sense of purpose, autonomy, peer relationships, and grades (Berzonsky & Kuk, 2005).

Identity style The different ways individuals seek out and deal with information that relates to questions of identity.

Two Approaches to Identity Intervention

The traditional view of identity development as put forward by Erikson (1968) and Marcia (1966) focuses on a process of rationally examining possible alternatives and constructing an identity by choosing among them. One alternative to this cognitively-oriented view sees identity exploration as more oriented to an emotional process of self-discovery (Waterman, 2004).

These views focus on different processes, but they may not really be as opposed as they sound. Self-construction and self-discovery may be *independent* but *overlapping* aspects of identity formation (Schwartz, 2002). According to this approach, "[s]ome individuals may see themselves as creating a sense of self, others may seek to find themselves, and still others may see themselves as doing both of these things simultaneously" (Schwartz et al., 2005, p. 313).

If both these processes contribute to identity development, can they be encouraged by intervention programs, and what sorts of intervention have more impact on one than on the other? These are among the questions that researchers Seth Schwartz, William Kurtines, and Marilyn Montgomery tried to answer in a recent (2005) study.

The participants in the study were college undergraduates. They were predominately women (85%) and Hispanic (70%), which reflected the makeup of the institution where the research was carried out. At the beginning, the participants responded to several identity-related measures, including identity processing style, critical problem solving, personal expressiveness and flow, and self-actualization. The participants were then randomly assigned to a *cognitively focused* intervention, an *emotionally focused* intervention, or a control group.

Participants met in small groups in weekly sessions. Each group member in turn was the focus of a single session. In the *cognitively focused* sessions, the member whose turn it was presented the identity-related life choice she or he had used for the critical problem-solving measure at the start of the study. The group then discussed the life choice, with the goals of identifying possible sources of information that might help solve the problem, encouraging active exploration, generating possible alternative solutions, and critically evaluating each alternative.

In the *emotionally focused* sessions, the member whose turn it was presented the three goal strivings from the pretest measure of personal expressiveness. With help from the group, the member then went through a series of steps that included breaking down the goal striving into its component activities, associating each activity with feeling words, generating a list of activities he or she associated with feelings of flow, and developing creative ways to integrate flow activities into goal strivings.

At the end of the study, participants again completed the four identity measures. As the investigators expected, the cognitively focused intervention had a positive effect on identity self-construction, while the emotionally focused intervention had more impact on self-discovery processes. Participants in both conditions felt that they had gained something valuable from the group experience. This suggests that programs to foster identity development should target both self-discovery *and* self-construction by including both types of intervention.

Source: Schwartz, Kurtines, & Montgomery, 2005.

Self-Construction and Self-Discovery. The research on identity styles that we just examined assumes that adolescents acquire their sense of self through a process of *self-construction.* They are motivated to seek out information in their social environment that may be identity related and to build a coherent self from it (Berzonsky, 2004a). In contrast, other theorists see identity formation as a process of *self-discovery* (Waterman, 2004). Achieving an authentic identity, in this view, means searching for one's intrinsic nature or "true self" and adopting values, beliefs, and goals that will develop one's inner potential.

The self-construction and self-discovery views of identity development are certainly different in emphasis, but they do not necessarily conflict with each other (Schwartz, Côté, & Arnett, 2005). For instance, students sometimes decide to take a course on an unfamiliar topic because their friends tell them they'll like it (self-construction), only to find that the material appeals to some passion they didn't even know they had (self-discovery).

Teens themselves find that their activities offer them ways both to try new things and to gain self-knowledge (Dworkin, Larson, & Hansen, 2003). This is especially the case with *self-defining activities*, those they consider important to who they are as a person (Coatsworth, Palen, Sharp, & Ferrer-Wreder, 2006). This suggests that both self-construction and self-discovery can encourage a consolidated sense of identity

(Schwartz, 2006). This chapter's Applications in the Spotlight on page 371 describes a program to help college students in their identity development using intervention strategies based on both these approaches.

Does Identity Come Later Today? As the intervention project by Schwartz and his colleagues (2005) indicates, today the process of identity development starts later and takes longer than Erikson originally thought. Erikson assumed that the identity crisis starts in early adolescence and is usually over by age 16 or 18. However, changing social conditions in the United States and other Western countries have led to a more extended transition to adulthood (Côté, 2000). Researchers who measure the identity status of adolescents at different ages find that most of them are in either the diffusion or foreclosure categories right through the high school years. It isn't until college age that identity achievement becomes more common (Archer, 1982; Kroger, 2000, 2007; Streitmatter, 1993).

The process also follows less of a straight-line course than might be expected. From the definitions and descriptions, it would seem that diffusion is the least-developed status, followed by foreclosure and moratorium, and then identity achievement, which is developmentally the most advanced (Kroger, 2003). By and large, young adolescents do shift out of the less mature statuses, and older adolescents do shift into the more mature statuses (Berzonsky & Adams, 1999; Bosma & Kunnen, 2001; Waterman, 1999). However, some people shift back and forth between diffusion and moratorium, while others go from moratorium to achievement and then back to moratorium (Archer, 1989; van Hoof, 1999).

Several explanations can be offered for this unexpected finding that teens do not always follow the predicted status sequence. One is a question of method. Critics say that Marcia's way of defining the identity statuses leaves out or minimizes some important aspects of Erikson's theory (Bosma & Kunnen, 2001; Kroger, 2003). For Erikson, the identity crisis meant going deep into the personality and its relationship to society, and commitment meant an investment of the self in an overarching meaning. In Marcia's approach, a teen can be classified as exploring for having read some articles about high-tech careers, and as making a commitment for saying, yes, he's made up his mind to major in computer sciences. When that is the level of commitment being measured, it should not surprise us if some people later decide they are not as committed as they thought. It may also be helpful to draw a distinction between *making* a commitment, after exploring a range of alternatives, and *identifying with* a commitment after exploring it in depth (Luyckx, Goossens, & Soenens, 2006). The latter is likely to be much more stable and long-lasting.

On a more fundamental level, the world has changed in the half-century since Erikson developed his ideas. Young people have to deal with increasing demands for a prolonged education, with a commercialized youth culture, and with the social and psychological impact of new media technologies. Developing a clear, coherent, satisfying conception of one's relation to such a fast-changing world is not easy, and even once achieved, it is always somewhat provisional. It's no wonder that identity formation now stretches beyond adolescence into the 20s (Côté, 2006a). Maybe that would not have come as such a surprise to Erikson after all. As he once wrote:

> Such a sense of identity is never gained nor maintained once and for all. Like a good conscience, it is constantly lost and regained, although more lasting and more economical methods of maintenance and restoration are evolved and fortified in late adolescence.
> —(ERIKSON, 1956, p. 74)

What Is Ethnic Identity?

▶ Learning Objective 11.5
How do parents, schools, and neighborhoods contribute to ethnic identity?

So far, we have been looking at how adolescents develop an individual sense of identity by exploring and making a commitment to their unique characteristics, talents, interests, and beliefs. But just as we are all individuals, we also all belong to social groups or categories that help define our place in society (Tajfel & Turner, 1979,

1986). One that continues to gain in importance, as modern societies become increasingly multicultural, is **ethnicity**. Ethnicity refers to the cultural background of a person's family (such as Cuban, Jamaican, Korean, and so on) and the customs, values, and attitudes that go along with it (Phinney, 2005). People from similar ethnic backgrounds tend to show similar patterns of attitudes and behaviors that distinguish them from those of other ethnicities, although cultural groups do change over time, influenced by the larger society (Fuligni, Tseng, & Lam, 1999).

Even in elementary school, children are able to say what their ethnicity is and have a basic notion that, like their gender, this is something about themselves that doesn't change (Bernal, Knight, Garza, Ocampo, & Cota, 1990; Brown & Bigler, 2005). As they approach adolescence, they also come to understand how their ethnic group differs from others. They become more aware of how their group is viewed and valued (or devalued) by the majority culture. This initiates a process that leads to the development of an ethnic identity. **Ethnic identity** has been defined as "a self-constructed understanding of oneself in terms of one's cultural and ethnic background and the attitudes and feelings associated with that background . . . an internalization of the meaning and implications of one's group membership" (Phinney, 2005, p. 189).

Who Needs an Ethnic Identity? As this definition makes clear, ethnic identity is a constituent part of a person's sense of identity as a whole. It might seem logical, then, to include ethnic identity as part of any research program on identity development. By and large, this has not happened. According to projections by the U.S. Census Bureau (2004), by the middle of this century more than half of all U.S. adolescents will be members of ethnic minorities (see Figure 11.4). Even today, more than one-third of those 11 to 18 regard themselves as Asian, Black, or Hispanic. Yet, when a team of researchers recently reviewed a decade's worth of published studies of identity status, they found that in almost three-quarters of the studies the participants were primarily White (Sneed, Schwartz, & Cross, 2006). Over one-third of the studies didn't even report the ethnic composition of the sample.

For adolescents who belong to non-dominant minorities, part of the challenge in understanding social relationships is to understand those in higher status groups (Phinney, 2006). By and large, those in positions of influence and authority—school officials, professionals, political officeholders, superiors at work—tend to be members of the dominant group, that is, White. Trying to figure them out makes one's own

> **Ethnicity** A person's cultural background and the customs, values, and attitudes that go along with it.
>
> **Ethnic identity** An understanding of oneself in terms of one's ethnic and cultural background.

Figure 11.4   Projected Proportions of U.S. Adolescents 11–18 by Ethnicity, 2000–2050

According to projections, by 2050 the proportions of Asian and Hispanic teens in the U.S. population will increase sharply, the proportion of Black teens will stay steady, and the proportion of White teens will decline.

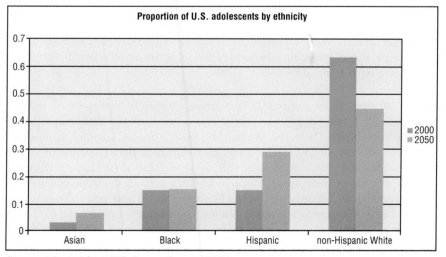

Source: Adapted from U.S. Census Bureau, 2004.

ethnic status stand out more. White teens, on the other hand, can usually get along without having to understand those in other groups, which makes their ethnic identity much less of an issue for them.

Developing an Ethnic Identity. The development of ethnic identity closely parallels the process of identity development described by Erikson (1968) and Marcia (1993) that we examined in the last section. The same four categories of diffused, foreclosed, moratorium, and achieved status show up in studies of ethnic identity (Yip, Seaton, & Sellers, 2006). The most widely used analysis of ethnic identity development has been put forward by Jean Phinney (1990, 1993). According to Phinney, those in the first stage of the process, the *unexamined* stage, show a lack of awareness or understanding of their ethnicity. Some young adolescents do identify with their ethnic group, but simply because they have been brought up to do so. This is similar to foreclosure status. Others say their ethnic status doesn't make much difference to them, which is equivalent to diffusion status.

During the second stage, typically in middle adolescence, teens embark on a process of active *exploration*. What does it mean to be a member of their ethnic group? What are the history, customs, and shared attitudes of the group? As part of the process, some adolescents get deeply involved in the language, music, and cultural traditions of their heritage. This exploration, which shares features with moratorium status, may be set off by the shock of an encounter with ethnic prejudice or discrimination (Cross, Strauss, & Fhagen-Smith, 1999) or may be one element in a wider search for personal identity. Ideally, this phase leads to an *achieved ethnic identity*, in which adolescents reach a secure, confident sense of their group membership and a clear understanding of the place of ethnicity in their lives (Phinney, 2003).

Benefits of Ethnic Identity. Achieving a solid sense of ethnic identity has many positive results, especially for teens whose ethnic groups are targets of prejudice and discrimination. Studies that included African American, Chinese, Mexican, and other Hispanic teens show that those with a stronger ethnic identity are more motivated and do better in school (Altschul, Oyserman, & Bybee, 2006; Chavous et al., 2003; Fuligni, Witkow, & Garcia, 2005; Oyserman, Harrison, & Bybee, 2001; Wong, Eccles, & Sameroff, 2003). In other studies, ethnic identity has been linked to less depression (Yasui, Dorham, & Dishion, 2004) and a stronger sense of psychological well-being (Kiang, Yip, Gonzales-Backen, Witkow, & Fuligni, 2006; Seaton, Scottham, & Sellers, 2006).

A well-developed sense of ethnic identity not only promotes a sense of well-being, it also helps to *protect* well-being. In one recent study, 9th graders from Chinese and Mexican backgrounds kept a diary in which they checked off daily activities that might be stressful, such as having a lot of work at home, a lot of schoolwork, and a lot of demands from parents and friends. They also gave daily ratings of their happiness and anxiety levels. As Figure 11.5 on page 375 shows, those with a strong ethnic identity were able to shrug off the effect of stressful events, both on the day they happened and the next day, while those lower in ethnic identity were brought down by stressful events both days (Kiang et al., 2006).

Between Two Cultures. Adolescents who by heritage are members of an ethnic minority grow up exposed in varying degrees to at least two cultures, that of their ethnic group and that of the wider society. Often the two cultures have attitudes, customs, and beliefs that are not only different, but in conflict, and each demands the allegiance of young people. How do minority teens cope with this dilemma? Do they identify with the majority culture and reject their ethnic culture? Identify with their ethnic culture and reject the majority culture? Identify with both? With neither? These possibilities, which we discussed earlier in Chapter 8, are presented again in Figure 11.6 on page 375.

When people hold on to the traditions and values of their ethnic culture and also develop an identification with the larger society, the outcome is called *integration* or *biculturalism*. Identifying with the majority culture at the cost of rejecting one's ethnic

Connect the Dots...

Some observers argue that a focus on ethnic identity dilutes adolescents' attachment to the broader society and potentially diverts them from paths that may lead to personal success. Given what you have learned so far about ethnic identity, how would you respond to this point? Why?

Figure 11.5 Ethnic Regard, Stressful Events, and Happiness
Ethnic regard, stressful events, and happiness.

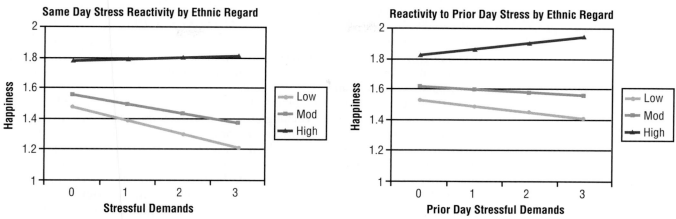

Source: L. Kiang, T. Yip, M. Gonzalez-Backen, M. Witkow, & A. J. Fuligni, 2006, "Ethnic identity and the daily psychological well-being of adolescents from Mexican and Chinese backgrounds," *Child Development, 77,* figure 1, p. 1344 and figure 3, p. 1346. Used by permission.

culture is called *assimilation*. Those who reject the majority culture for the sake of maintaining their ethnic culture are practicing *separation*. Finally, there are those who do not hold onto their ethnic heritage, but do not identify with the majority culture either; they are victims of *marginalization* (Berry, 1990).

It is helpful to distinguish between two types of bicultural individuals (Phinney & Devich-Navarro, 1997). An *alternating bicultural* moves between non-overlapping aspects of the two cultures, while a *blended bicultural* has developed a new identity that combines features of both cultures (Birman, 1994; LaFromboise, Coleman, & Gerton, 1993). For example, an African American adolescent who uses standard English grammar and a standard American accent in the classroom and switches to a more "Black" dialect and accent back home would be considered an alternating bicultural. One whose speech patterns usually have features typical of the language customs of the majority culture *and* the ethnic culture would be a blended bicultural.

Code Switching and Cultural Frames. Many adolescents are bilingual, for example in English and Spanish. When they move from one language to the other, it requires

Figure 11.6 A Model of Identification with Two Cultures
The cultural attitudes of teens are affected both by identification with their ethnic culture and identification with the majority culture.

| | | Identification with Majority Culture | |
		Yes	No
Identification with Ethnic Culture	Yes	Integration/ Biculturalism	Separation
	No	Assimilation	Marginalization

Source: Adapted from Berry, 1990.

what linguists call **code switching.** According to some recent research, when we switch languages it may serve as a cue to also switch our **cultural frames.** These are the attitudes, ways of thinking, and manners of relating to others that are associated with the culture of each of the languages (Hong, Morris, Chiu, & Benet-Martínez, 2000; Hull, 1996). For example, bilinguals score differently on personality tests, depending on whether they are responding in Spanish or English (Ramírez-Esparza, Gosling, Benet-Martínez, Potter, & Pennebaker, 2006). As a Czech proverb says, "Learn a new language and get a new soul."

It may be that teens who are bilingual are more likely to be alternating biculturals because of the effect of code switching on their cultural frames. In a study that looked at both Mexican American and African American adolescents, about two-thirds of the Mexican Americans were alternating biculturals and one-third were blended biculturals. The balance was quite different for the African Americans. Only one-quarter were alternating biculturals, and over half were blended biculturals. Some 17% of the African American teens were classified as separated, while only one Mexican American fit that category. No one in either group was considered assimilated or marginalized (Phinney & Devich-Navarro, 1997). These results suggest that biculturalism, by offering ways to be part of both cultures in different degrees, permits ethnic minority adolescents to avoid feeling pulled in two directions by competing cultural demands.

Family, School, Neighborhood. We have been looking at the form and content of ethnic identity, but what about its developmental course? Do adolescents from ethnic minorities simply wake up one morning, decide to explore their ethnicity, and start down a path that eventually leads to an achieved ethnic identity? Put that way, it sounds absurd, but we know surprisingly little about the specific factors that influence the development of ethnic identity (Umaña-Taylor, Bhanot, & Shin, 2006). An approach that has produced promising results finds that teens who get more family ethnic socialization are more likely to explore their ethnicity, feel good about their ethnic background, and make a strong commitment to their ethnic identity (Umaña-Taylor & Fine, 2004).

Ethnic socialization refers to behaviors in the family, such as talking about one's ethnic background, history, and customs; participating in cultural events and festivals; listening to ethnic music; and eating ethnic meals. One recent study looked at American high school students of Asian Indian, Chinese, Filipino, Salvadoran, and Vietnamese descent. The results indicated that ethnic socialization in the family is a central component of ethnic identity formation, regardless of ethnic background (Umaña-Taylor et al., 2006).

Code switching The cognitive and linguistic changes that take place when someone who is bilingual moves from speaking one language to another.

Cultural frame The attitudes, ways of thinking, and manners of relating to others that are associated with speaking a particular language.

▶ Ethnic socialization within the family is a central element in the development of ethnic identity.

Another recent study, of African American adolescents, found a close tie between ethnic socialization by parents and the teens' ethnic identity (McHale et al., 2006).

A major factor that motivates adolescents to explore their ethnic background is a heightened awareness of difference. This awareness, in turn, is affected by the amount of interaction an adolescent has with members of other groups. In recent decades, adolescents from minority groups are more and more likely to live in neighborhoods and attend schools that are homogeneous instead of ethnically diverse. The result is that they do not have much exposure to teens from other ethnic groups, and their development of an ethnic identity is slower. One recent study indicated that Hispanic high school students in schools with a high proportion of Hispanics have a weaker sense of ethnic identity than those in schools that are mostly non-Hispanic (Umaña-Taylor, 2004). Even in schools where different ethnic groups are represented, teens tend to spend their free time with others from their own ethnic group (Tatum, 1997), which may reduce their motivation to develop an ethnic identity.

Summing Up...

Identity is an integrated sense of one's character, beliefs, values, and hopes. It becomes a major psychosocial issue during adolescence. According to Erikson, teens benefit from being given a moratorium, in which they are free to explore their talents, inclinations, feelings, and ideas about possible futures. Some instead adopt a rigid definition of the self from parents and others in what is called foreclosure. Identity diffusion, in contrast, involves avoiding the issues of identity. Marcia's adaptation of Erikson's theory interprets an adolescent's identity status as the consequences of exploration and commitment. Ethnic identity, an understanding of one's relationship to ethnic background, promotes well-being, especially for teens of minority origin.

THE MORAL SELF

Choosing an occupation, a hobby, a political party, a set of friends, or an ethnic iden-tification is certainly part of constructing a personal identity. However, identity is much more than that. At the core of the process is the task of developing a system of moral values and beliefs (Erikson, 1963). A teen's personal values and beliefs affect everything from social relationships and occupational commitments to feelings of self-respect and ways of responding to crises. But where do these values and beliefs come from? How do they develop?

Social scientists who study moral development generally make two related points. The first is that parents and cultures obviously play an important role in communicat-ing specific beliefs and values to children and adolescents. The second is that the ways adolescents (as well as children and adults) *think about and decide* issues of morals and beliefs are grounded in a process of cognitive development that is common to all peo-ple everywhere. This second point was stressed particularly by Jean Piaget and Lawrence Kohlberg, whose ideas on the subject we turn to now.

Piaget and Moral Judgment

Early in his career, Piaget carried out a series of studies to find out how children think about questions of right and wrong. He reported the results in a book called, *The Moral Judgment of the Child* (Piaget, 1932/1965). This was his only venture into the area of moral development, but its impact on the way scholars think about children's moral reasoning continues to this day.

▶ **Learning Objective 11.6**
How did Piaget investigate and explain moral judgment in children?

Phases of Moral Development. As in his investigations of mental structures, which were discussed in Chapter 4, Piaget approached moral judgment by presenting children with situations and asking them questions about their thinking. To find out how they understood rules, he played marbles with them and asked such questions as where the rules of the game came from, whether everybody had to follow them, and whether players could change the rules if they wanted. To explore their ideas about justice, he told them stories that raised moral issues. In one of these stories, there are two children. One of them is helping to clear the table after dinner, but he trips and breaks six plates. The other has been told he can't have a cookie, but he climbs on the kitchen counter to reach the cookie jar and knocks over a plate, which breaks. Are either of them naughty, and if so, is one naughtier than the other?

The ways children answered him led Piaget to conclude that there are two distinct phases of moral development. The first, from around ages 4 to 7, is the phase of *moral realism* or **heteronomous morality.** Rules are seen as established by authority figures (parents, God, the cops) and fixed in stone. Following the rules is always the right thing to do, and breaking them is always wrong. As for the two children who broke plates, heteronomous children are likely to say that the one who broke more plates is naughtier. Why? Because he broke more plates, of course! In other words, the actor's intent is overlooked or considered less important than the objective consequences. Piaget also said that children during this phase believe in **immanent justice.** If someone breaks a rule, punishment will follow. A child who swipes an apple in the market may trip on the way out and hurt his arm. Why did he hurt his arm? Because he stole the apple!

After a transitional period from about ages 7 to 10, children enter the phase of *moral relativism* or **autonomous morality.** They now see rules as arbitrary conventions that can be changed if people agree and broken if there's some good reason. For example, if someone is really sick and has to get to the hospital, it would be okay to break the speed limit. In judging someone's actions, they pay more attention to the person's intent than to the outcome. Maybe the child who broke six dishes should have been more careful, but he wasn't naughty because he was just trying to help. The child who broke one dish while climbing on the counter, on the other hand, was doing something he knew he shouldn't. Morally autonomous children also move away from the concept of immanent justice. They come to realize that wrongdoing isn't always punished, and that sometimes people are punished even though they haven't done anything wrong.

The Role of Peers. An important factor in children's progress from heteronomous to autonomous moral thinking, according to Piaget, is their interactions with peers. As we saw earlier, in Chapter 6, peer relationships are based on roughly equal status and power, which means disagreements (about the rules of a game, for example) have to be settled through negotiation instead of by one person's "Because I said so!" This leads to a more flexible understanding of the nature of rules. Peer interactions also promote more advanced *role-taking*, the ability to look at situations from another person's point of view, which makes it possible to figure out what a person's intent may have been.

Since Piaget published his work on moral judgment, research has confirmed some aspects of his conclusions and cast doubt on others. Children in many different cultures do move from a more heteronomous to a more autonomous orientation, and this movement is linked to their level of cognitive development and role-taking skill (Lapsley, 1996). However, in several respects Piaget apparently underestimated the moral abilities of young children. Even 3-year-olds will take an actor's intentions into account, *if* the intentions are made clear enough (Nelson, 1980). Three-year-olds can also start to distinguish between *moral* rules, such as not hitting, stealing, or lying, and *social-conventional* rules, such as saying "please" and "thank you" and eating with a knife and fork instead of fingers (Turiel, 2006). Social-conventional rules are open to change, according to circumstance, but moral rules are not (Nucci & Turiel, 1993).

Kohlberg and Moral Reasoning

Some three decades after Piaget's investigation of moral development, Lawrence Kohlberg began a long project to revise and extend Piaget's theory (Colby &

Heteronomous morality Piaget's term for the earlier phase of moral development, in which authority figures determine what is right and wrong.

Immanent justice The belief that wrongdoing is always punished.

Autonomous morality Piaget's term for the later phase of moral development, in which rules are seen as changeable and an actor's intentions are given more weight than the outcome of an action.

Kohlberg, 1987; Kohlberg, 1963, 1984). Like Piaget, he tried to get at the moral reasoning of his participants by asking them to consider and discuss stories that had some relevance to moral issues. His participants, however, were older children, adolescents, and adults, and the stories he presented them with were correspondingly more complex, pitting different moral values against one another. Here is the best known:

> In Europe, a woman was near death from a special kind of cancer. There was one drug that the doctors thought might save her. It was a form of radium that a druggist in the same town had recently discovered. The drug was expensive to make, but the druggist was charging 10 times what the drug cost him to make. He paid $200 for the radium and charged $2,000 for a small dose of the drug. The sick woman's husband, Heinz, went to everyone he knew to borrow the money, but he could only get together $1,000, which is half of what it cost. He told the druggist that his wife was dying and asked him to sell it cheaper or let him pay later. But the druggist said, "No, I discovered the drug, and I am going to make money from it." So Heinz got desperate and broke into the man's store to steal the drug for his wife.
>
> —(Kohlberg, 1969, p. 379)

Those being interviewed are then asked a series of questions, such as: Should Heinz have stolen the drug? Why (or why not)? What if Heinz doesn't love his wife; does that make a difference? Why (or why not)? Should Heinz steal the drug to cure his dearly loved pet? If Heinz does steal the drug and gets caught, what should the judge do, and why?

Six Stages of Development. The answers Kohlberg received led him to describe moral development as a sequence of three levels and six stages:

Level 1. **Preconventional morality.** Morality is defined by external rewards and punishments, and only one point of view is taken into account.

> *Stage 1: Punishment orientation.* If those in charge punish an action, that means it is morally wrong. If it isn't punished, it isn't wrong.
>
> *Stage 2: Naive hedonism.* If an action leads to rewards, it is right. You are nice to people who may be nice to you.

Level 2. **Conventional morality** Morality is defined by the standards of others, such as parents or society, which one follows to gain approval. Other people's points of view become very important.

> *Stage 3: "Good boy/Good girl" orientation.* The morally right thing to do is to live up to the legitimate role expectations of significant others.
>
> *Stage 4: Social order orientation.* Morality is defined by rules put forward by legitimate authorities and aimed at preserving social order.

Level 3. **Postconventional morality** What is right is based on the individual's internalization of universal principles of ethics and justice.

> *Stage 5: Social contract orientation.* Systems of laws and rules are morally legitimate to the extent they preserve fundamental rights and values.
>
> *Stage 6: Universal ethical principles.* Moral right is based on universally applicable moral principles that transcend any rules that may be in conflict with them.

What is important in assessing an individual's stage of moral development is not the particular content of the answer ("Heinz should steal the drug" or "Heinz shouldn't steal the drug"), but rather the structure of the person's reasoning. Indeed, Kohlberg suggested that people at any of the stages might come down on either side of an issue, as shown by the responses in Figure 11.7 on page 380.

Different aspects of Kohlberg's theory have been tested in a wide variety of cultures around the world. The results indicate that, as Kohlberg predicted, the stage of moral

◄ **Learning Objective 11.7**
How did Kohlberg describe the stages and levels of moral reasoning?

Connect the Dots...

Before going on to the next section, ask yourself what *you* think Heinz should do. Should he steal the drug? Why, or why not? If a friend took the opposite view, what arguments would you put forward to change his or her mind?

Preconventional morality For Kohlberg, a level of judgment in which right and wrong are defined in terms of external punishments and rewards.

Conventional morality For Kohlberg, a level of judgment in which right and wrong are defined in terms of the standards of others, such as parents and society.

Postconventional morality For Kohlberg, a level of judgment in which right and wrong are defined in terms of internalizing universal principles of ethics and justice.

Figure 11.7 Stages of Moral Reasoning

In Kohlberg's view, moral reasoning develops in a sequence of three levels and six stages.

I. Preconventional Level	Heinz *should* steal the drug because:	Heinz *shouldn't* steal the drug because:
1. Punishment Orientation	If Heinz just lets his wife die, he could get in big trouble.	If he steals the drug, he could get put in jail.
2. Naïve Hedonism	If he saves his wife's life, she'll be really nice to him after that.	If he goes to jail, his wife won't be much use to him.
II. Conventional Level		
3. "Good boy/Good girl" Orientation	A good husband is supposed to take care of his wife.	If he becomes a thief, he'll bring shame on his family.
4. Social Order Orientation	He has a duty to save his wife, but he should pay back the money and take his punishment for stealing.	Breaking the law is wrong, it just encourages others to break the law.
III. Postconventional Level		
5. Social Contract Orientation	The underlying purpose of the law is to protect human rights, but in this case it doesn't protect the right of Heinz's wife to live, so he should disregard it.	Laws are our way of making sure we live together properly. Everyone would understand if Heinz stole the drug, but that doesn't make it right.
6. Universal Ethical Principles	Preserving human life is a higher value than protecting property. Even the druggist would tell Heinz to steal the drug if there was a chance that his own life was at stake.	In stealing the drug, Heinz is overlooking the rights of others who might need it just as badly as his wife.

reasoning increases with age (Colby & Kohlberg, 1987; Colby, Kohlberg, Gibbs, & Lieberman, 1983; Rest, Narvaez, Bebeau, & Thomas, 1999). Most children are at the preconventional level (stages 1 and 2). With adolescence, the numbers of those at stages 1 and 2 drop off, and stage 3 becomes the most common stage. Gradually across the adolescent years, more stage 4 reasoning is seen, but there is hardly any evidence of postconventional moral thinking before adulthood. Even then, only a small proportion of people are scored at stage 5. As for stage 6, Kohlberg came to believe that very few people attain it, and it was eliminated from the scoring manual for his Moral Judgment Interview.

Moving Through Stages. How did Kohlberg think people progress from one stage of moral reasoning to the next? True to his roots in Piaget's theory, he maintained that interactions with others, especially with peers, are crucial. Suppose you are discussing the Heinz story with classmates. Some of them will be at a less advanced stage of reasoning than you. You will easily recognize and set aside their arguments because they represent a form of reasoning you yourself were using not so long ago and then moved past. Others, maybe, will use reasoning that is a good deal more advanced than yours. Chances are, you will dismiss those arguments too, because your reasoning structure doesn't yet allow you to make sense of them. Some classmates will put forward reasoning that is a little more complex and morally adequate than yours. You will understand what they are saying, but you won't be able to counter it because you can *recognize* that it is more advanced. The result is that you move a bit closer to their way of thinking. At the same time, *your* reasoning will be having a similar impact on other classmates who are slightly less advanced in their moral thinking than you.

Evidence for this process comes from a study by Lawrence Walker and his co-workers (Walker, Hennig, & Krettenauer, 2000). Fifth and 10th graders discussed both hypothetical dilemmas, along the lines of the Heinz story, and real personal moral conflicts with a friend and also, separately, with one of their parents. The moral stage of the participants was measured each year for the next 4 years. The interactions with friends predicted the rate of the participants' moral development. As Kohlberg would have expected, the interactions that had the biggest effect were those in which friends felt free to argue directly with each other's reasoning.

The discussions with parents also predicted the children's moral development, but the quality of the discussions that had the most impact was quite different. The parents who had the greatest effect used a gentle Socratic approach of eliciting their child's reasoning, probing to be sure they understood before suggesting their own, more complex views. For both parent-child and peer discussions, presenting a lot of information was linked to slower moral development, probably because it felt like being lectured at.

Gender, Culture, and Moral Thought

Kohlberg's theory of moral development has been the most influential view of the topic for four decades, but it has also attracted its share of criticism. At least two major questions have been raised.

Is the theory biased against women?

Is it biased against people from non-Western cultures?

What is the basis for these questions, and what does the evidence suggest?

Gender Bias? Kohlberg's earliest research on moral judgment included only male participants, and when he extended it to include women, he found at first that they scored at a lower stage on average than men. This finding was questioned by Carol Gilligan (1982, 1993), on the ground that Kohlberg was imposing a male perspective on moral development. Women, she argued, have a typical way of considering moral questions that is different from the one men typically use, but every bit as valid. Boys, in her view, are brought up to be independent and assertive. This leads them to see moral questions as a matter of finding fair, objective resolutions to conflicts between separate individuals. Gilligan calls this a **justice orientation.** Girls, on the other hand, are raised to be expressive, kind, and responsive to the needs of others. This encourages them to develop a **care orientation,** in which morality implies special attention to the relationships among people.

Consider the story about Heinz and the drug. Someone with a justice orientation might argue that Heinz shouldn't steal the drug because theft infringes on an owner's right to his property. This would probably be considered a stage 4 response. Someone with a care orientation might talk about Heinz's feelings for his wife, his wife's belief that their connection will lead him to take care of her, and the druggist's heartlessness in the face of their plight. This would most likely be scored as a stage 3 response. The person with a justice orientation might dismiss this as irrelevant sentimentality—did he steal the drug, or didn't he? "Do the crime, do the time!" And someone with a care orientation might reject the other's argument as showing a level of heartlessness at least as cruel and cold as the druggist's.

Gilligan's ideas have a lot of immediate appeal. After all, "everybody knows" that males are supposed to be cool and rational, while females are supposed to be nurturing, sympathetic, and emotionally sensitive. Why shouldn't those qualities show up in their moral attitudes? Researchers have had a harder time finding evidence that supports her views, however (Brabeck & Shore, 2003; Turiel, 2006). One review found that in most of the studies examined, there were no sex differences in level of moral reasoning. Where there were differences, about the same number of studies found females scoring higher than males as found the opposite (Walker, 1991).

As for justice and care orientations, a longitudinal study of children and adolescents found no gender differences in the importance given to obligations versus intimacy in

◄ **Learning Objective 11.8**
How do gender, culture, and social status affect moral thinking?

Justice orientation For Gilligan, approaching moral questions with the primary goal of finding fair, objective resolutions to conflicts.

Care orientation For Gilligan, approaching moral questions with the primary goal of preserving positive relationships among people.

dealing with interpersonal conflicts (Keller & Edelstein, 1993). The fairest conclusion from the research seems to be that both men and women use both orientations, depending on the kind of situation they are considering, and that neither orientation is used mainly by women or men (Jaffee & Hyde, 2000; Pratt, Skoe, & Arnold, 2004).

Cultural Bias? Does Kohlberg's theory represent a specifically Western conception of morality, one that stresses individual rights as opposed to social harmony? And does it, as a result, underestimate or distort the moral thinking of those from non-Western societies? Critics have argued that the answer to these questions is "yes" (Shweder et al., 2006). As we saw in Chapter 8, many anthropologists and cultural psychologists have distinguished between *individualist* cultures, which stress personal autonomy, rights, and goals, and *collectivist* cultures, in which the relationship to the group (family, caste, country) is most important and people are expected to set aside personal goals in the interest of the group. Kohlberg's theory, it is claimed, falsely labels individualist ideas as morally superior to collectivist ideas.

In one study, children, adolescents, and adults from the United States and India were asked to judge a long list of actions that included:

A husband beats his wife black and blue for going to a movie without his permission.

A woman cooks a family meal during her menstrual period.

A man sees a dog sleeping by the side of the road and kicks it.

Indians and Americans agreed that kicking a dog for no reason is morally offensive, but they disagreed sharply about the other two examples. As you might expect, Americans disapproved of wife-beating and saw nothing wrong with cooking during one's menstrual period. For Indians, it was just the opposite (Shweder, Mahapatra, & Miller, 1987).

Why? The answer lies in certain Hindu religious beliefs that non-Hindu Americans do not share as a rule. One is that the head of a family (the husband/father) has a moral duty to preserve the natural order by enforcing his decisions, even if he would prefer not to. Another is that if a woman cooks during her period, it offends family members in the afterlife and causes them to avoid the household, bringing great harm to the family.

As experience tells us, and as the study just mentioned makes clear, moral and religious beliefs often differ widely between different cultures, subcultures, religious groups, and even individual families. For observant Moslems and Jews, avoiding bacon is a moral obligation. For Roman Catholic priests, abstaining from sex is a moral duty. In many families and many cultures, addressing your parents by their first names, or not addressing them as "sir" and "ma'am," is a sign of disrespect, which is morally wrong. What isn't clear is how much these examples cast doubt on Kohlberg's theory. As we saw, he found that adolescents, and most adults, reason morally at the conventional level. The *way* they reason, then, will be similar. But the *content* of their reasoning will be affected by the beliefs, customs, and conventions that are characteristic of their particular social setting.

Questions have also been raised about whether it even makes good psychological sense to type cultures as either individualist or collectivist (Oyserman, Coon, & Kemmelmeier, 2002). On closer examination, it appears that differences in moral judgment among individuals and across situations *within* cultures are of greater significance than the differences *between* cultures (Wainryb, 2006). In that case, it may make more sense to emphasize the similarities and differences in moral development among adolescents, whatever their cultural background, than to put too much stress on the possible role of their cultures.

Why Be Moral?

▶ **Learning Objective 11.9**
What is empathy and how may it be linked to brain structures?

Piaget's and Kohlberg's theories of moral development focus on the reasoning children, adolescents, and adults use to decide the moral thing to do in a particular situation. Critics charge that this approach leaves a crucial set of questions unanswered. Suppose you have decided that a certain action is the moral thing to do. What leads you to *do* it, especially if there is a personal cost involved? Are some people more likely to follow through on their moral judgments than others, and if so, why? What factors in an adolescent's life promote more consistent moral behavior, and what factors make this less likely?

The Role of Guilt. During much of the 20th century, ideas about morality in children were strongly influenced by the psychoanalytic theory of Sigmund Freud. As we saw in Chapter 2, Freud maintained that there is a built-in tension between what individuals want and what society requires. To protect people from one another's sexual and aggressive impulses, parents pass along to their children both a set of social rules and powerful reasons not to break those rules.

This happens primarily as a result of the child's fear of the parent during the Oedipus complex. Children also fear that if they are "bad," they will lose the love and support of the parents and be abandoned. As a defense against these fears, children *identify* with the parent and *internalize* the parent's moral code. This becomes the core of the personality structure called the **superego,** which includes both those things the child morally must do (the *ego ideal*) and those things the child morally must not do (the *conscience*). The most important tool the superego uses to enforce its standards is the emotion of *guilt*. If you do what the superego says you shouldn't, or fail to do what the superego says you should, you are punished by feeling guilty and worthless.

Most observers would agree with Freud that guilt feelings play an important role in moral behavior and that some people are plagued by guilt feelings that seem exaggerated or unjustified. However, the Freudian account of how these feelings develop has not held up well. Freud's theory implies that parents who are punitive and threatening will have children with stronger moral codes. It is hard to find evidence that supports this idea. In fact, harsh parents tend to have children who act up, misbehave, and seem immune to feelings of guilt and remorse. And children start to follow rules when no one is looking, and get upset when they break a rule, as early as age 2 (Kochanska, Aksan, Knaack, & Rhines, 2004; Kochanska, Gross, Lin, & Nichols, 2002). This is before the age when Freud said the Oedipus complex begins and long before it is supposed to be resolved with the formation of the superego.

The Role of Empathy. According to psychologist Martin Hoffman (1991, 2000), the development of moral responses begins with an infant's built-in capacity for **empathy,** or experiencing feelings similar to those someone else is experiencing. Babies less than 2 days old show more distress to the sound of another baby crying than to other noises (Dondi, Simion, & Caltran, 1999; Sagi & Hoffman, 1976), and toddlers will offer a toy to an upset playmate (Eisenberg, Fabes, & Spinrad, 2006). By late childhood, children are able to feel empathy, not just for those whose pain and pleasure they observe directly, but for more generalized groups of others, such as the poor, the handicapped, or the oppressed (Hoffman, 2000).

Recent research by neuroscientists has uncovered structures in the brain that may be a physical basis for empathy. These are "mirror neurons" that are activated in a similar way when the person observes someone else's distress as when they themselves are distressed. For example, seeing an expression of disgust on another person's face leads to the same sort of activation in a brain structure called the insula as having a foul-smelling substance waved under your nose (Gallese, 2005; Gallese, Keysers, & Rizzolatti, 2004). The insula and nearby structures are also activated when people listen to sad stories (Decety & Chaminade, 2003). Apparently, when people say, "I feel your pain," they just might be speaking the literal truth!

There is plenty of evidence that feelings of empathy contribute to moral and prosocial behavior and that adolescents have a more generalized ability to feel empathy than children. In part, this is a result of their more developed cognitive and role-taking skills (Eisenberg et al., 2006). Scholars point out, however, that the connection between empathy and moral actions is not always straightforward. If your empathic response leads to *sympathy*, that is, a feeling of concern for someone in distress, it is likely to set off an attempt to do something about the other person's distress. Empathy alone, in contrast, may shift the focus to ways to reduce *your own* empathic distress.

▲ The capacity to feel empathy for others becomes more generalized during adolescence.

Superego In Freud's theory, the structure of personality that incorporates the moral standards of parents and society and enforces them through feelings of guilt.

Empathy The capacity to experience similar feelings to those someone else is experiencing.

Connect the **Dots...**

Imagine that you are a parent who wants to encourage moral judgment and moral behavior in your child. What sorts of experiences, approaches, and practices do you think would be most helpful?

Along with helping, these could include such psychological mechanisms as denial, "blaming the victim," or simply turning away (Batson, 1991; Eisenberg et al., 1994). In effect, the person thinks, "I can't stand to see someone in pain—so I won't look!"

Parents and Moral Development.   As we saw earlier, both Piaget (1932) and Kohlberg (1984) put great stress on the role of peers in promoting moral development and hardly any on the role of parents. Piaget even suggested that parents who make too much use of their position of authority may slow down the child's progress toward more autonomous moral thinking. More recent research indicates that, in fact, parents play an important role in their children's moral development. Social cognitive theorists such as Albert Bandura (2002) point out that parents serve both as models for mature moral behavior and as sources of praise and criticism. In these ways, they help their children acquire and internalize standards of right and wrong, as well as standards for self-satisfaction and self-condemnation, depending on whether they live up to their personal moral standards.

On a more global level, teens who have warm and supportive relationships with their parents have higher levels of moral and prosocial development (Carlo, 2006). Not surprisingly, parents who take an authoritative approach, as discussed in Chapter 5, have children who are more likely to accept and internalize the parents' moral values.

One aspect of parenting that has particular links to moral development is the kind of disciplinary technique parents use. Martin Hoffman (1970, 2000) has described three major approaches to discipline:

Induction, in which parents explain the effects and implications of an action, stressing how it affected others and its connection to moral values. "Look, what you said hurt Jimmy's feelings and now he's sad."

Power assertion, in which parents use their dominant position to control the child's actions, for example, through physical punishment or taking away privileges. "If you don't stop teasing your brother, no TV time today!"

Love withdrawal, in which parents threaten the child with a loss of affection or approval. "When you act that way, I can't bear to have you around!"

As the descriptions suggest, induction is used more often by authoritative parents, and power assertion by authoritarian parents. Like authoritative parenting, induction is associated with more mature moral thinking and behavior. There are several possible reasons for this connection. First, parents who use induction give clear, relevant statements of their own moral values. Second, they typically encourage empathy and perspective-taking skills by asking the child to imagine how the other person feels. Third, they are likely to discuss the issue in a calm, well-regulated way that gives the adolescent the emotional room to listen without feeling forced into a self-defensive mode (Carlo, 2006).

Moral Identity.   Suppose a group of adolescents all have similar age-appropriate levels of cognitive functioning, perspective-taking skills, and moral judgment. Does that mean that their moral actions will also be similar? Probably not. The likelihood is that some of them are more consistent in the way they act on their moral principles and commitments. Why? In recent years, a number of scholars have suggested that just as people have different moral standards, beliefs, and ways of reasoning, they also differ in how *important* moral concerns are to them (Blasi, 2005; Hardy & Carlo, 2005; Hart, 2006; Moshman, 2005).

This characteristic is known as **moral identity:** To what extent does someone believe that being moral, and acting morally, is a central or essential characteristic of his or her sense of self? The stronger that belief, the stronger the moral identity. Because there is a "natural human tendency to want to live consistent with one's sense of self" (Hardy & Carlo, 2005, p. 235), those with a stronger moral identity are more likely to act in accord with their moral judgments and beliefs. Being faithful to one's core self is felt more and more as a necessity, and realizing that one has acted in a way that conflicts with one's principles and standards is quite painful.

One line of research that has helped to expand our understanding of moral identity studies **moral exemplars,** people who are considered by those who know them to be

Induction A disciplinary approach in which parents explain the effects of an action, stressing how it affected others and its connection to moral values.

Power assertion A disciplinary approach in which parents use their dominant position to control the child's actions.

Love withdrawal A disciplinary approach in which parents threaten the child with a loss of affection or approval.

Moral identity The extent to which someone believes that being moral and acting morally are essential characteristics of his or her sense of self.

Moral exemplar An individual whom others regard as outstanding in moral commitment, personality, and character.

◄ Adolescents with a strong moral identity are more likely to take actions that fit with their moral beliefs.

outstanding in their moral commitment, personality, and character (Colby & Damon, 1994). The key finding is that those who show high levels of commitment to moral causes "are more likely than others to construct their self-concept and identity around these moral concerns" (Hardy & Carlo, 2005, p. 240).

A recent study looked at inner-city adolescents who became deeply involved in community service projects (Reimer, 2003). One was a 15-year-old girl who lived with her mother and brother in a single room in a dangerous neighborhood. At 14, she organized other teens into a successful "adopt-a-grandparent" program at a nearby convalescent home. When she was asked how she came to think of herself as a caring person, she said,

> I would like to be a person like my mom. She doesn't let herself go by what people think of her. She lets herself go by what she thinks of herself and she doesn't do like most people and judge people by what she sees. She judges them by what they think and the way they are. This is how I learned to care.
>
> —(Reimer, 2003, p. 130)

Not everyone is blessed with a mother who is a source of personal inspiration, but in Chapter 14 we will examine a number of ways that adolescents can be encouraged to transform their personal goals into moral goals, see moral concerns with more clarity, develop a greater sense of responsibility for the welfare of their communities, and gain a sense of optimism that personal effort pays off and makes a difference (Lapsley & Narvaez, 2006).

Summing Up...

Personal values and beliefs emerge during the process of moral development. In Piaget's view, children's moral judgments change from heteronomous, or simply obeying rules, to autonomous, partly in response to interactions with peers. Kohlberg, building on Piaget's approach, described six stages of moral development from childhood through adolescence into adulthood. Gilligan argues that Kohlberg's theory favors a justice orientation, more common among men, over a care orientation, more common among women. On the issue of why people behave morally, Freud's theory stresses the role of guilt, while Hoffman and others emphasize the importance of empathy. The kind of discipline parents use has also been linked to moral behavior. Those adolescents who see their moral identity as a central aspect of the self are more likely to act according to their beliefs. A strong moral identity is encouraged by exposure to moral exemplars.

SUMMARY

The **self-concept**, an awareness of being separate from the world around and having one's own individual characteristics, begins to develop as early as infancy and takes an important step forward during adolescence.

Learning Objective 11.1 How does the self-concept change during adolescence?

Children usually describe themselves in terms of concrete aspects such as age, sex, physical characteristics, and personal likings. In late childhood and early adolescence, more psychological concepts make their appearance in the self-concept. During adolescence, the self-concept becomes more complex, more differentiated, more abstract, and more integrated.

The abstract reasoning powers of adolescence make it easier to imagine **possible selves** that play a role in planning, setting priorities, and self-regulation. The self-concept develops as children and adolescents think about themselves, but also as a **looking-glass self** based on noticing the ways others respond to them, leading to a sense of the **generalized other**.

Learning Objective 11.2 How do personal characteristics and experiences contribute to self-esteem?

Self-esteem is the term used for someone's feelings about the self, whether positive, negative, or both. **Baseline self-esteem** is reasonably stable over time, while **barometric self-esteem** goes up and down in response to particular incidents and experiences. During early and middle adolescence, baseline self-esteem drops sharply, and then levels off in late adolescence and rises slightly in early adulthood.

The adolescent drop in self-esteem is more severe for girls than for boys, creating a gender gap that continues through the adult years. The factor that contributes most strongly to self-esteem during adolescence is physical appearance, followed by feeling socially accepted. Sports and academics have less impact.

There are important individual differences among teens in the sources of their self-esteem. For adolescents from minority backgrounds, self-esteem is closely linked to community support and to a sense of ethnic identity. While low self-esteem is often cited as a cause of adolescent problems, the research evidence is mixed, suggesting that problems may also be a source of low self-esteem.

The quest for a sense of **identity**—the psychological structure that gives individuals a sense of coherence, continuity, and personal meaning—is considered one of the most urgent tasks of adolescence.

Learning Objective 11.3 Why is adolescence considered the period of the identity crisis?

Erikson proposed that adolescence sets off the **identity crisis,** in which childhood identifications with the goals, beliefs, and attitudes of parents may be brought into question. Many teens benefit from a **psychosocial moratorium**, in which they have greater freedom to explore their talents and interests and try out different, even unconventional, roles. Exploration typically results in choice, followed by commitment and consolidation. This sequence is often repeated in different domains, such as moral, political, and religious beliefs and career aspirations.

Instead of exploring, some teens take over a rigid definition of identity and roles prescribed for them by parents and community, in a process called **identity foreclosure.** Some who find it hard to face the process of identity exploration and construction fall into a state of **identity diffusion** and waste their energies in meaningless activities. Teens who feel that their social world ignores them may adopt a **negative identity** that forces others to acknowledge them.

Learning Objective 11.4 How are identity exploration and identity commitment linked to identity status?

Recent research on Erikson's theory is largely based on Marcia's work, which sees **identity status** as the product of two processes, **identity exploration** and **identity commitment**. Diffusion results when someone neither explores identity issues nor makes a commitment. Foreclosure results when someone makes commitments without exploration. Moratorium describes someone who is in the process of exploration, but has not yet made commitments. Identity achievement describes someone who, after exploration, has made a personal commitment.

Identity style reflects the ways people deal with identity relevant information. A *diffuse-avoidant* style is linked to diffusion status, a *normative* style is linked to foreclosure status, and an *informational* style is linked to moratorium and achieved status. Although Erikson maintained that the identity crisis begins in early adolescence and is usually completed by late adolescence, today the transition to adulthood is more extended in Western cultures.

Learning Objective 11.5 How do parents, schools, and neighborhoods contribute to ethnic identity?

Ethnic identity is an important part of an adolescent's sense of identity as a whole, especially for those who belong to a nondominant ethnic minority. Like identity development generally, the development of ethnic identity involves active exploration, choice, commitment, and consolidation. A well-developed sense of ethnic identity has been linked to less depression, a greater ability to shrug off stressful events, and a stronger sense of well-being.

Teens who are members of an ethnic minority are usually exposed to two cultures, that of their ethnic group and that of the wider society. Their response to this may be *biculturalism, assimilation, separation,* or *marginalization*. Bicultural adolescents may combine features of both cultures in their attitudes and behaviors (*blended biculturals*) or move between aspects of the two cultures (*alternating biculturals*). Moving between different languages or dialects involves **code switching**, which may also cue changes in **cultural frame**, the ways of thinking and relating that are typical of the different linquistic communities.

Adolescents are more likely to begin exploring their ethnic identity when they have frequent interactions with members of other ethnic groups, through living in ethnically diverse neighborhoods and attending ethnically diverse schools.

A central aspect of identity is a person's moral values, beliefs, and ways of dealing with moral issues.

Learning Objective 11.6   How did Piaget investigate and explain moral judgment in children?

Piaget approached moral development in terms of how children and adolescents think about moral issues. Piaget found that children's moral judgment goes through two phases. During the phase of **heteronomous morality** (ages 4 to 7), rules are seen as unbendable and offenses are judged by the amount of damage they cause. During the phase of **autonomous morality** (age 7 on), rules are seen as conventions that can be broken if there is good reason, and offenses are judged more in terms of the actor's good or bad intentions.

Learning Objective 11.7   How did Kohlberg describe the stages and levels of moral reasoning?

Kohlberg extended Piaget's theory by giving adolescents and adults more complex moral situations and analyzing the reasoning they use in resolving them. The best known of these concerns a man whose wife needs a certain drug to survive, and his decision whether to steal the drug for her. Kohlberg described moral reasoning in terms of six stages, at three levels.

Preconventional morality, which includes the *punishment* orientation and the stage of *naïve hedonism*, focuses on the external rewards and punishments for an action. **Conventional morality**, which includes the *"good boy/nice girl"* stage and the *social order* stage, focuses on the standards and expectations set up by others. **Postconventional morality**, which includes the *social contract* stage and the *universal principles* stage, focuses on internalized universal principles of ethics and justice.

Learning Objective 11.8   How do gender, culture, and social status affect moral thinking?

Kohlberg's work has been challenged by some, such as Gilligan, who see it as reflecting a masculine bias, and by others who believe it embodies a pro-Western concept of morality. For Gilligan, males are more likely to adopt a **justice orientation,** in which the goal of moral decisions is to reach fair, objective resolutions. Females, in contrast, are more likely to adopt a **care orientation,** in which the goal of moral decisions is to safeguard important relationships among people. Most research does not find the gender differences in orientation that Gilligan proposes. As for possible cultural bias, research suggests that the differences in moral judgment among people within cultures are more significant than those between cultures.

Learning Objective 11.9   What is empathy and how may it be linked to brain structures?

The goal of moral reasoning is to decide what is the right thing to do in a given situation. But what leads people to do the right thing, once they have decided what it is? For Freud, the primary reason to act morally is to avoid feelings of *guilt* imposed by the **superego.** Hoffman says that the precursors of **empathy,** the capacity to feel similar emotions to those of someone else, are present from birth. Empathy is linked to moral behavior in those for whom it leads to feelings of sympathy, but for some it may lead to nonmoral responses, such as denial or blaming the victim.

Parents affect the moral development of their children both as models of mature adult behavior and through the disciplinary techniques they use. In **induction,** parents explain the effects of an action and how it has affected others, and then suggest ways to repair any damage. In **power assertion,** parents use their dominant position to control what the child does, through the threat of punishment or loss of privileges. In **love withdrawal,** parents threaten the child with a loss of affection or approval. Authoritative parents are more likely to use induction, which is linked to more mature moral thinking and behavior, while authoritarian parents are more likely to rely on power assertion.

Moral identity reflects the extent to which individuals see acting morally as a central part of their sense of self. Those with a strong moral identity are more likely to act in accord with their moral judgments and beliefs. One source of moral identity is coming into contact with **moral exemplars,** individuals who are outstanding in their moral strength, commitment, and character.

KEY TERMS

Self-concept (359)	Psychosocial moratorium (368)	Ethnic identity (373)	Justice orientation (381)
Possible selves (361)	Identity foreclosure (368)	Code switching (376)	Care orientation (381)
Looking-glass self (361)	Identity diffusion (369)	Cultural frame (376)	Superego (383)
Generalized other (361)	Negative identity (369)	Heteronomous morality (378)	Empathy (383)
Self-esteem (362)	Identity exploration (369)	Immanent justice (378)	Induction (384)
Baseline self-esteem (362)	Identity commitment (369)	Autonomous morality (378)	Power assertion (384)
Barometric self-esteem (363)	Identity status (369)	Preconventional morality (379)	Love withdrawal (384)
Identity (367)	Identity style (370)	Conventional morality (379)	Moral identity (384)
Identity crisis (367)	Ethnicity (373)	Postconventional morality (379)	Moral exemplar (384)

Intimacy

Outline	Learning Objectives
FRIENDSHIP	
Friends in Adolescence	◀ **12.1** How do friendships change with adolescence?
How Friendships Develop	◀ **12.2** How do Sullivan and Erikson describe the stages of friendship?
"Who's Your Friend?"	◀ **12.3** What characteristics predict which teens will become close friends?
What Are Friends For?	◀ **12.4** What are the benefits and risks of adolescent friendships?
ROMANCE	
The Dating Game	◀ **12.5** What needs are met by dating at different points in adolescence?
"I'll Take Romance"	◀ **12.6** What phases do romantic relationships go through?
"Breaking Up Is Hard to Do"	◀ **12.7** Why is the end of a romantic relationship so painful?
SEX	
Adolescent Sexuality and Culture	◀ **12.8** How do different cultures deal with adolescent sexuality?
Sexual Activity in Adolescence	◀ **12.9** What is the usual sequence of sexual activity in adolescence?
Sexual Minorities in Adolescence	◀ **12.10** What special issues do sexual minority youth face?
Risks of Adolescent Sex	◀ **12.11** What are the risks of adolescent sex and how can they be reduced?

The title of this chapter, *intimacy*, is a term that takes on different colors in different contexts. Your *intimates* are those people you feel particularly close to, who know and like you well and whom you know and like well. An *intimate moment* suggests being alone with a special someone, preferably with moonlight, a soft breeze, and a distant murmur of music, surf, or both. *Intimate relations* is a polite way of referring to sex, even though many adolescents are intimate without sexual involvement or sexually active without real intimacy.

For most teens, the adolescent years are made memorable by the formation of close friendships, the delight and despair of romantic relationships, and the transition to sexual activity. In this chapter, we look at all of these and examine how they are interconnected in the experiences of adolescents.

FRIENDSHIP

Friendships are a central feature of social interactions from almost the beginning of life. Even 2-year-olds may have certain playmates whom they consistently choose in preference to others. These relationships have real implications, too. Preschool children are more affectionate, approving, and sympathetic with friends than with others, and their play together is more advanced cognitively (Howes, 1996). Those who form solid friendships at this age are more socially competent, too. They know how to play according to rules, such as taking turns, and they are better at following their friends' thoughts and understanding their emotions. When they reach school age, they find it easier to make new friends as well (Dunn, 2004).

Affection, approval, sympathy, and understanding are qualities essential to our concept of friendship, whether we are thinking of kindergarten children, adolescents, or adults. There are other aspects of friendship that are important throughout the lifespan, too. Among other things, a friend is someone who

likes to spend time with you and do the kinds of things you like to do;

has interesting, stimulating, and funny things to say and do;

lends a hand when you need help and sticks up for you with others; and

makes you feel more positive about yourself.

Yet, while friendships have a lot in common at different ages, they also go through important developmental changes. Around age 7, a friend is someone who is easy to get together with and fun to be with. A child down the block who has neat toys and likes the same games and activities fits the requirements very well. Later in the elementary school years, children start to put more emphasis on shared values and social attitudes, especially loyalty and mutual support. Someone who won't stand up for you when you're being teased or who makes fun of you behind your back is *not* a friend, no matter how much time you spend together or how close your families are.

► **Learning Objective 12.1**
How do friendships change with adolescence?

Self-disclosure The process in which individuals communicate to others intimate information about their experiences and feelings.

Intimacy An emotional sense of attachment to someone with whom one shares personal knowledge and a concern for one another's well-being.

Friends in Adolescence

As children approach puberty, the qualities of mutual trust, warmth, and understanding take on more and more importance in their friendships (Rubin, Bukowski, & Parker, 2006). Mutual trust is particularly crucial because of the emergence of **self-disclosure** as a feature of close friendships. Young adolescents begin to share their most personal thoughts and feelings with those they are close to (Berndt, 2002). They talk about their ambitions and doubts, the problems they are having with parents, siblings, and other peers, their hopes, dreams, and fears. In the process, they build a genuine sense of **intimacy**, the emotional attachment that is felt by those who share personal knowledge and understanding, concern for each other's welfare, and a joint commitment to maintaining and deepening the relationship.

A whole array of factors contributes to making adolescence such an important period in the development of intimate friendships. The physical changes of puberty, and the social and emotional changes that accompany them, confront children with a seemingly endless series of urgent questions, such as: What is happening to me? Is this normal? Am I okay? Yet, the sensitive nature of the questions and the social distancing from parents that often comes with puberty make most young adolescents shy away from discussing such topics with their parents. When they need information, and especially when they need reassurance and support, they are more likely to turn to a friend who is going through the same changes and confronting the same questions.

On a cognitive level, adolescence brings an increased ability to set one's own viewpoint to one side and look at things from another person's perspective (Selman, 1980). Teens understand themselves and others in a more complex, differentiated way. This makes them able to empathize with the other person more deeply and more accurately, which, in turn, makes them able to respond on a more intimate level (Soenens, Duriez, Vansteenkiste, & Goossens, 2007). We saw in Chapter 11 that with adolescence, children's self-concepts become more psychological and more attuned to the ways someone's personality interacts with features of the setting. In the same way, adolescents have a greater ability to understand how situational factors, such as a fight with one's parents, can lead friends to behave in ways that are "not like them."

The social changes of adolescence also contribute. As peer relationships take on increasing importance, having someone to talk over those relationships with—someone who really knows them—is vital. When teens begin to develop romantic interests, to whom can they turn to explore their feelings of attraction, insecurity, and all the rest? Their parents? Some random classmate? Of course not. It has to be someone they feel they can count on to understand, sympathize, and deserve their trust. Because parents give teens a greater degree of social independence, they are able to choose their friends more freely and spend more of their time with them (Brown & Klute, 2003).

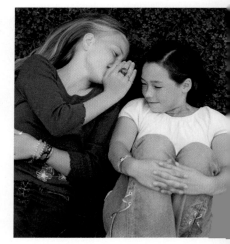

▲ Puberty is a time when children begin to develop a sense of intimacy with close friends.

How Friendships Develop

How do children acquire the understanding and skills that it takes to be a close friend to another person? What factors in their development are most crucial? Different theorists have advanced different answers to these questions. In this section, we look at three major points of view on the development of friendship—Sullivan's, Erikson's, and Bowlby's—and examine where they overlap and where they contrast with one another.

◀ **Learning Objective 12.2**
How do Sullivan and Erikson describe the stages of friendship?

Stages of Friendship: Sullivan. For the last half-century, thinking and research about the development of friendship and intimacy have been strongly influenced by the ideas of psychiatrist Harry Stack Sullivan. Like Freud and Erikson, Sullivan believed that all children pass through a sequence of stages, and that what happens to them during those stages is crucial to their psychological functioning as adults. As we have seen, Freud's theory described the psychosexual stages of childhood and Erikson's stressed the emergence of different psychosocial issues. Sullivan, in contrast, maintained that we should look at development in terms of changing *interpersonal needs* and *social relationships*. At each stage, children who are able to get their needs met build up a sense of interpersonal security that prepares them well for coping with the next stage. Those who do not get their needs met, on the other hand, are left with feelings of interpersonal insecurity and anxiety that make it more difficult to deal with later needs as they emerge (Sullivan, 1953).

The stages Sullivan described are shown in Figure 12.1 on page 392. During infancy, the most important need is for *tenderness*, and the interpersonal source for it is the parents. In the preschool years, another need emerges, for *companionship*. This is "the interest and participation of a significant adult in the child's play" (Sullivan, 1953, p. 291), and the parents continue as a preferred source. During the early school years,

Figure 12.1 Stages of Social Needs According to Sullivan
Sullivan described six stages of social needs across the childhood and adolescent years.

STAGE	SOCIAL NEED	KEY RELATIONSHIP
Infancy (0–2 years)	Tenderness	Parents
Childhood (2–6 years)	Companionship	Parents
Juvenile (6–9 years)	Acceptance	Peers
Preadolescence (9–12 years)	Intimacy	Same-sex friend ("Chum")
Early adolescence (12–16 years)	Sexuality	Romantic partner
Late adolescence (16 years–adulthood)	Integration into adult society	Significant adults

Source: Sullivan, 1953.

however, an important shift takes place. Playmates—same-age (and as a rule, same-sex) peers—increasingly fill the need for companionship. This brings the need for *acceptance* into sharp focus. Those children who are not able to be accepted, for whatever reason, suffer from feelings of exclusion and ostracism, and these feelings affect their confidence and sense of self as they approach the next stage.

Finding a Chum. The preadolescent years, from about age 9 to puberty, occupy a critical place in Sullivan's theory. These years mark the emergence of the **need for intimacy.** During this stage, children seek to escape loneliness and gain a sense of well-being by developing a "specific new type of interest in a *particular* member of the same sex who becomes a chum or a close friend" (Sullivan, 1953, p. 245; italics in original). These *chumships* are a child's first real experience of a close interpersonal relationship based on mutual caring, regard, reciprocity, and an exchange between equals. Within them,

> . . . [Y]our child begins to develop a real sensitivity to what matters to another person. And this is not in the sense of "what should I do to get what I want," but instead "what should I do to contribute to the happiness or to support the prestige and feeling of worth-whileness of my chum."
>
> —(Sullivan, 1953, p. 246)

Close friendships in the preadolescent period give the child the confidence to give and receive intimate thoughts and feelings and the sensitivity to understand and respond to someone else's needs and desires. Just as important, the experience of being known and liked by another person contributes to the child's emerging sense of self. Like Cooley (1902) and Mead (1934), whose ideas we encountered in Chapter 10, Sullivan held that our self-concept is shaped by our awareness of how others regard us. He went on, however, to suggest that chumships offer a unique chance to see ourselves through the eyes of an equal who knows us really well *and still cares for us.* This potent combination of appraisal, acceptance, and validation strengthens the child's self-esteem. At the same time, it helps the child construct a more realistic and adaptive self-concept. There are some things about yourself that you are better off knowing, but that only a best friend will dare tell you!

Finding a Partner. During early adolescence, the **need for sexuality** emerges, in response to both the biological changes of puberty and the social changes of the adolescent peer group. The intimacy needs that developed before adolescence and were met in the context of a chumship are as powerful as ever. Now, however, they begin to act in tandem with romantic and sexual desires. The goal becomes finding a romantic partner who can also be an intimate friend. Consider the assets that emerge during a chumship and make it work. They may include:

an ability to care deeply about another person;

a sensitivity to the other person's feelings and needs;

Connect the **Dots...**

As a child or young adolescent, did you have a "chum," a special friend with whom you did and shared everything and felt especially close? If not, did you have a sense that you were missing out on something important? How well does Sullivan's account fit with your own experiences and those of others you knew?

Need for intimacy According to Sullivan, a desire to develop a relationship with a close friend or *chum* that emerges during the preadolescent years.

Need for sexuality For Sullivan, a need that emerges in response to the biological changes of puberty and the social changes of the adolescent peer group.

◄ Sullivan stresses the importance of same-sex friends or "chums" in early adolescence.

a willingness to share very personal information; and

a commitment to mutuality and equality.

With adolescence, these become essential elements in achieving a satisfying romantic and sexual relationship. Chumships, then, are important not only for themselves, but also as essential preparation for intimate relationships later on.

In Sullivan's view, all adolescents face the challenge of coordinating the need for intimacy and the need for sexuality, but they do not all meet the challenge in the same way. As we will see later in this chapter, some become intimately involved with a romantic partner at an early point. Others go through a series of relationships that may become increasingly close. Still others look for intimacy and sexual expression in different people, for example, by maintaining an intimate nonsexual friendship while keeping an emotional distance from romantic partners. Some, unfortunately, find it hard to form intimate connections with either a close friend *or* a love interest.

As adolescents near adulthood, they move into the last stage in Sullivan's theory of interpersonal development. Ideally, they will have already consolidated their sexual identity and developed the ability to express both sexuality and intimacy with a single partner. Now their principal need becomes to integrate themselves with the adult world. This involves developing a network of mature interpersonal relationships that includes a committed love relationship that fuses the needs for intimacy and sexual gratification.

The Quest for Intimacy: Erikson. Erik Erikson's analysis of the quest for identity during adolescence was a major topic in Chapter 11. According to his general theory of psychosocial development across the lifespan, the next stage, during young adulthood, is defined by the crisis of **intimacy versus isolation** (Erikson, 1968). In his view, the main challenge young adults face is to develop an intimate relationship that can take on a life and identity of its own without submerging the individual identities of the partners. For this reason, only those who have *already* achieved a firm sense of identity are able to move on to develop a mature intimate relationship. How can you disclose your inner self to another person if you don't have a clear sense of who you are? Unless you have a clear sense of where you are going in your life, how deep a commitment can you make to someone else?

On the surface, the connection between identity and intimacy that Erikson describes seems like the exact opposite of the one Sullivan describes. Erikson sees adolescents struggling with the issue of identity so that, as young adults, they can deal with the issue

Intimacy versus isolation
According to Erikson, the most important psychosocial crisis that young adults face.

of intimacy. Sullivan sees adolescents, and even preadolescents, trying to express and gratify their need for intimacy and gaining a firmer sense of self by way of their intimate exchanges with chums and romantic partners. So who's right? Does intimacy come before identity, or identity before intimacy?

On closer examination, Erikson and Sullivan are discussing complementary issues that both come under the heading of intimacy. Erikson asks what it takes to achieve a mature intimate relationship and concludes that one of the preconditions is a firm sense of personal identity. Sullivan asks how people become able to make intimate connections with another person and concludes that the process begins as early as age 8 or 9. Erikson is describing an ideal destination and Sullivan is describing the route people take to get there. We should also keep in mind that as intimacy and identity develop, each may strengthen the other. Those adolescents with a clearer sense of identity will gain the self-confidence it takes to risk intimacy, and those who are more deeply involved in intimate relationships will get the external validation of their worth that is so essential to developing a firm sense of self.

Attachment to Friends: Bowlby. A third approach to understanding how close relationships develop is derived from John Bowlby's (1973) account of attachment. As we learned in Chapter 5, Bowlby says the experiences babies have with their parents lead them to develop internal **working models,** or ideas and expectations about interpersonal relationships. Caregivers who are sensitive and responsive foster secure attachment, which leads children to see themselves as lovable and others as responsive to their needs. Children with inconsistent or unresponsive caregivers, on the other hand, develop working models of themselves as unworthy and of others as rejecting or unresponsive to their needs (Ainsworth, Blehar, Waters, & Wall, 1978).

Bowlby maintained that these working models have an enduring effect. They influence the way children interact with their parents and shape the expectations children hold for other close relationships, including both friendships and romantic relationships. In turn, the expectations they hold about these relationships affect the ways they behave in them and the results they achieve.

More specifically, a child who formed a *secure* attachment as a baby will approach later relationships with a healthy, positive attitude. One who is *anxious-avoidant* or *dismissing* will hold back from getting into close relationships out of an expectation of rejection and failure. A child with an *anxious-ambivalent* or *preoccupied* attachment style will be eager, even desperate, to form close relationships, but may then undermine them by overinvolvement, fears of loss, and demands for reassurance (Sroufe, Egeland, Carlson, & Collins, 2005).

As for research evidence, a review of over 60 studies confirms the connection between early attachment to parents and close friendships in adolescence (Schneider, Atkinson, & Tardiff, 2001). Those teens who have more secure attachments to their parents are also likely to have more positive close friendships (Rubin et al., 2004). One recent study found that the working models adolescents have for parents and those they have for relationships with close friends and romantic partners are similar (Furman, Simon, Shaffer, & Bouchey, 2002).

This should not be taken to mean that what happens in infancy *determines* the course of later relationships, however. Bowlby saw infant attachment as setting the child on a particular pathway, but a pathway that has twists, turns, and branchings. At each point along the way, new experiences can lead to changes in the child's pattern of adaptation. At the same time, these new experiences themselves are understood and even shaped by the views the child formed while experiencing earlier relationships and trying to understand what they meant (Sroufe, 2005).

For example, a preschool child who developed an anxious-ambivalent attachment style as an infant may really want to join the children playing in the block corner, but hangs back out of fear of rejection. The odds are that the other children will ignore him or her, confirming and strengthening the child's feelings of unworthiness. But suppose one of them looks up and motions for the child to come play. The block corner, and the welcoming child, may now seem just a little safer. Each repetition of a positive peer

Working models According to Bowlby, implicit expectations about relationships that form in infancy and affect attitudes toward others.

experience helps the child's working model of *peer* relationships become less anxious and more positive, even if the attachment to the parents is still insecure.

"Who's Your Friend?"

Over 2,000 years ago, in the course of discussing the nature of friendship, the Greek philosopher Aristotle quoted a proverb that was well-known even back then, *Birds of a feather flock together.* More recent research confirms the accuracy of the saying. The best way of predicting whether two children or adolescents are likely to be close friends is to see how similar they are (Hartup, 1996).

◄ **Learning Objective 12.3**
What characteristics predict which teens will become close friends?

Similarities Among Friends. It may be true that occasionally "opposites attract," but most of the time children make and keep friends on the basis of common interests, common activities, and common ways of thinking and behaving. If one child is passionate about soccer and the child next door is an avid stamp collector, they may both be nice and friendly, but they are not going to find a lot of things to do together or much time to do them.

Among high school students, close friends tend to be similar on a long list of social and demographic characteristics. These characteristics include age, grade level, sex, ethnic background, socioeconomic status, and religion (Aboud & Mendelson, 1996). They are also more alike in school-related attitudes, academic achievement, and college plans (Berndt, 1996; Brown, 2004), as well as smoking, drinking, drug use, and antisocial behavior (Dishion, Andrews, & Crosby, 1995; Dishion & Owen, 2002). Best friends are similar in their identity status, too (Akers, Jones, & Coyl, 1998). What accounts for these pervasive similarities?

In Chapter 6 we examined the way the linked processes of *selection* and *socialization* affect peer relations generally. These processes have a powerful effect on friendships as well. Suppose you meet someone for the first time and discover that you both like inline skating, Thai food, and garage-band rock. You already have a lot to talk about and do together, if you both want to develop the acquaintance. You *select* each other because something, it almost doesn't matter what, makes you "click." To the extent that you continue to click on further contact, you will also start to influence or *socialize* one another. Your tastes, attitudes, preferences, even the way you dress and the slang phrases you use, will tend to become more similar as the friendship becomes more intimate.

Other-Sex Friends. One important exception to the rule that close friends are similar to each other is friendships between girls and boys. These are rare among preadolescents and early adolescents, in part because the gender segregation that is typical of childhood still holds sway (Sroufe, Bennett, Englund, Urban, & Shulman, 1993). Then too, girls this age are generally more mature, physically, socially, and emotionally, than their male classmates, which makes equal relationships problematical. Girls and boys also tend to have different approaches to friendship; girls are more relation-oriented and boys more activity-oriented (Rubin et al., 2006). Still another obstacle is that having *any* close relationship with someone of the other sex can set off sexually tinged teasing from peers (Jones, Newman, & Bautista, 2005).

Nevertheless, having a close other-sex friend is widespread by middle adolescence. In fact, according to one study, by age 17 more teens *do* have a close friend of the other sex than *don't* (Kuttler, La Greca, & Prinstein, 1999). Another study found that by late adolescence other-sex friendships are seen as closer and more cohesive than same-sex friendships (Johnson, 2004).

In middle childhood, having close other-sex friends has been linked to adjustment problems (Kovacs, Parker, & Hoffman, 1996). This is not at all the case during adolescence. Teens who have close friends of both sexes are as well-adjusted in their relationships as those who have only same-sex close friends. For boys (but not for girls), an other-sex close friend is more likely to make them feel good about themselves than a same-sex close friend is (Kuttler et al., 1999). In fact, boys see their friendship with their best female friend as more rewarding than their friendship with their best male

▶ Friendships between girls and boys become more common in mid-adolescence.

friend (Thomas & Daubman, 2001). Girls, on the other hand, rate their same- and other-sex friends about the same.

What Are Friends For?

▶ **Learning Objective 12.4**
What are the benefits and risks of adolescent friendships?

> A best friend to me is someone you can have fun with and you can also be serious with about personal things—about girls, or what you're going to do with your life or whatever. My best friend, Jeff, and I can talk about things. His parents are divorced too, and he understands when I feel bummed out about the fights between my mom and dad. A best friend is someone who's not going to make fun of you just because you do something stupid or put you down if you make a mistake. If you're afraid of something or someone, they'll give you confidence.
>
> —Sam, 13 (Bell, 1998, p. 80)

Sam's answer touches on many of the positive features that close friendships provide. A more formal list of these provisions would include:

companionship—someone to be with and have fun with;

intimacy—someone with whom to share personal thoughts and feelings;

trust—someone who keeps promises and doesn't divulge your secrets;

loyalty—someone who stands up for you;

warmth—someone with whom you share emotional closeness;

assistance—someone who lends a hand when needed;

acceptance—someone who likes you the way you are;

support—someone who affirms your competence and worth; and

guidance—someone who gives advice with your best interest in mind.

High-quality friendship A relationship that has many positive features and few negative features.

Low-quality friendship A relationship in which negative features, such as conflict, hostility, and rivalry, outweigh positive features such as trust, loyalty, and warmth.

On the dark side, even close friendships may also have negative features such as *domination, conflict, hostility, rivalry, belittlement,* and *betrayal*. If a relationship has many of the positive qualities and few of the negative, we can think of it as a **high-quality friendship.** If the negative qualities outweigh the positive qualities, it would be considered a **low-quality friendship** (Berndt, 2002; Burk & Laursen, 2005; Furman, 1989).

The Quality of Friendships. What determines whether the friendships a teen becomes involved in will be high quality or low quality? One factor that makes a difference is self-esteem. Whether they have high or low self-esteem, adolescents have very similar ideas about what friendship *should* be. What they think about their actual friendships, and the ways they manage them, are very different. Those with high self-esteem see their friendships as positive, intimate, and mutually satisfying (Azmitia, 2001; Thomas & Daubman, 2001).

Those with low self-esteem, in contrast, tend to mull over the negative aspects of their relationships. They may come to doubt whether their friends really like them and try to test the friendship, with predictably negative results (Rosenberg & Owens, 2001). When teens with high self-esteem have disappointing experiences with friends, they don't dwell on them, but attribute them to the normal ups and downs of friendships. Those with low self-esteem tend instead to see conflicts and betrayals as stemming from the general nature of the relationship and to expect them to continue (Azmitia, Ittel, & Radmacher, 2005).

Aspects of the teen's social environment also contribute importantly to the quality of close friendships. In a recent study of urban, ethnic minority adolescents, family relationships, teacher/student relations, and student/student relations were all related to increasing quality of friendships across the adolescent years (Way & Greene, 2006). One interesting finding in this study was that for boys, friendship quality increased more dramatically during adolescence than it did for girls, largely because the boys started out at such a lower level.

Support and Protection. High-quality friendships provide an array of benefits that includes higher self-esteem, greater involvement in school, and higher social acceptance (Berndt, 2002). Adolescents who have supportive friendships are better prepared to form positive relationships with other peers (Berndt, 2004). These relationships will not be as close as their friendships, of course, but they still make an important contribution to social adjustment.

In one study, 6th graders rated the quality of their friendships and also rated the leadership and sociability of their classmates. The following year, the same students, now in junior high school, provided similar ratings of themselves and their classmates. We saw in Chapter 7 that a great many adolescents have social problems following the transition from elementary school to junior high (Eccles, 2004). In this study, however, for those students whose friendships in 6th grade were higher in quality, classmates' ratings of their sociability and leadership improved from 6th to 7th grade, but *only* if most of their 6th-grade friendships had survived the transition to junior high (Berndt, Hawkins, & Jiao, 1999).

Friendships can also play a protective role. Canadian psychologist Ernest Hodges and his colleagues followed a large group of preadolescents over the course of a year, with a particular focus on those who were potential victims of bullying (Hodges, Boivin, Vitaro, & Bukowski, 1999). As a rule, children with internalizing problems such as high anxiety, emotionality, submissiveness, and low self-confidence are likely to experience increasing victimization. That was found in this study, too, but less so for those who had at least one high-quality friendship.

Those children with friends were protected in another way, too. Ordinarily, being victimized leads to an increase in the internalizing problems that make victimization more likely. Victims, in other words, are usually caught in a vicious circle. But in this study, among children who were equally victimized at the beginning, those with a close friend showed lower increases in emotional problems a year later. Friendship offered them some protection both against victimization itself and against the negative impact of being victimized.

Friendship Risks. Beneficial as they are, high-quality friendships sometimes have negative effects as well. The intimate self-disclosure that is such a feature of close relationships may take the form of *co-rumination*, in which the friends extensively discuss and rediscuss problems, bad situations, and negative feelings (Rose, 2002). Ironically, co-rumination has been linked both to closer, higher-quality friendships and to

Connect the **Dots...**

Among those you knew during adolescence, think of examples you would describe as high-quality friendships and as low-quality friendships. What characteristics—of the teens or of their relationships—lead you to label the friendships that way? What was the developmental course of the friendships, and how did they affect those involved?

increased depression and anxiety. As was discussed earlier, in Chapter 10, girls are more likely to engage in co-rumination than boys are. This may help explain both girls' more intimate friendships and their higher levels of depression and anxiety (Rose, 2002).

Some scholars have suggested another way that high-quality friendships might play a negative role. As we have seen, friends influence each other in many ways, and it seems reasonable to suppose that close friends have greater influence (Berndt & Murphy, 2002). What if one effect of close friendships is to *magnify* the influence a friend's characteristics have on a child, whether those characteristics are positive or negative? If you become best friends with someone who is a delinquent, doesn't that pose a risk that you will fall in with your friend's deviant behavior? There is not as much evidence for this effect as might be expected (Berndt, 2002), but there is some. For example, investigators have found a reciprocal relationship between friendship and substance use (Dishion & Owen, 2002). Having a friend who is a substance user predicts higher levels of substance use, and being a substance user predicts choosing friends who are, too.

Low-quality friendships—those high in such negative features as conflict, rivalry, and hostility—pose a different set of risks. One study that tracked 7th graders found that those who were involved in such friendships in the fall were more disruptive in school the following spring (Berndt & Keefe, 1995). One explanation is that friends who fight a lot with each other are practicing negative ways of behaving that carry over to their interactions with other children and adults. The unfavorable reactions these behaviors provoke make them pull away from other children and depend more on their friendship. The more adolescents see their friendships as being high in negativity, and the more they *agree* with each other on this, the more behavior problems they develop and the worse they do in school (Burk & Laursen, 2005).

> ### Summing Up...
>
> Friendships take on new importance and new features with the approach of adolescence. Mutual trust and understanding lead to greater self-disclosure, which, in turn, builds a sense of intimacy. Because teens can better take one another's point of view, their mutual understanding is more complex and differentiated. For Sullivan, puberty brings a need for intimacy that is met by making a chum, a close friend of the same sex. In middle adolescence, the need for sexuality shifts these intimacy goals to a romantic partner. Working models formed earlier in childhood affect a teen's close friendships as well. High-quality friendships offer support and protection, as well as companionship, trust, and other positive features. Low-quality friendships, in contrast, are marked by domination, rivalry, conflict, and other negative features.

ROMANCE

Like friendships, romantic relationships are ongoing interactions that two people voluntarily choose to keep active. Unlike most friendships, romances have a passionate intensity that sets them apart from everyday life. Who writes mournful songs about a friend leaving town on the morning train? Or tells stories about the rage and despair felt when a friend, even a best friend, spends an evening with someone else? Romance is different, and it is during adolescence that this difference makes itself obvious.

The Dating Game

▶ **Learning Objective 12.5**
What needs are met by dating at different points in adolescence?

For several generations of American adolescents, the social ritual that carried the greatest burden of meaning in their daily (and especially, weekend) lives was the *date*. The rules and customs of dating varied in different regions and across different decades, but there were always rules and customs that everyone knew and followed. In the classic mid-20th-century version, it was the boy who proposed a date and the girl who decided whether to say yes. The girl's parents were told where the teens were going, what they were planning to do, and what time the girl would be home. It was understood that the boy paid for the movie tickets, the snack afterwards, and whatever other expenses that came up. It was also understood that he would hope to get a goodnight kiss and that it was up to her to decide if he got one and, if so, how long and involved it became.

To adolescents today, this would probably all sound as quaint as dancing a minuet. Yet, if the ritual has changed in its details, if it's called *hanging out* instead of *going out*, it is still a central feature of social relationships during adolescence and beyond (Collins & Sroufe, 1999; Furman, Ho, & Low, 2007). Dating gives adolescents a socially recognized way to satisfy a variety of needs that are important to them, including:

> *recreation*—doing fun things with someone congenial;
>
> *socialization*—learning to get along with other-sex peers by trying it and learning from mistakes;
>
> *status*—associating with a desirable partner to raise one's own social standing;
>
> *companionship*—building a history of shared activities and exchanges with someone;
>
> *sexual experimentation*—exploring sexual activity;
>
> *intimacy*—establishing a uniquely close relationship with someone; and
>
> *courtship*—looking for a partner for a long-term relationship.
>
> —(Paul & White, 1990; Skipper & Nass, 1966)

One thing about this list is how much it overlaps the list earlier in the chapter of the qualities of close friendships. That shouldn't surprise us. All close relationships have features in common, as well as features that distinguish among them. Remember that Sullivan (1953), for one, saw the intimate "chumships" of preadolescence as an essential training ground for romantic relationships in adolescence.

Another thing to notice about the list, however, is what it leaves out. There is no mention of the intense attraction, euphoria, despair, obsessiveness, wild mood swings, and intrusive thinking that make romantic love such a cauldron of emotions (Fisher, 2006). Romeo and Juliet weren't dating, they were *in love*, and in the end, they were ready to die for it. We will have more to say about romantic love later in the chapter.

Different aspects of dating take on importance at different points across the adolescent years. In early adolescence, recreation and status needs are prominent (Collins & Sroufe, 1999; Connolly, Craig, Goldberg, & Pepler, 1999). Having fun with your date matters, but what matters even more is showing up at the party with somebody who is considered attractive and popular. Even if the two of you have nothing to say to each other, the fact that you're on a date together scores points and boosts egos.

Later in adolescence, mutual and reciprocal needs, such as companionship and intimacy, become more central. Partners are chosen in the hope both of their meeting those needs and of being able to meet the same needs for them. Socialization also takes on more importance, as older adolescents open themselves to the possibility of becoming a more sensitive partner and helping the other person toward the same goal. Parents sometimes warn adolescent girls that "boys only want one thing." Perhaps so; but a recent study of 10th-grade boys found that their most important motive for dating was the hope of getting to know their partner better (Smiler, 2008).

Development of Dating. As we saw earlier, in Chapter 6, as children approach adolescence, they typically hang out in groups of same-gender, same-age peers (Brown, 2004). Relationships with other-gender peers start when groups of boys or girls go places (the schoolyard, the mall) where they can expect to "accidentally" run into groups of the other gender. Later, mixed-gender group-oriented activities, such as parties, school functions, and sports events, become important (Pellegrini & Long, 2007). These mixed-gender group activities give adolescents a way to meet and get to know potential partners. These activities also offer a valuable opportunity to learn social skills from watching how other teens handle mixed-gender interactions (Feiring, 1999).

A recent study of Canadian early adolescents confirmed a sequence that went from same-gender activities, to hanging out in mixed-gender groups, to going on group

▶ Mixed-gender group activities offer a safe setting for getting to know potential partners.

dates, to having a boyfriend or girlfriend (Connolly, Craig, Goldberg, & Pepler, 2004). One big advantage young adolescents find in mixed-gender group activities is that interactions with potential partners are possible but *not* required. This means that each teen can take part at his or her own comfort level (Connolly et al., 2004). Even after teens start dating, they continue to participate in mixed-gender group activities, which serve as a familiar, secure base for exploring more intense and less familiar romantic involvements. Interestingly, since the early 1990s the percentage of older adolescents who say that are actively dating (at least one date a week) has dropped steadily, as shown in Figure 12.2 on page 401 (Child Trends, 2005). This may reflect a trend toward less formal socializing among teens.

Most of what has been said so far about the goals of dating and the ways dating develops applies as much to sexual-minority teens (gays, lesbians, bisexuals) as to those whose primary orientation is heterosexual. A date does not have to be a matter of boy-girl, and those that are not can serve the same social functions as those that are. However, sexual-minority adolescents face some particular problems that most other teens do not. These problems range from dealing with disapproval from parents, peers, and members of the community to coping with a much smaller pool of potential partners (Diamond, 2003). We will take a closer look at issues for gay, lesbian, and bisexual adolescents later in the chapter.

Who Dates and When. Does every American adolescent get involved in dating? Just about. A decade ago, Candice Feiring (1996) found that around 90% of 15-year-olds had dated, though a much smaller number were in an active dating relationship at the time. More recently, researchers asked a representative sample of almost 12,000 American adolescents, ages 12 to 18, "In the last 18 months, have you had a special romantic relationship with anyone?" Over half said yes, and another 10% reported acting in ways that most people would think of as indicating a romantic relationship (Carver, Joyner, & Udry, 2003).

As might be expected, dating and romantic relationships are much more common among older than younger teens. In the study just cited, about 25% of the 12-year-olds said they had been in a relationship in the previous 18 months (which, we should note, takes them back to age 10-1/2) (Carver et al., 2003). Across the teen years the proportions went up steadily, reaching 70–75% for 18-year-olds, as shown in Figure 12.3. Among different ethnic groups, the levels of relationship experience were much the same, with

Connect the **Dots...**

At what age did you and your friends start dating? How well does the description you just read fit with your own experience and observations? Do you think that the pattern or development of dating has changed in recent years? If so, how and why?

Figure 12.2 Changes in Active Dating, by Grade
Active dating by adolescents has declined somewhat in recent years.

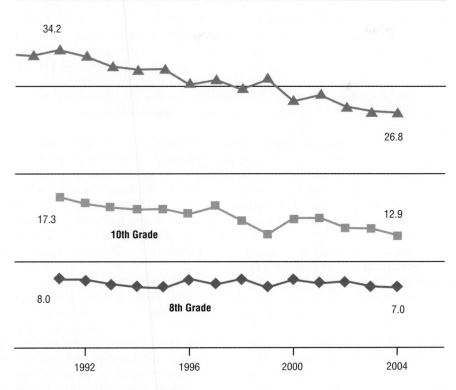

34.2

26.8

17.3

10th Grade

12.9

8.0   **8th Grade**   7.0

1992   1996   2000   2004

Source: Child Trends Data Bank, 2005.

Figure 12.3 Proportion of Adolescents in Romantic Relationships
The proportion of adolescents in romantic relationships climbs steadily with age.

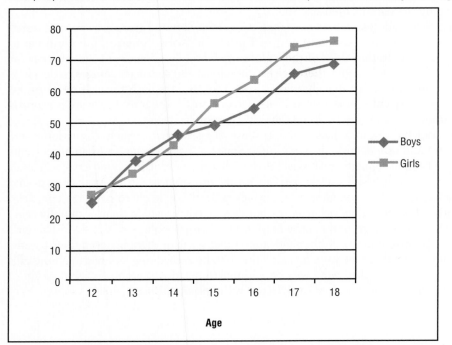

Percentage of adolescents who have experienced a romantic relationship in the last 18 months.
Source: Carver, Joyner, & Udry, 2003, p. 33.

one exception. Teens of Asian background were considerably less likely to have been in a relationship than Whites, African Americans, Hispanics, or Native Americans.

Culture and Courtship. An old saying tells us that "love makes the world go 'round." Maybe it does, but is dating a necessary part of it? Adolescents throughout the world do go through the same series of physical, sexual, and cognitive changes we have been discussing, and many of the same social changes as well. They also begin to look at their age mates—or rather, certain of their age mates—in a different way (Jankowiak & Fischer, 1998). What happens next, however, varies enormously according to culture and tradition. What *doesn't* happen, in most parts of the world, is that a boy asks a girl out on a date.

The countries of Western Europe are similar in a great many ways to Canada and the United States. The custom of adolescent dating, however, is known mostly from watching American movies and television shows (Alsaker & Flammer, 1999). European adolescents do get together, and they do pair off, but mostly in the context of informal mixed-gender groups. For example, a group of adolescents will meet and go to a movie or concert together. It is generally understood who will want to sit next to whom, but there is not the same sense that "she's here with him, so I shouldn't talk to her." Nor is there the same unspoken assumption that the boy will pay the costs and the girl will make it up to him in other ways.

Traditional societies generally keep a tight rein on adolescent socializing (Brown, Larson, & Saraswathi, 2002). The most important reason adolescents are allowed to interact with other-sex peers is courtship, and the goal of courtship is a suitable marriage. "Suitable," in this context, means that the prospective partner is of the right family background, religion, social class, and economic status. For most of human history, and even today in much of the world, marriage is a matter of deep economic and social significance to the entire family, and much too important to be trusted to the flighty emotions of adolescents (Coontz, 2005; Hatfield & Rapson, 2005). The notion that marriages should be based on romantic love is rather recent and still widely disputed, though with lots of help from the popular media it is gaining ground. For example, in India, the second most populous country on earth, "love marriages" are becoming more common and even rather fashionable, but most marriages are still arranged by the parents (Jensen, 2003).

What about adolescents whose families have immigrated from a more traditional society to the relative permissiveness of Europe or North America, but continue to hold onto the cultural values of their place of origin? In Chapter 11 we saw that for ethnic minority adolescents, there are psychological and social advantages to developing a bicultural identity, one that takes from and respects both the culture of origin and the majority culture. But what if the two cultures come into direct opposition? If your parents say you cannot go on dates, do you obey or disobey?

The available research, like common sense, suggests that in such a situation, some teens obey and others don't. In the United States, the percentage of Asian adolescents who have been in romantic relationships is smaller than for other ethnic groups (Carver et al., 2003), but it is still substantial. In Canada, too, adolescents of Asian background express less interest in romantic relationships and are less likely to participate in them than those of other ethnic backgrounds, but they do participate in them (Connolly et al., 2004). While middle ground may be hard to find, it is possible. A study of Moslem girls of Moroccan origin in the Netherlands found that some of them believed their parents were quite aware that they were breaking the rules by exchanging letters and phone calls with boys. However, they were very careful not to put their parents in the position of having to *acknowledge* that they knew (Ketner, Buitelaar, & Bosma, 2004).

"I'll Take Romance"

▶ **Learning Objective 12.6**
What phases do romantic relationships go through?

Why is going to a movie on a date different from going to the same movie with a close friend? Both involve spending time doing something interesting with someone you find it pleasant and rewarding to be with. Yet clearly there is a difference. You are not likely to find yourself holding your breath when your friend comes into view or when you accidentally brush against each other. If your friend declares, "We'll always be such good friends," you don't feel devastated, you feel pleased. The difference, of course, is that a friend is a friend and a date is (you hope) a romantic partner. If the twain sometimes meet, if a friend becomes a romantic interest or a former romantic interest stays a friend, the ways your emotions respond to them still make it fairly easy to tell which is which.

Poets and philosophers, along with ordinary people, have been thinking and talking about romance for centuries. Among the earliest surviving works of literature are love poems scratched on clay tablets in ancient Sumeria some 4,000 years ago (Wolkstein, 1991). One idea that comes up repeatedly is that love and romance are *mysterious and unpredictable*. It certainly feels that way to many people who become immersed in a romantic experience. However, without pretending to solve all the mysteries of love, the tools of social and behavioral science can help us better understand the process, why it goes the ways it goes, and why adolescence is such a crucial period for its development.

Romantic Development. Romantic relationships bring into play several different needs and behavioral systems that develop to meet those needs (Furman & Simon, 1999), including *attachment, romantic passion*, and *sexual gratification*. Each of these has been linked to particular brain structures and neurochemicals, and together they have a clear connection to mate selection, procreation, and child rearing (Fisher, 2004). Attachment involves wanting to stay close to the attachment figure, using the attachment figure as a safe base for exploration, and feeling anxious and unhappy when separated. The characteristics of romantic passion include high energy, wide mood swings, obsessive thinking, and a powerful urge to win and keep the desired person (Fisher, 2006). The need for sexual gratification, when aroused, creates a sense of urgency and a sort of "tunnel vision" in which other needs are temporarily ignored.

Adolescence is the first time that all three of these systems are fully active. The attachment system, as we have seen, dates back to early infancy, though its objects change across childhood (Bowlby, 1973). Elements of passion start to make their appearance in the "chumships" of late childhood (Sullivan, 1953), but become stronger in early adolescence. The sex drive is also somewhat evident during childhood, but it increases sharply with the hormonal changes of puberty and particularly with the increased levels of testosterone in both boys and girls (Savin-Williams & Diamond, 2004).

Attachment, passion, and sexual desire are typical of people everywhere, but the ways they are combined, and the ways they are understood and experienced, can vary a great deal from culture to culture and from person to person (Schwartz, 2006). In the following sections, we refer mainly to the familiar concept of romantic love that developed since the 14th century in Western culture and that is increasingly spreading its influence to other parts of the world as part of the process of globalization (Hatfield & Rapson, 2005).

The Course of Romance. In the most celebrated adolescent romance in literature, Romeo and Juliet meet for the first time, fall passionately in love, and immediately start making plans to stay together for the rest of their lives. It can happen like that, but most adolescents find that their experiences with romance develop much more gradually (and much less tragically). Jennifer Connolly and her colleagues have described four phases in the development of romantic relationships in adolescence that are discussed in the following paragraphs (Connolly & Goldberg, 1999; for a similar approach, see also Brown, 1999):

Initial infatuations. This phase first appears in early adolescence as "crushes" that combine passion and physical attraction, but usually lack any real interaction or attempt at intimacy. Adolescents in the grip of an infatuation may spend hours daydreaming of the desired one, talking about him or her with close friends, staring at the back of the other's head in class, and compulsively writing the person's name in their notebooks, but never so much as speak to the object of their longing.

Affiliative relationships. With the emergence of mixed-gender peer groups, teens initiate casual dating in a context that emphasizes companionship with partners and peers as much as passionate connections. This allows them to get more accustomed to interacting with a romantic partner within the safety and comfort of the peer group setting. As was mentioned earlier, one of the considerations in dating someone is the effect it will have on one's status within the peer group (Brown, 1999). Even if no one is looking, the increased ability adolescents have to see situations from multiple points of view leads to a stronger focus on how an "imaginary audience" will judge their attractiveness and romantic competence. Friends and peers also serve as go-betweens, passing the word that X is attracted to Y, finding out what Y's reaction is to this news, and passing that back to X, who can act on it without running as much risk of rejection.

Intimate relationships. As adolescents gain more confidence and experience in romantic relationships, they are better able to work toward achieving emotional closeness, sharing, and mutual support with a romantic partner. The emphasis shifts to couples, and the peer group becomes less important as a social context or as a source of evaluations of one's partner or relationship. If the people in your friendship group don't like your partner, you are more likely to look for a new group of friends than to change partners.

Committed relationships. Toward the end of adolescence, passion, affiliation, and intimacy are joined by commitment as defining features of romantic relationships. The partners make a mutual, conscious decision that they want to maintain the relationship over the long term and work through any difficulties that may get in the way of achieving that goal.

Recent research has confirmed the outlines of this sequence. As teens get older, there is a shift in the way they are most likely to approach romantic relationships. In early adolescence infatuation is most common, giving way to status-oriented relationships in mid-adolescence. Gradually, more intimate and committed relationships become more frequent (Connolly et al., 2004; Montgomery, 2005; Seiffge-Krenke, 2003).

A Theory of Love. The developmental sequence that Connolly and Goldberg propose was inspired in part by Robert Sternberg's (1986, 1988) "triangular" theory of love, shown in Figure 12.4 on page 405. Sternberg suggests that all love is made up of three basic components: *intimacy*, *passion*, and *commitment*. The *relative* strength of these components determines the *kind* of love in a relationship, and the *total* strength of the three determines the *amount* of love.

For example, intimacy alone, without passion or commitment, is linked to the sort of liking one might feel for a close friend, while passion alone, without intimacy or commitment, equals infatuation. When both passion and intimacy are present, but not commitment, the result is the physical and emotional bonding known as romantic love. For Sternberg, the ideal is a relationship that fully combines all three components into *consummate* love, and, as he points out, reaching that goal may be easier than maintaining it. The attainment of consummate love is no guarantee that it will last (Sternberg, 1986).

Sternberg's objective is to analyze different varieties of love, but we can also use his theory, together with that of Connolly and Goldberg (1999), to tell us something about how love *develops* across adolescence. In effect, young adolescents in the infatuation phase of romantic development are starting at the lower left of Sternberg's triangle. As they add increasing degrees of intimacy to their relationships, they move toward the area of romantic love. As commitment becomes part of the mix, it pulls them more and more into the center of the triangle, which stands for a mature love relationship. Not that all adolescents follow that sequence, of course. Some start with

Connect the Dots...

Recently, some observers have claimed that U.S. teens are wary of intimacy and commitment and instead prefer casual, temporary "hook-ups." Do your own observations of adolescents support that claim? If so, can you think of reasons that might be the case? What consequences do you think such a change in customs and attitudes might bring?

Figure 12.4 Sternberg's Triangular Theory of Love
Sternberg sees love as determined by the relative strength of intimacy, passion, and commitment.

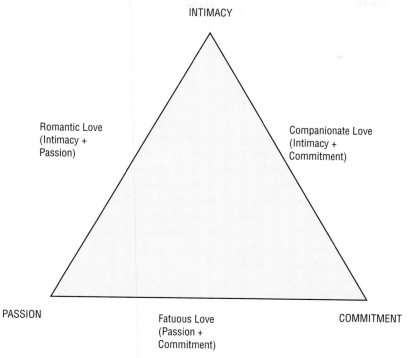

INTIMACY

Romantic Love
(Intimacy +
Passion)

Companionate Love
(Intimacy +
Commitment)

PASSION

Fatuous Love
(Passion +
Commitment)

COMMITMENT

Source: Sternberg's Triagular Theory of Love," in *The Psychology of Love,* by R. J. Sternberg and M. L. Barnes (Eds). © 1988 Yale University Press. Used by permission.

passion, add a hefty dash of commitment but no intimacy, and end up with fatuous love. This may lead to the sort of 2-week-long marriage that, if they happen to be pop stars, gets their photo on the cover of celebrity magazines.

A Fine Romance. Someone reading a description of the phases through which romantic relationships develop and progress might get a very rosy picture of adolescent romance. Common sense and a dash of personal experience tell us that it is not always that way. Yes, many teens become passionately attracted to someone, get to know the person better, develop a genuine sense of intimacy and caring, and progress to a mutual commitment. Even if the relationship does not last forever—and most don't—the former partners will probably think back on each other and their time together with affection, satisfaction, and maybe a touch of regret. But just as we have seen that close friendships may be of high quality or low quality, so may romantic relationships. Given the level of emotional investment adolescents make in romantic relationships, the consequences of being involved in a low-quality relationship can be much more damaging and long lasting than the effects of having a friendship that doesn't work out.

What makes the difference between high-quality and low-quality romantic relationships? When teens are asked what makes them happy or unhappy with a relationship, the features they list include:

passion;

mutual communication;

mutual caring;

commitment;

emotional support;

togetherness;

exhilaration;

feeling appreciated; and

feeling special.

—(COLLINS & SROUFE, 1999; LEVESQUE, 1993)

The more of these features a relationship has, the higher its quality, and the fewer of them, the lower its quality. Negative features, such as conflict, bad feeling, and doubts about commitment, also have an impact on the quality of the relationship.

Partners, Parents, and Peers. Many factors can influence the quality of an adolescent's romantic relationship. On a social level, what do parents and peers think a romantic relationship should be like, and who do they think would be an appropriate partner? The reactions of close friends count, too. More than one romance has suffered because a close friend of one of the partners felt threatened by the relationship and tried to undermine it. The degree to which the two partners are relatively similar or different in their personal characteristics, such as temperament and activity level, also matters (Berscheid & Regan, 2005). Most important, though, is the experiences of relationships each of the partners has had earlier with parents, peers, and friends. That history leaves a legacy of attitudes, expectations, and beliefs about relationships that shape how the partners act and react in the context of a romance (Brown, 2004, 2006; Collins, 2003; Collins & van Dulmen, 2006).

The most widely held view about how earlier relationships affect romantic relationships calls on attachment theory (Ainsworth et al., 1978; Bowlby, 1973) and the concept of *working models*. We discussed these earlier in the context of friendships. Briefly, securely attached infants are said to develop positive working models of the self and others, while those with anxious attachments develop negative working models of the self, others, or both. These working models are carried forward into childhood and affect the way the child approaches peers. In turn, the experiences the child has with peers can modify the working models, which then influence further behavior with peers and, later on, romantic partners (Mayseless & Scharf, 2007; Simpson, Collins, Tran, & Haydon, 2007). This chapter's Research in the Spotlight on page 407 takes a closer look at the connections between childhood attachment and adolescent romance.

Evidence continues to accumulate for these links between early experiences and the quality of adolescent romances. Recent studies have looked at longitudinal data collected from infancy, across the childhood years, to late adolescence. The results show that the quality of early attachment interacts with peer experiences over time to predict the quality of relationships in late adolescence (Carlson, Sroufe, & Egeland, 2004; Roisman, Collins, Sroufe, & Egeland, 2005; Simpson et al., 2007). Conflict resolution with parents predicts later conflict resolution with romantic partners (Reese-Weber & Marchand, 2002), and negative emotionality between parents and teens predicts poor quality interactions with romantic partners later (Kim, Conger, Lorenz, & Elder, 2001). Other research confirms the links between friendship quality and the quality of romantic relationships (Furman, Simon, Shaffer, & Bouchey, 2002). In short, most teens who have high-quality romantic relationships have high-quality relationships with parents and friends as well (Laursen & Mooney, 2007).

The Cost of Rejection. No one likes to be left out or rejected. It really hurts. In fact, neuroscientists have recently discovered that physical pain and the social pain of rejection activate related structures in the brain (Eisenberger & Lieberman, 2005). If children repeatedly feel the pain of being ignored or pushed away by parents, or later by playmates and peers, they may develop a persistent way of perceiving, understanding, and reacting to interpersonal events that is called **rejection sensitivity** (Downey, Bonica, & Rincón, 1999). This has major implications for romantic relationships in adolescence.

Teens who are rejection-sensitive approach social relationships carrying a burden of expectations that they will be rejected, along with anger or anxiety about the mere possibility. This may make romantic relationships seem so threatening that they avoid them altogether or put strict limits on the degree of involvement or investment they

Rejection sensitivity A tendency to be on the lookout for and to detect rejection in interpersonal relationships.

Working Models and Romantic Relationships

According to John Bowlby (1973), babies and children develop *working models* that reflect the quality of their attachment relationships and serve as a guide or *prototype* for future relationships. Working models can be modified by later interactions with parents and other attachment figures, but those earliest experiences leave a residue of secure or insecure feelings about what to expect from others in close relationships (Collins & Sroufe, 1999).

The working models hypothesis is one of the most widely used ideas about how early experience can continue to affect the way people relate to others. But does what happened years before, in infancy, really have an impact on how someone acts on a first date or in a marriage? And how would you know? To pin down a connection between what happened in someone's past and the way the person is now, you need information from both points in time. One way to get that information is to carry out a *longitudinal study*. In the research we are considering now, the participants were recruited even before they were born and followed through childhood and adolescence. At 12 months old and again at 18 months old, they and their mothers took part in what is called the Strange Situation test (Ainsworth et al., 1978). This involves seeing how much the baby uses the mother as a secure base from which to explore a new situation and how the baby reacts to the mother's departure and return. On the basis of these two assessments, the babies in this study were classified as *securely attached* or *insecurely attached*.

Twenty years later, the same participants were invited to complete a romantic relationship assessment with their current partners. This included a detailed interview and questionnaires about how they saw their relationship, plus a videotaped session in which they and their partners discussed a problem they were having and their concept of an ideal couple. This information was used to rate the closeness, security, positive feelings, and overall quality of the relationship.

The results showed that those young adults who had been securely attached as babies were more secure in, and more positive about, their current romantic relationship. In addition, trained observers who watched the videos of their discussions with their partners rated the relationships as of higher quality. Further analyses suggested that their secure attachments as babies predicted how secure they felt in their current relationship, even when the effect of current relationship quality was removed.

The conclusion the researchers drew from these results was that the way young adults think about their current relationships is affected both by the quality of those relationships *and* by attachment experiences in infancy. This does not prove that their current relationships were shaped by the expectations they formed in infancy, as the working models hypothesis claims, but it is certainly a step in that direction.

Source: Roisman, G. I., Collins, W. A., Srouge, L. A., & Egelund, B., 2005.

are willing to risk. Those who do get involved in relationships may use coercive measures to ward off the risk of rejection. They may threaten to harm a partner who shows signs of wanting to break off the relationship: "Stay with me or I don't know what I might do to you." Just as coercive, they may threaten to harm themselves: "If you ever leave me, I'll jump off a bridge." Some may go to the other extreme and put up with emotional, physical, or sexual abuse from their partner to preserve the relationship and avoid the worse pain of rejection.

Looking on the Bad Side. Within the context of a relationship, teens who are rejection-sensitive are constantly on the lookout for the slightest sign of rejection. They are also predisposed to interpret neutral or ambiguous cues as indicating that they are being, or are about to be, rejected. For example, if the partner has a casual conversation with a potential rival, this may be taken as a sure sign of looming faithlessness and betrayal. When they do convince themselves in this way that they are facing rejection, they tend to overreact. They may become intensely hostile or deeply despondent. They may make abject attempts to preserve or reestablish the relationship. They may even break off the relationship themselves, on the preemptive principle of, "Do unto others before they have a chance to do unto you."

There can be many reasons that children suffer the exclusions that lead to rejection sensitivity. Earlier rejections may have left them with an anxious or hostile way of approaching others, which makes rejection more likely. This rejection, in turn, increases their anxiety and hostility in an escalating spiral. Outgroup status, such as belonging to a racial or ethnic minority, often leads to experiences of discrimination that leave the child with a defensive sensitivity to rejection or a "chip on the shoulder." Even something as seemingly trivial as having a different accent or being the only one who wears glasses can result in being left on the sidelines or ignored. Because the experience of exclusion can damage a child's social relationships over many years, it is important for parents, teachers, and other adults who work with children to foster an inclusionary atmosphere and inclusionary attitudes (Paley, 1993).

Romantic Relationships of Sexual Minority Youth. Until quite recently, little could have been said specifically about the romantic relationships of nonheterosexual adolescents, for the simple reason that hardly any research had been done on the subject (Diamond, 2003a). Yet, one can argue that romantic relationships matter even more to sexual minority teens than to heterosexual teens. The special problems they face, of stigma, discrimination, victimization, and possibly family rejection, mean that they may be particularly in need of the companionship, emotional support, and personal validation that ideally come from a romantic partner.

One point to stress is that there is not a single typical course of development for sexual minority romantic relationships. The majority of adolescents with same-sex attractions also experience some degree of other-sex attractions (Garofalo, Wolf, Wissow, Woods, & Goodman, 1999) and participate in other-sex relationships at some point during adolescence (Diamond, Savin-Williams, & Dubé, 1999). Some find themselves sexually attracted to someone of one sex and emotionally attracted to someone of the other sex (Savin-Williams, 1998). Some pursue physical intimacy with one partner and emotional intimacy with another. And quite a few do not get involved in *any* romantic relationships during their teenage years (Diamond & Dubé, 2002). This may be for any of a number of reasons, including discomfort with their same-sex desires, a need to hide their orientation from peers and family members, and a shortage of potential sexual minority partners.

As we have seen, romantic relationships give adolescents a chance to practice and master important skills such as patience, mutuality, intimate self-disclosure, commitment, and trust (Brown, 1999). Learning to recognize, understand, and handle the intense emotions of romance is particularly critical (Larson, Clore, & Wood, 1999). Those who miss out on this training, whether they are same-sex attracted, other-sex attracted, or both, are at a disadvantage in their intimate relationships going forward. While this is not specifically a problem of sexual minority teens, it may have more impact on them because of the strain their "differentness" placed on peer relationships during childhood and early adolescence (Diamond, 2003a).

During childhood, girls focus much more on interpersonal and intimacy skills than boys do (Buhrmester & Prager, 1995). As a result, cross-sex adolescent romances have been described as giving girls a chance to *practice* intimacy and giving boys a chance to *learn* intimacy (Connolly & Johnson, 1996). These gender differences tend to be magnified in same-sex couples. When sexual minority adolescents are asked about their most significant same-sex relationship, boys typically say it began as a sexual liaison and then developed into a romance. Girls, in contrast, say it began as a close friendship, progressed to romantic involvement, and then became sexual (Diamond, 2003a). Even when the male-male relationships do become more romantic, they feature less interpersonal closeness, emotional attachment, and emotional support than the female-female relationships. Perhaps as a result of this relative lack of intimacy in their romantic relationships, sexual minority males are more likely than heterosexual males to have many female friends and to nominate a female as their best friend (Diamond & Dubé, 2002).

"Breaking Up Is Hard to Do"

▶ **Learning Objective 12.7**
Why is the end of a romantic relationship so painful?

No matter how intense, high-quality, or "made in heaven" adolescent romantic relationships may be, practically all of them end, and most end when one of the partners rejects the other (Battaglia, Richard, Datteri, & Lord, 1998). A study of college students revealed that more than 9 of 10, of both sexes, had been thrown over by someone they adored. Not only that, more than 9 of 10 reported that they had rejected someone who was in love with them (Baumeister, Wotman, & Stillwell, 1993)! The predictable result in many cases is an awful mixture of anger, pain, despair, and a deep sense of loss. A major cause of depression in teens, especially in girls, is a recent breakup (Monroe, Rohde, Seeley, & Lewinsohn, 1999; Welsh, Grello, & Harper, 2003).

What makes breaking up so painful? The list of reasons is long and predictable. A romantic relationship is a source of affection, comfort, support, pleasure, validation, and esteem (Schwartz, 2006). In the enclosed world of the adolescent peer group, it is often a source of social status as well. With the end of the relationship, all of these are threatened or lost. Bad enough, certainly, but it gets worse. First, the "personal fable" of adolescent egocentrism leads the bereft teen to believe that no one has ever felt this bad and that he or she will never, ever feel better again. Second, the breakup, like the relationship, has probably been played out on the public stage. Everyone in school knows who was going together and everybody knows who broke up. Most painful, there is no easy way to avoid coming into contact with the former romantic partner every day. As one 14-year-old boy put it,

> It hurts really bad. I see her with her new boyfriend and I want to run away and cry. We were going to get married. We were going to spend our lives together. I loved her so much.
>
> —(BELL, 1998, p. 86)

When a romantic relationship ends, both partners are affected, but the one who initiates the breakup usually suffers less distress (Welsh, Grello, & Harper, 2003). The initiator has a greater sense of personal control and a better chance to prepare mentally for being out of the relationship. It is also likely that the one who initiates the breakup was less committed to the relationship and may have other options. In addition, the one who is broken up with may feel a strong sense of responsibility and self-blame. This often takes the form of *rumination* ("Where did I go wrong? What could I have done to make him/her stay?"), which has been linked to increased depression (Little, Widman, Welsh, & Darling, 2006; Welsh et al., 2003).

For all that, going through a breakup often proves to be a valuable experience, even if it is one most teens would just as soon pass by (Larson et al., 1999). Negative emotions tell us that we did something we should try to avoid in the future, and mulling over where a romance left the tracks can offer lessons on how to avoid a similar disaster in the future. In one recent study, 12th graders who had been through a breakup in 10th grade were more satisfied with their current relationship than those who had *not* been through an earlier breakup (Barber, 2006). So maybe what the poet Tennyson said is true after all: "'Tis better to have loved and lost than never to have loved at all."

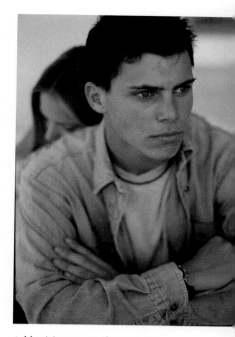

▲ Most teens go through the painful experience of breaking up with a romantic partner.

Summing Up...

Like friendships, romantic relationships are attachments that teens choose to keep active, but they also have a greater emotional intensity than most friendships. In the United States, unlike many other cultures, romance is linked to dating, which has functions ranging from recreation and social status to intimacy and courtship. Dating progresses from mixed-gender group activities, to group dates, to having a boyfriend or girlfriend. As for romance, it meets such needs as attachment, passion, and sexual desire. Sternberg sees love as being made up of intimacy, passion, and commitment, in different strengths and proportions. The quality of romantic relationships is linked to early attachment and to peer relations during childhood. Teens who have had bad experiences earlier may develop rejection sensitivity that makes romantic involvement seem threatening. For most teens, the end of a romantic relationship is a difficult and painful experience, but may have some positive effects.

SEX

When adults talk about "the facts of life," they are usually referring to sexuality. And sexuality is definitely a major fact of life. From birth on, the sexual organs are a potential source of pleasure (Ryan, 2000). Unless they are taught not to, young children engage in a variety of sexual activities, both alone and with playmates. However, sex play in children is often as much about play as it is about sex. Young children "playing doctor" may be just as interested in pretending to give each other shots as in examining each other's bodies.

That changes with adolescence, which should not surprise anyone. One of the basic ways to define adolescence is as the period of transition from childhood to sexual and reproductive adulthood. The physical and hormonal changes of puberty give sexual activities a different meaning and context. Sexual impulses take on a new, strange, and sometimes disturbing urgency (Fisher, 2006). Sexual maturation alters the way teens relate with parents and siblings. Sexual attractions and sexual experiences change the dynamic of social relations with peers.

The sexual changes of adolescence come to everyone, and the issues they raise are similar for many teens. Among these issues are:

whether to engage in sexual activity; and if so,

what sorts of activity;

with whom;

at what age;

under what circumstances; and

with what safeguards.

Families, communities, cultures, and adolescents themselves approach these questions in a huge variety of ways that reflect different social and religious beliefs, customs and values, and particular circumstances. They may also find themselves facing another crucial issue, how to deal with any consequences that may follow from adolescent sexual activity.

Adolescent Sexuality and Culture

▶ **Learning Objective 12.8**
How do different cultures deal with adolescent sexuality?

Half a century ago, social scientists Clellan Ford and Frank Beach (1951) studied first-hand accounts of the sexual practices of 190 cultures throughout the world. They documented an enormous range of differences in the way childhood and adolescent sexuality was treated.

Three Kinds of Cultures. One way to summarize the differences among cultures is to group them into three broad categories:

Restrictive societies Those societies that control or forbid any sexual expression before adulthood or marriage.

Semirestrictive societies Those societies that prohibit premarital sex, but do not strictly enforce this prohibition.

Permissive societies Those societies that take it for granted that children and adolescents will be active sexually.

Restrictive societies control or forbid any sexual expression before adulthood or marriage. Boys and girls may be kept apart from an early age or come in contact with one another only with a watchful chaperone nearby. Some restrictive societies place particular stress on female virginity. If it becomes known that a girl has lost her virginity, she may be beaten or even murdered by males in her family (Shaaban, 1991).

Semirestrictive societies, like restrictive societies, say that adolescents should not engage in premarital sex; however, these prohibitions are not taken very seriously or enforced very rigorously. As long as adults are not forced to notice adolescent sexual activity, they generally don't. If something makes such activity obvious, however, the rules come back into play. For example, if a girl becomes pregnant, she and her partner may be forced to marry.

Permissive societies expect children and adolescents to be active sexually. Families often sleep in one room, giving children an opportunity to observe adult sexual behavior, and children are allowed to take part in discussions of sexual matters. Their own sexual activities are simply ignored. By the time they reach puberty, they are already

◄ Sexually-tinged relationships are a "fact of life" for contemporary Western adolescents.

both knowledgeable and experienced. For example, among the Ifugao people of the Philippines,

> . . . unmarried individuals live in separate dormitories from early childhood. It is customary for each boy to sleep with a girl every night. The only check on promiscuity is that imposed by the girls themselves. Usually a girl is unwilling to form too prolonged an attachment to one boy until she is ready to be married. Boys are urged by their fathers to begin sexual activities early, and a man may shame his son if the latter is backward in this respect.
>
> —(FORD & BEACH, 1951, p. 190)

We should remember that these ethnographic records were compiled decades ago, at a time when many of the cultures being observed still had only limited contact with the rest of the world. As they have become increasingly exposed to global values and ideas about sexuality, and to the efforts of missionaries from more developed societies, their customs have started to shift in the direction of less permissive norms (Hatfield & Rapson, 2005).

Attitudes in the United States and the Developed World. Western societies today are flooded with sexual messages, mostly aimed at the young (Collins, 2005; Comstock & Scharrer, 2006; Ward, 2003). From billboards and posters, buff models of both sexes show off their low-cut jeans and brand-name underwear, along with quantities of bare, evenly tanned skin. Magazines offer detailed advice on sexual conduct, mostly with a "how-to" angle. On mainstream television, both shows and commercials portray recreational sex as universal and glamorous, while some music videos get downright kinky. As for the Internet, the hardest of hard-core pornography is just a few mouse clicks away.

Does this mean that we live in a permissive society? Well, no, not really. A better description might be *ambivalent, troubled, and confused* (Crockett, Raffaelli, & Moilanen, 2003; Ponton, 2001). Adolescents are sternly told to "Just say no," and then given long stretches of unsupervised time alone with their romantic partners. As one 16-year-old sarcastically remarked, "What do they think we're doing in my room together with the door closed—listening to old Frank Sinatra records?"

Figure 12.5 Attitudes About Teenage Sex
Attitudes about teenage sex vary greatly in different countries.

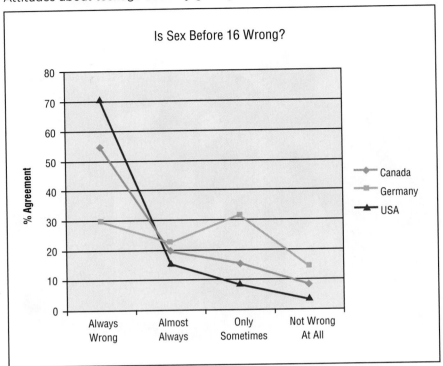

Source: Data from Widmer et al., 1998, Table 1, p. 351.

Adolescent sexuality is generally treated as a source of problems, rather than as an integral part of human development. This is especially so for girls (Diamond, 2006). Any sexual expression by teens is considered a dangerous activity that leads to pregnancy, sexually transmitted diseases, poor school achievement, lower educational aspirations, substance use, and deviant behavior (Savins-Williams & Diamond, 2004). As one widely read advice columnist put it, "That kind of behavior means moving into an intimacy that kids are simply not prepared for . . . and most experts believe that kids under 16 do not have the psychological and neurological development necessary to satisfactorily manage these feelings" (Pinsky, 2002, p. 6).

Not all developed countries are quite as upset by teen sex as is the United States. A 1994 survey looked at attitudes toward nonmarital sex among large, representative samples of adults in 24 countries (Widmer, Treas, & Newcomb, 1998). The United States was one of the most restrictive countries, along with Ireland, Northern Ireland, and Poland. To the question, "Is sex before age 16 wrong?" 71% replied that it is always wrong, and another 16% that it is *almost* always wrong. As Figure 12.5 shows, this is in sharp contrast to some other countries. In Germany, about 33% said that sex before age 16 is only sometimes wrong, and about 15% said that it is not wrong at all. The responses in Austria and Sweden (not shown) were similar. Most of the other countries surveyed, represented in the graph by Canada, fell in the middle—less permissive than the permissive group, but less restrictive than the restrictive group.

Sexual Activity in Adolescence

▶ **Learning Objective 12.9**
What is the usual sequence of sexual activity in adolescence?

Whether adults think adolescent sexual activity is wrong, right, or something in between, in Western societies today sex is the norm among adolescents (Savin-Williams & Diamond, 2004). About one in four American adolescents is sexually experienced before age 16. By age 18, the proportion rises to roughly 70% (Abma, Martinez, Mosher, & Dawson, 2004). Similar percentages have been found in other developed countries such as Britain, Canada, France, and Sweden (Darroch, Singh, & Frost, 2001).

In the studies that produced these statistics, *sexually experienced* refers to those of a given age who have taken part in penile-vaginal intercourse at least once at some point in their lives. We should notice some problems with this definition. First, it simply ignores teens who are sexually involved only with others of their own sex. Second, it leaves out those adolescents who engage in a variety of sexual activities, but are careful to avoid intercourse, because in their minds that is what counts as "having sex." Also, concentrating on heterosexual intercourse diverts researchers from examining the pathways along which sexuality develops before adolescents begin to have intercourse.

This limited focus has connections with a broader issue. There is a great deal we simply do not know about adolescent sexuality. This is mostly for political and social reasons (Gardner & Wilcox, 1993). Probably because so many American adults believe adolescent sex is always wrong, a lot of elected officials, school administrators, media commentators, and people who fund research shy away from approving studies on the topic. Apparently, just asking detailed questions about sexual activity is thought to run a risk of giving impressionable adolescents the idea that teen sex has some kind of official approval.

As a result of these concerns, much of the research that *does* get approved and funded focuses on teen pregnancy or sexually transmitted infections (STIs). Practically everyone agrees that these are serious social problems that must be investigated, understood, and addressed. Unfortunately, this leaves social scientists, and the rest of us as well, with less information than we might like about the sexual attitudes and activities of the large numbers of adolescents who do not get pregnant or contract an STI.

Solitary Sex. Many boys, maybe most of them, give themselves their first adolescent sexual experience through **masturbation.** Estimates vary widely, but possibly as many as 6 of 10 boys have masturbated by age 13. By age 19 the figure is more like 85% or 90% (Halpern, Udry, Suchindran, & Campbell, 2000; Schwartz, 1999). For girls, the estimates are much lower, about half of what they are for boys (King, 2005). In one study of college students, 63% of the women reported that they had *never* masturbated (Schwartz, 1999). A review that examined dozens of studies of gender and sexual behavior found that the biggest single difference between males and females was the percentage who said they had masturbated (Oliver & Hyde, 1993).

Why is our information so vague about a behavior that is so widespread? One reason is that adolescents, and adults as well, don't like to talk about masturbation (Savin-Williams & Diamond, 2004). Although attitudes have changed a great deal in recent decades, there is still an aura of shame surrounding solitary sex (Crooks & Baur, 2005). Teens responding to a questionnaire about their sexual experiences are more likely to skip items about masturbation than about any other sexual activity (Rodgers, Billy, & Udry, 1982). Traditional gender roles play a part in this. Boys may see masturbation as an admission that they are not grown up or "manly" enough to win a real sexual partner, while for girls, it is an admission that they have sexual impulses and desires, which "nice" girls are not supposed to have (Savin-Williams & Diamond, 2004).

Masturbation has also been the subject of many peculiar cultural myths (Laqueur, 2004). In the past, young adolescents were bombarded with totally unfounded warnings that practicing what was referred to as "self-pollution" would drain their physical strength, stunt their growth, promote depravity, and lead eventually to feeble-mindedness and hopeless lunacy. Nor are such baseless alarms totally gone and forgotten. As one boy recalled:

> My grandparents gave me this book about bad little kids who masturbate. One of the bad little kids went blind, and another one had his thumbs cut off. Can you believe that? There was no doubt about the message in that book: *Don't masturbate.* It was lucky for me that my parents were cool and didn't do that number on me.
>
> —(BELL, 1998, p. 98)

Masturbation Sexual self-stimulation.

Figure 12.6   Age at First Experience of Various Sexual Behaviors
The typical sequence of different sexual behaviors is similar for boys and girls.

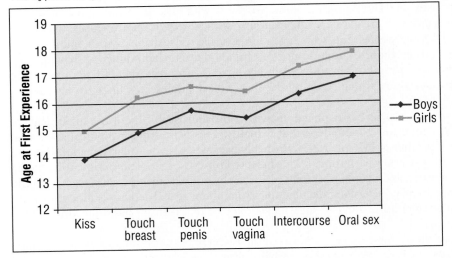

Source: Feldman et al., 1999.

Partnered Sex. Once adolescents begin to interact sexually with an other-sex partner, they tend to follow a fairly consistent sequence of increasingly intimate activities, which is shown in Figure 12.6 (Feldman, Turner, & Araujo, 1999). Teens usually use less clinical descriptions such as *necking, petting, heavy petting,* and *going all the way,* or adopt baseball terminology: *first base, second base,* and so on. As the graph indicates, the sequence is the same for girls and boys, but girls report engaging in each activity about 1 year later than boys do.

This presents something of a puzzle. It is well-established that girls generally choose sexual partners who are their own age or older, while boys choose those their own age or younger (Manlove, Franzetta, Ryan, & Moore, 2006). Given that, one might expect that girls would reach each milestone *earlier* than boys, not later. Once again, a likely explanation for the contradiction is traditional gender roles. Boys tend to *exaggerate* their sexual experience to seem more grown-up, and girls tend to *minimize* their sexual experience to avoid seeming promiscuous (Catania, 1999; Siegel, Aten, & Roghmann, 1998).

The way the information is collected also matters. Talking about your sexual activities face-to-face with an adult who writes down what you say is enough to make almost anyone reticent. Adolescents are more willing to report sensitive sexual behaviors when they listen to recorded questions over headphones and type their answers into a computer, a method called **CASI,** or computer-assisted self-interview (Copas et al., 2002). In line with our supposition about gender roles, one study found that when this technique was used, girls were more likely to admit that they were not virgins, and boys were more likely to admit that they *were* virgins (Catania, 1999).

Oral Sex. The information presented in Figure 12.6 indicates that adolescents first engage in **oral sex** several months after their first experience of intercourse (Feldman et al., 1999). Recent research suggests that this is changing in the United States. In one study, more 10th graders reported engaging in oral sex than in intercourse (Prinstein, Meade, & Cohen, 2003). They also reported having more oral sex partners than intercourse partners. Another study looked at 9th graders, average age 14-1/2. Almost 20% reported having had oral sex, as compared to 13.5% for vaginal sex. In addition, 31.5% of them said they *intended* to have oral sex in the next

CASI Computer-assisted self-interview, a research technique in which people are interviewed via computer, avoiding direct interpersonal contact.

Oral sex Oral stimulation of a partner's genitals.

◄ Most teens follow a fairly consistent sequence of increasingly intimate activities.

6 months, while 26.3% said they intended to have vaginal sex (Halpern-Felsher, Cornell, Kropp, & Tschann, 2005). According to a national survey conducted in 2002, about 20% of those 15- to 17-year-olds who have *not* had sexual intercourse have taken part in oral sex. For those who have had intercourse, the figure is over 80% (Child Trends, 2006b).

Why are more adolescents taking part in oral sex and at younger ages? When asked, the reasons they mention include curiosity, pleasure-seeking, and promoting greater intimacy with a romantic partner. Teens also believe oral sex poses fewer health risks than vaginal sex, and they see it as more acceptable than intercourse in both dating and non-dating relationships. Social pressure, both from partners and from peers in general, plays a role as well (Cornell & Halpern-Felsher, 2006).

Social attitudes are also important. In the United States, one common adult response to teenage sex has been to emphasize the value of *sexual abstinence* and *virginity* (Sonenstein, 2004). But in a recent survey of 14- to 19-year-olds, one-third of the participants said that a boy or girl who gives or receives oral sex is still being sexually abstinent. *Twice* that number said he or she is still a virgin (Bersamin, Fisher, Walker, Hill, & Grube, 2006). This suggests that another reason oral sex is becoming more common is that it offers teens a way to have sex and not have sex at the same time!

The Transition to Intercourse. A large majority of U.S. adolescents take part in heterosexual *intercourse* at some point before they turn 20. The average age for girls is 17 and for boys 16 (Savin-Williams & Diamond, 2004). Fewer than 10% of boys and girls have first intercourse before they turn 14, but as Figure 12.7 on page 416 shows, the percentage goes steadily up across the adolescent years. By their 19th birthday, about 65% of girls and 70% of boys will have had intercourse at least once (Abma et al., 2004). Historically, this represents a steady trend toward earlier sexual initiation (Centers for Disease Control, 2002; DeLamater & Friedrich, 2002).

Within this overall trend, there are some reliable ethnic differences. As Figure 12.8 on page 416 indicates, Black adolescents tend to first have intercourse at younger ages than either White or Hispanic adolescents. By age 18, roughly 70% of Black teens have had intercourse, as compared to between 50% and 60% for White and Hispanic teens. Other research indicates that Asian American adolescents are much less likely

Figure 12.7   Percent of U.S. Teens Who Have Had Intercourse, by Age
By age 19, about two-thirds of U.S. teens have had intercourse.

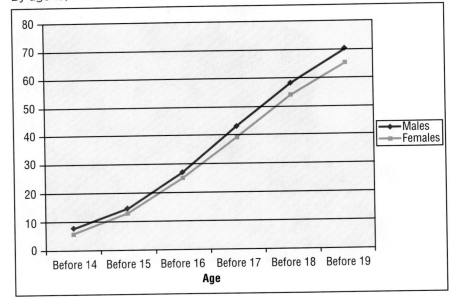

Source: Abma et al., 2004.

to engage in intercourse than those the same age from other ethnic backgrounds (Connolly et al., 2004; Feldman et al., 1999).

We should note that being "sexually experienced" (having had intercourse at least once) does not necessarily mean being sexually *active*. Some adolescents may have had sex that one time and never since, and others may begin, but then have sex only occasionally. In support of this, a national survey in 2002 revealed that among sexually experienced 15- to 19-year- olds, one in four girls and one in three boys had not had sex at all in the previous 3 months. During the previous 4 weeks,

Figure 12.8   Percent of Teens Who Have Had Intercourse, by Ethnic Group
The likelihood that an adolescent aged 15–17 has ever had intercourse varies by ethnic group.

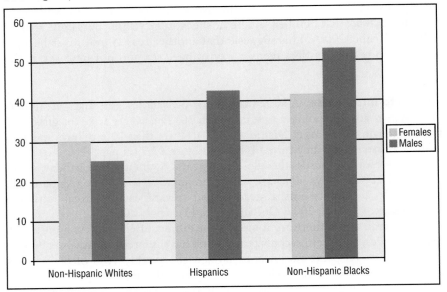

Source: Abma et al., 2004, Table 2.

39% of the girls and 46% of the boys had not had sex (Terry-Humen, ManTove, & Cottingham, 2006).

Sex and Relationships. In American culture, there is a conviction that romantic partners should become emotionally affectionate and intimate before expressing that intimacy in a sexual way (Miller & Benson, 1999). Adolescents themselves say that sexual relations are more acceptable when they take place in the context of a serious relationship (Feldman et al., 1999). What is less clear is how much impact this belief has on what teens actually do.

In one recent study, about 70% of girls and boys said that their first time was in the context of a romantic relationship. Maybe so, but in that same study 25% of the girls and 37% of the boys first had intercourse either before the relationship began or during the same month it began. For almost 20% of the girls and 30% of the boys, that first time was also the *only* time with that partner (Manlove et al., 2006). Another recent survey found that, while 75% of girls said that their first sex was in the context of going steady, only 52% of boys said the same (Abma et al., 2004). Fully one-third of the boys said their first time was with a friend or someone they had just met, as contrasted with 14% of the girls. It appears that sometimes, at least, a "serious relationship" turns out to mean one in which intercourse takes place.

Speeding Up and Slowing Down. Many factors have been linked to beginning intercourse earlier, including poverty, neighborhood characteristics, school underachievement, family structure, and involvement in other risk behaviors, such as alcohol and drug use (Cubbin, Santelli, Brindis, & Braveman, 2005; Miller, Benson, & Galbraith, 2001; Zimmer-Gembeck, & Helfand, 2008). In girls, early puberty is connected to early sexual initiation, probably because early-maturing girls tend to attract and hang out with older boys (Petersen, 1993). Among the strongest psychological predictors are personal beliefs about whether sexual activity is acceptable and whether one's friends believe sexual activity is acceptable (Santelli et al., 2004). If most of the teens in a friendship group are sexually experienced, those who are not feel a lot of social pressure to join the club (Sieving, Eisenberg, Pettingell, & Skay, 2006).

Other factors slow down the movement toward intercourse. Adolescents who believe their parents disapprove of adolescent sex tend to start later. However, the parental message does not necessarily get through. Among teens whose mothers strongly disapprove, almost one-third of the girls and almost one-half of the boys *don't* believe their mothers disapprove (Blum, 2002). Teens who take part in religious services on a regular basis, as well as those whose friends take part in religous services, wait longer to begin intercourse (Adamczyk & Felson, 2006; Rostowsky, Brian, Wright, & Randall, 2004). Girls who remain virgins through their adolescent years cite religious or moral beliefs more often than any other reasons (Moore, Driscoll, & Lindberg, 1998).

Since 1998, the U.S. government has provided major funding for school programs that teach abstinence from sexual activity as the only certain and socially approved way to avoid pregnancy and sexually transmitted diseases (STDs). Do such abstinence education programs work? To answer that question, a major federally funded study randomly assigned over 2,000 young adolescents to take part in abstinence education or not (Trenholm et al., 2007). Four to 6 years later, the teens were surveyed about their sexual activity, age at first intercourse, number of sexual partners, and rates of unprotected sex.

The results were strikingly clear. Those who went through the abstinence education programs were no more likely to have abstained from sex than those in the control group. In both groups, about half were abstinent and half sexually experienced. Among those who reported having had sex, the two groups were essentially identical in rates of unprotected sex, number of sexual partners, and age of sexual initiation (Trenholm et al., 2007). This chapter's Applications in the Spotlight on

Applications in the Spotlight

Reducing Adolescent Pregnancies and Sexually Transmitted Infections?

Compared to other countries of the developed world, the United States has shockingly high rates of pregnancies and sexually transmitted infections among adolescents (Panchaud, Singh, Feivelson, & Darroch, 2000; Singh & Darroch, 2000). As we have seen in this chapter, the numbers have improved somewhat in recent years, but they are still far out of line with those in Canada, Australia, and Western Europe. An overwhelming majority of Americans—90% or more—agree that a key element to improving this situation is giving children and adolescents a more thorough and accurate understanding of sexuality, its risks, and ways to avoid those risks. They also agree just as overwhelmingly that a logical place to give children this understanding is in school (National Public Radio, 2004).

One approach to sexuality education that has become increasingly widespread in the United States is *abstinence education*. As defined by federal law, this is a program that, among other qualifications:

has as its exclusive purpose, teaching the social, psychological, and health gains to be realized by abstaining from sexual activity;

teaches abstinence from sexual activity outside marriage as the expected standard for all school-age children;

teaches that abstinence from sexual activity is the only certain way to avoid out-of-wedlock pregnancy, sexually transmitted diseases, and other associated health problems;

teaches that a mutually faithful monogamous relationship in the context of marriage is the expected standard of human sexual activity...

—(Social Security Administration, 2005)

By law, these programs are not allowed to give students information about contraceptive services, to advocate contraceptive use, or even to discuss contraceptive methods, such as condoms, except to emphasize their failure rates. In fact, critics charge that students are often given negative information about condoms that is wildly inaccurate (SIECUS, 2005).

Recently, a team of researchers headed by Dr. John Santelli carried out a survey of research that evaluates abstinence-only and comprehensive sexuality education programs. Is either approach effective at encouraging adolescents to put off initiating sexual activity, and if so, how do they compare (Santelli et al., 2006)? For the comprehensive programs, one review looked at 28 evaluation studies. In 9 of them, the program led teens to delay intercourse, 18 had no effect on intercourse timing, and 1 actually speeded up the initiation of intercourse (Kirby, 2002). Another review examined evaluations of 20 comprehensive sexuality programs and found that 15 of them significantly delayed the onset of sexual activity (Manlove et al., 2006). In contrast, neither review found any scientific evidence that abstinence-only programs delayed intercourse.

A related line of research has looked at adolescents who have taken a public virginity pledge, often as a result of an abstinence-only program. Compared to non-pledgers, they are more likely to delay intercourse some 18 months on average. However, when they do initiate intercourse, they are less likely to use contraception (Bearman & Bruckner, 2001). A follow-up study found similar levels of STIs among those who had taken the abstinence pledge and those who hadn't (Bruckner & Bearman, 2005). In addition, pledgers were less likely to see a doctor about a possible STI or to receive STI testing.

One way to sum up the research on abstinence-only programs can be found in the official evaluation of such a program by the state of Pennsylvania. The authors concluded:

Beyond the eighth grade, abstinence-only programs can continue to play a valuable role in reinforcing and supporting youth who choose to remain sexually abstinent. For those youth who do not remain abstinent, however, the reduction of teenage pregnancies, STDs, and HIV/AIDS requires an alternative strategy.

(Smith, Dariotis, & Potter, 2003, p. 21)

page 418 takes a closer look at what kinds of educational programs for teens seem to work, and what kinds don't.

Age Differences in Partners. For most boys, the first time is with a partner the same age (33%) or a year or more younger (38%). The picture is quite different for most girls, whose first-time partners tend to be a year older (21%), 2–3 years older (34%), or 4+ years older (14%) (Manlove et al., 2006). Girls are also more likely to report that at the time, they had negative or mixed feelings about doing it. Only 34% of girls say, "I really wanted it to happen," compared to 62% of boys, and twice as many girls (13%) as boys (6%) say they really *didn't* want it to happen (Terry-Humen, Manlove,

Figure 12.9 Unwanted First Sexual Experience, by Gender and Age at First Sex
Younger girls are more likely to say that their first experience was unwanted.

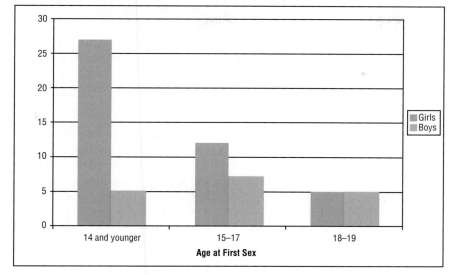

Source: Abma et al., 2004.

& Cunningham, 2006). The younger the girl was at the time, the more likely she is to report that she didn't want it (see Figure 12.9), while age makes no difference in boys' responses. Among girls 14 and under, more than one in four say they didn't want it to happen at the time (Abma et al., 2004).

Taken together, these statistics suggest that many young girls engage in sex the first time (and maybe thereafter as well) because their older, more experienced, partners want it and not because they themselves want it. Research shows that girls with older partners are more likely to have had intercourse, to have sex under the influence of alcohol or drugs, and to have been subjected to sexual coercion (Gowen, Feldman, Diaz, & Yisrael, 2004). They are also more likely to agree that "guys can't control their sexual urges." As we saw in Chapter 10, girls are traditionally taught to please others, defer to those of higher status, and work to maintain close relationships (Brown & Gilligan, 1993). This makes it more likely that they will think, "He really needs it. If I want to hold onto him, I'd better go along."

Sexual Minorities in Adolescence

Almost all the research we have looked at so far in this section deals with the majority of adolescents who are sexually attracted to, and engage in sexual activities with, only those of the other sex. A great many teens, however, have a different **sexual orientation.** They feel sexual attractions and engage in sexual activities with others of the same sex, either instead of or alongside other-sex attractions and activities. In the past, they would have been called *homosexual*, but because this term implies an either/or distinction that doesn't capture the complexities of human sexuality, and because it has long had negative connotations, many social scientists these days prefer to speak of **sexual minorities.**

How big a minority? The answer depends on how membership is defined. We need to distinguish among those who acknowledge:

Same-sex attraction, either exclusive or non-exclusive;

Same-sex behavior, again either exclusive or non-exclusive;

Same-sex identity as *gay* (males), *lesbian* (females), or *bisexual* (both).

Connect the Dots...

What explanations can you suggest for the fact that girls tend to have first-time sexual partners who are a good deal older than them? What consequences do you think this tendency may have for a girl and for her partner?

◀ **Learning Objective 12.10**
What special issues do sexual minority youth face?

Sexual orientation The sexual attraction a person feels toward those of the same or the other sex.

Sexual minorities Those whose sexual orientation is other than exclusively heterosexual.

Recent research suggests that many more adolescents experience some degree of same-sex attraction and engage in some form of same-sex behavior than personally identify themselves as gay, lesbian, or bisexual (GLB) (Savin-Williams, 2006).

For example, only 2% to 3% of adult males identify themselves as gay, but as many as *half* of heterosexual adult males can recall sexual incidents of some kind with another boy during childhood and adolescence (Bell, Weinberg, & Hammersmith, 1981). In a large, representative survey of American teens, over 8% of boys and 6% of girls reported either same-sex attractions or a same-sex relationship (Russell & Joyner, 2001), but fewer than 2% of teens identify themselves as gay, lesbian, or bisexual (Garofolo et al., 1999).

How Sexual Orientation Develops. There is a great deal we do not know about the development of sexual orientation, but one thing is clear. Because most children grow up to be oriented toward those of the other sex, that is usually assumed to be normal and obvious. It is those who are different who are seen as presenting a problem. However, the process of development is just as complex for the majority as it is for the minority (Graber & Archibald, 2001).

A minority sexual orientation usually begins to make itself known in late childhood and early adolescence, but its probable roots go back much farther. The evidence to date points to an interaction of genetic factors, prenatal factors, and childhood experiences (Mustankski, Chivers, & Bailey, 2003):

Genetic factors. Twin studies show a higher *concordance* for same-sex orientation among identical than fraternal twins, and both are higher than among non-twin and adopted siblings (Savin-Williams & Cohen, 2004). In other words, if one twin has a same-sex orientation, the likelihood is higher that the other twin will as well. This implies some element of genetic involvement.

Prenatal factors. During fetal development, underexposure to androgens (male sex hormones) in males, and overexposure to androgens in females, have been linked to atypical brain development and later atypical sexual attractions (Collaer & Hines, 1995).

Childhood experiences. Children whose temperaments and activity levels are not typical for their sex may be channeled toward gender-atypical games, interests, and companions, leading them to feel and to be treated by parents and peers as "different" or "odd" (Bem, 2001).

Recently, a team of researchers looked at childhood home movies of gay, lesbian, and heterosexual adults. Those who grew up to have a minority sexual orientation were rated as more gender nonconforming as children (Rieger, Linsenmeier, Gygax, & Bailey, 2008).

One curious finding is that boys who have older brothers are more likely to grow up to be gay, and the more older brothers they have, the greater the likelihood (Blanchard, 2001). One explanation that has been offered is that carrying a male fetus stimulates the mother's immune system to react against androgens. The more male babies she has, the more suppression of androgens takes place. However, there may also be some of the "niche-picking" discussed in Chapter 5. For a boy with several older brothers, it may be harder to find a behavioral niche that is both distinctive and stereotypically masculine.

Special Difficulties for Sexual Minority Teens. Dealing with the physical, social, and emotional changes of adolescence and the transition to sexual activity is not that easy for anyone. For sexual minority teens it is that much more difficult. All their lives they have been watching movies and reading stories about heterosexual love and sex. And for much of their lives they have been hearing, and maybe repeating, jokes and insults about "fags" and "dykes." Now they face the realization that, as one Gay Pride bumper sticker put it, "I am one of the people my parents warned me against." This is not just upsetting, it can be actively dangerous. One study found that a large majority of teens who were open about having same-sex orientations had been insulted and harassed by peers, more than one in three had been dumped by friends, and one in seven had suffered physical attacks (D'Augelli, 2002).

Keeping one's desires and activities secret is not much of a solution, either, though many sexual minority teens try it (D'Augelli, Grossman, & Starks, 2005). It does nothing to relieve feelings of loneliness and isolation. Usually, teens with a romantic problem can talk about it with a close friend and get some emotional support. But what if the problem is that you think you may be in love with your close friend? And to make it worse, you're afraid he or she will be totally disgusted and never speak to you again if you let slip even the slightest hint of your real feelings. Given all the pain sexual minority teens may be subjected to, both from others and from within themselves, it is not surprising to learn that they are more likely than other adolescents to attempt suicide (D'Augelli, 2002; Russell, 2006).

A bleak picture, perhaps, but there have been some positive changes in recent decades. Surveys show that acceptance of sexual minorities in the United States has risen steadily, especially among those who actually know someone who is gay, lesbian, or bisexual (Mangaliman, 2006; Pew Foundation, 2006). In many areas, schools and community organizations have set up gay-straight alliances, clubs, and coffeehouses where sexual minority youth can hang out, talk openly about their experiences and difficulties, and maybe meet prospective romantic partners (Diamond et al., 1999). For those in more isolated or rural areas, the Internet offers a way to discover that their feelings and problems are not unique and that there are many others who share them (Diamond, 2003a). In response to this improved psychological climate, larger numbers of sexual minority teens are *coming out*, that is, disclosing their sexual identity to friends, parents, and others (Savin-Williams, 2001).

Risks of Adolescent Sex

Sexual activity carries certain risks, whether one is 15 or 35. For sexually active adolescents, however, the risks are especially high. Adolescents may lack the experience or the mature judgment to assess risks and make good decisions under pressure. Because most are not very active sexually, they may find themselves unprepared emotionally or practically when sexual activity does occur. This is especially the case for younger adolescents. Unfortunately, a great many adolescents are misinformed or uninformed about sex, its possible risks, and ways they can reduce or avoid those risks.

Sexually Transmitted Infections. Any time people are close to one another, it gives disease-causing organisms a chance to move to a new host, and sexual activity brings people especially close. As the name implies, **sexually transmitted infections (STIs)** are spread mainly through sexual contact, and some of them spread very easily. Among American young people 15 to 24, at least 15 million have ongoing cases of STIs and an estimated 9 million more are infected each year (Weinstock, Berman, & Cates, 2004). The first large-scale national study of STIs by the U.S. Centers for Disease Control and Prevention found that *one in four* girls and young women ages 14 to 19 are infected with at least one of the more common STIs (Altman, 2008).

Two insidious features of STIs help to make the numbers of those infected so high. Some STIs, including HIV/AIDS and herpes, can have a very long **latency period,** during which the person has no symptoms, but can unknowingly infect others. In addition, active STIs often do not cause *any* easily noticeable symptoms. Neither the person who is infected nor a potential sexual partner is likely to realize that sex together poses a risk.

◄ **Learning Objective 12.11**
What are the risks of adolescent sex and how can they be reduced?

Sexually transmitted infections (STIs) Diseases, such as chlamydia, herpes, and HIV/AIDS, that are spread mainly through sexual contact.

Latency period For infections, a period of time after a person has contracted the disease, but before any noticeable symptoms appear.

Among the STIs that sexually active adolescents may be exposed to are chlamydia, gonorrhea, genital herpes, human papillomavirus, and HIV/AIDS. We will take a brief look at each of these.

Chlamydia. Chlamydia is so infectious that many people catch it from a single time with an infected partner (Cates, 1999). As many as 1.5 million young Americans contract chlamydia every year (Weinstock et al., 2004). The highest rate of infection is among girls ages 15 to 19, and African American women are much more affected than White women (CDC, 2005). Because many females do not experience any symptoms, chlamydia often goes undiagnosed and untreated. When symptoms do occur, they can include pain during intercourse and urination and disrupted menstrual periods. Treatment with antibiotics is usually effective, but if left untreated, chlamydia can cause pelvic inflammatory disease (PID), which can lead to infertility. In addition, women infected with chlamydia are up to five times more likely to contract HIV if exposed (CDC, 2005).

Gonorrhea. Often called "the clap," gonorrhea is a bacterial infection that first shows itself in males as a burning sensation during urination. In females, the early symptoms may be nothing more than a mild vaginal discharge. Over 400,000 young Americans contract gonorrhea each year (Weinstock et al., 2004). In the past, treatment with antibiotics was usually effective, but in recent years drug-resistant strains of the bacteria have become widespread. If left untreated, gonorrhea can lead to various serious complications.

Genital Herpes. Herpes is the medical name for a large family of viruses that cause an assortment of diseases including chicken pox, cold sores, and shingles. The genital form produces painful sores and blisters in the genital region that may last several weeks. During this time, the condition is highly contagious. The symptoms do go away, but they tend to come back at least once, and more frequently for some. Genital herpes has spread dramatically in recent decades. By one estimate, over 4 million young Americans are infected, and another 600,000 become infected every year (Weinstock et al., 2004). While there are treatments that can lessen the symptoms and shorten the episodes, so far there is no cure for herpes.

Human Papillomavirus (HPV). The human papillomavirus (HPV) is highly contagious, but difficult to test for and diagnose. As a result, it is the most common STI, infecting more than 9 million American youth (Weinstock et al., 2004). Sometimes HPV causes genital warts, but in most cases it has no obvious symptoms. Women who carry the virus are at much greater risk of developing cervical cancer, which is the second-leading cause of death among women worldwide. In the United States, the use of Pap smears to detect early signs of the cancer reduces the toll, but it still strikes some 13,000 American women a year and kills 4,500 (Ries et al., 2006). HPV has also been shown to cause cancer of the mouth and throat in those who have engaged in oral sex (D'Souza et al., 2007).

There is no cure for HPV, but there *is* some very good news for future generations. The U.S. Food and Drug Administration recently approved a vaccine that is almost 100% effective against the two dominant strains of HPV. Medical experts are urging that every girl be given the vaccine at age 11 or 12, before she is likely to be sexually active and possibly exposed to the virus. If adopted worldwide, such a program will eventually eliminate a major cause of cancer and save the lives of hundreds of thousands of women (Harris, 2006). It is likely that the vaccine against HPV will soon be approved and recommended for boys as well. However, because it is mostly the boys' future sexual partners who will benefit, observers wonder how much parents will go along with such a recommendation (Hoffman, 2008).

HIV/AIDS. The human immunodeficiency virus (HIV) that causes acquired immune deficiency syndrome (AIDS) came to the attention of the world in the

1980s and quickly became the best-known and most feared STI (King, 2005). HIV is transmitted by exposure to the bodily fluids of someone who is infected. Usually this means semen during sexual contact or blood from shared IV needles. Once contracted, HIV has an unusually long latency period. Someone can become HIV-positive and have no symptoms for 5 or even 10 years, but pass the virus on to others during that time. Eventually, HIV attacks and weakens the person's immune system, which becomes unable to fight off other debilitating or fatal diseases such as pneumonia and cancer. This is the phase called AIDS.

Around the world, some 12 million young people ages 15 to 24 are infected with HIV/AIDS, almost two-thirds of them female (UNAIDS, 2006). Every day, another 6,000 youths are infected. The crisis is worldwide, but unevenly so. The hardest hit region is Sub-Saharan Africa, where in some countries 20% of the young people are HIV-positive. Youth in the Caribbean, Latin America, Eastern Europe, and East Asia also have high or growing infection rates (UNAIDS, 2006). In the United States, there have been at least 40,000 cases among those aged 13 to 24, and over 10,000 in that age group have died of AIDS since the epidemic began (NIAID, 2006). Because of the very long latency period, it is practically certain that there are thousands more adolescents and young adults in the United States who are HIV-positive but do not yet realize it.

There is no cure for HIV/AIDS and no vaccine to ward it off. A combination of antiretroviral drugs can help keep someone with AIDS alive and reasonably healthy, but the treatment calls for unwavering discipline and attention and is far too expensive for most AIDS victims. There are some ways to slow the *spread* of HIV/AIDS, however. One is to abstain from sex and from sharing IV needles, the two main avenues of transmission. For those adolescents who are sexually active, the consistent use of latex condoms has been found to greatly reduce the risk that HIV will be passed between partners (CDC, 2002).

Pregnancy. Along with STIs, the other major risk that sexually active adolescents face is an unintended *pregnancy*. In the United States, about 780,000 girls ages 15 to 19 become pregnant every year, and some four out of five of these pregnancies were unintended (Upchurch & Kusunoki, 2006). About two-thirds of these pregnancies result in childbirth and one-third end in abortion (Singh & Darroch, 2000). In all, over one-third of girls who are sexually active get pregnant at some point during their teenage years (CDC, 2002).

Connect the Dots...

Suppose you set out to design a program to reduce the frequency of STIs among adolescents. What approach would you take? What features of the program do you think would be particularly effective? What would you try to avoid, and why?

◄ Preventing the spread of HIV/AIDS among sexually active teens is a major social concern.

Figure 12.10 Adolescent Pregnancy Rates by Year and Ethnic Group
Adolescent pregnancy rates have declined in each ethnic group in recent Years.

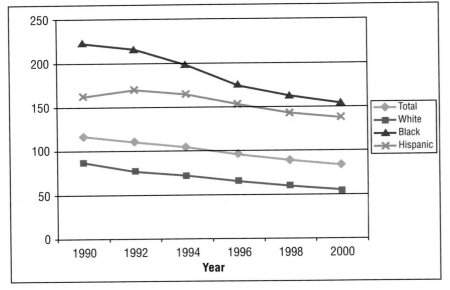

Source: Guttmacher Institute, 2004.

Any girl who has intercourse may get pregnant, but some are more likely to than others. Factors that place teens at greater risk for pregnancy include living in a dangerous neighborhood and in a lower-SES family, living with a single parent, having older sexually active siblings, and having teenage sisters who are pregnant or are already mothers (Miller et al., 2001). Girls who reach puberty early and start sex younger are also at greater risk, especially if, as is generally the case, their partners are older (Manlove et al., 2006). Ethnicity is an important factor as well. As Figure 12.10 shows, Black adolescents have the highest pregnancy rate and Whites the lowest, with Hispanics in between (Alan Guttmacher Institute, 2004).

In recent years, pregnancy and birth rates among adolescents in the United States have fallen considerably. Between 1990 and 2000, the teenage pregnancy rate fell by 28% and the birth rate by 21% (Alan Guttmacher Institute, 2004). This drop in pregnancy rate and the way it varied across ethnic groups can also be seen in Figure 12.10. The biggest drop, 32%, was among Black adolescents. For White teens, the pregnancy rate declined 28%, and for Hispanics, 15%. The birth rate among girls 15 to 19 continued to decline between 2000 and 2004, the most recent year for which information is available (Child Trends, 2006a).

International Comparisons. The marked decline of adolescent pregnancy and birth rates in the United States in recent years is good news, but those rates are still astonishingly higher than those in other developed countries (Singh & Darroch, 2000). As Figure 12.11 on page 425 shows, the U.S. teen pregnancy rate is nearly twice those in England, Canada, and Australia; three and a half times those in France, Denmark, and Sweden; and almost *seven times* those in Italy, Belgium, and the Netherlands. This is not because American teens are more active sexually. Adolescents in other developed countries tend to be just as sexually active as those in the United States or even more so (Teitler, 2002). Those in England, France, and Sweden, for example, are more likely than American teens to have had sex in the last 3 months (Darroch et al., 2001).

Why are U.S. teens so much more likely to get pregnant? The most obvious reason is that American adolescents are less likely to use contraception. Surveys show that 20% of American teens—one in five—did not use *any* method of contraception the most recent time they had intercourse. By comparison, only 11% of French

Figure 12.11   Birth, Pregnancy, and Abortion in Developed Countries

Birth, pregnancy, and abortion rates are sharply higher in the United States than in other developed countries.

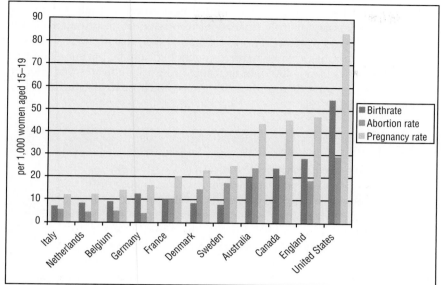

Source: Singh & Darroch, 2000.

teens, 6% of Swedish teens, and 4% of English teens failed to use contraception (Darroch et al., 2001). Contraceptive use by U.S. teens has improved in recent years (Santelli, Morrow, Anderson, & Lindberg, 2006), but it is still well behind that of European youth.

As for why American adolescents do not consistently use contraception, one reason is that their sexual activity tends to happen without advance planning (Morrison, 1985). That, in turn, has been linked to the American ambivalence about adolescent sex that we discussed earlier in the chapter. To plan for sex means to acknowledge an *intention* to have sex, which may arouse feelings of guilt. Those who don't plan, however, can tell themselves that they were simply carried away by the moment. In one study, teens who said they would feel "very guilty" about having sex were less likely than others to have sex, but when they *did* have sex, they were also less likely to use contraception (Gerrard, 1987).

Does that mean that European teens always schedule their sexual encounters in advance? No, but culturally they are better prepared for them when they do happen. Messages about safe sex are everywhere in the media. Children are taught about sex in school from an early age. Parents take it for granted that by late adolescence their children are likely to be sexually active and discuss with them the need to take responsibility for their actions. Teens have easy, unembarrassing, and inexpensive access to means of contraception (Berne & Huberman, 1999). As a result, not only are pregnancy rates strikingly lower among Western European teens, so are the rates of STIs (Panchaud et al., 2000).

Consequences of Teen Pregnancy.   Teen pregnancies are usually accompanied by a variety of physical, social, economic, and personal consequences, mostly negative. Pregnant adolescents are more likely than older pregnant women to suffer such physical complications as hemorrhage and miscarriage. If they carry through with the pregnancy, they are likely to drop out of school and have trouble finding employment (Leadbetter & Way, 2001). Their babies suffer, too. They are more likely to be born prematurely and to have a low birth weight, factors that are linked to a long list of problems during infancy and childhood (Miller, Bayley, Christensen, Leavitt, & Coyl, 2003).

About 30% of American adolescents who suffer an unintended pregnancy choose to end it through *abortion* (Singh & Darroch, 2000). Those who make this choice are disproportionately from middle-class and upper-middle-class families, have educated parents, and have high educational and occupational aspirations themselves (South & Baumer, 2001). Americans are sharply divided on the issue of abortion, especially when adolescents are involved. However, most experts agree that teenage girls who choose an abortion are not likely to be harmed psychologically by having made that decision (Adler, Ozer, & Tschann, 2003). In fact. some research indicates that later on they are better off in many ways than comparable girls who chose to give birth (Zabin, Hirsch, & Emerson, 1989).

Summing Up...

The physical, hormonal, and psychological changes of puberty make sexuality a major issue of adolescence, one on which different cultures impose restrictive, semirestrictive, or permissive customs. In Western societies today, sexual activity is the norm among teens. Partnered sex typically follows a sequence of increasing physical intimacy, leading to intercourse, usually in the context of a romantic relationship. Some adolescents feel sexual attraction to those of the same sex, either along with or instead of other-sex attraction. These sexual minority youth may experience special difficulties because of social stigma and harassment, as well as feelings of isolation resulting from a sense of "differentness." Adolescent sex carries a number of risks, ranging from sexually transmitted infections to pregnancy. These risks are heightened by a lack of information and education and by attitudes that discourage planning and taking precautions.

SUMMARY

Adolescence is marked by the development of close friendships, the emergence of romantic relationships, and the transition to sexual activity.

Learning Objective 12.1 How do friendships change with adolescence?

While even preschool children have friendships, several features of adolescence favor closer relationships. In **self-disclosure**, young adolescents begin to confide their most personal thoughts and feelings with age mates whom they like and trust. An increased ability to take the perspective of others helps teens understand and respond to close friends more deeply. The increased importance of the peer group makes it vital to have someone understanding, sympathetic, and trustworthy to talk with about social relationships and problems.

Learning Objective 12.2 How do Sullivan and Erikson describe the stages of friendship?

The leading theory about the development of friendship was put forth by Sullivan, who described stages at which different inter-personal needs become primary. The preadolescent years are marked by the **need for intimacy**, shown in the development of close same-sex friendships or chumships. In early adolescence, the **need for sexuality** leads to a search for a romantic partner who can also be a friend. The sensitivities that were encouraged through chumships contribute to this process.

Other viewpoints on friendship development include those of Erikson and Bowlby. Erikson maintained that only those who have resolved their identity crisis are able to form truly intimate relationships. Bowlby saw the **working models** formed by attachment relations in early childhood as shaping responses to others later in childhood and in adolescence.

Learning Objective 12.3 What characteristics predict which teens will become close friends?

Close friends are generally similar in age, grade, sex, ethnic and class background, social and school-related attitudes, religious beliefs, and problem behaviors. Teens select friends largely on the basis of similarities, and once they become friends, they socialize one another to become still more similar. By middle adolescence most teens have at least one close friend of the other sex.

Learning Objective 12.4 What are the benefits and risks of adolescent friendships?

High-quality friendships, which have many positive and few negative features, confer many benefits, but **low-quality friend-ships**, in which negative features predominate, have been linked to increased behavior problems.

Romantic attractions and romantic attachments come to the fore with adolescence.

In the United States, romantic feelings find an outlet in the custom of dating.

Learning Objective 12.5 What needs are met by dating at different points in adolescence?

Dating meets a variety of needs, including recreation, status, companionship, and intimacy. The development of dating patterns moves from mixed-gender groups, to group dates, to more exclusive couple relationships. Dating in the United States starts as young as 12 and is nearly universal by 18. Three-quarters of 18-year-olds have recently been in a romantic relationship.

Relationship experience is similar across ethnic groups in the United States, with the exception of Asian American teens, who are much less likely to have been in a relationship. Dating is much less common in Western Europe, where informal mixed-gender group activities are the rule. In more traditional societies, mixed-gender adolescent socializing is tightly controlled or even forbidden.

Learning Objective 12.6 What phases do romantic relationships go through?

Romantic relationships involve behavioral systems that include attachment, romantic passion, and sexual gratification. One account of romance outlines four phases: initial infatuation, affiliative relationships, intimate relationships, and committed relationships. Infatuation is more common in early adolescence, affiliation in middle adolescence, and intimacy and commitment in late adolescence.

As with friendships, the working models formed in early childhood affect the expectations and attitudes an adolescent brings to romantic relationships. Earlier difficulties with peers can lead to **rejection sensitivity**, a tendency to be alert for signs of rejection and to interpret ambiguous cues in a negative way.

The romantic relationships of sexual minority youth are similar in many ways to those of other adolescents, but with particular difficulties that may include discomfort with their own desires, social stigma, and a shortage of potential sexual minority partners.

Learning Objective 12.7 Why is the end of a romantic relationship so painful?

Practically all adolescent romances come to an end, generally when one partner rejects the other. For most teens the breakup of a romance is a deeply distressing experience. A recent breakup is a leading cause of adolescent depression, especially in girls.

The physical, hormonal, emotional, and social changes of puberty combine to give new impetus to sexual impulses.

Learning Objective 12.8 How do different cultures deal with adolescent sexuality?

Societies deal with adolescent sexuality in many different ways. **Restrictive societies** control or forbid any sexual expression before adulthood or marriage, often by keeping boys and girls apart from an early age. **Semirestrictive societies** officially frown on adolescent sexual activity, but generally do not enforce

prohibitions rigorously. **Permissive societies** expect children and adolescents to be active sexually. While Western societies, including the United States, feature pervasive sexual messages that target adolescents, sexual activity by adolescents is usually seen as a source of problems.

Learning Objective 12.9 What is the usual sequence of sexual activity in adolescence?

In the United States, sexual activity is the norm among adolescents. One-quarter of U.S. teens are sexually experienced before 16, and almost three-quarters by age 18. For most boys, the first adolescent sexual experience is through **masturbation**. Girls are much less likely to masturbate. Partnered sex typically follows a regular age-linked sequence of increasingly intimate activities leading to intercourse. This sequence is the same for girls and boys, but girls report engaging in each activity about a year later than boys do. Recent research indicates that **oral sex** is becoming more common, and at earlier ages, among U.S. teens.

The average age for transition to intercourse among U.S. adolescents is 16 for boys and 17 for girls. Among U.S. ethnic groups, Black teens tend to begin intercourse earlier than White or Hispanic teens, and Asian teens tend to begin later. Most adolescents say that their first experience of intercourse was in the context of a romantic relationship.

Among the factors that predict starting intercourse earlier are, for girls, early puberty, and for girls and boys, having friends who see sexual activity as acceptable. Those whose parents disapprove of adolescent sex are likely to start sexual activity later. Educational programs that teach total abstinence from sexual activity have been shown to have very little or no effect on age of sexual initiation or number of sexual partners.

Most boys start sexual activity with a partner of their own age. For girls, however, the first time is likely to be with a partner who is from 1 to 4 or more years older. Girls are more likely than boys to have mixed or negative feelings about initiating intercourse, and the younger they were at the time, the more negative their feelings.

Learning Objective 12.10 What special issues do sexual minority youth face?

Many adolescents have a **sexual orientation** that includes feelings of attraction to others of the same sex, either with or instead of feelings of attraction to those of the other sex. Many more teens experience some degree of same-sex attraction or engage in some form of same-sex behavior than identify themselves as gay, lesbian, or bisexual. The development of sexual orientation is complex for all adolescents and probably results from an interaction of genetic factors, prenatal influences, and childhood experiences. While **sexual minorities** face many difficulties in addition to those common to all adolescents, social acceptance of sexual minorities in the United States has risen steadily, especially among younger people.

Learning Objective 12.11 What are the risks of adolescent sex and how can they be reduced?

Sexual activity poses a variety of risks that are greater for adolescents because of their inexperience and lack of information about those risks and how to avoid them. **Sexually transmitted infections (STIs)**, such as chlamydia, gonorrhea, genital herpes, human papillomavirus, and HIV/AIDS, are spread by sexual contact. Some STIs have long **latency periods** before symptoms show themselves, and in some the symptoms are not easily noticed. This makes it more likely that someone who is infected will unknowingly infect others.

An unintended pregnancy is a major risk of sexual activity, affecting as many as one-third of sexually active teenage girls.

The teen pregnancy rate in the United States is much higher than in other developed countries, even though rates of teen sexual activity are comparable. The immediate cause is that American teens are much less likely to use contraception. More generally, cultural attitudes that discourage adolescents from planning to have sex mean they are less likely to be prepared to cope with its risks. Teen pregnancies generally carry a variety of negative consequences, whether they lead to an abortion or adolescent parenthood.

KEY TERMS

Self-disclosure (390)
Intimacy (390)
Need for intimacy (392)
Need for sexuality (392)
Intimacy versus isolation (393)

Working models (394)
High-quality friendship (396)
Low-quality friendship (396)
Rejection sensitivity (406)
Restrictive societies (410)

Semirestrictive societies (410)
Permissive societies (410)
Masturbation (413)
CASI (414)
Oral sex (414)

Sexual orientation (419)
Sexual minorities (419)
Sexually transmitted infections (STIs) (421)
Latency period (421)

Part 5 Adolescent Problems and Prospects

chapter 13

Problems

Outline	Learning Objectives
THE REALITY OF ADOLESCENT PROBLEMS	
Points to Remember	◄ 13.1 What are some reasons for hope when teens develop problems?
Two Kinds of Problems	◄ 13.2 What is the distinction between externalizing and internalizing problems?
EXTERNALIZING PROBLEMS	
Delinquency and Violence	◄ 13.3 What are the risk factors for delinquency and adolescent violence?
Substance Use	◄ 13.4 How many teens use which substances, how often, and why?
INTERNALIZING PROBLEMS	
Eating Problems	◄ 13.5 What are the major eating disorders and why are they more common among girls?
Depression	◄ 13.6 What are the causes of adolescent depression?
Suicide	◄ 13.7 What are the risk factors and warning signs for teen suicide?

O ne of the things that everyone in today's world takes for granted is that adolescents are especially likely to have problems themselves and to create problems for others. Adults who do not know the difference between G. Stanley Hall and Carnegie Hall will confidently tell you that adolescence is supposed to be a time of "storm and stress," probably caused by "raging hormones." And when was the last time you heard the word *gang* without *teenage* in front of it, or *delinquent* without *juvenile*?

One reason for this is a normal tendency we all have to notice and remember what sticks out. It is unremarkable, and unremarked, if 30 students sit quietly through a boring class. But suppose one of them slams his book on the desk, shouts, "This really sucks!" and stomps out. The incident gets talked about for days, maybe weeks, and leaves listeners with the impression that teenage students are generally disruptive.

Another factor is the sensationalism that seems built into the way the media approach adolescence. Try to imagine a television newscaster announcing, "This just in: Tonight more than 5,000 teenagers attended a rock concert, dispersed to area fast-food restaurants for snacks, and went home peacefully!" In novels and television dramas, when some teen is egged into committing a minor act of vandalism early on, you just know that by the end he is going to be fully embarked on a life of crime, or else dead from an overdose or a drive-by shooting.

THE REALITY OF ADOLESCENT PROBLEMS

The picture of tumultuous teens that the media present is not complete fiction, of course. Many adolescents do have problems, as do many children and adults. And some adolescents have more serious problems than others. Before we examine these problems in more detail, however, we should try to remember that they are not necessarily a sign of lifelong difficulties. There are several reasons to hold out hope even when problems do develop.

Points to Remember

▶ **Learning Objective 13.1**
What are some reasons for hope when teens develop problems?

Trying something out is not the same as engaging with it to the point that it becomes a serious problem. When we discussed identity development in Chapter 11, we saw that adolescence is very much a time for trying things out. Some of those things may not be prudent, socially approved, or even legal. For example, most American adolescents have tried alcohol at some point, even though underage drinking is against the law. In fact, about one-third of high school seniors say they have had five or more drinks in a row—the definition of binge drinking—within the previous *2 weeks* (Johnston, O'Malley, Bachman, & Schulenberg, 2006). Even so, only a few teens develop a serious ongoing drinking problem.

An adolescent's problems may have their origins well before adolescence. For example, many teens who become delinquent have shown various conduct problems as children and many who become depressed have had emotional problems as children (Cicchetti & Toth, 2006; Dodge, Coie, & Lynam, 2006). The fact that a problem shows up during adolescence does not necessarily mean that it is an "adolescent problem."

Many adolescents "grow out" of their problems. Among those teens who break the law, the great majority turn into law-abiding adults (McCurley, 2007). The few who do go on to be criminals as adults are generally those who showed problem behaviors in their childhood as well as adolescent years (Moffitt, 1993, 2003). Problems should still be addressed when they come up, of course, but they should not necessarily be taken as a dire warning of terrible things to come.

Some actions are considered problems mainly because it is adolescents who are doing them, as opposed to adults. For instance, if you decide to systematically skip class, it is almost certainly a bad idea, but it is not against the law. An adolescent below a certain age who skips school, however, is guilty of *truancy*. You are free to spend a few nights at a friend's place without asking anyone's permission (except your friend's, of course). A teen who does the same thing might be labeled a runaway. Truancy and leaving home without parental permission are examples of a **status offense**, something that is a violation of the law for people with the status of minors, but not for adults (Scott & Woolard, 2004). Other examples of status offenses include having sex and buying cigarettes and beer.

Two Kinds of Problems

Those who treat adolescent problems or do research on them generally draw a distinction between *externalizing problems* and *internalizing problems* (Frick & Kimonis, 2005; Ollendick, Shortt, & Sander, 2005).

Adolescents with **externalizing problems** turn their difficulties outward, toward the external world. For example, aggression, delinquency, and antisocial behavior are directed toward others. Many experts, though not all, put substance abuse in the category of externalizing problems as well. Those with externalizing problems tend to be *undercontrolled*; that is, they show a weak ability to control their impulses (Van Leeuwen, De Fruyt, & Mervielde, 2004). On average, externalizing problems are more common among boys than among girls (Frick & Kimonis, 2005).

Adolescents with **internalizing problems** turn their difficulties inward, toward themselves. Among the more common internalizing problems are depression, anxiety, and eating disorders. Those with internalizing problems tend to be *overcontrolled* and to repress their impulses (Van Leeuwen et al., 2004). On average, internalizing problems are more common among girls than among boys (Ollendick et al., 2005).

Distinguishing between externalizing and internalizing problems is helpful when we are trying to understand the origins, symptoms, and treatment of adolescent disorders. We should remember, though, that in real life the two sorts of problems are not always so separate. The term experts use when two or more problems tend to show up at the same time is **comorbidity**, and this is not uncommon among adolescents (Lilienfeld, 2003). Comorbid problems may be the product of underlying factors, such as a tendency toward negative emotionality or disinhibition (Clark, 2005; Kreuger & Markon, 2006). For example, adolescents with a conduct problem are often depressed as well (Beyers & Loeber, 2003; Rowe, Maughan, & Eley, 2006). While many teens with antisocial problems abuse drugs and alcohol, so do many who are depressed. There is clearly a difference between an adolescent who goes out, gets drunk, and looks for somebody to pick a fight with, and one who drinks alone at home to the point of passing out. Their drinking problem, however, is similar, and both, as we shall see, might benefit from similar treatment for that aspect of their problems.

Many protective and risk factors also cross the boundary between externalizing and internalizing problems. For example, a positive self-concept is important for adjustment and for protection against both sorts of problem behavior (Ybrandt, 2008). Having a negative self-concept is a major risk factor for *internalizing* problems in girls and for *externalizing* problems in boys. At this point we are going to turn our attention specifically to two of the major categories of externalizing problems in adolescents. What are they like? How common are they? What are their origins? What can be done to treat and prevent them? Later in the chapter we address the same questions about major categories of internalizing problems.

EXTERNALIZING PROBLEMS

In the eyes of many adults, externalizing problems are *the* problems of adolescence. "Kids these days" are seen as wild, violent, always getting high and having sex, thumbing their noses at adult rules, and taking crazy chances that endanger themselves and those around them. As we saw in Chapter 1, some version of this view of young people has been around for hundreds and even thousands of years. Widespread and enduring as it may be, however, is it at all accurate? To find that out, we need to turn to the less sensational world of objective information and testable propositions. In this section, we look first at research about delinquency and violence, then we examine the issue of adolescent substance use and abuse.

◄ **Learning Objective 13.2**
What is the distinction between externalizing and internalizing problems?

Status offense An action, such as truancy or buying cigarettes, that is against the law for those who are considered minors, but not for adults.

Externalizing problem Turning one's difficulties toward the external world, for example, in the form of aggressive or antisocial behavior.

Internalizing problem Turning one's difficulties inward, toward the self, for example, in the form of depression or an eating disorder.

Comorbidity Different problems that tend to show up at the same time in the same person.

Delinquency and Violence

▶ **Learning Objective 13.3**
What are the risk factors for delinquency and adolescent violence?

Delinquency is a legal term that can refer to a wide variety of actions. Social scientists are more likely to talk about *antisocial behavior*, and clinicians prefer the diagnostic category of *conduct disorder*, but on the whole the three terms refer to the same sorts of activities (Farrington, 2004). Delinquent behavior includes *status offenses* such as truancy and running away, misconduct such as being disruptive in school, and minor offenses such as gambling and spitting on the sidewalk. The greatest concern, however, is the two categories of serious violations known as **index crimes**, defined as:

> *Violent crimes:* murder, forcible rape, robbery, and aggravated assault; and
>
> *Property crimes:* burglary, larceny-theft, motor vehicle theft, and arson.

Figure 13.1 charts the ages of those younger than 25 arrested in the United States for violent crimes during the year 2004. A similar chart for property crimes is shown in Figure 13.2 on page 435. Both present a dismal picture, especially for adolescent males. Their arrest rate for both violent and property crimes climbs steeply and steadily across the teenage years, reaching a peak at 18 or 19. For females, the rate of violent crimes stays low across the adolescent years, while the rate for property crimes increases somewhat to age 16, then starts to drop. Among those younger than 18, boys are about twice as likely as girls to be arrested for property crimes and more than four times as likely to be arrested for violent crimes (Federal Bureau of Investigation, 2006).

Another way to think about this information is in proportion to the general population. In the United States, as of 2004, those ages 10 to 17 made up about 11.5% of the total population (U.S. Census Bureau, 2006). That same year, more than 15% of those arrested for violent crimes, and *28%* of those arrested for property crimes, were younger than 18. Across the two categories of serious crimes, *one of every four* arrests was of someone younger than 18, even though only a little more than 1 of 10 people belonged to that group.

On a slightly brighter note, although the rate of violent crimes by those younger than 18 increased steadily from the mid-1980s to the early 1990s, starting around 1994 it began to decline just as steadily. Figure 13.3 on page 435 shows both the number of juvenile arrests for index crimes (both violent and property crimes) and the

Delinquency The legal term for actions by juveniles that violate the law.

Index crimes Serious violations of the law, so called because they are included on official indexes of criminal activity.

Figure 13.1 Arrests for Violent Crimes, by Age and Sex, 2004
Arrests for violent crimes climb steeply for boys across adolescence.

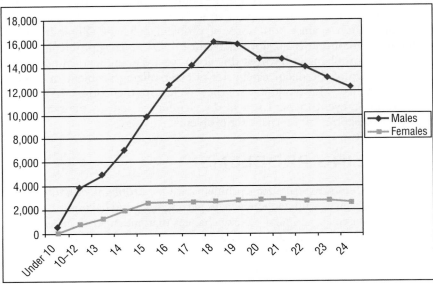

*Murder, forcible rape, robbery, and aggravated assault.
Source: Federal Bureau of Investigation, 2006.

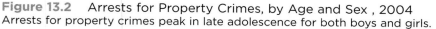

Figure 13.2 Arrests for Property Crimes, by Age and Sex , 2004
Arrests for property crimes peak in late adolescence for both boys and girls.

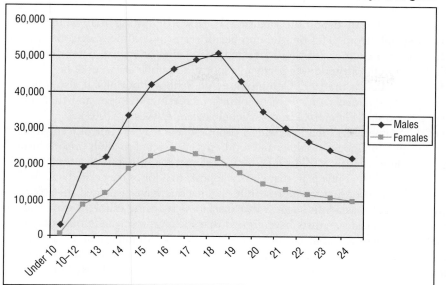

*Burglary, larceny-theft, motor vehicle theft, and arson.

Source: "And the Walls Keep Tumbling Down," by D. Mendal. *Advocasey*, pp. 18–27, 2003.
Used by permission.

Figure 13.3 Juvenile Arrests and Confinements, 1991–1999
Although juvenile arrests declined sharply after 1995, the number of
juveniles in confinement continued to rise.

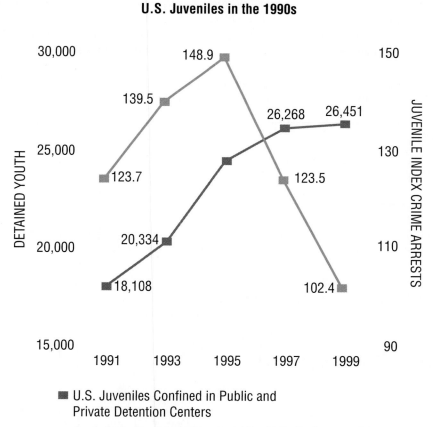

Source: Mendel, 2003, p. 20.

number of juveniles in detention facilities. It is worth noting that while arrests dropped off steeply from 1995 on, the number of teens in confinement continued to climb. In other words, more of those arrested were jailed or sent to detention facilities. This "get-tough" attitude was partly a response to public alarm over highly publicized incidents such as the 1999 Columbine High School shootings. It also reflected a general impression that teens were becoming increasingly violent and that something had to be done (Flannery, Hussey, Biebelhausen, & Wester, 2003).

One of the "somethings" that was widely proposed as a way to control teen violence was to try juvenile offenders as adults and send those convicted to adult prisons instead of juvenile facilities (Fagan & Zimring, 2000). A slogan for this approach was "Do the crime, do the time." A simple plan that clearly appeals to a lot of concerned people, but does it work? Not according to the research. Studies that have evaluated the effects of punishing adolescents as adults suggest that instead of reducing crime, it may actually increase it. Some social scientists have argued that locking up juvenile offenders with serious adult criminals is like giving them free higher education in crime. Compared to those committed to juvenile facilities, delinquent teens who are sent to adult prisons are *more* likely to get arrested again once they are out (Butts & Mears, 2001; Redding, 2005).

Delinquency and Ethnicity. Juvenile arrests and detentions in the United States are spread very unevenly across different ethnic groups (Snyder & Sickmund, 2006). The likelihood of getting caught up in the juvenile justice system for the same offense is significantly higher for youths of color than for their White counterparts (Farrington, Loeber, & Stouthamer-Loeber, 2003). In 2003, 190 of every 100,000 White adolescents were in custody in a juvenile facility. For Black teens, the rate was 754, almost four times as high (see Figure 13.4). Comparable rates for other ethnic categories were 348 for Hispanics, 496 for American Indians, and 113 for Asians.

These differences are at least partly the result of bias in the juvenile justice system (Juvenile Justice Evaluation Center, 2006). When teens describe their own delinquent activities with a promise that their answers will be kept confidential, there are many fewer ethnic differences than one would expect from the statistics about teens in custody (see Figure 13.5 on page 437). More Blacks and Hispanics than Whites say they are

▲ Growing numbers of adolescents are being tried and punished as adults.

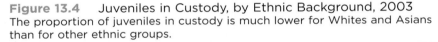

Figure 13.4 Juveniles in Custody, by Ethnic Background, 2003
The proportion of juveniles in custody is much lower for Whites and Asians than for other ethnic groups.

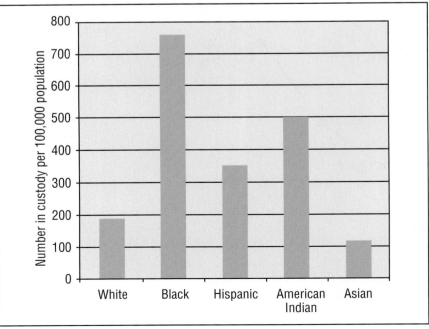

Source: Snyder & Sickmund, 2006, p. 213.

Figure 13.5   Self-Reported Delinquent Activities, by Ethnic Groups
Self-reported delinquent activities are roughly similar across ethnic groups.

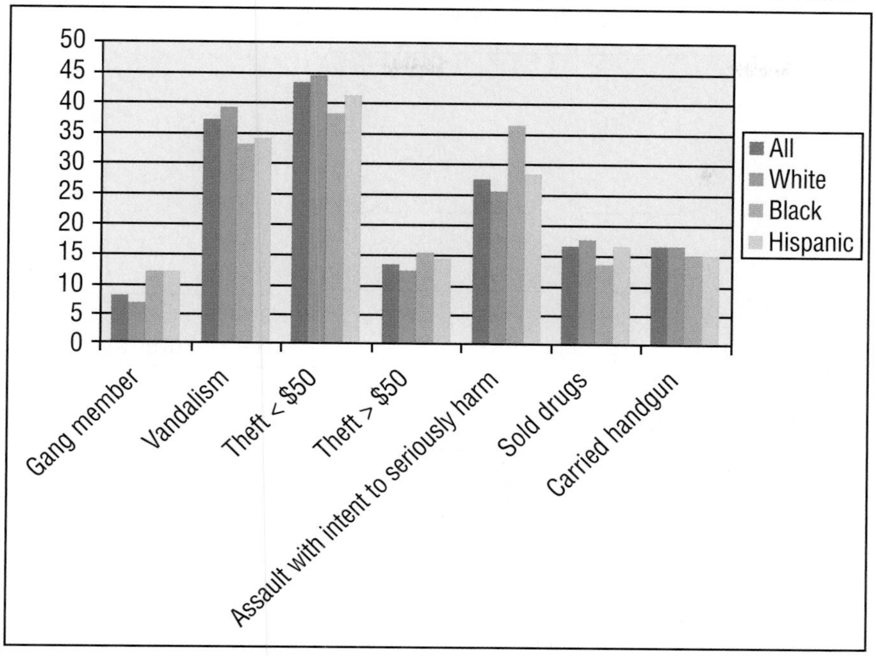

Source: Snyder & Sickmund, 2006, p. 70.

members of a gang, and Blacks are more likely to admit to assaulting someone with the intent of serious harm. However, there are no important differences in reported behaviors such as theft and carrying a handgun, and Whites are actually *more* likely to say they have committed acts of vandalism (McCurley, 2007; Snyder & Sickmund, 2006).

Delinquency and Class. The discrepancy between self-reported delinquency and the official statistics also reflects the influence of social class, which is closely intertwined with ethnicity in the United States. As of 2002, one of six Americans younger than age 18 lived below the official poverty line, as compared to 1 of 10 adults. As Figure 13.6 on page 438 illustrates, Black and Hispanic juveniles were three times as likely to live in poverty, and in extreme poverty, as White juveniles (Snyder & Sickmund, 2006). Low family income in childhood has been found to predict both self-reported delinquency and conviction rates in the teenage years (Farrington, 2004). One reason for this is that poverty is linked to greater family disruption, such as separation and divorce, which, in turn, influences juvenile violence (Dodge et al., 2006). Like minority teens, those from lower-income families are more likely to be arrested than those from middle-income families, and once arrested they are more likely to end up in confinement.

Another reason for the gap between self-reported delinquency and crime statistics is that a good deal of delinquency by middle-class adolescents never makes it into official records. Suppose a store manager catches a teen shoplifting. If the culprit seems to be from a "good home," the manager may be content to call the parents and let the teen off with a stiff warning. But what if the teen lives in the projects with a single parent who can't even be reached by phone? The odds just went up that the manager will file charges. Even if the store has a set policy of calling the cops for every incident of shoplifting, middle-class families are more likely to have the knowledge, resources, and social connections to get any charges reduced or dismissed.

Risk Factors for Delinquency. According to most surveys, about three of four adolescents are involved in some form of delinquent activity at some point during their teenage years (Moffitt, 2003). In this sense, simply being an adolescent could be thought of as a risk factor for delinquency. A personal example: During my senior year in high school, there was a brief craze for stealing highway signs. Not, I should add,

Figure 13.6   Americans Younger Than 18 in Poverty, by Ethnic Group
The proportion of American children and teens in poverty is much higher among Blacks and Hispanics than among Whites and Asians.

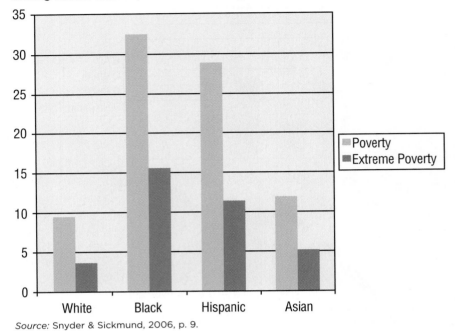

Source: Snyder & Sickmund, 2006, p. 9.

any whose absence we thought might create a safety hazard! These trophies decorated the senior study room until the school administration got alarmed about possible consequences and confiscated them. Among this group of middle-class, college-bound teens with concerned, mostly professional parents, practically all the boys and some of the girls carried out what was, after all, a criminal act. Yet, as far as I know, not one of them has been in trouble with the law as an adult.

If we are going to understand delinquency, we need to distinguish between those adolescents who occasionally break the law in some relatively minor way during their teenage years and those who commit more serious offenses over the long run. Psychologist Terrie Moffitt (1993, 2003) has proposed that these two sorts of delinquency involve different individuals, different sources and risk factors, and different trajectories.

Life-course-persistent offenders are mostly boys whose antisocial behavior, such as physical aggression and defiance, first shows up in childhood (Broidy et al., 2003; Farrington, 2004). They tend to be more impulsive and restless than their age mates, to have trouble controlling their anger, and to have low IQ scores and school grades. These characteristics may be linked to a reduced brain response following errors; in effect, they are less likely to learn from their mistakes (Hall, Bernat, & Patrick, 2007). At the same time, they tend to react with more stress to negative events (Hart, Eisenberg, & Valiente, 2007). More than their better-adjusted peers, they are also likely to come from disrupted families, with hostile or neglecting parents who provide poor supervision and punitive or erratic discipline. The interaction of a difficult environment and neuropsychological problems makes them more likely to develop problem behaviors, become involved in criminal behavior, and stay involved as adults (Hart et al., 2007; Moffit, 2003).

Adolescence-limited offenders, in contrast, do not seem that different from anyone else during infancy and childhood, or, for that matter, once they reach full adulthood. It is only during adolescence and emerging adulthood that they are involved in antisocial behavior, and whether they are labeled as delinquents depends mostly on whether they get caught doing whatever it is they do. While adolescence-limited offending is not associated with seriously disrupted families the way life-course-persistent offending is, it has been linked to less close monitoring by parents (Laird, Pettit, Bates, & Dodge, 2003). Parental monitoring is especially important for teens in families that live in dangerous neighborhoods (Pettit, Bates, Dodge, & Meece, 1999).

Life-course-persistent offenders Adolescents whose antisocial behavior first appears in childhood and tends to continue into adulthood.

Adolescence-limited offenders Adolescents who become involved in antisocial activities during adolescence and typically do not continue them into adulthood.

Individual Characteristics. Several aspects of individual personality and functioning have been shown to increase the risk of delinquency. We just mentioned that those antisocial adolescents who are most likely to continue as adult offenders are more impulsive and restless than their peers. Recent research suggests that this results from an interaction between genetic factors and events in childhood. Studies that have compared twins, siblings, and adopted children find a substantial genetic influence on antisocial behavior, along with a substantial environmental impact (Jaffee et al., 2005; Moffitt & Caspi, 2007; Rhee & Waldman, 2002). One line of research has examined the role of a specific gene linked to metabolizing neurotransmitters that are involved in self-control. Those adolescents who have the low-activity version of the gene *and* who were mistreated as children are at much greater risk to develop antisocial behavior (Caspi et al., 2002; Foley et al., 2004). So it is neither the gene itself, nor the childhood maltreatment, that is responsible, but the way the two factors interact.

The way a teen's hormonal system functions may also have a role in habitual aggressive behavior, at least in boys. Young adolescent boys whose resting levels of the stress hormone *cortisol* are consistently low show more externalizing problems (Shirtcliff, Granger, Booth, & Johnson, 2005). This connection does *not* show up in girls. One way in which cortisol levels may affect externalizing behavior is that boys with low cortisol may experience a lack of fear and anxiety in situations that would set off a stress reaction, and maybe a reluctance to go ahead, in other people (Raine, 2002). A related possibility is that boys with low cortisol need a higher level of stimulation to feel pleasurable excitement. This could make riskier, possibly antisocial, activities more attractive to them. One recent longitudinal study of young boys found that fearlessness at age 2 predicted conduct problems later in childhood, which is consistent with the link between low cortisol levels and externalizing problems (Shaw, Gilliom, Ingoldsby, & Nagin, 2003).

On a psychological level, antisocial teens are more likely to have a **hostile attributional bias** when they react to the words and actions of others (Dodge et al., 2006; Dodge & Pettit, 2003). These teens are quick to notice hostile features of others' behavior and at the same time may overlook or ignore non-hostile cues. If there is doubt or ambiguity about the meaning of the interaction, they tend to assume that the other person meant to be hostile. So if another teen makes a remark that might (or might not) be an insult or bumps into them in the hallway, they interpret the event as an intentional attack. In addition, they tend to react more quickly and automatically, giving less consideration to alternative responses. The result is that they are more likely to respond aggressively to even minor or unintentional clashes (Dodge et al., 2003).

The Role of Deviant Peers. We saw in Chapter 6 that peer influence becomes a powerful force during adolescence, for good or bad. In the case of antisocial or delinquent adolescents, that peer influence is bad. Quite simply, teens whose friends are deviant are at greater risk for deviant behavior themselves (Dishion & Dodge, 2006). Moreover, those who are unpopular with peers generally, for example, because of their aggressiveness, are more likely to take up with other deviant peers (Bukowsky, Vitaro, & Brendgen, 2007; Laird, Pettit, Dodge, & Bates, 2005). Antisocial teens also tend to overestimate how antisocial their friends are. As each tries to measure up to the other, there is a tendency for antisocial behavior to escalate (Prinstein & Wang, 2005). Deviant friends egg each other on, socially rewarding increasingly deviant behavior (Patterson, Dishion, & Yoeger, 2000). These friends also model antisocial activities and put social pressure on others to take part in them. If the teens you usually hang with decide to spray paint their tag on the side of a building, throw rocks at the windows of a grumpy neighbor, or break into a music store, it is very hard to feel like the only wuss in the bunch.

One study analyzed videotapes of boys interacting with a friend at ages 14, 16, and 18. Those boys whose antisocial behavior had started at an early age laughed more when their friend made an antisocial remark and didn't react when the friend made a more ordinary comment. The result, just as a learning psychologist would predict, was that the amount and degree of antisocial talk went up over the course of the conversation. In addition, those whose conversations were predictable and well-organized,

Connect the **Dots...**

If, as research suggests, boys with low levels of cortisol are at risk for antisocial aggression because they feel less fear in stressful situations, can you think of ways that this characteristic might be rechanneled in socially useful directions?

Hostile attributional bias A tendency to interpret ambiguous cues and situations as reflecting hostile intent and to respond aggressively to them.

but high in deviant content, were most likely to continue their antisocial behavior into adulthood (Dishion, Nelson, Winter, & Bullock, 2004).

Another indication of the influence deviant peers can exercise comes from a longitudinal study that followed adolescents who became members of a teenage gang. Before joining, their level of delinquency was no higher than that of others their age. After they became gang members, however, their delinquency rates increased substantially. Interestingly, once they left the gang, their likelihood of committing a violent offense dropped again (Thornberry, Krohn, Lizotte, Smith, & Tobin, 2003). It was only during the period of gang membership that their delinquency rates were high. In other words, while *self-selection* probably played a role in leading them to join the gang, once they were in, the other members *socialized* them in the direction of more deviant behavior.

Family and Neighborhood. When people consider the contexts of delinquency, such as the family, school, and neighborhood, it is tempting to ask how these affect the adolescent. However, a developmental systems approach (Lerner, 2006) reminds us that adolescents themselves are *active* participants in each of their contexts. Antisocial teens have an impact on the interlinked systems they are part of, just as these systems have an impact on them.

To illustrate this point, suppose a school has a high proportion of deviant students. This makes it more likely that other students will associate with deviant peers, because there are so many of them, and be influenced in the direction of deviancy themselves. This, in turn, increases the proportion of deviant students and the level of antisocial disruption and creates a climate in which deviant and antisocial behavior is seen as the norm. In a similar way, someone growing up in a high-crime neighborhood is exposed to successful deviant models and opportunities for deviant behavior, along with a scarcity of prosocial models and avenues for prosocial development. To the extent that adolescents are influenced either to engage in antisocial behavior or simply to tolerate and accept it, the neighborhood becomes that much more dangerous.

Not surprisingly, researchers have found that adolescents are more likely to develop antisocial problems in neighborhoods that have high poverty and unemployment, low educational levels, and large numbers of single-parent households (Beyers, Bates, Pettit, & Dodge, 2003). The characteristics of the neighborhood influence children's development both directly and through their impact on the family (Dodge et al., 2006).

Even when other factors are taken into account, family poverty predicts greater antisocial behavior in children. The stress on parents who are struggling to get by tends to make them less effective and more coercive toward their children, which, in turn, may lead to aggressiveness in the children (McLoyd, 1998). This can create a dynamic system in which attempts to control the child quickly escalate into confrontation (Granic & Patterson, 2006). Parents, especially overstretched single parents, may become so discouraged by the constant battles that they give up trying to monitor or control their deviant teens. If adolescents also see that the parents have externalizing problems of their own, such as substance use or antisocial conduct, the chances that the teens will develop antisocial problems increase significantly (Dogan, Conger, Kim, & Masyn, 2007).

A unique illustration of the link between family poverty and antisocial conduct comes from a "natural experiment" in the late 1990s. When a casino opened on an Indian reservation in North Carolina, poor families on the reservation received cash payments. This money moved some, but not all, of the families out of poverty. As it happened, many of their children were taking part in a longitudinal study that had started years before. Before the casino arrived, adolescents from poor families had a higher level of conduct disorders than others in the study whose families were not poor. Afterwards, adolescents whose families had been lifted out of poverty showed a *40% drop* in conduct disorders, but those whose families remained poor showed an *increase* in conduct problems (Costello, Compton, Keeler, & Angold, 2003).

Parents and Family Conflict. Poverty is far from being the only aspect of family life that predicts antisocial behavior. Parental monitoring was discussed at some length in

▲ Minor antisocial behaviors, such as shoplifting, are more common in teens with many deviant peers.

Chapter 5, but its complicated relationship to antisocial problems in adolescence should be pointed out again. Most parents gradually monitor their adolescents less because they recognize the teens' growing need for autonomy and greater maturity (Gutman & Eccles, 2007; Laird et al., 2003). Ironically, parents of antisocial boys who might actually benefit from *greater* parental monitoring and control tend not just to ease off gradually but to disengage rapidly. In effect, they give up trying to have a positive impact on their unruly teens. The result, not surprisingly, is that their children increasingly hang out with deviant peers and become more delinquent (Dishion, Nelson, & Bullock, 2004).

Everyday conflict between parents is also associated with more antisocial behavior in children and adolescents (Cummings, Goeke-Morey, & Papp, 2004). This is especially the case if the conflict includes domestic violence (Jaffee, Moffitt, Caspi, Taylor, & Arseneault, 2002). Because coping with a child who has conduct problems can increase tension and conflict between parents, it is possible to argue that the child's problems are increasing the parents' difficulties, more than the other way around. However, one long-term longitudinal study showed that in families that went through a divorce, boys had an increase in externalizing problems during the period *following* the divorce (Malone et al., 2004). This provides evidence that the change in the child's behavior was in response to the parents' difficulties.

Gangs. In June 2006, a suburban high school in eastern Pennsylvania held its annual graduation ceremonies under lockdown conditions. Students, family members, and guests had to pass through metal detectors to enter the stadium, which was patrolled by undercover police officers. The senior class president, an honor student and star athlete, delivered his speech to his classmates by closed-circuit television from a secret location. The reason for all this? Members of a street gang had threatened to kill him during the ceremony because his sister had agreed to testify in the murder trial of other gang members (Kocieniewski, 2006).

Adolescent street gangs have been part of the American urban scene for well more than a century. In the 1800s, bands of teenage boys in New York, Chicago, and other large cities hassled respectable passers-by, stole fruit from pushcarts, and served as lookouts and apprentices to adult criminals (Franzese, Covey, & Menard, 2006). In the mid-20th century, the American public learned a new meaning to the word "turf" when they went to see *West Side Story*, an updated musical version of the Romeo and Juliet tale set amid the battling teenage gangs of Manhattan.

Today, the notion of two teenage gangs meeting by prearrangement, somewhere along the border between their neighborhoods, to have it out with fists and a few switchblade knives is as antique as catching a horsedrawn streetcar to go downtown. Two new elements in particular have transformed the American street gang: drug dealing and guns.

Before the 1980s, gangs were groups of teenage boys, usually of the same ethnic background, in impoverished inner-city neighborhoods. Their reasons for joining were mostly social, and most of their activities involved hanging out, committing petty crimes, and making sure other gangs didn't infringe on their territory. If the leader of the gang carried a gun, it was more a mark of his prestige than a practical weapon. More recently, however, most gang activity is connected to drug trafficking: transporting and selling drugs, and trying to eliminate rival gangs of dealers (Franzese et al., 2006). As everyone knows from news reports and television dramas, the wars between youth gangs are no longer carried out with switchblades, but with military-grade automatic weapons.

Gangs are not only more violent than in the past, they are also much more widespread. In the mid-20th century, they were found mostly in the largest cities. Not any longer. In 2003, 21% of students ages 12–18—one of five nationwide—said that street gangs were a presence in their school (DeVoe, Peter, Noonan, Snyder, & Baum, 2005). A recent survey of law enforcement agencies throughout the United States showed that 80% of medium to large cities, 40% of suburban counties, 30% of small towns, and 12.5% of rural counties had a problem with delinquent youth gangs. Federal agencies estimate that nationwide there are more than 760,000 gang

▶ Gang activity has become more widespread and more violent in recent decades.

members in some 24,000 gangs, spread across more than 3,000 localities (Egley & Ritz, 2006).

One particularly chilling change: In a survey, gang members from before and since 1980 were asked whether, if forced to choose, they would protect their family or their gang. All of those who had been gang members during the earlier period said they would protect their families. Among the more recent group of gang members, however, four of five said they would choose to protect their gang instead of their family (Evans & Taylor, 1995).

Individual Violence. America is haunted by images of terrified students filing out of their school with their hands clasped on their heads, or worse, being wheeled out on gurneys. Violent incidents like the Columbine, Virginia Tech, or Northern Illinois shootings are in fact exceedingly rare, but their unpredictability makes them even more frightening. What is much more common in the experience of U.S. adolescents is their *daily* encounters with violence. These encounters do not make the evening news, but they are deeply disturbing all the same. According to the National Crime Victimization Survey, about half a million teens a year are victims of serious violent crimes—rape, sexual assault, robbery, and aggravated assault (DeVoe et al., 2005). One of three teens reports having been in a fight in the past year, and 1 of 10 reports having been threatened or injured with a gun, knife, or club on school property. Not surprisingly, some 5% of adolescents say they have avoided school activities in the previous 6 months because they were too scared to go (DeVoe et al., 2005).

As we saw in Chapter 8, one major factor in sustaining aggressive and antisocial attitudes among adolescents is the way the media glorify violence. From terminators to gangsta rap, by way of the NFL and NHL, graphic images of violent acts are presented as exciting, admirable, and sexy (Comstock & Scharrer, 2006). No wonder, then, that childhood exposure to television violence predicts later aggression, even when family and economic differences are taken into account (Huesmann, Moise-Titus, Podolski, & Eron, 2003). Even more threatening are the effects of playing the first-person shooter video games so popular among young adolescent boys (Anderson, 2004; Janz, 2005).

Another major factor is the easy availability of guns in the United States. According to recent data, 17% of students in grades 9–12 report that they have carried a weapon during the previous month (DeVoe et al., 2005). If we look just at boys, the rate climbs to 27%, more than one in four. Nor is this something that happens only among inner-city minority teens. In fact, the figure is much the same across ethnic groups. Most adolescents who admit to carrying a weapon say that they do it for self-protection, but having a weapon makes it that much more likely that any confrontation will escalate into violence.

The result is appalling. Homicide is the number two cause of death among 15- to 19-year-olds in the United States, across all races and both sexes. Among Black males it is by far the *leading* cause of death (Anderson & Smith, 2005). Four of five of these homicides are committed with guns (Snyder, Finnegan, & Kang, 2006). It is likely that many of these deaths would not have occurred if the killer had not been armed with a gun. Compared to nations that have stricter controls on firearms, the juvenile homicide rate in the United States is 5 to 10 times higher (Cukier, 1998). For victims younger than age 15, it is almost *16 times* higher than in other developed countries (Centers for Disease Control, 1997).

Substance Use

Throughout recorded history, and almost certainly long before, humans have used various substances to change the way they think, feel, and experience the world. Four thousand years ago, Egyptian pharaohs made sure their amphoras of fine wines were marked with the name of the vineyard and the vintage year. Poorer Egyptians contented themselves with a beverage made of fermented grains, what we today call beer. Ancient seers swallowed exotic mushrooms or inhaled the fumes from volcanic vents before pronouncing their prophecies. When Peruvian peasants got tired, they chewed the leaves of the coca plant for renewed energy. And the next time you see a notice for a symposium, you should know that originally the word meant a drinking party.

Modern society, with a lot of help from pharmaceutical science, has taken this practice to a new level. Feeling sleepy, but need to be alert? Take a pill. Need some sleep, but feeling wide awake? There's a pill for that, too. Anxious? Depressed? Jittery? Shy? Nervous about an exam? In physical pain? Bored to the point of tears? Want to lose weight? Or gain weight? Eager to explore inner space or plumb the secrets of the universe? For all of these conditions, and many more besides, there is some substance that someone, somewhere, will swear is exactly what you need to take into your system.

Adolescents today grow up surrounded by messages about substance use. Heavily financed advertising campaigns push the notion that real, sophisticated adults drink and smoke, and that they have more fun when they are doing it. Commercials for prescription drugs communicate the message that you can fix any physical, mental, and emotional problems through chemistry. Even illicit substances, such as "designer drugs," are discussed with that mixture of disapproval and fascination that adults so often use when talking about the latest trend among the young. No wonder so many teens are drawn into substance use, whether from curiosity, a desire to seem older, or a wish to go along with what they think those around them are doing (Levinthal, 2005).

Instrumental and Recreational Use. Researchers often draw a distinction between *instrumental* and *recreational* substance use. In **instrumental substance use**, a person takes a drug as a way of achieving some socially acceptable goal. Keeping awake, getting to sleep, alleviating pain, and losing weight are all goals that people often use drugs to help accomplish. **Recreational substance use**, on the other hand, is taking a drug in order to experience the effect of the drug itself. Whether it's drinking a martini before dinner or smoking a joint before a concert, the goal is to enjoy the state induced by the substance.

We should notice that legality is not the issue here. Both instrumental and recreational substance use may be *licit* (legal) or *illicit* (illegal), depending on circumstances. If a student has to study for an exam and gets some amphetamines from a friend, that is instrumental but illicit. If the same student relies on coffee or caffeine tablets instead, that is instrumental and licit. Taking a latte break because you enjoy the mild buzz is recreational and licit. Taking a hit of hash because you enjoy being high is recreational and illicit. As for that martini, drinking it is licit if the person is of legal drinking age and illicit if the person is underage. Social customs and attitudes also matter. In some parts of the world, marijuana is legal. In other parts of the world, alcohol is forbidden to everyone, not just to minors.

◀ **Learning Objective 13.4**
How many teens use which substances, how often, and why?

Instrumental substance use
Taking a drug as a means to reach some socially acceptable goal, such as relieving pain or falling asleep.

Recreational substance use
Taking a drug in order to experience the effects of the drug.

People use many substances for many reasons. For the most part, these are not a matter of social concern. On advice from my doctor, I swallow an aspirin tablet every morning. Is that a problem for me or anyone else? Not really. If I were told tomorrow to stop, I'd stop. Many people say they are addicted to chocolate, but all they mean is that they like it a lot. They could get by without it for a period of time and might not even notice its absence. It is different with what are called **psychoactive substances**, such as alcohol, nicotine, marijuana, and opiates. These substances affect a person's thoughts, feelings, perceptions, and behavior by influencing the way the brain works. The repeated use of psychoactive substances over a period of time poses a danger of leading to *drug dependence*.

Drug dependence is a condition in which the person develops a strong craving for the drug and often needs increasing amounts of it to achieve the same effect. Someone who has developed a drug dependence and tries to stop using the drug experiences unpleasant physical or mental **drug withdrawal** symptoms. One quick way to alleviate these symptoms is by taking the drug again, so a vicious circle comes into operation. This may lead to repeated unsuccessful attempts to quit. As a result, those who become drug dependent often feel that their lives are spinning out of control. They may give up important social and recreational activities because of substance use and spend much of their time and energy on getting and using the substance (American Psychiatric Association, 2000).

Of course, many people, both adolescents and adults, use various psychoactive substances from time to time without developing a strong physical or psychological dependence, but the risk of becoming drug dependent is an important factor to keep in mind when we consider the facts of adolescent substance use. It may be a cliché that it is easier to avoid bad habits than to break them once they're formed, but in the case of drug dependence, the cliché is absolutely right.

Adolescents and Substance Use. Ever since the 1960s, some social observers have claimed that all American teenagers care about is sex, drugs, and rock and roll. We already looked at adolescent sexuality in Chapter 12, and musical trends are mostly beyond the scope of this book. But what about drugs? Are they really a defining feature of adolescence today? Who uses them, what do they use, how frequently, and with what effects? In this section, we look at recent trends in substance use among American teens. We then take a more detailed look at the most commonly used substances. Finally, we consider some factors that either put teens at greater risk for substance use or help protect them against it.

Prevalence of Substance Use. How widespread is adolescent substance use? For an answer to that question, we can turn to an ongoing project called Monitoring the Future. Every year since 1975, researchers from the University of Michigan have asked large representative samples of American adolescents a series of detailed questions about substance use. Originally, only high school seniors were surveyed, but 8th and 10th graders were added in 1991. Recent surveys have included about 16,500 teens at each grade level, for a total of roughly 50,000 (Johnston, O'Malley, Bachman, & Schulenberg, 2006).

Figure 13.7 on page 445 shows the percentage of adolescents, year by year, who said they had used any illicit substance in the previous 12 months (not including alcohol or tobacco). In the late 1970s, more than half of 12th graders reported some illicit substance use. The percentage then declined steadily, to just more than 25% in 1992. At that point it started to climb again, and then leveled off in the mid-1990s. The figures for 8th and 10th graders show a peak in 1996, followed by a gradual decline. As of 2005, the percentage of teens who said they had *ever* tried an illicit drug was 21% for 8th graders, 38% for 10th graders, and 50% for 12th graders (Johnston et al., 2006b). In other words, exactly half of American teens have tried some illicit drug by the time they near high school graduation.

Which drugs? The answer shown in Figure 13.8 on page 445 may surprise those who have been alarmed by talk show discussions of "club drugs," "designer drugs," and the like. The substances used by American high school seniors fall into three distinct groups. The clear leader, used by almost half of 12th graders in the last 30 days, is alcohol. Competing for second place are tobacco (23%) and marijuana (20%). All the rest,

Psychoactive substances Those drugs that affect a person's psychological state by way of altering brain functions, for example, alcohol, opiates, and hallucinogens.

Drug dependence Developing a strong craving for a particular drug and, in many cases, needing growing amounts of it to achieve the same effect.

Drug withdrawal A set of unpleasant physical or mental symptoms that are experienced when someone with a drug dependence stops taking the drug.

Figure 13.7 8th-, 10th-, and 12th-Graders Who Have Used Any Illicit Drug in the Last 12 Months

In recent years, the percentage of teens who have used an illicit drug first rose, then began to decline.

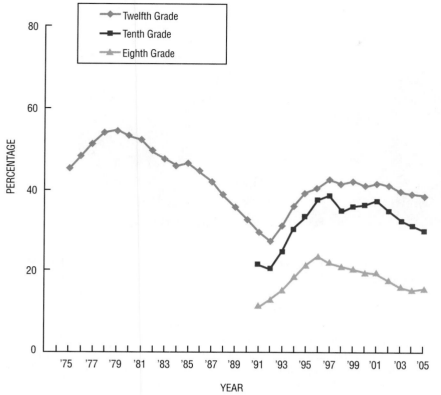

Source: Johnston et al., 2006.

Figure 13.8 Percentage of High School Seniors Who Have Used Various Substances in the Last Month

Among high school seniors, alcohol, cigarettes, and marijuana are by far the most frequently used substances.

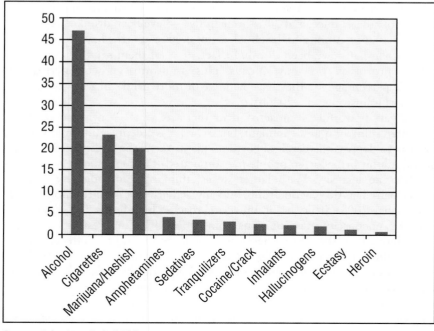

Source: Johnston et al., 2006.

▶ As many as one third of high school seniors regularly engage in binge drinking.

Connect the **Dots...**

Drinking games that encourage consuming a lot of alcohol in a short period of time are widespead and popular among adolescents and young adults. Why do you think they are popular, and what might be done to make teens more aware of the obvious dangers they present? Do you think teens may already know about the dangers but take part anyway?

from amphetamines to heroin, are at well less than 5% (Johnston et al., 2006b). What if we ask whether the teens have used various substances, not in the last month, but *ever* in their lives? Even then, there are only three substances in the last group that more than 1 of 10 high school seniors has ever tried. These are amphetamines (13%), inhalants such as glue (11%), and sedatives such as barbiturates (10%). By way of comparison, almost half of high school seniors—45%—have tried marijuana at least once.

One obvious reason that alcohol and tobacco are so far in the lead is that they are so easily available. Unlike other substances on the list, they are found in a great many homes. In most parts of the United States they can be bought legally, without a prescription, by anyone older than 21. With convincing ID or an older friend, even the "over 21" limitation is not much of an obstacle. As for marijuana, its possession and sale may be against the law in the United States, but three of four 10th graders and five of six 12th graders say they could get some easily if they wanted to. Even among 8th graders, 40% say the same (Johnston et al., 2006b).

Alcohol. By the time they are in 8th grade, more than 40% of American adolescents have tried alcohol at least once, and 20%—one in five—have been drunk at least once (Johnston et al., 2006b). Among high school seniors, three-fourths have tried alcohol and well more than half have been drunk. In fact, 30% of them say they have been drunk at least once in the previous 30 days. This is unsurprising, considering that almost the same percentage say they have had five or more drinks in a row within the previous *2 weeks* (Johnston et al., 2006b).

Alcohol is a very powerful psychoactive drug that acts on the central nervous system. People often think of it as a stimulant, but in fact it is a depressant. In low doses, its first effect is to depress the cerebral cortex. This weakens the ability of the cortex to control and inhibit behavior, so people *feel* stimulated. They talk more, gain confidence, and become less shy. With larger doses, thinking and judgment become increasingly impaired, as do reaction times and any activity that requires motor coordination (Levinthal, 2005). If alcohol in the blood reaches high levels, the person may lapse into stupor, unconsciousness, or coma, sometimes with lethal results.

Even more lethal than the direct effects of alcohol are the indirect effects. Among 15- to 20-year-olds, motor vehicle crashes are *the* leading cause of death. In 2004, teenage drivers were involved in almost 8,000 fatal automobile accidents. In one of four of those accidents, the driver was legally drunk (National Highway Traffic Safety Administration, 2005). Among 20-year-olds, one in three was drunk.

The cost in deaths and injuries of drinking is still higher than these statistics suggest. Even a single drink is enough to dull a person's coordination, attention, and perceptual functioning (Levinthal, 2005). In 2005, 1 of 10 high school students—almost twice that figure for 12th graders—admitted that just in the previous 30 days, they had driven while drinking. *Three* of 10 said they had ridden with a driver who was drinking (Centers for Disease Control and Prevention, 2006). Teens who have been drinking are also less likely to use seatbelts, which pushes the risk level still higher (National Highway Traffic Safety Administration, 2005).

Alcohol use poses long-term health risks as well. **Alcoholism** is a chronic condition that involves major psychological, physical, social, and occupational problems. According to one recent study, those who start drinking during adolescence are at higher risk of developing alcoholism, and the earlier they start, the higher the risk (Hingson, Heeren, & Winter, 2006).

Cigarettes. Cigarette smoking is the single biggest preventable cause of death in the United States. Every year more than 430,000 people die from tobacco-related illnesses (Centers for Disease Control and Prevention, 2004). That amounts to 1,200 people a day or 50 every hour. A person's life is shortened by 14 minutes with every cigarette smoked. If someone smokes two packs a day for 20 years, those minutes add up to 8 years off the person's lifespan (Levinthal, 2005). Tobacco use is responsible for a long list of serious or fatal conditions, including coronary heart disease, emphysema, lung cancer, and, for women who smoke during pregnancy, health risks to the developing fetus as well as the mother. In addition, a recent study indicates that for girls, cigarette use in early adolescence stunts the child's growth (Stice & Martinez, 2005). So it turns out that the warnings of generations of parents on this topic were at least half right!

The most important psychoactive compound in cigarettes is **nicotine**. This is a highly toxic substance that is absorbed into the blood extremely quickly. It begins to affect the brain in seconds, stimulating receptors in the central nervous system that cause the release of *adrenalin*, which increases the heart rate and blood pressure. At the same time, nicotine promotes the release of the neurotransmitter *dopamine* in the so-called reward center of the brain, reducing anxiety and tension.

These physiological effects, combined with a variety of behavioral and social rewards, give cigarettes a very great potential to create dependence. Ask any smoker or ex-smoker about quitting and you are likely to hear stories of heroic efforts, days and weeks of headaches, irritability, and other withdrawal symptoms, and, all too often, a shame-faced return to smoking. In one study, one in three smokers who were in treatment programs for drug abuse said it was much harder to quit smoking than to kick a drug habit (Koslowski et al., 1989).

Most people who smoke started in adolescence, and most adolescents who smoke start before high school. As early as 8th grade, more than one-quarter have tried cigarettes and almost 10% are regular smokers. By 12th grade, fully half have tried cigarettes and almost one-fourth are regular smokers (Johnston et al., 2006b). These percentages are high, but even so they represent an important decrease in teen smoking over the past decade. As shown in Figure 13.9 on page 448, cigarette use peaked in the mid-1990s, and then declined steadily. The most recent findings, however, suggest that the percentage of teens who smoke has now leveled off (Johnston et al., 2006b).

Marijuana. By far the most commonly used psychoactive substance among adolescents, after alcohol and tobacco, is marijuana. Almost half of high school seniors in the United States have tried marijuana at some point. One in five seniors has used it in the last month, and 5% use it on a daily basis (Johnston et al., 2006b). Even among 8th graders, one in six has tried marijuana and 7% have used it in the last month, although only 1 in 100 uses it daily.

Marijuana is the dried leaves of an incredibly hardy and prolific plant, *Cannabis sativa*. The plant has been known and cultivated since ancient times. Its fibrous stalks are the source of *hemp*, used for making rope. George Washington grew cannabis at Mount Vernon and was eager to improve the quality of his crop. As far as anyone knows, his aim was to make stronger rope, rather than any more questionable purpose. The chief psychoactive ingredient in marijuana, **THC**, is found in a resin that accumulates on

Alcoholism A medical condition that stems from alcohol dependence and carries serious risks to physical and psychological health.

Nicotine A highly toxic substance that is one of the principal active ingredients in cigarettes, snuff, and other forms of tobacco.

THC Tetrahydrocannabinol, the chief psychoactive ingredient in marijuana and hashish.

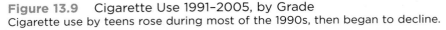

Figure 13.9 Cigarette Use 1991–2005, by Grade
Cigarette use by teens rose during most of the 1990s, then began to decline.

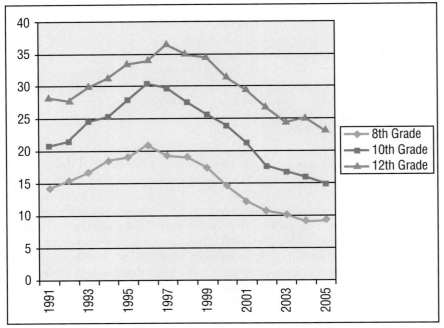

Source: Johnston et al., 2006.

the leaves of the plant. In some parts of the world, this resin is scraped off the leaves and dried to make a more potent substance known as *hashish*. Street marijuana in the United States usually contains between 2% and 6% THC. In comparison, the concentration of THC in hashish is between 8% and 14%, or more than twice as strong (Levinthal, 2005).

The psychoactive effects of marijuana are varied and rather hard to classify. They may include excitement, relaxation, increased sensitivity to colors and sounds, distorted perceptions, euphoria, a sense of increased creativity, a slowed sense of time, and a tendency to find almost anything wildly funny. Marijuana also reduces concentration, attention, short-term memory, and motor coordination. As a result, those who have been smoking marijuana are less competent as drivers (Gieringer, 1988), yet as many teens report driving under the influence of marijuana as under the influence of alcohol (O'Malley & Johnston, 2003). To make matters worse, low levels of THC linger in the body for several days. This means the negative effects on driving ability may persist well after the person no longer *feels* high.

Is chronic marijuana use a long-term risk? This is a very controversial topic that is argued as much on cultural and political grounds as on research-based evidence. Studies show that stopping after frequent use may be followed by physical and psychological withdrawal symptoms, which is one of the indications of drug dependence. However, the withdrawal symptoms from marijuana are considerably milder than those linked to alcohol or opiates (Duffy & Milin, 1996). Marijuana use is associated with lower grades and more conflict with parents, but this may well mean that children with problems at home and in school are more likely to start smoking marijuana, rather than the marijuana creating their problems (Pope, 2002). A recent study indicates that, though long-term marijuana users have problems with attention and memory, these symptoms clear up after a month without the drug (Grady, 2002).

One widespread concern is that marijuana use makes it more likely the person will use other, more dangerous substances. This is called the **gateway hypothesis** (Kandel, 1975, 2002). Surveys show that adolescents are likely to try alcohol first, followed by cigarettes, and then marijuana (Johnston et al., 2006b). Almost everyone who tries more "serious" drugs, such as amphetamines, cocaine, or heroin, has already tried marijuana.

Gateway hypothesis The idea that the use of relatively mild illicit drugs, such as marijuana, makes it more likely that a person will go on to use more dangerous hard drugs.

Figure 13.10   Substance Use Patterns, High Schools Seniors, 2005
More high school seniors have tried alcohol than cigarettes or marijuana,
but cigarettes are most likely to be used daily.

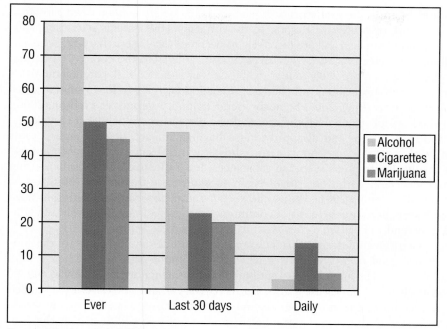

Source: Johnston et al., 2006.

However, this does not necessarily mean that using marijuana *causes* adolescents to move on to other illicit substances. Most adolescents who try marijuana, and even most who become chronic users, do not go on to use other illicit drugs (Kandel, 2002).

Risk Factors for Substance Use. As we have seen, the great majority of American adolescents say they have tried substances by the time they are in 12th grade. Half of them say they have used illicit substances such as marijuana (Johnston et al., 2006b). So in a sense, a major risk factor for adolescent substance use is simply being an adolescent! As was pointed out at the beginning of this chapter, we have to distinguish between experimentation and an ingrained pattern of behavior. For a clear illustration of this point, look at Figure 13.10. This figure shows the percentages of high school seniors who have ever tried alcohol, cigarettes, or marijuana; how many have used these substances in the last 30 days; and how many use them daily. Only about half of those who have tried these substances used them even a single time in the previous month. As for daily use, the only substance used by more than 1 in 20 adolescents was tobacco.

Generally, males tend to use alcohol, marijuana, and other illicit drugs more than females, but not by much (Johnston et al., 2006b). As for cigarettes, about the same proportion of male and female high school seniors use them either occasionally or daily, and among 8th graders, slightly more girls than boys smoke. Socioeconomic status, as indicated by parents' education, shows very little connection with substance use, but ethnic background does. Contrary to what many people might expect, African American teens report substantially *lower* use of most drugs than do Whites. That includes marijuana, alcohol, and cigarettes. In fact, African Americans' use of cigarettes is dramatically lower than Whites' use. Hispanics have rates of use that tend to fall between the other two groups (Johnston et al., 2006a).

Some personal factors that are associated with *high* levels of substance use, as opposed to occasional use, are aggression, disruptive behavior, and conduct problems. All these may be part of a syndrome with poor response inhibition and impulsiveness, which also predict substance use problems (Nigg et al., 2006). School misbehavior, especially if it gets encouragement from peers, is linked both to substance use and to increased use over time (Bryant, Schulenberg, O'Malley, Bachman, & Johnston, 2003). On the other hand, school bonding, school interest, school effort, academic achievement, and parental help with school are all associated with lower levels of substance use.

Parents and Friends. Several aspects of parents' behavior are connected to substance use, either as risk or protective factors. Teens with supportive parents start using substances later, use them less, and are less likely to become heavy users (Barnow, Schuckit, Lucht, John, & Freyberger, 2002; Marshal & Chassin, 2000). Hostile, coercive parenting, on the other hand, is more likely to lead to abuse of substances. Weak parental monitoring is linked to substance abuse and effective parental monitoring to lower substance use (Nash, McQueen, & Bray, 2005; Siebenbruner, Englund, Egeland, & Hudson, 2006). Parents who keep an eye on what their teens do have teens who watch what they do.

Parental expectations and disapproval also have an impact, even though parents may not think so at the time. Adolescents whose parents disapprove of substance use are less involved with peers who use substances, less influenced by substance-using peers, and less likely to become involved in substance use themselves (Nash et al., 2005; Sargent & Dalton, 2001). We should keep in mind, however, that with substance use, as with sexuality, parents may not communicate their feelings effectively and adolescents may tend to hear what they want to hear (Knafo & Schwartz, 2003).

A major factor in adolescent substance use is the attitudes and behaviors of the adolescent's friends and peers (Kiesner & Kerr, 2004; Simons-Morton & Chen, 2006). Those adolescents who are more susceptible to peer influence are also likely to engage in higher levels of substance use (Allen, Porter, & McFarland, 2006). As we discussed earlier, in Chapter 6, a teen may be affected by others through *socialization*, in which peers encourage or discourage some behavior; through *selection*, in which the teen associates more with peers who have similar attitudes and behaviors; or through some combination of the two (Dishion & Owen, 2002). Socialization may also take more subtle forms than direct influence. An adolescent may be swayed by beliefs about group norms and expectations, even if these are not accurate. This chapter's Research in the Spotlight on page 451 describes a longitudinal study that examines the balance between socialization and selection in affecting substance use.

How do parents and peers compare in their influence on substance use? The answer is complex. One recent study looked at the impact on smoking of having childhood friends who smoke, compared to the impact of having parents who smoke (Bricker et al., 2006). The results indicated that friends had more influence than parents over whether the adolescent *tried* cigarettes, and about the same influence on whether the adolescent started to smoke more than once a month. It was having parents who smoke, however, that was more closely linked to becoming a daily smoker. This strongly suggests that effective prevention programs need to target both parents *and* peers.

Summing Up...

Adolescents with externalizing problems, such as delinquency and substance use, tend to have poor impulse control and are more often boys. Delinquency rates climb steadily across the adolescent years, peaking at 18 or 19. Arrest and detention rates are much higher for youths of color than for Whites, and for those with low family incomes. Other risk factors include genetic and hormonal influences, conflict with parents, a tendency to interpret others' ambiguous actions as hostile, associating with deviant peers, and gang membership. Substance use also becomes increasingly common across the teen years, with fully half of 12th graders having tried some illicit drug. By far the most commonly used drugs are alcohol, tobacco, and marijuana, each of which presents its own particular risks. One in five 8th graders have been drunk at least once, and among 12th graders, about one in three has been drunk during the last month. While teen smoking has declined in recent years, 1 in 10 8th graders and one in four 12th graders are regular smokers. As for marijuana, 1 in 12 8th graders and one in five 12th graders have used it in the last month. A leading risk factor for substance use is peer attitudes and behaviors.

Socialization, Selection, and Substance Use

Why do adolescents start drinking and smoking? Once they start, why do they increase their substance use? For educators and social scientists to develop effective programs to prevent or reduce adolescent substance use, they need solid, objective information about the factors that lead adolescents to start using substances and to increase their usage once they have started.

One well-established finding is that teens who use substances are likely to associate with other teens who use substances. At the same time, teens who associate with others who use substances are likely to *increase* their substance use (Dishion & Owen, 2002). In Chapter 6, we got acquainted with two processes that might account for this result: *socialization* and *selection*.

In its most direct form, socialization involves open encouragement or discouragement from peers to behave in a certain way. If others at a party make fun of you for not drinking, or cheer when you down a can of beer without stopping for breath, the effect will be to push you toward drinking or drinking more. Socialization may also be more subtle and indirect. The way adolescents perceive the norms, expectations, and social status linked to a particular behavior will affect the way they think and the way they act. Selection, on the other hand, involves choosing to associate with peers who have similar attitudes, interests, beliefs, and behaviors.

To tease apart the effect of selection and socialization, Bruce Simons-Morton and Rusan Chen, of the National Institute of Child Health and Human Development, studied some 2,500 students in suburban Maryland from the beginning of 6th grade to the beginning of 9th grade. On five separate occasions students were asked how many times in the previous 30 days they had smoked a cigarette or drank alcohol. They were also asked on each occasion about how many of their five closest friends smoked or drank.

The investigators found that both substance use and number of substance-using friends went up steadily from 6th grade to 9th grade. When they looked at the associations from one time period to another, however, only the links from peers to substance use held up. Knowing how many of a teen's friends drank or smoked in 6th grade, for instance, you could predict whether that teen's drinking or smoking would increase by 7th grade, but not the reverse. This suggests that socialization is a more powerful factor than selection.

These findings do not necessarily mean that friends pressure one another into drinking and smoking. As the researchers point out,

> This relationship could also be explained in terms of perceived social norms, where adolescent use increases as adolescents perceive that it is more normative as the number of their friends who use these substances increase.

(Simons-Morton & Chen, 2006, p. 1221).

INTERNALIZING PROBLEMS

Now that we have a clearer understanding of the externalizing problems of delinquency and substance use, we turn our attention to the second type of adolescent problem, *internalizing problems*. We look first at *eating problems*, and then examine the most widespread serious adolescent problem, *depression*. Finally, we look at the prevalence and risk factors for *suicide*.

Eating Problems

> I really gotta start losing weight before spring break. Basically today I went 24 hours without food and then I ate green beans and a little baked ziti. Frankly I'm proud of myself, not to mention the 100 sit-ups on the yoga ball and the 100 I'll do before sleep . . . Yey for me.
>
> —from the blog of a 15-year-old girl (WILLIAMS, 2006)

▶ **Learning Objective 13.5**
What are the major eating disorders and why are they more common among girls?

American girls have grown up hearing the saying, "You can never be too rich or too thin." The women who are presented as attractive in magazines, ads, movies, and television shows may not be quite as extreme in their body proportions as Barbie, but they are definitely slimmer and less curvy than in the past, and much slimmer than the average healthy adult woman (Sypeck, Gray, & Ahrens, 2004). Barbie herself is still around, having a significant impact on the body images of young girls (Dittmar, Halliwell, & Ive, 2006).

▲ Influenced by media standards, many young adolescent girls want to change their bodies.

This relentless focus on female thinness poses an almost insoluble problem for adolescent girls. As we saw in Chapter 3, for girls the normal changes of puberty include significant weight gain, especially in the thighs, hips, and breasts, and an increase in the ratio of body fat to muscle. Those who enter puberty earlier tend to end up somewhat shorter and heavier than those who mature later (Brooks-Gunn, 1991). The result of this collision between nature and cultural standards is that a great many adolescent girls are unhappy with their bodies and desperately want to do something to change them.

At least 16% of adolescent girls in the United States are overweight (Ogden et al., 2006). Being overweight poses a variety of health risks that include Type II diabetes, asthma, and hypertension (Krishnamoorthy, Hart, & Jelalian, 2006). In addition, longitudinal research shows that girls who are overweight in childhood are much more likely to be obese as young adults (Thompson et al., 2007). All of these are serious problems that need to be faced. Just as alarming, a recent large-scale survey showed that almost 40% of adolescent girls *think* they are overweight, as opposed to the 16% who actually are, and 60%, a clear majority, are actively trying to *lose* weight (Centers for Disease Control and Prevention, 2006). Some of the means they use in their quest to take off pounds are exercise (67%), eating less (55%), not eating for 24 hours or more (17%), taking diet pills without a doctor's advice (8%), and vomiting or taking laxatives (6%).

Anorexia and Bulimia. As the statistics just cited show, having a distorted view of one's weight, being dissatisfied with one's body, and taking more or less drastic steps to change it, are common among adolescent girls. For a small minority, these cascade into a full-blown *eating disorder*. Two serious eating disorders that have received wide public attention in recent years usually appear first during adolescence and primarily affect girls.

Anorexia nervosa is a disorder in which people literally starve themselves in an attempt to become or stay impossibly thin. The symptoms of those with this disorder include:

Maintaining a weight of less than 85% of what would be expected for someone that age and height, or not gaining the weight that would be expected during a period of growth;

Having an intense fear of gaining weight or becoming fat;

Experiencing one's body weight or shape in a distorted way, so that even those who are dangerously thin see themselves as fat (Skrzypek, Wehmeier, & Remschmidt, 2001); and

Denying that there is anything unusual or serious about their abnormally low weight.

—(American Psychiatric Association, 2000)

Among girls who have had their first period, anorexia is also marked by *amenorrhea*, the absence of menstrual cycles.

Bulimia is a disorder in which people eat large quantities of food in a short time (*binge eating*), and then get rid of it by forcing themselves to vomit or by taking laxatives (*purging*). Like those with anorexia, bulimics are sharply focused on their body image and have a desperate desire to appear thin. However, they also feel they cannot control their urge to eat, even when they are in the middle of a binge. As a result, they are convinced that their only hope of staying thin is to purge what they have just eaten. Those diagnosed with bulimia follow this binge-and-purge pattern at least twice a week, or even more frequently, over a period of months (American Psychiatric Association, 2000). Unlike anorexics, whose thinness is very noticeable, those with bulimia typically have normal weights for their age and height. Unfortunately, this makes it less likely that parents and friends will detect their problem and persuade them to seek help.

If we go by strict clinical definitions, both anorexia and bulimia are fairly uncommon disorders. According to recent estimates, among females aged 15 to 24, about 3 in 1,000 develop anorexia and 10 in 1,000 develop bulimia (Hoek, 2006). These are small percentages, certainly, but even so they indicate that about 60,000 young American women suffer from anorexia and 200,000 from bulimia (National Center for Health Statistics, 2005). Experts say that in fact the problem is much more widespread than these numbers suggest. Up to 19% of young women—almost one in five—have some bulimic symptoms (Hoek, 2002).

Anorexia nervosa A serious, sometimes fatal, disorder in which a distorted view of one's weight and body shape and an intense fear of getting fat leads to starving oneself.

Bulimia An eating disorder in which the person alternates between binge overeating and purging.

Risk Factors for Eating Disorders. Studies of twins and families suggest that both anorexia and bulimia have some genetic basis (Bulik & Tozzi, 2004; Stroeber, Freeman, Lampert, Diamond, & Kaye, 2000). The genes involved in regulating the neurotransmitter *serotonin*, which is linked to eating behavior as well as variations in mood, are considered likely candidates.

On a personal level, adolescents who are dissatisfied with their bodies are at greater risk for eating problems (Johnson & Wardle, 2005). The more importance they give to body image, the greater the risk (McCabe & Ricciardelli, 2006). General mood also matters. Teens who feel bad tend to think negatively about their bodies as well (Sim & Zeman, 2006). They may try to relieve these bad feelings through binge-eating "comfort foods," but this can lead to feelings of helplessness and self-disgust that prolong the cycle (Butcher, Mineka, & Hooley, 2007; Stice, 2002). They often try dieting, but ironically, this can lead to still greater body dissatisfaction (Bearman, Presnell, Martinez, & Stice, 2006). A recent study that looked at over 5,700 adolescent girls found that those who saw themselves as less popular with peers were much more likely to have a higher increase in body mass over the following two years (Lemeshow et al., 2008). Another risk factor is **perfectionism**, a need to do things exactly right (Wonderlich, Lilenfeld, Riso, Engel, & Mitchell, 2005).

The risk of developing eating problems and disorders is linked to an adolescent's ethnic background as well. In the United States, anorexia and bulimia are less common among African American girls than among either Whites or Hispanics, reflecting ethnic differences in body-type preferences (Wildes, Emery, & Simons, 2001). Social class also makes a difference. Girls from middle-class and upper-middle-class families that stress high achievement and competition are more likely to develop anorexia (Schmidt, 2003). In a recent study of almost 1 million residents of Sweden, the girls most at risk for anorexia were those from wealthy White families (Lindberg & Hjern, 2003). Families can also play an important protective role. For example, the results of a large longitudinal study show that girls whose families have meals together at least five times a week are significantly less likely to develop eating problems (Neumark-Sztainer, Eisenberg, Fulkerson, Story, & Larson, 2008).

As we saw in Chapter 8, the media play a crucial role in transmitting cultural values to the young. This is certainly the case with body-type preferences (Shroff & Thompson, 2006). In one recent study, British girls were shown photos of either very thin or average-size magazine models. Those who saw the ultra-thin models later had lower body satisfaction and self-esteem (Clay, Vignoles, & Dittmar, 2005). These influences start very early. By the time they are 6, girls who watch music videos or look at appearance-related magazines say they want to diet and become thinner (Dohnt & Tiggemann, 2006).

Is it really possible that the media have such a strong impact on the body satisfaction and eating patterns of adolescents? An answer to this question comes from a dramatic "natural experiment" on the island of Fiji, in the South Pacific (Becker, Burwell, Gilman, Herzog, & Hamburg, 2002). Until recently, Fijians considered being fat as a sign of strength, kindness, and generosity, while those who were thin were seen as sickly and incompetent. Not surprisingly, a great many Fijians, especially women, were overweight by Western standards. Then, in the 1990s, Western television came to Fiji. After watching a lot of *Beverly Hills 90210*, *Melrose Place*, and *Zena the Warrior Princess*, Fijian girls began expressing dissatisfaction with their bodies and going on diets. As one explained,

> When I look at the characters on television, the way they act on television and I just look at the body, the figure of that body, so I say, "Look at them, they are thin and they all have this figure," so I myself want to become like that, to become thin.

> —(BECKER et al., 2002, p. 513)

Health Consequences. Anorexia nervosa has the highest mortality rate of any psychiatric disorder (Birmingham, Su, Hlynsky, Goldner, & Gao, 2005). Some 10% of those who develop anorexia inadvertently starve themselves to death or die of conditions brought on by the extreme stress the disorder puts on the body. Short of dying,

Connect the Dots...

As an adolescent, did you have friends who seemed to fit the description of those with a serious eating problem? Did you ever try to reason with them when they worried about being too fat? If so, how much effect do you think you had?

Perfectionism An exaggerated need to do things just right and to look just right that is a risk factor for eating disorders.

the health consequences include limp, brittle hair; dry skin; abnormally slow pulse; and an inability to tolerate cold. Over the long run, low calcium levels weaken the bones and increase the risk of osteoporosis, while low electrolyte levels may cause irregular heart rhythms and heart failure (Katzman, 2005). Bulimia has a less drastic effect on health, but the stomach acid brought up by frequent vomiting can damage the esophagus and eat away at tooth enamel.

Although eating disorders have severe and well-documented effects on health, some of those affected by anorexia reject the medical view and argue that anorexia is a "lifestyle choice." The Internet offers them a way to give one another emotional support, to swap weight-loss tips, and to exchange "pro-ana" motivational messages (Norris, Boydell, Pinhas, & Katzman, 2006).

Treatment. Adolescents with eating disorders often deny that there is anything wrong with them and fight against efforts to help them. A sizable number of those whose problem has become severe, possibly life-threatening, have to be committed to a hospital against their will (Watson, Bowers, & Andersen, 2000). Once their weight has been restored to a level that does not endanger their survival, *family therapy* is considered the most effective treatment for anorexia (le Grange & Lock, 2005). The therapist observes family meals and helps the parents learn how to encourage their child to eat again. Once the adolescent starts to gain weight, other problems in the family and in the patient are also addressed. Family treatment of this sort works particularly well for those whose anorexia developed before age 19 and has lasted less than 3 years (Dare & Eisler, 2002).

For teens who suffer from bulimia, an effective approach is *cognitive-behavioral therapy* (Fairburn & Harrison, 2003). This approach involves helping the adolescent change distorted beliefs about weight and food and confront such dysfunctional thought patterns as, "I might as well keep eating, since I already blew it by starting." Teens are also taught healthy habits, such as eating smaller portions more regularly. Antidepressant medications that affect serotonin regulation are said to help, both by improving the adolescent's mood and by reducing the urge to binge (Walsh, 2002).

And What About the Boys? This section has focused almost entirely on adolescent girls. The reason is straightforward: Girls are about 10 times more likely than boys to develop serious eating disorders during adolescence (Butcher et al., 2007). Being unhappy with one's body, which is a major risk factor for eating disorders (Stice, 2002), is something that is experienced by many boys as well as girls (Davison & McCabe, 2006). However, there are some important gender differences that are directly linked to cultural stereotypes.

Adolescent girls who have a poor body image generally focus on their figures and weight. Most boys are much more concerned about muscularity (Jones, 2004; Smolak & Stein, 2006). As a result, their strategies for dealing with body dissatisfaction include excessive exercise and, for some, use of anabolic steroids, rather than the fasting or bingeing and purging typical of eating disorders (Jones & Crawford, 2005). As we discussed in Chapter 3, puberty tends to alter girls' bodies in ways contrary to the cultural ideal of slimness. For boys, their bodies change *toward* the cultural ideal of broad shoulders and bulging muscles (think GI Joe). The result is that while the level of body dissatisfaction in girls increases significantly during early adolescence, for boys it *decreases* significantly (Bearman et al., 2006).

Depression

▶ **Learning Objective 13.6**
What are the causes of adolescent depression?

When I'm feeling depressed I go home and I just lie there. It feels like I've entered a black hole and am being buried alive. I don't do anything or say anything. I just lie there and stare at the ceiling.

—TRINITY (BELL, **1998, p. 173**)

Figure 13.11 Long-Term Sad or Hopeless Feelings, by Ethnic Group

Long-term sad or hopeless feelings are more common among Hispanic and Black teens than among White teens. In each ethnic group, girls are almost twice as likely to experience such feelings than boys.

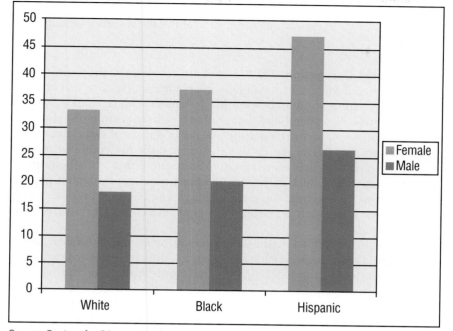

Source: Centers for Disease Control and Prevention, 2006.

According to a recent national survey, 29% of U.S. high school students felt sad or hopeless almost every day for 2 weeks or longer during the previous year. These feelings affected them so much so that they stopped doing some of their usual activities (Centers for Disease Control and Prevention, 2006). These are characteristics of **depression**, and the fact that almost 3 in 10 adolescents say they have experienced them recently indicates how widespread this problem is. In fact, depression is generally considered the most common psychological disturbance among adolescents (Graber, 2004; Ollendick et al., 2005).

We all have a pretty good idea of what it means to say "I feel depressed." Psychologists, however, distinguish among *depressed mood, depressive syndrome,* and *major depressive disorder* (Compas, Ey, & Grant, 1993). Many adolescents, perhaps even a majority, go through more or less lengthy stretches of depressed mood at some point. The more severe depressive syndrome and major depressive disorder are much less common, affecting about 3% to 6% of adolescents (Cheung, Emslie, & Mayes, 2005; Rushton, Forcier, & Schectman, 2002).

As was pointed out earlier, in Chapter 10, during childhood, boys are just as likely as girls to experience depressive symptoms. Once in adolescence, however, about twice as many girls as boys become depressed (Ge, Natsuaki, & Conger, 2006; Twenge & Nolen-Hoeksema, 2002). Some reasons for this gender difference that were described in Chapter 10 are summarized later in this section. Ethnic background also makes a difference, as shown in Figure 13.11. For both boys and girls, more Black teens have long-term sad feelings than Whites, and more Hispanics have these feelings than either of the other two groups (Centers for Disease Control and Prevention, 2006).

While deep, lasting sadness is a central feature of depression, the condition shows itself in other ways as well. Among these are:

Emotional—dejected or irritable mood, feelings of worthlessness;

Cognitive—pessimistic or hopeless bias in interpreting events, poor concentration, difficulty making decisions;

Depression A mood disturbance marked by lengthy periods of deep sadness.

Motivational—apathy, boredom, loss of interest in activities that used to be enjoyable; and

Physical—loss of appetite, low energy, sleep problems.

—(American Psychiatric Association, 2000)

Someone suffering from a depressive disorder may also have recurrent thoughts of death or suicide.

Causes of Adolescent Depression. What factors lead so many teens to sink into a depressed mood or even develop a depressive disorder? One widely-accepted explanation is the **diathesis-stress model** (Lewinsohn, Joiner, & Rohde, 2001). *Diathesis* refers to some condition or vulnerability that predisposes the person to developing a problem such as depression. *Stress* refers to the negative impact of circumstances or events in the person's life. According to this model, it takes the combination of a diathesis and stress to set off a depressive reaction. Someone *without* a diathesis might confront a terrible experience, such as the loss of a parent, and get through it without falling into depression. Meanwhile, someone *with* a diathesis might become deeply despondent after some event, such as getting a low grade in a course, that many others would be able to shrug off.

One source of vulnerability to depression is family background (Graber, 2004). Children of depressed parents are much more likely to develop depressive symptoms themselves. This is probably a result of both inherited vulnerabilities and the influence of the parents' own depression (Frye & Garber, 2005). On the biological level, we saw in Chapter 3 that the *HPA axis*, a hormonal system that involves the pituitary and adrenal glands, becomes more active just before and during puberty. It is responsible for producing the stress hormone *cortisol*, which is crucial to the stress response system (Walker, Walder, & Reynolds, 2001). Adolescents who continue to produce cortisol for longer after a stressful event are likely to have more internalizing problems (Klimes-Dougan, Hastings, Granger, Usher, & Zahn-Waxler, 2001; McEwen, 2000). Researchers have also found that girls are more susceptible to stress than boys, which may help explain their greater vulnerability to depression after puberty (Meadows, Brown, & Elder, 2006).

Stress Factors. What factors in a vulnerable adolescent's life might generate the sort of stress that leads to depression? Some are normative experiences that everyone goes through, such as entering puberty or graduating from middle school to high school. Others, such as moving to a new home or having one's parents get a divorce, are particular to the individual teen. A recent study shows that those who experience a parental divorce by age 15 have a sharply greater increase in depressive symptoms (Ge et al., 2006). Living in an impoverished, unsafe neighborhood increases depression and also intensifies the effects of other sources of stress (Cutrona, Wallace, & Wesner, 2006).

Because peers become so much more important during early adolescence, as we saw in Chapter 6, they also become a major source of stress. Those who do not manage to achieve good relationships with peers are more likely to become depressed. Worse, those who are depressed tend to be avoided or rejected by peers, who find them less fun to be around (Bukowsky et al., 2007; Kistner, 2006). This can generate a vicious circle of rejection and depression that is especially difficult for girls, whose self-esteem is so largely based on their personal relationships (Hankin, Mermelstein, & Roesch, 2007).

Another common source of stress in adolescence, especially for girls, is romantic relationships (Davila & Steinberg, 2006). As was discussed in Chapter 12, girls generally place more value on romantic attachments than boys and see any difficulties in their relationships as a reflection on themselves (Shulman & Sharf, 2000). They are also more likely to develop a *preoccupied* relational style, in which they desperately want a romantic involvement, but constantly worry about whether it is working out (Davila, Steinberg, Kachadourian, Cobb, & Fincham, 2004). This is also a risk factor for depression.

Diathesis-stress model The theory that depression results from a combination of a predisposing vulnerability (*diathesis*) and the impact of negative events (*stress*).

◀ Problems with romantic relationships are a major factor in setting off depression, especially for girls.

Cognitive Factors. The ways adolescents *think* about and *explain* the events that happen to them have also been linked to depression (Beck, 1967; Scher, Ingram, & Segal, 2005). Imagine that a teen has just been treated coldly by an old friend. He or she might think, "I wonder what's going on in my friend's life just now and how soon it'll pass." This would explain the event as *external* (something about the friend) and *unstable* (something that will not last for long). No particular reason to be depressed there.

Now imagine another adolescent in a similar situation who thinks, "There must be something about me that people don't like. I should have known so-and-so wasn't a real friend. I'll never manage to have any real friends." An explanation of this sort interprets the negative event as *internal* (something about me), *global* (not just about this situation), and *stable* (will go on happening). This pessimistic style of explanation leads to **learned helplessness** (Abramson, Seligman, & Teasdale, 1978; Buchanan & Seligman, 1995), which, in turn, is linked to depression.

Even if the cause of a negative event is external, if it seems uncontrollable and stable, it can create a sense of **hopelessness** that leads to depression (Abramson & Alloy, 2006). This pattern of thinking is more common in girls and helps explain why they are more susceptible to depression (Calvete & Cardeñoso, 2005). Girls are also more prone to **rumination** (Nolen-Hoeksema & Corte, 2004). They brood about the reasons they are depressed, talk about their mood with friends, and recall other negative events from the past or listen to negative feedback from friends, making them still more depressed (Borelli & Prinstein, 2006; Nolen-Hoeksema, 2002). Boys, in contrast, are more likely to distract themselves from their depression by playing sports, getting involved in a video game, or drinking (Nolen-Hoeksema & Corte, 2004).

Treatment. As we have seen, many parents, teachers, and other adults believe the stereotype that teens are generally moody, difficult, and at the mercy of their hormones, and that these problems will naturally pass with time. An adolescent who is deeply sad and pessimistic about the future may be told, "Cheer up, it's just a stage!" This is unlikely to do any good. In fact, the lack of sympathy and understanding from important others may even amplify the adolescent's depressed mood. Depression is fairly common among adolescents, yes, but that does not mean it can be safely ignored or treated lightly. In addition to the emotional distress it causes, adolescent depression increases the risk of other problems, from difficulties in school to suicide (Houston, Hawton, & Sheppard, 2001). Without effective treatment, depressed

Connect the Dots...

Can you think of steps that school or community authorities could take to reduce the frequency or severity of depression among adolescents?

Learned helplessness A deeply pessimistic attitude that results from interpreting negative events as stemming from internal, global, and stable causes.

Hopelessness A result of seeing negative events as uncontrollable and lasting that may lead to depression.

Rumination A process of dwelling on negative events, recalling other negative events from the past, and amplifying the long-term significance of negative factors.

adolescents often go on to become depressed young adults (Lewinsohn, Rohde, Seeley, Kline, & Gotlib, 2006).

In recent years, the most common form of treatment for adolescent depression has been a combination of medication and psychotherapy (Butcher et al., 2007). Research indicates that **cognitive-behavioral therapy**, which works on changing the adolescent's habitually pessimistic way of interpreting events, effectively reduces both current depressive symptoms and the likelihood of a relapse (Beck, 2005; Rohde, Lewinsohn, Clarke, Hops, & Seeley, 2005).

In adults, depression is often treated with antidepressant medications. These have helped many depressed adolescents as well, but may be dangerous for some (Cheung et al., 2005). Since 2004, the U.S. Food and Drug Administration has required antidepressants to carry a warning that they "increase the risk of suicidal thinking and behavior (suicidality) in children and adolescents . . . " (Food and Drug Administration, 2004). In 2007 the warning was extended to cover young adults as well (Food and Drug Administration, 2007). However, medical researchers point out that overall, antidepressant use reduces the suicide rate among adolescents and that the risk of suicide in *untreated* depression is many times higher than the risk from antidepressants (Friedman & Leon, 2007; Gibbons, Hur, Bhaurnik, & Mann, 2006). Physicians, parents, and adolescents who are taking antidepressants need to be alert to possible negative effects, but not at the cost of losing the benefits that treatment may bring.

Whatever the outcome of further research, antidepressant medications are very far from being the only source of suicidal thinking in adolescents. In the next section, we look at the facts about adolescent suicide, learn which teens are most at risk, and discuss some ways that adults and peers can detect and help a teen who may be considering suicide.

Suicide

▶ **Learning Objective 13.7**
What are the risk factors and warning signs for teen suicide?

Sometimes you get to the point where you don't really care how anyone else feels. You just want to get the hell out. You just want to escape. You feel the world is so cruel. When I felt that way, I didn't think about other people. I just thought about how much I wanted to get out, to get out of living. It's such a big pain in the ass. You feel like there's no other way out except death.

—BETH, 15 (BELL, 1998, p. 176)

A recent survey of high school students in the United States found that 17%—*one in six*—had seriously thought about suicide in the previous 12 months. That means that if you gathered a random group of a dozen teens, the odds are that one or two of them have recently considered killing themselves. Some 13% of those surveyed said they had gone beyond thinking to come up with a suicide plan, and 8.5%—1 in 12—had actually attempted to kill themselves at least once (Centers for Disease Control and Prevention [CDCP], 2006).

Far too many adolescents who try to commit suicide succeed. In 2003, 1,401 boys and 321 girls aged 11–19 died from deliberately self-inflicted injuries. This makes suicide the third leading cause of death among American teens (CDCP, 2005). More adolescents die from suicide than from cancer, heart disease, AIDS, birth defects, stroke, pneumonia, influenza, and chronic lung disease *combined* (U.S. Public Health Service, 1999). This may even be an underestimation. How many adolescent drownings, fatal drug overdoses, and single-passenger car crashes are not as accidental as family members would prefer to believe?

Cognitive-behavioral therapy An approach to treatment that focuses on changing the self-defeating ways an adolescent interprets and responds to life events.

Gender, Ethnicity, and Age. The risk of suicidal thoughts and behavior is not spread equally across all adolescents. Figure 13.12 on page 459 shows the percentage of U.S. high school students who have thought seriously about suicide, made a suicide plan, attempted suicide, and needed medical treatment after a suicide attempt. The most noticeable aspect of these charts is that, for every one of these measures, and across all

Figure 13.12 Suicidal Thoughts, Plans, and Actions, by Gender and Ethnic Groups
Suicidal thoughts, plans, and actions show similar variations by gender and ethnic group.

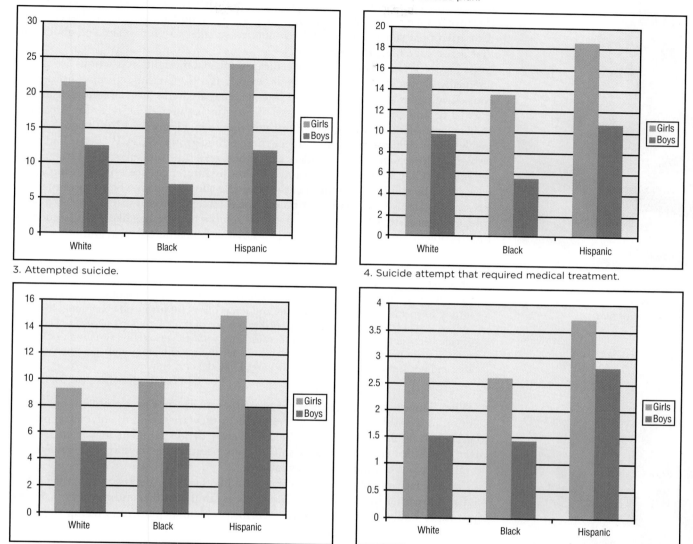

Source: Centers for Disease Control and Prevention, 2006.

ethnic categories, the rate for girls is roughly twice as high as that for boys (CDCP, 2006). Yet boys are about four times as likely to *die* from suicide as girls. Why this difference? One big reason is that most boys who attempt suicide either shoot or hang themselves, methods that are quick and reliably lethal. Girls are more likely to swallow pills or other harmful substances. These may take long enough to work to allow discovery and medical treatment to save their lives.

We should not take this difference to mean that boys are more earnest about killing themselves. A more likely explanation is that on the whole, they are more physically aggressive, more impulsive, and more accustomed to firearms than girls (Annest, Mercy, Gibson, & Ryan, 1995). Taking a lethal dose of a medication may mean planning and hoarding pills for days or weeks. During this time, the problems that inspired the suicide plan may start to seem less horrible, or the teen may reconsider. Pulling a trigger or looping a belt around your neck and tying it to a closet hook, however, takes hardly any time at all and gives you no chance to change your mind. This certainly

▲ Girls who attempt suicide are more likely to resort to a lethal overdose of pills.

does not mean that a girl's suicide attempt should be minimized as "not real," just because it was thwarted in time. Those girls who do complete a suicide, like the boys who do so, are likely to hang themselves or use a gun (CDCP, 2005), and one of the biggest risk factors for adolescent suicide is an earlier, unsuccessful suicide attempt (Spirito & Oberholser, 2003). In fact, one study found that among adolescent boys who attempted suicide, almost 9% completed suicide within 5 years, and about half that percentage for girls (King, 1997).

As Figure 13.12 on page 459 also indicates, suicidal thoughts and actions are spread unequally across ethnic groups as well. Among the three ethnic groups shown, and considering boys and girls together, Hispanic teens are highest on all four measures of suicidality, and Blacks are lowest, with Whites in between. The rates for American Indians and Alaska Natives, which are not shown in Figure 13.12 on page 459, are much higher than those of any of these three ethnic groups (CDCP, 2006). There are also grade differences. Ninth graders are highest on all the measures, and 12th graders are lowest (CDCP, 2006). The reasons for these differences are not clear, but as we have seen, the many transitions of early to middle adolescence can be a source of much stress. We can also speculate that the personal fable, discussed in Chapter 4, plays a role. Compared to 9th graders, high school seniors may be less likely to assume that their problems are unique and eternal and that death is the only way out.

Risk Factors.

That's what I refer to my suicide as, a place. I've got a whole universe of suicide that I enter every so often and it's got its own little villages where you kind of go, into wrist-slitting town and suffocate-yourselfville and jump-off-a-cliff town and everything. It's like being stuck in it and you work really hard to get out of it . . . kids don't necessarily commit suicide because they want to die, but because they want to get out of a situation that's causing them pain and god knows, I did. I was feeling very unhappy and very uncomfortable and not feeling worthy. So suicide looked like the only way out.

—TANIA, 17 (FULLAGAR, 2003, pp. 296–297)

What Tania is saying is that some teens see suicide, not as a problem, but as the solution to a problem. Most often the problem they are trying to solve is connected to *depression* (Holmes & Holmes, 2005). Severely depressed teens may even seem to cheer up a little once they make a suicide plan, because they believe they have finally found a way out of their emotional pain.

The risk factors for suicide are very much like those for depression that we examined a little earlier in this chapter. One factor is family conflict and disruption (Evans, Hawton, & Rodham, 2004). Another factor is problems with peers. Feeling alone and friendless can lead to thoughts of suicide. So can trying to cope with the breakup of an important relationship. Victims of bullying sometimes feel that they have no way out except killing themselves. Gay teens and those whose gender behavior is atypical or nonconforming may be particular targets of bullying, leading them to consider suicide (Friedman, Koeske, Silvestre, Korr, & Sites, 2006). Still another risk factor is a suicide attempt, whether completed or not, by a family member, friend, neighbor, or schoolmate (Bearman & Moody, 2004; Liu, 2006).

In this chapter's Applications in the Spotlight on page 461, we look at some warning signs for adolescent suicide and some steps that those who spot these warning signs can take to prevent a tragedy.

Anyone who comes into contact with adolescents should be acquainted with the problems we have been considering in this chapter. As parents, teachers, counselors, or simply members of the public who sympathize with the dreams and struggles of young people, we need to be aware of the risk factors, warning signs, and treatment options for externalizing and internalizing problems. We should also keep in mind, however, that even among those teens most at risk for serious problems, there are a great many who manage to stay healthy, confident, positive, and enthusiastic. In the final chapter of this book, we look at what social scientists are finding out about coping, caring, and developing in a positive direction across the adolescent years.

▲ Boys who attempt suicide are more likely to use very immediate means such as firearms.

A Applications in the Spotlight

Suicide: What to Look For, What to Do

What if something about the behavior of a friend or an adolescent you know makes you wonder if he or she is considering suicide? What signs should you be on the lookout for? If you do come to suspect that the person is thinking about suicide, what steps can you take to help?

Some signs to pay attention to are:

Being bullied, pushed around, or harassed;

Being in an abusive relationship;

Having problems with gender identity or sexual minority status;

Sudden worsening in school performance;

Withdrawal from friends and extracurricular activities;

A sudden decline in energy and enthusiasm;

Expressions of sadness and hopelessness, or anger and rage;

Excessive interest in death, expressed in reading, writing, artwork, music, video games; and

A fascination with weapons.

Warning signs that call for *immediate action* include:

Giving away prized possessions;

Talking or writing about suicide;

Expressing a belief that life is meaningless;

Saying things like:

I wish I were dead.

I'm going to end it all.

You'll all be better off without me.

Life sucks and I want out.

Who cares if I'm dead anyway?

Soon the pain will be over.

Announcing that he or she has planned "how to do it"; and

Obtaining a weapon or other means, such as prescription drugs.

If you come to believe that the adolescent is planning a suicide attempt, here are some steps to take:

Don't try to do it all yourself. Get support from someone who understands young people and can help—a teacher, guidance counselor, member of the clergy, or youth worker. Call the National Suicide Prevention Lifeline, (800) 273-TALK (8255) for advice and information about resources in your area.

Don't be afraid of being wrong. Adolescents who show the warning signs just listed may not be actively considering suicide, but they certainly have serious problems that they need help with. Talking about their situation and feelings with someone who will listen can make a big difference.

Explore the situation. Ask them outright if they are thinking about hurting or killing themselves. If they say yes, ask if they've made plans for how to do it, if they have whatever they need to carry it out, and if they have set a definite time. It is *not* the case that talking about suicide or suicidal thoughts will push someone to kill himself or herself. An open discussion can help decrease anxiety and give them the relief of knowing that someone cares and wants to help.

Don't minimize their problems, try to tell them everything will be all right, or offer too much advice. Acknowledge their fear, sadness, and other feelings.

Never promise to keep secret their plans to kill or hurt themselves. If you can't avoid promising, be prepared to break the promise. Keeping a promise counts for a lot less than saving a life.

Don't leave them alone if they say they've made a definite plan or decision. Stay with them until they are willing to go with you to get help, or until you can get help to come to them.

Once again, the National Suicide Prevention Lifeline is available 24/7 at (800) 273-TALK (8255).

Sources: U.S. Department of Health and Human Services, 2005; Suicide Prevention Resource Center, 2005.

Summing Up...

Adolescents with internalizing problems, such as eating problems, depression, and suicidal tendencies, tend to be overcontrolled and are more often girls. Many teenage girls in the United States are overweight, but more than twice as many *think* they are, and even more are trying to lose weight. The media play an important role in transmitting "super-thin" cultural standards to teens. For some, a distorted body image and obsession with weight control leads to the serious eating disorders of anorexia nervosa or bulimia. The most common internalizing problem for teens is depression, which strikes about twice as many girls as boys during adolescence. Depression may result from the interaction of some vulnerability or diathesis with the stressful impact of negative events or circumstances. Peer and romantic relationships are a common source of stress. Depression is often linked to suicide, the third leading cause of death among American teens. As many as one in six high school students has thought seriously about suicide in the last year, and 1 in 12 has actually attempted suicide. Girls are twice as likely to attempt suicide as boys, but boys are four times as likely to die because they tend to use more immediately lethal means. Risk factors for suicide include family conflict, disruption of a romantic relationship, and being bullied.

SUMMARY

Many adolescents have problems at some point, but the mistaken impression that such problems are nearly universal is encouraged by media sensationalism.

Learning Objective 13.1 What are some reasons for hope when teens develop problems?

Trying something is not necessarily the same as developing a serious problem. The problems an adolescent does have may date to well before adolescence. Many adolescents who have problems grow out of them, and many adolescent problems are **status offenses** that would not be considered problems in an adult.

Learning Objective 13.2 What is the distinction between externalizing and internalizing problems?

Experts on adolescent problems generally distinguish between externalizing and internalizing problems. Those with **externalizing problems**, such as aggression and delinquency, tend to be undercontrolled, that is, to have difficulty controlling their impulses. Boys are more likely than girls to develop externalizing problems. Those with **internalizing problems**, such as eating disorders and depression, tend to be overcontrolled, that is, to repress their impulses. Girls are more likely than boys to develop internalizing problems. Adolescent problems often occur together, in what is called **comorbidity**.

Many adults think of externalizing problems such as delinquency, violence, and substance use as being especially typical of adolescents.

Learning Objective 13.3 What are the risk factors for delinquency and adolescent violence?

Delinquency can range from status offenses, such as truancy and running away, to minor violations, such as gambling and disorderly conduct, to serious **index crimes**, including burglary, aggravated assault, rape, and murder. For boys, serious crimes increase sharply across the adolescent years, while for girls the rate of violent crimes stays low and the rate of property crimes

rises somewhat, then drops. Boys are much more likely than girls to be arrested for serious violent and property crimes.

The number of those younger than 18 in detention facilities has climbed steadily, even while the number of arrests dropped off. Some teens who are arrested are tried as adults and sent to adult prisons. Both ethnic background and social class are linked to how often delinquent acts lead to arrest and detention. It is important to distinguish between teens who occasionally break the law (**adolescence-limited offenders**) and those who commit more serious offenses over the long run (**life-course-persistent offenders**).

Risk factors for delinquency include gender (males), impulsiveness, a **hostile attributional bias**, association with deviant peers, living in high poverty, high-crime neighborhoods, and conflict within the family. Delinquent youth gangs have become more widespread and more violent, supported by drug trafficking.

More than one in four boys in the United States report that they have carried a weapon to school during the previous month. The rate of juvenile homicides in the United States is many times higher than in other developed countries. Homicide, mostly committed with guns, is the number two cause of death among older teens across ethnic groups and gender, and the leading cause of death among Black males.

Learning Objective 13.4 How many teens use which substances, how often, and why?

Substance use is widespread among adolescents, whether it is **instrumental**—a way of reaching some socially acceptable goal, or **recreational**—done for the sake of feeling the effects of the substance. Some substances are licit, such as coffee; some are illicit, such as marijuana; and some may be licit or illicit depending on the user's age and status (alcohol, tobacco). **Psychoactive substances**, which affect the user's thoughts, feelings, and behavior, may lead to a condition of **drug dependence**, in which attempts to stop using the substance create unpleasant **drug withdrawal** symptoms.

By age 18, half of U.S. adolescents have tried some illicit drug, not including alcohol or tobacco. Most often, this is marijuana. Other substances, such as amphetamines, barbiturates, and opiates, are much less commonly used.

Two in five 8th graders have tried alcohol at least once, and one in five has been drunk at least once. By 12th grade, three in four have tried alcohol and more than half have been drunk. One in 10 high school students say they have driven while drinking during the previous month, and 3 in 10 say they have ridden with a driver who was drinking. Motor vehicle crashes are the leading cause of death among 15- to 20-year-olds.

One in four 8th graders has tried cigarettes and almost 1 in 10 is a regular smoker. By 12th grade, one in two has tried cigarettes and one in four is a regular smoker. Most adults who smoke started in adolescence.

One in six 8th graders has tried marijuana, although very few use it daily. By 12th grade, almost half have tried it, one in five has used it in the previous month, and 1 in 20 uses it daily.

A major risk factor for substance use is the attitudes and behaviors of an adolescent's friends, schoolmates, and peers. A teen who believes everyone else smokes, drinks, or uses marijuana is more likely to try these substances.

Major internalizing problems among adolescents include eating problems, depression, and suicide.

Learning Objective 13.5 What are the major eating disorders and why are they more common among girls?

Distorted body image and body dissatisfaction are common among adolescent girls. Two girls in five believe they are overweight, and three in five are actively trying to lose weight. A small percentage of girls go on to develop a serious eating disorder such as **anorexia nervosa** or **bulimia**. Those with anorexia feel intense fear of getting fat and starve themselves to become or stay thin. Those with bulimia engage in binge eating, then purge themselves through vomiting or taking laxatives. Risk factors for eating disorders include body dissatisfaction, a **perfectionist** attitude, and exposure to very thin models in television shows, music videos, and appearance-related magazines.

Adolescent boys with body dissatisfaction are more likely to over-exercise and perhaps use steroids to become more muscular.

Learning Objective 13.6 What are the causes of adolescent depression?

Many, perhaps most, adolescents experience symptoms of **depression**, including sad or hopeless feelings severe and lasting enough to interfere with their lives. Childhood depression is equally common in girls and boys, but in adolescence twice as many girls as boys become depressed. One explanation for depression is that it is produced by the interaction of a predisposition or **diathesis**, and the *stress* of negative events or circumstances.

Children of depressed parents are more likely to develop depression, probably because of a combination of inherited vulnerability and the stress of dealing with depressed parents. Other risk factors include changing schools; moving to a new home; living in an impoverished, unsafe neighborhood; and experiencing a parental divorce. Poor relationships with peers and difficulties with romantic partners are a major source of stress that leads to depression.

Teens who interpret negative events as caused by permanent aspects of themselves may develop **learned helplessness**, which, in turn, may lead to depression. Treatment for depression frequently involves **cognitive-behavioral therapy**, possibly combined with antidepressant medications.

Learning Objective 13.7 What are the risk factors and warning signs for teen suicide?

Suicide is the third leading cause of death among U.S. adolescents. One in six high school students seriously considered suicide in the previous year, one in eight developed a suicide plan, and 1 in 12 attempted to kill themselves. Girls are twice as likely as boys to consider or attempt suicide, but boys are four times as likely to die from suicide as girls. One reason for the higher death rate among boys is that they are more likely to shoot or hang themselves, with immediate fatal results, while girls are more likely to swallow pills, which may leave enough time for them to be found and revived.

Hispanic teens are highest on measures of suicidality, and Blacks are lowest, with Whites in between. As for age, suicidal thoughts and actions are highest among 9th graders and lowest in 12th graders. Risk factors for suicide include family conflict and disruption, difficulties with peers and romantic partners, and being the victim of bullying.

Those who interact with adolescents, whether parents, teachers, coaches, or others, need to understand the warning signs for adolescent suicide and know how to respond in a helpful way.

KEY TERMS

Status offense (433)
Externalizing problem (433)
Internalizing problem (433)
Comorbidity (433)
Delinquency (434)
Index crimes (434)
Life-course-persistent offenders (438)

Adolescence-limited offenders (438)
Hostile attributional bias (439)
Instrumental substance use (443)
Recreational substance use (443)
Psychoactive substances (444)

Drug dependence (444)
Drug withdrawal (444)
Alcoholism (447)
Nicotine (447)
THC (447)
Gateway hypothesis (448)
Anorexia nervosa (452)
Bulimia (452)
Perfectionism (453)

Depression (455)
Diathesis-stress model (456)
Learned helplessness (457)
Hopelessness (457)
Rumination (457)
Cognitive-behavioral therapy (458)

Positive Prospects

They said, "You have a blue guitar,
You do not play things as they are."

The man replied, "Things as they are
Are changed upon the blue guitar."
—WALLACE STEVENS, **The Blue Guitar**

Most of the information we have learned about adolescence has been gathered using some combination of two general approaches:

The *scientific approach* involves trying to find the most accurate, useful, and economical ways to describe and understand what is.

The *medical approach* involves trying to describe and understand problems and to develop ways to correct them.

Both approaches have led to incredibly important and valuable insights. With each passing day and each new issue of a scientific journal on adolescence, we learn more about genetics, brain development, hormonal influences, family structure and functioning, peer relationships, and dozens of other factors that have a profound influence on adolescents and their development. As we saw in the last chapter, we constantly learn more about the problems that afflict adolescents as well. What factors lead to these problems? How can they be prevented or made less severe? If they do arise, how can they be treated and possibly cured?

In this chapter, the final chapter of the book, we get acquainted with a different way to look at adolescence, one that has become increasingly prominent in recent years. This approach focuses on **positive youth development** (Benson, Scales, Hamilton, & Sesma, 2006; Lerner, 2005). This represents a major shift in focus. Traditionally, social scientists, policymakers, parents, and adults generally have tended to think of *healthy* adolescence as the *absence* of such problems as substance use, antisocial behavior, early sexual activity, pregnancy, eating disorders, and suicide. It is easy to understand why this is so. No one can doubt that all of these are serious and widespread problems that blight the lives and futures of many, many teens. Finding ways to reduce them would greatly benefit both adolescents themselves and society as a whole.

On the individual level, the child who has problems obviously needs help and support. With luck, he or she will get it. But what about a child who doesn't have any obvious problems? Parents, teachers, and even friends the same age may simply assume that a child like that can get through adolescence successfully without any special attention or help. As an old saying points out, "It's the squeaky wheel that gets the grease." If the wheel doesn't squeak, people assume it is doing okay, unless a moment arrives when it doesn't. But what if there are ways to make the wheel, not just okay, but better?

In contrast to this focus on simply preventing problems, the positive youth development perspective

> aims at understanding, educating, and engaging children in productive activities rather than at correcting, curing, or treating them for maladaptive tendencies or so-called disabilities.
>
> —(DAMON, 2004, p. 15)

Positive youth development An approach to studying adolescence that focuses on factors that encourage young people to develop healthy attitudes and become engaged in productive, life-enhancing activities.

Problems do come up, of course. But when they do, they are considered part of a range of *possible* outcomes, many of which are not just un-negative, but actively life-enhancing. Young people are not thought of as incubators for problems that have to be averted, fixed, or managed. Nor are they stereotyped as blank slates on which a hostile environment may have scribbled rude graffiti with semipermanent marker. Instead, they are seen as active, capable individuals who are eager to explore and understand, become more competent, and develop their potential to enjoy productive, fulfilling lives and give back to their families, communities, and world (Damon, 2004; Roth & Brooks-Gunn, 2003).

Later in the chapter, we discuss this more confident approach to what adolescents are and can become in detail. We also examine the sources of support that can help them achieve their positive goals. First, however, we look at some ways adolescents deal with problems that come up in their lives. Why are some able to ride out stressful situations and rise above them, while others flounder or sink? What tools and resources might help teens confront difficult life issues more confidently and effectively? These questions are the focus of the next section.

STRESS, COPING, AND RESILIENCE

As a prominent government official once pointed out, "Stuff happens." The morning of an important exam, your car won't start. Your cell phone falls out of your pocket into a sink full of soapy water. Your romantic partner moves across the country, loses interest, or still worse, drops you for someone you know and can't stand. Some things that happen have still more serious implications. Your parents tell you they are splitting up. You find out you have a life-threatening medical condition. Your home burns to the ground. Your country is attacked or invaded.

Stress

When we confront events that we think pose some sort of threat, we respond by experiencing **stress**. The body's resources are mobilized, by way of the endocrine and sympathetic nervous systems, and placed on high alert. If the threat is averted or dealt with, the system returns to normal. Suppose you are about to cross the street when a car comes speeding around the corner, horn blaring. You jump back out of the way. For the next few minutes you probably feel edgy and short of breath, but gradually you are able to relax and put the incident out of your mind. This would be an example of *acute* stress, in response to a sudden and short-lived threat.

What if the source of the threat, the *stressor*, persists? The problems caused by poverty or discrimination, for example, come up every day in different ways, and an adolescent with diabetes is reminded of the condition with every meal and every blood test. Such ongoing threats may lead to *chronic* stress, which has consequences that can include a compromised immune system, high blood pressure, depression, and suicide (Brady & Matthews, 2006; Cole, Nolen-Hoeksema, Girgus, & Paul, 2006; Hampton, 2006; Nolen-Hoeksema, 2007).

◀ **Learning Objective 14.1**
How do adolescents deal with different sorts of stress?

Stress A physical, hormonal, and psychological response to the perception of danger or threat.

◀ Natural and social disasters such as Hurricane Katrina confront teens with high levels of chronic stress.

Recent research that uses neuroimaging to study the body's responses to stress indicates that with puberty, the biological stress system becomes more sensitive and reactive (Gunnar & Quevedo, 2007). This implies that adolescents may be at greater risk for the negative consequences of threats, even if the threats themselves were just as severe earlier, during childhood. How can adolescents deal with stress, whether it is acute or chronic? This is the focus of research on **coping**—what teens actually do when they have to handle specific difficulties in real-life contexts and how these encounters with adversity shape their development (Skinner & Zimmer-Gembeck, 2007).

Coping

▶ **Learning Objective 14.2**
How is gender linked to coping strategies?

Connect the **Dots...**

Can you recall occasions during adolescence when you found yourself facing (a) a situation that generated a moderate level of stress; and (b) a situation that generated a high level of stress? How did the level of stress affect the way you dealt with the situation?

It is useful to think of coping as two linked processes. The first is a quick, impulsive, "hot" system that reacts to situations almost automatically, with little conscious control. Its effect is to bring the person into readiness to do something in response to the situation. The second process is a "cool" regulatory system that plans, guides, and organizes the response to the situation (Compas, 2004).

Those who find themselves facing situations that create a moderate level of stress are more likely to mobilize the regulatory system. This gives them a chance to come up with ways to deal effectively with both their emotions and the situation itself. Successful responses, in turn, help the regulatory system become more efficient. High levels of stress, on the other hand, may disrupt or overwhelm the regulatory system (Skinner & Zimmer-Gembeck, 2007). The same adolescent who responds coolly and effectively to a moderate stressor may panic and react impulsively in a situation that causes a very high level of stress.

Kinds of Coping. There are practically as many sorts of coping responses as there are situations that evoke them and individuals who carry them out. One review found labels for more than 400 different types (Skinner, Edge, Altman, & Sherwood, 2003). Most of these can be put into one of about a dozen families of responses that range from *Problem-solving*, *Escape*, and *Support-seeking* to *Negotiation* and *Submission* (Skinner et al., 2003). Researchers also find it useful to distinguish between two broad strategies for coping (Lazarus, 1999; Lazarus & Folkman, 1984):

Problem-focused coping is more likely to be used when it seems possible to change a harmful, threatening, or challenging situation. It involves such techniques as confronting the situation and trying to manage it, giving oneself positive instructions, and seeking practical support. For instance, a student who is having trouble in a course might schedule more reading time, put notes around the house that say, "I can do it if I try," and ask the instructor for suggestions about more effective studying.

Emotion-focused coping is more likely to be used when it seems that nothing can be done to change a harmful, threatening, or challenging situation. It involves such techniques as minimizing the importance of the situation, seeing the causes as external and temporary, and framing the problem in a larger, more positive context. Getting emotional support from others may also be part of this approach. For instance, a student who has failed a final exam might argue that grades don't matter that much, that a bout of flu was the main reason for the failure, or that this is a needed wakeup call to take academics more seriously.

Coping The various ways adolescents develop to handle situations that create stress.

Problem-focused coping Trying to manage a stressful situation by analyzing it and mobilizing the means to change it in a positive direction.

Emotion-focused coping Trying to manage the negative psychological effects of a stressful situation that does not seem open to being changed.

If a situation really cannot be changed, emotion-focused coping strategies may be the most effective response (Cunningham, 2002; Skinner et al., 2003). For example, if you are stuck in a traffic jam on your way to an important meeting, telling yourself the meeting isn't *that* important or distracting yourself with music or an involving mental game may be the best way of dealing with the stress. Much of the time, however, problem-focused coping is more closely linked to competence, positive functioning, and healthy emotional states (Compas, Connor-Smith, Saltzman, Thomsen, & Wadsworth, 2001). Compared to children, adolescents show greater flexibility in switching between problem-focused and emotion-focused coping strategies, depending on the demands of the situation (Pincus & Friedman, 2004).

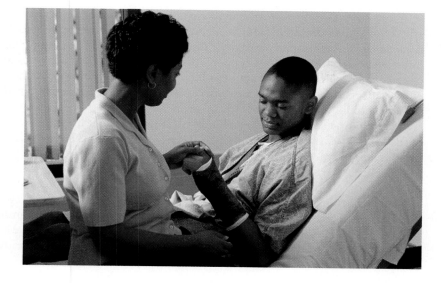

◄ Adolescents are able to switch among different coping strategies in response to different stressful situations.

Sources of Coping. Why are some adolescents able to call on more effective coping strategies when they are faced with stressful situations? Which adolescents are they? Scholars suggest that some of the answers to these questions go back as far as infancy and early childhood (Derryberry, Reed, & Pilkenton-Taylor, 2003). Some children react to new objects and situations with fearfulness and withdrawal, indicating higher levels of stress, while others show interest and attraction (Fox, Henderson, Marshall, Nichols, & Ghera, 2005). Some children react to even mild stressors, such as having to wait a few minutes for a snack, with high levels of anger and frustration (Calkins, Dedmon, Gill, Lomax, & Johnson, 2002). This sort of high reactivity can get in the way of developing an ability to control and regulate negative emotions, which is an important element in coping.

Both gender and gender identity have been linked to the sorts of coping strategy adolescents prefer. On the whole, girls are more likely to prefer emotion-focused strategies, and boys to prefer problem-focused strategies (Hampel & Petermann, 2005; Renk & Creasey, 2003). Among both male and female adolescents, those with higher femininity scores tend to prefer emotion-focused strategies and those with higher masculinity scores tend to prefer problem-focused strategies (Renk & Creasey, 2003). This may help explain an experience many people have had when they confided to a friend about some problem. A female friend may explore your feelings about the problem and perhaps suggest ways you could feel more positive about it. A male friend may be more likely to suggest practical steps you might take to solve the problem. Either response, of course, may or may not feel helpful.

Parents and Coping. The experiences children and adolescents have with caregivers and attachment figures play a vital role in the development of their coping abilities (Zimmer-Gembeck & Locke, 2007). Parents can help shield children from stressors and teach them to learn from their bad experiences. If parents themselves have problems—for instance, if they are not getting along well with one another—their problems may become a source of stressors for the child. In addition, the ways parents deal with their problems offer the child examples of more or less mature ways of coping with difficulties (Power, 2004; Skinner & Zimmer-Gembeck, 2007).

Parents can also be a major source of emotional and practical support (Sieffge-Krenke, 1995). Beginning in early adolescence, teens become increasingly skilled at figuring out where best to turn for support, depending on the sort of difficulty they face. For social and emotional problems, they tend to turn to peers for support. In situations that are uncontrollable or in which adults are in charge, however, they are more likely to seek support from parents and other adults (Skinner & Zimmer-Gembeck, 2007).

As we have already seen in our discussion of the family, in Chapter 5, two vital aspects of the relationships adolescents have with their parents are *responsiveness* and *demandingness*. Authoritative parents, those who are high on both these characteristics, offer teens warmth, care, and support, but also monitor their activities and provide clear guidelines. An approach that can help us understand the ways authoritative parenting affects coping is *self-determination theory* (Ryan & Deci, 2000b; Ryan, Deci, Grolnick, & La Guardia, 2006).

According to self-determination theory, all adolescents have basic psychological needs for *relatedness, competence,* and *autonomy*. When parents support these needs by giving teens warm, responsive relationships, a predictable environment, and the space to make decisions for themselves, the teens are more likely to use active, engaged coping behaviors. If the family environment is hostile, chaotic, and coercive, however, adolescents are more likely to adopt passive or avoidant coping strategies, such as denial or wishful thinking. A recent study examined the links between family relationships and coping in adolescents. The results confirm that those who have a more positive family climate use more active coping strategies when dealing with problems both at home and at school (Zimmer-Gembeck & Locke, 2007).

Coping is part of a complex adaptive system that helps the individual deal with threats and with the physical and psychological stress that threats set off (Masten, 2006). The coping strategies that adolescents use, and the outcomes that these strategies lead to, have both immediate effects and a long-term impact on individual functioning and development. As one expert in the field put it,

> Protection . . . resides, not in the evasion of risk, but in successful engagement with it . . . protection stems from the adaptive changes that follow successful coping.
>
> —(RUTTER, 1987, p. 318)

When an adolescent is able to cope effectively with a problem, that success strengthens the teen's confidence and sense of self-efficacy (Bandura, 2001). This increased confidence, in turn, reduces the level of stress the next time a similar problem comes up. In effect, the adolescent thinks, "I believe I can handle this, because I managed to deal with something like it before without falling apart."

Over time, adolescents who cope successfully with problems develop a more general ability to confront and rise above difficulties. This quality is often referred to as *resilience*. We now turn our attention briefly to an examination of adolescent resilience and some of the factors that encourage it.

Resilience

▶ **Learning Objective 14.3**
What adaptational systems help promote resilience?

In Chapter 13, we saw that a variety of risk factors have been linked to the emergence of problems during adolescence. Some are at the level of the individual. A few examples of this are low birth weight, complications during the birth process, impulsiveness, and a withdrawn or resistant temperament. Others are at the level of social interactions. These factors might include parenting style, family conflict, divorce, victimization, and association with deviant peers. Still others, such as family poverty, discrimination, lack of resources in schools and neighborhoods, and exposure to violence, are characteristics of the community and broader society. As we have discussed more than once, over time risk factors at one level act on, and are acted upon by, those at other levels, in a dynamic, developing system (Lerner & Castellino, 2002).

Social scientists have learned a lot about risk factors and the ways they are connected to adolescent problems. Along the way, they noticed something else as well. There are many children and adolescents who, according to the research, are clearly at risk for developing problems, and yet they turn out well. This capacity to develop normally under difficult conditions is called **resilience** (Masten, 2001; Masten & Reed, 2005). Surprisingly, most of those who possess it are *not* superkids with some extraordinary strength of character. Instead, they are normal teens whose most notable characteristic is the fact that there is nothing terribly unusual about them. And yet, in some fashion,

Resilience The capacity to develop normally and positively under difficult conditions.

◄ Many teens show resilience and avoid the negative effects of adversity.

they are able to dodge, throw off, or resist the negative effects of personal, family, and community adversities.

This realization has led psychologist Ann Masten, a leading expert on the subject, to call resilience *ordinary magic*. As she points out:

> Resilience appears to be a common phenomenon that results in most cases from the operation of basic human adaptational systems. If those systems are protected and in good working order, development is robust even in the face of severe adversity; if these major systems are impaired . . . then the risk for developmental problems is much greater . . . Resilience does not come from rare and special qualities, but from the everyday magic of ordinary, normative human resources in the minds, brains, and bodies of children, in their families and relationships, and in their communities.
>
> —(MASTEN, 2001, pp. 227, 235)

The adaptational systems Masten refers to have already come up in earlier chapters, but it is helpful to list them in this context. They include:

cognitive skills;

attachment relationships;

self-regulation of emotions and behavior;

positive self-regard;

self-efficacy; and

intrinsic motivation.

—(MASTEN, 2001)

Of these, the most basic is having warm, supportive connections to competent and caring adults in the family and community (Serbin & Karp, 2004). These connections, in turn, promote the other adaptational systems.

Even children who have suffered extreme deprivation and adversity can often be helped back onto a normal path of development if they receive good physical and psychological care from caregivers (Rutter & ERA Study Team, 1998; Wright & Masten, 2005). For example, research on children born with medical or physical disorders shows that those who experience harsh parenting have a low ability to cope with stress. Those who experience warm, supportive parenting, however, have an exceptional resilience and ability to adapt to stress (Bugental, 2004).

For adolescents, whose relationships outside the home take on increasing importance, experiences in school also play an important role in fostering resilience. Ideally, the educational system has a mission to develop young people who are, "knowledgeable,

Connect the Dots...

Why do you think there is such a close connection between the kind of parenting a child experiences and the child's ability to deal with chronic stress? Which of the adaptational systems listed might be especially affected by the parenting approach?

responsible, healthy, caring, connecting, and contributing" (Weissberg & O'Brien, 2004, p. 87). To do this, schools need to offer a safe environment, with supportive peers, positive teacher influences, and opportunities to experience success, both academic and otherwise. These conditions benefit the teen's self-regard, sense of self-efficacy, and intrinsic motivation. All of these, in turn, promote greater resilience.

Often, however, school reforms focus narrowly on raising standardized test scores and neglect the broader goal of positive youth development (Scales, Benson, Roehlkepartain, Sesma, & van Dulme, 2006). Later in this chapter, we discuss how school-based programs have succeeded in enhancing students' personal and social assets while improving the school-community environment.

Summing Up...

When threatening situations and events arouse stress, teens may react by using problem-focused and emotion-focused coping. On average, males use problem-focused coping more and females use emotion-focused coping more. Warm, responsive relationships with parents and a supportive home environment foster active, engaged coping behaviors. Teens with a history of coping successfully with problems may develop resilience, a general ability to confront and rise above difficulties.

FROM SURVIVING TO THRIVING

The attitudes, skills, and social supports that help adolescents cope successfully with stress and respond with resilience to adversities make important contributions to positive development. They are, however, only part of what is needed. Coping and resilience are qualities that help an adolescent avoid being submerged by problems and difficulties. However, keeping your head above water is not the same as enjoying a healthful, exhilarating swim. What does it mean for adolescents not simply to *survive* but to *thrive?* What qualities should they aspire to?

Five Cs and a Sixth

▶ **Learning Objective 14.4**
How do the Five Cs and the sixth C contribute to thriving?

Scholars and practitioners have summarized the basic goals of positive youth development as the **Five Cs**:

Competence—being aware that one can act effectively in specific domains. The *social* domain includes interpersonal skills such as conflict resolution. The *cognitive* domain involves such skills as making effective decisions. The *academic* domain includes study habits and school grades.

Confidence—an internal sense of overall positive self-worth and self-efficacy.

Character—having respect for social and cultural rules, a sense of right and wrong, and personal integrity.

Connection—developing positive bonds with peers, family members, school, and community that lead to exchanges in which both parties contribute to the growth of the relationship.

Caring—having a sense of sympathy and compassion for others.

—(Eccles & Gootman, 2002; Roth & Brooks-Gunn, 2003)

Five Cs The psychological qualities of Competence, Confidence, Character, Connection, and Caring that form the basic goals of positive youth development.

These goals are not static endpoints a teen tries to reach, but dynamic qualities that develop and expand in the process of expressing them. As young people act on their feelings of connection with their community, for example, they also change their community in ways that make those connections more possible and more rewarding.

A leading theoretician in the field, Richard Lerner, recently proposed that as adolescents develop and show the Five Cs over time, they are also on course toward a

"Sixth C." This takes the form of *Contributions* to the self, the family, the community, and the institutions of civil society (Lerner, 2005). Young people—*all* young people—have the capacity and potential to make an active and constructive contribution to the development of their selves, their community, and their society. They are not problems to be managed, but resources to be nurtured and helped to flourish (Benson et al., 2006). And they themselves are prime actors in shaping their own positive developmental trajectories.

Suppose an adolescent decides to devote part of a vacation to helping build homes for people in a devastated area. The main impulse may be a sense of compassion for the victims, but it probably matters that some friends are going too, and that it is a chance to do something new and different away from home. As the project continues, the teen may gain a stronger sense of self-confidence, greater self-respect, and a feeling of closer connection to the other volunteers and the people in the community.

At the same time, the example of young people offering their free time to help others will change the way adults in the community see adolescents. (They aren't all druggies and gang members after all!) This, in turn, may give the adults more respect for adolescents and make them more willing to support ideas and programs that draw adolescents more deeply into the life of the community.

This view puts special stress on the concept that adolescents are active participants in their own development. The arrow that joins them to their physical and social environment points both ways: person ↔ environment (Lerner, 2005). The choices they make, the actions they take, the settings they select, all potentially contribute to their well-being and effective functioning. And as they change, so does the effect they are able to have on their environment (Brandstädter, 2006).

For example, teens who join a youth organization may be shy and unconfident at first. If the organization is structured to build confidence, however, they will come to feel more comfortable offering ideas and taking an active part in the life of the organization. These contributions, in turn, may change the organization in a direction that makes future new members feel at home more quickly. As adolescents see that they are having a positive impact, their confidence and sense of empowerment become stronger.

The Language of Thriving

One of the obstacles to achieving a broader understanding of the sources and meaning of thriving in adolescence is that until recently, attention has been devoted mostly to adolescent *problems* and efforts to reduce them. This tendency reflects the longstanding and widespread belief that adolescence is necessarily a time of "storm and stress" (Hall, 1904). The news media often report that teen pregnancies, or teen drug use, or teen violence, are up or down. But when was the last time you heard a commentator announce that levels of teen competence or teen character had improved? The vocabulary of teen well-being and thriving is simply not as widely used as that of teen problems (Lerner et al., 2005). As a result, there are fewer positive indicators available to reflect the desirable, healthy, and valued behaviors and attitudes of adolescents.

Part of the difficulty is that scholars, parents, youth workers, and adolescents themselves do not agree completely on the qualities that are most important to teen well-being. In one recent study (King et al., 2005), people working in youth development programs nominated program participants whom they saw as good examples of thriving adolescents. These adolescents, their parents, and the youth workers themselves, were then asked questions such as, "How can you tell if a young person is thriving or doing really well?" Their answers generated a list of over 1,500 terms. A great many of these overlapped in meaning, such as "active thinker," "critical thinking," "reflective thinking," and "independent thinking," so expert raters condensed the list to 77 terms. These included such characteristics as *positive attitude*, *care for others*, *easy-going*, and *adaptable* (King et al., 2005).

Table 14.1 on page 474 lists the 10 characteristics that were named most often by practitioners, parents, and younger and older adolescents. Only three qualities appear on all

◀ **Learning Objective 14.5**
What qualities do parents and teens think are most important to well-being?

Connect the **Dots...**

Do you believe the stereotype of sullen, unruly teenagers is accurate? If not, why do you think it is so widespread in modern society? What benefits might come from changing the impressions adults hold of teens in a more positive direction, and what sorts of efforts might it take to bring about such a change?

Table 14.1 Different Perceptions of Thriving Adolescents

Parents, those who work with teens, and teens themselves have somewhat different views of what it means to thrive.

Rank	Practitioners	Parents	Younger Adolescents	Older Adolescents
1	Connected with others	Positive self-concept	Academic success	Positive self-concept
2	Support from outside	Communication skills	Extracurricular activities	Future orientation
3	Positive self-concept	Future orientation	Future orientation	Happy
4	Future orientation	Connected with others	Responsible	Academic success
5	Social skills	Support from outside	Academic commitment	Successful
6	Communication skills	Cognitive competence	Work ethic	Contribution
7	Engaged	Responsible	Positive self-concept	Positive attitude
8	Cognitive competence	Happy	Successful	Social skills
9	Resiliency	Successful	Leadership	Responsible
10	Care for others	Engaged	Communication skills	Communication skills

Source: Adapted from King et al., 2005, pp. 102–103.

four lists: *positive self-concept, future orientation,* and *communication skills.* Compared to the other groups, the younger adolescents (average age 13+) mentioned more school-related terms (*extracurricular activities, academic commitment, work ethic*), while the older adolescents (average age 17) included more psychological characteristics such as *happy* and *responsible.*

Neither age group of teens was as likely to mention some of the qualities youth workers and parents considered most important, such as *connection with others, engaged,* and *resiliency.* It is also worth noting that not one of the 77 terms on the reduced list was used consistently across all four groups, nor were any of the terms mentioned by a clear majority of those in any of the individual groups (King et al., 2005). This suggests that to build greater public awareness of the factors that promote thriving in adolescence, concepts such as the Five Cs need to be more widely known and discussed among teens, parents, and the community at large.

Thriving as a Dynamic Process

▶ **Learning Objective 14.6**
How can teens interact with their contexts to enhance both the self and the setting?

As we have seen, recent concepts of thriving in adolescence stress the dynamic interactions of the developing teen with his or her changing context. Factors in the person's context promote change in the person, but the person also promotes change in the context. To take an example we discussed in Chapter 7, school climate has a crucial influence on students' behavior, achievement, and well-being. A psychological climate that is both responsive and demanding promotes better behavior, higher achievement, and stronger identification with the school (Eccles, 2004). At the same time, the ways students behave, their attitudes toward achievement, and their degree of identification with the school have an impact on the climate of the school.

When an interaction between individual and context promotes positive change in both, it creates what is called an adaptive developmental regulation (Brandstädter, 2006). The ongoing presence of adaptive developmental regulations helps create a sense of well-being in the present, and over time it promotes thriving and a positive trajectory toward adulthood (Rathunde & Csikszentmihalyi, 2006). A thriving adolescent, then, is one who is able to interact with his or her various contexts or settings in ways that enhance both the self and the setting.

The "goodness of fit" between the person's behavior and the characteristics of the setting matter, too. Different settings and contexts often call for different behaviors. A

◀ Thriving teens seek out settings that allow them to enhance both themselves and those they interact with.

teen would be unlikely to dress, speak, or act the same way hanging out with friends as presenting arguments for a new program to the school principal. Yet, because this is a dynamic process, a student who dresses and speaks informally, but makes convincing points, may also help change the principal's viewpoint about the need for formality.

Of course, it is not only the individual adolescent who has to "fit" different settings. Ideally, settings will be responsive to the individual's characteristics as well. For example, some teens respond best to structured situations where the rules, goals, and limits are spelled out in detail. Others are more comfortable when they are allowed more individual latitude and responsibility.

What resources within the adolescent and in the adolescent's settings or contexts make it more likely that positive development will take place? This is the question we take up in the next section.

Summing Up...

Positive development is more than overcoming difficulties, it is also moving toward and expressing positive qualities such as the Five Cs of competence, confidence, character, connection, and caring. Over time these lead to the "Sixth C" of making contributions to the self, family, community, and society. Teens whose development is supported by their environment also change their environment in a positive way, creating a dynamic system that benefits both the individual and the setting or institution.

RESOURCES FOR POSITIVE DEVELOPMENT

What resources do adolescents need to flourish and thrive? How can these resources be provided and promoted? These questions have taken on increasing importance in recent years. One reason is straightforward: The way today's adolescents turn out will profoundly affect the shape of tomorrow's society. Another reason, more disturbing, is that so many recent social changes have challenged the ability of families and communities to provide resources that were largely taken for granted in the past.

Among these changes are:

reduced parental presence, as a result of changes in the workplace and the much greater number of mothers who work outside the home;

less civic engagement;

fewer shared ideals about the goals of development;

increased age segregation;

less neighborhood cohesion;

decreased teen involvement in structured programs; and

increased teen absorption in popular media.

—(BENSON et al., 2006)

Developmental scientists Urie Bronfenbrenner and Pamela Morris dramatically describe the current situation as one of,

. . . growing chaos in the lives of families, in child care settings, schools, peer groups, youth programs, neighborhoods, workplaces, and other everyday environments in which human beings live their lives. Such chaos, in turn, interrupts and undermines the formation and stability of relationships and activities that are necessary for psychological growth.

—(BRONFENBRENNER & MORRIS, 1998, p. 1022)

Pitted against this chaos are those who have become alerted to the danger and have committed themselves to creating positive settings for adolescent development. Among them are parents, teachers, researchers, religious and community leaders, concerned citizens, and adolescents themselves, who, after all, are the most directly affected.

Internal Resources

▶ **Learning Objective 14.7**
What internal resources help adolescents develop positively?

Some of the important resources that promote positive development in adolescents are qualities the adolescents themselves possess. For example, on a very basic level, those teens who have good health habits and good skills for managing health risks will be more able to engage in activities that foster their psychological growth. Further, taking full advantage of the opportunities and supports that are available involves both *selection* and *optimization* (Baltes, Lindenberger, & Staudinger, 2006). Adolescents must be able to recognize and choose those resources that best fit their own personal goals, then use them effectively to advance their development. This is more likely to happen when they have good reasoning and decision-making skills. To take on something new, they also need a sense of confidence in their ability to achieve their goals and a commitment to use their time well.

Suppose a local community center sends around a booklet describing its activities for teens in the coming months. The list of after-school programs includes workshops in writing, pottery, music, martial arts, and several sports. All of these may sound attractive and interesting. To choose effectively, though, teens must be able to make an objective assessment of their talents, interests, and goals. They must also take account of the amount of time and energy an activity may require and balance that against what they have available. Other factors—schedules, what friends are doing—also enter into the process. Those adolescents who are better equipped to weigh all the information coolly and carefully are more likely to make enriching choices and to avoid problem and risk behaviors (Gestsdóttir & Lerner, 2007).

Scholars and youth workers have described many personal resources that help adolescents develop positively and thrive, including:

critical thinking;

positive self-regard;

emotional self-regulation;

coping skills;

conflict resolution skills;

mastery motivation;

a sense of self-efficacy;

a sense of responsibility for the self;

optimism coupled with realism;

positive personal identity;

prosocial values;

a commitment to civic engagement;

a desire to plan for the future; and

a sense of purpose in life.

—(ECCLES & GOOTMAN, 2002)

Once again, it is important to keep in mind that these attributes are not fixed goals to be reached, checked off, and then forgotten about. They are elements in an ongoing dynamic process. The more of these attributes adolescents have, the more they are able to profit from the positive resources available in their families, schools, and communities. The experiences they have as they make use of resources promote and strengthen these qualities. At the same time, their actions strengthen the positive aspects of the context in a bidirectional relationship (Lerner, Dowling, & Anderson, 2003).

For example, speaking up at a student assembly calls for some minimum degree of self-confidence and courage. It also requires a belief, however shaky, that what one has to say is worth listening to. If the setting is one that embodies the positive values of openness, tolerance, and respect for differing views, teens will be more willing to contribute to the discussion. When they do, they will emerge with a still stronger belief in themselves and their ability to develop and express worthwhile opinions. This leaves them better able to take advantage of similar opportunities in the future. At the same time, their example—yes, you *can* speak up and live to tell the tale!—makes the setting more welcoming to participation by others.

Depending on the setting and activity in question, some of these personal resources may be more directly relevant than others. In school, for instance, intellectual and motivational assets are clearly important. However, so are such psychological factors as an orientation toward the future and a sense of purpose. If committing yourself to your schoolwork seems pointless, you are unlikely to do well, however bright you may be. As a result, experts suggest that personal resources simply add up—the more, the better (Benson et al., 2006).

A similar point can be made about external resources. Adolescents who have a greater number and variety of appropriate resources accessible to them are more likely to discover, connect with, and make good use of them. What are these external resources, and what qualities make them effective in promoting positive development in adolescents? We look at some answers to these questions in the next section.

◄ Settings that foster openness, tolerance, and respect encourage teens to examine and express their opinions.

External Resources

▶ **Learning Objective 14.8**
How do school and community resources contribute to positive development?

As we have stressed in earlier chapters, the closest, most intimate contexts of adolescent development are the family, the peer group, the school, and the community. Somewhat more distant, but still hugely important, are social and cultural values, beliefs, and practices. These are expressed and communicated, for example, by political and religious institutions and the media. All of these can potentially encourage—or discourage—positive development among adolescents. For example, if school officials and community leaders think of teens primarily as a source of problems that need to be controlled, the programs and measures they adopt are likely to work *against* the process of positive development instead of for it.

Each context has its own particular features that can help promote positive development. There are also more general features that are important to the effectiveness of *any* positive developmental setting (Eccles & Gootman, 2002). These include:

Physical and psychological safety. Both physical facilities and interactions with peers and adults are experienced as safe.

Appropriate structure. Clear, consistent rules and expectations, predictability, age-appropriate monitoring.

Supportive relationships. Warmth, caring, guidance, secure attachment, responsiveness.

Opportunity to belong. Meaningful inclusiveness, social engagement and integration, support for cultural competence.

Positive social norms. Prosocial expectations, ways of doing things, and values.

Support for efficacy and mattering. Practices that encourage autonomy, empowerment, responsibility, being taken seriously, and making a difference.

Opportunity for skill building. Exposure to physical, intellectual, emotional, and social learning experiences, opportunities to develop social and cultural capital.

Integration of efforts. Coordination and synergy among family, school, and community.

—(Eccles & Gootman, 2002)

Connect the Dots...

Were there times as an adolescent when you found yourself trying to do something that seemed beyond your capabilities because some feature of the setting encouraged you? Looking back, what was that feature? An adult—parent, teacher, mentor? Friendly and accepting peers? A strong internal need that pushed you past your usual boundaries?

The more a particular setting embodies these features, the more it is likely to foster positive development.

Family Contributions. For most adolescents, the relationships they have with their parents are the most influential relationships in their lives. Peers may have more obvious impact on personal habits and preferences, such as what to wear and what kind of music to listen to, but when it comes to seeking counsel and support on big, important matters most teens look to their parents (Collins & Laursen, 2004; Steinberg & Silk, 2002). As we have seen repeatedly, the parents who are particularly likely to have a positive influence on their adolescent children are those who take an *authoritative* approach. Authoritative parenting, which combines warmth, acceptance, and responsiveness with age-appropriate rules, goals, and expectations, has been consistently linked to more positive development in adolescents. This holds whether we look at school success, self-confidence, positive mood, or avoidance of risk behaviors (Steinberg, 2001).

Parents as Models. Parents can serve as *models* of positive development for their adolescent children (Bandura, 2001). To the degree that they themselves are competent, confident, caring, connected to others, and of solid character (the *Five C's*), they both encourage these qualities in their children and provide clear evidence that developing these qualities is possible and worthwhile. Adolescents who have watched their parents deal confidently with a problem or take an unpopular stand on a moral issue or go out of their way to help a friend or neighbor are more likely to value such behaviors *and* to believe they are capable of emulating them.

At the same time that parents model positive attitudes and actions, their praise and approval encourages teens to follow their example. In addition, parents themselves generally derive internal feelings of satisfaction from possessing and exercising their positive qualities. Seeing this helps adolescents develop an attitude of intrinsic motivation for positive actions (Ryan & Deci, 2000). The teen comes to think, "I *want* to do this [develop a skill, speak up on an issue, connect with others, show compassion] because I'm the sort of person who gets personal satisfaction from learning to do things well, acting on my beliefs and values, having close relationships, and doing good turns for others."

The priorities that parents set can affirm that it is important for adolescents to pursue a path to positive development. At the same time, the ways they allocate family resources can make that path more accessible. For example, the great American composer George Gershwin (*Porgy and Bess, Rhapsody in Blue*) was born into a poor immigrant family. His parents had to struggle to get by, but they placed great importance on culture and the arts and thought they saw musical talent in their children. When George was 13, they scrimped to buy a piano and to give him and his brother Ira music lessons. The rest, as they say, is history (Jablonski, 1987).

Sources of Social Capital. The parents of adolescents, by their position and associations in the community, also act as a source of *social capital* (Bourdieu, 1985; Coleman, 1990; Sampson, 2001). When there is an opportunity to be grasped, a barrier to be overcome, or resources to be found, the parents may be able to help directly. But even if they are not, they may be able to find out who can and enlist that person's help. Is it just a matter of luck when the child of some famous pop star is "discovered" and signed to a recording contract? Sure, he or she may have talent. But there are probably dozens, even hundreds, of other teens who are just as talented, accomplished, and ambitious. What they lack, however, is any easy way to connect with adults in the music business who can encourage them, give them advice, and open doors for them.

It is not only celebrated parents who can accumulate social capital. Take, for instance, parents who make special efforts to get acquainted with their children's teachers and school officials. They are more likely to learn about after-school programs, summer institutes, scholarships, internships, and other opportunities that might benefit their teenager. They are also likely to find out more quickly if a problem is developing and to know the best people to go to for help in solving it.

Other Parental Contributions. Parents contribute to the positive development of their adolescent children in many other ways as well. If they show they hold expectations for their adolescents that are both positive and within reach, the teens will tend to adopt those expectations for themselves and strive to fulfill them. One factor that helps make parental expectations more realistic, and that also makes its own independent contribution to positive development, is parental monitoring (Kerr & Stattin, 2003). Keeping up with what is going on in a teen's life is a way of showing that one cares. As we saw in Chapter 5, effective parental monitoring depends on open, active lines of communication between parents and adolescents. Communication, in turn, depends on the parents being accessible. Busy lives may make this difficult, but those who make the effort make a difference. To illustrate this point, a recent study found that one of the best ways to predict how parents affect their adolescents' positive outcomes is simply to ask how many nights a week the family eats dinner together (Theokas & Lerner, 2006).

The lifestyle choices parents make help determine the extent and potential impact of other resources as well. If a family lives within walking or biking distance of schools, libraries, community centers, and cultural facilities, or has access to public transportation to them, adolescents are more likely to use and benefit from these resources (Theokas & Lerner, 2006). Parents who are active in school, neighborhood, and community organizations, and who socialize with the parents of their children's friends and other adults in the neighborhood, help create a web of engagement that amplifies the positive effects of school, neighborhood, and the wider community.

Enlisting Peers. Few aspects of adolescence stand out as clearly as the increased social influence of peers and friends, and few aspects of adolescence have led to as

► Parents who make sure they are accessible on a regular basis contribute to the positive development of their adolescents.

much concern and foreboding among adults. As we saw earlier, some observers have worried that adolescents form a separate *youth culture* with customs and values that undermine the goals of adult society (Brake, 1985). One reason this concern is so widespread is that parents, as well as other adults who deal with adolescents, often see themselves as competing for social influence with the adolescent peer group. Still more alarming, they see themselves coming off second-best.

Current teen fashions in music, dress, manners, and slang can be disturbing to those whose expectations and tastes were formed 10 or 20 or 30 years ago. Social and cultural changes, such as the easy availability of illicit substances and the trend toward earlier sexual initiation, add to adult concern about peer influence. And of course, many parents would like to believe that if their own teen is having problems, it is mostly the result of getting in with the wrong crowd.

Parallel with the worries of parents, much of the research on peer influence during adolescence has focused on the negative effects of associating with deviant peers (Dishion, McCord, & Poulin, 1999). We discussed the results of some of this research earlier, in Chapters 6 and 13. Unsurprisingly, we saw that hanging out with teens who drink, do drugs, have sex, start fights, and break the law is indeed linked to getting involved in these and other problem behaviors. Does that mean the influence of peers in general should be a source of worry?

In a word, no. On the contrary—under the right conditions, peers can be enlisted as a powerful resource for *positive* development (Benson et al., 2006). The peer group in general has an effect because it generates a positive or negative social climate, but those peers who have the strongest and most direct effects are an adolescent's friends (Rubin, Bukowski, & Parker, 2006). As we saw in Chapter 12, friendships develop by way of the paired processes of selection and socialization. On the whole, adolescents are drawn to others who have similar interests, attitudes, and values. Once they are friends, they tend to become *more* similar because each one affects and serves as a model for the others. This dynamic helps explain why having deviant peers as friends might lead to increased deviant behavior. On the other hand, it also explains why making friends who have positive qualities, such as inclusiveness, good conflict resolution skills, and an identification with prosocial goals, leads to more positive development.

One important factor in determining the sorts of peers adolescents become friends with is their experiences in the family. A longitudinal study of over 12,000 young adolescents in an area near Washington, DC, found strong links between the family and the quality of friendships. Those teens who were from homes with authoritative parenting and extensive parent-child communication tended to have more stable friendships with peers who were less deviant and more involved in school activities (Cook, Herman, Phillips, & Settersten, 2002).

◄ Friends who work together toward shared community goals improve both their friendship and their community.

The way friends spend their time together matters, too. Hanging out, listening to music, playing games, and doing homework together have their value for building intimacy, but more structured activities are more closely tied to indicators of positive development (Fredricks & Eccles, 2006; Hirsch, 2005). When friends take part in extracurricular and community-based organizations, the positive effects of friendship are amplified by the effects of working side-by-side with other adolescents toward a shared goal. In the next section, we look at some of the ways youth activities contribute to personal and social growth.

Youth Activities and Positive Development. Adolescents who take part in structured extracurricular and community activities open themselves up to a wide range of experiences that promote personal growth and positive development (Larson et al., 2004; Mahoney, Eccles, & Larson, 2004). For a start, they have a chance to explore talents and interests and develop skills that may lie outside the standard school curriculum. As we saw in Chapter 11, this sort of exploration is essential to the identity work that is such a central part of adolescence. One high school freshman on Club Day joined a service club, a political organization, chorus, the photography club, the yearbook, the Spanish club, a humanitarian group, and a folkdance society. She explained that they all sounded interesting. How could she know which she would find most involving unless she tried them all? Besides, she added, it was a great way to meet other teens with similar interests.

Not only other teens. Youth activities offer adolescents a way to connect to involved, caring adults who are not part of their family context. As they interact with advisors, coaches, and others who work with youth organizations, teens improve their interpersonal and communications skills. The relationships they build add to their social capital by giving them access to adult resources such as information, assistance, support, and encouragement (Jarrett, Sullivan, & Watkins, 2005). This is especially important for those whose parents have less extensive or less effective social networks, but most adolescents can gain from contact with an adult perspective that is different from the one they have grown up with.

Structured youth activities give adolescents an opportunity to develop teamwork and leadership skills (Larson, 2007). Working effectively with others calls for the ability to understand different perspectives, engage in shared decision making, and subordinate individual inclinations for the sake of accomplishing a shared goal. As teens grapple with different viewpoints, skills, and levels of motivation, they improve their communication and conflict resolution skills, as well as their ability to appreciate diverse orientations (Hansen, Larson, & Dworkin, 2003). They also develop better action skills, such as planning, problem solving, and getting things done (Larson & Wood, 2006). This chapter's Applications in the Spotlight on page 482 looks at some ways youth activities can be designed to offer teens more effective training in teamwork skills.

Applications in the Spotlight

Encouraging a Capacity for Teamwork

"Plays well with others."

We all remember how important that was in kindergarten. For today's young people, *working* well with others is still more vital. In an increasingly interdependent world, they need to know how to collaborate and work in teams (Partnership for 21st Century Skills, 2003). This is not so easy. Egocentrism gets in the way, as does the task of understanding the viewpoints of others. Even when that is taken care of, there is the need to coordinate the intentions and actions of team members for the sake of accomplishing shared goals. This may be particularly hard for teens who have grown up in the more individualistic cultures of Europe and America. They are not used to sharing decision making and effort, much less the credit for success.

How can the capacity for teamwork best be fostered? In a recent book chapter, Reed Larson (2007) says the answer is *structured youth activities*. For example, a recent study of over 2,000 11th graders found much more teamwork learning in youth programs than during schoolwork (Larson, Hansen, & Moneta, 2006). What features of a program encourage the development of teamwork skills, and what are the steps by which those skills develop?

To answer these questions, Larson and his co-workers followed students in an urban high school who signed up for a program to learn video and computer skills. In the first days of the program, the participants were paired off at computers and given structured assignments. At first they were constantly asking the leaders for advice, but soon they began to turn to one another instead. In the process of giving and getting help, a new group identity began to emerge. During the last half of the program, each participant created a short video. This meant choos-

ing and directing a crew of four others, so all the teens had direct experience of being in both the leader's and the follower's role.

By the end of the program, participants said they had learned three types of reciprocity between self and other. These were:

Helping and being helped. "Help, getting people to help you was a pretty way to success. You will always accomplish it through teamwork. That's what I think I learned."

Getting and giving feedback. "When you're working independently, it's only you thinking about it. But working with other people, you get more chances of finding other ways to express what you're doing."

Leading and being led. "I learned that you need to talk to others, you need to explain to them what do you want so it all comes correctly. Because if we don't say what you want to do, they're never gonna understand."

In all three types of reciprocity, the teens came to recognize a relationship of symmetry and equality between self and other. They were *exchanging* help, information, and direction, and these exchanges made their own work easier and better.

As for the adults, they encouraged self-expression and creativity, but kept the work moving forward, giving manageable assignments and monitoring progress. They encouraged participants to seek help from one another and to be sensitive in how they gave help. As Larson says,

> . . . youth are most empowered to engage in developmental change when adults strike an optimal balance between encouraging youth agency and providing structure and support that keeps youth on track.

—(LARSON, 2007)

Choosing to Take Part. Another benefit of participating in structured youth activities is that, as a general rule, teens do so as a matter of free choice. School is compulsory, and the classes you take are more or less set, but individuals can decide for themselves about extracurricular and after-school activities. They make a voluntary decision to join one organization instead of another and to commit their energies to its activities. This increases their sense of engagement with the organization and gives them a feeling of empowerment. Because their participation is self-determined, they are more likely to see their contributions as intrinsically motivated (Ryan & Deci, 2000).

Intrinsic motivation leads to longer and more intense involvement in the organization and its activities. Ongoing involvement matters. One recent study surveyed 6,000 adolescents, equally distributed across six ethnic groups (Native American, Black, Asian, Hispanic, White, and Multiracial). The developmental resource that was most closely linked to thriving was 3 hours or more of weekly participation in structured youth activities (Scales, Benson, Leffert, & Blyth, 2000). Generally, involvement becomes more concentrated in particular sorts of activities from middle childhood to early adolescence, as interests crystallize (Jacobs, Vernon, & Eccles, 2005). Both intensity of involvement and the number of different types of activities a young person is involved in are related to measures of positive development (Rose-Krasnor, Busseri, Willoughby, & Chalmers, 2006).

Today, the great majority of adolescents participate in at least one school-based community service project at some point, often as part of the school curriculum (Corporation for National and Community Service [CNCS], 2006). What are the positive elements of such projects, and what do teens gain from them? One recent study followed two groups of 6th graders who undertook community service projects. One group decided to focus on animal neglect and the other on raising awareness of child abuse. What counted most for both groups was that the project was guided by their own initiative and strengths, and that it encouraged cooperation and collective decision making. Those who took part emerged with a stronger sense of empathy and an intention to be involved in future community action (Lakin & Mahoney, 2006).

Sometimes, of course, taking part is not purely a matter of free choice. Some adolescents sign up for community service projects because they have heard it looks good on college applications. Others are pushed into an activity, such as sports or academic clubs, by the ambitions of their parents. Still others see some activity mainly as a way to get closer to someone they take a romantic interest in. In such cases, the developmental benefits that might be gained by taking part may be reduced, especially if the activity is seen as extrinsically motivated. It does happen, however, that teens start an activity for extrinsic reasons and then discover they enjoy participating and want to continue.

Activity, Development, and the "Big Three". Not every youth activity can be described as a youth *development* activity (Roth & Brooks-Gunn, 2003). According to current research, three features are especially important in fostering positive youth development. These "Big Three" are:

positive and sustained relationships between young people and adults;

activities that build competencies and skills; and

opportunities to use these skills productively by participating in community-based activities.

—(Lerner, 2005)

For example, getting together with a few friends after school to learn and practice clown skills would certainly be fun, and it might count as developing a new competency. Its overall positive effects, however, would probably be fairly limited. Signing up for an ongoing clown workshop with a positive and experienced adult, or even organizing it oneself, would add major benefits. If the long-term goal involved developing a show and performing it in elementary schools and hospital children's wards, it might well turn out to be a life-changing experience for the teens who participate.

Organized activities that feature these three qualities are more likely to provide positive developmental experiences, but the specific sorts of experiences they provide differ across different types of activity. A recent study looked at more than 2,200 11th graders in a diverse selection of Illinois high schools (Larson et al., 2006). Teens who participated in faith-based activities reported more experiences linked to identity, emotional regulation, and interpersonal development. Those in service activities, such as tutoring and community service programs, were more likely to cite teamwork, positive relationships, and increased social capital as benefits. Both sports and arts programs fostered a sense of initiative, but participation in team sports was also associated with high stress (Larson et al., 2006; Scanlan, Babkes, & Scanlan, 2005).

School and Community Resources. Adolescents live and act within their schools, neighborhoods, and communities, and the resources they have available to them in these contexts make a difference in their positive development. In a real sense, though, these resources are more remote from them. Families, groups of friends, even youth organizations and activities, are affected by individual teens even as they have an effect

Connect the Dots...

What organized activities do you feel had the greatest influence on your experience as an adolescent? What were the positive features or qualities of these activities that still stand out in your mind?

on the teens. The relationship is immediate and reciprocal. This is less the case with schools and still less so with larger social institutions and contexts where the direction of influence is more one-way. For instance, whether the local public library is open or closed evenings and weekends is an important matter for teens. As individuals, however, teens are not likely to have much impact when library hours are being decided.

Earlier in the chapter, we looked at a list of desirable qualities that make positive developmental settings more effective (Eccles & Gootman, 2002). The very first item on the list was *safety*. This is as crucial in school and in the neighborhood as it is within the family. If moving from one class to the next or going to the store for a quart of milk means constantly glancing over your shoulder and staying alert for impending threats, you are not going to have much mental energy left for composing songs, planning your future, or thinking up exactly the right birthday present for your best friend. Even the most thoughtfully operated community center is not much use if young people are afraid to make the journey there or back home afterwards.

Schools and neighborhoods share something else with families, too. Like authoritative parents, schools and communities that combine age-appropriate rules and expectations with warmth, responsiveness, inclusiveness, and respect promote positive development in children and adolescents. A positive, authoritative school climate encourages students to feel connected to the school and helps them learn better (Eccles, 2004). A stable neighborhood in which people interact more often, trust one another more, and have similar ideas about how children should be treated gives adolescents the sense of groundedness they need to venture out and explore their interests and potentials (Sampson, 2001; Sampson, Morenoff, & Gannon-Rowley, 2002).

Hardly anyone lives in a perfect neighborhood and goes to a perfect school. In an imperfect world, what characteristics can make a difference? For schools, a crucial factor is a sense of engagement or membership (Anderman & Freeman, 2004; Furrer, Skinner, Marchand, & Kindermann, 2006). When adolescents feel connected to their school, they feel more positive about the other students, the teachers, and the activities of the school. They also have a greater feeling of responsibility for the school and its reputation in the community. As we discovered in Chapter 7, one factor that promotes a sense of membership is school size (Crosnoe, Johnson, & Elder, 2004). Another factor is the ratio of teachers to students. This is a rough indicator of how likely students are to develop a personal relationship with a teacher (Theokas & Lerner, 2006). Other factors include peer and family support for learning and future aspirations (Appleton, Christenson, Kim, & Reschly, 2006).

In neighborhoods, physical and institutional resources, such as libraries, sports facilities, and community centers, matter a great deal (Benson et al., 2006; Sampson et al., 2002), as does the accessibility of these resources. Are they within walking distance or reachable by public transportation? Are they staffed by welcoming, responsive adults? Do their hours of operation fit with the schedules and needs of adolescents? Are their programs specifically designed to promote positive youth development?

Another neighborhood feature that promotes positive development is collective activity (Flanagan, in press). Local organizations that draw in adolescents and represent the needs of the neighborhood benefit young people in several ways. When teens take action to better their physical and social environment, the activity builds teamwork, initiative, and leadership skills. To the extent they achieve their goal, they improve their surroundings. They also develop a stronger sense of self-efficacy and social power. Those who act now are more likely to act again in the future. They come to think of themselves as people who *do* act when it is called for. By their example, they encourage other young people to get involved and take action (Larson & Wood, 2006). As a prominent team of researchers put it:

> Human beings develop through active engagement with their environment; by making choices and shaping that environment, they also direct their own development.

—(Hamilton, Hamilton, & Pittman, 2004, p. 15)

Summing Up...

Both internal and external resources are necessary for positive development. Self-confidence helps teens choose and engage in activities that fit their talents, interests, and goals. Settings that are safe, supportive, inclusive, and prosocial help foster positive development, as do authoritative parents who model the Five Cs and devote family resources to their children's development. Prosocial peers, structured community activities, and schools that promote a sense of membership also play an important role.

INITIATIVE, ENGAGEMENT, AND THE PURSUIT OF HAPPINESS

Many adolescents today spend much of their time being bored. In one classic study, young adolescents carried pagers for a week and noted what they were doing and how they felt when signaled at random intervals. At over one-fourth of these moments, they reported feeling bored (Larson & Richards, 1991). School homework was considered boring 40% of the time, and school classwork 32% of the time. More surprisingly, even creative activities, listening to music, watching television, and socializing with friends were rated as boring at least 20% of the time. Teens gave different explanations for their boredom in school ("English stinks") and out of school ("I had nothing to do"), but the quality of the mood was similar. They were uninvolved, unengaged, unexcited, and simply getting through the day. This was as true of honor students as of those with delinquency problems.

Recent research indicates that the general level of boredom actually goes up across adolescence, while the general level of interest goes down (Sharp, Caldwell, Graham, & Ridenour, 2006; Wigfield & Eccles, 2002). This holds not only for schoolwork, but for free time or leisure activities as well (Caldwell, 2005; Sharp et al., 2006). There is a paradox here. As we have seen repeatedly, adolescence is a period that offers new possibilities for self-chosen, self-motivated explorations of interests, relationships, and the world at large. Yet it seems that the curiosity and fascination with new experiences that are so much a part of childhood (Izard, 1991) too often get bottled up just when we would expect them to be expanding freely.

High levels of boredom and alienation are unpleasant and unproductive in themselves. More ominously, they often lead to problem behaviors, including substance use, casual sex, dangerous thrill-seeking, and antisocial conduct such as vandalism (Sommers & Vodanovich, 2000)—anything that can help kill time and obscure the inner emptiness. Yet it would be misleading to think of this disconnection from meaningful activity as an emotional disturbance or psychological problem. It is less a matter of negative development than an absence of *positive* development. As psychologist Reed Larson points out, these bored young people,

> . . . are not invested in paths into the future that excite them or feel like they originate from within. A central question of youth development is how to get adolescents' fires lit, how to have them develop the complex of dispositions and skills needed to take charge of their lives.
>
> —(LARSON, 2000, p. 170)

What would it take to get adolescents' fires lit? For Larson, a key element is **initiative**, which he sees as *the ability to be motivated from within to direct attention and effort toward a challenging goal* (Larson, 2000, p. 170). As he points out, American and European adolescents spend the larger part of their waking hours either in schoolwork or in leisure activities, especially with friends (Larson & Verma, 1999). Neither of these contexts offers a very good training ground for initiative. Schoolwork certainly calls for directed attention and effort, but it is not experienced as being motivated from within. Leisure activities, in contrast, are felt as being motivated from within, but they generally do not call for much in the way of attention and effort.

Initiative The ability to motivate oneself to strive toward a challenging goal.

Taking part in structured voluntary activities, however, is different (Larson & Wood, 2006). Arts, hobbies, and community service projects call into play all three aspects of initiative: intrinsic motivation, directed attention, and a challenging goal. As a result, these activities can give teens the experience of successfully exercising initiative. They also provide the encouragement teens need to direct their actions toward accomplishing self-relevant goals.

Taking an Interest

We can think of **interest** as the opposite of boredom. Interest is a basic tool adolescents use to select information from their environment (Brandstädter, 2006). It focuses attention on some things, events, and activities and away from others. Not coincidentally, one effect of encountering something interesting is that the pupils of the eyes widen, as if to let in more information (Gregory, 1998). Interest also has an important motivating function. When activities are interesting, people find it easier to concentrate, to persist, to learn, and to recall (Renninger, 2000). They also enjoy the activities more. This leads them to look for ways they can act on their environment to discover still other sources of interest (Wigfield & Eccles, 2002). In this way, an attitude of interest is part of a dynamic system that generates continued and even greater interest.

Some adolescents habitually find they are really interested by what they are doing. Others typically find what they are doing really boring. How else do these two groups differ? That question was addressed by a recent study (Hunter & Csikszentmihalyi, 2003). A representative sample of teens filled out forms about their activities and moods several times a day over the course of a week. Those whose score on interest was in the top one-fourth were then compared to those with a score in the bottom one-fourth.

The teens in the high interest group, those who were chronically interested by the activity they were engaged in, had sharply higher self-esteem than those who were chronically bored. They also had a much more internal locus of control. In agreeing with statements such as, "When I make plans, I am certain they will work," they showed a belief that they were able to affect their outcomes. In contrast, the bored group endorsed such statements as, "I do not have enough control over my life." The two groups also differed on both optimism and pessimism. Asked about the future, the interested group felt more confident, curious, enthusiastic, and powerful. In contrast,

Interest The quality that focuses attention on certain activities and motivates the person to engage in them.

▶ Taking part in interesting activities is linked to greater confidence and enthusiasm.

the bored group felt more doubtful, lonely, angry, and empty (Hunter & Csikszentmihalyi, 2003).

These findings have a close relationship to some of the ideas about achievement that we discussed in Chapter 9. Adolescents who maintain a high level of interest in their lives and activities are more likely to believe that what they do has an impact on what happens to them. This belief encourages them to try harder because they are convinced trying harder will make a difference. It gives them higher expectations for the future and greater confidence that they will be able to realize these expectations. In turn, confidence in a bright future encourages teens to conceive of challenging but achievable long-term goals and to develop concrete plans for bringing them about. These goals and efforts may be individual or shared with others. Either way, they offer high levels of interest, intrinsic motivation, and realistic challenge. These are precisely the qualities that can give rise to the intense state of involvement called *flow* (Csikszentmihalyi, 1990).

An Extended Engagement

As we have seen so far in this chapter, much of the discussion of positive youth development centers on the individual adolescent. How can teens be encouraged to achieve more of their intellectual, emotional, and social potential? What would help them see themselves as active participants in creating more meaningful lives for themselves? These are real and important questions. Think of all the urgent tasks of adolescence we have discussed in different chapters. Coming to terms with a changing body, changing feelings, and changing ways of thinking. Coping with parents. Coping with peers. Developing a sense of oneself as a person, as a friend, as a romantic partner—and the list goes on.

What is sometimes neglected on this list is the role of the adolescent as part of civil society. Adults tend to be convinced that young people today have little knowledge, interest, or involvement in social ideas and politics (Galston, 2001). Yet political systems depend on the support of their members, and the teens of today are the adult members of tomorrow. To fulfill their civic roles responsibly, they will need to develop and examine their values, moral beliefs, and social standards. Just as important, they will need to see themselves as active, engaged participants in the ongoing evolution of the community and society (Flanagan, in press; Youniss & Hart, 2005). The welfare of everyone benefits when adolescents are encouraged to develop a long-term **engagement** with their society.

How is that sense of engagement to be brought about? One activity that is said to foster civic development in adolescents is **community service**. We need to be cautious, though, as this term covers a wide array of activities. Some teens might organize a raffle and send the proceeds to disaster victims in a distant land. Meanwhile, others might be serving meals and tutoring children in a homeless shelter near their school. Both are worthy efforts, but they involve very different commitments and experiences.

Heinz Reinders and James Youniss (2006a) have studied the effects of community service programs intensively. In their view, service experiences are most likely to have a lasting impact when:

there is direct interaction with people in need;

the organization provides a clear rationale for service;

participants are exposed to new ideas and beliefs during service; and

adolescents experience being actors who are capable of changing things and of reaching at least some of their goals.

Summarizing their findings, Reinders and Youniss argue that

. . . community service involving interaction with people in a state of need increases self-awareness in adolescents and gives them a feeling of being actively involved; this, in turn, leads to a more prosocial personality and the readiness for civic engagement.

Connect the Dots...

To what extent does taking an interest in activities appear to be a question of one's individual personality, of cultural attitudes ("Man, life's a drag!"), or of features of the setting? How would you go about helping a teen who is chronically bored to become more interested?

◄ **Learning Objective 14.10**
What do teens gain from engagement with society?

Engagement An outcome when teens see themselves as active and welcome participants in the development of their community.

Community service A wide array of organized activities intended to help link adolescents to broader circles of their society.

▶ Community service projects that let teens directly help people in need lead to greater involvement and more positive benefits.

Community service can provide an ideological and organisational framework that links adolescents to the broader sphere of society, and thereby helps them to regard themselves as part of a society's past, present and future.

—(REINDERS & YOUNISS, 2006a, p. 204)

This chapter's Research in the Spotlight on page 489 details a longitudinal study of high school students who took part in a variety of service projects and how being in direct contact with others in need affected the impact their experiences had on them.

Be Well, Be Happy

▶ **Learning Objective 14.11**
What factors promote happiness, and why is hope so central to striving for it?

Earlier in the chapter, we discussed the goals of positive youth development as encouraging the development of the Five Cs—Competence, Confidence, Character, Connection, and Caring—as well as a Sixth C, Contributions, that is said to follow from the exercise of the other five (Eccles & Gootman, 2002; Lerner, 2004; Roth & Brooks-Gunn, 2003). This is a useful way to describe the skills, attitudes, and virtues that adolescents need to acquire if they are to live a good life and thrive in a democratic society. As Lerner and his colleagues say,

An integrated moral and civic identity and a commitment to society beyond the limits of one's own existence enable thriving youth to be agents both in their own, healthy development and in the positive enhancement of other people and of society.

—(LERNER, DOWLING, & ANDERSON, 2003, p. 172)

The ultimate aim of positive youth development efforts can be expressed in another way, too. It is to offer adolescents, whatever their background, the possibility of gaining the resources they need to achieve **happiness**. This means not only living well, but living well the life that is *good for one to live* (Lapsley & Narvaez, 2006).

Understanding what that might be brings in profound moral and ethical questions. Some might argue that such questions are beyond the grasp of the social sciences. I certainly do not pretend to offer authoritative answers to them here. But we can take a look at what social scientists have learned about the nature and sources of happiness. We can also see what these findings tell us about optimal paths to positive youth development.

Since at least the time of Aristotle, philosophers have been concerned with how to achieve the good life (Russell, 1945). Over the centuries, two major conceptions of happiness have emerged. One, *hedonism*, sees happiness as resulting from the pursuit

Happiness Living a life that is good for one to live and that may include the pursuit of pleasure, the pursuit of meaning, and the pursuit of engagement.

Community Service and Civic Development

The great majority of middle schools and high schools in the United States make some form of community service available to their students, often as a required part of the curriculum. According to a national survey, 38% of young people, or some 10.6 million youth in the United States, report current or past participation in school-based service (CNCS, 2006). These programs are seen as a way to "build active citizens."

Does it work? When adolescents take part in a community service project, does the experience in fact lead to greater civic involvement? What features of community service give it more impact, and why? These questions were addressed in a recent longitudinal study by Heinz Reinders and James Youniss (2006b). The participants were students at two suburban Catholic high schools near Washington, DC. Most were White, with 19% Hispanic, Black, or Asian. Students had to put in 20 to 30 hours of service, such as tutoring, raising money, doing clerical tasks, working at soup kitchens, and visiting the elderly, each year.

At the end of 11th grade, students wrote a description of the service experience during that year that had given them the best moment. They also responded to questions about examining their attitudes and beliefs and feeling they had contributed to the service organization. Four months later, in the fall of 12th grade, they were given a survey that included questions about being helpful to a stranger. Near the end of 12th grade, another survey included items asking how likely they were to vote, work in a political campaign, and boycott a product or service.

Reinders and Youniss reasoned that two aspects of service experiences would have particular significance: whether students came in direct contact with recipients, and whether recipients were in obvious states of need. They then examined the ways type of service, increased self-awareness, and feelings of having contributed were related to helpfulness and civic engagement. Figure R14.1 shows the result. The solid arrows represent significant paths from one element to the next, and the dotted arrows are paths that were not supported by the analysis.

What this suggests is that:

those who interacted directly with the needy were more likely to feel they had made a contribution to the organization;

those who felt they had made a contribution were more likely to reexamine their ideas about themselves;

those who reexamined their ideas about themselves were more likely to be helpful to strangers; and

those who were helpful to strangers were more likely to say they intended to vote, work in political campaigns, and take part in boycotts.

This study has several important implications. The first is that even when community service is a school requirement, it can have a positive effect on the self-concept, civic attitudes, and future intentions of adolescents. It is most effective, however, when it gives them an opportunity to experience themselves as having the capacity to directly help others who clearly need help.

Figure R14.1   Links Between Service and Civic Engagement
Community service in high school has been linked to later civic engagement.

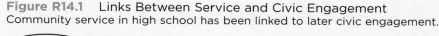
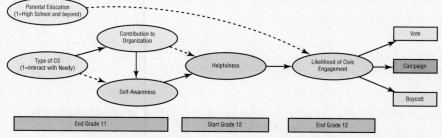

Source: Figure 1, "School-Based Required Community Service," by H. Reinders and J. Youniss. *Applied Developmental Science 10,* 2–12. © 2006. Used by permission.

of pleasure. The other, called *eudaimonia,* says that people are happiest when they give meaning to their lives by developing their potentials and using them for the greater good (Ryan & Deci, 2000a; Waterman, 1993). In recent years, a third possibility has also been described. This is the pursuit of *engagement,* the psychological state that accompanies highly involving activities and that we have been referring to as *flow* (Csikszentmihalyi, 1990; Seligman, 2002).

In one recent study (Peterson, Park, & Seligman, 2005), adults said how much they agreed with statements that represented these three approaches to happiness. They also rated their general satisfaction with life. Each of the orientations, pursuit of pleasure, pursuit of meaning, and pursuit of engagement, individually predicted life satisfaction. The highest life satisfaction scores, however, came from those who highly endorsed *all three* orientations, with meaning and engagement carrying the greatest weight. What this suggests is that these orientations do not necessarily conflict with one another. Ideally, they should complement one another.

In adolescents, a number of desirable psychological characteristics have been linked to higher life satisfaction, including internal locus of control, high self-esteem, intrinsic motivation, self-efficacy, mastery orientation, optimism, and prosocial attitudes (Park, 2004). If this list sounds familiar, or even redundant, it is because it is so similar to earlier descriptions of the benefits of positive youth development programs. We can add that supportive parenting, engagement in challenging activities, and positive interactions with significant others also contribute to the development of happiness (Park, 2004).

Some of these factors that promote happiness may be easier to change than others, but in principle all of them can be addressed. More generally, happiness levels can be altered by *intentional activity* (Lyubomirsky, Sheldon, & Schkade, 2005). This activity could be behavioral (starting an exercise program, doing deliberate acts of kindness), cognitive (pausing to count one's blessings), volitional (devoting effort to meaningful causes), or a combination of all three (Sheldon & Lyubomirsky, 2006). Increasing happiness matters; its positive byproducts benefit individuals, families, and communities. Those who are happier are also physically and psychologically healthier, more creative and productive, more cooperative, and more prosocial (Lyubomirsky, King, & Diener, 2005).

Can all adolescents benefit from activities and programs intended to increase their chances to achieve happiness? The evidence we have looked at says they could, but to take advantage of the opportunities, they must first be able to **hope**. They must allow themselves to imagine being happier, to want it, and to expect that it may actually come to pass (Gillham & Reivich, 2004; Valle, Huebner, & Suldo, 2006). Once they begin to believe they can exert some control over events, they will be better able to formulate goals, make plans, and begin to take charge of their lives—but first they must hope. Erik Erikson (1964, p. 115) said it well:

> Hope is both the earliest and the most indispensable virtue inherent in the state of being alive . . . [I]f life is to be sustained hope must remain, even where confidence is wounded, trust impaired.

Hope The capacity to imagine a better life, to want it, and to believe in the possibility that it can be achieved.

SUMMARY

The **positive youth development** approach sees a healthy adolescence as more than the absence of problems and considers adolescents to be capable, active individuals who contribute to the fulfillment of their potential.

Learning Objective 14.1 How do adolescents deal with different sorts of stress?

The changes of adolescence raise difficult life issues for many teens. These issues generate **stress** that may be acute or may become chronic. There is reason to believe that adolescents become biologically more sensitive to the effects of stress and its many negative consequences.

Learning Objective 14.2 How is gender linked to coping strategies?

Research on **coping** looks at how teens handle problems and the stress these problems create. **Problem-focused coping** is a more likely response when a threatening situation seems open to change. It involves trying to manage the threat and seeking practical support. **Emotion-focused coping** is a more likely response when a threatening situation seems impossible to change or avoid. It involves trying to reduce the negative emotions created by the threat and seeking emotional support.

Adolescents are flexible in switching between problem-focused and emotion-focused coping, depending on the situation.

Girls are more likely to prefer emotion-focused strategies and boys to prefer problem-focused strategies. Both parents and peers are important sources of encouragement and support in stressful situations. Teens with warm, responsive parents are more likely to use active, engaged coping behaviors.

Learning Objective 14.3 What adaptational systems help promote resilience?

Successful coping increases a teen's sense of self-efficacy and, over time, leads to a more general ability to rise above problems. This ability is called **resilience**.

Coping skills and resilience help an adolescent to survive in the face of difficulties, but what does it take not just to survive but to thrive?

Learning Objective 14.4 How do the Five Cs and the sixth C contribute to thriving?

The basic elements of thriving are the **Five Cs:** Competence, Confidence, Character, Connection, and Caring. As teens develop the Five Cs over time, they move toward expressing the Sixth C, Contributions, by having a positive impact on their family, their community, and their society.

Learning Objective 14.5 What qualities do parents and teens think are most important to well-being?

While parents, youth workers, and adolescents themselves agree on the importance of positive development, they differ in what qualities they consider most crucial. For teens, school-related and psychological characteristics ranked high, while adults stressed more social qualities such as engagement and connection with others.

Learning Objective 14.6 How can teens interact with their contexts to enhance both the self and the setting?

Thriving is a dynamic process in which positive elements in the context or setting encourage positive change in the individual, and those individual changes, in turn, have an impact on the setting.

To thrive, adolescents benefit from both internal and external resources.

Learning Objective 14.7 What internal resources help adolescents develop positively?

Internally, the ability to take advantage of opportunities through selection and effective use advances personal development. Qualities such as critical thinking, positive self-regard, mastery motivation, optimism, and prosocial values are elements in a dynamic process in which positive experiences strengthen the personal resources that make further positive experiences more likely.

Learning Objective 14.8 How do school and community resources contribute to positive development?

Externally, settings with such features as physical and psychological safety, clear rules and expectations, supportive relationships, and opportunities to belong and to build skills contribute more toward positive development.

Parents who are authoritative and who themselves exemplify the Five Cs encourage teens to develop intrinsic motivation for positive actions. Parents who give priority to the positive development of their teens and who make an effort to provide them with the benefits of social capital make thriving more likely. Peers contribute to one another's positive development when they take part in organized youth activities and work together toward shared positive goals.

Structured activities that include positive sustained relationships between teens and adults, activities that build competencies, and ways to use skills productively provide more positive developmental experiences. Schools that foster a sense of membership promote positive development, as do neighborhoods that make physical and institutional resources, such as libraries, sports facilities, and community centers, accessible and welcoming.

Positive development is more than a way of doing things, it is a way of being that includes initiative, interest, and engagement.

Learning Objective 14.9 How do initiative and interest combat boredom?

Initiative is an internal motivation that directs effort toward meaningful and challenging goals. Taking an **interest** in events and activities becomes part of a dynamic system that generates continued and increasing interest.

Learning Objective 14.10 What do teens gain from engagement with society?

For teens, **engagement** with civil society involves seeing themselves as active, involved members of their community whose own welfare, and that of their families, friends, and neighbors, is affected by their efforts and contributions.

Learning Objective 14.11 What factors promote happiness, and why is hope so central to striving for it?

The ultimate aim of positive youth development can be expressed as offering adolescents resources that increase their chances to achieve **happiness**, but to take advantage of their opportunities, they must first be able to **hope**.

KEY TERMS

Positive youth development (466)	Problem-focused coping (468)	Initiative (485)	Happiness (488)
Stress (467)	Emotion-focused coping (468)	Interest (486)	Hope (490)
Coping (468)	Resilience (470)	Engagement (487)	
	Five Cs (472)	Community service (487)	

Glossary

Acceptance/responsiveness. A dimension of child rearing that includes giving praise, warmth, and affection and paying attention to children's wants, needs, and concerns. **p 144**

Accommodation. For Piaget, the process of changing one's cognitive structures in response to new information or experiences. **p 107**

Achievement. The accomplishment of a goal, generally by using personal skills and resources to overcome difficulties. **p 292**

Achievement training. Encouraging children to strive to do things well. **p 293**

Active genotype-environment correlation. A situation in which children seek out settings that are congenial to their genetically influenced traits. **p 159**

Active learning. Interactions with new information, for example, by rephrasing material or trying to explain it to someone else. **p 6**

Adolescence-limited offenders. Adolescents who become involved in antisocial activities during adolescence and typically do not continue there into adulthood. **p 438**

Adolescent growth spurt. A period of rapid physical development that lasts from about 10 to 16 for girls and 12 to 18 for boys. **p 70**

Adoption study. Research that compares adopted children with their biological and adoptive parents to assess the effects of nature and nurture. **p 159**

Adrenarche. The time very early in puberty when the adrenal glands begin to produce a hormone called *DHEA*. **p 69**

Adult resemblance hypothesis. The idea that young adolescents who seem more adult-like will be treated more as adults, for better or worse. **p 86**

Age segregation. The social custom of grouping people, such as children and adolescents, on the basis of their chronological age. **p 177**

Age stratification. The process of defining groups, such as adolescents, on the basis of their age and treating them differently. **p 12**

Alcoholism. A medical condition that stems from alcohol dependence and carries serious risks to physical and psychological health. **p 447**

Androgens. Male sex hormones, principally *testosterone*, secreted mainly by the testes. **p 68**

Androgyny. Having both typically masculine and typically feminine psychological characteristics. **p 353**

Anorexia nervosa. A serious, sometimes fatal, disorder in which a distorted view of one's weight and body shape and an intense fear of getting fat leads to starving oneself. **p 452**

AP class. An intensive high school class that leads to a nationwide Advanced Placement exam in a subject; students who do well may get course credit in the subject when they reach college. **p 231**

Applications. Ways of taking knowledge about adolescents that is derived from research and putting it to practical use. **p 5**

Apprenticeship. A system in which adolescents divide their time between school and on-the-job training, leading to a certificate or diploma in their chosen career field. **p 246**

Assimilation. Piaget's term for the process by which one tries to understand a new experience by making it fit with existing knowledge or understandings. Also, a process in which members of an ethnic minority renounce their culture of origin and identify with the majority culture. **pp 107, 264**

Asynchronicity. The fact that, during early adolescence, different parts of the body change at different times and different rates. **p 72**

Attachment. The emotional bond that develops between parents and children; may include *secure, resistant, avoidant,* and *disorganized/disoriented* attachment. **p 153**

Attribution theory. An approach to achievement that focuses on the causes people see as responsible for their successes and failures. **p 308**

Authoritarian parents. Those who are demanding, but not responsive. **p 146**

Authoritative parents. Those who are both responsive and demanding. **p 145**

Autonomous morality. Piaget's term for the later phase of moral development, in which rules are seen as changeable and an actor's intentions are given more weight than the outcome of an action. **p 378**

Autonomy. An ability to act independently and a willingness to take responsibility for one's actions. **p 151**

Average. In nomination studies, a label for those who are near the middle on both social preference and social impact. **p 190**

Barometric self-esteem. Temporary changes in positive or negative feelings about the self that occur in response to particular incidents. **p 363**

Baseline self-esteem. A level of positive or negative feelings about the self that is fairly stable over time. **p 362**

Behavioral autonomy. The ability to make one's own decisions and take responsibility for them. **p 152**

Behavioral control. The rules and limits parents place on their child's activities. **p 152**

Behavioral genetics. A method for inferring the influence of genes and environment by studying people who are genetically related. **p 158**

Bicultural. A term for adolescents who have successfully integrated their identifications with both their culture of origin and the majority culture. **p 264**

Biological determinism. The idea that what we do is set or determined by our biological or genetic makeup. **p 32**

Body image. The ways people perceive, think of, and feel about their bodies. **p 94**

Bulimia. An eating disorder in which the person alternates between binge overeating and purging. **p 452**

Bullying. The deliberate victimization of another person through verbal, social, or physical attacks. **p 196**

Busing. The practice of shifting students of different racial backgrounds from one neighborhood to another in order to increase racial balance in schools. **p 227**

Capable self. An integrated description of the attitudes, habits, and characteristics that have been shown to positively affect achievement. **p 313**

Care orientation. For Gilligan, approaching moral questions with the primary goal of preserving positive relationships among people. **p 381**

Career maturity. A person's readiness to make informed, age-appropriate career decisions that depends on age, stage of career development, and situation. **p 317**

CASI. Computer-assisted self-interview, a research technique in which people are interviewed via computer, avoiding direct interpersonal contact. **p 414**

Causal stability. A belief that the cause of an outcome is relatively stable or variable. **p 309**

Cerebral cortex. The outermost layer of the brain that is the site of most higher-order brain functions. **p 91**

Charter schools. Publicly financed schools that function outside the ordinary public school structure. **p 229**

Clique. A small, close-knit group of friends, generally of the same age, sex, and social status. **p 200**

Code switching. The cognitive and linguistic changes that take place when someone who is bilingual moves from speaking one language to another. **p 376**

Cofigurative culture. A society in which social change is fairly rapid and both older and younger generations come to have knowledge and skills that the other needs to acquire. **p 179**

Cognitive-behavioral therapy. An approach to treatment that focuses on changing the self-defeating ways an adolescent interprets and responds to life events. **p 458**

Cognitive development. The ways the thinking process changes with age and experience. **p 106**

Cognitive stage. In Piaget's view, a distinctive way of thinking, typical of a particular age and based on a particular system of logic. **pp 35, 107**

Cohorts. Groups of people who were born at about the same time, such as in a particular calendar year. **p 52**

Collectivism. A worldview that focuses on the connectedness of the person to the family or group and stresses the importance of upholding the goals, norms, and beliefs of the group. **p 261**

Community service. A wide array of organized activities intended to help link adolescents to broader circles of their society. **p 487**

Comorbidity. Different problems that tend to show up at the same time in the same person. **p 433**

Competence motivation. The desire to control events and have an impact on the world that begins to show itself in early childhood. **p 292**

Competence-performance gap. The fact that people do not consistently do as well at some task as they are capable of doing. **p 108**

Comprehensive high school. High schools that try to educate the whole pool of adolescents by placing them in different *tracks* according to their presumed abilities and future economic roles. **p 211**

Concrete operations. Piaget's third stage, in which those in middle childhood become able to think about more than one aspect of a problem at a time and to solve it through mental operations. **p 107**

Conformity. Doing as others are doing or as others urge one to do, whether or not it fits with personal inclinations, values, and beliefs. **p 181**

Consumerism. A concern with having or getting the clothes, toys, and other stuff that are currently fashionable. **p 15**

Controllability. A belief that the cause of an outcome is something the person can deliberately affect. **p 310**

Controversial. In nomination studies, a label for those who are very high in social impact, but neutral in social preference. **p 190**

Conventional morality. For Kohlberg, a level of judgment in which right and wrong are defined in terms of the standards of others, such as parents and society. **p 379**

Coping. The various ways adolescents develop to handle situations that create stress. **p 468**

Correlational study. Research in which characteristics of the participants are observed or measured, and then the relationships among these characteristics are examined. **p 49**

Co-rumination. A process in which friends talk about their problems and negative feelings at length, sometimes prolonging or amplifying the feelings. **p 346**

Critical thinking. Connecting new information with existing understanding, analyzing points of agreement, and using the result to make effective decisions. **p 132**

Cross-cultural research. Research that involves comparing how the same process or phenomenon is expressed or experienced by people from different cultural groups. **p 260**

Cross-pressures. A situation in which someone is subject to competing social influences from different sources, such as parents and peers. **p 188**

Cross-sectional study. Research in which groups representing different ages are studied at the same point in time. **p 51**

Crowd. A social category for which membership is based largely on observed characteristics, reputation, and stereotypes. **p 202**

Crystallized intelligence. The ability to draw on accumulated knowledge and judgment. **p 124**

Cultural capital. The advantages young people gain from being introduced to art, music, libraries, museums, and other cultural resources. **p 300**

Cultural diversity. The variety of customs, beliefs, expectations, and behaviors that are typical of adolescents from different cultural and ethnic backgrounds. **p 5**

Cultural frame. The attitudes, ways of thinking, and manners of relating to others that are associated with speaking a particular language. **p 376**

Culture. A relatively stable system of shared norms, beliefs, values, and behaviors that is passed along across generations. **p 257**

Deep processing. The association of new information with material that is already in memory, especially material that has personal relevance. **p 6**

Defense mechanisms. According to Anna Freud, unconscious tools for controlling sexual and other dangerous psychological impulses. **p 33**

De-identification. A process in which siblings deliberately define themselves as different from one another by taking up different interests, activities, friends, and so on. **p 162**

Delinquency. The legal term for actions by juveniles that violate the law. **p 434**

Demandingness/control. A dimension of child rearing that includes setting rules, stating expectations clearly, and monitoring the child to make sure that rules are followed and expectations are met. **p 145**

Dependent variable. In an experiment, the factor that is observed or measured. **p 50**

Depression. A mood disturbance marked by lengthy periods of deep sadness. **p 455**

Detachment. The process by which adolescents break away from their parents. **p 156**

Developmental systems theory. Lerner's approach, which emphasizes the ways the adolescent plays an active role in dealing with social systems. **p 39**

Developmental tasks. The skills, attitudes, and social functions that a culture expects members to acquire at a particular point in their lives. **p 9**

Deviance hypothesis. The idea that those who enter puberty at a time noticeably different from their peers will be negatively affected. **p 86**

Diathesis-stress model. The theory that depression results from a combination of a predisposing vulnerability (*diathesis*) and the impact of negative events (*stress*). **p 456**

Disabled. Those students who have physical, cognitive, or developmental problems that interfere with their progress in school. **p 231**

Disequilibrium. In a family system, a situation in which there is significant change in a family member or in a relationship between family members. **p 141**

Distancing hypothesis. The idea that as children become more sexually mature, they have less contact with parents. **p 87**

Divided attention. Attending to more than one stimulus at the same time. **p 120**

Dropouts. Teens who leave high school before graduating and receiving a diploma. **p 232**

Drug dependence. Developing a strong craving for a particular drug and, in many cases, needing growing amounts of it to achieve the same effect. **p 444**

Drug withdrawal. A set of unpleasant physical or mental symptoms that are experienced when someone with a drug dependence stops taking the drug. **p 444**

Early adolescence. The period from ages 11 to 14 that roughly coincides with the middle or junior high school years. **p 9**

Ecological systems. The interacting structures both within the adolescent, such as physical, cognitive, and emotional functions, and in the adolescent's surroundings, such as family, peers, school, and the community. **p 4**

Ecological theory. Bronfenbrenner's view of development, which focuses on the ways an adolescent's social settings interact to influence development. **p 39**

Educated consumers. Those whose understanding of the field of adolescence and of the ways knowledge is gathered allows them to judge the strengths and weaknesses of new findings. **p 5**

Education vouchers. An approach that allows parents to use public education funds toward the cost of placing their children in private schools. **p 229**

Egocentrism. For Piaget, the process of assuming that other people's points of view are the same as one's own. **p 113**

Emotional autonomy. The ability to function without having to rely on others, such as parents, to provide a sense of comfort and security. **p 152**

Emotion-focused coping. Trying to manage the negative psychological effects of a stressful situation that does not seem open to being changed. **p 468**

Empathy. The capacity to experience similar feelings to those someone else is experiencing. **p 383**

Enculturation. The process by which children and adolescents acquire the attitudes, beliefs, and psychological aspects of their culture. **p 262**

Endocrine system. A system of glands that produce hormones, as well as parts of the brain and nervous system that regulate hormone production. **p 67**

Engagement. An outcome when teens see themselves as active and welcome participants in the development of their community. **p 487**

Estrogens. Female sex hormones, principally *estradiol*, secreted mainly by the ovaries. **p 68**

Ethnic group. A group of people who share characteristics such as race, religion, national origin, linguistic background, cultural heritage, and customs. **p 263**

Ethnic identity. An understanding of oneself in terms of one's ethnic and cultural background. **p 373**

Ethnicity. A person's cultural background and the customs, values, and attitudes that go along with it. **p 373**

Ethnocentrism. The tendency to see the world from the standpoint of one's own cultural values and assumptions. **p 258**

Ethnographic study. Research in which the investigator spends long periods of time in close contact with the people being studied. **p 47**

Evocative genotype–environment correlation. A situation in which a child has genetically influenced traits that evoke particular responses from others. **p 159**

Evolutionary psychology. An approach that tries to understand how current characteristics and behaviors may have been influenced by evolutionary forces. **p 32**

Executive control structures. Mental representations of goals, outcomes, and strategies that make it possible to approach problems more effectively. **p 118**

Expectancy. A subjective estimate of the likelihood that a particular action will lead to a particular result. **p 305**

Experience Sampling Method. A research approach in which participants record what they are doing, thinking, and feeling whenever they are signaled at random intervals. **p 47**

Experiment. Research in which some factor is varied and the effect on other factors is observed. **p 50**

Exploration stage. For Super, the period from mid-adolescence to young adulthood that involves translating knowledge and ideas about oneself into career leanings and occupational aims. **p 316**

Extended family. A family that includes grandparents, aunts and uncles, and other kin, as well as parents and children. **p 143**

Externalizing problem. Turning one's difficulties toward the external world, for example in the form of aggressive or antisocial behavior. **p 433**

Extracurricular activities. School sponsored and supported voluntary activities that are not part of the formal educational curriculum. **p 233**

Extrinsic motivation. Undertaking an activity for the sake of the expected outcome or consequence. **p 306**

Five Cs. The psychological qualities of Competence, Confidence, Character, Connection, and Caring that form the basic goals of positive youth development. **p 472**

Flow. A state of deep involvement and enjoyment that may occur when a task calls for solid skills and presents high but realistic challenges. **p 312**

Fluid intelligence. The ability to reason quickly and effectively about novel problems. **p 124**

Flynn effect. The trend for average scores on standardized intelligence tests to increase steadily over time. **p 129**

Forgotten Half. A term used to describe those adolescents, currently about one-third, who finish high school but do not go on to college. **p 246**

Formal operations. The fourth stage according to Piaget, which enables adolescents and adults to use an abstract system of logic to understand the world. **pp 35, 108**

Fuzzy-trace theory. The theory that we often store information in memory in inexact traces that preserve only the gist of the information. **p 121**

Gateway hypothesis. The idea that the use of relatively mild illicit drugs, such as marijuana, makes it more likely that a person will go on to use more dangerous hard drugs. **p 448**

Gender bias. A distortion that results from using habitual assumptions that reflect traditional gender roles. Similar distortions may arise from *ethnic, cultural,* and *class bias.* **p 55**

Gender consistency. A person's awareness that gender is a permanent or invariant characteristic of an individual. **p 332**

Gender difference. A difference between males and females that is thought to be based mainly on cultural and social factors. **p 328**

Gender identity. Those aspects of a person's sense of self that relate to masculinity or femininity. **p 332**

Gender intensification. The process in where young adolescents come under greater pressure to conform to traditional gender roles. **pp 87, 335**

Gender role. A set of shared cultural expectations that outlines the attitudes and behaviors a typical male or female should display. **p 328**

Gender schema theory. A set of ideas that concerns the ways children, adolescents, and adults gather and organize information about gender, and then use this information to guide their attitudes and actions. **p 332**

Gender typing. The process by which children come to take on the gender roles expected in their society. **p 329**

Gene-environment interaction. A situation in which a particular genetic predisposition is expressed in one environment but not in another, or in which a particular environment has a certain effect on those with one set of genes but not on those with a different set. **p 160**

Generalizable. A description of information gathered from a *representative sample* that can be extended to apply to the population as a whole. **p 46**

Generalized other. For G. H. Mead, someone's internalized summary of the ways others have responded to that person in social interactions. **p 361**

Generation gap. The idea that there is a sharp divide between the value systems and goals of adolescents and adults. **p 178**

Genotype. A person's genetic makeup, as contrasted with the *phenotype*, or the way that genetic makeup is expressed in the person. **p 158**

Gifted. Those students who are considered to have unusually strong talents or abilities that make more challenging educational efforts advisable. **p 231**

Globalization. The tendency for economic, social, and political events and trends in one part of the world to have an impact on lives in other, distant parts of the world. **p 5**

Gonads. The sex glands: the *ovaries* in females and the *testes* in males. **p 68**

Goodness of fit. The relationship between the demands and expectations of parents and the temperament of the child. **p 147**

Growth stage. For Super, the period during childhood and early adolescence that involves acquiring knowledge of work in general and particular occupations. **p 316**

Happiness. Living a life that is good for one to live and that may include the pursuit of pleasure, the pursuit of meaning, and the pursuit of engagement. **p 488**

Heteronomous morality. Piaget's term for the earlier phase of moral development, in which authority figures determine what is right and wrong. **p 378**

High-quality friendship. A relationship that has many positive features and few negative features. **p 396**

Home schooling. A situation in which parents educate their children at home, generally with some oversight from local or state education authorities. **p 230**

Homophobia. A pronounced attitude of fear or distaste for feelings of sexual attraction toward one's own sex or for those who are thought to have such feelings. **p 346**

Hope. The capacity to imagine a better life, to want it, and to believe in the possibility that it can be achieved. **p 490**

Hopelessness. A result of seeing negative events as uncontrollable and lasting that may lead to depression. **p 457**

Hormones. Chemical substances that circulate through the bloodstream and regulate many body functions. **p 67**

Hostile attributional bias. A tendency to interpret ambiguous cues and situations as reflecting hostile intent and to respond aggressively to them. **pp 190, 439**

HPG axis. A *feedback loop* that regulates the hormones involved in puberty and growth. **p 68**

Hypothalamus. A part of the brain that monitors and regulates many bodily functions, including hormone production. **p 67**

Hypothesis testing. A model for gaining knowledge that involves using a theory to generate a prediction or hypothesis, and then collecting information that bears on whether the prediction is correct or not. **p 43**

Hypothetico-deductive reasoning. A way of reasoning in which a person makes a logical prediction based on some supposition, and then checks the prediction against reality. **p 108**

Identity. The psychological structure that gives people a sense of personal continuity across situations and across their individual history. **p 367**

Identity commitment. Choosing a belief or course of action and making a personal investment in it. **p 369**

Identity crisis. For Erikson, an adolescent's response to the tension between the need to explore what is unique about oneself and the wish to become someone who will get respect and validation from family, friends, and community. **p 367**

Identity diffusion. A reluctance or refusal to consider identity issues; also called *identity confusion*. **p 369**

Identity exploration. For Marcia, examining alternatives in a particular area of activity, such as occupation or beliefs and values. **p 369**

Identity foreclosure. A process in which adolescents commit themselves to the identities assigned to them by their parents and community, while shutting off other possible paths of development. **p 368**

Identity status. For Marcia, the presence or absence, in different areas of activity, of *exploration* efforts and *commitment*. p 369

Identity style. The different ways individuals seek out and deal with information that relates to questions of identity. **p 370**

Idiosyncratic transitions. Changes take place at unpredictable points during adolescence, such as a parental divorce or a serious illness. **p 8**

Imaginary audience. For Elkind, an aspect of adolescent egocentrism that involves believing that one is the focus of others' attention and involvement. **p 113**

Immanent justice. The belief that wrongdoing is always punished. **p 378**

Independence training. Encouraging children to do things on their own. **p 293**

Independent variable. In an experiment, the factor that is varied. **p 50**

Index crimes. Serious violations of the law, so called because they are included on official indexes of criminal activity. **p 434**

Indifferent parents. Those who are neither responsive nor demanding. **p 146**

Individualism. A worldview that focuses on the uniqueness and independence of autonomous individuals and stresses the importance of personal rights, goals, and needs. **p 261**

Induction. A disciplinary approach in which parents explain the effects of an action, stressing how it affected others and its connection to moral values. **p 384**

Inductive reasoning. The process of drawing a general conclusion from particular facts or instances. **p 109**

Indulgent parents. Those who are responsive, but not demanding. **p 146**

Information processing. The ways information enters the person's cognitive system, gets processed, and is stored for future use. **p 35**

Informational social influence. Acting like others because of a belief that others have better information about the correct thing to do. **p 182**

Informed consent. The ethical requirement that research participants understand what they will be expected to do and freely agree to take part. **p 54**

Ingroup bias. The tendency to see members of one's own group more as individuals and those in other groups more in terms of a social stereotype. **p 55**

Initiative. The ability to motivate oneself to strive toward a challenging goal. **p 485**

Instrumental substance use. Taking a drug as a means to reach some socially acceptable goal, such as relieving pain or falling asleep. **p 443**

Insulin-like growth factor-I (IGF-I). A substance produced in the liver that may be linked to the onset of puberty. **p 70**

Integration. A process in which members of an ethnic minority retain their identification with their culture of origin while *also* identifying with the majority culture. **p 264**

Intelligence quotient (IQ). A score that represents how a person's performance on measures of school-related skills (or *IQ tests*) compared with the performance of others who are similar in age. **p 123**

Interest. The quality that focuses attention on certain activities and motivates the person to engage in them. **p 486**

Internal working models. The basic positive or negative concepts that children form about other people and about themselves. **p 154**

Internalizing problem. Turning one's difficulties inward, toward the self, for example, in the form of depression or an eating disorder. **p 433**

Intimacy. An emotional sense of attachment to someone with whom one shares personal knowledge and a concern for one another's well-being. **p 390**

Intimacy versus isolation. According to Erikson, the most important psychosocial crisis that young adults face. **p 393**

Intrinsic motivation. Undertaking an activity for the sake of the interest or enjoyment that the activity brings. **p 306**

Inventionism. The view that the concept of adolescence was promoted in the early 20th century as a way of setting off young people from the adult world. **p 8**

Junior high school. Typically, a school that includes grades 7, 8, and 9, intended to meet the special needs of young adolescents and be a bridge between elementary and high schools. **p 215**

Justice orientation. For Gilligan, approaching moral questions with the primary goal of finding fair, objective resolutions to conflicts. **p 381**

Latchkey teens. Adolescents who are without adult supervision after school and on vacation days, usually because parents work outside the home. **p 168**

Late adolescence. The period from ages 18 to 22 that roughly coincides with the college years, often referred to as *emerging adulthood*. **p 9**

Latency period. For infections, a period of time after a person has contracted the disease, but before any noticeable symptoms appear. **p 421**

Learned helplessness. A condition that may follow failure if the person comes to believe that the outcome is uncontrollable and that further efforts are pointless; also a deeply pessimistic attitude that results from interpreting negative trends as stemming from internal, global, and stable causes and hence uncontrollable. **pp 311, 457**

Leptin. A protein secreted by fat cells that may play a role in the timing of menarche. **p 70**

Libido. In Freud's theory, the life force that is responsible for such drives as hunger, thirst, and sex. **p 33**

Life-course-persistent offenders. Adolescents whose antisocial behavior first appears in childhood and tends to continue into adulthood. **p 438**

Life-cycle service. The custom in preindustrial Europe that sent young people to live and work away from their families during adolescence. **p 11**

Locus of causality. A belief that the cause of an outcome is something about the person (internal) or about the situation (external). **p 308**

Longitudinal study. Research in which the same participants are studied at several points over a length of time. **p 52**

Looking-glass self. Cooley's term to indicate that we find out about ourselves by observing the way others respond to us in our interactions. **p 361**

Love withdrawal. A disciplinary approach in which parents threaten the child with a loss of affection or approval. **p 384**

Low-quality friendship. A relationship in which negative features, such as conflict, hostility, and rivalry, outweigh positive features such as trust, loyalty, and warmth. **p 396**

Mainstreaming. The practice of integrating students with disabilities into regular classrooms. **p 231**

Marginalization. A process in which members of an ethnic minority reject both their culture of origin and the majority culture. **p 264**

Mastery orientation. A focus on learning and mastering tasks and on personal improvement. Also called *task-goal orientation*. **pp 218, 310**

Masturbation. Sexual self-stimulation. **p 413**

Media. The various means, such as books, magazines, radio, television, films, and the Internet, by which information, experiences, and entertainment are communicated to the public. **p 273**

Menarche. The time at which a girl has her first menstrual period. **p 70**

Mentor. A non-familial adult who provides a young person with guidance and support. **p 241**

Metabolism. The rate at which the body uses energy. **p 99**

Metacognition. The ability to think about one's own thinking and reflect on the mental tools one has available for learning and solving problems. **pp 36, 130**

Middle adolescence. The period from ages 14 to 18 that roughly coincides with the high school years. **p 9**

Middle school. A school that typically includes grades 6, 7, and 8, and that has become more common than junior high school in recent years. **p 215**

Moral exemplar. An individual whom others regard as outstanding in moral commitment, personality, and character. **p 384**

Moral identity. The extent to which someone believes that being moral and acting morally are essential characteristics of his or her sense of self. **p 384**

Motive. A stable, ongoing personal sensitivity to a particular sort of emotional consequence. **p 304**

Motive to avoid failure (M_{af}). A sensitivity to the negative feelings that arise from failing at a task and a need to avoid those feelings. **p 305**

Motive to succeed (M_s). A need for sensitivity to the positive feelings that arise from succeeding at a task. **p 305**

Multiple intelligences. In Gardner's view, different abilities that are specific to particular domains and that are not necessarily closely related to one another. **p 128**

Multiracial schools. The increasingly common schools in which three or more different racial/ethnic groups each make up at least 10% of the enrollment. **p 228**

Myelination. The development of sheaths of myelin insulation along the axons of brain cells, making their operation more sensitive and precise. **p 91**

Naturalistic observation. Watching and taking notes on people in real-life settings, sometimes without their awareness that they are being watched. **p 47**

Need for intimacy. According to Sullivan, a desire to develop a relationship with a close friend or *chum* that emerges during the preadolescent years. **p 392**

Need for sexuality. For Sullivan, a need that emerges in response to the biological changes of puberty and the social changes of the adolescent peer group. **p 392**

Need to belong. The drive to be part of the social group and to feel accepted by others. **p 185**

Negative correlation. A relationship in which the associated factors tend to move in the opposite direction from one another. **p 50**

Negative feedback loop. A system in which a change in one connected factor leads to a change in the opposite direction in the other connected factor. **p 140**

Negative identity. Acting in ways that are guaranteed to arouse disapproval, but that also guarantee attention and concern. **p 369**

Neglected. In nomination studies, a label for those who are very low in social impact and neutral in social preference. **p 190**

Nicotine. A highly toxic substance that is one of the principal active ingredients in cigarettes, snuff, and other forms of tobacco. **p 447**

Nocturnal emission. A spontaneous ejaculation of seminal fluid while asleep; a "wet dream." **p 83**

Normative social influence. Acting like others because there is a social norm that prescribes doing as others do. **p 182**

Normative transitions. Changes that most adolescents go through at roughly the same point in their development, such as puberty and entering high school. **p 8**

Nuclear family. A single set of parents and their children. **p 143**

Oedipus complex. The period in which a child develops a desire to gain sexual possession of the opposite-sex parent and to eliminate the rival parent of the same sex; in girls, often referred to as the Elektra complex. **p 33**

Operant conditioning. A basic form of learning in which the likelihood of a behavior being repeated is affected by its consequences. **p 38**

Oppositional peer culture. The rejection of values and goals of the majority culture based on a belief that discrimination makes it pointless to try to conform to the majority. **p 382**

Oral sex. Oral stimulation of a partner's genitals. **p 414**

Ovum. The female sex cell, or egg, located in the ovary within a structure called a *follicle*. **p 73**

Passive genotype–environment correlation. A situation in which parents create environments that are associated with their own genetically influenced traits, which are similar to those of their child. **p 159**

Peak height velocity. The fastest change in height, which occurs at around 12 for girls and 14 for boys. **p 71**

Peer. Someone who is at roughly the same level in age, social status, or level of functioning with another. **pp 15, 174**

Perfectionism. An exaggerated need to do things just right and to look just right that is a risk factor for eating disorders. **p 453**

Performance orientation. A focus on competitive success and a tendency to interpret outcomes as a sign of ability of lack of ability. Also called *ability-goal orientation*. **pp 218, 311**

Permissive societies. Those societies that take it for granted that children and adolescents will be active sexually. **p 410**

Personal epistemology. The different ways children, adolescents, and adults think about what knowledge is and what it is based on. **p 131**

Personal fable. In Elkind's view, believing that one's experiences are unique and that one is exempt from the usual consequences of one's actions. **p 114**

Phase transition. A period of change in a family system during which minor events may have far-reaching consequences. **p 141**

Pheromones. Airborne chemicals believed to signal emotional states to others. **p 75**

Pituitary. An endocrine gland that is considered the master gland of the endocrine system. **p 68**

Popular. In nomination studies, a label for those who are high in both social preference and social impact. **p 190**

Population. In a research project, the group that is the focus of the research. **p 45**

Population pyramids. A way of showing in graphic form the proportions of people in a society who fall into different age categories. **p 17**

Positive correlation. A relationship in which the associated factors tend to move in the same direction as one another. **p 50**

Positive feedback loop. A system in which an increase or decrease in one connected factor leads to a change in the same direction in the other connected factor. **p 140**

Positive youth development. An approach to studying adolescence that focuses on factors that encourage young people to develop healthy attitudes and become engaged in productive, life-enhancing activities. **p 466**

Possible selves. People's sense of the different selves they might become under various circumstances and with various courses of action. **p 361**

Postconventional morality. For Kohlberg, a level of judgment in which right and wrong are defined in terms of internalizing universal principles of ethics and justice. **p 379**

Postfigurative culture. A culture in which social change is slow and younger generations need to acquire the knowledge and skills of their elders. **p 179**

Power assertion. A disciplinary approach in which parents use their dominant position to control the child's actions. **p 384**

Preconventional morality. For Kohlberg, a level of judgment in which right and wrong are defined in terms of external punishments and rewards. **p 379**

Prefigurative culture. A culture in which social change is very rapid and older generations need to replace obsolete knowledge and skills with those of the younger generation. **p 179**

Premature affluence. The experience of having disposable income with few responsibilities, which may give adolescents unrealistic attitudes toward money. **p 246**

Preoperational stage. The second of Piaget's stages of cognitive development, marked by the emergence of an ability to represent objects and events symbolically. **p 107**

Problem-focused coping. Trying to manage a stressful situation by analyzing it and mobilizing the means to change it in a positive direction. **p 468**

Progressive education. An approach that sees equality and democratic citizenship as central goals of the educational system. **p 211**

Psychoactive substances. Those drugs which affect a person's psychological state by way of altering brain functions, for example alcohol, opiates, and hallucinogens. **p 444**

Psychological control. Trying to control children by acting on their thoughts and feelings. **p 152**

Psychosexual stages. According to Freud, changes in the source and target of the sex drive during childhood and adolescence that create the oral, anal, phallic, latency, and genital stages. **p 33**

Psychosocial moratorium. A period in which adolescents are given a degree of freedom to explore their impulses, talents, interests, social roles, and beliefs without fear that minor offenses against convention will bring drastic consequences. **p 368**

Psychosocial stages. For Erikson, distinctive ways that developmental changes in the child, adolescent, or adult interact with the social environment to make particular issues more salient. **p 34**

Puberty rites. Cultural rituals such as the Jewish *Bar* and *Bas Mitzvah* or the Hispanic *quinceañero* that mark a child's passage to adolescence. **p 88**

"Raging hormones." The belief that many of the problems of adolescents can be traced to their changing hormone levels. **p 93**

Reaction range. A biologically influenced spread in some characteristic, such as height, within which an individual will end up. **p 76**

Recreational substance use. Taking a drug in order to experience the effects of the drug. **p 443**

Reductionism. An approach to scientific explanation that reduces complex processes to more elementary components. **p 92**

Reference group. A set of people that someone looks to for information about what to do and what constitutes doing well, as well as evaluative comments and praise. **p 182**

Rejected. In nomination studies, a label for those who are low in social preference, but high in social impact. **p 190**

Rejection sensitivity. A tendency to be on the lookout for and to detect rejection in interpersonal relationships. **p 406**

Relational aggression. Trying to hurt someone by attacking their personal and social relationships, for example, through ridicule, exclusion, and malicious gossip. **p 193**

Representative sample. A sample that is basically similar to the intended population. **p 45**

Reproductive fitness. The Darwinian principle that genetic characteristics that make the survival of one's offspring more likely will gradually become more common in the population. **p 32**

Resilience. The capacity to develop normally and positively under difficult conditions. **p 470**

Restrictive societies. Those societies that control or forbid any sexual expression before adulthood or marriage. **p 410**

Rumination. A process of dwelling on negative events, recalling other negative events from the past, and amplifying the long-term significance of negative factors. **p 457**

Sample. A group, drawn from a population, on which research is conducted. **p 45**

Scaffolding. For Vygotsky, adapting one's guidance and support to the current level of knowledge and understanding of the learner. **p 117**

School choice. An approach that makes it easier for parents and students to change from one public school to another. **p 229**

School climate. The general learning atmosphere in a school, including attitudes of students and staff, order and discipline, and student participation. **p 219**

School membership. The sense that students have of being connected and committed to their school and its positive functioning. **p 220**

Secular trend. The tendency in recent centuries for puberty to occur at younger ages. **p 76**

Selection. A process by which adolescents tend to choose to associate with friends who are similar to them. **p 295**

Selective attention. Concentrating on one task or experience while blocking out awareness of others. **p 120**

Self-care. Adolescents who are left unsupervised during the hours after school lets out. **p 236**

Self-concept. The organized set of thoughts, ideas, and perceptions that people hold about themselves. **p 359**

Self-Directed Search. A measure of vocational type that yields a "Holland Code" representing the person's three most important types. **p 318**

Self-disclosure. The process in which individuals communicate to others intimate information about their experiences and feelings. **p 390**

Self-esteem. The set of positive or negative evaluations and feelings that people hold about themselves. **p 362**

Self-handicapping. Placing obstacles in the way of one's performance in order to avoid having to attribute a possible failure to low ability. **p 311**

Self-regulated learning. Exercising personal control over the steps that lead to developing skills and improving understanding. **p 130**

Self-reinforcement. Rewarding or punishing oneself for what one considers a good or bad outcome of one's actions. **p 184**

Semirestrictive societies. Those societies that prohibit premarital sex, but do not strictly enforce this prohibition. **p 410**

Sense of community. The feeling of close connection and shared purpose that unites the person with others in the group. **p 253**

Sensorimotor stage. The stage Piaget says is characteristic of infancy, in which experience of the world is based on perceptions and motor activity. **p 107**

Separation. A process in which members of an ethnic minority identify only with their culture of origin and reject the majority culture. **p 264**

Sequential study. Research in which participants from different age cohorts are studied at several points over time, in effect combining cross-sectional and longitudinal approaches. **p 53**

Sex difference. A difference between males and females that is thought to be based mainly on biological factors. **p 328**

Sexual minorities. Those whose sexual orientation is other than exclusively heterosexual. **p 419**

Sexual orientation. The sexual attraction a person feels toward those of the same or the other sex. **p 419**

Sexually transmitted infections (STIs). Diseases, such as chlamydia, herpes, and HIV/AIDS, that are spread mainly through sexual contact. **p 421**

Sibling collusion. A situation in which siblings form coalitions that encourage deviant or problem behavior. **p 162**

Social capital. A network of personal and social relationships that makes it easier to be effective in accomplishing one's goals. **p 241**

Social class. A person's place or status in society, as indicated by wealth, income, education, living conditions, prestige, and influence. **p 269**

Social cognition. The ability to reason effectively about people and social relationships. **p 194**

Social cognitive theory. An approach that sees observing what others do and what happens to them as important ways of learning. **p 38**

Social comparison. The process of comparing one's status or performance to that of a particular reference group. **p 184**

Social impact. The degree to which a person is chosen either as liked *or* disliked. **p 189**

Social perspective taking. The capacity to infer or imagine the thoughts, perceptions, and emotions of other people. **p 195**

Social preference. In nomination studies, the degree to which a person is chosen as liked (and not chosen as disliked) by others in the social group. **p 189**

Social sciences. Fields of investigation and knowledge, such as psychology, sociology, and anthropology, that use the scientific method to study questions about people and their societies. **p 41**

Socialization. The processes through which children acquire the attitudes, beliefs, behaviors, and skills that their parents, peers, and culture consider appropriate. **pp 138, 262, 295, 331**

Sociometric techniques. Research tools used to study the structure and inner connections of social groups. **p 189**

Sperm. The male sex cell, produced in huge quantities by the testes beginning at puberty. **p 74**

Spermarche. A boy's first ejaculation of seminal fluid. **p 83**

Stage-environment fit. The ways developmental changes in an adolescent interrelate with changes in the adolescent's social environment, such as parental rules and demands. **p 5**

Stage termination hypothesis. The idea that girls who enter puberty early suffer because they did not have time to accomplish the normal tasks of childhood. **p 86**

Standards-based education. An approach that sets society-wide educational standards that all schools and students are expected to meet. **p 212**

Statistical significance. A measure that indicates that a particular result or relationship is strong enough that it is unlikely to be the result of chance or accident. **p 58**

Status offense. An action, such as truancy or buying cigarettes, that is against the law for those who are considered minors, but not for adults. **p 433**

Stereotype threat. A factor that may interfere with the performance of those who belong to groups that are the target of negative stereotypes by arousing anxiety that they will fail and in this way confirm the stereotype. **p 302**

Storm and stress (in German, "Stürm und Drang"). The belief that adolescence is necessarily a very tumultuous period. **p 11**

Stress. A physical, hormonal, and psychological response to the perception of danger or threat. **p 467**

Superego. In Freud's theory, the structure of personality that incorporates the moral standards of parents and society and enforces them through feelings of guilt. **p 383**

Synaptic pruning. A process in which brain circuits that are less used are eliminated, leading to a faster, more efficient cognitive system. **p 91**

Tanner stages. A system used to rate the development of secondary sex characteristics during puberty. **p 74**

THC. Tetrahydrocannabinol, the chief psychoactive ingredient in marijuana and hashish. **p 447**

Tracking. The practice, now less common, of assigning students to a particular curriculum or set of courses on the basis of their presumed abilities. **p 218**

Triarchic theory of intelligence. Sternberg's notion that that practical, creative, and analytic intelligence represent different, independent abilities. **p 127**

Twin study. Research that compares identical and fraternal twins to assess the effects of nature and nurture. **p 158**

Urbanization. The trend for young people, especially those in developing countries, to leave the countryside and move to cities. **p 21**

Uses and gratifications. An approach to understanding how adolescents choose which media to attend to and what they get from their choices. **p 277**

Vocational type theory. The idea that people enjoy a career more and are more successful in it if their occupation is a good match with their personality and interests. **p 317**

Work ethic. The belief that working brings positive personal benefits, such as a strengthened character, in addition to whatever goods the work produces. **p 244**

Working models. According to Bowlby, implicit expectations about relationships that form in infancy and affect attitudes toward others. **p 394**

Youth culture. The idea that adolescents as a group have customs, values, and beliefs that separate them from the culture of adults. **p 180**

Zone of proximal development. Vygotsky's term for tasks that children cannot yet accomplish on their own but could succeed at with help from someone more skilled. **p 117**

References

Abbassi, V. (1998). Growth and normal puberty. *Pediatrics* (Suppl.), *102*(2), 507–511.

Abma, J. C., Martinez, G. M., Mosher, W. D., & Dawson, B. S. (2004). *Teenagers in the United States: Sexual activity, contraceptive use, and childbearing, 2002.* Hyattsville, MD: National Center for Health Statistics.

Aboud, F. E., & Mendelson, M. J. (1996). Determinants of friendship selection and quality: Developmental perspectives. In W. M. Bukowski, A. F. Newcomb, & W. W. Hartup (Eds.), *The company they keep: Friendships in childhood and adolescence.* New York: Cambridge University Press.

Abrams, L. S., & Stormer, C. C. (2002). Sociocultural variations in the body image perceptions of urban adolescent females. *Journal of Youth and Adolescence, 31,* 443–450.

Abramson, L. Y., & Alloy, L. B. (2006). Cognitive vulerability to depression: Current status and developmental origins. In T. E. Joiner, J. S. Brown, & J. Kistner (Eds.), *The interpersonal, cognitive, and social nature of depression.* Mahwah, NJ: Erlbaum.

Abramson, L. Y., Seligman, M. E. P., & Teasdale, J. D. (1978). Learned helplessness in humans: Critique and reformulation. *Journal of Abnormal Psychology, 87,* 49–74.

Abu-Lughod, L. (1993). *Writing women's worlds: Bedouin stories.* Berkeley, CA: University of California Press.

Adalbjarnardottir, S., & Hafsteinsson, L. G. (2001). Adolescents' perceived parenting styles and their substance use: Concurrent and longitudinal analyses. *Journal of Research on Adolescence, 11,* 401–423.

Adamczyk, A., & Felson, J. (2006). Friends' religiosity and first sex. *Social Science Research, 35,* 924–947.

Adams, G., & Berzonsky, M. (Eds.) (2002). *Handbook on adolescence.* New York: Blackwell.

Adamuti-Trache, M., & Andres, L. (2002). Issues of retention of B.C. young women through the science and engineering pipeline. In *Women in a knowledge-based society: Proceedings of the 12th International Congress on Women in Engineering and Science.* CD-ROM available from the International Network of Women in Engineering and Science, at www.inwes.org.

Adan, A. M., & Felner, R. D. (1995). Ecological congruence and adaptation of minority youth during the transition to college. *Journal of Community Psychology, 23,* 256–269.

Adelman, C. (1999). *Answers in the tool box: Academic intensity, attendance patterns and bachelor's degree attainment.* Washington, DC: U.S. Department of Education.

Adelson, J. (1979, January). Adolescence and the generalization gap. *Psychology Today,* 33–37.

Adler, N. E., Ozer, E. J., & Tschann, J. (2003). Abortion among adolescents. *American Psychologist, 58,* 211–217.

Adler, P. A., & Adler, P. (1998). *Peer power: Preadolescent culture and identity.* New Brunswick, NJ: Rutgers University Press.

Ainsworth, M. D. S., Blehar, M. C., Waters, E., & Wall, S. (1978). *Patterns of attachment: A psychological study of the Strange Situation.* Chicago: The University of Chicago Press.

Ainsworth-Darnell, J. W., & Downey, D. B. (1998). Assessing the oppositional culture explanation for racial/ethnic differences in school performance. *American Sociological Review, 63,* 536–553.

Ajrouch, A. J. (2004). Gender, race, and symbolic boundaries: Contested spaces of identity among Arab American adolescents. *Sociological Perspectives, 47,* 371–391.

Akers, J. F., Jones, R. M., & Coyl, D. D. (1998). Adolescent friendship pairs: Similarities in identity status development, behaviors, attitudes, and intentions. *Journal of Adolescent Research, 13,* 178–201.

Akos, P., & Levitt, D. H. (2002). Promoting healthy body image in middle school. *Professional School Counseling, 6,* 138–144.

Alan Guttmacher Institute. (2004). *U.S. teenage pregnancy statistics: Overall trends, trends by race and ethnicity, and state-by-state information.* New York: Author.

Alberts, A., Elkind, D., & Ginsberg, S. (2007). The personal fable and risk-taking in early adolescence. *Journal of Youth and Adolescence, 36,* 71–76.

Alderman, M. K. (2003). *Motivation for achievement: Possibilities for teaching and learning* (2nd ed.). Mahwah, NJ: Erlbaum.

Alexandre-Bidon, D., & Lett, D. (1999). *Children in the Middle Ages, fifth–fifteenth centuries.* Notre Dame, IN: University of Notre Dame Press.

Allen, J. P. (1989). Social impact of age mixing and age segregation in school: A context-sensitive investigation. *Journal of Educational Psychology, 81,* 408–416.

Allen, J. P., Marsh, P., McFarland, C., McElhaney, K. B., Land, D. J., Jodl, K. M., & Peck, S. (2002). Attachment and autonomy as predictors of the development of social skills and delinquency during midadolescence. *Journal of Consulting and Clinical Psychology, 70,* 56–66.

Allen, J. P., Porter, M. R., & McFarland, F. C. (2006). Leaders and followers in adolescent close friendships: Susceptibility to peer influence as a predictor of risky behavior, friendship instability, and depression. *Development and Psychopathology, 18,* 155–172.

Allen, R. J. (1992). Social factors associated with the amount of school week sleep lag for seniors in an early starting urban high school. *Sleep Research, 21,* 114.

Allgood-Merton, B., & Stockard, J. (1991). Sex-role identity and self-esteem: A comparison of children and adolescents. *Sex Roles, 25,* 129–139.

Alsaker, F. D. (1995). Timing of puberty and reactions to pubertal changes. In M. Rutter (Ed.), *Psychosocial disturbances in young people: Challenges for prevention.* Cambridge, UK: Cambridge University Press.

Alsaker, F. D., & Flammer, A. (1999). *The adolescent experience: European and American adolescents in the 1990s.* Mahwah, NJ: Erlbaum.

Alspaugh, J. W. (1998). Achievement loss associated with the transition to middle school and high school. *Journal of Educational Research, 92,* 20–25.

Alspaugh, J. W. (2000). The effect of transition grade to high school, gender, and grade level upon dropout rates. *American Secondary Education, 29,* 2–9.

Alt, N. M., & Peter, K. (2002). *Private schools: A brief portrait.* Washington, DC: National Center for Education Statistics.

Altschul, I., Oyserman, D., & Bybee, D. (2006). Racial-ethnic identity in mid-adolescence: Content and change as predictors of academic achievement. *Child Development, 77,* 1155–1169.

Alwin, D. F. (1988). From obedience to autonomy: Changes in traits desired in children, 1928–1978. *Public Opinion Quarterly, 52,* 33–52.

Amato, P. R., & Booth, A. (1996). A prospective study of divorce and parent-child relationships. *Journal of Marriage and the Family, 58,* 356–365.

Amato, P. R., & Keith, B. (1991). Parental divorce and the well-being of children: A meta-analysis. *Psychological Bulletin, 100,* 26–46.

Amato, P. R., Loomis, L. S., & Booth, A. (1995). Parental divorce, marital conflict, and offspring well-being during early adulthood. *Social Forces, 73,* 895–915.

Ambady, N., Paik, S. K., Steele, J., Owen-Smith, A., & Mitchell, J. P. (2004). Deflecting negative self-relevant stereotype activatiion: The effects of individuation. *Journal of Experimental Social Psychology, 40,* 401–408.

American Association of University Women. (1992). *The AAUW report: How schools short-change girls.* Washington, DC: Author.

American Council on Education. (2002). *Access and persistence.* Washington, DC: Author.

American Medical Association. (2003). *Healthy youth 2010.* Available: www.ama-assn.org/ama1/pub/upload/mm/39/hy2010revised.pdf.

American Psychiatric Association. (2000). *Diagnostic and statistical manual of mental disorders: DSM-IV-TR.* Washington, DC: Author.

American Psychological Association. (1992). Ethical principles of psychologists and code of conduct. *American Psychologist, 47,* 1597–1611.

American Psychological Association. (2004). *APA Policy Statement: Sexual orientation, parents, and children.* Available: www.apa.org/pi/lgbc/policy/parents.html.

American School Health Association. (1991). *Sexuality education within comprehensive school health education.* Kent, OH: Author.

American Social Health Association. (1996). *Gallup study: Teenagers know more than adults about STDs.* Durham, NC: Author.

Ames, C. (1992). Classrooms: Goals, structures, and student motivation. *Journal of Educational Psychology, 84,* 261–271.

Amrein, A. L., & Berliner, D. C. (2002). High-stakes testing, uncertainty, and student learning. *Education Policy Analysis Archives, 10*(18). Retrieved March 17, 2003 from http://epaa.asu.edu/epaa/v10n18/.

Amsel, E., Bowden, T., Cottrell, J., & Sullivan, J. (2005). Anticipating and avoiding regret as a model of adolescent decision-making. In J. E. Jacobs & P. A. Klaczynski (Eds.), *The development of decision-making: Cognitive, sociocultural, and legal perspectives.* Mahwah, NJ: Erlbaum.

Amundsen, S. W., & Diers, C. J. (1969). The age of menarche in Classical Greece and Rome. *Human Biology, 41,* 124–132.

Anderluh, M. B., Tchanturia, K., Rabe-Hesketh, S., & Treasure, J. (2003). Childhood obsessive-compulsive personality traits in adult women with eating disorders: Defining a broader eating disorder phenotype. *American Journal of Psychiatry, 160,* 242–247.

Anderman, E. M. (2002). School effects on psychological outcomes during adolescence. *Journal of Educational Psychology, 94,* 795–809.

Anderman, E. M., Austin, C. C., & Johnson, D. M. (2003). The development of goal orientation. In A. Wigfield & J. Eccles (Eds.), *Developmental perspectives on achievement motivation.* New York: Academic Press.

Anderman, E. M., Maehr, M. L., & Midgley, C. (1999). Declining motivation after the transition to middle school: Schools can make a difference. *Journal of Research and Development in Education, 32,* 131–147.

Anderman, L. H., & Anderman, E. M. (1999). Social predictors of changes in students' achievement goal orientations. *Contemporary Educational Psychology, 25,* 21–37.

Anderman, L. H., & Freeman, T. M. (2004). Students' sense of belonging in school. In P. R. Pintrich & M. L. Maehr (Eds.), *Motivating students, improving schools: The legacy of Carol Midgley.* New York: Elsevier.

Anderson, A., Hamilton, R. J., & Hattie, J. (2004). Classroom climate and motivated behaviour in secondary schools. *Learning Environments Research, 7,* 211–225.

Anderson, C. A. (2004). An update on the effects of violent video games. *Journal of Adolescence, 27,* 113–122.

Anderson, C. A., & Bushman, B. J. (2001). Effects of violent video games on aggressive behavior, aggressive cognition, aggressive affect, physiological arousal, and prosocial behavior: A meta-analytic review of the scientific literature. *Psychological Science, 12,* 353–359.

Anderson, D. A., & Hamilton, M. (2005). Gender role stereotyping of parents in children's picture books: The invisible father. *Sex Roles, 52,* 145–151.

Anderson, D. R., Huston, A. C., Schmitt, K. L., Linebarger, D. L., & Wright, J. C. (2001). Early childhood television viewing and adolescent behavior: The recontact study. *Monographs of the Society for Research in Child Development, 66*(1), Serial No. 264.

Anderson, E., Greene, S. M., Hetherington, E. M., & Clingempeel, W. G. (1999). The dynamics of parental remarriage: Adolescent, parent, and sibling influences. In E. M. Hetherington (Ed.), *Coping with divorce, single parenting, and remarriage: A risk and resiliency perspective.* Mahwah, NJ: Erlbaum.

Anderson, R. N., & Smith, B. L. (2005, March 7). Deaths: Leading causes for 2002. *National Vital Statistics Report, 53*(17).

Andersson, T., & Magnusson, D. (1990). Biological maturation in adolescence and the development of drinking habits and alcohol abuse among young males: A prospective longitudinal study. *Journal of Youth and Adolescence, 19,* 33–42.

Andreou, E. (2000). Bully/victim problems and their association with psychological constructs in 8- to 12-year-old Greek schoolchildren. *Aggressive Behavior, 26,* 49–56.

Angus, D. L. (1988). Historical development of age stratification in schooling. *Teachers College Record, 90,* 211–236.

Annest, J. L., Mercy, J. A., Gibson, D. R., & Ryan, G. W. (1995). National estimates of nonfatal firearm-related injury. Beyond the tip of the iceberg. *Journal of the American Medical Association, 273,* 1749–1754.

Anokhin, A. P., Lutzenberger, W., Nikolaev, A., & Birbaumer, N. (2000). Complexity of electrocortical dynamics in children: Developmental aspects. *Developmental Psychobiology, 36,* 9–22.

Anonymous (2001). Tracking Asia's teens: *Ad Age Global* and ACNielson assembled a panel of leading marketers in Hong Kong to discuss Asia's youth market. *Ad Age Global,* Dec. 1, 2001, 26.

Anselmi, D. L. (1998). *Questions of gender.* New York: McGraw-Hill.

Appleton, J. J., Christenson, S. L., Kim, D., & Reschly, A. L. (2006). Measuring cognitive and psychological engagement: Validation of the Student Engagement Instrument. *Journal of School Psychology, 44,* 427–445.

Archer, S. L. (1982). The lower age boundaries of identity development. *Child Development, 53,* 1551–1556.

Archer, S. L. (1989). The status of identity: Reflections on the need for intervention. *Journal of Adolescence, 12,* 345–359.

Archibald, A. B., Graber, J. A., & Brooks-Gunn, J. (2002). Pubertal processes and physiological growth in adolescence. In G. R. Adams & M. Berzonsky (Eds.), *The Blackwell handbook of adolescence.* Cambridge, MA: Blackwell.

Ariès, P. (1962). *Centuries of childhood.* New York: Knopf.

Armesto, J. C. (2002). Developmental and contextual factors that influence gay fathers' parental competence: A review of the literature. *Psychology of Men and Masculinity, 3,* 67–78.

Armstrong, T., & Costello, E. (2002). Community studies on adolescent substance use, abuse, or dependence and psychiatric comorbidity. *Journal of Consulting and Clinical Psychology, 70,* 1224–1239.

Arnett, J. (1992). Reckless behavior in adolescence: A developmental perspective. *Developmental Review, 12,* 339–373.

Arnett, J. J. (1995a). Adolescents' uses of media for self-socialization. *Journal of Youth & Adolescence, 24,* 519–533.

Arnett, J. J. (1995b). Broad and narrow socialization: The family in the context of a cultural theory. *Journal of Marriage and the Family, 57,* 617–628.

Arnett, J. J. (1999). Adolescent storm and stress, reconsidered. *American Psychologist, 54,* 317–326.

Arnett, J. (2000). Emerging adulthood: A theory of development from the late teens through the twenties. *American Psychologist, 55,* 469–480.

Arnett, J. J. (2000). Optimistic bias in adolescent and adult smokers and nonsmokers. *Addictive Behaviors, 25,* 625–632.

Arnett, J. J. (2002a). Adolescents in Western countries in the 21st century: Vast opportunities for all? In B. Brown, R. W. Larson, & T. S. Saraswathi (Eds.), *The world's youth: Adolescence in eight regions of the globe.* New York: Cambridge University Press.

Arnett, J. J. (2002b). The psychology of globalization. *American Psychologist, 57,* 774–783.

Arnett, J. J. (2002c). The sounds of sex: Sex in teens music and music videos. In J. Brown, K. Walsh-Childers, & J. Steele (Eds.), *Sexual teens, sexual media.* Hillsdale, NJ: Erlbaum.

Arnett, J. J. (2004). *Emerging adulthood: The winding road from the late teens through the twenties.* New York: Oxford University Press.

Arnett, J. J., & Balle–Jensen, L. (1993). Cultural bases of risk behavior: Danish adolescents. *Child Development, 64,* 1842–1855.

Aro, H., & Taipale, V. (1987). The impact of timing of puberty on psychosomatic symptoms among fourteen- to sixteen-year-old

Finnish girls. *Child Development, 58,* 261–268.

Aron, D. C., Findling, J. W., & Tyrrell, J. B. (2001). Hypothalamus & pituitary. In D. Gardner & F. S. Greenspan (Eds.), *Basic and clinical endocrinology* (6th ed.). E. Norwalk, CT: Appleton & Lange.

Aronson, J., Fried, C. B., & Good, C. (2002). Reducing the effects of stereotype threat on African American college students by shaping theories of intelligence. *Journal of Experimental Social Psychology, 38,* 113–125.

Aronson, J., & Good, C. (2002). The development and consequences of stereotype vulnerability in adolescents. In F. Pajares & T. Urdan (Eds.), *Academic motivation of adolescents.* Greenwich, CT: Information Age.

Asch, S. E. (1953). Effects of group pressure upon the modification and distortion of judgements. In D. Cartwright & A. Zander (Eds.), *Group dynamics.* New York: Harper & Row.

Aspy, C. B., Oman, R. F., Vesely, S. K., McLeroy, K., Rodine, S., & Marshall, L. (2004). Adolescent violence: The protective effects of youth assets. *Journal of Counseling and Development, 82,* 269–277.

Associated Press (1992, Oct. 2). Company news: Critics question Barbie's self-esteem (or lack thereof). *New York Times,* late edition, p. D3.

Associated Press (2003, March 25). Parents of hockey players accused of attacking third parent. New York: Author.

Astone, N., & McLanahan, S. (1991). Family structure, parental practices, and high school completion. *American Sociological Review, 56,* 309–320.

Astone, N. & McLanahan, S. S. (1995). Family structure, residential mobility, and school dropout: A research note. *Demography, 9,* 375–388.

Atkinson, J. W. (1964). *An introduction to motivation.* Princeton, NJ: Van Nostrand.

Atkinson, J. W., & Feather, N. T. (1966). *A theory of achievement motivation.* New York: Wiley.

Atkinson, R. C., & Schiffrin, R. M. (1968). Human memory: a proposed system and its control processes. In K. W. Spence & J. T. Spence (Eds.) *The psychology of learning and motivation Volume 2.* New York: Academic Press.

Attie, I., Brooks-Gunn, J., & Petersen, A. C. (1990). A developmental perspective on eating disorders and eating problems. In M. Lewis & S. M. Miller (Eds.), *Handbook of developmental psychopathology.* New York: Plenum.

Aubrey, J. S. (2002, April). *The sexual double standard in teen-oriented programming: A content analysis.* Paper presented at the Society for Research on Adolescence, New Orleans.

Aubrey, J. S. (2004). Sex and punishment: An examination of sexual consequences and the sexual double standard in teen programming. *Sex Roles, 50,* 505–514.

Azmitia, M. (2001). Self, self-esteem, conflicts, and best friendships in early adolescence. In T. M. Brinthaupt & R. P. Lipka (Eds.),

Understanding the self of the early adolescent. Albany, NY: SUNY Press.

Azmitia, M., Ittel, A. & Radmacher, K. (2005). Narratives of friendship and self in adolescence. *New Directions for Child and Adolescent Development* (no. 109), 23–39.

Bachman, J. G. (1983). Premature affluence: Do high school students earn too much money? *Economic Outlook USA, 10,* 64–67.

Bachman, J. G., & Schulenberg, J. (1993). How part-time work intensity relates to drug use, problem behavior, time use, and satisfaction among high school seniors: Are these consequences or merely correlates? *Developmental Psychology, 29,* 220–235.

Baddeley, A. (1992). Working memory. *Science, 255,* 556–559.

Badinter, E. (1980). *L'Amour en plus: Histoire de l'amour maternel, XVIIe–XXe siècle.* Paris: Flammarion.

Bahr, H. M. (1980). Changes in family life in Middletown, 1924–77. *Public Opinion Quarterly, 44,* 35–52.

Bailey, J. M., & Dawood, K. (1998). Behavior genetics, sexual orientation, and the family. In C. J. Patterson & A. R. D'Augelli (Eds.), *Lesbian, gay and bisexual identities in families: Psychological perspectives.* New York: Oxford University Press.

Bakan, D. (1972). Adolescence in America: From idea to social fact. In J. Kagan & R. Coles (Eds.), *Twelve to sixteen: Early adolescence.* New York: Norton.

Baker, E. R. (1985). Body weight and the initiation of puberty. *Clinical and Obstetrical Gynecology, 28,* 573–579.

Bakhtin, M. (1981). *The dialogic imagination.* M. Holquist (Ed). Austin, TX: University of Texas Press.

Baldry, A. C., & Farrington, D. P. (2000). Bullies and delinquents: Personal characteristics and parental styles. *Journal of Community and Applied Social Psychology, 10,* 17–31.

Balfanz, R., & Legters, N. (2001, January). *How many central city high schools have a severe dropout problem, where are they located, and who attends them? Initial estimates using the Common Core of Data.* Paper presented to the Conference on Drop Outs in America, Harvard University Civil Rights Project, Cambridge, MA.

Baltes, P. B., Lindenberger, U., & Staudinger, U. M. (2006). Life span theory in developmental psychology. In W. Damon & R. M. Lerner (Eds.), *Handbook of child psychology.* Hoboken, NJ: Wiley.

Bandura, A. (1986). *Social foundations of thought and action: A social cognitive theory.* Englewood Cliffs, NJ: Prentice Hall.

Bandura, A. (1989). Social cognitive theory. In R. Vasta (Ed.), *Annals of child development: Vol. 6. Theories of child development: Revised formulations and current issues.* Greenwich, CT: JAI Press.

Bandura, A. (1997). *Self-efficacy: The exercise of control.* New York: Freeman.

Bandura, A. (1998, August). *Swimming against the mainstream: Accentuating the positive aspects of humanity.* Paper presented at the meeting of the American Psychological Association, San Francisco.

Bandura, A. (2001). Social cognitive theory: An agentic perspective. *Annual Review of Psychology, 52,* 1–26.

Bandura, A. (2002a). Social cognitive theory of mass communication. In J. Bryant & D. Zillmann (Eds.), *Media effects: Advances in theory and research* (2nd ed.). Mahwah, NJ: Erlbaum.

Bandura, A. (2002b). Selective moral disengagement in the exercise of moral agency. *Journal of Moral Education, 31,* 101–119.

Bandura, A. (2006a). Going global with social cognitive theory: From prospect to paydirt. In S. I. Donaldson, D. E. Berger, & K. Pezdek (Eds.), *Applied psychology: New frontiers and rewarding careers.* Mahwah, NJ: Erlbaum.

Bandura, A. (2006b). Toward a psychology of human agency. *Perspectives on Psychological Science, 1,* 164–180.

Bandura, A., Barbarabelli, C., Caprara, G. V., & Pastorelli, C. (2001). Self-efficacy beliefs as shapers of children's aspirations and career trajectories. *Child Development, 72,* 187–206.

Bandura, A., & Bussey, K. (2004). On broadening the cognitive, motivational, and sociostructural scope of theorizing about gender development and functioning: Comment on Martin, Ruble, and Szkrybalo (2002). *Psychological Bulletin, 130,* 691–701.

Barber, B. K. (1996). Parental psychological control: Revisiting a neglected construct. *Child Development, 67,* 3296–3319.

Barber, B. K. (2002). Reintroducing parental psychological control. In B. K. Barber (Ed.), *Intrusive parenting: How psychological control affects children and adolescents.* Washington, DC: American Psychological Association.

Barber, B. K., & Harmon, E. L. (2002). Violating the self: Parental psychological control of children and adolescents. In B. K. Barber (Ed.), *Intrusive parenting: How psychological control affects children and adolescents.* Washington, DC: American Psychological Association.

Barber, B. K., & Olsen, J. A. (2004). Assessing the transitions to middle and high school. *Journal of Adolescent Research, 19,* 3–30.

Barber, B. K., Stolz, H. E., & Olsen, J. A. (2005). Parental support, psychological control, and behavioral control: Assessing relevance across time, culture, and method. *Monographs of the Society for Research in Child Development, 70*(4), Serial No. 282.

Barber, B. L. (2006). To have loved and lost: Adolescent romantic relationships and rejection. In A. Booth & A. Crouter (Eds.), *Romance and sex in adolescence and emerging adulthood: Risks and opportunities.* Mahwah, NJ: Erlbaum.

Barber, B. L., & Eccles, J. (1992). Long-term influence of divorce and single parenting on adolescent family- and work-related values, behaviors, and aspirations. *Psychological Bulletin, 111,* 108–126.

Barber, B. L., Eccles, J. S., & Stone, M. R. (2001). Whatever happened to the jock, the brain, and the princess? Young adult pathways linked to adolescent activity involvement and social identity. *Journal of Adolescent Research, 16,* 429–455.

Barber, B. R. (1995). *Jihad vs. McWorld: How globalism and tribalism are reshaping the world*. New York: Ballantine.

Barker, E. T., & Galambos, N. L. (2003). Body dissatisfaction of adolescent girls and boys: Risk and protective factors. *Journal of Early Adolescence, 23*, 141–165.

Barker, R., & Gump, P. (1964). *Big school small school: High school size and student behavior.* Stanford, CA: Stanford University Press.

Barnes, G. M., Reifman, A. S., Farrell, M. P., & Dintcheff, B. A. (2000). The effects of parenting on the development of adolescent alcohol misuse: A six-wave latent growth model. *Journal of Marriage and the Family, 62*, 175–186.

Barnes, H. V. (1975). Physical growth and development during puberty. *Medical Clinics of North America, 59*, 1305–1317.

Barnow, S., Schuckit, M. A., Lucht, M., John, U., & Freyberger, H. (2002). The importance of a positive family history of alcoholism, parental rejection and emotional warmth, behavioral problems and peer substance use for alcohol problems in teenagers: A path analysis. *Journal of Studies on Alcohol, 63*, 305–315.

Bartholomew, K., & Horowitz, L. M. (1991). Attachment styles among young adults: A test of a four-category model. *Journal of Personality and Social Psychology, 61*, 226–244.

Bartini, M. (2006). Gender role flexibility in early adolescence: Developmental change in attitudes, self-perceptions, and behaviors. *Sex Roles, 55*, 233–245.

Bartko, W. T., & Eccles, J. S. (2003). Adolescent participation in structured and unstructured activities: A person-oriented analysis. *Journal of Youth and Adolescence, 32*, 233–241.

Bateman, H. V. (2002). Sense of community in the school: Listening to students' voices. In A. T. Fisher, C. C. Sonn, & B. J. Bishop (Eds.), *Psychological sense of community: Research, applications, and implications.* New York: Plenum.

Batson, C. D. (1991). *The altruism question: Toward a social-psychological answer.* Hillsdale, NJ: Erlbaum.

Battaglia, D. M., Richard, F. D., Datteri, D. L., & Lord, C. G. (1998). Breaking up is (relatively) easy to do: A script for the dissolution of close relationships. *Journal of Social and Personal Relationships, 15*, 829–845.

Bauman, Z. (2001). *The individualized society.* Cambridge, UK: Polity Press.

Baumeister, R. F. (1998). The self. In D. Gilbert, S. T. Fiske, & G. Lindzey (Eds.), *Handbook of social psychology.* New York: Oxford University Press.

Baumeister, R. F., Campbell, J. D., Krueger, J. I., & Vohs, K. E. (2003). Does high self-esteem cause better performance, interpersonal success, happiness, or healthier lifestyles? *Psychological Science in the Public Interest, 4*, 1–44.

Baumeister, R. F., and Leary, M. R. (1995). The need to belong: Desire for interpersonal attachments as a fundamental human motivation. *Psychological Bulletin, 117*, 497–529.

Baumeister, R. F., Wotman, S. R., & Stillwell, A. M. (1993) Unrequited love: On heartbreak, anger, guilt, scriptlessness, and humiliation. *Journal of Personality and Social Psychology, 64*, 377–394.

Baumrind, D. (1978). Parental disciplinary patterns and social competence in children. *Youth and Society, 9*, 239–276.

Baumrind, D. (1987). A developmental perspective on adolescent risk taking in contemporary America. *New Directions for Child Development, 37*, 93–125.

Baumrind, D. (1991a). Effective parenting during the early adolescent transition. In P. A. Cowan & E. M. Hetherington (Eds.), *Family transitions.* Hillsdale, NJ: Erlbaum.

Baumrind, D. (1991b). The influence of parenting styles on adolescent competence and substance use. *Journal of Early Adolescence, 11*, 56–95.

Baumrind, D. (1998). From "ought" to "is": A neo-Marxist perspective on the use and misuse of the culture construct. *Human Development, 41*, 145–165.

Baumrind, D. (2005). Patterns of parental authority and adolescent autonomy. *New Directions for Child and Adolescent Development, 108*, 61–69.

Bayley, N. (1968). Behavioral correlates of mental growth: Birth to thirty-six years. *American Psychologist, 23*, 1–17.

Bayly, M. K., Sipplola, L. K., & Buchanan, C. M. (2006, March). *Attitudes towards gender conforming and non-conforming peers in early adolescence.* Presented at the meeting of the Society for Research on Adolescence, San Francisco.

Bayot, J. (2003, December 1). The teenage market: Young, hip, and looking for a bargain. *New York Times*, p. C8.

Beam, M. R., Chen, C., & Greenberger, E. (2002). The nature of adolescents' relationships with their "very important" nonparental adults. *American Journal of Community Psychology, 30*, 305–325.

Bean, R. A., Bush, K. R., McKenry, P. C., & Wilson, S. M. (2003). The impact of parental support, behavioral control, and psychological control on the academic achievement and self-esteem of African American and European American adolescents. *Journal of Adolescent Research, 18*, 523–541.

Bearman, P. S., & Bruckner, H. (2001). Promising the future: Virginity pledges and first intercourse. *American Journal of Sociology, 106*, 859–912.

Bearman, P. S., & Moody, J. (2004). Suicide and friendships among American adolescents. *American Journal of Public Health, 94*, 89–95.

Bearman, S. K., Presnell, K., Martinez, E., & Stice, E. (2006). The skinny on body dissatisfaction: A longitudinal study of adolescent boys and girls. *Journal of Youth and Adolescence, 35*, 217–229.

Beaumont, S. L., Vasconcelos, V. C. B., & Ruggeri, M. (2001). Similarities and differences in mother-daughter and mother-son conversations during preadolescence and adolescence. *Journal of Language and Social Psychology, 20*, 419–444.

Beausang, C. C., & Razor, A. G. (2000). Young Western women's experiences of menarche and menstruation. *Health Care for Women International, 21*, 517–529.

Beck, A. T. (1967). *Depression: Causes and treatment.* Philadelphia: University of Pennsylvania Press.

Beck, A. T. (2005). The current state of cognitive therapy: A 40-year retrospective. *Archives of General Psychiatry, 62*, 953–959.

Becker, A. E., Burwell, R. A., Herzog, D. B., Hamburg, P., & Gilman, S. E. (2002). Eating behaviours and attitudes following prolonged exposure to television among ethnic Fijian adolescent girls. *British Journal of Psychiatry, 180*, 509–514.

Becker, B. E., & Luthar, S. S. (2007). Peer-perceived admiration and social preference: Contextual correlates of positive peer regard among suburban and urban adolescents. *Journal of Research on Adolescence, 17*, 117–144.

Beger, R. (2003). The "worst of both worlds": School security and the disappearing Fourth Amendment rights of students. *Criminal Justice Review, 28*, 336–354.

Beilin, H., & Fireman, G. (2000). The foundation of Piaget's theories: Mental and physical action. In H. W. Reese (Ed.), *Advances in child development and behavior* (Vol. 27). San Diego: Academic Press.

Bell, A. P., Weinberg, M. S., & Hammersmith, S. K. (1981). *Sexual preference: Its development in men and women.* Bloomington, IN: Indiana University Press.

Bell, J. H., & Bromnick, R. D. (2000, March). *A grounded approach to understanding modern dilemmas of individuality.* Paper presented at the biennial meeting of the Society for Research on Adolescence, Chicago.

Bell, R. (1998). *Changing bodies, changing lives* (3rd ed.). New York: Times Books.

Bell, R. Q. (1979). Parent, child, and reciprocal influences. *American Psychologist, 34*, 821–826.

Bellamy, C. (2002). *The state of the world's children 2002.* New York: UNICEF.

Bellmore, A. D., & Cillessen, A. H. N. (2006). Reciprocal influences of victimization, perceived social preference, and self-concept in adolescence. *Self and Identity, 5*, 209–229.

Belmont, L., & Marolla, F. A. (1973). Birth order, family size, and intelligence. *Science, 182*, 1096–1101.

Belsky, J., Steinberg, L. D., Houts, R. M., Friedman, S. L., DeHart, G., et al. (2007). Family rearing antecedents of pubertal timing. *Child Development, 78*, 1302–1321.

Bem, D. J. (2001). Exotic becomes erotic: Integrating biological and experiential antecedents of sexual orientation. In A. R. D'Augelli & C. J. Patterson (Eds.), *Lesbian, gay, and bisexual identities and youth: Psychological perspectives.* New York: Oxford University Press.

Bem, S. L. (1977). On the utility of alternative procedures for assessing psychological androgyny. *Journal of Consulting and Clinical Psychology, 45*, 196–205.

Bem, S. L. (1981). Gender schema theory: A cognitive account of sex typing. *Psychological Review, 88,* 354–364.

Ben-Amos, I. K. (1994). *Adolescence and youth in early modern England.* New Haven, CT: Yale University Press.

Benbow, C. P., Lubinski, D., Shea, D. L., & Eftekhari-Sanjani, H. (2000). Sex differences in mathematical reasoning ability at age 13: Their status 20 years later. *Psychological Science, 11,* 474–480.

Bence, P. J. (1990). The experience of mood during adolescence. *Dissertation Abstracts International, 50*(11-B), 5342–5343.

Benedict, R. (1934). *Patterns of culture.* Boston: Houghton Mifflin.

Benedikt, R., Wertheim, E. H., & Love, A. (1998). Eating attitudes and weight-loss attempts in female adolescents and their mothers. *Journal of Youth and Adolescence, 27,* 43–57.

Benenson, J. F., & Christakos, A. (2003). The greater fragility of females' versus males' closest same-sex friendships. *Child Development, 74,* 1123–1129.

Benenson, J. F., Sinclair, N., & Dolenszky, E. (2006). Children's and adolescents' expectations of aggressive responses to provocation: Females predict more hostile reactions in compatible dyadic relationships. *Social Development, 15,* 65–80.

Benner, A. D., & Graham, S. (2007). Navigating the transition to multi-ethnic urban high schools: Changing ethnic congruence and adolescents' school-related affect. *Journal of Reearch on Adolescence, 17,* 207–220.

Bennett, K., & LeCompte, M. (1990). *The way schools work.* New York: Longman.

Bennett, N. (1998). Annotation: Class size and the quality of educational outcomes. *Journal of Child Psychology and Psychiatry, 39,* 797–804.

Bennett, W. J. (1992). *The de-valuing of America: The fight for our culture and our children.* New York: Simon & Schuster.

Benson, P. L., Scales, P. C., Hamilton, S. F., & Sesma, A., Jr. (2006). Positive youth development: Theory, research, and applications. In W. Damon & R. L. Lerner (Eds.), *Handbook of child psychology* (6th ed.). Hoboken, NJ: Wiley.

Benson, P. L., Scales, P. C., Leffert, N., & Roehlkpartain, E. C. (1999). *A fragile foundation: The state of developmental assets among American youth.* Minneapolis, MN: Search Institute.

Benveniste, L., Carnoy, M., & Rothstein, R. (2002). *All else equal: Are public and private schools different?* New York: RoutledgeFalmer.

Ben-Zeev, T., Carrasquillo C. M., Ching, A., Kliengklom, T. J., McDonald, K. L., Newhall, D. C., et al. (2005). "Math is hard!" (Barbie, 1994): Responses of threat vs. challenge mediated arousal to stereotypes alleging intellectual inferiority. In A. M. Gallagher & J. C. Kaufman (Eds.), *Gender differences in mathematics: An integrative psychological approach.* New York: Cambridge University Press.

Ben-Zeev, T., Fein, S., & Inzlicht, M. (2005). Arousal and stereotype threat. *Journal of Experimental Social Psychology, 41,* 174–181.

Berenbaum, S. A. (1999). Effects of early androgens on sex-typed activities and interests in adolescents with congenital adrenal hyperplasia. *Hormones and Behavior, 35,* 102–110.

Berenbaum, S. A. (2002). Prenatal androgen and sexual differentiation of behavior. In E. A. Eugster & O. H. Pescovitz (Eds.), *Developmental endocrinology: From research to clinical practice.* Totowa, NJ: Humana Press.

Berger, K. S. (2007). Update on bullying at school: Science forgotten? *Developmental Review, 27,* 90–126.

Berkowitz, L. (1990). On the formation and regulation of anger and aggression: A cognitive-neoassociationist analysis. *American Psychologist, 45,* 494–503.

Berman, A. M., Schwartz, S. J., Kurtines, W. M., & Berman, S. L. (2001). The process of exploration in identity formation: The role of style and competence. *Journal of Adolescence, 24,* 513–528.

Bernal, M. E., Knight, G. P., Garza, C. A., Ocampo, K. A., & Cota, M. K. (1990). The development of ethnic identity in Mexican-American children. *Hispanic Journal of Behavioral Sciences, 12,* 3–24.

Berndt, T. J. (1979). Developmental changes in conformity to peers and parents. *Developmental Psychology, 15,* 608–616.

Berndt, T. J. (1996). Exploring the effects of friendship quality on social development. In W. M. Bukowski, A. F. Newcomb, & W. W. Hartup (Eds.), *The company they keep: Friendships in childhood and adolescence.* New York: Cambridge University Press.

Berndt, T. J. (2002). Friendship quality and social development. *Current Directions in Psychological Science, 11,* 7–10.

Berndt, T. J. (2004). Children's friendships: Shifts over a half-century in perspectives on their development and their effects. *Merrill-Palmer Quarterly, 50,* 206–223.

Berndt, T. J., Hawkins, J. A., & Jiao, Z. (1999). Influences of friends and friendship on adjustment to junior high school. *Merrill-Palmer Quarterly, 45,* 13–41.

Berndt, T. J., & Keefe, K. (1995). Friends' influence on adolescents' adjustment to school. *Child Development, 66,* 1312–1329.

Berndt, T. J., & Murphy, L. M. (2002). Influences of friends and friendships: Myths, truths, and research recommendations. In R. V. Kail (Ed.), *Advances in child development and behavior* (Vol. 30). San Diego, CA: Academic Press.

Berndt, T. J., & Savin-Williams, R. C. (1993). Peer relations and friendships. In B. Tolan & B. Cohler (Eds.), *Handbook of clinical research and practice with adolescents.* New York: Wiley.

Berne, L., & Huberman, B. (1999). *European approaches to adolescent sexual behavior & responsibility.* Washington, DC: Advocates for Youth.

Berry, J. W. (1990). Psychology of acculturation. In J. Berman (Ed.), *Cross-cultural perspectives: Nebraska symposium on motivation.* Lincoln: University of Nebraska Press.

Berry, J. W. (1995). Psychology of acculturation. In N. R. Goldberger & J. B. Veroff (Eds.), *The culture and psychology reader.* New York: New York University Press.

Berry, J. W., Kim, U., Minde, T., & Mok, D. (1987). Acculturative stress in Canada. *International Migration Review, 21,* 491–511.

Berry, J. W., Poortinga, Y. H., Segall, M. H., & Dasen, P. R. (1992). *Cross-cultural psychology: Research and applications.* New York: Cambridge University Press.

Bersamin, M., Fisher, D. A., Walker, S., Hill, D. L., & Grube, J. W. (2006, March). *Defining virginity and abstinence: Adolescent interpretation of sexual behavior.* Presented at the meeting of the Society for Research on Adolescence, San Francisco.

Berscheid, E., & Regan, P. (2005). *The psychology of close relationships.* Upper Saddle River, NJ: Prentice-Hall.

Berzonsky, M. D. (2003a). Identity style and well-being: Does commitment matter? *Identity, 3,* 131–142.

Berzonsky, M. D. (2003b). The structure of identity: Commentary on Jane Kroger's view of identity status transition. *Identity, 3,* 231–246.

Berzonsky, M. D. (2004a). Identity processing style, self-construction, and personal epistemic assumptions: A social-cognitive perspective. *European Journal of Developmental Psychology, 1,* 303–315.

Berzonsky, M. D. (2004b). Identity style, parental authority, and identity commitment. *Journal of Youth and Adolescence, 33,* 213–220.

Berzonsky, M. D., & Adams, G. R. (1999) Reevaluating the identity status paradigm: Still useful after 35 years. *Developmental Review, 19,* 557–590.

Berzonsky, M. D., & Kuk, L. S. (2005). Identity style, psychosocial maturity, and academic performance. *Personality and Individual Differences, 39,* 235–247.

Best, D. L., & Thomas, J. J. (2004). Cultural diversity and cross-cultural perspectives. In A. H. Eagly, A. E. Beall, & R. J. Sternberg (Eds.), *The psychology of gender* (2nd ed.). New York: Guilford.

Beutler, L., & Martin, B. (1999). Scientific objectivity. In P. Kendall, J. Butcher, & C. Holmbeck (Eds.), *Handbook of research methods in clinical psychology.* New York: Wiley.

Beyers, J. M., Bates, J. E., Pettit, G. S., & Dodge, K. A. (2003). Neighborhood structure, parenting processes, and the development of youths' externalizing behaviors: A multilevel analysis. *American Journal of Community Psychology, 31,* 35–53.

Beyers, J. M., & Loeber, R. (2003). Untangling developmental relations between depressed mood and delinquency in male adolescents. *Journal of Abnormal Child Psychology, 31,* 247–266.

Beyth–Marom, R., Austin, L., Fischoff, B., Palmgren, C., & Jacobs–Quadrel, M. (1993). Perceived consequences of risky behaviors: Adults and adolescents. *Developmental Psychology, 29,* 549–563.

Bhanot, R., & Jovanovic, J. (2005). Do parents' academic gender stereotypes influence whether they intrude on their children's homework? *Sex Roles, 52,* 597–607.

Bianci, S. M. (2000). Maternal employment and time with children: Dramatic change or surprising continuity? *Demography, 37,* 401–414.

Biesecker, G., & Easterbrooks, M. A. (2002, April). *Attachments to mothers, fathers, and peers: Connections with emotion regulation and working models of self and world.* Paper presented at the meeting of the Society for Research on Adolescence, New Orleans.

Bigelow, B. J., Tesson, G., & Lewko, J. H. (1999). The contextual influences of sibling and dating relations on adolescents' personal relations and their close friends, dating partners, and parents: The Sullivan-Piaget-Hartup hypothesis considered. In J. A. McClellan & M. J. V. Pugh (Eds.), *The role of peer groups in adolescent social identity: Exploring the imporance of stability and change.* San Francisco: Jossey-Bass.

Bigler, R. S., Averhart, C. J., & Liben, L. S. (2003). Race and the workforce: Occupational status, aspirations, and stereotyping among African American children. *Developmental Psychology, 39,* 572–580.

Bigner, J. J., & Jacobsen, R. B. (1989). Parenting behaviors of homosexual and heterosexual fathers. In F. W. Bozett (Ed.), *Homosexuality and the family.* New York: Harrington Park Press.

Birman, D. (1994). Acculturation and human diversity in a multicultural society. In E. Trickett, R. Watts, & D. Birman (Eds.), *Human diversity: Perspective on people in context.* San Francisco: Jossey-Bass.

Birmingham, C. L., Su, J., Hlynsky, J. A., Goldner, E. M., & Gao, M. (2005). The mortality rate from anorexia nervosa. *International Journal of Eating Disorders, 38,* 143–146.

Biro, F. M., Lucky, A. W., Simbartl, L. A., Barton, B. A., Daniels, S. R., Striegel-Moore, R., et al. (2003). Pubertal maturation in girls and the relationship to anthropometric changes: Pathways through puberty. *Journal of Pediatrics, 142,* 643–646.

Bitar, A., Fellmann, N., Vernet, J., Coudert, J., & Vermorel, M. (1999). Variations and determinants of energy expenditure as measured by whole-body indirect calorimetry during puberty and adolescence. *American Journal of Clinical Nutrition, 69,* 1209–1216.

Bjork, R. A. (1989). Retrieval inhibition as an adaptive mechanism in human memory. In H. L. Roediger, III, & F. I. M. Craik (Eds.), *Varieties of memory and consciousness.* Hillsdale, NJ: Erlbaum.

Bjorklund, D. F. (2000). *Children's thinking: Developmental function and individual differences* (3rd ed.). Belmont, CA: Wadsworth.

Blackwell, L. S., Trzesniewski, K. H., & Dweck, C. S. (2007). Implicit theories of intelligence predict achievement across an adolescent transition: A longitudinal study and an intervention. *Child Development, 78,* 246–263.

Blair, S. L., Legazpi Blair, M. C., & Madamba, A. B. (1999). Racial/ethnic differences in high school students' academic performance: Understanding the interweave of social class and ethnicity in the family context. *Journal of Comparative Family Studies, 30,* 539–555.

Blakemore, J. E. O., Berenbaum, S. A., & Liben, L. S. (2005). *Gender development.* Mahwah, NJ: Erlbaum.

Blanchard, R. (2001). Fraternal birth order and the maternal immune hypothesis of male homosexuality. *Hormones and Behavior, 40,* 105–114.

Blasi, A. (2005). Moral character: A psychological approach. In D. K. Lapsley & F. C. Power (Eds.), *Character psychology and character education.* Notre Dame, IN: University of Notre Dame Press.

Block, J. H. (1984). *Sex role identity and ego development.* San Francisco: Jossey-Bass.

Blos, P. (1970). *The young adolescent.* New York: Free Press.

Blum, L. W. (2002). *Mothers' influence on teen sex: Connections that promote postponing sexual intercourse.* Minneapolis, MN: Center for Adolescent Health and Development, University of Minnesota.

Blume, J. (1970). *Are you there God? It's me, Margaret.* Engelwood Cliffs, NJ: Bradbury.

Blumenfeld, P. C. (1992). Classroom learning and motivation: Clarifying and expanding goal theory. *Journal of Educational Psychology, 84,* 272–281.

Blyth, D., Hill, J., & Thiel, K. (1982). Early adolescents' significant others: Grade and gender differences in perceived relationships with familial and non-familial adults and young people. *Journal of Youth and Adolescence, 11,* 425–450.

Bogaert, A. F. (2005). Age at puberty and father absence in a national probability sample. *Journal of Adolescence, 28,* 541–546.

Bogenschneider, K., & Steinberg, L. (1994). Maternal employment and adolescent academic achievement: A developmental analysis. *Sociology of Education, 67,* 60–77.

Bogenschneider, K., Wu, M., Raffaelli, M., & Tsay, J. C. (1998). Parent influences on adolescent peer orientation and substance use: The interface of parenting practices and values. *Child Development, 69,* 1672–1688.

Boivin, M., Hymel, S., & Bukowski, W. M. (1995). The roles of social withdrawal, peer rejection, and victimization by peers in predicting loneliness and depressed mood in childhood. *Development and Psychopathology, 7,* 765–785.

Booth, A., & Amato, P. R. (2001). Parental predivorce relations and offspring postdivorce well-being. *Journal of Marriage and the Family, 63,* 197–212.

Booth, M. (2002). Arab adolescents facing the future: Enduring ideals and pressures for change. In B. Brown, R. Larson, & T. S. Saraswathi (Eds.), *The world's youth: Adolescence in eight regions of the globe.* New York: Cambridge University Press.

Borbely, C. J., Graber, J. A., Nichols, T., Brooks-Gunn. J., & Botvin, G. J. (2005). Sixth graders' conflict resolution in role plays with a peer, parent, and teacher. *Journal of Youth and Adolescence, 34,* 279–291.

Borelli, J. L., & Prinstein, M. J. (2006). Reciprocal, longitudinal associations among adolescents' negative feedback-seeking, depressive symptoms, and peer relations. *Journal of Abnormal Child Psychology, 34,* 159–169.

Bornstein, M. H., & Bradley, R. H. (Eds.). (2003). *Socioeconomic status, parenting, and child development.* Mahwah, NJ: Erlbaum.

Bosma, H. A., & Kunnen, E. S. (2001). Determinants and mechanisms in ego identity development: A review and synthesis. *Developmental Review, 21,* 39–66.

Boswell, J. (1988). *The kindness of strangers: The abandonment of children in Western Europe from late Antiquity to the Renaissance.* New York: Pantheon.

Bouchey, H. A., & Harter, S. (2005). Reflected appraisals, academic self-perceptions, and math/science performance during early adolescence. *Journal of Educational Psychology, 97,* 673–686.

Bourdieu, P. (1997). The forms of capital. In A. H. Halsey, H. Lauder, P. Brown, & A. S. Wells (Eds.), *Education: Culture, economy, and society.* Oxford: Oxford University Press.

Bowker, A., Bukowski, W. M., Hymel, S., & Sippola, L. K. (2000). Coping with daily hassles in the peer group during early adolescence: Variations as a function of peer experience. *Journal of Research on Adolescence, 10,* 211–243.

Bowlby, J. (1969). *Attachment and loss: Vol. 1. Attachment.* New York: Basic Books.

Bowlby, J. (1973). *Attachment and loss. Vol. 2: Separation: Anxiety and anger.* New York: Basic Books.

Bowlby, J. (1988). *A secure base: Clinical applications of attachment theory.* New York: Basic Books.

Bowman, S. A., Gortmaker, S. L., Ebbeling, C. B., Pereira, M. A., & Ludwig, D. S. (2004). Effects of fast-food consumption on energy intake and diet quality among children in a national household survey. *Pediatrics, 113,* 112–118.

Boyes, M. C., & Chandler, M. J. (1992). Cognitive development, epistemic doubt, and identity formation in adolescence. *Journal of Youth and Adolescence, 21,* 277–304.

Brabeck, M. M., & Shore, E. L. (2003). Gender differences in intellectual and moral development? The evidence that refutes the claim. In J. Demick & C. Andreoletti (Eds.), *Handbook of adult development.* New York: Kluwer Academic/Plenum.

Bracey, J. R., Bámaca, M. Y., & Umaña-Taylor, A. J. (2004). Examining ethnic identity and self-esteem among biracial and monoracial adolescents. *Journal of Youth and Adolescence, 33,* 123–132.

Bradbard, M. R., Martin, C. L., Endsley, R. C., & Halverson, C. F. (1986). Influence of sex stereotypes on children's exploration and memory: A competence versus performance distinction. *Developmental Psychology, 22,* 481–486.

Bradley, C. B., McMurray, R. G., Harrell, J. S., & Deng, S. (2000). Changes in common activities of 3rd through 10th graders: The CHIC study. *Medicine & Science in Sports & Exercise, 32,* 2071–2078.

Brady, S. S., & Matthews, K. A. (2006). Chronic stress influences ambulatory blood pressure in adolescents. *Annals of Behavioral Medicine, 31,* 80–88.

Brainerd, C. J. (1996). Piaget: A centennial celebration. *Psychological Science, 7,* 191–195.

Brainerd, C. J., & Gordon, L. L. (1994). Development of verbatim and gist memory for numbers. *Developmental Psychology, 30,* 163–177.

Brainerd, C. J., & Reyna, V. F. (1990). Gist is the grist: Fuzzy-trace theory and the new intuitionism. *Developmental Review, 4,* 311–377.

Brainerd, C. J., & Reyna, V. F. (2001). Fuzzy-trace theory: Dual processes in memory, reasoning, and cognitive neuroscience. In H. W. Reese (Ed.), *Advances in child development and behavior* (Vol. 28). San Diego: Academic Press.

Brake, M. (1985). *Comparative youth culture: The sociology of youth cultures and youth subcultures in America, Britain, and Canada.* London: Routledge and Kegan Paul.

Brandstädter, J. (2006). Action perspectives on human development. In W. Damon & R. M. Lerner (Eds.), *Handbook of child psychology.* Hoboken, NJ: Wiley.

Bray, J. H., Adams, G. J., Getz, J. G., & McQueen, A. (2003). Individuation, peers, and adolescent alcohol use: A latent growth analysis. *Journal of Consulting and Clinical Psychology, 71,* 553–564.

Bray, J. H., & Kelly, J. (1998). *Stepfamilies: Love, marriage, and parenting in the first decade.* New York: Broadway Books.

Breedlove, S. (1994). Sexual differentiation of the human nervous system. *Annual Review of Psychology, 45,* 389–418.

Brendgen, M., Vitaro, F., & Bukowski, W. M. (2000). Stability and variability of adolescents' affiliation with delinquent friends: Predictors and consequences. *Social Development, 9,* 205–225.

Brendgen, M., Vitaro, F., Bukowski, W. M., Doyle, A. B., & Markiewicz, D. (2001). Developmental profiles of peer social preference over the course of elementary school: Associations with trajectories of externalizing and internalizing behavior. *Developmental Psychology, 37,* 308–320.

Brendgen, M., Vitaro, F., Doyle, A. B., Markiewicz, D., & Bukowski, W. M. (2002). Same-sex peer relations and romantic relationships during early adolescence: Interactive links to emotional, behavioral, and academic adjustment. *Merrill-Palmer Quarterly, 48,* 77–103.

Brenneis, D. (2002). Some cases for culture. *Human Development, 45,* 264–269.

Brent, D. A., & Mann, J. J. (2003). Familial factors in adolescent suicidal behavior. In R. A. King & A. Apter (Eds.), *Suicide in children and adolescents.* New York: Cambridge University Press.

Bretherton, I. (1990). Open communication and internal working models: Their role in the development of attachment relationships. In R. A. Thompson (Ed.), Socioemotional development. *Nebraska Symposium on Motivation* (Vol. 36). Lincoln: University of Nebraska Press.

Brewer, M. B., & Chen, Y.-R. (2007). Where (who) are collectives in collectivism? Toward conceptual clarification of individualism and collectivism. *Psychological Review, 114,* 133–151.

Bricker, J. B., Peterson, A. V., Jr., Andersen, M. R., Rajan, K. B., Leroux, B. G., et al. (2006). Childhood friends who smoke: Do they influence adolescents to make smoking transitions? *Addictive Behaviors, 31,* 889–900.

Briley, D. A., & Wyer, R. S., Jr. (2001). Transitory determinants of values and decisions: The utility (or nonutility) of individualism and collectivism in understanding cultural differences. *Social Cognition, 19,* 197–227.

Brockerhoff, M. P. (2000). An urbanizing world. *Population Bulletin, 55,* 3.

Brody, G. H., & Flor, D. L. (1998). Maternal resources, parenting practices, and child competence in rural single-parent African American families. *Child Development, 69,* 803–816.

Brody, G. H., Kim, S., Murry, V. M., & Brown, A. C. (2003). Longitudinal direct and indirect pathways linking older sibling competence to the development of younger sibling competence. *Developmental Psychology, 39,* 618–628.

Brody, G. H., & Neubaum, E. (1996). Family transitions as stressors in children and adolescents. In Cynthia R. Pfeffer (Ed.), *Severe stress and mental disturbance in children.* Washington, DC: American Psychiatric Press.

Brody, G. H., Stoneman, Z., & McCoy, J. (1994). Forecasting sibling relationships in early adolescence from child temperaments and family processes in middle childhood. *Child Development, 65,* 771–784.

Brody, L. R., & Hall, J. A. (2000). Gender, emotion, and expression. In M. Lewis & J. M. Haviland-Jones (Eds.), *Handbook of emotions: Part IV: Social/personality issues* (2nd ed.). New York: Guilford Press.

Broh, B. A. (2002). Linking extracurricular programming to academic achievement: Who benefits and why? *Sociology of Education, 75,* 69–91.

Broidy, L. M., Nagin, D. S., Tremblay, R. E., Brame, B., Dodge, K. A., Fergusson, D., et al. (2003). Developmental trajectories of childhood disruptive behaviors and adolescent delinquency: A six-site, cross-national study. *Developmental Psychology, 39,* 222–245.

Brokaw, T. (1998). *The greatest generation.* New York: Random House.

Bronfenbrenner, U. (1967). Response to pressure from peers versus adults among Soviet and American school children. *International Journal of Psychology, 2,* 199–207.

Bronfenbrenner, U. (1979). *The ecology of human development.* Cambridge, MA: Harvard University Press.

Bronfenbrenner, U. (1986). Ecology of the family as a context for human development: Research perspectives. *Developmental Psychology, 22,* 723–742.

Bronfenbrenner, U. (1989). Ecological systems theory. In R. Vasta (Ed.), *Six theories of child development: Revised formulations and current issues.* Greenwich, CT: JAI Press.

Bronfenbrenner, U. (1995). Developmental ecology through space and time: A future perspective. In P. Moen, G. H. Elder, & K. Ltiacher (Eds.), *Examining lives in context.* Washington, DC: American Psychological Association.

Bronfenbrenner, U., & Morris, P. A. (2006). The ecology of developmental processes. In W. Damon & R. M. Lerner (Eds.), *Handbook of child psychology.* Hoboken, NJ: Wiley.

Brook, C. (1999). Mechanism of puberty. *Hormone Research, 51*(suppl.), 52–54.

Brooks-Gunn, J. (1984). The psychological significance of different pubertal events to young girls. *Journal of Early Adolescence, 4,* 315–327.

Brooks-Gunn, J. (1991). Consequences of maturational timing variations in adolescent girls. In R. M. Lerner, A. C. Petersen, and J. Brooks-Gunn (Eds.), *Encyclopedia of adolescence* (Vol. 2). New York: Garland.

Brooks-Gunn, J., Duncan, G. J., & Maritato, N. (1997). Poor families, poor outcomes: The well-being of children and youth. In G. J. Duncan & J. Brooks-Gunn (Eds.), *Consequences of growing up poor.* New York: Russell Sage Foundation.

Brooks-Gunn, J., Graber, J. A., & Paikoff, R. L. (1994). Studying links between hormones and negative affect: Models and measures. *Journal of Research on Adolescence, 4,* 469–486.

Brooks-Gunn, J., Newman, D. L., Holderness, C., & Warren, M. P. (1994). The experience of breast development and girls' stories about the purchase of a bra. *Journal of Youth and Adolescence, 23,* 539–565.

Brooks-Gunn, J., & Paikoff, R. (1997). Sexuality and developmental transitions during adolescence. In J. Schulenberg, J. L. Maggs, & K. Hurrelmann (Eds.), *Health risks and developmental transitions during adolescence.* New York: Cambridge University Press.

Brooks-Gunn, J., & Reiter, E. O. (1990). The role of pubertal processes. In S. S. Feldman & G. R. Elliott (Eds.), *At the threshold: The developing adolescent.* Cambridge, MA: Harvard University Press.

Brooks-Gunn, J., & Ruble, D. N. (1982). The development of menstrual-related beliefs and behaviors during early adolescence. *Child Development, 53,* 1567–1577.

Brooks-Gunn, J., & Warren, M. P. (1988). The psychological significance of secondary sexual characteristics in nine- to eleven-year-old girls. *Child Development, 59,* 1061–1069.

Brooks-Gunn, J., & Warren, M. P. (1989). Biological and social contributions to negative affect in young adolescent girls. *Child Development, 60,* 40–55.

Brophy, J. (1998). *Motivating students to learn.* New York. McGraw-Hill.

Brosnan, M. J. (1998). Spatial ability in children's play with Lego blocks. *Perceptual and Motor Skills, 87,* 19–28.

Brown, B. B. (1990). Peer groups and peer cultures. In S. S. Feldman & G. R. Elliott (Eds.), *At the threshold: The developing adolescent.* Cambridge, MA: Harvard University Press.

Brown, B. B. (1999). "You're going out with *who?*" Peer group influences on adolescent romantic relationships. In W. Furman, B. B. Brown, & C. Feiring (Eds.), *The development of romantic relationships in adolescence.* New York: Cambridge University Press.

Brown, B. B. (2001). *Teens, jobs, and welfare: Implications for social policy.* Child Trends Research Brief. Washington, DC: Child Trends.

Brown, B. B. (2003). Crowds, cliques, and friendships. In G. R. Adams & M. Berzonsky (Eds.), *Blackwell handbook on adolescence.* New York: Blackwell.

Brown, B. B. (2004). Adolescents' relationships with peers. In R. Lerner & L. Steinberg (Eds.), *Handbook of adolescent psychology.* New York: Wiley.

Brown, B. B. (2006). A few "course corrections" to Collins and van Dulmen's "The course of true love." In A. Booth & A. Crouter (Eds.), *Romance and sex in adolescence and emerging adulthood: Risks and opportunities.* Mahwah, NJ: Erlbaum.

Brown, B. B., & Klute, C. (2003). Friends, cliques, and crowds. In G. R. Adams & M. D. Berzonsky (Eds.), *Blackwell handbook of adolescence.* Malden, MA: Blackwell.

Brown, B. B., & Larson, R. W. (2002). The kaleidoscope of adolescence: Experiences of the world's youth at the beginning of the 21st century. In B. B. Brown, R. W. Larson, & T. S. Saraswathi (Eds.), *The world's youth: Adolescence in eight regions of the globe.* New York: Cambridge University Press.

Brown, B. B., Larson, R., & Saraswathi, T. S. (2002). *The world's youth: Adolescence in eight regions of the globe.* New York: Cambridge University Press.

Brown, B. B., Mory, M., & Kinney, D. A. (1994). Casting adolescent crowds in relational perspective: Caricature, channel, and context. In R. Montemayor, G. R. Adams, & T. P. Gullotta (Eds.), *Advances in adolescent development: Vol. 6. Personal relationships during adolescence.* Newbury Park, CA: Sage.

Brown, B. B., & Mounts, N. (1989, April). *Peer group structures in single versus multiethnic high schools.* Paper presented at the meeting of the Society for Research in Child Development, Kansas City.

Brown, B. B., Mounts, N., Lamborn, S., & Steinberg, L. (1993). Parenting practices

and peer group affiliation in adolescence. *Child Development, 64,* 467–482.

Brown, C. S., & Bigler, R. S. (2005). Children's perceptions of discrimination: A developmental model. *Child Development, 76,* 533–553.

Brown, D. (1991). *Human universals.* New York: McGraw-Hill.

Brown, D. E., Koenig, T. V., Demorales, A. M., McGuire, K., & Mersai, C. T. (1996). Menarche age, fatness, and fat distribution in Hawaiian adolescents. *American Journal of Physical Anthropology, 99,* 239–247.

Brown, J. D. (2000). Adolescents' sexual media diets. *Journal of Adolescent Health,* supplement to *24*(2), 25–40.

Brown, J. D. (2002). Mass media influences on sexuality. *Journal of Sex Research, 39,* 42–55.

Brown, J. D., & Steele, J. R. (1995). *Sex and the mass media.* Menlo Park, CA: Kaiser Family Foundation.

Brown, J. D., Steele, J. R., & Walsh-Childers, K. (Eds.). (2001). *Sexual teens, sexual media: Investigating media's influence on adolescent sexuality.* Hillsdale, NJ: Erlbaum.

Brown, J. D., White A. B., & Nikopoulou, L. (1993). Disinterest, intrigue, resistance: Early adolescents girls' use of sexual media content. In B. S. Greenberg, J. D. Brown, & N. Buerkel-Rothfuss (Eds.), *Media, sex and the adolescent.* Cresskill, NJ: Hampton Press.

Brown, K. M., McMahon, R. P., Biro, F. M., Crawford, P., Schreiber, G. B., Similo, S. L., et al. (1998). Changes in self-esteem in black and white girls between the ages of 9 and 14 years: The NHLBI Growth and Health Study. *Journal of Adolescent Health, 23,* 7–19.

Brown, L. M. (2001). White working class girls, femininities, and the paradox of resistance. In D. Tolman & M. Brydon-Miller (Eds.), *From subjects to subjectivities: A handbook of interpretive and participatory methods.* New York: New York University Press.

Brown, L. M., & Gilligan, C. (1993). *Meeting at the crossroads: Women's psychology and girls' development.* Cambridge, MA: Harvard University Press.

Brown, L., Gardner, G., & Halweil, B. (1999). 16 impacts of population growth. *The Futurist, 33*(2), 36–41.

Bruce, M. L. (1986). *The usurper king: Henry of Bolingbroke, 1366–99.* London: Rubicon Press.

Bruckner, H., & Bearman, P. S. (2005). After the promise: The STD consequences of adolescent virginity pledges. *Journal of Adolescent Health, 36,* 271–278.

Brumberg, J. J. (1997). *The body project: An intimate history of American girls.* New York: Random House.

Bryant, A. L., Schulenberg, J. E., O'Malley, P. M., Bachman, J. G., & Johnston, L. D. (2003). How academic achievement, attitudes, and behaviors relate to the course of substance use during adolescence: A 6-year, multiwave national longitudinal study. *Journal of Research on Adolescence, 13,* 361–397.

Bryant, B. K., Zvonkovic, A. M., & Reynolds, P. (2006). Parenting in relation to child and adolescent vocational development. *Journal of Vocational Behavior, 69,* 149–175.

Bryk, A. S., Lee, V. E., & Holland P. B. (1993). *Catholic schools and the common good.* Cambridge, MA: Harvard University Press.

Buchanan, C. L., & Hughes, J. L. (2002, April). *Mothers' beliefs concerning adolescence: Links to feelings of efficacy, causal attributions, and parenting practices.* Paper presented at the meeting of the Society for Research on Adolescence, New Orleans.

Buchanan, C. M. (2000). The impact of divorce on adjustment during adolescence. In R. D. Taylor & M. Weng (Eds.), *Resilience across contexts: Family, work, culture, and community.* Mahwah, NJ: Erlbaum.

Buchanan, C. M. (2003). Mother's generalized beliefs about adolescents: Links to expectations for a specific child. *Journal of Early Adolescence, 23,* 29–50.

Buchanan, C. M., Eccles, J. S., & Becker, J. B. (1992). Are adolescents the victims of raging hormones? Evidence for activational effects of hormones on moods and behavior at adolescence. *Psychological Bulletin, 111,* 62–107.

Buchanan, C. M., Eccles, J. S., Flanagan, C., Midgley, C. Feldlaufer, H., & Harold, R. D. (1990). Parents' and teachers' beliefs about adolescents: Effects of sex and experience. *Journal of Youth and Adolescence, 19,* 363–394.

Buchanan, C. M., Maccoby, E. E., & Dornbusch, S. M. (1991). Caught between parents: Adolescents' experience in divorced homes. *Child Development, 62,* 1008–1029.

Buchanan, C. M., Maccoby, E. E., & Dornbusch, S. M. (1996). *Adolescents after divorce.* Cambridge, MA: Harvard University Press.

Buchanan, G. M., & Seligman, M. E. P. (Eds.). (1995). Afterword: The future of the field. In *Explanatory style.* Hillsdale, NJ: Erlbaum.

Buckley, T., & Gottlieb, A. (Eds.). (1988). A critical appraisal of theories of menstrual symbolism. In *Blood magic: The anthropology of menstruation.* Berkeley: University of California Press.

Buehler, C., Lange, G., & Franck, K. L. (2007). Adolescents' cognitive and emotional responses to marital hostility. *Child Development, 78,* 775–789.

Bugental, D. B. (2004). Thriving in the face of early adversity. *Journal of Social Issues, 60,* 219–235.

Buhle, M. J., Buhle, P., & Georgakas, D. (1998). *Encyclopedia of the American Left* (2nd ed.). New York: Oxford University Press.

Buhrmester, D., & Furman, W. (1987). The development of companionship and intimacy. *Child Development, 58,* 1101–1113.

Buhrmester, D., & Furman, W. (1990). Perceptions of sibling relationships during middle childhood and adolescence. *Child Development, 61,* 1387–1396.

Buhrmester, D., & Prager, K. (1995). Patterns and functions of self-disclosure during childhood and adolescence. In K. J. Rotenberg (Ed.), *Disclosure processes in children and adolescents*. New York: Cambridge University Press.

Buki, L. P., Ma, T., Strom, R. D., & Strom, S. K. (2003). Chinese immigrant mothers of adolescents; Self-perceptions of acculturation effects on parenting. *Cultural Diversity and Ethnic Minority Psychology, 8*, 127–140.

Bukowski, W. M., Gauze, C., Hoza, B., & Newcomb, A. F. (1993). Differences and consistency between same-sex and other-sex peer relationships during early adolescence. *Developmental Psychology, 29*, 253–263.

Bukowski, W. M., & Sippola, L. K. (2005). Friendship and development: Putting the most human relationship in its place. *New Directions for Child and Adolescent Development, 109*, 91–98.

Bukowski, W. M., Sippola, L. K., & Hoza, B. (1999). Same and other: Interdependency between participation in same-and other-sex friendships. *Journal of Youth and Adolescence, 28*, 439–459.

Bukowski, W. M., Vitaro, F., & Brendgen, M. (2007). Peers and socialization: Effects on externalizing and internalizing problems. In J. E. Grusec & P. D. Hastings (Eds.), *Handbook of socialization: Theory and research*. New York: Guilford.

Bulik, C. M., & Tozzi, F. (2004). Genetics in eating disorders: State of the science. *CNS Spectrums, 9*, 511–515.

Bullock, B. M., & Dishion, T. J. (2002). Sibling collusion and problem behavior in early adolescence: Toward a process model for family mutuality. *Journal of Abnormal Child Psychology, 30*, 143–153.

Bullough, V. L. (1981). Age at menarche: A misunderstanding. *Science, 213*, 365–366.

Bumpass, L. L., & Raley, R. K. (1995). Redefining single-parent families: Cohabitation and changing family reality. *Demography, 32*, 97–109.

Bumpus, M. F., Crouter, A. C., & McHale, S. M. (2001). Parental autonomy granting during adolescence: Exploring gender differences in context. *Developmental Psychology, 37*, 163–173.

Bureau of Labor Statistics. (2006a). *What do you like? BLS Career Information home page*. Available: www.bls.gov/k12.

Bureau of Labor Statistics. (2006b). *Occupational outlook handbook*. Washington, DC: Author. Available: www.bls.gov/oco/home.htm.

Burhans, K. K., & Dweck, C. S. (1995). Helplessness in early childhood: The role of contingent worth. *Child Development, 66*, 1719–1738.

Buriel, R., & Cardoza, D. (1993). Mexican American ethnic labeling: An introfamilial and intergenerational analysis. In M. Bernal & G. Knight (Eds.), *Ethnic identity: Formation and transmission among Hispanics and other minorities*. Albany, NY: State University of New York Press.

Burk, W. J., & Laursen, B. (2005). Adolescent perceptions of friendship and their associa-

tions with individual adjustment. *International Journal of Behavioral Development, 29*, 156–164.

Bush, G. W. (2001). *No child left behind*. Washington, DC: U.S. Government Printing Office.

Bushman, B. J., & Anderson, C. A. (2001). Media violence and the American public: Scientific facts versus media misinformation. *American Psychologist, 56*, 477–489.

Bushman, B. J., & Cantor, J. (2003). Media ratings for violence and sex: Implications for policymakers and parents. *American Psychologist, 58*, 130–141.

Bushman, B. J., & Huesmann, L. R. (2001). Effects of televised violence on aggression. In D. Singer & J. Singer (Eds.), *Handbook of children and the media*. Thousand Oaks, CA: Sage.

Buss, D. M. (1994). *The evolution of desire*. New York: Basic Books.

Buss, D. M. (Ed.) (2005a). *Handbook of evolutionary psychology*. Hoboken, NJ: Wiley.

Buss, D. M. (2005b). The strategies of human mating. In P. W. Sherman & J. Alcock (Eds.), *Exploring animal behavior*. Sunderland, MA: Sinauer.

Bussey, K., & Bandura, A. (1999). Social cognitive theory of gender development and differentiation. *Psychological Review, 106*, 676–713.

Butcher, J. N., Mineka, S., & Hooley, J. M. (2007). *Abnormal psychology* (13th ed.). Boston: Allyn & Bacon.

Butts, F. (1978). *Public education in the United States: From revolution to reform*. New York: Holt, Rinehart, & Winston.

Butts, J., & Mears, D. (2001). Reviving juvenile justice in a get-tough era. *Youth and Society, 33*, 169–198.

Byely, L., Archibald, A. B., Graber, J., & Brooks-Gunn, J. (2000). A prospective study of familial and social influences on girls' body image and dieting. *International Journal of Eating Disorders, 28*, 155–164.

Byrnes, J. P. (2002). Cognitive development during adolescence. In G. R. Adams & M. Berzonsky (Eds.), *Blackwell handbook on adolescence*. New York: Blackwell.

Cacciari, E., Frèjaville, E., Cicognani, A., Pirazzoli, P., Frank, G., Galsamo, A., et al. (1983). How many cases of true precocious puberty in girls are idiopathic? *Journal of Pediatrics, 102*, 357.

Cadinu, M., Maass, A., Rosabianca, A., & Kiesner, J. (2005). Why do women underperform under stereotype threat? Evidence for the role of negative thinking. *Psychological Science, 16*, 572–578.

Caldwell, L. L. (2005). Educating for, about and through leisure. In P. A. Witt & L. L. Caldwell (Eds.), *Recreation and youth development*. State College, PA: Venture.

Calkins, S. D., Dedmon, S. E., Gill, K. L., Lomax, L. E., & Johnson, L. M. (2002). Frustration in infancy: Implications for emotion regulation, physiological processes, and temperament. *Infancy, 3*, 175–197.

Call, K. T., Riedel, A. A., Hein, K., McLoyd, V., Petersen, A., & Kipke, M. (2002). Adolescent health and well-being in the

21st century: A global perspective. *Journal of Research on Adolescence, 12*, 69–98.

Calvete, E., & Cardeñoso, O. (2005). Gender differences in cognitive vulerability to depression and behavior problems in adolescents. *Journal of Abnormal Child Psychology, 33*, 179–192.

Cameron, J. A., Alvarez, J. M., Ruble, D. N., & Fuligni, A. J. (2001). Children's lay theories about ingroups and outgroups: Reconceptualizing research on "prejudice." *Personality and Social Psychology Review, 5*, 118–128.

Cameron, J. L. (1990). Factors controlling the onset of puberty in primates. In J. Bancroft & J. M. Reinisch (Eds.), *Adolescence and puberty*. New York: Oxford University Press.

Canedy, D. (2003, February 11). Florida struggles to find a way to achieve smaller classes. *The New York Times*, p. A18.

Cantor, J. (2000, August). *Media violence and children's emotions: Beyond the "smoking gun."* Paper presented at the annual convention of the American Psychological Association, Washington, DC.

Capaldi, D. M. (2003). Parental monitoring: A person-environment interaction perspective on this key parenting skill. In A. C. Crouter & A. Booth (Eds.), *Children's influence on family dynamics: The neglected side of family relationships*. Mahwah, NJ: Erlbaum.

Capaldi, D. M., & Patterson, G. (1991). Relation of parental transitions to boys' adjustment problems: I. A linear hypothesis. *Developmental Psychology, 27*, 489–504.

Capelli, C. A., Nakagawa, N., & Madden, C. M. (1990). How children understand sarcasm: The role of context and intonation. *Child Development, 61*, 1824–1841.

Caplow, T., & Bahr, H. M. (1979). Half a century of attitude change in Middletown. *Public Opinion Quarterly, 43*, 1–17.

Capon, N., & Kuhn, D. (1979). Logical reasoning in the supermarket: Adult females' use of a proportional reasoning strategy in an everyday context. *Developmental Psychology, 15*, 450–452.

Caporael, L. R., & Baron, R. M. (1997). Groups as the mind's natural environment. In J. Simpson & D. Kenrick (Eds.), *Evolutionary social psychology*. Mahwah, NJ: Erlbaum.

Carlo, G. (2006). Care-based and altruistically based morality. In M. Killen & J. G. Smetana (Eds.), *Handbook of moral development*. Mahwah, NJ: Erlbaum.

Carlson, E. A. (1998). A prospective longitudinal study of attachment disorganization/disorientation. *Child Development, 69*, 1107–1128.

Carlson, E. A., Sroufe, L. A., & Egeland, B. (2004). The construction of experience: A longitudinal study of representation and behavior. *Child Development, 75*, 66–83.

Carlson, M. J., & McLanahan, S. S. (2002). Fragile families, father involvement, and public policy. In C. S. Tamis-LeMonda & N. Cabrera (Eds.), *The handbook of father involvement*. Mahwah, NJ: Erlbaum.

Carnagey, N. L., & Anderson, C. A. (2005). The effects of reward and punishment in violent video games on aggressive affect, cognition, and behavior. *Psychological Science, 16,* 882–889.

Carnagey, N. L., Anderson, C. A., & Bushman, B. J. (2007). The effect of video game violence on physiological desensitization to real-life violence. *Journal of Experimental Social Psychology, 43,* 489–496.

Carnegie Council on Adolescent Development (1992). *A matter of time: Risk and opportunity in the after-school hours.* Washington, DC: Author.

Carnegie Council on Adolescent Development (1995). *Great transitions: Preparing adolescents for a new century.* Washington, DC: Author.

Carr, C. L. (2007). Where have all the tomboys gone? Women's accounts of gender in adolescence. *Sex Roles, 56,* 439–448.

Carraher, T. N., Carraher, D., & Schliemann, A. D. (1985). Mathematics in the streets and in schools. *British Journal of Developmental Psychology, 3,* 21–29.

Carskadon, M. A. (2002). Factors influencing sleep patterns of adolescents. In M. A. Carskadon (Ed.), *Adolescent sleep patterns: Biological, social, and psychological influences.* Cambridge, UK: Cambridge University Press.

Carskadon, M. A., Acebo, C., Richardson, G., Tate, B., & Seifer, R. (1997). Long nights protocol: Access to circadian parameters in adolescents. *Journal of Biological Rhythms, 12,* 278–289.

Carskadon, M. A., Harvey, M. K., & Duke, P. (1980). Pubertal changes in daytime sleepiness. *Sleep, 2,* 453–460.

Carskadon, M. A., Vieria, C., & Acebo, C. (1993). Association between puberty and delayed phase preference. *Sleep, 16,* 258–262.

Carskadon, M. A., Wolfson, A. R., Acebo, C., Tzischinsky, O., & Seifer, R. (1998). Adolescent sleep patterns, circadian timing, and sleepiness at a transition to early school days. *Sleep, 21,* 871–881.

Carver, K., Joyner, K., & Udry, J. R. (2003). National estimates of adolescent romantic relationships. In P. Florsheim (Ed.), *Adolescent romantic relations and sexual behavior: Theory, research, and practical implications.* Mahwah, NJ: Erlbaum.

Carver, P. R., Yunger, J. L., & Perry, D. G. (2003). Gender identity and adjustment in middle childhood. *Sex Roles, 49,* 95–109.

Case, R. (1992). *The mind's staircase: Exploring the conceptual underpinnings of children's thought and knowledge.* Hillsdale, NJ: Erlbaum.

Case, R. (1998). The development of conceptual structures. In W. Damon (Gen. Ed.), D. Kuhn, & R. S. Siegler (Vol. Eds.), *Handbook of child psychology* (Vol. 2). New York: Wiley.

CASEL—Collaborative for Academic, Social, and Emotional Learning. (2003). *Safe and sound: An educational leader's guide to evidence-based social and emotional learning programs.* Chicago: Author.

Casey, B. J., Getz, S., & Galvan, A. (2008). The adolescent brain. *Developmental Review, 28,* 62–77.

Casey, B. J., Giedd, J. N., & Thomas, K. M. (2000). Structural and functional brain development and its relation to cognitive development. *Biological Psychology, 54,* 241–257.

Casey, B. J., Trainor, R. J., Orendi, J. L., Schubert, A. B., Nystrom, L. E., Giedd, J. N., et al. (1997). A developmental functional MRI study of prefrontal activation during performance of a go-no-go task. *Journal of Cognitive Neuroscience, 9,* 835–847.

Casey, M. B. (1996). Understanding individual differences in spatial ability within females: A nature/nurture interactionist framework. *Developmental Review, 16,* 241–260.

Cash, T. F., & Henry, P. E. (1995). Women's body images: The results of a national survey in the USA. *Sex Roles, 33,* 19–28.

Cash, T. F., & Pruzinsky, T. (2002). *Body image: A handbook of theory, research, and clinical practice.* New York: Guilford Press.

Caspi, A., Lynam, D., Moffitt, T., & Silva, P. (1993). Unraveling girls' delinquency: Biological, dispositional, and contextual contributions to adolescent misbehavior. *Developmental Psychology, 29,* 19–30.

Caspi, A., McClay, J., Moffitt, T. E., Mill, J., Martin, J., Craig, A. W., et al. (2002). Role of genotype in the cycle of violence in maltreated children. *Science, 297,* 851–854.

Caspi, A., & Moffett, T. (1991). Individual differences and personal transitions: The sample case of girls at puberty. *Journal of Personality and Social Psychology, 61,* 157–168.

Caspi, A., Wright, B. R. E., Moffitt, T. E., & Silva, P. A. (1998). Early failure in the labor market: Childhood and adolescent predictors of unemployment in the transition to adulthood. *American Sociological Review, 63,* 424–451.

Catania, J. A. (1999). A framework for conceptualizing reporting bias and its antecedents in interviews assessing human sexuality. *The Journal of Sex Research, 36,* 25–38.

Cates, W. (1999). Chlamydial infections and the risk of ectopic pregnancy. *Journal of the American Medical Association, 281,* 117–118.

Cattell, R. B. (1998). Where is intelligence? Some answers from the triadic theory. In J. J. McArdle & R. W. Woodcock (Eds.), *Human cognitive abilities in theory and practice.* Mahwah, NJ: Erlbaum.

Cauffman, E., & Steinberg, L. (1996). Interactive effects of menarcheal status and dating on dieting and disordered eating among adolescent girls. *Developmental Psychology, 32,* 631–635.

Caufriez, A. (1997). The pubertal spurt: Effects of sex steroid on growth hormone and insulin-like growth factor I. *European Journal of Obstetrics & Gynecology and Biology, 71,* 215–217.

Ceballo, R., & McLoyd, V. C. (2002). Social support and parenting in poor, dangerous neighborhoods. *Child Development, 73,* 1310–1321.

Ceci, S. J. (2003). Cast in six ponds and you'll reel in something: Looking back on 25 years of research. *American Psychologist, 58,* 855–864.

Centers for Disease Control (CDC). (1997). Rates of homicide, suicide, and firearm-related death among children—26 industrialized countries. *Morbidity and Mortality Weekly Report, 46*(5), 101–105.

Centers for Disease Control (CDC). (2002a). *HIV/AIDS among U.S. women: Minority and young women at continuing risk.* Atlanta, GA: Author.

Centers for Disease Control (CDC). (2002b, September 27). Trends in sexual risk behaviors among high school student—United States, 1991–2001. *Morbidity and Mortality Weekly Report, 51*(38), 856–859.

Centers for Disease Control (CDC). (2005a). *Sexually transmitted disease surveillance 2004.* Available: www.cdc.gov/std/stats.

Centers for Disease Control (CDC). (2005b). *Trends in reportable sexually transmitted diseases in the United States, 2004: National surveillance data for chlamydia, gonorrhea, and syphilis.* Washington, DC: Government Printing Office.

Centers for Disease Control (CDC). (2006). *Health, United States, 2005: With chartbook on trends in the health of Americans.* Hyattsville, MD: Author.

Centers for Disease Control and Prevention [CDCP]. (2004). *The health consequences of smoking: A report of the Surgeon General.* Washington, DC: Government Printing Office.

Centers for Disease Control and Prevention [CDCP]. (2005). National Center for Injury Prevention and Control, *Web-based injury statistics query and reporting system (WISQARS).* Available: www.cdc.gov/ncipc/wisqars.

Centers for Disease Control and Prevention [CDCP]. (2006). Youth risk behavior surveillance—2005. *Morbidity and Mortality Weekly Report, 55*(No. SS-5), 2–108.

Chaiklin, S. (2003). The zone of proximal development in Vygotsky's analysis of learning and instruction. In A. Kozulin, B. Gindis, V. S. Ageyev, & S. M. Miller (Eds.), *Vygotsky's educational theory in cultural context.* New York: Cambridge University Press.

Champion, K., Vernberg, E., & Shipman, K. (2003). Nonbullying victims of bullies: Aggression, social skills, and friendship characteristics. *Applied Developmental Psychology, 24,* 535–551.

Chan, R. W., Brooks, R. C., Raboy, B., & Patterson, C. J. (1998). Division of labor among lesbian and heterosexual parents: Associations with children's adjustment. *Journal of Family Psychology, 12,* 402–419.

Chandler, M. J., Lalonde, C. E., Sokol, B. W., & Hallett, D. (2003). Personal persistence, identity development, and suicide: A study of Native and non-Native North American adolescents. *Monographs of the Society for Research in Child Development, 68* (2, Series No. 273).

Chao, R. (1994). Beyond parental control and authoritarian parenting style: Understanding Chinese parenting through the cultural notion of training. *Child Development, 65,* 1111–1119.

Chao, R. (2001). Extending research on the consequences of parenting style for Chinese Americans and European Americans. *Child Development, 72,* 1832–1843.

Chapin, J. R. (2000). Adolescent sex and mass media: A developmental approach. *Adolescence, 35,* 799–811.

Chase-Lansdale, P. L., Cherlin, A. J., & Kiernan, K. E. (1995). The long-term effects of parental divorce on the mental health of young adults: A developmental perspective. *Child Development, 66,* 1614–1634.

Chassin, L., Pitts, S. C., & Prost, J. (2002). Binge drinking trajectories from adolescence to emerging adulthood in a high-risk sample: Predictors and substance abuse outcomes. *Journal of Counseling and Clinical Psychology, 70,* 67–78.

Chavous, T. M., Bernat, D. H., Schmeelk-Cone, K., Caldwell, C. H., Kohn-Wood, L., & Zimmerman, M. A. (2003). Racial identity and academic attainment among African American adolescents. *Child Development, 74,* 1076–1090.

Cheek, D. B. (1974). Body composition, hormones, nutrition, and adolescent growth. In M. M. Grumbach, G. D. Grave, & F. E. Mayer (Eds.), *Control of the onset of puberty.* New York: Wiley.

Cheever, S. (2002, July 24). The working mom guilt trip: It's not academic. *Newsday,* B2.

Chen, C., & Stevenson, H. (1995). Motivation and mathematics achievement: A comparative study of Asian-American, Caucasian-American, and East Asian high school students. *Child Development, 66,* 1215–1234.

Chen, X., Rubin, K. H., & Li, D. (1997). Maternal acceptance and social and school adjustment: A four-year longitudinal study. *Merrill-Palmer Quarterly, 43,* 663–681.

Chen, X., Rubin, K. H., Li, B., & Li, D. (1999). Adolescent outcomes of social functioning in Chinese children. *International Journal of Behavioral Development, 23,* 199–223.

Cherlin, A. J. (1999). Going to extremes: Family structure, children's well-being, and social science. *Demography, 36,* 421–428.

Cherlin, A. J., Furstenberg, F., Jr., Chase-Lansdale, L., Kiernan, K., Robins, P., Morrison, D., & Teitler, J. (1991). Longitudinal studies of effects of divorce on children in Great Britain and the United States. *Science, 252,* 1386–1389.

Cheung, A. H., Emslie, C. J., & Mayes, T. L. (2005). Review of the efficacy and safety of antidepressants in youth depression. *Journal of Child Psychology and Psychiatry 46,* 735–754.

Child Trends. (2004). *Guide to effective programs for children and youth.* Washington, DC: Author. Available: www.childtrends.org/Lifecourse/index.htm.

Child Trends (2005). *Dating.* Available: www.childtrendsdatabank.org/indicators/73Dating.cfm.

Child Trends. (2006a). *Facts at a glance 2006: Teenage childbearing.* Washington, DC: Author.

Child Trends. (2006b). *Oral sex.* Available: www.childtrendsdatabank.org/indicators/95OralSex.cfm.

Children Now. (2001). *Fair play: Violence, gender and race in video games.* Oakland, CA: Author.

Chu, J. Y., Porche, M. V., & Tolman, D. L. (2005). The adolescent masculinity ideology in relationships scale: Development and validation of a new measure for boys. *Men and Masculinities, 8*(1), 93–115.

Chugani, H. T., Phelps, M. E., & Mazziotta, J. C. (1987). Positron emission tomography study of human brain functional development. *Annals of neurology, 22,* 487–497.

Church, R. (1976). *Education in the United States.* New York: Free Press.

Cicchetti, D., & Toth, S. (2006). Developmental psychopathology and preventive intervention. In W. Damon & R. Lerner (Eds.), *Handbook of child psychology* (6th ed.). New York: Wiley.

Cillessen, A. H. N., & Mayeux, L. (2004). From censure to reinforcement: Developmental changes in the association between aggression and social status. *Developmental Psychology, 75,* 1–17.

Cillessen, A. H. N., & Nukulkij, P. (2002, April). *Contextual factors moderate the effects of peer victimization in early adolescence.* Paper presented at the meeting the Society for Research on Adolescence, New Orleans.

Cillessen, A. H. N., & Rose, A. J. (2005). Understanding popularity in the peer system. *Current Directions in Psychological Science, 14,* 102–105.

Claes, M. (1998). Adolescents' closeness with parents, siblings, and friends in three countries: Canada, Belgium, and Italy. *Journal of Youth & Adolescence, 27,* 165–184.

Clark, L. A. (2005). Temperament as a unifying basis for personality and psychopathology. *Journal of Abnormal Psychology, 114,* 505–521.

Clark, L. A., Kochanska, G., & Ready, R. (2000). Mothers' personality and its interaction with child temperament as predictors of parenting behavior. *Journal of Personality and Social Psychology, 79,* 274–285.

Clark, R., Almeida, M., Gurka, T., & Middleton, L. (2003). Engendering tots with Caldecotts: An updated update. In E. S. Adler & R. Clark (Eds.), *How it's done: An invitation to social research* (2nd ed.). Belmont, CA: Wadsworth.

Clay, D., Vignoles, V. L., & Dittmar, H. (2005). Body image and self-esteem among adolescent girls: Testing the influence of sociocultural factors. *Journal of Research on Adolescence, 15,* 451–477.

Coatsworth, J. D., Palen, L., Sharp, E. H., & Ferrer-Wreder, L. (2006). Self-defining activities, expressive identity, and adolescent wellness. *Applied Developmental Science, 10,* 157–170.

Cohen-Bendahana, C. C. C., Buitelaarc, J. K., van Goozend, S. H. M., Orlebekee, J. F., & Cohen-Kettenis, P. T. (2005). Is there an effect of prenatal testosterone on aggression and other behavioral traits? A study comparing same-sex and opposite-sex twin girls. *Hormones and Behavior, 47,* 230–237.

Cohn, L., Millstein, S., Irwin, C., Jr., Adler, N., Kegeles, S., Dolcini, P., & Stone, G. (1988). A comparison of two measures of egocentrism. *Journal of Personality Assessment, 52,* 212–222.

Coie, J. D., Dodge, K. A., & Coppotelli, H. (1982). Dimensions and types of social status: A cross-age perspective. *Developmental Psychology, 18,* 557–570.

Coie, J. D., Dodge, K. A., & Kupersmidt, J. B. (1990). Peer group behavior and social status. In S. R. Asher & J. D. Coie (Eds.), *Peer rejection in childhood.* Cambridge UK: Cambridge University Press.

Colby, A., & Damon, W. (1994). *Some do care: Contemporary lives of moral commitment.* New York: Free Press.

Colby, A., & Kohlberg, L. (1987). *The measurement of moral judgment.* New York: Cambridge University Press.

Colby, A., Kohlberg, L., Gibbs, J., & Lieberman, M. (1983). A longitudinal study of moral judgment. *Monographs of the Society for Research in Child Development, 48*(21, Serial No. 201).

Cole, D. A., Nolen-Hoeksema, S., Girgus, J., & Paul, G. (2006). Stress exposure and stress generation in child and adolescent depression: A latent trait-state-error approach to longitudinal analyses. *Journal of Abnormal Psychology, 115,* 40–51.

Coleman, J. (1961). *The adolescent society.* Glencoe, IL: Free Press.

Coleman, J. C. (1974). *Relationships in adolescence.* Boston: Routledge & Kegan Paul.

Coleman, J. S. (1990). *Foundations of social theory.* Cambridge, MA: Belknap Press of Harvard University.

Coleman, J., & Hoffer, T. (1987). *Public and private high schools: The impact of communities.* New York: Basic Books.

Coleman, M., Ganong, L., & Fine, M. (2000). Reinvestigating remarriage: Another decade of progress. *Journal of Marriage and the Family, 62,* 1288–1307.

Coley, R. L. (1998). Children's socialization experiences and functioning in single-mother households: The importance of fathers and other men. *Child Development, 69,* 219–230.

Collaer, M. L., & Hines, M. (1995). Human behavioral sex differences: A role for gonadal hormones during early development? *Psychological Bulletin, 118,* 55–107.

College Board Commission on Precollege Guidance and Counseling. (1986). *Keeping the options open.* New York: College Entrance Examination Board.

Collins, R. L. (2005). Sex on television and its impact on American youth: Background and results from the RAND Television and Adolescent Sexuality Study. *Child and Adolescent Psychiatric Clinics of North America, 14,* 371–385.

Collins, W. A. (1990). Parent-child relationships in the transition to adolescence: Continuity and change in interaction, affect, and cognition. In R. Montemayor, G. Adams, & T. Gullotta (Eds.), *Advances in adolescent development, Vol. 2: The transition from childhood to adolescence.* Beverly Hills, CA: Sage.

Collins, W. A. (1995). Relationships and development: Family adaptation to individual change. In S. Shulman (Ed.), *Close relationships and socioemotional development.* New York: Ablex.

Collins, W. A. (2003). More than myth: The developmental significance of romantic relationships during adolescence. *Journal of Research on Adolescence, 13,* 1–24.

Collins, W. A., & Laursen, B. (2004). Changing relationships, changing youth: Interpersonal contexts of adolescent development. *Journal of Early Adolescence, 24,* 55–62.

Collins, W. A., Maccoby, E. E., Steinberg, L., Hetherington, E. M., & Bornstein, M. H. (2000). Contemporary research on parenting: The case for nature *and* nurture. *American Psychologist, 55,* 218–232.

Collins, W. A., & Repinski, D. J. (2001). Parents and adolescents as transformers of relationships: Dyadic adaptations to developmental change. In J. R. M. Gerris (Ed.), *Dynamics of parenting.* Leuven-Apeldoorn: Garant.

Collins, W. A., & Sroufe, L. A. (1999). Capacity for intimate relationships: A developmental construction. In W. Furman, B. B. Brown, & C. Feiring (Eds.), *The development of romantic relationships in adolescence.* New York: Cambridge University Press.

Collins, W. A., & van Dulmen, M. (2006). The course of true love(s): Origins and pathways in the development of romantic relationships. In A. Booth & A. Crouter (Eds.), *Romance and sex in adolescence and emerging adulthood: Risks and opportunities.* Mahwah, NJ: Erlbaum.

Colon, A. R. (2001). *A history of children: A socio-cultural survey across millennia.* Westport, CT: Greenwood Press.

Comings, D. E., Muhleman, D., Johnson, J. P., & MacMurray, J. P. (2002). Parent-daughter transmission of the androgen receptor gene as an explanation of the effect of father absence on age of menarche. *Child Development, 73,* 1046–1051.

Compas, B. E. (2004). Processes of risk and resilience during adolescence: Linking contexts and individuals. In R. M. Lerner & L. Steinberg (Eds.), *Handbook of adolescent psychology* (2nd ed.). Hoboken, NJ: Wiley.

Compas, B. E., Connor-Smith, J. K., Saltzman, H., Thomsen, A. H., & Wadsworth, M. E. (2001). Coping with stress during childhood and adolescence: Problems, progress, and potential in theory and research. *Psychological Bulletin, 127,* 87–127.

Compas, B. E., Ey, S., & Grant, K. E. (1993). Taxonomy, assessment, and diagnosis of depression during adolescence. *Psychological Bulletin, 114,* 323–344.

Compas, B. E., & Phares, V. (1991). Stress during childhood and adolescence: Sources of risk and vulnerability. In E. M. Cummings,

A. L. Greene, & K. H. Karraker (Eds.), *Life-span perspectives on stress and coping.* Hillsdale, NJ: Erlbaum.

Comstock, G., & Scharrer, E. (1999). *Television: What's on, who's watching, and what it means.* San Diego, CA: Academic Press.

Comstock, G., & Scharrer, E. (2006). Media and popular culture. In W. Damon & R. Lerner (Eds.), *Handbook of child psychology* (6th ed.). New York: Wiley.

Conant, J. B. (1959). *The American high school today.* New York: McGraw-Hill.

Condry, J., & Condry, S. (1976). Sex differences: A study of the eye of the beholder. *Child Development, 47,* 812–819.

Condon, R. G. (1987). *Inuit youth: Growth and change in the Canadian Arctic.* New Brunswick, NJ: Rutgers University Press.

Conger, K. J., Rueter, M. A., & Conger, R. D. (2000). The role of economic pressure in the lives of parents and their adolescents: The family stress model. In L. J. Crockett & R. J. Silbereisen (Eds.), *Negotiating adolescence in times of social change.* Cambridge, UK: Cambridge University Press.

Conger, K., & Conger, R. (1994). Differential parenting and change in sibling differences in delinquency. *Journal of Family Psychology, 8,* 287–302.

Conger, K., Conger, R., & Scaramella, L. (1997). Parents, siblings, psychological control, and adolescent adjustment. *Journal of Adolescent Research, 12,* 113–138.

Conger, R. D., Ge, X., Elder, G. H., Jr., Lorenz, F. O., & Simons, R. L. (1994). Economic stress, coercive family processes, and developmental problems of adolescents. *Child Development, 65,* 541–561.

Conger, R. D., Wallace, L. E., Sun, Y., Simons, R. L., McLoyd, V. C., & Brody, G. H. (2002). Economic pressure in African American families: A replication and extension of the family stress model. *Developmental Psychology, 38,* 179–193.

Connolly, J., Craig, W., Goldberg, A., & Pepler, D. (1999). Conceptions of cross-sex friendships and romantic relationships in early adolescence. *Journal of Youth and Adolescence, 28,* 481–494.

Connolly, J., Craig, W., Goldberg, A., & Pepler, D. (2004). Mixed-gender groups, dating, and romantic relationships in early adolescence. *Journal of Research on Adolescence, 14,* 185–207.

Connolly, J., & Goldberg, A. (1999). Romantic relationships in adolescence: The role of friends and peers in their emergence. In W. Furman, B. B. Brown, & C. Feiring (Eds.), *The development of romantic relationships in adolescence.* New York: Cambridge University Press.

Connolly, J., & Johnson, A. M. (1996). Adolescents' romantic relationships and the structure and quality of their close interpersonal ties. *Personal Relationships, 3,* 185–195.

Connor-Smith, J. K., Compas, B. E., Wadsworth, M. E., Thomsen, A. H., & Saltzman, H. (2000). Responses to stress in adolescence: Measurement of coping and

involuntary stress responses. *Journal of Consulting and Clinical Psychology, 68,* 976–992.

Conte, F. A., Grumbach, M. M., Kaplan, S. L., & Reiter, E. O. (1980). Correlation of luteinizing hormone-releasing factor-induced luteinizing hormone and follicle-stimulating hormone release from infancy to 19 years with the changing pattern of gonadotropin secretion in agonadal patients: Relation to the restraint of puberty. *Journal of Clinical Endrocrinology and Metabolism, 52,* 163.

Cook, T. D., Herman, M. R., Phillips, M., & Settersten, R. A. (2002). Some ways in which neighborhoods, nuclear families, friendship groups, and schools affect changes in early adolescent development. *Child Development, 73,* 1283–1309.

Cook, W. L. (2001). Interpersonal influence in family systems: A social relations model analysis. *Child Development, 72,* 1179–1197.

Cooksey, E., Mott, F., & Neubauer, S. (2002). Friendships and early relationships: Links to sexual initiation among American adolescents born to young mothers. *Perspectives on Sexual and Reproductive Health, 34,* 118–126.

Cooley, C. H. (1902). *Human nature and the social order.* New York: Charles Scribner & Sons.

Coolidge, F. L., Thede, L. L., & Young, S. E. (2002). The heritability of gender identity disorder in a child and adolescent twin sample. *Behavior Genetics, 32,* 251–257.

Coontz, S. (2005). *Marriage, a history: From obedience to intimacy, or how love conquered marriage.* New York: Viking-Penguin.

Cooper, H., Valentine, J. C., Nye, B., & Lindsay, J. J. (1999). Relationships between five after-school activities and academic achievement. *Journal of Educational Psychology, 91,* 369–378.

Copas, A. J., Wellings, K., Erens, B., Mercer, C. H., McManus, S., Fenton, K. A., et al. (2002). The accuracy of reported sensitive sexual behaviour in Britain: Exploring the extent of change 1990–2000. *Sexual Transmission and Infection, 78,* 26–30.

Corby, B. C., Hodges, E. V. E., & Perry, D. G. (2007). Gender identity and adjustment in Black, Hispanic, and White preadolescents. *Developmental Psychology, 43,* 261–266.

Cornell, J. L., & Halpern-Felsher, B. L. (2006). Adolescents tell us why teens have oral sex. *Journal of Adolescent Health, 38,* 299–301.

Corporation for National and Community Service [CNCS]. (2006). *Educating for active citizenship: Service-learning, school-based service, and civic engagement.* Washington, DC: Author.

Costello, E. J., Compton, S. N., Keeler, G., & Angold, A. (2003). Relationships between poverty and psychopathology: A natural experiment. *Journal of the American Medical Association, 290,* 2023–2029.

Costos, D., Ackerman, R., & Paradis, L. (2002). Recollections of menarche: Communication between mothers and daughters regarding menstruation. *Sex Roles, 46,* 49–59.

Côté, J. E. (2000). *Arrested adulthood: The changing nature of maturity and identity.* New York: New York University Press.

Côté, J. (2006a). Acculturation and identity: The role of individualization theory. *Human Development, 49,* 31–35.

Côté, J. (2006b). Identity studies: How close are we to developing a social science of identity?—An appraisal of the field. *Identity, 6,* 3–25.

Côté, J. E., & Levine, C. G. (1988). The relationship between ego identity status and Erikson's notions of institutionalized moratoria, value orientation state, and ego dominance. *Journal of Youth and Adolescence, 17,* 81–99.

Cotton, K. (1996). *School size, school climate, and student performance.* Close-Up #20. Portland, OR: Northwest Regional Educational Laboratory.

Cotton, K. (2001). *New small learning communities: Findings from recent literature.* Portland, OR: Northwest Regional Educational Laboratory.

Covington, M. V. (1992). *Making the grade: A self-worth perspective on motivation and school reform.* New York: Cambridge University Press.

Covington, M. V. (2002). Rewards and intrinsic motivation: A needs-based, developmental perspective. In F. Pajares & T. Urdan (Eds.), *Academic motivation of adolescents.* Greenwich, CT: Information Age.

Covington, M. V., & Müeller, K. J. (2001). Intrinsic versus extrinsic motivation: An approach/avoidance reformulation. *Educational Psychology Review, 13,* 157–176.

Cowan, N. (2001). The magical number 4 in short-term memory: A reconsideration of mental storage capacity. *Behavioral and Brain Sciences, 24,* 87–185.

Cowan, N., Wood, N. L., Wood, P. K., Keller, T. A., Nugent, L. D., & Keller, C. V. (1998). Two separate verbal processing rates contributing to short-term memory span. *Journal of Experimental Psychology: General, 127,* 141–160.

Cox, B. J., Enns, M. W., & Clara, I. P. (2004). Psychological dimensions associated with suicidal ideation and attempts in the National Comorbidity Study. *Suicide and Life-Threatening Behavior, 34,* 209–219.

Cox, M. J., & Paley, B. (1997). Families as systems. *Annual Review of Psychology, 48,* 243–267.

Craig, W. M. (1998). The relationship among bullying, victimization, depression, anxiety, and aggression in elementary school children. *Personality and Individual Differences, 24,* 123–130.

Crandall, V. C. (1969). Sex differences in expectancy of intellectual and academic reinforcement. In C. P. Smith (Ed.), *Achievement-related motives in children.* New York: Russell Sage Foundation.

Crawford, M. (2001). Gender and language. In R. K. Unger (Ed.), *Handbook of the psychology of women and gender.* New York: Wiley.

Creed, P. A., & Patton, W. (2003). Predicting two components of career maturity in school based adolescents. *Journal of Career Development, 29,* 277–290.

Creusere, M. A. (1999). Theories of adults' understanding and use of irony and sarcasm; Applications to and evidence from research with children. *Developmental Review, 19,* 213–262.

Crick, N. R. (1997). Engagement in gender normative versus nonnormative forms of aggression: Links to social-psychological adjustment. *Developmental Psychology, 33,* 610–617.

Crick, N. R., Casas, J. F., & Nelson, D. A. (2002). Toward a more comprehensive understanding of peer maltreatment: Studies of relational victimization. *Current Directions in Psychological Science, 11,* 98–101.

Crick, N. R., & Dodge, K. (1989). Children's perceptions of peer entry and conflict situations: Social strategies, goals and outcome expectations. In B. Schneider, J. Nadel, G. Attili, & R. Weissberg (Eds.), *Social competence in developmental perspective.* Boston: Kluwer.

Crick, N. R., & Dodge, K. (1994). A review and reformulation of social information-processing mechanisms in children's social adjustment. *Psychological Bulletin, 115,* 74–101.

Crick, N. R., & Dodge, K. (1996). Social information-processing mechanisms in reactive and proactive aggression. *Child Development, 67,* 993–1002.

Crick, N. R., & Grotpeter, J. K. (1995). Relational aggression, gender, and social-psychological adjustment. *Child Development, 66,* 710–722.

Crick, N. R., & Ladd, G. W. (1993). Children's perceptions of their peer experiences: Attributions, loneliness, social anxiety, and social avoidance. *Developmental Psychology, 29,* 244–254.

Criss, M. M., Pettit, G. S., Dodge, K. A., Bates, J. E., & Williams, D. H. (2006, March). *Monitoring behavior and knowledge: Distinct antecedents and behavioral outcomes?* Paper presented at the meeting of the Society for Research on Adolescence, San Francisco, CA.

Crockett, L. J., Raffaelli, M., & Moilanen, K. (2003). Adolescent sexuality: Behavior and meaning. In G. Adams & M. D. Berzonsky (Eds.), *Blackwell handbook of adolescence.* Malden, MA: Blackwell.

Croizet, J., & Claire, T. (1998). Extending the concept of stereotype and threat to social class: The intellectual underperformance of students from low socioeconomic backgrounds. *Personality and Social Psychology Bulletin, 24,* 588–594.

Crooks, R., & Baur, K. (2002). *Our sexuality* (8th ed.). Pacific Grove, CA: Wadsworth.

Crooks, R., & Baur, K. (2005). *Our sexuality* (9th ed.). Pacific Grove, CA: Wadsworth.

Crosnoe, R. (2001). Academic orientation and parental involvement in education during high school. *Sociology of Education, 74,* 210–230.

Crosnoe, R. (2002). High school curriculum track and adolescent association with delinquent friends. *Journal of Adolescent Research, 17,* 143–167.

Crosnoe, R., Cavanagh, S., & Elder, G. H., Jr. (2003). Adolescent friendships as academic resources: The intersection of friendship, race, and school disadvantage. *Sociological Perspectives, 46,* 331–352.

Crosnoe, R., Erickson, K. G., & Dornbusch, S. M. (2002). Protective functions of family relationships and school factors on the deviant behavior of adolescent boys and girls: Reducing the impact of risky friendships. *Youth and Society, 33,* 515–544.

Crosnoe, R., Johnson, M. K., & Elder, G. H., Jr. (2004). School size and the interpersonal side of education: An examination of race/ethnicity and organizational context. *Social Science Quarterly, 85,* 1259–1274.

Crosnoe, R., Mistry, R. S., & Elder, G. H., Jr. (2002). Economic disadvantage, family dynamics, and adolescent enrollment in higher education. *Journal of Marriage and Family, 64,* 690–702.

Crosnoe, R., Riegle-Crumb, C., Field, S., Frank, K., & Muller, C. (2008). Peer group contexts of girls' and boys' academic experiences. *Child Development, 79,* 139–155.

Cross, S. E., & Madson, L. (1997). Models of the self: Self-construals and gender. *Psychological Bulletin, 122,* 5–37.

Cross, W. E., Jr., Strauss, L., & Fhagen-Smith, P. (1999). African American identity development across the life span: Educational implications. In R. H. Sheets & E. R. Hollins (Eds.), *Racial and ethnic identity in school practices: Aspects of human development.* Mahwah, NJ: Erlbaum.

Crouch, G. (2006, March 15). A candid Dutch film may be too scary for immigrants. *New York Times,* p. A4.

Crouter, A. C., Bumpus, M. F., Davis, K. D., & McHale, S. M. (2005). How do parents learn about adolescents' experiences? Implications for parental knowledge and adolescent risky behavior. *Child Development, 76,* 869–882.

Crouter, A. C., Bumpus, M. F., Maguire, M. C., & McHale, S. M. (1999). Linking parents' work pressure and adolescents' well-being: Insights into dynamics in dual-earner families. *Developmental Psychology, 35,* 1453–1461.

Crouter, A. C., Manke, B. A., & McHale, S. M. (1995). The family context of gender intensification in early adolescence. *Child Development, 66,* 317–329.

Crozier, G. (2005). "There's a war against our children": Black educational underachievement revisited. *British Journal of Sociology of Education, 26,* 585–598.

Crystal, D. S., Watanabe, H., Weinfurt, K., & Wu, C. (1998). Concepts of human differences: A comparison of American, Japanese, and Chinese children and adolescents. *Developmental Psychology, 34,* 714–722.

Csikszentmihalyi, M. (1990). *Flow.* New York: Harper & Row.

Csikszentmihalyi, M., & Larson, R. (1984). *Being adolescent: Conflict and growth in the teenage years.* New York: Basic Books.

Csikszentmihalyi, M., Larson, R., & Prescott, S. (1977). The ecology of adolescent activity and experience. *Journal of Youth and Adolescence, 6,* 281–294.

Csikszentmihalyi, M., & Schmidt, J. A. (1998). Stress and resilience in adolescence: An evolutionary perspective. In K. Borman & B. Schneider (Eds.), *The adolescent years: Social influences and educational challenges.* Chicago: University of Chicago Press.

Csikszentmihalyi, M., & Schneider, B. (2000). *Becoming adult: How teenagers prepare for the world of work.* New York: Basic Books.

Cubbin, C., Santelli, J., Brindis, C. D., & Braveman, P. (2005). Neighborhood context and sexual behaviors among adolescents: Findings from the National Longitudinal Study of Adolescent Health. *Perspectives on Sexual and Reproductive Health, 37,* 125–134.

Cui, M., Conger, R. D., Bryant, C. M., & Elder, G. H., Jr. (2002). Parental behavior and the quality of adolescent friendships: A social-contextual perspective. *Journal of Marriage and the Family, 64,* 676–689.

Cukier, W. (1998). Firearms regulation: Canada in the international context. *Chronic Diseases in Canada, 19,* 25–35.

Cummings, E. M., & Davies, P. T. (1994). *Children and marital conflict: The impact of family dispute and resolution.* New York: Guilford.

Cummings, E. M., Goeke-Morey, M. C., & Papp, L. M. (2004). Everyday marital conflict and child aggression. *Journal of Abnormal Child Psychology, 32,* 191–202.

Cunningham, E. G. (2002). Developing a measurement model for coping research in early adolescence. *Educational and Psychological Measurement, 62,* 147–163.

Cutrona, C. E., Wallace, G., & Wesner, K. A. (2006). Neighborhood characteristics and depression: An examination of stress processes. *Current Directions in Psychological Science, 15,* 188–192.

Czarra, F. (2002). *Global education checklist.* New York: American Forum for Global Education.

D'Augelli, A. R. (2002). Mental health problems among lesbian, gay, and bisexual youths ages 14–21. *Clinical Child Psychology & Psychiatry, 7,* 433–456.

D'Augelli, A. R., Grossman, A. H., & Starks, M. T. (2005). Parents' awareness of lesbian, gay, and bisexual youths' sexual orientation. *Journal of Marriage and the Family, 67,* 474–482.

D'Souza, G., Kreimer, A. R., Viscidi, R., Pawlita, M., Fakhry, C., et al. (2007). Case-control study of human papillomavirus and oropharyngeal cancer. *New England Journal of Medicine, 356,* 1944–1956.

Dadisman, K., Vandell, D. L., & Pierce, K. (2002, April). *Experience sampling provides a window into after-school program experiences.* Paper presented at the Society for Research on Adolescence, New Orleans.

Dahl, R. E. (2004). Adolescent brain development: A period of vulnerabilities and opportunities. *Annals of the New York Academy of Sciences, 1021,* 1–22.

Damon, W. (1997). *The youth charter: How communities can work together to raise standards for all our children.* New York: Free Press.

Damon, W. (2004). What is positive youth development? *Annals of the American Academy of Political and Social Science, 591,* 13–24.

Daniels, D. H., & Shumow, L. (2003). Child development and classroom teaching: A review of the literature and implications for educating teachers. *Applied Developmental Psychology, 23,* 495–526.

Dare, C., & Eisler, I. (2002). Family therapy and eating disorders. In C. G. Fairburn & K. D. Brownell (Eds.,) *Eating disorders and obesity: A comprehensive handbook* (2nd ed.). New York: Guilford.

Darling, N. (2005). Participation in extracurricular activities and adolescent adjustment: Cross-sectional and longitudinal findings. *Journal of Youth and Adolescence, 34,* 493–505.

Darling, N., Hamilton, S. F., Toyokawa, T., & Matsuda, S. (2002). Naturally occurring mentoring in Japan and the United States: Social roles and correlates. *American Journal of Community Psychology, 30,* 245–270.

Darroch, J. E., Singh, S., Frost, J. J., & the Study Team (2001). Differences in teenage pregnancy rates among five developed countries: The roles of sexual activity and contraceptive use. *Family Planning Perspectives, 33,* 244–250, 281.

Daughaday, W. H. (1981). Growth hormone and the somatomedins. In W. H. Daughaday (Ed.), *Endocrine control of growth.* New York: Elsevier.

David, C. F., & Kistner, J. A. (2000). Do positive self-perceptions have a "dark side"? Examination of the link between perceptual bias and aggression. *Journal of Abnormal Child Psychology, 28,* 327–337.

Davies, P. G., & Spencer, S. J. (2005). The gender-gap artifact: Women's underperformance in quantitative domains through the lens of stereotype threat. In A. M. Gallagher & J. C. Kaufman (Eds.), *Gender differences in mathematics: An integrative psychological approach.* New York: Cambridge University Press.

Davila, J., & Steinberg, S. J. (2006). Depression and romantic dysfunction during adolescence. In T. E. Joiner, J. S. Brown, & J. Kistner (Eds.), *The interpersonal, cognitive, and social nature of depression.* Mahwah, NJ: Erlbaum.

Davila, J., Steinberg, S., Kachadourian, L., Cobb, R., & Fincham, F. (2004). Romantic involvement and depressive symptoms in early and late adolescence: The role of a preoccupied relational style. *Personal Relationships, 11,* 161–178.

Davis, M. (1992). The role of the amygdala in fear and anxiety. *Annual Review of Neuroscience, 15,* 353–375.

Davison, G. C. (2000). Case study. In A. Kazdin (Ed.), *Encyclopedia of psychology.* Washington, DC & New York: American Psychological Association and Oxford University Press.

Davison, K. K., & Birch, L. L. (2002). Processes linking weight status and self-concept among girls from ages 5 to 7 years. *Developmental Psychology, 38,* 735–748.

Davison, K. K., & Susman, E. J. (2001). Are hormone levels and cognitive ability related during early adolescence? *International Journal of Behavioral Development, 25,* 416–428.

Davison, T. E., & McCabe, M. P. (2006). Adolescent body image and psychosocial functioning. *Journal of Social Psychology, 146,* 15–30.

Dawson, D. A. (1988). Ethnic differences in female overweight: Data from the 1985 National Health Interview Survey. *American Journal of Public Health, 78,* 1326–1329.

de Bruyn, E. H., & Cillessen, A. H. N. (2006). Popularity in early adolescence: Prosocial and antisocial subtypes. *Journal of Adolescent Research, 21,* 607–627.

De Groot, A., Kaplan, J., Rosenblatt, E., Dews, S., & Winner, E. (1995). Understanding versus discriminating nonliteral utterances: Evidence for a disassociation. *Metaphor and Symbolic Activity, 10,* 255–273.

De Woolf, M. S., & van Ijzendoorn, M. H. (1997). Sensitivity and attachment: A meta-analysis of parental antecedents of infant attachment. *Child Development, 68,* 571–591.

Deater-Deckard, K. (2001). Annotation: Recent research examining the role of peer relationships in the development of psychopathology. *Journal of Child Psychology and Psychiatry, 42,* 565–579.

Deater-Deckard, K., & Dodge, K. A. (1997). Externalizing behavior problems and discipline revisited: Nonlinear effects and variation by culture, context, and gender. *Psychological Inquiry, 8,* 161–175.

Deater-Deckard, K., & O'Connor, T. G. (2000). Parent-child mutuality in early childhood: Two behavioral genetic studies. *Developmental Psychology, 36,* 561–570.

Decety, J., & Chaminade, T. (2003). Neural correlates of feeling sympathy. *Neuropsychologia, 41,* 127–138.

Deci, E. L. (1971). Effects of externally mediated rewards on intrinsic motivation. *Journal of Personality and Social Psychology, 18,* 105–115.

Deci, E. L. (1975). *Intrinsic motivation.* New York: Plenum.

Deci, E. L., Koestner, R., & Ryan, R. M. (2001). Extrinsic rewards and intrinsic motivation in education: Reconsidered once again. *Review of Educational Research, 71,* 1–51.

Deci, E. L., & Ryan, R. M. (1985). *Intrinsic motivation and self-determination in human behavior.* New York: Plenum.

Deci, E. L., & Ryan, R. M. (Eds.). (2002). *Handbook of self-determination research.* Rochester, NY: University of Rochester Press.

Deci, E. L., Vallerland, R. J., Pelletier, L. G., & Ryan, R. M. (1991). Motivation and education: The self-determination perspective. *Educational Psychologist, 26*, 325–346.

Decovic, M. (1999). Parent-adolescent conflict: Possible determinants and consequences. *International Journal of Behavioral Development, 23*, 977–1000.

Decovic, M. (2002, April). *Discrepancies between parental and adolescent developmental expectations*. Paper presented at the meeting of the Society for Research on Adolescence, New Orleans.

Decovic, M., Noom, M. J., & Meeus, W. (1997). Expectations regarding development during adolescence: Parental and adolescent perceptions. *Journal of Youth and Adolescence, 26*, 253–272.

Dees, L., Hiney, J. K., & Srivastava, V. (1998). Alcohol's effects on female puberty: The role of insulin-like growth factor I. *Alcohol Health & Research World, 22*, 165–167.

Degirmencioglu, S. M., Urberg, K. A., Tolson, J. M., & Richard, P. (1998). Adolescent friendship networks: Continuity and change over the school year. *Merrill-Palmer Quarterly, 44*, 313–337.

DeGroot, E. (1997). *The relations between perceptions of the school psychological environment and adaptive functioning among early adolescents: A longitudinal study*. Unpublished doctoral dissertation, University of Michigan, Ann Arbor.

Deke, J., & Haimson, J. (2006). *Valuing student competencies: Which ones predict postsecondary educational attainment and earnings, and for whom?* Princeton, NJ: Mathematica Policy Research.

Dekovic, M., & Meeus, W. (1997). Peer relations in adolescence: Effects of parenting and adolescents' self-concept. *Journal of Adolescence, 20*, 163–176.

DeLamater, J., & Friedrich, W. N. (2002). Human sexual development. *Journal of Sex Research, 39*, 10–14.

Delaney, C. (1988). Mortal flow: Menstruation in Turkish village society. In T. Buckley & A. Gottlieb (Eds.), *Blood magic: The anthropology of menstruation*. Berkeley: University of California Press.

Delaney, J., Lupton, M. J., & Toth, E. (1996). *The curse: A cultural history of menstruation*. New York: Dutton.

Delisi, R., & McGillicuddy-Delisi, A. (2002). Sex differences in mathematical ability and achievement. In A. McGillicuddy-Delisi & R. Delisi (Eds.), *Biology, society, and behavior: The development of sex differences in cognition*. Westport, CT: Ablex.

Dellasega, C., & Nixon, C. (2003). *Girl wars: 12 strategies that will end female bullying*. New York: Simon & Schuster.

DeLoache, J. S., Miller, K. F., & Pierroutsakos, S. L. (1998). Reasoning and problem solving. In W. Damon (Gen. Ed.), D. Kuhn, & R. S. Siegler (Vol. Eds.), *Handbook of child psychology* (Vol. 2). New York: Wiley.

DeMause, L. (1974). *The history of childhood*. New York: Psychohistory Press.

Demetriou, A., Christou, C., Spanoudis, G., & Platsidou, M. (2002). The development of mental processing: Efficiency, working memory, and thinking. *Monographs of the Society for Research in Child Development, 67*(1, Serial No. 268), 1–171.

Demetriou, A., & Raftoupoulos, A., (1999). Modeling the developing mind: From structure to change. *Developmental Review, 19*, 319–368.

Demo, D., & Acock, A. (1996). Family structure, family process, and adolescent well-being. *Journal of Research on Adolescence, 6*, 457–488.

Department of Health. (1991). *Dietary reference values for food energy and nutrients for the United Kingdom*. London: HMSO.

Derryberry, D., Reed, M. A., & Pilkenton-Taylor, C. (2003). Temperament and coping: Advantages of an individual differences perspective. *Developmental Psychopathology, 15*, 1049–1066.

Deutsch, M., & Gerard, H. B. (1955). A study of normative and informational influence upon individual judgment. *Journal of Abnormal and Social Psychology, 51*, 629–636.

Deutsch, N. L. (2003, April). *The space to be me: Benefits of youth organizations as less-structured spaces for adolescent development*. Presented at the biennial meeting of the Society for Research in Child Development, Tampa, FL.

Deutsch, N. L., & Hirsch, B. J. (2002). A place to call home: Youth organizations in the lives of inner city adolescents. In T. M. Brinthaupt & R. P. Lipka (Eds.), *Understanding early adolescent self and identity: Applications and interventions*. Albany, NY: SUNY Press.

DeVoe, J. F., Peter, K., Kaufman, P., Ruddy, S. A., Miller, A. K., Planty, M., et al. (2002). *Indicators of School Crime and Safety: 2002*. Washington, DC: U.S. Departments of Education and Justice.

DeVoe, J. F., Peter, K., Kaufman, P., Ruddy, S. A., Miller, A. K., Planty, M., et al. (2003). *Indicators of School Crime and Safety: 2003*. U.S. Departments of Education and Justice. Washington, DC: U.S. Government Printing Office.

DeVoe, J. F., Peter, K., Noonan, M., Snyder, T. D., & Baum, K. (2005). *Indicators of School Crime and Safety: 2005*. U.S. Departments of Education and Justice. Washington, DC: U.S. Government Printing Office.

DeWoskin, K. J. (1995). Famous Chinese childhoods. In A. B. Kenney (Ed.), *Chinese views of childhood*. Honolulu: University of Hawai'i Press.

DeZolt, D. M., & Hull, S. H. (2001). Classroom and school climate. In J. Worrell (Ed.), *Encyclopedia of women and gender*. San Diego: Academic Press.

Diamond, J. B. (2007). Where the rubber meets the road: Rethinking the connection between high-stakes testing policy and classroom instruction. *Sociology of Education, 80*, 285–309.

Diamond, J. B., Randolph, A., & Spillane, J. P. (2004). Teachers' expectations and sense of responsibility for student learning: The importance of race, class, and organizational habitus. *Anthropology and Education Quarterly, 35*, 75–99.

Diamond, L. M. (2003a). Love matters: Romantic relationships among sexual-minority adolescents. In P. Florsheim (Ed.), *Adolescent romantic relations and sexual behavior: Theory, research, and practical implications*. Mahwah, NJ: Erlbaum.

Diamond, L. M. (2003b). What does sexual orientation orient? A biobehavioral model distinguishing romantic love and sexual desire. *Psychological Review, 110*, 173–192.

Diamond, L. M. (2006). Introduction: In search of good sexual-developmental pathways for adolescent girls. *New Directions for Child and Adolescent Development, 112*, 1–7.

Diamond, L. M., & Dubé, E. M. (2002). Friendship and attachment among heterosexual and sexual-minority youth: Does the gender of your friend matter? *Journal of Youth and Adolescence, 31*, 155–166.

Diamond, L. M., Savin-Williams, R., & Dubé, E. M. (1999). Sex, dating, passionate friendships, and romance: Intimate peer relations among lesbian, gay, and bisexual adolescents. In W. Furman, B. B. Brown, & C. Feiring (Eds.), *The development of romantic relationships in adolescence*. New York: Cambridge University Press.

Dickson, J. W. (2002, April). *The association between the quality of sibling relationship and adolescents' individual and social functioning*. Paper presented at the meeting of the Society for Research on Adolescence, New Orleans.

Dinella, L. M., & Martin, C. L. (2003, April). *Gender stereotypes, gender identity, and preferences of self-identified tomboys and traditional girls*. Paper presented at the biennial meeting of the Society for Research in Child Development, Tampa, FL.

Dinkes, R., Cataldi, E. F., Kena, G., & Baum, K. (2006). *Indicators of school crime and safety: 2006*. Washington, DC: U.S. Government Printing Office.

Dishion, T. J., Andrews, D. W., & Crosby, L. (1995). Antisocial boys and their friends in early adolescence: Relationship characteristics, quality, and interactional process. *Child Development, 66*, 139–151.

Dishion, T. J., & Dodge, K. A. (2006). Deviant peer contagion in interventions and programs: An ecological framework for understanding influence mechanisms. In K. A. Dodge, T. J. Dishion, & J. E. Lansford (Eds.), *Deviant peer influences in programs for youth: Problems and solutions*. New York: Guilford.

Dishion, T. J., & Kavanagh, K. (2003). *Intervening in adolescent problem behavior: A family-centered approach*. New York: Guilford.

Dishion, T. J., & McMahon, R. J. (1998). Parental monitoring and the prevention of child and adolescent problem behavior: A conceptual and empirical formulation. *Clinical Child and Family Psychology Review, 1*, 61–75.

Dishion, T. J., McCord, J., & Poulin, F. (1999). When interventions harm: Peer groups and problem behavior. *American Psychologist, 54*, 755–764.

Dishion, T. J., Nelson, S. E., & Bullock, B. M. (2004). Premature adolescent autonomy: Parent disengagement and deviant peer process in the amplification of problem behavior. *Journal of Adolescence, 27,* 515–530.

Dishion, T. J., Nelson, S. E., Winter, C. E., & Bullock, B. M. (2004). Adolescent friendship as a dynamic system: Entropy and deviance in the etiology and course of male antisocial behavior. *Journal of Abnormal Child Psychology, 32,* 651–663.

Dishion, T. J., & Owen, L. D. (2002). A longitudinal analysis of friendships and substance use: Bidirectional influence from adolescence to adulthood. *Developmental Psychology, 38,* 480–491.

Dittmar, H., Halliwell, E., & Ive, S. (2006). Does Barbie make girls want to be thin? The effect of experimental exposure to images of dolls on the body image of 5- to 8-year-old girls. *Developmental Psychology, 43,* 283–292.

Dmitrieva, J., Chen, C., Greenberger, E., & Gil-Rivas, V. (2004). Family relationships and adolescent psychosocial outcomes: Converging findings from Eastern and Western cultures. *Journal of Research on Adolescence, 14,* 425–447.

Dodge, K. A., Coie, J. D., & Lynam, D. (2006). Aggression and antisocial behavior in youth. In W. Damon & R. M. Lerner (Eds.), *Handbook of child psychology* (6th ed.). New York: Wiley.

Dodge, K. A., Lansford, J. E., Burks, V. S., Bates, J. E., Pettit, G. S., Fontaine, R., et al. (2003). Peer rejection and social information-processing factors in the development of aggressive behavior problems in children. *Child Development, 74,* 374–393.

Dodge, K. A., & Pettit, G. S. (2003). A biopsychosocial model of the development of chronic conduct problems in adolescence. *Developmental Psychology, 39,* 349–371.

Dogan, S. J., Conger, R. D., Kim, K. J., & Masyn, K. E. (2007). Cognitive and parenting pathways in the transmission of antisocial behavior from parents to adolescents. *Child Development, 78,* 335–349.

Dohnt, H., & Tiggemann, M. (2006a). Body image concerns in young girls: The role of peers and media prior to adolescence. *Journal of Youth and Adolescence, 35,* 141–151.

Dohnt, H., & Tiggemann, M. (2006b). The contribution of peer and media influences to the development of body satisfaction and self-esteem in young girls: A prospective study. *Developmental Psychology, 42,* 929–936.

Dominick, J. R. (2001). *Dynamics of mass communication: Media in the Digital Age* (7th ed.). New York: McGraw-Hill.

Dondi, M., Simion, F., & Caltran, G. (1999). Can newborns discriminate between their own cry and the cry of another newborn infant? *Developmental Psychology, 35,* 418–426.

Donnellan, M. B., Trzesniewski, K. H., Robins, R. W., Moffitt, T. E., & Caspi, A. (2005). Low self-esteem is related to aggression, antisocial behavior, and delinquency. *Psychological Science, 16,* 328–335.

Dorn, L. D., Susman, E. J., & Ponirakis, A. (2003). Pubertal timing and adolescent adjustment and behavior: Conclusions vary by rater. *Journal of Youth and Adolescence, 32,* 157–167.

Dornbusch, S. M. (1994, April). *Off the track.* Presidential address at the meeting of the Society for Research on Adolescence, San Diego, CA.

Douvan, E., & Adelson, J. (1966). *The adolescent experience.* New York: Wiley.

Downey, D. B., & Ainsworth-Darnell, J. W. (2002). The search for oppositional culture among black students. *American Sociological Review, 67,* 156–165.

Downey, G., Bonica, C., & Rincón, C. (1999). Rejection sensitivity and adolescent romantic relationships. In W. Furman, B. B. Brown, & C. Feiring (Eds.), *The development of romantic relationships in adolescence.* New York: Cambridge University Press.

Downey, G., Lebolt, A., Rincon, C., & Freitas, A. L. (1998). Rejection sensitivity and children's interpersonal difficulties. *Child Development, 69,* 1074–1091.

Downs, A. C., & Fuller, M. J. (1991). Recollections of spermarche: An exploratory investigation. *Current Psychology, 10,* 93–102.

Dubas, J., Graber, J., & Petersen, A. (1991). A longitudinal investigation of adolescents' changing perceptions of pubertal timing. *Developmental Psychology, 27,* 580–586.

DuBois, D. L., Burk-Braxton, C., Swenson, L., Tevendale, H., & Hardesty, J. (2002). Race and gender influences on adjustment in early adolescence: Investigation of an integrative model. *Child Development, 73,* 1573–1592.

DuBois, D. L., Burk-Braxton, C., Swenson, L., Tevendale, H., Lockerd, E. M., & Moran, B. L. (2002). Getting by with a little help from self and others: Self-esteem and social support as resources during early adolescence. *Developmental Psychology, 38,* 822–839.

DuBois, D. L., Holloway, B. E., & Valentine, J. C. (2002). Effectiveness of mentoring programs for youth: A meta-analytic review. *American Journal of Community Psychology, 30,* 157–197.

DuBois, D. L., Lockerd, E. M., Reach, K., & Parra, G. R. (2003). Effective strategies for esteem-enhancement: What do young adolescents have to say? *Journal of Early Adolescence, 23,* 405–434.

DuBois, D. L., & Tevendale, H. D. (1999). Self-esteem in childhood and adolescence: Vaccine or epiphenomenon? *Applied and Preventive Psychology, 8,* 103–117.

DuBois, D. L., Tevendale, H. D., Burk-Braxton, C., Swenson, L. P., & Hardesty, J. L. (2000). Self-system influences during early adolescence: Investigation of an integrative model. *Journal of Early Adolescence, 20,* 12–43.

Duffy, A., & Milin, R. (1996). Case study: Withdrawal syndrome in adolescent chronic cannabis users. *Journal of the American Academy of Child and Adolescent Psychiatry, 35,* 1618–1621.

Dumais, S. A. (2002). Cultural capital, gender, and school success: The role of habitus. *Sociology of Education, 75,* 44–68.

Dumont, M., & Provost, M. A. (1999). Resilience in adolescents: Protective role of social support, coping strategies, self-esteem, and social activities on experience of stress and depression. *Journal of Youth and Adolescence, 28,* 343–363.

Duncan, G. J., & Brooks-Gunn, J. (2000). Family poverty, welfare reform, and child development. *Child Development, 71,* 188–196.

Duncan, P., Ritter, P., Dornbusch, S., Gross, R., & Carlsmith, J. (1985). The effects of pubertal timing on body image, school behavior, and deviance. *Journal of Youth and Adolescence, 14,* 227–236.

Duncan, R. M., & Cheyne, J. A. (1999). Incidence and functions of self-reported private speech in young adults: A self-verbalization questionnaire. *Canadian Journal of Behavioural Science, 31,* 133–136.

Dunn, J. (1993). *Young children's close relationships: Beyond attachment.* Newbury Park, CA: Sage.

Dunn, J. (2004). *Children's friendships: The beginnings of intimacy.* Malden, MA: Blackwell.

Dunn, J., Slomkowski, C., & Beardsall, L. (1994). Sibling relationships from the preschool period through middle childhood and early adolescence. *Developmental Psychology, 30,* 315–324.

Dunphy, D. (1963). The social structure of urban adolescent peer groups. *Sociometry, 26,* 230–246.

Durston, S., Hulshoff Pol, H. E., Casey, B. J., Giedd, J. N., Buitelaar, J. K., & van Engeland, H. (2001). Anatomical MRI of the developing human brain: What have we learned? *Journal of the American Academy of Child and Adolescent Psychiatry, 40,* 1012–1020.

Dweck, C. S. (1999). *Self-theories: Their role in motivation, personality, and development.* Philadelphia, PA: Psychology Press.

Dweck, C. S., & Elliot, E. S. (1983). Achievement motivation. In P. H. Mussen (Ed.), *Handbook of child psychology. Vol. 4: Socialization, personality, and social development.* New York: Wiley.

Dworkin, J. B., Larson, R., & Hansen, D. (2003). Adolescents' accounts of growth experiences in youth activities. *Journal of Youth and Adolescence, 32,* 17–26.

Dwyer, J. T., Evans, M., Stone, E. J., Feldman, H. A., Lytle, L., Hoelscher, D., et al. (2001). Adolescents' eating patterns influence their nutrient intakes. *Journal of the American Dietetic Association, 101,* 798–801.

Eanes, A. Y., Fletcher, A. C., & Brown, B. B. (2002, April). *Friends' shared participation in extracurricular activities as a predictor of adolescent activity continuation.* Paper presented at the Society for Research on Adolescence, New Orleans.

Eaton, D. K., Kann, L., Kinchen, S., Ross, J., Hawkins, J., Harris, W. A., et al. (2006). Youth Risk Behavior Surveillance—United States, 2005. *Morbidity and Mortality Weekly Report, 55*, No. SS-5.

Eaton, S. E. (2001). *The other Boston busing story: What's won and lost across the boundary line.* New Haven, CT: Yale University Press.

Eberly, M. B., & Montemayor, R. (1999). Adolescent affection and helpfulness toward parents: A 2-year follow-up. *Journal of Early Adolescence, 19*, 226–248.

Eccles, J. S. (1993). School and family effects on the ontogeny of children's interests, self-perceptions, and activity choices. In R. Dienstbier & J. E. Jacobs (Eds.), *Developmental perspectives on motivation.* Lincoln, NE: University of Nebraska Press.

Eccles, J. S. (2004). Schools, academic motivation, and stage-environment fit. In R. M. Lerner & L. Steinberg (Eds.), *Handbook of adolescent psychology.* New York: Wiley.

Eccles, J. S., & Barber, B. L. (1999). Student council, volunteering, basketball, or marching band: What kind of extracurricular involvement matters? *Journal of Adolescent Research, 14*, 10–43.

Eccles, J. S., Barber, B., & Jozefowicz, D. H. (1998). Linking gender to educational, occupational, and recreational choices: Applying the Eccles et al. model of achievement-related choices. In W. B. Swann, J. H. Langlois, & L. A. Gilbert (Eds.), *The many faces of gender: The multidimensional model of Janet Spence.* Washington, DC: APA Press.

Eccles, J. S., Buchanan, C., Flanagan, C., Fuligni, A., Midgley, C., & Yee, D. (1991). Control versus autonomy in adolescence. *Journal of Social Issues, 47*, 53–68.

Eccles, J. S., & Gootman, J. A. (Eds.). (2002). *Community programs to promote youth development.* Washington, DC: National Academy Press.

Eccles, J. S., Lord, S. F., Roeser, R. W., Barber, B. L., & Hernandez Jozefowicz, D. M. (1997). The association of school transitions in early adolescence with developmental trajectories through high school. In J. Schulenberg, J. L. Maggs, & K. Hurrelmann (Eds.), *Health risks and developmental transitions during adolescence.* New York: Cambridge University Press.

Eccles, J. S., Midgley, C., Wigfield, A., Buchanan, C. M., Reuman, D., Flanagan, C., & MacIver, D. (1993). Development during adolescence: The impact of stage-environment fit on adolescents' experiences in schools and families. *American Psychologist, 48*, 90–101.

Eccles, J. S., & Roeser, R. W. (2003). Schools as developmental contexts. In G. R. Adams & M. Berzonsky (Eds.), *Blackwell handbook on adolescence.* New York: Blackwell.

Eccles, J. S., & Wigfield, A. (1985). Teacher expectations and student motivation. In J. B. Dusek (Ed.), *Teacher Expectations.* Hillsdale, NJ: Erlbaum.

Eccles, J. S., Wigfield, A., & Byrnes, J. (2004). Cognitive development in adolescence. In R. M. Lerner, M. A. Easterbrooks, & J. Mistry (Eds.), *Comprehensive handbook of psychology. Vol. 6: Developmental psychology.* New York: Wiley.

Eccles, J. S., Wong, C. A., & Peck, S. C. (2006). Ethnicity as a social context for the development of African-American adolescents. *Journal of School Psychology, 44*, 407–426.

Eckerman, C. O., & Didow, S. M. (1996). Nonverbal imitation and toddlers' mastery of verbal means of achieving coordinated action. *Developmental Psychology, 32*, 141–152.

Eder, D. (1985). The cycle of popularity: Interpersonal relations among female adolescents. *Sociology of Education, 58*, 154–165.

Eder, D. (1995). *School talk: Gender and adolescent culture.* New Brunswick, NJ: Rutgers University Press.

Eder, D., & Kinney, D. A. (1995). The effect of middle school extracurricular activities on adolescents' popularity and peer status. *Youth & Society, 26*, 298–324.

Education Trust. (2001). *Youth at the crossroads.* Washington, DC: Author.

Egan, S. K., & Perry, D. G. (2001). Gender identity: A multidimensional analysis with implications for psychosocial adjustment. *Developmental Psychology, 37*, 451–463.

Eggebeen, D. (1992). Changes in sibling configurations for American preschool children. *Social Biology, 39*, 27–44.

Egley, A., Jr., & Ritz, C. E. (2006). *Highlights of the 2004 National Youth Gang Survey.* Washington, DC: Office of Juvenile Justice and Delinquency Prevention.

Ehrenberg, R. G., Brewer, D. J., Gamoran, A., & Willms, J. D. (2001). Class size and student achievement. *Psychological Science in the Public Interest, 2*, 1–30.

Ehrhardt, A. A., & Baker, S. W. (1977). Males and females with congenital adrenal hyperplasia: A family study of intelligence and gender-related behavior. In A. Lee, L. P. Plotnick, A. A. Kowarski, & C. J. Migeon (Eds.), *Congenital adrenal hyperplasia.* Baltimore: University Park Press.

Eichhorn, D. (1966). *The middle school.* New York: Center for Applied Research in Education.

Eichstedt, J. A., Serbin, L. A., Poulin-Dubois, D., & Sen, M. G. (2002). Of bears and men: Infants' knowledge of conventional and metaphorical gender stereotypes. *Infant Behavior and Development, 25*, 296–310.

Eisenberg, N., Fabes, R. A., & Guthrie, I. K. (1997). Coping with stress: The roles of regulation and development. In S. A. Wolchik & I. N. Sandler (Eds.), *Handbook of children's coping: Linking theory and intervention.* New York: Plenum.

Eisenberg, N., Fabes, R. A., Murphy, B., Karbon, M., Maszk, P., Smith, M., et al. (1994). The relations of emotionality and regulation to dispositional and situational empathy-related responding. *Journal of Personality and Social Psychology, 66*, 776–797.

Eisenberg, N., Fabes, R. A., & Spinrad, T. L. (2006). Prosocial development. In W. Damon & R. Lerner (Eds.), *Handbook of child psychology* (6th ed.). New York: Wiley.

Eisenberg, N., & Valiente, C. (2004). Elaborations on a theme: Beyond main effects in relations of parenting to children's coping and regulation. *Parenting: Science and Practice, 4*, 319–323.

Eisenberger, N. I., & Lieberman, M. D. (2005). Why it hurts to be left out: The neurocognitive overlap between physical and social pain. In K. D. Williams, J. P. Forgas, & W. von Hippel (Eds.). *The social outcast: Ostracism, social exclusion, rejection, and bullying.* New York: The Psychology Press.

Elbaum, B. (2002). The self-concept of students with learning disabilities: A meta-analysis of comparisons across different placements. *Learning Disabilities Research & Practice, 17*, 216–226.

Elder, G. H., Jr. (1980). Adolescence in historical perspective. In J. Adelson (Ed.), *Handbook of adolescent psychology.* New York: Wiley.

Elder, G. H., Jr., & Conger, R. D. (2000). *Children of the land.* Chicago: University of Chicago Press.

Elkind, D. (1967). Egocentrism in adolescence. *Child Development, 38*, 1025–1034.

Elkind, D. (1978). Understanding the young adolescent. *Adolescence, 13*, 127–134.

Elkind, D. (1981). *The hurried child.* Reading, MA: Addison-Wesley.

Elkind, D. (1985). Egocentrism redux. *Developmental Review, 5*, 218–226.

Elkind, D., & Bowen, R. (1979). Imaginary audience behavior in children and adolescents. *Developmental Psychology, 15*, 38–44.

Elliot, A., & Church, M. (1997). A hierarchical model of approach and avoidance achievement motivation. *Journal of Personality and Social Psychology, 72*, 218–232.

Elliot, A. J., & Dweck, C. S. (2005). Competence and motivation: Competence as the core of achievement motivation. In A. J. Elliot & C. S. Dweck (Eds.), *Handbook of competence and motivation.* New York: Guilford.

Elliott, J. G., & Bempechat, J. (2002). The culture and contexts of achievement motivation. *New Directions for Child and Adolescent Development, 96*, 7–26.

Elliott, J. G., Hufton, N., Illushin, L., & Willis, W. (2003). *Performance in context: Motivation and achievement from an international perspective.* New York: Palgrave Press.

Ellis, B. J. (2004). Timing of pubertal maturation in girls: An integrated life history approach. *Psychological Bulletin, 130*, 920–958.

Ellis, B., & Garber, J. (2000). Psychosocial antecedents of variation in girls' pubertal timing: Maternal depression, stepfather presence, and marital and family stress. *Child Development, 71*, 485–501.

Ellis, B., McFadyen-Ketchum, S., Dodge, K., Pettit, G., & Bates, J. (1999). Quality of early family relationships and individual differences in the timing of pubertal maturation in girls: A longitudinal test of an evolutionary model. *Journal of Personality and Social Psychology, 77,* 387–401.

Ellis, B. J., & Essex, M. J. (2007). Family environments, adrenarche, and sexual maturation: A longitudinal test of a life history model. *Child Development, 78,* 1799–1817.

Ellis, S., Rogoff, B., & Cromer, C. C. (1981). Age segregation in children's social interactions. *Developmental Psychology, 17,* 399–407.

Else-Quest, N. M., Hyde, J. S., Goldsmith, H. H., & Van Hulle, C. A. (2006). Gender differences in temperament: A meta-analysis. *Psychological Bulletin, 132,* 33–72.

Emery, R. E. (1999). *Marriage, divorce, and children's adjustment* (2nd ed.). Thousand Oaks, CA: Sage.

Engels, R. C. M. E., Dekovic, M., & Meeus, W. (2002). Parenting practices, social skills and peer relations in adolescence. *Social Behavior and Personality, 30,* 3–18.

Engels, R. C. M. E., Finkenauer, C., Meeus, W., & Dekovic, M. (2001). Parental attachment and adolescents' emotional adjustment: The associations with social skills and relational competence. *Journal of Counseling Psychology, 48,* 428–439.

Engle, R. W., Kane, M. J., & Tuholski, S. W. (1999). Individual differences in working memory capacity and what they tell us about controlled attention, general fluid intelligence, and functions of the prefrontal cortex. In A. Miyake & P. Shah (Eds.), *Models of working memory.* Cambridge, UK: Cambridge University Press.

Englund, M. M., Levy, A. K., Hyson, D. M., & Sroufe, L. A. (2000). Adolescent social competence: Effectiveness in a group setting. *Child Development, 71,* 1049–1060.

Ennett, S. T., & Bauman, K. E. (1996). Adolescent social networks: School, demographic, and longitudinal considerations. *Journal of Adolescent Research, 11,* 194–215.

Enright, R. D., Lapsley, D. K., & Shukla, D. G. (1979). Adolescent egocentrism in early and late adolescence. *Adolescence, 14,* 687–695.

Enright, R. D., Shukla, D. G., & Lapsley, D. K. (1980). Adolescent egocentrism–sociocentrism and self–consciousness. *Journal of Youth and Adolescence, 16,* 541–559.

Entwistle, N. (1990). Student learning and classroom environment. In N. Jones & N. Frederickson (Eds.), *Refocusing educational psychology.* Oxford, UK: Taylor & Francis.

Epstein, S. (1994). Integration of the cognitive and psychodynamic unconscious. *American Psychologist, 49,* 709–724.

Erchull, M. J., Chrisler, J. C., Gorman, J. A., & Johnston-Robledo, I. (2002). Education and advertising: A content analysis of commercially produced booklets about menstruation. *Journal of Early Adolescence, 22,* 455–474.

Erickson, F. (2002). Culture and human development. *Human Development, 45,* 299–306.

Ericson, N. (2001, May). *The YMCA's teen action agenda.* OJJDP Fact Sheet #14. Washington, DC: U.S. Department of Justice, Office of Juvenile Justice and Delinquency Prevention.

Erikson, E. H. (1950). *Childhood and society.* New York: Norton.

Erikson, E. H. (1956). The problem of ego identity. *Journal of the American Psychoanalytic Association, 4,* 56–121.

Erikson, E. H. (1959). *Identity and the life cycle.* New York: International Universities Press.

Erikson, E. H. (1963). *Childhood and society* (2nd ed.). New York: Norton.

Erikson, E. H. (1964). *Insight and responsibility.* New York: Norton.

Erikson, E. H. (1968). *Identity: Youth and crisis.* New York: Norton.

Etzioni, A. (1996). *The new golden rule: Community and morality in a democratic society.* New York: Basic Books.

Evans, E., Hawton, K., & Rodham, K. (2004). Factors associated with suicidal phenomena in adolescents: A systematic review of population-based studies. *Clinical Psychology Review, 24,* 957–979.

Evans, J. P., & Taylor, J. (1995). Understanding violence in contemporary and earlier gangs: An exploratory application of the theory of reasoned action. *Journal of Black Psychology, 21,* 71–81.

Eveleth, P. B., & Tanner, J. M. (1976). *Worldwide variation in human growth.* New York: Cambridge University Press.

Eveleth, P. B., & Tanner, J. M. (1990). *Worldwide variation in human growth.* New York: Cambridge University Press.

Experiment in International Living. (2004). *The Experiment in International Living 2004.* Brattleboro, VT: Author.

Fadiman, A. (1997). *The spirit catches you and you fall down: A Hmong child, her American doctors, and the collision of two cultures.* New York: Farrar, Straus, and Giroux.

Fagan, J., & Zimring, F. (2000). *The changing borders of juvenile justice: Transfer of adolescents to the criminal court.* Chicago: University of Chicago Press.

Fagot, B. I., Rodgers, C. S., & Leinbach, M. D. (2000). Theories of gender socialization. In T. Eckes & H. M. Trautner (Eds.), *The developmental social psychology of gender.* Mahwah, NJ: Erlbaum.

Fairburn, C. G., & Harrison, P. J. (2003, Feb.). Eating disorders. *Lancet, 361,* 407–416.

Faircloth, B. S., & Hamm, J. V. (2005). Sense of belonging among high school students representing 4 ethnic groups. *Journal of Youth and Adolescence, 34,* 293–309.

Falbo, T. (1992). Social norms and the one-child family: Clinical and policy implications. In F. Boer & J. Dunn (Eds.), *Children's sibling relationships.* Hillsdale, NJ: Erlbaum.

Farber, S. L. (1981). *Identical twins reared apart: A reanalysis.* New York: Basic Books.

Farkas, G., Lleras, C., & Maczuga, S. (2002). Does oppositional culture exist in minority and poverty peer groups? *American Sociological Review, 67,* 148–155.

Farkas, S., & Johnson, J., with Immerwahr, S., & McHugh, J. (1998). *Time to move on: African-American and White parents set an agenda for public.* New York: Public Agenda.

Farmer, T. W., Leung, M-C., Pearl, R., Rodkin, P. C., Cadwallader, T. W., & Van Acker, R. (2002). Deviant or diverse peer groups? The peer affiliations of aggressive elementary students. *Journal of Educational Psychology, 94,* 611–620.

Farrell, M., & Rosenberg, S. (1981). *Men at midlife.* Boston: Auburn House.

Farrington, D. P. (2004). Conduct disorder, aggression and delinquency. In R. M. Lerner & L. Steinberg (Eds.), *Handbook of adolescent psychology.* New York: Wiley.

Farrington, D. P., Loeber, R., & Stouthamer-Loeber, M. (2003). How can the relationship between race and violence be explained? In D. Hawkins (Ed.), *Violent crimes: Assessing race and ethnic differences.* New York: Cambridge University Press.

Farver, J. A. M., Narang, S. K., & Bhadha, B. R. (2002). East meets West: Ethnic identity, acculturation, and conflict in Asian Indian families. *Journal of Family Psychology, 16,* 338–350.

Faust, M. S. (1960). Development maturity as a determinant in prestige of adolescent girls. *Child Development, 31,* 173–184.

Faust, M. S. (1983). Alternative constructions of adolescent growth. In J. Brooks-Gunn & A. C. Petersen (Eds.), *Girls at puberty.* New York: Plenum.

Federal Bureau of Investigation. (2006). *Crime in the United States 2004.* Available: www.fbi.gov/ucr/cius_04/index.html.

Federal Trade Commission. (2007). *Marketing violent entertainment to children.* Washington, DC: Author.

Feinberg, M. E., & Hetherington, E. M. (2000). Sibling differentiation in adolescence: Implications for behavioral genetic theory. *Child Development, 71,* 1512–1524.

Feinberg, M. E., & Hetherington, E. M. (2001). Differential parenting as a within-family variable. *Journal of Family Psychology, 15,* 22–37.

Feiring, C. (1996). Concepts of romance in 15-year-old adolescents. *Journal of Research on Adolescence, 6,* 181–200.

Feiring, C. (1999a). Gender identity and the development of romantic relationships in adolescence. In W. Furman, B. B. Brown, & C. Feiring (Eds.), *Development of romantic relationships in adolescence.* Cambridge, UK: Cambridge University Press.

Feiring, C. (1999b). Other-sex friendship networks and the development of romantic relationships in adolescence. *Journal of Youth and Adolescence, 28,* 495–512.

Feldlaufer, H., Midgley, C., & Eccles, J. S. (1988). Student, teacher, and observer perceptions of the classroom environment before and after the transition to junior high school. *Journal of Early Adolescence, 8,* 133–156.

Feldman, A. F., & Matjasko, J. L. (2005). The role of school-based extracurricular activities in adolescent development: A comprehensive review and future directions. *Review of Educational Research, 75,* 159–210.

Feldman, A. F., & Matjasko, J. L. (2006). Profiles and portfolios of adolescent school-based extracurricular activity participation. *Journal of Adolescence, 30,* 313–332.

Feldman, S. S., Rosenthal, D. A., Mont-Reynaud, K., Lao, S., & Leung, K. (1991). Ain't misbehavin': Adolescent values and family environments as correlates of misconduct in Australia, Hong Kong, and the United States. *Journal of Research on Adolescence, 1,* 109–134.

Feldman, S. S., Turner, R. A., & Araujo, K. (1999). Interpersonal context as an influence on sexual timetables of youths: Gender and ethnic effects. *Journal of Research on Adolescence, 9,* 25–52.

Felner, R. D., Brand, S., DuBois, D. L., Adan, A., Mulhall, P. F., & Evans, E. G. (1995). Socioeconomic disadvantage, proximal environmental experiences, and socioemotional and academic adjustment in early adolescence: Investigation of a mediated effects model. *Child Development, 66,* 774–792.

Feng, J., Spence, I., & Pratt, J. (2007). Playing an action video game reduces gender differences in spatial cognition. *Psychological Science, 18,* 850–855.

Ferguson, A. N., Bowey, J. A., & Tilley, A. (2002). The association between auditory memory span and speech rate in children from kindergarten to sixth grade. *Journal of Experimental Child Psychology, 81,* 141–156.

Ferguson, R. F. (1998). Teachers' perceptions and expectations and the Black-White test score gap. In C. Jencks and M. Phillips (Eds.), *The Black-White test score gap.* Washington, DC: Brookings Institute Press.

Fergusson, D., Woodward, L., & Horwood, L. (1999). Childhood peer relationship problems and young people's involvement with deviant peers in adolescence. *Journal of Abnormal Child Psychology, 27,* 357–369.

Ferron, C. (1997). Body image in adolescence: Cross-cultural research—results of the preliminary phase of a quantitative survey. *Adolescence, 32,* 735–745.

Ferry, T. R., Fouad, N. A., & Smith, P. L. (2000). The role of family context in a social cognitive model for career-related choice behavior: A math and science perspective. *Journal of Vocational Behavior, 57,* 348–364.

Festinger, L. (1957). *A theory of cognitive dissonance.* Stanford, CA: Stanford University Press.

Field, A. E., Camargo, C. A., Jr., Taylor, C. B., Berkey, C. S., Roberts, S. B., & Colditz, G. A. (2001). Peer, parent, and media influences on the development of weight concerns and frequent dieting among preadolescent and adolescent girls and boys. *Pediatrics. 107,* 54–60.

Field, T., Diego, M., & Sanders, C. E. (2001). Exercise is positively related to adolescents' relationships and academics. *Adolescence, 36,* 105–110.

Figueira-McDonough, J. (1986). School context, gender, and delinquency. *Journal of Youth and Adolescence, 15,* 79–98.

Fine, M. (1991). *Framing dropouts: Notes on the politics of an urban public high school.* Albany, NY: State University of New York Press.

Fine, M., & Somerville, J. (Eds.). (1998). *Small schools, big imaginations: A creative look at urban public schools.* Chicago: Cross City Campaign for Urban School Reform.

Finkenauer, C., Engels, R. C. M. E., & Meeus, W. (2002). Keeping secrets from parents: Advantages and disadvantages of secrecy in adolescence. *Journal of Youth and Adolescence, 31,* 123–136.

Finn, J. D. (2002). Small classes in American schools: Research, practice, and politics. *Phi Delta Kappan, 83,* 551–560.

Finn, J. D., Gerber, S. B., Achilles, C. M., & Boyd-Zaharias, J. (2001). The enduring effects of small classes. *Teachers College Record, 103,* 145–183.

Fischer, K. W. (1980). A theory of cognitive development: The control and construction of hierarchies of skills. *Psychological Review, 87,* 477–531.

Fischer, K. W., & Bidell, T. (1998). Dynamic development of psychological structures in action and thought. In W. Damon (Gen. Ed.) & R. M. Lerner (Vol. Ed.), *Handbook of child psychology,* Vol 1. New York: Wiley.

Fisher, H. E. (2004). *Why we love: The nature and chemistry of romantic love.* New York: Henry Holt.

Fisher, H. E. (2006). Broken hearts: The nature and risks of romantic rejection. In A. C. Crouter & A. Booth (Eds.), *Romance and sex in adolescence and emerging adulthood: Risks and opportunities.* Mahwah, NJ: Erlbaum.

Fisher, W., Branscombe, N., & Lemery, C. (1983). The bigger the better? Arousal and attributional responses to erotic stimuli that depict different size penises. *Journal of Sex Research, 19,* 377–396.

Fiske, A. P. (2002). Using individualism and collectivism to compare cultures—A critique of the validity and measurement of the constructs: Comment on Oyserman et al. (2002). *Psychological Bulletin, 128,* 78–88.

Flaks, D. K., Ficher, I., Masterpasqua, F., & Joseph, G. (1995). Lesbians choosing motherhood: A comparative study of lesbian and heterosexual parents and their children. *Developmental Psychology, 31,* 105–114.

Flammer, A., & Schaffner, B. (2003). Adolescent leisure across European nations. *New Directions for Child and Adolescent Development, 90,* 65–77.

Flanagan, C. (2009). Young people's civic engagement and political development. In A. Furlong (Ed.), *Handbook of youth and young adulthood.* New York: Routledge.

Flanagan, C. A. (2003). Volunteerism, leadership, political socialization, and civic engagement. In R. M. Lerner & L. Steinberg (Eds.), *Handbook of adolescent psychology.* New York: Wiley.

Flannery, D. J., Hussey, D., Biebelhausen, L., & Wester, K. (2003). Crime, delinquency, and youth gangs. In G. Adams & M. Berzonsky (Eds.), *Blackwell handbook of adolescence.* Malden, MA: Blackwell.

Flavell, J. H. (1996). Piaget's legacy. *Psychological Science, 7,* 200–203.

Flavell, J. H., Miller, P. H., & Miller, S. A. (2002). *Cognitive development* (4th ed.). Upper Saddle River, NJ: Prentice Hall.

Flieller, A. (1999). Comparison of the development of formal thought in adolescent cohorts aged 10 to 15 years (1967–1996 and 1972–1993). *Developmental Psychology, 35,* 1048–1058.

Floud, R. (1994). The heights of Europeans since 1750: A new source for European economic history. In J. Komlos (Ed.), *Stature, living standards, and economic development: Essays in anthropometric history.* Chicago: University of Chicago Press.

Flouri, E., & Buchanan, A. (2002). The role of work-related skills and career role models in adolescent career maturity. *Career Development Quarterly, 51,* 36–43.

Flynn, J. (1987). Massive IQ gains in 14 nations: What IQ tests really measure. *Psychological Bulletin, 101,* 171–191.

Flynn, J. (1999). Searching for justice: The discovery of IQ gains over time. *American Psychologist, 54,* 5–20.

Flynn, K., & Fitzgibbon, M. (1996). Body image ideals of low-income African American mothers and their preadolescent daughters. *Journal of Youth and Adolescence, 25,* 615–630.

Foehr, U. G. (2006). *Media multitasking among American youth: Prevalence, predictors and pairings.* Washington, DC: Henry J. Kaiser Family Foundation.

Foley, D. L., Eaves, L. J., Wormley, B., Silberg, J., Maes, H., Kuhn, J., et al. (2004). Childhood adversity, monoamine oxidase A genotype, and risk for conduct disorder. *Archives of General Psychiatry, 61,* 738–744.

Food and Drug Administration. (2004, October 15). *Suicidality in children and adolescents being treated with antidepressant medications.* FDA Public Health Advisory. Available: www.fda.gov/CDER/drug/antidepressants/SSRIPHA200410.htm.

Food and Drug Administration. (2007, May 2). *FDA proposes new warnings about suicidal thinking, behavior in young adults who take antidepressant medications.* Available: www.fda.gov/bbs/topics/NEWS/2007/NEW01624.html.

Ford, C. S., & Beach, F. A. (1951). *Patterns of sexual behavior.* New York: Harper.

Fordham, S., & Ogbu, J. U. (1986). Black students' school success: The "burden of 'acting white'." *Urban Review, 18,* 176–206.

Forum on Child and Family Statistics. (2002). *America's children: Key national indicators of well-being, 2002.* Washington, DC: U.S. Government Printing Office.

Fouts, G., & Burggraf, K. (2000). Television situation comedies: Female weight, male negative comments, and audience reactions. *Sex Roles, 42,* 925–932.

Fox, C. L., & Boulton, M. J. (2006). Friendship as a moderator of the relationship between social skills problems and peer victimization. *Aggressive Behavior, 32,* 110–121.

Fox, N. A., Calkins, S., Schmidt, L., Rubin, K. H., & Coplan, R. J. (1996). The role of frontal activation in the regulation and dysregulation of social behavior during the preschool years. *Development and Psychopathology, 8,* 89–102.

Fox, N. A., Henderson, H. A., Marshall, P. J., Nichols, K. E., & Ghera, M. M. (2005). Behavioral inhibition: Linking biology and behavior within a developmental framework. *Annual Review of Psychology, 56,* 235–262.

Fox, V. (1978). Is adolescence a phenomenon of modern times? *History of childhood quarterly, 5,* 271–290.

Frankenberg, E., Lee, C., & Orfield, G. (2003). *A multiracial society with segregated schools: Are we losing the dream?* Cambridge, MA: The Civil Rights Project, Harvard University.

Franquart–Declercq, C., & Gineste, M.–D. (2001). L'enfant et la métaphore. *L'Année Psychologique, 101,* 723–752.

Franzese, R. J., Covey, H. C., & Menard, S. W. (2006). *Youth gangs* (3rd ed.). Springfield, IL: Charles C. Thomas.

Fredericks, J. A., & Eccles, J. S. (2005). Developmental benefits of extracurricular involvement: Do peer characteristics mediate the link between activities and youth outcomes? *Journal of Youth and Adolescence, 34,* 507–520.

Fredricks, J. A., & Eccles, J. S. (2006). Is extracurricular participation associated with beneficial outcomes? Concurrent and longitudinal relations. *Developmental Psychology, 42,* 698–713.

Fredrickson, B. L., & Roberts, T.-A. (1997). Objectification theory: Toward understanding women's lived experiences and mental health risks. *Psychology of Women Quarterly, 21,* 173–206.

Fredriksen, K., Rhodes, J., Reddy, R., & Way, N. (2004). Sleepless in Chicago: Tracking the effects of adolescent sleep loss during the middle school years. *Child Development, 75,* 84–95.

Freedman, J. L. (1984). Effects of television violence on aggressiveness. *Psychological Bulletin, 96,* 227–246.

Freeman, D. (1983). *Margaret Mead and Samoa.* Cambridge, MA: Harvard University Press.

Freeman, H., & Brown, B. B. (2001). Primary attachment to parents and peers during adolescence: Differences by attachment style. *Journal of Youth and Adolescence, 30,* 653–674.

French, S. E., Seidman, E., Allen, L., & Aber, J. L. (2006). The development of ethnic identity during adolescence. *Developmental Psychology, 42,* 1–10.

Freud, A. (1936/1946). *The ego and the mechanisms of defense.* New York: International Universities Press.

Freud, A. (1958). Adolescence. *Psychoanalytic Study of the Child, 13,* 255–278.

Freud, S. (1938). *An outline of psychoanalysis.* London: Hogarth Press.

Frey, K. S., Hirschstein, M. K., Snell, J. L., Edstrom, L. V. S., MacKenzie, E. P., & Broderick, C. J. (2005). Reducing playground bullying and supporting beliefs: An experimental trial of the *Steps to Respect* program. *Developmental Psychology, 41,* 479–491.

Frick, P. J., & Kimonis, E. R. (2005). Externalizing disorders of childhood and adolescence. In J. E. Maddux & B. A. Winstead (Eds.), *Psychopathology: Foundations for a contemporary understanding.* Mahwah, NJ: Erlbaum.

Friedman, M. S., Koeske, G. F., Silvestre, A. J., Korr, W. S., & Sites, E. W. (2006). The impact of gender-role nonconforming behavior, bullying, and social support on suicidality among gay male youth. *Journal of Adolescent Health, 38,* 621–623.

Friedman, R. A., & Leon, A. C. (2007, May 7). Expanding the black box—Depression, antidepressants, and the risk of suicide. *New England Journal of Medicine,* Article #10.1056/NEJMp078015. Available: www.nejm.org.

Frisbie, C. J. (1967). *Kinaaldá: A study of the Navaho girl's puberty ceremony.* Middletown: Wesleyan University Press.

Frisch, R. E. (1984). Body fat, puberty, and fertility. *Biology Review, 59*(2), 161–188.

Frisch, R. E. (1991). Puberty and body fat. In R. M. Lerner, A. C. Petersen, & J. Brooks-Gunn (Eds.), *Encyclopedia of adolescence* (Vol. 2). New York: Garland.

Frost, J., & McKelvie, S. (2004). Self-esteem and body satisfaction in male and female elementary school, high school, and university students. *Sex Roles, 51,* 45–54.

Fry, A. F., & Hale, S. (2000). Relationships among processing speed, working memory, and fluid intelligence in children. *Biological Psychology, 54,* 1–34.

Frye, A. A., & Garber, J. (2005). The relations among maternal depression, maternal criticism, and adolescents' externalizing and internalizing symptoms. *Journal of Abnormal Child Psychology, 33,* 1–11.

Fuligni, A. J. (1997). The academic achievement of adolescents from immigrant families: The roles of family background, attitudes, and behavior. *Child Development, 68,* 261–273.

Fuligni, A. J. (1998). Authority, autonomy, and parent-adolescent conflict and cohesion: A study of adolescents from Mexican, Chinese, Filipino, and European backgrounds. *Developmental Psychology, 34,* 782–792.

Fuligni, A. J. (2001). Family obligation and the academic motivation of adolescents from Asian, Latin American, and European backgrounds. *New Directions for Child and Adolescent Development,* Serial No. 94, 61–75.

Fuligni, A. J., & Eccles, J. (1993). Perceived parent-child relationships and early adolescents' orientation toward peers. *Developmental Psychology, 29,* 622–632.

Fuligni, A. J., Eccles, J. S., & Barber, B. L. (1995). The long-term effects of seventh-grade ability grouping in mathematics. *Journal of Early Adolescence, 15,* 58–89.

Fuligni, A. J., Eccles, J. S., Barber, B. L., & Clements, P. (2001). Early adolescent peer orientation and adjustment during high school. *Developmental Psychology, 37,* 28–36.

Fuligni, A. J., & Stevenson, H. (1995). Time-use and mathematics achievement among American, Chinese, and Japanese high school students. *Child Development 66,* 830–842.

Fuligni, A. J., Tseng, V., & Lam, M. (1999). Attitudes toward family obligations among American adolescents from Asian, Latin American, and European backgrounds. *Child Development, 70,* 1030–1044.

Fuligni, A. J., Witkow, M., & Garcia, C. (2005). Ethnic identity and the academic adjustment of adolescents from Mexican, Chinese, and European backgrounds. *Developmental Psychology, 41,* 799–811.

Fuligni, A. J., Yip, T., & Tseng, V. (2002). The impact of family obligation on the daily activities and psychological well-being of Chinese American adolescents. *Child Development, 73,* 302–314.

Fuligni, A. J., & Zhang, W. (2004). Attitudes toward family obligation among adolescents in contemporary urban and rural China. *Child Development, 75,* 180–182.

Fullagar, S. (2003). Wasted lives: The social dynamics of shame and youth suicide. *Journal of Sociology, 39,* 291–308.

Fuller, B., Gawlik, M., Gonzales, E. K., & Park, S., with Gibbings, G. (2003). Charter schools and inequality: National disparities in funding, teacher quality, and student support. Working Paper Series 03-2. Berkeley, CA: Policy Analysis for California Education.

Furman, W. (1989). The development of children's social networks. In D. Belle (Ed.), *Children's social networks and social supports.* New York: Wiley.

Furman, W., & Buhrmester, D. (1985). Children's perceptions of the qualities of sibling relationships. *Child Development, 56,* 448–461.

Furman, W., & Buhrmester, D. (1992). Age and sex differences in perceptions of networks of personal relationships. *Child Development, 63,* 103–115.

Furman, W., Ho, M. J., & Low, S. M. (2007). The rocky road of adolescent romantic experience: Dating and adjustment. In R. C. M. E. Engels, M. Kerr, & H. Stattin (Eds.), *Friends, lovers and groups: Key relationships in adolescence.* New York: Wiley.

Furman, W., & Simon, V. A. (1999). Cognitive representations of adolescent romantic relationships. In W. Furman, B. B. Brown, & C. Feiring (Eds.), *The development of romantic relationships in adolescence.* New York: Cambridge University Press.

Furman, W., Simon, V. A., Shaffer, L., & Bouchey, H. A. (2002). Adolescents' working models and styles for relationships with parents, friends, and romantic partners. *Child Development, 73,* 241–255.

Furrer, C. J., Skinner, E., Marchand, G., & Kindermann, T. A. (2006, March). *Engagement vs. disaffection as central constructs in the dynamics of motivational development.* Paper presented at the Annual Meeting of the Society for Research on Adolescence, San Francisco, CA.

Furstenberg, F. E., Jr., & Harris, K. M. (1992). The disappearing American father? Divorce and the waning significance of biological parenthood. In S. J. South & S. E. Tolnay (Eds.), *The changing American family: Sociological and demographic perspectives*. Boulder, CO: Westview Press.

Fussell, E. (2002). Youth in aging societies. In J. Mortimer & R. Larson (Eds.), *The future of adolescent experience: Societal trends and the transition to adulthood*. New York: Cambridge University Press.

Fussell, E., & Greene, M. E. (2002). Demographic trends affecting youth around the world. In B. B. Brown, R. W. Larson, & T. S. Saraswathi (Eds.), *The world's youth: Adolescence in eight regions of the globe*. New York: Cambridge University Press.

Gaddis, A., & Brooks-Gunn, J. (1985). The male experience of pubertal change. *Journal of Youth and Adolescence, 14*, 61–69.

Gaines, S., Jr., Marelich, W., Bledose, K., Steers, W., Henderson, M., Granrose, C., et al. (1997). Links between race/ethnicity and cultural values as mediated by racial/ethnic identity and moderated by gender. *Journal of Personality and Social Psychology, 72*, 1460–1476.

Galambos, N. L. (2004). Gender and gender role development in adolescence. In R. M. Lerner & L. Steinberg (Eds.), *Handbook of adolescent psychology*. New York: Wiley.

Galambos, N. L., Almeida, D. M., & Petersen, A. C. (1990). Masculinity, femininity, and sex role attitudes in early adolescence: Exploring gender intensification. *Child Development, 61*, 1905–1914.

Galambos, N. L., Barker, E. T., & Almeida, D. M. (2003). Parents do matter: Trajectories of change in externalizing and internalizing problems in early adolescence. *Child Development, 74*, 578–594.

Galambos, N. L., & Ehrenberg, M. F. (1997). The family as health risk and opportunity: A focus on divorce and working families. In J. Schulenberg, J. L. Maggs, & K. Hurrelmann (Eds.), *Health risks and developmental transitions during adolescence*. New York: Cambridge University Press.

Galambos, N. L., Kolaric, G., Sears, H., & Maggs, J. (1999). Adolescents' subjective age: An indicator of perceived maturity. *Journal of Research on Adolescence, 9*, 309–337.

Galambos, N. L., Leadbeater, B. J., & Barker, E. T. (2004). Gender differences in and risk factors for depression in adolecence: A 4-year longitudinal study. *International Journal of Behavioral Development, 28*, 16–25.

Gallagher, W. (1993, May). Midlife myths. *The Atlantic Monthly*, 51–68.

Gallese, V. (2005). "Being like me": Self-other identity, mirror neurons, and empathy. In S. Hurley & N. Chater (Eds.), *Perspectives on imitation: From neuroscience to social science: Vol. 1: Mechanisms of imitation and imitation in animals*. Cambridge, MA: MIT Press.

Gallese, V., Keysers, C., & Rizzolatti, G. (2004). A unifying view of the basis of

social cognition. *Trends in Cognitive Sciences, 8*, 396–403.

Gallup Organization. (1999, September 27). Poll analysis: Americans want integrated schools, but oppose school busing. Available: www.gallup.com.

Galotti, K. M., Komatsu, L. K., & Voelz, S. (1997). Children's differential performance on deductive and inductive syllogisms. *Developmental Psychology, 33*, 70–78.

Galston, W. A. (2001). Political knowledge, political engagement, and civic education. *Annual Review of Political Science, 4*, 217–234.

Galvin, A., Hare, T. A., Parra, C. E., Penn, J., Voss, H., Glover, G., & Casey, B. J. (2006). Earlier development of the accumbens relative to orbitofrontal cortex might underlie risk-taking behavior in adolescents. *Journal of Neuroscience, 26*, 6885–6892.

Ganahl, D. J., Prinsen, T. J., & Netzley, S. B. (2003). A content analysis of prime time commercials: A contextual framework of gender representation. *Sex Roles, 49*, 545–551.

Garandeau, C. F., & Cillessen, A. H. N. (2006). From indirect aggression to invisible aggression: A conceptual view on bullying and peer group manipulation. *Aggression and Violent Behavior, 11*, 612–625.

Garcia Coll, C. G., Meyer, E. C., & Brillon, L. (1995). Ethnic and minority parenting. In M. H. Bornstein (Ed.), *Handbook of parenting: Vol. 2. Biology and ecology of parenting*. Mahwah, NJ: Erlbaum.

Gardner, H. (1983). *Frames of mind: The theory of multiple intelligences*. New York: Basic Books.

Gardner, H. (1993). *Multiple intelligences: The theory in practice*. New York: Basic Books.

Gardner, H. (1999). *Intelligence reframed: Multiple intelligences for the 21st century*. New York: Basic Books.

Gardner, R. M., Friedman, B. N., & Jackson, N. A. (1999). Body size estimations, body dissatisfaction, and ideal size preferences in children six through thirteen. *Journal of Youth and Adolescence, 28*, 603–618.

Gardner, W., & Wilcox, B. L. (1993). Political intervention in scientific peer review: Research on adolescent sexual behavior. *American Psychologist, 48*, 972–983.

Garn, S. M. (1992). Physical growth and development. In S. B. Friedman, M. Fisher, & S. K. Schonberg (Eds.), *Comprehensive Adolescent Health Care*. St. Louis: Quality Medical Publishing.

Garner, R., Bootcheck, J., Lorr, M., & Rauch, K. (2006). The adolescent society revisited: Cultures, crowds, climates, and status structures in seven secondary schools. *Journal of Youth and Adolescence, 35*, 1023–1035.

Garofolo, R., Wolf, R. C., Wissow, L. S., Woods, E. R., & Goodman, E. (1999). Sexual orientation and risk of suicide attempts among a representative sample of youth. *Archives of Pediatrics and Adolescent Medicine, 153*, 487–493.

Gartrell, N., Deck, A., Rodas, C., Peyser, H., & Banks, A. (2005). The national lesbian

family study: 4. Interviews with the 10-year-old children. *American Journal of Orthopsychiatry, 75*, 518–524.

Gathercole, S. E., Pickering, S. J., Ambridge, B., & Wearing, H. (2004). The structure of working memory from 4 to 15 years of age. *Developmental Psychology, 40*, 177–190.

Gauze, C., Bukowski, W. M., Aquan-Assee, J., & Sippola, L. K. (1996). Interactions between family environment and friendship and associations with self-perceived well-being during early adolescence. *Child Development, 67*, 2201–2216.

Gavin, L., & Furman, W. (1989). Age differences in adolescents' perceptions of their peer groups. *Developmental Psychology, 25*, 827–834.

Gazelle, H., & Ladd, G. W. (2003). Anxious solitude and peer exclusion: A diathesis-stress model of internalizing trajectories in childhood. *Child Development, 74*, 247–258.

Ge, X., Best, K. M., Conger, R. D., & Simons, R. L. (1996). Parenting behaviors and the occurrence and co-occurrence of adolescent depressive symptoms and conduct problems. *Developmental Psychology, 32*, 717–731.

Ge, X., Brody, G. H., Conger, R. D., & Simons, R. L. (2006). Pubertal transition and African American children's internalizing and externalizing symptoms. *Journal of Youth and Adolescence, 35*, 531–540.

Ge, X., Brody, G. H., Conger, R. D., Simons, R. L., & Murry, V. M. (2002). Contextual amplification of pubertal transmission effects on deviant peer affiliation and externalizing behavior among African-American children. *Developmental Psychology, 38*, 42–54.

Ge, X., Conger, R. D., & Elder, G. H., Jr. (2001a). Pubertal transition, stressful life events and the emergence of gender differences in adolescent depressive symptoms. *Developmental Psychology, 37*, 404–417.

Ge, X., Conger, R. D., & Elder, G. H., Jr. (2001b). The relation between puberty and psychological distress in adolescent boys. *Journal of Research on Adolescence, 11*, 49–70.

Ge, X., Conger, R., & Elder, G. H., Jr. (1996). Coming of age too early: Pubertal influences on girls' vulnerability to psychological distress. *Child Development, 67*, 3386–3400.

Ge, X., Natsuaki, M. N., & Conger, R. D. (2006). Trajectories of depressive symptoms and stressful life events among male and female adolescents in divorced and nondivorced families. *Development and Pychopathology, 18*, 253–273.

Geary, D. C. (1996). Sexual selection and sex differences in mathematical abilities. *Behavioral and Brain Sciences, 19*, 229–284.

Geary, D. C. (1998). *Male, female: The evolution of human sex differences*. Washington, DC: American Psychological Association.

Gelbard, A., Haub, C., & Kent, M. M. (1999). World population beyond six billion. *Population Bulletin, 54*(1), 3–45.

Gennep, A. van (1960). *The rites of passage*. Chicago: University of Chicago Press. (Original French edition, 1909.)

Gentner, D., Holyoak, K. J., & Kokinov, B. N. (Eds.). (2001). *The analogical mind: Perspectives from cognitive science.* Cambridge, MA: MIT Press.

George, P. S., & Alexander, W. M. (2003). *The exemplary middle school* (3rd ed.). Belmont, CA: Wadsworth/Thomson Learning.

George, P. S., McEwin, C. K., & Jenkins, J. M. (2000). *The exemplary high school.* Fort Worth, TX: Harcourt.

Gerbner, G., Gross, L., Morgan, M., Signorielli, N., & Shanahan, J. (2002). Growing up with television: Cultivation processes. In J. Bryant & D. Zillman (Eds.), *Media effects: Advances in theory and research* (2nd ed.). Mahwah, NJ: Erlbaum.

Geronimus, A. T., & Korenman, S. (1992). The socioeconomic consequences of teen childbearing reconsidered. *Quarterly Journal of Economics, 107,* 1187–1214.

Gerrard, M. (1987). Sex, sex guilt, and contraception revisited: The 1980s. *Journal of Personality and Social Psychology, 52,* 975–980.

Gestsdóttir, S., & Lerner, R. M. (2007). Intentional self-regulation and positive youth development in early adolescence: Findings from the 4H Study of Positive Youth Development. *Developmental Psychology, 43,* 508–521.

Giang, M. T., Ghavami, N., Gonzalez, C., & Wittig, M. A. (2002, April). *Peer harassment, friendship, and self worth: A mediational model.* Paper presented at the meeting of the Society for Research on Adolescence, New Orleans.

Gibbons, R. D., Hur, K., Bhaurnik, D. K., & Mann, J. J. (2006). The relationship between antidepressant prescription rates and rate of early adolescent suicide. *American Journal of Psychiatry, 163,* 1898–1904.

Gibbs, R. W., Jr. (2000). Irony in talk among friends. *Metaphor and Symbolic Activity, 15,* 5–27.

Gibson-Cline, J. (Ed.). (2000). *Youth and coping in twelve nations. Surveys of 18–20-year-old young people.* New York: Routledge.

Giedd, J. N., Blumenthal, J., Jeffries, N. O., Castellanos, F. X., Liu, H., Zijdenbos, A., et al. (1999). Brain development during childhood and adolescence: A longitudinal MRI study. *Nature Neuroscience, 2*(10), 861–863.

Gieringer, D. H. (1988). Marijuana, driving, and accident safety. *Journal of Psychoactive Drugs, 20,* 93–101.

Gillham, J., & Reivich, K. (2004). Cultivating optimism in childhood and adolescence. *Annals of the American Academy of Political and Social Science, 591,* 146–163.

Gilliam, F. D., Jr., & Bales, S. N. (2001). Strategic frame analysis: Reframing America's youth. *Social Policy Report, XV*(3), 1–16.

Gilligan, C. (1982). *In a different voice: Psychological theory and women's development.* Cambridge, MA: Harvard University Press.

Gilligan, C. (1993). Joining the resistance: Psychology, politics, and girls. In L. Weis & M. Fine (Eds.), *Beyond silenced voices.* Albany, NY: SUNY Press.

Gilligan, C., Rogers, A. G., & Tolman, D. L. (Eds.). (1991). *Women, girls and psychotherapy: Reframing resistance.* New York: Haworth.

Ginzberg, E. (1977). The job problem. *Scientific American, 237,* 43–51.

Gladwell, M. (2005). *Blink: The power of thinking without thinking.* New York: Little, Brown.

Glazer, N. (1997). *We are all multiculturists now.* Cambridge, MA: Harvard University Press.

Gneezy, U., Niederle, M., & Rustichini, A. (2003). Performance in competitive environments: Gender differences. *Quarterly Journal of Economics, 110,* 1049–1074.

Goldberg, W. A., Prause, J-A், Lucas-Thompson, R., & Himsel, A. (2008). Maternal employment and children's achievement in context: A meta-analysis of four decades of research. *Psychological Bulletin, 134,* 77–108.

Golden, M. (1990). *Children and childhood in classical Athens.* Baltimore: Johns Hopkins University Press.

Goldfien, A. (2001). Adrenal medulla. In D. Gardner & F. S. Greenspan (Eds.), *Basic and clinical endocrinology* (6th ed.). E. Norwalk, CT: Appleton & Lange.

Goldhaber, D. D., & Eide, E. R. (2002). What do we know (and need to know) about the impact of school choice reforms on disadvantaged students? *Harvard Educational Review, 72,* 157–176.

Goldstein, H., Yang, M., Omar, R., Turner, R., & Thompson, S. (2000). Meta analysis using multilevel models with an application to the study of class size effects. *Journal of the Royal Statistical Society, Series C, 49,* 399–412.

Goldston, D. B., Molock, S. D., Whitbeck, L. B., Murakami, J. L., Zayas, L. H., & Hall, G. C. N. (2008). Cultural considerations in adolescent suicide prevention and psychosocial treatment. *American Psychologist, 63,* 14–31.

Golombok, S., Perry, B., Burston, A., Murray, C., Mooney-Somers, J., Stevens, M., & Golding, J. (2003). Children with lesbian parents: A community study. *Developmental Psychology, 39,* 20–33.

Golombok, S., & Tasker, F. (1996). Do parents influence the sexual orientation of their children? Findings from a longitudinal study of lesbian families. *Developmental Psychology, 32,* 3–11.

Gonzalez, A. R., Doan Holbein, M. F., & Quilter, S. (2002). High school students' goal orientations and their relationship to perceived parenting styles. *Contemporary Educational Psychology, 27,* 450–470.

Gonzalez, N., Cauce, A., Friedman, R., & Mason, C. (1996). Family, peer, and neighborhood influences on academic achievement among African-American adolescents: One-year prospective effects. *American Journal of Community Psychology, 24,* 365–387.

Good, C., Aronson, J., & Harder, J. A. (2008). Problems in the pipeline: Stereotype threat and women's achievement in high-level math courses. *Journal of Applied Developmental Psychology, 29,* 17–28.

Good, C., Aronson, J., & Inzlicht, M. (2003). Improving adolescents' standardized test performance: An intervention to reduce the effects of stereotype threat. *Applied Developmental Psychology, 24,* 645–662.

Goodman, P. (1966). A social critic on "moral youth in an immoral society." In *The young Americans.* New York: Time Books.

Goodyer, I. M., Herbert, J., Tamplin, A., & Altham, P. M. E. (2000). First-episode major depression in adolescents: Affective, cognitive and endocrine characteristics of risk status and predictors of onset. *British Journal of Psychiatry, 176,* 142–149.

Goossens, L. (1995). Identity status development and students' perception of the university environment: A cohort-sequential study. In A. Oosterwegel & R. A. Wicklund (Eds.), *The self in European and North American culture: Development and processes.* New York: Kluwer.

Goossens, L., & Beyers, W. (2002, April). *'Naturally occurring' types of parenting and adolescent adjustment and competence: Aggregated and disaggregated approaches.* Paper presented at the meeting of the Society for Research on Adolescence, New Orleans.

Goossens, L., Beyers, W., Emmen, M., & van Aken, M. A. G. (2002). The imaginary audience and personal fable: Factor analyses and concurrent validity of the "New Look" measures. *Journal of Research on Adolescence, 12,* 193–215.

Goossens, L., Seiffge-Krenke, L., & Marcoen, A. (1992). The many faces of adolescent egocentrism: Two European replications. *Journal of Adolescent Research, 7,* 43–58.

Gootman, E. (2007, Jan. 3). Trying to find solutions in chaotic middle schools. *New York Times,* pp. A1, B7.

Gordon-Larsen, P., Nelson, M. C., & Popkin, B. M. (2004). Longitudinal physical activity and sedentary behavior trends: Adolescence to adulthood. *American Journal of Preventive Medicine, 27,* 277–283.

Gorman, A. H., Schwartz, D., Nakamoto, J., Abou-ezzeddine, T., & Toblin, R. L. (2003, March). *Peer perceived popularity and adolescents' academic engagement.* Paper presented at the meeting of the Society for Research in Child Development, Tampa, FL.

Goswami, U. (2001). Analogical reasoning in children. In D. Gentner, K. J. Holyoak, & B. N. Kokinov (Eds.), *The analogical mind: Perspectives from cognitive science.* Cambridge, MA: MIT Press.

Gottfredson, G. D., & Holland, J. L. (1996). *Dictionary of Holland occupational codes* (3rd ed.). Odessa, FL: Psychological Assessment Resources.

Gottfried, A. E., Fleming, J. S., & Gottfried, A. W. (1998). Role of cognitively stimulating home environment in children's academic intrinsic motivation: A longitudinal study. *Child Development, 69,* 1448–1460.

Gottfried, A. E., Fleming, J. S., & Gottfried, A. W. (2001). Continuity of academic intrinsic motivation from childhood through late adolescence: A longitudinal study. *Journal of Educational Psychology, 93,* 3–13.

Gottfried, A. E., Gottfried, A. W., & Bathurst, K. (2002). Maternal and dual-earner employment status and parenting. In M. H. Bornstein (Ed.), *Handbook of parenting* (2nd ed., Vol. 2). Mahwah, NJ: Erlbaum.

Gottman, J. S. (1990). Children of gay and lesbian parents. In F. W. Bozett & M. B. Sussman (Eds.), *Homosexuality and family relations*. New York: Harrington Park Press.

Gould, S. J. (2002). *The structure of evolutionary theory*. Cambridge, MA: Harvard University Press.

Gowen, L. K., Feldman, S. S., Diaz, R., & Yisrael, D. S. (2004). A comparison of the sexual behaviors and attitudes of adolescent girls with older vs. similar-aged boyfriends. *Journal of Youth and Adolescence, 33,* 167–175.

Graber, J. A. (2004). Internalizing problems during adolescence. In R. Lerner & L. Steinberg (Eds.), *Handbook of adolescent psychology*. New York: Wiley.

Graber, J. A., & Archibald, A. B. (2001). Psychosocial change at puberty and beyond: Understanding adolescent sexuality and sexual orientation. In A. R. D'Augelli & C. J. Patterson (Eds.), *Lesbian, gay, and bisexual identities and youth: Psychological perspectives*. New York: Oxford University Press.

Graber, J. A., & Brooks-Gunn, J. (1996). Transitions and turning points: Navigating the passage from childhood through adolescence. *Developmental Psychology, 32,* 768–776.

Graber, J. A., & Brooks-Gunn, J. (1999). "Sometimes I think that you don't like me": How mothers and daughters negotiate the transition into adolescence. In M. J. Cox & J. Brooks-Gunn (Eds.), *Conflict and cohesion in families: Causes and consequences*. Mahwah, NJ: Erlbaum.

Graber, J. A., Brooks-Gunn, J., & Petersen, A. C. (1996). Adolescent transitions in context. In J. A. Graber, J. Brooks-Gunn, & A. C. Petersen (Eds.), *Transitions through adolescence: Interpersonal domains and contexts*. Mahwah, NJ: Erlbaum.

Graber, J. A., Brooks-Gunn, J., & Warren, M. (1995). The antecedents of menarcheal age: Heredity, family environment, and stressful life events. *Child Development, 66,* 346–359.

Graber, J. A., Brooks-Gunn, J., & Warren, M. P. (2006). Pubertal effects on adjustment in girls: Moving from demonstrating effects to identifying pathways. *Journal of Youth and Adolescence, 35,* 391–401.

Graber, J. A., Lewinsohn, P., Seeley, J., & Brooks-Gunn, J. (1997). Is psychopathology associated with the timing of pubertal development? *Journal of the American Academy of Child and Adolescent Psychiatry, 36,* 1768–1776.

Grady, M. (2002). Cognitive deficits associated with heavy marijuana use appear to be reversible. *NIDA Notes, 17*(1), 8–9.

Graham, S. (2006). Peer victimization in school: Exploring the ethnic context. *Current Directions in Psychological Science, 15,* 317–321.

Graham, S., & Juvonen, J. (2001). An attributional approach to peer victimization. In J. Juvonen & S. Graham (Eds.), *Peer harassment in school: The plight of the vulnerable and victimized*. New York: Guilford.

Graham, S., & Juvonen, J. (2002). Ethnicity, peer harassment, and adjustment in middle school: An exploratory study. *Journal of Early Adolescence, 22,* 173–199.

Graham, S., & Weiner, B. (1996). Theories and principles of motivation. In D. C. Berliner & R. C. Calfee (Eds.), *Handbook of educational psychology*. New York: Macmillan.

Granic, I. (2000). The self-organization of parent-child relations: Beyond bidirectional models. In M. D. Lewis & I. Granic (Eds.), *Emotion, development, and self-organization: Dynamic systems approaches to emotional development*. New York: Cambridge University Press.

Granic, I., Dishion, T. J., & Hollenstein, T. (2002). The family ecology of adolescence: A dynamic systems perspective on normative development. In G. R. Adams & M. Berzonsky (Eds.), *The Blackwell handbook of adolescence*. Cambridge, MA: Blackwell.

Granic, I., Hollenstein, T., Dishion, T. J., & Patterson, G. R. (2003). Longitudinal analysis of flexibility and reorganization in early adolescence: A dynamic systems study of family interactions. *Developmental Psychology, 39,* 606–617.

Granic, I., & Patterson, G. R. (2006). Toward a comprehensive model of antisocial development: A dynamic systems approach. *Psychological Review, 113,* 101–131.

Grant, B. F., & Dawson, D. A. (1997). Age at onset of alcohol use and its association with *DSM–IV* alcohol abuse and dependence: Results from the national longitudinal alcohol epidemiologic survey. *Journal of Substance Abuse, 9,* 103–110.

Gray, P., & Feldman, J. (1997). Patterns of age mixing and gender mixing among children and adolescents at an ungraded democratic school. *Merrill-Palmer Quarterly, 43,* 67–86.

Gray, W. M. (1990). Formal operational thought. In W. F. Overton (Ed.), *Reasoning, necessity, and logic: Developmental perspectives*. Hillsdale, NJ: Erlbaum.

Gray-Little, B., & Hafdahl, A. (2000). Factors influencing racial comparisons of self-esteem: A quantitative reivew. *Psychological Bulletin, 126,* 26–54.

Green, R. L., Hoffman, L. T., Morse, R., Hayes, M. E., & Morgan, R. F. (1964). *The educational status of children in a district without public schools*. Washington, DC: Office of Education, U.S. Department of Health, Education, and Welfare.

Greenberg, M. T., Weissberg, R. P., O'Brien, M. U., Zins, J. E., Fredericks, L., Resnik, H., et al. (2003). Enhancing school-based prevention and youth development through coordinated social, emotional, and academic learning. *American Psychologist, 58,* 466–474.

Greenberger, E., & Chen, C. (1996). Perceived family relationships and depressed mood in early and late adolescence: A comparison of European and Asian Americans. *Developmental Psychology, 32,* 707–716.

Greenberger, E., Chen, C., & Beam, M. (1998). The role of "very important" non-parental adults in adolescent development. *Journal of Youth and Adolescence, 27,* 321–343.

Greenberger, E., & Steinberg, L. (1986). *When teenagers work: The psychological and social costs of adolescent employment*. New York: Basic Books.

Greene, M. L., & Way, N. (2005). Self-esteem trajectories among ethnic minority adolescents: A growth curve analysis of the patterns and predictors of change. *Journal of Research on Adolescence, 15,* 151–178.

Greenfield, P. M. (1998). The cultural evolution of IQ. In U. Neisser (Ed.), *The rising curve: Long-term gains in IQ and related measures*. Washington, DC: American Psychological Association.

Greenough, W. T., & Black, J. E. (1999). Experience, neural plasticity, and psychological development. In N. A. Fox, L. A. Leavitt, & J. G. Warhol (Eds.), *The role of early experience in infant development*. Pompton Plains, NJ: Johnson and Johnson Pediatric Institute.

Gregory, A., & Weinstein, R. S. (2004). Connection and regulation at home and in school: Predicting growth in achievement for adolescents. *Journal of Adolescent Research, 19,* 405–427.

Gregory, R. L. (1998). *Eye and brain: The psychology of seeing* (5th ed.). Princeton, NJ: Princeton University Press.

Gregory, T. (2000). *School reform and the no-man's-land of high school size*. Seattle, WA: Center on Reinventing Public Education.

Greif, E. B., & Ulman, K. J. (1982). The psychological impact of menarche on early adolescent females: A review of the literature. *Child Development, 53,* 1413–1430.

Grigorenko, E. L., Jarvin, L., & Sternberg, R. J. (2002). School-based tests of the triarchic theory of intelligence: Three settings, three samples, three syllabi. *Contemporary Educational Psychology, 27,* 167–208.

Grilo, C. M., & Pogue-Geile, M. F. (1991). The nature of environmental influences on weight and obesity: A behavior-genetic analysis. *Psychological Bulletin, 110,* 520–537.

Grolnick, W. S., & Slowiaczek, M. L. (1994). Parents' involvement in children's schooling: A multidimensional conceptualization and motivational model. *Child Development, 65,* 237–252.

Grossman, J. B. (2003, April). *Student outcomes and after-school program participation*. Paper presented at the Society for Research in Child Development, Tampa, FL.

Grossman, J. B., Price, M. L., Fellerath, V., Jucovy, L. Z., Kotloff, L. J., Raley, R., & Walker, K. E. (2002). *Multiple choices after school: Findings from the Extended-Service Schools initiative*. Philadelphia, PA: Public/Private Ventures.

Grossman, J. B., & Rhodes, J. E. (2002). The test of time: Predictors and effects of duration in youth mentoring relationships. *American Journal of Community Psychology, 30,* 199–219.

Grumbach, M. M., & Styne, D. M. (2003). Puberty: Ontogeny, neuroendocrinology, physiology and disorders. In P. R. Larsen, H. M. Kronenberg, S. M. Melmed, & K. S. Polonsky (Eds.), *Williams textbook of endocrinology* (10th ed.). Philadelphia: Saunders.

Guerin, B. (1986). Mere presence effects in humans: A review. *Journal of Experimental Social Psychology, 22,* 38–77.

Guernsey, L. (2003, May 8). Telling tales out of school: As Web sites traffic in teenage gossip, campuses feel the sting. *New York Times,* pp. G1, G6.

Guillen, E., & Barr, S. (1994). Nutrition, dieting, and fitness messages in a magazine for adolescent women, 1970–1990. *Journal of Adolescent Health, 15,* 464–472.

Gunnar, M., & Quevedo, K. (2007). The neurobiology of stress and development. *Annual Review of Psychology, 58,* 145–173.

Guo, S. S., Roche, A. F., Chumlea, W. C., Gardner, J. D., & Siervogel, R. M. (1994). The predictive value of childhood body mass index values for overweight at age 35 years. *American Journal of Clinical Nutrition, 59,* 810–819.

Gutiérrez, E. C. Z., & Kendall, C. (2000). The globalization of heath and disease: The health transition and global change. In G. L. Albrecht, R. Fitzpatrick, & S. C. Scrimshaw (Eds.), *Handbook of social studies in health and medicine.* London: Sage Publications.

Gutman, L. M., & Eccles, J. S. (1999). Financial strain, parenting behaviors, and adolescents' achievement: Testing model equivalence between African American and European American single- and two-parents families. *Child Development, 70,* 1464–1476.

Gutman, L. M., & Eccles, J. S. (2007). Stage-environment fit during adolescence: Trajectories of family relations and adolescent outcomes. *Developmental Psychology, 43,* 522–537.

Gutman, L. M., Sameroff, A. J., & Eccles, J. S. (2002). The academic achievement of African American students during early adolescence: An examination of multiple risk, promotive, and protective factors. *American Journal of Community Psychology, 30,* 367–399.

Haefeli, K. (2000, August). *Vocational education in Switzerland: Facts, figures and prospects.* Paper presented at the National Dissemination Center for Career and Technical Education, Ohio State University, Columbus, OH.

Haffner, D. W., & Wagoner, J. (1999). Vast majority of Americans support sexuality education. *SIECUS Report, 27*(6), 22–23.

Hafner, K. (2003, June 5). On video games, the jury is out and confused. *New York Times,* pp. G1, G7.

Halford, G. S. (1993). *Children's understanding: The development of mental models.* Hillsdale, NJ: Erlbaum.

Halford, G. S. (1999). The properties of representations used in higher cognitive processes: Developmental implications. In I. E. Sigel (Ed.), *Development of mental representations: Theories and applications.* Mahwah, NJ: Erlbaum.

Hall, G. S. (1904). *Adolescence: Its psychology and its relation to physiology, anthropology, sociology, sex, crime, religion, and education* (Vols. 1 & 2). Englewood Cliffs, NJ: Prentice-Hall.

Hall, J. R., Bernat, E. M., & Patrick, C. J. (2007). Externalizing psychopathology and the error-related negativity. *Psychological Science, 18,* 326–333.

Hallahan, D. P., & Kauffman, J. M. (1999). *Exceptional learners: Introduction to special education* (8th ed.). Boston, MA: Allyn & Bacon.

Halperin, S. (1998). *The forgotten half revisited: American youth and young families, 1988–2008.* Washington, DC: American Youth Policy Forum.

Halpern, C. J. T., Udry, J. R., Suchindran, C., & Campbell, B. (2000). Adolescent males' willingness to report masturbation. *Journal of Sex Research, 37,* 327–332.

Halpern, D. F. (2000). *Sex differences in cognitive abilities* (3rd ed.). Mahwah, NJ: Erlbaum.

Halpern, R. (2002). A different kind of child development institution: The history of after-school programs for low-income children. *Teachers College Record, 104,* 178–211.

Halpern-Felsher, B. L., Cornell, J. L., Kropp, R. Y., & Tschann, J. M. (2005). Oral versus vaginal sex among adolescents: Perceptions, attitudes, and behaviors. *Pediatrics, 115,* 845–851.

Halpern-Felsher, B. L., & Schinnerer, J. (2002, April). *Will it happen to you or me? Optimistic bias among adolescents and young adults.* Paper presented at the biennial meeting of the Society for Research on Adolescence, New Orleans.

Hamilton, C. E. (2000). Continuity and discontinuity of attachment from infancy through adolescence. *Child Development, 71,* 690–694.

Hamilton, J. A. (1983). Development of interest and enjoyment in adolescence: I. Attentional capacities. *Journal of Youth and Adolescence, 12,* 355–362.

Hamilton, M. C., Anderson, D., Broaddus, M., & Young, K. (2006). Gender stereotyping and under-representation of female characters in 200 popular children's picture books: A twenty-first century update. *Sex Roles, 55,* 757–765.

Hamilton, S. F., & Darling, N. (1996). Mentors in adolescents' lives. In K. Hurrelmann & S. F. Hamilton (Eds.), *Social problems and social contexts in adolescence: Perspectives across boundaries.* Hawthorne, NY: Aldine de Gruyter.

Hamilton, S. F., & Hamilton, M. A. (2003). Contexts for mentoring: Adolescent-adult relationships in workplaces and communities. In R. M. Lerner & L. Steinberg (Eds.), *Handbook of adolescent psychology.* New York: Wiley.

Hamilton, S. F., Hamilton, M. A., & Pittman, K. (2004). Principles for youth development. In S. F. Hamilton & M. A. Hamilton (Eds.), *The youth development handbook: Coming of age in American communities.* Thousand Oaks, CA: Sage.

Hamilton, S. F., & Hurrelmann, K. (1994). The school-to-career transition in Germany and the United States. *Teachers College Record, 96,* 329–344.

Hampel, P., & Petermann, F. (2005). Age and gender effects on coping in children and adolescents. *Journal of Youth and Adolescence, 34,* 73–83.

Hampton, T. (2006). Effects of stress on children examined. *Journal of the American Medical Association, 295,* 1888.

Hanawalt, B. A. (1986). *The ties that bound: Peasant families in medieval England.* New York: Oxford University Press.

Hanish, L. D., & Guerra, N. G. (2002). A longitudinal analysis of patterns of adjustment following peer victimization. *Development and Psychopathology, 14,* 69–89.

Hankin, B. L., Mermelstein, R., & Roesch, L. (2007). Sex differences in adolescent depression: Stress exposure and reactivity models. *Child Development, 78,* 279–295.

Hansen, D. M., Larson, R. W., & Dworkin, J. B. (2003). What adolescents learn in organized youth activities: A survey of self-reported developmental experiences. *Journal of Research on Adolescence, 13,* 25–35.

Harackiewicz, J. M., Barron, K. E., Tauer, J. M., Carter, S. M., & Elliot, A. J. (2000). Short-term and long-term consequences of achievement goals: Predicting interest and performance over time. *Journal of Educational Psychology, 92,* 316–330.

Harackiewicz, J. M., Pintrich, P. R., Barron, K. E., Elliot, A. J., & Thrash, R. M. (2002). Revision of achievement goal theory: Necessary and illuminating. *Journal of Educational Psychology, 94,* 638–645.

Hardy, S. A., & Carlo, G. (2005). Identity as a source of moral motivation. *Human Development, 48,* 232–256.

Harlan, W. R., Harlan, E. A., & Grillo, G. P. (1980). Secondary sex characteristics of girls 12 to 16 years of age: The U. S. Health examination survey. *Journal of Pediatrics, 96,* 1074–1078.

Härnqvist, K. (1968). Changes in intelligence from 13 to 18. *Scandinavian Journal of Psychology, 9,* 50–82.

Harold, G. T., & Conger, R. D. (1997). Marital conflict and adolescent distress: The role of adolescent awareness. *Child Development, 68,* 333–350.

Harold, G. T., Fincham, F. D., Osborne, L. N., & Conger, R. D. (1997). Mom and Dad are at it again: Adolescent perceptions of marital conflict and adolescent psychological distress. *Developmental Psychology, 33,* 333–350.

Harris, G. (2006, June 9). U.S. approves use of vaccine for cervical cancer. *New York Times,* p. A1.

Harris, J. R. (1998). *The nurture assumption: Why children turn out the way they do.* New York: Free Press.

Harris, J. R. (2006). *No two alike: Human nature and human individuality.* New York: Norton.

Harrison, A., Wilson, M., Pine, C., Chan, S., & Buriel, R. (1990). Family ecologies of ethnic minority children. *Child Development, 61,* 347–362.

Harrison, K. (2001). Ourselves, our bodies: Thin-ideal media, self-discrepancies, and eating disorder symptomatology in adolescents. *Journal of Social & Clinical Psychology, 20,* 289–323.

Harrison, K., & Cantor, J. (1997). The relationship between media consumption and eating disorders. *Journal of Communication, 47,* 40–67.

Hart, D. (2006). The development of moral identity. In G. Carlo & C. P. Edwards (Eds.), *Nebraska Symposium on Motivation: Moral development through the lifespan: Theory, research, and application* (Vol. 51). Lincoln: University of Nebraska Press.

Hart, D., & Atkins, R. (2002). Civic competence in urban youth. *Applied Developmental Science, 6,* 227–236.

Hart, D., Eisenberg, N., & Valiente, C. (2007). Personality change at the intersection of autonomic arousal and stress. *Psychological Science, 18,* 492–497.

Harter, S. (1988). Developmental and dynamic changes in the nature of the self-concept: Implications for child psychotherapy. In S. Shirk (Ed.), *Cognitive development and child psychotherapy.* New York: Plenum.

Harter, S. (1989). *Self-perception profile for adolescents.* Unpublished manuscript, University of Denver.

Harter, S. (1990). Self and identity development. In S. S. Feldman & G. R. Elliott (Eds.), *At the threshold: The developing adolescent.* Cambridge, MA: Harvard University Press.

Harter, S. (1999). *The construction of the self: A developmental perspective.* New York: Guilford.

Harter, S. (2006). The self. In W. Damon & R. Lerner (Eds.), *Handbook of child psychology* (6th ed.). New York: Wiley.

Harter, S., Bresnick, S., Bouchey, H. A., & Whitesell, N. R. (1997). The development of multiple role-related selves during adolescence. *Development and Psychopathology, 9,* 835–853.

Harter, S., Marold, D. B., Whitesell, N. R., & Cobbs, G. (1996). A model of the effects of parent and peer support on adolescent false self behavior. *Child Development, 67,* 160–174.

Harter, S., & Monsour, A. (1992). Developmental analysis of conflict caused by opposing attributes in the adolescent self-portrait. *Developmental Psychology, 28,* 251–260.

Harter, S., Waters, P. L., & Whitesell, N. R. (1997). Lack of voice as a manifestation of false self-behavior among adolescents: The school setting as a stage upon which the drama of authenticity is enacted. *Educational Psychologist, 32,* 153–173.

Harter, S., Waters, P. L., Whitesell, N. R., & Kastelic, D. (1998). Level of voice among female and male high school students: Relational context, support, and gender orientation. *Developmental Psychology. 34,* 892–901.

Hartman, H., & Hartman, M. (2002). *Comparing female and male experiences in the Rowan undergraduate engineering program.* In Women in a knowledge-based society: Proceedings of the 12th International Congress on Women in Engineering and Science. CD-ROM available from the International Network of Women in Engineering and Science, www.inwes.org.

Hartup, W. W. (1983). Peer relations. In P. H. Mussen (Series Ed.) & E. M. Hetherington (Vol. Ed.), *Handbook of child psychology* (Vol. 4). New York: Wiley.

Hartup, W. W. (1996). The company they keep: Friendships and their developmental significance. *Child Development, 67,* 1–13.

Hartup, W. W. (2005). The development of aggression: Where do we stand? In R. E. Tremblay, W. W. Hartup, & J. Archer (Eds.), *Developmental origins of aggression.* New York: Guilford.

Hartup, W. W., & Stevens, N. (1997). Friendships and adaptation in the life course. *Psychological Bulletin, 121,* 355–370.

Harvey, E. (1999). Short-term and long-term effects of early parental employment on children of the National Longitdinal Survey of Youth. *Developmental Psychology, 35,* 445–459.

Harwood, R. L., Schoelmerich, A., Ventura-Cook, E., Schulze, P. A., & Wilson, S. P. (1996). Culture and class influences on Anglo and Puerto Rican mothers' beliefs regarding long-term socialization goals and child behavior. *Child Development, 67,* 2446–2461.

Hastings, P. D., & Rubin, K. H. (1999). Predicting mothers' beliefs about preschool-aged children's social behavior: Evidence for maternal attitudes moderating child effects. *Child Development, 70,* 722–741.

Hatfield, E., & Rapson, R. L. (2005). *Love and Sex: Cross-Cultural Perspectives.* Lanham, MD: University Press of America.

Haub, C., & Rogers, M. (2002). *Kids count international data sheet.* Washington, DC: Population Reference Bureau.

Havighurst, R. (1972). *Developmental tasks and education* (3rd ed.). New York: McKay.

Hawker, D. S. J., & Boulton, M. J. (2000). Twenty years' research on peer victimization and psychosocial maladjustment: A meta-analytic review of cross-sectional studies. *Journal of Child Psychology and Psychiatry, 41,* 441–455.

Hawley, P. H., Little, T. D., & Card, N. A. (2007). The allure of a mean friend: Relationship quality and processes of aggressive adolescents with prosocial skills. *International Journal of Behavioral Development, 31,* 170–180.

Hayes, D. & Grether, J. (1982). The school year and vacations: When do students learn? *Cornell Journal of Social Relations, 17,* 56–71.

Haynes, N. M., Emmons, C., & Ben-Avie, M. (1997). School climate as a factor in student adjustment and achievement. *Journal of Educational and Psychological Consultation, 8,* 321–329.

Haynie, D. L., Nanszel, T., Eitel, P., Crump, A. D., Saylor, K., Yu, K., & Simons-Morton, B. (2001). Bullies, victims, and bully/victims: Distinct groups of at-risk youth. *Journal of Early Adolescence, 21,* 29–49.

Hays, T. E., & Hays, P. H. (1982). Opposition and complementarity in Ndumba initiation. In G. H. Herdt (Ed.), *Rituals of manhood: Male initiation in Papua New Guinea.* Berkeley: University of California Press.

Hayward, C., Gotlib, I., Schraedley, P., & Litt, I. (1999). Ethnic differences in the association between pubertal status and symptoms of depression in adolescent girls. *Journal of Adolescent Health, 25,* 143–149.

Hayward, C., Killen, J., Wilson, D., Hammer, L., Litt, I., Kraemer, H., et al. (1997). Psychiatric risk associated with early puberty in adolescent girls. *Journal of the American Academy of Child and Adolescent Psychiatry, 36,* 255–261.

Heaviside, K., Rowand, L., Williams, F., & Farris, K. (1998). *Violence and discipline problems in U.S. public schools: 1996–1997.* Washington, DC: National Center for Education Statistics.

Hedden, T., Ketay, S., Aron, A., Markus, H. R., & Gabrieli, J. D. E. (2008). Cultural influences on neural substrates of attentional control. *Psychological Science, 19,* 12–17.

Heider, F. (1958). *The psychology of interpersonal relations.* New York: Wiley.

Helm, P., & Grolund, L. (1998). A halt in the secular trend towards earlier menarche in Denmark. *Acta Obstetrica Gyncologica Scandinavia, 77,* 198–200.

Helms, J. E. (1992). Why is there no study of cultural equivalence in standardized cognitive ability testing? *American Psychologist, 47,* 1083–1101.

Helms, J. E. (1997). The triple quandary of race, culture, and social class in standardized cognitive ability testing. In D. P. Flanagan, J. Genshaft, & P. L. Harrison (Eds.), *Contemporary intellectual assessment: Theories, tests, and issues.* New York: Guilford.

Helwig, C. C., Arnold, M. L., Tan, D., & Boyd, D. (2003). Chinese adolescents' reasoning about democratic and authority-based decision making in peer, family, and school contexts. *Child Development, 74,* 783–800.

Helwig, C. C., & Kim, S. (1999). Children's evaluations of decision-making procedures in peer, family, and school contexts. *Child Development, 70,* 502–512.

Henderlong, J., & Lepper, M. R. (2002). The effects of praise on children's intrinsic motivation: A review and synthesis. *Psychological Bulletin, 128,* 774–795.

Henrich, C. C., Blatt, S. J., Kuperminc, G. P., Zohar, A., & Leadbeater, B. J. (2001). Levels of interpersonal concerns and social functioning in early adolescent boys and girls. *Journal of Personality Assessment, 76,* 48–67.

Henrich, C. C., Kuperminc, G. P., Sack, A., Blatt, S. J., & Leadbeater, B. J. (2000). Characteristics and homogeneity of early adolescent friendship groups: A comparison of male and female clique and non-clique members. *Applied Developmental Science, 4,* 15–26.

Henry, C. S., Robinson, L. C., Neal, R. A., & Huey, E. L. (2006). Adolescent perceptions of overall family system functioning and parental behaviors. *Journal of Child and Family Studies, 15,* 319–329.

Henry, D. B., Schoeny, M. E., Deptula, D. P., & Slavick, J. T. (2007). Peer selection and socialization effects on adolescent intercourse without a condom and attitudes about the cost of sex. *Child Development, 78,* 825–838.

Herdt, G. H. (1982). Editor's preface. In G. H. Herdt (Ed.), *Rituals of manhood: Male initiation in Papua New Guinea.* Berkeley: University of California Press.

Herdt, G. H. (1990). Mistaken gender. *American Anthropologist, 92,* 433–446.

Herdt, G. H., & McClintock, M. (2000). The magical age of 10. *Archives of Sexual Behavior, 29,* 587–606.

Herman-Giddens, M., Slora, E., Wasserman, R., Bourdony, C., Bhapkar, M., Koch, G., & Hasemeier, C. (1997). Secondary sexual characteristics and menses in young girls seen in office practice: A study from the Pediatric Research in Office Settings Network. *Pediatrics, 88,* 505–512.

Hernandez, D. J (1997). Child development and the social demography of childhood. *Child Development, 68,* 149–169.

Herrnstein, R. J., & Murray, C. (1994). *The bell curve: Intelligence and class structure in American life.* New York: Free Press.

Herszenhorn, D. M. (2003, July 23). Basic skills forcing cuts in art classes: New curriculum leaves little room in schedule. *The New York Times,* pp. B1, B6.

Hertsgaard, L., Gunnar, M., Erickson, M. F., & Nachmias, M. (1995). Adrenocortical responses to the Strange Situation in infants with disorganized-disoriented attachment relationships. *Child Development, 66,* 1100–1106.

Hetherington, E. M. (1993). An overview of the Virginia longitudinal study of divorce and remarriage with a focus on early adolescence. *Journal of Family Psychology, 7,* 39–56.

Hetherington, E. M. (1999). Social capital and the development of youth from nondivorced, divorced, and remarried families. In W. A. Collins & B. Laursen (Eds.), *Relationships as developmental contexts: The Minnesota Symposia on Child Psychology* (Vol. 30). Mahwah, NJ: Erlbaum.

Hetherington, E. M., Bridges, M., & Insabella, G. M. (1998). What matters? What does not? Five perspectives on the association between marital transitions and children's adjustment. *American Psychologist, 53,* 167–184.

Hetherington, E. M., Henderson, S. H., & Reiss, D., with Anderson, E. R., Bridges, M., Chan R. W., et al. (1999). Adolescent siblings in stepfamilies: Family functioning and adolescent adjustment. *Monographs of the Society for Research in Child Development, 64* (4, Serial No. 259).

Hetherington, E. M., & Jodl, K. M. (1994). Stepfamilies as settings for child development. In A. Booth & J. Dunn (Eds.), *Stepfamilies: Who benefits? Who does not?* Hillsdale, NJ: Erlbaum.

Hetherington, E. M., & Kelly, J. (2002). *For better or for worse: Divorce reconsidered.* New York: Norton.

Hetherington, E. M., & Stanley-Hagan, M. (2002). Parenting in divorced and remarried families. In M. H. Bornstein (Ed.), *Handbook of parenting* (2nd ed., Vol. 3). Mahwah, NJ: Erlbaum.

Heyman, G. D., & Legare, C. H. (2004). Children's beliefs about gender differences in the academic and social domains. *Sex Roles, 50,* 227–239.

Hickman, M., Roberts, C., & Gaspar de Matos, M. (2000). Exercise and leisure-time activities. In C. Currie, K. Hurrelmann, W. Settertobulte, R. Smith, & J. Todd (Eds.), *Health and health behavior among young people.* Copenhagen: World Health Organization.

Hill, J., & Holmbeck, G. (1986). Attachment and autonomy during adolescence. In G. Whitehurst (Ed.), *Annals of child development.* Greenwich, CT: JAI Press.

Hill, J., & Holmbeck, G. (1987). Disagreements about rules in families with seventh-grade girls and boys. *Journal of Youth & Adolescence, 16,* 221–246.

Hill, J. P., & Lynch, M. E. (1983). The intensification of gender-related role expectations during early adolescence. In J. Brooks-Gunn & A. C. Petersen (Eds.), *Girls at puberty: Biological and psychosocial perspectives.* New York: Plenum.

Hine, T. (1999). *The rise and fall of the American teenager.* New York: Bard Books.

Hines, A. (1997). Divorce-related transitions, adolescent development, and the role of the parent-child relationship: A review of the literature. *Journal of Marriage and the Family, 59,* 375–388.

Hines, M. (2002). Sexual differentiation of human brain and behavior. In D. W. Pfaff, A. P. Arnold, A. M. Etgen, S. E. Fahrbach, & R. T. Rubin (Eds.), *Hormones, brain and behavior.* New York: Academic Press.

Hines, M. (2004). *Brain gender.* New York: Oxford University Press.

Hines, M., Brook, C., & Conway, G. S. (2004). Androgen and psychosexual development: Core gender identity, sexual orientation, and recalled childhood gender role behavior in women and men with congenital adrenal hyperplasia (CAH). *Journal of Sex Research, 41,* 75–81.

Hines, M., Fane, B. A., Pasterski, V. L., Mathews, G. A., Conway, G. S., & Brook, C. (2003). Spatial abilities following prenatal androgen abnormality: Targeting and mental rotations performance in individuals with congenital adrenal hyperplasia. *Psychoneuroendochrinology, 28,* 1010–1026.

Hines, M., Golombok, S., Rust, J., Johnston, J. K., and Golding, J., & the ALSPAC Team (2002). Testosterone during pregnancy and

gender role behavior in preschool children: A longitudinal, population study. *Child Development, 73,* 1678–1687.

Hiney, J. K., Srivastava, V., Nyberg, C. L., Ojeda, S. R., & Dees. W. L. (1996). Insulin-like growth factor I of peripheral origin acts centrally to accelerate the initiation of female puberty. *Endrocrinology, 137,* 3717–3728.

Hingson, R. W., Heeren, T., & Winter, M. R. (2006). Age at drinking outset and alcohol dependence: Age at onset, duration, and severity. *Archives of Pediatric and Adolescent Medicine, 160,* 739–746.

Hirsch, B. (2005). *A place to call home: After-school programs for urban youth.* Washington, DC: American Psychological Association.

Hodges, E. V. E., Boivin, M., Vitaro, F., & Bukowski, W. M. (1999). The power of friendship: Protection against an escalating cycle of peer victimization. *Developmental Psychology, 35,* 94–101.

Hodges, E. V. E., & Perry, D. G. (1999). Personal and interpersonal antecedents and consequences of victimization by peers. *Journal of Personality and Social Psychology, 76,* 677–685.

Hoek, H. W. (2002). Distribution of eating disorders. In C. G. Fairburn & K. D. Brownell (Eds.), *Eating disorders and obesity: A comprehensive handbook* (2nd ed.). New York: Guilford.

Hoek, H. W. (2006). Incidence, prevalence and mortality of anorexia nervosa and other eating disorders. *Current Opinion in Psychiatry, 19,* 389–394.

Hofer, B. K., & Pintrich, P. R. (Eds.) (2002). *Personal epistemology: The psychology of beliefs about knowledge and knowing.* Mahwah, NJ: Erlbaum.

Hofer, B., & Pintrich, P. (1997). The development of epistemological theories: Beliefs about knowledge and knowing and their relation to learning. *Reivew of Educational Research, 67,* 88–140.

Hoffman, J. (2008, February 24). Vaccinating boys for girls' sake? *New York Times,* pp. ST1, ST10.

Hoffman, L. (1996). Progress and problems in the study of adolescence. *Developmental Psychology, 32,* 777–780.

Hoffman, L. W. (1989). Effects of maternal employment in the two-parent family. *American Psychologist, 44,* 283–292.

Hoffman, M. L. (1970). Moral development. In P. H. Mussen (Ed.), *Carmichael's manual of child psychology.* New York: Wiley.

Hoffman, M. L. (1991). Empathy, social cognition, and moral action. In W. M. Kurtines & J. L. Gewirtz (Eds.), *Handbook of moral behavior and development: Vol. 1. Theory.* Hillsdale, NJ: Erlbaum.

Hoffman, M. L. (2000). *Empathy and moral development: Implications for caring and justice.* New York: Cambridge University Press.

Hofschire, L. J., & Greenberg, B. S. (2002). Media's impact on adolescents' body dissatisfaction. In J. D. Brown & J. R. Steele (Eds.), *Sexual teens, sexual media: Investigating media's influence on adolescent sexuality.* Mahwah, NJ: Erlbaum.

Hoglund, W. L. G. (2007). School functioning in early adolescence: Gender-linked responses to peer victimization. *Journal of Educational Psychology, 99,* 683–699.

Holden, S. (2003, June 11). A grim high wire for Indian girls. *New York Times,* p. E5.

Holland, D., Lachicotte, W., Jr., Skinner, D., & Cain, C. (2001). *Identity and agency in cultural worlds.* Cambridge, MA: Harvard University Press.

Holland, J. L. (1973). *Making vocational choices: A theory of careers.* Englewood Cliffs, NJ: Prentice Hall.

Holland, J. L. (1987). Current status of Holland's theory of careers: Another perspective. *Career Development Quarterly, 36,* 24–30.

Holland, J. L. (1996). Exploring careers with a typology: What we have learned and some new directions. *American Psychologist, 51,* 397–406.

Holland, J. L. (1997). *Making vocational choices: A theory of vocational personalities and work environments* (3rd ed.). Odessa, FL: Psychological Assessment Resources.

Hollos, M., & Leis, P. E. (1989). *Becoming Nigerian in Ijo society.* New Brunswick, NJ: Rutgers University Press.

Holmes, L. D. (1987). *Quest for the real Samoa: The Mead-Freeman controversy and beyond.* South Hadley, MA: Bergin & Garvey.

Holmes, R. M., & Holmes, S. T. (2005). *Suicide.* Thousand Oaks, CA: Sage.

Holt, J. (1964). *How children fail.* New York: Pitman Press.

Holt, J. (1967). *How children learn.* New York: Pitman Press.

Hong, Y.-Y., Morris, M. W., Chiu, C.-Y., & Benet-Martínez, V. (2000). Multicultural minds: A dynamic constructivist approach to culture and cognition. *American Psychologist, 55,* 709–720.

Hooper, C. J., Luciana, M., Conklin, H. M., & Yarger, R. S. (2004). Adolescents' performance on the Iowa gambling task: Implications for the development of decision making and ventromedial prefrontal cortex. *Developmental Psychology, 40,* 1148–1158.

Hopper, B. R., & Yen, S. S. (1975). Circulating concentrations of dehydroepiandrosterone and dehydroepiandrosterone sulfate during puberty. *Journal of Clinical Endocrinology and Metabolism, 40,* 458–461.

Hopwood, N. J., Kelch, R. P., Hale, P. M., Mendes, T. M., Foster, C. M., & Beitins, I. Z. (1990). The onset of human puberty: Biological and environmental factors. In J. Bancroft & J. M. Reinisch (Eds.), *Adolescence and puberty.* New York: Oxford University Press.

Horan, P., & Hargis, P. (1991). Children's work and schooling in the late nineteenth-century family economy. *American Sociological Review, 56,* 583–596.

Horlick, M. B., Rosenbaum, M., Nicolson, M., Levine, L. S., Fedun, B., Wang, J., et al. (2000). Effect of puberty on the relationship between circulating leptin and body composition. *Journal of Clinical Endocrinology & Metabolism, 85,* 2509–2518.

Horn, J. L. (1998). A basis for research on age differences in cognitive abilities. In J. J. McArdle & R. Woodcock (Eds.), *Human cognitive abilities in theory and practice.* Mahwah, NJ: Erlbaum.

Horn, S. (2003). Adolescents' reasoning about exclusion from social groups. *Developmental Psychology, 39,* 71–84.

Horn, S. (2006). Group status, group bias, and adolescents' reasoning about the treatment of others in school contexts. *International Journal of Behavioral Development, 30,* 208–218.

Houston, K., Hawton, K., & Sheppard, R. (2001). Suicide in young people aged 15–24: A psychological autopsy study. *Journal of Affective Disorders, 63,* 159–170.

Howe, N., Aquan-Assee, J., Bukowski, W. M., Rinaldi, C., & Lehoux, P. M. (2000). Sibling self-disclosure in early adolescence. *Merrill-Palmer Quarterly, 46,* 653–671.

Howes, C. (1996). The earliest friendships. In W. M. Bukowski, A. F. Newcomb, & W. W. Hartup (Eds.), *The company they keep: Friendships in childhood and adolescence.* New York: Cambridge University Press.

Howley, C. (1994). The academic effectiveness of small-scale schooling (an update). ERIC Digest. Charleston, WV: ERIC Clearinghouse on Rural Education and Small Schools.

Howley, C., & Bickel, R. (2000). *School size, poverty, and student achievement.* Washington, DC: The Rural School and Community Trust.

Howley, C., Strange, M., & Bickel, R. (2000). *Research about school size and school performance in impoverished communities.* ERIC Digest. Charleston, WV: ERIC Clearinghouse on Rural Education and Small Schools.

Hua, C. (2001). *A society without fathers or husbands: The Na of China.* New York: Zone Books.

Huesmann, L. R., Moise-Titus, J., Podolski, C.-L., & Eron, L. D. (2003). Longitudinal relations between children's exposure to TV violence and their aggressive and violent behavior in young adulthood: 1977–1992. *Developmental Psychology, 39,* 201–221.

Hughes, J. N. (2002). Authoritative teaching: Tipping the balance in favor of school versus peer effects. *Journal of School Psychology, 40,* 485–492.

Hull, P. V. (1996). Bilingualism: Some personality and cultural issues. In D. I. Slobin, J. Gerhardt, A. Kyratzis, & J. Guo (Eds.), *Social interaction, social context, and language: Essays in honor of Susan Ervin-Tripp.* Mahwah, NJ: Erlbaum.

Hundert, J., Boyle, M. H., Cunningham, C. E., Duku, E., Heale, J., McDonald, J., et al. (1999). Helping children adjust—a Tri-Ministry Study: II. Program effects. *Journal of Child Psychology and Psychiatry, 40,* 1061–1073.

Hunt, D. P. (1999). Emotions in early puberty: Sex differences in affect patterns across pubertal phases from a developmental neuropsychology perspective. *Dissertation Abstracts International, 59* (10-B), 5599.

Hunter, J. P., & Csikszentmihalyi, M. (2003). The positive psychology of interested adolescents. *Journal of Youth and Adolescence, 32,* 27–35.

Hunter, S. C., & Boyle, J. M. E. (2004). Appraisal and coping strategy use in victims of school bullying. *British Journal of Educational Psychology, 74,* 83–107.

Huntington, S. P. (1993). The clash of civilizations. *Foreign Affairs, 72*(3), 22–50.

Huntsinger, C. S., Jose, P. E., & Larson, S. L. (1998). Do parent practices to encourage academic competence influence the social adjustment of young European American and Chinese American children? *Developmental Psychology, 34,* 747–756.

Huston, A. C., Donnerstein, E., Fairchild, H., Feshbach, N. D., Katz, P. A., Murray, J. P., et al. (1992). *Big world, small screen: The role of television in American society.* Lincoln, NE: University of Nebraska Press.

Huston, A. C., McLoyd, V. C., & Coll, C. G. (1994). Children and poverty: Issues in contemporary research. *Child Development, 65,* 275–282.

Huttenlocher, P. R. (1999). Synaptogenesis in human cerebral cortex and the concept of critical periods. In N. A. Fox, L. A. Leavitt, & J. G. Warhol (Eds.), *The role of early experience in infant development.* Pompton Plains, NJ: Johnson and Johnson Pediatric Institute.

Hyde, J. S. (2005). The gender similarities hypothesis. *American Psychologist, 60,* 581–592.

Hyde, J. S. (2007). New directions in the study of gender similarities and differences. *Current Directions in Psychological Science, 16,* 259–263.

Hyde, J. S., Fennema, E., & Lamon, S. J. (1990). Gender differences in mathematics performance: A meta-analysis. *Psychological Bulletin, 107,* 139–155.

Hymel, S., Bowker, A., & Woody, E. (1993). Aggressive versus withdrawn unpopular children: Variations in peer and self-perceptions in multiple domains. *Child Development, 64,* 879–896.

Iceland, J., Weinberg, D. H., & Steinmetz, E. (2002). *Racial and ethnic residential segregation in the United States: 1980–2000.* Washington, DC: U.S. Census Bureau.

iEARN (2003). What is iEARN? Available: www.iearn.org/about/index.html.

Iervolino, A. C., Hines, M., Golombok, S. E., Rust, J., & Plomin, R. (2005). Genetic and environmental influences on sex-typed behavior during the preschool years. *Child Development, 76,* 826–840.

Iervolino, A. C., Pike, A., Manke, B., Reiss, D., Hetherington, E. M., & Plomin, R. (2002). Genetic and environmental influences on adolescent peer socialization: Evidence from two genetically sensitive designs. *Child Development, 73,* 162–174.

Illich, I. (1971). *Deschooling society.* New York: Harper & Row.

Inhelder, B., & Piaget, J. (1958). *The growth of logical thinking from childhood to adolescence.* New York: Basic Books.

Interactive Digital Software Association. (2003). *Essential facts about the computer and video game industry.* Washington, DC: Author.

Inter-University Consortium for Political and Social Research. (2001). *Historical, demographic, economic, and social data: U.S., 1790–1970.* Ann Arbor, MI: Author.

Inzlict, M., & Ben-Zeev, T. (2003). Do high-achieving female students underperform in private? The implications of threatening environments on intellectual processing. *Journal of Educational Psychology, 95,* 796–805.

Irwin, M. (1981). Diagnosis of anorexia nervosa in children and the validity of DSM-III. *American Journal of Psychiatry, 138,* 1382.

Irwin-Chase, H., & Burns, B. (2000). Developmental changes in children's abilities to share and allocate attention in a dual task. *Journal of Experimental Child Psychology, 77,* 61–85.

Isaacs, J., Card, N. A., & Hodges, E. V. E. (2000, June). *Aggression, peer victimization, social cognitions, and weapon carrying in schools.* Paper presented at the convention of the American Psychological Society, Miami Beach, FL.

Isabella, R. A. (1993). Origins of attachment: Maternal interactive behavior across the first year. *Child Development, 64,* 605–621.

Isabella, R. A., & Belsky, J. (1991). Interactional synchrony and the origins of infant-mother attachment. *Child Development, 62,* 373–384.

Isakson, K., & Jarvis, P. (1999). The adjustment of adolescents during the transition into high school: A short-term longitudinal study. *Journal of Youth and Adolescence, 28,* 1–26.

Ivie, R., & Stowe, K. (2002). *U.S. women in academic physics.* In Women in a knowledge-based society: Proceedings of the 12th International Congress on Women in Engineering and Science. CD-ROM available from the International Network of Women in Engineering and Science, at www.inwes.org.

Izard, C. E. (1991). *The psychology of emotions.* New York: Plenum.

Jablonski, E. (1987). *Gershwin.* New York: Doubleday.

Jacobs, J. E., Davis-Kean, P., Bleeker, M., Eccles, J. S., & Malanchuk, O. (2005). "I can, but I don't want to": The impact of parents, interests, and activities on gender differences in math. In A. M. Gallagher & J. C. Kaufman (Eds.), *Gender differences in mathematics: An integrative psychological approach.* New York: Cambridge University Press.

Jacobs, J. E., Lanza, S., Osgood, D. W., Eccles, J. S., & Wigfield, A. (2002). Changes in children's self-competence and values: Gender and domain differences across grades one through twelve. *Child Development, 73,* 509–527.

Jacobs, J. E., & Narloch, R. H. (2001). Children's use of sample size and variability to make social inferences. *Applied Developmental Psychology, 22,* 311–331.

Jacobs, J. E., Vernon, M. K., and Eccles, J. (2005). Activity choices in middle childhood: The roles of gender, self-beliefs, and parents' influence. In J. L. Mahoney, R. W. Larson, & J. S. Eccles (Eds.), *Organized activities as contexts of development: Extracurricular activities, after-school and community programs.* Mahwah, NJ: Erlbaum.

Jacobsen, T., & Hofmann, V. (1997). Children's attachment representations: Longitudinal relations to school behavior and academic competency in middle childhood and adolescence. *Developmental Psychology, 33,* 703–710.

Jacobson, K. C., & Crockett, L. J. (2000). Parental monitoring and adolescent adjustment: An ecological perspective. *Journal of Research on Adolescence, 10,* 65–97.

Jaffee, S. R., Caspi, A., Moffitt, T. E., Dodge, K. A., Rutter, M., & Taylor, A. (2005). Nature X nurture: Genetic vulnerabilities interact with physical maltreatment to promote conduct problems. *Development and Psychopathology, 17,* 67–84.

Jaffee, S. R., & Hyde, J. H. (2000). Gender differences in moral orientation: A meta-analysis. *Psychological Bulletin, 12,* 703–726.

Jaffee, S. R., Moffitt, T. E., Caspi, A., Taylor, A., & Arseneault, L. (2002). Influence of adult domestic violence on children's internalizing and externalizing problems: An environmentally informative twin study. *Journal of the American Academy of Child and Adolescent Psychiatry, 41,* 1095–1103.

Jahns, L., Siega-Riz, A. M., & Popkin, B. M. (2001). The increasing prevalence of snacking among U.S. children from 1977 to 1996. *Journal of Pediatrics, 138,* 493–498.

James, W. (1890). *The principles of psychology.* New York: Holt.

Jankowiak, W. R., & Fischer, E. F. (1998). A cross-cultural perspective on romantic love. In J. M. Jenkins, K. Oatley, & N. L. Stein (Eds.), *Human emotions: A reader.* Malden, MA: Blackwell.

Janosz, M., Le Blanc, M., Boulerice, B., & Tremblay, R. E. (2000). Predicting different types of school dropouts: A typological approach with two longitudinal samples. *Journal of Educational Psychology, 92,* 171–190.

Jansz, J. (2005). The emotional appeal of violent video games for adolescent males. *Communication Theory, 15,* 219–241.

Janveau–Brennan, G., & Markovits, H. (1999). The development of reasoning with causal conditionals. *Developmental Psychology, 35,* 904–911.

Jarrett, R. L., Sullivan, P. J., & Watkins, N. D. (2005). Developing social capital through participation in organized youth programs: Qualitative insights from three programs. *Journal of Community Psychology, 33,* 41–55.

Jejeebhoy, S. J. (1995). *Women's education, autonomy, and reproductive behaviour: Experience from developing countries.* Oxford: Clarendon Press.

Jekielek, S. (1998). Parental conflict, marital disruption and children's emotional well-being. *Social Forces, 76,* 905–936.

Jensen, A. R. (1980). *Bias in mental testing.* New York: Free Press.

Jensen, L. A. (2003). Coming of age in a multicultural world: Globalization and adolescent cultural identity formation. *Applied Developmental Science, 7,* 189–196.

Jessor, R., Colby, A., & Shweder, R. A. (1996). *Ethnography and human development: Context and meaning in social inquiry.* Chicago: University of Chicago Press.

Jessor, R., & Jessor, S. (1977). *Problem behavior and psychosocial development.* New York: Academic Press.

Jessor, R., Turbin, M. S., & Costa, F. M. (1998). Protective factors in adolescent health behavior. *Journal of Personality and Social Psychology 75,* 788–800.

Jodl, K. M., Michael, A., Malanchuk, O., Eccles, J. S., & Sameroff, A. (2001). Parents' roles in shaping early adolescents' occupational aspirations. *Child Development, 72,* 1247–1265.

Johns, M., Schmeder, T., & Martens, A. (2005). Knowing is half the battle: Teaching stereotype threat as a means of improving women's math performance. *Psychological Science, 16,* 175–179.

Johnson, D., & Lino, M. (2000). Teenagers: Employment and contributions to family spending. *Monthly Labor Review* Online, *123*(9). Available: http://stats.bls.gov/OPUB/MLR/2000/09/contents.htm.

Johnson, F., & Wardle, J. (2005). Dietary restraint, body dissatisfaction, and psychological distress: A prospective analysis. *Journal of Abnormal Psychology, 114,* 119–125.

Johnson, H. D. (2004). Gender, grade, and relationship differences in emotional closeness within adolescent friendships. *Adolescence, 39,* 243–255.

Johnson, J. (2002). Do communities want smaller schools? *Educational Leadership, 59,* 42–45.

Johnson, J. G., Cohen, P., Smailes, E. M., Kasen, S., & Brook, J. S. (2002). Television viewing and aggressive behavior during adolescence and adulthood. *Science, 295,* 2468–2471.

Johnson, M. H. (1999). Developmental cognitive neuroscience. In M. Bennett (Ed.), *Developmental psychology: Achievements and prospects.* Philadelphia: Psychology Press.

Johnson, M. K., Crosnoe, R., & Elder, G. H., Jr. (2001). Student attachment and academic engagement: The role of race and ethnicity. *Sociology of Education, 74,* 318–40.

Johnson, O. (1912). *Stover at Yale.* New York: Frederick A. Stokes.

Johnston, L. D., O'Malley, P. M., Bachman, J. G., & Schulenberg, J. E. (2006a). *Demographic subgroup trends for various licit and illicit drugs, 1975–2005.* Ann Arbor, MI: Institute for Social Research. Available: monitoringthefuture.org/

Johnston, L. D., O'Malley, P. M., Bachman, J. G., & Schulenberg, J. E. (2006b). *Monitoring the future national results on adolescent drug use: Overview of key findings, 2005.* Bethesda, MD: National Institute on Drug Abuse.

Jones, D. C. (2004). Body image among adolescent girls and boys: A longitudinal study. *Developmental Psychology, 40*, 823–835.

Jones, D. C., & Crawford, J. K. (2005). Adolescent boys and body image: Weight and muscularity concerns as dual pathways to body dissatisfaction. *Journal of Youth and Adolescence, 34*, 629–636.

Jones, D. C., Newman, J. B., & Bautista, S. (2005). A three-factor model of teasing: The influence of friendship, gender, and topic on expected emotional reactions to teasing during early adolescence. *Social Development, 14*, 421–439.

Jones, J. M. (1999). Cultural racism: The intersection of race and culture in intergroup conflict. In D. A. Prentice & D. T. Miller (Eds.), *Cultural divides: Understanding and overcoming group conflict*. New York: Russell Sage Foundation.

Jones, M. C. (1965). Psychological correlates of somatic development. *Child Development, 36*, 899–911.

Jones, M. C., & Bailey, N. (1950). Physical maturing among boys as related to behavior. *Journal of Educational Psychology, 41*, 129–148.

Jones, R. E. (1996). *Human reproductive biology* (2nd ed.). New York: Academic Press.

Joyner, K., & Udry, J. R. (2000). You don't bring me anything but down: Adolescent romance and depression. *Journal of Health and Social Behavior, 41*, 369–391.

Juang, L. P., & Silbereisen, R. K. (2002). The relationship between adolescent academic capability beliefs, parenting and school grades. *Journal of Adolescence, 25*, 3–18.

Jussim, L., & Eccles, J. S. (1992). Teacher expectations II: Construction and reflection of student achievement. *Journal of Personality and Social Psychology, 63*, 947–961.

Jussim, L., Eccles, J. S., & Madon, S. (1996). Social perception, social stereotypes, and teacher expectations: Accuracy and the quest for the powerful self-fulfilling prophecy. In L. Berkowitz (Ed.), *Advances in experimental social psychology*. New York: Academic Press.

Juvenile Justice Evaluation Center. (2006). *Disproportionate minority contact (DMC)*. Available: www.jrsa.org/jjec/programs/dmc/index.html.

Juvonen, J., Nishina, A., & Graham, S. (2006). Ethnic diversity and perceptions of safety in urban middle schools. *Psychological Science, 17*, 393–400.

Kagan, J., Reznick, J. S., & Snidman, N. (1987). The physiology and psychology of behavioral inhibition in children. *Child Development, 58*, 1459–1473.

Kagitcibasi, C. (2003). Autonomy, embeddedness and adaptability in immigration contexts. *Human Development, 46*, 145–150.

Kahne, J., Nagaoka, J., Brown, A., O'Brien, J., Quinn, T., & Thiede, K. (2001). Assessing after-school programs as settings for youth development. *Youth and Society, 32*, 421–446.

Kail, R. (1991). Developmental change in speed of processing during childhood and adolescence. *Psychological Bulletin, 109*, 490–501.

Kail, R. (1997). Processing time, imagery, and spatial memory. *Journal of Experimental Child Psychology, 64*, 67–78.

Kail, R. (2000). Speed of information processing: Developmental change and links to intelligence. *Journal of School Psychology, 38*, 51–61.

Kail, R. V., & Ferrer, E. (2007). Processing speed in childhood and adolescence: Longitudinal models for examining developmental change. *Child Development, 78*, 1760–1770.

Kail, R., & Hall, L. K. (2001). Distinguishing short-term memory from working memory. *Memory & Cognition, 29*, 1–9.

Kaiser Family Foundation. (1999). *Kids & media @ the new millennium*. Menlo Park, CA: Author.

Kaiser Family Foundation. (2001a). *Generation Rx.com: How young people use the Internet for health information*. Menlo Park, CA: Author.

Kaiser Family Foundation. (2001b). *Parents and the V-chip 2001: How parents feel about TV, the TV ratings system, and the V-chip*. Menlo Park, CA: Author.

Kakar, S. (1998). Asian Indian families. In R. L. Taylor (Ed.), *Minority families in the United States: A multicultural perspective*. Upper Saddle River, NJ: Prentice Hall.

Kan, M. L., & McHale, S. M. (2007). Clusters and correlates of experiences with parents and peers in early adolescence. *Journal of Research on Adolescence, 17*, 565–586.

Kandel, D. B. (1975). Stages in adolescent involvement in drug use. *Science, 190*, 912–914.

Kandel, D. B. (2002). Examining the gateway hypothesis. In D. B. Kandel (Ed.), *Stages and pathways of drug involvement: Examining the gateway hypothesis*. New York: Cambridge University Press.

Kane, E. W. (2000). Racial and ethnic variations in gender-related attitudes. *Annual Review of Sociology, 26*, 419–439.

Kane, E. W. (2006). "No way my boys are going to be like that!" Parents' responses to children's gender nonconformity. *Gender & Society, 20*, 149–176.

Kann, L. (2001). The youth risk behavior surveillance system: Measuring health-risk behaviors. *American Journal of Health Behavior, 25*, 272–277.

Kann, L., Kinchen, S. A., Williams, B. I., Ross, J. G., Lowry, R., Grunbaum, J. A., & Kolbe, L. J. (2000). Youth risk behavior surveillance—United States, 1999. *Morbidity and Mortality Weekly Report, 49*(SS-5), 1–98.

Kantor, H. (1994). Managing the transition from school to work: The false promise of youth apprenticeship. *Teachers College Record, 95*, 442–461.

Kao, G. & Tienda. (1995). Asian Americans as model minorities? A look at their academic performance. *American Journal of Education, 103*, 121–159.

Kaplan, A., & Maehr, M. L. (2002). Adolescents' achievement goals: Situating motivation in sociocultural contexts. In F. Pajares & T. Urdan (Eds.), *Academic motivation of adolescents*. Greenwich, CT: Information Age.

Kaplan, R. M., & Saccuzzo, D. P. (2001). *Psychological testing: Principles, applications, and issues* (5th ed.). Belmont, CA: Wadsworth.

Kaplan, S. L., Grumbach, M. M., & Aubert, M. L. (1975). The ontogenesis of pituitary hormone and hypothalamic factors in the human fetus: Maturation of central nervous system regulation of anterior pituitary function. In R. O. Greep (Ed.), *Recent progress in hormone research* (Vol. 32). New York: Academic Press.

Kaprio, J., Rimpela, A., Winter, T., Viken, R. J., Rimpela, M., & Rose, R. J. (1995). Common genetic influence on BMI and age at menarche. *Human Biology, 67*, 739–753.

Karen, D. (2002). Changes in access to higher education in the United States: 1980–1992. *Sociology of education, 75*, 191–210.

Katchadourian, H. (1977). *The biology of adolescence*. San Francisco: W. H. Freeman.

Katz, M. A. (1998). Women, children and men. In P. Cartledge (Ed.), *The Cambridge illustrated history of ancient Greece*. Cambridge, UK: Cambridge University Press.

Katzman, D. K. (2005). Medical complications in adolescents with anorexia nervosa: A review of the literature. *International Journal of Eating Disorders, 37* (Supplement), S52–S59.

Kaufman, P., Chen, X., Choy, S. P., Ruddy, S. A., Miller, A. K., & Fleury, J. K. (2000). *Indicators of school crime and safety*. Washington, D.C.: National Center for Education Statistics.

Kazdin, A. (Ed.) (2000). *Encyclopedia of psychology*. Washington, DC & New York: American Psychological Association and Oxford University Press.

Keating, D. P. (1990). Adolescent thinking. In S. S. Feldman & G. R. Elliott (Eds.), *At the threshold: The developing adolescent*. Cambridge, MA: Harvard University Press.

Keating, D. P. (1996). Habits of mind for a learning society: Educating for human development. In D. Olsen & N. Torrance (Eds.), *Handbook of education and human development: New models of learning, teaching, and schooling*. Cambridge, MA: Basil Blackwell.

Keating, D. P. (2004). Cognitive and brain development. In R. M. Lerner & L. Steinberg (Eds.), *Handbook of adolescent psychology*. New York: John Wiley.

Keating, D. P., & Sasse, D. K. (1996). Cognitive socialization in adolescence: Critical period for a critical habit of mind. In G. R. Adams, R. Montemayer, & T. Guilotta (Eds.), *Psychosocial development during adolescence*. Thousand Oaks, CA: Sage.

Keisner, J., & Pastore, M. (2005). Differences in the relations between antisocial behavior and peer acceptance across contexts and across adolescence. *Child Development, 76*, 1278–1293.

Keller, J., & Dauenheimer, D. (2003). Stereotype threat in the classroom: Dejection mediates the disrupting threat effect on women's math performance. *Personality & Social Psychology Bulletin, 29,* 371–381.

Keller, M., & Edelstein, W. (1993). The development of the moral self from childhood to adolescence. In G. G. Noam & T. E. Wren (Eds.), *The moral self: Building a better paradigm.* Cambridge, MA: MIT Press.

Keller, S. N., & Brown, J. D. (2002). Media interventions to promote responsible sexual behavior. *Journal of Sex Research, 39,* 67–72.

Kelly, A. M., Wall, M., Eisenberg, M. E., Story, M., & Neumark-Sztainer, D. (2005). Adolescent girls with high body satisfaction: Who are they and what can they teach us? *Journal of Adolescent Health, 37,* 391–396.

Keniston, K. (1965). *The uncommitted.* New York: Harcourt, Brace, & World.

Keniston, K. (1968). *Young radicals.* New York: Harcourt, Brace, & World.

Keniston, K. (1970). Youth: A "new" stage of life. *American Scholar, 39,* 631–641.

Kennedy, J. H. (1990). Determinants of peer social status: Contributions of physical appearance, reputation, and behavior. *Journal of Youth and Adolescence, 19,* 233–244.

Kenney, A. B. (1995). *Chinese views of childhood.* Honolulu: University of Hawai'i Press.

Kenney, A. B. (2003). *Representations of children and youth in early China.* Stanford, CA: Stanford University Press.

Kenney-Benson, G. A., Pomerantz, E. M., Ryan, A. M., & Patrick, H. (2006). Sex differences in math performance: The role of children's approach to schoolwork. *Developmental Psychology, 42,* 11–26.

Kerckhoff, A. C. (2002). The transition from school to work. In J. T. Mortimer & R. W. Larson (Eds.), *The changing adolescent experience: Societal trends and the transition to adulthood.* New York: Cambridge University Press.

Kerns, K. A., & Berenbaum, S. A. (1991). Sex differences in spatial ability in children. *Behavioral Genetics, 21,* 383–396.

Kerr, M., & Stattin, H. (2000). What parents know, how they know it, and several forms of adolescent adjustment: Further evidence for a reinterpretation of monitoring. *Developmental Psychology, 36,* 366–380.

Kerr, M., & Stattin, H. (2003) Parenting of adolescents: Action or reaction? In A. C. Crouter & A. Booth (Eds.), *Children's influence on family dynamics: The neglected side of family relationships.* Mahwah, NJ: Erlbaum.

Kerr, M., Stattin, H., Biesecker, G., & Ferrer-Wreder, L. (2002). Parents and peers as developmental contexts. In R. M. Lerner, M. A. Easterbrooks, & J. Mistry (Eds.), *Comprehensive handbook of psychology: Vol. 6, Developmental psychology.* New York: Wiley.

Ketner, S. L., Buitelaar, M. W., & Bosma, H. A. (2004). Identity strategies among adolescent girls of Moroccan descent in the Netherlands. *Identity, 4,* 145–169.

Kett, J. (1977). *Rites of passage: Adolescence in America, 1790 to the present.* New York: Basic Books.

Khaleque, A., & Rohner, R. P. (2002). Perceived parental acceptance-rejection

and psychological adjustment: A meta-analysis of cross-cultural and intracultural studies. *Journal of Marriage and the Family, 64,* 54–64.

Kiang, L., Yip, T., Gonzales-Backen, M., Witkow, M., & Fuligni, A. J. (2006). Ethnic identity and the daily psychological well-being of adolescents from Mexican and Chinese backgrounds. *Child Development, 77,* 1338–1350.

Kiefer, A. K., & Sekaquaptewa, D. (2007). Implicit stereotypes, gender identification, and math-related outcomes: A prospective study of female college students. *Psychological Science, 18,* 13–18.

Kieren, D. K., & Morse, J. M. (1992). Preparation factors and menstrual attitudes of pre– and postmenarcheal girls. *Journal of Sex Education and Therapy, 18,* 155–174.

Kiesner, J., & Kerr, M. (2004). Families, peers, and contexts as multiple determinants of adolescent problem behavior. *Journal of Adolescence, 27,* 493–495.

Kim, J.-Y., McHale, S. M., Osgood, D. W., & Crouter, A. C. (2006). Longitudinal course and family correlates of sibling relationships from childhood through adolescence. *Child Development, 77,* 1746–1761.

Kim, K. J., Conger, R. D., Lorenz, F. O., & Elder, G. H., Jr. (2001). Parent-adolescent reciprocity in negative affect and its relation to early adult social development. *Developmental Psychology, 37,* 775–790.

Kimball, M. M. (1989). A new perspective on women's math achievement. *Psychological Bulletin, 105,* 198–214.

Kimmel, A. (1996). *Ethical issues in behavioral research.* Cambridge, MA: Blackwell.

Kindermann, T. A., McCollam, T., & Gibson, E. (1996). Peer networks and students' classroom engagement during childhood and adolescence. In J. Juvonen & K. Wentzel (Eds.), *Social motivation: Understanding children's school adjustment.* Cambridge, UK: Cambridge University Press.

King, B. M. (2005). *Human sexuality today* (5th ed.). Upper Saddle River, NJ: Prentice Hall.

King, C. A. (1997). Suicidal behavior in adolescence. In R. W. Maris, M. M. Silverman, & S. S. Canetoon (Eds.), *Review of suicidology, 1997.* New York: Guilford.

King, K. A. (1997). Self-concept and self-esteem: A clarification of terms. *Journal of School Health, 67,* 68–73.

King, P. E., Dowling, E. M., Mueller, R. A., White, K., Schultz, W., Osborn, P., et al. (2005). Thriving in adolescence: The voices of youth-serving practitioners, parents, and early and late adolescents. *Journal of Early Adolescence, 25,* 94–112.

King, P. M., & Kitchener, K. S. (2002). The reflective judgment model: Twenty years of research on cognition. In B. K. Hofer & P. R. Pintrich (Eds.), *Personal epistemology: The psychology of beliefs about knowledge and knowing.* Mahwah, NJ: Erlbaum.

King, S., & Jones, D. C. (2006, March). *Appearance magazines and adolescents: Age*

and gender differences. Presented at the meeting of the Society for Research on Adolescence, San Francisco.

Kinney, D. A. (1993). From nerds to normals: The recovery of identity among adolescents from middle school to high school. *Sociology of Education, 66,* 21–40.

Kinney, D. A. (1999). From "headbangers" to "hippies": Delineating adolescents' active attempts to form an alternative peer culture. *New Directions for Child Development, 84,* 21–35.

Kipke, M. D. (1999). *Adolescent development and the biology of puberty.* Washington, DC: National Academy Press.

Kirby, D. (2002). The impact of schools and school programs upon adolescent sexual behavior. *The Journal of Sex Research, 39,* 27–33.

Kirschner, B., Strobel, K., & Fernández, M. (2002, April). *Civic involvement among urban youth: A qualitative study of "critical engagement."* Presented at the Society for Research on Adolescence, New Orleans.

Kistner, J. (2006). Children's peer acceptance, perceived acceptance, and risk for depression. In T. E. Joiner, J. S. Brown, & J. Kistner (Eds.), *The interpersonal, cognitive, and social nature of depression.* Mahwah, NJ: Erlbaum.

Kitayama, S., & Markus, H. R. (2000). The pursuit of happiness and the realization of sympathy: Cultural patterns of self, social relations, and well-being. In E. Diener & E. M. Suh (Eds.), *Culture and subjective well-being.* Cambridge, MA: MIT Press.

Kitson, G. C., & Holmes, W. M. (1992). *Portrait of divorce: Adjustment to marital breakdown.* New York: Guilford.

Klaczynski, P. A. (2000). Motivated scientific reasoning biases, epistemological beliefs, and theory polarization: A two–process approach to adolescent cognition. *Child Development, 71,* 1347–1366.

Klaczynski, P. A. (2001). Analytic and heuristic processing influences on adolescent reasoning and decision-making. *Child Development, 72,* 844–861.

Klaczynski, P. A. (2005). Metacognition and cognitive variability: A dual-process model of decision making and its development. In J. E. Jacobs & P. A. Klaczynski (Eds.), *The development of decision-making: Cognitive, sociocultural, and legal perspectives.* Mahwah, NJ: Erlbaum.

Klaczynski, P. A., & Narasimham, G. (1998). Development of scientific reasoning biases: Cognitive versus ego–protective explanations. *Developmental Psychology, 34,* 175–187.

Klassen, R. (2002). Writing in early adolescence: A review of the role of self-efficacy beliefs. *Educational Psychology Review, 14,* 173–203.

Klebanov, P. K., Brooks-Gunn, J., McCarton, C., & McCormick, M. C. (1998). The contribution of neighborhood and family income to developmental test scores over the first three years of life. *Child Development, 69,* 1420–1436.

Kleiber, D., Larson, R., & Csikszentmihalyi, M. (1986). The experience of leisure in adolescence. *Journal of Leisure Research, 18,* 169–176.

Kleijwegt, M. (1991). *Ancient youth: The ambiguity of youth and the absence of adolescence in Greco-Roman society.* Amsterdam: J. C. Gieben.

Klein, M. (1998). Teen green. *American Demographics, 20* (2), 39.

Klein, M. W. (2006). Peer effects in naturally occurring groups: The case of street gangs. In Dodge, K. A., Dishion, T. J., & Lansford, J. E. (Eds.), *Deviant peer influences in programs for youth: Problems and solutions.* New York: Guilford.

Klein, T. A. (1999). Puberty, in humans. In E. Knobil & J. Neill (Eds.), *The encyclopedia of reproduction* (Vol. 4). New York: Academic Press.

Klimes-Dougan, B., Hastings, P. D., Granger, D. A., Usher, B. A., & Zahn-Waxler, C. (2001). Adrenocorticol activity in at-risk and normally developing adolescents: Individual differences in salivary cortisol basal levels, diurnal variation, and responses to social challenges. *Development and Psychopathology, 13,* 695–719.

Kling, K. C., Hyde, J. S., Showers, C. J., & Buswell, B. N. (1999). Gender differences in self-esteem: A meta-analysis. *Psychological Bulletin, 125,* 470–500.

Kluckhohn, C. (1954). Culture and behavior. In G. Lindzey (Ed.), *Handbook of social psychology,* Vol. 2. Cambridge, MA: Addison-Wesley.

Knafo, A., Iervolino, A. C., & Plomin, R. (2005). Masculine girls and feminine boys: Genetic and environmental contributions to atypical gender development in early childhood. *Journal of Personality and Social Psychology, 88,* 400–412.

Knafo, A., & Schwartz, S. H. (2003). Parenting and adolescents' accuracy in perceiving parental values. *Child Development, 74,* 595–611.

Knickmeyer, R., Baron-Cohen, S., Raggatt, P., & Kevin Taylor, K. (2005). Foetal testosterone, social relationships, and restricted interests in children. *Journal of Child Psychology and Psychiatry, 46,* 198–210.

Koch, J. (2003). Gender issues in the classroom. In I. B. Weiner (Ed.), *Handbook of psychology* (Vol. 7). New York: Wiley.

Kochanska, G., Aksan, N., Knaack, A., & Rhines, H. M. (2004). Maternal parenting and children's conscience: Early security as a moderator. *Child Development, 75,* 1229–1242.

Kochanska, G., Gross, J. N., Lin, M., & Nichols, K. E. (2002). Guilt in young children: Development, determinants, and relations with a broader system of standards. *Child Development, 73,* 461–482.

Kochenderfer-Ladd, B., & Wardrop, J. L. (2001). Chronicity and instability of children's peer victimization experiences as predictors of loneliness and social satisfaction trajectories. *Child Development, 72,* 134–151.

Kocieniewski, D. (2006, June 9). After gang threat, it's cap, gown and lockdown. *New York Times,* p. A1.

Koerner, S., Jacobs, S., & Raymond, M. (2000). When mothers turn to their adolescent daughters: Predicting daughters' vulnerability to negative adjustment outcomes. *Family Relations, 49,* 301–309.

Koff, E., & Rierdan, J. (1996). Premenarcheal expectations and postmenarcheal experiences of positive and negative menstrual related changes. *Journal of Adolescent Health, 18,* 286–291.

Kohl, G. O., Lengua, L. J., McMahon, R. J., & Conduct Problems Prevention Research Group. (2000). Parent involvement in school: Conceptualizing multiple dimensions and their relations with family and demographic risk factors. *Journal of School Psychology, 38,* 501–523.

Kohlberg, L. (1963). The development of children's orientations toward a moral order: I. Sequence in the development of moral thought. *Vita Humana, 6,* 11–33.

Kohlberg, L. (1966). A cognitive-developmental analysis. In E. Maccoby (Ed.), *The development of sex differences.* Stanford, CA: Stanford University Press.

Kohlberg, L. (1969). Stage and sequence: The cognitive-developmental approach to socialization. In D. A. Goslin (Ed.), *Handbook of socialization theory and research.* Skokie, IL: Rand McNally.

Kohlberg, L. (1984). *Essays on moral development. Vol 2: The psychology of moral development.* San Francisco: Harper & Row.

Kohn, A. (2000). *The case against standardized testing: Raise the scores, ruin the schools.* Portsmouth, NH: Heineman.

Kolata, G. (2008, Feb. 18). Big-time injury strikes little players. *New York Times,* pp. A1, A10.

Korner, M. (1991). Universals of behavioral development in relation to brain myelination. In K. R. Gibson & A. C. Petersen (Eds.), *Brain maturation and cognitive development: Comparative and cross-cultural perspectives.* New York: Aldine de Gruyter.

Koslowski, L. T., Wilkinson, A., Skinner, W., Kent, C., Franklin, T., & Pope, M. (1989). Comparing tobacco cigarette dependence with other drug dependencies. *Journal of the American Medical Association, 261,* 898–901.

Kovacs, D. M., Parker, J. G., & Hoffman, L. W. (1996). Behavioral, affective, and social correlates of involvement in cross-sex friendship in elementary school. *Child Development, 67,* 2269–2286.

Kowalski, R. M., & Chapple, T. (2000). The social stigma of menstruation: Fact or fiction? *Psychology of Women Quarterly, 24,* 74–80.

Kracke, B. (2002). The role of personality, parents and peers in adolescents career exploration. *Journal of Adolescence, 25,* 19–30.

Krebs-Smith, S. M., Cook, A., Subar, A. F., Cleveland, L., Friday, J., & Kahle, L. L. (1996). Fruit and vegetable intakes of children and adolescents in the United States. *Archives of Pediatrics & Adolescent Medicine, 150,* 81–86.

Kreuger, R. F., & Markon, K. E. (2006). Reinterpreting comorbidity: A model-based approach to understanding and classifying psychopathology. *Annual Review of Clinical Psychology, 2,* 111–133.

Kreuz, R. J., & Roberts, R. M. (1995). Two cues for verbal irony: Hyperbole and the ironic tone of voice. *Metaphor and Symbolic Activity, 10,* 21–31.

Kring, A. M. (2000). Gender and anger. In A. H. Fischer (Ed.), *Gender and emotion: Social psychological perspectives.* New York: Cambridge University Press.

Kring, A. M., & Gordon, A. H. (1998). Sex differences in emotion: Expression, experience, and physiology. *Journal of Personality and Social Psychology, 74,* 686–703.

Krishnamoorthy, J. S., Hart, C., & Jelalian, E. (2006). The epidemic of childhood obesity: Review of research and implications for public policy. *Social Policy report, 19,* 3–18.

Kroger, J. (1998). Adolescence as a second separation-individuation process: Critical review of an object relations approach. In E. E. A. Skoe & A. L. von der Lippe (Eds.), *Personality development in adolescence: A cross-national and life span perspective.* New York: Routledge.

Kroger, J. (2000). *Identity development: Adolescence through adulthood.* Thousand Oaks, CA: Sage.

Kroger, J. (2003). What transits in an identity status transition? *Identity, 3,* 197–220.

Kroger, J. (2007). Why is identity achievement so elusive? *Identity, 7,* 331–348.

Krug, E. (1966). *Salient dates in American education: 1635–1964.* New York: Harper & Row.

Krug, E. A. (1971). *The shaping of the American high school.* Madison, WI: University of Wisconsin Press.

Kuczmarski, R. J., Ogden, C. L., Grummer-Strawn, L. M., Flegal, K. M., Guo, S. S., Wei, R., et al. (2000). *CDC Growth Charts: United States.* Hyattsville, MD: National Center for Health Statistics.

Kuczynski, L., & Kochanska, G. (1995). Function and content of maternal demands: Developmental significance of early demands for competent action. *Child Development, 66,* 616–628.

Kuczynski, L., & Parkin, C. M. (2006). Agency and bidirectionality in socialization: Interactions, transactions, and relational dialectics. In J. E. Grusec & P. D. Hastings (Eds.), *Handbook of socialization: Theory and research.* New York: Guilford.

Kuhn, D. (1999). Metacognitive development. In L. Balter & C. Tamis-LeMonda (Eds.), *Child psychology: A handbook of contemporary issues.* Philadelphia: Psychology Press.

Kuhn, D. (2006). Do cognitive changes accompany developments in the adolescent brain? *Perspectives on Psychological Science, 1,* 59–67.

Kuhn, D., & Franklin, S. (2006). The second decade: What develops (and how)? In W. Damon & R. M. Lerner (Eds.), *Handbook of child psychology* (6th ed.). Hoboken, NJ: Wiley.

Kuhn, D., Garcia-Mila, M., Zohar, A., & Anderson, C. (1995). Strategies of knowledge acquisition. *Monographs of the Society for Research in Child Development, 60,* Serial No. 245.

Kulin, H. E., Bwibo, N., Mutie, D., & Santner, S. J. (1982). The effect of chronic childhood malnutrition on pubertal growth and development. *American Journal of Clinical Nutrition, 36,* 527.

Kulin, H. E., Bwibo, N., Mutie, D., & Santner, S. J. (1984). Gonadotropin excretion during puberty in malnourished children. *Journal of Pediatrics, 105,* 325.

Kulin, H. E., & Muller, J. (1996). The biological aspects of puberty. *Pediatric Review, 17,* 75–86.

Kumar, R. (2006). Students' experiences of home-school dissonance: The role of school academic culture and perceptions of classroom goal structures. *Contemporary Educational Psychology, 31,* 253–279.

Kunkel, D., Cope-Farrar, K., Biely, E., Farinola, W., & Donnerstein, E. (2001). *Sex on TV.* Biennial report to the Kaiser Family Foundation. Menlo Park, CA: Kaiser Family Foundation.

Kunnen, E., & Bosma, H. A. (2003). Fischer's skill theory applied to identity development: A response to Kroger. *Identity, 3,* 247–270.

Kuperminc, G. P., Leadbetter, B. J., & Blatta, S. J. (2001). School social climate and individual differences in vulnerability to psychopathology among middle school students. *Journal of School Psychology, 39,* 141–159.

Kupersmidt, J., Burchinal, M., & Patterson, C. (1995). Developmental patterns of childhood peer relations as predictors of externalizing behavior problems. *Development and Psychopathology, 7,* 825–843.

Kurdek, L., & Fine, M. (1994). Family acceptance and family control as predictors of adjustment in young adolescents: Linear, curvilinear, or interactive effects. *Child Development, 65,* 1137–1146.

Kurman, J. (2004). Gender, self-enhancement, and self-regulation of learning behaviors in junior high school. *Sex Roles, 50,* 725–735.

Kuttler, A. F., La Greca, A. M., & Prinstein, M. J. (1999). Friendship qualities and social-emotional functioning of adolescents with close, cross-sex friendships. *Journal of Research on Adolescence, 9,* 339–366.

Kwak, K. (2003). Adolescents and their parents: A review of intergenerational family relations for immigrant and non-immigrant families. *Human Development, 46,* 115–136.

Kwak, K., & Berry, J. W. (2001). Generational differences in acculturation among Asian families in Canada: A comparison of Vietnamese, Korean, and East-Indian groups. *International Journal of Psychology, 36,* 152–162.

La Fontaine, J. S. (Ed.). (1972). Ritualization of women's life-crises in Bugisu. In *The interpretation of ritual: Essays in honour of A. I. Richards.* London: Tavistock.

La Fontaine, J. S. (1985). *Initiation.* New York: Viking Penguin.

La Greca, A. M., Prinstein, M. J., & Fetter, M. D. (2001). Adolescent peer crowd affiliation: Linkages with health-risk behaviors and close friendships. *Journal of Pediatric Psychology, 26,* 131–143.

La Sage, E., & Ye, R. (2000, January). *A study on the relationship between students' achievement, school size, and gender.* Paper presented at the Southwest Educational Research Association, Dallas, TX.

Labaree, D. (1997). Public goods, private goods: The American struggle over educational goals. *American Educational Research Journal, 34,* 39–81.

Laberge, L., Petit, D., Simard, C., Vitaro, F., Tremblay, R. E., & Montplaisir, J. (2001). Development of sleep patterns in early adolescence. *Journal of Sleep Research, 10,* 59–67.

Labre, M. P. (2002). Adolescent boys and the muscular male body ideal. *Journal of Adolescent Health, 30*(4, Suppl), 233–242.

Lacey, M. (2003, November 14). U.S. trade law gives Africa hope and hard jobs. *New York Times,* p. A1.

Lachman, M. E. (2001). *Handbook of midlife development.* New York: Wiley.

Ladurie, E. L. R. (1975). *Montaillou, village occitan de 1294 à 1324.* Paris: Gallimard.

LaFontana, K. M., & Cillessen, A. H. N. (2002). Children's perceptions of popular and unpopular peers: A multi-method assessment. *Developmental Psychology, 38,* 635–647.

LaFromboise, T., Coleman, H. L. K., & Gerton, J. (1993). Psychological impact of biculturalism: Evidence and theory. *Psychological Bulletin, 114,* 395–412.

Lahey, B. B., Loeber, R., Burke, J., Rathouz, P. J., & McBurnett, K. (2002). Waxing and waning in concert: Dynamic comorbidity of conduct disorder with other disruptive and emotional problems over seven years among clinic-referred boys. *Journal of Abnormal Psychology, 111,* 556–567.

Laird, R. D., Jordan, K. Y., Dodge, K. A., Pettit, G. S., & Bates, J. E. (2001). Peer rejection in childhood, involvement with antisocial peers in early adolescence, and the development of externalizing behavior problems. *Development and Psychopathology, 13,* 337–354.

Laird, R. D., Pettit, G. S., Bates, J. E., & Dodge, K. A. (2003). Parents' monitoring-relevant knowledge and adolescents' delinquent behavior: Evidence of correlated developmental changes and reciprocal influences. *Child Development, 74,* 752–768.

Laird, R. D., Pettit, G. S., Dodge, K. A., & Bates, J. E. (2003). Change in parents' monitoring knowledge: Links with parenting, relationship quality, adolescent beliefs, and antisocial behavior. *Social Development, 12,* 401–419.

Laird, R. D., Pettit, G. S., Dodge, K. A., & Bates, J. E. (2005). Peer relationship antecedents of delinquent behavior in late adolescence: Is there evidence of demographic group differences in developmental processes? *Development and Psychopathology, 17,* 127–144.

Lakin, R., & Mahoney, A. (2006). Empowering youth to change their world: Identifying key components of a community service program to promote positive development. *Journal of School Psychology, 44,* 513–531.

Lamborn, S., Dornbusch, S., & Steinberg, L. (1996). Ethnicity and community context as moderators of the relation between family decision-making and adolescent adjustment. *Child Development, 66,* 283–301.

Landis, D. (2002). Cuts won't be pleasant; Plains preparing to drop activities. Springfield, IL: *The State Journal-Register,* November 25, p. 1.

Landry, D. J., Singh, S., & Darroch, J. E. (2000). Sexuality education in fifth and sixth grades in U.S. public schools, 1999. *Family Planning Perspectives, 32,* 212–219.

Lapan, R. T., Hinkelman, J. M., Adams, A., & Turner, S. (1999). Understanding rural adolescents' interests, values, and efficacy expectations. *Journal of Career Development, 26,* 107–124.

Lapan, R. T., Kardash, C., & Turner, S. (2002). Empowering students to become self regulated learners. *Professional School Counseling, 5*(4), 257–265.

Lapsley, D. K. (1996). Toward an integrated theory of adolescent ego development: The "new look" at adolescent egocentrism. *American Journal of Orthopsychiatry, 63,* 562–571.

Lapsley, D. K., Enright, R., & Serlin, R. (1985). Toward a theoretical perspective on the legislation of adolescence. *Journal of Early Adolescence, 5,* 441–466.

Lapsley, D. K., Milstead, M., Quintana, S. M., Flannery, D., & Buss, R. R. (1986). Adolescent egocentrism and formal operations: Tests of a theoretical assumption. *Developmental Psychology, 22,* 800–807.

Lapsley, D. K., & Narvaez, D. (2006). Character education. In W. Damon & R. Lerner (Eds.), *Handbook of child psychology* (6th ed.). New York: Wiley.

Laqueur, T. W. (2004). *Solitary sex: A cultural history of masturbation.* New York: Zone.

Larson, M. (1996). Sex roles and soap operas: What adolescents learn about single motherhood. *Sex Roles, 35,* 97–121.

Larson, R. W. (2000). Toward a psychology of positive youth development. *American Psychologist, 55,* 170–183.

Larson, R. W. (2002a). Globalization, societal change, and new technologies: What they mean for the future of adolescence. *Journal of Research on Adolescence, 12,* 1–30.

Larson, R. W. (2002b). Constructing social science (please read all warnings before, during, and after use). *Journal of Marriage and the Family, 64,* 1058–1062.

Larson, R. W. (2007). From "I" to "we": Development of the capacity for teamwork in youth programs. In R. Silbereisen & R. M. Lerner (Eds.), *Approaches to positive youth development.* Thousand Oaks, CA: Sage.

Larson, R. W., Clore, G. L., & Wood, G. A. (1999). The emotions of romantic relationships: Do they wreak havoc on adolescents? In W. Furman, B. B. Brown, & C. Feiring (Eds.), *The development of romantic relationships in adolescence.* New York: Cambridge University Press.

Larson, R. W., Hansen, D. M., & Moneta, G. (2006). Differing profiles of developmental experiences across types of organized youth activities. *Developmental Psychology, 42,* 849–863.

Larson, R. W., & Ham, M. (1993). Stress and "storm and stress" in early adolescence: The relationship of negative events with dysphoric affect. *Developmental Psychology, 29,* 130–140.

Larson, R. W., Hansen, D., & Walker, K. (2005). Everybody's gotta give: Development of initiative and teamwork within a youth program. In J. L. Mahoney, R. W. Larson, & J. S. Eccles (Eds.), *Organized activities as contexts of development: Extracurricular activities, after-school and community programs.* Mahwah, NJ: Erlbaum.

Larson, R. W., Jarrett, R., Hansen, D., Pearce, N., Sullivan, P., et al. (2004). Organized youth activities as contexts for positive development. In P. A. Linley & S. Joseph (Eds.), *Positive psychology in practice.* New York: Wiley.

Larson, R. W., Moneta, G., Richards, M. H., & Wilson, S. (2002). Continuity, stability, and change in daily emotional experience across adolescence. *Child Development, 73,* 1151–1165.

Larson, R. W., & Richards, M. H. (1991a). Boredom in the middle school years: Blaming schools versus blaming students. *American Journal of Education, 99,* 418–443.

Larson, R. W., & Richards, M. H. (1991b). Daily companionship in late childhood and early adolescence: Changing developmental contexts. *Child Development, 62,* 284–300.

Larson, R. W., & Richards, M. H. (1994). *Divergent realities: The emotional lives of mothers, fathers, and adolescents.* New York: Basic Books.

Larson, R. W., & Richards, M. H. (1998). Waiting for the weekend: Friday and Saturday nights as the emotional climax of the week. *New Directions for Child and Adolescent Psychology, 82,* 37–52.

Larson, R. W., Richards, M. H., Moneta, G., Holmbeck, G., & Duckett, E. (1996). Changes in adolescents' daily interactions with their families from ages 10 to 18: Disengagement and transformation. *Developmental Psychology, 32,* 744–754.

Larson, R. W., & Seepersad, S. (2003). Adolescents' leisure time in the United States: Partying, sports, and the American Experiment. *New Directions for Child and Adolescent Development, 90,* 53–64.

Larson, R. W., & Verma, S. (1999). How children and adolescents spend time across the world: Work, play, and developmental opportunities. *Psychological Bulletin, 125,* 701–736.

Larson, R. W., Wilson, S., Brown, B. B., Furstenberg, F. F., Jr., & Verma, S. (2002). Changes in adolescents' interpersonal experiences: Are they being prepared for adult relationships in the twenty-first century? *Journal of Research on Adolescence, 12,* 31–68.

Larson, R. W., & Wood, D. (2006). Positive development. In L. R. Sherrod, C. A.

Flanagan, R. Kassimir, & A. K. Syvertsen (Eds.), *Youth activism: An international encyclopedia.* Westport, CT: Greenwood.

Lashbrook, J. T. (2000). Fitting in: Exploring the emotional dimension of adolescent peer pressure. *Adolescence, 35,* 747–757.

Laursen, B. (1995). Conflict and social interaction in adolescent relationships. *Journal of Research on Adolescence, 5,* 55–70.

Laursen, B., & Collins, W. A. (1994). Interpersonal conflict during adolescence. *Psychological Bulletin, 115,* 197–209.

Laursen, B., Coy, K. C., & Collins, W. A. (1998). Reconsidering changes in parent-child conflict across adolescence: A meta-analysis. *Child Development, 69,* 817–832.

Laursen, B., & Mooney, K. S. (2007). Individual differences in adolescent dating and adjustment. In R. C. M. E. Engels, M. Kerr, & H. Stattin (Eds.), *Friends, lovers and groups: Key relationships in adolescence.* New York: Wiley.

Laursen, B., & Williams, V. (1997). Perceptions of interdependence and closeness in family and peer relationships among adolescents with and without romantic partners. In S. Shulman & W. A. Collins (Eds.), *Romantic relationships in adolescence: New directions for child development.* San Francisco: Jossey-Bass.

Lazarus, R. S. (1999). *Stress and emotion: A new synthesis.* New York: Springer.

Lazarus, R. S., & Folkman, S. (1984). *Stress, appraisal, and coping.* New York: Springer.

le Grange, D., & Lock, J. (2005). The dearth of psychological treatment studies for anorexia nervosa. *International Journal of Eating Disorders, 37,* 79–91.

Leadbeater, B. J. R., & Way, N. (2001). *Growing up fast: Transitions to early adulthood of inner-city adolescent mothers.* Mahwah, NJ: Erlbaum.

Leaper, C. (2000). The social construction and socialization of gender during development. In P. H. Miller & E. K. Scholnick (Eds.), *Toward a feminist developmental psychology.* New York: Routledge.

Leaper, C. (2002). Parenting girls and boys. In M. H. Bornstein (Ed.), *Handbook of parenting: Vol. 1. Children and parenting* (2nd ed.). Mahwah, NJ: Erlbaum.

Leaper, C., Anderson, K. J., & Sanders, P. (1998). Moderators of gender effects on parents' talk to their children: A meta-analysis. *Developmental Psychology, 34,* 3–27.

Leaper, C., & Friedman, C. K. (2006). The socialization of gender. In J. E. Grusec & P. D. Hastings (Eds.), *Handbook of socialization: Theory and research.* New York: Guilford.

Leaper, C., & Valin, D. (1996). Predictors of Mexican American mothers' and fathers' attitudes toward gender equality. *Hispanic Journal of Behavioral Sciences, 18,* 343–355.

Leary, M. R., & Tangney, J. P. (2002). The self as an organizing construct in the behavioral and social sciences. In M. R. Leary & J. P. Tangney (Eds.), *Handbook of self and identity.* New York: Guilford.

Lease, A. M., Kennedy, C. A., & Axelrod, J. L. (2002). Children's social constructions of popularity. *Social Development, 11,* 87–109.

Lee, C. B. T. (1970). *The campus scene, 1900–1970: Changing styles in undergraduate life.* New York: McKay.

Lee, F. R. (2002, November 30). Why are black students lagging? A new theory in a thorny debate points to the minorities themselves. *New York Times,* pp. B1, B11.

Lee, J. (1994). Menarche and the (hetero) sexualization of the female body. *Gender and Society, 8,* 343–362.

Lee, J. M., Appugliese, D., Kaciroti, N., Corwyn, R. F., Bradley, R. H., & Lumeng, J. C. (2007). Weight status in young girls and the onset of puberty. *Pediatrics, 119,* 624–630.

Lee, K., Cameron, C. A., Xu, F., & Board, J. (1997). Chinese and Canadian children's evaluation of lying and truth-telling: Similarities and differences in the context of pro- and antisocial behaviors. *Child Development, 68,* 924–934.

Lee, M. (2003). Korean adolescents' "Examination Hell" and their use of free time. *New Directions for Child and Adolescent Development, 90,* 9–35.

Lee, P. A., Kulin, H. E., & Guo, S. S. (2001). Age of puberty among girls and the diagnosis of precocious puberty. *Pediatrics, 107,* 1493.

Lee, V. E., & Smith, J. B. (1997). High school size: Which works best and for whom? *Educational Evaluation and Policy Analysis, 19,* 205–228.

Lee, V. E., & Smith, J. B. (2001). *Restructuring high schools for equity and excellence: What works.* New York: Teachers College Press.

Lemeshow, A. R., Fisher, L., Goodman, E., Kawachi, I., Bekey, C. S., & Colditz, G. A. (2008). Subjective social status in the school and change in adiposity in female adolescents. *Archives of Pediatric and Adolescent Medicine, 162,* 23–28.

Lemke, M., Sen, A., Pahlke, E., Partelow, L., Miller, D. et al. (2004). *International outcomes of learning in mathematics literacy and problem solving: PISA 2003, results from the U. S. perspective.* Washington, DC: U.S. Department of Education.

Lenhart, A., & Madden, M. (2005). *Teen content creators and consumers.* Washington, DC: Pew Foundation.

Lenhart, A., Madden, M., & Hitlin, P. (2005). *Teens and technology: Youth are leading the transition to a fully wired and mobile nation.* Washington, DC: Pew Foundation.

Lent, R. W., & Brown, S. D. (2002). Social cognitive career theory and adult career development. In S. G. Niles (Ed.), *Adult career development: Concepts, issues and practices* (3rd ed.). Columbus, OH: National Career Development Association.

Lent, R. W., Brown, S. D., Brenner, B., Chopra, S. B., Davis, T., Talleyrand, R., & Suthakaran, V. (2001). The role of contextual supports and barriers in the choice of math/science educational options: A test of social cognitive hypotheses. *Journal of Counseling Psychology, 48,* 474–483.

Lepper, M. R., Corpus, J. H., & Iyengar, S. S. (2005). Intrinsic and extrinsic motivational orientations in the classroom: Age differences and academic correlates. *Journal of Educational Psychology, 97*, 184–196.

Lepper, M. R., & Greene, D. (1975). Turning play into work: Effects of adult surveillance and extrinsic rewards on children's intrinsic motivation. *Journal of Personality and Social Psychology, 31*, 479–486.

Lepper, M. R., Greene, D., & Nisbett, R. E. (1973). Undermining children's intrinsic interest with extrinsic rewards: A test of the "overjustification" hypothesis. *Journal of Personality and Social Psychology, 28*, 129–137.

Lerner, J. V., & Noh, E. R. (2000). Maternal employment influences on early adolescent development: A contextual view. In R. D. Taylor & M. C. Wang (Eds.), *Resilience across contexts: Family, work, culture, and community.* Mahwah, NJ: Erlbaum.

Lerner, R. M. (1992). *Final solutions: Biology, prejudice, and genocide.* University Park, PA: Penn State Press.

Lerner, R. M. (2002). *Concepts and theories of human development* (3rd ed.). Mahwah, NJ: Erlbaum.

Lerner, R. M. (2005, September). *Promoting positive youth development: Theoretical and empirical bases.* White paper prepared for the Workshop on the Science of Adolescent Health and Development, National Research Council/Institute of Medicine. Washington, DC: National Academies of Science.

Lerner, R. M. (2006). Developmental science, developmental systems, and contemporary theories of human development. In W. Damon & R. M. Lerner (Eds.), *Handbook of child psychology.* Hoboken, NJ: Wiley.

Lerner, R. M., Almerigi, J. B., Theokas, C., & Lerner, J. V. (2005). Positive youth development: A view of the issues. *Journal of Early Adolescence, 25*, 10–16.

Lerner, R. M., & Castellino, D. R. (2002). Contemporary developmental theory and adolescence: Developmental systems and applied developmental science. *Journal of Adolescent Health, 31*, 122–135.

Lerner, R. M., Dowling, E. M., & Anderson, P. M. (2003). Positive youth development: Thriving as the basis of personhood and civil society. *Applied Developmental Science, 7*, 172–180.

Lerner, R. M., Lerner, J. V., Almerigi, J. B., Theokas, C., Phelps, E., Gestsdottir, S., et al. (2005). Positive youth development, participation in community youth development programs, and community contributions of fifth-grade adolescents: Findings from the first wave of the 4-H Study of Positive Youth Development. *Journal of Early Adolescence, 25*, 17–71.

Lerner, R. M., & Steinberg, L. (Eds.). (2004). *Handbook of adolescent psychology.* New York: Wiley.

Leve, L. D., & Fagot, B. I. (1997). Gender-role socialization and discipline processes in one- and two-parent families. *Sex Roles, 36*, 1–21.

Leventhal, T., & Brooks-Gunn, J. (2000). The neighborhoods they live in: The effects of neighborhood residence on child and adolescent outcomes. *Psychological Bulletin, 126*, 309–337.

Leventhal, T., & Brooks-Gunn, J. (2003). Moving on up: Neighborhood effects on children and families. In M. H. Bornstein & R. H. Bradley (Eds.), *Socioeconomic status, parenting, and child development.* Mahwah, NJ: Erlbaum.

Leventhal, T., & Brooks-Gunn, J. (2004). A randomized study of neighborhood effects on low-income children's educational outcomes. *Developmental Psychology, 40*, 488–507.

Levesque, R. J. R. (1993). The romantic experience of adolescents in satisfying love relationships. *Journal of Youth and Adolescence, 22*, 219–251.

Levine, M. P., & Smolak, L. (2001). Primary prevention of body image disturbance and disordered eating in childhood and early adolescence. In J. K. Thompson & L. Smolak (Eds.), *Body image, eating disorders, and obesity in youth: Assessment, prevention, and treatment.* Washington, DC: American Psychological Association.

Levine, S. C., Vasilyeva, M., Lourenco, S. F., Newcombe, N. S., & Huttenlocher, J. (2005). Socioeconomic status modifies the sex difference in spatial skill. *Psychological Science, 16*, 841–845.

LeVine, R. A. (1974). Parental goals: A cross-cultural view. *Teachers College Record, 76*, 226–239.

Levinthal, C. F. (2005). *Drugs, behavior, and modern society* (4th ed.). Boston: Allyn & Bacon.

Lévy-Strauss, C. (1963). *Structural anthropology.* Garden City, NY: Doubleday.

Lewin, T. (1999, May 2). Arizona high school provides glimpse inside cliques' divisive webs. *New York Times*, p. A1.

Lewin, T. (2002a, July 17). Study links working mothers to slower learning. *New York Times*, p. A14.

Lewin, T. (2002b, July 21). Ideas & trends: A child study is a peek. it's not the whole picture. *New York Times*, p. D3.

Lewin-Epstein, N. (1981). *Youth employment during high school.* Washington, DC: National Center for Education Statistics.

Lewinsohn, P. M., Joiner, T. E., Jr., & Rohde, P. (2001). Evaluation of cognitive diathesis-stress models in predicting major depressive disorder in adolescents. *Journal of Abnormal Psychology, 110*, 203–215.

Lewinsohn, P. M., Rohde, P., Seeley, J. R., Kline, D. N., & Gotlib, I. H. (2006). The psychosocial consequences of adolescent major depressive disorder on young adults. In T. E. Joiner, J. S. Brown, & J. Kistner (Eds.), *The interpersonal, cognitive, and social nature of depression.* Mahwah, NJ: Erlbaum.

Lewis, C. J., Crane, N. T., & Hubbard, V. S. (1994). Healthy people 2000: Report on the 1994 nutrition progress review. *Nutrition Today, 29*, 6–14.

Lewis, M., & Brooks-Gunn, J. (1979). *Social cognition and the acquisition of self.* New York: Plenum.

Lewis, M., Feiring, C., & Rosenthal, S. (2000). Attachment over time. *Child Development, 71*, 707–720.

Lewis, M. D. (2000). The promise of dynamic systems approaches for an integrated account of human development. *Child Development, 71*, 36–43.

Lewis, M. D., & Douglas, L. (1998). A dynamic systems approach to cognition-emotion interactions in development. In M. F. Mascolo & S. Griffin (Eds.), *What develops in emotional development?* New York: Plenum Press.

Lewontin, R. C. (1976). Race and intelligence. In N. J. Block & G. Dworkin (Eds.), *The IQ controversy.* New York: Pantheon.

Liang, B., Tracy, A. J., Taylor, C. A., & Williams, L. M. (2002). Mentoring college-age women: A relational approach. *American Journal of Community Psychology, 30*, 271–288.

Liben, L. S. (2004). Cultural development and gender development: Shared concepts, methodologies, and challenges. *Human Development, 47*, 179–184.

Liben, L. S., & Bigler, R. S. (2002). The developmental course of gender differentiation. *Monographs of the Society for Research in Child Development, 67*, vii–147.

Lickliter, R., & Honeycutt, H. (2003). Developmental dynamics: Toward a biologically plausible evolutionary psychology. *Psychological Bulletin, 129*, 819–835.

Lilienfeld, S. O. (2003). Comorbidity between and within childhood externalizing and internalizing disorders: Reflections and directions. *Journal of Abnormal Child Psychology, 31*, 285–292.

Limber, S. P., & Flekkoy, M. G. (1995). The U.N. Convention on the Rights of the Child: Its relevance for social scientists. *Social Policy Report, IX*(2), 1–15.

Lincoln, B. (1981). *Emerging from the chrysalis: Studies in rituals of women's initiation.* Cambridge, MA: Harvard University Press.

Lindberg, L., & Hjern, A. (2003). Risk factors for anorexia nervosa: A national cohort study. *International Journal of Eating Disorders, 34*, 397–408.

Lindsey, B. B., & Evans, W. (1925). *The revolt of modern youth.* New York: Boni & Liveright.

Linn, M., & Petersen, A. (1985). Emergence and characterization of sex differences in spatial skill: A meta-analysis. *Child Development, 56*, 1479–1498.

Linville, P. W., & Jones, E. E. (1980). Polarized appraisals of out-group members. *Journal of Personality and Social Psychology, 38*, 689–703.

Lippa, R. A. (2002). *Gender, nature, and nurture.* Mahwah, NJ: Erlbaum.

Lips, H. M. (2004). The gender gap in possible selves: Divergence of academic self-views among high school and university students. *Sex Roles, 50*, 357–371.

Lissau, I., Overpeck, M. D., Ruan, W. J., Due, P., Holstein, B. E., Hediger, M. L., et al. (2004). Body mass index and overweight in adolescents in 13 European countries, Israel, and the United States. *Archives of Pediatrics & Adolescent Medicine, 158,* 27–33.

Little, K., Widman, L., Welsh, D. P., & Darling, N. (2006, March). *Predictors of adolescent romantic relationship trajectories: Break-up and recover.* Presented at the biennial meeting of the Society for Research on Adolescence, San Francisco.

Liu, R. X. (2006). Vulnerability to friends' suicide influence: The moderating effects of gender and adolescent depression. *Journal of Youth and Adolescence, 35,* 479–489.

Liu, W. M., Pope-Davis, D. B., Nevitt, J., & Toporek, R. L. (1999). Understanding the function of acculturation and prejudicial attitudes among Asian Americans. *Cultural Diversity and Ethnic Minority Psychology, 5,* 317–328.

Livson, N., & Peskin, H. (1980). Perspectives on adolescence from longitudinal research. In J. Adelson (Ed.), *Handbook of adolescent psychology.* New York: Wiley.

Loeber, R., & Dishion, T. J. (1984). Boys who fight at home and school: Family conditions influencing cross-setting consistency. *Journal of Consulting and Clinical Psychology, 52,* 759–768.

Logan, G. (2000). Information processing theories. In A. Kazdin (Ed.), *Encyclopedia of psychology.* Washington, DC and New York: American Psychological Association and Oxford University Press.

Lohman, B. J., & Newman, B. M. (2002, April). *Connectedness to family, school, and peers: A cumulative risk perspective on adolescents' academic and psychological adjustment.* Paper presented at the meeting of the Society for Research on Adolescence, New Orleans.

Lorsbach, T. C., & Reimer, J. F. (1997). Developmental changes in the inhibition of previously relevant information. *Journal of Experimental Child Psychology, 64,* 317–342.

Lucas, S. R. (1999). *Tracking inequality: Stratification and mobility in American high schools.* New York: Teachers College Press.

Luyckx, K., Goossens, L., & Soenens, B. (2006). A developmental contextual perspective on identity construction in emerging adulthood: Change dynamics in commitment formation and commitment evaluation. *Developmental Psychology, 42,* 366–380.

Lyman, P. (1987). The fraternal bond as a joking relationship: A case study of the role of sexist jokes in male group bonding. In M. Kimmel (Ed.), *Changing Men.* Newbury Park, CA: Sage.

Lynd, R. S., & Lynd, H. M. (1929). *Middletown, a study in contemporary American culture.* New York: Harcourt, Brace, & World.

Lynd, R. S., & Lynd, H. M. (1937). *Middletown in transition, a study in cultural conflicts.* New York: Harcourt, Brace, & World.

Lytton, H., & Romney, D. M. (1991). Parents' differential socialization of boys and girls: A meta-analysis. *Psychological Bulletin, 109,* 267–297.

Lyubomirsky, S., King, L., & Diener, E. (2005). The benefits of frequent positive affect: Does happiness lead to success? *Psychological Bulletin, 131,* 803–855.

Lyubomirsky, S., Sheldon, K. M., & Schkade, D. (2005). Pursuing happiness: The architecture of sustainable change. *Review of General Psychology, 9,* 111–131.

Maccoby, E. E. (1980) *Social development: Psychological growth and the parent-child relationship.* New York: Harcourt Brace Jovanovich.

Maccoby, E. E. (1998). *The two sexes: Growing up apart, coming together.* Cambridge, MA: Harvard University Press.

Maccoby, E. E. (2000). Parenting and its effects on children: On reading and misreading behavior genetics. *Annual Review of Psychology, 51,* 1–27.

Maccoby, E. E. (2002). Gender and group processes: A developmental perspective. *Current Directions in Psychological Science, 11,* 54–58.

Maccoby, E. E. (2006). Historical overview of socialization research and theory. In J. E. Grusec & P. D. Hastings (Eds.), *Handbook of socialization: Theory and research.* New York: Guilford.

Maccoby, E. E., & Jacklin, C. N. (1974). *The psychology of sex differences.* Palo Alto, CA: Stanford University Press.

Maccoby, E. E., & Martin, J. A. (1983). Socialization in the context of the family: Parent-child interaction. In P. H. Mussen (Ed.), E. M. Hetherington (Vol. Ed.), *Handbook of child psychology:* Vol. 4. *Socialization, personality, and social development* (4th ed.). New York: Wiley.

MacKelvie, K. J., Khan, K. M., Petit, M. A., Janssen, P. A., & McKay, H. A. (2003). A school-based exercise intervention elicits substantial bone health benefits: A 2-year randomized controlled trial in girls. *Pediatrics, 112,* e447–e452.

MacKinnon-Lewis, C., Starnes, R., Volling, B., & Johnson, S. (1997). Perceptions of parenting as predictors of boys' sibling and peer relations. *Developmental Psychology, 33,* 1024–1031.

Macklon, N., & Fauser, B. (1999). Aspects of ovarian follicle development throughout life. *Hormone Research, 52,* 161–170.

MacPhee, D., Fritz, J., & Miller-Heyl, J. (1996). Ethnic variations in personal social networks and parenting. *Child Development, 67,* 3278–3295.

Madon, S., Jussim, L., & Eccles, J. (1997). In search of the powerful self fulfilling prophecy. *Journal of Personality and Social Psychology, 72,* 791–809.

Maehr, M. L., & Meyer, H. A. (1997). Understanding motivation and schooling: Where we've been, where we are, and where we need to go. *Educational Psychology Review, 9,* 371–409.

Maehr, M. L., & Midgley, C. (1996). *Transforming school cultures to enhance student motivation and learning.* Boulder, CO: Westview Press.

Maggs, J. L, Schulenberg, J., & Hurrelmann, K. (1997). Developmental transitions in adolescence: Health promotion implications. In J. Schulenberg, J. L. Maggs, & K. Hurrelmann (Eds.), *Health risks and developmental transitions during adolescence.* New York: Cambridge University Press.

Mahoney, J. L., & Cairns, R. B. (1997). Do extracurricular activities protect against early school dropout? *Developmental Psychology, 33,* 241–253.

Mahoney, J. L., Cairns, B. D., & Farmer, T. (2003). Promoting interpersonal competence and educational success through extracurricular activity participation. *Journal of Educational Psychology, 95,* 409–418.

Mahoney, J. L., Eccles, J. S., & Larson, R. W. (2004). Processes of adjustment in organized out-of-school activities: Opportunities and risks. *New Directions in Youth Development, 101,* 115–144.

Major, B., Spencer, S. J., Schmader, T., Wolfe, C., & Crocker, J. (1998). Coping with negative stereotypes about intellectual performance: The role of psychological disengagement. *Personality and Social Psychology Bulletin, 24,* 34–50.

Malamuth, N. M., & Impett, E. A. (2001). Research on sex in the media: What do we know about effects on children and adolescents? In. D. G. Singer & J. L. Singer (Eds.), *Handbook of children and the media.* Thousand Oaks, CA: Sage.

Malina, R. M. (1985). Menarche in athletes: A synthesis and hypothesis. *Annals of Human Biology, 10,* 1–24.

Malina, R. M. (1989). Growth and maturation: Normal variations and the effects of training. In C. V. Gisolfi & D. R. Lamb (Eds.), *Perspectives in exercise science and sports medicine: Vol II. Youth, exercise, and sport.* Indianapolis, IN: Benchmark Press.

Malina, R. M., Bouchard, C., & Beunen, G. (1988). Human growth: Selected aspects of current research on well-nourished children. *Annual Review of Anthropology, 17,* 187–219.

Malone, P. S., Lansford, J. E., Castellino, D. R., Berlin, L. J., Dodge, K. A., Bates, J. E., et al. (2004). Divorce and child behavior problems: Applying latent change score models to life event data. *Structural Equation Modeling, 11,* 401–423.

Mangaliman, J. (2006, March 22). Poll: Tolerance of gays growing: Survey indicates familiarity breeds acceptance. San Jose (CA) *Mercury News,* p. A1.

Manlove, J., Franzetta, K., Ryan, S., & Moore, K. (2006). Adolescent sexual relationships, contraceptive consistency, and pregnancy prevention approaches. In A. C. Crouter & A. Booth (Eds.), *Romance and sex in adolescence and emerging adulthood: Risks and opportunities.* Mahwah, NJ: Erlbaum.

Manset, G., & Semmel, M. I. (1997). Are inclusive programs for students with mild disabilities effective? A comparative review of model programs. *The Journal of Special Education, 31,* 155–180.

Marcia, J. E. (1966). Development and validation of ego identity status. *Journal of Personality and Social Psychology, 3,* 551–558.

Marcia, J. E. (1980). Identity in adolescence. In J. Adelson (Ed.), *Handbook of adolescent psychology.* New York: Wiley.

Marcia, J. E. (1993). The ego identity status approach to ego identity. In J. E. Marcia, A. S. Waterman, D. R. Matteson, S. L. Archer, & J. L. Orlofsky (Eds.), *Ego identity: A handbook for psychosocial research.* New York: Springer-Verlag.

Markovits, H., & Barrouillet, P. (2002). The development of conditional reasoning: A mental model account. *Developmental Review, 22,* 5–36.

Markovits, H., & Dumas, C. (1999). Developmental patterns of understanding social and physical transitivity. *Journal of Experimental Child Psychology, 73,* 95–114.

Markovits, H., Venet, M., Janveau–Brennan, G., Malfait, N., Pion, N., & Vadeboncoeur, I. (1996). Reasoning in young children: Fantasy and information retrieval. *Child Development, 67,* 2857–2872.

Markstrom, C. A., & Iborra, A. (2003). Adolescent identity formation and rites of passage: The Navajo Kinaaldá ceremony for girls. *Journal of Research on Adolescence, 13,* 399–425.

Markus, H., & Kitiyama, S. (1991). Culture and the self: Implications for cognition, emotion, and motivation. *Psychological Review, 98,* 224–253.

Marsh, H. W. (1991). Employment during high school: Character building or a subversion of academic goals? *Sociology of Education, 64,* 172–189.

Marsh, H. W. (1992). Extracurricular activities: Beneficial extension of the traditional curriculum or subversion of academic goals? *Journal of Educational Psychology, 84,* 553–562.

Marsh, P., McFarland, F. C., Allen, J. P., Boykin McElhaney, K., & Land, D. (2003). Attachment, autonomy, and multifinality in adolescent internalizing and risky behavioral symptoms. *Development and Psychopathology, 15,* 451–467.

Marshal, M. P., & Chassin, L. (2000). Peer influence on adolescent alcohol use: The moderating role of parental support and discipline. *Applied Developmental Science, 4,* 80–88.

Marshall, N. L., Coll, C. G., Marx, F., McCartney, K., Keefe, N., & Ruh, J. (1997). After-school time and children's behavioral adjustment. *Merrill-Palmer Quarterly, 43,* 497–514.

Marshall, W., & Tanner, J. M. (1970). Variations in the pattern of pubertal changes in boys. *Archives of Disease in Childhood, 45,* 13–23.

Marshall, W., & Tanner, J. M. (1986). Puberty. In F. Falkner & J. Tanner (Eds.), *Human growth* (2nd ed., Vol. 2). New York: Plenum.

Martin, A. J., Marsh, H. W., & Debus, R. L. (2001). Self-handicapping and defensive pessimism: Exploring a model of predictors and outcomes from a self-protection perspective. *Journal of Educational Psychology, 93,* 87–102.

Martin, C. L. (2000). Cognitive theories of gender development. In T. Eckes & H. M.

Trautner (Eds.), *The developmental social psychology of gender* (pp. 91–121). Mahwah, NJ: Erlbaum.

Martin, C. L., & Dinella, L. (2002). Children's gender cognitions, the social environment, and sex differences in cognitive domains. In A. V. McGillicuddy-De Lisi & R. De Lisi (Eds.), *Biology, society, and behavior: The development of sex differences in cognition* (pp. 207–239). Westport, CT: Ablex.

Martin, C. L., Eisenbud, L., & Rose, H. (1995). Children's gender-based reasoning about toys. *Child Development, 66,* 1453–1471.

Martin, C. L., & Fabes, R. A. (2001). The stability and consequences of young children's same-sex peer interactions. *Developmental Psychology, 37,* 431–446.

Martin, C. L., & Halverson, C. F. (1981). A schematic processing model of sex typing and stereotyping in children. *Child Development, 52,* 1119–1134.

Martin, C. L., & Halverson, C. F. (1983). The effects of sex-typing schemas on young children's memory. *Child Development, 54,* 563–574.

Martin, C. L., & Halverson, C. F. (1987). The roles of cognition in sex role acquisition. In D. B. Carter (Ed.), *Current conceptions of sex roles and sex typing: Theory and research.* New York: Praeger.

Martin, C. L., & Ruble, D. (2004). Children's search for gender cues. *Current Directions in Psychological Science, 13,* 67–70.

Martin, C. L., Ruble, D. N., & Szkrybalo, J. (2002). Cognitive theories of early gender development. *Psychological Bulletin, 128,* 903–933.

Martin, C. L., Ruble, D. N., & Szkrybalo, J. (2004). Recognizing the centrality of gender identity and stereotype knowledge in gender development and moving toward theoretical integration: Reply to Bandura and Bussey (2004). *Psychological Bulletin, 130,* 702–710.

Martin, C. L., Wood, C. H., & Little, J. K. (1990). The development of gender stereotype components. *Child Development, 61,* 1891–1904.

Martin, K. A. (1996). *Puberty, sexuality, and the self: Boys and girls at adolescence.* Florence, KY: Taylor & Frances.

Marx, M. H., & Henderson, B. (1996). A fuzzy trace analysis of categorical inferences and instantial associations as a function of retention interval. *Cognitive Development, 11,* 551–569.

Marzano, R., Pickering, D., & Pollock, J. (2001). *Classroom instruction that works: Research-based strategies for increasing student achievement.* Alexandria, VA: Association for Supervision and Curriculum Development.

Maslow, A. H. (1954). *Motivation and personality.* New York: Harper & Brothers.

Massad, C. (1981). Sex role identity and adjustment during adolescence. *Child Development, 66,* 1290–1298.

Masten, A. S. (2001). Ordinary magic: Resilience processes in development. *American Psychologist, 56,* 227–238.

Masten, A. S. (2006). Developmental psychopathology: Pathways to the future.

International Journal of Behavioral Development, 30, 47–54.

Masten, A. S., & Reed, M.-G. J. (2005). Resilience in development. In C. R. Snyder & S. J. Lopez (Eds.), *Handbook of positive psychology.* New York: Oxford University Press.

Masters, W. H., Johnson, V. E., & Kolodny, R. C. (1988). *Human sexuality* (3rd ed.). Boston: Little, Brown.

Mastropieri, M. A., Scruggs, T. E., Spencer, V., & Fontana, J. (2003). Promoting success in high school world history: Peer tutoring versus guided notes. *Learning Disabilities Research & Practice, 18,* 52–65.

Matsumoto, D. (2000). *Culture and psychology: People around the world.* (2nd ed.) Belmont, CA: Wadsworth.

Mayeux, L., Bellmore, A. D., & Kaplan, A. M. (2002, April). *Stability and correlates of perceived popularity in adolescence.* Paper presented at the meeting of the Society for Research on Adolescence, New Orleans.

Mayeux, L., & Cillessen, A. H. N. (2007). Peer influence and the development of antisocial behavior. In R. C. M. E. Engels, M. Kerr, & H. Stattin (Eds.), *Friends, lovers, and groups: Key relationships in adolescence.* Hoboken, NJ: Wiley.

Mayo, Y. Q., & Resnick, R. P. (1996). The impact of machismo on Hispanic women. *Journal of Women & Social Work, 11,* 257–277.

Mayseless, O., & Scharf, M. (2007). Adolescents' attachment representations and their capacity for intimacy in close relationships. *Journal of Research on Adolescence, 17,* 23–50.

McArdle, J. J., Ferrer-Caja, E., Hamagami, F., & Woodcock, R. W. (2002). Comparative longitudinal structural analyses of the growth and decline of multiple intellectual abilities over the life span. *Developmental Psychology, 38,* 115–142.

McCabe, M. P., & Ricciardelli, L. A. (2006). A prospective study of extreme weight change behaviors among adolescent boys and girls. *Journal of Youth and Adolescence, 35,* 425–434.

McCall, R. B., Appelbaum, M. I., & Hogarty, P. S. (1973). Developmental changes in mental performance. *Monographs of the Society for Research in Child Development, 38* (Serial No. 150).

McClelland, D. C. (1961). *The achieving society.* Princeton, NJ: Van Nostrand.

McClintock, M., & Herdt, G. (1996). Rethinking puberty: The development of sexual attraction. *Psychological Sciences, 5,* 178–183.

McClintock, M. K. (1996). Menstrual synchrony and suppression. In L. D. Houck & L. C. Drickamer (Eds.), *Foundations of animal behavior: Classic papers with commentaries.* Chicago: University of Chicago Press.

McCurley, C. (2007). *Self-reported law-violating behavior from adolescence to early adulthood in a modern cohort.* Philadelphia: National Center for Juvenile Justice.

McDougall, P., Vaillancourt, T., & Hymel, S. (2002, April). *What does it take to maintain popularity during the transition to high school?* Paper presented at the meeting of the

Society for Research on Adolescence, New Orleans.

McEwen, B. S. (2000). The neurobiology of stress: From serendipity to clinical relevance. *Brain Research, 886,* 172–189.

McGee, T. (2001). Urbanization takes on new dimensions in Asia's population giants. *Population Today, 29*(7), 1–2.

McGhee, P. E. (1976). Children's appreciation of humor: A test of the cognitive congruency principle. *Child Development, 47,* 420–426.

McGhee, P. E. (1979). *Humor: Its origins and development.* San Francisco: W. H. Freeman.

McGinnis, J. M., & Foege, W. H. (1993). Actual causes of death in the United States. *Journal of the American Medical Association, 270,* 2207–2212.

McGrath, D. J., Swisher, R. R., Elder, G. H., Jr., & Conger, R. D. (2001). Breaking new ground: Diverse routes to college in rural America. *Rural Sociology, 66,* 244–267.

McHale, S. M., Corneal, D. A., Crouter, A. C., & Birch, L. L. (2001). Gender and weight concerns in early and middle adolescence: Links with well-being and family characteristics. *Journal of Clinical Child Psychology, 30,* 338–348.

McHale, S. M., & Crouter, A. C. (1996). The family contexts of children's sibling relationships. In G. Brody (Ed.), *Sibling relationships: Their causes and consequences.* Norwood, NJ: Ablex.

McHale, S. M., Crouter, A. C., Kim, J.-Y., Burton, L. M., Davis, K. D., et al. (2006). Mothers' and fathers' racial socialization in African American families: Implications for youth. *Child Development, 77,* 1387–1402.

McHale, S. M., Crouter, A. C., & Tucker, C. J. (2001). Free-time activities in middle childhood: Links with adjustment in early adolescence. *Child Development, 72,* 1764–1778.

McHale, S. M., Crouter, A. C., & Whiteman, S. D. (2003). The family contexts of gender development in childhood and adolescence. *Social Development, 12,* 125–148.

McHale, S. M., Updegraff, K. A., Helms-Erikson, H., & Crouter, A. C. (2001). Sibling influence on gender development in middle childhood and early adolescence: A longitudinal study. *Developmental Psychology, 37,* 115–125.

McKnight Foundation. (1994). *The McKnight Foundation program for research and training in the diagnosis, treatment, and prevention of eating disorders.* Minneapolis, MN: Author.

McKown, C., & Weinstein, R. S. (2003). The development and consequences of stereotype consciousness in middle childhood. *Child Development, 74,* 498–515.

McLanahan, S., & Sandefur, G. (1994). *Growing up with a single parent: What hurts, what helps?* Cambridge, MA: Harvard University Press.

McLoyd, V. C. (1990). The impact of economic hardship on Black families and children: Psychological distress, parenting, and socioemotional development. *Child Development, 61,* 311–346.

McLoyd, V. C. (1998). Socioeconomic disadvantage and child development. *American Psychologist, 53,* 185–204.

McMahan, I. D. (1996). *Get it done: A guide to motivation, determination, and achievement.* New York: Avon.

McMahan, I. D. (1998). *Secrets of the pharaohs.* New York: Avon.

McMillan, S. J., & Morrison, M. (2006). Coming of age with the Internet: A qualitative exploration of how the Internet has become an integral part of young people's lives. *New Media & Society, 8,* 73–95.

McNeal, R. B. (1995). Extracurricular activities and high school dropouts. *Sociology of Education, 68,* 62–81.

McNeal, R. B. (1999). Parent involvement as social capital: Differential effectiveness on science achievement, truancy, and dropping out. *Social Forces, 78,* 117–144.

McNeal, R. B. (1999). Participation in high school extracurricular activities: Investigating school effects. *Social Science Quarterly, 80,* 291–309.

McNeely, C. A., Nonnemaker, J. M., & Blum, R. W. (2002). Promoting school connectedness: Evidence from the National Longitudinal Study of Adolescent Health. *Journal of School Health, 72,* 138–146.

McNelles, L. R., & Connolly, J. A. (1999). Intimacy between adolescent friends: Age and gender differences in intimate affect and intimate behaviors. *Journal of Research on Adolescence, 9,* 143–159.

McPartland, J., & Jordan, W. (2001, January). *Essential components of high school dropout prevention reforms.* Paper presented to the Conference on Drop Outs in America, Harvard University Civil Rights Project, Cambridge, MA.

McWhirter, E. H., Hackett, G., & Bandalos, D. L. (1998). A causal model of the educational plans and career expectations of Mexican American high school girls. *Journal of Counseling Psychology, 45,* 166–181.

Mead, G. H. (1934). *Mind, self, and society.* Chicago: University of Chicago Press.

Mead, M. (1928). *Coming of age in Samoa.* New York: Morrow.

Mead, M. (1935). *Sex and temperament in three primitive societies.* New York: William Morrow.

Mead, M. (1978). *Culture and commitment: The new relationships between the generations in the 1970s.* New York: Columbia University Press.

Meadows, S. O., Brown, J. S., & Elder, G. H., Jr. (2006). Depressive symptoms, stress, and support: Gendered trajectories from adolescence to young adulthood. *Journal of Youth and Adolescence, 35,* 93–103.

Mecca, A. M., Smelser, N. J., & Vasconcellos, J. (Eds.). (1989). *The social importance of self-esteem.* Berkeley: University of California Press.

Meece, J. L., Anderman, E. M., & Anderman, L. H. (2006). Classroom goal structure, student motivation, and academic achievement. *Annual Review of Psychology, 57,* 487–503.

Meece, J. L., Glienke, B. B., & Burg, S. (2006). Gender and motivation. *Journal of School Psychology, 44,* 351–373.

Meeks, C. B. (1998). Factors influencing adolescents' income and expenditures. *Journal of Family and Economic Issues, 19,* 131–150.

Meeus, W., & Dekovic, M. (1995). Identity development, parental, and peer support: Results of a national Dutch survey. *Adolescence, 30,* 931–944.

Meeus, W., Iedema, J., Helsen, M., & Vollebergh, W. (1999). Patterns of adolescent identity development: Review of literature and longitudinal analysis. *Developmental Review, 19,* 419–461.

Meier, D. W. (1996). The big benefits of smallness. *Educational Leadership, 54,* 12–15.

Mendel, D. (2003, Spring). And the walls keep tumbling down. *Advocasey,* pp. 18–27. Available: www.aecf.org/publications/advocasey/spring2003.

Mendle, J., Turkheimer, E., & Emery, R. E. (2007). Detrimental psychological outcomes associated with early pubertal timing in adolescent girls. *Developmental Review, 27,* 151–171.

Mensch, B. S., Bruce, J., & Greene, M. E. (1998). *The uncharted passage: Girls' adolescence in the developing world.* New York: Population Council.

Menschik, D., Ahmed, S., Alexander, M. H., & Blum, R. W. (2008). Adolescent physical activities as predictors of young adult weight. *Archives of Pediatric and Adolescent Medicine, 162,* 29–33.

Mercer, R. J., Merritt, S. L., & Cowell, J. M. (1998). Differences in reported sleep needs among adolescents. *Journal of Adolescent Health, 23,* 259–263.

Mernissi, F. (1994). *Dreams of trespass: Tales of a harem girlhood.* Reading, MA: Addison-Wesley.

Merten, D. E. (1996). Visibility and vulnerability: Responses to rejection by nonaggressive junior high school boys. *Journal of Early Adolescence, 16,* 5–26.

Merten, D. E. (1997). The meaning of meanness: Popularity, competition, and conflict among junior high school girls. *Sociology of Education, 70,* 175–191.

Merton, R. K. (1948). The self-fulfilling prophecy. *Antioch Review, 8,* 193–210.

Metz, E., & Youniss, J. (2005). Longitudinal gains in civic development through school-based required service. *Political Psychology, 26,* 413–437.

Michels, T. M., Kropp, R. Y., Eyre, S. L., & Halpern-Felsher, B. L. (2005). Initiating sexual experiences: How do young adolescents make decisions regarding early sexual activity? *Journal of Research on Adolescence, 15,* 583–607.

Mickelson, R. (1990). The attitude-achievement paradox among black adolescents. *Sociology of Education, 63,* 44–61.

Middleton, M., & Midgley, C. (1997). Avoiding the demonstration of lack of ability: An underexplored aspect of goal theory. *Journal of Educational Psychology, 89,* 710–718.

Midgley, C., Anderman, E., & Hicks, L. (1995). Differences between elementary and middle school teachers and students: A goal theory approach. *Journal of Early Adolescence, 15*, 90–113.

Midgley, C., Feldlaufer, H., & Eccles, J. (1989a). Student/teacher relationships and attitudes toward mathematics before and after the transition to junior high. *Child Development, 60*, 981–992.

Midgley, C., Feldlaufer, H., & Eccles, J. (1989b). Changes in teacher efficacy and student self- and task-related beliefs during the transition to junior high school. *Journal of Educational Psychology, 81*, 247–258.

Midgley, C., Kaplan, A., Middleton, M., Maehr, M. L., Urdan, T., Anderman, L. H., et al. (1998). The development and validation of scales assessing students' achievement goal orientations. *Contemporary Educational Psychology, 23*, 113–131.

Midgley, C., Middleton, M., Gheen, M., & Kumar, R. (2002). Stage/environment fit revisited: A goal theory approach to examining school transitions. In C. Midgley (Ed.), *Goals, goal structures, and patterns of adaptive learning.* Mahwah, NJ: Erlbaum.

Mihalic, S. W. & Elliot, D. (1997). Short- and long-term consequences of adolescent work. *Youth & Society, 28*, 464–498.

Miller, B. C., Bayley, B. K., Christensen, M., Leavitt, S. C., & Coyl, D. D. (2003). Adolescent pregnancy and childbearing. In G. R. Adams & M. D. Berzonsky (Eds.), *Blackwell handbook of adolescence.* Malden, MA: Blackwell.

Miller, B. C., & Benson, B. (1999). Romantic and sexual relationship development during adolescence. In W. Furman, B. B. Brown, & C. Feiring (Eds.), *The development of romantic relationships in adolescence.* New York: Cambridge University Press.

Miller, B. C., Benson, B., & Galbraith, K. A. (2001). Family relationships and adolescent pregnancy risk: A research synthesis. *Developmental Review, 21*, 1–38.

Miller, D., & Byrnes, J. (1997). The role of contextual and personal factors in children's risk taking. *Developmental Psychology, 33*, 814–823.

Miller, L. (1995). Children of the dream: The adolescent world in Cao Xueqin's *Honglou meng.* In A. B. Kenney (Ed.), *Chinese views of childhood.* Honolulu: University of Hawai'i Press.

Miller, P. H. (2001). *Theories of developmental psychology* (4th ed.). New York: Worth.

Miller, P. H., & Bjorklund, D. F. (1998). Contemplating fuzzy-trace theory: The gist of it. *Journal of Experimental Child Psychology, 71*, 184–193.

Miller, S. A., Custer, W. L., & Nassau, G. (2000). Children's understanding of the necessity of logically necessary truths. *Cognitive Development, 15*, 383–403.

Millstein, S. G. (1993). Perceptual, attributional, and affective process in perceptions of vulnerability through the life span. In N. J. Bell & R. W. Bell (Eds.), *Adolescent risk taking.* Thousand Oaks, CA: Sage.

Minuchin, P. P. (1988). Relationships within the family: A systems perspective on development. In R. A. Hinde & J. Stevenson-Hinde (Eds.), *Relationships within families: Mutual influences.* New York: Oxford University Press.

Mistry, R. S., Vandewater, E. A., Huston, A. C., & McLoyd, V. C. (2002). Economic well-being and children's social adjustment: The role of family process in an ethnically diverse low-income sample. *Child Development, 73*, 935–951.

Mitchell, G. (1981). *Human sex differences: A primatologist's perspective.* New York: Van Nostrand Reinhold.

Mitterauer, M. (1992). *A history of youth.* Cambridge, MA: Blackwell.

Miyanaga, K. (1992). *The creative edge: Emerging individualism in Japan.* New Brunswick, NJ: Transaction Publishers.

Mize, J., & Pettit, G. S. (1997). Mother's social coaching, mother-child relationship style, and children's peer competence: Is the medium the message? *Child Development, 68*, 312–322.

Modell, J., & Goodman, M. (1990). Historical perspectives. In S. S. Feldman & G. Elliott (Eds.), *At the threshold: The developing adolescent.* Cambridge, MA: Harvard University Press.

Moffitt, T. E. (1993). Adolescence-limited and life-course-persistent antisocial behavior: A developmental taxonomy. *Psychological Review, 100*, 674–701.

Moffitt, T. E. (2003). Life-course-persistent and adolescence-limited antisocial behavior: A 10-year research review and a research agenda. In B. B. Lahey, T. E. Moffitt, & A. Caspi (Eds.), *Causes of conduct disorder and juvenile delinquency.* New York: Guilford.

Moffitt, T. E., & Caspi, A. (2007). Evidence from behavioral genetics for environmental contributions to antisocial conduct. In J. E. Grusec & P. D. Hastings (Eds.), *Handbook of socialization: Theory and research.* New York: Guilford.

Moffitt, T. E., Caspi, A., Belsky, J., & Silva, P. A. (1992). Childhood experience and onset of menarche: A test of a sociobiological model. *Child Development, 63*, 47–58.

Moje, E., & Wade, S. (1997). What case studies reveal about teacher thinking. *Teaching and Teacher Education, 13*, 691–712.

Molden, D., & Dweck, C. S. (2000). Meaning and motivation. In C. Sansone & J. Harackiewicz (Eds.), *Intrinsic and extrinsic motivation: The search for optimal motivation and performance.* San Diego, CA: Academic Press.

Molgaard, V. K., Spoth, R. L., & Redmond, C. (2000, August). Competency training: The Strengthening Families Program: For parents and youth 10–14. *OJJDP Juvenile Justice Bulletin*, 1–11.

Molina, B. S. G., & Chassin, L. (1996). The parent-adolescent relationship at puberty: Hispanic ethnicity and parent alcoholism as moderators. *Developmental Psychology, 32*, 675–686.

Moller, J. (2003, December 12). No apology for Lafayette gay mom; School board decides child's discipline valid. *New Orleans (LA) Times-Picayune*, p. 1.

Money, J. (1980). *Love and love sickness.* Baltimore: Johns Hopkins.

Money, J., & Ehrhardt, A. (1972). *Man and woman, boy and girl.* Baltimore: Johns Hopkins University Press.

Monroe, S. M., Rohde, P., Seeley, J. R., & Leinsohn, P. M. (1999). Live events and depression in adolescence: Relationship loss as a prospective risk factor for first onset of major depressive disorder. *Journal of Abnormal Psychology, 108*, 606–614.

Montemayor, R. (1983). Parents and adolescents in conflict: All families some of the time and some families most of the time. *Journal of Early Adolescence, 3*, 83–103.

Montemayor, R. (1984). Maternal employment and adolescents' relations with parents, siblings, and peers. *Journal of Youth and Adolescence, 13*, 543–557.

Montemayor, R. (1986). Family variation in parent-adolescent storm and stress. *Journal of Adolescent Research, 1*, 15–31.

Montemayor, R. (2000). Paths to adulthood: Adolescent diversity in contemporary America. In R. Montemayor, G. R. Adams, & T. P. Gullotta (Eds.), *Adolescent diversity in ethnic, economic, and cultural contexts.* Newbury Park, CA: Sage.

Montemayor, R., & Eisen, M. (1977). The development of self-conceptions from childhood to adolescence. *Developmental Psychology, 13*, 314–319.

Montgomery, M. J. (2005). Psychosocial intimacy and identity: From early adolescence to emerging adulthood. *Journal of Adolescent Research, 20*, 346–374.

Moore, J. W. (1993, December 18). Lights! Camera! It's gun control time. *National Journal*, 3007.

Moore, K. A., Driscoll, A. K., & Lindberg, L. D. (1998). *Statistical portrait of adolescent sex, contraception, and childbearing.* Washington, DC: National Campaign to Prevent Teen Pregnancy.

Moore, K. A., Guzman, L., Hair, E., Lippman, L., & Garrett, S. (2004). Parent-teen relationships and interactions: Far more positive than not. *Child Trends Research Brief*, No. 2004–2025.

Morabia, A., & Costanza, M. C. (1998). The World Health Organization collaborative study of neoplasia and steroid contraceptives: International variability in ages at menarche, first livebirth and menopause. *American Journal of Epidemiology, 148*, 1195–1205.

Morrison, D. M. (1985). Adolescent contraceptive behavior: A review. *Psychological Bulletin, 9*, 538–568.

Morrison, D. N., McGee, R., & Stanton, V. V. R. (1992). Sleep problems in adolescence. *Journal of the American Academy of Child and Adolescent Psychiatry, 31*, 94–99.

Morrison, M. M., & Shaffer, D. R. (2003). Gender-role congruence and self-referencing as determinants of advertising effectiveness. *Sex Roles, 49*, 265–275.

Morse, J. M., & Doan, H. M. (1987). Growing up at school: Adolescents' response to menarche. *Journal of School Health, 57,* 385–389.

Mortimer, J. T., Finch, M., Ryu, S., Shanahan, M., & Call, K. (1996). The effects of work intensity on adolescent mental health, achievement, and behavioral adjustment: New evidence from a prospective study. *Child Development, 67,* 1243–1261.

Mortimer, J. T., & Shanahan, M. J. (1994). Adolescent work experience and family relationships. *Work and Occupations, 21,* 369–384.

Mortimer, J. T., & Larson, R. W. (Eds.) (2002). *The changing adolescent experience: Societal trends and the transition to adulthood.* New York: Cambridge University Press.

Mortimer, J. T., Zimmer-Gemback, M. J., Holmes, M., & Shanahan, M. J. (2002). The process of occupational decision-making: Patterns during the transition to adulthood. *Journal of Vocational Behavior, 61,* 439–465.

Moshman, D. (2005). *Adolescent psychological development: Rationality, morality, and identity* (2nd ed.). Mahwah, NJ: Erlbaum.

Mosteller, F., Light, R., & Sachs, J. (1996). Sustained inquiry in education: Lessons from skill grouping and class size. *Harvard Educational Review, 66,* 797–842.

Mounts, N. S. (2002). Parental management of adolescent peer relationships in context: The role of parenting style. *Journal of Family Psychology, 16,* 58–69.

Mueller, C. M., & Dweck, C. S. (1998). Praise for intelligence can undermine children's motivation and performance. *Journal of Personality and Social Psychology, 75,* 33–52.

Muller, C. (1998). Gender differences in parental involvement and adolescents' mathematics achievement. *Sociology of Education, 71,* 336–356.

Murdock, T. B., Anderman, L. H., & Hodge, S. A. (2000). Middle-grade predictors of students' motivation and behavior in high school. *Journal of Adolescent Research, 15,* 327–352.

Murnane, R. J., & Levy, F. (1997). *Teaching the new basic skills: Principles for educating children to thrive in a changing economy.* New York: Free Press.

Murphy, B. C., & Eisenberg, N. (2002). An integrative examination of peer conflict: Children's reported goals, emotions, and behaviors. *Social Development, 11,* 534–557.

Murphy, M. C., Steele, C. M., & Gross, J. J. (2007). Signaling threat: How situational cues affect women in math, science, and engineering settings. *Psychological Science, 18,* 879–885.

Musgrove, F. (1964). *Youth and the social order.* Bloomington, IN: Indiana University Press.

Mussell, M., Binford, R., & Fulkerson, J. (2000). Eating disorders: Summary of risk factors, prevention programming, and prevention research. *The Counseling Psychologist, 28,* 764–796.

Mussen, P., & Jones, M. (1958). The behavior-inferred motivations of late- and early-maturing boys. *Child Development, 29,* 61–67.

Mustanski, B. S., Chivers, M. L., & Bailey, J. M. (2003). A critical review of recent biological research on human sexual orientation. *Annual Review of Sex Research, 13,* 89–140.

Mustanski, B. S., Viken, R. J., Kaprio, J., Pulkkinen, L., & Rose, R. J. (2004). Genetic and environmental influences on pubertal development: Longitudinal data from Finnish twins at ages 11 and 14. *Developmental Psychology, 40,* 1188–1198.

Nakamura, I., Shimura, M., Nonaka, K., & Miura, T. (1986). Changes of recollected menarcheal age and month among women in Tokyo over a period of 90 years. *Annals of Human Biology, 13,* 547–554.

Nakamura, J., & Csikszentmihalyi, M. (2002). The concept of flow. In C. R. Snyder & S. J. Lopez (Eds.), *Handbook of positive psychology.* London: Oxford University Press.

Nansel, T. R., Overpeck, M. D., Haynie, D. L., Ruan, W. J., & Scheidt, P. C. (2003). Relationships between bullying and violence among U.S. youth. *Archives of Pediatrics and Adolescent Medicine, 157,* 348–353.

Nansel, T. R., Overpeck, M., Pilla, R. S., Ruan, W. J., Simons-Morton, B., & Scheidt, P. (2001). Bullying behaviors among U.S. youth: Prevalence and association with psychosocial adjustment. *JAMA: Journal of the American Medical Association, 285,* 2094–2100.

Nash, R. A. (1996). The serotonin connection. *Journal of Orthomolecular Medicine, 11,* 327–328.

Nash, S. G., McQueen, A., & Bray, J. H. (2005). Pathways to adolescent alcohol use: Family environment, peer influence, and parental expectations. *Journal of Adolescent Health, 37,* 19–28.

National Center for Education Statistics [NCES]. (2000). *The Condition of Education 2000.* Washington, DC: U.S. Government Printing Office.

National Center for Education Statistics [NCES]. (2001). *The Condition of Education 2001.* Washington, DC: U.S. Government Printing Office.

National Center for Education Statistics [NCES]. (2002). *The Condition of Education 2002.* Washington, DC: U.S. Government Printing Office.

National Center for Education Statistics [NCES]. (2003). *The Condition of Education 2003.* Washington, DC: U.S. Government Printing Office.

National Center for Education Statistics [NCES]. (2004). *The Condition of Education 2004.* Washington, DC: U.S. Government Printing Office.

National Center for Education Statistics [NCES]. (2005). *The Condition of Education 2005.* Washington, DC: U.S. Government Printing Office.

National Center for Education Statistics [NCES]. (2006). *The Condition of Education 2006.* Washington, DC: U.S. Government Printing Office.

National Center for Health Statistics. (2001). *Health, United States, 2001.* Atlanta, GA: Centers for Disease Control and Prevention.

National Center for Health Statistics. (2002). *Health, United States, 2002.* Atlanta, GA: Centers for Disease Control and Prevention.

National Center for Health Statistics. (2005). *Health, United States, 2005: With chartbook on trends in the health of Americans.* Hyattsville, MD: Author.

National Commission on Excellence in Education. (1983). *A nation at risk: The imperative for educational reform.* Washington, DC: U.S. Department of Education.

National Commission on Youth. (1980). *The transition to adulthood: A bridge too long.* New York: Westview Press.

National Council for Research on Women. (2002). *Balancing the equation: Where are women and girls in science, engineering, and technology?* New York: Author.

National Highway Traffic Safety Administration. (2005). Young drivers. *Traffic Safety Facts: 2004 Data.* Washington, DC: Author.

National Institute on Student Achievement, Curriculum, and Assessment. (1999). *The educational system in the United States: Case study findings.* Washington, DC: NISACA, Office of Educational Research and Improvement, U.S. Department of Education. Available: www.ed.gov/PDFDocs/UScasestudy.pdf.

National Public Radio, Henry J. Kaiser Foundation, & Kennedy School of Government. (2004). *Sex education in America.* Washington, DC: Author.

Neff, K. D. (2001). Judgments of personal autonomy and interpersonal responsibility in the context of Indian spousal relationships: An examination of young people's reasoning in Mysore, India. *British Journal of Developmental Psychology, 19,* 233–257.

Neisser, U. (Ed.). (1999). *The rising curve: Long-term gains in IQ and related measures.* Washington, DC: American Psychological Association.

Neisser, U., Boodoo, G., Bouchard, T. J., Boykin, A. W., Brody, N., Ceci, S. J., et al. (1996). Intelligence: Knowns and unknowns. *American Psychologist, 51,* 77–101.

Neleman, H. (1999). *Moko: Maori tattoos.* Zurich: Editions Stemmle.

Nelson, M. C., Gordon-Larsen, P., Adair, L. S., & Popkin, B. M. (2005). Adolescent physical activity and sedentary behavior: Patterning and long-term maintenance. *American Journal of Preventive Medicine, 28,* 259–266.

Nelson, S. A. (1980). Factors influencing young children's use of motives and outcomes as moral criteria. *Child Development, 51,* 823–829.

Néraudau, J.–P. (1984). *Être enfant à Rome.* Paris: Les Belles Lettres.

Neumark-Sztainer, D., Eisenberg, M. E., Fulkerson, J. A., Story, M., & Larson, N. I. (2008). Family meals and disordered eating in adolescents. *Archives of Pediatric and Adolescent Medicine, 162,* 17–22.

Newcomb, A. F., & Bukowski, W. M. (1984). A longitudinal study of the utility of social preference and social impact sociometric classification schemes. *Child Development, 55,* 1434–1447.

Newcomb, A. F., Bukowski, W. M., & Pattee, L. (1993). Children's peer relations: A meta-analytic review of popular, rejected, neglected, controversial, and average sociometric status. *Psychological Bulletin, 113,* 99–128.

Newcomb, M. D., Abbott, R. D., Catalano, R. F., Hawkins, J. D., Battin Pearson, S., & Hill, K. (2002). Mediational and deviance theories of late high school failure: Process roles of structural strains, academic competence, and general versus specific problem behaviors. *Journal of Counseling Psychology, 49,* 172–186.

Newman, B. M., & Newman, P. R. (2001). Group identity and alienation: Giving the we its due. *Journal of Youth & Adolescence, 30,* 515–538.

Newman, S. A., Fox, J. A., Flynn, E. A., & Christeson, W. (2000). *America's after-school choice: The prime time for juvenile crime, or youth enrichment and achievement.* Washington, DC: Fight Crime: Invest in Kids.

Newmann, F. M., Wehlage, G. G., & Lamborn, S. D. (1992). The significance and sources of student engagement. In F. M. Newmann (Ed.), *Student engagement and achievement in American secondary schools.* New York: Teachers College Press.

NIAID. (2006). *HIV infection in adolescents and young adults in the U.S.* Available: www.niaid.nih.gov/factsheets/hivadolescent.htm.

Nichols, J. D. (1996). The effects of cooperative learning on student achievement and motivation in a high school geometry class. *Contemporary Educational Psychology, 21,* 467–476.

Niederle, M., & Vesterlund, L. (2005). *Do women shy away from competition? Do men compete too much?* NBER Working Paper No. 11474. Stanford, CA: National Bureau of Economic Research.

Nieman, D. C., & Pedersen, B. K. (1999). Exercise and immune function: Recent developments. *Sport Medicine, 27,* 73–80.

Nigg, J. T., Wong, M. M., Martel, M. M., Jester, J. M., Puttler, L. I., Glass, J. M., et al. (2006). Poor response inhibition as a predictor of problem drinking and illicit drug use in adolescents at risk for alcoholism and other substance use disorders. *Journal of the American Academy of Child and Adolescent Psychiatry, 45,* 468–475.

Nishina, A., & Juvonen, J., (2005). Daily reports of witnessing and experiencing peer harassment in middle school. *Child Development, 76,* 435–450.

Nishino, H. J., & Larson, R. (2003). Japanese adolescents' free time: *Juku, Bukatsu,* and government efforts to create more meaningful leisure. *New Directions for Child and Adolescent Development, 90,* 23–36.

Noguera, P. (1995). Preventing and producing violence: A critical analysis of responses to school violence. *Harvard Educational Review, 65,* 189–212.

Nolen-Hoeksema, S. (2002). Gender differences in depression. In I. H. Gotlib & C. L. Hammen (Eds.), *Handbook of depression.* New York: Guilford.

Nolen-Hoeksema, S. (2007). *Abnormal psychology* (4th ed.). New York: McGraw-Hill.

Nolen-Hoeksema, S., & Corte, C. (2004). Gender and self-regulation. In R. F. Baumeister & K. D. Vohs (Eds.), *Handbook of self-regulation: Research, theory, and applications.* New York: Guilford.

Norris, M. L., Boydell, K. M., Pinhas, L., & Katzman, D. K. (2006). Ana and the Internet: A review of pro-anorexia websites. *International Journal of Eating Disorders, 39,* 443–447.

Nosek, B. A., Banaji, M. R., & Greenwald, A. G. (2002). Math ≠ male, me = female, therefore math ? me. *Journal of Personality and Social Psychology, 83,* 44–59.

Nottelmann, E. D., Susman, E. J., Blue, J. H., Inoff-Germain, G., Dorn, L. D., Loriaux, D. L., et al. (1987). Gonadal and adrenal hormone correlates of adjustment in early adolescence. In R. M. Lerner & T. T. Foch (Eds.), *Biological-psychological interactions in early adolescence.* Hillsdale, NJ: Erlbaum.

Nsamenang, B. (2002). Adolescence in sub-Saharan Africa. In B. Brown, R. Larson, & T. S. Saraswathi (Eds.), *The world's youth: Adolescence in eight regions of the globe.* New York: Cambridge University Press.

Nucci, L., Hasebe, Y., & Lins-Dyer, M. T. (2005). Adolescent psychological well-being and parental control of the personal. *New Directions for Child and Adolescent Development, 108,* 17–30.

Nucci, L., & Turiel, E. (1993). God's word, religious rules, and their relation to Christian and Jewish children's concepts of morality. *Child Development, 64,* 1475–1491.

Nuttal, R. L., Casey, M. B., & Pezaris, E. (2005). Spatial ability as a mediator of gender differences on mathematics tests: A biological-environmental framework. In A. M. Gallagher & J. C. Kaufman (Eds.), *Gender differences in mathematics: An integrative psychological approach.* New York: Cambridge University Press.

O'Brien, K. M., Friedman, S. M., Tipton, L. C., & Linn, S. G. (2000). Attachment, separation, and women's vocational development: A longitudinal analysis. *Journal of Counseling Psychology, 47,* 301–315.

O'Connor, T. G., Plomin, R., Caspi, A., & DeFries, J. C. (2000). Are associations between parental divorce and children's adjustment genetically mediated? An adoption study. *Developmental Psychology, 36,* 429–437.

O'Dea, J. A. (1995). Body image and nutritional status among adolescents and adults: A review of the literature. *Australian Journal of Nutrition and Diet, 52,* 56–67.

O'Dea, J. A., & Abraham, S. (1999). Onset of disordered eating attitudes and behaviors in early adolescence: Interplay of pubertal status, gender, weight, and age. *Adolescence, 34,* 671–679.

O'Hare, W. P. (2001). *The child population: First data from the 2000 census.* Washington, DC: Population Reference Bureau.

O'Malley, P., & Johnston, L. (2003). Unsafe driving by high school seniors: National trends from 1976 to 2001 in tickets and accidents after alcohol, marijuana and other illegal drugs. *Journal of Studies on Alcohol, 64,* 305–312.

O'Moore, M., & Kirkham, C. (2001). Self-esteem and its relationship to bullying behaviour. *Aggressive Behavior, 27,* 269–283.

O'Shea, L. J., O'Shea, D. J., & Algozzine, B. (2002). *Learning disabilities: From theory towards practice.* Upper Saddle River, NJ: Pearson Education.

O'Sullivan, L. F., Meyer-Bahlburg, H. F. L., & Watkins, B. X. (2000). Social cognitions associated with pubertal development in a sample of urban, low-income, African-American and Latina girls and mothers. *Journal of Adolescent Health, 27,* 227–235.

Oakes, J., Gamoran, A., & Page, R. N. (1992). Curriculum differentiation: Opportunities, outcomes, and meanings. In P. Jackson (Ed.), *Handbook of research on curriculum.* New York: Macmillan.

Obeidallah, D. A., Brennan, R. T., Brooks-Gunn, J., Kindlon, D., & Earls, F. (2000). Socioeconomic status, race, and girls' pubertal maturation: Results from the Project on Human Development in Chicago Neighborhoods. *Journal of Research on Adolescence, 10,* 443–464.

OBLEMA. (2000). *Survey of states' limited English proficient students and available educational programs and services: 1997–98.* Washington, DC: U.S. Department of Education.

Offer, D. (1969). *The psychological world of the teenager.* New York: Basic Books.

Office on Women's Health. (2000). *BodyWise: Eating disorders information for middle school personnel* (2nd ed.). Washington, DC: U.S. Department of Health and Human Services.

Ogbu, J. U. (1994). From cultural differences to differences in cultural frames of reference. In P. M. Greenfield & R. R. Cocking (Eds.), *Cross-cultural roots of minority child development.* Hillsdale, NJ: Erlbaum.

Ogbu, J. U. (2002). *Black American students in an affluent suburb: A study of academic disengagement.* Mahwah, NJ: Erlbaum.

Ogden, C. L., Carroll, M. D., Curtin, L. R., McDowell, M. A., Tabak, C. J., & Flegal, K. M. (2006). Prevalence of overweight and obesity in the United States, 1999–2004. *Journal of the American Medical Association, 295,* 1549–1555.

Ogden, C. L., Kuczmarski, R. J., Flegal, K. M., Mei, Z., Guo, S., Wei, R. et al. (2002). Centers for Disease Control and Prevention 2000 growth charts for the United States: Improvements to the 1977 National Center for Health Statistics version. *Pediatrics, 109,* 45–60.

Olafsen, R. N., & Viemero, V. (2000). Bully/victim problems and coping with stress in school among 10- to 12-year-old pupils in Aland, Finland. *Aggressive Behavior, 26,* 57–65.

Olivardia, R., Pope, H. G., Borowiecki, J. J., & Cohane, G. H. (2004). Biceps and body image: The relationship between muscularity and self-esteem, depression and eating disorder symptoms. *Psychology of Men and Masculinity, 5,* 112–120.

Oliver, M. B. (1994). Portrayals of crime, race, and aggression in "reality-based" police shows: A content analysis. *Journal of Broadcasting and Electronic Media, 38,* 179–192.

Oliver, M. B., & Hyde, J. S. (1993). Gender differences in sexuality: A meta-analysis. *Psychological Bulletin, 114,* 29–51.

Ollendick, T. H., Shortt, A. L., & Sander, J. B. (2005). Internalizing disorders of childhood and adolescence. In J. E. Maddux & B. A. Winstead (Eds.), *Psychopathology: Foundations for a contemporary understanding.* Mahwah, NJ: Erlbaum.

Olson, E. T. (1999). There is no problem of the self. In S. Gallagher & J. Shear (Eds.), *Models of the self.* Thorverton, UK: Imprint Academic.

Olweus, D. (1993). *Bullying at school: What we know and what we can do.* Cambridge, MA: Blackwell.

Olweus, D. (1995). Bullying or peer abuse at school: Facts and interventions. *Current Directions in Psychological Science, 4,* 196–200.

Olweus, D., Limber, S., & Mihalic, S. (1999). *Blueprints for violence prevention, Book Nine: Bullying Prevention Program.* Boulder, CO: Center for the Study and Prevention of Violence.

Orfield, G. (1999). Conservative activists and the rush toward resegregation. In J. P. Heubert (Ed.), *Law and school reform: Six strategies for promoting educational equity.* New Haven, CT: Yale University Press.

Orfield, G., Losen, D., Wald, J., & Swanson, C. (2004). *Losing our future: How minority youth are being left behind by the graduation rate crisis.* Cambridge, MA: The Civil Rights Project at Harvard University.

Osgood, D. W., Anderson, A. L., & Shaffer, J. N. (2005). Unstructured leisure in the after-school hours. In J. L. Mahoney, R. W. Larson, & J. S. Eccles (Eds.), *Organized activities as contexts of development: Extracurricular activities, after school and community programs.* Mahwah, NJ: Erlbaum.

Osgood, D. W., Wilson, J. K., O'Malley, P. M., Bachman, J. G., & Johnston, L. D. (1996). Routine activities and individual deviant behavior. *American Sociological Review, 61,* 635–655.

Ottenberg, S. (1994). Initiations. In P. K. Bock (Ed.), *Handbook of psychological anthropology.* Westport, CT: Greenwood.

Overton, W. (1990). Competence and procedures: Constraints on the development of logical reasoning. In W. Overton (Ed.), *Reasoning, necessity, and logic: Developmental perspectives.* Hillsdale, NJ: Erlbaum.

Owens, L., Shute, R., & Slee, P. (2000). "I'm in and you're out. . .": Explanations for teenage girls' indirect aggression. *Psychology, Evolution & Gender, 2,* 19–46.

Owens, L., Slee, P., & Shute, R. (2000). 'It hurts a hell of a lot. . .' : The effects of indirect aggression on teenage girls. *School Psychology International, 21,* 359–376.

Oyserman, D., Brickman, D., & Rhodes, M. (2007). Racial-ethnic identity in adolescence: Content and consequences for African American and Latino youth. In A. Fuligni (Ed.), *Contesting stereotypes and creating identities: Social categories, social identities, and educational participation.* New York: Russell Sage Foundation.

Oyserman, D., Coon, H. M., & Kemmelmeier, M. (2002). Rethinking individualism and collectivism: Evaluation of theoretical assumptions and meta-analyses. *Psychological Bulletin, 128,* 3–72.

Oyserman, D., & Fryberg, S. (2006). The possible selves of diverse adolescents: Content and function across gender, race, and national origin. In C. Dunkel & J. Kerpelman (Eds.), *Possible selves: Theory, research and applications.* Hauppauge, NY: Nova Science.

Oyserman, D., Gant, L., & Ager, J. (1995). A socially contextualized model of African American identity: Possible selves and school persistence. *Journal of Personality and Social Psychology, 69,* 1216–1232.

Oyserman, D., Harrison, K., & Bybee, D. (2001). Can racial identity be promotive of academic efficacy? *International Journal of Behavioral Development, 25,* 379–385.

Ozer, E. M., Macdonald, R., & Irwin, Jr., C. E. (2002). Adolescent health care: Implications and projections for the new millennium. In J. Mortimer & R. Larson (Eds.), *The future of adolescent experience: Societal trends and the transition to adulthood.* New York: Cambridge University Press.

Paikoff, R. L., & Brooks-Gunn, J. (1991). Do parent–child relationships change during puberty? *Psychological Bulletin, 110,* 47–66.

Pajares, F. (1992). Teachers' beliefs and educational research: Cleaning up a messy construct. *Review of Educational Research, 62,* 307–332.

Pakaslahti, L., & Keltigangas-Jarvinen, L. (2000). Comparison of peer, teacher, and self-assessments on adolescent direct and indirect aggression. *Educational Psychology, 20,* 177–190.

Paley, V. G. (1993). *You can't say you can't play.* Cambridge, MA: Harvard University Press.

Pallas, A. M., Entwisle, D. R., Alexander, K. L., & Stluka, M. F. (1994). Ability group effects: Instructional, social, or institutional? *Sociology of Education, 67,* 27–46.

Panchaud, C., Singh, S., Feivelson, D., & Darroch, J. E. (2000). Sexually transmitted diseases among adolescents in developed countries. *Family Planning Perspectives, 32*(1), 24–32, 45.

Paris, S. G., & Paris, A. H. (2001). Classroom applications of research on self-regulated learning. *Educational Psychologist, 36,* 89–101.

Park, N. (2004). The role of subjective well-being in positive youth development. *Annals of the American Academy of Political and Social Science, 591,* 25–39.

Park, S., Belsky, J., Putnam, S., & Crnic, K. (1997). Infant emotionality, parenting, and 3-year inhibition: Exploring stability and lawful discontinuity in a male sample. *Developmental Psychology, 33,* 218–227.

Parker, D. L. (1997). Child labor: The impact of economic exploitation on the health and welfare of children. *Minnesota Medicine, 80,* 55.

Parker, J. G., & Gottman, J. M. (1989). Social and emotional development in a relational context: Friendship interaction from early childhood to adolescence. In T. J. Berndt & G. W. Ladd (Eds.), *Peer relationships in child development.* Oxford, UK: Wiley.

Parker, S., Nichter, M., Nichter, M., Vuckovic, N., et al. (1995). Body image and weight concerns among African American and White adolescent females: Differences that make a difference. *Human Organization, 54,* 103–114.

Parkhurst, J. T., & Hopmeyer, A. (1998). Sociometric popularity and peer-perceived popularity: Two distinct dimensions of peer status. *Journal of Early Adolescence, 18,* 125–144.

Parra, G. R., DuBois, D. L., Neville, H. A., & Pugh-Lilly, A. O. (2002). Mentoring relationships for youth: Investigation of a process-oriented model. *Journal of Community Psychology, 30,* 367–388.

Parsons, T. (1964). *Essays in sociological theory.* Chicago: Free Press.

Partnership for 21st Century Skills (2003). *Learning for the 21st century.* Tucson, AZ: Author.

Pascoe, C. J. (2005). 'Dude, you're a fag': Adolescent masculinity and the fag discourse. *Sexualities, 8,* 329–346.

Pascual-Leone, J., & Johnson, J. (1999). A dialectical constructivist view of representation: Role of mental attention, executives, and symbols. In I. E. Sigel (Ed.), *Development of mental representations: Theories and applications.* Mahwah, NJ: Erlbaum.

Patrick, H. (2004). Re-examining classroom mastery goal structure. In M. L. Maehr & P. R. Pintrich (Eds.), *Advances in motivation, Vol. 13: Motivating students, improving schools: The legacy of Carol Midgley.* Greenwich, CT: Elsevier.

Patrick, H., Anderman, L. H., Ryan, A. M., Edelin, K. C., & Midgley, C. (2001). Teachers' communication of goal orientations in four fifth-grade classrooms. *Elementary School Journal, 102,* 35–58.

Patrick, H., & Pintrich, P. (2001). Conceptual change in teacher's intuitive conceptions of learning, motivation, and instruction: The role of motivational and epistemological beliefs. In R. Torff & R. Sternberg (Eds.), *Understanding and teaching the intuitive mind: Student and teacher learning.* Mahwah, NJ: Erlbaum.

Patrick, H., Ryan, A. M., & Kaplan, A. (2007). Early adolescents' perceptions of the classroom social environment, motivational beliefs, and engagement. *Journal of Educational Psychology, 99,* 83–98.

Patrick, H., Turner, J. C., Meyer, D. K., & Midgley, C. (2003). How teachers establish psychological environments during the first days of school: Associations with avoidance in mathematics. *Teachers College Record, 105,* 1521–1558.

Patterson, C. J. (2002). Lesbian and gay parenthood. In M. H. Bornstein (Ed.), *Handbook of parenting* (2nd ed., Vol. 3). Mahwah, NJ: Erlbaum.

Patterson, C. J. (2006). Children of lesbian and gay parents. *Current Directions in Psychological Science, 15*, 241–244.

Patterson, C. J., & Hastings, P. D. (2006). Socialization in the context of family diversity. In J. E. Grusec & P. D. Hastings (Eds.), *Handbook of socialization: Theory and research.* New York: Guilford.

Patterson, G. R., Dishion, T. J., & Yoeger, K. (2000). Adolescent growth in new forms of problem behavior: Macro- and micro-peer dynamics. *Prevention Science, 1*, 3–13.

Patton, W., & Lokan, J. (2001). Perspectives on Donald Super's construct of career maturity. *International Journal of Educational and Vocational Guidance, 1*, 31–48.

Paul, E. L., & White, K. M. (1990). The development of intimate relationships in late adolescence. *Adolescence, 25*, 375–400.

Paul, J. J., & Cillessen, A. H. N. (2003). Dynamics of peer victimization in early adolescence: Results from a four-year longitudinal study. In M. J. Elias & J. E. Zins (Eds.), *Bullying, peer harassment, and victimization in the schools: The next generation of prevention.* Binghamton, NY: Haworth.

Pearce, N. J., & Larson, R. W. (2006). How teens become engaged in youth development programs: The process of motivational change in a civic activism organization. *Applied Developmental Science, 10*, 121–131.

Pederson, S. (2005). Urban adolescents' out-of-school activity profiles: Associations with youth, family, and school transition characteristics. *Applied Developmental Science, 9*, 107–124.

Peets, K., & Kikas, E., (2006). Aggressive strategies and victimization during adolescence: Grade and gender differences, and cross-informant agreement. *Aggressive Behavior, 32*, 68–79.

Pellegrini, A. D., Bartini, M., & Brooks, F. (1999). School bullies, victims, and aggressive victims: Factors relating to group affiliation and victimization in early adolescence. *Journal of Educational Psychology, 91*, 216–224.

Pellegrini, A. D., & Long, J. D. (2002). A longitudinal study of bullying, dominance, and victimization during the transition from primary school through secondary school. *British Journal of Developmental Psychology, 20*, 259–280.

Pellegrini, A. D., & Long, J. D. (2007). An observational study of early heterosexual interaction at middle school dances. *Journal of Research on Adolescence, 17*, 613–638.

Pelto, P. J. (1968, April). The differences between "tight" and "loose" societies. *Transaction*, pp. 37–40.

Perry, A. C., Rosenblatt, E. B., & Wang, X. (2004). Physical, behavioral, and body image characteristics in a tri-racial group of adolescent girls. *Obesity Research, 12*, 1670–1679.

Peskin, H. (1967). Pubertal onset and ego functioning. *Journal of Abnormal Psychology, 72*, 1–15.

Peskin, H., & Livson, N. (1972). Pre-and post-pubertal personality and adult psychologic functioning. *Seminars in Psychology, 4*, 343–355.

Petersen, A. (1985). Pubertal development as a cause of disturbance: Myths, realities, and unanswered questions. *Genetic, Social, and General Psychology Monographs, 111*, 205–232.

Petersen, A. C. (1993). Creating adolescents: The role of context and process in developmental trajectories. *Journal of Research on Adolescence, 3*, 1–18.

Petersen, A. C., Compas, B. E., Brooks-Gunn, J., Stemmler, M., Ey, S., & Grant, K. E. (1993). Depression in adolescence. *American Psychologist, 48*, 155–168.

Petersen, A. C., Sarigiani, P. A., & Kennedy, R. E. (1991). Adolescent depression: Why more girls? *Journal of Youth and Adolescence, 20*, 247–271.

Petersen, A., & Taylor, B. (1980). The biological approach to adolescence: Biological change and psychological adaptation. In J. Adelson (Ed.), *Handbook of adolescent psychology.* New York: Wiley.

Peterson, C., Park, N., & Seligman, M. E. P. (2005). Orientations to happiness and life satisfaction: The full life versus the empty life. *Journal of Happiness Studies, 6*, 25–41.

Pettit, G. S., Bates, J. E., & Dodge, K. A. (1997). Supportive parenting, ecological context, and children's adjustment: A seven-year longitudinal study. *Child Development, 68*, 908–923.

Pettit, G. S., Bates, J. E., Dodge, K. A., & Meece, D. W. (1999). The impact of after-school peer contact on early adolescent externalizing problems is moderated by parental monitoring, neighborhood safety, and prior adjustment. *Child Development, 70*, 768–778.

Pettit, G. S., Laird, R. D., Dodge, K. A., Bates, J. E., & Criss, M. M. (2001). Antecedents and behavior-problem outcomes of parental monitoring and psychological control in early adolescence. *Child Development, 72*, 583–598.

Pew Foundation. (2006, March 22). *Less opposition to gay marriage, adoption and military service.* Available at: http://peoplepress.org/reports/display.php3?ReportID=273.

Phelan, P., Davidson, A. L., & Yu, H. C. (1998). *Adolescents' worlds: Negotiating family, peers, and school.* New York: Teachers College Press.

Phillips, M. (1997). What makes schools effective? A comparison of the relationships of communitarian climate and academic climate to mathematics achievement and attendance during middle school. *American Educational Research Journal, 34*, 633–662.

Phinney, J. S. (1990). Ethnic identity in adolescents and adults: A review of research. *Psychological Bulletin, 108*, 499–514.

Phinney, J. S. (1993). A three-stage model of ethnic identity development. In M. Bernal & G. Knight (Eds.), *Ethnic identity: Formation and transmission among Hispanics and other minorities.* Albany: State University of New York Press.

Phinney, J. S. (1996). When we talk about American ethnic groups, what do we mean? *American Psychologist, 51*, 918–927.

Phinney, J. S. (2003). Ethnic identity and acculturation In K. Chun, P. Ball, & G. Marin (Eds.), *Acculturation: Advances in theory, measurement, and applied research.* Washington, DC: American Psychological Association.

Phinney, J. S. (2005). Ethnic identity in late modern times: A response to Ratttansi and Phoenix. *Identity, 5*, 187–194.

Phinney, J. S. (2006). Ethnic identity exploration in emerging adulthood. In J. J. Arnett & J. L. Tanner (Eds.), *Emerging adults in America: Coming of age in the 21st century.* Washington, DC: American Psychological Association.

Phinney, J. S., & Alipuria, L. L. (2006). Social categorization among multicultural, multiethnic, and multiracial individuals: Processes and implications. In R. J. Crisp & M. Hewstone (Eds.), *Multiple social categorization: Processes, models, and applications.* Hove, UK: Psychology Press.

Phinney, J. S., & Devich-Navarro, M. (1997). Variations in bicultural identification among African American and Mexican American adolescents. *Journal of Research on Adolescence, 7*, 3–32.

Phinney, J. S., & Flores, J. (2002). "Unpackaging" acculturation: Aspects of acculturation as predictors of traditional sex role attitudes. *Journal of Cross-Cultural Psychology, 33*, 320–331.

Phinney, J. S., Ong, A., & Madden, T. (2000). Cultural values and intergenerational value discrepancies in immigrant and non-immigrant families. *Child Development, 71*, 528–539.

Piaget, J. (1952). *The child's conception of number.* New York: Humanities Press.

Piaget, J. (1965). *The moral judgment of the child.* New York: Free Press. (Originally published 1932.)

Piaget, J. (1970). Piaget's theory. In P. H. Mussen (Ed.), *Carmichael's manual of child psychology* (Vol. 1). New York: Wiley.

Piaget, J. (1971). *Biology and knowledge.* Chicago: University of Chicago Press.

Piaget, J. (1972). Intellectual evolution from adolescence to adulthood. *Human Development, 15*, 1–12.

Piaget, J., & Inhelder, B. (1969). *The psychology of the child.* New York: Basic Books.

Pickering, L. E., & Vazsonyi, A. T. (2002). The impact of adolescent employment on family relationships. *Journal of Adolescent Research, 17*, 196–218.

Pickles, A., Pickering, K., Simonoff, E., Silberg, J., Meyer, J., & Maes, H. (1998). Genetic "clocks" and "soft" events: A twin model for pubertal development and other recalled sequences of developmental milestones, transitions, or ages at onset. *Behavior Genetics, 28*, 243–253.

Pigeon, P., Oliver, I., Charlet, J. P., & Rochioccioli, P. (1997). Intensive dance practice: Repercussions on growth and puberty. *American Journal of Sports Medicine, 25*, 243–247.

Pillow, B. H. (2002). Children's and adults' evaluation of the certainty of deductive inferences, inductive inferences, and guesses. *Child Development, 73,* 779–792.

Pincus, D. B., & Friedman, A. G. (2004). Improving children's coping with everyday stress: Transporting treatment interventions to the school setting. *Clinical Child and Family Psychology Review, 7,* 223–240.

Pinquart, M., Juang, L. P., & Silbereisen, R. K. (2003). Self-efficacy and successful school-to-work transition: A longitudinal study. *Journal of Vocational Behavior, 63,* 329–346.

Pinsky, D. (2002, August 23–25). The sex life of kids. *USA Weekend,* pp. 6–7.

Pintrich, P. R. (2000). An achievement goal theory perspective on issues in motivation terminology, theory, and research. *Contemporary educational psychology, 25,* 92–104.

Pintrich, P. R., & Schunk, D. H. (2002). *Motivation in education: Theory, research, and applications* (2nd ed.). Englewood Cliffs, NJ: Merrill Prentice-Hall.

Pipher, M. (1994). *Reviving Ophelia.* New York: Putnam.

Plant, E. A., Hyde, J. S., Keltner, D., & Devine, P. G. (2000). The gender stereotyping of emotions. *Psychology of Women Quarterly, 24,* 81–92.

Plant, T. M. (1988). Puberty in primates. In E. Knobil & J. Neill (Eds.), *The physiology of reproduction.* Vol 2. New York: Raven Press.

Plomin, R., & Daniels, D. (1987). Why are children in the same family so different from one another? *Behavioral and Brain Sciences, 10,* 1–60.

Plotsky, P. M., & Meaney, M. J. (1993). Early, postnatal experience alters hypothalamic corticotropin-releasing factor (CRF) mRNA, median eminence CRF content and stress-induced release in adult rats. *Brain Research: Molecular Brain Research, 18,* 195–200.

Poinsett, A. (1996). *The role of sports in youth development.* New York: Carnegie Corporation.

Polce-Lynch, M. (2001). Adolescent self-esteem and gender: Exploring relations to sexual harrassment, body image, media influence, and emotional expression. *Journal of Youth and Adolescence, 30,* 225–244.

Polce-Lynch, M., Myers, B. J., Kliewer, W., & Kilmartin, C. (2001). Adolescent self-esteem and gender: Exploring relations to sexual harassment, body image, media influence, and emotional expression. *Journal of Youth and Adolescence, 30,* 225–244.

Pollack, W. (1998). *Real boys: Rescuing our sons from the myths of boyhood.* New York: Random House.

Pomerantz, E. M., Ruble, D. N., Frey, K. S., & Grenlich, F. (1995). Meeting goals and confronting conflict: Children's changing perceptions of social comparison. *Child Development, 66,* 723–728.

Ponton, L. (2001). *The sex lives of teenagers: Revealing the secret world of adolescent boys and girls.* New York: Penguin Putnam.

Poole, F. J. P. (1982). The ritual forging of identity: Aspects of person and self in Bimin-Kuskusmin male initiation. In G. H. Herdt (Ed.), *Rituals of manhood: Male initiation in Papua New Guinea.* Berkeley: University of California Press.

Pope, H. (2002). Cannabis, cognition, and residual confounding. *Journal of the American Medical Association, 287,* 1172–1174.

Pope, H. G., Olivardia, R., Gruber, A., & Borowiecki, J. (1999). Evolving ideals of male body image as seen through action toys. *International Journal of Eating Disorders, 26,* 65–72.

Portes, A. (1997). Immigration theory for a new century: Some problems and opportunities. *International Migration Review, 31,* 799–825.

Posner, J. K., & Vandell, D. L. (1994). Low-income children's after-school care: Are there beneficial effects of after-school programs? *Child Development, 65,* 440–456.

Posner, J. K., & Vandell, D. L. (1999). After school activities and the development of low-income children: A longitudinal study. *Developmental Psychology, 35,* 868–879.

Poteat, V. P., & Espelage, D. L. (2007). Predicting psychosocial consequences of homophobic victimization in middle school students. *Journal of Early Adolescence, 27,* 175–191.

Poulin-Dubois, D., Serbin, L. A., & Derbyshire, A. (1998). Toddlers' intermodal and verbal knowledge about gender. *Merrill-Palmer Quarterly, 44,* 338–354.

Poulin-Dubois, D., Serbin, L. A., Eichstedt, J. A., Sen, M. G., & Beissel, C. F. (2002). Men don't put on make-up: Toddlers' knowledge of the gender stereotyping of household activities. *Social Development, 11,* 166–181.

Power, R., Taylor, C. L., & Nippold, M. A. (2001). Comprehending literally–true versus literally–false proverbs. *Child Language Teaching & Therapy, 17,* 1–18.

Power, T. G. (2004). Stress and coping in childhood: The parents' role. *Parenting: Science and Practice, 4,* 271–317.

Powlishta, K. K. (2004). Gender as a social category: Intergroup processes and gender-role development. In M. Bennett & F. Sani (Eds.), *The development of the social self.* New York: Psychology Press.

Pratt, M. W., Skoe, E. E., & Arnold, M. L. (2004). Care reasoning development and family socialization patterns in later adolescence: A longitudinal analysis. *International Journal of Behavioral Development, 28,* 139–147.

Preskill, S. (1989). Educating for democracy: Charles W. Eliot and the differentiated curriculum. *Educational Theory, 39,* 351–358.

Preti, G., Cutler, W. B., Garcia, C. R., Huggins, G. R., & Lawley, H. J. (1986). Human axillary secretions influence women's menstrual cycles: The role of donor extract of females. *Hormones and Behavior, 20,* 474–482.

Priel, B., & deSchonen, S. (1986). Self-recognition: A study of a population without mirrors. *Journal of Experimental Child Psychology, 41,* 237–250.

Prinstein, M. J., & Cillessen, A. H. N. (2003). Forms and functions of adolescent peer aggression associated with high levels of peer status. *Merrill-Palmer Quarterly, 49,* 310–342.

Prinstein, M. J., & La Greca, A. (2002). Peer crowd affiliation and internalizing distress in childhood and adolescence: A longitudinal follow-back study. *Journal of Research on Adolescence, 12,* 325–351.

Prinstein, M. J., Meade, C. S., & Cohen, G. L. (2003). Adolescent oral sex, peer popularity, and perceptions of best friends' sexual behavior. *Journal of Pediatric Psychology, 28,* 243–249.

Prinstein, M. J., & Wang, S. S. (2005). False consensus and adolescent peer contagion: Examining discrepancies between perceptions and actual reported levels of friends' deviant and health risk behaviors. *Journal of Abnormal Child Psychology, 33,* 293–306.

Psacharopoulos, G. (1997). Child labor versus educational attainment: Some evidence from Latin America. *Journal of Population Economics, 10,* 377–386.

Public Agenda. (2002). *Sizing things up.* New York: Author.

Public Health Service. (1988). *The Surgeon General's report on nutrition and health.* Washington, DC: U.S. Department of Health and Human Services.

Pulliam, J., & Van Patten, J. (1995). *History of education in America.* Englewood Cliffs, NJ: Prentice Hall.

Putnam, R. (2000). *Bowling alone: The collapse and revival of American community.* New York: Simon and Schuster.

Quadrel, M., Fischoff, B., & Davis, W. (1993). Adolescent (in)vulnerability. *American Psychologist, 48,* 102–116.

Quaiser-Pohl, C., Geiser, C., & Lehmann, W. (2006). The relationship between computer-game preference, gender, and mental-rotation ability. *Personality and Individual Differences, 40,* 609–619.

Quartz, S. R., & Sejnowski, T. J. (1997). The neural basis of cognitive development: A constructivist manifesto. *Behavioral and Brain Sciences, 20,* 537–596.

Raffaelli, M., & Ontai, L. L. (2004). Gender socialization in Latino/a families: Results from two retrospective studies. *Sex Roles, 50,* 287–299.

Raine, A. (2002). Biosocial studies of antisocial and violent behavior in children and adults: A review. *Journal of Abnormal Child Psychology, 30,* 311–326.

Ramírez-Esparza, N., Gosling S. D., Benet-Martínez, V., Potter, J. P., & Pennebaker, J. W. (2006). Do bilinguals have two personalities? A special case of cultural frame switching. *Journal of Research in Personality, 40,* 99–120.

Rankin, J. L., Lane, D. J., Gibbons, F. X., & Gerrard, M. (2004). Adolescent self-consciousness: Longitudinal age changes and gender differences in two cohorts. *Journal of Research on Adolescence, 14,* 1–21.

Rathunde, K., & Csikszentmihalyi, M. (2006). The developing person: An experiential perspective. In W. Damon & R. M. Lerner (Eds.), *Handbook of child psychology.* Hoboken, NJ: Wiley.

Rattermann, M. J., & Gentner, D. (1998). More evidence for a relational shift in the development of analogy: Children's performance on a causal–mapping task. *Cognitive Development, 13,* 453–478.

Räty, H., Vänskä, J., Kasanen, K., & Kärkkäinen, R. (2002). Parents' explanations of their child's performance in mathematics and reading: A replication. *Sex Roles, 46,* 121–128.

Raven, J. C., Court, J. H., & Raven, J. (1983). *Manual for Raven's progressive matrices and vocabulary scales.* London: H. K. Lewis.

Raywid, M. A. (1999). *Current literature on small schools.* ERIC Digest. Charleston, WV: ERIC Clearinghouse on Rural Education and Small Schools.

Reardon, S. F., & Yun, J. T. (2001). Suburban racial change and suburban school segregation, 1987–95. *Sociology of Education, 74,* 79–101.

Reber, A. S., & Reber, E. S. (2001). *The Penguin dictionary of psychology* (3rd ed.). New York: Penguin.

Redding, R. E. (2005). Adult punishment for juvenile offenders: Does it reduce crime? In N. E. Dowd, D. G. Singer, & R. F. Wilson (Eds.), *Handbook of children, culture, and violence.* Thousand Oaks, CA: Sage.

Redmond, C., Spoth, R., Shin, C., & Lepper, H. (1999). Modeling long-term parent outcomes of two universal family-focused preventive interventions: One year followup results. *Journal of Consulting and Clinical Psychology, 67,* 975–984.

Reese-Weber, M., & Marchand, J. F. (2002). Family and individual predictors of late adolescents' romantic relationships. *Journal of Youth and Adolescence, 31,* 197–206.

Reich, C. A. (1970). *The greening of America: How the youth revolution is trying to make America livable.* New York: Random House.

Reicher, S., Levine, R. M., & Gordijn, E. (1998). More on deindividuation, power relations between groups, and the expression of social identity: Three studies on the effects of visibility to the in-group. *British Journal of Social Psychology, 37,* 15–40.

Reimer, K. (2003). Committed to caring: Transformation in adolescent moral identity. *Applied Developmental Science, 7,* 129–137.

Reinders, H., & Youniss, J. (2006a). Community service and civic development in adolescence: Theoretical considerations and empirical evidence. In A. Sliwka, M. Diedrich, & M. Hofer (Eds.), *Citizenship education: Theory, research, practice.* London: Waxmann.

Reinders, H., & Youniss, J. (2006b). School-based required community service and civic development in adolescents. *Applied Developmental Science, 10,* 2–12.

Reisner, E. R., Russell, C. A., Welsh, M. E., Birmingham, J., & White, R. N. (2002). *Supporting quality and scale in after-school services to urban youth: Evaluation of program implementation and student engagement in the TASC After-School Program's third year.* Washington, DC: Policy Studies Associates.

Reiss, D., & Neiderhiser, J. M. (2000). The interplay of genetic influences and social processes in developmental theory: Specific mechanisms are coming into view. *Development and Psychopathology, 12,* 357–374.

Reiss, D., Neiderhiser, J. M., Hetherington, E. M., & Plomin, R. (2000). *The relationship code: Deciphering genetic and social patterns in adolescent development.* Cambridge, MA: Harvard University Press.

Renk, K., & Creasey, G. (2003). The relationship of gender, gender identity, and coping strategies in late adolescents. *Journal of Adolescence, 26,* 159–168.

Rennebohm-Franz, K. (1996). Towards a critical social consciousness in children: Multicultural peace education in a first grade classroom. *Theory Into Practice, 35,* 264–279

Renninger, K. A. (2000). Individual interest and its implications for understanding intrinsic motivation. In C. Sansone & J. M. Harackiewicz (Eds.), *Intrinsic and extrinsic motivation: The search for optimal motivation and performance.* San Diego, CA: Academic Press.

Repucci, N. (1999). Adolescent development and juvenile justice. *American Journal of Community Psychology, 27,* 307–326.

Rest, J. R., Narvaez, D., Bebeau, M. J., & Thomas, S. J. (1999). *Postconventional moral thinking.* Mahwah, NJ: Erlbaum.

Reyna, V. F., & Brainerd, C. J. (1995). Fuzzy-trace theory: An interim synthesis. *Learning and Individual Differences, 7,* 1–75.

Reyna, V. F., & Farley, F. (2006). Risk and rationality in adolescent decision making: Implications for theory, practice, and public policy. *Psychological Science in the Public Interest, 7,* 1–44.

Rhee, S. H., & Waldman, I. D. (2002). Genetic and environmental influences on antisocial behavior: A meta-analysis of twin and adoption studies. *Psychological bulletin, 128,* 490–529.

Rhodes, J. E. (2002). *Stand by me: The risks and rewards of mentoring today's youth.* Cambridge, MA: Harvard University Press.

Rhodes, J. E., Grossman, J. B., & Resch, N. L. (2000). Agents of change: Pathways through which mentoring relationships influence adolescents' academic adjustment. *Child Development, 71,* 1662–1671.

Ricciardelli, L. A., & McCabe, M. P. (2001). Self-esteem and negative affect as moderators of sociocultural influences on body dissatisfaction, strategies to decrease weight, and strategies to increase muscles among adolescent boys and girls. *Sex Roles, 44,* 189–207.

Ricciardelli, L. A., McCabe, M. P., Holt, K. E., & Finemore, J. (2003). A biopsychosocial

model for understanding body image and body change strategies among children. *Journal of Applied Developmental Psychology, 24,* 475–495.

Richards, A. I. (1982). *Chisungu: A girls' initiation ceremony among the Bemba of Zambia.* New York: Tavistock.

Richards, M., & Duckett, E. (1994). The relationship of maternal employment to early adolescent daily experience with and without parents. *Child Development, 65,* 225–236.

Richardson, V. (1996). The role of attitudes and belief in learning to teach. In J. Sikula, T. Buttery, & E. Guyton (Eds.), *Handbook of research on teacher education* (2nd ed.). New York: Prentice-Hall.

Ridderinkhof, K. R., van der Molen, M. W., & Band, G. P. H. (1997). Sources of interference from irrelevant information: A developmental study. *Journal of Experimental Child Psychology, 65,* 315–341.

Riegel, K. F. (1976). The dialectics of human development. *American Psychologist, 31,* 689–700.

Rieger, G., Linsenmeier, J. A. W., Gygax, L., & Bailey, J. M. (2008). Sexual orientation and childhood gender nonconformity: Evidence from home videos. *Developmental Psychology, 44,* 46–58.

Rierdan, J., Koff, E., & Flaherty, J. (1983). Clinical experiences: Guidelines for preparing girls for menstruation. *Journal of the American Academy of Child Psychiatry, 22,* 480–486.

Rierdan, J., Koff, E., & Stubbs, M. L. (1989). Timing of menarche, preparation, and initial menstrual experience: Replication and further analyses in a prospective study. *Journal of Youth and Adolescence, 18,* 413–426.

Ries, L. A. G., et al. (Eds.). (2006). *SEER cancer statistics review, 1975–2003.* Bethesda, MD: National Cancer Institute.

Rigsby, L. C., & McDill, E. L. (1975). Value orientations of high school students. In H. R. Stub (Ed.), *The sociology of education: A sourcebook* (3rd ed.). Homewood, IL: Dorsey.

Rimer, S. (2003, April 8). Study finds charter schools lack experienced teachers. *New York Times,* p. A14.

Ritchie, K. L. (1999). Maternal behaviors and cognitions during discipline episodes: A comparison on power bouts and single acts of noncompliance. *Developmental Psychology, 35,* 580–589.

Ritts, V., Patterson, M., & Tubbs, M. (1992). Expectations, impressions, and judgments of physically attractive students: A review. *Review of Educational Research, 62,* 413–426.

Rivkin, S. G. (1994). Residential segregation and school integration. *Sociology of Education, 67,* 279–292.

Roberts, D. F. (2003). From Plato's Republic to Hillary's village: Children and the changing media environment. In R. Weissberg, C. Kuster, H. Walbert, & O. Reyes (Eds.), *Trends in the well-being of children and youth.* Washington, DC: Child Welfare League of America Press.

Roberts, D. F., & Foehr, U. G. (2004). *Kids and media in America: Patterns of use at the millennium*. New York: Cambridge University Press.

Roberts, D. F., Foehr, U. G., & Rideout, V. (2005). *Generation M: Media in the lives of 8–18 year-olds*. Washington, DC: Henry J. Kaiser Family Foundation.

Roberts, D. F., Henriksen, L., & Foehr, U. G. (2004). Adolescents and media. In R. M. Lerner & L. Steinberg (Eds.), *Handbook of adolescent psychology*. New York: Wiley.

Roberts, M., & Steinberg, L. (1999). Unpacking authoritative parenting: Reassessing a multidimensional construct. *Journal of Marriage and the Family, 61*, 574–587.

Robertson, T., & Vaishnav, A. (2004, January 3). No easy answers as school killings increase: Officials stunned as precautions fail to curb attacks. *Boston Globe*, p. A3.

Robins, R. W., & Trzesniewski, K. H. (2005). Self-esteem development across the lifespan. *Current Directions in Psychological Science, 14*, 158–162.

Robins, R. W., Trzesniewski, K. H., Tracy, J. L., Gosling, S. D., & Potter, J. (2002). Global self-esteem across the lifespan. *Psychology and Aging, 17*, 423–434.

Rochat, P., & Striano, T. (2002). Who's in the mirror? Self-other discrimination in specular images by four- and nine-month old infants. *Child Development, 73*, 35–46.

Roche, A. F. (1986). Bone growth and maturation. In F. Falkner & J. Tanner (Eds.), *Human growth* (2nd ed., Vol. 2). New York: Plenum.

Rodgers, J. E., Billy, J. O. G., & Udry, J. R. (1982). The rescission of behaviors: Inconsistent responses in adolescent sexuality data. *Social Science Research, 11*, 280–296.

Rodkin, P. C. (2004). Peer ecologies of aggression and bullying. In D. L. Espelage & S. M. Swearer (Eds.), *Bullying in American schools: A social-ecological perspective on prevention and intervention*. Mahwah, NJ: Erlbaum.

Rodkin, P. C., Farmer, T. W., Pearl, R., & Van Acker, R. (2000). Heterogeneity of popular boys: Antisocial and prosocial configurations. *Developmental Psychology, 36*, 14–24.

Rodkin, P. C., Farmer, T. W., Pearl, R., & Van Acker, R. (2002, April). *Short-term longitudinal analysis of popular-aggressive boys from spring 3rd to spring 4th grade*. Paper presented at the meeting of the Society for Research on Adolescence, New Orleans.

Roeser, R. W. (2004). Competing schools of thought in achievement goal theory? In P. R. Pintrich & M. L. Maehr (Eds.), *Motivating students, improving schools: The legacy of Carol Midgley (Advances in motivation and achievement, Vol. XIII)*. Greenwich, CT: JAI.

Roeser, R. W., & Eccles, J. S. (1998). Adolescents' perceptions of middle school: Relation to longitudinal changes in academic and psychological adjustment. *Journal of Research on Adolescence, 8*, 123–158.

Roeser, R. W., Eccles, J. S., & Freedman-Doan, C. (1999). Academic functioning and mental health in adolescence: Patterns, progressions, and routes from childhood. *Journal of Adolescent Research, 14*, 135–174.

Roeser, R. W., Eccles, J.S., & Sameroff, J. (1998). Academic and emotional functioning in early adolescence. Longitudinal relations, patterns, and prediction by experience in middle school. *Development and Psychopathology, 10*, 321–352.

Roeser, R. W., & Midgley, C.M. (1997). Teachers' views of aspects of student mental health. *Elementary School Journal, 98*(2), 115–133.

Roeser, R. W., Midgley, C. M., & Urdan, T. C. (1996). Perceptions of the school psychological environment and early adolescents' psychological and behavioral functioning in school: The mediating role of goals and belonging. *Journal of Educational Psychology, 88*, 408–422.

Rogers, C. R. (1951). *Client-centered therapy*. Boston: Houghton Mifflin.

Rogers, K. N., Buchanan, C. M., & Winchell, M. E. (2003). Psychological control during early adolescence: Links to adjustment in differing parent/adolescent dyads. *Journal of Early Adolescence, 23*, 349–383.

Rogoff, B. (1990). *Apprenticeship in thinking: Cognitive development in social context*. New York: Oxford University Press.

Rogoff, B. (1998). Cognition as a collaborative process. In D. Kuhn & R. Siegler (Eds.), W. Damon (Series Ed.), *Handbook of child psychology (5th ed): Vol. 2: Cognition, perception, and language*. New York: Wiley.

Rogoff, B., Turkanis, C. G., & Bartlett, L. (Eds.). (2001). *Learning together: Children and adults in a school community*. New York: Oxford University Press.

Rogol, A. D., Clark, P. A., & Roemmich, J. N. (2000). Growth and pubertal development in children and adolescents: Effects of diet and physical activity. *American Journal of Clinical Nutrition, 72*, 521S–528S.

Rogol, A. D., Roemmich, J. N., & Clark, P. A. (2002). Growth at puberty. *Journal of Adolescent Health, 31*, 192–200.

Rohde, P., Lewinsohn, P. M., Clarke, G. N., Hops, H., & Seeley, J. R. (2005). The adolescent coping with depression course: A cognitive-behavioral approach to the treatment of adolescent depression. In E. D. Hibbs & P. S. Jensen (Eds.), *Psychosocial treatments for child and adolescent disorders: Empirically based strategies for clinical practice* (2nd ed.). Washington, DC: American Psychological Association.

Roisman, G. I., Collins, W. A., Sroufe, L. A., & Egeland, B. (2005). Predictors of young adults' representations of and behavior in their current romantic relationship: Prospective tests of the prototype hypothesis. *Attachment & Human Development, 7*, 105–121.

Roscigno, V. J. (2000). Family/school inequality and African-American/Hispanic achievement. *Social Problems, 47*, 266–290.

Rose, A. J. (2002). Co-rumination in the friendships of girls and boys. *Child Development, 73*, 1830–1843.

Rose, A. J., & Asher, S. R. (2004). Children's strategies and goals in response to help-giving and help-seeking tasks within a friendship. *Child Development, 75*, 749–763.

Rose, A. J., & Rudolph, K. D. (2006). A review of sex differences in peer relationship processes: Potential trade-offs for the emotional and behavioral development of girls and boys. *Psychological Bulletin, 132*, 98–131.

Rose, L. C., & Gallup, A. M. (2002). The 34th annual Phi Delta Kappa/Gallup poll of the public's attitudes toward the public schools. *Phi Delta Kappan, 84*, 41–56.

Rose-Krasnor, L., Busseri, M. A., Willoughby, T., & Chalmers, H. (2006). Breadth and intensity of youth activity involvement as contexts for positive development. *Journal of Youth and Adolescence, 35*, 385–399.

Rosen, B. C., & D'Andrade, R. (1959). The psychological origins of achievement motivation. *Sociometry, 22*, 185–218.

Rosenbaum, J. (1995). Changing the geography of opportunity by expanding residential choice: Lessons from the Gautreaux Program. *Housing Policy Debate, 6*(1), 231–269.

Rosenbaum, M. (1979). The changing body image of the adolescent girl. In M. Sugar (Ed.), *Female adolescent development*. New York: Bruner/Mazel.

Rosenberg, M. (1986). *Conceiving the Self*. Malabar, FL: Krieger.

Rosenberg, M., & Owens, T. J. (2001). Low self-esteem people: A collective portrait. In T. J. Owens, S. Stryker, & N. Goodman (Eds.), *Extending self-esteem theory and research: Sociological and psychological currents*. Cambridge, UK: Cambridge University Press.

Rosenblum, G. D., & Lewis, M. (1999). The relations among body image, physical attractiveness, and body mass in adolescence. *Child Development, 70*, 50–64.

Rosenthal, R., & Jacobson, L. (1968). *Pygmalion in the classroom*. New York: Holt, Rinehart & Winston.

Rosner, B. A., & Rierdan, J. (1994, February). *Adolescent girls' self-esteem: Variations in developmental trajectories*. Paper presented at the meeting of the Society for Research on Adolescence, San Diego.

Rosnow, R. L. (2000). Longitudinal research. In A. Kazdin (Ed.), *Encyclopedia of psychology*. Washington, DC & New York: American Psychological Association and Oxford University Press.

Rostosky, S., Brian, W., Wright, M., & Randall, B. (2004). The impact of religiosity on adolescent sexual behavior: A review of the evidence. *Journal of Adolescent Research, 19*, 677–697.

Roth, J. L., & Brooks-Gunn, J. (2000). What do adolescents need for healthy development? Implications for youth policy. *Social Policy Report, XIV*(1), 1–16.

Roth, J. L., & Brooks-Gunn, J. (2003). What exactly is a youth development program? Answers from research and practice. *Applied Developmental Science, 7*, 94–111.

Rothbart, M. K., & Posner, M. I. (2005). Genes and experience in the development of executive attention and effortful control.

New Directions for Child and Adolescent Development, 109, 101–108.

Rothbaum, F., Pott, M., Azuma, H., Miyake, K., & Weisz, J. (2000). The development of close relationships in Japan and the United States: Paths of symbiotic harmony and generative tension. *Child Development, 71,* 1121–1142.

Rousseau, J.-J. (1762/1972). *Emile.* New York: Dutton.

Rowan, B., Chiang, F., & Miller, R. (1997). Using research on employees' performance to study the effects of teachers on students' achievement. *Sociology of Education, 70,* 256–284.

Rowe, D. C. (1994). *The limits of family influence: Genes, experience, and behavior.* New York: Guilford.

Rowe, D. C. (1999). Genetic and environmental influences on vocabulary IQ: Parental education level as a moderator. *Child Development, 70,* 1151–1162.

Rowe, D. C. (2000). Environmental and genetic influences on pubertal development: Evolutionary life history traits? In J. L. Rodgers, D. C. Rowe, & W. B. Miller (Eds.), *Genetic influences on human fertility and sexuality.* Boston, MA: Kluwer.

Rowe, R., Maughan, B., & Eley, T. C. (2006). Links between antisocial behavior and depressed mood: The role of life events and attributional style. *Journal of Abnormal Child Psychology, 34,* 293–302.

Rubin, A. M. (2002). The uses-and-gratifications perspective of media effects. In J. Bryant & D. Zillmann (Eds.), *Media effects: Advances in theory and research* (2nd ed.). Mahwah, NJ: Erlbaum.

Rubin, K. H. (1998). Social and emotional development from a cultural perspective. *Developmental Psychology, 34,* 611–615.

Rubin, K. H., Bukowski, W., & Parker, J. (2006). Peer interactions, relationships, and groups. In W. Damon & R. Lerner (Eds.), *Handbook of child psychology* (6th ed.). Hoboken, NJ: Wiley.

Rubin, K. H., Chen, X., McDougall, P., Bowker, A., & McKinnon, J. (1995). The Waterloo Longitudinal Project: Predicting adolescent internalizing and externalizing problems from early and mid-childhood. *Development and Psychopathology, 7,* 751–764.

Rubin, K. H., Dwyer, K. M., Booth, C. L., Kim, A. H., Burgess, K. B., & Rose-Krasnor, L. (2004). Attachment, friendship, and psychosocial functioning in early adolescence. *Journal of Early Adolescence, 24,* 326–356.

Ruble, D. N., Alvarez, J. M., Bachman, M., Cameron, J. A., Fuligni, A. J., Garcia Coll, C., & Rhee, E. (2004). The development of a sense of "we": The emergence and implications of children's collective identity. In M. Bennett & F. Sani (Eds.), *The development of the social self.* New York: Psychology Press.

Ruble, D. N., & Brooks-Gunn, J. (1982). The experience of menarche. *Child Development, 53,* 1557–1566.

Ruble, D. N., Martin, C. L., & Berenbaum, S. (2006). Gender development. In W.

Damon & R. Lerner (Eds.), *Handbook of child psychology* (6th ed.). New York: Wiley.

Rudman, L. A, Feinberg, J., & Fairchild, K. (2002). Minority members' implicit attitudes: Automatic ingroup bias as a function of group status. *Social Cognition, 20,* 294–320.

Rudolph, K. D. (2002). Gender differences in emotional responses to interpersonal stress during adolescence. *Journal of Adolescent Health, 30,* 3–13.

Rumberger, R. (1995). Dropping out of middle school: A multilevel analysis of students and schools. *American Educational Research Journal, 32,* 583–625.

Rumberger, R. W. (2001, January). *Why students drop out of school and what can be done.* Paper presented to the Conference on Drop Outs in America, Harvard University Civil Rights Project, Cambridge, MA.

Rushton, J., Forcier, M., & Schectman, R. (2002). Epidemiology of depressive symptoms in the National Longitudinal Study of Adolescent Health. *Journal of the American Academy of Child and Adolescent Psychiatry, 41,* 199–205.

Russell, B. (1945). *A history of western philosophy, and its connection with political and social circumstances from the earliest times to the present day.* New York: Simon & Schuster.

Russell, S. (2006). Substance use and abuse and mental health among sexual minority youths: Evidence from Add Health. In A. Omoto & H. Kurtzman (Eds.), *Sexual orientation and mental health.* Washington, DC: American Psychological Association.

Russell, S., & Joyner, K. (2001). Adolescent sexual orientation and suicide risk: Evidence from a national study. *American Journal of Public Health, 91,* 1276–1281.

Rutter, M. (1983). School effects on pupil progress: Research findings and policy implications. *Child Development, 54,* 1–29.

Rutter, M. (1987). Psychosocial resilience and protective mechanisms. *American Journal of Orthopsychiatry, 57,* 316–331.

Rutter, M. (2002). Nature, nurture, and development: From evangelism through science toward policy and practice. *Child Development, 73,* 1–21.

Rutter, M., & the English and Romanian Adoptees (ERA) Study Team. (1998). Developmental catch-up and deficit, following adoption after severe global early privation. *Journal of Child Psychology and Psychiatry, 39,* 465–476.

Rutter, M., Graham, P., Chadwick, F., & Yule, W. (1976). Adolescent turmoil: Fact or fiction? *Journal of Child Psychology and Psychiatry, 17,* 35–56.

Rutter, M., & Maughan, B. (2002). School effectiveness findings 1979–2002. *Journal of School Psychology, 40,* 451–475.

Ryan, A. M. (2001). The peer group as a context for the development of young adolescent motivation and achievement. *Child Development, 72,* 1135–1150.

Ryan, A. M., Pintrich, P. R., & Midgley, C. (2001). Avoiding seeking help in the classroom: Who and why? *Educational Psychology Review, 13,* 93–114.

Ryan, G. (2000). Childhood sexuality: A decade of study. Part I—Research and curriculum development. *Child Abuse and Neglect, 24,* 33–48.

Ryan, K. E., & Ryan, A. M. (2005). Psychological processes underlying stereotype threat and standardized math test performance. *Educational Psychologist, 40,* 53–63.

Ryan, M. K. (2003). Gender differences in ways of knowing: The context dependence of the Attitudes Toward Thinking and Learning Survey. *Sex Roles, 49,* 11–12.

Ryan, R. M., & Deci, E. L. (2000a). Intrinsic and extrinsic motivations: Classic definitions and new directions. *Contemporary Educational Psychology, 25,* 54–67.

Ryan, R. M., & Deci, E. L. (2000b). On happiness and human potentials: A review of research on hedonic and eudaimonic well-being. *Annual Review of Psychology, 52,* 141–166.

Ryan, R. M., & Deci, E. L. (2000c). Self-determination theory and the facilitation of intrinsic motivation, social development, and well-being. *American Psychologist, 55,* 68–78.

Ryan, R. M., Deci, E. L., Grolnick, W. S., & La Guardia, J. G. (2006). The significance of autonomy and autonomy support in psychological development and psychopathology. In D. Cicchetti & D. J. Cohen (Eds.), *Developmental psychopathology* (2nd ed.). Hoboken, NJ: Wiley.

Sabatier, C. (2008). Ethnic and national identity among second-generation immigrant adolescents in France: The role of social context and family. *Journal of Adolescence, 31,* 185–205.

Sadeh, A., & Gruber, R. (2002). Stress and sleep in adolescence: A clinical-developmental perspective. In M. A. Carskadon (Ed.), *Adolescent sleep patterns: Biological, social, and psychological influences.* Cambridge, UK: Cambridge University Press.

Sadker, D., Sadker, M. P., & Zittleman, K. (2008). *Teachers, schools, and society* (8th ed.). New York: McGraw-Hill.

Sagestrano, L. M., McCormick, S. H., Paikoff, R. L., & Holmbeck, G. N. (1999). Pubertal development and parent–child conflict in low-income, urban, African American adolescents. *Journal of Research on Adolescence, 9,* 85–107.

Sagi, A., & Hoffman, M. L. (1976). Empathic distress in newborns. *Developmental Psychology, 12,* 175–176.

Saguaro Seminar. (2001). *Better together: Report of the Saguaro Seminar on Civic Engagement in America.* Cambridge, MA: John F. Kennedy School of Government, Harvard University. Available: www.bettertogether.org.

Salem, D., Zimmerman, M., & Notaro, P. (1998). Effects of family structure, family process, and father involvement on psychosocial outcomes among African American adolescents. *Family Relations, 47,* 331–341.

Sallis, J. F., Prochaska, J. J., Taylor, W. C., Hill, J. O., & Geraci, J. C. (1999). Correlates of physical activity in a national sample of girls and boys in grades 4 through 12. *Health Psychology, 18,* 410–415.

Salmivalli, C., Kaukiainen, A., & Lagerspetz, K. (2000). Aggression and sociometric status among peers: Do gender and type of aggression matter? *Scandinavian Journal of Psychology, 41,* 17–24.

Salti, R., Galluzzi, F., Bindi, G., Perfetto, F., Tarquini, R., Halberg, F., & Cornelissen, G. (2000). Nocturnal melatonin patterns in children. *Journal of Clinical Endocrinology & Metabolism, 85,* 2137–2144.

Sam, D. L., & Berry, J. W. (1995). Acculturative stress among young immigrants in Norway. *Scandinavian Journal of Psychology, 36,* 10–24.

Sampson, R. J. (2002). How do communities undergird or undermine development? Relevant contexts and social mechanisms. In A. Booth & A. C. Crouter (Eds.), *Does it take a village? Community effects on children, adolescents, and families.* Mahwah, NJ: Erlbaum.

Sampson, R. J., Morenoff, J. D., & Gannon-Rowley, T. (2002). Assessing "neighborhood effects": Social processes and new directions in research. *Annual Review of Sociology, 28,* 443–478.

Sanders, M. G. (1998). The effect of school, family, and community support on the academic achievement of African-American adolescents. *Urban Education, 33,* 385–409.

Sandstrom, M. J., & Cillessen, A. H. N. (2003). Sociometric status and children's peer experiences: Use of the daily diary method. *Merrill-Palmer Quarterly, 49,* 427–452.

Sandstrom, M. J., Cillessen, A. H. N., & Eisenhower, A. (2003). Children's appraisal of peer rejection experiences: Impact on social and emotional adjustment. *Social Development, 12,* 530–550.

Santa Maria, M. (2002). Youth in Southeast Asia: Living within the continuity of tradition and the turbulence of change. In B. Brown, R. Larson, & T. S. Saraswathi (Eds.), *The world's youth: Adolescence in eight regions of the globe.* New York: Cambridge University Press.

Santelli, J. S., Kaiser, J., Hirsch, L., Radosh, A., Simkin, L., & Middlestadt, S. (2004). Initiation of sexual intercourse among middle school adolescents: The influence of psychosocial factors. *Journal of Adolescent Health, 34,* 200–208.

Santelli, J. S., Morrow, B., Anderson, J. E., & Lindberg, L. D. (2006). Contraceptive use and pregnancy risk among U.S. high school students, 1991–2003. *Perspectives on Sexual and Reproductive Health, 38,* 106–111.

Santelli, J., Ott, M. A., Lyon, M., Rogers, J., Summers, D., & Schleifer, R. (2006). Abstinence and abstinence-only education: A review of U.S. policies and programs. *Journal of Adolescent Health, 38,* 72–81.

Sargent, J. D., & Dalton, M. (2001). Does parental disapproval of smoking prevent adolescents from becoming established smokers? *Pediatrics, 108,* 1256–1262.

Sarigiani, P. A., & Petersen, A. C. (2000). Adolescence: Puberty and biological maturation. In A. Kazdin (Ed.), *Encyclopedia of psychology.* Washington, DC & New York: American Psychological Association and Oxford University Press.

Sarrel, L. J., & Sarrel, P. M. (1979). *Sexual unfolding: Sexual development and sex therapies in late adolescence.* Boston: Little, Brown.

Saul, N. (1997). *Richard II.* New Haven, CT: Yale University Press.

Savin-Williams, R. C. (1979). Dominance hierarchies in groups of early adolescents. *Child Development, 50,* 923–935.

Savin-Williams, R. C. (1998). *". . . And then I became gay": Young men's stories.* New York: Routledge.

Savin-Williams, R. C. (2001). *Mom, Dad, I'm gay.* Washington, DC: American Psychological Association.

Savin-Williams, R. C. (2006). Who's gay? Does it matter? *Current Directions in Psychological Science, 15,* 40–44.

Savin-Williams, R. C., & Cohen, K. M. (2004). Homoerotic development during childhood and adolescence. *Child and Adolescent Psychiatric Clinics of North America, 13,* 529–549.

Savin-Williams, R. C., & Diamond, L. M. (2004). Sex. In R. M. Lerner & L. Steinberg (Eds.), *Handbook of adolescent psychology.* New York: Wiley.

Savin-Williams, R. C., & Esterberg, K. G. (2000). Lesbian, gay, and bisexual families. In D. H. Demo, K. R. Allen, & M. A. Fine (Eds.), *Handbook of family diversity.* New York: Oxford University Press.

Scales, P. C., Benson, P. L., Leffert, N., & Blyth, D. A. (2000). Contribution of developmental assets to the prediction of thriving among adolescents. *Applied Developmental Science, 4,* 27–46.

Scales, P. C., Benson, P. L., Roehlkepartain, E. C., Sesma, A., Jr., & van Dulmen, M. (2006). The role of developmental assets in predicting academic achievement: A longitudinal study. *Journal of Adolescence, 29,* 691–708.

Scanlan, T., Babkes, M., & Scanlan, L. (2005). Participation in sport: A developmental glimpse at emotion. In J. L. Mahoney, R. W. Larson, & J. S. Eccles (Eds.), *Organized activities as contexts of development: Extracurricular activities, after-school and community programs.* Mahwah, NJ: Erlbaum.

Scaramella, L. V., Conger, R. D., Spoth, R., & Simons, R. L. (2002). Evaluation of a social contextual model of delinquency: A cross-study replication. *Child Development, 73,* 175–195.

Scarr, S. (1993). Biological and cultural diversity: The legacy of Darwin for development. *Child Development, 64,* 1333–1353.

Scarr, S., & McCartney, K. (1983). How people make their own environments: A theory of genotype-environment effects. *Child Development, 54,* 424–435.

Scarr, S., & Weinberg, R. A. (1983). The Minnesota adoption studies: Genetic dif-

ferences and malleability. *Child Development, 54,* 260–267.

Schacter, F. F. (1985). Sibling deidentification in the clinic: Devil vs. Angel. *Family Process, 24,* 415–427.

Schaefer, E. S. (1965). A configurational analysis of children's reports of parent behavior. *Journal of Consulting Psychology, 29,* 552–557.

Schaie, K. W. (1977). Quasi-experimental research designs in the psychology of aging. In J. E. Birren & K. W. Schaie (Eds.), *Handbook of the psychology of aging* (pp. 39–58). New York: Van Nostrand Reinhold.

Scher, C. D., Ingram, R. E., & Segal, Z. V. (2005). Cognitive reactivity and vulnerability: Empirical evaluation of construct activation and cognitive diatheses in unipolar depression. *Clinical Psychology Review, 25,* 487–510.

Schieffelin, B. (1990). *The give and take of everyday life: Language socialization of Kaluli children.* New York: Cambridge University Press.

Schiff, A., & Knopf, I. (1985). The effects of task demands on attention allocation in children of different ages. *Child Development, 56,* 621–630.

Schlegel, A. (1995). A cross-cultural approach to adolescence. *Ethos, 23,* 5–32.

Schlegel, A. (2000). The global spread of adolescent culture. In L. J. Crockett & R. K. Silbereisen (Eds.), *Negotiating adolescence in times of social change.* Cambridge, UK: Cambridge University Press.

Schlegel, A., & Barry, H., III (Eds.). (1980). Adolescent initiation ceremonies: A cross-cultural code. In *Cross-cultural samples and codes.* Pittsburgh: University of Pittsburgh Press.

Schlegel, A., & Barry, H., III (1991). *Adolescence: An anthropological inquiry.* New York: Free Press.

Schmader, T., & Johns, M. (2003). Converging evidence that stereotype threat reduces working memory capacity. *Journal of Personality and Social Psychology, 85,* 440–452.

Schmader, T., Johns, M., & Barquissau, M. (2004). The costs of accepting gender differences: The role of stereotype endorsement in women's experience in the math domain. *Sex Roles, 50,* 835–850.

Schmidt, U. (2003). Aetiology of eating disorders in the 21st century: New answers to old questions. *European Child and Adolescent Psychiatry, 12*(Supp. 1), 1130–1137.

Schneider, B. H., Atkinson, L., & Tardif, C. (2001). Child-parent attachment and children's peer relations: A quantitative review. *Developmental Psychology, 37,* 86–100.

Schofield, J. W. (2001). Maximizing the benefits of student diversity: Lessons from school desegregation research. In G. Orfield (Ed.), *Diversity challenged: Evidence on the impact of affirmative action.* Cambridge, MA: Harvard Education Publishing Group.

Schwartz, D., Gorman, A. H., Nakamoto, J., & Toblin, R. L. (2005). Victimization in the peer group and children's academic functioning. *Journal of Educational Psychology, 97,* 425–435.

Schwartz, I. M. (1999). Sexual activity prior to coital initiation: A comparison between males and females. *Archives of Sexual Behavior, 28,* 63–69.

Schwartz, P. (2006). What elicits romance, passion, and attachment, and how do they affect our lives throughout the life cycle? In A. C. Crouter & A. Booth (Eds.), *Romance and sex in adolescence and emerging adulthood: Risks and opportunities.* Mahwah, NJ: Erlbaum.

Schwartz, S. J. (2001). The evolution of Eriksonian and neo-Eriksonian identity theory and research: A review and integration. *Identity, 1,* 7–58.

Schwartz, S. J. (2002). An examination of change processes in identity: Integrating the constructivist and discovery perspectives on identity. *Identity, 2,* 317–339.

Schwartz, S. J. (2006). Predicting identity consolidation from self-construction, eudaimonistic self-discovery, and agentic personality. *Journal of Adolescence, 29,* 777–793.

Schwartz, S. J., Côté, J. E., & Arnett, J. J. (2005). Identity and agency in emerging adulthood: Two developmental routes in the individualization process. *Youth and Society, 37,* 201–229.

Schwartz, S. J., Kurtines, W. M., & Montgomery, M. J. (2005). A comparison of two approaches for facilitating identity exploration processes in emerging adults: An exploratory study. *Journal of Adolescent Research, 20,* 309–345.

Schwartz, S. J., Montgomery, M. J., & Briones, E. (2006). The role of identity in acculturation among immigrant people: Theoretical propositions, empirical questions, and applied recommendations. *Human Development, 49,* 1–30.

Scott, C. S., Arthur, D., Panizo, M. I., & Owen, R. (1989). Menarche: The black experience. *Journal of Adolescent Health Care, 10,* 363–368.

Scott, D. M. (1997). *Contempt and pity: Social policy and the image of the damaged Black psyche 1880–1996.* Chapel Hill: University of North Carolina Press.

Scott, E., & Woolard, J. (2004). The legal regulation of adolescence. In R. M. Lerner & L. Steinberg (Eds.), *Handbook of adolescent psychology.* New York: Wiley.

Scott-Little, C., Hamann, M. S., & Jurs, S. G. (2002). Evaluations of after school programs: A meta-evaluation of methodologies and narrative synthesis of findings. *American Journal of Evaluation, 23,* 387–419.

Seaton, E. K., Scottham, K. M., & Sellers, R. M. (2006). The status model of racial identity development in African American adolescents: Evidence of structure, trajectories, and well-being. *Child Development, 77,* 1416–1426.

Sebald, H. (1986). Adolescents' shifting orientation toward parents and peers: A curvilinear trend over recent decades. *Journal of Marriage and the Family, 48,* 5–13.

Seginer, R. (1998). Adolescents' perception of relationships with older siblings in the context of other close relationships. *Journal of Research on Adolescence, 8,* 287–308.

Seidman, E., Aber, J. L., & French, S. E. (2003). Restructuring the transitions to middle/junior high school: A strengths-based approach to the organization of schooling. In K. Maton, C. Schellenbach, B. Leadbeater, & A. Solarz (Eds.), *Investing in children, families, and communities: Strengths-based research and policy.* Washington, DC: American Psychological Association.

Seidman, E., Allen, L., Aber, J. L., Mitchell, C., & Feinman, J. (1994). The impact of school transitions in early adolescence on the self-esteem and perceived social context of poor urban youth. *Child Development, 65,* 507–522.

Seiffge-Krenke, I. (2003). Testing theories of romantic develoopment from adolescence to young adulthood: Evidence of a developmental sequence. *International Journal of Behavioral Development, 27,* 519–531.

Seiffge-Krenke, I., & Stemmler, M. (2002). Factors contributing to gender differences in depressive symptoms: A test of three developmental models. *Journal of Youth and Adolescence, 31,* 405–417.

Seiffge-Krenke, I. (1995). *Stress, coping, and relationships in adolescence.* Hillsdale, NJ: Erlbaum.

Seligman, M. E. P. (1975). *Helplessness: On depression, development, and death.* New York: W. H. Freeman.

Seligman, M. E. P. (2002). *Authentic happiness: Using the new positive psychology to realize your potential for lasting fulfillment.* New York: Free Press.

Selman, R. L. (1976). Social-cognitive understanding: A guide to educational and clinical practice. In T. Lickona (Ed.), *Moral development and behavior: Theory, research, and social issues.* New York: Holt, Rinehart, and Winston.

Selman, R. L. (1980). *The growth of interpersonal understanding.* Orlando, FL: Academic Press.

Serbin, L. A., & Karp, J. (2004). The intergenerational transfer of psychosocial risk: Mediators of vulnerability and resilience. *Annual Review of Psychology, 55,* 333–363.

Shaaban, B. (1991). *Both right and left handed: Arab women talk about their lives.* Bloomington, IN: Indiana University Press.

Shanahan, M. J., Mortimer, J. T., & Krüger, H. (2002). Adolescence and adult work in the twenty-first century. *Journal of Research on Adolescence, 12,* 99–120.

Sharp, E. H., Caldwell, L. L., Graham, J. W., & Ridenour, T. A. (2006). Individual motivation and parental influence on adolescents' experiences of interest in free time: A longitudinal examination. *Journal of Youth and Adolescence, 35,* 359–372.

Sharp, E. H., Coatsworth, J. D., Darling, N., Cumsille, P., & Ranieri, S. (2007). Gender differences in the self-defining activities and identity experiences of adolescents and emerging adults. *Journal of Adolescence, 30,* 251–269.

Shaw, D. S., Gilliom, M., Ingoldsby, E. M., & Nagin, D. S. (2003). Trajectories leading to
school-age conduct problems. *Developmental Psychology, 39,* 189–200.

Shaw, P., Greenstein, D., Lerch, J., Clasen, L., Lenroot, R., Gogtay, N., et al. (2006). Intellectual ability and cortical development in children and adolescents. *Nature, 440,* 676–679.

Shearer, C. L., Crouter, A. C., & McHale, S. M. (2005). Parents' perceptions of changes in mother-child and father-child relationships during adolescence. *Journal of Adolescent Research, 20,* 662–684.

Sheeber, L., Hops, H., & Davis, B. (2001). Family processes in adolescent depression. *Clinical Child and Family Psychology Review, 4,* 19–35.

Shek, D. T. (1996). Mental health of Chinese adolescents. In S. Lau (Ed.), *Growing up the Chinese way: Chinese child and adolescent development.* Hong Kong: Chinese University Press.

Sheldon, K. M., & Lyubomirsky, S. (2006). Achieving sustainable gains in happiness: Change your actions, not your circumstances. *Journal of Happiness Studies, 7,* 55–86.

Sheley, J. F., & Wright, J. D. (1998). High school youths, weapons, and violence: A national survey. *Research in brief.* Washington, DC: National Institute of Justice.

Shepher, J. (1983). *Incest: A biosocial view.* New York: Academic Press.

Sherif, M., Harvey, O. J., White, B. J., Hood, W. R., & Sherif, C. R. (1961). *Intergroup conflict and cooperation: The Robber's Cave experiment.* Norman, OK: University of Oklahoma Institute of Group Relations.

Sherman, J. D., Honegger, S. D., & McGivern, J. L. (2003). *Comparative indicators of education in the United States and other G-8 countries: 2002.* Washington, DC: U.S. Department of Education, National Center for Education Statistics.

Shipman, G. (1968). The psychodynamics of sex education. *Family Coordinator, 17,* 3–12.

Shipman, K. L., Zeman, J. L., & Stegall, S. (2001). Regulating emotionally expressive behavior: Implications of goals and social partner from middle childhood to adolescence. *Child Study Journal, 31,* 249–268.

Shirtcliff, E. A., Granger, D. A., Booth, A., & Johnson, D. (2005). Low salivary cortisol levels and externalizing behavior problems in youth. *Development and Psychopathology, 17,* 167–184.

Shorter, E. (1975). *The making of the modern family.* New York: Basic Books.

Shroff, H., & Thompson, J. K. (2006). The tripartite influence model of body image and eating disturbance: A replication with adolescent girls. *Body Image, 3,* 17–23.

Shrum, L. J. (2002). Media consumption and perceptions of social reality: Effects and underlying processes. In J. Bryant & D. Zillmann (Eds.), *Media effects: Advances in theory and research* (2nd ed). Mahwah, NJ: Erlbaum.

Shulman, S., Elicker, J., & Sroufe, L. A. (1994). Stages of friendship growth in preadolescence as related to attachment history. *Journal of Social and Personal Relationships, 11,* 341–361.

Shulman, S., & Scharf, M. (2000). Adolescent romantic behaviors and perceptions: Age- and gender- related differences, and links with family and peer relationships. *Journal of Research on Adolescence, 10,* 99–118.

Shultz, T. R., & Horibe, F. (1974). Development of the appreciation of verbal jokes. *Developmental Psychology, 10,* 13–20.

Shweder, R. A. (Ed.). (1998). *Welcome to middle age! (And other cultural fictions).* Chicago: University of Chicago Press.

Shweder, R. A. (2000). The psychology of practice and the practice of the three psychologies. *Asian Journal of Social Psychology, 3,* 207–222.

Shweder, R. A., Goodnow, J., Hatano, G., LeVine, R. A., Markus, H., & Miller, P. (2006). The cultural psychology of development: One mind, many mentalities. In W. Damon & R. Lerner (Eds.), *Handbook of child psychology* (6th ed.). Hoboken, NJ: Wiley.

Shweder, R. A., Mahapatra, M., & Miller, J. (1987). Culture and moral development. In J. Kagan & S. Lamb (Eds.), *The emergence of morality in young children.* Chicago, IL: University of Chicago Press.

Siebenbruner, J., Englund, M. M., Egeland, B., & Hudson, K. (2006). Developmental antecedents of late adolescence substance use patterns. *Development and Psychopathology, 18,* 551–571.

Sieber, J. E., Iannuzzo, R., & Rodriguez, B. (1995). Deception methods in psychology: Have they changed in 23 years? *Ethics and Behavior, 5,* 67–85.

SIECUS. (2005). In their own words: What abstinence-only-until-marriage programs say. Washington, DC: Author.

Siega-Riz, A. M., Cavadini, C., & Popkin, B. M. (2001). U.S. Teens and the nutrient contribution and differences of their selected meal patterns. *Family Economics and Nutrition Review, 13,* 15–26.

Siegel, D. M., Aten, M. J., & Roghmann, K. J. (1998). Self-reported honesty among middle and high school students responding to a sexual behavior questionnaire. *Journal of Adolescent Health, 23,* 20–28.

Siegel, J. M., Yancey, A., Aneshensel, C. S., & Schuler, R. (1999). Body image, perceived pubertal timing and adolescent mental health. *Journal of Adolescent Health, 25,* 155–165.

Siegel-Hinson, R. I., & McKeever, W. F. (2002). Hemispheric specialisation, spatial activity experience, and sex differences on tests of mental rotation ability. *Laterality, 7,* 59–74.

Siegler, R. S. (1998). *Children's thinking* (3rd ed.). Englewood Cliffs, NJ: Prentice-Hall.

Sieving, R. E., Eisenberg, M. E., Pettingell, S., & Skay, C. (2006). Friends' influence on adolescents' first sexual intercourse. *Perspectives on Sexual and Reproductive Health, 38,* 13–19.

Signorielli, N., & Kahlenberg, S. (2001). Television's world of work in the nineties. *Journal of Broadcasting & Electronic Media, 45,* 4–22.

Silbereisen, R., Petersen, A., Albrecht, H., & Kracke, B. (1989). Maturational timing and the development of problem behavior: Longitudinal studies in adolescence. *Journal of Early Adolescence, 9,* 247–268.

Silberman, C. (1970). *Crisis in the classroom.* New York: Random House.

Silk, J. S., Morris, A. S., Kanaya, T., & Steinberg, L. (2003). Psychological control and autonomy granting: Opposite ends of a continuum or distinct constructs? *Journal of Research on Adolescence, 13,* 113–128.

Silverberg, S. B., & Gondoli, D. M. (1996). Autonomy in adolescence: A contextual perspective. In G. R. Adams, R. Montemayor, & T. P. Gullotta (Eds.), *Psychosocial development during adolescence.* Thousand Oaks, CA: Sage.

Silverberg, S., & Steinberg, L. (1990). Psychological well-being of parents at midlife: The impact of early adolescent children. *Developmental Psychology, 26,* 658–666.

Sim, L., & Zeman, J. (2006). The contribution of emotion regulation to body dissatisfaction and disordered eating in early adolescent girls. *Journal of Youth and Adolescence, 35,* 219–228.

Simmons, R. (2002). *Odd girl out: The hidden culture of aggression in girls.* New York: Harcourt.

Simmons, R. G., & Blyth, D. A. (1987). *Moving into adolescence: The impact of pubertal change and school context.* Hawthorn, NY: Aldine de Gruyler.

Simmons, R. G., Blythe, D. A., Van Cleave, E. F., & Bush, D. M. (1979). Entry into early adolescence: The impact of school structure, puberty, and early dating on self-esteem. *American Sociological Review, 44,* 948–967.

Simons, R. L., & Johnson, C. (1996). Mother's parenting. In R. L. Simons & Associates (Eds.), *Understanding differences between divorced and intact families: Stress, interaction, and child outcome.* Thousand Oaks, CA: Sage.

Simons, R. L., Johnson, C., Beaman, J. J., Conger, R. D., & Whitbeck, L. B. (1996). Parents and peer group as mediators of the effect of community structure on adolescent behavior. *American Journal of Community Psychology, 24,* 145–171.

Simons-Morton, B., & Chen, R. S. (2006). Over time relationships between early adolescent and peer substance use. *Addictive Behaviors, 31,* 1211–1223.

Simpson, J. A., Collins, W. A., Tran, S., & Haydon, K. C. (2007). Attachment and the experience and expression of emotions in romantic relationships: A developmental perspective. *Journal of Personality and Social Psychology, 92,* 355–367.

Singer, E. (1981). Reference groups and social evaluation. In M. Rosenberg & R. Turner (Eds.), *Social psychology: Sociological perspectives.* New York: Basic Books.

Singh, K. (1998). Part-time employment in high school and its effect on academic achievement. *Journal of Educational Research, 91,* 131–139.

Singh, K., & Ozturk, M. (2000). Effect of part-time work on high school mathematics and science course taking. *Journal of Educational Research, 94,* 67–74.

Singh, S., & Darroch, J. E. (2000). Adolescent pregnancy and childbearing: Levels and trends in developed countries. *Family Planning Perspectives, 32*(1), 14–23.

Sipe, C. L. (2002). Mentoring programs for adolescents: A research summary. *Journal of Adolescent Health, 31,* 251–260.

Sippola, L., Bukowski, W. M., & Noll, R. B. (1997). Age differences in children's and early adolescents' liking for same-sex and other-sex peers. *Merrill-Palmer Quarterly, 43,* 547–561.

Sirin, S. R., & Rogers-Sirin, L. (2005). Components of school engagement among African-American adolescents. *Applied Developmental Science, 9,* 5–13.

Skaalvik, S., & Skaalvik, E. M. (2004). Gender differences in math and verbal self-concept, performance expectations, and motivation. *Sex Roles, 50,* 241–252.

Skinner, B. F. (1953). *Science and human behavior.* New York: Free Press.

Skinner, E. A., Edge, K., Altman, J., & Sherwood, H. (2003). Searching for the structure of coping: A review and critique of category systems for classifying ways of coping. *Psychological Bulletin, 129,* 216–269.

Skinner, E. A., & Zimmer-Gembeck, M. J. (2007). The development of coping. *Annual Review of Psychology, 58,* 119–144.

Skipper, J. K., Jr., & Nass, G. (1966). Dating behavior: A framework for analysis and an illustration. *Journal of Marriage and the Family, 28,* 412–420.

Skorikov, V., & Vondracek, F. W. (2007). Positive career orientation as an inhibitor of adolescent problem behaviour. *Journal of Adolescence, 30,* 131–146.

Skrzypek, S., Wehmeier, P. M., & Remschmidt, H. (2001). Body image assessment using body size estimation in recent studies on anorexia nervosa: A brief review. *European Child and Adolescent Psychiatry, 10,* 215–221.

Slicker, E. (1998). Relationship of parenting style to behavioral adjustment in graduating high school seniors. *Journal of Youth and Adolescence, 27,* 345–372.

Sloman, S. A. (1996). The empirical case for two systems of reasoning. *Psychological Bulletin, 119,* 3–22.

Slomkowski, C., Rende, R., Conger, K. J., Simons, R. L., & Conger, R. D. (2001). Sisters, brothers, and delinquency: Evaluating social influence during early and middle adolescence. *Child Development, 72,* 271–283.

Smerdon, B. A. (2002). Students' perceptions of membership in their high schools. *Sociology of Education, 75,* 287–305.

Smetana, J. (2000). Middle-class African American adolescents' and parents' conceptions of parental authority and parenting practices: A longitudinal investigation. *Child Development, 71,* 1672–1686.

Smetana, J., & Asquith, P. (1994). Adolescents' and parents' conceptions of parental authority and personal autonomy. *Child Development, 65,* 1147–1162.

Smetana, J., & Chuang, S. (2001). Middle-class African American parents' conceptions of parenting in early adolescence. *Journal of Research on Adolescence, 11,* 177–198.

Smetana, J. G., & Daddis, C. (2002). Domain-specific antecedents of parental psychological control and monitoring: The role of parenting beliefs and practices. *Child Development, 73,* 563–580.

Smetana, J., & Gaines, C. (1999). Adolescent-parent conflict in middle-class African-American families. *Child Development, 70,* 1447–1463.

Smetana, J. Metzger, A., Gettman, D. C., & Campione-Barr, N. (2006). Disclosure and secrecy in adolescent–parent relationships. *Child Development, 77,* 201–217.

Smiler, A. P. (2008). "I wanted to get to know her better": Adolescent boys' dating motives, masculinity ideology, and sexual behavior. *Journal of Adolescence, 31,* 17–32.

Smith, A. L. (1999). Perceptions of peer relationships and physical activity participation in early adolescence. *Journal of Sport & Exercise Psychology, 21,* 329–350.

Smith, E., Dariotis, J., & Potter, S. (2003). *Evaluation of the Pennsylvania Abstinence Education and Related Services Initiative: 1998–2002.* Philadelphia, PA: Maternal and Child Health Bureau of Family Health, Pennsylvania Department of Health.

Smith, E. R., Murphy, J., & Coats, S. (1999). Attachment to groups: Theory and measurement. *Journal of Personality and Social Psychology, 77,* 94–110.

Smith, K. (2002). *Who's minding the kids? Child care arrangements: Spring 1997.* Washington, DC: U.S. Census Bureau.

Smith, N. J. (1980). Excessive weight loss and food aversion in athletes simulating anorexia nervosa. *Pediatrics, 66,* 139.

Smith, P. K., & Brain, P. (2000). Bullying in schools: Lessons from two decades of research. *Aggressive Behavior, 26,* 1–9.

Smith, P. K., Pepler, D., & Rigby, K. (Eds.). (2004). *Bullying in schools: How successful can interventions be?* New York: Cambridge University Press.

Smith, P. K., Shu, S., & Madsen, K. (2001). Characteristics of victims of school bullying: Developmental changes in coping strategies and skills. In J. Juvonen & S. Graham (Eds.), *Peer harassment in school: The plight of the vulnerable and victimized.* New York: Guilford Press.

Smith, T. E., & Leaper, C. (2006). Self-perceived gender typicality and the peer context during adolescence. *Journal of Research on Adolescence, 16,* 91–103.

Smolak, L. (2004). Body image in children and adolescents: Where do we go from here? *Body Image: An International Journal of Research, 1,* 15–28.

Smolak, L., Levine, M., & Gralen, S. (1993). The impact of puberty and dating on eating problems among middle school girls. *Journal of Youth and Adolescence, 22,* 355–368.

Smolak, L., Murnen, S. K., & Thompson, J. K. (2005). Sociocultural influences and muscle building in adolescent boys. *Psychology of Men & Masculinity, 6,* 227–239.

Smolak, L., & Stein, J. A. (2006). The relationship of drive for muscularity to sociocultural factors, self-esteem, physical attributes gender role, and social comparison in middle school boys. *Body Image, 3,* 121–129.

Sneed, J. R., Schwartz, S. J., & Cross, W. E., Jr. (2006). A multicultural critique of identity status theory and research: A call for integration. *Identity, 6,* 61–84.

Snell, E. K., Adam, E. K., & Duncan, G. J. (2007). Sleep and the body mass index and overweight status of children and adolescents. *Child Development, 78,* 309–323.

Snyder, H., Finnegan, T., & Kang, W. (2006). *Easy access to the FBI's Supplementary Homicide Reports: 1980–2003.* Available: http://ojjdp.ncjrs.org/ojstatbb/ezashr.

Snyder, H. N., & Sickmund, M. (2006). *Juvenile offenders and victims: 2006 national report.* Washington, DC: U.S. Department of Justice.

Snyder, T. D., & Hoffman, C. M. (2002). *Digest of education statistics 2001.* Washington, DC: National Center for Education Statistics.

Social Security Administration. (2005). *Social Security Act: Title V: Maternal and Child Health Services Block Grant.* Separate Program for Abstinence Education, SEC 510 [42 U.S.C. 710].

Soenens, B., Duriez, B., Vansteenkiste, M., & Goossens, L. (2007). The intergenerational transmission of empathy-related responding in adolescence: The role of maternal support. *Personality and Social Psychology Bulletin, 33,* 299–311.

Soenens, B., Vansteenkiste, M., Luyckx, K., & Goossens, L. (2006). Parenting and adolescent problem behavior: An integrated model with adolescent self-disclosure and perceived parental knowledge as intervening variables. *Developmental Psychology, 42,* 305–318.

Sommers, C. (2000). *The war against boys.* New York: Simon & Schuster.

Sommers, J., & Vodanovich, S. (2000). Boredom proneness: Its relationship to psychological- and physical-health symptoms. *Journal of Clinical Psychology, 56,* 149–155.

Sonenstein, F. L. (2004). What teenagers are doing right: Changes in sexual behavior over the past decade. *Journal of Adolescent Health, 35,* 77–78.

Sothern, M. S., Loftin, M., Suskind, R. M., Udall, J. N., & Blecker, U. (1999). The health benefits of physical activity in children and adolescents: Implications for chronic disease prevention. *European Journal of Pediatrics, 158,* 271–274.

South, S., & Baumer, E. (2001). Community effects on the resolution of adolescent premarital pregnancy. *Journal of Family Issues, 22,* 1025–1043.

Sowell, T. (1978). Race and IQ reconsidered. In T. Sowell (Ed.), *American ethnic groups.* Washington, DC: Urban Institute.

Spear, L. P. (2000). The adolescent brain and age-related behavioral manifestations. *Neuroscience and biobehavioral reviews, 24,* 417–463.

Spence, J. T., & Helmreich, R. L. (1978). *Masculinity and femininity: Their psychological dimensions, correlates, and antecedents.* Austin, TX: University of Texas Press.

Spencer, R. (2007). "It's not what I expected" A qualitative study of youth mentoring relationship failures. *Journal of Adolescent Research, 22,* 331–354.

Spencer, S. J., Steele, M., & Quinn, D. M. (1999). Stereotype threat and women's math performance. *Journal of Experimental Social Psychology, 35,* 4–28.

Spera, C. (2006). Adolescents' perceptions of parental goals, practices, and styles in relation to their motivation and achievement. *Journal of Early Adolescence, 26,* 456–490.

Spindler, G. D. (1970). The education of adolescents: An anthropological perspective. In D. Ellis (Ed.), *Adolescents: Readings in behavior and development.* Hillsdale, IL: Dryden Press.

Spirito, A., & Oberholser, J. C. (2003). *Evaluating and treating adolescent suicide attempters: From research to practice.* San Diego, CA: Academic Press.

Spiro, M. (1993). Is the Western conception of the self "peculiar" within the context of the world cultures? *Ethos, 21,* 107–153.

Spoth, R. L., Redmond, C., & Shin, C. (2001). Randomized trial of brief family interventions for general populations: Adolescent substance use outcomes 4 years following baseline. *Journal of Consulting and Clinical Psychology, 69,* 627–642.

Sroufe, L. A. (2005). Attachment and development: A prospective, longitudinal study from birth to adulthood. *Attachment & Human Development, 7,* 349–367.

Sroufe, L. A., Bennett, C., Englund, M., Urban, J., & Shulman, S. (1993). The significance of gender boundaries in preadolescence: Contemporary correlates and antecedents of boundary violation and maintenance. *Child Development, 64,* 455–466.

Sroufe, L. A., Egeland, B., Carlson, E., & Collins, W. A. (2005). *The development of the person: The Minnesota study of risk and adaptation from birth to adulthood.* New York: Guilford.

St. George, I. M., Williams, S., & Silva, P. A. (1994). Body size and menarche: The Dunedin study. *Journal of Adolescent Health, 15,* 573–576.

Staffieri, J. R. (1967). A study of social stereotype of body image in children. *Journal of Personality and Social Psychology, 7,* 101–104.

Stanger, C., & Lange, J. E. (1994). Mental representations of social groups: Advances in understanding stereotypes and stereotyping. *Advances in Experimental Social Psychology, 26,* 357–416.

Stanovich, K. E. (1999). *Who is rational?* Mahwah, NJ: Erlbaum.

Starr, L. R., & Davila, J. (in press). Clarifying co-rumination: Associations with internalizing symptoms and romantic involvement among adolescent girls. *Journal of Adolescence, 31.*

Stattin, H., & Magnusson, D. (1990). *Pubertal maturation in female development.* Hillsdale, NJ: Erlbaum.

Steele, C. M. (1997). A threat in the air: How stereotypes shape intellectual identity and performance. *American Psychologist, 52,* 613–629.

Steele, C. M., & Aronson, J. (1995). Stereotype threat and the intellectual test performance of African-Americans. *Journal of Personality and Social Psychology, 69,* 797–811.

Steele, C. M., Spencer, S., & Aronson, J. (2002). Contending with images of one's group: The psychology of stereotype and social identity threat. In M. Zanna (Ed.), *Advances in experimental social psychology.* New York: Academic Press.

Steele, J. R., & Ambady, N. (2006). "Math is hard!" The effect of gender priming on women's attitudes. *Journal of Experimental Social Psychology, 42,* 428–436.

Stein, J. H., & Reiser, L. W. (1994). A study of white middle-class adolescent boys' responses to "semenarche" (the first ejaculation). *Journal of Youth and Adolescence, 23,* 373–384.

Steinberg, L. (1987a, September). Bound to bicker: Pubescent primates leave home for good reasons. Our teens stay with us and squabble. *Psychology Today,* 36–39.

Steinberg, L. (1987b). Single parents, stepparents, and the susceptibility of adolescents to antisocial peer pressure. *Child Development, 58,* 269–275.

Steinberg, L. (1988). Reciprocal relation between parent-child distance and pubertal maturation. *Developmental Psychology, 24,* 122–128.

Steinberg, L. (1989). Pubertal maturation and parent–adolescent distance: An evolutionary perspective. In G. Adams, R. Montemayor, & T. Gullotta (Eds.), *Advances in adolescent development* (Vol. 1). Beverly Hills, CA: Sage.

Steinberg, L. (1990). Autonomy, conflict, and harmony in the family relationship. In S. Feldman & G. Elliott (Eds.), *At the threshold: The developing adolescent.* Cambridge, MA: Harvard University Press.

Steinberg, L. (1996). *Beyond the classroom: Why school reform has failed and what parents need to do.* New York: Simon & Schuster.

Steinberg, L. (2001). We know some things: Parent-adolescent relationships in retrospect and prospect. *Journal of Research on Adolescence, 11,* 1–19.

Steinberg, L. (2005). Psychological control: Style or substance? *New Directions for Child and Adolescent Development, 108,* 71–78.

Steinberg, L. (2007). Risk taking in adolescence: New perspectives from brain and behavioral science. *Current Directions in Psychological Science, 16,* 55–59.

Steinberg, L. (2008). A social neuroscience perspective on adolescent risk-taking. *Developmental Review, 28,* 78–106.

Steinberg, L., Blatt-Eisengart, I., & Cauffman, E. (2006). Patterns of competence and adjustment among adolescents from authoritative, authoritarian, indulgent, and neglectful homes: A replication in a sample of serious juvenile offenders. *Journal of Research on Adolescence, 16,* 47–58.

Steinberg, L., Brown, B. B., & Dornbusch, S. (1996). *Beyond the classroom: Why school reform has failed and what parents need to do.* New York: Simon & Schuster.

Steinberg, L., & Cauffman, F. (1995). The impact of employment on adolescent development. In R. Vasta (Ed.), *Annals of Child Development* (Vol. 11). London: Jessica Kingsley Publishers.

Steinberg, L., Fegley, S., & Dornbusch, S. M. (1993). Negative impact of part time work on adolescent adjustment: Evidence from a longitudinal study. *Developmental Psychology, 29,* 171–180.

Steinberg, L., Lamborn, S., Darling, N., Mounts, N., & Dornbusch, S. (1994). Over-time changes in adjustment and competence among adolescents from authoritative, authoritarian, indulgent, and neglectful families. *Child Development, 65,* 754–770.

Steinberg, L., & Scott, E. (2003). Less guilty by reason of adolescence: Developmental immaturity, diminished responsibility, and the juvenile death penalty. *American Psychologist, 58,* 1009–1018.

Steinberg, L., & Silk, J. S. (2002). Parenting adolescents. In M. Bornstein (Ed.), *Handbook of parenting* (2nd ed., Vol. 1). Mahwah, NJ: Erlbaum.

Steinberg, L., & Silverberg, S. B. (1986). The vicissitudes of autonomy in early adolescence. *Child Development, 57,* 841–851.

Steinberg, L., & Steinberg, W. (1994). *Crossing paths: How your child's adolescence triggers your own crisis.* New York: Simon & Schuster.

Stephens, W. N. (1967). A cross-cultural study of menstrual taboos. In C. S. Ford (Ed.), *Cross-cultural approaches: Readings in comparative research.* New Haven: Human Relations Area Files Press.

Stephenson, J. (2000). AIDS in South Africa takes center stage. *Journal of the American Medical Association, 284,* 165–167.

Stern, K., & McClintock, M. K. (1998). Regulation of ovulation by human pheromones. *Nature, 392,* 177–179.

Sternberg, R. J. (1985). *Beyond IQ: A triarchic theory of human intelligence.* Cambridge: Cambridge University Press.

Sternberg, R. J. (1986). A triangular theory of love. *Psychological Review, 93,* 119–135.

Sternberg, R. J. (1988a). *The triarchic mind: A new theory of human intelligence.* New York: Viking.

Sternberg, R. J. (1988b). Triangulating love. In R. J. Sternberg & M. L. Barnes (Eds.), *The psychology of love.* New Haven, CT: Yale University Press.

Sternberg, R. J. (1997). *Successful intelligence.* New York: Plume.

Sternberg, R. J. (2002). Raising the achievement of all students: Teaching for successful intelligence. *Educational Psychology Review, 14,* 383–393.

Sternberg, R. J., Grigorenko, E. L., & Bundy, D. A. (2001). The predictive value of IQ. *Merrill-Palmer Quarterly, 47,* 1–41.

Sternberg, R. J., Grigorenko, E. L., & Kidd, K. K. (2005). Intelligence, race, and genetics. *American Psychologist, 60,* 46–59.

Sternberg, R. J., & Nigro, G. (1980). Developmental patterns in the solution of verbal analogies. *Child Development, 51,* 27–38.

Sternberg, R. J., Torff, B., & Grigorenko, E. L. (1999). Teaching triarchically improves school achievement. *Journal of Educational Psychology, 90,* 374–384.

Sternberg, R. J., & Williams, W. M. (2002). *Educational Psychology.* Boston: Allyn-Bacon.

Stevens, R. J., & Slavin, R. E. (1995). Effects of a cooperative learning approach in reading and writing on academically handicapped and nonhandicapped students. *Elementary School Journal, 95,* 241–262.

Stevens, T., Wang, K., Olivárez, A., Jr., & Hamman, D. (2007). Use of self-perspectives and their sources to predict the mathematics enrollment intentions of girls and boys. *Sex Roles, 56,* 351–363.

Stevenson, D., & Baker, D. (1987). The family-school relation and the child's school performance. *Child Development, 58,* 1348–1357.

Stevenson, H. W., Chen, C., & Lee, S. (1993). Mathematics achievement of Chinese, Japanese, and American children: Ten years later. *Science, 259,* 53–58.

Stevenson, H. W., & Lee, S. Y. (1990). Contexts of achievement: A study of American, Chinese, and Japanese children. *Monographs of the Society for Research in Child Development, 55*(1–2), serial no. 221.

Stevenson, H. W., & Stigler, J. (1992). *The learning gap: Why our schools are failing and what we can learn from Japanese and Chinese education.* New York: Simon & Schuster.

Stewart, S. M., Bond, M. H., Ho, L. M., Zaman, R. M., Dar, R., & Anwar, M. (2000). Perceptions of parents and adolescent outcomes in Pakistan. *British Journal of Developmental Psychology, 18,* 335–352.

Stewart, S. M., Kennard, B. D., Lee, P. W. H., Hughes, C. W., Mayes, T. L., Emslie, G. J., & Lewinsohn, P. M. (2004). A cross-cultural investigation of cognitions and depressive symptoms in adolescents. *Journal of Abnormal Psychology, 113,* 248–257.

Stice, E. (2002). Risk and maintenance factors for eating pathology: A meta-analytic review. *Psychological Bulletin, 128,* 825–848.

Stice, E., & Martinez, E. E. (2005). Cigarette smoking prospectively predicts retarded physical growth among female adolescents. *Journal of Adolescent Health, 37,* 363–370.

Stice, E., Presnell, K., & Bearman, S. K. (2001). Relation of early menarche to depression, eating disorders, substance abuse, and comorbid psychopathology among adolescent girls. *Developmental Psychology, 37,* 608–619.

Stice, E., Presnell, K., & Spangler, D. (2002). Risk factors for binge eating onset in adolescent girls: A 2-year prospective study. *Health Psychology, 21,* 131–138.

Stiefel, L., Latarola, P., Fruchter, N. A., & Berne, R. (1998). *The effects of size of student body on school costs and performance in NYC high schools.* New York: Institute for Education and Social Policy.

Still, B. (2002). *Officials under assault—Update 2002.* NASO Special report. Racine, WI: National Association of Sports Officials.

Stipek, D. (2002). *Motivation to learn: From theory to practice* (4th ed.). Needham Heights, MA: Prentice-Hall.

Stocker, C. M., Burwell, R. A., & Briggs, M. L. (2002). Sibling conflict in middle childhood predicts children's adjustment in early adolescence. *Journal of Family Psychology, 16,* 50–57.

Stodghill, R. (1998, June 15). Where'd you learn that? *Time,* pp. 52–59.

Stone, L. B., & Hankin, B. L. (2007, March). *Co-rumination, stress generation, and internalizing symptoms during adolescence.* Presented at the meeting of the Society for Research in Child Development, Boston.

Stone, M. R., Barber, B. L., & Eccles, J. S. (2002, April). *Adolescent "crowd" clusters: An adolescent perspective on persons and patterns.* Paper presented at the meeting of the Society for Research on Adolescence, New Orleans.

Stone, M. R., & Brown, B. B. (1998). In the eye of the beholder: Adolescents' perceptions of peer crowd stereotypes. In R. Muuss (Ed.), *Adolescent behavior and society: A book of readings* (5th ed.). San Francisco: Jossey-Bass.

Stone, M. R., & Brown, B. B. (1999). Identity claims and projections: Descriptions of self and crowds in secondary school. In J. A. McLellan & M. J. V. Pugh (Eds.), *The role of peer groups in adolescent social identity: Exploring the importance of stability and change.* San Francisco: Jossey-Bass.

Stoneman, Z., Brody, G. H., & MacKinnon, C. E. (1986). Same-sex and cross-sex siblings: Activity choices, roles, behavior, and gender stereotypes. *Sex Roles, 15,* 495–511.

Stonequist, E. V. (1935). The problem of marginal man. *American Journal of Sociology, 7,* 1–12.

Storch, E. A., Brassard, M. R., & Masia-Warner, C. L. (2003). The relationship of peer victimization to social anxiety and loneliness in adolescence. *Child Study Journal, 33,* 1–18.

Streitmatter, J. (1993). Gender differences in identity development: An examination of longitudinal data. *Adolescence, 28,* 55–66.

Stringer, C. B., & McKie, R. (1996). *African exodus: The origins of modern humanity.* New York: Henry Holt.

Strober, M., Freeman, R., Lampert, C., Diamond, J., & Kaye, W. (2000). Controlled family study of anorexia nervosa and bulimia nervosa: Evidence of shared liability and transmission of partial syndromes. *American Journal of Psychiatry, 157,* 393–401.

Strough, J., & Berg, C. A. (2000). Goals as a mediator of gender differences in high-affiliation dyadic conversations. *Developmental Psychology, 36,* 117–125.

Styne, D. (2001). Puberty. In D. Gardner & F. S. Greenspan (Eds.), *Basic and clinical endocrinology* (6th ed.). E. Norwalk, CT: Appleton & Lange.

Suarez-Orozco, C., & Suarez-Orozco, M. (1996). *Transformations: Migration, family life and achievement motivation among Latino adolescents.* Palo Alto, CA: Stanford University Press.

Sue, S., & Okazaki, S. (1990). Asian-American educational achievements: A phenomenon in search of an explanation. *American Psychologist, 45,* 913–920.

Suh, E. M. (2002). Culture, identity consistency, and subjective well-being. *Journal of Personality and Social Psychology, 83,* 1378–1391.

Suicide Prevention Resource Center (2005). *Teens.* Available: www.sprc.org/featured_resources/customized/pdf/teens.pdf.

Sullivan, H. S. (1953). *Conceptions of modern psychiatry.* New York· Norton.

Suls, J., & Wheeler, L. (Eds.). (2000). *Handbook of social comparison: Theory and research.* New York: Kluwer.

Summers-Effler, E. (2004). Little girls in women's bodies: Social interaction and the strategizing of early breast development. *Sex Roles, 51,* 29–44.

Sun, Y. (2001). Family environment and adolescents' well-being before and after parents' marital disruption: A longitudinal analysis. *Journal of Marriage and the Family, 63,* 697–713.

Suomi, S. J. (2000). A biobehavioral perspective on developmental psychopathology: Excessive aggression and serotonergic dysfunction in monkeys. In A. J. Sameroff, M. Lewis, & S. M. Miller, (Eds.), *Handbook of developmental psychopathology* (2nd ed.). New York: Plenum.

Super, D. (1957). *The psychology of careers.* New York: Harper.

Super, D. (1990). A life span, life-space approach to career development. In D. Brown & L. Brooks (Eds.), *Career choice and development: Applying contemporary theories to practice* (2nd ed.). San Francisco: Jossey-Bass.

Surbey, M. (1990). Family composition, stress, and human menarche. In F. Bercovitch & T. Zeigler (Eds.), *The socioendocrinology of primate reproduction.* New York: Alan R. Liss.

Surgeon General. (1999). Children and mental health. In *Mental health: A report of the Surgeon General.* Washington, DC: Government Printing Office.

Susman, E. J. (1997). Modeling developmental complexity in adolescence: Hormones and behavior in context. *Journal of Research on Adolescence, 7,* 283–306.

Susman, E. J., Dorn, L. D., & Schiefelbein, V. L. (2003). Puberty, sexuality, and health. In R. M. Lerner, M. A. Easterbrooks, & J. Mistry (Eds.), *Handbook of psychology: Vol 6, Developmental psychology.* New York: Wiley.

Susman, E. J., & Rogol, A. (2004). Puberty and psychological development. In R. M. Lerner & L. Steinberg (Eds.), *Handbook of adolescent psychology.* New York: Wiley.

Sutton, M. J., Brown, J. D., Wilson, K. M., & Klein, J. D. (2002). Shaking the tree of knowledge for forbidden fruit: Where adolescents learn about sexuality and contraception. In J. D. Brown, J. R. Steele, & K. Walsh-Childers (Eds.), *Sexual teens, sexual media.* Mahwah, NJ: Erlbaum.

Svenson, O. (1981). Are we all less risky and more skillful than our fellow drivers? *Acta Psychologica, 47,* 143–148.

Swanson, H. L. (1999). What develops in working memory? A life span perspective. *Developmental Psychology, 35,* 986–1000.

Sypeck, M. F., Gray, J. J., & Ahrens, A. H. (2004). No longer just a pretty face: Fashion magazines' depictions of ideal female beauty from 1959–1999. *International Journal of Eating Disorders, 36,* 342–347.

Szkrybalo, J., & Ruble, D. N. (1999). "God made me a girl": Sex-category constancy judgments and explanations revisited. *Developmental Psychology, 35,* 392–402.

Tajfel, H. (1981). *Human groups and social categories: Studies in social psychology.* Cambridge, UK: Cambridge University Press.

Tajfel, H., & Turner, J. C. (1979). An integrative theory of intergroup relations. In W. G. Austin & S. Worchel (Eds.), *The social psychology of intergroup relations.* Monterey, CA: Brooks/Cole.

Tajfel, H., & Turner, J. C. (1986). The social identity theory of intergroup behavior. In S. Worchel & W. G. Austin (Eds.), *Psychology of intergroup relations* (2nd ed.). Chicago: Nelson-Hall.

Takanishi, R. (2000). Preparing adolescents for social change. In L. J. Crockett & R. K. Silbereisen (Eds.), *Negotiating adolescence in times of social change.* New York: Cambridge University Press.

Talbot, M. (2002, February 24). Girls just want to be mean. *New York Times Magazine,* pp. 24–65.

Tamis-LeMonda, C. S., Way, N., Hughes, D., Yoshikawa, H., Kalman, R. K., & Niwa, E. Y. (2008). Parents' goals for children: The dynamic coexistence of individualism and collectivism in cultures and individuals. *Social Development, 17,* 183–209.

Tannen, D. (1990). *You just don't understand!* New York: Ballantine.

Tanner, J. M. (1965). The relationship of puberty to other maturity indicators and body composition in man. *Symposia of the Society for the Study of Human Biology, 6,* 211.

Tanner, J. M. (1972). Sequence, tempo, and individual variation in growth and development of boys and girls aged twelve to sixteen. In J. Kagan & R. Coles (Eds.), *Twelve to sixteen: Early adolescence.* New York: Norton.

Tanner, J. M. (1978). *Fetus into man: Physical growth from conception to maturity.* Cambridge, MA: Harvard University Press.

Tanner, J. M. (1991). Menarche, secular trend in age of. In R. M. Lerner, A. C. Petersen, & J. Brooks-Gunn (Eds.), *Encyclopedia of adolescence* (Vol. 2). New York: Garland.

Tappan, M. B. (1998). Sociocultural psychology and caring psychology: Exploring Vygotsky's "hidden curriculum." *Educational Psychologist, 33,* 23–33.

Tarrant, M. (2002). Adolescent peer groups and social identity. *Social Behavior, 11,* 110–123.

Tasker, F. L., & Golombok, S. (1998). The role of co-mothers in planned lesbian-led families. In G. A. Dunne (Ed.), *Living difference: Lesbian perspectives on work and family life.* New York: Harrington Park Press.

Tattersall, I. (1997). *The fossil trail: How we know what we think we know about human evolution.* New York: Oxford University Press.

Tatum, B. (1997). *"Why are all the Black kids sitting together in the cafeteria?" and other conversations about race.* New York: Basic Books.

Taylor, C. A., Liang, B., Tracy, A. J., Williams, L. M., & Seigle, P. (2002). Gender differences in middle school adjustment, physical fighting, and social skills: Evaluation of a social competency program. *Journal of Primary Prevention, 23,* 259–272.

Taylor, R. D. (1996). Adolescents' and perceptions of kinship support and family management practices: Association with adolescent adjustment in African American families. *Developmental Psychology, 32,* 687–695.

Taylor, R. D. (1997). The effects of economic and social stressors on parenting and adolescent adjustment in African-American families. In R. D. Taylor & M. C. Wang (Eds.), *Social and emotional adjustment and family relations in ethnic minority families.* Mahwah, NJ: Erlbaum.

Taylor, R. D., & Roberts, D. (1995). Kinship support and maternal and adolescent well-being in economically disadvantaged African-American families. *Child Development, 66,* 1585–1597.

Teitler, J. O. (2002). Trends in youth sexual initiation and fertility in developed countries: 1960–1995. *Annals of the American Academy of Political Science Studies, 580,* 134–152.

Tenenbaum, H. R., & Leaper, C. (2003). Parent-child conversations about science: The socialization of gender inequities? *Developmental Psychology, 39,* 34–47.

Tenenbaum, H. R., Snow, C. E., Roach, K. A., & Kurland, B. (2005). Talking and reading science: Longitudinal data on sex differences in mother-child conversations in low-income families. *Applied Developmental Psychology, 26,* 1–19.

Terry, R., & Coie, J. D. (1991). A comparison of methods for defining sociometric status among children. *Developmental Psychology, 27,* 867–880.

Terry-Humen, E., Manlove, J., & Cottingham, S. (2006). *Trends and recent estimates: Sexual activity among U.S. teens.* Washington, DC: Child Trends.

Teti, D. M. (2002). Retrospect and prospect in the study of sibling relationships. In J. P. McHale & W. S. Grolnick (Eds.), *Retrospect and prospect in the study of families.* Mahwah, NJ: Erlbaum.

Thatcher, R. W., Lyon, G. R., Rumsey, J., & Krasnegor, N. (Eds.). (1996). *Developmental neuroimaging: Mapping the development of brain and behavior.* San Diego, CA: Academic Press.

Theokas, C., Almerigi, J. B., Lerner, R. M., Dowling, E. M., Benson, P. L., Scales, P. C., & von Eye, A. (2005). Conceptualizing and modeling individual and ecological asset components of thriving in early adolescence. *Journal of Early Adolescence, 25,* 113–143.

Theokas, C., & Lerner, R. M. (2006). Observed ecological assets in families, schools, and neighborhoods: Conceptualization, measurement, and relations with positive and negative developmental outcomes. *Applied Developmental Science, 10,* 61–74.

Thomas, A., & Chess, S. (1986). The New York longitudinal study: From infancy to early adult life. In R. Plomin & J. Dunn (Eds.), *The study of temperament: Changes, continuities, and challenges.* Hillsdale, NJ: Erlbaum.

Thomas, F., Renaud, F., Benefice, E., de Meeüs, T., & Guegan, J.-F. (2001). International variability of ages at menarche and menopause: Patterns and main determinants. *Human Biology, 73,* 271–290.

Thomas, J. J., & Daubman, K. A. (2001). The relationship between friendship quality and self-esteem in adolescent girls and boys. *Sex Roles, 45,* 53–65.

Thomas, K. M., Drevets, W. C., Dahl, R. E., Ryan, N. D., Birmaher, B., Eccard, C. H., et al. (2001). Amygdala response to fearful faces in anxious and depressed children. *Archives of General Psychiatry, 58,* 1057–1063.

Thompson, D. R., Obarzanek, E., Franko, D. L., Barton, B. A., Morrison, J., Biro, F. M., et al. (2007). Childhood overweight and cardiovascular disease risk factors: The National Heart, Lung, and Blood Institute Growth and Health Study. *Journal of Pediatrics, 150,* 18–25.

Thompson, J. K., & Smolak, L. (2001). *Body image, eating disorders, and obesity in childhood and adolescence.* Washington, DC: American Psychological Association.

Thompson, K., & Haninger, K. (2001). Violence in E-rated video games. *Journal of the American Medical Association, 286,* 591–598.

Thompson, S. H., Corwin, S. J., Rogan, T. J., & Sargent, R. G. (1999). Body size beliefs and weight concerns among mothers and their adolescent children. *Journal of Child & Family Studies, 7,* 91–108.

Thompson, S. H., Corwin, S. J., & Sargent, R. G. (1997). Body size beliefs and weight concerns of fourth-grade children. *International Journal of Eating Disorders, 21,* 279–284.

Thompson, S. H., Sargent, R. G., & Kemper, K. A. (1996). Black and White adolescent males' perceptions of ideal body size. *Sex Roles, 34,* 391–406.

Thomsen, S., Weber, M., & Brown, L. (2001). The relationship between health and fitness magazine reading and eating-disordered weight-loss methods among high school girls. *American Journal of Health Education, 32,* 133–138.

Thornberry, T. P., Krohn, M. D., Lizotte, A. J., Smith, C. A., & Tobin, K. (2003). *Gangs and delinquency in developmental perspective.* New York: Cambridge University Press.

Thorndike, R. L., Hagen, E. P., & Sattler, J. M. (1986). *The Stanford-Binet Intelligence Scale (4th edition): Guide for administering and scoring.* Chicago: Riverside.

Thorne, B. (1993). *Gender play: Girls and boys in school.* New Brunswick, NJ: Rutgers University Press.

Tienari, P., Wynne, L. C., Laksy, K., Moring, J., Nieminen, P., Sorri, A., et al. (2003). Genetic boundaries of the schizophrenia spectrum: Evidence from the Finnish adoptive family study of schizophrenia. *American Journal of Psychiatry, 160,* 1587–1594.

Tienari, P., Wynne, L. C., Moring, J., Lahti, I., Maarala, M., Sorri, A., et al. (1994). The Finnish adoption family study of schizophrenia: Implications for family research. *British Journal of Psychiatry, 164* (Suppl. 23), 20–26.

Tierney, J. (2001, August 5). Here come the alpha pups. *New York Times Magazine,* p. 38.

Tierney, J. P., Grossman, J. B., & Resch, N. L. (1995). *Making a difference: An impact study of Big Brothers/Big Sisters.* Philadelphia: Public/Private Ventures.

Tilton-Weaver, L. C., & Galambos, N. (2002, August). *Parents' peer management, adolescents' friendships, and the parent-adolescent relationship.* Paper presented at the meeting of the International Society for the Study of Behavioral Development, Ottawa, Ontario, Canada.

Tilton-Weaver, L. C., & Galambos, N. L. (2003). Adolescents' characteristics and parents' beliefs as predictors of parents' peer management behaviors. *Journal of Research on Adolescence, 13,* 269–300.

Tilton-Weaver, L. C., & Marshall, S. K. (2003). *Parents' knowledge and adolescents' problem behaviors: Linkages mediated by adolescents' information management.* Paper presented at the meeting of the Society for Research in Child Development, Tampa, FL.

Timmer, S. G., Eccles, J., & O'Brien, K. (1985). How children use time. In F. T. Juster & F. P. Stafford (Eds.), *Time, goods, and well-being.* Ann Arbor, MI: Institute for Social Research.

TIMSS. (1997). *TIMSS highlights of international results.* Chestnut Hill, MA: TIMSS International Study Center, Boston College.

Tizon, A. (1996, February 6). Sharp surge in teen violence puzzles town. *Seattle Times,* pp. B1–B2.

Tobin-Richards, M. H., Boxer, A. M., & Petersen, A. C. (1983). The psychological significance of pubertal change: Sex differences in perceptions of self during early adolescence. In J. Brooks-Gunn & A. C. Petersen (Eds.), *Girls at puberty: Biological and psychosocial perspectives.* New York: Plenum.

Tolkien, J. R. R. (1965). Foreword. *The fellowship of the ring* (rev. ed.). Boston: Houghton Mifflin.

Tolman, D. L., Impett, E. A., Tracy, A. J., & Michael, A. (2006). Looking good, sounding good: Femininity ideology and adolescent girls' mental health. *Psychology of Women Quarterly, 30,* 85–95.

Tolman, D. L., Spencer, R., Harmon, T., Rosen-Reynoso, M., & Striepe, M. (2004). Getting close, staying cool: Early adolescent boys' experiences with romantic relationships. In N. Way & J. Y. Chu (Eds.), *Adolescent boys: Exploring diverse cultures of boyhood.* New York: New York University Press.

Torney-Purta, J., Lehmann, R., Oswald, H., & Schulz, W. (2001). *Citizenship and education in twenty-eight countries: Civic knowledge and engagement at age fourteen.* Amsterdam, Netherlands: International Association for the Evaluation of Educational Achievement.

Tracey, T. J. G., & Robbins, S. B. (2005). Stability of interests across ethnicity and gender: A longitudinal examination of grades 8 through 12. *Journal of Vocational Behavior, 67,* 335–364.

Tracy, D. M. (1987). Toys, spatial ability, and science and mathematics achievement: Are they related? *Sex Roles, 17,* 115–138.

Trautner, H. M., Ruble, D. N., Cyphers, L., Kirsten, B., Behrendt, R., & Hartmann, P. (2005). Rigidity and flexibility of gender stereotypes in childhood: Developmental or differential? *Infant and Child Development, 14,* 365–381.

Trebay, G. (2003, September 2). The skin wars start earlier and earlier. *New York Times,* p. B8.

Treffert, D. A., & Wallace, G. L. (2002, June). Islands of genius. *Scientific American, 286,* 76–85.

Tremblay, R. E., & Nagin, D. S. (2005). The developmental origins of physical aggression in humans. In R. E. Tremblay, W. W. Hartup, & J. Archer (Eds.), *Developmental origins of aggression.* New York: Guilford.

Trenholm, C., Devaney, B., Fortson, K., Quay, L., Wheeler, J., & Clark, M. (2007). *Impacts of four Title V, Section 510 abstinence education programs: Final report.* Princeton, NJ: Mathematica Policy Research.

Triandis, H. C. (1995). *Individualism and collectivism.* Boulder, CO: Westview Press.

Triandis, H. C. (1996). The psychological measurement of cultural syndromes. *American Psychologist, 51,* 407–415.

Triandis, H. C. (2001). Individualism-collectivism and personality. *Journal of Personality, 69,* 907–924.

Triandis, H. C., & Gelfand, M. (1998). Converging measurements of horizontal and vertical individualism and collectivism. *Journal of Personality and Social Psychology, 74,*118–128.

Triandis, H. C., & Suh, E. M. (2002). Cultural influences on personality. *Annual Review of Psychology, 53,* 133–160.

Troiano, R. P., Briefel, R. R., Carroll, M. D., & Bialostosky, K. (2000). Energy and fat intakes of children and adolescents in the United States: Data from the National Health and Nutrition Examination Surveys. *American Journal of Clinical Nutrition, 72* (5 Suppl), 1343S–1353S.

Troiano, R. P., & Flegal, K. M. (1998). Overweight children and adolescents: Description, epidemiology, and demographics. *Pediatrics, 101,* 497–504.

Tryggvadottir, L., Tulinius, H., & Larusdottir, M. A. (1994). Decline and a halt in mean age at menarche in Iceland. *Annals of Human Biology, 21,* 179–186.

Trzesniewski, K. H., Donnellan, M. B., Moffitt, T. E., Robins, R. W., Poulton, R., & Caspi, A. (2006). Low self-esteem during adolescence predicts poor health, criminal behavior, and limited economic prospects during adulthood. *Developmental Psychology, 42,* 381–390.

Trzesniewski, K. H., Donnellan, M. B., & Robins, R. W. (2003). Stability of self-esteem across the life span. *Journal of Personality and Social Psychology, 84,* 205–220.

Tucker, C. J., McHale, S. M., & Crouter, A. C. (2001). Conditions of sibling support in adolescence. *Journal of Family Psychology, 15,* 254–271.

Tucker, C. J., Updegraff, K. A., McHale, S. M., & Crouter, A. C. (1999). Older siblings as socializers of younger siblings' empathy. *Journal of Early Adolescence, 19,* 176–198.

Tucker, C. J., & Winzeler, A. (2007). Adolescent siblings' daily discussions: Connections to perceived academic, athletic, and peer competency. *Journal of Research on Adolescence, 17,* 145–152.

Turiel, E. (2002). *The culture of morality: Social development, context, and conflict.* Cambridge, UK: Cambridge University Press.

Turiel, E. (2006). The development of morality. In W. Damon & R. Lerner (Eds.), *Handbook of child psychology* (6th ed.). New York: Wiley.

Turing, A. M. (1963). Computing machinery and intelligence. In E. A. Feigenbaum & J. Feldman (Eds.), *Computers and thought.* New York: McGraw-Hill.

Turkheimer, E., & Waldron, M. (2000). Nonshared environment: A theoretical, methodological, and quantitative review. *Psychological Bulletin, 126,* 78–108.

Turnage, B. F. (2004). Influences on adolescent African American females' global self-esteem: Body image and ethnic identity. *Journal of Ethnic & Cultural Diversity in Social Work, 13*(4), 27–45.

Turner, J. C. (1995). The influence of classroom contexts on young children's motivation for literacy. *Reading Research Quarterly, 30,* 410–441.

Turner, J. C., Midgley, C., Meyer, D. K., Gheen, M., Anderman, E. M., Kang, Y., & Patrick, H. (2002). The classroom environment and students' reports of avoidance strategies in mathematics: A multimethod study. *Journal of Educational Psychology, 94,* 88–106.

Turner, S., & Lapan, R. T. (2002). Career self-efficacy and perceptions of parent support in adolescent career development. *Career Development Quarterly, 51,* 44–55.

Turner, S. L., Hamilton, H., Jacobs, M., Angood, L. M., & Dwyer, D. H. (1997). The influence of fashion magazines on the body image satisfaction of college women: An exploratory analysis. *Adolescence, 32,* 603–614.

Turner, V. W. (1969). *The ritual process.* Chicago: Aldine.

Twenge, J. M., & Crocker, J. (2002). Race and self-esteem: Meta-analyses comparing Whites, Blacks, Hispanics, Asians, and American Indians and comment on Gray-Little and Hafdahl (2000). *Psychological Bulletin, 128,* 371–408.

Twenge, J. M., & Nolen-Hoeksema, S. (2002). Age, gender, race, socioeconomic status, and birth cohort differences on the Children's Depression Inventory: A meta-analysis. *Journal of Abnormal Psychology, 111,* 578–588.

Tyack, D. B. (1990). *The one best system: A history of American urban education.* Cambridge, MA: Harvard University Press.

U.S. Bureau of the Census. (1999). *Current population survey.* Washington, DC: Government Printing Office.

U.S. Bureau of the Census. (2000). *Current population survey, March 2000.* Washington, DC: Government Printing Office.

U.S. Bureau of the Census. (2001, March). *CPS Annual Demographic Survey, March Supplement.* Available: ferret.bls.census.gov/macro/032001/perinc/new03_001.htm.

U.S. Bureau of the Census. (2001a). Families, by presence of own children under 18: 1960 to present. Washington, DC: Government Printing Office. (Internet release date: June 29, 2001).

U.S. Bureau of the Census. (2001b). Living arrangements of children under 18 years old: 1960 to present. Washington, DC: Government Printing Office. (Internet release date: June 29, 2001).

U.S. Bureau of the Census. (2002). *Statistical abstract of the United States* (122nd ed.). Washington, DC: Government Printing Office.

U.S. Bureau of the Census. (2003). Married couples by labor force status of spouse: 1986 to present. Washington, DC: Government Printing Office. (Internet release date: June 12, 2003).

U. S. Bureau of the Census. (2004). *U.S. interim projections by age, sex, race, and Hispanic origin.* Washington, DC: Government Printing Office.

U.S. Bureau of the Census. (2006a). *Current population survey: Annual social and economic supplement.* Washington, DC: Government Printing Office.

U.S. Bureau of the Census. (2006b). *Educational attainment in the United States: 2005.* Washington, DC: U.S. Government Printing Office.

U.S. Bureau of the Census. (2006c). *Statistical abstract of the United States, 2007.* Washington, DC: U.S. Government Printing Office.

U.S. Bureau of the Census. (2006d). *National population estimates: Characteristics.* Available: www.census.gov/popest/national/asrh/NC-EST2005-sa.htm.

U.S. Department of Commerce. (2002). *A nation online: How Americans are expanding their use of the Internet.* Washington, DC: Author.

U.S. Department of Commerce, Bureau of the Census. (1940). *Characteristics of the population.* Washington, DC: U.S. Government Printing Office.

U.S. Department of Education, Office of the Under Secretary. (2003). *When schools stay open late: The national evaluation of the 21st-Century Learning Centers program, first year findings.* Washington, DC: Author.

U.S. Department of Health and Human Services. (2000a). *Healthy people 2010: Understanding and improving health* (2nd ed.). Washington, DC: U.S. Government Printing Office.

U.S. Department of Health and Human Services. (2000b). *Physical activity and health.* Washington, DC: U.S. Government Printing Office.

U.S. Department of Health and Human Services. (2005a). *Dietary guidelines for Americans 2005.* Washington, DC: Author.

U.S. Department of Health and Human Services. (2005b). *Suicide warning signs.* Available: www.mentalhealth.samhsa.gov/publications/allpubs/walletcard/_pdf/nsple.pdf.

U.S. Department of Health and Human Services, Office of the Assistant Secretary for Planning and Evaluation. (2001). *Trends in the well-being of America's children and youth—2000.* Washington, DC: Author.

U.S. Department of Labor. (2000). *Report on the youth labor force.* Washington, DC: Author.

U.S. Department of Labor, Wage and Hour and Public Contracts Division. (1968). *Child labor laws historical development.* Washington, DC: Author.

U.S. Public Health Service. (1999). *The Surgeon General's call to action to prevent suicide.* Washington, DC: Author.

Ueda, R. (1987). *Avenues to adulthood: The origins of the high school and social mobility in an American suburb.* New York: Cambridge University Press.

Ullrich, M., & Kreppner, K. (2002, April). *Family communication during transition to adolescence: Parent-parent relationship and communication dynamics in the coparenting setting.* Paper presented at the meeting of the Society for Research on Adolescence, New Orleans.

Umaña-Taylor, A. J. (2004). Ethnic identity and self-esteem: Examining the role of social context. *Journal of Adolescence, 27,* 139–149.

Umaña-Taylor, A. J., Bhanot, R., & Shin, N. (2006). Ethnic identity formation during adolescence: The critical role of families. *Journal of Family Issues, 27,* 390–414.

Umaña-Taylor, A. J., & Fine, M. A. (2004). Examining ethnic identity among Mexican-origin adolescents living in the United States. *Hispanic Journal of Behavioral Sciences, 26,* 36–59.

UNAIDS. (2001a). *Children and young people in a world of AIDS.* Geneva: Author.

UNAIDS. (2001b). *AIDS epidemic update, December 2001.* Geneva: Author.

UNAIDS. (2006). *2006 report on the global AIDS epidemic.* Geneva, Switzerland: Author.

Underwood, M. K. (2003). *Social aggression among girls.* New York: Guilford Press.

UNESCO. (1999). *Statistical yearbook.* New York: United Nations.

UNESCO. (2003a). *Literacy skills for the world of tomorrow.* Montreal: UNESCO Institute for Statistics.

UNESCO. (2003b). *Literacy skills for the world of tomorrow: Further results from PISA 2000.* Paris: Author.

UNESCO. (2005). *Global education digest 2005: Comparing education statistics across the world.* Montreal: UNESCO Institute for Statistics.

UNICEF. (2000). *A league table of child poverty in rich nations.* Innocenti Report Card No. 1. Florence, Italy: UNICEF Innocenti Research Centre.

UNICEF. (2001). *Profiting from abuse: An investigation into the sexual exploitation of our children.* New York: Author.

UNICEF. (2002). *Children on the edge: Protecting children from sexual exploitation and trafficking in East Asia and the Pacific.* Bangkok: Author.

UNICEF. (2003). *Africa's orphaned generations.* New York: Author.

UNICEF. (2005). *Child poverty in rich countries, 2005.* Innocenti Report Card No. 6. Florence, Italy: UNICEF Innocenti Research Centre.

UNICEF. (2007). *The state of the world's children 2007.* New York: Author.

United Nations. (2004). *World population prospects: The 2004 revision.* New York: Author.

Upchurch, D. M., & Kusunoki, Y. (2006). Adolescent sexual relationships and reproductive health outcomes: Theoretical and methodological challenges. In A. Booth & A. Crouter (Eds.), *Romance and sex in adolescence and emerging adulthood: Risks and opportunities.* Mahwah, NJ: Erlbaum.

Updegraff, K. A., Booth, A., & Thayer, S. M. (2002, April). *Hormones and adolescents' peer experiences: The moderating role of the parent-adolescent relationship.* Paper presented at the meeting of the Society for Research on Adolescence, New Orleans.

Updegraff, K. A., McHale, S. M., & Crouter, A. C. (2000). Adolescents' sex-typed friendship experiences: Does having a sister versus a brother matter? *Child Development, 71,* 1597–1610.

Urberg, K. A, Degirmencioglu, S. M., Tolson, J. M., & Halliday-Scher, K. (1995). The structure of adolescent peer networks. *Developmental Psychology, 31,* 540–547.

Urberg, K. A., Degirmencioglu, S. M., Tolson, J. M., & Halliday-Scher, K. (2000). Adolescent social crowds: Measurement and relationship to friendships. *Journal of Adolescent Research, 15,* 427–445.

Urdan, T. (2004). Can achievement goal theory guide school reform? In P. R. Pintrich & M. L. Maehr (Eds.), *Motivating students, improving schools: The legacy of Carol Midgley (Advances in motivation and achievement, Vol. XIII).* Greenwich, CT: JAI.

Urdan, T., & Midgley, C. (2003). Changes in the perceived classroom goal structure and pattern of adaptive learning during early adolescence. *Contemporary Educational Psychology, 28,* 524–551.

Urdan, T., & Schoenfelder, E. (2006). Classroom effects on student motivation: Goal structures, social relationships, and competence beliefs. *Journal of School Psychology, 44,* 331–349.

Vaillancourt, T. (2005). Indirect aggression among humans: Social construct or evolutionary adaptation? In R. E. Tremblay, W. W. Hartup, & J. Archer (Eds.), *Developmental origins of aggression.* New York: Guilford.

Valentine, S., & Mosley, G. (2000). Acculturation and sex-role attitudes among Mexican Americans: A longitudinal analysis. *Hispanic Journal of Behavioral Sciences, 22,* 104–113.

Valkenburg, P. M., & Peter, J. (2007). Preadolescents' and adolescents' online communication and their closeness to friends. *Developmental Psychology, 43,* 267–277.

Valle, M. F., Huebner, E. S., & Suldo, S. M. (2006). An analysis of hope as a psychological strength. *Journal of School Psychology, 44,* 393–406.

van de Vliert, E., & Janssen, O. (2002). "Better than" performance motives as roots of satisfaction across more and less developed countries. *Journal of Cross-Cultural Psychology, 33,* 380–397.

van den Boom, D. C. (1995). Do first-year intervention effects endure? Follow-up during toddlerhood of a sample of Dutch irritable infants. *Child Development, 66,* 1798–1816.

Van Hoof, A. (1999). The identity status field re-reviewed: An update of unresolved and neglected issues with a view on some alternative approaches. *Developmental Review, 19,* 497–565.

Van Leeuwen, K., De Fruyt, F., & Mervielde, I. (2004). A longitudinal study of the utility of the resilient, overcontrolled, and undercontrolled personality types as predictors of children's and adolescents' problem behaviour. *International Journal of Behavioral Development, 28,* 210–220.

Vandell, D. L., & Mueller, E. C. (1995). Peer play and friendships during the first two years. In H. C. Smith, A. J. Chapman, & J. R. Smith (Eds.), *Friendship and social relations in children.* New Brunswick, NJ: Transaction.

Vander Ven, T. M., Cullen, F. T., Carrozza, M. A., & Wright, J. P. (2001). Home alone: The impact of maternal employment on delinquency. *Social Problems, 48,* 236–257.

Vartanian, L. R. (2000). Revisiting the imaginary audience and personal fable constructs of adolescent egocentrism: A conceptual review. *Adolescence, 35,* 639–661.

Vartanian, L. R. (2001). Adolescents' reactions to hypothetical peer group conversations: Evidence for an imaginary audience? *Adolescence, 36,* 347–380.

Vartanian, L. R. (2003, April). *A look at parents' contributions to facets of "adolescent egocentrism."* Presented at the Society for Research in Child Development, Tampa, FL.

Veenstra, R., Lindenberg, S., Oldehinkel, A. J., De Winter, A. F., Verhulst, F. C., & Ormel, J. (2005). Bullying and victimization in elementary schools: A comparison of bullies, victims, bully/victims, and uninvolved preadolescents. *Developmental Psychology, 41,* 672–682.

Venezia, A., Kirst, M. W., & Antonio, A. L. (2003). *Betraying the college dream: How disconnected K-12 and postsecondary education systems undermine student aspirations.* Stanford, CA: Stanford Institute for Higher Education Research.

Ventura, S. J., Martin, J., Curtin, S., Menacker, F., & Hamilton, B. (2000). Births: Final data for 1999. *National Vital Statistics Reports 49*(1). Hyattsville, MD: National Center for Health Statistics.

Verma, S., Sharma, D., & Larson, R. W. (2002). School stress in India: Effects on time and daily emotions. *International Journal of Behavioral Development, 26,* 500–508.

Vieno, A., Perkins, D. D., Smith, T. M., & Santinello, M. (2005). Democratic school climate and sense of community in school: A multilevel analysis. *American Journal of Community Psychology, 36,* 327–341.

Villanueva-Abraham, S. (2002, April). *Mother-daughter disagreement during the entry into puberty: Patterns of individuual differences in girls.* Paper presented at the meeting of the Society for Research on Adolescence, New Orleans.

Vondracek, F. W., & Porfeli, E. (2002). Integrating person- and function-centered approaches in career development theory and research. *Journal of Vocational Behavior, 61,* 386–397.

Vondracek, F. W., & Porfeli, E. J. (2003). The world of work and careers. In G. R. Adams & M. Berzonsky (Eds.), *Blackwell handbook on adolescence.* New York: Blackwell.

Vossekuil, B., Fein, R. A., Reddy, M., Borum, R., & Modzeleski, W. (2002). *The final report and findings of the Safe School Initiative: Implications for the prevention of school attacks in the United States.* Washington, DC: U.S. Secret Service and Department of Education.

Vuchinich, S., Bank, L. & Patterson, G. R. (1992). Parenting, peers, and the stability of antisocial behavior in preadolescent boys. *Developmental Psychology, 28,* 510–521.

Vuchinich, S., Hetherington, E. M., Vuchinich, R. A., & Clingempeel, W. G. (1991). Parent-child interaction and gender differences in early adolescents' adaptation to stepfamilies. *Developmental Psychology, 27,* 618–626.

Vygotsky, L. S. (1962). *Thought and language.* Cambridge, MA: MIT Press.

Vygotsky, L. S. (1978). *The mind in society: The development of higher psychological processes.* Cambridge, MA: Harvard University Press.

Vygotsky, L. S. (1987). *Thinking and speech.* In R. Rieber & A Carton (Eds.), *The collected works of L. S. Vygotsky* (Vol. 1). New York: Plenum. (Original work published 1934.)

Waber, D. P., De Moor, C., Forbes, P. W., Almli, C. R., Botteron, K. N., et al. (2007). The NIH MRI study of normal brain development: Performance of a population based sample of healthy children aged 6 to 18 years on a neuropsychological battery. *Journal of International Neuropsychological Society, 13,* 1–18.

Wade, T., Cairney, J., & Pevalin, D. (2002). Emergence of gender differences in depression during adolescence: National panel results from three countries. *Journal of the American Academy of Child and Adolescent Psychiatry, 41,* 190–198.

Wagner, B. M., Cohen, P., & Brook, J. S. (1996). Parent/adolescent relationships: Moderators of the effects of stressful life events. *Journal of Adolescent Research, 11,* 347–374.

Wahlstrom, K. L. (Ed.). (1999). *Adolescent sleep needs and school starting times.* Washington, DC: Phi Delta Kappan Educational Foundation.

Wahlstrom, K. L. (2002). Accommodating the sleep patterns of adolescents within current educational structures: An uncharted path. In M. A. Carskadon (Ed.), *Adolescent sleep patterns: Biological, social, and psychological influences.* Cambridge, UK: Cambridge University Press.

Wainryb, C. (2006). Moral development in culture: Diversity, tolerance, and justice. In M. Killen & J. G. Smetana (Eds.), *Handbook of moral development.* Mahwah, NJ: Erlbaum.

Wainwright, J. L., & Patterson, C. J. (2006). Delinquency, victimization, and substance use among adolescents with female same-sex parents. *Journal of Family Psychology, 20,* 526–530.

Wainwright, J. L., & Patterson, C. J. (2008). Peer relations among adolescents with female same-sex parents. *Developmental Psychology, 44,* 117–126.

Wainwright, J. L., Russell, S. T., & Patterson, C. J. (2004). Psychosocial adjustment and school outcomes of adolescents with same-sex parents. *Child Development, 75,* 1886–1898.

Waldman, I. D., Weinberg, K. A., & Scarr, S. (1994). Racial-group differences in IQ in the Minnesota Transracial Adoption Study: A reply to Levin and Lynn. *Intelligence, 19,* 29–44.

Walker, E. F., Walder, D. J., & Reynolds, F. (2001). Developmental changes in cortisol secretion in normal and at-risk youth. *Development and Psychopathology, 13,* 721–732.

Walker, L. J. (1991). Sex differences in moral reasoning. In W. M. Kurtines & J. L. Gewirtz (Eds.), *Handbook of moral behavior and development: Vol. 2. Research.* Hillsdale, NJ: Erlbaum.

Walker, L. J., & Hennig, K. H. (2004). Differing conceptions of moral exemplarity: Just, brave, and caring. *Journal of Personality and Social Psychology, 86,* 629–647.

Walker, L. J., Hennig, K. H., & Krettenauer, T. (2000). Parent and peer contexts for children's moral reasoning development. *Child Development, 71,* 1033–1048.

Walsh, B. T. (2002). Pharmacological treatment of anorexia nervosa and bulimia nervosa. In C. G. Fairburn & K. D. Brownell (Eds.), *Eating disorders and obesity: A comprehensive handbook* (2nd ed.). New York: Guilford.

Walsh, D., & Gentile, D. (2001). A validity test of movie, television, and video-game ratings. *Pediatrics, 107,* 1302–1308.

Walsh-Childers, K., Gotthoffer, A., & Lepre, C. R. (2002). From "Just the Facts" to "Downright Salacious": Teens' and women's magazines' coverage of sex and sexual health. In J. D. Brown, J. R. Steele, & K. Walsh-Childers (Eds.), *Sexual teens, sexual media.* Mahwah, NJ: Erlbaum.

Ward, L. M. (2002). Does television exposure affect emerging adults' attitudes and assumptions about sexual relationships? Correlational and experimental confirmation. *Journal of Youth and Adolescence, 24,* 595–615.

Ward, L. M. (2003). Understanding the role of entertainment media in the sexual socialization of American youth: A review of empirical research. *Developmental Review, 23,* 347–388.

Ward, L. M., & Friedman, K. (2006). Using TV as a guide: Associations between television viewing and adolescents' sexual attitudes and behavior. *Journal of Research on Adolescence, 16,* 133–156.

Ward, L. M., Hansbrough, E., & Walker, E. (2005). Contributions of music video exposure to Black adolescents' gender and sexual schemas. *Journal of Adolescent Research, 20,* 143–166.

Ward, S., & Overton, W. (1990). Semantic familiarity, relevance, and the development of deductive reasoning. *Developmental Psychology, 26,* 488–493.

Warren, M. P. (1983). Physical and biological aspects of puberty. In J. Brooks-Gunn & A. C. Petersen (Eds.), *Girls At Puberty.* New York: Plenum.

Wasley, P. A., Fine, M., King, S. P., Powell, L. C., Holland, N. E., Gladden, R. M., & Mosak, E. (2000). *Small schools: Great strides. A study of new small schools in Chicago.* New York: Bank Street College of Education.

Waterman, A. S. (1993). Two conceptions of happiness: Contrasts of personal expressiveness (eudaimonia) and hedonic enjoyment. *Journal of Personality and Social Psychology, 64,* 678–691.

Waterman, A. S. (1999). Identity, the identity statuses, and identity status development: A contemporary statement. *Developmental Review, 19,* 591–621.

Waterman, A. S. (2004). Finding someone to be: Studies on the role of intrinsic motivation in identity formation. *Identity, 4,* 209–228.

Waterman, A. S. (2007). Doing well: The relationship of identity status to three conceptions of well-being. *Identity, 7,* 289–307.

Waters, E., Merrick, S., Treboux, D., Crowell, J., & Albersheim, L. (2000). Attachment security in infancy and early adulthood: A twenty-year longitudinal study. *Child Development, 71*, 684–689.

Waters, E., Weinfield, N. S., & Hamilton, C. E. (2000). The stability of attachment security from infancy to adolescence and early adulthood: General discussion. *Child Development, 71*, 703–706.

Waters, E., Wippman, J., & Sroufe, L. A. (1979). Attachment, positive affect, and competence in the peer group: Two studies in construct validation. *Child Development, 50*, 821–829.

Waters, M. (1990). *Ethnic options: Choosing identity in America.* Berkeley: University of California Press.

Watson, T. L., Bowers, W. A., & Andersen, A. E. (2000). Involuntary treatment of eating disorders. *American Journal of Psychiatry, 157*, 1806–1810.

Way, N., & Greene, M. L. (2006). Trajectories of perceived friendship quality during adolescence: The patterns and contextual predictors. *Journal of Research on Adolescence, 16*, 293–320.

Weber, M. (1946). Class, status, and party. In H. Gerth & C. W. Mills (Eds.), *From Max Weber.* New York: Oxford University Press.

Weber, R., Ritterfeld, U., & Mathiak, K. (2006). Does playing violent video games induce aggression? Empirical evidence of a functional magnetic resonance imaging study. *Media Psychology, 8*, 39–60.

Wechsler, D. (1981). *Manual for the Wechsler Adult Intelligence Scale.* New York: Psychological Corporation.

Wechsler, D. (1991). *Wechsler Intelligence Scale for Children* (3rd ed.). San Antonio, TX: Psychological Corporation.

Weinberg, M. (1977). The relationship between school desegregation and academic achievement: A review of the research. In B. Levin & W. D. Hawley (Eds.), *The courts, social science and school desegregation.* New Brunswick, NJ: Transaction Books.

Weiner, B. (1985). An attributional theory of achievement motivation and emotion. *Psychological Review, 92*, 548–573.

Weiner, B. (1992). *Human motivation: Metaphors, theories, and research.* Newbury Park, CA: Sage.

Weiner, B. (1994). Integrating social and personal theories of achievement striving. *Review of Educational Research, 64*, 557–573.

Weinfield, N. S., Sroufe, L. A., & Egelund, B. (2000). Attachment from infancy to early adulthood in a high-risk sample: Continuity, discontinuity, and their correlates. *Child Development, 71*, 695–702.

Weinstein, N. D. (1998). Accuracy of smokers' risk perceptions. *Annals of Behavioral Medicine, 20,*135–140.

Weinstock, H., Berman, S., & Cates, W., Jr. (2004). Sexually transmitted diseases among American youth: Incidence and prevalence estimates, 2000. *Perspectives on Sexual and Reproductive Health, 36*, 6–10.

Weisbrot, M., Baker, D., Kraev, E., & Chen, J. (2002). *The scorecard on globalization 1980–2000: Twenty years of diminished progress.* Washington, DC: Center for Economic and Policy Research.

Weisfeld, G. (1997). Puberty rites as clues to the nature of human adolescence. *Cross-Cultural Research: The Journal of Comparative Social Science, 31*, 27–54.

Weisner, T. S. (1989). Comparing sibling relationships across cultures. In P. Goldring-Zukow (Ed.), *Sibling interaction across cultures.* New York: Springer-Verlag.

Weissberg, R. P., & O'Brien, M. U. (2004). What works in school-based social and emotional learning programs for positive youth development. *Annals of the American Academy of Political and Social Science, 591*, 86–97.

Weller, W., Weller, A., & Roizman, S. (1999). Human menstrual synchrony in families and among close friends: Examining the importance of mutual exposure. *Journal of Comparative Psychology, 113*, 261–268.

Wells, A. S., & Crain, R. L. (1994). Perpetuation theory and the long-term effects of school desegregation. *Review of Educational Research, 64*, 531–555.

Welsh, D. P., Grello, C. M., & Harper, M. S. (2003). When love hurts: Depression and adolescent romantic relationships. In P. Florsheim (Ed.), *Adolescent romantic relations and sexual behavior: Theory, research, and practical implications.* Mahwah, NJ: Erlbaum.

Wenger, E. (1998). *Communities of practice: Learning, meaning, and identity.* New York: Cambridge University Press.

Wenglinsky, H. (2002). How schools matter: The link between teacher classroom practices and student academic performance. *Education Policy Analysis Archives, 10* (12). Retrieved March 23, 2003 from http://epaa.asu.edu/epaa/v10n12/.

Wentzel, K. (1998). Social relationships and motivation in middle school: The role of parents, teachers, and peers. *Journal of Educational Psychology, 90*, 202–209.

Wentzel, K. R. (2000). What is it that I'm trying to achieve? Classroom goals from a content perspective. *Contemporary Educational Psychology, 25*, 105–115.

Wentzel, K. R. (2002). Are effective teachers like good parents? Teaching styles and student adjustment in early adolescence. *Child Development, 73*, 287–301.

Wentzel, K. R., Monzo, J. C., Williams, A. Y., & Tomback, R. M. (2007, March). *Teacher and peer influences on academic motivation in adolescence: A cross-sectional study.* Presented at the biennial conference of the Society for Research in Child Development, Boston.

Westen, D. (2000). Psychoanalysis: Psychoanalytic theories. In A. Kazdin (Ed.), *Encyclopedia of psychology.* Washington, DC & New York: American Psychological Association and Oxford University Press.

White, L., & Gilbreth, J. G. (2001). When children have two fathers: Effects of relationships with stepfathers and non-custodial fathers on adolescent outcomes. *Journal of Marriage and the Family, 63*, 155–167.

White, M. (2001). *The material child: Coming of age in Japan and America.* New York: Free Press.

White, R. W. (1959). Motivation reconsidered: The concept of competence. *Psychological Review, 66*, 297–333.

Whiteman, S. D., & Buchanan, C. M. (2002). Mothers' and children's expectations for adolescence: The impact of perceptions of an older sibling's experience. *Journal of Family Psychology, 16*, 157–171.

Whiting, B. B., & Edwards, C. P. (1988). *Children of different worlds: The formation of social behavior.* Cambridge, MA: Harvard University Press.

Whitlock, J. L. (2002, April). *School and community contexts for positive youth development: Adolescent perceptions of stage-environment fit.* Paper presented at the meeting of the Society for Research on Adolescence, New Orleans.

Wichstrøm, L. (1999). The emergence of gender difference in depressed mood during adolescence: The role of intensified gender socialization. *Developmental Psychology, 35*, 232–245.

Wichstrøm, L. (2000). Predictors of adolescent suicide attempts: A nationally representative longitudinal study of Norwegian adolescents. *Journal of the American Academy of Child and Adolescent Psychiatry, 39*, 603–610.

Wichstrøm, L. (2001). The impact of pubertal timing on adolescents' alcohol use. *Journal of Research on Adolescence, 11*, 131–150.

Widmer, E. D., Treas, J., & Newcomb, R. (1998). Attitudes toward nonmarital sex in 24 countries. *Journal of Sex Research, 35*, 349–358.

Wiedemann, T. (1989). *Adults and children in the Roman Empire.* London: Routledge.

Wigfield, A., Battle, A., Keller, L., & Eccles, J. S. (2002). Sex differences in motivation, self-concept, career aspirations, and career choice: Implications for cognitive development. In A. McGillicuddy DeLisi & R. DeLisi (Eds.), *Biology, society, and behavior: The development of sex differences in cognition.* Greenwich, CT: Ablex.

Wigfield, A., & Eccles, J. S. (1989). Test anxiety in elementary and secondary school students. *Educational Psychologist, 24*, 159–183.

Wigfield, A., & Eccles, J. S. (1992). The development of achievement task values: A theoretical analysis. *Developmental Review, 12*, 265–310.

Wigfield, A., & Eccles, J. S. (2000). Expectancy-value theory of achievement motivation. *Contemporary Educational Psychology, 25*, 68–81.

Wigfield, A., & Eccles, J. S. (2002). Students' motivation during the middle school years. In J. Aronson (Ed.), *Improving academic achievement: Impact of psychological factors on education.* San Diego, CA: Academic Press.

Wigfield, A., Eccles, J. S., Schiefele, U., Roeser, R., & Davis-Kean, P. (2006). Development of achievement motivation. In W. Damon & R. M. Lerner (Eds.), *Handbook of child psychology* (6th ed.). Hoboken, NJ: Wiley.

Wigfield, A., & Wagner, A. L. (2005). Competence, motivation, and identity development during adolescence. In A. J. Elliot &

C. S. Dweck (Eds.), *Handbook of competence and motivation*. New York: Guilford.

Wikan, U. (1991). Toward an experience-near anthropology. *Cultural Anthropology, 6*, 285–305.

Wildes, J. E., Emery, R. E., & Simons, A. D. (2001). The role of ethnicity and culture in the development of eating disturbance and body dissatisfaction: A meta-analytic review. *Clinical Psychology Review, 21*, 521–551.

Wilgenbusch, T., & Merrill, K. W. (1999). Gender differences in self-concept among children and adolescents: A meta-analysis of multidimensional studies. *School Psychology Quarterly, 14*, 101–120.

William T. Grant Foundation Commission on Work, Family, and Citizenship (1988). *The forgotten half: Noncollege-bound youth in America*. New York: William T. Grant Foundation.

Williams, A. (2006, April 2). Before spring break, the anorexic challenge. *New York Times*, section 9, pp. 1, 6.

Williams, D. T. (1990). The dimensions of education: Recent research on school size. Working Paper Series. Clemson, SC: Clemson University.

Williams, J. E., & Best, D. L. (1990). *Sex and psyche: Gender and self viewed cross-culturally*. Newbury Park, CA: Sage.

Williams, J. K. Y., Goebert, D., Hishinuma, E., Miyamoto, R., Anzai, N., Izutsu, S., et al. (2002). A conceptual model of cultural predictors of anxiety among Japanese American and part-Japanese American adolescents. *Cultural Diversity and Ethnic Minority Psychology, 8*, 320–333.

Williams, J. M., & Currie, C. (2000). Self-esteem and physical development in early adolescence: Pubertal timing and body image. *Journal of Early Adolescence, 20*, 129–149.

Williams, J. M., & Dunlop, L. C. (1999). Pubertal timing and self-reported delinquency among male adolescents. *Journal of Adolescence, 22*, 155–171.

Williams, W. M., & Ceci, S. J. (1997). Are Americans becoming more or less alike? Trends in race, class, and ability differences in intelligence. *American Psychologist, 52*, 1226–1235.

Willis, B. M., & Levy, B. S. (2002). Child prostitution: Global health burden, research needs, and interventions. *Lancet, 359*, 1417–1422.

Willoughby, P. R. (1993). The Middle Stone Age in East Africa and modern human origins. *African Archaeological Review, 11*, 3–20.

Wilson, S. P., & Kipp, K. (1998). The development of efficient inhibition: Evidence from directed-forgetting tasks. *Developmental Review, 18*, 86–123.

Wines, M. (2003, November 27). AIDS blamed for legions of orphans in Africa. *New York Times*, p. A6.

Winne, P. H. (2001). Self-regulated learning viewed from models of information processing. In B. J. Zimmerman & D. H. Schunk (Eds.), *Self-regulated learning and academic achievement: Theoretical perspectives* (2nd ed.). Mahwah, NJ: Erlbaum.

Wiseman, C. V., Gray, J., Mosimann, J. E., & Ahrens, A. H. (1992). Cultural expectations of thinness in women: An update. *International Journal of Eating Disorders, 11*, 85–89.

Wiseman, R. (2002). *Queen bees and wannabes: Helping your daughter survive cliques, gossip, boyfriends, and other realities of adolescence*. New York: Crown.

Wolak, J., Mitchell, K. J., & Finkelhor, D. (2003). Escaping or connecting? Characteristics of youth who form close online relationships. *Journal of Adolescence, 26*, 105–119.

Wolchik, S., Tein, J.-Y., Sandler, I. & Doyle, K. (2002). Fear of abandonment as a mediator of the relations between divorce stressors and mother-child relationship quality and children's mental health problems. *Journal of Abnormal Child Psychology, 30*, 401–418.

Wolchik, S., Wilcox, K., Tein, J.-Y. & Sandler, I. (2000). Maternal acceptance and consistency of discipline as buffers of divorce stressors on children's psychological adjustment problems. *Journal of Abnormal Child Psychology, 28*, 87–102.

Wolfradt, U., Hempel, S., & Miles, J. N. V. (2002). Perceived parenting styles, depersonalisation, anxiety, and coping behaviour in adolescents. *Personality and Individual Differences, 34*, 521–532.

Wolfson, A. R., & Carskadon, M. A. (1998). Sleep schedules and daytime functioning in adolescents. *Child Development, 69*, 875–887.

Wolkstein, D. (1991). *The first love stories*. New York: Harper Perennial.

Wonderlich, S. A., Lilenfeld, L. R., Riso, L. P., Engel, S., & Mitchell, J. E. (2005). Personality and anorexia nervosa. *International Journal of Eating Disorders, 37* (Suppl.), S68–S71.

Wong, C. A., Eccles, J. S., & Sameroff, A. (2003). The influence of ethnic discrimination and ethnic identification on African American adolescents' school and socioemotional adjustment. *Journal of Personality, 71*, 1197–1232.

World Resources Institute. (2000). *World resources 2000–2001*. Washington, DC: Author.

Worthman, C. M. (1999). Evolutionary perspectives on the onset of puberty. In W. Trevethan, E. O. Smith, & J. J. McKenna (Eds.), *Evolutionary medicine*. New York: Oxford University Press.

Wright, M. O., & Masten, A. S. (2005). Resilience processes in development: Fostering positive adaptation in the context of adversity. In S. Goldstein & R. B. Brooks (Eds.), *Handbook of resilience in children*. New York: Kluwer.

Wudy, S. A., Dorr, H. G., Solleder, C., Djalali, M., & Homoki, J. (1999). Profiling steroid hormones in amniotic fluid of midpregnancy by routine stable isotope dilution/gas chromatography-mass spectrometry: Reference values and concentrations in fetuses at risk for 21-hydroxylase deficiency. *Journal of Clinical Endocrinology and Metabolism, 84*, 2724–2728.

Yasui, M., Dorham, C. L., & Dishion, T. J. (2004). Ethnic identity and psychological adjustment: A validity analysis for European American and African American adolescents. *Journal of Adolescent Research, 19*, 807–825.

Ybrandt, H. (2008). The relation between self-concept and social functioning in adolescence. *Journal of Adolescence, 31*, 1–16.

Yeates, K. O., & Selman, R. L. (1989). Social competence in the schools: Toward an integrative developmental model for intervention. *Developmental Review, 9*, 64–100.

Yip, T., Seaton, E. K., & Sellers, R. M. (2006). African American racial identity across the lifespan: Identity status, identity content, and depressive symptoms. *Child Development, 77*, 1504–1517.

Young, F. (1965). *Initiation ceremonies: A cross-cultural study of status dramatization*. Indianapolis, IN: Bobbs-Merrill.

Young, H., & Ferguson, L. (1979). Developmental changes through adolescence in the spontaneous nomination of reference groups as a function of decision context. *Journal of Youth and Adolescence, 8*, 239–252.

Young, R. A. (1994). Helping adolescents with career development: The active role of parents. *Career Development Quarterly, 42*, 195–203.

Youniss, J., Bales, S., Christmas-Best, V., Diversi, M., McLaughlin, M., & Silbereisen, R. (2002). Youth civic engagement in the twenty-first century. *Journal of Research on Adolescence, 12*, 121–148.

Youniss, J., & Hart, D. (2005). Intersection of social institutions with civic development. *New Directions for Child and Adolescent Development, 109*, 73–81.

Youniss, J., McLellan, J. A., & Yates, M. (1997). What we know about engendering civic identity. *American Behavioral Scientist, 40*, 620–631.

Youniss, J., & Smollar, J. (1985). *Adolescent relations with mothers, fathers, and friends*. Chicago: University of Chicago Press.

Yunger, J. L., Carver, P. R., & Perry, D. G. (2004). Does gender identity influence children's psychological well-being? *Developmental Psychology, 40*, 572–582.

Zabin, L., Hirsch, M., & Emerson, M. (1989). When urban adolescents choose abortion: Effects on education, psychological status, and subsequent pregnancy. *Family Planning Perspectives, 21*, 248–255.

Zajonc, R. B., & Mullally, P. R. (1997). Birth order: Reconciling conflicting effects. *American Psychologist, 52*, 685–699.

Zakriski, A. L., & Coie, J. D. (1996). A comparison of aggressive-rejected and nonaggressive-rejected children's interpretations of self-directed and other-directed rejection. *Child Development, 67*, 1048–1070.

Zand, D. H., Thomson, N., Cervantes, R., Espiritu, R., Klagholz, D., LaBlanc, L., & Taylor, A. (in press). The mentor-youth alliance: The role of mentoring relationships in promoting youth competence. *Journal of Adolescence, 31*.

Zhou, M., & Bankston, C. L. (1998). *Growing up American: How Vietnamese children adapt to life in the United States*. New York: Russell Sage Foundation.

Zillmann, D. (2000). Influence of unrestrained access to erotica on adolescents' and young adults' dispositions toward sexuality. *Journal of Adolescent Health, 27*(2, Suppl. 1), 41–44.

Zillmann, D. (2002). Exemplification theory of media influence. In J. Bryant & D. Zillmann (Eds.), *Media effects: Advances in theory and research* (2nd ed.). Mahwah, NJ: Erlbaum.

Zimmer-Gembeck, M. J., Chipuer, H. M., Hanisch, M., Creed, P. A., & McGregor, L. (2006). Relationships at school and stage-environment fit as resources for adolescent engagement and achievement. *Journal of Adolescence, 29*, 911–933.

Zimmer-Gembeck, M. J., Geiger, T. C., & Crick, N. R. (2005). Relational and physical aggression, prosocial behavior, and peer relations: Gender moderation and bidirectional associations. *Journal of Early Adolescence, 25*, 421–452.

Zimmer-Gembeck, M. J., & Helfand, M. (2008). Ten years of longitudinal research on U. S. adolescent sexual behavior: Developmental correlates of sexual intercourse, and the importance of age, gender, and ethnic background. *Developmental Review, 28*, 153–224.

Zimmer-Gembeck, M. J., & Locke, E. M. (2007). The socialization of adolescent coping behaviours: Relationships with families and teachers. *Journal of Adolescence, 30*, 1–16.

Zimmerman, B. J. (2000). Attaining self-regulation: A social cognitive perspective. In M. Boekarts, P. Pintrich, & M. Zeidner (Eds.), *Self-regulation: Theory, research, and applications*. Orlando, FL: Academic.

Zimmerman, B. J. (2002). Achieving academic excellence: A self-regulatory perspective. In M. Ferrari (Ed.), *The pursuit of excellence through education*. Mahwah, NJ: Erlbaum.

Zimmerman, M. A., Bingenheimer, J. B., & Notaro, P. C. (2002). Natural mentors and adolescent resiliency: A study with urban youth. *American Journal of Community Psychology, 30*, 221–243.

Zukow-Goldring, P. (2002). Sibling caregiving. In M. Bornstein (Ed.), *Handbook of parenting* (2nd ed., Vol. 2). Mahwah, NJ: Erlbaum.

Name Index

Subject Index

Roman "t" following page number indicates table, roman "f" indicates figure.

Photo Credits